KT-154-886

The International Handbook of Applied Research in Intellectual Disabilities

The International Handbook of Applied Research in Intellectual Disabilities

Edited by

Eric Emerson
Lancaster University, UK
Chris Hatton
Lancaster University, UK
Travis Thompson
University of Minnesota, USA
and
Trevor R. Parmenter
University of Sydney, Australia

John Wiley & Sons, Ltd

Telephone (+44) 1243 779777

Email (for orders and customer service enquiries): cs-books@wiley.co.uk
Visit our Home Page on www.wileyeurope.com or www.wiley.com

Other Wiley Editorial Offices

John Wiley & Sons Inc., 111 River Street, Hoboken, NJ 07030, USA

Jossey-Bass, 989 Market Street, San Francisco, CA 94103-1741, USA

Wiley-VCH Verlag GmbH, Boschstr. 12, D-69469 Weinheim, Germany

John Wiley & Sons Australia Ltd, 33 Park Road, Milton, Queensland 4064, Australia

John Wiley & Sons (Asia) Pte Ltd, 2 Clementi Loop #02-01, Jin Xing Distripark, Singapore 129809

John Wiley & Sons Canada Ltd, 22 Worcester Road, Etobicoke, Ontario, Canada M9W 1L1

Wiley also publishes its books in a variety of electronic formats. Some content that appears in print may not be available in electronic books.

Library of Congress Cataloging-in-Publication Data

The international handbook of applied research in intellectual disabilities / edited by Eric Emerson . . . [et al.].
p. cm.
Includes bibliographical references and index.
ISBN 0-471-49709-6 (cloth : alk. paper)
1. People with mental disabilities—Research. 2. Learning disabilities—Research. I. Emerson, Eric.
HV3004.I5485 2004
362.2′072—dc22 2003021195

British Library Cataloguing in Publication Data

A catalogue record for this book is available from the British Library

ISBN 0-471-49709-6

Typeset in 10/12pt Times by TechBooks Electronic Services, New Delhi, India
Printed and bound in Great Britain by TJ International Ltd, Padstow, Cornwall
This book is printed on acid-free paper responsibly manufactured from sustainable forestry in which at least two trees are planted for each one used for paper production.

Contents

About the Editors

Eric Emerson, Ph.D., is Professor of Clinical Psychology at the Institute for Health Research at Lancaster University, UK. Prior to this, he held posts at the Hester Adrian Research Centre at the University of Manchester, the Tizard Centre (University of Kent at Canterbury) and the South East Thames Regional Health Authority, and as a clinical psychologist in the UK and Canada. He has written several books and over 140 articles in academic and professional journals on issues related to supported accommodation, challenging behaviour and health/social care services for children and adults with intellectual disabilities.

Chris Hatton, Ph.D., is Professor of Psychology, Health and Social Care at the Institute for Health Research at Lancaster University, UK, having previously held research posts at the Hester Adrian Research Centre, University of Manchester, UK. He has written or edited several books and almost 100 articles in academic and professional journals on a range of issues concerning people with intellectual disabilities, including the assessment of service quality, supported accommodation, staffing issues, and the experiences of people with intellectual disabilities and their families from minority ethnic communities in the UK.

Travis Thompson, Ph.D., is Executive Program Director of the Minnesota Autism Center and Professor, Department of Pediatrics, University of Minnesota School of Medicine, Minneapolis, USA. He has published 24 books and more than 240 articles, chapters in journals and monographs. He has served on numerous national and international committees concerned with research, ethics, and policy. His research has focused on the environmental and biological factors underlying the challenging behaviour of people with developmental disabilities, including communication, architectural design, and genetics variables.

Trevor R. Parmenter, Ph.D., holds the Foundation Chair of Developmental Disability in the Faculty of Medicine, and the Adjunct Chair in the Faculty of Education, at the University of Sydney, Australia. He is the Director of the Centre for Developmental Disability Studies in the Royal Rehabilitation Centre, Sydney. His former positions include Professorial Fellow and Director of the Unit for Community Integration Studies at Macquarie University, Australia, prior to which he held teaching and administrative positions in the New South Wales Department of Education and Training. Currently, he is the Immediate Past President of the International Association for the Scientific Study of Intellectual Disabilities. His publications include 80 articles in professional journals and 45 book chapters in the areas of disability policy, quality of life, dual diagnosis, and vocational training.

List of Contributors

Michael V. Angrosino, *Department of Anthropology, University of South Florida, Tampa, FL 33620, USA*

Susan Balandin, *School of Communication Sciences and Disorders, Faculty of Health Sciences, University of Sydney, NSW 2006, Australia*

Nigel Beail, *Psychological Health Care, Barnsley CPS Trust, 11/12 Keresforth Close, Off Broadway, Barnsley, S70 6RS, UK*

Christine Bigby, *Department of Social Work and Social Policy, La Trobe University, Bundoora, Victoria 3083, Australia*

Jan Blacher, *School of Education, University of California, Riverside, CA 92521, USA*

Audrey Blakeley-Smith, *Department of Psychology, SUNY at Stony Brook, Stony Brook, NY 11794-2500, USA*

Nancy C. Brady, *Institute for Life Span Studies, University of Kansas, 1052 Dole, Lawrence, KS 66045, USA*

Edward G. Carr, *Department of Psychology, SUNY at Stony Brook, Stony Brook, NY 11794-2500, USA*

Sally-Ann Cooper, *Section of Psychological Medicine, University of Glasgow, Academic Centre, Gartnavel Royal Hospital, 1055 Great Western Road, Glasgow, G12 0XH, UK*

Dave Dagnan, *Department of Psychological Services, West Cumberland Hospital, Hensingham, Whitehaven, Cumbria, CA28 8JG, UK*

Elisabeth M. Dykens, *John F. Kennedy Center for Research on Human Development and Peabody College, Vanderbilt University, Peabody Box 328, 230 Appleton Place, Nashville, TN 37203-5701, USA*

Eric Emerson, *Institute for Health Research, Alexandra Square, Lancaster University, Lancaster, LA1 4YT, UK*

David Felce, *Welsh Centre for Learning Disabilities, Centre for Health Sciences Research, University of Wales, Heath Park, Cardiff, CF14 4XN, UK*

Marc E. Fey, *Hearing and Speech Department, University of Kansas Medical Center, 3901 Rainbow Blvd, Kansas City, KS 66160, USA*

Frank J. Floyd, *Georgia State University, Department of Psychology, MSC 2A1155, 33 Gilmer St, Unit 2, Atlanta, GA 30303-3082, USA*

Margaret Flynn, *School of Nursing and Midwifery, University of Sheffield, Samuel Fox House, Northern General Hospital, Herries Road, Sheffield, S5 7AU, UK*

Gordon Grant, *School of Nursing and Midwifery, University of Sheffield, Samuel Fox House, Northern General Hospital, Herries Road, Sheffield, S5 7AU, UK*

Tim Griffin, *School of Applied Social and Human Sciences, University of Western Sydney, Locked Bag 1797, Penrith South, NSW 1797, Australia*

Dorothy M. Griffiths, *Brock University, 500 Glenridge Avenue, St Catharines, Ontario, L2S 3A1, Canada*

Angela Hallam, *Health and Community Care Research Team, 2nd Floor East Rear, St Andrew's House, Edinburgh, EH1 3DG, UK*

Chris Hatton, *Institute for Health Research, Alexandra Square, Lancaster University, Lancaster, LA1 4YT, UK*

Susan Hayes, *Centre for Behavioural Sciences in Medicine, D06, University of Sydney, NSW 2006, Australia*

Lora Tuesday Heathfield, *Department of Special Education, Graduate School of Education, Salt Lake City, UT 84112, USA*

Andrea R. Hindes, *Georgia State University, Department of Psychology, MSC 2A1155, 33 Gilmer St, Unit 2, Atlanta, GA 30303-3082, USA*

Robert M. Hodapp, *John F. Kennedy Center for Human Development and Peabody College, Vanderbilt University, Peabody Box 328, 230 Appleton Place, Nashville, TN 37203-5701, USA*

Robert H. Horner, *Department of Special Education and Community Resources, College of Education, University of Oregon, Eugene, OR 97403, USA*

John Innis, *Department of Psychology, SUNY at Stony Brook, Stony Brook, NY 11794-2500, USA*

Mark Jakowski, *School of Education, Indiana University, 201 N Rose Ave, Bloomington, IN 47405-1006, USA*

Craig H. Kennedy, *Department of Special Education and Kennedy Center, Vanderbilt University, Peabody Box 328, 230 Appleton Place, Nashville, TN 37203-5701, USA*

Katherine Klingerman, *School of Education, Indiana University, 201 N Rose Ave, Bloomington, IN 47405-1006, USA*

Martin Knapp, *Centre for the Economics of Mental Health, Institute of Psychiatry, De Crespigny Park, London SE5 8AF and Personal Social Services Research Unit, London School of Economics, Houghton Street, London WC2A 2AE, UK*

K. Charlie Lakin, *Centre on Residential Services and Community Living, Institute on Community Integration, College of Education and Human Development, 214 Pattee Hall, 150 Pillsbury Drive SE, Minneapolis, MN 55455-0223, USA*

Tanya Lewis, *Brock University, 500 Glenridge Avenue, St Catharines, Ontario, L2S 3A1, Canada*

William R. Lindsay, *University of Abertay, Wedderburn House, 1 Edward Street, Dundee, DD1 5NS, UK*

Iris Tan Mink, *UCLA Psychiatry and Biobehavioral Science, Box 9517549, 760 Westwood Plaza Box 62, Los Angeles, CA 90095-1759, USA*

J. Stephen Newton, *Department of Special Education and Community Resources, College of Education, University of Oregon, Eugene, OR 97403, USA*

Samuel L. Odom, *School of Education, Indiana University, 201 N Rose Ave, Bloomington, IN 47405-1006, USA*

Robert E. O'Neill, *Department of Special Education, Graduate School of Education, Salt Lake City, UT 84112, USA*

Trevor R. Parmenter, *Centre for Developmental Disability Studies, The University of Sydney, PO Box 6, Ryde, NSW 1680, Australia*

Jonathan Perry, *Welsh Centre for Learning Disabilities, University of Wales, Meridian Court, North Road, Cardiff, CF4 3BL, UK*

Paul Ramcharan, *School of Nursing and Midwifery, University of Sheffield, Samuel Fox House, Northern General Hospital, Herries Road, Sheffield, S5 7AU, UK*

David Rose, *Psychology Department, Ridge Hill, Brierley Hill Rd, Stourbridge, West Midlands, DY8 5ST, UK*

John Rose, *Department of Clinical Psychology, University of Birmingham, Edgbaston, Birmingham, B15 2TT, UK*

Robert L. Schalock, *Department of Psychology, Hastings College, Hastings, NE 68901, USA*

Marsha Mailick Seltzer, *Waisman Center, University of Wisconsin–Madison, 1500 Highland Avenue, Madison, WI 53705, USA*

Katherine Short-Meyerson, *University of Wisconsin–Oshkosh, 800 Algoma Boulevard, Oshkosh, WI 54901-9988, USA*

Roger J. Stancliffe, *Centre for Developmental Disability Studies, The University of Sydney, PO Box 6, Ryde, NSW 1680, Australia*

Karen Stoner, *Brock University, 500 Glenridge Avenue, St Catharines, Ontario, L2S 3A1, Canada*

Frank Symons, *College of Education, University of Minnesota, Room 238 BuH 3171, 178 Pillsbury Drive SE, Minneapolis, MN 55455, USA*

Jon Tapp, *John F. Kennedy Center, Peabody College, Vanderbilt University, Nashville, TN 37203, USA*

Travis Thompson, *Minnesota Autism Center, 3001 Broadway Street NE, Suite 185, Minneapolis, MN 55413, USA*

Shawn Vasdev, *Department of Psychology, SUNY at Stony Brook, Stony Brook, NY 11794-2500, USA*

Steven F. Warren, *Bureau of Child Research, Institute for Life Span Studies, University of Kansas, 1052 Dole, Lawrence, KS 66045, USA*

Shelley L. Watson, *University of Alberta, 114 St – 89 Ave, Edmonton, Alberta, T6G 2E1, Canada*

Paul J. Yoder, *John F. Kennedy Center, Peabody College, Vanderbilt University, Nashville, TN 37203, USA*

Jennifer Zarcone, *Department of Psychiatry and Behavioral Sciences, University of Kansas Medical Center, 3901 Rainbow Blvd, Kansas City, KS 66160, USA*

Preface

Research has the potential to generate knowledge that our societies can use to address the disadvantage faced by children and adults with intellectual disabilities. Of course, this potential is not always realised. Poorly conducted research may generate false knowledge or simply waste scarce resources by failing to generate any new knowledge. Researchers may address issues that are tangential or irrelevant to the social situation of people with intellectual disabilities. Our societies may choose not to implement the knowledge that has been generated.

The primary aim of the present text is to address the first of these potential failings. To do this, we have gathered together contributions from a range of active researchers of international standing in their particular field and asked them to summarise current thinking in relation to key conceptual and methodological issues.

Section I of the text addresses broader aspects of the historical and social context within which research is undertaken. An appreciation of where we have come from (Parmenter, Chapter 1) provides an important foundation for our current efforts. In this section, we also address the importance of incorporating an appreciation of culture into research (Hatton, Chapter 2), the ethics of applied research involving people with intellectual disabilities (Griffin and Balandin, Chapter 3), and contemporary movements towards more participatory or emancipatory research paradigms (Ramcharan, Grant and Flynn, Chapter 4).

In Section II, we turn to the discussion of particular approaches to measurement. These include interviews undertaken with people with intellectual disabilities (Perry, Chapter 5) and members of their families (Blacher and Mink, Chapter 6), participant observation (Angrosino, Chapter 7), and behavioural "non-participant" observation (Yoder, Short-Meyerson and Tapp, Chapter 8). While the examples given in these chapters may be specific to particular areas of investigation, the issues raised cut across the full range of research activity.

Section III addresses the application of applied research methods to understanding the nature, characteristics, and social context of intellectual disability. Research undertaken in these areas opens up the possibility of identifying areas of need (and the nature of that need) in which people with intellectual disabilities may benefit from support. Here we cover an array of more specific issues, ranging from measuring genetic contributions to behaviour (Hodapp and Dykens, Chapter 9) to contemporary understanding of the nature and measurement of quality of life (Schalock and Felce, Chapter 12). Contributors in this section address methodological issues relating to the family context within which the vast majority of children with intellectual disabilities (and the majority of adults) live (Seltzer, Floyd and Hindes, Chapter 11), social inclusion (Odom, Klingerman and Jakowski, Chapter 13), and social relationships (Kennedy, Chapter 14). The other chapters in this section address aspects of personal functioning such as adaptive behaviour (Schalock, Chapter 18), communication and language (Warren, Brady and Fey, Chapter 19), choice making (Hatton, Chapter 16), engagement in activity (Felce and Emerson, Chapter 17), sexuality (Griffiths, Watson, Lewis and Stoner, Chapter 15), ageing (Bigby and Balandin, Chapter 10), mental health (Cooper, Chapter 20), and challenging behaviour (Carr, Innis, Blakeley-Smith and Vasdev, Chapter 21).

In Section IV, we turn to more evaluative research methods used to investigate the impact of support systems and services. In this section, contributors discuss conceptual and methodological issues relating to the evaluation of educational supports (O'Neill and Heathfield, Chapter 22), residential supports (Stancliffe, Emerson and Lakin, Chapter 23), the criminal justice system (Hayes, Chapter 24), staff performance (Hatton, Rose and Rose, Chapter 29), and a range of therapeutic approaches, including behavioural (Newton and Horner, Chapter 25), cognitive behavioural (Dagnan and Lindsay, Chapter 26), psychotherapeutic (Beail, Chapter 27), and psychopharmacological (Thompson, Zarcone and Symons, Chapter 28). We conclude with a chapter on health economics (Hallam and Knapp, Chapter 30), an often ignored aspect of evaluative research.

We hope that the experience and knowledge of our contributors will be of value to all who are contemplating or currently undertaking research involving people with intellectual disabilities, and also to people who act as the "consumers" of research. Sorting the wheat from the chaff can be a complex and difficult task. We believe that the contributions in this volume also provide some useful ideas and pointers for all who are involved in considering the potential value of the outputs of the research process.

It is, of course, impossible to focus simply on methodological and conceptual issues. Research, and particularly applied research, in such an area as intellectual disabilities takes place in a political and social context. It is inevitable, then, that along the way our contributors have also drawn attention to the social and applied relevance of research questions or topics in their particular fields. As such, they have also addressed the second potential failing of the research process we noted above (researchers addressing issues that are tangential or irrelevant to the social situation of people with intellectual disabilities). We sincerely hope that by collecting together an international cast of experienced researchers to address these two areas we will have made a modest contribution to improving the quality and relevance of research that addresses the disadvantage faced by children and adults with intellectual disabilities.

Eric Emerson
Chris Hatton
Travis Thompson
Trevor R. Parmenter

SECTION I

The Historical and Social Context of Research

CHAPTER 1

Historical Overview of Applied Research in Intellectual Disabilities: The Foundation Years

Trevor R. Parmenter
University of Sydney, Australia

INTRODUCTION

In 1958, Jack Tizard, one of the pioneer giants in the field of the study of intellectual disabilities, wrote:

> What are most needed today are properly controlled experimental studies and surveys designed to answer particular questions about the social costs of various types of administrative arrangements for dealing with mentally subnormal individuals. On the psychological side, we need to discover the most efficient methods of teaching or training those who are grossly subnormal in intelligence, or handicapped in other ways. The efficacy of different forms of treatment, including the psychological effects of medical treatments, must be studied, and new methods developed. How to teach social skills to dull, badly educated people has hardly been studied at all as yet, nor has the treatment of emotional maladjustment or psychopathic instability. (Tizard, 1958, p. 448)

While we would now use more acceptable terminology when referring to people with an intellectual disability, Tizard's injunction remains relevant. Indeed, the following chapters of this book represent a timely response to contemporary challenges that are not at all dissimilar to the core issues identified by Tizard almost half a century ago. In the same year, other pioneers in our field, Ann and Alan Clarke from the UK and later Norman Ellis from the USA, highlighted the need for applied research that recognises "the intimate reciprocal and enriching relationship between theory and practice and the use of experimental method in both cases" (Clarke & Clarke, 1958, p. xiv). Ellis (1963c, p. xi) commented: "Since mental retardation is a social problem, it would seem that the main thrust... would have only applied significance. Such is not the case... research findings and the related theories

The International Handbook of Applied Research in Intellectual Disabilities. Edited by E. Emerson, C. Hatton, T. Thompson and T.R. Parmenter ISBN 0-471-49709-6.

usually have implications for training or educating the retarded." Clarke and Clarke (1958, p. xiv) further suggested that "mental deficiency is a social-administrative rather than a scientific concept, varying in different countries and within a given country at different times".

This chapter will touch upon these issues in the context of the main historical research developments in the field of intellectual disabilities in the period from the late 1950s to the late 1980s. It will trace events that saw applied behavioural research challenge the exclusivity of the medical research that had dominated the field in the first half of the twentieth century. Later chapters, however, demonstrate the present situation, where multidisciplinary research teams are characterised by their interweaving of biomedical, psychological, social, and educational theories and practices. While the emphasis will be upon applied research developments, one needs to be reminded that all research sits within social, philosophical, ideological, economic, and political contexts. This is especially the case in the field of intellectual disability, given the long history of discrimination this population has experienced (Parmenter, 1991, 2001).

Origins of the International Association for the Scientific Study of Intellectual Disability

This review will draw heavily upon a small number of resources that are representative of research activities in essentially English-speaking industrialised countries. A rich source of the trends in the field is the *Proceedings* of the regular congresses of the International Association for the Scientific Study of Intellectual Disabilities (IASSID)[1] that was formally constituted in 1964. This association was born out of three international congresses held in Europe in the period 1960–63. The first, held in London in 1960 in observation of World Mental Health Year, was sponsored by the Royal Medico-Psychological Association, the Royal Society of Medicine, and the British Psychological Society, in cooperation with the National Association on Mental Health and the American Association on Mental Deficiency. A second congress was held in Vienna in 1961 and a third in Copenhagen in 1964, at which the International Association was duly formalised with a constitution that was published in the *American Journal of Mental Deficiency* (1965, vol. 69, p. 599) and the *Journal of Mental Deficiency Research* (1965, vol. 9, p. 150). The inaugural president was Harvey A. Stevens, the then president of the American Association on Mental Deficiency and Director of the Waisman Center, Wisconsin, USA; he was followed by Alexander Shapiro of Harperbury Hospital, Hertfordshire, UK. In honour of these outstanding leaders, the IASSID awards Stevens–Shapiro Fellowships to enable young researchers to present papers at its regular congresses. These were held every three years subsequent to the Copenhagen meeting until 1988, when the cycle went to every fourth year to coordinate with the quadrennial congresses of Inclusion International.[2] The first official congress of the Association was held in Montpellier, France, in 1967. The Twelfth Congress returns to Montpellier in 2004.

[1] Formerly International Association for the Scientific Study of Mental Deficiency (IASSMD).
[2] Formerly International League of Societies for the Mentally Handicapped (ILSMH).

Major Reviews in the Field

A second important resource is the several editions of *Mental Deficiency. The Changing Outlook*, first edited by Ann and Alan Clarke in 1958, with further editions in 1965, 1974, and 1985. While the majority of contributors are from the UK, Ann and Alan Clarke's international perspective is strongly evident in each of the editions.

Across the Atlantic, Norman Ellis's editorial contributions, such as the *Handbook of Mental Deficiency, Psychological Theory and Research* (1963c, 1979) and the *International Review of Research in Mental Retardation*,[3] are relevant. Other publications have been accessed to a lesser extent. For instance, detailed analyses of significant, long-standing journals, such as the *American Journal of Mental Retardation*,[4] *Mental Retardation*, the *British Journal of Mental Subnormality*, the *Journal of Applied Behaviour Analysis*, and the *Journal of Intellectual Disability Research*,[5] have not been made. The regular Gatlinburg Conferences held in the USA, and the symposia of the American Academy on Mental Retardation that coincide with the annual conferences of the American Association on Mental Retardation, are also indicative of applied research trends in this field. Wherever possible, primary resources have been accessed.

Development of University Research Centres in Intellectual Disability

A significant feature of the last 50 years has been the increase in the sharing of research efforts across the world, stimulated in large part by the growth of scientific journals, international conferences, and the sophistication of information technology. The field has also benefited enormously from the establishment of major university-affiliated research centres dedicated to the study of intellectual disabilities in Europe, North America, and Australasia. Arguably, two of the most significant developments that have bolstered the research output in the area of intellectual disability in the English-speaking world were the establishment of the Hester Adrian Research Centre at the University of Manchester in 1967 and the establishment of the National Institute of Child Health and Human Development (NICHD) through the energies of President John Kennedy and Dr John Cooke in the USA in the early 1960s (Alexander, 1988).

A Period of Optimism

The significant initiatives of the Kennedy Administration in the field of intellectual disability resulted from the appointment of a special President's Panel on Mental Retardation on 11 October 1961. The Panel's first report, submitted in 1962, made 112 recommendations under eight headings, the first of which called for a vigorous research effort into the causes of intellectual disability and in methods of care, rehabilitation, and learning. The Panel's report also resulted in the passing of far-reaching legislation by the US Congress that authorised significant Federal funds for research, training, and services in the field of intellectual

[3] Norman Ellis was editor from 1966 to 1987, followed by Norman Bray and subsequently Loraine Masters Glidden in 1997.
[4] Formerly *American Journal of Mental Deficiency*.
[5] Formerly *Journal of Mental Deficiency Research*.

disability. These developments have had a profound impact on our field, especially in the way they focused attention not only on the research and training of researchers, but also upon the place of people with intellectual disabilities in a civil society.

In a sense, at this time, there was a recapturing of the optimism of the mid-1800s for the improvement of the functioning of people with intellectual disabilities, exemplified by figures such as Guggenbuhl, Seguin, and H.B. Wilbur, that was replaced by the darker days of institutionalisation and the eugenics movement of the late 1800s and early 1900s. Lest we are carried away by a sense of triumphalism for the advances we have seen, it is salutary to be reminded that the demise of the nineteenth-century optimism was possibly brought about because, in the words of Murray (1988, p. 101), "they attempted to do too much with too few in the face of too much need".

Despite the exponential growth of research in recent decades, the gap between research and practice remains a significant problem to be tackled. Obviously, the ecological validity of the various research outputs is a key issue. For instance, the research conducted in controlled environments has not always been translated into applied settings. As indicated above, political and economic forces have a direct bearing upon the takeup of evidence-based practices in the service sectors. A further moderating factor relates to the waxing and waning of what Ellis (1963c) termed the "public conscience" (p. ix) and its impact upon the social and political scene.

Subsequent sections of the chapter trace in greater detail the historical development of applied research that laid the foundations for the rich variety of research initiatives described in later chapters.

DEVELOPMENTS IN THE LATE 1950s AND THE 1960s

Prior to this period, the dissemination of knowledge of intellectual disability had been relatively meagre when compared to advances in knowledge of other disabilities. In the USA in particular, the 1950s saw a quickening of resolve to tackle the gaps in knowledge covering this disability (Stevens & Heber, 1964). A significant imperative that was recognised early in this period, and one that would continue throughout the rest of the century, was the importance and interrelationship of research in the biological, psychological, educational, and sociocultural aspects of intellectual disability. However, it is only in recent years that the biopsychosocial approach to disability has gained stronger focus (WHO, 2001).

This principle was highlighted by the grant made by the National Institute for Mental Health in 1955 to the American Association on Mental Deficiency for a project entitled "Technical Planning in Mental Retardation". The brief of this project was as follows:

> The basic purpose of this project was seen as the delineation of current needs, the stimulation of creative thinking, integration and organization of work which had already been done, the improvement of liaison between interested groups and individuals—professional, government, lay and parents. For functional and organizational structure the broad general problems were thought to fall into three categories: research, training of personnel, and programming. (US Department of Health, Education, and Welfare, 1955, p. 20)

One of the outcomes of this project was the publication *Mental Retardation. A Review of Research* (Stevens & Heber, 1964), which brought together, in the US context, the knowledge

Table 1.1 Distribution of papers presented to world congresses of IASSMD/IASSID (percentage of total papers)

Year	Biomedical	Epidemiological/ classification	Philosophy, policy, service models	Applied research	Early intervention	Vocational
1967	33	8	16	37	4	2
1970	41	6	13	33	1	7
1973	29	5	15	45	2	4
1976	24	6	16	46	5	3
1979	19	8	14	50	4	5
1982	12	7	27	48	2	4
1985	24	8	12	51	2	3
1988	13	5	10	66	1	5
1992	15	6	10	61	2	6
1996	18	5	14	57	2	4
2000	10	9	17	58	2	4

obtained from research in all the major scientific disciplines that had contributed to a better understanding of the complexities of intellectual disability.

In the 1950s and 1960s, a distinguishing feature between the triennial conferences of IASSMD and the editorial work of Clarke and Clarke (1958) and Ellis (1963c) was that the former covered both the broad areas of medical and behavioural research, while the latter was essentially behavioural in focus. In the case of Clarke and Clarke, later editions acknowledged the need for a more integrated approach. However, Ellis, in both the *Handbook of Mental Deficiency* and *The International Review of Research in Mental Retardation*, maintained a heavy emphasis upon behavioural/psychological research issues. As Table 1.1 indicates, over the period of the 11 world congresses of IASSMD/IASSID,[6] the relative percentage of biomedical presentations fell significantly, with a concomitant increase in the percentage of applied research presentations. The percentages of subsections such as epidemiology/classification, philosophy/policy/service models, early intervention, and vocational remained fairly stable.

Both Clarke and Clarke (1958) and Ellis (1963c) observed that until the mid-1950s intellectual disability was a relatively neglected field of study except for some outstanding work in neuropathology and genetics. There had been little change in approaches to support this population since the turn of the century. Basically, the teaching techniques, vocational training, psychological treatments, and socialisation programmes employed were the same as those used with the non-disabled population. Behavioural science was essentially employed in the area of psychometric testing and diagnosis, where the emphasis was upon documenting the nature of the defect. These processes were generally used to exclude disabled persons from a service rather than to provide a programme that might enhance their competence and lifestyle.

Clarke and Clarke (1958) contended that the legacy of the eugenics movement, and the depression and resultant high unemployment between the two world wars, produced a social climate that was not conducive to positive alternatives for these people. In the introductory

[6] At the London conference held in 1960, 37 of the 97 presentations were from non-medical disciplines, principally psychology and education (Richards, Clarke & Shapiro, 1962).

chapter of Clarke and Clarke (1958), Tizard (1958) supported this assessment of the relative neglect of intellectual disability as a field of study. He observed that

> physicians have tended to neglect it as a field because of the seeming hopelessness of effecting specific cures; educationists and psychologists have been primarily concerned with problems of normal children; society as a whole has viewed the social problem of mental defect with a mixture of alarm and embarrassment. (p. 20)

Impact of Operant Psychology

On the other hand, the extremist behaviourist views of J.B. Watson (1913, 1924) began to attract researchers to the field of intellectual disability research, possibly because they appeared to be an antidote to the equally absolutist views of those who maintained that heredity was the sole determinant of intelligence. Watson, a former student of the revered American educational philosopher John Dewey, left his footprint solidly on the operant conditioning branch of behaviourism, the legacy of which permeated much of the applied research work in the area of those with severe and profound levels of intellectual disability in the early 1970s and beyond. His influence continues to be reflected in the applied behaviour-analysis approach to ameliorating severely challenging behaviours.

Watson's first public statement on behaviourism, made in 1913, was that "psychology as the behaviorist views it is a purely objective experimental branch of natural science. Its theoretical goal is the prediction and control of behaviour" (1913, p. 158). In 1924, he asserted:

> Give me a dozen healthy infants, well-formed, and my own specified world to bring them up in and I'll guarantee to take anyone at random and train him [*sic*] to become any type of specialist I might select—doctor, lawyer, artist, merchant—chief, and, yes, even beggar-man and thief, regardless of his talents, penchants, tendencies, abilities, vocations, and race of his ancestors. (1924, p. 104)

While Watson may have been the progenitor of behaviourism of the operant school, the theoretical work of figures such as Edward L. Thorndike, Edward R. Guthrie, Edward C. Tolman, Clarke L. Hall, and O. Hobart Mowrer provided a source of inspiration for psychologists who were searching for answers to the complex problems people with intellectual disabilities were presenting. However, it was B.F. Skinner (1938), in outlining his principles of operant conditioning, who laid the foundation for many of the practices that were instituted in the 1960s and 1970s and continue to be applied in this field of research and practice (Scheerenberger, 1987).

The oft-quoted classical study by Fuller (1949), in which a person with a profound intellectual disability was taught to raise his hand via a reinforcement procedure, has been heralded as a social and educational revolution in the area of intellectual disability (Whitman & Scibak, 1979). In the 1960s, significant research was conducted in the areas of language (Schiefelbusch, 1963; Baer & Sherman, 1964; Guess, Sailor, Rutherford & Baer, 1968; Bricker & Bricker, 1970), stereotypic movements (Berkson & Mason, 1963), punishment (Birnbrauer, 1968), toilet training (Ellis, 1963b), autism (Lovaas, 1966), tantrum behaviour (Sailor, Guess, Rutherford & Baer, 1968), functional speech in echolalic children (Risley & Wolf, 1967), and behaviour shaping of people in an institutional setting (Watson, 1968). Spradlin and Girardeau (1966) and Baer, Wolf and Risley (1968) provided a comprehensive review of this field of research that was primarily conducted with people with severe to profound intellectual disability in institutional settings.

Need for a Theoretical Base to Drive Research

A more coordinated approach to the study of intellectual disability began to emerge in this period. Ellis's first edition of *The Handbook* (1963c) was characterised by two principles. The first was that this field of study should not be an isolated study, for it was proposed that its special problems ought to be formulated in general behaviour theory terms. Reciprocally, the second principle was that the field of intellectual disability had much to offer behavioural scientists in their quest to understand the full complexities of human development and behaviour. There also emerged the realisation that theory and behavioural research needed to be closely integrated.

Ellis (1963c) suggested that behavioural science assumed two roles in the area of intellectual disability, service, and research. In the service area, the role operated mainly in the areas of evaluation and diagnosis, guidance, and a small but unsuccessful approach to psychotherapeutic interventions. He further suggested that the clinical psychology of intellectual disability "had consisted of little more than psychometric procedures, quite often applied indiscriminately, and without clear purpose" (p. 2). Psychologists would typically spend over 50% of their time administering intelligence tests, leaving relatively little of their time to support the needs of the clients. At this time, there was also emerging some dissatisfaction with the use of intelligence tests as a clinical tool.

Impact of Research on Clinical Practice

At this time, there was scant evidence that research was of benefit to the clinician, possibly because much of the research had been conducted by individuals trained in a service role rather than in the techniques required by a trained experimentalist. However, there were encouraging signs that this situation was changing. There were also exemplary programmes of medical and genetic research in the field, which provided a model for the development of programmes dedicated to the rigorous scientific analysis of abnormal behaviour. Changing social attitudes toward persons with intellectual disability led governments to provide increased support for research in this field. For instance, as indicated above, the President's Panel on Mental Retardation, appointed in October 1961 and its subsequent report in 1962, heralded a new era in both service and research in the USA. To a lesser extent, the UK Royal Commission on the Law relating to Mental Illness and Mental Deficiency, 1954–57, reflected a change in attitude towards people with an intellectual disability in the UK. However, Tizard (1958) was trenchant in his criticism of the Royal Commission's Report, arguing that it overemphasised the psychopathy of people with intellectual disability and maintained the prevalent medical view that little could be done to improve the competence of these people.

In this period, two, sometimes competing, streams of research began to emerge. The first was primarily concerned with establishing general laws of behaviour that may inform practice. Significant figures included Sidney Bijou, Herman Spitz, Norman Ellis, David Zeaman, Rue Cromwell, and Joseph Spradlin in the USA, and Ann Clarke, Alan Clarke,

Jack Tizard, N. O'Connor, and N.C. Gunzburg in the UK. The works of Luria (1963) and Piaget (cf. Inhelder, 1968) also impacted upon the theoretical and conceptual developments in the study of intellectual disability. The second emerging stream was more pragmatically inclined and enthusiastically sought to apply the results of laboratory research to practical situations. Often, insufficient recognition was given to the need for a careful examination of the means by which laboratory results could be generalised to the "real-world" situations. Ellis (1963) suggested that the application of the results of laboratory work usually demands research in which successive approximations to the practical setting are explored in order to establish ecological validity. He deplored the approach of many researchers who made "overgeneralized statements based on narrow research findings" (p. 2). He also pointed out that while there were many critics of pure or basic research in the field of intellectual disability, the solution to the practical problem often comes about through pure rather than applied research.

The tension between the discoverers of new knowledge and the potential users of the knowledge was later highlighted by Begab (1977) in his welcoming address to the Fourth Congress of IASSMD, held in Washington, DC, in 1978. As a result of the communication gap between researchers and practitioners, Begab suggested that "questions are not target oriented; laboratory findings fail to find expression in naturalistic settings; programs are implemented on a massive scale without adequate scientific base; and competition for limited resources is generated" (p. A-2). Begab also pointed out that we need to recognise that many of our most significant discoveries in science were serendipitous in nature.

There was a failure to consider the important variables that were operating in either or both the laboratory or applied situations. The exaggerated and overenthusiastic claims for the success of this approach led McClelland (1978) to comment later that the

> American public has come to question whether psychological knowledge can be used to improve the human condition. The main reason for this disillusionment is that in the 1960s we set grandiose goals for ourselves to transform society in a hurry, applied massive doses of inappropriate behavioural technology, and, by and large, failed to reach these goals. (p. 201)

Despite this later judgement, significant ground work was being laid in this period that resulted in important developments in both policy and practice. Undoubtedly, the growing dissatisfaction with the deplorable conditions in large institutions provided the engine for social policy change and concomitant investment in research across a wide range of areas.

Impact of the Revision of the Definition and Classification of Intellectual Disability

A further important influence was the revision of the definition and classification of intellectual disability by the American Association on Mental Deficiency (Heber, 1958), which included "impairment in adaptive behaviours" in addition to subaverage general intellectual functioning. This new definition, linked with the optimism of new pedagogical techniques, supported the proposition that the effects of intellectual disability could be reversed or ameliorated. There was a striking similarity between the educational initiatives of this period and those of the medicopsychologists of the nineteenth century. Simpson (1998) observed that the basic difference between the two periods was that, whereas the nineteenth-century reformers established pedagogical institutions for intellectually deficient children, their twentieth-century counterparts were using similar arguments to close them.

While there was a shift from a medical to a psychomedical theoretical model of intellectual disability, both approaches concentrated upon the intrinsic impairments and skill deficits of the person. This approach emphasised the utilitarian nature of programmes and treatments that would make disabled people more functional for society, a position challenged by the later emergence of the social system model of disability (Mercer, 1992).

Study of Learning

In this period, the foundations were laid for a serious consideration by experimental scientists of perception (Spivack, 1963), attention (Zeaman & House, 1963; Bryant, 1967), memory (Belmont, 1966), motivation (Haywood, 1967), language (Spradlin, 1958; Semmel, Bateman, O'Connor & Miller, 1967), self-concept (Cobb, 1966), discrimination learning (Stevenson, 1963; Ross, 1966), problem solving and conceptual behaviour (O'Connor, 1958, 1965; Rosenberg, 1963), and functional analysis of behaviour (Bijou, 1966), the building blocks of learning. Investigations were also under way in the areas of personality (Zigler, 1966), problem behaviour (Spradlin & Girardeau, 1966), early intervention (Skodak, 1967), psychotherapy (Gunzburg, 1958), and social development (Gunzburg, 1967).

While biomedical research continued to explore the aetiologies of intellectual disability with the view of prevention, behavioural research was developing a theoretical and applied base upon which to build more adequate educational programmes. Areas included adaptive behaviour, early intervention, special education, social development, communication, and vocational training. This period also saw the instigation of longitudinal studies of adult adjustment of people with intellectual disabilities (Tizard, 1958; Cobb, 1967; Edgerton, 1967).

Issues Impacting upon Research

In his presidential address to the First Congress of IASSID, Harvey Stevens (1967) highlighted a number of important issues that related to the study of intellectual disability. The first concerned the human rights of this population. Stevens commented that in the not-too-distant past the person with an intellectual disability "was viewed not as a second-class citizen but, rather, as one who possessed *no citizenship*" (p. xxxii). The proclamation by the United Nations, in 1971, of the Declaration of the Rights of Mentally Retarded Persons provided an impetus for countries to re-examine their laws to ensure that the rights of people with an intellectual disability were being safeguarded. To a large degree, human rights issues provided the cultural framework in which research could prosper, not the least reason being the need for government resources to fund it.

A second and related area concerned the participation of people with disabilities in research. Stevens called for IASSMD to assume an aggressive leadership role in developing guidelines for the involvement of people with an intellectual disability as research subjects. While university and hospital ethics committees have monitored this in the areas of social and health-related research over subsequent years, IASSID is about to adopt a set of International Multi-Centre Research Ethics Guidelines that refer specifically to this population. Griffin and Balandin (Chapter 3) present a comprehensive analysis of this critical issue.

Two further issues of particular international significance were raised; first, the need for an international uniformity in terminology and classification that could inform the establishment of a uniform international statistical reporting system. Here Stevens highlighted the need for international epidemiological studies. The second issue was the need to focus on the relationship between nutrition and intellectual disability, especially the effects of malnutrition on the physical and intellectual growth and development of children. Malnutrition and other environmental hazards continue to be among the greatest causes of intellectual disability worldwide.

The dehumanising effects of institutionalisation and particularly the size of residential facilities were issues that required immediate research attention. The assault upon the dignity of individuals in the large congregate facilities was starkly described, a theme later taken up by Nirje (1969) and Wolfensberger (1969). However, in this period, calls for downscaling still saw facilities of 50–1000 beds as reasonable (American Association on Mental Deficiency, 1964). Stevens cited a paper presented by George Tarjan in 1965, in which he said, with some prescience, given current efforts to improve the quality of service delivery in much smaller residential settings, together with the remaining larger ones:

> Today we are preoccupied with the bigness of institutions.... I hope that this concern will not lead us to the construction of a series of small facilities without providing adequate resources for programming in the traditional as well as the newer settings. (cited in Stevens, 1967, p. xxxvi)

An ongoing challenge for research is the exploration of how people with intellectual disabilities become an integral part of a community irrespective of where they live.

Other points touched upon by Stevens were professionalism and workforce issues related to the need to translate research into practice. He recognised the importance of a multidisciplinary approach to scientific research, as no single discipline can take sole responsibility for the lifelong needs of a person with an intellectual disability. However, the principle of the interdependence of disciplines in order to effect better outcomes for the individual has been slow in being realised. The continued growth of university-affiliated programmes on developmental disability, and mental retardation research centres in the USA and similar centres in other countries, has been instrumental in the movement towards this goal. Finally, he asserted that major advances in the areas of prevention and the provision of evidence-based services would not come from new knowledge generated by research over the succeeding 10 years. Rather, they would come from the application of existing knowledge. This, he suggested, can be done through multidisciplinary training and an increasing emphasis upon intellectual disability in existing professional educational programmes. It was this development, it is suggested, that marked the transition of research and practice from the excitement of the 1960s to their consolidation in the 1970s and 1980s.

Summary

In summary, this period saw the significant development of behavioural studies in the area of intellectual disability to complement and, to some degree, replace the emphasis upon medical research. This development was fostered by important social, human rights, and policy initiatives that were spreading across the West. There was a recognition that theories of human cognitive development were needed to underpin the growing demands for applied research to meet the pressing needs of people with intellectual disabilities. Foundations were laid for a more detailed analysis of human learning. The results of applied studies in controlled situations gave rise to a new-found optimism that people with an intellectual disability could learn to meet many of the demands of everyday living. An overarching phenomenon was the growing pressure to downscale the large, congregate care facilities that had burgeoned in the first six decades of the twentieth century.

INTO THE 1970s AND 1980s

Undoubtedly, the major underlying forces that drove applied research in this period were related to the deinstitutionalisation movement and community-living initiatives, as evidenced by significant legislative reforms in many industrialised countries. To a degree, social policy initiatives outstripped the capacity of the research community to inform policies and practices in this period (Parmenter, 1991). This was the case, despite the optimistic belief that research should play a conceptual role in providing a framework of concepts, orientations, and generalisations that can inform policy, identify problems and potential solutions, and set the agenda for future policy formulations (Beyer & Trice, 1982). Unfortunately, as Emerson (1985) observed, one needs to be reminded that the major use of research is symbolic; that is, it entails the non-functional use of data to justify predetermined positions. However, earlier in this period, Clarke and Clarke (1974) asserted that the general message of their review of research in this field was that

> careful empirical work in all disciplines pays off both in the short and long term. It has implications for prevention and the amelioration of subnormality, as well as a more general understanding of man [*sic*] as a biosocial organism. (p. xix)

This more optimistic view was certainly reinforced by the pronouncement of the President's Committee on Mental Retardation (1975) that, by using present knowledge and techniques in the biomedical and behavioural sciences, it is possible to reduce the incidence of mental retardation by half by the end of the century.

In his presidential address to the Fourth Congress of IASSID, Clarke (1977) emphasised the phrases "present knowledge and techniques" and "it is possible", and suggested that whether or not the possible becomes probable would be dependent upon the resources that would be made available. In the context of the theme of this congress, "Research to Practice in Mental Retardation", he questioned whether there was any sign of the impact of research upon practice. Begab (1977), programme chair for the congress, pointed out that society's response to the problems of intellectual disability was largely practice-directed, a situation, it would be fair to say, that still obtains in most countries. In the 1970s in the USA, for instance, he indicated that of the five billion dollars spent annually on service and income maintenance programmes for this population, three-quarters was expended on residential care and education, while only 1.5% was to support research. Braddock (1987) also highlighted a decline, in real terms, of US federal funds spent on disability research.

As indicated earlier, intellectual disability is a social and administrative rather than a scientific concept, being subjected to and influenced by social, political, and economic issues. Begab (1977) took up this theme in his remarks as the programme chair:

> The application of knowledge derived from research in service programs requires more than a free flow of information between scientist and practitioner.... It is imperative, therefore, that we recognize the broad social context that may impede the implementation of scientific discovery. The notion that we already know enough to reduce the incidence of mental retardation by half by the year 2000 may or may not be valid. But if we are to achieve this goal we will need to modify our social values, upgrade the economy and resolve some of our moral and ethical conflicts. Only then will the fruits of science be fully harvested. (p. A-5)

The applied research themes in this period were those of continual exploration of human learning including language, burgeoning of operant research with concomitant emphasis upon people with severe to profound levels of disability, and studies of the effects of deinstitutionalisation. Other issues that emerged towards the end of the period were vocational options, transition from school to work and adult living, ageing, family studies, and mental health. It is acknowledged that in this period, there was also an extensive literature in the areas of early intervention and special education, but, for the purposes of this review, it will not be examined.

Study of Human Behaviour and Learning

Two discrete traditions in the study of human behaviour and learning emerged in this period. The first, which will be termed "cognitive", tended to study the behaviour of those with moderate to mild levels of intellectual disability. The second, applied analysis of behaviour, influenced by Skinnerian principles, found enthusiastic followers among both researchers and practitioners. This approach helped to shift attention from research efforts in the area of those with moderate to mild levels of intellectual disability to those with more severe and profound levels. This trend had begun in the late 1960s, but accelerated in the 1970s. Acknowledging this trend in 1979, Carl Haywood, then editor of the *American Journal of Mental Deficiency*, asked, "What happened to mild and moderate mental retardation?" (Haywood, 1979, p. 429). He noted that from 1969 to 1973 most of the articles published in the journal were concerned with mild to moderate levels of intellectual disability. However, from 1974 to 1978, the majority of papers were devoted to people with severe and profound degrees of disability. While supporting the continuing study of those with more severe disabilities, he advocated that researchers should not ignore exploring the needs of those with milder levels of intellectual disability. However, despite Haywood's admonitions, behaviour-modification studies involving primarily the more severely disabled continued to predominate. As Ellis (1979) pointed out, few "basic" research findings in the cognitive area of research had been translated into applicable principles, except possibly for the work of Mercer and Snell (1977). On the other hand, the use of behaviour modification from the principles of operant conditioning demonstrated the application of laboratory findings to real-world behaviours.

Learning and Memory

Two of the most significant figures in this field were Edward Zigler of Yale University and Norman Ellis of the University of Alabama, both of whom built on basic learning theories developed much earlier. Zigler (1982), who grounded his position in Kurt Lewin's field theory of the 1930s, postulated a developmental approach to understanding the learning characteristics of the largest group of people with intellectual disability, those whose impairment was the result of polygenic inheritance, as against those with definite organic pathology.

Zigler's developmental theory proposed that children at the same cognitive levels, as measured by mental age (MA) on an intelligence test, are similar cognitively and do not differ in performance of cognitive tasks. Exceptions would occur when motivation or some other cognitive variable produced differences. In contrast, other scientists, whom Zigler labelled "difference" or "defect" theorists, maintained that "retarded and non-retarded persons even of equivalent developmental levels should differ in cognitive performance because of intrinsic differences over and above intellectual slowness" (Zigler & Balla, 1982, p. 4). Notable among these was Norman Ellis, whose work involved the stimulus trace theory that he formulated in the early 1960s (Ellis, 1963a). This theory proposed that the memory stimulus trace is shortened and the intensity of the stimulus is diminished among people with an intellectual disability. As a result, behaviour involving short-term memory, which is critical to much learning, would be impaired. He also suggested a possible neurological basis for his stimulus trace hypothesis, thus including all aetiological groups, and not excluding those with organic impairments, as did Zeaman and his colleagues.

Other deficit theorists included Alexander Luria, who suggested that people with an intellectual disability had a major deficit in their ability to utilise their verbal systems effectively to mediate and regulate behaviour (Luria, 1963). David Zeaman and Betty House demonstrated attention deficits in people with intellectual disabilities, but normal rates of learning once learning begins (Zeaman & House, 1979).

The cortical satiation theory of Spitz (1979) and the social learning theory of Cromwell (1963) also led to systematic research efforts. A number of researchers studied strategies in laboratory settings that were directed to improving memory and learning in people with intellectual disabilities. These included clustering and list retention (Evans & Bilsky, 1979), maintenance and generalisation of skills and strategies (Borkowski & Cavanaugh, 1979), learning and memory (Glidden, 1979), imaging and verbal elaboration (Taylor & Turnure, 1979), strategy production (Brown, 1974), information processing (Stanowich, 1978), and paired associate learning (Baumeister & Kellas, 1971). In this period, the study of social intelligence by Stephen Greenspan (1979) laid firm foundations for subsequent decades of research that has examined the nature of intelligence and intellectual processes in people with intellectual disability.

Assessment of Cognitive Processes and Strategy Training

Research into the assessment of cognitive processes and strategy training was strongly represented in this period. The work of J.P. Das (Das, 1973, 1977; Das, Kirby & Jarman, 1979), who proposed a model of information integration based on the theories of Luria (1973), stimulated experiments that attempted to improve cognitive functioning and educational performance (Kirby & Das, 1977; Das & Cummins, 1978; Kaufman & Kaufman, 1979; Das, Smart & Mulcahy, 1982; Parmenter, 1984, 1986b; Ashman & Conway, 1990). Das's model of simultaneous and successive processing was also the basis for the development of new tests of intelligence (Kaufman & Kaufman, 1983).

In Israel, Reuven Feuerstein (Feuerstein et al., 1972) developed the learning potential assessment device (LPAD), which assessed the process of learning across a large number of cognitive operations that are necessary for relative complex learning. He related performance in these areas to specific educational intervention techniques. After assessment by LPAD, a programme of institutional enrichment (IE) would be devised to remedy cognitive deficiencies (Rand, Feuerstein, Tannenbaum, Jensen & Hoffman, 1977), by the principles of mediated learning experience (MLE). Feuerstein (1977) contended that it is through MLE that normal learning processes occur through complex interactions with stimuli.

In a critical appraisal of Feuerstein's model and research, Bradley (1983) was wary of a repetition of the over-optimism generated during the 1960s and early 1970s by diagnostic-remedial approaches to the training of abilities, a position echoed by Ysseldyke (1982). Bradley concluded that the results, in terms of improved intellectual and school subject performances and measures of attitudes, classroom behaviours, and motivation, were very modest and at best clouded.

Other significant contributions in the area of research were in the area of metacognition (Brown, 1974; Justice, 1985), the assessment of and theories of intelligence (Silverstein, 1970; Campione & Brown, 1978; Sternberg & Sheer, 1985), and motivation (Haywood & Switzky, 1986).

While these research directions developed a greater theoretical understanding of the cognitive processes of people with intellectual disabilities, it would be fair to say that they had little impact upon practices in the field. With the movement towards community living both for those who had been institutionalised and for those who remained in the family home, the everyday living needs of these persons were of paramount importance to practitioners. The assessment of adaptive behaviours, the teaching of independent living skills, and the management of challenging behaviours were critical issues that confronted practitioners including professional staff, such as teachers, psychologists, therapists, and social workers, many of whom had little professional training in the field of intellectual disability.

Measurement of Adaptive Behaviour

Following the introduction of the classification of adaptive behaviour in the area of intellectual disability in 1959 (Heber, 1958), the definition and label of intellectual disability (or mental retardation) were based on elements besides the IQ or psychometric test results, including evidence of a "deficit in adaptive behaviour" (Grossman, 1973). Subsequently, Nihira, Foster, Shellhaas and Leland (1969, 1974) developed the AAMD Adaptive Behavior Scale (ABS), which has undergone several revisions and translations (e.g., Magerotte, 1977; Tomiyasu, 1977). The original version was constructed for and normalised on an institutionalised, intellectually disabled population. Later versions included more representative samples. There was a proliferation of development of other adaptive scales, and, by 1980, there were well over 100 published scales, formal and informal (Scheerenberger, 1987). These scales were not without their critics. For instance, Clausen (1972) was particularly sceptical and preferred retaining the priority of intelligence tests. He was especially concerned about the validity of estimates of developmental potential and judgement of social inadequacy, which may vary with examiner and circumstances. Bortner (1978) provided a detailed review of the 1974 version of the AAMD ABS and concluded that the scale identified the existence of meaningful factors or aspects of adjustment and was able to discriminate successfully between variously labelled groups.

Research in adaptive behaviour burgeoned in this period, two significant instruments being the Scales of Independent Behavior (SIB), an in-depth measure of adaptive and problem behaviours (Bruininks, Woodcock, Weatherman & Hill, 1984) and the Inventory for Client and Agency Planning (ICAP) (Bruininks et al., 1986). These instruments have found wide use in diagnosis, programme planning, and evaluation.

Clarke and Clarke (1985, p. 50) concluded:

> The development of scales designed to measure adaptive behaviour is to be welcomed . . . these scales at the very least mark a major advance from the vague and often unreliable statements concerning "social incompetence". . . . An important question . . . is how to arrive at a sensible taxonomy for scientific use which will enable research workers and others to communicate. . . . Multi-axial classification, pioneered by WHO, is to be commended.

Schalock (Chapter 18) discusses contemporary practices in the measurement of adaptive behaviours, particularly in the context of the merging of the constructs of intelligence and adaptive behaviour.

Applied Behaviour Analysis (ABA)

The more contemporary term has been chosen to head this section, but in the period under discussion the popular term was "behaviour modification" (BM). It would not be extravagant to assert that in the field of applied research into intellectual disability BM has played the pre-eminent role. It is not difficult to discover reasons for this phenomenon. For instance, as Chris Kiernan (1991) has suggested, the conditions in impoverished institutional environments in earlier decades provided a fertile ground for the promise of BM techniques. As indicated above, they were an antidote to the deep pessimism of professionals regarding the learning potential of people with severe and profound disabilities. There was also a confluence with emerging philosophical, social, and legislative forces that began the journey towards citizenship and the realisation of basic human rights for this population. The educability of these people had been demonstrated, albeit in reasonably controlled environments; the challenge lay in ensuring that inhumane neglect was not replaced by equally inhumane behaviour-management procedures that the principles of BM could also deliver.

It is also not surprising that in this period BM research was directed almost exclusively towards people with severe and profound levels of disability. They obviously presented the greater intellectual challenge, but the presence of large numbers of these people in the restricted environment of an institution provided a ready opportunity for both researchers and professional staff to explore the application of BM techniques.

Advocacy groups,[7] who were strongly promoting the devolution of large institutions, were energetic in their support for the more severely disabled, who, it was feared, would be

[7] One of the earliest was the American Association for the Education of the Severely/Profoundly Handicapped, formed in 1974. In 1980, the name was changed to the Association for the Severely Handicapped (TASH), reflecting the Association's broader vision. The name was changed to the Association for Persons with Severe Handicaps in 1983, but the acronym was retained. In 1995, the Association voted to maintain the acronym because it was widely recognised, but to stop using the full name of the organisation, as it did not reflect current values and directions. These were summed up as "equity, diversity, social justice and inclusion".

left to languish in the institutions owing to their extremely high and costly support needs. If it could be shown that these people could perform self-help and other adaptive behaviour skills with a degree of independence, policy planners would be more likely to support community living options for them. In the event, it was the strength of the human rights argument that prevailed, rather than research options per se.

It is not the intent of this analysis to provide an exhaustive examination of the literature on BM/ABA, given its breadth and depth. In his keynote address to the 33rd Annual Congress of the Australian Society for the Study of Intellectual Disability (ASSID), Bob Remington (1998) indicated that there were some 580 articles relating to behaviour analysis of developmental disabilities in the *Journal of Applied Behavior Analysis* (*JABA*) alone. However, in the period under discussion, there was an expansion of the settings in which BM/ABA research was conducted, including schools, community living programmes, families, and vocational settings. There were also important developments in the technology itself. Its greatest impact, and the most lasting it is suggested, was in the management of what are popularly termed "challenging behaviours". Its use also raised some important ethical and methodological issues.

The following appraisal of the impact of BM/ABA technology and unresolved issues that remained to be addressed following the 1980s draws, in part, upon the reviews by Kiernan (1985, 1991), Whitman and Scibak (1979), and Schroeder, Mulick and Schroeder (1979).

Throughout the 1970s, research settings were usually either laboratories or the relatively controlled environments of institutions. Areas targeted for study followed a similar pattern to those reported earlier, although, by the end of the 1970s, studies were being conducted in more natural environments such as places of work (cf. Bellamy, Horner & Inman, 1979). The challenges presented by practitioners, who were strongly influenced by the continuing political, social, and legislative developments, put increasing pressure upon researchers to demonstrate the ecological or social validity of their findings. The possible weaknesses in BM/ABA research at this time identified by Whitman and Scibak (1979) included:

- a lack of reliability in the measurement of behaviours and inadequate experimental control
- insufficient demonstration of clinically meaningful changes in behaviour
- interventions not always cost-effective or cost-efficient
- lack of demonstration of maintenance and generalisation effects (cf. Stokes & Baer, 1977)
- the need to demonstrate that procedures not only produce increases in adaptive behaviours, but also decreases in inappropriate behaviours not directly treated; possible "side effects" of a particular treatment procedure needed to be made known
- insufficient methodological details provided, making replication difficult.

These issues were echoed by Schroeder, Mulick and Schroeder (1979) in the context of research into the management of severe behaviour problems. They added consumer satisfaction and social validity to their three criteria to judge the effectiveness of behaviour-management procedures: degree and rapidity of suppression, durability of suppression, and covariation (that is, positive or negative side effects).

Single-Subject Designs

The advent of BM/ABA studies gave rise to single-subject designs (cf. Herson & Barlow, 1976) that took some time to be accepted by journal editors that were committed to traditional group designs. It was not surprising, therefore, that a number of new journals emerged that extensively published BM/ABA research. Despite their power to demonstrate experimental control, single-subject designs are restricted in the types of questions they can answer. To make comparisons of different techniques, as well as analyse the components of treatment packages, as, for instance, in the area of the treatment of inappropriate behaviours, group designs may be more efficient.

Emphasis upon Contingencies

In the 1970s, the majority of interventions utilised rewards to increase behaviours or punishment to reduce behaviours. The techniques included shock and verbal prohibition, physical restraint, over-correction, time out, differential reinforcement of other behaviour (DRO), reinforcement of specific incompatible responses, and differential stimulus-control procedures. Despite an increase in community living provisions for people with severe and profound intellectual disabilities, their needs for professional support in areas such as self-help skills, social behaviours, toilet training, language, and modification of inappropriate behaviours were not diminished. While moves to a less restrictive environment and greater opportunities for a more stimulating lifestyle brought about positive changes, there is evidence that environmental change, in and of itself, does not reduce the incidence of challenging behaviours (Young, Sigafoos, Suttie, Ashman & Grevell, 1998). In areas such as toilet training and severe challenging behaviours, the results of the research in this decade remain especially relevant. The problem that was evident 30 years ago remains today; the lack of professional expertise to implement BM/ABA strategies faithfully, a problem identified by Kiernan in 1985 and Emerson and Emerson in 1987. Kiernan (1985) outlined a number of challenges facing this technology. One was the "bad press" received by electroshock. He commented further,

> The 1980s have witnessed the emergence of what has been referred to as a "new realism", accepting the difficulties in ameliorating the basic deficits of mentally handicapped people and of successfully integrating them into society. It is undoubtedly a part-manifestation of a general social and political mood which has little to do with scientific principles or teaching techniques. However, it is also partly a function of the failure of intervention techniques, primarily behavioural in nature, to produce radical change in the behaviour of mentally handicapped individuals. (pp. 470–471)

A number of significant research initiatives in the 1980s provided firm foundations for future work. These included developments to increase maintenance and generalisation effects (Horner, Dunlap & Koegel, 1985), and to reduce behaviour problems through functional communication training (Carr & Durand, 1985). The need for well-constructed and detailed programmes based on sound BM/ABA principles to inform practitioners was supported by publications such as *Alternatives to Punishment: Solving Behavior Problems with Non-aversive Strategies* (LaVigna & Donnellan, 1986), *An Educative Approach to Behaviour Problems* (Evans & Meyer, 1985), and *Non-Aversive Intervention for Behaviour Problems* (Meyer & Evans, 1989).

Horner et al. (1985) provided an overview of generalisation and maintenance strategies that have empirical support in applied settings. These included the modification of environments, self-management procedures, community intensive instruction, functional competence, general case programming, and functional equivalence as a mechanism of response generalisation. The drawing together of well-researched findings into a single volume was a welcome initiative that supported practitioners in translating research into practice.

The seminal work of Carr and Durand (1985) brought a new insight into the possible causes of child behaviour problems. This study lent support to the hypothesis that some of these undesirable behaviours may be seen as a non-verbal means of communication. Teaching more acceptable means of communicating the same need or desire helps to eliminate the undesirable non-verbal behaviour. This work has had a profound impact in achieving more effective and efficient intervention strategies. However, there is a concomitant need for practitioners and families to be trained in how to determine the communicative intent of the child's non-verbal behaviours.

Research to Practice

La Vigna and Donnellan (1986) produced a textbook that essentially outlined the basic steps to be followed in the implementation of BM/ABA principles. The procedures were supported by reference to a wide range of empirical research findings. Likewise, Evans and Meyer (1985) and Meyer and Evans (1989) based their training manuals on established empirical work. Their strategies emphasised the manipulation of antecedent events, particularly environmental control. They especially targeted teachers, families, and community-living support workers, who work under administrative situations quite dissimilar to clinicians. Teachers and support workers were increasingly required to comply with mandatory individual programming procedures that involved the families, the child with the disability, and other professionals. In these situations, the use of aversive consequences, such as physical punishment, was prohibited. A key principle of their approach was not to target undesirable behaviours as the focus of the interventions, but to focus on desirable behaviours that may replace them. Their aim was to build sound behavioural principles into the overall educational planning. This position, they suggested,

> involves an extension and elaboration of standard behavior modification methods. It is a "second generation" of behavior modification in which the focus is no longer simply on the derivation of techniques from learning principles, but on how these principles may be most effectively adapted to the institutional situation and extended to deal with the total educational needs of the child. (Evans & Meyer, 1985, p. 2)

A comprehensive review of a pilot project that incorporated these principles in group and family homes indicated that there needed to be a significant input into staff and parent training. Fidelity to the principles was achieved by experienced practitioners working beside the less experienced. Within the family setting, it was found that the procedures needed to be supplemented by family therapy (Parmenter & Gray, 1990; Wiese, 1993).

The need for a systems approach to implementing sound practices in service organisations was recognised by Kushlick (1975), who suggested that it is important to consider whole organisations as systems controlled by behavioural principles. For instance, there was a need for compatibility of the practices with the organisational philosophy of the agency (Kiernan & Jones, 1980). Innovative work in the UK in the late 1980s involved the development of service models that adopted this approach (Emerson et al., 1987; Mansell et al., 1987; Felce, 1989).

Emerging Issues

The 1970s and 1980s undoubtedly built on and expanded earlier research in this area. However, a number of challenges in later developments became apparent. There was a continuing need to narrow the gap between theoretical work in the research centres and applications in field settings. A close relationship between experimental analysis of behaviour and applied behaviour analysis was seen as a priority (Morris, 1991). For example, Remington (1991) commented: "There has not been a shortage of research reporting the success of particular interventions, but there is a shortage of more analytical work aimed at developing behaviour analysis in applied contexts" (p. 8). Kiernan (1985) also recognised the need for application to get back to basic science; in particular, to "a closer examination of the central Skinnerian concept of the operant as a *functional* unit of behaviour" (Remington, 1991, p. 7).

There was, too, a growing awareness of the need for ethical guidelines for professionals to ensure that "the behaviour of people working with those with mental handicap should further their legitimate interests and not cause them harm (beneficence)" (Kiernan, 1991, p. 773). Van Houten et al. (1988) also emphasised that the individual has a basic right to a therapeutic environment that is safe, humane, and responsive to human needs. The recognition of this right presaged developments in the area of choice and self-determination (Wehmeyer, Abery, Mithang & Stancliffe, 2003). Kiernan (1985a) deplored the separation of the operant and non-operant research and thinking. He suggested that there were signs of a rapprochement in the area of language and communication, "but an almost total theoretical divide in others" (p. 496).

The challenges this period offered to later work in this area was best summed up by Kiernan (1985a, p. 496):

> It seems clear that the general pressure during the next decade should be to disseminate sophisticated behavioural techniques and, at the same time, to correct oversimplifications. This means that dissemination to direct care personnel must be complemented by an increase in the effort to develop management-level staff who are in direct touch with sophisticated ideas and who can be skilled and creative in using them well with direct care staff in developing programs.

Carr, Innis, Blakeley-Smith and Vasdev (Chapter 21) and Newton and Horner (Chapter 25) explore contemporary design, measurement, and evaluation issues.

Language and Communication

In the 1970s, a behavioural technology of language development had begun to emerge to meet the challenge that up to 55% of people with intellectual disability had deficiencies in both receptive and expressive language (President's Committee on Mental Retardation, 1975). In people with IQs of less than 50, the absence or near absence of speech could be found in 75–80%. Much of the earlier work in receptive language research had focused upon gaining verbal control over a person's motor behaviour, in particular, through the establishment of instruction-following behaviour. In the area of expressive speech development, operant approaches generally adopted a two-step process of establishing imitative verbal behaviour followed by attempts to develop functional and spontaneous speech in natural settings. However, Whitman and Scibak (1979) noted that, while investigations had generally examined the effects of their intervention strategies in a systemic way, the research had been "narrow in its focus . . . examining for change only within the confines of restricted and well-controlled experimental environments" (p. 310).

It was possibly the burgeoning of empirical studies of normal development in the linking of language to cognitive development, and the linking of the growth of language to social context and social development, that had the greatest impact upon language and communication in the latter part of this period. A diverse range of theoretical approaches to normal language development influenced applied research in the area of intellectual disability. A common theme among these approaches was that language was embedded within the context of communication and social behaviour, a key factor being that language is learned as a way of relating to other people and controlling to some extent one's environment. When translated to the area of intellectual disability, studies tended to pursue either the delay hypothesis or the difference hypothesis discussed above. In his detailed examination of this area, Kiernan (1985a) noted that the delay or similar sequence hypothesis was more strongly supported by published data.

A significant factor in the study and remediation of delayed language development in children with an intellectual disability was the sharp division between the trajectories of researchers and practitioners. For instance, in the practical early intervention and school programmes, practitioners experimented with the use of non-verbal systems, including signing, graphic symbol systems, and aided systems such as speech synthesisers. Researchers were slow, however, to follow these innovations with studies of their effectiveness, an example, suggested Kiernan (1985b), "of researchers not absorbing and investigating what practitioners are revealing" (p. 632). It was interesting to note in this context that Lloyd and Fuller (1990) presented a paper, "The Role of Iconicity in Augmentative and Alternative Communication-Symbol Learning", to the Eighth Congress of IASSID held in Dublin in 1988. Disappointingly, there was little evidence of practitioners applying research outcomes in other areas of their remediation programmes.

The gap between research and practice in this area is to some extent quite understandable, for language acquisition and communication in people with an intellectual disability is one of the most complex problems faced by practitioners and researchers alike. Applied research generally has focused on specific aspects of language acquisition, often in controlled rather than natural environments. Practitioners in this period were bombarded by a proliferation of language programme packages, the majority of which were outdated by the time they were published. Of more pressing concern was that such packages so often ignored the basic principle that language and communication-skills development essentially relies upon transactions between individuals in real-life settings. Warren, Brady and Fey (Chapter 19) explore more recent methodological and measurement issues in communication and language.

Deinstitutionalisation and Community Living

At the Fourth Congress of IASSID held in Washington, DC, in 1976, Stephen Richardson reported that there had been no follow-up or longitudinal studies that dealt with the total population of all subtypes of children with an intellectual disability living in the community who were followed through adolescence to adulthood,[8] but there had been studies dealing with people who had been released or escaped from institutions (Cobb, 1972; Goldstein, 1964; Tizard, 1965; Rosen, Clarke & Kivitz, 1977). The results showed that these people, in many cases, were able to function in the community, find and hold jobs, and marry and raise families. From the research perspective, there were major difficulties in interpreting the results, as there was an absence of data on the levels of functioning of the people studied and a lack of information on whether or not they were in any way representative of the populations in the residential institutions. For instance, placement in institutions occurred for many reasons other than clear evidence of severe intellectual disability. It is suspected, then, that the focus of these studies was largely on adults with mild degrees of intellectual disability for whom, on criteria established at the time, institutional care was inappropriate.

With the increasing pace of deinstitutionalisation in Western countries in the 1970s and 1980s, there was a similar increase of studies that examined the outcomes for the people involved. A variety of methodologies were employed, including traditional group designs that measured the relative impact of the process on outcomes (Malony & Taplin, 1988), studies that sought to determine predictor variables for successful outcomes (Heal, Lakin, Bruininks, Hill & Best-Sigford, 1984), and life-history interviewing (Edgerton, 1977). Studies have also examined community attitudes towards community residences for people with intellectual disabilities (Seltzer & Litchfield, 1984).

Before examining these developments, it is important to recognise a number of issues raised by Clarke, Clarke and Berg (1985) in their review on lifespan development and psychosocial intervention. In particular, they suggested that an important question was "the extent to which the mentally retarded show behavioural consistency over time, requiring special support services of either a formal or an informal nature" (p. 440). Furthermore, they pointed out further that this question was related to the general issue of discontinuities in development that was reviewed in depth by Emde and Harmon (1985) and Clarke and Clarke (1984). Their evaluation was summarised as follows:

> Neither genetic programmes nor social influences necessarily unfold in a constant way and their interactions are complex. The role of chance events adds a further and sometimes potent uncertainty in prediction equations. Both constancies and changes in ordinal position and/or level occur for most characteristics in normal circumstances, but following significant ecological improvement, personal changes among the disadvantaged can be much larger. Recent research emphasizes the inadequacy of considering either genetic or environmental effects during one period of development outside the context of preceding and subsequent influences. It is to long-term consistent influences that importance must be ascribed. (pp. 440–441)

As noted earlier, the lifespan development and support needs of those with moderate to mild levels of intellectual disability and those with more severe to profound levels may be quite dissimilar, an issue not always acknowledged in the studies reported in this period.

It had been recognised for some time that the administratively defined prevalence of intellectual disability reached its peak during the later years of schooling and declined shortly thereafter, largely due to those with milder levels of disability merging into the general community (Cobb, 1972). The situation for those with more severe disabilities,

[8] However, 20 years later, Richardson and Koller (1996) reported a 22-year longitudinal study of such a population in Aberdeen, Scotland.

even in times of full employment, indicated that they require ongoing levels of support (Kushlick & Blunden, 1974), a position that remains unchanged in more recent times.

The increased number and range of studies of deinstitutionalisation in this period were characterised by relatively inadequate, or absence of, definitions of what constituted "institutional living" and "community living". In the case of the former, many studies assumed that the populations and the quality of supports were homogeneous. As Bachrach (1981) noted, the word "community" was used in the literature concerning people with an intellectual disability so loosely that it became synonymous with "noninstitution". She also warned against the danger of proposing a geographical relocation, from a residential facility funded directly by the state to one funded indirectly by the community, on the assumption of better or more appropriate care.

Effects of Institutionalisation

An issue that has been underestimated in more recent years has been the effects of institutionalisation on people with intellectual disability. In 1979, Zigler and Balla suggested that the impact of institutional experience on the behaviour and development of people with intellectual disability was important for a number of reasons, not the least being that if policy-makers cannot demonstrate that community-based residentials are cost-effective, "it may well be that central institutions will be rediscovered" (1977, p. 268). As indicated above, in large measure, the movement to deinstitutionalisation was more motivated by social, moral, and political forces than empirical research. Nevertheless, reliable knowledge of the effects of institutionalisation on resident behaviours, Zigler and Balla suggested, would help providers whether people were in institutions or community placements. After receiving several studies, they concluded that it was not the size of the setting that was the determinant of care practices.

In a detailed analysis of the development of intellectually disabled persons in a sample of community and institutional settings, Eyman, Silverstein, McLean and Miller (1977) concluded that the social-psychological characteristics of a residence, rather than its setting or location, influenced the behaviours of the residents. A later study of placement type and client functional level suggested that there were systemic differences among large care facilities and community placements. In the former, there appeared to be a greater emphasis upon components of client normalisation while in the latter the emphasis was on environmental normalisation. Aspects of client normalisation were deficient. It was concluded that the primary emphasis in the deinstitutionalisation process appeared to have been an environmental normalisation, with an inadequate community-based, comprehensive, interdisciplinary service system that would support better client outcomes (Bjaanes, Butler & Kelly, 1981). Butler and Bjaanes (1977) had emphasised the point earlier when they categorised community care facilities into three types: custodial, therapeutic, and maintaining. Custodial facilities were those in which little or nothing was done to achieve normalisation and where residents may regress. Therapeutic facilities were those in which there was an active, ongoing attempt at enhancing the normalisation process. The maintaining type was characterised by little change in resident outcomes. They concluded,

> It cannot and should not be assumed that a community care facility is *a priori* a normalizing environment. That assumption is much too likely to result in a shift from larger total institutions to smaller dispersed community-based total institutions. (p. 346)

Evaluation of Quality Outcomes

In terms of quality outcomes for community-living support services, two not incompatible directions emerged. One related to conformity to service standards against which organisations could be assessed. In the UK in 1977, for instance, the Royal Society for Mentally Handicapped Children and Adults published a series of Stamina documents, specifying minimum standards for services such as special schools, adult training centers, and residential services (NSMHC, 1977). In the USA, the Accreditation Council for Services for Mentally Retarded and Other Developmentally Disabled Persons published detailed guidelines for public accreditation of services (ACMRDD, 1983). The Australian Commonwealth Government promulgated a set of Disabled Service Standards in association with its Disability Service Act (1986).

The second initiative, developed in the late 1980s, addressed quality-of-life outcomes for the individual with a disability (Emerson, 1985; Landesman, 1986; Brown, 1988; Goode, 1988; Schalock, 1990; Parmenter, 1992a). This development was a harbinger of future initiatives that provided opportunities for a greater consumer voice in disability policy directions. For instance, people with intellectual disabilities now play an active role in service management committees and national advocacy organisations, and serve on government committees, confirming their increasing progress towards full personhood and citizenship. Another initiative of this period was the development of *individual service plans*, which were possibly borrowed from the concept of the *individual education plans* mandated by special education legislation in the USA in the mid-1970s. Other countries soon followed this practice, but, as Emerson (1990) pointed out, "local ownership of the plans was considered crucial to ensuring their adoption" (p. 401).

Methodological Issues

Studying residential alternatives for people with intellectual disabilities has produced a variety of sophisticated methodologies. In this period, one of the most sophisticated approaches was that of Heal and Fujima (1984). Their insightful exploration of issues related to internal and external validity, the validity of measurement instruments, social validity, and the ethics of research provided an excellent model for prospective researchers. In their review of studies, they deplored the low response rate to surveys and the lack of true experiments where there had been a random allocation of individuals to experimental and control conditions. On the other hand, more qualitative methodologies, including anthropological and ethnographical ones, were beginning to emerge, illustrating that there are many paths to scientific "truth". There was a common plea for a greater number of longitudinal studies that would explore the long-term effects of specific interventions, such as early childhood programmes, special education provisions, and alternative residential placements.

New Directions

Research in vocational options for people with mild disabilities (Ward, Parmenter, Debenham & Miller, 1972; Parmenter, 1980; Rusch, 1986; Richardson, Koller & Katz, 1990) and for those with severe disabilities (Gold, 1973; Bellamy, Horner & Inman, 1979) demonstrated that people at all levels of intellectual disability can be taught to perform relatively complex vocational tasks in natural settings. This is one area where research possibly did have a direct effect upon legislative and equal opportunity provisions, given the rapid growth of competitive and supported employment options for people with disabilities in the industrialised world in the late 1980s and early 1990s. However, in many countries, little impact has been made on reducing the relative proportion of people with intellectual disabilities in segregated employment settings (Parmenter, 1992b). In fact, the situation for those with high support needs is currently far from optimistic, despite the earlier research that demonstrated their potential for obtaining and sustaining integrated employment (Parmenter, 1999a).

The related area of research into the transition from school to adult life of young people with intellectual disabilities began in the mid-1970s (Brolin, Durrand, Cromer & Muller, 1975; Richardson, 1977) and expanded in the 1980s (Halpern, 1985; Parmenter, 1986a; Bruininks, Thurlow, McGrew & Lewis, 1990; Lewis, Bruininks, Thurlow & McGrew, 1990), providing detailed analyses of the effects of transitional planning on vocational and community-living adjustments for this population. This research confirmed the critical importance of social skills and social relationships for successful community integration, especially in the vocational area.

Interestingly, in 1988, Steven Reiss, in a report to the Illinois Governor's Planning Council on Developmental Disabilities, estimated that for every intellectually disabled person in the USA who needed treatment for a severe behaviour disorder, there were 10 who needed training in social skills, and two who needed treatment for depression (Reiss, 1988). In the previous year, Reiss had convened an International Research Conference on Mental Health Aspects in Evanston, Illinois, USA, the purpose of which was to discuss research and clinical issues pertinent to the growing international demand for mental health services for people with intellectual disability. Menolascino (1988) suggested at the conference that it was generally recognised that people with intellectual disability were nearly twice as likely to develop mental illness as those in the general population. There had been earlier research in the UK in the area of forensic psychiatry that indicated that people with mild intellectual disability were over-represented in the criminal justice system through involvement in sexual offences and arson (Walker & McCabe, 1973; Gibbens & Robertson, 1983). The following decade was to see a rapid increase in applied research endeavours into the psychopathology of this population, especially those with mild intellectual disabilities.

With increasing emphasis upon community options for people with intellectual disabilities, including remaining in the family home, it was not surprising that aspects of support for families and family adjustments emerged as a focus of research studies (Turnbull, Brotherson & Summers, 1985; Blacher & Bromley, 1990; Richardson, Gouldron, Koller & Katz, 1990). Research into the effects of ageing had its beginnings in biomedical studies of the early onset of dementia in people with Down syndrome in the late 1980s. The exploration of service provision (Hogg, 1990; Janicki, 1990) for people with an intellectual disability who were ageing gave rise to later research efforts that saw a much stronger relationship between biomedical and applied work.

Summary

In many respects, applied research in the 1970s and 1980s continued to build up the major themes that had emerged in the previous period. Researchers from different theoretical, philosophical, and methodological perspectives were concerned with aspects of human behaviour and learning in the context of intellectual disability. The infectious optimism generated in the late 1960s was confronted with the realities of the challenges thrown up by the deinstitutionalisation movement. The promises predicted by strong research initiatives in the field of applied behaviour analysis were to some extent realised, but the end of the 1980s still saw researchers grappling with the complexities of the maintenance and generalisation of training.

Research on the outcomes of deinstitutionalisation employed a variety of methodologies to examine specific issues, including the effects of institutionalisation, predictor variables of outcomes, and community attitudes towards community residences for people with intellectual disabilities. Practices to ensure quality outcomes were initiated in this period. Community living threw up new problems, such as those of mental health provisions, family adjustment, and ageing, that became the focus of research initiatives into the next decade.

THE FOUNDATION YEARS IN RETROSPECT AND BEYOND

The period of the late 1950s through to the late 1980s was exciting and significant in many respects, not only for the dramatic changes in philosophies, attitudes, and social policy developments that impinged on the lives of all people with disabilities, including those with intellectual disability, but also for the rich array of applied research that sought to discover new knowledge to inform both policies and practices. While this analysis has been concerned with applied behavioural research in the field of intellectual disability, a strong parallel movement in biomedical research was also proceeding. In many respects, its efforts demonstrated a multidisciplinary approach to pushing the frontiers of knowledge more than did the applied behavioural area. But there were emerging signs that the applied behavioural scientists were coming to recognise the importance of an integration of the biological and behavioural sciences. For instance, Stephen Schroeder (1991) suggested that neuroscience represents a fusion of several scientific disciplines—biophysics, biochemistry, physiology, anatomy, pharmacology, genetics, and psychology. It also focuses on understanding the relationships between brain and behaviour. Begab (1981) echoed these comments when he called for a greater interdependence of basic and targeted research.

Social, political, and economic factors continued to provide the context in which research was located. There appeared to be a definite lessening of social and political commitment to the field in the late 1980s that translated into a more parsimonious financial commitment to the needs of people with disabilities in general. This coincided with, or was directly caused by, the commitment of the governments of industrialised countries to neoliberal economic policies that were in the ascendancy throughout the 1990s and beyond (Parmenter, 1999b).

Paradigm shifts were under way in the field of disability in general, and in the area of intellectual disability in particular. The deinstitutionalisation movement precipitated the denigration of the medical model of disability and saw the growth of a variety of scientific paradigms, including cognitive and psychomedical models, social-system models, and the conflict model (Mercer, 1992). As predicted by Mercer and suggested above, there emerged a recognition of the need to study the interactions between biomedical and behavioural/environmental approaches. A further shift was about to occur in the area of the definition and classification of intellectual disability, as evidenced by the 1992 publication of the American Association on Mental Retardation (AAMR), *Definition and Classification of Mental Retardation* (AAMR, 1992). This development, not without some controversial comment at the time, emphasised the concept of "person–environment fit" and the notion of supports that became the focus for the classification of intellectual disability, rather than levels of IQ.

A persistent theme throughout the period was the need to translate research into practice, but, as was reported earlier in this chapter, Clarke and Clarke (1958) and Ellis (1963c) indicated that intellectual disability is a social and administrative problem rather than a scientific concept. Therefore, the way ahead should involve a stronger emphasis on research that analyses macro-level service systems compared to the more micro-level investigation of human behaviour. Indeed, the challenge goes beyond research to a large degree, for, as Michael Begab, in his presidential address to the Fifth Congress of IASSMD held in Jerusalem in 1979, commented,

> Knowledge is not a guarantee of action. We have known from time immemorial that poverty and its correlates, in industrial and underdeveloped nations alike, are festering places for many of the world's social ailments and deterrents to optimal development and self-fulfilment. We know, too, that malnutrition and inadequate health care resources, endemic in many parts of the world, are breeding grounds for infant mortality and morbidity. . . . the implementation of knowledge goes well beyond the purview of science and service. Only as we make an impact on the political process and provide an empirical base for rational decision-making can significant inroads to the global and complex problem of mental retardation be expected. (Begab, 1981, p. xxii)

This challenge is as relevant today as it was over two decades ago. Now more than ever before, we also need to acknowledge that knowledge is not the sole province of the scientist. Again, as Begab (1981) admonished,

> We have much to learn from professional practitioners, from caregivers . . . and from parents whose individual and collective efforts to cope successfully with family problems and societal prejudices have inspired new insights into the resilience of the human personality and the capacity of even the least fortunate among us to change and grow. (p. xxii)

Not only did the foundation years pave the way for the discovery of new insights into intellectual disability; they also helped to contribute, through the application of knowledge, to the continuing emancipation of people with an intellectual disability, who now have been able to contribute as partners rather than subjects in many of the processes of scientific enquiry. It is hoped that this historical analysis will set the scene for the following chapters that address many of the issues raised from a more contemporary perspective. Undoubtedly, there was a sense of excitement on the part of the researchers in the period reviewed. As in all areas of scientific enquiry, there were some false leads and disappointments, but there were also many significant advances made. Above all, they were inspired by the same desire as those of us who have followed; to push forward the boundaries of knowledge in order to help people with intellectual disabilities live a more satisfying and enjoyable life as full citizens in society.

REFERENCES

ACMRDD (Accreditation Council for Services to Mentally Retarded and Other Developmentally Disabled Persons) (1983). *Standards for Services for Developmentally Disabled Individuals* (2nd edn). Washington, DC: Author.

Alexander, D. (1988). The impact of national policies on research in mental retardation—a United States perspective. *Australia and New Zealand Journal of Developmental Disabilities*, **14**, 183–188.

American Association on Mental Deficiency (1964). *Standards for State Residential Facilities for the Mentally Retarded, a Manual of Minimal Standards.* Washington, DC: Author.

American Association on Mental Retardation (1992). *Mental Retardation. Definition, Classification and Systems of Supports* (9th edn). Washington, DC: Author.

Ashman, A.F. & Conway, R.N.F. (1990). A model for integrating processing strategies and curriculum content. In W.I. Fraser (Ed.) *Key Issues in Mental Retardation Research* (pp. 327–335). Proceedings from the Eighth Congress of the International Association for the Scientific Study of Mental Deficiency. London: Routledge.

Australian Government (1986). *Disability Services Act.* Canberra: Australian Government Printer.

Bachrach, L.L. (1981). A conceptual approach to deinstitutionalization of the mentally retarded: a perspective from the experience of the mentally ill. In R.H. Bruininks, C. Edward Meyers, B.B. Sigford & K.C. Lakin (Eds) *Deinstitutionalization and Community Adjustment of Mentally Retarded People* (pp. 51–67). AAMD Monograph No. 4. Washington, DC: American Association on Mental Deficiency.

Baer, D.M. & Sherman, J.A. (1964). Reinforcement control of generalized imitation in young children. *Journal of Experimental Child Psychology*, **1**, 37–49.

Baer, D.M., Wolf, M.M. & Risley, T.R. (1968). Current dimensions of applied behaviour analysis. *Journal of Applied Behavior Analysis*, **1**, 91–97.

Baumeister, A. (1981). Mental retardation policy and research: the unfulfilled promise. *American Journal of Mental Deficiency*, **85**, 449–456.

Baumeister, A. & Berkson, G. (1982). Mental retardation research funding trends of the National Institute of Child Health and Human Development. *American Journal of Mental Deficiency*, **87**, 119–121.

Baumeister, A.A. & Kellas, G. (1971). Process variation paired-associate learning of retardates. In N.R. Ellis (Ed.) *International Review of Research in Mental Retardation*, vol. 4 (pp. 221–270). New York: Academic Press.

Begab, M.J. (1977). Barriers to the application of knowledge. In P. Mittler (Ed.) *Research to Practice in Mental Retardation*, vol. 1. *Care and Intervention* (pp. A1–5). Proceedings of the Fourth Congress of the International Association for the Scientific Study of Mental Deficiency. Baltimore, MD: University Park Press.

Begab, M.J. (1981). Presidential address: frontiers of knowledge in mental retardation. In P. Mittler (Ed.) *Frontiers of Knowledge in Mental Retardation* (pp. xxi–xxxv). Proceedings of the Fifth Congress of the International Association for the Scientific Study of Mental Deficiency, vol. II. Baltimore, MD: University Park Press.

Bellamy, G.T., Horner, R.H. & Inman, D.P. (1979). *Vocational Habilitation of Severely Retarded Adults. A Direct Service Technology.* Baltimore, MD: University Park Press.

Belmont, J.M. (1966). Long-term memory in mental retardation. In N.R. Ellis (Ed.) *International Review of Research in Mental Retardation*, vol. 1 (pp. 219–255). New York: Academic Press.

Berg, J.M. (Ed.) (1984). *Perspectives and Progress in Mental Retardation.* Proceedings of the Sixth Congress of the International Association for the Scientific Study of Mental Deficiency, vols I and II. Baltimore, MD: University Park Press.

Berg, J.M. (Ed.) (1986). *Science and Service in Mental Retardation.* Proceedings of the Seventh Congress of the International Association for the Scientific Study of Mental Deficiency. London: Methuen.

Berkson, G. & Mason, W.A. (1963). Stereotyped movements in mental defectives. III. Situation effects. *American Journal of Mental Deficiency*, **68**, 409–412.

Beyer, J.M. & Trice, H.H. (1982). The utilization process: a conceptual framework and syntheses of empirical findings. *Administration Science Quarterly*, **27**, 591–622.

Bijou, S. (1963). Theory and research in mental (developmental) retardation. *Psychological Record*, **134**, 95–110.

Bijou, S.W. (1966). A functional analysis of retarded development. In N.R. Ellis (Ed.) *International Review of Research in Mental Retardation*, vol. 1 (pp. 1–18). New York: Academic Press.

Birnbrauer, J.S. (1968). Generalization of punishment effects—a case study. *Journal of Applied Behaviour Analysis*, **1**, 201–211.

Bjaanes, A.T., Butler, E.W. & Kelly, B.R. (1981). Placement type and client functional level as factors in provision of services aimed at increasing adjustment. In R.H. Bruininks, C.E. Meyers, B.B. Sigford & K.C. Lakin (Eds) *Deinstitutionalization and Community Adjustment of Mentally Retarded People* (pp. 337–350). AAMD Monograph No. 4. Washington, DC: American Association on Mental Deficiency.

Blacher, J. & Bromley, B. (1990). Factors influencing and factors preventing placement of severely handicapped children: perspectives from mothers and fathers. In W.I. Frazer (Ed.) *Key Issues in Mental Retardation Research* (pp. 222–235). Proceedings of the Eighth Congress of the International Association for the Scientific Study of Mental Deficiency. London: Routledge.

Borkowski, J.C. & Cavanaugh, J.C. (1979). Maintenance and generalization of skills and strategies by the retarded. In N.R. Ellis (Ed.) *Handbook of Mental Deficiency, Psychological Theory and Research* (2nd edn) (pp. 569–617). Hillsdale, NJ: Erlbaum.

Bortner, M. (1978). AAMD Adaptive Behavior Scale, 1974 revision. In O.K. Buros (Ed.) *The Eighth Mental Measurements Yearbook* (pp. 492–493). Highland Park, NJ: Gryphon.

Braddock, D. (1987). *Federal Policy Toward Mental Retardation and Developmental Disabilities.* Baltimore, MD: Brookes.

Bradley, T.B. (1983). Remediation of cognitive deficits: a critical appraisal of the Feuerstein model. *Journal of Mental Deficiency Research*, **27**, 79–82.

Bricker, W.A. & Bricker, D.D. (1970). Development of receptive vocabulary in severely retarded children. *American Journal of Mental Deficiency*, **74**, 599–607.

Brolin, D., Durrand, R., Cromer, K. & Muller, P. (1975). Post-school adjustment of educable retarded students. *Education and Training of the Mentally Retarded*, **10**, 144–149.

Brown, A.L. (1974). The role of strategic behaviour in retardate memory. In N.R. Ellis (Ed.) *International Review of Research in Mental Retardation*, vol. 7 (pp. 55–111). New York: Academic Press.

Brown, A.L. (1978). Knowing when, where, and how to remember: a problem of metacognition. In R. Glaser (Ed.) *Advances in Instructional Psychology*, vol. 1 (pp. 77–165). Hillsdale, NJ: Erlbaum.

Brown, R.I. (Ed.) (1988). *Quality of Life for Handicapped People.* London: Croom Helm.

Bruininks, R., Woodcock, R.W., Weatherman, R.F. & Hill, B.H. (1984). *Scales of Independent Behaviour.* Allen, TX: DLM Teaching Resources.

Bruininks, R., Woodcock, R.W., Weatherman, R.F. & Hill, B.H. (1986). *Inventory for Client and Agency Planning*. Allen, TX: DLM Teaching Resources.

Bruininks, R.H., Meyers, C.E., Sigford, B.B. & Lakin, K.S. (Eds) (1981). *Deinstitutionalization and Community Adjustment of Mentally Retarded People.* AAMD Monograph No. 4. Washington, DC: American Association on Mental Deficiency.

Bruininks, R.H., Thurlow, M.L., McGrew, K.S. & Lewis, D.R. (1990). Dimensions of community adjustment among young adults with intellectual disabilities. In W.I. Frazer (Ed.) *Key Issues in Mental Retardation Research* (pp. 435–448). Proceedings from the Eighth Congress of the International Association for the Scientific Study of Mental Deficiency. London: Routledge.

Bryant, P.E. (1967). Selective attention and learning in severely subnormals. In B.W. Richards (Ed.) *Proceedings of the First Congress of the International Association for the Scientific Study of Mental Deficiency* (pp. 264–269). London: Michael Jackson.

Butler, E.W. & Bjaanes, A.T. (1977). A typology of community care facilities and differential normalization outcomes. In P. Mittler (Ed.) *Research into Practice in Mental Retardation*, vol. 1. *Care and Intervention* (pp. 337–347). Proceedings of the Fourth Congress of International Association for the Scientific Study of Mental Deficiency. Baltimore, MD: University Park Press.

Campione, J.C. & Brown, A.L. (1978). Toward a theory of intelligence: contributions for research with retarded children. *Intelligence*, **2**, 279–304.

Carr, E.G. & Durand, V.M. (1985). Reducing behaviour problems through functional communication training. *Journal of Applied Behaviour Analysis*, **18**, 111–126.

Clarke, A.D.B. (1977). Presidential address: from research to practice. In P. Mittler (Ed.) *Research to Practice in Mental Retardation*, vol. 1. *Care and Intervention* (pp. A-7–19). Proceedings of the Fourth Congress of the International Association for the Scientific Study of Mental Deficiency. Baltimore, MD: University Park Press.

Clarke, A.D.B. & Clarke, A.M. (1984). Constancy and change in the growth of human characteristics: the first Jack Tizard Memorial Lecture. *Journal of Child Psychiatry*, **25**, 191–208.

Clarke, A.M. & Clarke, A.D.B. (Eds) (1958). *Mental Deficiency. The Changing Outlook.* London: Methuen.

Clarke, A.M. & Clarke, A.D.B. (Eds) (1965). *Mental Deficiency. The Changing Outlook* (2nd edn). London: Methuen.

Clarke, A.M. & Clarke, A.D.B. (Eds) (1974). *Mental Deficiency. The Changing Outlook* (3rd edn). London: Methuen.

Clarke, A.M., Clarke, A.D.B. & Berg, J.M. (Eds) (1985). *Mental Deficiency. The Changing Outlook* (4th edn). London: Methuen.

Clausen, J. (1972). *Quo Vadis*, AAMD? *Journal of Special Education*, **6**, 51–60.

Cobb, H.V. (1966). The attitude of the retarded person toward himself. In International League of Societies for the Mentally Handicapped (Ed.) *Stress on Families of the Mentally Handicapped* (pp. 62–74). Brussels: International League of Societies for the Mentally Handicapped.

Cobb, H.V. (1967). The prediction of adult adjustment of the retarded. In B.W. Richards (Ed.) *Proceedings of the First Congress of the International Association for the Scientific Study of Mental Deficiency* (pp. 314–322). London: Michael Jackson.

Cobb, H.V. (1972). *The Forecast of Fulfillment: A Review of Research on Predictive Assessment of the Adult Retarded for Social and Vocational Adjustment.* New York: Teachers College Press.

Cromwell, R.L. (1963). A social learning approach to mental retardation. In N.R. Ellis (Ed.) *Handbook of Mental Deficiency, Psychological Theory and Research* (pp. 41–90). New York: McGraw-Hill.

Das, J.P. (1973). Structure of cognitive abilities: evidence for simultaneous successive processing. *Journal of Educational Psychology*, **65**, 103–108.

Das, J.P. (1977) . Understanding intellectual dysfunctions. In P. Mittler (Ed.) *Research into Practice in Mental Retardation*, vol. II. *Education and Training* (pp. 63–66). Proceedings of the Fourth Congress of the International Association for the Scientific Study of Mental Deficiency.

Das, J.P. & Cummins, J. (1978). Academic performance and cognitive processes in EMR children. *American Journal of Mental Deficiency*, **83**, 197–199.

Das, J.P., Kirby, J. & Jarman, R.F. (1979). *Simultaneous and Successive Cognitive Processes.* New York: Academic Press.

Das, J.P., Smart, F. & Mulcahy, R.F. (1982). Reading disability and its relation to information integration. In J.P. Das, R. Mulcahy & A. Wall (Eds) *Theory and Research in Learning Disabilities* (pp. 85–109). New York: Plenum.

Edgerton, R. (1967). *The Cloak of Competence.* Berkeley, CA: University of California Press.

Edgerton, R.B. (1977). The study of community adaptation. Toward an understanding of lives in progress. In P. Mittler (Ed.) *Research to Practice in Mental Retardation*, vol. 1. *Care and Intervention* (pp. 371–378). Proceedings of the Fourth Congress of the International Association for the Scientific Study of Mental Deficiency. Baltimore, MD: University Park Press.

Ellis, N.R. (1963a). The stimulus trace and behavioural inadequacy. In N.R. Ellis (Ed.) *Handbook of Mental Deficiency, Psychological Theory and Research* (pp. 134–158). New York: McGraw-Hill.

Ellis, N.R. (1963b). Toilet training in the severely defective patient. *American Journal of Mental Deficiency*, **68**, 98–103.

Ellis, N.R. (Ed.) (1963c). *Handbook of Mental Deficiency, Psychological Theory and Research.* New York: McGraw-Hill.

Ellis, N.R. (Ed.) (1979). *Handbook of Mental Deficiency, Psychological Theory and Research* (2nd edn). Hillsdale, NJ: Erlbaum.

Ellis, N.R. & Cavalier, A.R. (1982). Research perspectives in mental retardation. In E. Zigler & D. Balla (Eds) *Mental Retardation. The Developmental-Difference Controversy* (pp. 121–152). Hillsdale, NJ: Lawrence Erlbaum Associates.

Emde, R. & Harman, R. (1985). *Continuities and Discontinuities in Development.* New York: Plenum.

Emerson, E.B. (1985). Evaluating the impact of deinstitutionalization on the lives of mentally retarded people. *American Journal of Mental Deficiency*, **90**, 277–288.

Emerson, E. (1990). Designing individual community-based placements as an alternative to institutions for people with severe mental handicap and severe behaviour problems. In W.I. Frazer (Ed.) *Key Issues in Mental Retardation Research* (pp. 395–404). Proceedings of the Eighth Congress of the International Association for the Scientific Study of Mental Deficiency. London: Routledge.

Emerson, E., Barrett, S., Bell, C., Cummings, R., McCool, C., Toogood, A., et al. (1987). *Developing Services for People with Severe Learning Difficulties and Challenging Behaviours.* Canterbury: Institute of Social and Applied Psychology, University of Kent.

Emerson, E. & Emerson, C. (1987). Barriers to the implementation of habilitation behaviour programs in an institutional setting. *Mental Retardation*, **25**, 101–106.

Evans, I.M. & Meyer, L.H. (1985). *An Educative Approach to Behavior Problems. A Practical Decision Model for Interventions with Severely Handicapped Learners.* Baltimore, MD: Brookes.

Evans, R.A. & Bilsky, L.H. (1979). Clustering and categorical list retention of mental deficiency in the mentally retarded. In N.R. Ellis (Ed.) *Handbook of Mental Deficiency, Psychological Theory and Research* (pp. 533–567). Hillsdale, NJ: Erlbaum.

Eyman, R.K., Silverstein, R., McLean, R. & Miller, C. (1977). Effects of residential setting on development. In P. Mittler (Ed.) *Research to Practice in Mental Retardation*, vol. I. *Care and Intervention* (pp. 305–314). Proceedings of the Fourth Congress of the International Association for the Scientific Study of Mental Deficiency. Baltimore, MD: University Park Press.

Felce, D. (1989). *Staffed Housing for Adults with Severe or Profound Mental Handicaps: The Andover Project.* Kidderminster: British Institute of Mental Handicap.

Feuerstein, R. (1977). Moderate learning experience. In P. Mittler (Ed.) *Research into Practice in Mental Retardation*, vol. II. *Education and Training* (pp. 105–116). Proceedings of the Fourth Congress of the International Association for the Scientific Study of Mental Deficiency. Baltimore, MD: University Park Press.

Feuerstein, R., Shalom, H., Narrol, H., Hoffman, M., Keram L., Katz, D., et al. (1972). *Studies in Cognitive Modifiability: The Dynamic Assessment of Retarded Performers*, vol. 1. *Clinical LPAD Battery.* Jerusalem: Hadassah-Wizo-Canada Research Institute.

Fraser, W.I. (Ed.) (1990). *Key Issues in Mental Retardation Research.* Proceedings of the Eighth Congress of the International Association for the Scientific Study of Mental Deficiency. London: Routledge.

Fuller, P. (1949). Operant conditioning of a vegetative human organism. *American Journal of Psychology*, **62**, 587–590.

Gibbens, T.C.N. & Robertson, G. (1983). A survey of the criminal careers of hospital order patients. *British Journal of Psychiatry*, **143**, 362–369.

Glidden, L.M. (1979). Training of learning and memory in retarded persons: strategies, techniques, and teaching tools. In N.R. Ellis (Ed.) *Handbook of Mental Deficiency, Psychological Theory and Research* (2nd edn) (pp. 619–657). Hillsdale, NJ: Erlbaum.

Gold, M. (1973). Research on the vocational habilitation of the retarded: the present, the future. In N.R. Ellis (Ed.) *International Review of Research in Mental Retardation*, vol. 6 (pp. 97–147). New York: Academic Press.

Goldstein, H. (1964). Social and occupational adjustment. In H.A. Stevens & R. Huber (Eds) *Mental Retardation. A Review of Research* (pp. 214–258). Chicago: University of Chicago Press.

Goode, D.A. (1988). *Quality of Life for Persons with Disabilities: A Review and Synthesis of the Literature.* New York: Westchester County Medical Center.

Greenspan, S. (1979). Social intelligence in the retarded. In N.R. Ellis (Ed.) *Handbook of Mental Deficiency, Psychological Theory and Research* (2nd edn) (pp. 483–531). New York: McGraw-Hill.

Grossman, H. (Ed.) (1973). *A Manual on Terminology and Classification in Mental Retardation.* Washington, DC: American Association on Mental Deficiency.

Guess, D., Sailor, W., Rutherford, G. & Baer, D.M. (1968). An experimental analysis of linguistic development: the productive use of the plural morpheme. *Journal of Applied Behaviour Analysis*, **1**, 297–306.

Gunzberg, H.S. (1958). Psychopathology with the feeble minded. In A.M. Clarke & A.D.B. Clarke (Eds) *Mental Deficiency. The Changing Outlook* (pp. 365–392). London: Methuen.

Gunzberg, H.S. (1967). The assessment and evaluation of social development in the mentally handicapped child. In B.W. Richards (Ed.) *Proceedings of the First Congress of the International Association for the Scientific Study of Mental Deficiency* (pp. 236–245). London: Michael Jackson.

Halpern, A.S. (1985). Transition: a look at the foundations. *Exceptional Children*, **61**, 479–486.

Haywood, H.C. (1967). Psychometric motivation and the efficiency of learning and performance in the mentally retarded. In B.W. Richards (Ed.) *Proceedings of the First Congress of the International Association for the Scientific Study of Mental Deficiency* (pp. 276–283). London: Michael Jackson.

Haywood, H.C. (1977). The ethics of doing research... and of not doing it. *American Journal of Mental Deficiency*, **81**, 311–317.

Haywood, H.C. (1979). What happened to mild and moderate mental retardation? *American Journal of Mental Deficiency*, **83**, 429–431.

Haywood, H.C. & Switzky, H.N. (1986). Intrinsic motivation and behaviour effectiveness in retarded persons. In N.R. Ellis & N.W. Bray (Eds) *International Review of Research in Mental Retardation*, vol. 14 (pp. 1–46). New York: Academic Press.

Heal, L.W. & Fujima, G.T. (1984). Toward a valid methodology for research on residential alternatives for developmentally disabled citizens. In N.R. Ellis (Ed.) *International Review of Research in Mental Retardation*, vol. 12 (pp. 205–244). New York: Academic Press.

Heal, L.W., Lakin, K.C., Bruininks, R.H., Hill, B.K. & Best-Sigford, B. (1984). Placement of mentally retarded residents from public residential facilities in the United States. In J.M. Berg (Ed.) *Perspectives and Progress in Mental Retardation*, vol. 1. *Social, Psychological and Educational Aspects* (pp. 351–361). Proceedings of the Sixth Congress of the International Association for the Scientific Study of Mental Deficiency. Baltimore, MD: University Park Press.

Heber, R. (Ed.) (1958). *A Manual on the Terminology and Classification in Mental Retardation.* Monograph (Suppl.). *American Journal of Mental Deficiency*, **64**, No. 2.

Herson, M. & Barlow, D.H. (1976). *Single Case Experimental Designs; Strategies for Studying Behaviour Change.* New York: Permagon Press.

Hogg, J. (1990). Mental handicap, ageing and the community. In W.I. Frazer (Ed.) *Key Issues in Mental Retardation Research* (pp. 460–473). Proceedings of the Eighth Congress of the International Association for the Scientific Study of Mental Deficiency. London: Routledge.

Horner, R.L., Dunlap, G. & Koegel, R.L. (Eds) (1985). *Generalisation and Maintenance. Lifestyle Changes in Applied Settings.* Baltimore, MD: Brookes.

Inhelder, B. (1968). *The Diagnosis of Reasoning in the Mentally Retarded.* New York: John Day.

Janicki, M.P. (1990). Service provision for ageing/aged persons with mental retardation. In W.I. Frazer (Ed.) *Key Issues in Mental Retardation Research* (pp. 466–473). Proceedings of the Eighth Congress of the International Association for the Scientific Study of Mental Deficiency. London: Routledge.

Justice, E.M. (1985). Metamemory: an aspect of metacognition in the mentally retarded. In N.R. Ellis & N.W. Bray (Eds) *International Review of Research in Mental Retardation*, vol. 13 (pp. 79–107). New York: Academic Press.

Kaufman, A.S. & Kaufman, P. (1983). *Kaufman Assessment Scale for Children.* Circle Plains, MN: American Guidance Service.

Kaufman, D. & Kaufman, P. (1979). Strategy training and remedial techniques. *Journal of Learning Disabilities*, **12**, 416–419.

Kiernan, C. (1985a). Behaviour modification. In A.M. Clarke & A.D.B. Clarke (Eds) *Mental Deficiency. The Changing Outlook* (4th edn) (pp. 465–511). London: Methuen.

Kiernan, C. (1985b). Communication. In A.M. Clarke & A.D.B. Clarke (Eds) *Mental Deficiency. The Changing Outlook* (4th edn) (pp. 584–638). London: Methuen.

Kiernan, C. (1991). Professional ethics: behaviour analysis and normalization. In B. Remington (Ed.) *The Challenge of Severe Mental Hardship. A Behaviour Analytic Approach* (pp. 369–390). Chichester: Wiley.

Kiernan, C.C. & Jones, M.C. (1980). The behaviour assessment battery for use with the profoundly retarded. In J. Hogg & P. Mittler (Eds) *Advances in Mental Handicap Research* (pp. 27–53). New York: Wiley.

Kirby, J.R. & Das, J.P. (1977). Reading achievement, IQ and simultaneous successive processing. *Journal of Educational Psychology*, **69**, 54–70.

Kushlick, A. (1975). Improving the services for the mentally handicapped. In C.C. Kiernan & F.P. Woodford (Eds) *Behaviour Modification with the Severely Retarded* (pp. 263–291). Amsterdam: Elsevier.

Kushlick, A. & Blunden, R. (1974). The epidemiology of mental subnormality. In A.M. Clarke & A.D.B. Clarke (Eds) *Mental Deficiency. The Changing Outlook* (3rd edn) (pp. 31–81). London: Methuen.

Landesman, S. (1986). Quality of life and personal life satisfaction: definition and measurement issues. *Mental Retardation*, **24**, 141–143.

La Vigna, G. & Donnellan, A. (1986). *Alternatives to Punishment: Solving Behavior Problems with Non-aversive Strategies*. New York: Irvington.

Lewis, D.R., Bruininks, R.H., Thurlow, M.L. & McGrew, K.S. (1990). Assessing post school effects of special education for youth with mental retardation through economic analysis. In W.I. Fraser (Ed.) *Key Issues in Mental Retardation Research* (pp. 426–434). Proceedings of the Eighth Congress of the International Association for the Scientific Study of Mental Deficiency. London: Routledge.

Lloyd, L.L. & Fuller, D.R. (1990). The role of iconicity and augmentative and alternative communicative-symbol learning. In W.I. Fraser (Ed.) *Key Issues in Mental Retardation Research* (pp. 295–306). Proceedings of the Eighth Congress of the International Association for the Scientific Study of Mental Deficiency. London: Routledge.

Lovaas, O.I. (1966). Program for establishment of speech in schizophrenic and autistic children. In J.K. Wing (Ed.) *Early Childhood Autism: Clinical Educational and Social Aspects* (pp. 115–144). London: Permagon Press.

Luria, A.R. (1963). Psychological studies of mental deficiency in the Soviet Union. In N.R. Ellis (Ed.) *Handbook of Mental Deficiency, Psychological Theory and Research* (pp. 353–390). New York: McGraw-Hill.

Luria, A.R. (1973). *The Working Brain*. Harmondsworth: Penguin.

Magerotte, G. (1977). Assessment of adaptive behaviour in Belgian schools. In P. Mittler (Ed.) *Research into Practice in Mental Retardation*, vol. II. *Education and Training* (pp. 191–195). Proceedings of the Fourth Congress of the International Association for the Scientific Study of Mental Deficiency. Baltimore, MD: University Park Press.

Malony, H. & Taplin, J. (1988). Deinstitutionalization of people with developmental disability. *Australia and New Zealand Journal of Developmental Disability*, **14**, 109–122.

Mansell, J., Brown, H., McGill, P., Hoskin, S., Lindley, P. & Emerson, E. (1987). *Bringing People Back Home: A Staff Training Initiative in Mental Handicap*. Bristol and Bexhill-on-Sea: National Health Service Training Authority and South East Thames Regional Health Authority.

Mau, F.C. & Wacker, D.P. (1994). Toward greater integration of basic and applied behavioural research: an introduction. *Journal of Applied Behaviour Analysis*, **27**, 569–574.

McClelland, D. (1978). Managing motivation to expand human freedom. *American Psychologist*, **33**, 201–210.

McConkey, R. (1990). Community reactions to group homes: contrasts between people living in areas with and without a group home. In W.I. Fraser (Ed.) *Key Issues in Mental Retardation Research* (pp. 415–425). Proceedings of the Eighth Congress of the International Association for the Scientific Study of Mental Deficiency. London: Routledge.

Menolascino, F.J. (1988). Guest editorial. *Australia and New Zealand Journal of Developmental Disabilities*, **14**, 1–2.

Mercer, C.D. & Snell, M.E. (1977). *Learning Theory Research in Mental Retardation: Implications for Teaching*. Columbus, OH: Merrill.

Mercer, J. (1992). The impact of changing paradigms of disability on mental retardation in the year 2000. In L. Rowitz (Ed.) *Mental Retardation in the Year 2000* (pp. 15–38). New York: Springer-Verlag.

Meyer, L.H. & Evans, I.M. (1989). *Non-aversive Intervention for Behavior Problems. A Manual for Home and Community*. Baltimore, MD: Brookes.

Mittler, P. (Ed.) (1977). *Research to Practice in Mental Retardation*. Proceedings of the Fourth Congress of International Association for the Scientific Study of Mental Deficiency, vols I, II and III. Baltimore, MD: University Park Press.

Mittler, P. (Ed.) (1981). *Frontiers of Knowledge in Mental Retardation.* Proceedings of the Fifth Congress of the International Association for the Scientific Study of Mental Deficiency, vols I and II. Baltimore, MD: University Park Press.

Morris, E.K. (1991). Deconstructing "technological to a fault". *Journal of Applied Behavior Analysis*, **24**, 411–416.

Murray, P. (1988). The study of the history of disability services: examining the past to improve the present and the future. *Australia and New Zealand Journal of Developmental Disabilities*, **14**, 93–102.

Nihira, K., Foster, R., Shellhaas, M. & Leland, H. (1969). *AAMD Adaptive Behaviour Scale.* Washington, DC: American Association on Mental Deficiency.

Nihira, K., Foster, R., Shellhaas, M. & Leland, H. (1974). *AAMD Adaptive Behaviour Scale, 1974 Revision.* Washington, DC: American Association on Mental Deficiency.

Nirje, B. (1969). The normalization and its human management implications. In R. Kugel & W. Wolfensberger (Eds) *Changing Patterns in Residential Services for the Mentally Retarded* (pp. 181–194). Washington, DC: President's Committee on Mental Retardation.

NSMHC (National Society for Mentally Handicapped Children) (1977). *STAMINA: Minimum Standards for ESN(S), Schools. ATCs and Residential Homes.* London: MENCAP.

O'Connor, N. (1958). Learning and mental defect. In A.M. Clarke & A.D.B. Clarke (Eds) *Mental Deficiency. The Changing Outlook* (pp. 43–64). London: Methuen.

O'Connor, N. (1965). Learning and mental defect. In A.M. Clarke & A.D.B. Clarke (Eds) *Mental Deficiency. The Changing Outlook* (2nd edn) (pp. 188–223). London: Methuen.

Oliver, C. (1995). Annotation: self-injurious behaviour in children with learning disabilities: recent advances in assessment and intervention. *Journal of Child Psychology and Psychiatry*, **36**, 909–927.

Parmenter, T.R. (1980). *Vocational Training for Independent Living.* New York: World Rehabilitation Fund.

Parmenter, T.R. (1984). Comparisons of the effects of teaching direct and indirect strategies on acquisition of reading skills by mildly developmentally disabled adolescents. In J.M. Berg (Ed.) *Perspectives and Progress in Mental Retardation*, vol. 1. *Social, Psychological and Educational Aspects* (pp. 293–301). Proceedings of the Sixth Congress of the International Association for the Scientific Study of Mental Deficiency. Baltimore, MD: University Park Press.

Parmenter, T.R. (1986a). *Bridges from School to Working Life for Handicapped Youth: The View from Australia.* New York: World Rehabilitation Fund.

Parmenter, T.R. (1986b). The relationship between selected information processing variables and reading skills in a sample of mildly retarded adolescents. In J.M. Berg (Ed.) *Science and Service in Mental Retardation* (pp. 205–215). Proceedings of the Seventh Congress of the International Association for the Scientific Study of Mental Deficiency. London: Methuen.

Parmenter, T.R. (1991). Has social policy left research behind? *Australia and New Zealand Journal of Developmental Disabilities*, **17**, 1–6.

Parmenter, T.R. (1992a). Quality of life for people with developmental disabilities. In N.W. Bray (Ed.) *International Review of Research in Mental Retardation*, vol. 18 (pp. 246–288). New York: Academic Press.

Parmenter, T.R. (1992b). International perspectives of vocational options for people with mental retardation. The promise and reality. *Mental Retardation*, **31**, 359–367.

Parmenter, T.R. (1999a). Effecting a system change in the delivery of employment services for people with disabilities: a view from Australia. *Journal of Vocational Rehabilitation*, **13**, 117–229.

Parmenter, T.R. (1999b). Implications of social policy for service delivery: the promise and the reality. Are we getting real? *Journal of Intellectual and Developmental Disability*, **24**, 321–331.

Parmenter, T.R. (2001). Intellectual disabilities—*Quo vadis?* In G.A. Albrecht, K.D. Seelman & M. Bury (Eds) *Handbook of Disability Studies* (pp. 267–296). New York: Sage.

Parmenter, T.R. & Gray, C. (1990). *Evaluation of the Training Resource Unit for Children and Adolescence with Severe Behavioural and Intellectual Disabilities.* Sydney: Unit for Rehabilitation Studies, Macquarie University.

President's Committee on Mental Retardation (1975). *Mental Retardation... the Known and Unknown.* Washington, DC: Government Printing Office.

President's Committee on Mental Retardation (1992). *Entering the Era of Human Ecology.* Department of Health, Education and Welfare. Publication No. (OS) 72–77.

Primrose, D.A.A. (Ed.) (1971). *Proceedings of the Second Congress of the International Association for the Scientific Study of Mental Deficiency*. Warsaw: Polish Medical Publishers.

Primrose, D.A.P. (Ed.) (1975). *Proceedings of the Third Congress of the International Association for the Scientific Study of Mental Deficiency*, vols I and II. Larbert, Stirlingshire: Royal Scottish National Hospital.

Rand, Y., Feuerstein, R., Tannerbaum, A.J., Jensen, M.R. & Hoffman, M.B. (1977). An analysis of the effects of instrumental enrichment on disadvantaged adolescents. In P. Mittler (Ed.) *Research into Practice in Mental Retardation*, vol. II. *Education and Training* (pp. 117–128). Proceedings of the Fourth Congress of the International Association for the Scientific Study of Mental Deficiency. Baltimore, MD: University Park Press.

Reiss, S. (1988). Dual diagnosis in the United States. *Australia and New Zealand Journal of Developmental Disabilities*, **14**, 43–48.

Remington, B. (1991). Behaviour analysis and severe mental handicap: the dialogue between research and application. In B. Remington (Ed.) *The Challenge of Severe Mental Handicap* (pp. 1–22). Chichester: Wiley.

Remington, B. (1998). Applied behaviour analysis and intellectual disability: a long-term relationship. *Journal of Intellectual and Developmental Disability*, **23**, 121–135.

Richards, B.W. (Ed.) (1968). *Proceedings of the First Congress of the International Association for the Scientific Study of Mental Deficiency*. London: Michael Jackson.

Richards, B.W., Clarke, A.D.B. & Shapiro, A. (1962). *Proceedings of the London Conference on the Scientific Study of Mental Deficiency.* Dagenham: May & Baker.

Richardson, S.A. (1977). Mental retardation in the community. The transition from childhood to adulthood. In P. Mittler (Ed.) *Research to Practice in Mental Retardation*, vol. 1. *Care and Intervention* (pp. 363–369). Proceedings of the Fourth Congress of the International Association for the Scientific Study of Mental Deficiency. Baltimore, MD: University Park Press.

Richardson, S.A., Gouldron, K.J., Koller, H. & Katz, M. (1990). The long term influence of the family of upbringing on young adults with mild mental retardation. In W.I. Frazer (Ed.) *Key Issues in Mental Retardation Research* (pp. 190–202). Proceedings of the Eighth Congress of the International Association for the Scientific Study of Mental Deficiency. London: Routledge.

Richardson, S.A. & Koller, H. (1996). *Twenty-Two Years. Carers and Consequence of Mental Retardation.* Cambridge, MA: Harvard University Press.

Richardson, S.A., Koller, H. & Katz, M. (1990). Job histories in open employment of a population of young adults with mental retardation. In W.I. Frazer (Ed.) *Key Issues in Mental Retardation Research* (pp. 449–459). Proceedings of the Eighth Congress of the International Association for the Scientific Study of Mental Deficiency. London: Routledge.

Risley, T.R. & Wolf, M.M. (1967). Establishing functional speech in echolalic children. *Behavior Research and Therapy*, **5**, 73–88.

Rosen, M., Clarke, G.R. & Kivitz, M.S. (1977). *Habilitation of the Handicapped. New Dimensions in Programs for the Developmentally Disabled.* Baltimore, MD: University Park Press.

Rosenberg, S. (1963). Problem-solving and conceptual behaviour. In N.R. Ellis (Ed.) *Handbook of Mental Deficiency, Psychological Theory and Research* (pp. 439–462). New York: McGraw-Hill.

Ross, L.E. (1966). Classical conditioning and discrimination learning research with the mentally retarded. In N.R. Ellis (Ed.) *International Review of Research in Mental Retardation*, vol. 1 (pp. 21–54). New York: Academic Press.

Rusch, F. (Ed.) (1986) *Competitive Employment Issues and Strategies.* Baltimore, MD: Brookes.

Sailor, W., Guess, D., Rutherford, G. & Baer, D.M. (1968). Control of tantrum behaviour by operant techniques during experimental verbal training. *Journal of Applied Behavior Analysis*, **1**, 237–243.

Scheerenberger, R.C. (1987). *A History of Mental Retardation. A Quarter Century of Promise.* Baltimore, MD: Brookes.

Schiefelbusch, R.L. (Ed.) (1963). Language studies in mentally retarded children. *Journal of Speech and Hearing Disorders*, Monograph Suppl. No. 10.

Schalock, R.L. (Ed.) (1990). *Quality of Life: Perspectives and Issues.* Washington, DC: American Association on Mental Retardation.

Schroeder, S. (1991). Biological and behavioural interaction in mental retardation research. *Psychology on Mental Retardation and Developmental Disabilities*, **17**, 1–6.

Schroeder, S.R., Malick, J.A. & Schroeder, C.S. (1979). Management of severe behavior problems of the retarded. In N.R. Ellis (Ed.) *Handbook of Mental Deficiency, Psychological Theory and Research* (2nd edn) (pp. 341–366). Hillsdale, NJ: Erlbaum.

Seltzer, M.M. & Litchfield, L.C. (1984). Community reaction to community residences. A study of factors related to community response. In J.M. Berg (Ed.) *Perspectives and Progress in Mental Retardation*, vol. 1. *Social, Psychological and Educational Aspects* (pp. 393–399). Proceedings of the Sixth Congress of the International Association for the Scientific Study of Mental Deficiency. Baltimore, MD: University Park Press.

Semmel, M.I., Bateman, B., O'Connor, N. & Miller, M.B. (1967). Research on the language behaviour of mentally retarded children. In B.W. Richards (Ed.) *Proceedings of the First Congress of the International Association for the Scientific Study of Mental Deficiency* (pp. 715–726). London: Michael Jackson.

Silverstein, A.B. (1970). The measurement of intelligence. In N.R. Ellis (Ed.) *International Review of Research in Mental Retardation*, vol. 4 (pp. 194–221). New York: Academic Press.

Simpson, M.K. (1998). The roots of normalization: a reappraisal. *Journal of Intellectual Disability Research*, **42**, 1–7.

Skinner, B. (1968). *The Technology of Teaching.* New York: Appleton-Century-Crofts.

Skinner, B. (1975). The steep and theory way to a science of behaviour. *American Psychologist*, **30**, 42–49.

Skinner, B. (1983). Origins of a behaviourist. *Psychology Today*, **17**, 22–38.

Skinner, B.F. (1938). *The Behaviour of Organisms.* New York: Appleton-Century-Crofts.

Skodak, M. (1967). Adult status of individuals who experienced early intervention. In B.W. Richards (Ed.) *Proceedings of the First Congress of the International Association for the Scientific Study of Mental Deficiency* (pp. 11–18). London: Michael Jackson.

Spitz, H.H. (1979). Beyond field theory in the study of mental deficiency. In N.R. Ellis (Ed.) *Handbook of Mental Deficiency, Psychological Theory and Research* (pp. 121–141). Hillsdale, NJ: Erlbaum.

Spivack, G. (1963). Perceptual processes. In N.R. Ellis (Ed.) *Handbook of Mental Deficiency, Psychological Theory and Research* (pp. 480–511). New York: McGraw-Hill.

Spradlin, J.E. (1958). Language and communication of mental defectives. In N.R. Ellis (Ed.) *Handbook of Mental Deficiency, Psychological Theory and Research* (pp. 512–555). New York: McGraw-Hill.

Spradlin, J.E. & Girardeau, F.L. (1966). The behaviour of moderately and severely retarded persons. In N.R. Ellis (Ed.) *International Review of Research in Mental Retardation*, vol. 1 (pp. 257–298). New York: Academic Press.

Stanovich, K.E. (1978). Information processing in mentally retarded individuals. In N.R. Ellis (Ed.) *International Review of Mental Retardation*, vol. 9 (pp. 29–56). New York: Academic Press.

Sternberg, R.J. & Sheer, L.C. (1985). A triarchic theory of mental retardation. In N.R. Ellis & N. Bray (Eds) *International Review of Research in Mental Retardation*, vol. 13 (pp. 301–326). New York: Academic Press.

Stevens, H. (1967). Mental deficiency in an international perspective. In B.W. Richards (Ed.) *Proceedings of the First Congress of the International Association for the Scientific Study of Mental Deficiency* (pp. xxxi–xli). London: Michael Jackson.

Stevens, H. (1985). American Association on Mental Deficiency: participation in international activities. *Mental Retardation*, **23**, 215–218.

Stevens, H.A. & Heber, R. (Eds) (1964). *Mental Retardation. A Review of Research.* Chicago: University of Chicago Press.

Stevenson, H.W. (1963). Discrimination learning. In N.R. Ellis (Ed.) *Handbook of Mental Deficiency, Psychological Theory and Research*, vol. 1 (pp. 424–438). New York: McGraw-Hill.

Stokes, T.F. & Baer, D.M. (1977). An implicit technology of generalization. *Journal of Applied Behavior Analysis*, **10**, 349–369.

Taylor, A.M. & Turnure, J.E. (1979). Imaging and verbal elaboration with retarded children: effects on learning and memory. In N.R. Ellis (Ed.) *Handbook of Mental Deficiency, Psychological Theory and Research* (2nd edn) (pp. 391–423). New York: McGraw-Hill.

Thorndike, E. (1898). Animal intelligence: an experimental study of the associative processes in animals. *Psychological Review*, Monograph Suppl. No. 8.

Thorndike, E. (1913). The psychology of learning. *Educational Psychology*, **2**, 19–23.

Tizard, J. (1958). Longitudinal and follow-up studies. In A.M. Clarke & A.D.B. Clarke (Eds) *Mental Deficiency. The Changing Outlook* (pp. 422–449). London: Methuen.

Tizard, J. (1965). Longitudinal and follow-up studies. In A.M. Clarke & A.D.B. Clarke (Eds) *Mental Deficiency. The Changing Outlook* (2nd edn) (pp. 478–509). London: Methuen.

Tomiyasu, Y. (1977). Measurement of adaptive behaviour in Japan. In P. Mittler (Ed.) *Research into Practice in Mental Retardation*, vol. II. *Education and Training* (pp. 177–183). Proceedings of the Fourth Congress of the International Association for the Scientific Study of Mental Deficiency. Baltimore, MD: University Park Press.

Turnbull, A.P., Brotherson, M.J. & Summers, J.A. (1985). The impact of deinstitutionalization on families. A family systems approach. In R.H. Bruininks & K.C. Lakin (Eds) *Living and Learning in the Least Restrictive Environment* (pp. 115–140) Baltimore, MD: Brookes.

United Nations (1971). *On the Declaration on the Rights of Mentally Retarded Persons.* General Assembly Resolution 2857 (xxvi). New York: Author.

US Department of Health, Education, and Welfare (1955). Mental retardation. In *Activities of the US Department of Health, Education, and Welfare.* Washington, DC: US Government Printing Office.

Van Houten, R., Atelrod, S., Bailey, J.S., Farell, J.E., Foxx, R.M., Iwata, B.A., et al. (1988). The rights to behavioural treatment. *Journal of Applied Behavior Analysis*, **21**, 381–384.

Walker, N. & McCabe, S. (1973). *Crime and Insanity in England*, vol. II. *New Solutions and New Problems*. Edinburgh: Edinburgh University Press.

Ward, J., Parmenter, T.R., Debenham, D. & Miller, V. (1972). Vocational preparation for the mildly retarded—an investigation into employment patterns and related factors. *National Rehabilitation Digest*, **1**, 29–45.

Watson, J.B. (1913). Psychology as the behaviourist views it. *Psychological Review*, **20**, 158–177.

Watson, J.B. (1924). *Behaviourism.* Chicago: People's Institute.

Watson, L.S. (1968). Application of behaviour-shaping devices to training severely and profoundly mentally retarded children in an institutional setting. *Mental Retardation*, **6**, 21–23.

Wehmeyer, M.L., Abery, B.H., Mithang, D.E. & Stancliffe, R. (2003). *Theory in Self Determination.* Springfield, IL: Charles C. Thomas.

Whitman, T.L. & Scibak, J.W. (1979). Behavior modification research with the severely and profoundly retarded. In N.R. Ellis (Ed.) *Handbook of Mental Deficiency, Psychological Theory and Research* (2nd edn) (pp. 289–340). Hillsdale, NJ: Erlbaum.

Wiese, M. (1993). Stress and mental health of the family with a child with an intellectual disability and challenging behaviour. Unpublished master's thesis. Sydney: Macquarie University.

Wolfensberger, W. (1969). The origin and nature of our institutional models. In R. Kugel & W. Wolfensberger (Eds) *Changing Patterns in Residential Services for the Mentally Retarded* (pp. 59–177). Washington, DC: President's Committee on Mental Retardation.

World Health Organization (WHO) (2001). *The International Classification of Function, Disability and Health.* Geneva: Author.

Young, L., Sigafoos, J., Suttie, J., Ashman, A. & Grevell, P. (1998). Deinstitutionalisation of persons with intellectual disabilities: a review of Australian studies. *Journal of Intellectual and Developmental Disability*, **23**, 155–170.

Ysseldyke, J.E. (1982). Planning instructional interventions: what does research say? Paper presented to the Annual Committee of the American Psychological Association. Washington, DC.

Zeaman, D. & House, B.J. (1958). The role of attention in retardate discrimination learning. In N.R. Ellis (Ed.) *Handbook of Mental Deficiency, Psychological Theory and Research* (pp. 391–423). New York: McGraw-Hill.

Zeaman, D. & House, B.J. (1963). The role of attention in retardate discrimination learning. In N.R. Ellis (Ed.) *Handbook of Mental Deficiency, Psychological Theory and Research* (pp. 159–222). Hillsdale, NJ: Erlbaum.

Zeaman, D. & House, B. (1979). A review of attention theory. In N.R. Ellis (Ed.) *Handbook of Mental Deficiency, Psychological Theory and Research* (2nd edn) (pp. 163–170). Hillsdale, NJ: Erlbaum.

Zigler, E. (1966). Research on personality structure in the retardate. In N.R. Ellis (Ed.) *International Review of Research in Mental Retardation*, vol. 1 (pp. 77–108). New York: Academic Press.

Zigler, E. (1978). National crisis in mental retardation research. *American Journal of Mental Deficiency*, **83**, 1–8.

Zigler, E. (1982). Developmental versus difference theories of mental retardation and the problem of motivation. In E. Zigler & D. Balla (Eds) *Mental Retardation. The Developmental-Difference Controversy* (pp. 163–188). Hillsdale, NJ: Erlbaum.

Zigler, E. & Balla, D. (1979). The social policy implications of a research program on the institutionalization on retarded persons. In P. Mittler (Ed.) *Research to Practice in Mental Retardation*, vol. 1. *Care and Intervention* (pp. 267–274). Proceedings of the Fourth Congress of the International Association for the Scientific Study of Mental Deficiency. Baltimore, MD: University Park Press.

Zigler, E. & Balla, D. (Eds) (1982). *Mental Retardation. The Developmental-Difference Controversy.* Hillsdale, NJ: Erlbaum.

CHAPTER 2

Cultural Issues

Chris Hatton
Lancaster University, UK

OVERVIEW

Increasing research attention is being paid to the influence of culture on the lives of people with intellectual disabilities, although the quantity of research activity devoted to cultural issues is still comparatively small and marginal. This chapter has two major aims, with the combined purpose of stimulating research examining the role of culture in the lives of people with intellectual disabilities. The first aim is to outline some basic conceptual, methodological, and practical issues underpinning cross-cultural research concerning people with intellectual disabilities. The second major aim of the chapter is to argue that a cultural perspective is crucial for all research concerning people with intellectual disabilities, not just those research projects focusing on specific cultural groups.

The chapter will begin by briefly surveying the current state of research concerning culture with people with intellectual disabilities. The constructs of race, ethnicity, and culture will be discussed and differentiated in terms of their potential as explanatory constructs when investigating cross-cultural differences among people with intellectual disabilities. Next, three competing paradigms will be outlined which have very different consequences for cross-cultural research; the absolutist, relativist, and universalist positions. The chapter will then focus on methodological issues when conducting research with a cultural focus. First, issues involved in conducting emic research, designed to build up a detailed picture of a particular cultural group, will be outlined. Second, issues involved in conducting etic research, designed to compare different cultures, will be discussed. Finally, some general recommendations for cultural research involving people with intellectual disabilities will be made.

Culture and People with Intellectual Disabilities: The State of the Research Literature

The role of culture in the lives of people with intellectual disabilities is becoming increasingly visible, both to service professionals and researchers. Many countries that in their recent past have been relatively homogeneous in terms of ethnicity (an obvious marker of

The International Handbook of Applied Research in Intellectual Disabilities. Edited by E. Emerson, C. Hatton, T. Thompson and T.R. Parmenter © 2004 John Wiley & Sons, Ltd. ISBN 0-471-49709-6.

certain aspects of culture; see below) are becoming more ethnically diverse and complex (e.g., Shinagawa & Jang, 1998), with a corresponding increase in the ethnic diversity of populations of people with intellectual disabilities (e.g., Emerson & Hatton, 1999).

However, as with social science research generally (e.g., Graham, 1992), research concerning people with intellectual disabilities has largely focused on white, middle-class populations, neglecting lower socio-economic status groups and minority ethnic groups (Mink, 1997). A recent review of research concerning persons of colour with intellectual disabilities in the USA and the UK (Hatton, 2002) identified a sparse and patchy published research literature. For example, even basic epidemiological research concerning the prevalence of intellectual disabilities across ethnic groups is rare and methodologically problematic, with few attempts to establish the cross-cultural equivalence of constructs such as intelligence or adaptive behaviour, or the measures required to test these constructs. There is also very little research concerning the experiences of adults of colour with intellectual disabilities. The bulk of the existing research literature focuses on families with a child with intellectual disabilities (for reviews, see Mink, 1997; Glidden, Rogers-Dulan & Hill, 1999; Hatton, 2002; Chapter 6, this volume), including topics such as the use of education and other services, the material and social resources of families, familial coping, and parental distress. Understandably, much of this research has been concerned with documenting inequalities in resources and access to services, although the result of this focus has been research that is sometimes atheoretical and methodologically limited.

This lack of attention to cultural issues is also illustrated by an examination of the leading journals concerned with people with intellectual disabilities. Table 2.1 presents a content analysis of three journals (*American Journal on Mental Retardation* [*AJMR*], *Mental Retardation* [*MR*], and *Journal of Intellectual Disability Research* [*JIDR*]) for the years 2000–2002, focusing on the reporting of the ethnicity of study samples, the ethnic composition of study samples where reported, the number of studies reporting cross-cultural comparisons or within-culture variations, and the number of countries reported as author affiliations.

As Table 2.1 shows, a minority of empirical studies in *AJMR* (27%) reported the ethnic composition of the participant samples employed. Of those that did report the ethnicity of participants, most participants (80%) were white. Only two studies reported planned cross-cultural comparisons (Naglieri & Rojahn, 2001; Edeh & Hickson, 2002), and one study focused exclusively on Hispanic families (Skinner, Correa, Skinner & Bailey, 2001). No other studies conducted cross-cultural subgroup comparisons or separate analyses within cultural subgroups.

A higher proportion of empirical studies in *MR* reported the ethnic composition of their samples (44%), with an average lower proportion of white participants (66%). Only one study reported a planned cross-national comparison (Shin, 2002), and three studies focused exclusively on Hispanic or Latino families (Blue-Banning, Turnbull & Pereira, 2000; Magana, 2000; Turnbull, Blue-Banning & Pereira, 2000). Most notably, a number of studies reported the collection or secondary analysis of large-scale data sets (Olney & Kennedy, 2001; Oswald, Coutinho, Best & Nguyen, 2001; Rhoades & Altman, 2001; Yamaki & Fujiura, 2002); all these studies reported the ethnic composition of their samples and conducted cross-cultural analyses. Perhaps surprisingly, qualitative studies designed to produce a rich picture of the lives of people with intellectual disabilities rarely mentioned ethnicity or culture as issues (e.g., Peter, 2000; Kahn-Freedman, 2001; Smith, 2001; Cooney, 2002).

Table 2.1 Reporting of ethnicity and ethnic composition of samples in the *American Journal on Mental Retardation, Mental Retardation,* and *Journal of Intellectual Disability Research,* 2000–2002

	American Journal on Mental Retardation (AJMR)[a]		*Mental Retardation (MR)*[b]		*Journal of Intellectual Disability Research (JIDR)*	
	n	%	*n*	%	*n*	%
Total empirical articles concerning individual participants	93		70		138	
Empirical articles reporting sample ethnicity	25	27	31	44	19	14
Total proportion of white ethnic populations in studies reporting ethnicity data		80		66		89
Studies reporting cross-cultural comparisons	2		5		2	
Studies reporting within-culture analyses	1		3		0	
Country of author affiliation: total	14		10		21	

a: Number 5, 2000 missing.
b: Number 5, 2000 missing.

Very few empirical studies in *JIDR* (14%) reported the ethnic composition of participant samples; where ethnicity was reported, samples were overwhelmingly white (89%). Only two studies in *JIDR* reported planned cross-cultural comparisons within one country (Molteno, Molteno, Finchilescu & Dawes, 2001; McGrother, Bhaumik, Thorpe, Watson & Taub, 2002), and one study used ethnicity as a covariate (Joyce, Ditchfield & Harris, 2001). In addition, three papers in *JIDR*, although not reporting the ethnicity of their samples, were concerned with evaluating the applicability of measures in a different country from the country where the measure was developed (e.g., Dekker, Nunn & Coot, 2002; Gonzalez-Gordon, Salvador-Carulla, Romero, Gonzalez-Sais & Romero, 2002; Gustafson & Sonnander, 2002).

For all three journals, although the research work published is international in scope (from 14, 10, and 21 countries, respectively, in *AJMR*, *MR*, and *JIDR*), it is clearly not routinely addressing culture as a potentially important aspect of the lives of people with intellectual disabilities. In all three journals, most papers did not report the ethnicity of their participant samples, the implicit assumption being either that such samples were ethnically homogeneous or that culture was not relevant. Given that almost all the constructs and measures used in intellectual disability research have been derived from white, English-speaking populations, this lack of attention to culture assumes the cross-cultural applicability of these constructs and measures rather than testing this applicability empirically.

Where the ethnicity of participant samples was reported, the majority of samples were white, and cross-ethnic group comparisons or within-ethnic group analyses were rarely conducted. In many studies, this was a function of the relative ethnic homogeneity of participant samples (as in administratively defined samples), although such studies again often implicitly assume either the cross-cultural applicability of constructs and measures or the irrelevance of culture.

With such culturally and ethnically homogeneous samples, cultural and ethnic variations are extremely unlikely to be identified and therefore investigated, with the consequence that much theory in intellectual disability research ignores the roles of culture or ethnicity as influences on behaviour. Similar issues apply to measures developed with homogeneous samples—such measures also rarely take into account linguistic, cultural, or ethnic variation. The risk of such a restricted research endeavour is that such culturally limited theories are assumed to be universally applicable, making the issue of cross-cultural variation invisible and leading to a self-perpetuating cycle of lack of research attention to cultural issues.

RESEARCHING CULTURE: BASIC ISSUES

Clearly, the current research endeavour concerning the role of culture in the lives of people with intellectual disabilities is severely limited. To increase the quality as well as the quantity of research including cultural issues, researchers need to be clear about the basic assumptions underpinning their research activity. The most basic issue researchers need to address is that of definition.

Defining Race, Ethnicity, and Culture

The terms "race", "ethnicity", and "culture" are often used interchangeably in research concerning people with intellectual disabilities, with considerable confusion and inconsistency in the terms used (for example, in the sample of journals reported above, US studies used the terms "white", "white non-Hispanic", "Caucasian", "Euro-American", "majority", and "non-minority" for presumably similar ethnic communities). However, distinguishing between these terms is crucial when conducting research (see Mink, 1997, for a thorough review in relation to people with intellectual disabilities). Whether one uses race, ethnicity, or culture as an explanatory variable in research entails very different assumptions about which underlying factors determine variations in the prevalence, circumstances, or life experiences of people with intellectual disabilities. Similar issues arise when considering service provision and professional practice concerning people with intellectual disabilities; assumptions of the importance of race, ethnicity, or culture will lead to very different conclusions about the volume and nature of appropriate service provision, with potentially harmful consequences for people with intellectual disabilities.

Race is commonly defined as a population distinguished as a discrete group on the basis of genetically transmitted physical features, such as skin colour (Betancourt & Lopez, 1995). As the genetic characteristics used to distinguish racial groups are comparatively small and arbitrary (relating to a small number of physical characteristics), the concept of race has very little validity as an explanatory construct. For example, 85.4% of all human genetic variation is accounted for by variations within a specific nation or tribe, with 8.3% accounted for by national or tribal differences within major racial groups and only 6.3% accounted for by differences between major racial groups (Lewontin, 1995). When one considers that specific genetic or chromosomal syndromes can result in widely different abilities and behaviours, as illustrated by behavioural phenotype research (see Chapter 9, this volume), the relatively small and arbitrary set of genes underpinning racial differences are unlikely to account for variations in abilities or behaviour among people with intellectual disabilities. The eugenic political uses of racist explanations of behaviour (Herrnstein & Murray, 1994) illustrate the negative consequences of using race as an explanatory construct for many people with intellectual disabilities (Smith, 1995).

Ethnicity is often used interchangeably with race, yet the construct of ethnicity is essentially socio-political rather than biological (Betancourt & Lopez, 1995). Ethnicity refers to a set of individuals who share a common and distinctive heritage, and who have a sense of identity as a group. However, ethnicity is not necessarily a monolithic construct. For example, as Mink (1997) notes, behavioural ethnicity (distinctive beliefs, values, norms, and languages that underpin social behaviour) and ideological ethnicity (customs and beliefs that are observed, but are not central to the person's daily life) may be quite different. Thus, identification with an ethnic group may be associated with diverse beliefs and behaviours, which are subject to change over time as different ethnic communities interact with each other (see, for example, research using the concept of "acculturation"; Berry, 1995). Although there is a substantial overlap between the constructs of ethnicity and culture, there are some factors that specifically relate to ethnicity rather than culture, such as ethnic identification, perceived discrimination, and bilingualism (Betancourt & Lopez, 1995). Therefore, when considering ethnicity as an explanatory variable, it is important to specify which aspects of ethnicity are considered to be important and the hypothesised mechanisms through which ethnicity accounts for any observed differences or similarities.

Culture is a frequently used but often poorly defined construct, and is frequently confused with ethnicity and race. Most definitions of culture emphasise aspects of individuals' physical and social environments that are shared by a group, and are learned or transmitted across generations (Betancourt & Lopez, 1995). Of particular importance here is subjective culture—collective beliefs, values, and social norms identified by individuals as shared. Cultures may be multiple or overlapping for an individual, although it is likely that subjective subcultures are nested within a broad cultural framework that contains the self-evident, unspoken assumptions, or worldviews, of a cultural group (Kluckhohn, 1956). While ethnicity is an important dimension of cultural difference, it is important to note that there are many other sources of cultural variation across individuals, such as local or regional affiliations and perceived social class. There have also been recent changes in theoretical conceptions of culture from something that is "given" (that is, predates and determines individual behaviour) to something that is "created" (culture exists as a set of appraisals which are created) (Berry, 1999). As with ethnicity, the construct of culture is of little value as an explanatory construct without specifying which aspects of culture are hypothesised to be important, and the mechanisms through which these aspects of culture operate.

Paradigms of Cross-Cultural Research

Cross-cultural researchers in social science (see Berry, Poortinga & Pandey, 1997; Berry, Poortinga, Segall & Dasen, 2002) have not reached a consensus on the feasibility of constructing valid cross-cultural theories of behaviour. In a review, Berry (1999) discusses the variety of perspectives on culture assumed by different approaches to psychological research. Berry (1999) identifies three theoretical orientations within cross-cultural psychology that are equally applicable to all social science disciplines: absolutism, relativism, and universalism.

Absolutism assumes that human phenomena are basically the same, in a qualitative sense, across all cultures. Thus, culture is assumed to play little or no role in either the meaning or display of human characteristics, with biology or economic circumstances usually assumed to underpin cross-cultural differences. The wholesale adoption of concepts such as "depression" across cultures, along with the use of (translated) standardised measures, is assumed to be unproblematic on this view (but see Helman, 2000).

In contrast to the absolutist approach is relativism, which assumes that all human behaviour is culturally determined. Thus, each culture is unique and incommensurable with other cultures, and must be understood "on its own terms" (often called an emic approach). On this view, cross-cultural comparisons are theoretically indefensible and inevitably ethnocentric, and attempts to look for cross-cultural universals should not be made.

The third approach, universalism, lies somewhere between the absolutist and relativist positions. This approach assumes that basic human characteristics are universal, and that culture influences the development and display of these characteristics. The degree to which particular characteristics and behaviours are cross-culturally universal or culturally patterned will vary, and can be tested empirically (often called an etic approach). For example, cross-cultural variations in mental health are likely to be accounted for by a combination of biological, economic, and cultural factors, with some mental health problems specific to particular cultures at particular times and others being less culture-specific (see Berrios, 1996; Nazroo, 1997; Hacking, 1999; Helman, 2000). While research using this approach aims to develop cross-culturally valid theories and research methods, researchers must establish the cross-cultural equivalence of the constructs existing within a particular theoretical framework (such as stress, coping, social support, and resources), and develop corresponding cross-culturally equivalent measures.

These three paradigms have very different implications for research activity involving people with intellectual disabilities, as shown in Figure 2.1. This figure represents the research strategies associated with the absolutist, relativist, and universalist paradigms. In this figure, emic refers to research conducted within one cultural group, and etic refers to comparative research across cultural groups.

As an absolutist paradigm assumes no role for culture, it is not surprising that absolutist research strategies reflect this lack of interest. Constructs, measures, and theories are developed with reference only to the culture of the researchers (typically white). If other cultures are investigated at all, these constructs, measures, and theories are imposed upon them in a manner assumed to be unproblematic. By default, the vast majority of research activity concerning people with intellectual disabilities implicitly takes an absolutist stance.

As the relativist position assumes that cross-cultural comparisons are indefensible, only emic research within one's own culture is possible. According to this paradigm, researchers cannot even engage in emic research with other cultural groups from themselves, as this would involve a de facto imposition of the researcher's cultural worldview on another cultural group. Very little, if any, research concerning people with intellectual disabilities seems to have explicitly taken this stance.

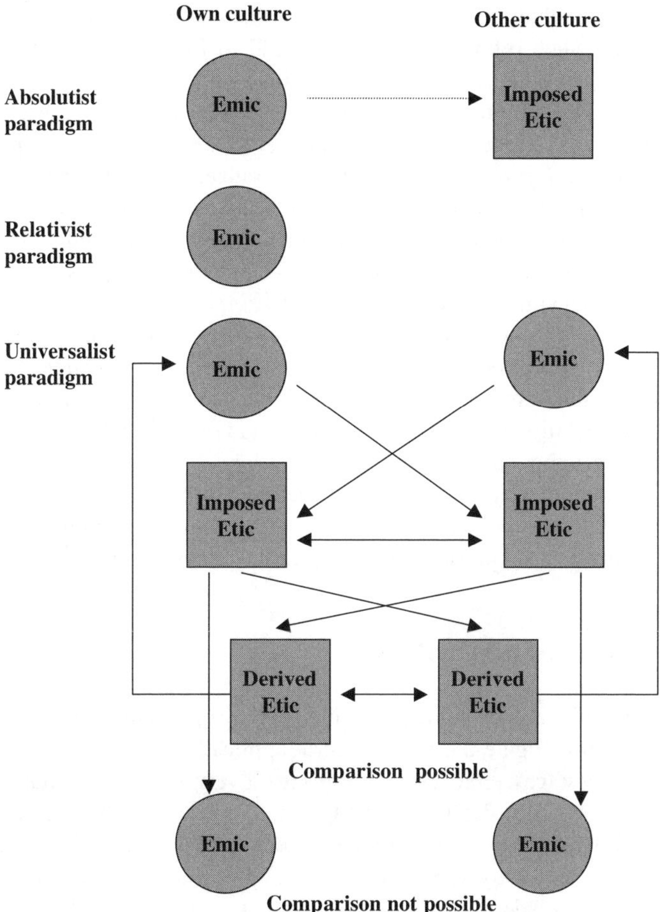

Figure 2.1 Research activity associated with paradigms of cross-cultural research

As Figure 2.1 illustrates, the research strategies involved in adopting a universalist stance are much more complex and demanding than those involved in taking either an absolutist or a relativist stance. Indeed, the difficulty and cost of conducting methodologically rigorous cross-cultural research projects is likely to be an important factor hindering the conduct of such research with people with intellectual disabilities. Figure 2.1 presents a schematic illustration of an ideal universalist research strategy involving two cultures. The first stage is to conduct emic research separately within the two cultures to establish constructs, measures, and theories grounded within the experience of each culture. The second stage involves an attempt to transport these constructs, measures, and theories to the culture other than the one in which they were derived (imposed etic). The findings of the emic research and the imposed etic research stages are then compared and integrated. There may be constructs, measures, and theories derived from emic research that are not comparable across cultures; further emic research within each culture may then further investigate these within the terms of each cultural group separately. Where constructs, measures, and theories may be applicable to both cultures under study, further studies may refine and test them cross-culturally (the derived etic stage). Such refinement may then lead to further questions requiring emic research within each culture, and the process begins again.

Clearly, this is an ideal for universalist research, and one that has not yet been fully realised in any area of the social sciences (see Berry et al., 2002). Berry (1999) has proposed a less demanding set of research strategies to underpin a universalist paradigm: (1) to transport and test current psychological knowledge and perspectives by using them in other cultures; (2) to explore and discover new aspects of the phenomenon being studied in local cultural terms; (3) to integrate what has been learned from the first two strategies to generate theories of cross-cultural applicability which can be tested.

To me, a universalist paradigm offers the best way forward for research investigating the role of culture in the lives of people with intellectual disabilities. Research strategies underpinned by a universalist stance allow for the empirical testing of the culture-dependence or cross-cultural applicability of constructs, measures, and theories, where absolutist and relativist paradigms presuppose an answer to such questions. Adopting a universalist approach is, however, methodologically and theoretically demanding for researchers. The next section of this chapter will discuss issues involved in conducting the two major research strategies underpinning a universalist approach, emic research strategies and etic research strategies.

EMIC RESEARCH STRATEGIES

Emic research strategies aim to build up a detailed picture of a culture on its own terms, rather than attempting to investigate the cross-cultural applicability of constructs, theories, and measures. In its early stages, emic research lends itself very easily to qualitative approaches, as such approaches are specifically designed to build accounts or hypotheses grounded in the data obtained, while minimising the preconceptions researchers bring to the study in obtaining, recording, and analysing the data (see Chapter 7, this volume, for an example of a qualitative approach). Readers are referred elsewhere to the many excellent texts describing qualitative research methods in detail (e.g., Creswell, 1998; Denzin & Lincoln, 2000). For many researchers, a qualitative emic research phase may be followed by a quantitative emic research phase, involving the development of quantitative measures for relevant constructs identified within that culture and the statistical testing of hypotheses relating to within-culture variation. For example, both qualitative and quantitative studies have identified the importance of religion to families with a person with intellectual disabilities in separate studies involving US Latino or African-American families (e.g., Heller, Markwardt, Rowitz & Farber, 1994; Rogers-Dulan, 1998; Skinner, Rodriguez & Bailey, 1999; Skinner et al., 2001).

This section will briefly outline some of the basic steps involved in emic research, and some of the decisions researchers need to take at each step; Magana (2000) provides some detailed and useful guidance for those conducting research concerning people with intellectual disabilities in US Latino communities.

Step 1: Decide on the Focus of the Study

Clearly, no single study can explore every aspect of a culture. Unless there is previous research to indicate that a construct is present within the culture being studied, researchers must try to avoid framing the research question in terms of constructs imported from another culture (for example, framing a study in terms of maternal depression).

Step 2: Try to Minimise Researchers' Preconceptions

Emic research studies can adopt one of two general strategies to reduce the influence of the researchers' preconceptions on the data obtained. The first is for the researchers to be members of the cultural group being studied, so that preconceptions from other cultures are less likely to be present and researchers will have an implicit "insider" understanding of relevant constructs. The second strategy is for the researchers to be members of a different culture, with the idea that a "cultural stranger" will ask about aspects of a culture that might remain implicit and unspoken between members of the same culture. There are advantages and disadvantages of both approaches, and it may be useful for research teams to include both insiders and cultural strangers to enable the fruitful comparison of data obtained from different sources.

Step 3: Sampling/Gaining Access

Whether we are conducting qualitative or quantitative research, the sampling issue is crucial for emic research as well as etic research (see below). Researchers must ensure that their procedures for gaining access to participants are not culturally biased, so that those who take part are representative of the cultural group being studied rather than those who are easy to access.

Step 4: Collecting Data

Whichever research method is being employed, it is important that the method is acceptable to the cultural group taking part in the study. Practical issues here may include the location of data collection, times and days when data collection is or is not possible, who is present when data are collected, and what support participants may require to participate in the study. Researchers also need to consider whether the methods being employed have equivalent meanings for the cultural group participating in the study. For example, cultural groups may differ in their understanding of the construct of a research interview or a participant observation study (Greenfield, 1997).

Step 5: Analysing Data

Clearly, data-analysis methods will vary according to the data collected. However, emic research is always concerned with accounting for within-culture variation and invariants. Data analysis needs to include checks on the consistency and validity of the data obtained, particularly in terms of possible cultural bias operating in the data-collection phase. Researchers also need to ensure that their preconceptions or knowledge of constructs and theories drawn from other cultures do not unduly influence data analysis. Any similarities between the culture being studied and other cultures must be rigorously demonstrated through the data analysis rather than assumed. Member checking, where the researchers' interpretations of the data are checked with study participants, can be a useful procedure at this point.

Step 6: Reporting

Given the pervasive discrimination and disadvantage experienced by people in many cultural groups, researchers may feel a responsibility to the participants in the study, in terms of providing accessible versions of the project's findings and using the findings to attempt to improve policy and practice.

ETIC RESEARCH STRATEGIES

Etic research strategies are those involving cross-cultural comparisons. Although this section will largely discuss issues involved in quantitative cross-cultural research, it is worth noting that qualitative etic research strategies are also possible (see Berry et al., 2000). Researchers wanting to engage in etic research need to consider a number of theoretical and methodological issues, including:

- specifying which aspects of culture are relevant to the study
- sampling issues
- establishing the cross-cultural equivalence of constructs, measures, and theories.

Specifying Culture

As mentioned earlier, cross-cultural research involving people with intellectual disabilities has rarely been strongly driven by theoretical concerns (see Glidden et al., 1999; Blacher, 2001, for exceptions); instead, studies have largely been concerned with highlighting inequalities across cultural groups rather than rigorously testing theories designed to explain such cultural inequalities (see Hatton, 2002, for a review). In attempting to explain differences between cultural groups, it is vital for researchers to specify the aspect of culture that is hypothesised to be important, and to conduct planned comparisons of cultural groups to test the hypothesis. The logic of such planned comparison is quasi-experimental; comparison groups should ideally vary according to the aspect of culture of interest, while being similar in all other aspects of culture. Potential aspects of culture that might be relevant include the following factors.

The Nation

It is possible that international differences in the lives of people with intellectual disabilities may be partly accounted for by national differences in policy and practice (e.g., Hatton,

Table 2.2 Acculturation theory: summary of strategies used by ethnocultural groups and wider societies

		Maintenance of heritage, culture, and identity			
		High maintenance		Low maintenance	
Relationships sought among groups		Group strategy	Societal strategy	Group strategy	Societal strategy
	Yes	Integration	Multiculturalism	Assimilation	Melting pot
	No	Separation	Segregation	Marginalisation	Exclusion

Emerson & Kiernan, 1995). Socio-political variations between smaller geographical units may also be relevant (as in the states of the USA; Hemp, Rizzolo & Braddock, 2002).

Self-Identified Ethnicity Within Plural Societies

A considerable body of research has developed acculturation theory to account for the experiences of different cultural groups (typically ethnic groups) within a multicultural society (see Berry et al., 2002, for a review). Basically, acculturation theory proposes that ethnic groups can vary in their relationships to each other along two independent dimensions; the extent to which the heritage, culture, and identity are maintained, and the extent to which relationships are sought with other ethnic groups. As Table 2.2 outlines, depending on these dimensions, different strategies are adopted by ethnocultural groups and by the wider society within which the ethnocultural group are living. Of course, some ethnocultural groups may have restrictions placed upon them in the strategies they can adopt by the strategies of the wider society, and strategies can also change over time.

Although proxy indicators of ethnic identity (such as the extent to which UK South Asian parents of a child with severe intellectual disabilities identify themselves as Asian and British; Hatton, Akram, Shah, Robertson & Emerson, in press) are beginning to be used, research using acculturation theory involving people with intellectual disabilities has not yet taken off. It is also important to note the view of some theorists that people with intellectual disabilities constitute an almost ethnocultural group with their wider societies, and have begun to use acculturation theories to understand the position of people with intellectual disabilities within society (e.g., Minnes, Buell, Feldman, McColl & McCreary, 2002). Acculturation theory is clearly a promising framework for comparing the lives of people with intellectual disabilities from different ethnic groups within one country, particularly in terms of interactions with instruments of wider society, such as access to service supports.

Specific Cultural Mechanisms

Although little researched with people with intellectual disabilities, there are likely to be a host of specific cultural factors that affect the lives of people with intellectual disabilities. One example is language; certainly language differences between families with a person with intellectual disabilities and service professionals have been consistently associated with lower awareness, uptake, and satisfaction with services across a range of ethnocultural groups in the USA and the UK (e.g., Smith & Ryan, 1987; Sontag & Schacht, 1994; Hatton, Azmi, Caine & Emerson, 1998; Bailey et al., 1999; Hatton et al., in press). Researchers interested in the specific role of language differences between families and professionals could compare:

- families within the same cultural group who do and do not speak the same language as professionals (for example, UK South Asian families who do and do not speak English)
- families within the same cultural group where professionals do and do not speak the same language as families (for example, Spanish-speaking Latino families accessing English-speaking versus Spanish-speaking professionals)
- families within a locality who are part of cultural groups that do and do not speak the same language as professionals (for example, English-speaking African-American families and Spanish-speaking Latino families, both accessing the same English-speaking professionals).

Another example of a specific cultural practice is family religiosity, a construct that has been found to be associated with positive outcomes for African-American and Latino families in the USA (Rogers-Dulan, 1998; Skinner et al., 2001). The construct of religiosity could be tested cross-culturally; research questions may include whether positive associations between family religiosity and outcomes apply to other Christian traditions and to other religions, and whether the mechanisms through which religiosity influences families are similar across cultural groups.

Whichever aspect of culture is hypothesised to be important by the researcher, it is crucial to measure additional variables which may confound or interact with the cultural variable of interest. For example, in the UK, English-language use among South Asian families with a person with intellectual disabilities is associated with economic, employment, housing, and social-class differences (Hatton et al., 1998, in press).

Sampling Issues

As mentioned earlier, studies involving people with intellectual disabilities rarely describe their participants in cultural terms, and where samples are described they are mainly white. More diverse participant samples are clearly required if the cross-cultural applicability of many widely used constructs, theories, and methods are to be tested (see Okazaki & Sue, 1995; Leung & van de Vijver, 1996, for discussions of sampling issues in cross-cultural research). The sampling strategy adopted will vary according to the research question being asked. For example, research concerning the uptake of service supports by different cultural communities (e.g., the uptake of residential services; Meyers, Borthwick & Eyman, 1985; Emerson & Hatton, 1998) may find very small numbers of participants in particular cultural groups as a finding of the study. Research investigating the experiences of different cultural groups (for example, concerning family support services; e.g., Chamba, Ahmad, Hirst, Lawson & Beresford, 1999), however, may need to over-sample cultural groups that would appear in negligible numbers if random sampling strategies were to be employed. If over-sampling still yields very small numbers, an option for researchers is to combine groups that appear to share some characteristics (for example, UK research with South

Asian participants, combining people with very diverse languages, religions, and cultures), although such combinations are often based more on racial grounds than the grounds of cultural similarity. Combining cultural groups in this way may be the only way to gain a sample sufficient for analysis purposes, although there are likely to be serious limits to the interpretability of the data.

Research involving a planned comparison of cultural groups on theoretical grounds (for example, interpersonal problem-solving between Nigerian, African-American, and European-American samples; Edeh & Hickson, 2002) requires either an attempt to match samples on potentially relevant secondary variables (such as socio-economic variables; schooling) or an attempt to measure potentially relevant secondary variables across unmatched samples and use them for covariance analysis.

Identifying the cultural groups that participants belong to is becoming a more complex issue as societies become more pluralist. Ethnicity is a good example of the dilemmas researchers face when attempting to identify a cultural variable. Historically, ethnicity has been treated as a categorical variable (equivalent to race), whereby a person can be assigned to any one of a number of mutually exclusive categories (as in census surveys). Such assignment may assume that ethnicity is a fixed attribute of the person, as, for example, by assigning ethnicity on the basis of surname, which may be the only option for researchers using archival data. Categorical assignment may also be attempted through self-report, where participants are offered a series of categories from which one category has to be selected. However, self-reported ethnic identity may not easily fit into a single category. First, participants in plural societies may have family backgrounds involving several ethnicities (for example, in 1990, multiethnic Americans constituted more than 35% of the population in 20 US states; Shinagawa & Jang, 1998), and they may wish to define themselves in terms of several ethnic identities. Second, acculturation research demonstrates that perceived ethnicities may not be exclusive; for example, a person may feel simultaneously Asian and British. These considerations suggest a multidimensional model of assessing self-identified ethnicities, although the data derived from such assessments would be more complex for researchers to handle.

Establishing Cross-Cultural Equivalence

For cross-cultural studies, establishing the cross-cultural equivalence of constructs, measures, and theories is a necessary (although demanding) part of the research endeavour. Many cross-cultural psychology texts describe the issues involved in establishing cross-cultural equivalence in great depth (see Berry et al., 1997, 2002); this section will briefly outline some of the issues researchers need to consider when trying to establish cross-cultural equivalence and avoid cultural bias. A number of types of cultural bias are possible; Table 2.3 outlines some of these types of cultural bias, some possible sources of these types of cultural bias, and examples of bias from a hypothetical study investigating the cross-cultural equivalence of the construct of adaptive behaviour between European-Americans and European-Britons (adapted from Berry et al., 2002).

Methods of analysing cultural bias include judgemental approaches (where experts and/or participants from all cultures under investigation give their opinion on the measure and the construct it is supposed to measure) and psychometric approaches. Psychometric approaches may include establishing structural equivalence (do the items in the measure relate to each

Table 2.3 Types and sources of cultural bias

Type of bias	Source of bias	Example
Construct	Incomplete overlap of definitions of the construct across cultures	Adaptive behaviour construct includes knowledge of self in USA, but includes lack of knowledge of self in UK
	Differential appropriateness of item content	Item refers to playing football
	Poor sampling of all relevant behaviours	Self-help domain does not include items on donning a monocle, top hat, and frock coat for British participants
	Incomplete coverage of the psychological construct	Measure only assesses basic developmental skills
Method	Differential social desirability	For British respondents, socially desirable response is to minimise their competence; for US respondents, the opposite
	Differential response styles such as extreme scoring and acquiescence	British respondents acquiescent to be polite
	Differential stimulus familiarity	British respondents more likely to have completed forms in the past (while queueing for things)
	Lack of comparability of samples	British respondents made physically weak through excessive tea drinking
	Differences in physical testing conditions	Form more difficult to read in permanently cloudy British weather
	Tester effects	British testers too diffident to ask questions concerning personal care
	Communication problems between participant and tester in either cultural group	British participants want to spell words wrongly, including adaptive behaviour
Item	Poor item translation	Item on participation in sports refers to playing baseball
	Inadequate item formulation	Wording of questions too direct for Britons to understand
	One or a few items may invoke additional traits or abilities	British version includes items on keeping a stiff upper lip—a British personality trait rather than component of adaptive behaviour
	Incidental differences in appropriateness of the item content	British respondents regard questions concerning money as vulgar

other and to other variables in the same way in both cultures?) or, more demandingly, measurement unit equivalence (does a unit increase in a scale score have the same meaning in both cultures?) (see Berry et al., 2002, for more details).

For much cross-cultural research, the translation of measures into other languages will be required. Standard practice in cross-cultural research is to translate the measure (for example, English to Spanish), back-translate the measure (for example, Spanish to English) with a different translator, then compare the original and back-translated versions. If the measures are identical or very similar, this indicates that the measure can successfully be translated into the other language. Areas where the measures are different indicate problems either in the specific translation or in the translatability of the measure. Guidelines to optimise the translatability of a measure are listed below (adapted and abridged from Brislin, 1986, pp. 143–150):

- Use short and simple sentences and avoid unnecessary words.
- Employ the active rather than the passive voice because the former is easier to comprehend.
- Repeat nouns instead of using pronouns because the latter may have vague referents; thus, "you" can refer to a single person or to a group of persons.
- Avoid metaphors and colloquialisms. In many cases, their translations will not be equally concise, familiar, and captivating.
- Avoid verbs and prepositions telling "where" and "when" that do not have a precise meaning, such as "soon" and "often".
- Avoid possessive forms where possible because it may be difficult to determine the ownership. The ownership such as "his" in "his dog" has to be derived from the context of the sentence, and languages vary in their system of reference.
- Use specific rather than general terms. Who is included in "members of your family" greatly differs across cultures; more precise terms are less likely to run into this problem.

Although a measure may meet the criterion of translatability, broader issues of construct bias may still apply, and all measures should be rigorously piloted with participants across all relevant cultural groups. For example, although the terms used to anchor Likert scale items may be easily translatable (for example, *agree*, *somewhat agree*, *somewhat disagree*, and *disagree*), these anchor points may be placed in a different order in different languages (for example, in some languages the translation of "somewhat" may act as an intensifier). International consensus guidelines on good practice in test translation are available (van de Vijver & Hambleton, 1996).

CULTURAL RESEARCH WITH PEOPLE WITH INTELLECTUAL DISABILITIES

This chapter has hopefully demonstrated that the role of culture in the lives of people with intellectual disabilities needs to be seriously addressed by the research community, and has provided some guidance for researchers on how to begin cultural research with people with intellectual disabilities. In this final section, I want to outline briefly some examples of how a cultural approach might have an impact on researchers working with people with intellectual disabilities.

Classification

Although current classification systems (e.g., Luckasson et al., 2002) mention the importance of culture in the classification and definition of intellectual disability, assessment tools used for classification purposes have not yet demonstrated cross-cultural equivalence.

Of the major components of the definition of intellectual disability, the first is intelligence. The cross-cultural assessment of intelligence has a long and controversial history. Although it is clear that the construct of general intelligence, as measured by IQ tests, does not apply cross-culturally (Berry et al., 2002), some authors argue that trying to establish the cross-cultural equivalence of general intelligence assessments is fundamentally misguided (e.g., Greenfield, 1997). The issue of IQ testing is particularly important for research with people with intellectual disabilities, as most epidemiological studies of prevalence rely on IQ test scores alone (McLaren & Bryson, 1987; Roeleveld, Zielhuis & Gabreels, 1997), and the application of standard IQ cutoffs results in over-representations of people of colour within intellectual disability categories and special education systems (see Heflinger, Cook & Thackrey, 1987; Oswald et al., 2001).

Similar issues apply to the definition and assessment of adaptive behaviour, another fundamental aspect of current classification systems. As the construct of adaptive behaviour is defined in terms of person–environment fit, cultural differences may require fundamentally different skills and behaviours for a person to fit with their environment.

Researchers urgently need to investigate the applicability of current classification systems cross-culturally. This may mean attempting to develop cross-culturally valid measures of intelligence (whether general intelligence or a more plural model of intelligences) and adaptive behaviour (either a measure of a common subset of "core" adaptive behaviours, or different sets of adaptive behaviours assessing the same core set of required skills). Alternatively, a more fundamental revision of classification systems may be attempted to gain a cross-culturally valid classification system, or it may even be that different constructs and classification systems are required for different cultures. All these strategies will require much greater attention to emic research strategies within cultures other than white, English-speaking cultures.

Demonstrating the Cross-Cultural Applicability of Theories, Constructs, and Measures

There are many theories concerning people with intellectual disabilities in which culture is not hypothesised to be relevant, such as the opioid neurobiological model of the maintenance of self-injury (see Emerson, 2001). Rather than assuming the cross-cultural applicability of such theories, researchers could demonstrate this empirically by building cultural diversity routinely into their samples, and reporting both within-culture and cross-cultural comparisons.

Emic research within hitherto uninvestigated cultural groups, followed by etic research gaining insights from several cultural groups, could strengthen many theories and constructs concerning people with intellectual disabilities. For example, theories of the development of self-injury in childhood proposing that behaviours associated with a routine developmental stage are shaped into chronic self-injury by the child's social environment (e.g., Hall, Oliver & Murphy, 2001) could be strengthened by cross-cultural investigation. Etic research could establish whether the hypothesised developmental stage is universal across cultures, and emic research within cultures could investigate whether the same relationships between social environments and child behaviours exist cross-culturally. More fundamental emic research could investigate the applicability of constructs such as self-injury cross-culturally.

Routine Collection and Reporting of Cultural Variables

As mentioned earlier in this chapter, researchers in leading journals rarely report cultural aspects of their samples, include culturally diverse samples in their studies, or analyse their data in terms of cultural groups. The routine reporting of the ethnicity of samples (ideally according to standard categorical or dimensional guidelines suggested by journal editors) and descriptive data by ethnicity would enable future meta-analyses and systematic reviews focusing on ethnicity. For example, if such data were available, meta-analyses of the effectiveness of behavioural interventions for people with intellectual disabilities and challenging behaviours would be able to analyse the effectiveness of such interventions for different ethnic groups.

Specifying the Role of Culture

For theories where culture is hypothesised to be important, it is vital for researchers to specify the aspect of culture hypothesised to be relevant, and the mechanisms through which culture is hypothesised to operate. Research designs need to be explicitly designed to test specific theories, and also need to build in potentially confounding non-cultural variables.

Perhaps most importantly, emic research on cultures other than white, English-speaking cultures need to be conducted. Such emic research may yield a number of important constructs and theories yet to be investigated, which could be widely applicable cross-culturally. Such strategies could greatly enrich our theoretical understanding of people with intellectual disabilities within all cultural groups, although they will require culturally diverse research groups and much greater attention paid to unexciting methodological issues.

For researchers working with people with intellectual disabilities, routinely building a cultural perspective is demanding but, I believe, essential. The increasing diversity of nations demands a response from researchers if repeated calls for services to become culturally competent (e.g., Baxter, Poonia, Ward & Nadirshaw, 1990; Harry et al., 1995; Robinson & Rathbone, 1999) are to be grounded in research evidence.

REFERENCES

Bailey, D.B. Jr, Skinner, D., Correa, V., Arcia, E., Reyes-Blanes, M.E., Rodriguez, P., et al. (1999). Needs and supports reported by Latino families of young children with developmental disabilities. *American Journal on Mental Retardation*, **104**, 437–451.

Baxter, C., Poonia, K., Ward, L. & Nadirshaw, Z. (1990). *Double Discrimination: Issues and Services for People with Learning Difficulties from Black and Ethnic Minority Communities*. London: King's Fund Centre.

Berrios, G.E. (1996). *The History of Mental Symptoms: Descriptive Psychopathology Since the Nineteenth Century*. Cambridge: Cambridge University Press.

Berry, J.W. (1995). Psychology of acculturation. In N.R. Goldberger & J.B. Veroff (Eds) *The Culture and Psychology Reader* (pp. 457–488). New York: New York University Press.

Berry, J.W. (1999). On the unity of the field of culture and psychology. In J. Adamopoulos & Y. Kashima (Eds) *Social Psychology and Cultural Context* (pp. 7–15). London: Sage.

Berry, J.W., Poortinga, Y.H. & Pandey, J. (Eds) (1997). *Handbook of Cross-Cultural Psychology*, vol. 1. *Theory and Method*. Boston, MA: Allyn & Bacon.

Berry, J.W., Poortinga, Y.H., Segall, M.H. & Dasen, P.R. (2002). *Cross-Cultural Psychology: Research and Applications* (2nd edn). Cambridge: Cambridge University Press.

Betancourt, H. & Lopez, S.R. (1995). The study of culture, ethnicity and race in American psychology. In N.R. Goldberger & J.B. Veroff (Eds) *The Culture and Psychology Reader* (pp. 87–107). New York: New York University Press.

Blacher, J. (2001). Transition to adulthood: mental retardation, families, and culture. *American Journal on Mental Retardation*, **106**, 173–188.

Blue-Banning, M.J., Turnbull, A.P. & Pereira, L. (2000). Group action planning as a support strategy for Hispanic families: parent and professional perspectives. *Mental Retardation*, **38**, 262–275.

Brislin, R.W. (1986). The wording and translation of research instruments. In W.J. Lonner & J.W. Berry (Eds) *Field Methods in Cross-Cultural Research* (pp. 137–164). Newbury Park, CA: Sage.

Chamba, R., Ahmad, W., Hirst, M., Lawton, D. & Beresford, B. (1999). *On the Edge: Minority Ethnic Families Caring for a Severely Disabled Child*. Bristol: Policy Press.

Cooney, B.F. (2002). Exploring perspectives on transition of youth with disabilities: voices of young adults, parents, and professionals. *Mental Retardation*, **40**, 425–435.

Creswell, J. (1998). *Qualitative Inquiry and Research Design: Choosing Among Five Traditions*. London: Sage.

Dekker, M.C., Nunn, R. & Koot, H.M. (2002). Short report: psychometric properties of the revised Developmental Behaviour Checklist scales in Dutch children with intellectual disability. *Journal of Intellectual Disability Research*, **46**, 61–75.

Denzin, N.K. & Lincoln, Y.S. (2000). *The Handbook of Qualitative Research* (2nd edn). London: Sage.

Edeh, O.M. & Hickson, L. (2002). Cross-cultural comparison of interpersonal problem-solving in students with mental retardation. *American Journal on Mental Retardation*, **107**, 6–15.

Emerson, E. (2001). *Challenging Behaviour: Analysis and Intervention with People with Severe Intellectual Disabilities* (2nd edn). Cambridge: Cambridge University Press.

Emerson, E. & Hatton, C. (1998). Residential provision for people with intellectual disabilities in England, Wales and Scotland. *Journal of Applied Research in Intellectual Disabilities*, **11**, 1–14.

Emerson, E. & Hatton, C. (1999). Future trends in the ethnic composition of British society and among British citizens with learning disabilities. *Tizard Learning Disability Review*, **4**, 28–32.

Gatrell, A.C. (2002). *Geographies of Health: An Introduction*. Oxford: Blackwell.

Glidden, L.M., Rogers-Dulan, J. & Hill, A.E. (1999). "The child that was meant?" or "punishment for sin?": religion, ethnicity, and families with children with disabilities. In L.M. Glidden (Ed.) *International Review on Research in Mental Retardation*, vol. 22 (pp. 267–288). San Diego, CA: Academic Press.

Gonzalez-Gordon, R.G., Salvador-Carulla, L., Romero, C., Gonzalez-Sais, F. & Romero, D. (2002). Feasibility, reliability and validity of the Spanish version of Psychiatric Assessment Schedule for Adults with Developmental Disability: a structured psychiatric interview for intellectual disability. *Journal of Intellectual Disability Research*, **46**, 209–217.

Graham, S. (1992). "Most of the subjects were white and middle class": trends in published research on African-Americans in selected APA journals, 1970–1989. *American Psychologist*, **47**, 629–639.

Greenfield, P.M. (1997). You can't take it with you: why ability assessments don't cross cultures. *American Psychologist*, **52**, 1115–1124.

Gustafson, C. & Sonnander, K. (2002). Psychometric evaluation of a Swedish version of the Reiss Screen for Maladaptive Behavior. *Journal of Intellectual Disability Research*, **46**, 218–229.

Hacking, I. (1999). *Mad Travellers: Reflections on the Reality of Transient Mental Illnesses*. London: Free Association Books.

Hall, S., Oliver, C. & Murphy, G. (2001). Early development of self-injurious behavior: an empirical study. *American Journal on Mental Retardation*, **106**, 189–199.

Harry, B., Grenot-Scheyer, M., Smith-Lewis, M., Park, H.-S., Xin, F. & Schwartz, I. (1995). Developing culturally inclusive services for individuals with severe disabilities. *Journal of the Association of Severe Handicaps*, **20**, 99–109.

Hatton, C. (2002). People with intellectual disabilities from ethnic minority communities in the US and the UK. In L. Masters-Glidden (Ed.) *International Review on Research in Mental Retardation*, vol. 25 (pp. 209–239). San Diego, CA: Academic Press.

Hatton, C., Akram, Y., Shah, R., Robertson, J. & Emerson, E. (in press). *Supporting South Asian Families with a Child with Severe Disabilities*. London: Jessica Kingsley.

Hatton, C., Azmi, S., Caine, A.& Emerson, E. (1998). People from the South Asian communities who care for adolescents and adults with intellectual disabilities: family circumstances, service support and carer stress. *British Journal of Social Work*, **28**, 821–837.

Hatton, C., Emerson, E. & Kiernan, C. (1995). Trends and milestones: people in institutions in Europe. *Mental Retardation*, **33**, 132.

Heflinger, C.A., Cook, V.J. & Thackrey, M. (1987). Identification of mental retardation by the System of Multicultural Pluralistic Assessment: non-discriminatory or nonexistent? *Journal of School Psychology*, **25**, 177–183.

Heller, T., Markwardt, R., Rowitz, L. & Farber, B. (1994). Adaptation of Hispanic families to a member with mental retardation. *American Journal on Mental Retardation*, **99**, 289–300.

Helman, C.G. (2000). *Culture, Health and Illness* (4th edn). London: Butterworth Heinemann.

Hemp, R., Rizzolo, M.C. & Braddock, D. (2002). Trends and milestones: selected trends in public spending for MR/DD services and the state economies. *Mental Retardation*, **40**, 418–422.

Herrnstein, R. & Murray, C. (1994). *The Bell Curve: Intelligence and Class Structure in American Life*. New York: Free Press.

Joyce, T., Ditchfield, H. & Harris, P. (2001). Challenging behaviour in community services. *Journal of Intellectual Disability Research*, **45**, 130–138.

Kahn-Freedman, E. (2001). Finding a voice: poetry and people with developmental disabilities. *Mental Retardation*, **39**, 195–200.

Kleinman, A. (1995). Do psychiatric disorders differ in different cultures? The methodological questions. In N.R. Goldberger & J.B. Veroff (Eds) *The Culture and Psychology Reader* (pp. 631–651). New York: New York University Press.

Kluckhohn, C. (1956). Toward a comparison of value-emphases in different cultures. In L.D. White (Ed.) *The State of Social Sciences* (pp. 116–132). Chicago, IL: University of Chicago Press.

Leung, K. & van de Vijver, F. (1996). Cross-cultural research methodology. In F.T.L. Leong & J.T. Austin (Eds) *The Psychology Research Handbook* (pp. 351–358). Thousand Oaks, CA: Sage.

Lewontin, R. (1995). *Human Diversity*. New York: Scientific American Library.

Luckasson, R., Borthwick-Duffy, S., Buntinx, W.H.E., Coulter, D.L., Craig, E.M., Reeve, A., et al. (2002). *Mental Retardation: Definition, Classification, and Systems of Supports* (10th edn). Washington, DC: American Association on Mental Retardation.

Magana, S.M. (2000). Mental retardation research methods in Latino communities. *Mental Retardation*, **38**, 303–315.

McGrother, C.W., Bhaumik, S., Thorpe, C.F., Watson, J.M. & Taub, N.A. (2002). Prevalence, morbidity and service need among South Asian and white adults with intellectual disability in Leicestershire, UK. *Journal of Intellectual Disability Research*, **46**, 299–309.

McLaren, J. & Bryson, S.E. (1987). Review of recent epidemiological studies of mental retardation: prevalence, associated disorders, and etiology. *American Journal of Mental Retardation*, **92**, 243–254.

Meyers, C.E., Borthwick, S.A. & Eyman, R.K. (1985). Place of residence by age, ethnicity, and level of retardation of the mentally retarded/developmentally disabled population of California. *American Journal of Mental Deficiency*, **90**, 266–270.

Mink, I.T. (1997). Studying culturally diverse families of children with mental retardation. In N.W. Bray (Ed.) *International Review on Research in Mental Retardation*, vol. 20 (pp. 75–98). San Diego, CA: Academic Press.

Minnes, P., Buell, K., Feldman, M., McColl, M.A. & McCreary, B. (2002). Community integration as acculturation: preliminary validation of the AIMS interview. *Journal of Applied Research in Intellectual Disabilities*, **15**, 377–387.

Molteno, G., Molteno, C.D., Finchilescu, G. & Dawes, A.R.L. (2001). Behavioural and emotional problems in children with intellectual disability attending special schools in Cape Town, South Africa. *Journal of Intellectual Disability Research*, **45**, 515–520.

Naglieri, J.A. & Rojahn, J. (2001). Intellectual classification of black and white children in special education programs using the WISC-III and the Cognitive Assessment System. *American Journal on Mental Retardation*, **106**, 359–367.

Nazroo, J.Y. (1997). *The Health of Britain's Ethnic Minorities*. London: Policy Studies Institute.

Okazaki, S. & Sue, S. (1995). Methodological issues in assessment research with ethnic minorities. *Psychological Assessment*, **7**, 367–375.

Olney, M.F. & Kennedy, J. (2001). National estimates of vocational service utilization and job placement rates for adults with mental retardation. *Mental Retardation*, **39**, 32–39.

Oswald, D.P., Coutinho, M.J., Best, A.M. & Nguyen, N. (2001). Impact of sociodemographic characteristics on the identification rates of minority students as having mental retardation. *Mental Retardation*, **39**, 351–367.

Peter, D. (2000). Dynamics of discourse: a case study illuminating power relations in mental retardation. *Mental Retardation*, **38**, 354–362.

Rhoades, J.A. & Altman, B.M. (2001). Personal characteristics and contextual factors associated with residential expenditures for individuals with mental retardation. *Mental Retardation*, **39**, 114–129.

Robinson, E.G. & Rathbone, G.N. (1999). Impact of race, poverty, and ethnicity on services for persons with mental retardation: call for cultural competence. *Mental Retardation*, **37**, 333–338.

Roeleveld, N., Zielhuis, G.A. & Gabreels, F. (1997). The prevalence of mental retardation: a critical review of recent literature. *Developmental Medicine and Child Neurology*, **39**, 125–132.

Rogers-Dulan, J. (1998). Religious connectedness among urban African-American families who have a child with disabilities. *Mental Retardation*, **36**, 91–103.

Shin, J.Y. (2002). Social support for families of children with mental retardation: comparison between Korea and the United States. *Mental Retardation*, **40**, 103–118.

Shinagawa, L.H. & Jang, M. (1998). *Atlas of American Diversity*. Walnut Creek, CA: AltaMira.

Skinner, D., Rodriguez, P. & Bailey, D.B. Jr (1999). Qualitative analysis of Latino parents' religious interpretations of their child's disability. *Journal of Early Intervention*, **22**, 271–285.

Skinner, D.G., Correa, V., Skinner, M. & Bailey, D.B. Jr (2001). Role of religion in the lives of Latino families of young children with developmental delays. *American Journal on Mental Retardation*, **106**, 297–313.

Smith, J.D. (1995). For whom the bell curve tolls: old texts, mental retardation, and the persistent argument. *Mental Retardation*, **33**, 199–202.

Smith, M.J. & Ryan, A.S. (1987). Chinese-American families of children with developmental disabilities: an exploratory study of reactions to service providers. *Mental Retardation*, **25**, 345–350.

Smith, P. (2001). Inquiry cantos: poetics of developmental disability. *Mental Retardation*, **39**, 379–390.

Sontag, J.C. & Schacht, R. (1994). An ethnic comparison of parent participant and information needs in early intervention. *Exceptional Children*, **60**, 422–433.

Turnbull, A.P., Blue-Banning, M. & Pereira, L. (2000). Successful friendships of Hispanic children and youth with disabilities: an exploratory study. *Mental Retardation*, **38**, 138–153.

Van de Vijver, F. & Hambleton, R.K. (1996). Translating tests: some practical guidelines. *European Psychologist*, **1**, 89–99.

Yamaki, K. & Fujiura, G.T. (2002). Employment and income status of adults with developmental disabilities living in the community. *Mental Retardation*, **40**, 132–141.

CHAPTER 3

Ethical Research Involving People with Intellectual Disabilities

Tim Griffin
University of Western Sydney, Australia
and
Susan Balandin
University of Sydney, Australia

ethics
The study of morals and values; that is, the study of right and wrong, justice and injustice, virtue and vice, good and bad, and related concepts and principles. (National Health and Medical Research Council—NHMRC, 1999, p. 63)

To decree that "researchers must behave ethically" is uncontentious, not least as the alternative, to behave unethically, is unacceptable. Perhaps a few researchers knowingly practise unethically, but here we are not concerned with these recalcitrants. Others have described the egregious abuse of vulnerable individuals in the name of science (see Clements, Rapley & Cummins, 1999; Freedman, 2001; Iacono & Murray, 2003). Ethical guidelines for researchers originated in the recognition of such breaches and with the intention of preventing future abuses. Our aim is to provide guidance to relatively inexperienced researchers about how to think ethically and to offer some challenges for the experienced.

Fundamentally, ethical research is a matter of safeguarding the rights of participants (Sergejew, 1996). The right to choose, informed and free from coercion, whether to participate in research or not, and to have privacy respected and personal information treated confidentially and used only for the purpose for which consent was given, is a basic principle. Adherence to ethical principles is a matter of vigilance by researchers, agencies charged with assessing ethical conduct, and sometimes the participants themselves. Even research that is benevolent involves inherent costs and potential risks of harm for participants. Ethical research is a balance between "doing good" and "avoiding (physical and psychological) harm".

In our experience, which spans submissions of research proposals to ethics committees, advising students and researchers, supporting participants in research projects, and sitting on ethics committees, even well-meaning researchers can sometimes overlook potential

The International Handbook of Applied Research in Intellectual Disabilities. Edited by E. Emerson, C. Hatton, T. Thompson and T.R. Parmenter ISBN 0-471-49709-6.

ethical problems in their research plans. For example, one proposal reviewed was for a health service to interview recently widowed women about available community supports; yet the probability that they would feel emotional distress during the interviews was ignored by the researcher. This is an obvious omission, but ethical issues often surface more subtly. If researchers cannot identify and predict the obvious emotional or physical costs of their projects for participants, they will be unable to plan appropriate responses and will almost certainly overlook the less obvious implications. We do not believe that ethical infringements are due to researchers' malevolence. Lack of attention to submissions to ethics committees is more likely. Sometimes researchers have difficulty in viewing their projects from the participants' perspective. Immersed in their own agendas, processes, imperatives, and deadlines, they may not give sufficient depth of consideration to the impact on participants. Sensitivity to ethical issues requires the researcher to attempt to see research from the participant's point of view.

A chapter on research ethics in a book about research cuts across the entire research process, from design to dissemination. There is no aspect of research practice that is outside ethical consideration. We have tried to be as comprehensive as possible in expounding ethical principles and raising related issues. Despite the definition of ethics provided at the start of this chapter, we will not be prescriptive about what is "right" and "wrong", "good" and "bad". Our focus is on ethical issues and problems and suggested resolutions.

Generally, people with intellectual disabilities have cognitive limitations in expressive and receptive communication in written and spoken forms. Their vulnerability to unethical practice is compounded by life circumstances, especially if they have little experience in acting as autonomous persons, making decisions for themselves in their own best interests. People with significant cognitive disabilities, perhaps with severe communication impairments or medical fragility, are likely to need someone to decide for them about participation in research.

The growing respect for people with intellectual disabilities is reflected in current practices, such as individual planning based on choice, self-determination, and self-advocacy, and the empowerment movements that have enabled people with intellectual disabilities to become more involved in determining the trajectory of their lives (Freedman, 2001). Ethical research practice is compatible with these contemporary philosophies.

THE ROLE OF ETHICS COMMITTEES

In most Western countries, a specially constituted committee must vet research proposals prior to commencement (Frew, 2001). As committees vary in membership and processes, the generic term "institutional ethics committee" (IEC) is used here to refer to university, government, and non-government committees constituted to assess the ethics of proposed research. The IEC weighs up the gain versus pain of a proposed project—the gain must justify the pain (and vice versa) (Sergejew, 1996).

Submitting detailed proposals to ethics committees can be onerous. Some researchers charge IECs with being too pedantic or overstepping their bounds of responsibility and competence (McNeil, 1996), or as yet another barrier to prevent researchers from actually doing research. There is no avoiding IECs, however, as "ethics clearance" is mandated, at least by universities and often by research funding bodies. In some contexts, researchers require clearance from a scientific committee. Moreover, if access to clients of a service is required, the provider may have a committee to assess applications. Each level of committee is likely to have a different focus.

Scientific committees are concerned with methodological soundness and rigour with respect to the aims and rational of the research. Ethics committees are also interested in scientific diligence, because

> scientific inadequacies have ethical implications. Projects without scientific merit are wasteful of resources and needlessly subject participants to risks. Accordingly, an essential condition of the ethical acceptability of research is the determination of the scientific quality of a proposal and the skill and experience of the researchers are such that the objectives of the proposal can reasonably be expected to be achieved. (National Health and Medical Research Council—NHMRC, 1999, p. 5; see also Portney & Watkins, 2000)

IECs often focus on the research methods. Here, in the guts of the research, are details of what is going to be done to (or with) whom and how. IECs are particularly interested in how voluntary, informed consent will be obtained, privacy protected, data kept confidential, and participants anonymous.

If a service is going to provide access to clients and provide other resources (perhaps just time and a setting) to support the researcher, it may require the research to benefit its current or future clients. Service-based committees might ask: "What's in it for us?"

Processes for IEC scrutiny will be influenced by local regulations and conventions Sergejew, 1996; Iacono & Murray, 2003). Regardless of these variations, the researcher has to factor in the time needed to prepare, submit, and respond to an IEC that may meet only every month or so. IECs cannot presciently determine all the potential ethical issues and nuances in a particular study. A tick by an IEC is merely a signal to proceed with caution, exercise the greatest care of participants, and deal ethically with problems that arise. In this, we concur with Swain, Heyman & Gillman (1998, p. 22), who question:

> exclusive reliance on formal procedures commonly adopted in addressing ethical issues, ... [we] argue that ethical actions cannot be judged entirely on the principles by which research is planned and conducted, or on the final outcomes ... the pursuit of ethical ideals is founded on reflections on the decision making processes themselves, the differing vested interests of those involved and the social relations within specific contexts.

Reflection has to be grounded in understanding and testing of ethical principles. We cannot stipulate how to be reflective, but we can expound those principles and provide examples that aid transition to specific practices (see Kvale, 1996).

FOUNDATIONS OF ETHICAL CODES

Acting ethically is a basic tenet of research, yet guidance is based on principles the research community agrees are ethical practice. Ethics evolve as the roles of the researcher and the "researched" are conceptualised and reconceptualised. This is illustrated by using the term "participant" rather than "subject". While "participant" has various connotations (such as "participatory action research"), it is not a synonym for "subject". "Participant" implies ethical inclusion in research projects based on "respect for persons" and that research is being conducted *with* rather than *on* people, or at least, minimally, with their consent.

The atrocities perpetrated by Nazis during World War II on prisoners in the name of science precipitated the Nuremberg Code of 1947. Voluntary consent to being a subject, based on knowledge of the purposes, procedures, inconveniences, and potential hazards of the research, was enshrined in this code, as was the requirement that researchers be competent and scientifically qualified (Annas & Grodin, 1989; see also Portney & Watkins, 2000). The World Medical Association developed an influential code in 1964 (revised in 1975, 1983, and 1989), which contained, for the first time, the idea of independent review of experimental protocols, and stipulated that unethical research should not be published (World Medical Association, 1989). Current codes of ethical conduct are based on these foundational documents (Portney & Watkins, 2000).

There is a high concordance between ethical professional practice and research. Codes of ethical practice have been developed for specific professions or for members of broader professional bodies (e.g., American Association on Mental Retardation, 2001). Codes have been developed for ethical application of specific tools (such as the World Health Organisation's International Classification of Functioning, Disability, and Health [ICF]; WHO, 2001). This recognises that every scientific tool can be misused and that users have an obligation to minimise the risks that it will be used in ways that are disrespectful or harmful to people with disabilities. In social terms, the ICF should be used to enhance choices and control by people with disabilities and to inform social policy and political action to influence participation in society.

Ethical Frameworks

To emphasise the point that there are no absolute ethical codes, even an ethics of "rights" can be challenged (see Clegg, 2000). Kvale (1996) compared three frameworks for ethical practice: a duty ethics of principles; a utilitarian ethics of consequences; and a virtue ethics of values (see Miles & Huberman, 1994, for a slightly different slant).

A duty stance holds that action can be judged independently of its consequences. Research that adheres to ethical principles is "good" research, regardless of the outcome. The logical end point is that the means justify the ends. Conversely, a utilitarian ethics of consequences is concerned with the "greatest good for the greatest number", and, in logical extension, it is just as problematic because the ends justify the means. It is unlikely that modern-day researchers would strongly espouse either of these opposing philosophies, as, clearly, both the means (principles) and outcomes (harms and benefits) deserve equal consideration.

An ethics of values is less concerned with ethical principles per se than with how researchers internalise moral values and apply them in context. Practice is informed by the researcher's personal integrity in interaction with participants and other relevant "communities" and in relation to held ethical values (Clegg, 1999; 2000). For example, Kvale (1996) used the ethically contentious technique of deception of participants. A duty approach would emphasise honesty and disallow deception as a "greater good", regardless of the benefits (a different "greater good") that might accrue. A utilitarian would cite those benefits to justify the use of deception. A researcher using a "contextual-virtue" perspective would not have a ready answer, but would apply ethical skills and reasoning and confer with others who might be affected by the research or who have relevant experiences, to arrive at a judgement of ethical practice in given circumstances.

The "value" position appears implicitly in the reflections of a number of authors (e.g., Brigham, 1998; McCarthy, 1998; Stalker, 1998; Swain et al., 1998) and is advocated by Clements, Rapley and Cummins (1999), by whom ethical problems and issues are grappled with during the entire research process and in interaction with participants. A values approach implies learning by doing and observing (Kvale, 1996). However, in our reading, the authors cited above are deeply concerned with the reasoned application of ethical principles in conducting research with people with intellectual disabilities. Reasoned practice, as already stated, is grounded in understanding, working with and testing ethical principles in various research contexts.

ETHICAL ISSUES RELATED TO SCIENTIFIC ENDEAVOUR AND RESPECT FOR PERSONS

Ethical principles apply to the bigger picture of the overall goals and rationale of research as well as the methods and procedures that have direct impact on participants. If we ask whom the research benefits, our concern is with the "beneficence" of the project and its potential to serve either individuals, now or in the future, or society more broadly. On the other hand, gaining informed consent has direct impact on the individual participant: "Do I sign up or not?"

The instrumental Belmont Report (National Commission for the Protection of Human Subjects of Biomedical and Behavioural Research, 1978) identified three ethical principles, justice, beneficence, and respect for persons, that provide an ethical justification for research.

Distributive Justice

Research involving humans is conducted "to contribute to knowledge to ameliorate the human condition and enhance human dignity" (Kvale, 1996, p. 109). Alternative agendas may compete, such as the attainment of qualifications or furthering one's career. Researchers need to understand the changes their research creates and for whom. This is not as simple as it might seem, as there is an unpredictable relationship between research, policy, and practice, and positive and negative effects may be clear only with hindsight. For instance, research that focuses on factors of quality service provision may or may not articulate with government or provider policy directions and may or may not be adopted as good practice. Ethical researchers carefully consider the potential benefits of their research (and for whom) and the potential for harm or misuse, and conduct and disseminate research in ways that maximise the positive effects and minimise the negative effects.

The notion of justice goes beyond the single research project to consider whether the benefits and burdens of research are equitably distributed in society. For example, a number of ethical transgressions involved "captive" participants (such as people in institutions—see Clements et al., 1999). This research was not designed for their benefit, but for the good of people outside these settings. The participants bore the burden (sometimes life-threatening), but received none of the benefits.

Injustice can be found when some groups are disproportionately selected in research samples (such as people in institutions, who are easier to recruit) without regard to whether the findings will yield proportionate benefits (see Clements et al., 1999). Similarly, injustice may be charged if groups are systematically selected *out* of research (Fraser, 1999). The extent that, in ascending order of exclusion, people with disabilities, people with intellectual disabilities, and people with severe intellectual disabilities are not represented in research studies, is the extent to which the relevance of findings for these groups is compromised. In our own context, there is concern that people with intellectual disabilities and families from indigenous and other cultural minorities are under-represented in research. Indeed, mainstream social, behavioural, and medical research often explicitly excludes such human characteristics and diversity in its sampling frames. Justice is a matter of distributing across groups for whom the research is intended both the benefits and the burdens; some of these are explicated under the next heading.

Beneficence—"Doing Good"

Beneficence applies to research in progress and the intent of the researcher for future enterprises. Researchers who are motivated to "do good" have an obligation to maximise the benefits of their research and minimise the harm (maleficence). Acting beneficently requires sensitive assessment of the potential for physical or psychological stress, including any discomfort or economic or social disadvantage. For example, a significant burden on people who are economically disadvantaged is travelling to and from a setting expressly to participate in research. This in itself may be difficult if the person does not use public transport, requires wheelchair-accessible vehicles, or needs a support person in attendance. Defraying expenses and payments for time minimise the material costs of participation. Another cost is if people were to miss preferred activities or social interactions because they have consented to participate in the research.

Social and cultural implications of research should be considered. For example, an educational intervention for students with intellectual disabilities in a mainstream setting might have unintended consequences of further emphasising difference and special needs. An interview with elderly parents about the future of their son with intellectual disabilities may bring to the surface distress and concern that might otherwise have remained submerged. These projects might have laudable aims but also have concomitant harms. More broadly, research in institutions might inadvertently condone their existence, and research that ignores the "voice" of people with intellectual disabilities may have unintended social costs. Clements et al. (1999, p. 112) state that researchers should beware of "adding to the burden of stigma".

Recognising costs does not preclude research from proceeding. However, researchers can anticipate possible harms, reduce them where possible, and design responses to ameliorate them should they occur. An intervention plan in the case of the elderly parents above might, prior to interview, alert a local parent support group, trusted person, or counsellor. The researcher could then offer support and connect the participant with these supports if necessary. It is reasonable to assume that the more sensitive the research topic, the more potential there is for emotional distress (McCarthy, 1998) and the more reason for such a plan.

In most cases, some sort of "counselling" support would be required if a person becomes distressed. The researcher has an inherent conflict of interest (as well as a power "advantage") in the transaction of research *and* in recognising distress and providing support. The urge to collect data may desensitise the researcher to participants' discomfort. McCarthy

(1998) took another view. As she was an experienced counsellor and developed a close relationship with her participants in discussing a sensitive topic (their sexuality), she had not "compartmentalised [her] identity into counsellor, researcher and woman" (p. 141). She asserted that, should any conflict of interest arise, the counselling role would take precedence in the best interests of the participants.

It is not inevitable that research will cause or elicit discomfort. Rather than finding it a burden, many participants are positive about their involvement and find it an interesting and worthwhile contribution or a therapeutic and liberating experience (Alm, 1994; McCarthy, 1998; Balandin & Raghavendra, 1999). Although these positives should not be underestimated, the main point is that *potential* for harm should be considered and responses planned.

Some participants invest hope in a research project for a benefit implied, or perceived, if not promised by the researcher. Swain et al. (1998) described a participant who hoped that talking about her experiences of abuse would prevent it from happening to others. Researchers should foster realistic expectations in participants rather than overstating the benefits.

Beneficence goes beyond individual projects to the "greater good". Acting unethically (perhaps by betraying the trust of participants) has consequences for the research community and future participation (see NHMRC, 1999). Balandin has conducted research using people who use augmentative communication in employment settings. As there are only a small number of potential participants, unethical practice would jeopardise the goodwill they might have had (Balandin & Raghavendra, 1999).

Respect for Persons

The third principle in the Belmont Report is the keystone of ethical interaction with research participants. "Respect for persons" is to be accorded regardless of their capacities, social status, and values, and people should not be used as a means to an end (NHMRC, 1999). Research has to be justified by more than the acquisition of qualifications, promotions, kudos or status, or some other "good" that does not relate to the participants. Research has to serve loftier purposes (that is, beneficence and justice).

"Autonomy" upholds the right to decide whether or not to participate in research. Many people with intellectual disabilities have diminished autonomy and are entitled to protection from unethical practices. However, caution dictates that we should not *assume* that people with intellectual disabilities have diminished autonomy. In this section, we outline the related ethical issues of informed consent, privacy, anonymity and confidentiality, sampling and recruitment, and power relations.

Voluntary, Informed Consent

"Perhaps the most important ethical tenet in human studies is the individual's ability to agree to participate with full understanding of what will happen to them" (Portney & Watkins, 2000, p. 40). Voluntary, informed consent raises potential ethical problems in research with people with intellectual disabilities, as it is in these processes that their vulnerability is most obvious. In some circumstances, for people who are highly dependent on medical care, and in research areas such as epidemiology, tissue and genetic research might have special consent regulations (see NHMRC, 1999). In this chapter, we proceed with situations in which personal or proxy consent is required.

Although voluntary, informed consent is sometimes divided into information elements (participants must understand the risks and benefits of the research) and consent elements (autonomy, voluntariness, and competence to consent) (see NHMRC, 1999; Portney & Watkins, 2000), the concepts are interrelated. For example, limited capacity to understand information in turn limits autonomy and compromises voluntariness. The following discussion reflects the inherent conflation of concepts.

Participants Must Be Fully Informed

A written information sheet is often used to obtain consent. It should state the purpose of the research; its methods and demands on participants, including potential risks, inconveniences, or discomforts; the potential benefits to the participant or others; procedures for ensuring confidentiality; and the voluntariness of consent and the right to withdraw (NHMRC, 1999; Iacono & Murray, 2003). Participants should be assured that voluntary consent means that their support, programme, or intervention will not be compromised if they refuse to participate or later withdraw.

Informing people does not mean that they will either comprehend the content or consent to participate. People may even consent when they do not understand the information. Researchers should convey the essential components of research in plain language, free from jargon or unnecessary complexity. (We have seen information sheets so complex that academics themselves would be unable to provide informed consent.) Clearly, informed consent is a major issue for people with intellectual disabilities, and there is the added risk that the ubiquitous information sheet will be just another piece of paper. (Some alternative formats will be mentioned under the next subheading.)

There is a tension in all this. The researcher *wants* people to consent. This inherent bias may diminish informed consent when there is lack of dissent, or acquiescent or compliant response, or when, due to information overload, people consent when they do not understand what is required of them.

The development of guidelines regarding language levels for understanding of consent processes involving people with intellectual disabilities has not been wholly successful (see Iacono & Murray, 2003). One reason is individual variation in understanding written or spoken information. Presenting comprehensible information has tested researchers' ingenuity. McCarthy (1998), for example, was requested by an IEC to tape-record consent. An ethical conundrum was how to tape-record consent when consent had not yet been obtained to record the meeting. (A separate consent session, with verbal agreement to record it; or a discussion of consent followed by a taped session might work, but add to participants' confusion.) Another reason why the language level of information is difficult to prescribe is that the type of research influences (if not determines) the level of consent that should be obtained. Although consent is fundamental to all research involving humans, projects with high risks and no immediate benefits for the participants should, in principle, require a high level of direct, competent, informed consent by the participant. It could be argued that these consent factors should be mitigated for research with minimal (or not foreseeable) risks and significant benefits for the individual. This principle is also discussed later in relation to proxy decision making.

Autonomy, Voluntariness, and Competence

Iacono and Murray (2003) found definitional uncertainty of "incapacity" for voluntary, informed consent. They added that this is reflected in the extant literature, and there are no general guidelines to determine capacity to consent to participate in research.

Arscott, Dagnan and Kroese (1998) investigated competence for voluntary, informed consent by people with intellectual disabilities to participate in a psychological study. Not surprisingly, the understanding of aurally presented information was positively related to assessed comprehension levels. The general nature of the research seemed to be understood, but not the risks and benefits, or the right to refuse to participate or later to withdraw consent (see also Heller, Pederson & Miller, 1996).

The technique used by Arscott et al. (1998), reading plain language information, followed by a question–answer session, repeated if necessary, could be adopted by other researchers to gauge capacity for the voluntary, informed consent of people with intellectual disabilities. Capacity to consent, however, is a function of a person's competence and experience. Training in decision making, prior to information about the research, is a crucial step for people who have had limited opportunity to exercise choice. Information should be tailored to the individuals whose participation is being sought. It may be necessary to repeat information or break it up over a longer time period; visual materials such as pictures or a video that explains the purpose of the research and what will happen will make the choice less abstract, as will role-plays and other experiential activities (see Freedman, 2001). These techniques not only inform, but also build trust between researchers and participants.

People with intellectual disabilities are especially vulnerable when their ability to provide informed consent is compromised (Roberts & Roberts, 1999). Vulnerability is compounded if the person tends to be acquiescent or compliant, or lacks experience in assertive decision making. People who are socially impoverished may welcome the intrusion of a researcher, or the researcher may just be another in the procession of workers through a person's life. These issues are difficult to determine beforehand, unless the researcher already knows the potential participants. The potential participant might need a trusted support person or advocate to assist in understanding the information and deciding to participate or not.

Consent is an interactive construct and will vary according to the complexity of the information presented, whom it is presented by, the effort put into communicating it, and the setting in which the information is conveyed. Acquiescence, for example, may be particularly problematic, as the "expert" researcher is in a relatively powerful position (Clements et al., 1999). Other factors, such as anxiety or concomitant mental illness, also need to be taken into account. (See Iacono & Murray, 2003, for discussion of these points.) Caution should be exercised, therefore, in deeming a person incapable of consent.

A minimum requirement for consent (Dresser, 1996) is that the person is able to communicate a preference (that is, whether to participate or not). A conservative approach is to proceed as if choice can be expressed, verbally or behaviourally. However, ethical research is an abstract construct, and it is with such abstractions that people with intellectual disabilities have the most trouble (Stalker & Harris, 1998). Researchers promise intangible benefits and caution about possible risks of things that may never happen. Consent may be given but later withdrawn because of something that may change a person's mind in the future. "Data" will be recorded and taken away for analysis. A long time in the future, results will be used in a thesis, publications, or conferences. Even though the researcher and participants know each other, privacy, confidentiality, and anonymity will be protected (they may disclose something that might cause them embarrassment when they say it). The demands on the researcher for educational efforts and ingenuity of disclosure are substantial.

Proxy Consent

If a person lacks capacity to consent, a substitute decision maker (proxy) has to decide. Different jurisdictions have different legal requirements. (In our home State of New South Wales, Australia, a legally appointed guardian does not usually have authority to consent to research.) The proxy should be a trusted, independent person who will make an informed decision based on what the person would prefer and in the person's best interests. Freedman (2001) noted that parents are often the proxies for adults with intellectual disabilities.

"Preference" is predicated on a person's stated inclination prior to loss of capacity (for example, due to injury or illness). People with intellectual disabilities may also lose capacity, but many will not have expressed a preference for participation in research. Judging what they would have decided in a similar situation is impossible.

"Acting in the person's best interests" does not assume knowledge of preference. The proxy should know the person well; understand that person's needs, likes, and dislikes; and be willing to act on that knowledge. Based on the information provided, the proxy's responsibility is to weigh the potential benefits and risks and make a decision. A proxy should not expose people to risks greater than those that they face in their daily life (NHMRC, 1999). The more risk involved, the less willing the proxy should be to consent on a person's behalf. It would be very troubling if, for example, consent were given to take blood if the person is usually distressed at the sight of a needle. A researcher faced with this protest should immediately deem it withdrawn from the project.

Consent and Assent

When a proxy has consented for a person with intellectual disabilities to participate in a study, the person should also assent. We have often gained permission from a legal guardian to ask a person to agree to participate. Acquiescence needs to be considered, but lack of assent may be verbal or behavioural refusal or protest. It is also possible that the person may assent even though consent has not been given, in which case Freedman (2001) advocates supported conciliative discussion between person and proxy.

Consent by a parent or guardian, followed by assent, applies to the nascent capacity of young children and adolescents. Because capacity is central to voluntary, informed consent, some ethical issues related to adults with intellectual disabilities are also relevant to children (see Grodin & Glantz, 1994; NHMRC, 1999).

Withdrawal of Consent

If consent is freely given (by the person or a proxy), it may be withdrawn, at any time, without penalty. As with consent and assent, withdrawal may be expressed in various ways, from assertive discontinuation to silence. Withdrawal should be worry-free, but two implicit elements need to be dealt with.

Although withdrawal does not have to be justified, there may be circumstances when the researcher asks the person or advocate the reasons for the decision. Feedback about the conduct of the research might have implications for the other participants. The researcher may be able to ameliorate any problems the person had (for example, "everyone talks, but no one listens to me"). However, even subtle coercion is unethical.

Withdrawal of consent has implications for the fate of the data. People may withdraw yet be content for their data to remain in the study, especially if confidentiality and anonymity are assured. Or the person may have disclosed more than intended and wish the data to be erased. Within group interviews, an undertaking might be given to erase the person's data from the transcripts (or other data files).

As withdrawal may be expressed in various ways, when data gathering goes over several sessions, consent or assent could be checked at the start of each. In effect, this is consent to continue and might just require verbal agreement to this effect. Withdrawal from groups requires a reasonable level of assertion, and continuation of consent should be routinely monitored with the individuals as well the group as a whole.

In our experience, at least three levels of informed consent (after approval from various IECs) are required to access the clients of a service: central managers' (or board), field managers' or practitioners', and, finally, that of the participant (or an advocate or guardian, followed by the assent of the participant—see Stalker, 1998). Different levels of an organisation might have different issues with the research. Management, for example, may be sensitive about what might be "discovered" about the service during the research and later reported. We were temporarily blocked from approaching participants in group homes by staff who were involved in an industrial dispute and saw providing access as beyond "working to rule". In this case, the intervention of management, who had consented to accessing the service and its clients, was required. The active refusal or passive resistance by an organisation and its staff to allow the conduct of research is an ethical dilemma for researchers, who may have the willing, informed consent of participants, or when they have not been given the opportunity to consider consent. The solutions to these problems are context-specific. Building positive relationships with the various levels of services and perhaps advocacy organisations, and seeking their involvement in research planning, reduces the potential for later problems. Nonetheless, withdrawal of consent (or assent) could occur at any stage of the research at any of these organisational levels and jeopardise a project; the further down the track, the more problematic for the researcher.

Privacy, Confidentiality, and Anonymity

Respect for persons involves protecting their right to choose what to disclose to whom and when (privacy), shielding data from public or unauthorised scrutiny by securely storing identifying data (confidentiality), and de-identifying disseminations (anonymity). IECs like to see how researchers will protect privacy, confidentiality, and anonymity in their proposals. Sometimes this is difficult. For example, participatory action research might involve all participants agreeing on confidentiality and anonymity protocols. Moreover, the principle of anonymity might sometimes be more important for the researcher and IEC than for the participants, who may wish to share their experiences with their communities (see McCarthy, 1998; Swain et al., 1998). Privacy is more difficult to ensure with methods based on self-disclosure (as in interviews about personal topics), as neither the researcher nor participants can be sure what will be disclosed.

Confidentiality can be carelessly guaranteed. The NHMRC (1999) distinguishes three types of data. In ascending order of confidentiality, these are identified, potentially identifiable, and de-identified. Identified data may include name, date of birth, or other information that may identify participants. Much research falls into the "potentially identifiable" category. Here identifiers (such as name) are replaced by a code or pseudonym and can therefore be decoded to re-identify the participants. Only de-identified data are truly confidential and cannot be re-identified because identifiers have been permanently removed, or were never included (as in an anonymous questionnaire).

Confidentiality and anonymity are closely linked. A common way of guarding the anonymity of participants in qualitative research is to give them pseudonyms and change some demographic details (as Swain et al., 1998, did). The richer the description, or the more personalised the presentation of data, the less anonymity can be promised. This is particularly so with research that uses small pools of participants (Balandin & Raghavendra, 1999).

Like so many areas of ethical research, how to preserve participants' privacy, confidentiality, and anonymity cannot be prescribed. For example, participants may agree to reveal personal aspects of their lives if the researcher can justify that depth of disclosure. Conversely, if consent has not been obtained for personal disclosures that are not essential to the research aims, delving is very dubious. Researchers need to try to set boundaries, and not have participants who, "fuelled by doses of empathy and eye-contact, are left wondering whether they disclosed too much" (Kellehear, 1996, p. 102).

Anonymity is designed into some methods, such as questionnaire research. In some jurisdictions, the return of an anonymous questionnaire implies consent; in others, an explicit indication is necessary. If confidentiality and anonymity are promised, no identifying information should be elicited; if identifying information is required (as for a follow-up survey), explicit consent for this must be obtained. A questionnaire returned to the researcher's hand compromises confidentiality and anonymity. Participants also define their own privacy boundaries by implicitly or explicitly refusing to answer a question or engage in an activity. Researchers should not pressure this "zone of exclusivity", in which participants are free from scrutiny (NHMRC, 1999, p. 65).

A vexed area of confidentiality is when participants reveal compromising information about themselves or other people. What if, for example, a mother reveals that she is being abused? What if she reports that her child is being abused? Under what circumstances would a researcher breach confidentiality and trust in the interests of the mother and child? (see McCarthy, 1998; Swain et al., 1998, for a discussion of this issue). Researchers must consider their legal context as well as ethical values. The primary concern for researchers is protection of participants, broadly defined as those people who engage in the research and others affected by it (NHMRC, 1999).

Confidentiality is protection of information from people or agencies not authorised by consent to have access. Researchers often state that data and related documents are kept in a locked filing cabinet or a password-protected computer file. Researchers who have negotiated joint ownership of the research materials with participants should have protocols for appropriate access (e.g., Kellett & Nind, 2001).

Researches who conduct group interviews need to be particularly sensitive to privacy and confidentiality issues within the group, particularly if the topic is delicate. A blanket assurance of privacy and confidentiality is misleading when they are impossible to achieve within the group. Privacy and confidentiality should be discussed within the group, and ground rules established (for example, matters discussed in the group are not to be discussed outside it).

Sampling and Recruitment

Ethical issues related to selection of participants from a justice perspective have been discussed. Various sampling techniques carry with them ethical cautions, especially those related to obtaining voluntary, informed consent and confidentiality. The main issue is how the study is introduced to potential participants.

Achieving a representative, population-based sample is often difficult. Direct approaches such as "cold canvassing" (as in door knocking) are problematic, as the recipient may have limited opportunity to consider informed involvement. A more ethical way to obtain a community sample might be an information "drop" with contact information for those interested. However, there are no hard ethical rules for these sampling techniques. An information drop may disadvantage people with limited literacy and those whose language is not used in the content. Alternatively, a cold canvass might identify potential participants that may later, with appropriate permission, be approached to consider informed consent.

"Snowball" or "chain" sampling (also favoured by sales people, especially in the insurance industry), in which recruits are encouraged to provide contact details of other potential participants they know, is especially compromising (NHMRC, 1995). Contact details should not be given directly to the researcher; rather, an information sheet should be provided for the participants to forward to the new person, who is then left to consider involvement and to contact the researcher if interested.

Confidentiality of information is a prime consideration in obtaining lists of contact details of potential participants: the more personal this contact information, the more ethically problematic. Community service providers keen to have research conducted in their settings may inadvertently breach confidentiality conventions by providing contact details of clients and families. The researcher's right to this information is contentious. In ethical terms, information about the study and facilitation of entrée to participants should be arranged by the service provider, person, or agency with legitimate access to contact details.

Purposeful sampling has its own problems, as it is more likely that the researcher knows the potential participants. Subtle social pressure or a feeling of obligation to participate need to be taken into account.

A final consideration is inducement to participate. Inducement could be in cash or kind. Incentives carry a potential pressure to participate. This is linked to, but does not preclude, payment of participants for their time and effort. A double-edged sword, payment can be a hedge against exploitation of people with intellectual disabilities, but may be a suspect inducement to participate, especially if compensation encourages engagement in research that would otherwise be avoided.

Power Relations and Conflict of Interest

"One of the dilemmas in researching vulnerable people whose status in society is marginal is that the research may be conducted in a way which reproduces their marginality" (Wyn,

Lumley & Daly, 1996, p. 171). Many researchers are rightly concerned with the inherent power imbalance between researchers (who often enjoy relatively high status) and participants. This balance is tilted further towards the researcher when studies involve people with limited ability to process verbal information. The researcher, as an elite "word worker", has immense advantages (Kellehear, 1996, p. 103).

Power imbalance is present from consent, through data gathering (as in face-to-face interviews) and analyses, to dissemination of the research findings (Wyn et al., 1996) and is implicit in most of the ethical issues raised so far (and relevant to the discussion of "participatory approaches" later).

A conflict of interest is a clash of demands. Clements et al. (1999) observed that researchers can be "careless with the lives of powerless people" (p. 105) due to conflicting academic imperatives, including the need to meet required outputs.

The Practitioner as Researcher

There is an impetus for practitioners to become researchers of their own practice in the interests of the development of professional bodies of knowledge and evidence-based practice (Guyatt, 1996). McDonald (1996) argued that practitioners' responsibilities extend beyond individual clients, and that their participation in research is essential for improving client care and support. The interest here is in the potential for conflict of interest in the dual roles of practitioner and researcher. As previously mentioned, there is significant overlap of professional and research codes of ethical conduct.

If practice and research can be conceptualised as two ends of a continuum, when does practice *become* research? According to Guyatt (1996), "usual care" is considered practice, as are activities associated with quality assurance. Intent to publish or curiosity that takes the practitioner beyond optimal practice falls into the realms of research where conflict of interest is more likely and IECs become involved. The practitioner-researcher may introduce extra procedures in the interests of "good" research that carry additional burdens for the client-participant. Guyatt (1996) argues that because of competing demands, practitioner-researchers require external monitoring so that clients' rights are protected.

ETHICAL ISSUES RELATED TO RESEARCH METHODS

To a large extent, research methods determine the tenor of interactions with participants. Ethical problems find different expression in different approaches.

Quantitative Methods

The quantitative tradition has been charged with doing research *on* subjects. The ethical principles expounded in this chapter are incompatible with this attitude and reinforce the requirement that all researchers, regardless of their methods, must respect participants and safeguard their well-being.

Randomised Control Trials

The flagship design in quantitative research is the randomised control trial (RCT), which compares the results of an "experimental" group with a "control" group that receives either the usual "intervention" (drug, educational programme, etc.) or, in the case of drug trials, a placebo control. To avoid bias in the sample being studied, participants are selected at random from a population of interest and then randomly assigned to either the intervention or control group or groups. By statistically comparing the effects of the intervention group with a control group, strong evidence can be provided for the efficacy of the intervention. Studies that are designed for similar comparisons, but cannot select or assign people at random, are called "quasi-experimental" (see Iacono & Murray, 2003, for an example regarding the investigation of pica, the ingestion of inedible objects).

The main ethical problem of RCTs is that some participants (perhaps half of them) receive no intervention. Consent must be obtained before they know whether they will receive the intervention or not. Presumably, the study has a strong rationale that the intervention will have the desired effect. So, ethically, how can some people be excluded? The answers to this question solve some ethical problems but raise others.

The first response refers to the "larger picture" of beneficence and holds that RCTs establish the efficacy of interventions and will benefit those in the intervention group *and* future people in similar circumstances: the greater good is therefore served. (It is noted that interventions have their costs—they may not work or may be associated with unwanted side effects.)

Modification of the design to compare two interventions, thereby avoiding a control group, is another way forward. However, a conclusion that the intervention is better than no intervention cannot be drawn. If receiving *no* intervention (that is, control) is as effective as the intervention, using it would be unethical (Portney & Watkins, 2000).

Another approach is to give the control group the intervention after the study, should it prove to be effective. A more sophisticated variation is to provide intervention to the control group *when* it proves to be effective, not necessarily when the course of the study has run (Nolan, 1996).

When a new intervention is to be compared to a usual intervention, a control condition (the usual intervention) is implied. Zelen (referred to in Nolan, 1996) proposed a model where recruits for the novel intervention are randomly selected from those getting usual intervention. Consent is obtained only from those selected for the new intervention. This approach remains somewhat contentious and has not been routinely accepted by IECs (Nolan, 1996).

The assumption of "equipoise", a state of genuine uncertainty about the value of the intervention, underpins RCTs. "After considering the weight of all the available evidence, equipoise exists if the [researcher] cannot *reasonably* determine the efficacy or safety of the innovation" (Nolan, 1996, p. 60). This places RCTs in an ethical fix. If the researcher aims to *demonstrate* that an intervention works, there is *less* justification for a control group (Royall, 1991). However, uncertainty (if this is realistic) about the efficacy and risks of the intervention means the researcher may be hard-pressed to justify investigation, as there must be a "realistic possibility that the interventions being studied will be at least as effective as standard intervention" (NHMRC, 1999, p. 35).

Yet, Nolan (1996) claimed that practitioners have often been convinced about the safety and efficacy of their interventions only to be proven wrong after rigorous evaluation. An example in the field of intellectual disabilities can be found in the facilitated communication (FC) controversy. FC is a technique in which a "facilitator" supports the hand or arm of a person with a disability, who then uses a keyboard to communicate. It has been used to disclose the verbal communications of people with autism and severe intellectual disabilities that were previously mute. In 1994, the American Psychological Association was perturbed by the proliferation of FC and disclosed accusations of abuse (by caregivers) of the communicator, despite the absence of evidence of its efficacy, to form a resolution. The resolution concluded that "facilitated communication is a controversial and unproved communication procedure with no scientifically demonstrated support for its efficacy" (American Psychological Association, 1994, in Jacobson & Mulick, 1996, p. 431). Duchan and colleagues (Duchan, 1999; Duchan, Calculator, Sonnenmeier, Diehl & Cumley, 2001) summarised the dilemma for professionals when asked to consider FC as a communication technique. While professionals should respect the rights of clients and families to choose a controversial approach, they also have the responsibility to keep up to date and provide interventions based on the best evidence. Duchan et al. (2001) suggested that consent processes similar to those outlined in this chapter be applied prior to the clinical use of FC and other controversial approaches.

Other Controlled Designs

"Single-subject" designs in which participants are their own controls are commonly used with people with intellectual disabilities. An initial baseline is compared to a subsequent intervention to determine whether it has been successful. Removal of the intervention to see whether measurements return to baseline is further evidence of efficacy. Typically, there is a return to intervention if it can be shown to work (the so-called ABAB design). (See Zhan & Ottenbacher, 2001, for an overview of "single-subject" designs.)

The ethical problem with this design is that an intervention that appears to be working needs to be withdrawn to establish that fact. However, not withdrawing the intervention compromises the design; maybe something that occurred contemporaneously with the intervention (but not related to it) produced the improvement.

Kellett and Nind (2001) dealt with this issue in their evaluation of an intervention designed to enable "people with profound or complex learning disabilities to be more effective communicators, and those who work with and care for them to be more effective 'listeners' " (p. 52). A "multiple baseline" design obviated withdrawal of the intervention. The baseline period was staggered; as one person moved to the intervention condition, others remained on the baseline. With this design, an effective intervention should show a change for the person receiving the intervention, but not others. Similar, successive changes should be observed as each participant moves from baseline to intervention.

Kellett and Nind (2001) found an ethical issue in the duration of the baseline. In the "community special schools" where the intervention occurred, teachers enthusiastic about the potential of the intervention were keen to start. From their perspective, a prolonged baseline represented lost opportunities. The application of the design (for a compelling justification for its wider use) was pressured by immediate gains for children in the study.

Qualitative Methods

Although there is a range of qualitative methods (NHMRC, 1995), we concentrate on in-depth, open-ended individual or group interviews. Participatory approaches that use in-depth interviews may reduce some ethical risks, but others are more acute because of the close relationship between researcher and participant. It is argued, for example, that, when using participatory approaches, researchers are less likely to exercise power relations and control. Yet, the very closeness of the relationship between participants (the researcher included), the dynamism of the interactions, and the potential competition of agendas means that vigilance is necessary to recognise and avoid subtle manipulations.

Problems with personal disclosure have been flagged (see above). Intrusiveness can be a privacy issue, especially if the interviews are being conducted in the person's home. Close relationships engendered by in-depth interviewing can cause confusion about ongoing friendships (Stalker, 1998), which might be exacerbated when researchers reciprocate the sharing of experiences (see McCarthy, 1998; Swain et al., 1998). Indeed, no one may have ever spent so much time talking about feelings and issues with a participant as the researcher (Balandin & Raghavendra, 1999). Although a privileged bond may have formed, the researcher must be clear and realistic about continuing friendships. This relationship could be more important for the participant (who could be relatively socially isolated) than the researcher (Stalker, 1998).

A talking method with participants with intellectual disabilities raises the obvious consideration of limited verbal skills. Researchers are resourceful in working with participants with limited conceptual understanding and verbal expression. Balandin and Raghavendra (1999) described the intense effort required to interview people with severe communication impairments who are using communication technologies.

Deceptions and Other Covert Operations

The first author, as a psychology student, was raised on descriptions of compelling yet unethical studies that used the technique of deception. The research is undermined if participants know the real purpose; false pretence is required. For example, the dramatic experiments of Stanley Milgram on "obedience to authority" could not be repeated today (see Milgram, 1974). Deception, along with concealment and covert observations (NHMRC, 1999), is ethically tricky, as it disallows informed consent. The researcher must defend deception with a compelling statement that the research is necessary and there are no alternative techniques for the purpose. If deception will do no lasting harm (beyond the deception itself), the researcher should debrief the participants about the real purpose of the research and the need for deception as soon as practicable (see NHMRC, 1999).

One covert activity is data analysis. For most participants, quantitative data analysis is a "black box"—data go in and results come out. Covert operations occur in qualitative analysis in which verbal data are transformed, perhaps interpreted for meaning, and re-formed into themes. Participants may not recognise these transformations as their contributions. One safeguard is to validate the outcomes of analyses with participants (Brigham, 1998).

APPROACHES THAT MINIMISE RISK

Participative Approaches

Research ethics is concerned with how participants are treated while research politics assesses the social value of a piece of research. "Participatory" and especially "emancipatory" research are often overtly political, aiming to influence researchers to include people with intellectual disabilities as meaningful participants in research that empowers and liberates (see Stalker, 1998). Strident voices have sensitised researchers to the relationship between the researcher and "researched" (e.g., Kellett & Nind, 2001).

Sincere participatory approaches are less likely to exploit the power imbalance between researchers and participants with intellectual disabilities in the planning, conduct, and dissemination of research. (See Heller et al., 1996; Stalker, 1998; Balandin & Raghavendra, 1999; Chappell, 2000; Kellett & Nind, 2001, for the role of non-disabled researchers in intellectual disabilities research.) As previously noted, technical aspects of analyses may remain covert, but these can be validated with participants, who may also be involved in disseminations.

As participatory research mostly uses in-depth interviewing, ethical issues related to this method are relevant. The costs of participatory research are not often stated. Much time is required to do research with people with intellectual disabilities, with related output costs for the researcher, which may also be related to loss of control of the process. Researchers may compromise the quality of their research in the interests of participatory processes (see Ward & Trigler, 2001). Of course, the more significant their disability, the less able people are to participate. While people with intellectual disabilities appear to wish to move from "recipients" to partners and stakeholders, there is a fine line between supporting participation and overburdening them (Heller et al., 1996).

Ethics of Dissemination

Balandin (2003) argued that access to findings is a litmus test of who the beneficiaries of research really are. Participants should be given appropriate access to findings (Heller et al., 1996; Stalker, 1998). Participatory approaches are likely to include plans for dissemination for multiple purposes and audiences, including academics, practitioners, families, and people with intellectual disabilities. The formats and level of detail will be dictated by the purpose.

IECs are, in general, interested in how research findings will be publicised, regardless of the methodology, because, as alluded to above, the researcher's motives and application of ethical principles, such as "respect for persons" (that is, not using people as a means to an end), are revealed. The larger principle of "distributive justice" is also relevant here, as the benefits of research for participants (now or in the future) are at least more explicitly conveyed to them. In our judgement, it is becoming more common to find researchers preparing plain language summaries of their research and making these accessible to participants. Referring to people with developmental disabilities, Balandin and Morgan (1997) stated that few read for information or have access to journals or conferences. Just as researchers whose participants have intellectual disabilities need to tailor information for informed consent, they need to modify summaries of the outcomes. Potentially accessible formats include short written summaries, text-reading software, short audiotapes, videos or compact discs, graphic symbols, or line-drawings, although there is as yet little information on how best to impart outcome effectively (Balandin, 2003).

Balandin (2003) identified the benefits for both researchers and participants of providing feedback about the outcome of research. For example, a meeting with participants to discuss findings is likely to reinforce their valued contribution, and they may ask questions and provide feedback about their experiences to the researcher, which may then help to refine future projects. Importantly, this process may also give closure to the participants, and they may be able to share their experiences and the outcomes with friends, families, and others.

Least Intrusive Methods

The fundamental question for a researcher is, "Should this research be done?" McCarthy (1998) canvassed this question in interviewing women about a personal topic (their sexuality). It was argued that the benefits for the women would outweigh any distress. More broadly, McCarthy argued against putting private issues beyond research bounds, provided that people were "willing to share their experiences and certain conditions are in place to ensure their contributions are respected as individuals and they are not exploited" (p. 141). Indeed, McCarthy cited the positive consequences of involvement in the interviews. Participants may feel valued, that they have "had their say", or the process may be "therapeutic", in identifying and sharing concerns and feelings (see Kvale, 1996).

Proceeding with research that has potential for significant harm, regardless of anticipated benefits, is not always defensible. It is unethical to conduct research that is not essential to answer the questions posed, or to employ methods more taxing of participants than essential. Kellehear (1993, 1996) proposed a series of steps to find the least intrusive method. First, does the research have to be empirical? The answers may be found in the literature, or other data sources (such as social indicators). Second, would "indirect" methods do the job? These include analysis of artefacts or media images, and so on. Kellehear (1996) claims that indirect methods range "from simple tallying-type content analysis to the type of semiotic analysis that might impress even Foucault at a café near you" (p. 101).

Combining indirect and direct methods could be considered; perhaps in "action research" or "participant observation". Are there ways in which interviews, if necessary, could be more structured and prevent respondents from wondering whether they disclosed too much (Kellehear, 1996). Methods that limit intrusiveness and place less burden on participants should be in the researcher's kit.

CONCLUSIONS

As stated at the start of this chapter, ethical issues permeate all aspects of research. Ethical practice is underpinned by ensuring that vulnerable people are not exploited in the research relationship. Exploitation can be intended or unintended, obvious or subtle. The ethical issue of informed consent illustrates this point. It is in the researcher's best interest to assume consent, even when it is not obviously freely given. In this simple statement are the hallmarks of power imbalance and potential lack of due process.

There is always a tension between principles and practice. This is reflected in the approach implicitly adopted by many of the researchers cited in this chapter, value ethics. Researchers should internalise ethical standards and apply them to the contexts in which they work. However, IECs have a legal and moral imperative independently to weigh putative benefits and harms, and are unlikely to be convinced by applicants who state they are experienced in researching with people with intellectual disabilities and will work out how to deal with ethical issues when they arise. This is not necessarily a dilemma, because, of course, ethical sensitivity is also in the prediction of problems. For practical and ethical necessity, researchers must demonstrate how they will apply the principles of ethical research.

Our purpose has not been to vex inexperienced researchers into reconsidering their vocations. Ethical issues can be found in all aspects of research, with all methods. Rather than being paralysed into inaction, we must accept the challenge to work with people with intellectual disabilities in conducting research that answers important questions in ways that respect their rights and are as ethically benign as possible.

ACKNOWLEDGEMENT

We acknowledge the assistance of Dr Teresa Iacono in providing a key paper that was in press at the time of writing this chapter.

REFERENCES

Alm, N. (1994). Ethical questions in AAC research. In J. Brodin & E. Bjorck-Akesson (Eds) *Proceedings from the Third ISAAC Research Symposium in Augmentative and Alternative Communication* (pp. 98–104). Jonkoping, Sweden: Jonkoping University Press.

American Association on Mental Retardation (2001). *Guidelines on Professional Conduct* [Online]: www.aamr.org/Policies/guidelines.shtml

American Psychological Association (1994). Resolution on facilitated communication by the American Psychological Association. In J.W. Jacobson & J.A. Mulick (Eds) (1996) *Manual of Diagnosis and Professional Practice in Mental Retardation* (pp. 431–433). Washington, DC: American Psychological Association.

Annas, G.J. & Grodin, M.A. (1989). *The Nazi Doctors and the Nuremberg Code*. New York: Oxford University Press.

Arscott, K., Dagnan, D. & Kroese, B.S. (1998). Consent to psychological research by people with an intellectual disability. *Journal of Applied Research in Intellectual Disabilities*, **11**, 77–83.

Balandin, S. (2003). Happily ever after: communicating results to participants in research. *Journal of Intellectual and Developmental Disability*, **28**, 85–87.

Balandin, S. & Morgan, J. (1997). Adults with cerebral palsy: what's happening? *Journal of Intellectual and Developmental Disability*, **22**, 109–124.

Balandin, S. & Raghavendra, P. (1999). Challenging oppression: augmented communicators' involvement in AAC research. In F. Loncker, J. Clibbens & L. Lloyd (Eds) *Augmentative and Alternative Communication: New Directions in Research and Practice* (pp. 262–277). London: Whurr.

Brigham, L. (1998). Representing the lives of women with learning difficulties: ethical dilemmas in the research process. *British Journal of Learning Disabilities*, **26**, 146–150.

Chappell, A.L. (2000). Emergence of participatory methodology in learning difficulty research: understanding the context. *British Journal of Learning Disabilities*, **28**, 38–43.

Clegg, J. (1999). Ethics and intellectual disability. *Current Opinion in Psychiatry*, **12**, 537–541.

Clegg, J. (2000). Beyond ethical individualism. *Journal of Intellectual Disability Research*, **44**, 1–11.

Clements, J., Rapley, M. & Cummins, R.A. (1999). On, to, for, with— vulnerable people and practices of the research community. *Behavioural and Cognitive Psychotherapy*, **27**,103–115.

Dresser, R. (1996). Research involving persons with mental disabilities. In D. Evans & M. Evans (1996) *A Decent Proposal: Ethical Review of Clinical Research*. Chichester: Wiley.

Duchan, J.F. (1999). Views of facilitated communication: what's the point? *Language, Speech, and Hearing Services in Schools*, **30**, 401–408.

Duchan, J.F., Calculator, S., Sonnenmeier, R., Diehl, S. & Cumley, G.D. (2001). A framework for managing controversial practices. *Language, Speech, and Hearing Services in Schools*, **32**, 133–141.

Fraser, W.I. (1999). Ethical and evidential issues in mental retardation. *Current Opinion in Psychiatry*, **12**, 535–536.

Freedman, R.I. (2001). Ethical challenges in the conduct of research involving persons with mental retardation. *Mental Retardation*, **39**, 130–141.

Frew, R. (2001). Research ethics committees: what can we learn from the Western European and United States experience? *Monash Bioethics Review*, **20**, 61–77.

Grodin, M.A. & Glantz, L.H. (Eds) (1994). *Children as Research Subjects: Science, Ethics and Law*. Oxford: Oxford University Press.

Guyatt, G. (1996). Clinical care and clinical research: a false dichotomy. In J. Daly (Ed.) *Ethical Intersections: Health Research, Methods and Researcher Responsibility* (pp. 66–73). Sydney: Allen & Unwin.

Heller, T., Pederson, E.L. & Miller, A.B. (1996). Guidelines from the consumer: improving consumer involvement in research and training for persons with mental retardation. *Mental Retardation*, **34**, 141–148.

Iacono, T. & Murray, V. (2003). Issues of informed consent in conducting medical research involving people with intellectual disability. *Journal of Applied Research in Intellectual Disabilities*, **16**, 41–52.

Kellehear, A. (1993). *The Unobtrusive Researcher: A Guide to Methods*. Sydney: Allen & Unwin.

Kellehear, A. (1996). Unobtrusive methods in delicate situations. In J. Daly (Ed.) *Ethical Intersections: Health Research, Methods and Researcher Responsibility* (pp. 97–105). Sydney: Allen & Unwin.

Kellett, M. & Nind, M. (2001). Ethics in quasi-experimental research on people with severe learning disabilities: dilemmas and compromises. *British Journal of Learning Disabilities*, **29**, 51–55.

Kvale, S. (1996). *Interviews: An Introduction to Qualitative Research Interviewing*. London: Sage.

McCarthy, M. (1998). Interviewing people with learning disabilities about sensitive topics: a discussion of ethical issues. *British Journal of Learning Disabilities*, **26**, 140–145.

McDonald, I. (1996). Clinicians studying their own practice: an introduction. In J. Daly (Ed.) *Ethical Intersections: Health Research, Methods and Researcher Responsibility* (pp. 193–202). Sydney: Allen & Unwin.

McNeil, P.M. (1996). Research ethics committees: is the tail wagging the dog? In J. Daly (Ed.) *Ethical Intersections: Health Research, Methods and Researcher Responsibility* (pp. 15–23). Sydney: Allen & Unwin.

Miles, M.B. & Huberman, A.M. (1994). *Qualitative Data Analysis* (2nd edn). Thousand Oaks, CA: Sage.

Milgram, S. (1974). *Obedience to Authority*. New York: Harper & Row.

National Commission for the Protection of Human Subjects of Biomedical and Behavioural Research (1978). *The Belmont Report: Ethical Principles and Guidelines for the Protection of Human Subjects of Research*. Department of Health, Education and Welfare Publication No. (OS) 78-0012. Washington, DC: US Government Printing Office.

National Health and Medical Research Council (1995). *Ethical Aspects of Qualitative Methods in Health Research: An Information Paper of Institutional Ethics Committees*. Canberra: Australian Government Publishing Service.

National Health and Medical Research Council (1999). *National Statement on Ethical Conduct in Research Involving Humans*. Canberra: AusInfo.

Nolan, T. (1996). Traditional scientific designs and ethics. In J. Daly (Ed.) *Ethical Intersections: Health Research, Methods and Researcher Responsibility* (pp. 58–65). Sydney: Allen & Unwin.

Portney, L.G. & Watkins, M.P. (2000). *Foundations of Clinical Research: Applications to Practice*. (2nd edn). Upper Saddle River, NJ: Prentice-Hall.

Roberts, L. W. & Roberts, B. (1999). Psychiatric research ethics: an overview of evolving guidelines and current ethical dilemmas in the study of mental illness. *Biological Psychiatry*, **46**, 1025–1038.

Royall, R.M. (1991). Ethics and statistics in randomised clinical trials. *Statistical Science*, **6**, 52–88.

Sergejew, A. (1996, September). The research ethics process: an overview and tips for applicants. Paper presented at Research Ethics Seminars, Deakin University, Geelong, Australia [Online]: http://ecco.bsee.swin.edu.au/studes/ethics/ethics-tips.html.

Stalker, K. (1998). Some ethical and methodological issues in research with people with learning difficulties. *Disability and Society*, **13**, 5–19.

Stalker, K. & Harris, P. (1998). The exercise of choice by adults with intellectual disabilities: a literature review. *Journal of Applied Research in Intellectual Disabilities*, **11**, 60–76.

Swain, J., Heyman, B. & Gillman, M. (1998). Public research, private concerns: ethical issues in the use of open-ended interviews with people who have learning difficulties. *Disability and Society*, **13**, 21–36.

Ward, K. & Trigler, J.S. (2001). Reflections on participatory action research with people who have developmental disabilities. *Mental Retardation*, **39**, 57–59.

World Health Organisation (2001). *International Classification of Functioning and Disability and Health: ICF*. Geneva: Author.

World Medical Association. (1989). *The World Medical Association Declaration of Helsinki*: Recommendations Guiding Medical Doctors in Biomedical Research Involving Human Subjects [Online]: http://ecco.bsee.swin.edu.au/studes/ethics/Helsinki.html.

Wyn, J., Lumley, J. & Daly, J. (1996). Women's health: methods and ethics. In J. Daly (Ed.) *Ethical Intersections: Health Research, Methods and Researcher Responsibility* (pp. 166–179). Sydney: Allen & Unwin.

Zhan, S. & Ottenbacher, K.J. (2001). Single subject research designs for disability research. *Disability and Rehabilitation*, **23**, 1–8.

CHAPTER 4

Emancipatory and Participatory Research: How Far Have We Come?

Paul Ramcharan
University of Sheffield, UK
Gordon Grant
University of Sheffield, UK
and
Margaret Flynn
University of Sheffield, UK

INTRODUCTION

Research involving people with intellectual disabilities is evolving at a rapid pace. Barely 20 years ago, it was an exception for social research to use people with intellectual disabilities as respondents. Indeed, Simons, Booth and Booth (1989) identify only 20 British studies to have done so during the 1980s, but they argue that there is an "acceptance . . . that the views of people labelled as mentally handicapped . . . constitute a valid perspective" (1989, p. 9). This argument pales when set against the calls in the last decade for people with intellectual disabilities both to participate in and to undertake research.

We outline below the historical development of these ideas, pointing to differing trajectories in the development of the participatory and the emancipatory research paradigms, together with the distinctive interests they represent. As we proceed, we shall characterise each approach and, using examples, point to some of the successes of these approaches but also to some of their conceptual stumbling blocks and pitfalls. We do not seek to take a partisan position in relation to either position but, rather, critically to address contemporary arguments in relation to these approaches. Our view, summarised in the conclusion, is that much remains to be done to refine and test these approaches, so in concluding the chapter we consider such prospects in more detail.

The International Handbook of Applied Research in Intellectual Disabilities. Edited by E. Emerson, C. Hatton, T. Thompson and T.R. Parmenter ISBN 0-471-49709-6.

THE DEVELOPMENT OF EMANCIPATORY RESEARCH

Emancipatory research represents the *overt* "politicisation" of research in which the researcher struggles for "transformative change" (Barnes, 2003, p. 6) as a direct product of the research experience. Emancipation in and through research has been around at least since the seminal work in relation to the "emancipatory interests" of Habermas (1972) in his *Knowledge and Human Interests* and in the seminal writings of Paulo Freire (1968), who sought to encourage people to take power and find solutions to their problems through joint action. These approaches represented a radical response to the demise of "grand theory", that is, theories which sought to describe the large-scale structural forces that shape our social world and, as a result, our lives. There was a move within the social sciences away from such theorising towards postmodern theorising, in which societies were seen as multiply varied and resistant to categorisation as unitary structures. These approaches provided an alternative radical vehicle for social movements in supporting their cause, and seeking to give voice to groups who shared a sense of oppression. The emancipatory paradigm can also be seen as the logical conclusion of the position that research and the research process are inherently value-laden. It was no longer a case of whether or not researchers take sides, as in the debates of the 1970s (Becker, 1970; Gouldner, 1973), but, rather, how to organise research around particular value positions that seek to challenge oppression itself as part of the research process. It is in this sense that "emancipatory research is as much a form of political action as it is research" (Walmsley, 2001, p. 195).

The adoption of the emancipatory research paradigm within the disability movement has largely been a by-product of the "social model" of disability (see Barnes, 2003). At its heart the social model distinguishes between "impairment" and "disability":

> Impairment is the functional limitation within the individual caused by physical, mental or sensory impairment. Disability is the loss or limitation of opportunities to take part in a normal life of the community on an equal level to others due to physical and social barriers. (Barnes, 1991, p. 2)

But the social model is perhaps not as unitary a theory as the term suggests:

> Social model theory has been developing in Britain since the Union of the Physically Impaired Against Segregation (UPIAS) published their *Fundamental Principles of Disability* (1976), followed shortly afterwards by Finkelstein's seminal exposition of the oppression that disabled people face (1980). Since then, various competing positions have been elaborated from this original starting point. (Tregaskis, 2002, p. 457)

However, in this model, disability is seen as a social product, one that is culturally produced and one that is oppressive. It is not an "individual attribute" but a result of "exclusionary processes". For Oliver (1992), disability has been individualised through the medical model, which has "pathologised" the individual with its singular focus on impairment, as if such impairment were synonymous with disability. This, he argues, has suited the needs of the capitalist system, in which a "disablist" society sustains the intention of the nineteenth-century Poor Laws, which sought to distinguish between the employed, unemployed, and unemployable. As Bury remarks,

> If disability, from a "social oppression" viewpoint, is self-evidently entirely "social" and therefore "political" in character (Oliver, 1992) a social movement espousing such a position might well be expected to concern itself primarily with political action

against a "disablist" society and use research findings, wherever possible, for these purposes. (1996, p. 27)

Proponents of the social model assert that disabled people should not be treated as research subjects but, rather, as the authors of research; that is, they are to transform the social and material relations of research production. They make this claim against what they term "traditional" research within the medical and social research fields. Traditional research has served the interests of professionals and researchers rather than disabled people. It has reproduced the system of oppression; that is, it is iatrogenic. Or, as Dowson (1997) argues, it remains a "comfortable delusion" to think that anything will change if the present system is maintained. There is very little evidence, say social-model theorists, that traditional research has in any way changed the lives of people with disabilities or had any positive impact on policy (a point we discuss later in considering the links between research, policy, and positive change for intellectually disabled people). Because of this,

> Researchers should be espousing commitment not value-freedom, engagement not objectivity and solidarity not independence. There is no independent haven or middle ground when researching oppression: academics and researchers can only be with the oppressors or the oppressed. (Barnes, 1996, p. 110)

The Emancipatory Model and Intellectual Disability

Up to this point, we have referred to disabled people in discussing the emancipatory model. So, of what relevance is this to people with intellectual disabilities? It appears relevant in three distinct ways.

First, there is a growing alliance between self-advocacy (through the People First movement involving people with intellectual disabilities) and groups of disabled people, such as the British Council of Disabled People (BCODP). Over the past few years, a number of articles have prompted people with intellectual disabilities to see the similarities of their own position to that of disabled people. For example, Ward has argued:

> As organisations of people with learning difficulties become stronger, alliances between them and organisations of other disabled people will continue to grow as they jointly campaign against discrimination that all disabled people encounter in our society. (Ward, 1995, p. 16)

Aspis (1999) has gone one stage further. Reviewing publications by organisations of people with intellectual disabilities, she notes that recommendations are almost always stated in terms of "individual rights" rather than collective:

> History . . . tells us that it is when groups of people identify with each other and collectively define their oppression that they become successful in claiming their rights. The denial of this in the lives of disabled people with the learning difficulties label, through language omission and the reinforcement of ignorance, is the cruellest infringement of rights. (p. 181)

The converging agendas of these arms of a singular disability movement are therefore setting the grounds for an emancipatory research enterprise shared by disabled people, including those with intellectual disabilities. The extent to which the People First movement represents people with intellectual disabilities in Britain is important here, given the alliance that is being forged.

At the same time, Chappell (2000), reviewing the contributions of Zarb, Morris and Oliver, points to a number of features of emancipatory research:

- being a tool for improving the lives of disabled people
- providing opportunities for disabled people to be researchers themselves
- involving a more reflexive stance in relation to their work
- being commissioned by democratic organisations of disabled people
- having an accountability to democratic organisations of disabled people.

Yet, Chappell argues that the majority of research undertaken by disabled people has not only ignored the interests of people with intellectual disabilities, but has failed to meet social model theorists' own criteria, as, for example, in not being funded by or accountable to organisations of disabled people.

Second, researchers in the intellectual disability field have sought to measure the success of their research against the criteria of emancipatory research. This is not insignificant, since it marks an *aspiration* to emancipatory research principles.

Rodgers (1999), for example, sets out in confessional style to review her research about the health needs of people with intellectual disabilities against Zarb's (1992) four criteria for emancipatory research, which share a similarity to those of Chappell (2000) outlined above: that disabled people control the research, are involved in the research process, are in a position to criticise research and develop the future research agenda, and use the products of research for social change. However, in terms of her own research, Rodgers tells us :

> In contrast to an emancipatory framework, the research did not arise from questions raised by disabled people. The initial area of interest, health, was my own and fitted with the interests of the Regional Health Authority funders. (Rodgers, 1999, p. 422)

Seemingly, people with intellectual disabilities agreed to participate because this interest in health struck a chord with their own. They were involved as consultants to the project by helping to develop questions for an interview, giving new insights into the meaning of health to people with intellectual disabilities, and helping to develop plain language or picture summaries of the research and its findings. They also took part in interviewing with Rodgers, though she attests to the fact that they seldom took a lead role. In terms of analysis, Rodgers tells us that she used a grounded theory (analysis) concurrently with interviewing so that future interviews might be informed by emergent themes. She admits, "I found it hard to contemplate how the methodological considerations that I found challenging could be made more accessible to people with learning difficulties" (Rodgers, 1999, p. 431).

Perhaps the one area of self-avowed success for Rodgers' work relates to her experience that "apparently complex ideas can be expressed plainly and understood by people with learning difficulties" (Rodgers, 1999, p. 431). Rodgers asserts that if ideas are too sophisticated for people with intellectual disabilities to understand, they cannot be used to change their lives. Or, to qualify this, such ideas cannot be used meaningfully by people with intellectual disabilities *themselves* in seeking to change their lives. And, of course, changing lives through informal action is at the heart of the emancipatory research approach. The problem with this is highlighted in a review of a project aimed at evaluating the benefits of participation in performing arts for people with intellectual disabilities (Goodley & Moore, 2000). As the authors say,

> the parameters of the contract we signed up to with the funding bodies emphasised our roles as "consultants" and "experts" investigating an area of potential service provision. This prohibited adopting an emancipatory position. (p. 862)

The ideals of emancipatory research are therefore still to be accomplished by people with intellectual disabilities despite the enthusiasm of some non-intellectually disabled researchers. But what, then, of people with intellectual disabilities themselves as the originators and authors of their own research?

Finally, self-advocacy groups around Britain are developing a huge range of products, but it is not clear whether these might count as research, emancipatory research, or the outcome of local consultancy.

There has been a significant growth in products developed by self-advocacy groups in the last decade or so. For example,

> documents have been written on community care assessment (People First, 1993); how to have a say in services (Leeds Coalition, 1996); person-centred planning (Liverpool and Manchester People First, 1996; Speak Up Self Advocacy, 1998); how to make written information more accessible to people with learning disabilities (Change, 1997; People First, 1997) an Access First Directory (People First, 1998); how to get the services that you want (People First, 1994); safety issues and prevention of abuse (Walsall Women's Group, 1999). People First have also collaborated in a project to bring the findings of a study on housing to publication in an accessible format (People First, 1994). (Ramcharan & Grant, 2001, 352–353)

As yet, the evidence base upon which many of these products have drawn and the methods by which they have been put together are unclear. However, the self-advocacy movement has made their products far more accessible than have academic researchers.

Not only has the issue of accessibility been laid out in great detail (CHANGE, 1997), but picture banks have also been developed (People First, 1997; CHANGE, 2001) and products distributed in a number of formats, including videos, tapes, and Braille. Moreover, the self-advocacy movement has accomplished this work at a fraction of the cost of funding academic researchers.

There is a substantial debate about what methods are most appropriate for either emancipatory or participatory research. However, in her article on "Researching Together", Williams (1999) tells us that, for the group, research was "finding things out" (p. 49). If this is a sufficient definition, it might be argued that the vast array of products from the self-advocacy movement might be construed as research. Though such groups are supported in the development of their products, one might say that these products best represent the priorities and interests of the self-advocacy movement and, as such, of people with intellectual disabilities in Britain.

But this leaves a difficult problem. A substantial group of these products concern making the best of the service system as it exists, for example, in relation to person-centred planning or assessment; that is, from a social-model perspective, people with intellectual disabilities are colluding with organisations that disempower and oppress them. They are, as Aspis (1999) notes, concentrating on issues of importance to them as individuals rather than on those that warrant action as a common group pressing for political change. In arguing about accountability and the emancipatory paradigm, Barnes (2003) has pointed out that "many people with impairments do not consider themselves 'disabled' or members of an oppressed group" (p. 7). However, he points out that other oppressed groups do not recognise their oppression. For Barnes, "researchers making themselves accountable to organisations controlled and run by disabled people has gone some way in resolving this problem" (p. 7). Yet, from the products of the self-advocacy movement in the intellectual disability field, it is not clear that their products fit entirely with the social model. The question here is whether these voices have a legitimacy, given their origin, or whether those who do not adopt the social model "should not be thought of as exhibiting signs of false consciousness" (Davis, 2000, p. 194). The irony of this, as Davis asserts, is that "we run the risk within our field of using the very systems of exclusion and censorship that, it is claimed, exist within medical model driven research" (p. 194).

In addition, the work of the self-advocacy movement has not had the ascendancy of other products because publishers, with their avenues for formal dissemination, advertisement, and distribution, have, by and large, not published their products. While this is beginning to change in the UK, through publishers such as BILD and Pavilion, the odds are against their voice being heard as loudly as those of the academic and service development sphere.

Overall, then, a number of questions remain in relation to the development of emancipatory research and work produced by people with intellectual disabilities in their own representative groups.

Further Questions for Emancipatory Research

Unless we take the products of the self-advocacy movement to represent an "emancipatory research voice", there have, as yet, been no studies, as far as we are aware, owned and led by people with intellectual disabilities using an emancipatory research paradigm. Given that this ownership represents perhaps a primary characterising feature required for research to be termed "emancipatory", what are the prospects for the future?

Bury (1996) suggests that many proponents of the social model claim that disability theorists have previously been non-disabled and that this has added to their exclusion. Bury says that from here it is a short step to argue that research on disability should be carried out or controlled only by disabled people themselves (Zarb, 1992). Now that the People First movement is forging closer alliances with the disability movement in Britain, the foundations are being laid for a shared agenda for action. In emancipatory research, the success of this enterprise may be assessed against potentially differing criteria. If the disability lobby asserts that the interests of people with intellectual disabilities are shared with those of disabled people, intellectual disability as a discrete research category would be unnecessary. Perhaps this is why, despite emancipatory research by disabled people, none to date has been concerned with people with intellectual disabilities per se. Walmsley warns against this approach:

> Who should undertake research is a question which needs a more complex answer than "disabled people". Disabled people, like others, vary in the degree of power they may wield, and most people with learning difficulties are particularly disadvantaged even in comparison with other disabled people. (Walmsley, 2001, p. 199)

It is also worth noting the response of Gramlich et al. (2002), a group of researchers with intellectual disabilities:

> He [a direct payments coordinator] wanted to include people with learning difficulties with everyone else who was disabled. Other people from the Centres for Independent

> Living said the same.... We agree that it's a good idea to get together, because we know what it's like to be in this world with a label. But we think our self advocacy groups are very important.... We are in charge ourselves, we have respect and we can get our confidence. That is what we need. That is why self-advocacy can help us. (Stop 10, p. 96)

Social-model theorists are themselves none too clear on this score, Barnes (1991) recognising that the heterogeneity of disabled people in social class, culture, or economic status adds conceptual and experiential gaps between the researcher and the researched. Meanwhile, Oliver (1992) seems to suggest that disabled people have not yet developed research knowledge and skills, as, at present, they rely on non-disabled researchers, who do not have their experiential base upon which to understand fully the experience of disability.

In their consideration of the development of self-advocacy, Downer and Walmsley (1997) also talk about the ways in which groups of self-advocates are allying themselves along lines relating to ethnicity, gender, and more severe impairments. This gives rise to a multitude of groupings which, while sharing some forms of oppression, are also demonstrating differing forms of oppression in their multiple alliances. The question then arises as to whether such alliances are too diversified to be simply incorporated under the label "disabled people".

The more cynical observer might claim of emancipatory research that a university-based intelligentsia of disabled people is now seeking to privilege its own voice at the expense of others. In particular, for those whose impairments are in the use of concepts and ideas, the work of this intelligentsia is no less disempowering and oppressive than that of other forms of academic theorising:

> In disability studies, the privileging of the "social model" by researchers has been criticised on the basis that the theory may not be part of the research participants' own understanding of disability (Stone and Priestley, 1996; Priestley, 1997) and on the basis that it may inhibit the work of the researcher (Shakespeare, 1997). (Davis, 2000, p. 193)

The social-model theorists provide a preordained theoretical framework for research in opposition to other approaches and

> By creating "them" and "us" groups these writers reduce the importance of people as social actors, reifying the role of structure and ignoring the diverse ways in which individuals and social groups relate to and resist such structures. (Davis, 2000, p. 196)

A case in point here may be the emergence of life-history and biographical work within the intellectual disability field that has been developing for a number of years. In this arena, it has been claimed that this is "empowerment through knowledge. There is no better, nor more enduring kind" (Atkinson, 1998, p. 125). Can *individuals* challenge their disempowerment or oppression through such means? Or is it always necessary to see oppression as unidimensionally caused by exploitative structures and policies imposed over socially oppressed *groups*? What is the relationship between individual empowerment and group activism? For many social-model theorists, all of these issues are subsumed within the explanatory framework of the social model of disability and, seemingly, do not need to be addressed.

However, there are differing shades of opinion within the social movement, as intimated earlier. Focusing more on the need for reflexivity in emancipatory research, for example, Davis (2000) draws on a range of anthropological writings to substantiate the idea that there must be some "cultural exchange" within research where researchers confront their own values and beliefs against those of the groups they are studying:

> The cultural exchange form of ethnography supports the aims of emancipatory research because the researcher is required to be a reflexive participant.... This process complements the contention that disabled people should be able to influence the direction of a research project. (Davis, 2000, p. 192)

Thus, the aim is to represent "the contrasting and conflicting relations between individuals who inhabit a social location" (Davis, 2000, p. 96) or give room to voices operating within any social sphere or domain. Priestley (1997) suggests that such an approach recognises the importance of distinguishing between the researcher's research skills and the experience of disabled people as "knowers". In this view, reflexivity is associated with a developing methodology wrought out of the research relationships themselves. Such research is likely to have emergent rather than "scientific" designs. However, whether such "reflexivity" need necessarily be the sole preserve of the emancipatory paradigm remains open to question.

Whatever the chosen model of emancipatory research, such approaches would be possible only if we accept one of either two positions: (1) that people with intellectual disabilities can be represented by the broader framework and interests of disabled people, some issues about which we have raised above; or (2) that people with intellectual disabilities can undertake research independently of support, a further defining feature of such research. For the second position, Kiernan (1999) summarises a further problem that is encountered for the emancipatory paradigm.

> Given that the research process relies heavily on intellectual skills, it is less easily accessible to people with learning disabilities than to groups of people with disabilities who do not experience intellectual impairments. (1999, p. 46)

In this assertion, Kiernan is making a number of presuppositions: despite the distinction between disability and impairment in the social model, there is a point at which impairment itself provides the barrier to participation. Thus, it is asserted that intellectual proficiency to a certain level is a prerequisite to research. Associated with this is the presupposition that research is a specialist and highly technical task and must be expert-led.

Zarb (1992) has argued that participatory research is a "staging post" to emancipatory research while Oliver contends that "participatory research certainly seeks to improve the nature of the social and material relations of research production ... but it does not seek to revolutionise them by challenging and ultimately eradicating them" (1997, p. 26). But, in our view, social-model theorists such as Oliver and Zarb are yet to show how the move from participatory to emancipatory research is to be accomplished by people with intellectual disabilities. Apart from seeking to place intellectual disability within a wider social-model framework relating to disabled people, a contentious issue as outlined above, they have failed thus far to respond to the point that impairment itself is the barrier to ownership of research by people with intellectual disabilities. Indeed, some would argue that the emphasis of disabled theorists in relation to research has largely served to exclude those with impairment of "cognitive functioning" in favour of those whose impairments are of "the body" (Chappell, 1998).

We are therefore left to appraise participatory research and, in particular, the relationships of support and cooperation that characterise this enterprise, since these not only distinguish such research from emancipatory research, but also characterise the majority of studies within the participatory research paradigm.

THE HISTORICAL EMERGENCE OF PARTICIPATORY RESEARCH

Unlike emancipatory research, the heritage of participatory research is unclear in most texts. There have been recent attempts by some writers to give participatory research a history. For example, Kiernan (1999) argues that participatory research (e.g., Reason, 1994) has gained currency within academia and has been adopted by those working in the field of intellectual disability research. In contrast, Walmsley argues, "To the influence of normalisation can be attributed the rapid development of inclusive styles of research in the late 1980s and early 1990s" (Walmsley, 2001, p. 188).

These views offer seemingly logical explanations for the emergence of the approach, though they reconstruct the motives of those who implemented the approach. It can be argued that the academic backdrop to the emancipatory research interest and postmodern and post-positivist approaches might also be taken as equally good motives for the development of a participatory research paradigm. In their early paper on "user studies", Simons et al. (1989) point to the importance and value of studies involving client opinion within social work at that time. They argue that this interest should expand to include people with intellectual disabilities and that their voice represents "a valid perspective comparable with but distinct from ... direct care staff, managers, relatives and even researchers" (p. 9). The centrality of the client view might be conceived as a product of consumerism or the development of social movements such as the self-advocacy movement, which grew steadily from the 1980s onwards (Longhurst, 1994; Whittell & Ramcharan, 1999). Moreover, it was not only those in the self-advocacy movement who were taken to have a voice. Illuminating contributions from feminist ways of knowing and changing reality have been instrumental in strengthening participatory research (Tandon, 1996). As Simons et al. (1989) say, "People using mental handicap [*sic*] services, given the right context, can make perfectly sensible and illuminating comments on their experiences" (p. 16).

However, though a complex range of motives may explain the emergence of participatory research,

> the civil rights movement for people with learning difficulties took a strikingly different turn from that which it took for other groups where taking control of their own destiny was a leitmotif. (Walmsley, 2001, p. 191)

Instead, there was a place for those advocating for or supporting people with intellectual disabilities to have a voice within civil rights and research. As with emancipatory research, the potential areas for participation in research are identified through a critique of "traditional research" in which:

> The researcher decides on the research question, develops and employs what are felt to be suitable measures, analyses the ensuing data and interprets the results.... This is essentially research on people rather than research with people. (Kiernan, 1999, p. 43)

From here, it is easy to argue that it is therefore vital for people with intellectual disabilities to participate in *each part* of the research process. However, the participatory framework has also recently been extended beyond that process to both the commissioning and reviewing of research proposals in a national research initiative (see Grant & Ramcharan, 2002) associated with the new government policy for people with intellectual disabilities in England, set forth in a publication entitled *Valuing People* (Department of Health, 2001).

To reiterate, the idea of "participation" in research differs from the "ownership" model of emancipatory research. For closer examination of this, it is worth scrutinising one of the few theoretical outlines of participatory research. Registering a debt to Wolfensberger's account of social devaluation, Cocks and Cockram (1995) encourage us:

> to devise strategies in which research and action are closely linked . . . we advocate a participatory research paradigm as a powerful and liberating strategy to deliver meaningful services to people with disabilities. Through the participatory process the sharing of clients benefits both clients . . . and those who deliver services to them. (p. 25)

The above authors identify three processes in participatory research: a research question *being brought to the attention* of disabled people or being identified by disabled people themselves; disabled people and researchers *working together* to achieve a collective analysis; and *alliances formed* between disabled people, researchers, and others to seek to make change following the research. In this version, note that the place of the academic researcher is ensured and is central to the whole enterprise, a factor that distinguishes the participatory from the emancipatory research paradigm.

The Nature of Participation in the Participatory Research Paradigm

Once again, most of the discussion about the participation of people with intellectual disabilities in the research process has been reported by academics, and largely in academic journals. Ward (1998), for example, provides a useful review of the ways in which people with intellectual disabilities have extended their roles within the research process in terms of helping to shape the research agenda, advising and assisting in research, doing research themselves, and being involved in research dissemination.

In seeking to set the research agenda, Ward (1998) points out that funding bodies such as the Joseph Rowntree Foundation and Community Fund in the UK have established the grounds for voluntary organisations, including those run by and for people with intellectual disabilities, to submit proposals in collaboration with academics. A different approach has been that relating to a national research initiative in Britain (Grant & Ramcharan, 2002) that has provided funding from the Department of Health to examine lessons learned through the implementation of *Valuing People*, the White Paper relating to the lives and services for people with intellectual disabilities. In this initiative, people with intellectual disabilities were involved as reviewers of research proposals and as members of the commissioning group that made final decisions about which research proposals should be funded. The same participation is being afforded in relation to advising the commissioned research and in establishing relevant information and findings to suitable audiences. For this work, people with intellectual disabilities are being paid a full consultancy wage. Such mechanisms represent means through which power in setting the research agenda can be devolved to people with intellectual disabilities. However, it remains a long way off the ideal of the emancipatory model in which organisations of people with intellectual disabilities can themselves fund research, were they to choose to do so over their other competing priorities!

Moreover, from reports within the public domain, it is not clear that researchers within the participatory research framework have necessarily achieved one of the other ideals of the emancipatory model and responded to the interests of people with intellectual disabilities themselves. We have already shown how Rodgers (1999) reports using an already established research idea. In an article written by people with intellectual disabilities about their research experiences, March, Steingold and Justice (1997) also report:

> We wanted to take part in this to help ourselves, and help others . . . Paula [a PhD student] thought we would be the proper people to do it so people with learning difficulties can be in control for a change. We know a lot about self-advocacy and families, so we are the experts for this research. (p. 77)

The majority experience is that academic researchers or funding bodies have come up with their own ideas prior to inviting the participation of people with intellectual disabilities (e.g., Flynn with Liverpool Self Advocates, 1994; Minkes, Townsley, Weston & Williams, 1995; Northway, 1998). The national research initiative launched by the Department of Health in England, while being written after consultation with people with intellectual disabilities, was also a product of a number of other voices, not least those representing government, professional, family carer, and academic interests. The agenda, then, is not being drawn wholly from people with intellectual disabilities themselves. Rather, it accepts an alternative view that accords voice to "stakeholders"; that is, not only people with intellectual disabilities themselves but also their families and those who seek to provide services and support.

In terms of representing the interests of people with intellectual disabilities themselves, the work of Swindon People First and the Norah Fry Research Centre on Direct Payments (Gramlich et al., 2002) stands out as an exception to the examples outlined above, though it is not clear how much they contributed to writing the research proposal initially. However, this project is also, as far as we know, unique in that the researchers with intellectual disabilities were paid researchers' salaries.

Like many organisations of disabled people, the self-advocacy movement is so poorly funded as to make its sponsorship of research impossible even were it to choose such a use for its funds, a point alluded to by Barnes in relation to emancipatory research also (2003, p. 8). Placing people with intellectual disabilities and their organisations at the forefront of setting research priorities is therefore largely dependent upon the goodwill of funding agencies and advocates of the participatory research position. This remains precarious and maintains the status quo in terms of the power relations that have historically characterised the disbursement of funds for research. However, the majority of funding bodies still maintain their almost singular commitment to funding academics working in academic ways and in academic environments. At the same time, although the self-advocacy movement is becoming increasingly involved in research (Atkinson, 2002), no coherent framework or agenda for research has emerged from the self-advocacy movement itself in Britain. The Roeher Institute in Canada, taking a different approach, has consulted with Canada People First about the things that they felt were important as a means of letting them set their research agenda, out of which a number of publications have flowed from subsequent research (Roeher Institute, 1990a,b, 1991a,b, 1994, 1995, 1997a,b).

The material relations of research funding have seen a movement in some areas towards supporting the interests and agenda of local groups of people with intellectual disabilities. However, *the social relations* between funders and receivers of research funds have largely remained in the hands of the funding agencies. Researchers working in the participatory research paradigm may want to reflect these agendas and funding relations in writing their research reports.

What, then, of participation by people with intellectual disabilities in the research process itself? In recent years, researchers have broadly begun to accept managerialist assumptions about project management. These assumptions are based on the ideals of securing an independent voice to guide the research, drawing on experts more widely in the field, and having in place a system of checks and balances to provide governance in all its forms (ethical, financial, project, and methodological, for example). It is now increasingly accepted that project management and advisory groups should include people with intellectual disabilities. Within services, there is now not only a moral imperative for such participation but also a recognition that this makes for better participation and has benefits for the people involved (Simons, 2000, p. 3).

On such advisory committees, members with intellectual disabilities have variously contributed to the design of research questions and letters, developed accessible materials, and lent fresh insights to the research issues. In addition, they have acted as a sounding board for results, contributed to dissemination, and in some cases continued to operate together after the work has been completed (Minkes et al., 1995; McIntosh & Whittaker, 1998; Rodgers, 1999; Gramlich et al., 2002). Each of 12 projects presently funded under the Department of Health's English research initiative was reviewed by people with intellectual disabilities in terms of the relevant participation of people with intellectual disabilities among other things. Each project involves users on its project management group. There are plans to assess the success of the participatory frameworks for the projects and the effect such participation has on the projects and their outcomes. This should prove interesting, since, in other areas, participation has not been found to be either simple or straightforward (e.g., Welsh Office, 1989; All Wales Advisory Panel, 1991; Felce et al., 1998, especially Chapter 5).

Outside the management of projects, there have been growing examples of participation in other aspects of undertaking research. In some cases, participation has greatly affected the development of the research methods and the ways in which research has been carried out. In an early example (Whittaker, Gardner & Kershaw, 1990), people with intellectual disabilities developed a questionnaire to evaluate services. In other projects, people with intellectual disabilities have developed appropriate and relevant interview themes and questions (e.g., Minkes et al., 1995; March et al., 1997). In another approach, visits to respite care services were undertaken with self-advocates, who made their own observations independently of the researcher (Flynn with Liverpool Self Advocates, 1994).

There is a problem in many of the accounts where participation in the research process was said to have been undertaken, in that detailed information is seldom reported about what people actually did or how they were supported, and what the "division of labour" between them and academics actually involved. In regard to support, for example, there is little evidence about the roles of advocates, allies, or proxies that speak with or for the person, the conditions under which they become involved, the ethical and operational challenges faced, and whether the experience is enabling. This represents a not inconsiderable research agenda in itself.

In an exception to the above, March et al. (1997) report how they developed their research ideas about areas relating to self-advocacy and families and how they planned and undertook data collection. Importantly, they also received training about research methods, as did the Swindon People First Research Group (Gramlich et al., 2002), who undertook six half-day training sessions. Indeed, the latter research was the only one in which the intellectually disabled authors say, categorically, "We thought of the questions ourselves, and spent some time doing this" (Appendix, Part 2, p. 112). There are indications, then, that with the correct training and support it is possible for *at least some* people with intellectual disabilities to be involved in the collection of data through talking with people.

But if there are few studies in which people with intellectual disabilities have collected data, there are even fewer in which they have gone on to analyse that data, and, where this is claimed, even less evidence about what this actually involved. Gramlich et al. (2002) are an exception. After undertaking their interviews, they viewed videos and photographs taken at the localities in which the research was done. The academic adviser had the audiotapes of interviews transcribed. They then went over what interviewees said and put findings into boxes in which the "themes came from our own ideas" (Gramlich et al., 2002, Appendix, Part 6, p. 119). From the themes, picture charts were developed for each location visited, and the researchers read what each interviewee had said. Then the research group "made up stories" about what might happen to people with intellectual disabilities in relation to direct payments in that locality:

> We decided to do our report as a journey.... We have had support to write this report...and from our People First supporter.... Sometimes we have dictated our bits, sometimes put them on tape...[name of academic supporter] has helped to put it in order, but we have checked it all back through to make sure it is what we want to say. (Appendix, Part 7, p. 120)

However, in many other cases, the possibility of participation in analysis has proved very difficult (Minkes et al., 1995; Stalker, 1998; Rodgers, 1999). Northway (1998) found that transcribed tapes were too information-rich and therefore summarised the data in an accessible way herself. Williams (1999) argues that in supporting participative analysis there is merit in having concentrated periods of time to look at data.

The argument over analysis by people with intellectual disabilities also raises the issue of what has been referred to as "the ethics of representation" (Booth, 1996, in Stalker, 1998, p. 12) relating to informants with intellectual disabilities. To what extent is it ethical to present an academic analysis of themes for *confirmation* by co-researchers with intellectual disabilities? How legitimate is it to create one pastiche from what several people with intellectual disabilities have said in research interviews? (Booth, 1996). And as Stalker (1998) suggests, is a "respondent validation exercise" or are "member checks" (Acker, Barry & Esseveld, 1983; Rodgers, 1999) sufficient to confer some "validity" on reports of what research participants have said? Answers to these key questions about the status, validity, and even ethicality of how the voices of people with intellectual disabilities are recorded and published remain to be addressed. The debate would be helped by more transparency about how participation in the research process was organised.

But there are other issues that arise out of the above discussion. It is assumed that research method and analysis should indeed mirror the ways in which academics might usually treat data; that is, in a systematic way in a search for "validity" in the scientific sense. However, the above examples of analysis all seem to be based on some form of "thematic content analysis", an approach associated largely with "grounded theory" analysis. If they are produced by this approach, their worth is likely to be assessed against accepted criteria for judging such research approaches. Moreover, participation as a prerequisite may privilege specific styles of research. Indeed, in their early discussion of the participatory research paradigm, Cocks and Cockram (1995) see the potential methods as consisting of:

> discussion groups, public meetings, the establishment of investigative research teams, community seminars, fact-finding tours, the collective production of educational materials, the use of popular theatre, and educational camps or retreats. (1995, p. 32)

It may be that thematic analysis fits better with these methodological approaches, thus explaining their preponderance in the participatory studies so far undertaken. Two further associated points are worthy of note. The research enterprise will be constrained by the capacity of the researcher's skills. This is true for all research. As such, to make meaningful participation in analysis of research data a prerequisite also means that the form of analysis chosen may be limited by the researcher's and co-researcher's analytic capabilities.

In this way, the most appropriate choice of methods is not based upon theoretical or epistemological grounds, nor necessarily in relation to the specific phenomenon that is being investigated. Rather, methods are seemingly chosen on pragmatic grounds; that is, they can be accomplished by the researchers involved. And where the repertoire of research methods and analytic approaches is reduced, so, too, is the range of social phenomena that can be intercepted. Despite the seeming antipathy towards a host of approaches they term as "traditional", no attempt seems as yet to have been made by proponents of participatory research to develop or apply a system to judge the merits of that approach with anything nearing the sophistication applied to "traditional" approaches. Ironically, a further danger of participatory research also operates in the opposite direction. Here, people with intellectual disabilities who are more able may be advantaged in becoming involved in research. This has the potential to over-represent their interests against people with more profound or severe intellectual disabilities.

Moreover, the methods suggested by Cocks and Cockram (1995) seem to stand between research method and forms of activity that can prompt activism and lead to social change; that is, they seem to link directly information and activism. In this sense, they would require a wholly different approach to measuring their efficacy and validity. These would be less related to the standard of the research method and more associated with the outcomes for those involved. We can see movement towards these forms of argument in some contemporary research; for example, in their study of people with intellectual disabilities in the performing arts, Goodley and Moore argue:

> It is perhaps worth pointing out that qualitative research is exactly the same as quantitative research in terms of having a means to ensure rigour (Taylor and Bogdan, 1984; Hollway and Jefferson, 2000). Readers can be reassured of the rigour of this research precisely *because* we make no attempt to deny our own commitments . . . we make no claims for the data beyond its potential for rich and stimulating interpretation. (Goodley & Moore, 2002, p. 28)

And:

> Whether the accounts we present are regarded as "reliable" or "valid" simply depends on personal beliefs about the utility of objectivity anyway. A frank consideration of these criteria brings us to the realisation that all research is political in the sense that it is always undertaken to further someone's interests; it is never value free. (Goodley & Moore, 2002, p. 29)

The question here would be whether those who hold power in terms of services, practice, and policy would be more likely to accept these views from people with intellectual disabilities, their representative organisations, or academics over competing knowledge claims. Again, the links between theory, policy, and practice are implicated in this regard.

All research, information, and knowledge claims are made against beliefs about what is valid and correct, and the extent to which such claims are grounded in a rigorous approach.

As with all other research, participatory research should seek to make clear the grounds for rigour when making knowledge claims. Such rigour may not accord with academic standards relating to both qualitative and quantitative research, but, if not by those of the academy, by what standards will they be measured? There is still work to be done in developing this area of participatory research and in linking the complex decision-making contexts of practice, policy, and political change to competing knowledge claims.

Participation in data collection and analysis not only have been difficult in practice but also raise theoretical and epistemological issues. However, there have been other approaches to participation in data collection and analysis. For example, in one study (Flynn with Liverpool Self Advocates, 1994), self-advocates visited respite services to observe alongside the researcher and were able to reflect their observations and feelings about what they had seen. Their views are expressed throughout the report in italicised quotations. In this latter approach, the contribution to analysis is not one that requires research analysis to be viewed as systematic. Here, the ex-users or potential users of various respite services have paid these services a visit. They are reflecting what they feel about places that have had or may have a direct relevance in their lives, somewhat as we all do when making a decision about which hotel to stay at or school to attend. So when they use terms to describe these services such as "sad, strange, nervous, different staff, not nice, awful, lousy, upset, worried" (p. 30), these are exceptionally powerful and meaningful. These views can verify more academic analysis of the same phenomena, pose questions that academic researchers may have to address in their analysis, make academic researchers reflect upon their own observations, or substantiate for findings generated through a more formal and systematic analysis. Mostly, they provide a voice that would otherwise remain unheard.

This review work shares some "immediacy" and relevance for the participants. It shares some of the characteristics of techniques of rapid appraisal, a technique used in underdeveloped countries since the work of Freire (1968). Such participatory rural appraisal provides "a family of approaches and methods to enable rural people to share, enhance or analyse their knowledge of life and conditions, to plan and to act" (Chambers, 1994, p. 953). The work therefore supports what Freire (1968) calls the "conscientisation" of people to look at their life experiences, reflect upon them, produce knowledge, and act to change their situation. However, as we noted earlier, many of the products of the self-advocacy movement have arisen in relation to the question of how best to get the most out of the service system as it presently exists. If one accepts conscientisation as the arbiter of the self-advocates with intellectual disabilities, it is hard to see how this would square with attributing to them "false consciousness" for not having pursued more radical political or collective change.

We have so far avoided discussing all research in which people with intellectual disabilities are simply respondents or key informants or interviewees, in favour of approaches where there is a contribution to participation in the research process. More recently, however, some authors are making a case that some such studies may be viewed as participatory in nature. For example, life-story research or what has more recently been termed "participatory life-story research" (Atkinson, 2002, p. 127) has also squarely placed life-history work within the participatory research paradigm. In method, it is based upon people talking about and reflecting on their lives and life experiences. Few life histories have been published without support, usually from academics (for a brief history of life-history research, see Atkinson, Jackson & Walmsley, 1997; Atkinson & Walmsley, 1999). Atkinson (2002) makes a case that life-story research and self-advocacy are dependent upon each other. She argues:

> Life story research was made possible through self advocacy, and the interest of people within the movement in telling their stories. Although people with learning disabilities are able to articulate their experience... theorising from that experience has proved more problematic.... On the whole this means that non-disabled people are still needed as allies.... This is in contrast to emancipatory research where the demand is for the research to be owned and controlled by disabled people. (p. 126)

Atkinson argues that in telling their life stories people with intellectual disabilities were occupying research roles—for example, as "historical witness, critical commentator, and research partner".

In another approach relating to disability arts and people with intellectual disabilities, authors use critical ethnography, group discussions, and interviews (Goodley & Moore, 2002, pp. 24–27). Academics were involved in some performances but were on the whole collecting the data through these more formal academic means. They produced accessible summaries in the full report on all five performing-arts projects (Goodley & Moore, 2002) and a conference report in pictures and plain language of one of the projects in another article (Goodley & Moore, 2000). In their view, the approach was not "emancipatory" in that they were the "authors" and the "experts", not least because of the source of their funding. However, they also reject "pseudo-scientific ambitions in favour of critical engagement with participatory qualitative research" (Goodley & Moore, 2000, p. 862). This, we should point out, is not participation by people with intellectual disabilities within the research process but, rather, in performing their art, which becomes the artefact of academics' observations. The authors "went in firmly on the side of the performers—we wanted to represent their achievements, their ambitions and to present encouraging stories of people with the label of 'learning difficulties'" (Goodley & Moore, 2000, p. 862).

Indeed, the reports are unquestionably positive about the gains of people with intellectual disabilities involved in the performing arts. However, here it is the *products* of the research that are taken as the driving force of change and *not* participation in the research process itself. This raises the strong possibility that non-participatory approaches that provide information in an accessible way can be sufficient to establish the grounds for change among self-advocacy and other disabled people's groups.

In this short review, it will be clear that there are potentially many ways in which people with intellectual disabilities may participate in research. We have tried to demonstrate the sea change that is taking place in these terms. But where can the line be drawn between what is or is not participatory? For example, can one term an academic research project that has people with intellectual disabilities on its project management or advisory group as the only form of involvement, a participatory research project? If not, how can such a participatory project be distinguished from others?

The uncharitable view of the participatory research paradigm which uses academics as supporters would be that

> we as researchers gain but mainly at the expense of those whose lives we have researched. While our intentions have been honourable, we remain on the wrong side of the social and material relations of research production. (Oliver, 1997, p. 26)

In short, in this view, participatory research is just another form of colonisation and disempowerment. How, one can hear some radical thinkers argue, is it possible for so many products to keep academics in work and leave people with intellectual disabilities back where they started after their participation? As Chappell asks:

> If people with learning difficulties need non-disabled allies in the research process in order to convey their experiences in a way that is acceptable to the research community and its gatekeepers, how can the integrity of their accounts be maintained? How can we prevent non-disabled researchers . . . from assuming a dominant role in the research process? (Chappell, 2000, p. 41)

There are therefore good reasons to consider further ideas that distinguish participatory from other research in terms of the power relations between academics and co-researchers. A useful starting point here might be that, in reporting research in which people with intellectual disabilities have been involved, the relationship between the academic and co-researchers/participants should be detailed. It is only through this disclosure that others might make judgements about the degree of participation involved, its appropriateness, and its potential benefits.

As well as participation in the research process, it is also important to look at the *outcomes* of participatory research in changing people's lives. Once again, while "we need to hear more about the views and experiences of people with learning difficulties who have been involved in research in this way" (Stalker, 1998, p. 16), many of the discussions remain wholly located within academic debate.

If we look at the area of life histories and people with intellectual disabilities as a form of participatory research, the potential outcomes are wide and varied. Among these, it has variously been argued that such research helps people make sense of their lives through an understanding of their past (Gillman et al., 1997), acts as a treasured possession (Whittell & Ramcharan, 1999), is a demonstration of resilience against the odds (Goodley, 1996), or is a way of fighting back (Potts & Fido, 1991; Goodley, 1996).

These seem to constitute personal gains that are hard to deny. It is also the case that these may lead to conscientisation and to political affiliation and struggle, though this is by no means inevitable. However, while

> Some proponents of narrative inquiry would assert that stories are the central component of experience and reality (Didion, 1979; Sarbin, 1986; Bruner, 1987; Gergen and Gergen, 1988; Hoffman, 1993). . . . Alternatively, other proponents use narrative as a medium through which to present and reflect upon some of the experiences and realities of people (Allport, 1947; Parker, 1963, 1990, 1994; Plummer, 1983, 1995; Langness and Levine, 1986; Fairclough, 1989, 1992). Here reality and narrative are not necessarily seen as synonymous. (Goodley, 2000, p. 47)

Or, as McClimens (2003) argues, there is a dual merit of narrative analysis and analysis of narrative. In a previous article (Ramcharan & Grant, 2001), the two of us have argued that life histories without additional analysis pose some difficulties in terms of policy relevance, given the substantial additional work that is required to filter the messages through to policy from the text. However, at the point where additional analysis is undertaken, the product is one step removed from the voices of people with intellectual disabilities and is "owned" by the academic interpreter. We will return to this shortly, but it is worth noting that the relationship between research and social change at personal, social-movement, political, or policy levels is by no means straightforward.

So, what of the outcomes from other studies? Perhaps the most participatory of the projects discussed in previous sections has been that by Gramlich et al. (2002) on direct payments, that is, a payment made to and managed by disabled people themselves to buy the support services they need and want. The research starts with the assumption that direct payments have been positive for people with intellectual disabilities and the researchers sought to discover what people had gained from them and how to improve access to such payments. Their work goes into detail about how best to plan for a direct payment, how families might help, how participants gain the confidence to speak out, how best to provide information, how those gain who have had a direct payment, and, finally, how direct payments can transfer control into the lives of people with intellectual disabilities. After each section written by the researchers with intellectual disabilities, a supplementary discussion of the relevance of the findings to present government policy is written by academic advisers to the group. The group has presented seminars, fed back to localities in which the research was undertaken, and produced plain-language summaries of their work. In short, there has been an attempt to make the findings available to a number of audiences and in a number of ways. There are also plans to publish the work within academic journals. There have been gains for the researchers, not only in terms of their salaried posts, but also in terms of gaining the experience of research upon which to base future funding applications.

While much of the research in the participatory field finds its way into academic journals, there have been moves to develop an alternative dissemination approach—for example, the development of the *Plain Facts* documents by the Norah Fry Research Centre (see Townsley, 1998, for a review) and the books-without-words publications of St George's Hospital Medical School (Hollins, Murphy & Clare, 1996; Hollins, Clare & Murphy, 1996; Hollins, Bernal & Gregory, 1996; Hollins, Horrocks & Sinason, 1998; Hollins, Bernal & Gregory, 1998). If "collective action" is a vital feature of participatory research, it is essential to make findings available in ways that might be used by such collectives. This, we would argue, applies not only to participatory research, but also to all research about people with intellectual disabilities.

But there have been some difficulties for academics in using a plain-language approach. The position is well outlined by Goodley and Moore (2000) in their consideration of the conflicts between the "academy" and "the personal and political" aims of people with intellectual disabilities. They argue that the more academics do to make research meaningful to disabled people, the more such work is seen as "wasting time" and "unworthy within academic circles"; that plain-language summaries are dismissed by academic peers; that funding agencies seek reports and research that are at odds with the values and wishes of people with intellectual disabilities; acceptable academic writing is esoteric and elitist; and that research findings within academia tend to provide no grounds for "meaningful praxis-orientated developments" or social change by people with intellectual disabilities. They conclude that

> in attempting to bridge the artificially created divide between "activism" and the "academy" one of the first steps is to create research agendas that document resistance and disablement in ways that are sensitive to those who are resisting. (Goodley & Moore, 2000, p. 880)

But it should also be noted that it is the *products or outcomes* of research to which these authors are pointing. If so, this implies that participatory research should be characterised by a commitment to producing research findings that are in a form that can be appraised and used by people with intellectual disabilities and their representative organisations. Moreover, such work should state clearly how it is likely to challenge oppression or contribute to knowledge.

While it is too early to judge fully the outcomes of participatory research, it shares with the emancipatory paradigm the commitment to people with intellectual disabilities improving their own lives through research. This implies that there must be some need to know at least how the information is being used and by whom. Unfortunately, this is perhaps the nemesis of *all* research. Researchers have largely launched their products into the void and assumed that they have made a positive difference. The relationship between knowledge and social action, the relevance of research knowledge to complexities of decision making at policy and political level—in short, the link between *theoria* and *praxis*—remains a thorny issue, as we discuss in the next section.

Participatory and emancipatory research does not accept this assumption and yet, as argued below, it has still to produce a suitable alternative set of assumptions and criteria for measurement of the success of such research as "interventions".

DISCUSSION AND CONCLUSIONS

There is an oft-cited truism among proponents of the emancipatory model that traditional research "makes very little difference" (Goodley & Moore, 2002, p. 23) or is a "waste of time" to disabled people (Oliver, 1992). Minkes et al. go so far as to assert:

> From a quick review of the research listed in the BILD Current Awareness Service, it is difficult to see how a significant proportion of it will make much (if any) difference to the lives of people with learning difficulties. (1995, pp. 94–95)

We are not sure we necessarily agree with these blanket assertions. These views assume at least two distinguishing features of emancipatory or participatory research in contradistinction to all other approaches; (1) such research is singularly successful in changing policy and improving lives, and (2) it is the only research with "noble intent". This is not the place to debate these contentions in depth, but a cursory examination seems appropriate.

Success in Changing Policy and Improving Lives

Just 20 years ago, debates on the gap between theory and practice focused on the lack of a direct or instrumental link between research and policy (see Bulmer, 1982, p. 152). If research was not simply adopted and implemented, this meant there was some "translation" required by policy makers or practitioners who sought to draw upon research findings. Implicated here were "forms of influence" or the link between researchers and policy makers. Thomas (1987), for example, conceptualises these in terms of the "limestone model", in which findings are simply left to filter through to policy; the "gadfly" model, in which researchers seek to influence administrators and government; and the "insider" model, in which researchers maintain direct links with administrators or government officials.

While these may still be relevant, the unfolding of the consumerist and participatory agendas supported by successive governments have led to a different agenda in linking information to social, policy, and political change. Arguments are now more to do with how to harness the talents of people to make a difference (social capital) and about how communication can be formulated to force for change ("deliberative democracy"). This means that research is seeking to influence not only those in politics and political administrators but also additional groups that have a seat at the table or potential influence in that process, such as pressure groups and activists. This emphasises further the point made earlier that consumers as "an additional tier of influence on the political agenda" should be a legitimate target for research dissemination meaningful to them. This, we would argue, applies whatever the research approach. However, there are some who would argue otherwise.

In his editorial for a Special Issue of *Policy and Politics*, Colin Barnes (2002) makes a number of claims about the ways in which organisations of disabled people have effected change—for example, a major contribution to the UN's equality of opportunity and the classification of functioning, and a strong role in advising the UK government in relation to a number of Acts relating to disability discrimination, direct payments, carers, and disabled children.

Barnes argues that "there is little doubt that these policy initiatives would not have occurred without the politicisation of disability by disabled people and their organizations" (Barnes, C., 2002, p. 313). Yet, in the same volume, there are a number of problems raised with this interpretation. Marian Barnes (2002), for example, shows the difficulties of seeking to balance the sometimes differing views of relatives, informal carers, and those for whom they provide care within the policy agenda. A similar issue is the growing heterogeneity of the voluntary sector without a single united voice. This raises questions of how one voice is established over another; that is, of the representativeness of the voice of disabled activists and of representation (whom they have the right to claim to be representing). In seeking to privilege one voice, Colin Barnes (2002) makes it clear that positive changes have been achieved through organisations run *by* disabled people, and not those run *for* them.

In his editorial, Barnes alludes to being involved in relevant working groups or in advisory positions, somewhat like the "insider model" identified by Thomas (1987). And such incorporation, as Armstrong (2002) asserts in his review of self-advocacy, can be interpreted as a mechanism for managing and controlling a "troublesome minority". Moreover, Barnes does not establish the degree to which *emancipatory* or any other *research* has been brought to bear in pursuit of the interests of disabled people, and in not doing so conflates the voice of research with those of activists, as if the two were necessarily one and the same. Having taken these issues into account, however, we are still left with the difficult problem of *how* research has made a difference, how it has been drawn upon or illuminated decision making and hence affected policy, practice, and outcome. This takes us back to Bulmer's dilemma; that is, that research is seldom "instrumental" or couched in terms of an "engineering" model that can simply be implemented once it is complete. Rather, research tends to be "enlightening" with results filtering into policy and practice in a tangential way. Therefore, the burden of proof about the "degree of influence" still remains for emancipatory as for other research. Moreover, if the gap between research and policy remains problematic, so, too, does the relationship between research and professional practice aimed at improving the lives of people with intellectual disabilities as individuals, clients, service users, patients, or simply citizens.

Noble Intent

We have outlined above how traditional research is often taken to be less well intentioned than emancipatory research. In some texts, such traditional research is largely tied up with quantitative methods (Goodley & Moore, 2002) and in others with methods that do not fit the criteria for emancipatory research or social models. The twentieth century marked an important watershed in the extent to which social research established its central place in influencing government policy. The survey work of Booth (1889–1903) and Rowntree (1901) on poverty can be said to have had a huge impact on politics, as has the far later and equally impressive work of Townsend (1979) on poverty. Can such studies be taken to lack "noble intent"? Bury (1996) has also pointed out that OPCS (UK census) data helped to pave the way for welfare benefits payments, such as the Disability Living Allowance—in this case, large-scale surveys and categorisations of disability not fashionable to proponents of the social model led to these improvements. To be fair, in recognising some of these contributions, some social-model theorists go on to advocate the legitimacy of a range of methods. "It is not the research methods themselves that are the problem, it is the uses to which they are put" (Barnes, 2003, p. 12).

Additionally, the social model of disability, which claims the emancipatory research model as its vehicle, criticises the individualised and pathologised medical model and would dismiss it as self-serving and ignoble. Some examples of so-called traditional research help to make the case: health and medical technology research that seeks to develop aids and adaptations such as wheelchairs, footwear, and lifts that improve accessibility; pharmacological studies that have advanced anticonvulsant therapies; medical research that, recognising the disproportionately early onset of Alzheimer's disease among people with Down's syndrome, seeks, in the absence of other evidence, to establish causation with magnetic resonance imaging (Natarajan, Rolfe, Shah & Haque, 2003); and studies that examine the relative merits, costs, and outcomes of different residential options for people with intellectual disabilities (Emerson et al., 1999). It might finally be observed that social-model theorists are themselves not immune from using broad-level statistical data in identifying the extent of issues relating to disabled people and, in doing so, relying upon the very categories they seek to criticise (Bury, 1996).

If such studies are not of themselves ignoble or self-serving, perhaps the central questions that remain are as follows: when is quantitative and/or medical research relevant; when is "impairment" legitimate grounds for a research interest; where is the limit to be placed on the relevance of impairment to defining the situation and lives of people with intellectual disabilities; what place has a social model when set against the answers to these questions; and, finally, what is the place of participatory or emancipatory research in this rather complex context?

There are further issues associated with the arguments set out above. A yawning gap has emerged between science as evidence and evidence as conviction and values. While values within science remain a recognised problem, *conviction* within science is based upon a sophisticated set of arguments about the validity of the information it produces. But within the emancipatory model in particular, *conviction* and *personal values* seem to act as the sole arbiter of validity. The result seems to be a range of strategies that seek to privilege one voice over another. For example, there is a claim that *expertise* is a product of *experience*; thus, only disabled people can be experts on disabled people. It is a sad outcome here that collecting data from research is not seen to be a valid window on experience; this potentially undermines a substantial portion of the qualitative research enterprise. There are ironies here, too. Given diversity, it might be argued from a reductionist perspective that each individual is a product of his or her own singular experience and, as such, there is no commonality between any two people. In contrast, it might be argued from an organisational perspective that those who have not experienced a service cannot comment upon another's experience of that service, whether they are both disabled people or not. Can any of the above really be true? And if so, then where does that leave us in terms of giving due regard to competing voices? Barnes (2003) begins to recognise this in accepting positivist and "post-positivist" epistemologies. However, he argues that the distinguishing feature of emancipatory research is that it does not claim political neutrality. Despite this, it does claim to be correct. The present solution would seem therefore to be a preciousness and posturing by some emancipatory theorists where the main aim is to dismiss other voices as a means of substantiating their own position over all others. But even were other voices to be wrong, this does not necessarily make the voice or values of the emancipatory theorist right. Such attempts at substantiation are not based on epistemological grounds but on a Hobbesian-style war of all against all. And while there may be nothing wrong with the nature, intent, and outcomes of such "*conviction policy*", there is something wrong in the denial that others may bring with them a legitimate voice and equally strong convictions too.

There are further issues about the issue of validity. It has been argued that

> The extent to which disabled people and their allies have their opportunity to have their say, be listened to and have their views taken seriously within the research process is now regarded as probably the most important indicator of the validity of any piece of disability related research. (Goodley & Moore, 2002, p. 23)

But to what extent is it possible for the views of all people with intellectual disabilities to be taken into account? As part of a wider study of civil rights in a hospital for people with intellectual disabilities (Ramcharan, 1998, p. 13), a review of the communication of 151 residents indicated that a substantial amount of communication took place non-verbally or through augmented communication strategies. Although not generalisable and limited by being undertaken in a hospital, it was reported that only 57% of residents could ask questions, 59% label objects, and 68% make comments about or appraise experiences. In this light, and on the basis of this selective review of emancipatory and participatory research, we would argue that it would be *an exception* to find people with intellectual disabilities fully able to undertake research. This means that people with profound or multiple intellectual disabilities are less likely to be included in research or have their views represented.

We have also raised some issues about whether the agenda of "disabled researchers" or the disability lobby is shared with people with intellectual disabilities. Walmsley (1997) warns that the normalising agenda is

> an agenda which maintains that to take part in society on equal terms people with learning difficulties must rise above the impairment and join in a conspiracy to deny that their intellectual limitations matter. Or maybe these limitations are not real, maybe they are socially created and can be undone. Every form of disability gives rise to a particular set of restrictions on what the disabled person can do, and it is in the area of political and academic debate that people with learning difficulties will always be at a disadvantage. (p. 75)

Therefore, we have also suggested that emancipatory research needs, in our view, to address issues about the limitations of "impairment" in relation to the role of people with intellectual disabilities in the research.

In a notably acerbic article entitled "Final Accounts and the Parasitic People", Oliver argues that a

> second approach calls for participatory strategies involving research subjects. It attempts to deal with the problem of emancipation by sharing or attempting to share responsibility and indeed blame with the research participants. The worst exemplar of this is the attempt to do participation by employing a few disabled people as researchers, often without much support or understanding of what that means. Next worse comes involving disability organisations (often non-representative ones) in the process of research production. Least worst involves commitment to involving organisations of disabled people at all stages in the research process, short of overall control over resources and agendas. (Oliver, 1999, p. 187)

We would argue that there is a case for academics and supporters to work *with* people with intellectual disabilities. We would argue that this *can* be more of a "symbiotic relationship" than a parasitic one. For us, there is a case for a participatory paradigm in which people with intellectual disabilities are supported to undertake research and in which they collaborate with other researchers. And we accept the vitally important role of the self-advocacy movement in setting the research agenda itself. But we have also argued that there are seemingly legitimate ways of establishing the voice, views, values, and experiences of people with intellectual disabilities through other non-participatory research approaches. This is possible not only in relation to people with intellectual disabilities who can speak for themselves, but also for those whose communication requires us to attempt to understand their world through a different approach. That such an argument is being made implies that involvement in the management or the process of undertaking research should not be enjoined gratuitously. It must at all times be possible to say what is being gained by undertaking research in a participatory manner. Nor should academic researchers rationalise their research as worthwhile simply on the grounds that people with intellectual disabilities have been "involved".

Rather, together with their co-researchers, they should explain the ways in which their research interest has been guided by people with intellectual disabilities and their allies; show how and why the research will challenge oppression; explain how the research funding will affect their work; make clear the nature of the research relationships and the division of labour involved; explain the mechanisms that have been involved in making the participation of people with intellectual disabilities meaningful; state clearly the values underpinning their research; and, most importantly, in our view, publish their work in ways that are meaningful and useful not only to academics, but also to people with intellectual disabilities and their allies, who may judge its merits in making their political or other cases. It is the means through which information is used for social and political change that are very much at issue in this regard.

Finally, we draw attention to the results of Kitchin's interviews with 35 disabled people, in which he concluded:

> The ideal model [of research] forwarded by respondents was one of inclusivity: an equal-based, democratic, partnership between disabled people and disabled/non-disabled academics. The model did not preclude non-disabled researchers, but positively welcomed them. (2000, p. 45)

In listening to these disabled people, we would agree with their sentiments and, in doing so, would seek through reflection in the work we do to be on the side of people with intellectual disabilities. This involves a commitment to challenging oppression and disadvantage, a recognition of the power relations in research and the importance of informing people with intellectual disabilities and their allies, and a commitment to hearing their voice and understanding their values and culture. Yes, we are "for" people with intellectual disabilities, but to be "for" them is not the sole preserve of a few academics working within one model with a unidimensional view of the research process nor adopting to one theoretical perspective at all costs, even if the cost for people with intellectual disabilities is further oppression.

If there has been a natural evolution to a paradigm shift or the emergence of a new research idea, then, for emancipatory and participatory research, it started with the recognition that virtually the most important voice had been systematically excluded from research and the research process. The interests of individuals, people with intellectual disabilities included, are tied to their social world, their interactions with others, and with formal service organisations. It should therefore not be a revelation to see the relevance of their voice in making sense of and seeking to change the nature of that social world.

In the title of this chapter, we asked about emancipatory and participatory research, "How far have we come?", and have sought to answer this in what has been written. However, it is worth noting, too, that, to date, the participatory research paradigm within the intellectual disability field has been largely insular. More recently, proponents of the social model, operating with an emancipatory research paradigm, have prompted those wishing to work within the participatory paradigm to reappraise their approach in this light. However, participatory research is by no means confined to these approaches. There may still be much to learn from examining participatory research areas such as development studies (e.g., Bell & Stokes, 2001; Riley, Jossy, Nkinsi & Buhi, 2001), health and health issues research (e.g., Street, 1998; Dias & Simmons, 1999; Gray, Fitch, Davis & Phillips, 2000; Mullings et al., 2001), or in other specialisms (e.g., Macleod, 1997; Fenton, Chinouya & Davidson, 2002; Lazenbatt, Lynch & O'Neill, 2001).

The preliminary phase in the evolution of participatory and emancipatory research has been further characterised by an optimism about its potential and by generously uncritical spectators and commentators. However, there comes a point in the evolution of such a new paradigm when the knowledge base, theoretical substantiation, ethics, cost, and practicalities of the new approach need to be further elaborated and addressed. It is perhaps now appropriate to enter this second phase of the debate. There remain questions with this about how possible it would be for academics to support people with learning disabilities in this debate and about whether they have the capacity or desire to engage with these abstractions.

REFERENCES

Acker, J., Barry, K. & Esseveld, J. (1983). Objectivity and truth: problems in doing feminist research. *Women's Studies International Forum*, **6**, 423–435.

Allport, G.W. (1947). *The Use of Personal Documents in Psychological Science*. New York: Social Sciences Research Council.

All Wales Advisory Panel (1991). *Consumer Involvement and the All Wales Strategy: Report to the All Wales Advisory Panel from the Consumer Involvement Sub-group*. Cardiff: Welsh Office.

Armstrong, D. (2002). The politics of self-advocacy and people with learning difficulties. *Policy and Politics*, **30**, 333–345.

Aspis, S. (1999). What they don't tell disabled people with learning difficulties. In M. Corker & S. French (Eds) *Disability Discourse* (pp. 173–182). Buckingham: Open University Press.

Atkinson, D. (1998). Reclaiming our past: empowerment through oral history and personal stories. In L. Ward (Ed.) *Innovations in Advocacy and Empowerment: Innovations in Advocacy and Empowerment for People with Intellectual Disabilities* (pp. 115–126). Chorley: Lisieux Hall.

Atkinson, D. (2002). Self-advocacy and research. In B. Gray & R. Jackson (Eds), *Advocacy and Learning Disability* (pp. 120–136). London: Jessica Kingsley.

Atkinson, D., Jackson, M. & Walmsley, J. (Eds) (1997). *Forgotten Lives. Exploring the History of Learning Disability.* Kidderminster: BILD.

Atkinson, D. & Walmsley, J. (1999). Using autobiographical approaches with people with learning difficulties. *Disability and Society*, **14**, 203–216.

Barnes, C. (1991). *Disabled People in Britain and Discrimination: A Case Study for Anti-discrimination Legislation.* London: Hurst.

Barnes, C. (1996). Disability and the myth of the independent researcher. *Disability and Society*, **11**, 107–110.

Barnes, C. (2002). Introduction: disability, policy and politics. *Policy and Politics*, **30**, 311–318.

Barnes, C. (2003). What a difference a decade makes: reflections on doing "emancipatory" disability research. *Disability and Society*, **18**, 3–17.

Barnes, M. (2002). Bringing difference into deliberation? Disabled people, survivors and local governance. *Policy and Politics*, **30**, 319–331.

Becker, H. (1970). Whose side are we on? *Social Problems*, **14**, 239–247.

Bell, P.D. & Stokes, C.C. (2001). Melding disparate cultures and capacities to create global health partnerships. *American Journal of Public Health*, **91**, 1552–1554.

Booth, C. (1889–1903). *Life and Labour of People in London*, 17 vols. London: Macmillan.

Booth, T. (1996). Sounds of still voices: issues in the use of narrative methods with people who have learning difficulties. In L. Barton (Ed.) *Society and Disability: Emerging Issues and Insights.* (pp. 241–255). London: Longman.

Bruner, J. (1987). Life as narrative. *Social Research*, **54**, 11–32.

Bulmer, M. (1982). *The Uses of Social Research: Social Investigation in Public Policy-Making.* London: Allen & Unwin.

Bury, M. (1996). Defining and researching disability: challenges and responses. In C. Barnes & G. Mercer (Eds) *Exploring the Divide: Illness and Disability* (pp. 17–38). Leeds: Disability Press.

Chambers, R. (1994). Participatory Rural Appraisal (PRA): challenges, potentials and paradigm. *World Development*, **22**, 1437–1454.

CHANGE (1997). *MAP (More Access Please): The Right Track.* London [No place of publication identified].

CHANGE (2001). *CHANGE Picture Bank.* London: Hatcham Park Mews.

Chappell, A.L. (1998). Still out in the cold: people with learning difficulties and the social model of disability. In T. Shakespeare (Ed.) *The Disability Reader: Social Science Perspectives.* London: Cassell.

Chappell, A.L. (2000). Emergence of participatory methodology in learning disability research: understanding the context. *British Journal of Learning Disabilities*, **28**, 38–43.

Cocks, E. & Cockram, J. (1995). The participatory research paradigm and intellectual disability. *Mental Handicap Research*, **8**, 25–37.

Crawley, B. (1988). *The Growing Voice: A Survey of Self-Advocacy Groups in Adult Training Centres and Hospitals in Britain.* London: Values into Action.

Davis, J.M. (2000). Disability studies as ethnograpohic research and text: research strategies and roles for promoting social change? *Disability and Society,* **15**, 191–206.

Department of Health (2001). *Valuing People: A New Strategy for Learning Disability for the 21st Century.* Cm 5086. London: HMSO.

Dias, M. & Simmons, R. (1999). When is research participatory? Reflections on a reproductive health project in Brazil. *Journal of Women's Health*, **8**, 175–184.

Didion, J. (1979). *The White Album.* New York: Simon and Schuster.

Downer, J. & Walmsley, J. (1997). Shouting the loudest: self-advocacy, power and diversity. In P. Ramcharan, G. Roberts, G. Grant & J. Borland (Eds) *Empowerment in Everyday Life: Learning Disability* (pp. 35-47). London: Jessica Kingsley.

Dowson, S. (1997). Empowerment within services: a comfortable delusion. In P. Ramcharan, G. Roberts, G. Grant & J. Borland (Eds) *Empowerment in Everyday Life: Learning Disability* (pp. 101–120). London: Jessica Kingsley.

Emerson, E., Robertson, J., Gregory, N., Hatton, C., Keasissoglou, S., Hallam, A., et al. (1999). *A Comparative Analysis of Quality and Costs in Group Homes and Supported Hiring Schemes*. London: London School of Economics.

Fairclough, N. (1989). *Language and Power*. London: Longman.

Fairclough, N. (1992). *Discourse and Social Change*. Cambridge: Polity Press.

Felce, D., Grant, G., Todd, S., Ramcharan, P., Beyer, S., McGrath, M., et al. (1998). *Towards a Full Life: Researching Policy Innovation for People with Learning Disabilities*. London: Butterworth Heinemann.

Fenton, K.A., Chinouya, M. & Davidson, O. (2002). HIV testing and high risk sexual behaviour among London's migrant African communities: a participatory research study. *Sexually Transmitted Infections*, **78**, 241–245.

Flynn, M. with Liverpool Self Advocates (1994). *Taking a Break: Liverpool's Respite Services for Adult Citizens with Learning Disabilities*. Manchester: National Development Team.

Freire, P. (1968). *Pedagogy of the Oppressed*. New York: Seabury Press.

Gergen, K. & Gergen, M. (1988). Narrative and the self as relationship. *Advances in Experimental Psychology*, **21**, 17–56.

Gillman, M., Swain, J. & Heyman, B. (1997). "Life" history or "case" history; the objectification of people with learning difficulties through the tyranny of professional discourse. *Disability and Society*, **12**, 675–693.

Goodley, D. (1996). Tales of hidden lives: a critical examination of life history research with people who have learning difficulties. *Disability and Society*, **11**, 333–348.

Goodley, D. (2000). *Self-Advocacy in the Lives of People with Learning Difficulties*. Buckingham: Open University Press.

Goodley, D. & Moore, M. (2000). Doing disability research: activist lives and the academy. *Disability and Society*, **6**, 861–882.

Goodley, D. & Moore, M. (2002). *Disability Arts Against Exclusion: People with Learning Difficulties and Their Performing Arts*. Kidderminster: BILD.

Gouldner, A. (1973). The sociologist as partisan: sociology and the Welfare State. In A. Gouldner (Ed.) *For Sociology: Renewal and Critique in Sociology Today*. London: Allen & Unwin.

Gramlich, S., McBride, G., Snelham, N. & Myers, B.; with Williams, V. & Simons, K. (2002). *Journey to Independence: What Self Advocates Tell Us About Direct Payments*. Kidderminster, BILD.

Grant, G. & Ramcharan, P. (2002). Researching 'Valuing people'. *Tizard Learning Disability Review*, **7**, 27–33.

Gray, R.E., Fitch, M., Davis, C. & Phillips, C. (2000). Challenges of participatory research: reflections on a study with breast cancer self-help groups. *Health Expectations*, **3**, 243–252.

Habermas, J. (1972). *Knowledge and Human Interests*. London: Heinemann Educational.

Hoffman, L. (1993). *Exchanging Voices: A Collaborative Approach to Family Therapy*. London: Karnak.

Hollins, S., Bernal, J. & Gregory, M. (1996). *Going to the Doctor*. London: Gaskell.

Hollins, S., Bernal, J. & Gregory, M. (1998). *Going to Out-Patients*. London: Gaskell.

Hollins, S., Clare, I. & Murphy, G. (1996). *You're Under Arrest*. London: Gaskell.

Hollins, S., Horrocks, C. & Sinason, V. (1998). *I Can Get Through It*. London: Gaskell.

Hollins, S., Murphy, G. & Clare, I. (1996). *You're on Trial*. London: Gaskell.

Kiernan, C. (1999). Participation in research by people with learning disability: origins and issues. *British Journal of Learning Disabilities*, **27**, 43–47.

Kitchin, R. (2000). The researched opinions on research: disabled people and disability research. *Disability and Society*, **15**, 25–47.

Langness, L.L. & Levine, H.G. (1986). *Culture and Retardation*. Dordrecht: D. Reidel.

Lazenbatt, A., Lynch, U. & O'Neill, E. (2001). Revealing the hidden "troubles" in Northern Ireland: the role of participatory rapid appraisal. *Health Education Research*, **16**, 567–578.

Leeds Coalition (1996). *Working to Make Services Better for People with Learning Disabilities*. Leeds: Leeds Coalition.

Liverpool and Manchester People First (1996). *Our Plan for Planning*. Manchester: People First.

Longhurst, N.A. (1994). *The Self-Advocacy Movement and People with Developmental Disabilities: A Demographic Study and Directory of Self-Advocacy Groups in the United States*. Washington, DC: American Association on Mental Retardation.

Macleod, C. (1997). Research as intervention within community mental health. *Curationis*, **20**, 53–56.

March, J., Steingold, B. & Justice, S. (1997). Follow the yellow brick road! people with learning difficulties as co-researchers. *British Journal of Learning Disability*, **25**, 77–79.

McClimens, A. (2003). The Organisation of Difference: Meaning and Identity in the Lives of Four Individuals with a Learning Difficulty. Unpublished Ph.D. Thesis, University of Sheffield.

McIntosh, B. & Whittaker, A. (1998). *Days of Change: A Practical Guide to Developing Better Day Opportunities with People with Learning Difficulties*. London: King's Fund.

Minkes, J., Townsley, R., Weston, C. & Williams, C. (1995). Having a voice. Involving people with learning difficulties in research. *British Journal of Learning Disabilities*, **23**, 94–98.

Mullings, L., Wali, A., McLean, D., Mitchell, J., Prince, S., Thomas, D., et al. (2001). Qualitative methodologies and community participation in examining reproductive experiences: the Harlem Birth Right Project. *Maternal and Child Health Journal*, **5**, 85–93.

Natarajan, K., Rolfe, E., Shah, S. & Haque, M.S. (2003). Magnetic resonance imaging, Down's syndrome and Alzheimer's disease: research and clinical implications. *Journal of Intellectual Disability Research*, **47**, 90–100.

Northway, R. (1998). Engaging in participatory research: some personal reflections. *Journal of Learning Disabilities for Nursing, Health and Social Care*, **2**, 144–149.

Oakley, A. (2000). *Experiments in Knowing: Gender and Method in Social Sciences*. Cambridge: Polity Press.

Oliver, M. (1992). Changing the social relations of research production. *Disability and Society*, **7**, 101–115.

Oliver, M. (1993). Re-defining disability: a challenge to research. In J. Swain, V. Finkelstein, S. French & M. Oliver (Eds) *Disabling Barriers—Enabling Environments* (pp. 61–68). London: Sage.

Oliver, M. (1997). Emancipatory research: realistic goal or impossible dream? In C. Barnes and G. Mercer (Eds) *Doing Disability Research* (pp. 15–31). Leeds: Disability Press.

Oliver, M. (1999). Final accounts and the parasite people. In M. Corker & S. French (Eds) *Disability Discourse* (pp. 183–191). Buckingham: Open University Press.

People First (1993). *Oi! It's My Assessment—Why Not Listen to Me?* London: People First.

People First (1994). *Helping You Get the Services You Want: A Guide for People with Learning Difficulties to Help Them through their Assessment and Get the Services They Want.* London: People First.

People First (1997). *Access First. A Guide on How to Give Written Information to People with Learning Difficulties.* London: People First.

People First (1998). *Access First: Directory*. London: People First.

Potts, M. & Fido, R. (1991). *A Fit Person to be Removed: Personal Accounts of Life in a Mental Deficiency Institution*. Plymouth: Northcote House.

Priestley, M. (1997). Whose research? A personal audit. In C. Barnes & G. Mercer (Eds) *Doing Disability Research* (pp. 89–106). Leeds: Disability Press.

Ramcharan, P. (1998). *Fostering a Culture of Civil Rights in a Learning Disability Hospital*. Bangor: CSPRD, University of Wales Bangor.

Ramcharan, P. & Grant, G. (2001). Views and experiences of people with intellectual disabilities and their families. I. The user perspective. *Journal of Applied Research in Intellectual Disabilities*, **14**, 348–363.

Reason, P. (Ed.) (1994). *Participation in Human Enquiry*. London: Sage.

Riley, P.L., Jossy, R., Nkinsi, L. & Buhi, L. (2001). The CARE-CDC health initiative: a model for global participatory research. *American Journal of Public Health*, **91**, 1549–1552.

Rodgers, J. (1999). Trying to get it right: undertaking research involving people with learning difficulties. *Disability and Society*, **14**, 421–433.

Roeher Institute (1990a). *The Right to Have Enough Money: A Straightforward Guide to the Disability Income in Canada.* Ontario: Roeher Institute.

Roeher Institute (1990b). *The Right to Read and Write: A Straightforward Guide to Literacy and People with a Mental Handicap in Canada.* Ontario: Roeher Institute.

Roeher Institute (1991a). *The Right to Control What Happens to Your Body: A Straightforward Guide to Issues of Sexuality and Sexual Abuse.* Ontario: Roeher Institute.

Roeher Institute (1991b). *The Right to Fair and Equal Treatment: A Straightforward Guide to the Canadian Human Rights Act.* Ontario: Roeher Institute.

Roeher Institute (1994). *The Right to Have a Job: A Straightforward Guide to Canada's Employment-Related Programs for Persons with Disabilities.* Ontario: Roeher Institute.

Roeher Institute (1995). *Just Technology? Plain Language Summary. From Principles to Practice in Bio-Ethical Issues.* Ontario: Roeher Institute.

Roeher Institute (1997a). *Out of Harm's Way: A Safety Kit for People with Disabilities Who Feel Unsafe and Want to Do Something About It.* Ontario: Roeher Institute.

Roeher Institute (1997b). *The Power of Language: Guide to Plain Language* Writing. Ontario: Roeher Institute.

Rowntree, S. (1901). *Poverty: A Study of Town Life.* London: Longman.

Sarbin, T.R. (1986). *Narrative Psychology: The Storied Nature of Human Conduct.* New York: Praeger.

Shakespeare, T. (1997). Researching disabled sexuality. In C. Barnes & G. Mercer (Eds) *Doing Disability Research* (pp. 177–189). Leeds: Disability Press.

Simons, K. (2000). *A Place at the Table.* Kidderminster: BILD.

Simons, K., Booth, T. & Booth, W. (1989) Speaking out: user studies and people with learning difficulties. *Research Policy and Planning*, **7**, 9–17.

Speak Up Self Advocacy (1998). *It's My IPP.* Brighton: Pavilion.

Stalker, K. (1998). Some ethical and methodological issues in research with people with learning difficulties. *Disability and Society*, **13**, 5–19.

Stone, E. & Priestley, M. (1996). Parasites, pawns and partners: disability research and the role of non-disabled researchers. *British Journal of Sociology*, **47**, 699–716.

Street, A. (1998). From soulmates to stakeholders: issues in creating quality postmodern participatory research relationships. *Social Sciences in Health*, **4**, 119–129.

Tandon, R. (1996). The historical roots and contemporary tendencies in participatory research: implications for health care. In K. de Konig & M. Martin (Eds) *Participatory Research in Health* (pp. 24–59). London: Zed Books.

Taylor, S.J. & Bogdan, R. (1984). *Introduction to Qualitative Research Methods: The Search for Meaning* (2nd edn). New York: Wiley.

Thomas, P. (1987). The use of social research: myths and models. In M. Bulmer (Ed.) *Social Science Research and Government: Comparative Essays on Britain and the United States* (pp. 51–60). Cambridge: Cambridge University Press.

Townsend, P. (1979). *Poverty in the United Kingdom.* London: Allen Lane.

Townsley, R. (1998). Information is power: the impact of accessible information on people with learning difficulties. In L. Ward (Ed.) *Innovations in Advocacy and Empowerment for People with Intellectual Disabilities* (pp. 77–90). Chorley: Lisieux Hall.

Tregaskis, C. (2002). Social model theory: the story so far... *Disability and Society*, **17**, 457–470.

Walmsley, J. (1997). Including people with learning difficulties: theory and practice. In L. Barton & M. Oliver (Eds) *Disability Studies: Past, Present and Future* (pp. 62–77). Leeds: Disability Press.

Walmsley, J. (2001). Normalisation, emancipatory research and inclusive research in learning disability. *Disability and Society*, **16**, 187–205.

Walsall Women's Group (1999). *No Means No.* Brighton: Pavilion.

Ward, L. (1995). Equal citizens: current issues for people with learning difficulties and their allies. In T. Philpot & L. Ward (Eds) *Values and Visions: Changing Ideas in Services for People with Learning Difficulties* (pp. 3–19). Oxford: Butterworth Heinemann.

Ward, L. (1998). Practising partnership: involving people with learning difficulties in research. *British Journal of Learning Disabilities*, **26**, 128–134.

Welsh Office (1989). *Still a Small Voice: Consumer Involvement in the All Wales Strategy.* Cardiff: Welsh Office.

Whittaker, A. (1997). *Looking at Our Services: Service Evaluation by People with Learning Difficulties*. London: King's Fund.
Whittaker, A., Gardner, G. & Kershaw, J. (1990). *Service Evaluation by People with Learning Difficulties*. London: King's Fund.
Whittell, B. & Ramcharan, P. (1999). *Everyday Lives: Final Report to the Wales Office of Research and Development*. Bangor: CSPRD, University of Wales Bangor.
Williams, V. (1999). Researching together. *British Journal of Learning Disabilities*, **27**, 48–51.
Zarb, G. (1992). On the road to Damascus: first steps towards changing the relations of disability research production. *Disability, Handicap and Society*, **7**, 125–138.

SECTION II

Approaches to Measurement

CHAPTER 5

Interviewing People with Intellectual Disabilities

Jonathan Perry
University of Wales, UK

This chapter considers some of the reasons why it has become increasingly common to interview people with intellectual disabilities as part of research studies. Ethical issues related to interviewing this client group are discussed and strategies for facilitating effective interviewing are presented. The potential pitfalls and difficulties which one should be aware of are also highlighted. Responsiveness is considered first; that is, the limitations imposed on one's ability to respond to interview items by one's capacity for comprehension and expression. Related to this, there is a discussion of factors, such as acquiescence, which may result in biased or invalid responses. Problems associated with the consistency of responses over time are also considered. Following this, there is discussion of the use of proxy respondents as a strategy sometimes adopted to overcome response bias. In a similar vein, the degree to which responses to interviews agree with data gained by objective measurement is examined. Finally, consideration is given to the potential impact on interviewee responses of issues such as interviewer status, the way questions are framed, interviewee experience, and personal temperament. The chapter draws heavily on research on the quality of residential services because, arguably, it is in this field that there has been most debate about the issue of eliciting the views of people with intellectual disabilities. In addition, frequent reference is made to a study recently completed by researchers at the Welsh Centre for Learning Disabilities, because it examined in detail several fundamental issues in the research interviewing of people with intellectual disabilities. In conclusion, emphasis is given to the need to continue eliciting the views of people with intellectual disabilities while striving for and adopting methods which attempt to overcome the difficulties discussed.

DEFINITION OF TERMS

People's views can be ascertained directly through their verbal or written responses to verbal or written questions. For the purposes of this chapter, a research interview is defined as the verbal questioning of one person by another, whether using a predetermined set of questions or encouraging open discussion around a particular theme. The term implies

The International Handbook of Applied Research in Intellectual Disabilities. Edited by E. Emerson, C. Hatton, T. Thompson and T.R. Parmenter © 2004 John Wiley & Sons, Ltd. ISBN 0-471-49709-6.

a degree of verbal interaction between the questioner and the person being questioned, compared to a questionnaire (a set of written questions to which respondents are asked to provide written answers). However, it can be argued that a verbal response from the person being questioned is not necessary for an interview to have occurred. For example, some interview schedules allow the interviewee to respond to verbal questions by pointing to one of a number of options. While the focus of this chapter is on research interviewing, to the extent that interviews and questionnaires differ only with respect to whether questions and responses are verbal or written, the chapter is also relevant to questionnaire design for people with intellectual disabilities.

WHY INTERVIEW PEOPLE WITH INTELLECTUAL DISABILITIES?

The process of the deinstitutionalisation of residential services for people with intellectual disabilities has occurred throughout the UK, Scandinavia, and the USA over the last few decades (e.g., Mansell & Ericsson, 1996). Deinstitutionalisation has been accompanied by an increased prominence of the voice of people with intellectual disabilities. In the UK, the origin of this trend, which has been particularly evident since the early 1990s, can be traced back to the exposure of the abominable conditions which existed within institutions until at least the 1970s (e.g., Goffman, 1961), which demonstrated the imperative to monitor service quality. Wherever deinstitutionalisation and service reform have occurred, indicators of service process and outcome have been developed to investigate the effect of services on the lives of service users. The evolution of these indicators has tended to reflect the prevailing philosophies underlying services. For example, in response to the philosophies underlying reform, such as the principle of normalisation (Wolfensberger, 1972; Nirje, 1980), service evaluations began to take an holistic view of the quality of life (QOL) of service recipients.

In the field of residential service evaluation, there has been a tendency to focus on measurement of the objective life conditions of residents; for example, the number of possessions people have, the frequency of visits to the community, or the range of domestic tasks which people undertake. However, in line with the emerging consensus that QOL spans several life domains and is multidimensional, techniques for assessing residents' satisfaction with various aspects of their lives have gained increasing prominence since the early 1990s (e.g., Heal & Chadsey-Rusch, 1985; Cummins, 1992; Harner & Heal, 1993; Schalock & Keith, 1993).

The increasing tendency to seek the views of people with disabilities also reflects the emergence of a new research paradigm in which participants become co-workers in the research process (Heron, 1992; Oliver, 1992; Zarb, 1992; Ramcharan & Grant, 1994; Reason & Heron, 1995; Sample, 1996; Reason, 1998; Ramcharan, Grant & Flynn, Chapter 4, this volume). Kiernan (1999) has stated that intellectual disabilities research has tended to be "research *on* rather than research *with* people" (p. 43). Recently, distinctions have been drawn between emancipatory research, where people with intellectual disabilities have complete control over the entire research enterprise, and participatory research, where people with intellectual disabilities are involved in the research process as co-researchers. However, at this point, the most common form of research involvement for people with intellectual disabilities is as research participants rather than as researchers (Chapter 4, this volume).

Together, increased interest in monitoring the quality of services, calls for participatory and emancipatory research paradigms, and the expansion of the self-advocacy movement have acted as catalysts for the increased interest in, and adoption of, techniques to elicit the views of people with intellectual disabilities.

THE ETHICS OF INTERVIEWING PEOPLE WITH INTELLECTUAL DISABILITIES FOR RESEARCH

The ethical issues of interviewing this population should be considered at an early stage in the research process, preferably at the point of designing the study. Interviews demand the interviewee's time, and involve the divulgence of information or opinions which may be of a personal nature. It might not be necessary for the research to have a direct positive impact on the person or people being interviewed. However, it would be unethical to request the participation of people with intellectual disabilities in research which did not, at least, have the ultimate aim of improving the situation of people with intellectual disabilities in general. An exception to this might be a study aimed at building a theory. Generally, research on this population is not funded unless it has some applied value, whether directly or indirectly (as in theory building). In addition to the purpose of the research, one of the prime ethical considerations is the procedure by which the consent of research participants is gained. Gaining the consent of people with intellectual disabilities poses certain difficulties because the concept of consent is not simple. For example, a study of the capacity of 40 people with intellectual disabilities to give informed consent to taking part in a research study found that the majority of people appeared to understand the nature of the research project, but had a limited understanding of the risks and benefits involved or of their right to refuse to participate or to drop out of the study (Arscott, Dagnan & Kroese, 1998). However, a number of steps can be taken to facilitate the process. Before consent is requested, it is vital that potential participants understand the purpose of the research, what will be required of them, what impact participation in the research might have on themselves and others, and what impact not participating might have. Approval of research from ethical bodies is generally also dependent on a declaration that the researchers will not attempt to induce potential participants to consent; that they are made aware that non-participation will have no adverse consequences; that they can withdraw from the study at any time, without giving reason and without negative consequences; and that they be given reasonable time to consult with others and consider whether or not to participate.

In the case of people with intellectual disabilities, this information should be conveyed in as simple and straightforward a way as possible. A first step might be to establish whether the potential participant is literate, in which case it may be possible to convey the above information in a written format. If the person is unable to read or write, the information should be presented verbally. The person should have the option to ask questions. The person seeking consent should also ask questions to establish whether the information has been understood. If the person is able to write, they should be able to give written consent. If not, verbal consent should be sought. The whole process should take place in the presence of the person's carer or advocate so that if verbal consent is given, the third party can complete a written consent form on behalf of the person who has given it.

If the person is considered by their carer or advocate to be unable to understand what would be involved, or if this becomes clear during the process of giving information, it may be possible for consent to be sought from the person's carer, advocate, and/or responsible medical officer. However, as will be discussed below, in such cases the person might well be unable to participate in the interview process.

A further issue which relates to the consent procedure is the protection of privacy. Unless there are very good reasons not to, it is generally the case that potential participants are informed that all data collected will be treated confidentially and that they will not be identified in the course of disseminating the results. However, there are exceptional circumstances when confidentiality and anonymity cannot be preserved. For example, in cases where abuse is disclosed in the course of the interview process, it would be unethical for the researcher not to report the information to those who might be able to take action to end the abuse. Participants should be informed of such exceptions to confidentiality and anonymity at the start of the interview.

This raises a further issue. Some interviews might cause anxiety or distress to the interviewee. Sometimes the subject matter is clearly of a sensitive nature, and such reactions might be predicted. In other cases, the interviewer might inadvertently ask a question which provokes an adverse reaction in the interviewee. In either situation, the interviewer should have a strategy for dealing with this distress. For example, sometimes it may be sufficient to steer the discussion away from the distressing subject towards a neutral or positive topic. Where the interviewee remains distressed at the close of the interview, it may be possible to arrange some form of post-interview support.

FACILITATING EFFECTIVE INTERVIEWING

It is possible to conduct perfectly satisfactory interviews with many people with intellectual disabilities. However, there are certain difficulties which one should be aware of before undertaking interviews with people with intellectual disabilities. In general, the "rules of engagement" are not dissimilar from those applied in interviews with the general population. Generally applicable interviewing techniques can be found in texts such as Shea (1988). However, by virtue of the particular cognitive deficits associated with intellectual disabilities, there are certain steps which can be taken to maximise the likelihood of a successful interview. These techniques are described by Prosser and Bromley (1998). A brief summary follows.

Venue

Many people with intellectual disabilities are unable to travel independently. The cost of travelling might be prohibitive, especially for those who rely on state benefits for their income. Complicated procedures for reclaiming expenses would be unlikely to be understood or well received. Therefore, it is important that the venue for the interview is easily accessible to the interviewee. Ideally, the interviewer should travel to the interviewee's day-time or residential setting. Having decided on the most appropriate setting, one should find a suitable room within it. It is important that the room is as quiet and free from interruptions as possible. This safeguards privacy and confidentiality; moreover, it is particularly important to minimise the number of competing stimuli when introducing potentially complicated concepts to people with cognitive deficits. For example, one should avoid the situation, frequently encountered in residential settings, where one has to compete with a television set for a person's attention.

Opening the Interview

Clearly, it would be unwise to launch straight into the interview. Whether or not people have an intellectual disability, there is usually a certain amount of trepidation at the beginning of the interview. It may help to relax the potentially anxious respondent if the interview is started with a couple of minutes of "idle chat" about some neutral topic such as the weather!

Although the interviewer might have met the interviewee during the consent procedure and explained the purpose of the research, several days might have passed since this occurred, and the interviewee may have had only a brief explanation from staff about who the interviewer is and the purpose of the interview. Furthermore, the interview content is unlikely to have been discussed in detail during the consent procedure. Therefore, the interviewee will probably be wondering what kind of person you are, and will need to be reminded about who you represent, what the purpose of the interview is, what questions are about to be asked, and what the consequences of the interview are likely to be. It is important that the person is clear about this because people with intellectual disabilities are often dependent on services, and they might think that these services will be jeopardised by their responses during the interview. They should be put at their ease about this. They may also have doubts about their ability to answer the questions. It may help to bolster the interviewee's confidence if they are reassured that the questions are not difficult and that it is their opinions which are sought (assuming this is the case) and that, as such, there can be no "wrong" answers. In addition, if time and resources permit, it may be possible to "spread" the interview over two or more occasions. This gives greater scope for flexibility and can reduce the pressure on both interviewee and interviewer. If this is not feasible, it may be possible to have breaks "within" the interview. The timing of such breaks may be determined by requests from the interviewee, or be dependent on the interviewer's awareness of interviewee fatigue or waning concentration.

Once all this has been explained, the interview can proceed. During the interview the interviewer should be aware of a number of potential problems. These are covered below. Finally, as mentioned above, it may be useful to end the interview by talking about some neutral or uncontroversial topic.

Questioning Style

Whatever question format is adopted, questions should be short, simple, and unambiguous. Complex vocabulary and jargon should be avoided, and the interviewer should speak reasonably slowly and clearly. Prosser and Bromley (1998) provide the following 10 guidelines on how questioning can be simplified:

(1) Use short words and sentences, simplifying sentences if the respondent's comprehension is poor.
(2) Use single-clause sentences.
(3) Use active verbs as in "Did you make the bed?"
(4) When possible, use the present tense.

(5) Avoid questions about abstract concepts.
(6) Avoid double negatives.
(7) Avoid jargon.
(8) Avoid figurative language.
(9) Avoid colloquialisms.
(10) With these points in mind, prepare questions in advance and assess readability of written questionnaires.

Having asked a question, the interviewer should wait patiently for a reply, which might take longer than would be typical for a person who does not have an intellectual disability. However, waiting too long for a response might raise the interviewee's anxiety if they genuinely have not understood the question. Apart from the suggestion that, in general, allowances should be made for people with intellectual disabilities, it is inappropriate to be prescriptive about how much time should be allowed before rephrasing the question or moving on to another. Ultimately, the interviewer will have to make a judgement in each interview according to how he or she perceives issues such as the respondent's receptive and expressive language skills, anxiety levels, and so on.

Question Format

Clearly, there are various ways of asking questions. Research has demonstrated that responses may be affected by question format. The most common question formats are presented in Table 5.1, together with their respective advantages and disadvantages. Evidence from research, some of which is described below, suggests that, however questions are posed, one needs to be aware of the potential for biased responses. Some interview schedules have integral checks for response bias. Where they do not, it may be necessary to cross-check responses, perhaps by asking the interviewee to illustrate his or her response with an example. Alternatively, or in addition, one might seek third-party "validation" of responses, although this is useful only when questions concern objectively verifiable information, such as whether or not a person goes to church. As will be shown later, the latter strategy may be difficult if one attempts to use third-party validation to verify responses about emotions or satisfaction.

Open questions may be appropriate for individuals with higher levels of cognitive and communicative skill. They have the advantage of being unlikely to elicit response bias and may yield information which might be missed with closed questions. Open questions are the preferred format for qualitative interviewing. Closed questions tend to achieve a higher response rate than open questions (Sigelman, Budd, Winer, Schoenrock & Martin, 1982), although high response rates might not always be the prime consideration, especially if achieved at the expense of increased response bias. There are three basic types of closed question. Yes/no questions are probably both the easiest to understand and to respond to. However, they frequently elicit acquiescent responses. Multiple-choice questions permit a greater range of responses but are more complicated as a consequence. Furthermore, respondents have a tendency to "over-select" the last of the choices offered. Some life-satisfaction scales employ Likert-type scales that are, effectively, multiple-choice questions. As might be expected, marked inconsistencies have been reported among the responses of people with intellectual disabilities to such scales (Sigelman et al., 1983).

Table 5.1 Advantages and disadvantages of different question formats

	Question format	Advantages	Disadvantages
Closed	Yes/no	Increases responsiveness May increase test–retest reliability (especially if topic is not subjective)	Increases acquiescence Limits range of responses
	Multiple choice	Increases range of possible responses	Decreases responsiveness Increases recency bias May decrease test–retest reliability
	Multiple choice with icons	Increases range of possible options Icons may reduce recency bias Icons may increase responsiveness	Decreases responsiveness (icons tend to help with expression, not understanding)
	Either/or	Increases responsiveness Decreases acquiescence	Limits range of responses
Open	Qualitative interviewing	Minimises researcher-imposed "agenda" Allows relevant issues to be explored in greater depth Increases likelihood of appropriate vocabulary being used	Decreases responsiveness More time-consuming Possibly, more complicated to interpret/analyse responses

Quantitative multiple-choice scales may be presented verbally or iconically (for example, using a series of progressively "happier" faces). Some studies have found that, although all such scales are unreliable to some extent, the adoption of pictures to illustrate response alternatives both reduces "recency" (see below) and increases responsiveness (Sigelman & Budd, 1986; March, 1992). A few scales, developed specifically for people with intellectual disabilities, not only use iconic Likert-type scales, but also incorporate procedures designed to assess conceptual understanding and identify the most appropriate level of Likert-scale complexity. The most commonly used measure of this type is the Comprehensive Quality of Life Scale (ComQol) (Cummins, 1992), in which there are three phases of pretesting designed to determine whether the person can (a) identify items in order of magnitude, (b) use a scale by matching to a concrete reference, and (c) use a scale with an abstract reference. Within each phase, the tasks progress in complexity from binary choice to a choice involving five elements. For example, the binary choice for the first phase is between a picture of a large cube (or block) and a small one. The most complex task of the second phase is to match five blocks of varying sizes to five steps of varying sizes. The tasks of the third (abstract reference) phase use two, three, and five steps, respectively, each accompanied by a pictorial representation of the concept of importance. Respondents are required to demonstrate that they can associate these with varying levels of importance.

At each phase, respondents have to respond correctly, at least using the binary choice, in order to proceed to the next phase. Thus, if they do not respond correctly to all three phases, they do not complete the scale. For those who pass the pretest, the maximum level of discriminative competence displayed during the third phase determines the level of choice provided in the Likert scales used to rate importance of various life domains. A similar procedure is used to select an appropriate scale on which to rate satisfaction.

The third type of closed question uses an "either/or" format. There is evidence that this type of question is the least prone to response bias.

It is clear from the preceding discussion that it is not really possible to recommend a particular approach to asking questions. When designing an interview schedule, one should be mindful of the advantages and disadvantages of each approach, and their suitability to the question content and respondent characteristics. Some of the issues discussed above are considered in a little more depth in the remainder of this chapter.

RESPONSIVENESS

By virtue of their cognitive and language deficits (such as comprehension, memory, and expression), gaining the views of people with intellectual disabilities, particularly about complex abstract issues, has obvious difficulties. Sigelman and colleagues (1982) identified standards which could be applied in judging the validity of information gained directly from people with intellectual disabilities.

The first standard is responsiveness—the proportion of interviewees who could answer a question, regardless of the truth or falsity of answers. Sigelman et al. found that responsiveness varied as a function of both the level of respondent IQ and the way questions were framed. For example, yes/no questions about activities yielded higher responses than yes/no questions about subjective phenomena such as happiness. The latter type of question was answered more frequently than verbal multiple-choice questions or open-ended questions, both of which are more cognitively demanding.

ACQUIESCENCE

Another of Sigelman's standards is consistency—correspondence between responses to questions whose wording or format differed but whose meaning remained the same. The most common form of inconsistency among people with intellectual disabilities is the tendency to acquiesce, that is, to say yes to questions regardless of their content. High levels of acquiescence among people with intellectual disabilities are frequently reported (e.g., Heal & Chadsey-Rusch, 1985; Novak, Heal, Pilewski & Laidlaw, 1989; Harner, 1991; Heal & Rubin, 1993). Heal and Sigelman (1995) suggested that people with intellectual disabilities may say yes to many yes/no questions in order to be agreeable and may say no to questions that mention socially undesirable behaviours to deny any association with these taboos.

Another form of systematic response bias is recency bias, whereby the respondent has a tendency to choose the second of two parallel either/or questions in which only the order was altered. Sigelman, Budd, Spanhel & Schoenrock (1981a,b) reported that recency bias characterised an average of 21% of paired answers in three samples. Heal and Rubin (1993) reported recency bias at 10% in their study of 91 adults with intellectual disabilities.

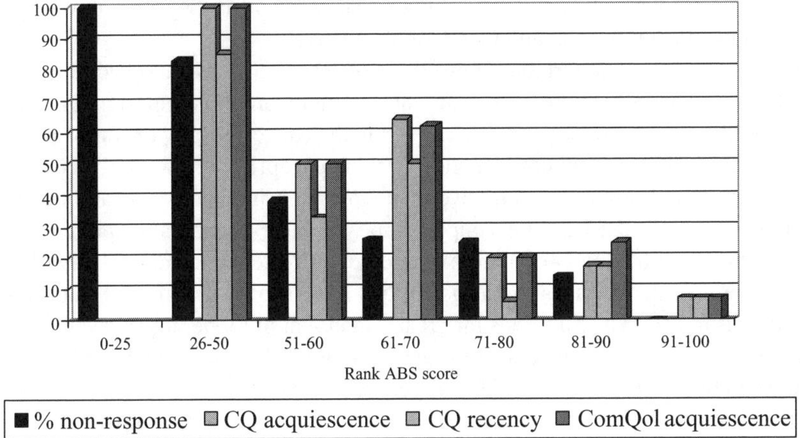

Figure 5.1 Percentage of residents who exhibited response bias, during pretesting on the Choice Questionnaire (CQ) and the ComQol

Perry and Felce (2002) examined responsiveness and response bias in a random sample of 154 people with a range of ability levels. They used scores on the Adaptive Behavior Scale (ABS) to indicate ability and two self-report measures of QOL that included pretests to check for presence of response bias. The two self-report scales were the Choice Questionnaire (CQ) (Stancliffe, 1995) and the Comprehensive Quality of Life Scale–Intellectual/Cognitive Disability (ComQol) (Cummins, 1997). Figure 5.1 shows the percentage of respondents at different ABS levels who were unable to respond to the pretest items of the CQ and ComQol, and the percentage of those who did who exhibited response bias. The horizontal axis represents residents grouped by rank ABS scores. The first two groups comprise residents whose scores were in the first or second quartile of rank ABS scores. The other groups comprise residents whose scores fell within subsequent deciles. All 20 residents in the bottom quartile (rank ABS scores up to 25%, mean raw score = 75) did not respond to the questions on either the CQ or the ComQol. Of the second quartile group (rank ABS scores between 26 and 50, mean raw score = 130), 83% also did not respond, and all of the remainder showed acquiescence bias, most showing recency bias. In the five upper deciles (mean raw scores = 181, 198, 227, 246, and 275, respectively), non-response rates declined progressively from 38% through 26%, 25%, and 14% to 0%. Acquiescence bias affected between a half and two-thirds of the remaining respondents with ABS scores in the two deciles between 51 and 70. Above this level, response biases were shown by only a small minority. Respondents were, on the whole, slightly less vulnerable to the recency effect than to acquiescence.

Perry and Felce also found that there was a significant difference between those who acquiesced in the ComQol and those who did not, in terms of total rank ABS scores, and scores on the language development domain of the ABS and BPVS scores. The same was true for those who acquiesced on the CQ and those who did not, and those who exhibited response bias on the CQ and those who did not.

In this sample, then, only people whose ABS scores were in the top three deciles were likely to be able to complete these scales without acquiescing. The average non-response rate for this group was 14%, and the average "pass" rates for the remaining respondents were 85% and 81% on the CQ and ComQol, respectively.

While not all authors report such low levels of responsiveness and such high levels of response bias, all agree that this is a significant problem, and it is important that continued efforts should be made to develop strategies which reduce the proportion of people with intellectual disabilities for whom interviews are inappropriate. However, it is also important to note that, although representative of people with intellectual disabilities who use residential services in the UK, the sample from which the above data were collected was not representative of the total population of people with intellectual disabilities. Population studies of the prevalence of learning disabilities have shown that the prevalence of mild intellectual disabilities (IQ 50–70) is far greater than that of moderate or severe intellectual disabilities. For example, in the UK, the prevalence of mild intellectual disabilities has been found to be in the region of 25–30/1000 (Fryers & Russell, 1997), whereas an overall crude rate of just 3.2–3.8/1000 has been estimated for severe learning disabilities (Welsh Office NHS Directorate, 1992). Therefore, failure to interview people with intellectual disabilities would disenfranchise the majority of people, who should be able to respond to questions without bias.

CONSISTENCY OVER TIME

Sigelman's third standard was test–retest reliability—correspondence between answers to the same questions on two occasions. Sigelman et al. (1983) reported extremely variable test–retest reliability figures for respondents who were interviewed twice with an interval of approximately a week. On average, a sample of institutionalised children gave consistent responses to yes/no questions about activities, asked on two occasions, 87% of the time. However, the consistency of answers to multiple-choice questions presenting four levels of happy and sad faces and enquiring about satisfaction with living circumstances was only 46%. Heal and Sigelman (1996) comment that it is difficult to isolate levels of test–retest reliability from levels of validity. For example, the higher levels of test–retest reliability found in the first sample may be evidence of a tendency to answer yes/no questions affirmatively rather than evidence of good test–retest reliability. Therefore, consistency appears to vary according to the way questions are framed.

Framing of Questions

Heal and Sigelman (1995) managed to circumvent acquiescence among people with intellectual disabilities by recasting yes/no questions into an either/or or multiple-choice format. However, this was at the expense of increasing the bias associated with recency. The potential influence on responses to different question formats was referred to in the earlier discussion on acquiescence. Further examples of this were highlighted by Antaki and Rapley (1996), who used conversation analysis to examine the interactions between interviewer and interviewee during administration of a QOL assessment interview. They reported distortions of the questions resulting from the interviewer's need to paraphrase complex items, the use of pre-questions, and the way in which response lists were presented. For example, some interviewees responded to questions when the interviewer paused between response options.

That is, the interviewee interpreted the pause as the end of the question. Furthermore, Antaki and Rapley reported a tendency for interviewers to pursue "legitimate" answers and to ignore matters raised by interviewees if they were not directly relevant to the questionnaire schedule. The authors concluded that such issues made it difficult to draw conclusions from the simple aggregation of responses to questionnaires with a fixed-response schedule.

Some authors have argued for the advantage of open-ended qualitative interviews over formal interviews as a way of resolving these difficulties, although, as has been mentioned, this may be at the expense of reducing responsiveness. There is also evidence that opportunities to discuss areas of dissatisfaction may reveal concerns that people have about their circumstances or lifestyle that are not reflected in their often high ratings of satisfaction (Holland, 1990).

INTERVIEWEE EXPERIENCE

The preceding sections have shown how people's responses, or lack of responses, may be influenced by interviewer behaviour. Attitudes, opinions, expectations, and therefore responses to certain interview questions are also influenced by factors unrelated to the interviewer's behaviour. It may be useful to be aware of these factors so that people's responses can be contextualised. For example, this applies particularly to interviews concerning personal satisfaction, which, according to theorists such as Michalos (1985), is related to the "gap" between one's expectations and one's actual situation. In turn, expectations are shaped by experience and reference groups, and experience of constrained opportunities and autonomy, together with reference groups which are restricted to peers with similar life experiences, may lead to low expectations or even the inability to make the comparisons necessary for subjective evaluations (Fabian, 1991). As lower expectations are more easily fulfilled, this is likely to result in high reported levels of satisfaction, even when objective life conditions are poor. Research on people with intellectual disabilities has provided a picture consistent with low expectation; individuals say they are satisfied despite experiencing many adverse conditions, including poverty, poor housing, threats to health and safety, victimisation, social isolation, experience of loss, and failure to gain or retain employment (Edgerton, Bollinger & Herr, 1984; Close & Halpern, 1988; Flynn, 1989). Consistent with the role that expectations might play, comparative studies of residents in markedly different environments have found that they report similar high levels of satisfaction (e.g., Holland, 1990; Emerson et al., 1999).

Therefore, where possible, interview responses should be seen in the context of a person's background and social network. Furthermore, a safeguard to "invalid" responses may be provided by supplementing interview data with objective data collected from other sources. These sources might include interviews with third parties, although, as will be shown below, this strategy has its own problems.

PERSONAL TEMPERAMENT

Another reason why gathering data from multiple sources might be useful is that, both among the general population and people with intellectual disabilities, subjective opinion often does not reflect objective conditions. Therefore, sole reliance on data derived from interviewing people with intellectual disabilities might fail to safeguard their interests. For example, research among the general population has tended to show that life satisfaction bears only a modest relationship to objective life circumstances (for a review, see Diener, 1984). The lack of correlation between satisfaction and objective conditions may be influenced by the extent to which people adjust to changing conditions. As Edgerton (1990; 1996) has pointed out, there is an increasingly convincing body of longitudinal research which testifies to the intrapersonal stability of subjective well-being, despite changing circumstances. As individuals adapt to circumstances and events, statements of satisfaction with life may be largely independent of the person's experience, deriving rather from personality, disposition, or temperament (Costa, McCrae & Zonderman, 1987; Costa & McCrae, 1988; Diener, Sandvik, Pavot & Fujita, 1992; Cummins, 1995; Suh, Diener & Fujita, 1996).

SOCIAL DESIRABILITY AND INTERVIEWER STATUS

Heal and Sigelman (1995) suggested that people may say "yes" to many yes/no questions in order to be agreeable and may say "no" to questions that mention socially undesirable behaviours to deny any association with these taboos. Investigations of social desirability have tended to measure the phenomenon directly by scales such as the Marlowe–Crowne Social Desirability Scale (Crowne & Marlowe, 1960) or the Balanced Inventory of Desirable Responding (Paulhus, 1998). For example, Sabourin, Laferriere, Sicuro and Coallier (1989) suggested that the scores on a satisfaction questionnaire completed by 82 clients who were undergoing therapy for mental health problems were contaminated by socially desirable responding. This conclusion was based on significant correlations between measures of satisfaction and social desirability.

In a meta-analysis of 61 studies of social desirability distortion, Richman, Kiesler, Weisband and Drasgow (1999) reported that there was less social desirability distortion in studies which used computerised versions of interviews than in those involving face-to-face interviews. This implies that social desirability may be partly a consequence of a perceived imbalance in the status of interviewer and interviewee. To date, there have been few investigations of the impact on response bias of reducing the perceived interviewer/interviewee status differential. However, in a pilot study exploring the impact of peer interviewing, Perry and Felce (2002) found that levels of responsiveness and response bias had far more to do with interviewee characteristics, particularly ability level, than the characteristics of the interviewer. They also reported that among people who responded without bias, responses were not tailored to the characteristics of the interviewer. Perry's sample was relatively small (23 people), and data were collected by only one non-disabled interviewer and one interviewer with intellectual disabilities; therefore, the results should be treated with caution. However, the study did at least demonstrate the possibility of involving people with intellectual disabilities as interviewers as well as interviewees.

THIRD-PARTY RESPONSES

The use of proxy respondents, such as staff or parents, is one possible solution to the problems mentioned above. Several studies have attempted to evaluate resident/proxy agreement by comparing proxy responses about residents who *can* respond for themselves with self-reports from these same people. Research on this issue has failed to conclude the debate. For example, in their analysis of resident/staff agreement, Budd, Sigelman and Sigelman (1981) reported agreement at only 52% for a yes/no checklist and 60% for an open-ended question about participation in various sports. Other research has also cast doubt on the accuracy of proxy responses, particularly in the case of questions about resident satisfaction with various aspects of their lives (e.g., Berkson & Romer, 1980; Burnett, 1989; Voelker, Shore, Brown-More, Hill & Perry, 1990; Stancliffe, 1995; Rapley, Ridgeway & Beyer, 1998). There is some evidence that proxy responses in relation to interviews which solicit objective data are considerably more likely to be consistent with the responses of people with intellectual disabilities than proxy appraisals of satisfaction (e.g., Perry & Felce, 2002). It might be concluded from these studies that research should be confined to objective methods for those individuals who are unable to voice their own opinions.

However, several studies have produced evidence of consumer/proxy agreement (e.g., Voelker et al., 1990; Schalock & Keith, 1993; Stancliffe, 1999; McVilly, Burton-Smith & Davidson, 2000). Furthermore, additional research is required to investigate whether consumer/proxy concordance varies as a function of the nature of the relationship between consumers and proxies. For example, it may be that more accurate proxy responses would be made by people such as family members or citizen advocates who have had long-term relationships with those on behalf of whom they are responding. As Stancliffe (2000) has pointed out, "It remains an open question as to whether findings of agreement between proxies and self-reports from verbal individuals can be generalized to non-verbal people with more profound intellectual disability who cannot respond for themselves" (p. 90). A judgement also has to be made as to whether proxy responses which might not reflect consumers' views accurately are preferable to a total absence of responses. Although it might not be appropriate to interview third parties at the expense of interviewing people with intellectual disabilities themselves, their responses should provide a valuable supplement.

CONCLUSIONS

The prospective interviewer of people with intellectual disabilities should not be disheartened by the difficulties which have been raised in this chapter. They have been raised so that interviews can be conducted in such a way as to maximise their validity, and so that interviewees' responses are considered in the appropriate context. It is also important to highlight the role of supplementing interviews with alternative methods of data collection. However, it remains the case that it should be possible to conduct perfectly valid and reliable interviews with many people with intellectual disabilities, and adoption of the techniques discussed here should help to maximise the likelihood of successful interviews.

REFERENCES

Antaki, C. & Rapley, M. (1996). Questions and answers to psychological assessment schedules: hidden troubles in "quality of life" interviews. *Journal of Intellectual Disability Research*, **40**, 421–437.

Arscott, K., Dagnan, D. & Kroese, B.S. (1998). Consent to psychological research by people with an intellectual disability. *Journal of Applied Research in Intellectual Disabilities*, **11**, 77–83.

Berkson, G. & Romer, D. (1980). Social ecology of supervised communal facilities for mentally disabled adults. I. Introduction. *American Association on Mental Deficiency*, **85**, 219–228.

Brown, R. (Ed.) (1995). *Quality of Life for Handicapped People*. London: Chapman & Hall.

Budd, E.C., Sigelman, C.K. & Sigelman, L. (1981). Exploring the outer limits of response bias. *Sociological Focus*, **14**, 297–307.

Burnett, P. (1989). Assessing satisfaction in people with an intellectual disability living in community based residential settings. *Australian Disability Review*, **1**, 14–19.

Close, D. & Halpern, A. (1988). Transitions to supported living. In M. Janicki, M. Krauss & M. Seltzer (Eds) *Community Residences for Persons with Developmental Disabilities: Here to Stay* (pp. 159–171). Baltimore, MD: Brookes.

Costa, P., McCrae, R. & Zonderman, A. (1987). Environmental and dispositional influences on well-being: longitudinal follow-up of an American national sample. *British Journal of Psychology*, **78**, 299–306.

Costa, P. & McCrae, R. (1988). Personality in adulthood: a six-year longitudinal study of self-reports and spouse-ratings on the NEO personality inventory. *Journal of Personality and Social Psychology*, **54**, 853–863.

Crowne, D. & Marlowe, D. (1960). A new scale of social desirability independent of psychopathology. *Journal of Consulting Psychology*, **24**, 349–354.

Cummins, R. (1992). *Comprehensive Quality of Life Scale: Intellectual Disability*. Melbourne: Deakin University.

Cummins, R. (1995). On the trail of the gold standard for subjective well-being. *Social Indicators Research*, **35**, 179–200.

Cummins, R. (1997). *The Comprehensive Quality of Life Scale: Intellectual Disability* (5th edn). Melbourne: Deakin University.

Department of Health and Social Security (DHSS) (1971). *Better Services for the Mentally Handicapped*. London: HMSO.

Diener, E. (1984). Subjective well-being. *Psychological Bulletin*, **95**, 542–575.

Diener, E., Sandvik, E., Pavot, W. & Fujita, F. (1992). Extraversion and subjective well-being in a US national probability sample. *Journal of Research in Personality*, **26**, 205–215.

Edgerton, R. (1990). Quality of life from a longitudinal research perspective. In R. Schalock (Ed.) *Quality of Life Perspectives and Issues* (pp. 149–160). Washington, DC: American Association on Mental Retardation.

Edgerton, R. (1996). A longitudinal-ethnographic research perspective on quality of life. In R. Schalock (Ed.) *Quality of Life*, vol. 1. *Conceptualization and Measurement* (pp. 83–90). Washington, DC: American Association on Mental Retardation.

Edgerton, R.B., Bollinger, M. & Herr, B. (1984). The cloak of competence—after 2 decades. *American Journal of Mental Deficiency*, **88**, 345–351.

Emerson, E., Robertson, J., Gregory, N., Hatton, C., Kessissoglou, S., Hallam, A., et al. (1999). *1. A Comparative Analysis of Quality and Costs in Village Communities, Residential Campuses and Dispersed Housing Schemes. 2. Quality and Costs of Residential Supports for People with Learning Disabilities: Predicting Variation in Quality and Costs. 3. An Observational Study of Supports Provided to People with Severe and Complex Disabilities in Residential Campuses and Dispersed Housing Schemes.* Manchester: University of Manchester, Hester Adrian Research Centre.

Fabian, E. (1991). Using quality of life indicators in rehabilitation program evaluation. *Rehabilitation Counseling Bulletin*, **34**, 344–356.

Felce, D., Lowe, K., Perry, J., Baxter, H., Jones, E., Hallam, A., et al. (1998). Service support to people in Wales with severe intellectual disability and the most severe challenging behaviours: processes, outcomes and costs. *Journal of Intellectual Disability Research*, **42**, 390–408.

Flynn, M. (1989). *Independent Living for Adults with a Mental Handicap: A Place of My Own*. London: Cassell.

Fryers, T. & Russell, O. (1997). Applied epidemiology. In O. Russell (Ed.) *Seminars in the Psychiatry of Learning Disabilities*. London: Royal College of Psychiatrists.

Goffman, E. (1961). *Asylums*. New York: Doubleday.

Goode, D. (Ed.) (1994). *Quality of Life for Persons with Disabilities: International Perspectives and Issues*. Cambridge, MA: Brookline Books.

Gordon, S., O'Connor, N. & Tizard, J. (1954). Some effects of incentives on the performance of imbeciles. *British Journal of Psychology*, **45**, 277.

Gunzburg, H. (1957). Therapy and social training for the feebleminded youth. *British Journal of Medical Psychology*, **30**.

Harner, C. (1991). *Assessing the Satisfaction of Adults with Mental Retardation Living in the Community*. Urbana, IL: University of Illinois Press.

Harner, C.J. & Heal, L.W. (1993). The Multifaceted Life-Style Satisfaction Scale (MLSS)—psychometric properties of an interview schedule for assessing personal satisfaction of adults with limited intelligence. *Research in Developmental Disabilities*, **14**, 221–236.

Hatton, C. & Emerson, E. (1996). *Residential Provision for People with Learning Disabilities: A Research Review*. Manchester: University of Manchester, Hester Adrian Research Centre.

Heal, L. & Rubin, S. (1993). Biases in responses during the interviews of individuals with mental retardation. Annual meeting of the American Association on Mental Retardation, Washington, DC.

Heal, L. & Sigelman, C. (1996). Methodological issues in quality of life measurement. In R. Schalock (Ed.) *Quality of Life*, vol. 1. *Conceptualization and Measurement* (pp. 91–104). Washington, DC: American Association on Mental Retardation.

Heal, L.W. & Chadsey-Rusch, J. (1985). The Lifestyle Satisfaction Scale (LSS)—assessing individuals' satisfaction with residence, community setting, and associated services. *Applied Research in Mental Retardation*, **6**, 475–490.

Heal, L.W. & Sigelman, C.K. (1995). Response biases in interviews of individuals with limited mental ability. *Journal of Intellectual Disability Research*, **39**, 331–340.

Heron, J. (1992). *Psychology and Personhood: Psychology in Another Key*. London: Sage.

Hilliard, L. & Mundy, L. (1954). Diagnostic problems in the feeble-minded. *Lancet*, **2**, 655.

Holland, A. (1990). *People with Mental Retardation Living in Community Homes: Their Views and the Quality of the Service*. Loughborough: University of Loughborough.

Keith, K. & Schalock, R. (Eds) (2000). *Cross-Cultural Perspectives on Quality of Life*. Washington, DC: American Association on Mental Retardation.

Kiernan, C. (1999). Participation in research by people with learning disability: origins and issues. *British Journal of Learning Disabilities*, **27**, 43–47.

Mansell, J. & Ericsson, K. (1996). *Deinstitutionalization and Community Living. Intellectual Disabilities Services in Britain, Scandinavia and the USA*. London: Chapman & Hall.

March, P. (1992). Do photographs help adults with severe mental handicaps make choices? *British Journal of Mental Subnormality*, **38**, 122–128.

McVilly, K., Burton-Smith, R. & Davidson, J. (2000). Concurrence between subject and proxy ratings of quality of life for people with and without intellectual disabilities. *Journal of Intellectual Disability Research*, **25**, 19–39.

Michalos, A. (1985). Multiple Discrepancies Theory (MDT). *Social Indicators Research*, **16**, 347–443.

Nirje, B. (1980). The normalisation principle. In R. Flynn & K. Nitsch (Eds) *Normalization, Social Integration and Community Services* (pp. 31–49). Baltimore, MD: University Park Press.

Novak, A., Heal, L., Pilewski, M. & Laidlaw, T. (1989). Apartment placement from a community ICFMR. Annual meeting of the American Association on Mental Retardation, San Francisco.

Oliver, M. (1992). Changing the social relations in research production. *Disability, Handicap and Society*, **7**, 157–169.

Paulhus, D. (1998). *The Balanced Inventory of Desirable Responding*. Toronto/Buffalo, Multi-Health Systems.

Perry, J. & Felce, D. (1994). Outcomes of ordinary housing services in Wales—objective indicators. *Mental Handicap Research*, **7**, 286–311.

Perry, J. & Felce, D. (2002). Subjective and objective quality of life assessment: responsiveness, response bias and agreement between the responses of people being supported and those of staff responding on their behalf. *Mental Retardation*, **40**, 445–456.

Prosser, H. & Bromley, J. (1998). Interviewing people with intellectual disabilities. In E. Emerson, C. Hatton, J. Bromley & A. Caine (Eds) *Clinical Psychology and People with Intellectual Disabilities* (pp. 99–113). Chichester: Wiley.

Ramcharan, P. & Grant, G. (1994). Setting one agenda for empowering persons with a disadvantage within the research process. In M. Rioux & M. Bach (Eds) *Disability Is Not Measles: New Research Paradigms in Disability* (pp. 227–244). Ontario: Roeher Institute.

Rapley, M., Ridgeway, J. & Beyer, S. (1998). Staff : staff and staff : client reliability of the Schalock and Keith (1993) Quality of Life Questionnaire. *Journal of Intellectual Disability Research*, **42**, 37–42.

Reason, P. (1998). *Human Inquiry in Action: Developments in New Paradigm research*. London: Sage.

Reason, P. & Heron, J. (1995). Cooperative inquiry. In J. Smith, R. Harre & L. van Hangenhove (Eds) *Rethinking Psychology*, vol. 2. *Evolving Methods* (pp. 122–142). London: Sage.

Richman, W., Kiesler, S., Weisband, S. & Drasgow, F. (1999). A meta-analytic study of social desirability distortion in computer-administered questionnaires, traditional questionnaires and interviews. *Journal of Applied Psychology*, **84**, 754–775.

Sabourin, S., Laferriere, N., Sicuro, F. & Coallier, J.-C. (1989). Social desirability, psychological distress, and consumer satisfaction with mental health treatment. *Journal of Counselling Psychology*, **36**, 352–356.

Sample, P. (1996). Beginnings: participatory action research and adults with developmental disabilities. *Disability and Society*, **11**, 317–332.

Schalock, R. (Ed.) (1990). *Quality of life: Perspectives and Issues*. Washington, DC: American Association on Mental Retardation.

Schalock, R. (Ed.) (1996). *Quality of Life*, vol. 1. *Conceptualization and Measurement*. Washington, DC: American Association on Mental Retardation.

Schalock, R. (Ed.) (1996). *Quality of Life*, vol. 2. *Application to Persons with Disabilities*. Washington, DC: American Association on Mental Retardation.

Schalock, R., Bonham, G. & Marchand, C. (2000). Consumer based quality of life assessment: a path model of perceived satisfaction. *Evaluation and Program Planning*, **23**, 75–85.

Schalock, R. & Keith, K. (1993). *Quality of Life Questionnaire*. Worthington, OH: IDS Publishing.

Shea, S. (1988). *Psychiatric Interviewing: The Art of Understanding*. New York: Harcourt Brace Jovanovich.

Sigelman, C. & Budd, E. (1986). Pictures as an aid in questioning mentally retarded persons. *Rehabilitation Counselling Bulletin*, **29**, 173–181.

Sigelman, C.K., Budd, E.C., Spanhel, C. & Schoenrock, C. (1981a). Asking questions of retarded persons—a comparison of yes no and either or formats. *Applied Research in Mental Retardation*, **2**, 347–357.

Sigelman, C.K., Budd, E.C., Spanhel, C. & Schoenrock, C. (1981b). When in doubt, say yes—acquiescence in interviews with mentally retarded persons. *Mental Retardation*, **19**, 53–58.

Sigelman, C.K., Budd, E.C., Winer, J., Schoenrock, C. & Martin, P. (1982). Evaluating alternative techniques of questioning mentally retarded persons. *American Journal of Mental Deficiency*, **86**, 511–518.

Sigelman, C., Schoenrock, C., Budd, E., Winer, J., Spanhel, C., Martin, P., et al. (1983). *Communicating with Mentally Retarded Persons: Asking Questions and Getting Answers*. Lubbock: Texas Tech. University, Research and Training Center in Mental Retardation.

Sigelman, C., Winer, J. & Schoenrock, C. (1982). The responsiveness of mentally retarded persons to questions. *Education and Training of the Mentally Retarded*, **17**, 120–124.

Stancliffe, R. (1995). *Choice and Decision Making and Adults with Intellectual Disability*. Sydney: Macquarie University.

Stancliffe, R. & Parmenter, T. (1999). The Choice Questionnaire: a scale to assess choices exercised by adults with intellectual disability. *Journal of Intellectual and Developmental Disability*, **24**, 107–132.

Stancliffe, R.J. (1995). Assessing opportunities for choice-making—a comparison of self-reports and staff reports. *American Journal on Mental Retardation*, **99**, 418–429.

Stancliffe, R.J. (1999). Proxy respondents and the reliability of the Quality of Life Questionnaire empowerment factor. *Journal of Intellectual Disability Research*, **43**, 185–193.

Stancliffe, R.J. (2000). Proxy respondents and quality of life. *Evaluation and Program Planning*, **23**, 89–93.

Suh, E., Diener, E. & Fujita, F. (1996). Events and subjective well-being: only recent events matter. *Journal of Personality and Social Psychology*, **70**, 1091–1102.

Voelker, S., Shore, D., Brown-More, C., Hill, L. & Perry, J. (1990). Validity of self-report of adaptive behavior skills by adults with mental retardation. *Mental Retardation*, **28**, 305–309.

Wehmeyer, M. & Metzler, C. (1995). How self-determined are people with mental retardation? The national consumer survey. *Mental Retardation*, **33**, 111–119.

Welsh Office NHS Directorate (1992). *Protocol for Investment in Health Gain: Mental Handicap (Learning Disabilities)*. Cardiff: Welsh Office.

Wolfensberger, W. (1972). *Normalization: The Principle of Normalization in Human Services.* Toronto: National Institute of Mental Retardation.

Zarb, G. (1992). On the road to Damascus: first steps toward changing the relations of disability research production. *Disability and Society*, **11**, 125–138.

CHAPTER 6

Interviewing Family Members and Care Providers: Concepts, Methodologies, and Cultures

Jan Blacher
University of California (Riverside), USA
and
Iris Tan Mink
University of California (Los Angeles), USA

INTRODUCTION

How does one ascertain what transpires in families of children with intellectual disabilities (ID)? An obvious answer is simply to ask the children's parents. As frequently happens, though, the simple solution is not the one employed. Perusal of the last hundred years or so of literature on families who have children with ID or mental retardation reveals that, for many years, families were ignored altogether. Parents were generally viewed as the "cause" of their child's ID and not deemed worthy to be informants or even the focus of study (Blacher & Baker, 2002). It followed that out-of-home placement was viewed as therapeutic for the child, and was frequently recommended. In the mid-twentieth century, families began to capture professional interest, though parents were still viewed as damaged or disturbed, and in need of "fixing", usually through psychotherapy (Wardell, 1952; Schonell & Watts, 1956), and they were still not typically informants. As the published literature in the USA revealed greater interest in family members, the professional view changed to children with disabilities exerting a devastating influence on the family. Parents were increasingly interviewed about their experiences, but the focus of questions was mainly on the "negative impact" of their children. Out-of-home placement was still recommended, but now to alleviate the crisis or stress on other family members.

Currently, the literature reflects a more balanced view (Baker, Blacher, Kopp & Kraemer, 1997). The acknowledgment that some negative impact comes from parenting a child with

The International Handbook of Applied Research in Intellectual Disabilities. Edited by E. Emerson, C. Hatton, T. Thompson and T.R. Parmenter ISBN 0-471-49709-6.

disabilities (Baxter, Cummins & Yiolitis, 2000) is offset by the recognition of positive impact as well (Glidden, Valliere & Herbert, 1988; Hong, Seltzer & Krauss, 2001). Additionally, parents have become partners with professionals in better serving their child's educational, therapeutic, and social-emotional needs (Walker & Singer, 1993). Indeed, a cadre of researchers has recognized parents, family members, and other care providers as potential participants in the research process (Turnbull et al., 1993).

Approach to the Chapter

This chapter addresses the research method of interviewing family members and care providers of children (and in some cases, adult children) with ID. The focus is on conceptual areas that have served as the content of such interviews, and on methodological issues that challenge most researchers who interview families. While we illustrate these with a description of some instruments currently used in studies of families with typically developing children or with children having disabilities, we do not attempt a comprehensive review.

A primary focus of this chapter is on considerations of culture in the choice and use of measures to assess family experiences. Three ongoing research projects that involve families from diverse cultures are presented as the context for understanding family interviews: the Families Project at the University of California–Riverside, and the Asian-American Family Project and the Chinese-American Fathers Project at the University of California–Los Angeles. These will be drawn on to illustrate some of the methodological, clinical, and design issues in doing research with family care providers, and findings from these projects will be interwoven throughout the chapter. We include an overview of some available measures or instruments that can be used with family members. We conclude with a summary of current critical concerns in interviewing families and suggestions for future research.

FAMILY INTERVIEWS: PURPOSES, TYPES, AND CAUTIONS

Family assessment, for clinical or research purposes, typically involves parents as informants. The aim is to obtain information about the child with ID and/or to obtain information about broader family functioning. Most early involvement of parents was for the purpose of clinical assessment, to determine the extent of psychopathology in the child, parent, or other family member. Shaffer, Lucas and Richters (1999) trace early sources of techniques used in interviews for the purpose of psychiatric diagnosis. These were traditionally conducted by trained clinicians who had knowledge of clinical conditions. The clinicians typically observed the patient, interviewed the patient or a proxy respondent (a person close enough to the patient to answer for him or her), and/or administered specific tests. Today, with psychiatric syndromes and diagnostic criteria codified in systems such as the American Psychiatric Association's *Diagnostic and Statistical Manual of Mental Disorders (DSM)* (2000), interviewers with less specialized clinical training can obtain and record information from parents. The purpose may be to establish specific psychiatric diagnoses or, more generally, to assess the adjustment and well-being of the child or family members, focusing on dimensions such as stress, depression, or child-care burden.

Types of Family Interviews

Shaffer et al. (1999) outline four ways in which information can be recorded from parents: the respondent-based interview (RBI), the use of symptom questionnaires, clinician rating scales, and the interviewer-based interview (IBI). The RBI is a face-to-face interview (Shaffer, Fisher & Lucas, 1999). It uses a predetermined script that is carefully worded; the interviewer must present questions in a precise order. Furthermore, answers are in the form of predefined alternatives. For example, the Diagnostic Interview Schedule for Children (DISC) (Costello, Edelbrock & Costello, 1985) is a highly structured diagnostic interview schedule covering current *DSM* criteria for child psychiatric disorders. Respondents, usually mothers, are asked about the presence or absence of symptoms that fall under the major diagnostic categories. The symptom questionnaire, although it can be administered in a face-to-face interview format, is more likely a paper-and-pencil measure completed by the parent respondent. It is generally less broad-ranging than the RBI, usually consisting of a set of questions in a linear format, one followed by the next. A widely used symptom questionnaire is the Child Behavior Checklist (Achenbach, 1991). Symptom questionnaires might also probe for information in order to make a diagnosis. Another way to determine a diagnosis or to draw final conclusions about a symptom picture is through the use of clinician rating scales. These scales may be used to help to standardize a clinician's rating or conclusion (e.g., the Center for Epidemiological Studies Depression Scale [CES–D] [Radloff, 1977], or the Symptom Checklist [SCL-35] [Derogatis, 1993]). This type of scale is also known as a diagnostic checklist. Before a psychiatric diagnosis is made, however, findings from such short checklists need to be corroborated by a longer and more intensive interview by a trained clinician.

In contrast to the RBI, the IBI allows the interviewer to vary the order of the questions. Moreover, respondents do not have to restrict their answers to "yes", "no", "sometimes", or some other predetermined scale. The interviewer can interpret answers, and then rate them according to a scale. In order to avoid interviewer "rating drift", there need to be frequent reliability checks; this is best done by recording interviews. IBIs allow cross-checking of the information that is confusing or discrepant (Angold & Fisher, 1999). Investigators of large-scale family research projects, such as those we will present later in this chapter, have developed IBIs unique to their research foci.

Family assessment that is for research purposes and/or is aimed at a broader understanding of family functioning has been influenced by theories and techniques from other fields, such as the survey research methods used in sociology and political science (Fowler, 1993). More recently, and perhaps more importantly, there are family interviews that employ the open-ended methods and techniques used by anthropology and social psychology (Patton, 1990). Survey research questionnaires are constructed in much the same manner as the above-described RBI. As in the RBI, the goal is description, and the questionnaires help the interviewers to obtain numerical or quantitative results that can be easily analyzed and presented.

Anthropological techniques also seek accurate description, but through different means. Here, the objective is to obtain information that captures the individual's experiences and perceptions without predetermining the response categories. Individuals are allowed to speak freely on topics that the interviewer presents, much like the IBI. This technique, though, requires a very high degree of interviewer training and the development of probes or strategies for the redirection of respondents who "go off topic". The response categories that will be used in the data-analysis phase are derived from the individual's free responses, which are coded after all interviews are completed. In addition, one should record and transcribe interviews with all respondents in order to develop the coding categories. This is a labor-intensive and expensive procedure.

Current qualitative methods in anthropology and social psychology have been strongly influenced by Bronfenbrenner's (1979) *The Ecology of Human Development: Experiments by Nature and Design*. This seminal work emphasized the interconnections between the developing individual and the contexts in which the development occurs. Stated simply, the conditions under which human beings live have powerful effects on how they develop. The research paradigm that evolved from this work is known as the ecological approach, and with this focus on "development in context" (Bronfenbrenner, 1979, p. 13), it necessarily excludes response-based interviews and emphasizes gathering information through in-depth, open-ended interviews or by direct observation—methods that allow free responses.

Beyond selecting interview methods that are appropriate for one's clinical or research purposes, there are two broad categories of concerns, or cautions, in developing a family or care-provider interview protocol: the logistics of the interview, and dilemmas in interviewing. There are many logistical decisions to be made; we will mention five primary ones. First, we have *reading level*. Will the respondents read well enough to complete paper-and-pencil measures? If all measures must be read to the respondents, and thus essentially converted to interview format, this will influence the choice of questionnaire measures. If these are used, they will need to be short and to have easily remembered response categories. For example, the two most common self-report measures of depression are of equal length, but the Beck Depression Inventory (BDI) (Beck, Ward, Mendelson, Mock & Erbaugh, 1961; Beck, Steer & Brown, 1996) has sentence-long response alternatives and is quite difficult to follow in an interview format. The CES–D (Radloff, 1977) uses the same numerical scale for every item and translates well into an interview.

The second decision is *interview length*. What is likely to be an acceptable interview length for both respondent and the interviewer? This decision, like the reading level, will delimit the measures to be obtained.

The third decision is *language*. In what language will the interview be conducted? Does the respondent use English as well as his or her native language (if different)? It is vital that the interviewer speak the same language as the respondent, and exercise care not to translate extemporaneously any item, response, or measure that might distort or change the original meaning.

The fourth decision is *multiple informants*. What will be done in the event that there is more than one respondent, especially when this is unexpected? For example, if the interview was set up in advance to be conducted solely with the mother, and the father or an older sibling (one involved in caregiving) arrives home unannounced, from whom should the interviewer gather data?

The fifth decision is the *honorarium*. If respondents are paid as a "thank you" for their participation, when and how is that distributed? Interviewers need to be sensitive to whether or not payment influences the content and affective atmosphere of the interview. Few instruments that we know of systematically record these kinds of data, so investigators may want to keep track of these issues by keeping a log or taking thorough notes during the interview.

Dilemmas abound in doing research with families, far too many to cover in this chapter. Several will be discussed here. First are issues of privacy and protection. Respondents need to know that their confidentiality will be maintained and that their data will be stored anonymously and will be protected; in research studies, these are basic assurances that are required in the USA by Human Subjects Protection Committees or Institutional Review Boards. However, if there are two or more respondents present during the interview, and if sensitive questions are part of the interview protocol, the investigator may have to give some thought to protecting each respondent's privacy. When the person with a disability is present, there are not only privacy but also courtesy issues; interviewers should be sensitive to speaking to children or persons with ID, rather than about them, when they are present.

Second are issues of safety, particularly the safety of the interviewers. Research ethics and institutional review boards strongly protect the research participants, but they rarely have a protocol for maintaining the safety of interviewers. We conduct regular training sessions for interviewers focused on safety concerns; we instruct them, for example, on how to terminate interviews in situations where the participant is intoxicated, there is evidence of violence in the family, or someone in the home behaves inappropriately toward them. A good rule of thumb is that if the interviewers feel their own safety is at risk or jeopardized, it probably is, and they should leave the premises. As a precaution, we have followed the practice of having two interviewers present, at least on the initial visit.

Third are issues of interviewer responsibility. Interviewers need to be trained in what types of family behavior require reporting, first to the person responsible for the research and, perhaps subsequently, to the appropriate agency. Examples include any evidence of child abuse, neglect, or endangerment; drug abuse; or alarmingly high clinical levels of psychiatric problems, such as depression, in a respondent. This could result in some compromise of the data collection; for example, most respondents reported to child-welfare agencies for potential abuse or neglect, as mandated by law, are unlikely to stay with an ongoing study. At a more general level, interviewers are responsible for recording, and reporting to the investigator, events that raise questions about the accuracy of any data obtained.

Finally, the age, life stage, and maturity of the interviewers can be an issue for older respondents. This is a particular concern in the USA when interviewing Latino or Hispanic families. In the University of California–Riverside (UCR) Families Project's Latino Study, interviewers are usually graduate students or even recent college graduates, who are interviewing parents of 16- to 26-year-olds with ID. In such cases, the respondents are roughly the same age as the interviewers' own parents. This raises issues of deference and respect, which make it difficult for some interviewers to control the timing and pace of the interview. A two-hour interview has been known to last for five hours!

Thus, interviewing families involves systematic consideration of the different kinds of interview techniques available, as well as considerations and cautions about their use. In embarking on a family research study, there is a further question that must first be confronted: what is a family?

Interviewing family members in the twenty-first century is a lot more complicated than it was even a few years ago. Simply defining "a family" can be tricky. Patterson (1996) advocates using the US Census Bureau definition: that a family is two or more persons living together who are related by blood, marriage, or adoption. "Significant others" would be included in this definition, as long as they live together. Usually, one finds that researchers let subject families determine which individuals are, and are not, part of the family. Biological relationships are no longer the sole criterion.

Indeed, today there are a number of other types of family constellations, which confuse participant or respondent selection. For example, in the case of same-sex couples, it is often necessary to determine who is the primary care provider. When household and child-care roles are divided in a nontraditional manner, some research measures may appear unsuitable or awkward. Most of this can be overcome with some adaptation of the measures, but it is important to keep the goals of the research study in mind so that the interview procedures have integrity.

MAJOR FAMILY CONSTRUCTS AND MEASURES

As noted, it is not our purpose to review all extant measures for interviewing family care providers and parents; for that, the reader is referred to the excellent compendia available for this purpose (e.g., Touliatos, Perlmutter & Strauss, 2001). Rather, we will consider the major constructs that have been the focus of family researchers within the last decade, and mention several instruments that address each of these constructs or concerns. Even though the focus is on family processes, it is still necessary to have an adequate assessment of the child, so we begin with sections on child adaptive behavior, maladaptive behaviors, and quality of life. We then consider a perennial research concern, the impact of the child on the parents, examining domains of stress, burden, health, and well-being. Moving to a broader perspective on families, we next consider the domains of the marital relationship and the family environment. A major construct in current family research is life-span development; in considering assessment here, we emphasize a critical period, the child's transition to adulthood. We conclude this section with a consideration of the ecological context and issues of ethnicity.

Child Adaptive Behavior

Family issues must be understood, of course, in relationship to characteristics of the "target child". In many cases, the child may be too young, or too impaired, for direct testing (for example, a measure of intelligence). Most investigators utilize some kind of standardized adaptive behavior measure, obtained from caregivers, to describe both positive and negative behaviors. In the USA, there are a variety of adaptive behavior scales (e.g., National Research Council, 2002), but one very widely used is the Vineland Adaptive Behavior Scales (Sparrow, Balla & Cicchetti, 1984). The Vineland is administered via a structured interview, usually with an adult (such as mother or care provider) who knows the child well. There is an adaptive behavior composite score, as well as subscales in the areas of communication, daily living skills, socialization, and motor skills.

Child Maladaptive Behavior

The Vineland also has a checklist for maladaptive behavior, although researchers may want to consider the use of questionnaires that have more comprehensive assessment of maladaptive behavior. There are several examples specific to ID: the Scales of Independent Behavior–Revised (SIB–R) (Bruininks, Woodcock, Weatherman & Hill, 1996), the Reiss Screen for Maladaptive Behavior (2nd edn) (Reiss, 1994), and the Developmental Behaviour Checklist (DBC) (Einfeld & Tonge, 1995). The SIB–R asks about behavior problems and yields a general maladaptive index, that is, the sum of three subscales assessing internalizing, externalizing, and asocial maladaptive behavior. If there is suspicion of a dual diagnosis (psychiatric disorder in addition to the ID), the researcher may want to assess the child with the Reiss Screen. This 38-item screening tool is used to identify mental health problems in adolescents and adults across the full range of ID. There is also a version for assessing dual diagnosis in children. The DBC is another widely used instrument completed by parents, teachers, or other carers. It yields a total problem behavior score as well as subscales in five areas of maladaptive behavior (such as disruptive or antisocial behavior, communication disturbance, self-absorbed behavior, and problems in anxiety and social relating) and a profile of individual behavior items.

Also useful are questionnaires normed on normally developing populations that evaluate child behaviors, emotions, and relationships. The best known instrument in family studies is the Child Behavior Checklist 4-16 (CBCL) (Achenbach, 1991), which assesses the child's social and academic competence as well as 113 specific problem behaviors. The CBCL yields a total score, broad-band externalizing and internalizing problems scores, and seven narrow-band scores (such as aggression, anxiety, and depression). There are parent, teacher, and child versions; extensive norms; good reliability and validity; and computer scoring programs that make the Achenbach scales particularly useful for researchers. Also useful are the Rutter Parents' and Teachers' Scales (Rutter, 1967; Elander & Rutter, 1996). These have a history of good usage in clinical and educational settings and are often employed in research studies. An easy-to-administer instrument with a more balanced focus is the Strengths and Difficulties Questionnaire (Goodman, 1997). This is a short, 25-item questionnaire that focuses on both positive and negative child behaviors and can be administered to the child, the parents, teachers, and others who work with the child. This instrument is appropriate for children and adolescents aged 4–16 years. The items are divided between five scales of five items each and cover conduct problems, hyperactivity, emotional symptoms, peer problems, and prosocial behavior. A strength of the measure, as with the CBCL scales, is that comparisons can be made between parents, teachers, and children on their respective perceptions of the child's behavior. The Strengths and Difficulties Questionnaire correlates highly with the Rutter scales and was developed on children drawn from both dental and psychiatric clinics. Currently, it does not have norms for groups other than English-speaking children, although there are Japanese and Chinese versions of the instrument.

Quality of Life

There are two distinctly different approaches to assessing an individual's quality of life. One involves objective economic and social indicators, such as income, home quality, and neighborhood quality. The other focuses on the individual's general sense of well-being, and involves determining his or her satisfaction with various domains of life, such as place of residence, family relationships, friends, and employment. We focus on this more subjective perspective of quality of life.

Often families who have a young adult with ID are asked to comment on their son or daughter's quality of life, regardless of whether the young adult lives in the family home or elsewhere. The concept of quality of life is multifaceted, and much has been written about it. Hensel, Rose, Kroese and Banks-Smith (2002) quote Emerson, Cullen, Hatton and Ross's (1996) statement "that a high quality of life is one in which people receive individually tailored support to become full participants in the life of the community, develop skills and independence, be given appropriate choice and control over their lives, be treated with respect in a safe and secure environment".

There are several instruments solely designed to assess quality of life from the perspective of the person with ID. One of the most widely used measures in the USA is the Quality of Life Questionnaire (QOL-Q) (Schalock & Keith, 1993). This measure has 40 criterion-referenced items that reflect four domains of a person's quality of life: satisfaction, competence/productivity, empowerment/independence, and social belonging/community integration. The Quality of Life Index is a sum score that can range from 40 (low quality of life) to 120 (high quality of life). This scale can be completed by the young adult alone, or, if the young person is not cognitively able to complete the form, by a parent or caregiver. Another similar measure is the Comprehensive Quality of Life Scale (ComQol) (Cummins, 1993). This, too, assesses quality of life across a number of domains (seven), and it yields information on both importance and satisfaction of quality of life.

Stress/Burden of Care

Without question, family researchers in the field of ID have focused primarily on family burden and stress. This approach broadened after Crnic, Friedrich and Greenberg published a model of family coping in 1983 that incorporated an ecological perspective, recognized perspectives of other family members besides mothers, and emphasized positive as well as negative impact. Nonetheless, the proliferation and use of instruments that assess dimensions of stress contribute to a growing literature with this as an outcome (or conversely, with well-being—conceived as the absence of stress—as an outcome).

A stress measure developed specifically in reference to children with ID that is often incorporated into family assessment batteries is the self-report Questionnaire on Resources and Stress (QRS); this is most often used in a 52-item form, the QRS-F (Friedrich, Greenberg & Crnic, 1983). A popular stress measure developed without reference to disability is the Parenting Stress Index (PSI) (Abidin, 1986). A difficulty that pervades these and many other measures purporting to assess parenting stress is that they do not directly assess parents' reactions; many items ask about the child's level of functioning or problem behaviors, and responses indicating greater child challenges are then presumed to indicate parenting stress. Thus, continued findings of greater parenting stress in families of children with more severe disabilities are circular, an artifact of the questions asked. This confound motivated Donenberg and Baker (1993) to develop the Family Impact Questionnaire (FIQ), a 50-item measure that directly asks respondents about the impact that their child has on family life relative to the impact they perceive other children his or her age to have. A further advantage of the FIQ is that it yields a positive impact scale as well as several negative impact scales.

Child-care burden is also assessed subjectively, and most often by mothers. The Zarit Burden Interview, or scale, although developed for caretakers of aging nondisabled individuals, has been widely used in the ID literature (Zarit, Reever & Bach-Peterson, 1980). This scale has been used to address issues such as the relationship between the person with a disability and the caregiver, as well as the caregiver's health, social life, and overall well-being.

There is much current interest in how parental coping and adaptation vary across the life span (Krauss, 1993; Heller, Hsieh & Rowitz, 1997; Seltzer & Heller, 1997; Blacher, Baker & Feinfield, 1999; Blacher & Hatton, 2001). Researchers are beginning to recognize the need for instruments to address domains such as stress and burden of care at different offspring ages, at different parental ages, and in different situations.

Health and Well-Being of Caregiver

Many large-scale research projects that involve families of children with ID focus on maternal well-being. Recently, fathers are of increased research interest in the USA (e.g., Phares, 1996; Simmerman, Blacher & Baker, 2001), but the majority of published research still focuses on the impact of the child on mothers. There are many dimensions of the health and well-being of mothers or caregivers; here we mention just two and give sample instruments for their assessment. First, in aging caregivers of persons with ID, the physical health of the caregiver is paramount. Several investigators (Seltzer & Krauss, 1989; Magana, 1999) use a single question taken from the Older Americans' Resources Services Multidimensional Functional Assessment. Respondents are simply asked to rate their own health on a four-point scale: excellent (4), good (3), fair (2), or poor (1). The criterion-related validity of this item with an entire physical examination has been reported to be 0.70 (Center for the Study of Aging and Human Development, 1978).

Second, as one dimension of well-being, depression is a construct that has been of widespread interest to family researchers. The two most popular instruments for assessing depressive symptomatology are the 21-item Beck Depression Inventory (Beck et al., 1961) and the 20-item CES–D (Radloff, 1977). Both of these short measures assess the frequency of common depressive symptoms. The CES–D has been shown to be reliable and valid with Spanish-speaking populations as well, though researchers need to be cautious because there is evidence that Latinos may report more elevated symptoms than other groups (Blacher, Lopez, Shapiro & Fusco, 1997a; Magana, 1999).

Marital Relationship

One instrument that addresses marital adjustment is the Marital Satisfaction Subscale of Enrich (Olson, Fournier & Druckman, 1987). This is a 10-item self-report measure of satisfaction; it covers personality, role responsibilities, conflict resolution, and the interpersonal and sexual relationship. A more process-oriented instrument is the 32-item Dyadic Adjustment Scale (DAS), a self-report measure of marital adjustment; it examines the quality of the marital relationship and the extent to which the adults agree or disagree on issues of married life (Spanier, 1976). One more specific domain that is often of interest to family researchers is the extent to which a parent perceives that his or her spouse is supportive in child rearing. Indeed, there is evidence that a mother's perception of the father's support is more important to her marital adjustment than the actual extent to which the father helps in child rearing (Simmerman et al., 2001). The Spousal Agreement and Support Scale (SASS) (Baker & Heller, 1996) is a 13-item measure developed to assess perceived spousal agreement about child problems and perceived support in child rearing; it has high internal reliability and stability over time.

Family Environment

In measuring family context, a frequently employed instrument is the Family Environment Scale (FES) (Moos & Moos, 1986). This paper-and-pencil instrument measures family values, attitudes, and behaviors and consists of nine scales: cohesion, conflict, control, expressiveness, independence, achievement orientation, intellectual-cultural orientation, moral-religious orientation, and active-recreational orientation. This measure has been shown to be quite stable over time in families with children with severe ID (Rousey, Wild & Blacher, 2002). Since it was developed and normed on a sample of the general US population, some of its subscales do not appear to be suitable for individuals from cultures other than European-American (Mink & Nihira, 1992). Furthermore, some subscales do not correlate well with other measures of the same construct (Russell, 1980). Nevertheless, the FES has been used successfully with families who had children at all levels of ID (Mink, Nihira & Meyers, 1983; Mink, Meyers & Nihira, 1984; Mink, Blacher & Nihira, 1988).

Another instrument that seeks to ascertain the context of the family environment is the Home Observation for Measurement of the Environment (HOME) (Bradley, 1999). This is an interviewer-completed rating scale that measures the quality and quantity of stimulation and support available to children residing within families. It is typically completed after the researcher has conducted a face-to-face interview in the family's home. Age-appropriate versions for children across the life span are available, as are norms for various ethnic groups (Bradley et al., 2000). All versions have the same or similar age-appropriate subscales. For example, in the early adolescent version, the subscales are physical environment, learning materials, modeling, fostering self-sufficiency, regulatory activities, variety of experiences and acceptance, and responsivity (Bradley et al., 1992). While the original version of this instrument was used with families of children without disabilities, it has been widely used with families of children who have ID (Mink et al., 1983; Mink & Nihira, 1986; Lamb et al., 1988; Amme & Takayama, 1989). More recently, a version of the HOME was developed specifically for use with families of children with disabilities (Bradley, Rock, Caldwell & Brisby, 1989).

Other measures used to assess the family environment are the Family Inventories from the University of Minnesota (Olson et al., 1986). Among this battery of instruments are FACES, which measures family adaptability and cohesion; ENRICH, which includes measures of marital satisfaction, communication, and religious orientation; and a quality of life measure. These instruments are based on Olson's theory of family life and were rigorously developed; however, while they were normed on a stratified (for life stage) sample, they were designed for the US middle class—primarily in the Midwest. These measures, then, may not be appropriate in the study of individuals from non-European-American cultures. Moreover, no mention is made of the inclusion in the normative sample of families with a child with ID.

Family quality of life is emerging as a new way to conceptualize the impact of a child with ID on the family. The overall emphasis is on the positive contributions of the child with ID to the family's quality of life, rather than on negative aspects, such as stress or burden of care (Blacher & Hatton, 2001). Instruments tailored to this concept are not in wide use, though assessments of overall "family quality of life" could certainly be made after doing a comprehensive interview with parents or caregivers and interpreting the data gathered. This approach has been used by Glidden and colleagues (Flaherty & Glidden, 2000; Glidden, 2000) in work with birth and adoptive families of children with ID.

A broader perspective is to examine the ecological or social context—that is, the surround in which the family functions and copes with problems associated with raising a child with disabilities—as well as functioning within the family. The Ecocultural Family Interview (EFI) (Nihira, Weisner & Bernheimer, 1994) was developed to do this—that is, to ascertain the family context of children with disabilities. This focused interview assesses 12 ecocultural factors describing environmental resources, opportunities, and constraints; goals and values of the family; and accommodation to the child with delayed development. The interviewer's manual, response rating, and coding system, and factor-scoring method were initially developed for European-American families of children with disabilities, and were later adapted for Asian and Latino immigrant families. For families with typically developing children, domains pertinent only to families of children with disabilities are omitted.

The EFI covers defined participants but within an open interview format. It is designed to be a focused conversation concerned with how family members achieve and sustain a meaningful daily routine and how parents manage to care for the child. The interview also provides parents with the opportunity to "tell their story". The resulting information is then analyzed by a comprehensive coding procedure (Weisner, Coots, Bernheimer & Arzubiaga, 1997). For more specific research questions and for open-ended questions, the accompanying transcripts are analyzed by a coding procedure developed for nonnumerical, unstructured material (Lieber, Weisner & Presley, 2003). The specific ecocultural variables covered in the EFI include family subsistence and economic base; safety, health, and education for the child; domestic and child-care workloads; familial and extrafamilial support networks; and sociocultural influence on the parents and children (Nihira et al., 1994; Weisner & Gallimore, 1994; Gallimore, Coots, Weisner, Garnier & Guthrie, 1996).

Transition

With increased attention to life-span issues, researchers have paid considerable attention to aging and are beginning to study earlier transitions. Most research on transition from adolescence to adulthood has been comprised of large-scale survey studies, whereby parents, or high-functioning young adults themselves, reported on broad transition outcomes, such as vocational status, number of hours worked, wages earned, or place of residence (Gallivan-Fenlon, 1994). No such comparable instruments were available to address transition issues for students with severe ID, the participants in the University of California–Riverside Families Project (Blacher, 1992). Thus, we designed an IBI as described earlier, the Transition Experiences Survey (TES), to gain an understanding of the transition experience for this particular population and their parents (Kraemer & Blacher, 2001).

The TES is a 48-item guided interview protocol through which we examined the young adult's current and previous involvement in programming related to the transition from school to adult life. There are both closed-ended (such as dichotomous yes/no or Likert-scale items) and open-ended questions. The domains surveyed included employment (for example, types of paid and unpaid work experiences of the young adult while still in school; community living (such as level of involvement in programming designed to increase independent and functional living skills); socialization (such as level of involvement and access to social/recreational activities); and family life (for example, level of involvement in family activities, such as going out to dinner and visiting relatives). Although the questions have face validity, the TES does not contain scales appropriate for reliability analyses.

The process of moving from adolescence to adulthood, or from secondary school to the world beyond, is probably universal in families from the diverse cultures that have emigrated to the USA or in countries and cultures that have moved from their nomadic or agrarian roots. However, family perceptions of this transition process—the focus of the interviews described above—may differ widely and be subject to a number of cultural concerns. For example, in the USA, there is a large population of monolingual and bilingual Spanish-speaking families. In these families, the cultural values of *familism* (such as interdependence among family members lending support) and *cohesion* may conflict with policies promoting inclusion in the community, which is a key component of most transition plans (Blacher et al., 1997a). Religious beliefs, attitudes, and practices might also be compatible or incompatible with transition goals or strategies (McAdoo, 1995; Rogers-Dulan & Blacher, 1995). Others suggest that Latino families may not face the same types and degree of transition challenges (Atkins, 1992), nor view behavior challenges in their children in the same way as Anglo families (Chavira, Lopez, Blacher & Shapiro, 2000).

MEASURES SPECIFICALLY FOR CULTURALLY DIVERSE FAMILIES

Many of the individuals in families termed "culturally diverse" are recent immigrants from regions other than Western Europe. Consequently, the culture of these individuals may be at some variance with the predominant culture of the USA, and the individuals themselves may experience shock or dissonance in their attempts to lead productive lives. The severity of their dissonance and life of apartness depends on a multitude of factors, chief among which are level of education, economic status, and facility with spoken English. Another factor of importance is the condition under which individuals left their country of origin—whether as routine emigrants or as refugees (Mink, 1997).

To ascertain the individual's level of dissonance/apartness in American culture, researchers working with recent immigrant families should consider employing a measure of acculturation. Measuring acculturation, though, tends to be complex, since these diverse groups have different immigrant experiences and concerns. Of necessity, then, acculturation measures are often designed for a particular culture. One widely used scale for use with Hispanic or Latino families is the Acculturation Scale of Marin, Sabogal, Marin, Otero-Sabogal and Perez-Stable (1987). The measure contains three subscales: media (use of and preference for language-specific electronic and print media), ethnic social relations (ethnicity of friends for oneself and one's children), and language use (current language use, language use as a child, and preference for language). Higher scores on each subscale indicate more acculturation. A newer version of this instrument is the Bidimensional Acculturation Scale for Hispanics (BAS) (Marin & Gamba, 1996). This scale version assesses Hispanicism or culture of origin, Americanism, and biculturalism.

However, some prefer the ARSMA-II (Acculturation Rating Scale for Mexican Americans-II). The ARSMA-II categorizes respondents into one of five categories that range from "very Latino oriented" to "very assimiliated, Anglicized". Although this measure is culture specific for Mexican-Americans, it may have utility with other Hispanic groups. The authors define acculturation as "those phenomena which result when groups of individuals having different cultures come into continuous first-hand contact, with subsequent changes in the original cultural patterns of either or both groups" (Cuellar, Arnold & Maldonado, 1995).

In studying acculturation in Asian groups, the most widely used scale is the Suinn-Lew Self-Identity Acculturation Scale (Suinn, Rickard-Figueroa, Lew & Vigil, 1987; Suinn, Ahuna & Khoo, 1992). This scale was developed and normed on Asian college-age students and may not be appropriate for adult samples. This Asian sample did not focus on particular ethnic groups; it included all students who identified themselves as Asian. Recently, a parent version of this instrument was developed with Chinese and Japanese parents of children with and without mental disabilities—the Asian Identity and Acculturation Scales (Lee & Nihira, 1999). The scales in this form are general acculturation, American values, Asian identity, and Asian holidays.

CULTURE AND RESEARCH

Before proceeding further, it is advisable to visit the concept of culture—what it is, and how it affects the research enterprise. An accepted definition of culture is "a shared organization of ideas that includes the intellectual, moral, and aesthetic standards prevalent in a community and the meaning of communicative actions" (LeVine, 1984, p. 67). Now, recall from developmental psychology that an individual's behavior depends on personal characteristics, the type of social environment in which he/she develops, and the interaction between these two components. Therefore, how an individual comes to construe the world is partially dependent on the culture in which the individual lives. If cultures are different from each other in intellectual, moral, and aesthetic standards, it follows that individuals from different cultures will structure the world differently.

It is this difference in worldview that has implications for the research enterprise when it is applied to individuals from a "diverse culture". For example, the investigator is usually from the USA or Western Europe, regions that are technically advanced with a well-developed research tradition. Theories of behavior, which are the bedrock of psychological research, are generally based on observations of individuals similar to the researchers—observations that are filtered through the worldview of the researchers. We can state with some certainty, then, that the research enterprise as we know it is a Western research enterprise. Now, contrast the above with the participants in a cross-cultural study, individuals from a "diverse culture". Suppose these individuals are Hmong refugees from the highlands of Vietnam, a culture that has been described as animist, nonrationalistic, and nonscientific (Fadiman, 1997). One can surmise that the worldview of the Hmong differs from that of the American researcher's psychological theories and instruments, and that the constructs and concepts the Hmong developed to explain their world are different. As Shweder (1986) notes, ideas about spirits and witches in animistic cultures—like the Hmong—are not unlike our scientific theories, as they are attempts to "explain" the workings of the world from "the native point of view".

Returning to the Western research enterprise, in its determined search for universal concepts, investigators have not always attended to the uniqueness of other cultures—with the result that in conducting research with individuals from a culture different from the investigator's own, there has been the tendency to take Western concepts of personality and family process and transport them unchanged to the study of the "diverse" culture. But, in view of differing worldviews, some instruments that were developed within the Western conceptualization of human behavior will not be appropriate for individuals from the other culture. Moreover, some concepts that are central to the other culture may be omitted entirely from the instruments the investigator plans to employ.

Such is the case in societies that are based on Confucian philosophy. In Confucian cultures, the central tenet is that "man exists in relationship to others". In contrast, Western culture, particularly American culture, conceives of "man as an individual". Clearly, these basic assumptions about man's place and relationship in the world are variant and may well be associated with different values. For example, in Confucian society, the central family relationship is that of child to parent, particularly, the son to the father. The guiding principle governing this intergenerational relationship is termed "filial piety".

> It prescribes how children should behave towards their parents, living or dead.... It makes stringent demands: that one should provide for the material and mental well-being of one's aged parents ... take care to avoid harm to one's body, ensure the continuity of the family line, and in general conduct oneself so as to bring honour and avoid disgrace to the family name. (Ho, 1996, p. 155)

To some, filial piety may resemble an amalgam of the Western concepts of obedience and loyalty. But on closer inspection, and in readings and discussions with individuals from Confucian cultures, it is clearly a much more powerful and encompassing concept. This conceptual absence from the research enterprise has implications for the study of Asians from Confucian societies living in the USA (see below).

As noted, there are stages in the research process where investigators considering the study of cultures different from their own must be particularly careful. Most important are the initial stages of research, which include the statement of the research question and the definition and operationalization of constructs, including those constructs that may be absent from, or have definitions different from, those used in the Western research enterprise.

Additionally, Tanaka, Ebreo, Linn and Morera (1998) have stated that desired outcomes for cultural research come about only if the investigator is able to "parse a research question into its fundamental components"; that is, to question the implicit assumptions (p. 22). For example, he considers the study of Asian-Americans and academic achievement. The first assumption that he questions is whether membership in a particular category, Asian-American, has specific behavioral correlates—that is, success in tests of academic achievement. From here, he proceeds to question whether the aggregation of different Asian-American groups is warranted, asking, is there a "core experience" among these different Asian groups? Tanaka then expounds on construct validity and measurement equivalence; the reader is referred to his chapter for a lucid presentation.

INTERVIEWS IN A CULTURAL CONTEXT

We next consider the convergence of family assessment and cultural issues, as illustrated by the authors' major programs of research focusing on the impact of a child with intellectual impairment on the family. These projects involve assessment of family well-being, though in very different ways and across different cultures (Euro-American or Anglo, Latino, and Asian-American). We note that there are other similar projects conducted by our colleagues in the USA that incorporate many of the same measures, using the same combination of open-ended and directed questions. For example, Glidden has studied both birth mothers and adoptive mothers of children with ID, and examined coping and adjustment across both samples and over time (Glidden, 2000). Researchers focusing on aging parents of adult sons or daughters with ID have also utilized an adjustment framework (Seltzer & Krauss, 1989; Hong et al., 2001) in the study of mothers, as well as of grandparents (Heller, Hsieh & Rowitz, 2000) and siblings (Orsmond & Seltzer, 2000).

The University of California–Riverside (UCR) Families Project

The University of California–Riverside Families Project was begun in 1982 by Jan Blacher and C. Edward Meyers (Meyers & Blacher, 1982). The original research emphasis was primarily on the impact of a child with severe ID on the family, mainly the mother. The 100 children in the study ranged in age from three to nine years. Today the original sample of children are leaving mandated schooling and making the transition to young adulthood. Over the past 20 years, we have studied over 600 additional families for various time periods.

Focus of the Research

While we have tracked the adaptive and maladaptive behavior of the children, adolescents, and young adults over the years, our main foci have been the parents and family—coping with the challenges of ID and even dual diagnosis; adjustment at different stages of the life course; involvement of mother, father, siblings; and the correlates and consequences of out-of-home placement. In the mid-1990s, we added a sample of monolingual and bilingual Spanish-speaking families, in order to study the processes of coping within a cultural context. Ultimately, we are concerned about parent and family well-being, particularly as their sons or daughters move from the aegis of the public schools to the adult service delivery system, presumably to lives in the community.

Applicability of Family Interview Methods

The cornerstone of this project has been the family interview process. At roughly 18-month intervals, parents have been interviewed in their own home about their life with a child with severe ID. At each stage of the life span, an IBI anchored the visit. For example, during the early childhood years, we asked about parent–child attachment (Blacher & Meyers, 1983; Blacher, 1984); during the school years, we focused on parents' perceptions of schooling for their child (Blacher, 1985; Meyers & Blacher, 1987); during adolescence, we focused on out-of-home placement (Blacher et al., 1999); and, currently, we focus on the transition to adulthood (Blacher, 2001; Kraemer & Blacher, 2001).

During the actual visits to the family home, parents complete paper-and-pencil measures, answer questions in an RBI format, and respond to open-ended questions, which often elicit candid, unsolicited remarks or responses. In almost all cases, two interviewers visit the home (to satisfy both safety and reliability concerns). One interviewer records parents' remarks to open-ended questions verbatim; portions of the interviews are also audiotaped for later coding. Interviews range in length from two to six hours.

Despite interest in other family members, mothers are most often interviewed (Blacher & Hatton, 2001). One issue that plagues family researchers is that of "shared method variance", whereby the same respondent (that is, the mother) completes a variety of different measures tapping interrelated constructs. For example, a mother who is highly stressed, due to challenges related to her child with ID, may score high on a measure of stress or negative impact, high on a measure of depressive symptomatology, and low on marital harmony. It would be difficult to sort out the true source of the stress, as a depressed mother might perceive more negativity from her child and her husband. One way to avoid this shared method variance problem is to administer the same measures to two different family members, as has been done with research on fathers (e.g., Simmerman et al., 2001). Another is to use observational data to back up some of the parent report data. For example, if the child or young adult is present, an interviewer can validate many of the adaptive behavior items that parents report on the Vineland. Finally, the use of interviewer-completed instruments can also support, or mitigate, parent reports. Both the Home Observation and Measurement of the Environment (Bradley, 1999) and the Home Quality Rating Scale (Meyers, Mink & Nihira, 1981) are examples of such measures (Blacher, Nihira & Meyers, 1987; Rousey et al., 2002). The gathering of qualitative as well as quantitative data can also validate the information obtained from the family interview. Finally, family interviewers can be trained to write detailed field notes describing the tone, affect, and perceived veracity of the parents' reports during the home visit.

What We Have Learned from Interviewing Families

Over the last 20 years, we have developed a large database on our participant families, and we are grateful to them for their willingness to participate so freely and openly. Here, we will note just four general findings or observations related to our assessment interviews that we hope will inform subsequent researchers in their work.

Studying Families of Children with Severe Disabilities Over Time Reveals Their Resiliency

While, at any one time, our measures certainly reveal the trials such families face, an advantage of interviewing over an extended number of years is that we come to know our families well. We come to appreciate the essential normalcy of their lives and, along with the stressors (often not related to the child with handicaps), we can share in their triumphs. Overcoming obstacles and living lives of relative normalcy is a consistent theme in our interviewers' field notes. Although we have studied the process of out-of-home placement of children and adolescents with severe ID, relatively few families, overall, do opt for placement; those who do place the child remain involved and adapt well to the change. The rest cope well with the challenges present at each new stage of the life course. Indeed, in many of our published studies, the intact marriage rate is above 70%, a fact which attests to some level of resiliency.

Using Multiple Child Measures Affords a Better Understanding of Parenting Stress

Using some of the measures described in this chapter, we have assessed not only child adaptive behavior but also maladaptive behavior and psychiatric disorder. In several studies with these multiple child measures, we have found that parenting stress is highly related to the extent of child behavior problems (Baker, Blacher, Crnic & Edelbrock, 2002; McIntyre, Blacher & Baker, 2002). Having accounted for the effects of behavior problems on parents, the child's level of ID, or even the presence of ID, does not further explain parenting stress. Moreover, longitudinal analyses have revealed that increased parenting stress may, over time, actually exacerbate the challenging behaviors displayed by the child (Baker et al., 2003).

Family Environments, in the Presence of a Child with Severe Intellectual Disability, Are Highly Stable

We recently examined family environments across three time points over about nine years, using the Family Environment Scale, the HOME, and the Home Quality Rating Scale, instruments mentioned above. We found a remarkable degree of stability, particularly for the Family Environment Scale (Rousey et al., 2002). However, it is possible that the families who were least stable were more likely to place their child and thus were not included in that particular study. Moreover, the sample in which we assessed stability of home environment comprised predominantly white, middle-class families, and we do not know whether the high stability would also hold with culturally diverse families who have a member with a disability.

While these measures of family environment have high face validity for the dominant US culture, they were not designed to take cultural context into account. We have successfully used the FES with Latino families who had children with ID, where the cohesion subscale served as one indicator of the key construct of familism (Blacher et al., 1997a; Blacher, Shapiro, Lopez, Diaz & Fusco, 1997b). Yet, as we examine below, there may be some limitations to the validity with non-Western cultures.

Family Interview Methods Do Have Applicability Across Cultures

Overall, our interview procedures worked well in our studies of monolingual and bilingual Spanish-speaking families. However, about 40% of the Latina mothers we interviewed were single parents, as opposed to the 20% who were single, as revealed in census data (Blacher et al., 1997a). Furthermore, when fathers were present, Latina mothers tended to be less forthcoming. In addition, the findings from some measures do differ according to the cultural context, and interpretations should be made with caution. For example, we have documented alarmingly high rates of depressive symptomatology among Latina mothers (Blacher et al., 1997a,b). On the other hand, the impact of specific child-related maladaptive behavior on Latina mothers appears to be similar, and can be interpreted according to prevailing theories about attributions of behavior (Chavira et al., 2000) or behavioral phenotypes (McIntyre & Blacher, 2002).

The University of California–Los Angeles (UCLA) Asian-American Family and Chinese-American Fathers Projects

The study of diverse cultures has long been the focus of research emanating from the Center for Culture and Health in the Department of Psychiatry and Biobehavioral Sciences at UCLA. The center is headed by Robert B. Edgerton and is focused on the study of diverse cultures within the USA—African-American, Asian-American, Caribbean, Euro-American, and Latino. Both the Asian-American Family Project (Edgerton, 1993) and the Chinese-American Fathers Project (Mink, 1994) are housed under these auspices.

Focus of the Research

The main objective of the Asian-American Families and Chinese-American Fathers projects was to ascertain the parenting behavior and acculturation of immigrant mothers and fathers from countries having a Confucian heritage. That is, what are the beliefs, values, and behaviors that these parents bring to rearing their children—both those with developmental disabilities and those who are typically developing? Moreover, is the acculturation experience different for these two groups of families? Another objective of the studies was to determine whether techniques and findings from previous studies of American families (Mink et al., 1983, 1984; Nihira, Mink & Meyers, 1985; Mink & Nihira, 1986, 1987) could be applied to the study of immigrant parents of Chinese descent.

Applicability of Family Interview Methods

As not infrequently happens in the course of research, the basic question addressed in the two studies—what characterizes Chinese-American parenting behaviors—was overshadowed by the secondary question—whether the concepts, and hence the instruments, developed to measure American values were appropriate for the study of Chinese-Americans. That is, are American theories, concepts, and the concomitant instruments transportable across cultures; is there measurement equivalence?

An earlier finding by Mink and Nihira (1991) indicated that definitions of certain concepts were not analogous in the Chinese and the general US samples. Moreover, other investigations and reviews indicate that Chinese culture, with its emphasis on collective responsibility, is at some variance with individualistic Euro-American culture (Marsella, Murray & Golden, 1974; Yang, 1986; Schwartz, 1994; Triandis, 1994; Bond, 1996).

What We Have Learned from Interviewing Families

The results of our study focusing on home environment differences between Chinese-American and Euro-American families of children having developmental disabilities illuminate some of the problems investigators encounter when they utilize instruments that were developed and normed on undifferentiated samples of the US population. Here, we review findings regarding four different instruments and techniques used in interviewing Asian-American families.

Family Environment

We measured family environment with the Family Environment Scale (Moos & Moos, 1986). An examination of our battery of instruments, wherein all interviews were conducted in either Mandarin or Cantonese, and all instruments were translated into Chinese, revealed more problems with the FES than with the other instruments in the back-translation phase

(Mink & Nihira, 1991). Scales that were particularly problematic were cohesion and moral religious orientation. Given Confucian tradition with its emphasis on the family (Hsu, 1967; Yang, 1986), we expected higher cohesion scores for Chinese-American families than for Euro-Americans. We found the opposite. The determination of whether the lower scores were the result of many Chinese dual-wage-earner families (with mothers having limited time for child care and the domestic workload), long working hours for fathers, immigrant status, or some combination of these factors, remains for further exploration. But it may also be that the items that comprise cohesion in the FES do not adequately assess cohesion as conceived by Chinese-American parents. Also problematic is the subscale of moral–religious emphasis. Here, the scale is clearly inappropriate for Chinese-Americans (unless they have converted to Christianity). Items that refer to church attendance, belief in heaven and hell, and the importance of the Bible are clearly inappropriate for Chinese-Americans who adhere to Buddhist, Taoist, and/or Confucian precepts.

HOME

We also assessed family environment with the Home Observation for Measurement of the Environment (HOME). We did not anticipate or encounter definitional problems, as this is an interviewer-completed behavior rating scale, and either the family has or does what the item describes, or it does not. We did note that certain behaviors, such as obedience and reticence, which are important to traditional Chinese parents, are not included in the scale. This absence was handled in our open-ended questions that inquired about these behaviors. We also did not intend to use the HOME scale to measure any area of affect, since earlier work by Nihira, Tomiyasu and Oshio (1987) had found that the pattern of correlation between the child's developmental status and measures of family environment was similar between Japanese and Euro-Americans in the cognitive–educational domain, but dissimilar in the affective–emotional domain. This finding was also noted in a comprehensive review of the use of HOME in cultures across the world, in which Bradley, Corwyn and Whiteside-Mansell (1996) concluded: "In general, there seemed greater cross-cultural equivalence for items assessing cognitively stimulating aspects of the environment than for items assessing socioemotional support" (p. 251).

Olson Scales

We assessed marital satisfaction with a scale developed by Olson et al. (1986). The same lack of socioemotional equivalence that was discovered on the HOME was also apparent here, in that Chinese-American mothers scored significantly lower on marital satisfaction than did Euro-American mothers. Several factors may contribute to this difference. First, in traditional Chinese families, the reason for marriage is procreation, not love. Thus, the parent–child relationship is central to the family, unlike Euro-American families, where the marital dyad is central. Second, although only approaching significance in this study, more Chinese-American than Euro-American mothers are employed full-time. This has implications for the complexity of the Chinese-American mother's schedule. This complexity, coupled with fewer child-care helpers (immigrants are often separated from extended family members) and the lack of active assistance from the father, may contribute to the lower score on marital satisfaction (Mink & Nihira, 1991). Third, the mothers may have acculturated more rapidly than the fathers, and thus modified their views of the woman's role in the family. Until further research is done on Chinese definitions of "marital satisfaction" along with the development of scales and norms that incorporate such definitions, it would be wise to restrict comparisons on marital satisfaction to "within-the-culture" samples rather than "across-culture" samples.

A Measure of Filial Piety

As previously mentioned, the standard repertoire of instruments developed to measure concepts salient to middle-class Americans often does not include instruments that address concepts that are key to understanding behavior in a diverse culture. Recall, that in Confucian cultures filial piety is a pivotal concept; however, a search of the literature revealed no American instruments that measured this concept. Fortunately, such an instrument was discovered in a study of Chinese families (Ho & Kang, 1984). We adapted this instrument that was originally developed for Hong Kong residents, so that it was appropriate for current behavior patterns and the Chinese immigrant experience in America. Chinese Fathers Project personnel (bilingual researchers of Chinese descent) adapted the instrument with pretesting, translation, back translation, and retesting. A factor analysis revealed four factors: *core* classic views on principles, *caring* for parents and parent–child relations, *nonconfrontational* filial piety, and the *right* to spousal choice (Lieber, Nihira & Mink, submitted).

Focus Groups

One of the goals of the Chinese-American Fathers Study was to assemble a lexicon of salient concepts for the study of Chinese families in America. For that purpose, focus groups were assembled that comprised fathers and mothers of typically developing children (Mink & Chang, 2002). Focus groups provided another method for obtaining information from families that was not covered in any standard family interview measures. The topics discussed were what defines good family life; the characteristics of a good marriage; the characteristics of "good" parenting behaviors, goals, and aspirations for children; and definitions and attributions of ID and mental illness.

In our study of definitions and attributions concerning ID, we discovered that both mothers and fathers describe "mental retardation" as below-average intellectual capacity that is accompanied by significant limitations in adaptive functioning. This definition is similar to that of the American Association on Mental Retardation. However, a major difference emerged in attributions regarding ID. Here, even though they acknowledged the contributions of genetic factors and accidents in causing ID, Chinese-American mothers and fathers tended to blame parents for making irresponsible decisions regarding the pregnancy and choice of mate, failing to care adequately for children's health and well-being, and engaging in high-risk behaviors such as substance abuse during the pregnancy (Mink & Chang, 2002). This finding is at some variance with accepted American attributions for ID and has implications for both the measure of child impact on the parents and the design of programs for Chinese parents of such children.

CONCLUSIONS

What has been learned about the "transportability" of our measures and techniques for interviewing families? Specifically, how do we transport our experiences and knowledge across families who have children with different disabilities, and across cultures? Assuming that in the "other" culture, some form of the nuclear family is the prevailing family type, that the culture shares some of our basic worldview beliefs, that it is at least at a moderate level of industrialization, or that the individuals to be studied have been exposed to Western-style advanced education, we can employ measures that assess the family environment, with some degree of confidence in their validity. However, stronger empirical evidence exists for their applicability if the measures focus more on cognitive stimulation, or the learning environment of the home. It is with measures in the affective–emotional domain that we must be cautious. These may be more culture-specific. Furthermore, we know little about the transportability of many measures that assess other domains in families, such as coping, adjustment, or reactions, to social policies affecting children with ID.

When we design home interview procedures, awareness of particular disabilities is paramount. For example, if the parents have a son or daughter with a chronic or even progressive disorder, some questions about the future may be perceived as irrelevant or particularly upsetting. More commonly, though, researchers need to be sensitive to the range of ID, and to the lack of variance which might be found on some items related to high, as opposed to low, functioning individuals. Instruments can easily be examined for their applicability across the levels of ID to be studied. Having established applicability of instruments, we have emphasized consideration of the cultural context.

Establishing cultural validity of constructs can be daunting, but it needs to begin in the design phase of the study. The same can be said of establishing validity across levels and types of disabilities. The first step requires the investigator to be knowledgeable about the culture, or the disability, that is to be studied. If the investigator is not from the culture, or has not lived in the culture, it is important that knowledgeable informants be included at a decision-making level in this phase of the study. Next, concepts salient to the culture need to be compiled. Then, the task is to discover the definitions of these concepts. This can be done through focus-group discussion or individual interviews.

Finally, we must ask whether it is desirable to develop measures that transcend differences between cultures and only measure areas in which cultures are similar—with the consequent loss of specificity and the ability to tap into the unique contributions of each culture. Or, we must consider whether it is better to address each culture separately. Perhaps, with thought and effort, it will be possible to attain some middle position that allows researchers to do both—measure cultural similarities and ascertain the uniqueness of culture—with applicability to families with children at any level of ID.

ACKNOWLEDGMENTS

Preparation of this chapter was supported in part by National Institute of Child Health and Human Development Grant no. HD21324 (University of California–Riverside Families Project, J. Blacher, principal investigator) and no. HD34879-1459 (Collaborative Family Study, J. Blacher, co-principal investigator). Research findings for Chinese-American families were supported by NICHD Grant no. HD11944 (Community Adaptation of Mildly Retarded Persons, I. Mink, key investigator) and no. HD31856 (Chinese-American Fathers of Children with MR/DD, I. Mink, principal investigator). We gratefully acknowledge the participation and support of the families in their research projects, from whom we have learned so much.

REFERENCES

Abidin, R. (1986). *Parenting Stress Index*. Charlottesville, VA: Pediatric Psychology Press.

Achenbach, T.M. (1991). *Manual for the Child Behavior Checklist 4–18*. Burlington, VT: University of Vermont, Department of Psychiatry.

American Psychiatric Association (2000). *Diagnostic and Statistical Manual of Mental Disorders*, 4th edn, Text Revision. Washington, DC: American Psychiatric Association.

Amme, T. & Takayama, T. (1989). Evaluation of home stimulation for normal and handicapped children in Japan. In P. Chan & M. Smilansky (Eds) *Early Childhood Toward the 21st Century: A Worldwide Perspective* (pp. 427–430). Hong Kong: Yew Chung Education Publishing Company.

Angold, A. & Fisher, P.W. (1999). Interviewer-based interviews. In D. Shaffer, C.P. Lucas & J.E. Richters (Eds) *Diagnostic Assessment in Child and Adolescent Psychopathology* (pp. 34–64). New York: Guilford.

Atkins, B. J. (1992). Transition for individuals who are culturally diverse. In F.R. Rusch, L. Destefano, J. Chadsey-Rusch, L.A. Phelps & E. Szymanski (Eds) *Transition from School to Adult Life. Models, Linkages, and Policy* (pp. 443–457). Sycamore, IL: Sycamore.

Baker, B.L., Blacher, J., Crnic, K.A. & Edelbrock, C. (2002). Behavior problems and parenting stress in families of three year old children with and without developmental delay. *American Journal on Mental Retardation*, **107**, 433–444.

Baker, B.L., Blacher, J., Kopp, C.B. & Kraemer, B. (1997). Parenting children with mental retardation. In N.W. Bray (Ed.) *International Review of Research in Mental Retardation*, vol. 20 (pp. 1–45). Orlando, FL: Academic Press.

Baker, B.L. & Heller, T.L. (1996). Preschool children with externalizing behaviors: impact on fathers and mothers. *Journal of Abnormal Child Psychology*, **24**, 513–532.

Baker, B.L., McIntryre, L.L., Blacher, J., Crnic, K., Edelbrock, C. & Low, C. (2003). Preschool children with and without developmental delay: behavior problems and parenting stress over time. *Journal of Intellectual Disability Research*, **47**, 217–230.

Baxter, C., Cummins, R. & Yiolitis, L. (2000). Parental stress attributed to family members with and without disability: a longitudinal study. *Journal of Intellectual and Developmental Disability*, **25**, 105–118.

Beck, A.T., Steer, R.A. & Brown, G.K. (1996). *Beck Depression Inventory* (2nd edn, *Manual*). San Antonio, TX: Psychological Corporation.

Beck, A.T., Ward, C.H., Mendelson, M., Mock, J. & Erbaugh, J. (1961). An inventory for measuring depression. *Archives of General Psychiatry*, **4**, 561–571.

Blacher, J. (1984). Attachment and severely handicapped children: implications for intervention. *Journal of Developmental and Behavioral Pediatrics*, **5**, 178–183.

Blacher, J. (1985). Evaluating the impact of schooling on families of severely impaired children. *Studies in Educational Evaluation*, **11**, 63–74.

Blacher, J. (1992). *Transition to Adulthood: MR, Families, and Culture*. National Institute of Child Health and Human Development Grant no. RO1HD21324 (1998–2003).

Blacher, J. (2001). The transition to adulthood: mental retardation, families, and culture. *American Journal on Mental Retardation*, **106**, 173–188.

Blacher, J. & Baker, B.L. (2002). *The Best of AAMR: Families and Mental Retardation: A Collection of Notable AAMR Journal Articles Across the 20th Century*. Washington, DC: Monographs of the American Association on Mental Retardation.

Blacher, J., Baker, B.L. & Feinfield, K.A. (1999). Leaving or launching? Continuing family involvement with children and adolescents in placement. *American Journal on Mental Retardation*, **104**, 452–465.

Blacher, J. & Hatton, C. (2001). Current perspectives on family research in mental retardation. *Current Opinion in Psychiatry*, **14**, 477–482.

Blacher, J., Lopez, S., Shapiro, J. & Fusco, J. (1997a). Contributions to depression in Latina mothers with and without children with retardation: implications for caregiving. *Family Relations*, **46**, 325–334.

Blacher, J. & Meyers, C.E. (1983). A review of attachment formation and disorder in handicapped children. *American Journal of Mental Deficiency*, **87**, 359–371.

Blacher, J., Nihira, K. & Meyers, C.E. (1987). Characteristics of home environment of families with mentally retarded children: comparison across levels of retardation. *American Journal of Mental Deficiency*, **91**, 313–320.

Blacher, J., Shapiro, J., Lopez, S., Diaz, L. & Fusco, J. (1997b). Depression in Latina mothers of children with mental retardation: a neglected concern. *American Journal on Mental Retardation*, **5**, 483–496.

Bond, M.H. (1996). Chinese values. In M.H. Bond (Ed.) *The Handbook of Chinese Psychology* (pp. 208–226). Hong Kong: Oxford University Press.

Bradley, R.H. (1999). The home environment. In S.L. Friedman & T.D. Wachs (Eds) *Measuring Environment Across the Life Span* (pp. 31–58). Washington, DC: American Psychological Association.

Bradley, R.H., Caldwell, B.M., Brisby, J., Magee, M., Whiteside, L. & Rock, S.L. (1992). The HOME inventory: a new scale for families of pre- and early-adolescent children with disabilities. *Research in Developmental Disabilities*, **13**, 313–333.

Bradley, R.H., Corwyn, R.F., Caldwell, B.M., Whiteside-Mansell, L., Wasserman, G.A. & Mink, I.T. (2000). Measuring the home environments of children in early adolescence. *Journal of Research on Adolescence*, **10**, 247–288.

Bradley, R.H., Corwyn, R.F. & Whiteside-Mansell, L. (1996). Life at home: same time, different places—an examination of the HOME inventory in different cultures. *Early Development and Parenting*, **5**, 251–269.

Bradley, R.H., Rock, S.L., Caldwell, B.M. & Brisby, J.A. (1989). Uses of the HOME inventory for families with handicapped children. *American Journal of Mental Retardation*, **94**, 313–333.

Bronfenbrenner, U. (1979). *The Ecology of Human Development: Experiments by Nature and Design*. Cambridge, MA: Harvard University Press.

Bruininks, R.H., Woodcock, R.W., Weatherman, R.F. & Hill, B.K. (1996). *Scales of Independent Behavior—Revised Comprehensive Manual*. Itasca, IL: Riverside Publishing.

Center for the Study of Aging and Human Development (1978). *Multidimensional Functional Assessment: The OARS Methodology. A Manual* (2nd edn). Durham, NC: Duke University.

Chavira, V., Lopez, S., Blacher, J. & Shapiro, J. (2000). Latina mothers' attributions, emotions and reactions to the behavior problems of their children with developmental disabilities. *Journal of Child Psychology and Psychiatry*, **41**, 245–252.

Costello, E.J., Edelbrock, C. & Costello, A.J. (1985). Validity of the NIMH Diagnostic Interview Schedule for Children: a comparison between pediatric and psychiatric referrals. *Journal of Abnormal Child Psychology*, **13**, 579–595.

Crnic, K.A., Friedrich, W.N. & Greenberg, M.T. (1983). Adaptation of families with mentally retarded children: a model of stress, coping, and family ecology. *American Journal of Mental Deficiency*, **88**, 125–138.

Cuellar, I., Arnold, B. & Maldonado, R. (1995). Acculturation Rating Scale for Mexican American-II: a revision of the original ARSMA scale. *Hispanic Journal of Behavioral Sciences*, **17**, 275–304.

Cummins, R.A. (1993). *The Comprehensive Quality of Life Scale-Intellectual Disability, 4th edn (ComQol-ID4)*. Melbourne: School of Psychology, Deakin University.

Derogatis, L.R. (1993). *BSI Brief Symptom Inventory: Administration, Scoring, and Procedures Manual*. Minneapolis, MN: National Computer Systems.

Donenberg, G. & Baker, B.L. (1993). The impact of young children with externalizing behaviors on their families. *Journal of Abnormal Child Psychology*, **21**, 179–198.

Edgerton, R.B. (1993). *The Community Adaptation of Mildly Retarded Persons*. National Institute of Child Health and Human Development (Grant no. HD11944). Bethesda, MD.

Einfeld, S.L. & Tonge, B.J. (1995). The Developmental Behaviour Checklist: the development and validation of an instrument to assess behavioural and emotional disturbance in children and adolescents with mental retardation. *Journal of Autism and Developmental Disorders*, **25**, 81–104.

Elander, J. & Rutter, M. (1996). Use and development of the Rutter Parents' and Teachers' Scales. *International Journal of Methods in Psychiatric Research*, **6**, 63–78.

Emerson, E., Cullen, C., Hatton, C. & Cross, B. (1996). *Residential Provision for People with Learning Disabilities: Summary Report*. Manchester: University of Manchester, Hester Adrian Research Centre.

Fadiman, A. (1997) *"The Spirit Catches You and You Fall Down": A Hmong Child, Her American Doctors and the Collision of Two Cultures*. New York: Farrar, Straus & Giroux.

Flaherty, E.M. & Glidden, L.M. (2000). Positive adjustment in parents rearing children with Down syndrome. *Early Education and Development*, **11**, 407–422.

Fowler, F.J. (1993). *Survey Research Methods* (2nd edn). Newbury Park, CA: Sage.

Friedrich, W.N., Greenberg, M.T. & Crnic, K. (1983). A short form of the Questionnaire on Resources and Stress. *American Journal on Mental Deficiency*, **88**, 41–48.

Gallimore, R., Coots, J.J., Weisner, T.S., Garnier, H. & Guthrie, G. (1996). Family responses to children with early developmental delays. II. Accommodation intensity and activity in early and middle childhood. *American Journal of Mental Retardation*, **101**, 215–232.

Gallivan-Fenlon, A. (1994). "Their senior year": family and service provider perspectives on the transition from school to adult life for young adults with disabilities. *Journal of the Association for Persons with Severe Handicaps*, **19**, 11–23.

Glidden, L.M. (2000). Adopting children with developmental disabilities: a long-term perspective. *Family Relations*, **49**, 397–405.

Glidden, L.M., Valliere, V.N. & Herbert, S.L. (1988). Adopted children with mental retardation: positive family impact. *Mental Retardation*, **26**, 119–125.

Goodman, R. (1997). The Strengths and Difficulties Questionnaire: a research note. *Journal of Child Psychology and Psychiatry*, **38**, 581–586.

Heller, T., Hsieh, K. & Rowitz, L. (1997). Maternal and paternal caregiving of persons with mental retardation across the life span. *Family Relations*, **46**, 407–415.

Heller, T., Hsieh, K. & Rowitz, L. (2000). Grandparents as support to mothers of persons with intellectual disability. *Journal of Gerontological Social Work*, **33**, 23–34.

Hensel, E., Rose, J., Kroese, B.S. & Banks-Smith, J. (2002). Subjective judgements of quality of life: a comparison study between those with intellectual disability and those without disability. *Journal of Intellectual Disability Research*, **46**, 95–107.

Ho, D.Y.F. (1996). Filial piety and its psychological consequences. In M.H. Bond (Ed.) *The Handbook of Chinese Psychology* (pp. 155–165). Hong Kong: Oxford University Press.

Ho, D.Y.F. & Kang, T.K. (1984). Intergenerational comparisons of child-rearing attitudes and practices in Hong Kong. *Developmental Psychology*, **20**, 1004–1016.

Hong, J., Seltzer, M.M. & Krauss, M.W. (2001). Change in social support and psychological well-being: a longitudinal study of aging mothers of adults with mental retardation. *Family Relations*, **50**, 154–163.

Hsu, F.L.K. (1967). Under the ancestors' shadow: kinship, personality, and social mobility in village China. New York: Doubleday.

Kraemer, B.R. & Blacher, J. (2001). Transition for young adults with severe mental retardation: school preparation, parent expectations, and family involvement. *Mental Retardation*, **39**, 423–435.

Krauss, W.M. (1993). Child-related and parenting stress: similarities and differences between mothers and fathers of children with disabilities. *American Journal on Mental Retardation*, **97**, 393–404.

Lamb, M.E., Hwang, C., Bookstein, F.L., Broberg, A., Hult, G. & Frodi, M. (1988). Determinants of social competence in Swedish preschoolers. *Developmental Psychology*, **24**, 58–70.

Lee, S. & Nihira, K. (1999). Acculturation in Asian-American families. *Pacific State Archives*, vol. 22, UCLA Developmental Disabilities Immersion Program (pp. 73–81).

LeVine, R.A. (1984). Properties of culture: an ethnographic view. In R.A. Shweder & R.A. LeVine (Eds) *Culture Theory: Essays on Mind, Self, and Emotion* (pp. 67–87). Cambridge: Cambridge University Press.

Lieber, E., Nihira, K. & Mink, I.T. (submitted). Filial piety in Chinese immigrant parents—quantitative and qualitative evidence.

Lieber, E., Weisner, T.S. & Presley, M. (2003). EthnoNotes: an internet-based field note management tool. *Field Methods*, **15**, 405–425.

Magana, S.M. (1999). Puerto Rican families caring for an adult with mental retardation: role of familism. *American Journal on Mental Retardation*, **104**, 466–482.

Marin, G. & Gamba, R.J. (1996). A new measurement of acculturation for Hispanics: the Bidimensional Acculturation Scale for Hispanics (BAS). *Hispanic Journal of Behavioral Sciences*, **18**, 297–316.

Marin, G., Sabogal, F., Marin, B.V., Otero-Sabogal, R. & Perez-Stable, E.J. (1987). Development of a short acculturation scale for Hispanics. *Hispanic Journal of Behavioral Sciences*, **9**, 183–205.

Marsella, A.J., Murray, M.D. & Golden, C. (1974). Ethnic variations in the phenomenology of emotions. I. Shame. *Journal of Cross-Cultural Psychology*, **5**, 312–328.
McAdoo, H.P. (1995). Stress levels, family help patterns, and religiosity in middle- and working-class African-American single mothers. *Journal of Black Psychology*, **21**, 424–449.
McIntryre, L.L. & Blacher, J. (2002, June). Behavioral disorders, syndrome specificity, and family impact. Paper given at the Inaugural SID-Europe Conference, Dublin, Ireland.
McIntyre, L.L., Blacher, J. & Baker, B.L. (2002). Behavior/mental health problems in young adults with intellectual disability: the impact on families. *Journal of Intellectual Disability Research*, **46**, 239–249.
Meyers, C.E. & Blacher, J. (1982). *The Effect of Schooling the Severely Impaired Child on the Family*. National Institute of Child Health and Human Development Grant no. RO1HD1468, 1982–1985.
Meyers, C.E. & Blacher, J. (1987). Parents' perceptions of schooling for their severely handicapped child: relationships with home and family variables. *Exceptional Children*, **53**, 441–449.
Meyers, C.E., Mink, I.T. & Nihira, K. (1981). *Home Quality Rating Scale Manual*. Pomona, CA: UCLA/Neuropsychiatric Institute-Lanterman State Hospital Research Group.
Mink, I.T. (1994). *Chinese-American Fathers with Children with MR/DD*. National Institute of Child Health and Human Development Grant no. HD31856. Bethesda, MD.
Mink, I.T. (1997). Studying culturally diverse families of children with developmental disabilities. In N.W. Bray (Ed.) *International Review on Research in Mental Retardation* (pp. 75–98). Orlando, FL: Academic Press.
Mink, I.T., Blacher, J. & Nihira, K. (1988). Taxonomy of family lifestyles. III. Replication with families with severely mentally retarded children. *American Journal on Mental Retardation*, **93**, 250–264.
Mink, I.T. & Chang, D.F. (2002). What is Mental Retardation? Definitions and Attributions of Chinese-American Parents. Unpublished manuscript, University of California at Los Angeles.
Mink, I.T., Meyers, C.E. & Nihira, K. (1984). Taxonomy of family lifestyles. II. Homes with slow-learning children. *American Journal of Mental Deficiency*, **89**, 111–123.
Mink, I.T. & Nihira, K. (1986). Family lifestyles and child behaviors: a study of direction of effects. *Developmental Psychology*, **22**, 610–616.
Mink, I.T. & Nihira, K. (1987). Direction of effects: family lifestyles and behavior of TMR children. *American Journal of Mental Deficiency*, **92**, 57–64.
Mink, I.T. & Nihira, K. (1991, August). Families with developmentally delayed children: Chinese-American and Euro-American. Paper presented at the meeting of the American Psychological Association, San Francisco, CA.
Mink, I.T. & Nihira, K. (1992, September). Measuring families across cultures. Presented at the Sixth International Conference on Children at Risk, Santa Fe, NM, USA.
Mink, I.T., Nihira, K. & Meyers, C.E. (1983). Taxonomy of family lifestyles. I. Homes with TMR children. *American Journal of Mental Deficiency*, **87**, 484–497.
Moos, R.H. & Moos, B.S. (1986). *Family Environment Scale Manual* (2nd edn). Palo Alto, CA: Consulting Psychologists Press.
National Research Council (2002). *Disability Determination for Mental Retardation*. Committee on Disability Determination for Mental Retardation. D.J. Reschly, T.G. Myers & C.R. Hartel (Eds). Division of Behavioral and Social Sciences and Education. Washington, DC: National Academy Press.
Nihira, K., Mink, I.T. & Meyers, C. E. (1985). Home environment and development of slow-learning adolescents: reciprocal relations. *Developmental Psychology*, **21**, 784–794.
Nihira, K., Tomiyasu, Y. & Oshio, C. (1987). Homes of TMR children: comparison between American and Japanese families. *American Journal of Mental Deficiency*, **91**, 486–495.
Nihira, K., Weisner, T. & Bernheimer, L. (1994). Ecocultural assessment in families of children with developmentally delays: construct and concurrent validities. *American Journal of Mental Retardation*, **98**, 551–566.
Olson, D.H., Fournier, D.G. & Druckman, J.M. (1987). *Counselor's Manual for PREPARE/ENRICH* (rev. edn). Minneapolis, MN: PREPARE/ENRICH, Inc.
Olson, D.H., McCubbin, H.I., Barnes, H., Larsen, A., Muxen, M. & Wilson, M. (1986). *Family Inventories*. St Paul, MN: Family Social Sciences.

Orsmond, G.I. & Seltzer, M.M. (2000). Brothers and sisters of adults with mental retardation: gendered nature of the sibling relationship. *American Journal on Mental Retardation*, **105**, 486–508.

Patterson, J. (1996). Family research methods: issues and strategies. In C.A. Heflinger & C.T. Nixon (Eds) *Families and the Mental Health System for Children and Adolescents: Policy, Services, and Research* (pp. 117–144). Thousand Oaks, CA: Sage.

Patton, M.Q. (1990). *Qualitative Evaluation and Research Methods* (2nd edn). Newbury Park, CA: Sage.

Phares, V. (1996). *Fathers and Developmental Psychopathology*. New York: Wiley.

Phillips, M.R., West, C.L., Shen, Q. & Zheng, Y. (1998). Comparison of schizophrenic patients' families and normal families in China, using Chinese versions of FACES-II and the Family Environment Scales. *Family Process*, **37**, 95–106.

Radloff, L. (1977). The CES-D scale: a self-report depression scale for research in the general population. *Applied Psychological Measurement*, **1**, 385–401.

Reiss, S. (1994). *Reiss Screen for Maladaptive Behavior: Test Manual* (2nd edn). Columbus, OH: IDS Publishing.

Rogers-Dulan, J. & Blacher, J. (1995). African-American families, religion, and disability: a conceptual framework. *Mental Retardation*, **33**, 226–238.

Rousey, A.M., Wild, M. & Blacher, J. (2002). Stability of measures of the home environment for families of children with severe disabilities. *Research in Developmental Disabilties*, **23**, 17–35.

Russell, C.W. (1980). A methodological study of family cohesion and adaptability. *Journal of Marital and Family Therapy*, **6**, 459–470.

Rutter, M. (1967). A children's behaviour questionnaire for completion by teachers: preliminary findings. *Journal of Child Psychology and Psychiatry*, **8**, 1–11.

Schalock, R.L. & Keith, K.D. (1993). *Quality of Life Questionnaire Manual.* Columbus, OH: IDS Publishing.

Schonell, F.J. & Watts, B.H. (1956). First survey of the effects of a subnormal child on the family unit. *American Journal of Mental Deficiency*, **61**, 210–219.

Schwartz, S.H. (1994). Beyond individualism/collectivism: new cultural dimensions of values. In U. Kim, H.C. Triandis, C. Kagitcibasi, S.C. Choi & G. Yoon (Eds) *Individualism and Collectivism: Theory, Method and Applications* (pp. 85–119). Thousand Oaks, CA: Sage.

Seltzer, M.M. & Heller, T. (1997). Families and caregiving across the life course: research advances on the influence of context. *Family Relations*, **46**, 321–323.

Seltzer, M.S. & Krauss, M.W. (1989). Aging parents with adult mentally retarded children: family risk factors and social support. *American Journal on Mental Retardation*, **94**, 303–312.

Shaffer, D., Fisher, P.W. & Lucas, C.P. (1999). Respondent-based interviews. In D. Shaffer, C.P. Lucas & J.E. Richters (Eds) *Diagnostic Assessment in Child and Adolescent Psychopathology* (pp. 3–33). New York: Guilford.

Shaffer, D., Lucas, C.P. & Richters. J.E. (Eds) (1999) *Diagnostic Assessment in Child and Adolescent Psychopathology*. New York: Guilford.

Shweder, R.A. (1986). Divergent realities. In D.A. Fiske & R.A. Shweder (Eds) *Metatheory in Social Science: Pluralisms and Subjectivities* (pp. 163–196). Chicago: University of Chicago Press.

Simmerman, S., Blacher, J. & Baker, B.L. (2001). Fathers' and mothers' perceptions of father involvement in families with young children with disability. *Journal of Intellectual and Developmental Disability*, **26**, 325–338.

Spanier, G.B. (1976). Measuring dyadic adjustment: new scales for assessing quality of marriage and similar dyads. *Journal of Marriage and Family Therapy*, **38**, 15–28.

Sparrow, S., Balla, D. & Cicchetti, D. (1984). *Vineland Adaptive Behavior Scales*. Circle Pines, MN: American Guidance Service.

Suinn, R.M., Ahuna, C. & Khoo, G. (1992). The Suinn-Lew Asian Self-Identity Acculturation Scale: concurrent and factorial validation. *Educational and Psychological Measurement*, **52**, 1041–1046.

Suinn, R.M., Rickard-Figueroa, K., Lew, S. & Vigil, P. (1987). The Suinn-Lew Self-Identity Acculturation Scale: an initial report. *Education and Psychological Measurement*, **47**, 401–407.

Tanaka, J.S., Ebreo, A., Linn, N. & Morera, O.F. (1998). Research methods: the construct validity of self-identity and its psychological implications. In L.C. Lee & N.W.S. Zane (Eds) *Handbook of Asian American Psychology* (pp. 21–79). Thousand Oaks, CA: Sage.

Touliatos, B.F., Perlmutter, B.F. & Strauss, M.A. (Eds) (2001). *Handbook of Family Measurement Techniques*. Thousand Oaks, CA: Sage.

Triandis, H.C. (1994). Major cultural syndromes and emotion. In S. Kitayama & H.R. Markus (Eds) *Emotion and Culture: Empirical Studies of Mutual Influence* (pp. 285–306). Washington, DC: American Psychological Association.

Turnbull, A.P., Patterson, J.M., Behr, S.K., Murphy, D.L., Marquis, J.G. & Blue-Banning, M.J. (1993). *Cognitive Coping, Families, and Disability.* Baltimore, MD: Brookes.

Walker, B. & Singer, G.H.S. (1993). Improving collaborative communication between professionals and parents. In G.H.S. Singer & L.E. Powers (Eds) *Families, Disability, and Empowerment* (pp. 285–315). Baltimore, MD: Brookes.

Wardell, W. (1952). The mentally retarded in family and community. *American Journal of Mental Deficiency*, **57**, 229–242.

Weisner, T.S., Coots, J.J., Bernheimer, L.P. & Arzubiaga, A. (1997). *The Ecocultural Family Interview Manual* (available from the Ecocultural Scale Project, Center for Culture and Health, Department of Psychiatry and Biobehavioral Science, UCLA, Los Angeles, CA 90024-1758).

Weisner, T.S. & Gallimore, R.G. (1994). Ecocultural studies of families adapting to childhood developmental delays: unique features, defining differences, and applied implications. In M. Leskinen (Ed.) *Family in Focus. New Perspectives on Early Childhood Special Education* (pp. 11–25). Jyvaskyla, Finland: University of Jyvaskyla.

Yang, K.-S. (1986). Chinese personality and its change. In M.H. Bond (Ed.) *The Psychology of the Chinese People* (pp. 106–170). Hong Kong: Oxford University Press.

Zarit, S., Reever, K. & Bach-Peterson, J. (1980). Relatives of the impaired elderly: correlates of feelings of burden. *Gerontologist*, **20**, 649–655.

CHAPTER 7

Participant Observation and Research on Intellectual Disabilities

Michael V. Angrosino
University of South Florida, USA

INTRODUCTION

This essay reviews participant-observation research, with particular attention to studies of people with intellectual disabilities.[1] Participant observation is not itself a data-collection technique; it is better understood as the context in which data collection can be conducted. Several selected studies will be reviewed to illustrate major genres of participant-observation research applied to people with mental retardation, in preference to a broad overview of the entire literature. Current concerns of scholars engaged in participant-observation research in the field of intellectual disabilities will be assessed.

Definitional Issues

Social scientists observe human activities and their physical settings in a presumably organized and objective manner. When they do so in *natural* (as opposed to laboratory or clinical) contexts, it is expected that they participate in those activities, the better to achieve rapport and approximate the insiders' perspective. The natural setting may be referred to as the *field* of research, and the process of conducting such research as *fieldwork*. The delicate balance between objective observation of and subjective immersion in the lifeways of a selected community is known as *participant observation*. According to Schensul, Schensul and LeCompte (1999, p. 91), "participant observation refers to a process of learning through exposure to or involvement in the day-to-day or routine activities of participants in the research settings", and it may be thought of as the starting point of ethnographic research.

[1] In this paper, the term "intellectual disabilities" will be treated as synonymous with "mental retardation", and the two will be used interchangeably, even though, in other contexts, there are recognized nuances of difference. It is my preference to refer to "people with mental retardation", or "people with intellectual disabilities", rather than to "mentally retarded people" or "intellectually disabled people", so that the people, rather than their condition, come first in their identification.

The International Handbook of Applied Research in Intellectual Disabilities. Edited by E. Emerson, C. Hatton, T. Thompson and T.R. Parmenter ISBN 0-471-49709-6.

In the ideal, therefore, participant observation helps fieldworkers identify and build relationships, understand how material objects and social relationships in the community are arranged, and discern the principles by which decisions are made. The approach is as much intuitive as intellectual. Adopting the stance of participant observation validates the presence of the researcher in the community, and provides him/her with cultural experiences that can be discussed in greater depth in interviews or surveys conducted in the course of the project. Participant observation may also give the researcher privileged access to events or other situations to which ordinary outsiders might not be invited.

The degree to which participation is feasible depends largely on the setting of research, some cultures being more receptive than others to the active presence of strangers in their midst. It also depends on the nature of the research question: a project that aims to produce a complete ethnography of a community requires a near-total experience of that community's daily round of life, while one that focuses on a particular group within that larger community, or on a particular event, may be conducted by a researcher who is not a full-time resident. In some public settings, the researcher may participate merely by accompanying local people, making unobtrusive observations, and asking general questions. In private or otherwise privileged settings, he/she must earn the right to exhibit more active involvement as a prelude to being allowed to do more structured, systematic observations and interviews. Some researchers endeavor to insert themselves into a community by making themselves useful (for example, minding children, helping to procure food, or driving people around) as a way of reinforcing their right to be included when other community activities are conducted.

Above all, participant observation demands *time*; one cannot successfully immerse oneself in a social setting, and achieve the degree of rapport described above, without committing oneself to an extended period of fieldwork. In traditional anthropological fieldwork, the researcher was expected to spend at least a year in the field, on the assumption that most significant events in the life of a community come around on a roughly annual cycle. Such an extended stay may, in fact, not be possible due to financial or other constraints; a variety of "rapid ethnographic" techniques have been devised to accommodate shortened time frames (Ervin, 2000, pp. 188–198), although even a rapid ethnographer is still expected to be more than a visiting outsider.

Once participation has secured the researcher a more or less trusted place in the community, it becomes possible to conduct detailed observations. Observation in the field is not a haphazard process, although it may seem so in the beginning (Fetterman, 1998, p. 35). Werner and Schoepfle (1987, pp. 262–264) suggest a three-step approach in which research begins with the fieldworker taking in great amounts of undigested information as he/she gets oriented to the setting. This stage of "descriptive observation" requires the researcher to adopt a childlike pose, knowing nothing and taking nothing for granted. In this early stage of fieldwork, it is necessary to document observations carefully and accurately, using concrete descriptive detail rather than categorical, inferential, or value-laden terminology (for example, "The people in the meeting tent were singing and jumping up and down", rather than "The people in the meeting tent were going wild with religious fervor"). Over time, repeated observations permit the researcher to discern patterns and layers of meaning in specific items, behavioral acts, relationships, and events.

As the project progresses, the researcher moves on to "focused observation", in which certain things, deemed irrelevant, can be ignored. Focused observation necessarily involves interviewing, since relevance is determined by a compromise between that which is salient to the researcher's own theoretical and methodological interests and that which local people consider to be important. Focused observation typically concentrates on well-defined types of group activities (such as religious rituals, with an emphasis on material content and personnel). Finally, there is the most systematic stage of research, "selective observation", in which the participant observer concentrates on the attributes of different types of activities (for example, what does this ritual *mean* to those who take part?). Doing so, however, requires that the researcher asks culturally appropriate questions—a sensitivity that can come only after a period of immersion in that culture.

Participant observation is "not really a method at all" (Bernard, 1988, p. 150). It is, rather, a strategy that facilitates a variety of data-collection techniques in the field, in part because it reduces the problem of people changing their behavior because they know they are the objects of study by an obtrusive stranger. The less "reactivity" there is in a field setting, the more valid the resulting data are likely to be. Since participant observation is a foundation for other field methods, it is important to develop a set of skills, insofar as one does not automatically become an effective participant observer simply by showing up and hanging out. The most important of these skills include:

(1) learning the local language (which may not be technically a foreign language—it could be just a different jargon that distinguishes members of an in-group from outsiders)
(2) building "explicit awareness" (Spradley, 1980, p. 55) of the minute details of ordinary life that we generally gloss over
(3) building memory, which is especially important when reconstructing an event, since participant observers, as opposed to outsider observers, may not be in a position to take notes on the spot
(4) maintaining naiveté, so that one does not become a total insider who is apt to take too much for granted.

Bernard (1988, p. 160) also emphasizes developing one's skills as a writer, since good participant observation depends on making highly detailed notes, and then being able to weave a reasonable analysis (narrative or quantified) from them.

THE EVOLUTION OF A PERSPECTIVE

Although participant observation, by definition, requires some subjectivity in fieldwork, its practitioners have long insisted on scientific rigor (Stocking, 1983, p. 8). Failure to give objectivity the upper hand might mean that the researcher had "gone native", rendering his/her work suspect as data (Pelto & Pelto, 1978, p. 69). Indeed, without objectivity, one would not be a "social *scientist*". Because we privilege eyewitness testimony, it is very important for social scientists to be able to hold such testimony to the most exacting standards. Observation must therefore rest on "something researchers can find constant" (Adler & Adler, 1994, p. 389), which means "their own direct knowledge".

Participant observers have usually been aware that their mere presence can change the situations they are trying to understand. But they have, at the same time, believed that it is both possible and desirable to develop standardized procedures that can, in the words of Gold (1997, p. 397),

> maximize observational efficacy, minimize investigator bias, and allow for replication and/or verification to check out the degree to which these procedures have enabled the investigator to produce valid, reliable data that, when incorporated into his or her published reports, will be regarded by peers as objective findings.

Several influential commentaries on social research (Kirk & Miller, 1986; Bernard 1988; Silverman, 1993; Altheide & Johnson, 1994; Miles & Huberman 1994) have, in fact, been dedicated in part or in sum to the task of clarifying and refining those standardized procedures. One of the hallmarks of scientific fieldwork is that multiple data-collection techniques are employed whenever feasible so that the bias in any one of them might be averaged out. Participant observation as a source of eyewitness testimony has been seen as the ultimate reality check on "all the other, more refined, research techniques" (Pelto & Pelto, 1978, p. 69). Moreover, social scientists have believed that the quality of what is *recorded* is the appropriate measure of usable data derived from participant observation (because it can be monitored and replicated), rather than the quality of the observation itself (which is, by definition, idiosyncratic and not subject to replication) (Werner & Schoepfle, 1987, p. 259).

These positivistic assumptions have been called into question by a variety of scholars, often lumped together as "postmodernists". Most postmodernist critics share the conviction that a fieldworker's "situation" (such as his or her gender, socioeconomic class, ethnicity, or sexual orientation) must always be taken into account in evaluating what purports to be eyewitness testimony. In other words, there can never be a completely (or even nearly) objective account of a people and its way of life; ethnography is inevitably the record of the encounter of a particular researcher with a particular community at a particular point in time. In its most radical form, this point of view implies that any research based on participant-observation fieldwork is a species of autobiography, and not an objective record of a way of life that transcends the specific encounter that produces it. In effect, the objective facts about a society or its culture can never be firmly established, since different people conducting observations at different points in time will inevitably produce accounts that reflect their own situations. Reality is always contested, never firmly established. According to Marcus (1997, p. 92), the published result of fieldwork based on participant observation, far from being the ultimate validation of data, "is never reducible to a form of knowledge that can be packaged in the monologic voice of the ethnographer alone".

Participant observation was once thought of as a part of a continuum of data-collection techniques that as a whole defined ethnographic methodology. It is now more likely to be thought of as a context in which the researcher's personal characteristics can be played out in dialogue with those being studied (see Angrosino & Mays de Pérez, 2000, for a critical analysis of this shift). In this redefined context, the people under study are no longer "subjects" but "collaborators", since the resulting ethnographic report is ideally a joint effort of the researcher and those in whose lives he/she participates. Regardless of where one stands on this evolving dichotomy, researchers who are participant observers tend to agree that it entails more than research—it is almost a philosophy of life. According to Bohannan (1992, p. 41),

> [A researcher] who does fieldwork learns culture twice. We can apply the same principles to our own journey through life—to participate actively in that journey as opposed to passively absorbing whatever comes our way. We can begin by looking carefully at

what goes on around us. What is that person telling me? What in my own training and experience makes it difficult for me to understand what is going on? You begin to see all around you the interplay of culture and character, of differentness, of discourse. You see with a new awareness. "Fieldwork", once you become familiar with it, becomes a way of life, a sort of sixth sense that broadens you as you respond to any environment, familiar or strange. Ultimately, you are never out of the field, no matter where you go.

PARTICIPANT OBSERVATION AND THE STUDY OF PEOPLE WITH MENTAL RETARDATION

Neither positivistic nor postmodern participant observation has been a common feature in the research about, for, or with people with mental retardation. The traditional practitioners of participant-observation research were cultural and social anthropologists, who left the study of people with mental retardation to clinical psychologists or special educators, whose methodological toolkits did not, until relatively late in the day, include participant observation. Moreover, it is difficult to immerse oneself in the day-to-day lives of people with mental retardation in the same way that one could enter into the cognitive and affective space of "normal", albeit "exotic", people. As a result, participant observation, if adopted at all, was likely to be conducted among professional and clinical staff, domestic caregivers, or public advocates, groups that were believed to "speak for" the supposedly inarticulate client population.

Nevertheless, several important studies demonstrate the feasibility and desirability of participant observation among people with mental retardation—not just in the professional spaces that impinge on their lives. They also illustrate different approaches to the understanding of the nature and function of participant observation itself.

The Traditional Ethnographic Approach

Participant observation historically developed in tandem with the ethnographic method, the aim of which was to provide as complete as possible a description of a people and its way of life. It is certainly possible to use specific ethnographic methods for more limited research purposes, but the classic ethnography aimed at the comprehensive and holistic treatment of a living community. Such an approach would be meaningful when studying people with intellectual disabilities only when such people actually live in community with one another, as in the pioneering ethnographic study of Geel, Europe's first "therapeutic community" (Roosens, 1979).

Since the thirteenth century, residents of the town of Geel in Belgium have taken in boarders with mental disabilities, who participate fully in the life of the town. The practice began because of the town's proximity to a shrine dedicated to St Dympna, a princess who, according to legend, resisted unto death her father's insanely incestuous demands. In medieval times, she was venerated as the patroness of the "senseless". Since madness was then believed to be the work of evil spirits, exorcisms were performed at her shrine, and the town opened its doors to the pilgrims who came seeking relief. Although exorcisms are no longer officially performed, the town has continued to cherish its status as a haven for the "senseless", and at the time of Roosens' study, some 1300 intellectually disabled and otherwise mentally disordered people from institutions in various parts of Belgium were living in Geel, a town with a total population of about 30 000.[2]

The research in Geel involved extensive participant observation conducted by two psychologists, an anthropologist, and a sociologist. The latter was a native of Geel, and one of the psychologists had lived there for many years with his family. They concentrated on public spaces, including "106 visits to 43 of the 143 bars of Geel" (Roosens, 1979, p. 62). The overall aim of the study was to ascertain the "crystallized average behavior and norms in the Geel system of caring" (1979, p. 65) with particular emphasis on the interactions between the people of Geel and their boarders outside the context of the host families. A purely clinical study might have charted changes in various standardized indices of patients' mental functioning, but would have missed the larger social context in which those changes were played out. It was in providing a descriptive account of the totality of life in Geel, as it encompasses both hosts and boarders, that participant observation proved its worth.

Roosens (1979, p. 189) concludes that there are significant therapeutic benefits to bringing intellectually disabled people into regular contact with "normal" people (other than clinical professionals). He points out that the benefits accrue not only to the patients themselves but also to the townspeople, who have learned to become tolerant of difference. It is not so much that the people of Geel no longer see the differences (in fact, they are quite clear about what constitutes "normal" and "abnormal" behavior); but they no longer, as a group, feel threatened by the "abnormal", and, furthermore, are able to make fairly sophisticated judgments about "good" and "bad" abnormal behavior (the latter being essentially that of people who constitute a danger to themselves or to others, which is a nearly universally recognized criterion for involuntary commitment). Since a therapeutic community is, by definition, a kind of partnership between those with disabilities and those considered mainstream, participant observation in the town itself—as opposed to the tracking of individual patients—allowed the research team to understand what makes such communities work.

Another important example of a holistic study in the participant-observation tradition is Evans' (1983) ethnography of the New Morning School, a "special" school for "mentally handicapped" students that is geographically isolated from schools for "normal" students in the same district.[3] Evans, a sociologist, chose a participant-observation approach because he believed that it could enhance our understanding of the "distant provinces of our social web of interdependency" (1983, p. 3). In other words, although the USA is huge and extremely diverse, all of the "small worlds" that make up the larger whole affect each other both

[2] The Geel model inspired a limited vogue for "therapeutic communities" in the 1970s and 1980s—the golden age of "deinstitutionalization". Perhaps its most enduring offshoot is the international network of L'Arche communities (Vanier, 1979; Daybreak International, 1981), where people with mental retardation and "normal" companions live together in small cooperatives. The main difference is that the L'Arche communities are deliberately founded for that purpose and have no official connection to the larger towns or cities in which they are located, whereas Geel was, and is, a town in its own right. Moreover, historically, Geel has never made a clear-cut distinction between those with mental retardation and those with psychiatric illness, whereas L'Arche is designed specifically for those with retardation.

[3] Evans is describing a setting, prevalent while he was conducting research in the 1970s, that has largely disappeared in the USA. By the time his book was published in the early 1980s, the Education for All Handicapped Children Act of 1975 had been widely implemented. This legislation mandated that a child with mental handicaps be educated in the "least restrictive environment", which, for all intents and purposes, has meant "mainstreaming" them whenever feasible in the same schools (and even, in many cases, in the same classrooms) attended by "normal" children.

directly and indirectly. It would obviously be impossible to conduct an ethnography of the USA as a whole; but one can study the "small worlds" that are its component parts, and, through them, get a sense of the whole. Fieldwork allowed Evans to go beyond the "thumbnail sketches" of the popular media; it "aims at demystifying small worlds everyone probably knows about, but does not really know" (1983, p. 3).

Although centered in a school, Evans' research ultimately took him into the homes and workplaces of the students. He interacted not only with the students and their teachers, but also with their parents, siblings, employers, friends, "and all manner of other advocates, hangers-on, and adversaries" (1983, p. 3). He describes the various ways in which people with mental retardation are educated, how they earn their livings, where they live, how they relate to families and significant others, and how they interface with various health and human service systems. He was primarily interested in learning how people with mental retardation form and sustain relationships and how they both affect and are affected by society at large. Unlike the Geel researchers, who had entrée into the community because of long-standing ties of kinship and residence, Evans began his participant observation as a complete outsider. So he began by explaining his intentions to the nonhandicapped "gatekeepers", who seem to have been remarkably open to the idea of having him just "watch what was going on" (1983, p. 4). His "just watching" quickly evolved into active participation, to the extent that he eventually was asked to serve on local boards of directors of agencies that served clients with mental handicaps; he was even recruited to serve on a statewide task force responsible for planning services. He expresses some misgivings about becoming "too earnest" in his role as an advocate, fearing that in the process he had broken some of the cardinal rules of scientific detachment; he nevertheless concludes that "although I played fast and loose with bias, it is my belief that the scope of the work was broadened" (1983, p. 4). Evans considers his fieldwork to be an ongoing experience—his involvement with the specific agencies and their clients continued for many years beyond the official end of the research project.

Evans' richly detailed monograph demonstrates a point that we may nowadays take for granted, but that was probably new to many scholars three decades ago, and that is probably still not widely grasped by the public at large: people with mental retardation are not a uniform group who can be pigeon-holed by their clinical label. They are, in fact, as diverse as any population with regard to behaviors, attitudes, abilities, preferences, and personality types. Moreover, their cognitive deficits limit in some ways, but do not prevent their interaction with members of the "mainstream". The presentation of the members of this "small world" in all their human diversity is a direct result of Evans' participant observation. It is clear that had he focused on the clinical diagnoses that were common to all, and not on their lived experience in both sheltered and nonsheltered environments, he would never have been able to document this diversity so persuasively.

The Case Approach

More common and influential than holistic ethnographies of settings in which people with mental retardation live are participant-observation studies conducted in a case-focused rather than a community-focused design. The standard for this genre of research has long been set by the Socio-Behavioral Group at the Mental Retardation Research Center at the

University of California at Los Angeles, a joint effort of the departments of anthropology and psychiatry, founded by Robert Edgerton.

Edgerton's own research began in the 1960s, at the very dawn of deinstitutionalization, when he followed a group of adults with mental retardation who had been discharged from a state institution and who were taking their first tentative steps to adjust to life in the community beyond the hospital walls. His classic monograph, *The Cloak of Competence*, details "the ways in which mentally retarded persons manage their lives and perceive themselves when left to their own devices in a large city" (1967, p. 9). Their condition (or, at least, the label) is of central importance in delineating the research population, but Edgerton's approach is not at all clinical, since he is concerned neither with the etiology nor with the treatment of their condition. Rather, his aim was to follow the people so labeled to see what they made of "real life". He was therefore a participant observer in their several and diverse lives, albeit not in a single, bounded community.

Edgerton and his research associates candidly told the study participants that they were part of a research project, but they also made it clear that they were not clinical staff and that nothing they learned would be used to send anyone back to the hospital. The researchers conducted semistructured interviews and accompanied their subjects as they went about their daily lives—shopping, sightseeing, going on social visits, doing housework, and joining in recreational activities. The researchers found that establishing rapport was relatively easy once they became part of the mundane round of life; they found terminating relationships to be more of a problem for, like Evans, they had been drawn into long-term commitments that extended beyond the boundaries of pure research.

The Socio-Behavioral Group defined two key components to its approach (Edgerton, 1984, p. 2). First, the lives of people with mental retardation are to be studied in their entirety; even in the absence of a community as such, the individual subjects are to be observed in every facet of their daily lives. Second, the lives of such people—like those of anyone else—are subject to various environmental demands; as those demands change, so do the people adapt. Their lives are not fixed clinical entities, but always works in process. Representative monographs in the case-approach style by members of the Socio-Behavioral Group include those by Kernan, Turner, Langness and Edgerton (1978), Koegel (1978), Whittemore and Koegel (1978), Whittemore, Koegel and Langness (1980), Mink, Meyers and Nihira (1981), and Sabsay and Platt (1985).[4]

Edgerton (1984, p. 2) is critical of that genre of research that looks at the community adaptation of people with mental retardation mainly in terms of "prognostic variables", readily quantifiable measures of success. This approach, he believes, ignores the possibility that success is a "multiplex process marked by change and contradiction" (1984, p. 2). The Socio-Behavioral Group therefore prefers a methodology based on three fundamental principles: that phenomena be seen in their relevant context; that these phenomena be seen not only through the observer's eyes, but those of the subjects as well; and that reactive procedures be avoided at the same time that investigators regard themselves as part of the phenomenon under investigation (Edgerton & Langness, 1978). This strategy, which Edgerton (1984, p. 3) terms "ethnographic naturalism", is predicated on prolonged contact with people. The researcher becomes a "natural" part of the lives of those people; since

[4] The Socio-Behavioral Group has also produced some studies that fit more nearly into the traditional ethnographic model, in which participant observation was carried out in defined settings. See, for example, Turner (1982) and Platt (1984). See Brenneis (1982) for a conceptual discussion of the two ways in which both individualized cases and localized settings have been used by the group members.

he/she is not, by any ordinary definition, a natural part of the subjects' lives, he/she must achieve that status through sustained participant observation. By virtue of that prolonged presence in the lives of their subjects, the researchers hope to be able to see more than the obvious. Edgerton (1984, p. 3) describes the process as follows:

> We attend important events in the lives of the people (and their parents, caretakers, and friends), going to weddings, family gatherings, or weekend outings, and we introduce them to new recreational experiences. We videotape some of these encounters so that we and the participants themselves can discuss and interpret the behavior that took place (we also erase these videotapes if the people find anything in them that is objectionable).

The Normative Ethnographic Approach

Participant-observation research among people with mental retardation in the era of deinstitutionalization and normalization, whether it follows the model of the traditional holistic ethnography in a defined community or that of the individualized case cohort, runs the paradoxical risk of dehumanizing mainstream culture even as it humanizes the people with intellectual disabilities. That is, the ethnographic approaches discussed above document the lives of people with mental retardation in rich detail, but implicitly assume that we already know enough about the "mainstream" culture into which deinstitutionalized people have been inserted. To deal with this imbalance, which tends to paint the mainstream as a monolith of normality, some researchers have reversed the process by first conducting a thorough participant-observation ethnography of a selected mainstream community, and only then exploring the lives of people with mental retardation within that community.

For example, Devlieger (1998, p. 55) bases his research on a "simple proposition", namely, "To understand the people [with mental disabilities], we need first to understand Americans and their culture." The people in his study population had all lived in similar environments in small towns in the US Midwest, and all deal in one way or another with a core aspect of American culture and identity: a perception of "the vastness of the country, and the capacity to overcome the inconvenience of *not* being able to master this vastness" (1998, p. 57). It is important for Americans to see themselves as in control, as making things happen, and to have things happen quickly and efficiently. People with mental retardation who are less than capable of acting in such a manner (or who are unable even to conceive of themselves acting in such a manner) are well and truly disabled, in ways that would not be salient in cultures that tend to see individuals as relatively passive pawns of fate. These ideas are explored ethnographically in Devlieger's doctoral dissertation (1995). In a similar vein, van Maastricht (1998) compares and contrasts two European societies, Greece and Wales. She discovered that Greek culture (unlike the American culture discussed by Devlieger with its apparent certitude about what a "real American" is supposed to be like, and unlike the Welsh, with its rather formal, vestigially hierarchical class structure) is disinclined to make sweeping categorical judgments, and even a matter such as "incompetence" is evaluated on an ad hoc basis. Persons may be excluded from certain activities, but included in others, with decisions reflecting the relatively fluid, informal nature of economic opportunities in a still largely rural society. The Greek villagers studied by van Maastricht believe that a successful adult is one who can contribute to the upkeep of his or her family and who, if at all possible, marries and starts a family of his/her own. Such goals are not beyond the reach of people with intellectual disabilities. It is ironic, van Maastricht (1998, p. 152) notes, that "in a country where formal interest in, and care of, incompetent people is minimal, incompetent people, because of local social and economic structures and a different model of competence, do have a chance to be a part of their society".

Implying that we label as mentally deficient those who are merely socially inappropriate, Whyte (1997) takes a similar tack in her studies in East Africa. She demonstrates that it is quite possible for people who would be considered to have mental retardation, were they evaluated in the USA or Western Europe, to be fully functioning members in local families and neighborhoods. In the communities she studied, the people who were kept at arm's distance were those who were considered disruptive troublemakers (often heavy drinkers); their IQs were not a consideration.

Nuttall (1992) captures a society in transition in his ethnography of Greenland. The skills needed for survival as a hunter in the traditional economy (which include learning about and understanding the extensively ramified network of kinship) are quite different from those required in a modern state, where one is expected to be formally "employed". Contemporary authorities in Greenland (which achieved home rule from Denmark in 1979) insist that the country must develop, and that this requires formal education according to the standard European model. That educational process, however, inevitably sets up categories of competence and incompetence in areas that the traditional culture did not even recognize. Vestiges of the traditional culture survive in isolated villages such as the one that was the center of Nuttall's participant observation. In that community, modern education is scorned as irrelevant, indeed harmful, as children stuck in school are unable to learn how to hunt and fish. It is further interesting to note that even in the traditional village, the incompetent person (that is, someone who, for whatever reason, is not a successful hunter) is not ostracized, but is taken care of by relatives. One retains one's full social personhood despite deficiencies in the ability to function in an acceptable adult manner.

These "normative" ethnographies demonstrate quite clearly that the diversity in life experiences exhibited by people with mental retardation is a factor of culture (rather than of organic, clinical deficits). The research in this genre suggests that if we want to understand the conditions of people with mental retardation, we do well to begin with as complete as possible an ethnographic description of the culture that shapes their lives. In other words, participant observation among people with mental retardation can and should also include participant observation in the larger community.[5]

An Alternative Approach

In recent years, "alternative" approaches to ethnographic research have come to prominence, in part the result of the postmodernist critique that has called the authority of the ethnographer into question. The traditional notion that participant observation allowed the researcher to capture objective reality through subjective immersion in the lives of others is now very much in doubt. Ethnography is now apt to be seen as the text recording a specific encounter between a particular researcher and a given group of people at a definite

[5] The Roosens study (1979) dealt with Geel as a whole, but always through the lens of the "boarders" with mental disabilities. There was no attempt, analogous to those described in this section, to describe traditional provincial Belgian culture—only the ways in which the "normal" townspeople interacted with their guests.

moment in time, rather than as a straightforward account of a timeless and verifiably factual truth. Denzin and Lincoln (2000, p. 3) define the "postmodern moment" by a concern for literary and rhetorical tropes and a turn to narrative ("storytelling") that goes hand in hand with a refusal to privilege any one method or theory (for examples, see Ellis & Bochner, 1996).

There is an obvious, albeit implicit association of studies of people with mental retardation with clinical and public policy concerns that would seem inappropriate for "alternative" styles of reporting. After all, clinical judgments and the formulation of public policy are both based on the presumed authority of the researcher and on the factuality of the situations and events being described and analyzed. This assumption, however, is in need of some modification.

My own research, for example, was moved in an alternative direction in part by an offhand comment by Edgerton (1984, p. 3), who, in describing the efforts of the Socio-Behavioral Group, remarked:

> Our procedures do not "break down" all deception (efforts to deceive are, after all, part of the reality we hope to study) nor do they reduce the complexities of human life to a clear and simple truth. However, they do lessen the likelihood that . . . the contradictory complexity of a human life—even a retarded life—will be seen as simple and straightforward. The method is not intended to provide simple answers; instead, it is intended to provide the grounds for rejecting simple answers in favor of more full and accurate understanding.

Like members of the Socio-Behavioral Group, I was using the life-history method (Frank, 1978) as a way to illuminate the individual experiences of the deinstitutionalized "dually diagnosed"[6] adults among whom I was conducting participant observation. But I had grown frustrated with the imprecision of the resulting data. My subjects either could not or would not tell a straightforward story. I was emotionally prepared to forgive the lapses that obviously resulted from cognitive deficits, but I was at a loss as to how to deal with what were just as clearly deliberate deceptions. Edgerton's comments suggested that it might not be necessary to scrap the data just because they could not be held up as objectively verifiable facts in the scientific sense. Indeed, lying is a social act; it implies that the deceiver and the deceived are working within the same narrative/communicative frame of reference. Over the course of nearly two decades of sustained participant observation in the community I have called "Opportunity House",[7] I have increasingly focused on the form of the stories the people have shared with me, rather than on the manifest content thereof. I have become convinced that even people who have difficulty (deliberate or otherwise) in communicating information on the superficial level are still conveying a great deal of information at the level of *how* they tell their stories (see Kernan & Sabsay, 1979; Angrosino, 1992, for a fuller treatment of the semantics of "retarded" discourse).

Like Evans, I moved from being someone just hanging out at the agency to one who was drawn into the life of the program and its clients. Like him, I was recruited for boards of directors of several other programs serving clients with intellectual disabilities. My most productive area of participation, however, was as a classroom volunteer. Opportunity House

[6] This designation refers to those who have been diagnosed with both mental retardation and chronic mental illness. When I began my research, there was only one agency in my region that served this population, and it became the focus of my participant observation.

[7] While based on the original agency noted above, "Opportunity House" as it appears in my published work is a composite of the programs and agencies in several states where I have done comparative ethnography over the years.

provided, among other services, adult special education classes, where basic academic skills (as well as "life skills") were taught by a certified instructor provided by the county school system. As I assisted the students with their daily lessons on a one-to-one basis, I became increasingly familiar with them as individuals, as well as with the world they inhabited. It was rarely practical to conduct formal interviews as a traditional ethnographer might understand that method. But we were constantly sharing stories. The very act of doing so with a sympathetic other (even one you were attempting to deceive just to see whether you *could*) had unintended therapeutic consequences. It also gave me insight into what I have come to see as the great unmet programmatic need in the range of services offered to clients with mental retardation: sexuality training. (See Angrosino & Zagnoli, 1992; Angrosino, 1997, for a fuller treatment of the development of a sexuality education policy for adults with mental disabilities.) I believe that because I was able to convey my impressions in the form of fictionalized stories (Angrosino, 1998) that linked up with common experience—as opposed to the expected charts and graphs of a standard positivistic presentation—I had more impact on policy makers and therapists than might otherwise have been expected from a "postmodern" or "alternative" genre.

An even more autobiographical example of the "postmodern moment" is Ronai's (1996) account of growing up with a mentally retarded mother. Ronai, a sociologist, essentially treats herself as a participant observer of her own life. But rather than present her memoirs as if they were a species of objective historical truth (the traditional stance of the autobiographer), she deliberately fractures the narrative into anecdotal shards, offering them as stories without formal scholarly analysis. Like a traditional participant observer, Ronai takes us into the world inhabited by people with mental retardation (and those whose lives they affect), and allows her subject to speak in her own words; what is missing is the overlay of the academic's authoritative voice. What gives Ronai authority in this case is the fact that she was there (as a decidedly intimate participant observer), not that she is a trained social scientist. And what makes us pay attention is the compelling nature of her narrative, not her ability to marshal objective statistics.

ISSUES AND PROSPECTS

As noted earlier, participant observation is less a data-collection technique than a strategy for conducting research in naturalistic settings; it is a platform on which data collection by other, more specific methods can be conducted. Nevertheless, some issues may be suggested for the consideration of those interested in using participant observation as the basis for their other data-collection techniques.

First, participant observation is a strategy for naturalistic inquiry in the field. It requires the researcher to have the time (and other resources) to spend on the research project, and to be prepared to spend a good part of that time simply establishing rapport rather than in the conduct of "productive" data collection. This stipulation would suggest that for researchers interested in studying people with mental retardation, a "field" be selected that allows for intensive and long-term immersion. Group homes, sheltered workshops, classrooms, supervised apartments, and the like are the obvious venues for such research. Much contemporary ethnography has been explicitly decoupled from geographic locale (e.g., Gupta & Ferguson, 1996); in the age of cybercommunication, people no longer need to be in face-to-face contact with one another in order to constitute a meaningful community.

This shift, however, is not entirely feasible when working with those with intellectual disabilities, since the likelihood of their surviving at large and disconnected in a larger society is not great. Even if a researcher is, like Edgerton, particularly interested in those who have established more or less independent lives, it is probably a good idea to use as a base of operations one of the agencies that anchor their scattered clients. Doing so has the disadvantage of identifying the researcher with that agency, and its staff and programs, which, depending on circumstances, may or may not be desirable. It also has the disadvantage of immediately labeling the study population in terms of its client status. Those drawbacks must therefore be balanced on a case-by-case basis by the difficulties inherent in locating a sufficiently large study population without beginning with a site with an identifiable clientele.

Second, participant observation is predicated on an important philosophical assumption with very real methodological implications—that it is both desirable and feasible to seek the "insider" perspective. Participant-observation research has not always been a reasonable option for those studying intellectual disability, since the people identified as having that condition were believed to be incapable of speaking for themselves or of forming anything like a meaningful community in which a researcher could truly participate. The selected studies briefly reviewed above demonstrate clearly that both of these fears are unfounded. While one should neither disregard nor disparage the insights of professional and lay caretakers, neither should one assume that theirs are the only insights that can be reasonably ascertained; after 20 years of deinstitutionalization and normalization, it is certainly an opportune time to hear from people with mental retardation themselves. The very real communicative deficits that mark many such people do, however, make it highly unlikely that standard, objective methods of data collection (such as surveys and key-informant interviews) will be sufficient to elicit information. Rather than a strategy for which people with intellectual disabilities are by definition unsuited, participant observation would seem to be the only truly effective way of ascertaining their insider's perspective, gleaned from extended association, casual conversation, and everyday observation. Indeed, "the rich holistic descriptions which are passed over by survey methods but which are developed through participant observation facilitate truly adequate assessments of a handicapped populations' abilities, disabilities, and needs" (Frank, 1980, p. 2).

Third, participant observation casts the researcher in multiple roles, some of which might not be automatically comfortable or easy to assimilate. Because the participant observer lives in a study community and is actively engaged in its daily life, he or she must be prepared to take on duties that are not, strictly speaking, those of a professional researcher. Participant observers often become chauffeurs, babysitters, liaisons with higher-ups, and so forth; in sum, they function as friends, in all the myriad capacities that term entails. This situation is especially delicate when working with people with mental retardation, who may not have much experience with "normal" friendships, and who may have emotional needs for which the researcher is not fully prepared. They may also be awkward in their expressions of friendship, resulting in embarrassingly, or even dangerously, inappropriate behavior. The researcher may therefore be called upon to play the additional roles of advocate (like Evans) or "benefactor" (a term encompassing both the financial and emotional support that several members of the Socio-Behavioral Group have discussed).[8] The researcher

[8] Frank (1980, p. 3) prefers the term "therapist" to that of "benefactor". In her view, a researcher who acts as a therapist helps the members of the study population "to cope socially and emotionally by providing an ear for problems, insight, advice, or direct aid, and sometimes even guiding the sample member's behavior through strategic interaction".

should also be sufficiently self-aware to spot his/her own emotional needs, and the degree to which he/she leans on an acquiescent, needy "friend" to gratify his/her own ego. We cannot undo our own personalities, but we should think very carefully about entering into participant-observation research if we are not really equipped to do so without damaging ourselves or others.

Fourth, while participant observation was developed as a way of learning about exotic cultures in other parts of the world, research with people with mental retardation is often conducted close to home. Even researchers who are interested in cultures outside the USA or Western Europe usually end up being immersed in our own culture, since in most parts of the world nowadays people with intellectual disabilities are involved to one degree or another in the discourse of Western medicine or social service. This situation can be problematic in that the standardized, objectified instruments by which we typically keep from taking too much for granted when studying our own society are absent in participant observation; the researcher must be careful not to become too much the unobservant insider.

Fifth, the ideal (one might almost say idealized) relationship in field research was one in which the researcher was naive, childlike, culturally incompetent, the better to learn the culture from scratch (Brenneis, 1982, p. 2). Native informants were the experts in their own world, and already had reasonably satisfying networks of kin and other associations, in addition to their own economic resources. Their willingness to tolerate, to indulge, and ultimately to accept the childlike foreigner in their midst was something akin to an act of grace. This romantic picture is turned upside down when working with people with mental retardation. In such research, it is the "natives" who are officially (albeit not necessarily functionally) incompetent, and who lack both social capital and economic resources. The researcher is, by contrast, "a certified, competent adult who [is] interested in the minute details of the sample member's daily experiences, feelings, thoughts, pleasures, and problems" (Frank, 1980, p. 3). This disparity is given added poignancy when the researcher is distinguished from "other staff" of the home agency and is recognized as someone without formal authority but who still provides a semblance of understanding, caring, or even love. For people with mental retardation, the mere fact that such a "real person"[9] is interested enough to hang out with them is a powerful validation that they are, after all, just as good as anyone else.

Sixth, the adoption of any of these friendship roles raises ethical issues that overshadow methodology. Whether one becomes an advocate, benefactor, or "therapist", one is, by definition, actively intervening in the lives of those one studies. One is no longer simply "participating" in their lives—one is taking a more or less active hand in shaping those lives. At best, such intervention involves merely supplying the resources that might help a person with mental retardation accomplish some goals he/she had already formulated. At worst, it might entail taking a directive stance which, even if it leads to a positive outcome, certainly compromises the respect for individual dignity that is supposedly at the heart of contemporary research on populations with intellectual disabilities. There is no single pat resolution to this dilemma; it can only be hoped that by raising awareness that such a dilemma is almost inherent in participant-observation research with people with mental

[9] I encountered this term with great frequency in my own research. It always grated on me because it implied that the people who used it had assimilated the lesson that they themselves were somehow less than real. However untrue in the existential sense, the phrase nonetheless encapsulates a sad, perceived reality in the lives of people with mental retardation.

retardation, researchers will engage in careful, critical reflection (within themselves and with trusted others) of their own feelings and values before casually launching into the research setting. After all, it is perhaps only in research with such a population that "the personal interaction of the researcher [is] so actively desired, so persistently solicited, and so potentially influential upon the daily subsistence and worldview of the research participant" (Frank, 1980, p. 12). As such, "the ethical dilemma was not so much whether to intervene, but when and how to do so responsibly" (Frank, 1980, p. 12).

REFERENCES

Adler, P.A. & Adler, P. (1994). Observational techniques. In N.K. Denzin & Y.S. Lincoln (Eds) *Handbook of Qualitative Research* (pp. 377–392). Thousand Oaks, CA: Sage.

Altheide, D.L. & Johnson, J.M. (1994). Criteria for assessing interpretive validity in qualitative research. In N.K. Denzin & Y.S. Lincoln (Eds) *Handbook of Qualitative Research* (pp. 485–499). Thousand Oaks, CA: Sage.

Angrosino, M.V. (1992). Benjy's tale: Faulkner and the sociolinguistics of mental retardation. *RE Arts and Letters*, **18**, 5–22.

Angrosino, M.V. (1997). The ethnography of mental retardation: an applied perspective. *Journal of Contemporary Ethnography*, **26**, 98–109.

Angrosino, M.V. (1998). *Opportunity House: Ethnographic Stories of Mental Retardation*. Walnut Creek, CA: AltaMira.

Angrosino, M.V. & Mays de Pérez, K.A. (2000). Rethinking observation: from method to context. In N.K. Denzin & Y.S. Lincoln (Eds) *Handbook of Qualitative Research* (2nd edn) (pp. 673–702). Thousand Oaks, CA: Sage.

Angrosino, M.V. & Zagnoli, L.J. (1992). Gender constructs and social identity: implications for community-based care of retarded adults. In T. Whitehead & B. Reid (Eds) *Gender Constructs and Social Issues* (pp. 40–69). Urbana, IL: University of Illinois Press.

Bernard, H.R. (1988). *Research Methods in Cultural Anthropology*. Newbury Park, CA: Sage.

Bohannan, P. (1992). *We, the Alien: An Introduction to Cultural Anthropology*. Prospect Heights, IL: Waveland.

Brenneis, D. (1982). *Making Sense of Settings: An Ethnographic Approach*. Los Angeles, CA: Mental Retardation Research Center, University of California.

Daybreak International (1981). *The Challenge of L'Arche*. Ottawa: Novalis.

Denzin, N.K. & Lincoln, Y.S. (2000). Introduction: the discipline and practice of qualitative research. In N.K. Denzin & Y.S. Lincoln (Eds) *Handbook of Qualitative Research* (2nd edn) (pp. 1–28). Thousand Oaks, CA: Sage.

Devlieger, P.J. (1995). On the Threshold of Adult Life: Life Course and the Discourse of Mental Retardation in American Culture. Ph.D. dissertation, University of Illinois.

Devlieger, P.J. (1998). (In)competence in America in comparative perspective. In R. Jenkins (Ed.) *Questions of Competence: Culture, Classification and Intellectual Disability* (pp. 54–76). Cambridge: Cambridge University Press.

Edgerton, R.B. (1967). *The Cloak of Competence: Stigma in the Lives of the Mentally Retarded*. Berkeley, CA: University of California Press.

Edgerton, R.B. (1984). Introduction. In R.B. Edgerton (Ed.) *Lives in Process: Mildly Retarded Adults in a Large City* (pp. 1–7). Washington, DC: American Association on Mental Deficiency.

Edgerton, R.B. & Langness, L.L. (1978). Observing mentally retarded persons in community settings: an anthropological perspective. In G.P. Sackett (Ed.) *Observing Behavior: Theory and Applications in Mental Retardation* (pp. 335–348). Baltimore, MD: University Park Press.

Ellis, C. & Bochner A.P. (Eds) (1996). *Composing Ethnography: Alternative Forms of Qualitative Writing*. Walnut Creek, CA: AltaMira.

Ervin, A.M. (2000). *Applied Anthropology: Tools and Perspectives for Contemporary Practice*. Needham Heights, MA: Allyn & Bacon.

Evans, D.P. (1983). *The Lives of Mentally Retarded People*. Boulder, CO: Westview.

Fetterman, D.M. (1998). *Ethnography* (2nd edn). Thousand Oaks, CA: Sage.

Frank, G. (1978). *Finding the Common Denominator: A Phenomenological Critique of Life History Method*. Los Angeles, CA: Mental Retardation Research Center, University of California.

Frank, G. (1980). *Intervention: Ethics and Objectivity in Participant Observation with the Mildly Retarded*. Los Angeles, CA: Mental Retardation Research Center, University of California.

Gold, R.L. (1997). The ethnographic method in sociology. *Qualitative Inquiry*, **3**, 388–402.

Gupta, A. & Ferguson, J. (1996). Culture, power, place: ethnography at the end of an era. In A. Gupta & J. Ferguson (Eds) *Culture, Power, Place: Explorations in Critical Anthropology* (pp. 1–32). Durham, NC: Duke University Press.

Kernan, K.T. & Sabsay, S. (1979). *Semantic Deficiencies in the Narratives of Mildly Retarded Speakers*. Los Angeles, CA: Mental Retardation Research Center, University of California.

Kernan, K.T., Turner, J.L. Langness, L.L. & Edgerton, R.B. (1978). *Issues in the Community Adaptation of Mildly Retarded Adults*. Los Angeles, CA: Mental Retardation Research Center, University of California.

Kirk, J. & Miller, M.L. (1986). *Reliability and Validity in Qualitative Research*. Beverly Hills, CA: Sage.

Koegel, P. (1978). *The Creation of Incompetence: Socialization and Mildly Retarded Persons*. Los Angeles, CA: Mental Retardation Research Center, University of California.

Marcus, G.E. (1997). The uses of complicity in the changing mise-en-scène of anthropological fieldwork. *Reflections*, **59**, 85–108.

Miles, M.B. & Huberman, A.M. (1994). *Qualitative Data Analysis: An Expanded Sourcebook* (2nd edn). Thousand Oaks, CA: Sage.

Mink, I.T., Meyers, C.E. & Nihira, K. (1981). *Lifestyles in Families with Slow-Learning Children*. Los Angeles, CA: Mental Retardation Research Center, University of California.

Nuttall, M. (1992). *Arctic Homeland: Kinship, Community and Development in Northwest Greenland*. Toronto: University of Toronto Press.

Pelto, P.J. & Pelto, G.H. (1978). *Anthropological Research: The Structure of Inquiry* (2nd edn). New York: Cambridge University Press.

Platt, M. (1984). *Displaying Competence: Peer Interaction in a Group Home for Retarded Adults*. Los Angeles, CA: Mental Retardation Research Center, University of California.

Ronai, C.R. (1996). My mother is mentally retarded. In C. Ellis & A.P. Bochner (Eds) *Composing Ethnography: Alternative Forms of Qualitative Writing* (pp. 109–131). Walnut Creek, CA: AltaMira.

Roosens, E. (1979). *Mental Patients in Town Life*. Beverly Hills, CA: Sage.

Sabsay, S. & Platt, M. (1985). *Weaving the Cloak of Competence*. Los Angeles, CA: Mental Retardation Research Center, University of California.

Schensul, S.L., Schensul, J.J. & LeCompte, M.D. (1999). *Essential Ethnographic Methods: Observations, Interviews, and Questionnaires*. Walnut Creek, CA: AltaMira.

Silverman, D. (1993). *Interpreting Qualitative Data: Strategies for Analyzing Talk, Text and Interaction*. London: Sage.

Spradley, J.P. (1980). *Participant Observation*, New York: Holt, Rinehart and Winston.

Stocking, G.W. (1983). History of anthropology: whence/whither. In G.W. Stocking (Ed.) *Observers Observed: Essays on Ethnographic Fieldwork* (pp. 3–12). Madison, WI: University of Wisconsin Press.

Turner, J.L. (1982). *Workshop Society: Ethnographic Observations in a Work Setting for Retarded Adults*. Los Angeles, CA: Mental Retardation Research Center, University of California.

Vanier, J. (1979). *Community and Growth*. Toronto: Griffin House.

van Maastricht, S. (1998). Work, opportunity and culture: (in)competence in Greece and Wales. In R. Jenkins (Ed.) *Questions of Competence: Culture, Classification and Intellectual Disability* (pp. 125–152). Cambridge: Cambridge University Press.

Werner, O. & Schoepfle, G.M. (1987). *Systematic Fieldwork*, vol. I. *Foundations of Ethnography and Interviewing*. Newbury Park, CA: Sage.

Whittemore, R.D. & Koegel, P. (1978). *Living Alone Is Not Helpful: Sexuality and Social Context among the Mildly Retarded.* Los Angeles, CA: Mental Retardation Research Center, University of California.

Whittemore, R.D., Koegel, P. & Langness, L.L. (1980). *The Life History Approach to Mental Retardation.* Los Angeles, CA: Mental Retardation Research Center, University of California.

Whyte, S.R. (1997). *Questioning Misfortune: The Pragmatics of Uncertainty in Eastern Uganda.* Cambridge: Cambridge University Press.

CHAPTER 8

Measurement of Behavior with a Special Emphasis on Sequential Analysis of Behavior

Paul J. Yoder
Vanderbilt University, USA
Katherine Short-Meyerson
University of Wisconsin–Oshkosh, USA
and
Jon Tapp
Vanderbilt University, USA

This book is focused on research methods relevant to studying people with intellectual disabilities. One issue is particularly salient in studies of this population. People with intellectual disabilities frequently need significant support or intervention from professionals to maximize their potential development. Therefore, we frequently need to identify the antecedents of desired and undesired behavior. For example, we may want to identify the antecedents of self-injurious behavior (e.g., Emerson, Hatton, Robertson, Henderson & Cooper, 1999; Hall & Oliver, 2000) so we can reduce the incidence of these antecedents. Or we may want to identify the antecedents of conversational participation (e.g., Yoder, Davies & Bishop, 1994) so we can increase the incidence of these antecedents. Sequential analysis of social interactions helps us reduce the number of probable antecedents by controlling for chance occurrence of the potential antecedent and target behaviors of interest. However, it is recognized that many readers of this book may not be familiar with some of the introductory concepts of observing behavior. Therefore, the introductory content of this chapter will be covered in a rather cursory fashion with references for appropriate sources for this information.[1] In this introductory section, we will cover (a) why researchers

[1] In the interests of focusing on issues rarely discussed, we had to choose to omit important information that is relevant to behavioral observation. Fortunately, this information is available elsewhere. Information relevant to (a) selecting specific research questions, (b) designing a behavioral coding system, (c) selecting a sampling method, and (d) deciding on the recording and representation

The International Handbook of Applied Research in Intellectual Disabilities. Edited by E. Emerson, C. Hatton, T. Thompson and T.R. Parmenter ISBN 0-471-49709-6.

observe behavior and the typical measurement contexts for observational measures, (b) the advantages of count data over qualitative ratings of behavior, and (c) the types of count data relevant to sequential analysis. After this introductory section, we will address topics relevant to the analysis of sequences of behavior: (a) the types of research questions that are best addressed by lag sequential analysis, (b) the types of lag sequential analysis, (c) a recommended method of organizing sequential data into a 2 × 2 table, (d) two suggested indices of sequential association, (e) two methods to test a sequential association for significance, (f) two methods to test the difference between sequential associations, and (g) a method to determine how large the behavior sample needs to be to conduct a reasonable sequential analysis of behavior. Whenever possible, we will use empirical data (that is, Monte Carlo studies) to support our recommendations. Finally, the chapter will briefly summarize some of the most frequently confronted issues relevant to reliability and validity of behavioral observations.

INTRODUCTION TO BEHAVIORAL OBSERVATIONS

Rationale and Typical Measurement Contexts

The primary reasons researchers observe behavior, instead of using responses to a test, are (a) they want a detailed description of how an individual typically behaves, and (b) they wish to reveal the reasons (that is, antecedent and consequences) people do the things they do (Thompson, Symons & Felce, 2000). The key words "detailed", "typical", "antecedents", and "consequences" reflect an important use of behavioral observation: designing and evaluating treatments that affect people's everyday lives. Behavioral observations have the potential to provide sensitive measures of behavioral change or individual differences in ecologically valid (that is, typical) contexts.

However, many studies have shown that different values on observational variables reflect, not just within-person factors (such as learning or development), but also the context in which the behavior has been measured (see Gardner, 2000, for review). There are three ways to address this issue. First, we need to be clear about what we are intending to measure. If the motivating purpose for the research is to learn how context affects behavior, we can measure and test which aspects of the naturally occurring measurement context covary with differences in behavior. However, many research questions are motivated by needs that require us to make inferences about the ways individuals usually act across contexts or the way an individual usually acts before and after treatment.

In such cases, a second option appears most appropriate: use multiple coders per session and multiple sessions per research participant. The use of multiple sessions helps address the effects of context of behavior, particularly when behavior is observed in different contexts. Multiple coders are used to reduce the measurement error due to disagreement between coders. The measurement error due to context differences is compounded by between-coder disagreements (Cronbach, Gleser, Nanda & Rajaratnam, 1972). The number of observations or coders one needs to measure a stable estimate of individual differences in the natural environment will vary according to the construct being measured. A dependability study is an empirical method for determining the length and number of observation sessions and

---

of intermittent (that is discontinuous) behavioral data can be found in Bakeman and Gottman (1997), Martin and Bateson (1993), Rosenblum (1978), and Sackett (1978).

the number of coders needed to estimate individual differences of a behavioral tendency at a given level of reliability (McWilliam & Ware, 1994). For example, McWilliam and Ware (1994) found that it would take eight 15-minute sessions *per child* to yield a reliable (that is, above .79) measure of undifferentiated engagement using only one coder. McWilliam and Ware (1994) showed that by using four coders for each session, one could reduce the number of sessions needed to three. As expensive as this sounds, it is helpful to keep in mind that attempts to measure behavioral tendencies from observations in the natural environment without attention to using an adequate number of sessions or coders elevates the probability of type II errors (McWilliam & Ware, 1994).

This trade-off between resources and generalizability across contexts could explain why many observational studies in the mental retardation literature use highly structured (as in Ainsworth's strange situation) or semistructured (such as meal time) contexts instead of less structured and more varying contexts (Sackett, 2000). The third strategy attempts to design a controlled measurement context that evokes the behavior of interest with the belief that doing so reflects individual differences in behavioral tendencies across many contexts. The extent to which this strategy yields valid, generalizable data varies by construct and needs to be empirically determined for each construct. We test the validity of such measures by using methods reviewed at the end of this chapter. The tendency to use carefully designed and implemented contexts as opposed to naturally occurring measurement contexts has been, and probably will continue to be, an area of disagreement among obervational researchers.

Why Focus on "Count" Data?

There are three major types of observational data: checklists, rating scales, and count data. Checklists guide the observer to make a "yes" or "no" decision regarding whether a particular type or quality of behavior occurred in the entire observation session (for example, whether the child used at least one instance of self-injury). Rating scales guide the observer to select a value on, for instance, a 5-point scale to indicate the extent to which targeted behaviors occur or have particular characteristics. Count data involve detailed records of the sequence, frequency, rate, duration, or latency of relevant behaviors in a behavior sample. Their level of detail provides the type of information that is not available in rating scales or checklist, and often involves less rater judgment about the qualitative nature of the target behavior. It is the only one of the three types of observational data that allows analysis of sequences of behavior. Thus, count data are the topic of this chapter.

Types of Count Data Relevant to Sequential Analyses: Continuously Recorded Data

To analyze the sequence of behaviors, we need continuous recording of behavior sequences (Bakeman & Gottman, 1997), rather than intermittent recording. Therefore, we will focus on the various types of continuously recorded data in this chapter. These types of count data are differentiated by how we record and represent relevant behaviors (Sackett, 1978; Martin & Bateson, 1993; Bakeman & Gottman, 1997). Bakeman and Gottman (1997) categorize the types of behaviors as interval, event, and timed-event data.

Interval data are the result of coding whether a relevant behavior occurred within a particular interval of time (such as 10 seconds). Interval data are usually represented as a single stream of codes. Each code represents a single interval and at least one instance of the type of relevant behavior observed within the interval. Therefore, we lose information when more than one instance of the relevant behavior occurs in the same interval. The probability that this problem will occur increases as the frequency of the relevant behaviors and duration of the interval increases. Although interval data can be analyzed sequentially, doing so results in a relatively low degree of precision compared to the other two types of sequentially analyzable count data. Additionally, computers and videotape machines have enabled collection of the following two types of data for almost any behavior in almost any context, thus eliminating the need for interval data collection in many situations.

Event data indicate only the presence and sequence of coded events; no time of occurrence is recorded. When we represent streams of event data, we can do so with a single stream of codes from a mutually exclusive coding system (no two coded behaviors categories can co-occur). Therefore, only research questions in which the relevant behaviors rarely or never co-occur can be addressed with event data. For example, conversations are often analyzed with event data.

Timed-event data record the presence of events and their onset and offset time (Bakeman & Gottman, 1997). For example, many research questions relevant to studying the social behavior of people with intellectual disabilities involve behaviors from two more actors in which one actor's behaviors can and do overlap in time with another actor's behaviors. Computer software designed to collect timed-event data usually represents the data as a single stream of codes with accompanying onset and offset times in which the codes indicate which actor produced the behavior.

In fact, it is almost always advisable to use computers to help collect data that are to be sequentially analyzed. The reason for this will become clear when we talk about how sequential behavioral data are organized and analyzed. Virtually all of the available software designed to aid behavioral data collection can produce any of the three types of count data reviewed here. For information about computer-aided data collection, see Kahng and Iwata (2000).

SEQUENTIAL ANALYSIS OF BEHAVIOR

Throughout this paper, the terms "antecedent" and "target" will be used to talk about the two behaviors in the sequence of interest. Although antecedent refers to the "first behavior" in the sequence and target refers to the "second behavior" in the sequence, it should be noted that we do not mean to imply that a relation between the two behaviors is assumed a priori. Rather, we have chosen the terms "antecedent" and "target" because they are conventionally used when exploring the relation between two behaviors in a sequence. The sequential analysis is conducted to determine whether a relation exists between antecedent and target behaviors. In this paper, we refer to analysis of behavior sequences, but the concepts are applicable to analysis of concurrent behaviors as well.

The Types of Research Questions That Sequential Analyses Can Address

The types of research questions that are appropriately addressed by sequential analysis are clarified by understanding the difference between *nonsequential* and *sequential* variables.

To aid this discussion, suppose that we hypothesize that teacher instructions have an immediate effect on student self-injuries. Before conducting an expensive experiment to determine whether reducing instructions results in fewer self-injury bouts, suppose we want to test whether there is a close temporal association between teacher instruction and student self-injury.

An approach that uses *nonsequential* variables to address this question might test whether there is a positive correlation between total number of teacher instructions and total number of student self-injuries. These two variables are nonsequential variables because each concerns only one behavior and neither variable expresses anything about the sequence of teacher instruction and student self-injury within a particular behavior sample.

Testing the same hypothesis with *sequential* variables in a group design, one might test whether the extent to which self-injury occurred immediately after teacher instruction was greater than one would expect by chance in the majority of teachers and students. The aspect of our theory that predicts that teacher instruction has an *immediate* effect on self-injury is reflected in our choice of a sequential level variable.

The main point is that sequential variables reflect a temporal association within an observation session. That is, the sequential variable quantifies the extent to which the target behavior (such as self-injury) occurs within a specified number of coded behaviors or time units from the antecedent behavior (such as teacher instruction). The reader should note that sequential analysis requires that the time period (such as within 5 seconds) or the number of coded behaviors (for example, the next coded behavior) from the antecedent behavior be specified. Because sequential variables require the investigator to predict the number of events after which, or the time window in which, the target behavior will occur after the antecedent behavior, very specific temporal relationships can be tested. The degree of specificity implicit in sequential variables reduces the number of alternative explanations for the association of interest.

However, statistically significant or large sequential associations do not necessarily mean that the antecedent behavior *caused* the target behavior to occur. Like other indices of association, indices of sequential association can be high because of some previously occurring or simultaneously occurring event (that is, a spurious association). For example, student self-injury may stimulate the teacher to provide instructions in an attempt to "redirect the student", and the student who is engaging in self-injury may continue doing so. Such a pattern would produce a large positive sequential association between teacher instruction and student self-injury, but the direction of effect would be from the student to the teacher, not vice versa.

Three Major Types of Sequential Analysis

The three major types of sequential analysis are defined by how the immediate temporal relationship between potential antecedent and the target behaviors is specified. One may ask whether self-injury follows teacher instruction by (a) a specified number of events (event-lag sequential analysis), (b) a specified number of time units (such as seconds) (that is, timed-lag sequential analysis), or (c) within a specific time window (such as within 5 seconds) (time-window sequential analysis).

For example, an event-lag sequential analysis might test whether the extent to which student self-injury follows teacher instruction is more than expected by chance. In event-lag sequential analysis, we are coding and considering the onset of all "relevant" behaviors.

By "relevant", we mean all target behaviors of interest and all of their potential antecedents. For example, we conducted a sequential analysis of parent and child verbal conversations in which each spoken utterance was coded and analyzed to determine which type of parent utterance had the strongest sequential association with child conversational participation (Yoder, Davies & Bishop, 1994). The relevant behaviors were adult and child utterances in the observation session. However, it is not usually obvious what constitutes the "relevant" behaviors. For example, it is not clear what the complete set of relevant behaviors is when testing whether teacher instruction elicits student self-injury. Later, it will become apparent that our definition of the "relevant" behaviors to code is extremely important in estimating the chance sequential occurrence of the antecedent and target behaviors. Our uncertainty about what constitutes the complete set of relevant behaviors is probably one reason why timed-lag sequential analysis was created.

A timed-lag sequential analysis might test whether the onset of student self-injury occurs *exactly* 1 second after the onset of teacher instruction more than is expected by chance. In timed sequential analysis, each time unit (such as second) is coded for presence and type of a behavior of interest. In data that are to be analyzed by timed-lag sequential analysis, it is quite acceptable to code only the potential antecedent and the target behavior of interest. For example, we might code an hour-long behavior sample as to when the onset of teacher instruction and self-injury occurs. Therefore, timed-lag sequential analysis enables us to circumvent the problem of defining all behaviors that should be considered "relevant to code". Later in the chapter, it will become apparent why all seconds within the behavior sample are considered to determine whether self-injury occurred after teacher instruction more than expected by chance.

A time-window sequential analysis might test whether the onset of student self-injury *occurs within* 5 seconds of the onset of teacher instruction. As in timed sequential analysis, each time unit (such as second) is coded for presence and type of a behavior of interest. Also like timed sequential analysis, all time units are analyzed to determine whether the occurrence of self-injury within 5 seconds of teacher instruction could have occurred by chance. However, the way the data are organized for analysis alters how chance is estimated in an important way that will become apparent when we discuss "contingency tables for time-window sequential analyses".

The time-window sequential analysis is a relative newcomer to the scene. It has some definite advantages over event-lag and timed-lag sequential analyses. Note that the time-window lag sequential analysis allows less precision than the timed-lag or event-lag sequential analysis in the prediction of the exact time or number of events that the target (such as self-injury) is expected to occur after the antecedent (such as teacher instruction). Therefore, time-window sequential analysis matches the complexity of human behavior and our limited state of knowledge of human interactions better than timed-lag or event-lag sequential analysis. Like timed-lag sequential analysis, the time-window analysis does not require that the investigator "correctly" decide all of the behaviors that are relevant to code to estimate chance correctly. In our opinion, time-window sequential analysis is likely to become the favored of the three methods as it becomes better known to investigators.

The Need to "Control for Chance"

Sequential frequency has been considered and discarded as a measure of the relation between behaviors that occur in a sequence because it does not control for chance occurrences of the sequence of interest (Bakeman & Gottman, 1997). In the example about parent–child conversations, the sequential frequency would be the number of times the child's topic-continuing utterances occurred after the adult's questions. Suppose that two children, Joe and Lisa, continued the topic after adult questions 5 times and 10 times, respectively, in a given period. Suppose further that the adult that interacted with Joe used 10 questions and the adult that interacted with Lisa used 20 questions. Even though Lisa's sequential frequency is twice that of Joe's, it is not clear what this means because Lisa's adult provided twice as many opportunities for the sequence of interest. This illustrates that the rate of occurrence of the antecedent, in this case adult questions, needs to be taken into account to know whether a sequential association between antecedent and target behaviors exists.

One way to control for the base rate of the antecedent behavior is to use the transitional probability. The transitional probability is the sequential frequency divided by the total number of antecedent events (Bakeman & Gottman, 1997). In the example above, the transitional probability of interest for both Joe and Lisa is .5 (that is, 5/10 and 10/20, respectively). Unfortunately, interpreting transitional probabilities on their own is problematic, too. A certain number of antecedent-target behavior sequences occur by chance (Bakeman & Gottman, 1997). The greater the frequency of the target event, the greater the transitional probability that is expected by chance. Note that Lisa has many more total instances of topic continuations than does Joe. In such a case, it would be "easier" for Lisa to attain a transitional probability of .5 than it would be for Joe. This makes comparing the transitional probabilities problematic because Lisa's transitional probability might be at chance level and Joe's might be much above chance. For more information on the inadequacies of transitional probability as an index of sequential association, see Yoder and Fearer (2000). The main point is that we need to estimate the chance occurrence of the sequence of interest to interpret correctly a transitional probability.

Most currently accepted estimates of chance occurrence of a sequence are estimated from the base rates of *both* the antecedent and target behaviors. For example, one index of sequential association estimates chance as the following: (simple probability of target) × (simple probability of antecedent) × (total number of events) (Bakeman & Gottman, 1997). A "simple probability" in event-lag sequential is the number of times a behavior occurs divided by the total number of coded events in the behavior sample. For example, if we have 100 utterances in a conversation and 20 of these are child topic-continuing utterances and 20 are adult questions, the chance estimate of the adult question-child continuing utterance sequence is $(.2)(.2)(100) = 4$. Therefore, a sequential frequency of 5 is greater than one would expect by chance, but not by much. A 2×2 contingency table is useful in organizing sequential data because such a table clarifies whether the estimate of chance occurrence of the sequence of interest really considers all of the instances of the antecedent and target behaviors.

Contingency Tables

In the sequential analysis literature, a contingency table is frequently used to illustrate how the raw sequential data are used to compute the index of sequential association (Bakeman & Gottman, 1997). Although there are more complex contingency tables, we present the simplest case to illustrate the principles used to construct a proper contingency table for sequential analysis.

The reader is asked to consider the example in Figure 8.1 carefully while reading the general procedure by which pairs of behaviors are tallied into the cells of the 2×2 table.

A convention used in the sequential analysis literature is to use the rows to categorize each pair of behaviors according to whether or not the antecedent behavior is the first behavior in the pair and to use the columns to categorize the same pair of behaviors according to whether the target behavior is the second behavior in the pair. That is, all coded behaviors are represented in both the rows and all columns. The cell labels (A–D) for the four cells in the 2×2 table in Figure 8.1 should be noted. In Figure 8.1, each behavior pair is labeled by the label for the cell into which it is tallied. It should be noted that behavior pairs are tallied into the 2×2 table in such a way that one behavior pair "overlaps" with the following behavior pair. That is, except for the first and last behavior, each behavior is considered both a "first behavior" and a "second behavior" (that is, the second behavior in one behavior pair is the first behavior in the next behavior pair). We refer to the 2×2 table in Figure 8.1 as Table A.

Bakeman and Doral (1989) have demonstrated empirically that the type I error rates for sequential analysis results are extremely similar regardless of whether one uses non-overlapping or overlapping pairs of behavior. A happy consequence of using overlapping behavior pairs is a doubling of the number of tallies in the 2×2 table (that is, the behavior sample size).

When one person uses the antecedent behavior and another person uses the target behavior and the data undergo an event-lag sequential analysis, a controversy exists concerning how to construct the 2×2 table. Some researchers (e.g., Rocissano, Slade & Lynch, 1987; Wampold & Kim, 1989) have constructed 2×2 tables in which the teacher behavior is tallied on the rows and the student behavior is tallied on the columns. This method is illustrated in Table B.

For behavior streams in which behaviors cannot follow themselves or other coded behaviors from the same actor, the two types of 2×2 tables yield exactly the same cell tallies. However, in many situations, behaviors *can and do* follow themselves. Therefore, to accurately reflect the *total* number of target and antecedent behaviors, not just those that occur in the hypothesized position in the behavior pair, the method of tallying behaviors into 2×2 tables must result in all instances of the target and antecedent behaviors being tallied, including those that occur after themselves and after other behaviors from the same actor. For example, in Figure 8.1, the first instance of student topic-continuing utterance follows an instance of "other student utterances". In a 2×2 table in which only teacher behaviors are counted in the first behavior position, there is no place to tally this behavior pair. Next we investigate the consequence of using 2×2 tables such as Table B when codes can follow themselves and other codes from the same actor.

Monte Carlo Simulation to Compare Results from Table A and Table B

We ran a Monte Carlo simulation to illustrate that the type of contingency table one constructs matters when events can follow themselves and other behavior from the same actor (Yoder, Short-Meyerson & Tapp, 2000). There were 1000 streams of data (which are analogous to subjects), all generated from the same algorithm (which is analogous to a population) where the true sequential link between behaviors was at chance level (that is, the null condition). The data were tallied into a 2×2 table like Table A and into one like Table B. An index of sequential association (that is, Yule's Q) was computed for each table for each data stream. The range of the difference scores between Yule's Q scores from each table was from $-.9$ to 1.0, thus illustrating that the indices of sequential association for Table A

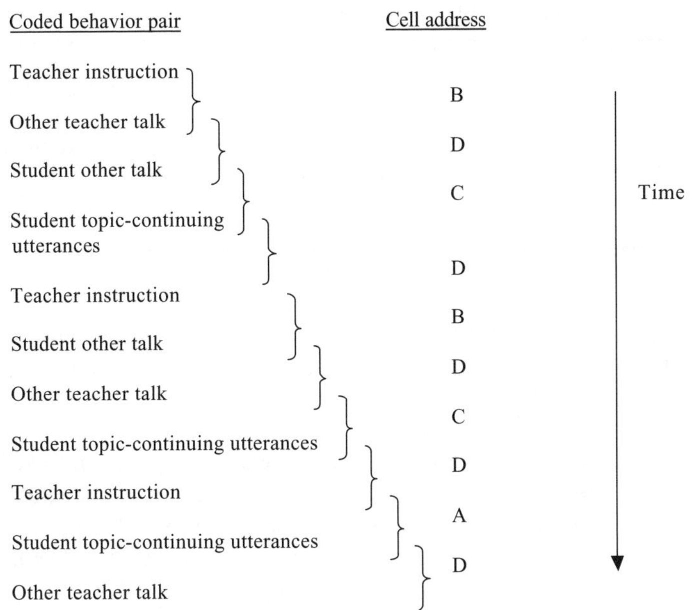

These pairs of behaviors are tallied into a 2 × 2 table as follows:

Table A — Behavior II

		Student topic-continuing utterances	Not topic-continuing utterances (teacher talk or other student talk)	Total for rows
Behavior I	Teacher instruction	1 pair A	2 pairs B	3 pairs
	Not teacher instruction (other teacher talk or student behavior)	2 pair C	5 pairs D	7 pairs
	Total for columns	3 pairs	7 pairs	Total of 10 observed pairs *

* These data are presented for illustrative purposes only. This would not be sufficient data to compute a reliable Yule's Q.

Figure 8.1 Tallying behavior pairs into a 2 × 2 table

Table B Contingency table organized by actor

		Child	
		Topic continuations	Not topic continuations
Adult	Questions	A	B
	Not questions	C	D

were sometimes very different from those for Table B. In fact, an agreement index (that is, kappa) for whether the sequential association is significant when computed from Table A versus Table B was quite low (.23). Thus, whether data are tallied into Table A or Table B does affect the results of sequential analysis.

The question then becomes, "Which 2 × 2 contingency table should be used?" We focused on those behavior streams for which the difference in sequential association from the two different methods of tallying the data into 2 × 2 tables exceeded .20 (n = 505 behavior streams). Because the population sequential association was known to be zero, the data from the more accurate table should be about zero. The mean sequential association for Table A was not significantly different from zero (mean Yule's $Q = .0006$; SD = .24; $t = .054$; $p = .96$), whereas the mean sequential association for Table B approached significance (mean Yule's $Q = .04$; SD = .45; $t = 1.92$; $p = .055$). Thus, Table A is more accurate than Table B.

Contingency Tables for Time-Window Lag Sequential Analysis

The reader is referred to Figure 8.2 to illustrate how time-window lag sequential data are tallied into a 2 × 2 table. The label for the first row is the primary difference between the table in Figure 8.2 (time-window lag sequential analysis) and the table in Figure 8.1 (event-lag and timed-lag sequential analysis). By asking whether student self-injurious behavior occurs within 5 seconds of the onset of teacher instruction, we have subtly changed the research question to one that is a bit less specific than that posed for event-lag or timed-lag sequential analysis. No longer does student self-injury have to occur a specified number of coded behaviors or an exact number of seconds after the onset of teacher instruction to be tallied in the A cell (that is, the cell for the sequence of interest). It should be noted that the base rate of the antecedent in time-window lag sequential analysis is the number of time units *within the specified time window*, not the number of antecedent events. Therefore, the larger the time window, the larger the chance estimate of targets in the time window. Therefore, the reduced precision allowed by time-window analysis is offset by the reduced sensitivity of the analysis.

Appropriate Measures of Sequential Association

Regardless of what 2 × 2 table we use to organize sequential data, we need an index of sequential association that (a) compares the observed frequency the target follows the antecedent with that expected by chance and (b) is not influenced by other aspects of the

The data:

Time of onset	Teacher behavior	Student behavior	Cell address
00:01	na	na	D
00:02	instruction	na	B
00:03	na	na	B
00:04	na	self-injury	A
00:05	na	na	B
00:06	na	na	D
00:07	na	na	D
00:08	na	self-injury	C
00:09	instruction	na	B
00:10	na	na	B
00:11	na	na	B
00:12	na	na	B

The contingency table:

		Second II	
		Student self-injury	Other
Second I	At or within 5 seconds of onset of teacher instruction	1 pair A	B 7 pairs
	Other	1 pair C	D 3 pairs

Figure 8.2 Contingency table for time-window lag sequential analysis

data that are not relevant to understanding the magnitude of the sequential association (for example, total number of coded events or time units in the behavior samples). The magnitude of a *sequential association* reflects the extent to which a sequence of interest occurs at a different rate than one would expect by chance.

The odds ratio is one such index of sequential association (Bakeman, McArthur & Quera, 1996a). The possible range of the odds ratio is zero to infinity, with 1.0 representing a null association. With the cell labels for the 2×2 table in Figure 8.2, the odds ratio equals AD/BC. The odds ratio of the table in Figure 8.1 is $5/4 = 1.25$. In the context of sequential analysis, the meaning of an odds ratio of 1.25 is that the target is 25% more likely to occur as the next event if the antecedent has just occurred. Put generally, an odds ratio above 1.0 is consistent with the antecedent facilitating the occurrence of the target event. In contrast, an odds ratio below 1.0 is consistent with the hypothesis that the antecedent inhibits occurrence of the target behavior. For example, an odds ratio of 0.5 means that the probability (that is, odds) of the target behavior is reduced by half if the antecedent behavior occurs. Audiences without training in the statistics that educators and psychologists use may relate to the odds ratio. For audiences that are familiar with Pearson's correlation coefficient, the asymmetry around 1 as an indication of statistical independence (that is, no association) may result in confusion.

Fortunately, the odds ratio can be transformed to Yule's Q without loss of information (Reynolds, 1984). Yule's Q has a possible minimum of -1.0 and a possible maximum of 1.0, with zero representing the null relationship between the antecedent and the target behaviors. A negative Yule's Q means that the target occurs after the antecedent less than is estimated by chance processes alone. A positive Yule's Q means that the target occurs after the antecedent behavior more than is estimated by chance processes alone. Using the cell labels for the 2×2 table in Figure 8.2, Yule's Q is computed as follows:

$$\text{Yule's } Q = (\text{AD} - \text{BC})/(\text{AD} + \text{BC})$$

Using the 2×2 table in Figure 8.1 as an example (although this data set is too small to render Yule's Q interpretable), Yule's Q is computed as follows:

$$\text{Yule's } Q = (5 - 4)/5 + 4) = 1/9 = .11$$

We conducted a Monte Carlo study to illustrate that Yule's Q is only minimally affected, whereas transitional probabilities are greatly affected, by the simple probability of the target behavior or antecedent behaviors. We randomly generated a set of 1000 data streams of 100 events each that represent four different behaviors. The behavior streams were generated by a computer program that generated sequences that had a mean Yule's Q of .5 for a hypothetical antecedent-target pair. We correlated the transitional probability, Yule's Q scores, and the simple probabilities of the target and antecedent behaviors from each of the 1000 behavior streams. The correlations between the Yule's Q scores and the corresponding simple probabilities of the target and antecedent behaviors were $-.02$ and .08, respectively. The correlations between the transitional probabilities and the corresponding simple probabilities for the target and antecedent behaviors were .70 and $-.04$, respectively. These data indicate that the simple probability of the target behaviors has a small effect on Yule's Q, but a large effect on transitional probabilities.

Testing the Significance of a Sequential Association

One needs to test the significance of sequential associations because almost any observed value for the sequential association of interest can occur by sampling error under the right circumstances. One can test significance of sequential associations by group research design logic or single-subject research design logic. The choice should be made according to what one wants to know. If one wants to test whether a single sequential association could have occurred by chance sampling of an unusually favorable behavior sample, one should test the significance of the sequential association on a single-subject level. If one wants to test whether a mean sequential association could have occurred by chance sampling of an especially favorable sample of people, one should test the significance of the sequential association on a group level.

When testing a sequential association on a group level, we test whether the mean Yule's Q score is different from zero by a one-sample t-test or similar analysis. The procedure is to compute a Yule's Q for each participant (such as student–teacher pair) and use the Yule's Q scores as the dependent variable in the analysis. Bakeman, Robinson and Quera (1996b) found that Yule's Q tends to have characteristics that match the assumptions of parametric analyses (for example, it is normally distributed with a mean of zero under the null condition).

When testing a sequential association on a single-subject level, we use one of three methods. We can use a log-linear analysis (Bakeman & Quera, 1995) or very similar method that uses a variant of the z-score that Allison and Liker (1982) put forth. Alternatively, we can use a sampled permutation test (Bakeman et al., 1996b). The log-linear analysis and z-score methods yield almost identical results (Bakeman & Quera, 1995). The permutation test yields very similar results to the z-score method (Bakeman et al., 1996b). The relative statistical power of these methods has not been tested. The z-score is the most commonly used method and the log-linear analysis a close second. However, the permutation test method is perhaps more readily understood by a lay audience. Therefore, there is a trade-off between familiarity and comprehensibility.

Comparing Sequential Associations

When comparing sequential associations in which the base rate of the target behavior for the two sequential associations to be compared is different, it is critical that the index of sequential association controls for such differences. Yule's Q will accomplish this task. Transitional probabilities will not (Yoder & Fearer, 2000). This is particularly important to note when one is doing a backward sequential analysis. Backward sequential analysis came about because of the popularity of functional assessment. Functional assessment of behavior involves asking significant others what events or behaviors "usually" occur before a particularly desirable (such as conversational participation) or undesirable (such as self-injury) behavior. Those events that occur most often before the behavior of interest are hypothesized to influence the occurrence of the behavior of interest. These hypotheses are then tested in interventions that are designed to reduce the occurrence of such prior events to alter the occurrence of the behavior of interest. Backward sequential analysis was designed to make this process more systematic and objective.

Backward Sequential Analysis

Because there is much potential for miscommunication and misinterpretation of backward sequential analyses, we will expand on the pitfalls of comparing transitional probabilities from backward sequential analysis. By backward sequential analysis, we mean that the investigator tallies the number of times certain behaviors occur *before* the behavior of interest. For example, let us say that we use theory to guide our decision to code several teacher behaviors that may increase the probability of self-injury (such as instructions, active ignoring, or talking to other students) because we ultimately want to reduce the instances of the associated teacher behaviors as part of an intervention to reduce self-injury. Just as one application of functional assessment requires that we ask teachers what tends to occur before student injury, we might sequentially analyze which of these teacher behaviors tends to *precede* self-injury most often.

The primary source of the miscommunication of backward sequential analysis results in the mismatch between the motivating theory of the study, the terms used in sequential analysis, and the backward sequential analysis process. The motivating theory of most studies employing sequential analysis presumes a causal relationship between the antecedent and target behaviors. Causality progresses forward in time. The terms "target" or "second behavior" typically apply to behaviors that occur *after* an "antecedent" or "first behavior".

For example, assume that we conduct a backward and forward analysis to identify the best candidates for antecedents of self-injury. The reason to conduct the study is eventually to reduce self-injury by reducing the occurrence of the antecedent behaviors of self-injury. However, the second behaviors in a backward analysis are the *possible antecedents.* In contrast, the second behavior in a forward analysis to address the same question is *self-injury*. That is, the target behavior in the two or more sequences compared in a similar forward sequential analysis is the same. But in the backward sequential analysis, the target behaviors in the sequential associations to be compared are different. If the target behaviors are different, their base rates are almost always different. As always, differences in the transitional probabilities are not interpretable when we compare transitional probabilities for sequences with different target behavior base rates. The implication of this is that backward sequential analyses that compare transitional probabilities can produce apparent differences that have nothing to do with the relative strength of association between the potential antecedents and the behavior of interest. Fortunately, Yule's Q provides an index that can be used to compare sequential associations derived from forward and backward sequential analyses because Yule's Q controls for the base rates of the antecedent and target behaviors. In fact, Yule's Q from a forward analysis is identical to that from a backward analysis of the same data.

Methods for Comparing Sequential Dependencies

We can compare sequential associations on a group or single-subject level. When we compare sequential associations on a single-subject level, we are testing whether the degree of difference in sequential associations could have occurred by a random process. We are not trying to generalize to a population of people. Instead, we are asking whether the differences are likely to replicate in similar behavior samples from the same subject. Yoder, Bruce and Tapp (2001) indicated that log-linear analysis can be used to compare sequential associations in a single participant with the proper alpha level in cases where the lengths of the behavior streams being compared are not grossly different. See Bakeman and Quera (1995b) for details on how these may be run.

When we compare sequential associations within persons for a group (such as injury after instructions in the classroom as opposed to on the playground), we are testing whether the mean difference between Yule's Q scores differs from zero. Unlike tests of the difference in sequential associations at the single-subject level, we are wanting to generalize to a population of people. We are asking whether the differences are likely to replicate in a different but similar sample of participants. This type of question could be addressed by using a one-sampled t-test. When we compare sequential associations between independent groups (such as injury after instructions in persons with severe mental retardation as opposed to persons with autism), we are testing whether the mean Yule's Q scores differ between groups. This can be tested with an independent t-test.

When Do We Have "Enough" Observational Data to Test Our Research Questions?

One needs a "sufficiently" large behavior sample for Yule's Q (or any other index of sequential association) to be reliable, and the behavior sample size must be sufficiently large to detect a particular sequential association or difference in sequential associations as statistically significant. When we attempt to address our research questions with "too few" coded behaviors or "too brief" a behavior sample, we make it more difficult to detect a sequential association, particularly if the sequence does not occur frequently in our behavior sample.

Measurement theory tells us that when a behavior sample is small, it will probably contain more measurement error than will longer samples. This point has been empirically demonstrated (Bakeman, Quera, McArthur & Robinson, 1997). There is evidence that a relatively short behavior sample can produce a reliable Yule's Q if (a) the individual codes are coded with great accuracy (such as above .80 kappa with a perfectly coded session), (b) the number of categories in the behavioral coding system is small (two or three), and the simple probabilities of the antecedent and target behaviors are approximately equal (Bakeman et al., 1997). Similarly, a much longer sample is needed to produce an acceptably reliable Yule's Q score when the number of codes is 10 or more and the simple probabilities of the antecedent and target events are very different from each other (Bakeman et al., 1997). Unfortunately, the simple probabilities of the target and antecedents are *usually* different, and we *usually* have more than two or three categories of behaviors in our coding systems. Of course, an index can be reliable, but still not have sufficient statistical power to detect a significant sequential association or difference in sequential associations.

If we are conducting our significance tests on the group level, we can use traditional power analyses to estimate the number of subjects needed for a sample of people. To determine how long or how many times one needs to observe each participant, it is advisable to conduct a power analysis at the single-subject level with pilot data from a representative participant. StatXact (Version 5) (Mehta & Patel, 2001) has power analysis for binomial tables that can be used to conduct power analyses at the single-subject level. This way of doing a power analysis requires that we indicate our proposed effect size and population characteristics in the form of a 2×2 table like Figure 8.1. For example, we may have a pilot behavior sample that has been coded and tallied into cells A – D with counts of 100, 200, 50, and 400, respectively. The Yule's Q for this 2×2 table is the effect size (that is, .6). The software program creates many (for example, 10 000) bootstrapped samples by randomly selecting with replacement the number of "behaviors" (that is, total tallies in the 2×2 table) that match a particular sample size (such as 500 behaviors) from the pilot "population" (that is, 2×2 table of pilot data). The computer program uses an iterative process to find the sample size of these bootstrapped samples that is necessary to attain the desired statistical power, given the effect size and population characteristics represented in the pilot data. This is implicitly the process we use when we use the effect size from pilot data in any power analysis. That is, we use the data from a limited sample and assume that it represents the effect size and population characteristics of the population from which we are sampling. The more representative the original "pilot" data, the more accurate the resulting power analysis.

RELIABILITY AND VALIDITY

This section takes a step back to issues that include both sequential and nonsequential variables: reliability and validity of variables derived from behavioral observations. Reliability refers to whether the variable is reproducible or consistent across observers, measurement contexts, and time. Validity refers to whether a variable measures the ability or characteristic it purports to measure. In general, coding systems or measurement procedures are not "reliable" or "valid". Instead, variables that are derived from coding systems are "reliable" or "valid" for a particular sample of people for a particular purpose. This means that we cannot just demonstrate reliability and validity for one sample and purpose and assume that it is reliable and valid for others.

Reliability

Classical measurement theory tells us that a variable is composed of a "true score" plus "measurement error" (Suen & Ary, 1989). The true score represents accurate differences between analysis units on some characteristic or ability (such as communication ability). The measurement error is the sum of all of the reasons one score is higher than another that do not have to do with differences in true ability. We can only estimate measurement error. The different types of reliability represent the primary ways we estimate different sources of measurement error.

Types of Reliability

There are three primary types of reliability that are relevant to observational data: across context (that is, representativeness), across measurement periods (that is, stability), and between observers. Reliability across context is relevant when the research question implicitly assumes that the observational data are measuring individual differences among participants that are assumed to be present in many or all contexts. Reliability across time is relevant when the research question implicitly assumes that the observational data are measuring individual differences among participants (or within a single participant) that are assumed to be present across a given interval of time. These two types of reliability are less frequently estimated for observational data than is interobserver reliability because (a) not all research questions require them, and (b) these types of reliability depend on interobserver reliability. Interobserver reliability is always necessary when using observational data, but it is insufficient to demonstrate representativeness and stability. Given the primary importance of interobserver reliability to the topic of this chapter, the rest of this section will focus on issues relevant to its estimation.

Interobserver Reliability Versus Interobserver Agreement

Conceptually, interobserver reliability refers to whether results are consistent between two or more observers. Typically, we estimate reliability by having two or more observers code about 20% of the real data. For example, if the data collected to address a research question are on 20 sessions, five of these sessions would be coded by two observers to estimate reliability. To increase the probability that the sessions will be representative, we sample them randomly from all relevant conditions. The "reliability sample" for this hypothetical study would be 10 data points (that is, five sessions times two observers).

Operationally, interobserver reliability refers to the ratio defined as the following: between-participant or between-session variance divided by total variance in the reliability sample (Suen & Ary, 1989). Differences between participants are relevant to group designs, and differences between sessions are relevant to single-case designs. Note that we did not say that interobserver reliability refers to whether two or more observers see the same thing from the same observation session. Suen and Ary (1989) distinguish the second meaning from the first by calling the latter "interobserver agreement" and the former "interobserver reliability". The two concepts are related, but they are different in ways that have practical consequences.

Interobserver agreement is important during the training and retraining phases of data collection. That is, we want to be recording that the same thing occurred at the same time during the training and retraining phases because it helps us fine-tune our understanding of the coding system and the coding system manual. This level of agreement is called "point-by-point" agreement. The most common index for this type of agreement is percentage agreement (that is, number of agreements/number of agreements plus disagreements). Unfortunately, percentage agreement does not control for chance agreement. That is why Cohen's (1960) kappa is a frequently recommended index of point-by-point interobserver agreement (Bakeman & Gottman, 1997). Kappa is conceptually defined as "observed agreement minus estimated chance agreement". Bakeman and Gottman (1997) discuss how to compute kappa.

However, after the data collection has been completed, we are ready to estimate the reliability of the variable scores that we wish to analyze to address our research question. At this stage, Suen and Ary (1989) and Bakeman and Gottman (1997) recommend intraclass correlation coefficients, or G coefficients, to estimate interobserver reliability. The conceptual meaning of such coefficients is true score/(true score plus measurement error). Because we cannot measure either directly, we estimate them by examining sources of variance in the reliability sample. True score is estimated by variance between the participants (or sessions) averaged across the coders. The measurement error due to differences between coders' judgments is variance between coders averaged across sessions (or participants) (Bakeman & Gottman, 1997). Thinking of reliability in this way allows us to judge the seriousness of the observed degree of disagreement between coders by considering the magnitude of variance between participants (or sessions). Given two data sets with the same amount of between-coder variance, reliability will be higher for a data set with much variance between participants than for a data set with little variance between participants. The G coefficient reflects this fact. Point-by-point agreement indices do not.

The reader's attention should be on the reliability of the *variable* that is to be analyzed, not on the reliability of a particular behavior category or the coding system as a whole. Bakeman et al. (1997) provided empirical evidence that the kappa for individual behaviors can be quite high, and the index of sequential association can still be unacceptably low. Similarly, individual behaviors can be coded at point-by-point interobserver agreement levels of .80, and proportions derived from summary counts of the behaviors can still be unreliable. For example, we want to know whether the proportion of acts to which mothers respond is reliable, not just whether the numerator and denominator (that is, number of communication acts and number of maternal responses, respectively) of this proportion are reliable.

Additionally, we need to know whether the variable is reliable at the unit of analysis we are analyzing. By units of analysis, we mean participants in a group design and sessions in a single-subject experimental design. For example, if the interobserver agreement of .80 for self-injury is derived from data that have been pooled across several participants because self-injury is such a low-frequency behavior in any one participant, the interobserver agreement estimate tells us little about the level of reliability of individual participant's variable scores. In reality, if the behavior is very low frequency in any one participant, it is extremely difficult to have enough variance between individuals or sessions to have high reliability. When behaviors of interest occur infrequently, many sessions for each individual may need to be collected.

We should care about the reliability of variables scores for the units whose variance we want to explain because it is reliability at this level of detail that affects the magnitude of effects we are able to detect (Suen & Ary, 1989). The G coefficient can estimate the reliability of any type of variable—frequency, rate, proportion, Yule's Q, etc.—and any type of reliability (such as stability across context, stability over time, or interobserver reliability). For information on how to compute G coefficients, see Suen and Ary (1989) or Bakeman and Gottman (1997).

The Consequence of Using Variables with Low Reliability

The consequence of low reliability is usually a reduced probability of detecting an effect or relationship involving the variable of interest, even when the predicted effect is really present (that is, a type II error). This occurs because measurement error is usually uncorrelated with levels of the other variables in the research question (that is, it is randomly distributed). Randomly distributed measurement error is noise, and noise makes it harder to perceive a pattern in the data. For example, assume I want to know whether children with intellectual disabilities intentionally communicate better with their teacher than with their parent. Further assume that the disagreements of the primary observer with the secondary observer favor the teacher half the time and favor the parent the other half of the time. In the analysis that tests the research question, variance due to observer measurement error is considered "unexplained variance". We detect relationships and differences by maximizing variance explained by the relationship or difference and reducing the variance that is "unexplained". Empirical studies of measurement error show that measurement error is usually randomly distributed (Thompson, 1994).

The exception to this rule is when the measurement error is correlated with levels or values of another variable named in the research question (that is, "correlated measurement error"). In such cases, the measurement error can cause the investigator to find an effect that is not really present in the population (that is, a type I error). For example, assume I want to know whether women with intellectual disabilities stay on topic better than do men with intellectual disabilities. Assume further that the primary observer is biased in favor of women due to positive past experience with women and negative past experience with men. Also assume that the reliability observer is not as biased toward either gender. Their disagreements on the relative number of on-topic utterances would reveal measurement error that was systematically associated with gender, a variable in the research question. This type of very specific bias is fortunately less common than randomly distributed error, particularly in observational data (Thompson, 1994).

Validity

Types of Validity

There are three primary types of validity: criterion-related, content, and construct. By criterion-related validity, we mean that the observational variable is moderately to strongly correlated with an accepted measure (that is, a "gold" standard) of the ability or characteristic that the observational measure is purported to measure (Suen & Ary, 1989). For example, a correlation of .75 between the number of different words used per minute in a free-flowing conversation and the raw score on the Expressive One Word Picture Vocabulary Test (EOWPVT) is evidence supporting the criterion-related validity of number of different words as a measure of productive vocabulary.

By content validity, we mean the degree to which experts agree that a particular operational definition of behavioral category represents what the field generally means when using the category's label (Kerlinger, 1979). For example, Baird, Hass, Carruth, McCormick and Turner (1991) sent out a coding system to many experts in mother–child interaction to determine the degree to which they agreed that the definitions for constructs such as "parent directiveness" in their coding system matched the expert's notion of the construct. Only 57% of the experts said the definition for parent directiveness was "extremely valid". After revising the definition, the second set of evaluations indicated that 71% of the experts considered the definition "extremely valid". The high agreement among the experts that the definition very closely matched their understanding of the "directiveness" construct was evidence of content validity.

Perhaps the most important type of validity is construct validity. Conceptually, this means that the variable in question correlates with measures of abilities that are theoretically associated with the construct in question, and does not correlate with measures of abilities that are theoretically unrelated to the construct of interest (Cronbach & Meehl, 1955). For example, we found that the number of prelinguistic comments from an evocative communication sample predicted who is likely to talk one year later in a sample of toddlers with developmental disabilities; however, the former variable was not related to chronological age (Yoder, Warren & McCathren, 1998). This supported the hypothesis that number of prelinguistic comments from this procedure is a valid measure of the ability because such an ability is predicted by theory to be related to later language, but not to chronological age in children with intellectual disabilities (Sigman & Ruskin, 1999).

CONCLUSION

Observing behavior can result in a rich description of what occurs in a particular context. There are two general types of variables derived from these observational data:

nonsequential and sequential. This chapter focused primarily on the latter. When one's research questions are motivated by a theory that poses a close temporal relationship between one behavior and another behavior, sequential analysis is likely to be useful. We recommend using the odds ratio or Yule's Q as the index of sequential association for most purposes. Methods of testing the significance of sequential associations and for testing the difference between sequential associations were discussed. Such significance tests can be carried out on the single-subject level or at the group level. We also discussed an approach to conducting a power analysis at the single-subject level to determine how large the behavioral sample needs to be to detect a sequential association of a given magnitude. Finally, we discussed several important issues relevant to estimating reliability and determining the validity of observational variables.

REFERENCES

Allison, P.D. & Liker, J.K. (1982). Analyzing sequential categorical data on dyadic interaction: a comment on Gottman. *Psychological Bulletin*, **91**, 393–403.

Baird, S., Hass, L., Carruth, C., McCormick, K. & Turner, K. (1991). The prelinguistic infant–parent communicative interaction code: a system for observation and measurement [unpublished manuscript]. Auburn University.

Bakeman, R. & Doral, B. (1989). The distinction between sampling independence and empirical independence in sequential analysis. *Behavioral Assessment*, **11**, 31–37.

Bakeman, R. & Gottman, J. (1997). *Observing Interaction: An Introduction to Sequential Analysis* (2nd edn). Cambridge: Cambridge University Press.

Bakeman, R., McArthur, D. & Quera, V. (1996a). Detecting group differences in sequential association using sampled permutations: log odds, kappa, and phi compared. *Behavior Research Methods, Instruments, and Computers*, **28**, 446–457.

Bakeman, R. & Quera, V. (1995). Log-linear approaches to lag-sequential analysis when consecutive codes may and cannot repeat. *Psychological Bulletin*, **118**, 272–284.

Bakeman, R., Quera, V., McArthur, D. & Robinson, B. (1997). Detecting sequential patterns and determining their reliability with fallible observers. *Psychological Methods*, **2**, 357–370.

Bakeman, R., Robinson, B. & Quera, V. (1996b). Testing sequential association: estimating exact *p* values using sampled permutations. *Psychological Methods*, **1**, 4–15.

Cohen, J. (1960). A coefficient of agreement for nominal scales. *Educational and Psychological Measurement*, **20**, 37–46.

Cronbach, L.J., Gleser, G.C., Nanda, H. & Rajaratnam, N. (1972). *The Dependability of Behavioral Measurements: Theory of Generalizability for Scores and Profiles*. New York: Plenum.

Cronbach, L. & Meehl, P. (1955). Construct validity in psychological tests. *Psychological Bulletin*, **52**, 281–302.

Edgington, E.S. (1995). *Randomization Tests* (3rd edn). New York: Marcel Dekker.

Emerson, E., Hatton, C., Robertson, J., Henderson, D. & Cooper, J. (1999). A descriptive analysis of the relationships between social context, engagement and stereotypy in residential services for people with severe and complex disabilities. *Journal of Applied Research in Intellectual Disabilities*, **12**, 11–29.

Gardner, F. (2000). Methodological issues in the direct observation of parent–child interaction: do observational findings reflect the natural behavior of participants? *Clinical Child and Family Psychology Review*, **3**, 185–198.

Hall, S. & Oliver, C. (2000). An alternative approach to the sequential analysis of behavioral interactions. In T. Thompson, D. Felce & F. Symons (Eds) *Behavioral Observation: Technology and Applications in Developmental Disabilities* (pp. 335–348). Baltimore, MD: Brookes.

Kahng, S. & Iwata, B. (2000). Computer systems for collecting real-time observational data. In T. Thompson, D. Felce & F. Symons (Eds) *Behavioral Observation: Technology and Applications in Developmental Disabilities* (pp. 35–46). Baltimore, MD: Brookes.

Kerlinger, F. (1979). *Behavioral Research: A Conceptual Approach*. New York: Holt, Rinehart and Winston.

Martin, P. & Bateson, P. (1993). *Measuring Behavior: An Introductory Guide* (2nd edn). New York: Cambridge University Press.

McWilliam, R. & Ware, W. (1994). The reliability of observations of young children's engagement: an application of generalizability theory. *Journal of Early Intervention*, **18**, 34–48.

Mehta, C. & Patel, N. (2001). *StatXact* (Version 5). Cambridge, MA: Cytel Software Corporation.

Reynolds, H.T. (1984). *Analysis of Nominal Data*. Beverly Hills, CA: Sage.

Rocissano, L., Slade, A. & Lynch, V. (1987). Dyadic synchrony and toddler compliance. *Developmental Psychology*, **23**, 698–704.

Rosenblum, L. (1978). The creation of a behavioral taxonomy. In G.P. Sackett (Ed.) *Observing Behavior*, vol. II. *Data Collection and Analysis Methods* (pp. 15–24). Baltimore, MD: University Park Press.

Sackett, G. (1978). Measurement in observational research. In G.P. Sackett (Ed.) *Observing Behavior*, vol. II. *Data Collection and Analysis Methods* (pp. 25–44). Baltimore, MD: University Park Press.

Sackett, G. (2000). Observational research in mental retardation. In T. Thompson, D. Felce & F. Symons (Eds) *Behavioral Observation: Technology and Applications in Developmental Disabilities* (pp. 17–31). Baltimore, MD: Brookes.

Sigman, M. & Ruskin, E. (1999). Continuity and change in the social competence of children with autism, Down syndrome, and developmental delays. *Monographs of the Society for Research in Child Development*, **64**.

Suen, H. & Ary, D. (1989). *Analyzing Quantitative Behavioral Observation Data*. Hillsdale, NJ: Erlbaum.

Thompson, B. (1994). Guidelines for authors. *Educational and Psychological Measurement*, **54**, 837–847.

Thompson, T., Symons, F. & Felce, D. (2000). Principles of behavioral observation. In T. Thompson, D. Felce & F. Symons (Eds) *Behavioral Observation: Technology and Applications in Developmental Disabilities* (pp. 3–16). Baltimore, MD: Brookes.

Wampold, B.E. & Kim, K.H. (1989). Sequential analysis applied to counseling process and outcome: a case study revisited. *Journal of Counseling Psychology*, **36**, 357–364.

Yoder, P.J., Bruce, P. & Tapp, J. (2001). Comparing sequential associations within a single dyad. *Behavior Research Methods, Instruments, and Computers*, **33**, 331–338.

Yoder, P.J., Davies, B. & Bishop, K. (1994). Reciprocal sequential dependencies in conversations with parents and children with developmental delays. *Journal of Early Intervention*, **18**, 362–379.

Yoder, P. & Fearer, I. (2000). Quantifying the magnitude of sequential association between events and behaviors. In T. Thompson, D. Felce & F. Symons (Eds) *Behavioral Observation: Technology and Applications in Developmental Disabilities* (pp. 317–334). Baltimore, MD: Brookes.

Yoder, P., Short-Meyerson, K. & Tapp, J.T. (2000, April). *Sequential analysis of adult–child interactions: issues that are rarely discussed*. Poster presented at the Conference on Treatment Efficacy, Nashville.

Yoder, P.J., Warren, S.F. & McCathren, R. (1998). Determining the spoken language prognosis in children with developmental disabilities. *American Journal of Speech-Language Pathology*, **7**, 77–87.

SECTION III

Researching the Nature, Characteristics, and Social Context of Intellectual Disability

CHAPTER 9

Studying Behavioral Phenotypes: Issues, Benefits, Challenges

Robert M. Hodapp
Vanderbilt University, USA
and
Elisabeth M. Dykens
Vanderbilt University, USA

A quiet revolution is influencing behavioral research in intellectual disabilities. Simply stated, researchers and practitioners have begun to realize that specific genetic disorders affect behavior. This growing appreciation, a process that continues to this day, nevertheless leaves many questions unanswered.

Before tackling these issues, some background seems necessary on the revolution itself, as well as the current state of disability studies vis-à-vis this revolution. A first point of entry involves human genetics. Probably more than any scientific field, human genetics has advanced rapidly over the past few years. Using modern molecular techniques, geneticists are now able to "see" parts of individual chromosomes and, increasingly, each individual gene on all 23 pairs of human chromosomes. The best-known result of these efforts is the Human Genome Project, which recently announced that geneticists have chemically mapped the entire human genome. Increasingly over the next few years, genetic causes and predispositions will be discovered for a wide variety of human diseases.

For our purposes, over 750 genetic disorders have now been associated with intellectual disabilities (Opitz, 1996). While a few of these syndromes are well known (such as Down syndrome), most occur only rarely. Overall, approximately 1/3 to 1/2 of all cases of intellectual disabilities are probably due to genetic disorders (Matalainen, Airaksinen, Mononen, Launiala & Kaarianen, 1995). More persons of lower IQ levels (IQ <50) show genetic etiologies, but substantial percentages of persons with mild intellectual disabilities are also now being diagnosed with genetic disorders (Rutter, Simonoff & Plomin, 1996). Though probably not the cause of intellectual disabilities in all cases, genetic disorders seem much more common than previously thought.

The International Handbook of Applied Research in Intellectual Disabilities. Edited by E. Emerson, C. Hatton, T. Thompson and T.R. Parmenter ISBN 0-471-49709-6.

What has been the response from behavioral workers to these genetic advances? In a word, mixed. On the one hand, many behavioral workers have persisted in the field's traditional, long-held views that "rarely have behavioral differences characterized different etiological groups" (Ellis, 1969). Similarly, in a review of intellectual disabilities journals from 1985 to 1990, we noted relatively small percentages (6–34%) of etiology-based behavioral research articles in journals such as *Mental Retardation*, the *American Journal on Mental Retardation*, and the *Journal of Intellectual Disabilities* (Hodapp & Dykens, 1994).

On the other hand, as the 1990s progressed, a steady increase occurred in the numbers of etiology-based articles. Comparing the 1990s to the 1980s, we recently documented this increase (Dykens & Hodapp, 2001). Over the past two decades, the numbers of behavioral research articles on Williams syndrome increased from 10 to 81; on Prader-Willi syndrome, from 24 to 86; and on fragile X syndrome, from 60 to 149. Even in Down syndrome, the sole etiology featuring a long-standing tradition of behavioral research, the amount of behavioral research almost doubled—from 607 to 1140 articles—from the 1980s to the 1990s.

Is the glass half-full or half-empty? Although one could argue either way, several facts seem clear. A first fact involves the unevenness in what we know about which syndromes. To this day, many more studies are performed on Down syndrome (over 1000 during the 1990s) than on almost all other syndromes combined. In addition, we know a fair amount about behavior in persons with Williams syndrome, Prader-Willi syndrome, and fragile X syndrome (see Dykens, Hodapp & Finucane, 2000, for a review). We also know a little, but not enough, about a few other genetic disorders such as the Rett, velocardiofacial, Rubenstein-Taybi, Smith-Magenis, Angelman, and 5p- syndromes. For most of the 750 or more genetic etiologies of intellectual disabilities, however, we do not possess even a single behavioral study. These disorders are the subject of only a few articles, usually in genetics or clinical genetics journals. In the midst of information about the disorder's genetics, prevalence, physical appearance, and medical-health issues, most such articles also provide basic behavioral descriptions, usually of IQ level or any salient maladaptive behavior. Though better than no information at all, such behavioral descriptions nevertheless need to be fleshed out by more sophisticated behavioral research.

The issues, though, transcend the need for more behavioral research per se. We also require more thinking about how to study the influences on behavior of different genetic disorders. In short, we continue to need a greater amount of *and* more sophisticated, etiology-based behavioral research.

This chapter examines several of these research issues. We begin by examining "behavioral phenotypes", providing our own definition of this controversial term. With this definition as background, we next explore design issues. Such issues include how to identify research subjects of a particular etiology, how to compare these subjects to control or contrast groups, and how to think about various types of within-syndrome variability. A second major issue concerns measurement. How does one even know, across a host of behavioral domains, that one has found an "etiology-related" behavior? We end this chapter by linking design-measurement concerns to three goals of etiology-based behavioral research.

"BEHAVIORAL PHENOTYPES": DEFINITION AND IMPLICATIONS

As the title of this chapter suggests, the behavioral effects of genetic syndromes have come to be considered under the term "behavioral phenotypes". At its most basic meaning, the term highlights the outcomes (that is, phenotypes)—in this case concerning behavior—that result from a particular genotype.

Beyond such general statements, however, the term "behavioral phenotype" has elicited many different definitions. At the risk of muddying already murky waters, we, too, offer a definition of "behavioral phenotype". Before doing so, however, it is instructive to cite another, also commonly used definition. Although clashing in several important ways, the two definitions highlight both practical and theoretical concerns that deserve our attention.

The first definition, by Flynt and Yule (1994), states that "a behavioral phenotype should consist of a distinct behavior that occurs in almost every case of a genetic or chromosomal disorder, and rarely (if at all) in other conditions" (p. 666). This definition thus reserves the term for behaviors that are distinctive, occur very commonly among individuals with a genetic syndrome ("in almost every case"), and are unique to a single syndrome ("rarely . . . in other conditions"). Not surprisingly, perhaps, given this definition—which Flynt and Yule (1994) admit is fairly strict—behavioral phenotypes exist in very few genetic disorders.

In contrast, we propose a less stringent definition, but one that may ultimately prove to be more useful for both research and intervention. Thus, according to Dykens (1995), a behavioral phenotype involves "the heightened probability or likelihood that people with a given syndrome will exhibit certain behavioral and developmental sequelae relative to those without the syndrome" (p. 523). This more probabilistic definition advances behavioral research by highlighting three basic facts, as follows.

Many, But Not All, Individuals with a Given Syndrome Will Show the Syndrome's "Characteristic" Behaviors

A more probabilistic definition acknowledges the large amount of variance within specific etiologies. Indeed, rarely are etiology-related behaviors found in every person with a particular syndrome. Consider the case of Down syndrome. Even compared to their overall mental ages, children and adults with Down syndrome generally show deficits in linguistic grammar (Fowler, 1990) and often show receptive language abilities in advance of expressive abilities (Miller, 1992, 1999). In addition, approximately 95% of mothers of children with Down syndrome report that others have difficulty in understanding their child's articulation of words and phrases (Kumin, 1994).

Despite such commonly observed deficits, not every person with Down syndrome shows particular difficulties with grammar, articulation, or expressive language. Rondal (1995) recently reported on the case of Françoise, a 32-year-old woman whose IQ is 64. Although Françoise has trisomy 21, she utters long and complex sentences. Rondal (1995, p. 117) reports her saying (translated), "And that does not surprise me because dogs are always too warm when they go outside" ("Et ça m'étonne pas parce que les chiens ont toujours trop chaud quand ils vont à la port"). Thus, while grammatical, articulatory, and expressive language problems may be common in Down syndrome, not every person with the syndrome shows such behavioral characteristics.

Some Etiology-Related Behaviors Will Be Unique to a Single Syndrome, Whereas Others Are Common to Two or More Syndromes

The second corollary of a more probabilistic definition considers whether an etiology-related distinctive behavior must occur "rarely (if at all) in other conditions". Again, we take issue with such a strict definition, mostly because recent research strongly implies that etiology-related behaviors are often not unique to a single syndrome.

In fact, connections between genetic syndromes and specific outcomes appear to be of at least two types. The first type involves connections that are unique, that appear in one and only one genetic syndrome. The second involves connections that are "partially specific" (Hodapp, 1997), in that a few syndromes show a particular behavior that is not generally found in others with intellectual disabilities.

In the first, unique pattern, a genetic syndrome often results in a particular outcome that is simply not seen in other genetic disorders. At present, the following behaviors seem unique to one and only one syndrome:

- extreme hyperphagia (overeating) (Dykens, 1999) in Prader-Willi syndrome
- the "cat cry" (Gersh et al., 1995) in 5p- syndrome
- extreme self-mutilation (Anderson & Ernst, 1994) in Lesch-Nyhan syndrome
- stereotypic "hand washing" or "hand-wringing" (Van Acker, 1991) in Rett syndrome
- body "self-hugging" (Finucane, Konar, Haas-Givler, Kurtz & Scott, 1994) and putting objects into body orifices (Greenburg et al., 1996) in Smith-Magenis syndrome.

Obviously, this list is fairly short; there are probably only a few instances in which a genetic disorder is unique in its behavioral effects. Flynt and Yule (1994) also noted this peculiarity, nominating as unique (in their term, as examples of a behavioral phenotype) only the self-mutilating behaviors in Lesch-Nyhan syndrome, the overeating and abnormal food-seeking behavior in Prader-Willi syndrome, and the hand-wringing in Rett syndrome (p. 667). Although Flynt and Yule also propose a few other examples in which a behavior might be unique to one syndrome, such 1:1 relationships are relatively rare.

In contrast, it now appears that many more instances will be discovered in which partial specificity is at work. To give but a few examples, a particular advantage in simultaneous (that is, holistic, Gestalt-like) processing compared to sequential (step-by-step) processing has now been found in boys with fragile X syndrome (Kemper, Hagerman & Altshul-Stark, 1988; Dykens, Hodapp & Leckman, 1987) and in children with Prader-Willi syndrome (Dykens, Hodapp, Walsh & Nash, 1992). Similarly, compared to groups with intellectual disabilities in general, hyperactivity is more frequently found in children with 5p- syndrome (Dykens & Clarke, 1997) and in boys with fragile X syndrome (Baumgardner, Reiss, Freund & Abrams, 1995). In both instances, a pattern of strengths and weaknesses or a particular type of maladaptive behavior-psychopathology is found in a few genetic disorders to much greater degrees (or in higher percentages of individuals) than is commonly noted among others with intellectual disabilities.

As these examples also demonstrate, the situation is further complicated in that both unique and partially specific behaviors often co-exist within the same syndrome. Groups with Prader-Willi syndrome are unique in that most individuals display hyperphagia, but persons with Prader-Willi syndrome join boys with fragile X syndrome in showing simultaneous over sequential processing (which is not seen in groups with intellectual disabilities due to heterogeneous causes) (Naglieri, 1985; Obrzut, Nelson & Obrzut, 1987).

Finally, partially specific behavioral effects seem more in line with many areas of genetics, child psychiatry, and psychiatry. Across these different disciplines, researchers are now discussing the many pathways—both genetic and environmental—by which one comes to have one or another psychiatric disorder. The clinical geneticist John Opitz (1985) put it well when he noted, "The causes are many, but the common developmental pathways are few" (p. 9).

Etiology-Related Behaviors Occur Across Many Behavioral Domains

When considering behavioral phenotypes, most researchers probably think of salient maladaptive behaviors such as hyperphagia in Prader-Willi syndrome or extreme self-mutilation in Lesch-Nyhan syndrome. At the same time, however, behavioral phenotypes can be found in many different domains. In the growing numbers of detailed studies of the language of children with Williams syndrome, for example, psycholinguists are gaining insights into whether language is indeed a "modular" system (Fodor, 1983). Such studies compare or correlate levels of functioning across different linguistic and nonlinguistic domains (e.g., Bellugi, Mills, Jernigan, Hickok & Galaburda, 1999; Mervis, Morris, Bertrand & Robinson, 1999). Etiology-related behaviors, then, can be found in linguistic and nonlinguistic functioning, but also in many other areas of human psychological functioning.

The point is that behavioral phenotypes need not be limited to maladaptive behavior or psychopathology. Instead, many behavioral domains and even individual behaviors (such as the self-hug) can be seen more often among persons with a particular etiology. Similarly, at times, what is of interest is not a single behavior per se, but a pattern of strengths and weaknesses, connected or disconnected behaviors, or other patterns seen in one or a few syndromes more often than in others with intellectual disabilities.

DESIGN ISSUES IN STUDIES OF BEHAVIORAL PHENOTYPES

Using this probabilistic definition as our starting point, we now consider how one studies behavioral phenotypes. The issues here seem threefold: identifying one's sample, comparing these samples to the appropriate control or contrast group, and considering various sources of within-syndrome variability.

Identifying or Documenting Cases with a Specific Syndrome

In most research in psychiatry and even in psychiatric genetics, one starts with behavior and tries to determine the underlying cause or causes of that behavior. Thus, one examines groups with depression, autism, or conduct disorder and attempts to determine which genetic or environmental factors helped bring about that disorder. In contrast, etiology-based researchers go in the opposite direction, starting with the person's genetic status and working forward to resultant behaviors. This sense that one "goes forward" from genetic diagnosis to resulting behaviors is, for us, one attraction of the etiology-based approach to behavioral research.

Examined closer, however, the situation is not so straightforward. Consider genetic diagnoses. For many syndromes, genetic diagnoses are relatively new. For example, even though Williams syndrome was first described in the early 1960s (Williams, Barrett-Boyes & Lowe, 1961; Beuren, Apitz & Harmjanz, 1962), the cause of this disorder remained unknown until the mid-1990s. Only at that time did Ewart et al. (1993) find that all cases of Williams syndrome had a very small deletion on the long arm of one of the person's chromosome 7s. Not visible by classic cytogenetic techniques, such microdeletions became detectable only due to developments in molecular genetics. Indeed, many molecular genetics techniques—including fluorescent in situ hybridization (FISH)—are less than a decade old (Dykens et al., 2000).

A further complication involves the various subtypes of genetic disorders. For certain genetic disorders, more than one genetic anomaly seems responsible. Whereas most (95%) persons with Down syndrome show trisomy 21, small percentages have either mosaicism (trisomy 21 in only some cells) or translocations (swapping of material from part of chromosome 21 and another chromosome). Similarly, Prader-Willi syndrome has two major subtypes: the first, occurring in about 2/3 of the population, has a deleted portion of chromosome 15 (15q11-q13), whereas the remainder show two chromosome 15s from the mother (maternal uniparental disomy).

Such issues bring about several practical problems. One involves the degree to which all subjects do indeed have any particular syndrome. To this day, most adults with Prader-Willi syndrome have been diagnosed either by cytogenetic studies (which can often show the deletion) or by "clinical criteria" (Holm et al., 1993). Such criteria are in some sense circular: experts with decades of experience in a disorder have decided that certain physical, medical, and behavioral indices make the person extremely likely to have the syndrome of interest. Although such clinical criteria have usually been borne out as more sensitive molecular methods have been developed, many individuals have been diagnosed by older cytogenetic or clinical criteria. Often, adults were diagnosed years ago (using the older criteria), and parents see little advantage in going back to have their offspring rediagnosed with the latest, state-of-the-art molecular techniques. As a result, although almost all persons diagnosed as having a particular genetic intellectual disability syndrome will actually have the syndrome, a few may not.

How can one ensure that all persons thought to have a particular genetic syndrome do indeed have that syndrome? Although time, money, and access to genetic laboratories can all be problematic, certain safeguards can be helpful. The first one involves collaborating with geneticists such that all subjects can be genetically diagnosed. At the very least, behavioral researchers can often obtain diagnostic information from newly performed genetic tests, pre-existing records, or even the parents themselves. One can then compare those subjects who, by genetic diagnosis, possess a specific genetic disorder to those who have the disorder on clinical grounds alone.

A final issue concerns whether one's subjects are typical of persons with the disorder. We here refer to the problem of parent groups. Simply stated, genetic disorders, such as the Prader-Willi, Williams, Smith-Magenis, and 5p- syndromes, are relatively rare, occurring only once in several thousand births. Researchers in most Western countries have therefore relied on subjects identified through membership in the appropriate parent group. But are parent-group parents—and their offspring—typical of the population of parents–offspring with a particular syndrome? At present, we do not know. Our suspicion, though, is that such parents are more often middle-class, well educated, and from the dominant culture; in the USA, such subjects are more often Caucasian, first (or only) English-speaking, and college educated.

If so, certain findings may be skewed. For example, although parents of, say, children with Prader-Willi syndrome show high levels of stress and stress levels relate to the child's degree of behavior problems (Hodapp, Dykens & Masino, 1997), those families that are non-Caucasian, non-English-speaking, and less highly educated, and that have lower incomes may show even more difficulties. Conversely, other issues would seem less

Table 9.1 Strengths and weaknesses of some common etiology-based research approaches

Control group	Characteristics	Strengths–weaknesses
A. *Strategies to determine whether a specific disorder has strengths–weaknesses*		
(1) *None*	Performance "against self"	Shows etiology strength
(2) *Typical*	Equated on MA	Shows relative strength (vs. MA) or intact functioning (vs. CA); unclear if equated on CA profile is unique, partially shared, or similar to all persons with intellectual disabilities (ID)
B. *Strategies to determine whether behavioral characteristics differ from others with intellectual disabilities*		
(3) *Mixed ID*	Mixed causes of ID	Shows that etiology strength–weakness is not due to ID. Weaknesses = hard to find; control group changes across studies; mixed ≠ nonspecific
(4) *Down*	DS	Shows behavior not due to any syndrome, but DS has its own behavioral *syndrome* characteristics (may lead to inaccurate conclusions if DS ≠ "all ID")
C. *Strategies to delineate further etiology-specific behaviors*		
(5) *Same-but-different ID*	Etiology similar in behavior to group	Highlights fine-grained differences in behavior if two or more etiologies have similar behaviors to make contrast meaningful
(6) *Special*	Group with special behavior	Shows ways that etiology is similar or different from group with special problem or profile (but without intellectual disabilities)

Notes: DS = Down Syndrome; MA = Mental Age; CA = Chronological Age
Source: reprinted (and adapted) from Hodapp and Dykens (2001)

influenced by such demographic variables. Parent education, ethnicity, and family income should, intuitively, have less of an effect on the child's type of maladaptive behavior-psychopathology or degree of simultaneous over sequential processing advantage.

Comparing to Others: The Control-Contrast Group Issue

After a group with a specific etiology is selected, who should be the control or comparison group? Reviewing research over the past decade, we conclude that most researchers use one of six different techniques (Hodapp & Dykens, 2001). These techniques, outlined in Table 9.1, revolve around three research questions.

Question 1: Does the Particular Etiology Group Show a Specific Strength or Weakness?

The first research question involves the presence of a particular strength or weakness. As shown in Table 9.1, two specific research techniques have generally been used. In the first, no control group is used. To determine whether children with Williams syndrome show strengths in language versus visuospatial processing, for example, Bellugi et al. (1999) compared each child's functioning on a language domain to that same child's performance on another domain. Similarly, we have found simultaneous processing strengths both in boys with fragile X syndrome (Dykens et al., 1987) and in children with Prader-Willi syndrome (Dykens et al., 1992) by comparing each child's performance on domains of simultaneous processing versus sequential processing on the Kaufman Assessment Battery for Children (K-ABC) (Kaufman & Kaufman, 1983). In Down syndrome, higher-level performance has been shown on tasks involving visual (as opposed to auditory) short-term memory (Pueschel, Gallagher, Zartler & Pezzullo, 1986; Hodapp et al., 1992; Hodapp, Evans & Gray, 1999).

Although widely used, this self-as-control technique has several limitations. One obvious problem is that, technically, one can only compare the person's performance on one versus another domain of a single test. Different tests have been standardized on different samples, and intelligence test scores tend to increase from decade to decade (the so-called "Flynn effect") (Flynn, 1999). As a result, it is probably better to stick to a single test when comparing any one individual's performance on different domains. Another problem involves the existence of such psychometric instruments. Many well-normed, standardized tests measure intellectual, adaptive, and linguistic functioning; many fewer assess mother–child interaction, emotions, or other areas.

A second commonly used technique within this class compares persons with intellectual disabilities to typically developing groups of either the same mental age (MA matches) or chronological age (CA matches). For almost four decades, developmentally oriented researchers have argued for MA matches, whereas "defect theorists" have advocated CA matches (cf. Hodapp & Zigler, 1995). Given recent etiology-based findings, both MA and CA matches may now be required. When certain etiological groups perform above MA matches, one has evidence that the group shows a relative strength in that area of behavior. But it is only in comparison to CA matches that one can determine whether certain groups are "spared" in their functioning in one or more areas of behavior. The best example involves Williams syndrome, long thought to be spared in certain areas of language. To determine whether language in Williams syndrome is indeed spared, one needs a CA-matched group or, through the use of the standardization sample, average or near-average performance in the domain of interest. Although "sparing" now seems unlikely for groups (as opposed to a few select individuals) with Williams syndrome (Karmiloff-Smith et al., 1997; Mervis et al., 1999), its test involves comparing to typically developing age-mates either explicitly (using a typical CA-matched group) or implicitly (using standard scores derived from a typically developing standardization sample).

Finally, showing that a particular etiological group has a specific strength or weakness does not, by itself, show a behavioral phenotype. It may instead be that all (or most) persons with intellectual disabilities show a particular pattern of cognitive, linguistic, adaptive, or other strengths and weaknesses. If so, then lowered intellectual ability is the problem, and the profile is not etiology-related per se. Such determinations require our second set of specific research techniques, to which we now turn.

Question 2: Does the Particular Etiology Group Show a Specific Profile or Behavior Compared to "Others with Intellectual Disabilities"?

As Table 9.1 shows, this second general research question also features two often-used techniques. In the first, researchers compare persons with a particular syndrome to a mixed or nonspecific group who are equated on both mental age and chronological age. If behavioral phenotypes do indeed involve "the heightened probability or likelihood that people with a given syndrome will exhibit certain behavioral and developmental sequelae relative to those without the syndrome" (Dykens, 1995, p. 523), such a "mixed group" would seem the best approximation to "those without the syndrome".

Even here, however, several issues arise. The first concerns the proper mixture of the mixed group, and how to ensure that one's sample does indeed approximate the larger population of persons with intellectual disabilities. Unfortunately, in contrast to many psychiatric disorders, the field of intellectual disabilities has performed few such epidemiological studies, and such issues become particularly problematic at mild levels of intellectual disabilities. Among all persons with intellectual disabilities, what percentage have Down syndrome? What percentage of those with mild intellectual disabilities have Prader-Willi syndrome? At present, we do not have precise answers.

Ironically, given current controversies, we may never know. Thus, the number of persons with intellectual disabilities overall will be greatly influenced by whether the IQ cutoff is considered to be "less than 70" or "less than 70 or 75" (Gresham, MacMillan & Siperstein, 1995). In the same way, percentages of the population with intellectual disabilities, and the numbers of persons at different levels of functioning (particularly with mild intellectual disabilities), will change according to whether the IQ cutoff is 70 or 75, as well as whether one includes (and how one defines) deficits in adaptive behavior. In short, if we cannot agree upon the makeup of the population of persons with intellectual disabilities, how can we ever possibly decide what the appropriate mix should be in samples with heterogeneous causes for their intellectual disabilities?

A second technique within this class compares one etiological group against persons with Down syndrome. Although groups with Down syndrome are often used as a "control group with intellectual disabilities", we consider this strategy to be inappropriate. Given findings from the past decade, persons with Down syndrome cannot constitute a stand-in for all persons with intellectual disabilities. As a group, persons with Down syndrome show deficits in grammar (Fowler, 1990) and in expressive language (Miller, 1992, 1999) that are much more severe than their overall mental-age levels; most persons with Down syndrome also show articulation problems (Kumin, 1994). Similarly, compared to others with intellectual disabilities, children with Down syndrome more often show "sociable" behaviors such as more looking and smiling at others (Kasari, Freeman, Mundy & Sigman, 1995; Kasari & Freeman, 2001). So, too, may these children show psychopathology less often and less severely than others with intellectual disabilities (Meyers & Pueschel, 1991; Dykens & Kasari, 1997). Especially in studies involving language, social skills, or maladaptive behavior-psychopathology, then, using samples with Down syndrome as a control group seems particularly ill advised.

Question 3: How Does the Particular Etiological Group Compare to Persons Without Intellectual Disabilities, But with Similar Conditions or Behaviors?

In contrast to the prior two general research approaches, this final approach compares persons who have a genetic syndrome to "specialized" groups. Here again, the general approach can be seen through the use of two specific research techniques. In the first, persons with a particular syndrome are compared to persons without intellectual disabilities who have one or another psychiatric disorder. Dykens, Leckman and Cassidy (1996) compared persons with Prader-Willi syndrome to outpatients with obsessive-compulsive disorder (OCD). With very few exceptions, the two groups were very similar in their mean number of compulsions, severity of compulsions, and the percentages within each group displaying such behaviors as cleaning, ordering/arranging, and repeating rituals. Although the two groups differed in a few behaviors, persons with Prader-Willi syndrome were remarkably similar in their obsessions and compulsions compared to a clinically diagnosed group with OCD.

Such a specialized-group strategy can also be shown in a second technique, this one comparing to persons without intellectual disabilities but who show particular cognitive-linguistic profiles. How, for example, might persons with Prader-Willi or fragile X syndrome—who show simultaneous-over-sequential processing abilities—compare to (typically developing) persons who similarly show such "simultaneous advantages"? Are the two groups approaching problems in the same way? How might children with Down syndrome compare to typical children who also show relative strengths in visual (versus auditory) short-term memory tasks?

In using the two specific techniques within this approach, one is trying to know more about the processes underlying behaviors. As such, one should be able to attain knowledge of specific behavioral processes that is far in advance of our current knowledge. The single drawback concerns the overall design of these studies. Essentially, using specialized groups without intellectual disabilities may often bring about no-difference findings. Though interesting, such results are always more problematic statistically.

Within-Syndrome Variability: All Persons with a Syndrome Are Not Alike

Although etiology-related behaviors are more common among persons with a particular syndrome, not every person will show the specific behavior of interest. But why not? Why doesn't every person with Prader-Willi syndrome show hyperphagia or the simultaneous-over-sequential processing advantage? Why does Françoise go against the "Down syndrome pattern" of extra deficits in language? To us, within-syndrome variability is equally as interesting as syndrome-related behaviors or profiles (Dykens, 1995; Fidler & Hodapp, 1999). Moreover, within-group variability opens up questions that so far remain almost totally unresolved.

To review a few of these issues, behavioral phenotypes change with age in several syndromes. Take the finding that boys with fragile X syndrome show higher-level abilities in simultaneous processing than in sequential processing. Although seen early on, older boys with fragile X syndrome show this simultaneous over sequential pattern to a much more pronounced degree (Hodapp, Dykens, Ort, Zelinsky & Leckman, 1991). Similarly, the percentage of young children with Down syndrome showing receptive language abilities in advance of expressive abilities goes up over the toddler years (Miller, 1992; 1999), and children with Williams syndrome show more pronounced language over visuospatial abilities as they get older (Bellugi et al., 1999; Jarrold, Baddeley, Hewes & Phillips, 2001).

In at least a few syndromes, then, areas of strength develop over age, whereas areas of weakness develop either very slowly or not at all. As a result, already strong domains become relatively stronger with age; conversely, weak ones become relatively weaker. But why such a finding occurs remains unclear. It may be that children themselves are "playing to their strengths", using pre-existing propensities toward their stronger areas to compensate for areas that, even at earlier ages, are already slightly weaker. Conversely, strengths (or weaknesses) may "kick in" at certain ages, or some combination of environmental and/or genetically mediated factors serve to turn on the development of strengths (and further slow the development of weaknesses). Whatever the explanation, developmental issues need to be included within etiology-related research more often and more explicitly (Bishop, 1999; Hodapp & Dykens, 2001).

Similarly, we only barely understand the different variants of genetic disorders. Prader-Willi syndrome, for example, occurs either through a deletion at a certain part of the father's chromosome 15 or from receiving two chromosome 15s from the mother (maternal uniparental disomy). For the most part, these two variants are similar, although those with deletions show higher levels of certain maladaptive behaviors and, possibly, lower IQs (possibly only verbal IQs; Dykens, Cassidy & King, 1999; Roof et al., 2000). Why such differences occur remains unknown.

Ultimately, within-group variation may be one key to understanding so-called "gene–brain–behavior" connections. Certain behavioral sequelae may result from having more versus less deleted material, or deleted material at one specific location and not another (as in the cat cry in 5p- syndrome; Gersh et al., 1995). Such genetic material, in turn, may lead to the production of either more or less of a particular protein, with changed distributions of such proteins resulting in different parts of the brain. So, too, may etiology-related behaviors change with age, with causes due to different environmental conditions or to different interactions between a child already predisposed to show certain profiles and specific environments. Within-group variation seems likely to produce tomorrow's most interesting etiology-related findings.

MEASUREMENT ISSUES IN STUDYING BEHAVIORAL PHENOTYPES

Just as the rise of science in the West was helped enormously by advances in the measurement of various natural phenomena (Crosby, 1997), so, too, is measurement important for etiology-based behavioral research. In past years, etiology-related measurement issues often concerned genetic diagnoses. Many syndromes had yet to be identified and, among those that were, reliable and valid diagnostic techniques were often not available. Over the past decade, FISH and other molecular genetic techniques have taken away such measurement issues in etiology-related research.

But still unresolved are many measurement issues concerning the best ways to identify and characterize etiology-related behaviors. This measurement issue arises partly due to the history of research on many genetic syndromes. Across many different etiologies, the original, more genetically oriented studies provided only general descriptions of behavior. Boys with fragile X syndrome were described as having speech that is "sing-songy"; children with Williams syndrome were said to have "cocktail party speech". Personality and maladaptive behavior were also described in global, impressionistic terms.

In subsequent years, behavioral workers have desired to measure these initial descriptors more precisely. Such approaches have generally fallen into one of the following three classes of measurement instrument.

A Comprehensive Checklist of Etiology-Related Behaviors

One approach has been to develop a single, comprehensive scale of behavioral measurement. Such a scale would capture individual behaviors, often those occurring in only one disorder. Rosen (1993) proposes the development of a checklist including "a finite number of stereotyped or ritualistic behaviors that have been observed in a broad group of biologically driven syndromes as well as in those individuals with developmental disorders with no known chromosomal or genetic determination" (p. 177). Such an approach, also supported by many members of the Society for the Scientific Study of Behavioural Phenotypes (O'Brien, 1993), would seem useful for studying certain types of etiology-related behaviors.

Several problems, however, arise with this approach. First, certain etiology-related behaviors occur in only a few syndromes and are unlikely to be included beforehand in any all-encompassing behavioral checklist. Would such a checklist include the self-hugging behavior in Smith-Magenis syndrome, or the cat cry in 5p- syndrome? Probably not. In fact, only behaviors already known or suspected to occur in a certain etiology would be placed on a comprehensive checklist.

A second problem concerns qualitative differences in behavior from one group to the next. Consider perseverative behavior. Although present in several genetic disorders, perseverative behaviors may differ markedly from one syndrome to another. As Dykens (1995) notes, males with fragile X syndrome often perseverate on unusual stimuli such as license plates, cartoons, or airplane engines, while the perseveration of persons with Smith-Magenis syndrome often involves repetitive questions (Where are you from? What's your name?). Individuals with Prader-Willi syndrome, in contrast, often perseverate on food. Using only a single, all-encompassing checklist, one could only describe each of these distinctive behaviors as "perseveration".

Third, one must address the idea of etiology-related behaviors that go beyond maladaptive behaviors per se. Higher language than visuospatial skills (Williams syndrome); better visual than auditory short-term memory (Down syndrome); higher simultaneous versus sequential processing (Prader-Willi syndrome; boys with fragile X syndrome)—all occur more often and to greater degrees in specific syndromes, yet are hard to capture using a single comprehensive checklist.

Overall, then, a single, comprehensive checklist may be acceptable when the etiology-related behavior is already known or suspected. In that case, the researcher can examine whether that single behavior occurs more frequently in one syndrome versus others with intellectual disabilities. This approach is limited, however, to individual behaviors that are already thought to occur more often in that particular syndrome.

Observational Methods

Judicious use of observational methods may circumvent some of the problems with a single, comprehensive checklist. By examining mother–child or experimenter–child interactions using time- or event-sampling coding, one can determine whether certain behaviors are indeed more common in a particular etiological group. Finucane et al. (1994), for example, noted a "self-hugging" behavior that probably occurs among individuals with Smith-Magenis syndrome much more often than among others with intellectual disabilities.

Similarly, the cat cry seems restricted to those with 5p- syndrome (Gersh et al., 1995). However, since neither study used control or contrast groups, one cannot say for sure that neither behavior occurs among others with intellectual disabilities. But, in principle, this more observational approach can usefully describe such behaviors.

In a similar way, one should be able to use observational methodology to examine more qualitative aspects of etiology-related behaviors. If, indeed, groups with fragile X syndrome, Smith-Magenis syndrome, and Prader-Willi syndrome show "perseveration" in different, etiology-related ways, it should be possible to capture such differences by observational methodology. To date, few studies have approached this level of refinement.

Measurement Issues Involving Psychometric Instruments

Another issue concerns psychometric instruments, usually of psychopathology-maladaptive behavior and cognition and language. As these issues also concern studies involving persons with intellectual disabilities in general, we deal with them only briefly.

A first concern arises when one examines etiology-related maladaptive behavior and psychopathology. To determine whether persons with a specific genetic syndrome differ from others with intellectual disabilities, many investigators have used standardized measures such as Achenbach's (1991) Child Behavior Checklist (CBCL), Aman and Singh's (1994) Aberrant Behavior Checklist (ABC), or Einfeld and Tonge's (1992) Developmental Behavioral Checklist (DBC). Such instruments incorporate many commonly occurring problems of childhood, and are often well normed on either typical populations (CBCL) or populations with intellectual disabilities (ABC; DBC). One can thereby determine whether children or adults with a genetic syndrome show higher levels of overall maladaptive behavior, of different types of behavior (the CBCL's wide- and narrow-band factors), and even of individual behaviors (e.g., Dykens & Kasari, 1997).

But such measures also have limitations. Specifically, measures normed on typically developing children may not always be appropriate for children or adults with intellectual disabilities. Conversely, the ABC, DBC, and instruments normed on populations with intellectual disabilities often have different items and factor structures compared to the CBCL and other measures of "typical" maladaptive behaviors (Dykens, 2000). In essence, one has difficulties in going back and forth between the two types of measures. How such measures then map onto psychiatric diagnoses—if they do—comprises yet another concern (Dykens, 1995). Each problem, though not specific to etiology-based research, still causes problems for those studying maladaptive behavior-psychopathology in persons with different genetic syndromes.

An additional variant of this problem arises when one considers etiology-related intellectual, linguistic, or adaptive profiles. Given the functioning levels of persons with many syndromes, researchers are often forced to rely on tests that have been normed on children younger than the study's subjects. In our studies of simultaneous and sequential processing in fragile X syndrome and Prader-Willi syndrome, we have often found it necessary to use the age-equivalent scores on the K-ABC, a test originally designed for $2\frac{1}{2}$- to 12-year-old children. Such age-equivalent scores are not as well normed as are standard scores (Sattler, 1992). Still, given that our goal was to examine intellectual strengths and weaknesses in groups with these syndromes, employing such age-equivalent scores seemed necessary.

Though not unique to groups with genetic syndromes, such measurement concerns nonetheless make more difficult studies in these areas. But until better measures are developed, many etiology-oriented behavioral workers will be forced to employ measures that, while useful to some degree, are not ideal for examining behavior in groups with different syndromes of intellectual disability.

FUTURE RESEARCH ON BEHAVIORAL PHENOTYPES

In considering the future of etiology-based behavioral research, one acknowledges three goals. The first involves simple, basic description. This function, which might be referred to as providing "demographic information", tells parents, families, educators, and group home workers basic information about a specific disorder. How often, for example, does severe psychosis occur in Prader-Willi syndrome, what does it look like, and how does it resolve itself (Clarke, 1993, 1998)? What percentage of children with 5p- syndrome show hyperactivity, what are prevalence levels at different ages, and are different subtypes of this disorder prone to different types or amounts of maladaptive behavior (Dykens & Clarke, 1997)? Answers to such questions provide parents and practitioners with some basic benchmarks—they can now compare their child or adult with a particular genetic syndrome to others with the same disorder.

Note that such descriptive information often occurs without much worry about behavioral phenotypes. For parents, families, and practitioners, it may not be all that informative to know that a certain etiology-related behavior is or is not often seen in others at a certain level of functioning, or in children or adults with one or another different disorder. Instead, this information provides useful benchmarks for clinical practice, and should be judged as such.

A second, more theoretical goal of etiology-based behavioral research involves connecting gene, brain, and behavior. This second goal acknowledges, in many ways, the unique position of modern genetics. As Comings (1980) noted years ago, with modern genetic techniques, "we now have the ironic situation of being able to jump to the bottom line without reading the rest of the page". In essence, we now have the beginnings (genes) and endings (physical or behavioral outcomes) of a wide variety of genetically related disorders.

Unfortunately, the middle of the page does matter, and researchers in a variety of disciplines are increasingly realizing just how much lies between genes and behavior. Genetic syndromes may well provide one good way to link genes at conception to full-fledged behavioral functioning in adulthood. Granted, much remains unknown, probably more than anyone now realizes. Still, the use of genetic disorders of intellectual disability—in which one does know the "beginning" and the "ending"—is a promising way to learn about the operations of and connections among different levels of the human system.

Finally, etiology-based research is important for more specific, targeted interventions. Such interventions may come about in a variety of areas. For example, it may now be possible to tailor educational interventions that target children with Down syndrome (Buckley, 1999; Hodapp & Ly, 2003), as well as those with fragile X, Prader-Willi, and Williams syndromes (Hodapp & Fidler, 1999). Similarly, attention to an individual's etiology may lead to specific psychotherapeutic and pharmacological recommendations (Dykens & Hodapp, 1997). Professionals across a variety of disciplines are beginning to consider such etiology-based approaches toward therapy.

Given these advances, what is the future of etiology-based approaches? Again, is the glass half-empty or half-full? The answer seems a little of both. We continue to know too little about behaviors in all but a handful of syndromes. Similarly, our knowledge of gene–brain–behavior connections is rudimentary, and most etiology-oriented interventions have yet to be either tried or evaluated. At the same time, however, behavioral knowledge proliferates on at least a few specific groups. Moreover, for syndromes such as the Williams, fragile X, and Prader-Willi syndromes, incredible research advances have occurred within the past decade, dwarfing all previous information. Overall, then, cautious optimism seems the best approach. Although we remain unsure precisely how etiology-based behavioral research will proceed, we remain hopeful that this "quiet revolution" will continue to aid in both understanding and helping persons with all genetic syndromes of intellectual disability.

REFERENCES

Achenbach, T.M. (1991). *Manual for the Child Behavior Checklist—4–18—and 1991 Profiles.* Burlington, VT: University of Vermont, Department of Psychiatry.

Aman, M.G. & Singh, N.N. (1994). *Aberrant Behavior Checklist—Community Supplementary Manual.* East Aurora, NY: Slosson Educational Publications.

Anderson, L. & Ernst, M. (1994). Self-injury in Lesch-Nyan disease. *Journal of Autism and Developmental Disorders*, **24**, 67–81.

Baumgardner, T.L., Reiss, A.L., Freund, L.S. & Abrams, M.T. (1995). Specification of the neurobehavioral phenotype in males with fragile X syndrome. *Pediatrics*, **95**, 744–752.

Bellugi, U., Mills, D., Jernigan, T., Hickok, G. & Galaburda, A. (1999). Linking cognition, brain structure, and brain function in Williams syndrome. In H. Tager-Flusberg (Ed.) *Neurodevelopmental Disorders* (pp. 111–136). Cambridge, MA: MIT Press.

Beuren, A.J., Apitz, J. & Harmjanz, D. (1962). Supravalvular aortic stenosis in association with mental retardation and a certain facial appearance. *Circulation*, **26**, 1235–1240.

Bishop, D.V.M. (1999). Cognition: an innate basis for language? *Science*, **286**, 2283–2284.

Buckley, S. (1999). Promoting the cognitive development of children with Down syndrome: the practical implications of recent psychological research. In J.A. Rondal, J. Perera & L. Nadel (Eds) *Down's Syndrome: A Review of Current Knowledge* (pp. 99–110). London: Whurr.

Clarke, D.J. (1993). Prader-Willi syndrome and psychoses. *British Journal of Psychiatry*, **163**, 680–684.

Clarke, D.J. (1998). Prader-Willi syndrome and psychotic symptoms. II. A preliminary study of prevalence using the Psychopathology Assessment for Adults with Developmental Disability Checklist. *Journal of Intellectual Disability Research*, **42**, 451–454.

Comings, D.E. (1980). Presidential address. American Society of Human Genetics 31st Annual Meeting, New York.

Crosby, A.W. (1997). *The Measure of Reality: Quantification and Western Society.* Cambridge: Cambridge University Press.

Dykens, E.M. (1995). Measuring behavioral phenotypes: provocations from the "new genetics". *American Journal on Mental Retardation*, **99**, 522–532.

Dykens, E.M. (1999). Prader-Willi syndrome. In H. Tager-Flusberg (Ed.) *Neurodevelopmental Disorders* (pp. 137–154). Cambridge, MA: MIT Press.

Dykens, E.M. (2000). Psychopathology in children with intellectual disability. *Journal of Child Psychology and Psychiatry*, **41**, 407–417.

Dykens, E.M., Cassidy, S.B. & King, B.H. (1999). Maladaptive behavior differences in Prader-Willi syndrome due to paternal deletion versus maternal uniparental disomy. *American Journal on Mental Retardation*, **104**, 67–77.

Dykens, E.M. & Clarke, D.J. (1997). Correlates of maladaptive behavior in individuals with 5p- (cri du chat) syndrome. *Developmental Medicine and Child Neurology*, **39**, 752–756.

Dykens, E.M. & Hodapp, R.M. (1997). Treatment issues in genetic mental retardation syndromes. *Professional Psychology: Research and Practice*, **28**, 263–270.

Dykens, E.M. & Hodapp, R.M. (2001). Research in mental retardation: toward an etiologic approach. *Journal of Child Psychology and Psychiatry*, **42**, 49–71.

Dykens, E.M., Hodapp, R.M. & Finucane, B.M. (2000). *Genetics and Mental Retardation Syndromes: A New Look at Behavior and Interventions*. Baltimore, MD: Brookes.

Dykens, E.M., Hodapp, R.M. & Leckman, J.F. (1987). Strengths and weaknesses in intellectual functioning of males with fragile X syndrome. *American Journal of Mental Deficiency*, **92**, 234–236.

Dykens, E.M., Hodapp, R.M., Walsh, K.K. & Nash, L. (1992). Profiles, correlates, and trajectories of intelligence in Prader-Willi syndrome. *Journal of the American Academy of Child and Adolescent Psychiatry*, **31**, 1125–1130.

Dykens, E.M. & Kasari, C. (1997). Maladaptive behavior in children with Prader-Willi syndrome, Down syndrome, and nonspecific mental retardation. *American Journal on Mental Retardation*, **102**, 228–237.

Dykens, E.M., Leckman, J.F. & Cassidy, S.B. (1996). Obsessions and compulsions in Prader-Willi syndrome. *Journal of Child Psychology and Psychiatry*, **37**, 995–1002.

Einfeld, S.L. & Tonge, B.J. (1992). *Manual for the Developmental Behaviour Checklist: Primary Carer Version*. School of Psychiatry, University of New South Wales.

Ellis, N.R. (1969). A behavioral research strategy in mental retardation: defense and critique. *American Journal on Mental Deficiency*, **73**, 557–566.

Ewart, A.K., Morris, C.A., Atkinson, D., Jin, W., Sternes, K., Spallone, P., et al. (1993). Hemizygosity at the elastin locus in a developmental disorder, Williams syndrome. *Nature Genetics*, **5**, 11–16.

Fidler, D.J. & Hodapp, R.M. (1999). Importance of typologies for science and service in mental retardation. *Mental Retardation*, **36**, 489–495.

Finucane, B.M., Konar, D., Haas-Givler, B., Kurtz, M.D. & Scott, L.I. (1994). The spasmodic upper-body squeeze: a characteristic behavior in Smith-Magenis syndrome. *Developmental Medicine and Child Neurology*, **36**, 78–83.

Flynn, J.R. (1999). IQ gains over time: toward finding the causes. In U. Neisser (Ed.) *The Rising Curve: Long-Term Gains in IQ and Related Measures* (pp. 25–66). Washington, DC: American Psychological Association.

Flynt, J. & Yule, W. (1994). Behavioural phenotypes. In M. Rutter, E. Taylor & L. Hersov (Eds) *Child and Adolescent Psychiatry: Modern Approaches* (3rd edn) (pp. 666–687). London: Blackwell Scientific.

Fodor, J. (1983). *Modularity of Mind: An Essay in Faculty Psychology*. Cambridge, MA: MIT Press.

Fowler, A.E. (1990). Language abilities in children with Down syndrome: evidence for a specific syntactic delay. In D. Cicchetti & M. Beeghly (Eds) *Children with Down Syndrome: A Developmental Approach* (pp. 302–328). New York: Cambridge University Press.

Gersh, M., Goodart, S.A., Pasztor, L.M., Harris, D.J., Weiss, L. & Overhauser, J. (1995). Evidence for a distinct region causing a cat-like cry in patients with 5p- deletions. *American Journal of Human Genetics*, **56**, 1404–1410.

Greenberg, F., Lewis, R.A., Potocki, L., Glaze, D., Parke, J., Killian, J., et al. (1996). Multidisciplinary clinical study of Smith-Magenis syndrome: (deletion 17p11.2). *American Journal of Medical Genetics*, **62**, 247–254.

Gresham, F.M., MacMillan, D.L. & Siperstein, G.N. (1995). Critical analysis of the 1992 AAMR definition: implications for school psychology. *School Psychology Quarterly*, **10**, 1–19.

Hodapp, R.M. (1997). Direct and indirect behavioral effects of different genetic disorders of mental retardation. *American Journal on Mental Retardation*, **102**, 67–79.

Hodapp, R.M. & Dykens, E.M. (1994). Mental retardation's two cultures of behavioral research. *American Journal on Mental Retardation*, **98**, 675–687.

Hodapp, R.M. & Dykens, E.M. (2001). Strengthening behavioral research on genetic mental retardation disorders. *American Journal on Mental Retardation*, **106**, 4–15.

Hodapp, R.M., Dykens, E.M. & Masino, L.L. (1997). Families of children with Prader-Willi syndrome: stress-support and relations to child characteristics. *Journal of Autism and Developmental Disorders*, **27**, 11–24.

Hodapp, R.M., Dykens, E.M., Ort, S.I., Zelinsky, D.G. & Leckman, J.F. (1991). Changing patterns of intellectual strengths and weaknesses in males with fragile X syndrome. *Journal of Autism and Developmental Disorders*, **21**, 503–516.

Hodapp, R.M., Evans, D. & Gray, F.L. (1999). What we know about intellectual development in children with Down syndrome. In J.A. Rondal, J. Perera & L. Nadel (Eds) *Down's Syndrome: A Review of Current Knowledge* (pp. 124–132). London: Whurr.

Hodapp, R.M. & Fidler, D.J. (1999). Special education and genetics: connections for the 21st century. *Journal of Special Education*, **33**, 130–137.

Hodapp, R.M., Leckman, J.F., Dykens, E.M., Sparrow, S.S., Zelinsky, D. & Ort, S.I. (1992). K-ABC profiles in children with fragile X syndrome, Down syndrome, and nonspecific mental retardation. *American Journal on Mental Retardation*, **97**, 39–46.

Hodapp, R.M. & Ly, T.M. (2003). Visual processing strengths in Down syndrome: a case for reading instruction? In S. Soraci & W.J. McIlvane (Eds) *Visual Information Processing* (pp. 155–169). Westport, CT: Praeger.

Hodapp, R.M. & Zigler, E. (1995). Past, present, and future issues in the developmental approach to mental retardation and developmental disabilities. In D. Cicchetti & D. Cohen (Eds) *Manual of Developmental Psychopathology*, vol. 2. *Risk, Disorder, and Adaptation* (pp. 299–331). New York: Wiley.

Holm, V.A., Cassidy, S.B., Butler, M.G., Hanchett, J.M., Greenswag, L.R., Whitman, B.Y., et al. (1993). Prader-Willi syndrome: consensus diagnostic criteria. *Pediatrics*, **91**, 398–402.

Jarrold, C., Baddeley, A.D., Hewes, A.K. & Phillips, C. (2001). A longitudinal assessment of diverging verbal and non-verbal abilities in the Williams syndrome phenotype. *Cortex*, **37**, 423–431.

Karmiloff-Smith, A., Grant, J., Berthoud, I., Davies, M., Howlin, P. & Udwin, O. (1997). Language and Williams syndrome: how intact is "intact"? *Child Development*, **68**, 246–262.

Kasari, C. & Freeman, S.F.N. (2001). Task-related social behavior in children with Down syndrome. *American Journal on Mental Retardation*, **106**, 253–264.

Kasari, C., Freeman, S.F.N., Mundy, P. & Sigman, M. (1995). Attention regulation by children with Down syndrome: coordinated joint attention and social referencing. *American Journal on Mental Retardation*, **100**, 128–136.

Kaufman, A.S. & Kaufman, N.L. (1983). *Kaufman Assessment Battery for Children*. Circle Pines, MN: American Guidance Service.

Kemper, M.B., Hagerman, R.J. & Altshul-Stark, D. (1988). Cognitive profiles of boys with fragile X syndrome. *American Journal of Medical Genetics*, **30**, 191–200.

Kumin, L. (1994). Intelligibility of speech in children with Down syndrome in natural settings: parents' perspective. *Perceptual and Motor Skills*, **78**, 307–313.

Matalainen, R., Airaksinen, E., Mononen, T., Launiala, K. & Kaarianen, R. (1995). A population-based study of the causes of severe and profound mental retardation. *Acta Paediatrica*, **84**, 261–266.

Mervis, C.B., Morris, C.A., Bertrand, J. & Robinson, B.F. (1999). Williams syndrome: findings from an integrated program of research. In H. Tager-Flusberg (Ed.) *Neurodevelopmental Disorders* (pp. 65–110). Cambridge, MA: MIT Press.

Meyers, B.A. & Pueschel, S.R. (1991). Psychiatric disorders in persons with Down syndrome. *The Journal of Nervous and Mental Disease*, **179**, 609–613.

Miller, J. (1992). Lexical development in young children with Down syndrome. In R. Chapman (Ed.) *Processes in Language Acquisition and Disorders* (pp. 202–216). St Louis, MO: Mosby.

Miller, J.F. (1999). Profiles of language development in children with Down syndrome. In J.F. Miller, M. Leddy & L.A. Leavitt (Eds) *Improving the Communication of People with Down Syndrome* (pp. 11–39). Baltimore, MD: Brookes.

Naglieri, J.A. (1985). Assessment of mentally retarded children with the Kaufman Assessment Battery for Children. *American Journal of Mental Deficiency*, **89**, 367–371.

O'Brien, G. (1993). Behavioral phenotypes and their measurement. *Developmental Medicine and Child Neurology*, **34**, 365–367.

Obrzut, A., Nelson, R.B. & Obrzut, J.E. (1987). Construct validity of the Kaufman Assessment Battery for Children with mildly mentally retarded students. *American Journal of Mental Deficiency*, **92**, 74–77.

Opitz, J.M. (1985). Editorial comment: the developmental field concept. *American Journal of Medical Genetics*, **21**, 1–11.

Opitz, J.M. (1996). Historiography of the causal analysis of mental retardation. Speech to the 29th Gatlinburg Conference on Research and Theory in Mental Retardation and Developmental Disabilities, Gatlinburg, TN, March.

Pueschel, S.R., Gallagher, P.L., Zartler, A.S. & Pezzullo, J.C. (1986). Cognitive and learning profiles in children with Down syndrome. *Research in Developmental Disabilities*, **8**, 21–37.

Rondal, J. (1995). *Exceptional Language Development in Down Syndrome*. New York: Cambridge University Press.

Roof, E., Stone, W., MacLean, W., Feurer, I.D., Thompson, T. & Butler, M.G. (2000). Intellectual characteristics of Prader-Willi syndrome: comparison of genetic subtypes. *Journal of Intellectual Disability Research*, **44**, 25–30.

Rosen, M. (1993). In search of the behavioral phenotype: a methodological note. *Mental Retardation*, **31**, 177–178.

Rutter, M., Simonoff, E. & Plomin, R. (1996). Genetic influences on mild mental retardation: concepts, findings, and research implications. *Journal of Biosocial Science*, **28**, 509–526.

Sattler, J. (1992). *Assessment of Children* (3rd edn, revised). San Diego, CA: J.M. Sattler.

Van Acker, R. (1991). Rett syndrome: a review of current knowledge. *Journal of Autism and Developmental Disorders*, **21**, 381–406.

Williams, J.C., Barrett-Boyes, B.G. & Lowe, J.B. (1961). Supravalvular aortic stenosis. *Circulation*, **24**, 1311–1318.

CHAPTER 10

Issues in Researching the Ageing of People with Intellectual Disability

Christine Bigby
La Trobe University, Australia
and
Susan Balandin
University of Sydney, Australia

Research into the ageing processes of people with intellectual disability is a relatively new phenomenon. Intellectual disability was a problem associated only with childhood when the World Health Organisation convened the first international conference on this issue in 1953. Recognition that adulthood brought with it significant changes to the status of people with intellectual disability did not occur until the mid-1960s, when policy makers were forced to confront the challenges this posed (Dybwad, 1985). However, until the late 1970s, ageing and old age were not acknowledged as part of the life course of people with intellectual disability. At this time, the increased life expectancy of people with intellectual disability, coupled with demographic changes in Western countries, meant the challenges of ageing became an issue for families, service providers, and policy makers. Consequently, a new area of research, that of ageing and intellectual disability, began to emerge. However, despite its short history, the breadth and sophistication of enquiry has grown considerably (Janicki & Deb, 1994), and a remarkable body of knowledge and a high level of international collaboration have been established (Janicki, 2001).

Drawing on key studies as illustrations, this chapter provides an overview of the focus and different perspectives on design found in the field of research on ageing with intellectual disability over the past three decades. Methodological challenges confronted by researchers are discussed and, finally, key issues for the next decade's research agenda are suggested.

Ageing research, like much of the field of disability, is characterised by its multidisciplinary nature and reference to normative life-course development, which in this case is found in the field of gerontology. Strong links between researchers and practitioners, together with an emphasis on the use of research to inform policy and service developments, also characterise this field (Bigby, 1999; Janicki & Ansello, 2000). Indications of

The International Handbook of Applied Research in Intellectual Disabilities. Edited by E. Emerson, C. Hatton, T. Thompson and T.R. Parmenter ISBN 0-471-49709-6.

progress in the field include the increase from one to more than a dozen books dedicated to older people with intellectual disability, since 1985 (Janicki & Wisniewski, 1985; Bigby, 2000); the inclusion of chapters on later life issues for this group in texts from the disciplines of gerontology, social work, psychology, and intellectual disability (Seltzer, 1992; Heller, 1993; Bigby, 2001); the development of specific policies on ageing in various countries (Moss, 1993); and the positioning of this issue on international health policy agendas (World Health Organisation, 2001).

DOMINANT RESEARCH THEMES

Initially, research concentrated on increased life expectancy, identification of the emergent group of older people with intellectual disability, and the challenges this posed for families (Richards & Sylvester, 1969; Forssman & Akesson, 1970; Anglin, 1981; Dybwad, 1985). The studies of life expectancy mean that startling comparisons can be made of such changes during the twentieth century (although the comparability is indicative only as initial studies were confined to institutional populations). For example, whereas the average age at death for people with intellectual disability living in institutions in 1931 was 22 years, by 1993, the average age at death was 66.1 years (Janicki, Dalton, Henderson & Davidson, 1999).

Other key questions posed by the pioneer researchers and advocates about ageing centred on how to prepare adults with intellectual disabilities and their families for old age and the inevitable loss of parents, and the likely transitions in provision of support, place of residence, nature of occupation, and types of services required (Anglin, 1981; Campaign for Mentally Handicapped People, 1981; Dybwad, 1985). These early issues are reflected in the three research themes noted at the first research roundtable on ageing and developmental disabilities in 1990 and are broadly characteristic of research in this field since that time. These themes are the responsiveness of human services to those who are ageing with an intellectual disability, the impact of extended caregiving and ageing on families, and the exploration of differences in the domains of human development among people who are ageing with and without an intellectual disability (Seltzer, Krauss & Janicki, 1994).

Early studies identified gaps in knowledge about the characteristics of older people and highlighted both their needs and possible directions for service provision (Segal, 1977; Di Giovanni, 1978). An enduring early theme has been the question whether the needs of older people with intellectual disabilities can be accommodated by mainstream aged person's services or whether specialist services are required (Anglin, 1981; Janicki, Otis, Puccio, Rettig & Jacobson, 1985; Seltzer & Krauss, 1987; Walker & Walker, 1998). Inevitably, the varying nature of existing specialist disability and mainstream aged services in different countries has resulted in differing conclusions about these issues across the world. A related strand of research activity has been the documentation and evaluation of innovative programmes and collaborative efforts between the aged care and disability sectors (Heller & Factor, 1994; Hogg, 1995; Janicki & Ansello, 2000). This has resulted in a greater awareness of how these two sectors can work together to improve the quality of life of all older people.

Through the use of large-scale surveys, the characteristics of service systems have been mapped, and a substantial body of epidemiological and demographic knowledge has been developed (Janicki & MacEarchron, 1984; Janicki & Jacobson, 1986; Seltzer & Krauss, 1987; Anderson, 1989; Haveman, Maaskant & Sturmans, 1989; Moss, Hogg & Horne,

1992; Ashman, Suttie & Bramley, 1993; Hand, 1994; Cooper, 1997). An offshoot of the epidemiological research has been biomedical research into the high prevalence of Alzheimer's disease in people with Down syndrome and issues relating to its diagnosis and treatment (Wisniewski, 1994; Janicki & Dalton, 1999; Holland, 2000).

Studies adopting a life-course perspective have focused on ageing parental carers of people with intellectual disability, and their caring experiences, expectations, and planning for the future care of their adult child with intellectual disability (e.g., Grant, 1989; Roberto, 1993; Walsh, Concliffe & Birkbeck, 1993; Seltzer & Krauss, 1994; Smith, 1997). Seltzer and Krauss (1994) suggested that life-course studies need to be broader than the traditional focus on the effects of the parent on the person with disability, and should include consideration of the adaptability and well-being of families and individual members involved in caring over an extended period. They also stressed the importance of comparative studies to document the diversity of family and caring experiences stemming from different cultural, ethnic, religious, cohort, or class experiences. However, to date, few such studies have been undertaken (see McCallion, Janicki & Grant-Griffin, 1997; Heller & Factor, 1988). The challenges and dilemmas of working with older carers of adults with an intellectual disability have also been examined (McCallion & Tobin, 1995; Bigby, Ozanne & Gordon, 2002).

Much of the research in the field of ageing and intellectual disability has adopted the traditional perspective in which older people with disabilities have been the subjects of study rather than informants, participants, or partners. Relatively few studies have focused on the perspective of older people themselves, their understanding, experiences, preferences, and concerns about the ageing experience (Erickson, Krauss & Seltzer, 1989; Edgerton & Gaston, 1991; Grant, McGrath & Ramcharan, 1995; Mahon & Mactavish, 2000). However, the influence of developments in the broader disability research arena (Booth & Booth, 1996; Moore, Beazley & Maelzer, 1998) are now becoming evident, and new, more inclusive approaches using qualitative research designs, such as narrative, life history, and emancipatory and participatory action research, are beginning to be used in ageing research.

DESIGN ISSUES

Research on ageing and intellectual disability draws on the long research tradition in gerontology, such that the quality of studies "can be improved by incorporating the relevant wisdom and techniques of gerontological researchers along with this field's own methodological tradition" (Seltzer, 1985, p. 172). Nevertheless, several complex issues arise in designing research about older people with intellectual disability. These include defining what is meant by an "older" person and "intellectual disability", operationalising definitions, determining the size of the population in question, and selecting and locating appropriate samples.

Defining Old Age

Gerontologists define old age by chronological age, usually 60 or 65 years. Concepts such as the "third age" and "fourth age" or "young old", "old old", and "oldest old" are used to differentiate the broad age span of being an older person (Laslett, 1989). As ageing is a relatively new phenomenon for people with intellectual disability, and some groups, such as those with Down syndrome and cerebral palsy, age prematurely, a younger age than that used for the general population has been taken to denote an older person. No consensus exists on exactly what this age should be. Reviewing 35 early studies, Seltzer and Krauss (1987) found 11 different age cut-offs, ranging from 40 to 75 years, with varying terms, including "older adults", "aged", "ageing", and "elderly adults", being used. This trend has continued; for example, 50 years was used in a national survey of older people with an intellectual disability in New Zealand (Hand, 1994), and in the UK Oldham survey (Moss, Hogg & Horne, 1992). Fifty-five years was used in both the Australian national survey (Ashman et al., 1993) and a Victorian study (Bigby, 2000), and 65 years for a study using the UK Leicestershire register (Cooper, 1997).

Any chronological cut-off point is arbitrary and may result in either the inclusion of some individuals who, on the basis of their current physical, psychological, and social abilities, would not be considered elderly in a functional sense or in the exclusion of younger individuals who already exhibit signs of premature ageing (Seltzer & Krauss, 1987). It may never be possible to obtain consensus on this issue internationally, as definitions of old age selected by researchers should reflect differences in culture and life expectancy within and between developing and developed nations. Therefore, it may be more important to use common age banding, such as five-year intervals from 50 upwards to facilitate comparability of studies.

Defining Intellectual Disability

The terms used to refer to and define intellectual disability vary historically, geographically, and culturally. Establishing and ensuring a consistent definition of intellectual disability within a study, as well as achieving comparability with other studies, poses some difficulties (Begun, 1987). Researchers have relied on a variety of means to identify a person as having an intellectual disability. Some designs incorporate the administration of a comprehensive set of tests (Haveman et al., 1989), whereas others have used registration with formal service systems as the criterion for having intellectual disability (Cooper, 1997). Researchers that utilise case-finding strategies have used other informants, such as family members or service providers, to identify people with intellectual disability (Horne, 1989; Bigby, 1995). Reliance on such informants can be particularly problematic given the confusion that often occurs between intellectual disability and psychiatric disability and the confounding effects of age-related disabilities. When using such strategies, it is preferable to seek confirmation from another source or by the examination of a person's educational or vocational history.

Sampling and Locating Older People with Intellectual Disability

Locating older people with intellectual disability and estimating the size of this population also poses difficulties. Reliance cannot be placed on administrative registers of people identified as having intellectual disability or on current client lists of specialist services alone. Some estimates suggest that as many as 60–70% of older people with intellectual disability are unknown to specialist services and that they are more likely than their younger counterparts to be unknown to services (Di Giovanni, 1978; Jacobson, Sutton & Janicki,

1985; Seltzer & Krauss, 1987). Horne (1989) suggested that older people are hidden to varying degrees, or in different ways; some just lose touch with services while others, often at the instigation of their families, deliberately choose to remain "hidden".

However, both large-scale surveys and smaller studies have relied on samples drawn only from those people who are in touch with specialist disability services. Such sampling can be criticised as being too narrow or exclusive in focus. This results in the suggestion that commonly no systematic sampling procedure is used, and non-probability samples of convenience (that is, those in touch with specialist service systems) predominate in ageing research methodology (Duffy, Widaman & Eyman, 1991; Seltzer, Begun, Seltzer & Krauss, 1991). Such samples are biased against people with a milder intellectual disability, who are less likely to be in touch with services, and mean that findings can be generalised to only the service population (Duffy et al., 1991; Seltzer, Krauss & Heller, 1991).

Locating and including the "hidden" population of older people with intellectual disability is a major challenge for researchers. However, just as administrative systems differ between countries and states, and across time, so, too, do the extent and nature of the hidden population and the ease or willingness with which they can be identified. Various methods of outreach or case finding have been adopted to locate both older people with intellectual disabilities and older carers of middle-aged people (Horne, 1989; Hand, 1994; Smith, Fullmer & Tobin, 1994). Although many of these methods are successful, case finding is a resource-intensive method of locating a sample. An ideal sampling frame is that found in Leicestershire, UK, where an administrative register is supported by regular updating to ensure accuracy, and outreach strategies are actively used to locate people for inclusion on the register (Cooper, 1997).

Most outreach strategies have sought the cooperation of personnel from a range of health, aged, and community services; housing agencies; and voluntary community groups to identify older people with intellectual disability. Horne (1989) suggested that there is a need to prioritise the potential sources of identification, as they tend to expand continuously as a study progresses. It is also clear that strategies must take account of cultural and geographical variations. For example, both Horne (1989) and Bigby (1997) used outreach strategies in metropolitan areas, finding that front-line personnel in mainstream aged services were the most promising group for identifying older people with intellectual disability. Such personnel are in touch with many older people and, even if not providing services directly to an older person with intellectual disability, are often providing them to other family members. Horne reported that asking general practitioners to identify older people with intellectual disability was less successful, as they had low response rates and when they did respond were not very good at identifying this group of people. In contrast, Hand and Reid (1989), who conducted much of their New Zealand national survey in rural and sparsely populated locations, found that local organisations and personal contacts were more useful sources for identifying older people with intellectual disability than formal service providers. Gow and Balla (1994) noted that the problems they encountered in Hong Kong were not only in locating people but also in the group's preference to remain "hidden" and not to participate in research once found by the researchers. This raises the ethical issues of researchers "finding" families for research purposes alone without offering any solution or support for the problems they may identify.

Various innovative methods have been used to locate and engage older carers of middle-aged people with disabilities. For example, Smith and his colleagues (1994) worked through mainstream, aged-care networks, initially offering workshops on future planning for carers.

In addition, they used non-traditional referral sources, such as postmen and chemists, as well as including a flyer about their project in utility bills.

The results of Horne's study (1989) demonstrated the extent of the hidden population of older people with intellectual disability in Oldham and the success of case-finding strategies. Ninety individuals were identified by various community informants (79 of these were found to have intellectual disability), of whom only 33 were already known to specialist intellectual disability services. Studies such as this suggest that populations not in touch with specialist services have different characteristics from those who use services; they are more likely to have remained at home with family, more likely to be using mainstream, aged-care services, and more likely to have a lower level of community activities and individual programming (Moss & Hogg, 1989; Bigby, 1995).

These variations between "hidden" and "known" older people suggest that important intracohort differences may exist that pose other sampling issues for researchers. The current cohort of older people includes various subgroups with quite distinct life experiences. These include those who have lived at home with parents for most of their life, those who were placed in institutions from an early age, and those who moved into supported accommodation during early adulthood. For example, various studies have indicated that the informal social networks of older adults with intellectual disability are affected by earlier life experiences, and those who have lived many years with parents have more extensive family ties in later life. This group, more so than others, experience later life as a time of opportunity, when for the first time they are treated as adults rather than children (Skeie, 1989; Bigby, 1997). Thus, different life experiences affect ageing processes and experiences. Consequently, it may be wise for researchers to take account of these different subgroups by, for instance, stratifying samples according to earlier life experiences.

Longitudinal or Cross-Sectional Designs

Researchers investigating the process and experiences of ageing must grapple with the issue of whether characteristics identified in an older population that differ from those found in a younger population are due to generational/cohort-related effects, differential mortality, or ageing processes. The cohort effect is based on the recognition that each aged cohort lives through a different historic period, and experiences a unique set of events and changes in their environment, such as those relating to social policies, health care, community attitudes, social conventions, and educational opportunities. Differential mortality or the healthy survivor effect is the phenomenon whereby the difference between older and younger populations may reflect not the ageing process per se, but, rather, differences in the composition of the sample groups (that is, some of those in the younger group may not live long enough to become the older group). Thus, the older group is composed of the healthy survivors. Another example of healthy survivor effect can be seen in the research into Alzheimer's disease. Research findings on the incidence of Alzheimer's disease have varied considerably. Zigman, Seltzer and Silverman (1994) suggested that this is partly due to the cross-sectional design of studies, which results in an apparently low incidence of Alzheimer's disease because of the healthy survivor effect. This effect can mask health problems and lead to an underestimation of risk among older people.

Another illustration of this effect is found in other health-related studies. No conclusive evidence exists on the relative health status of older people with intellectual disability in comparison to their younger peers. Moss (1991) found that older people with intellectual disabilities had fewer health problems, less incidence of epilepsy, and fewer challenging behaviours than their younger peers. In addition, their self-care skills continued to improve right up to the age of 60 years. Moss suggested that this might be accounted for by the higher mortality rate of people with more severe disabilities. He speculated that people with intellectual disability who have lived to be 50 or more are healthier than younger groups of people with intellectual disability. In contrast, however, the results of more comprehensive studies by Sally Cooper (1997, 1998), who used diagnostic instruments rather than data derived from an administrative register, suggested that the effect of old age on physical health means that, as in the general population, older people have poorer health than their younger counterparts. In particular, she noted that incontinence, reduced mobility, hearing impairment, arthritis, hypertension, and cerebrovascular disease are all more common among older than younger people with intellectual disability.

Both cross-sectional and longitudinal designs are associated with research that attempts to map age-related changes. Cross-sectional designs are those in which different cohorts are compared on one or more variables at one point in time. They make the assumption that ageing accounts for the differences found between age groups, but should take into account the healthy survivor effect in order to be valid. Longitudinal designs, in contrast, include measures of the same variable on the same individuals across time. In these studies, three factors limit the ability to infer ageing effects: current environmental influences, such as changes in policy or eligibility for services; testing effects, from administration of repeated measures; and the effects of drop-outs from the study which may threaten internal validity (Seltzer, 1985). Another drawback of longitudinal designs is the inclusion of only one age cohort; consequently, caution must be exercised when attempting to generalise the findings to other cohorts who may have had different life experiences.

Separation of age and cohort effect may be assisted by more complex designs based on a general developmental model. These involve the inclusion of at least two separate age cohorts that are tested over a period of time on at least two variables (Seltzer, 1985).

A longitudinal study that stands out in the research literature because of its comprehensive and ground-breaking nature is the body of work instigated by Seltzer and Krauss. The study was based on a prospective sample of 461 older mothers, aged 55–85 years, caring for an adult with intellectual disability residing in either Massachusetts or Wisconsin. It was conducted over a period of 12 years from 1988 to 2000, during which eight sets of interviews, each 18 months apart, were conducted with the mothers. In addition, at the time of the third and sixth interview, an additional interview was conducted with the most involved sibling of the person with a disability. A range of standard scales was used to collect data on factors such as functional ability, family involvement, maternal well-being, family and social climate, maternal burden, and social networks (see Seltzer et al., 1991). The adults with intellectual disability, the family, mothers, and siblings were all used as units of analysis. This study has provided insights into the continuity and discontinuity of family involvement following transition from parental care (Seltzer, Krauss, Hong & Orsmond, 2001), sibling relationships and their role in maternal well-being (Seltzer et al., 1991; Krauss, Seltzer, Gordon & Friedman, 1996), factors affecting the psychological and social well-being of parents (Krauss & Seltzer, 1993), and the benefit and challenges of long-term care for family members (Essex, Seltzer & Krauss, 1999).

This study has been able to disagregate individual change from family level change, take into account the view of various family members, and thus bring a multidimensional perspective to family well-being. Its prospective nature means that continuities and changes have been assessed across time. The retention rate was remarkably high, with 88.6% of participants still involved at the time of the seventh interview. One drawback of the design was reliance on mothers as informants in respect of the social networks of their adult son or daughter with intellectual disability, resulting in a lack of perspective or voice from these adults.

The other longitudinal study that stands out in this field is the seminal work by Edgerton and his colleagues in the "Cloak of Competence" studies. This research followed a cohort of people released from a large institution (then named Pacific Colony) over a period of 25 years. Edgerton graphically described the experiences of the ageing process for 16 of the original cohort. His work provided tremendous insights into the vulnerability of older people with intellectual disability who live in the community, particularly in terms of maintaining a healthy lifestyle and procuring quality health care (Edgerton & Gaston, 1991). The study used an ethnographic approach, relying on researchers spending considerable time both talking with and just spending time with the participants.

Measurement Issues

It can be argued that the use of standard measures designed for the general ageing population (such as assessments for physical function, instrumental activities of daily living, cognitive function, and social networks) have the benefit of facilitating comparison between the two populations when used with ageing people with an intellectual disability. However, obstacles exist to applying some measures across these two populations. For example, difficulties are likely to be encountered if measures relying on self-report are used with older people with severe disabilities or communication impairments. Moreover, scales that measure independence in activities of daily living among the general population tend to assume consistency of performance across various items, whereas people with intellectual disability show less consistency across items, as they may never have acquired mastery of some skills (Widaman, Borthwick-Duffy & Powers, 1994). Alternatively, the tasks may be outside their life experiences (Morse, 1988). Thus, this type of scale may have to be modified for people with intellectual disabilities, consequently invalidating the score.

Studies into all aspects of Alzheimer's disease in people with intellectual disability have occupied a significant place on the research agenda over the last decade, primarily because of the increased prevalence of Alzheimer's disease in people with Down syndrome. However, attention has been drawn to the lack of consistency of assessment tools and diagnostic criteria used in studies (Aylward, Burt, Thorpe, Lai & Dalton, 1997; Prasher, 1997). Diagnostic tools based on an assumed level of baseline functioning, which are used for the general population, are not appropriate for use with people with intellectual disabilities who may not have attained baseline function in all domains.

It is with Alzheimer's disease that significant international collaboration has occurred. For example, Evenhuis (1992, 1996) developed a tool for screening people with intellectual disability for dementia, the Dementia Questionnaire for Persons with Mental Retardation (DMR). This has subsequently been evaluated by other researchers (Prasher, 1997) and found to be appropriate for use with this population. However, Prasher warns that it must be used in conjunction with clinical assessments, including interviews with carers, review of medical and psychiatric history, a mental state assessment, and laboratory investigations for different diagnosis (1997). An international colloquium convened in 1994 drew together clinicians and researchers in the field of Alzheimer's disease and intellectual disability, and developed standardised criteria and procedures for the diagnosis of dementia in this population. This includes comprehensive recommendations as to scales that can be used to measure the various domains (see Aylward et al., 1997).

Assessing changes to physical functioning as people age is important, particularly for people with physical as well as intellectual disability who rely on the support of attendant carers. Balandin and her colleagues suggest that the Functional Independence Measure (FIM) is a reliable and valid tool for describing severity of physical disability and calculating attendant care needs that is not discipline specific (Uniform Data Set for Medical Rehabilitation, 1994). The tool is accepted worldwide, and is well known and widely used in Australia, New Zealand, and the USA (Balandin, Alexander & Hoffman, 1997).

The concept of quality of life is used to create a vision of the life possibilities for people with disabilities and as a tool for measuring changes in life satisfaction and outcomes of services. Quality-of-life measures involve both objective and subjective perspectives and comprise eight core dimensions: emotional well-being, interpersonal relationships, material well-being, personal development, physical well-being, self-determination, social inclusion, and rights (Schalock, DeVries & Lebsack, 1999). Aggregate scores across the eight core dimensions have been used to measure changes in the level of life satisfaction of older people with intellectual disabilities. The scale most commonly used for this purpose is the 40-item Quality of Life Questionnaire developed by Schalock and Keith (1993).

Studies of older carers of middle-aged adults with intellectual disability have drawn on various dimensions of quality of life and utilised instruments from mainstream psychology. For example, in their longitudinal study, Seltzer and Krauss have used the Positive Affect Scale (Bengston & Black, 1973) to measure the quality and nature of family relationships and the Zarit Burden Interview (Zarit, Reever & Bach-Peterson, 1980) to measure caregiver well-being. Grant and his colleagues have developed three instruments to measure aspects of caregiving; the Carers Assessment of Difficulties Index, the Carers Assessment of Satisfaction Index, and the Carers Assessment of Managing Index (Nolan, Grant & Keady, 1998). These tools provide both quantitative and qualitative data and can be used by researchers and practitioners to assess family coping. They can also be used as the basis for decisions regarding the most appropriate kind of support required by families.

Including the Voice of Older People with Intellectual Disabilities in Research

A small but growing trend is the use of methodologies that include the perspectives of people with intellectual disabilities as "insiders" and informants in the ageing experience. This reflects recent values and policy directions that emphasise empowerment and inclusion of people with disabilities (Department of Health, 2001; Department of Health and Community Services, 2001). It also allows valuable comparisons to be made between the views of other groups such as service providers, family members, and supporters (Biklen & Moseley, 1988).

Many studies of older adults with intellectual disability, particularly where people do not live with family members, have relied on formal service providers as informants (Hand & Reid, 1989; Moss et al., 1989; Maaskant & Haveman, 1990). A major drawback to this approach is that service providers often have a poor knowledge about the background of the older person with intellectual disability (Horne, 1989; Green & Wunsch, 1994). In addition, it silences the very people who have an intimate knowledge of their own ageing process.

Most studies of middle-aged and older adults with intellectual disability living with relatives have relied on the primary caregiver, usually a parent or sibling, to act as informant (Grant, 1989; Seltzer et al., 1991). Although this approach ensures that the informant is likely to have a good knowledge of the person's background, it has been criticised for relying on the perspective of one informant (Seltzer et al., 1991). The drawback of this approach is demonstrated by the marked differences between the perspectives of different informants. For example, in regard to social networks, family members are likely to disregard friendships between older adults and co-participants at day programmes, yet it is clear the adults themselves value these friendships (Bigby, 2000). In another study, older adults were found to have active positive views of activities they wished to do in later life, whereas day-service staff held much more pessimistic and passive views of activities that should be offered to older people (Bigby et al., in press).

Research that has directly involved older people with intellectual disability as informants gives credence to the premise that people with intellectual disability are a valid source of information who can speak for themselves, and some of whom can provide complex and moving accounts of their experiences (Erickson et al., 1989; Edgerton & Gaston, 1991; Grant, McGrath & Ramcharan, 1995). Some researchers suggest that the most effective designs for research about people with intellectual disability use a combination of data-collection strategies to allow for checking and cross-referencing of data (Atkinson, 1988; Mactavish, Mahon & Lutfiyya, 2000). This approach is particularly important where biographical information is sought, as people with intellectual disability may have difficulty in providing details about their past, often confusing sequences of events (Flynn, 1986). There are examples of studies that have used a mix of methodologies, comprising large-scale surveys complemented by intensive qualitative case studies (e.g., Grant, 1986).

Although the importance of involving people with intellectual disability in the research processes is recognised, the challenge still remains for researchers to involve individuals effectively (Atkinson, 1988; Ward, 1998). A small literature has addressed the most appropriate methods to involve people with an intellectual disability in the research process. This indicates that people with intellectual disabilities who have a mild to moderate disability are responsive in interview situations, and, if attention is paid to the appropriate format of questions and structure of interviews, they can provide reliable valid information (Sigelman, Budd, Winer, Schoenrock & Martin, 1982; Booth & Booth, 1996; Mactavish et al., 2000). However, there can be little doubt that a single interview with an unknown interviewer provides a very limited opportunity for persons with intellectual disability to give an account of their feelings, experiences, or insight into their personal world. As the work of Edgerton and his colleagues demonstrated, such opportunities and insights often occur only in the context of a long-term relationship between the researcher and the subject after many hours of discussion and observation (Edgerton & Gaston, 1991).

An Agenda for Future Research

Priestley (2001) challenged the concept of a "normal" life-course progression in the modern world and suggested that the globalising world is characterised by diversity of life experience and lifestyle. Future research must begin to delve into the diversity of the ageing experience for people with intellectual disability and the manner it is shaped by external economic and social factors such as gender, culture, location, and class. In particular, gender is a concept seldom applied to people with intellectual disabilities. There is a strong suggestion that this should be redressed in future research; for example, Walsh, Heller, Schupf and van Schrojenstein Lantman-de Valk (2001) stated that "understanding of the distinctive needs, vulnerabilities and sources of well-being for women with intellectual disabilities must be addressed vigorously" (p. 215). To date, there has been a major focus on developed nations; however, research must begin to identify the special issues pertaining to developing nations, where survival itself is still a key issue that must be achieved alongside movements for social change for people with disabilities (Stone, 2001).

A focus on the diversity and subgroups of ageing people is one aspect of the hefty research agenda put forward in the collection of WHO position papers on ageing and intellectual disability (2001). Another key direction suggested for future research is an exploration of the broader ecological context in which people age and the factors that may improve longevity and promote healthy ageing. At the microlevel, research is needed into the conditions and professional or therapeutic practices that best meet the health and social needs of older people with intellectual disabilities in the context of mainstream services, and the extent to which additional specialist service provisions may be required (Hogg, Lucchino, Wang & Janicki, 2001). In addition, a greater understanding of interactions and barriers that exist between ageing people with disabilities and health-care systems, including the development of adapted diagnostic and therapeutic methods for those with difficulties in cooperation or communication, is important (Balandin & Morgan, 2001; Evenhuis, Henderson, Beange, Lennox & Chicoine, 2001). In tune with current policy directions, it is also important to identify factors that promote inclusion and ways of combating the discriminatory attitudes still experienced by many older people with intellectual disability.

Despite the advances in policy and service provision in the last two decades, families still occupy a central place in the provision of support for people with intellectual disability. However, the experiences of families whose children will age over the next decades will be very different from those of previous generations. Continued research is required into the nature of the family life course where a family member has intellectual disability. This includes the challenge of effectively supporting families from successive generational cohorts, each of whom experience a unique set of factors that affect their coping mechanisms and the demands they encounter. Finally, future research must reflect the values of empowerment and inclusion by including the voices of "insiders"—older people with an intellectual disability themselves—in research. The field must continue to develop and experiment with ways of including this group, not only as informants and participants in research but also as partners in setting and implementing future research agendas.

REFERENCES

Anderson, D. (1989). Healthy and institutionalised: health and related conditions among older persons with developmental disabilities. *Journal of Applied Gerontology*, **8**, 228–241.

Anglin, B. (1981). *They Never Asked for Help. A Study of the Needs of Elderly Retarded People in Metro Toronto*. Maple, Ontario: Belster.

Ashman, A., Suttie, J. & Bramley, J. (1993). *Older Australians with an Intellectual Disability* (A Report to the Department of Health, Housing and Community Services, Research and Development

Grants Committee). Fred and Eleanor Schonnell Special Education Research Centre, University of Queensland, Queensland.

Atkinson, D. (1988). Research interviews with people with mental handicaps. *Mental Handicap Research*, **1**, 75–90.

Aylward, E., Burt, D., Thorpe, L., Lai, F. & Dalton, A. (1997). Diagnosis of dementia in individuals with intellectual disability. *Journal of Intellectual Disability Research*, **41**, 152–164.

Balandin, S., Alexander, B. & Hoffman, D. (1997). Using the functional independence measure to assess adults with cerebral palsy: an exploratory report. *Journal of Applied Research in Intellectual Disabilites*, **10**, 323–332.

Balandin, S. & Morgan, J. (2001). Preparing for the future: aging and AAC. *Augmentative and Alternative Communication*, **17**, 99–108.

Begun, A. (1987). Sibling relationships with developmentally disabled people. Unpublished Ph.D. thesis. University of Michigan, Michigan.

Bengston, V. & Black, K. (1973). Intergenerational relations and continuities in socialisation. In P. Baltes & W. Schaie (Eds) *Life-span Development Psychology: Personality and Socialisation* (pp. 207–234). New York: Academic Press.

Bigby, C. (1995). Is there a hidden group of older people with intellectual disability and from whom are they hidden? Lessons from a recent casefinding study. *Australia and New Zealand Journal of Developmental Disabilities*, **20**, 15–24.

Bigby, C. (1997). When parents relinquish care. The informal support networks of older people with intellectual disability. *Journal of Applied Intellectual Disability Research*, **10**, 333–344.

Bigby, C. (1999). Policy and programs for older people with an intellectual disability. In E. Ozanne, C. Bigby, S. Forbes, C. Glennen, M. Gordon & C. Fyffe (Eds) *Reframing Opportunities for People with an Intellectual Disability*. A report funded by the Myer Foundation. Melbourne: University of Melbourne.

Bigby, C. (2000). *Moving on Without Parents: Planning, Transitions and Sources of Support for Older Adults with Intellectual Disabilities*. New South Wales/Baltimore, MD: Mclennan & Petty/Brookes.

Bigby, C. (2001). Sustaining supportive networks: the challenge of continued community living for older people with intellectual disability. In T. Clunning (Ed.) *Practical Approaches to Community Aged Care*. Melbourne: Ausmed.

Bigby, C., Balandin, S., Fyffe, C., McCubbery, J. & Gordon, M. (in press). Retirement or just a change of pace: an Australian national survey of disability day services used by older people with disabilities. *Journal of Intellectual and Developmental Disabilites.*

Bigby, C., Ozanne, E. & Gordon, M. (2002). Facilitating transition: elements of successful case management practice for older parents of adults with intellectual disability. *Journal of Gerontological Social Work*, **37** (3/4), 25–44.

Biklen, J. & Moseley, C. (1988). "Are you retarded?" "No, I'm a Catholic": qualitative methods in the study of people with severe handicaps. *Journal of the Association for Persons with Severe Handicaps*, **13**, 155–162.

Booth, T. & Booth, W. (1996). Sounds of silence: narrative research with inarticulate subjects. *Disability and Society*, **11**, 55–70.

Campaign for Mentally Handicapped People (1981). *Living for the Present: Older Parents with a Mentally Handicapped Person Living at Home*. London: Author.

Cooper, S. (1997). Epidemiology of psychiatric disorders in elderly as compared with young adults with learning disabilities. *British Journal of Psychiatry*, **170**, 375–380.

Cooper, S. (1998). A population-based cross-sectional study of social networks and demography in older compared to younger adults with learning disabilities. *Journal of Learning Disabilities, Nursing Health and Social Care*, **2**, 212–220.

Department of Health (2001). *Valuing People: A New Strategy for Learning Disabilities for the 21st Century*. London: Stationery Office.

Department of Health and Community Services (2001). *Draft State Disability Plan*. Melbourne: Author.

Di Giovanni, L. (1978). Elderly mentally retarded. A little-known group. *Gerontologist*, **18**, 262–266.

Duffy, S., Widaman, K. & Eyman, R. (1991). Life-span development and age related trends in adaptive behaviour and mortality. In M. Janicki & M. Seltzer (Eds) *Aging and Developmental Disabilities:*

Challenges for the 1990s (Proceedings of the Boston Roundtable on Research Issues and Applications in Aging and Developmental Disabilities) (pp. 76–100). Washington, DC: Special Interest Group on Aging, American Association on Mental Retardation.

Dybwad, G. (1985). Aging and mental retardation. An international perspective. In C. Gaitz & T. Samorajski (Eds) *Aging 2000: Our Health Care Destiny* (pp. 465–475). New York: Springer-Verlag.

Edgerton, R. & Gaston, M. (1991). *"I've Seen It All." Lives of Older Persons with Mental Retardation in the Community*. Baltimore, MD: Brookes.

Erickson, M., Krauss, M. & Seltzer, M. (1989). Perceptions of old age among a sample of mentally retarded persons. *Journal of Applied Gerontology*, **8**, 251–260.

Essex, E., Seltzer, M. & Krauss, M. (1999). Differences in coping effectiveness and well-being among aging mothers and fathers of adults with mental retardation. *American Journal on Mental Retardation*, **104**, 545–563.

Evenhuis, H. (1992). Evaluation of a screening instrument for dementia in aging mentally retarded persons. *Journal of Intellectual Disability Research*, **36**, 337–347.

Evenhuis, H. (1996). Further evaluation of the Dementia Questionnaire for persons with mental retardation (DMR). *Journal of Intellectual Disability Research*, **40**, 369–373.

Evenhuis, H., Henderson, C., Beange, H., Lennox, N. & Chicoine, B. (2001). Healthy ageing—adults with intellectual disabilities: physical health issues. *Journal of Applied Research in Intellectual Disabilities*, **14**, 175–194.

Flynn, M. (1986). Adults who are mentally handicapped as consumers: issues and guidelines for interviewing. *Journal of Mental Deficiency Research*, **30**, 369–377.

Forssman, H. & Akesson, H. (1970). Mortality of the mentally deficient. A study of 12,903 institutionalised subjects. *Journal of Mental Deficiency Research*, **14**, 274–294.

Gow, L. & Balla, J. (1994). Methodological difficulties encountered in determining the service needs of a hidden population. *Journal of Intellectual Disability Research*, **38**, 329–339.

Grant, G. (1986). Older carers, interdependence and the care of mentally handicapped adults. *Ageing and Society*, **6**, 333–351.

Grant, G. (1989). Letting go: decision making among family carers of people with mental handicap. *Australia and New Zealand Journal of Developmental Disabilities*, **15**, 189–200.

Grant, C., McGrath, M. & Ramcharan, P. (1995). Community inclusion of older adults with learning disabilities. Care in place. *International Journal of Network and Community*, **2**, 29–44.

Green, J. & Wunsch, A. (1994). The lives of six women. *Interaction*, **7**, 11–15.

Hand, J. (1994). Report of a national survey of older people with lifelong intellectual handicap in New Zealand. *Journal of Intellectual Disability Research*, **38**, 275–287.

Hand, J. & Reid, P. (1989). Views and recollections of older people with intellectual handicaps in New Zealand. *Australia and New Zealand Journal of Developmental Disabilities*, **15**, 231–240.

Haveman, M., Maaskant, M. & Sturmans, F. (1989). Older Dutch residents of institutions with and without Down syndrome: comparisons of mortality and morbidity trends and motor/social functioning. *Australia and New Zealand Journal of Developmental Disabilities*, **15**, 241–255.

Heller, T. (1993). Mastery and control strategies throughout the life course among families of persons with mental retardation. In A. Turnbull, J. Patterson, S. Behr, D. Murphy, J. Marquis & M. Blue-Banning (Eds) *Cognitive Coping in Families Who Have a Member with Developmental Disability* (pp. 195–206). Baltimore, MD: Brookes.

Heller, T. & Factor, A. (1988). Permanency planning among black and white family caregivers of older adults with mental retardation. *Mental Retardation*, **26**, 203–208.

Heller, T. & Factor, A. (1994). Facilitating future planning and transisitions out of the home. In M. Seltzer, M. Krauss & M. Janicki (Eds) *Life Course Perspectives on Adulthood and Old Age.* (pp. 39–52). Washington, DC: American Association on Mental Retardation.

Hogg, J. (1995). *Their Face to the Wind: Service Developments for Older People with Learning Disabilities in Grampian*. Glasgow: Enable.

Hogg, J., Lucchino, R., Wang, K. & Janicki, M. (2001). Healthy ageing—adults with intellectual disabilities: ageing and social policy. *Journal of Applied Research in Intellectual Disabilities*, **14**, 229–255.

Holland, A. (2000). Incidence and course of dementia in people with Down's syndrome: findings from a population based study. *Journal of Intellectual Disability Research*, **44**, 138–146.

Horne, M. (1989). Identifying "hidden" populations of older adults with mental handicap: outreach in the UK. *Australia and New Zealand Journal of Developmental Disabilities*, **15**, 207–218.

Jacobson, J., Sutton, M. & Janicki, M. (1985). Demography and characteristics of aging and aged mentally retarded persons. In M. Janicki & H. Wisniewski (Eds) *Aging and Developmental Disabilities: Issues and Approaches* (pp. 115–143). Baltimore, MD: Brookes.

Janicki, M. (2001). Toward a rational strategy for promoting healthy ageing among people with intellectual disabilities. *Journal of Applied Research in Intellectual Disabilities*, **14**, 171–173.

Janicki, M. & Ansello, E. (2000). *Community Supports for Aging Adults with Lifelong Disabilities*. Baltimore, MD: Brookes.

Janicki, M. & Dalton, A. (1999). *Dementia, Aging and Intellectual Disabilities*. Philadelphia: Brunner/Mazel.

Janicki, M., Dalton, A., Henderson, C. & Davidson, P. (1999). Mortality and morbidity among older adults with intellectual disability: health services considerations. *Disability and Rehabilitation*, **21** (5–6), 284–294.

Janicki, M. & Deb, S. (1994). Ageing: our continuing challenge. *Journal of Intellectual Disability Research*, **38**, 229–232.

Janicki, M. & Jacobson, J. (1986). Generational trends in sensory, physical and behavioural abilities among older mentally retarded persons. *American Journal of Mental Deficiency*, **90**, 490–500.

Janicki, M. & MacEarchron, A. (1984). Residential, health and social service needs of elderly developmentally disabled persons. *Gerontologist*, **24**, 128–137.

Janicki, M., Otis, J., Puccio, P., Rettig, J. & Jacobson, J. (1985). Service needs among older developmentally disabled persons. In M. Janicki & H. Wisniewski (Eds) *Aging and Developmental Disabilities: Issues and Approaches* (pp. 289–304). Baltimore, MD: Brookes.

Janicki, M. & Wisniewski, H. (1985). *Aging and Developmental Disabilities. Issues and Approaches*. Baltimore, MD: Brookes.

Kaufman, A., Glicken, M. & de Weaver, K. (1989). The mentally retarded aged: implications for social work practice. *Journal of Gerontological Social Work*, **14**, 93–110.

Krauss, M. & Erickson, M. (1988). Informal support networks among aging persons with mental retardation. A pilot study. *Mental Retardation*, **26**, 197–201.

Krauss, M. & Seltzer, M. (1993). Coping strategies among older mothers of adults with retardation: a lifespan developmental perspective. In A. Turnbull, J. Patterson, S. Behr, D. Murphy, J. Marquis & M. Blue-Banning (Eds) *Cognitive Coping, Families and Disability* (pp. 173–182). Baltimore, MD: Brookes.

Krauss, M., Seltzer, M. & Goodman, S. (1992). Social support networks of adults with mental retardation who live at home. *American Journal on Mental Retardation*, **96**, 432–441.

Krauss, M., Seltzer, M., Gordon, R. & Friedman, D. (1996). Binding ties: the roles of adult siblings of persons with mental retardation. *Mental Retardation*, **34**, 83–93.

Laslett, P. (1989). *A Fresh Map of Life*. London: Weidenfeld and Nicolson.

Maaskant, M. & Haveman, M. (1990). Elderly residents in Dutch mental deficiency institutions. *Journal of Mental Deficiency Research*, **34**, 475–482.

Mactavish, J., Mahon, M. & Lutfiyya, Z. (2000). "I can speak for myself": involving individuals with intellectual disabilities as research participants. *Mental Retardation*, **38**, 216–227.

Mahon, M. & Mactavish, J. (2000). A sense of belonging: older adults' perspectives on social integration. In M. Janicki & E. Ansello (Eds) *Community Supports for Aging Adults with Lifelong Disabilities* (pp. 41–54). Baltimore, MD: Brookes.

McCallion, P., Janicki, M. & Grant-Griffin, L. (1997). Exploring the impact of culture and acculturation on older families' caregiving for persons with development disabilities. (Family caregiving for persons with disabilities). *Family Relations*, **46**, 347–358.

McCallion, P. & Tobin, S. (1995). Social workers' perceptions of older adults caring at home for sons and daughters with developmental disabilities. *Mental Retardation*, **33**, 153–162.

Moore, M., Beazley, S. & Maelzer, J. (1998). *Researching Disability Issues*. Buckingham: Open University Press.

Morse, J.L. (1988). Assessment procedures for people with mental retardation: the dilemma and suggested adaptive procedures. In S.N. Calculator & J.L. Bedrosian (Eds) *Communication Assessment and Intervention for Adults with Mental Retardation* (pp. 109–138). London: Taylor & Francis.

Moss, S. (1991). Age and functional abilities of people with mental handicap: evidence from the Wessex Mental Handicap Register. *Journal of Mental Deficiency Research*, **35**, 430–445.

Moss, S. (1993). *Aging and Developmental Disabilities: Perspectives from Nine Countries*. Durham, NH: International Exchange of Experts and Information in Rehabilitation.

Moss, S. & Hogg, J. (1989). A cluster analysis of support networks of older people with severe intellectual impairment. *Australia and New Zealand Journal of Developmental Disabilities*, **15**, 169–188.

Moss, S., Hogg, J. & Horne, M. (1989). *Residential Provision and Service Patterns in a Population of People Over the Age of 50 Years and with Severe Intellectual Impairment. A Demographic Study of Older People with Mental Handicap in Oldham Metropolitan Borough. Part 2*. Manchester: Hester Adrian Research Centre.

Moss, S., Hogg, J. & Horne, M. (1992). Demographic characteristics of a population of people with moderate, severe and profound intellectual disability (mental handicap) age structure, IQ and adaptive skills. *Journal of Intellectual Disability Research*, **36**, 387–401.

Nolan, M., Grant, G. & Keady, J. (1998). *Assessing the Needs of Family Carers: A Guide for Practitioners*. Brighton: Pavilion.

Prasher, V. (1997). Dementia questionnaire for persons with mental retardation (DMR): modified criteria for adults with Down's syndrome. *Journal of Intellectual Disability Research*, **10**, 54–60.

Priestley, M. (2001). *Disability and the Life Course: Global Perspectives*. Cambridge: University of Cambridge Press.

Richards, B. & Sylvester, P. (1969). Mortality trends in mental deficiency institutions. *Journal of Mental Deficiency Research*, **13**, 276–292.

Roberto, K. (1993). Family caregivers of aging adults with disabilities. A review of the caregiving literature. In K. Roberto (Ed.) *The Elderly Caregiver: Caring for Adults with Developmental Disabilities* (pp. 3–21). Newbury Park, CA: Sage.

Schalock, R., DeVries, D. & Lebsack, J. (1999). Enhancing quality of life. In S. Herr & G. Weber (Eds) *Aging, Rights and Quality of Life* (pp. 81–92). Baltimore, MD: Brookes.

Schalock, R. & Keith, K. (1993). *Quality of Life Questionnaire*. Worthington, OH: IDS Publishing.

Segal, R. (1977). Trends in services for the aged mentally retarded. *Mental Retardation*, **15**, 25–27.

Seltzer, M. (1983). Non-experimental field research methods. In J. Matson & J. Mulick (Eds) *Handbook of Mental Retardation* (pp. 557–570). New York: Pergamon.

Seltzer, M. (1985). Research in social aspects of aging and developmental disabilities. In M. Janicki & H. Wisniewski (Eds) *Aging and Developmental Disabilities: Issues and Approaches* (pp. 161–176). Baltimore, MD: Brookes.

Seltzer, M. (1992). Aging in persons with developmental disabilities. In J. Birren, R. Sloane & G. Cohen (Eds) *Handbook of Mental Health and Aging* (2nd edn, pp. 583–599). New York: Academic Press.

Seltzer, G., Begun, A., Seltzer, M. & Krauss, M. (1991). Adults with mental retardation and their aging mothers: impacts of siblings. *Family Relations*, **40**, 310–317.

Seltzer, M. & Krauss, M. (1987). *Aging and Mental Retardation. Extending the Continuum*. Washington, DC: American Association on Mental Retardation.

Seltzer, M. & Krauss, M. (1994). Aging parents with co-resident adult children: the impact of lifelong caregiving. In M. Seltzer, M. Krauss & M. Janicki (Eds) *Life Course Perspectives on Adulthood and Old Age* (pp. 3–18). Washington, DC: American Association on Mental Retardation.

Seltzer, M., Krauss, M. & Heller, T. (1991). Family caregiving over the life course. In M. Janicki & M. Seltzer (Eds) *Aging and Developmental Disabilities: Challenges for the 1990s* (Proceedings of the Boston Roundtable on Research Issues and Applications in Aging and Developmental Disabilities) (pp. 3–24). Washington, DC: Special Interest Group on Aging, American Association on Mental Retardation.

Seltzer, M., Krauss, M., Hong, J. & Orsmond, G. (2001). Continuity and discontinuity of family involvement following residential transitions of adults who have mental retardation. *Mental Retardation*, **39**, 181–194.

Seltzer, M., Krauss, M. & Janicki, M. (1994). *Life Course Perspectives on Adulthood and Old Age*. Washington, DC: American Association on Mental Retardation.

Sigelman, C., Budd, E., Winer, J., Schoenrock, C. & Martin, P. (1982). Evaluating alternative techniques of questioning mentally retarded persons. *American Journal of Mental Deficiency*, **86**, 511–518.

Skeie, G. (1989). Contact between elderly people with mental retardation living in institutions and their families. *Australia and New Zealand Journal of Developmental Disabilities*, **15**, 201–206.

Smith, G. (1997). Aging families of adults with mental retardation: patterns and correlates of service use, need and knowledge. *American Journal on Mental Retardation*, **102**, 13–26.

Smith, G., Fullmer, E. & Tobin, S. (1994). Living outside the system: an exploration of older families who do not use day programmes. In M. Seltzer, M. Krauss & M. Janicki (Eds) *Life Course Perspectives on Adulthood and Old Age* (pp. 19–38). Washington, DC: American Association on Mental Retardation.

Stone, E. (2001). A complicated struggle: disability, survival and social change in a majority world. In M. Priestley (Ed.) *Disability and the Life Course: Global Perspectives* (pp. 50–66). Cambridge: University of Cambridge Press.

Uniform Data Set for Medical Rehabilitation (1994). *Functional Independence Measure (FIM)* (Australian Version 4.0). Buffalo, NY: UB Foundation Activities.

Walker, A. & Walker, C. (1998). Age or disability? Age based disparities in service provision for older people with intellectual disabilities in Great Britain. *Journal of Intellectual and Developmental Disability*, **23**, 25–40.

Walsh, P., Concliffe, C. & Birbeck, G. (1993). Permanency planning and material well-being. A study of caregivers of people with intellectual disability in Ireland and Northern Ireland. *Irish Journal of Psychology*, **14**, 176–188.

Walsh, P., Heller, T., Schupf, N. & van Schrojenstein Lantman-de Valk, H. (2001). Healthy ageing—adults with intellectual disabilities: women's health and related issues. *Journal of Applied Research in Intellectual Disabilities*, **14**, 195–217.

Ward, L. (1998). Practicing partnerships: involving people with learning difficulties in research. *British Journal of Learning Disabilities*, **26**, 128–131.

Widaman, K., Borthwick-Duffy, S. & Powers, J. (1994). Methodological challenges in the study of life span development of persons with mental retardation. In M. Seltzer, M. Krauss & M. Janicki (Eds) *Life Course Perspectives on Adulthood and Old Age* (pp. 187–212). Washington, DC: American Association on Mental Retardation.

Wisniewski, H. (1994). Ageing, Alzheimer's disease and mental retardation. *Journal of Intellectual Disability Research*, **38**, 233–239.

World Health Organisation (2001). Healthy ageing—adults with intellectual disabilities: summative report. *Journal of Applied Research in Intellectual Disabilities*, **14**, 256–275.

Zarit, S., Reever, K. & Bach-Peterson, J. (1980). Relatives of the impaired elderly: correlates of feelings of burden. *Gerontologist*, **20**, 649–655.

Zigman, W., Seltzer, G. & Silverman, W. (1994). Behavioral and mental health changes associated with aging in adults with mental retardation. In M. Seltzer, M. Krauss & M. Janicki (Eds) *Life Course Perspectives on Adulthood and Old Age* (pp. 67–92). Washington, DC: American Association on Mental Retardation.

CHAPTER 11

Research Methods in Intellectual Disabilities: The Family Context

Marsha Mailick Seltzer
University of Wisconsin–Madison, USA
Frank J. Floyd
Georgia State University, USA
and
Andrea R. Hindes
Georgia State University, USA

INTRODUCTION

The family context is the most prominent and, arguably, the most important influence on the lives of persons with intellectual disabilities. Currently, all but a small minority of children with intellectual disabilities in the USA live in their family household, and most continue to live with a family member through adulthood (Fujiura, 1998; Braddock, 1999). US estimates for individuals with developmental disabilities, including mental retardation, indicate that of the 2.63 million persons with disabilities across all ages, 61% live with their families, and 63% of these families support children with disabilities who are under 22 years old (Fujiura, 1998). This pattern is evident in Canada, Australia, and the UK (Braddock, Emerson, Felce & Stancliffe, 2001). For example, in a Welsh sample, 88–94% of children under the age of 18 were estimated to live at home, and over 50% of people aged 18–34 continued to live at home (Todd, Shearn, Beyer & Felce, 1993). Furthermore, even when adults live in supported or independent homes, contacts with family members persist and continue to influence their well-being (Blacher & Baker, 1994; Seltzer, Krauss, Hong & Orsmond, 2001). Thus, families are the primary socialization agents for children who have disabilities, and their influence persists into and throughout adulthood.

The family context of persons with intellectual disabilities involves many features that distinguish them from other families. Notably, in the USA, the occurrence of developmental disabilities in a family member is associated with sociodemographic trends which suggest

The International Handbook of Applied Research in Intellectual Disabilities. Edited by E. Emerson, C. Hatton, T. Thompson and T.R. Parmenter © 2004 John Wiley & Sons, Ltd. ISBN 0-471-49709-6.

that there are socioeconomic strains for these families. As compared to the population in general, the families of persons with developmental disabilities tend to be larger, have lower incomes, have more households below the poverty level, are more likely to receive financial support from the government, and are more likely to be headed by single mothers (Fujiura, 1998). Similarly, within the Welsh sample (Todd et al., 1993), 25% of people with mental retardation were living in single-parent families in 1990. Moreover, for this group, the older the person with mental retardation, the fewer the number of parental caregivers and the number of other relatives within the household, further diminishing the family's ability to provide care for the member with mental retardation. It is impossible to discern the extent to which these family circumstances either contribute to or result from the occurrence of developmental disabilities. It is also important to recognize that despite these population-wide trends, families of children with intellectual disabilities come from all segments of society.

The need to provide lifelong support for the person with disabilities influences family development and family life-cycle patterns (Seltzer & Ryff, 1994). As compared to normative family life-cycle stages (Carter & McGoldrick, 1980), families of children with intellectual disabilities progress more slowly than others through the school-age years (Turnbull, Brotherson & Summers, 1986), and the launching and empty-nest phases may be postponed, prolonged, or completely precluded (Seltzer & Krauss, 1994). Moreover, parents' developmental trajectories often show unique patterns where, for example, mothers may delay seeking employment out of the home, and social contacts may be limited due to extensive demands for the care of the child with disabilities (Seltzer, Greenberg, Floyd, Pettee & Hong, 2001). Siblings also tend to have reduced contacts with friends and greater child-care responsibilities for the sister or brother with intellectual disabilities (cf. Stoneman & Berman, 1993). As adults, siblings are likely to assume the role of primary caretaker when the parents can no longer do so (Orsmond & Seltzer, 2000).

The nature and quality of relationships within the family also may be influenced by the presence of intellectual disability in a family member. For example, parent–child interactions differ for parents with children who have intellectual disabilities as compared to parents of typically developing children. In general, parents tend to be more directive and less playful with children who have intellectual disabilities, both when children are preschoolers (Marfo, 1990) and school-aged (Floyd & Phillippe, 1993). This difference suggests that the roles of teacher and behavior manager are relatively more important components of the parents' relationships with their children who have intellectual disabilities. Similarly, sibling relationships tend to be more asymmetrical and less egalitarian in these families, with both older and younger siblings who do not have disabilities taking on more dominant, parent-like roles with the children who have disabilities (Stoneman & Brody, 1993). Some studies show that families of children with intellectual disabilities report higher levels of cohesiveness and spousal closeness, as well as less conflict among all family members, than normative groups (Abbott & Meredith, 1986; Beavers, Hampson, Hulgus & Beavers, 1986). In contrast, the presence of a child with intellectual disabilities can be a stress on the parents' marriage, at least for couples who are vulnerable because of pre-existing marital strains (Benson & Gross, 1989), and married couples with children who have intellectual disabilities tend to have more difficulty than other couples resolving problems together in mutually supportive ways (Floyd & Zmich, 1991).

Finally, in addition to these unique aspects of family relationships, these families also must establish and maintain connections with formal service systems in order to arrange and facilitate support services for the family member with intellectual disabilities. The need for formal support networks begins as early as infancy (Bailey, Blasco & Simeonsson, 1992) and often persists throughout the lifetime of the person with disabilities. Thus, for example, decisions about schooling and day care for children, or employment for adults, often involve extensive collaboration with the social service system, which may undermine individual and family autonomy in these domains. Dyson (1996) reports that a common complaint of parents of children with mental retardation is the prolonged process of waiting for an assessment and school placement. Moreover, these parents are dissatisfied with their children's experiences in school, such as negative report cards, absence of appropriate reading material, and limited teacher attention.

The purpose of this chapter is to describe important methodological concerns and the range of methodological options available for studying persons with intellectual disabilities within the context of their families. The complexity of family structures, the multifaceted nature of family relationships, and the bidirectional patterns of influence among family members make research on the family context a challenging task under any set of circumstances. The unique circumstances for families of persons who have intellectual disabilities compound these complexities. This chapter focuses on design, sampling, and measurement issues relevant to research on the family context of persons with intellectual disabilities. Within each of these domains, we outline key concepts and illustrate them with research examples drawn from our own work and from other lines of investigation. Our goal is to encourage greater use of sophisticated methods that will more readily advance knowledge about the family context. We conclude with both recommendations for state-of-the-art research and proposals for future research endeavors.

DESIGN ISSUES

There are four key design decisions that researchers who study the family context of individuals with intellectual disabilities must confront. These involve selecting the optimal source or sources of data about the family, examining the extent to which these families are distinct from and similar to the norm, modeling the heterogeneity within the population of families of children with intellectual disabilities, and studying changes in individual families over time.

Sources of Data About the Family

The primary concern when selecting a source of data about the family is to obtain the most valid data possible about the family and its associations with the person with intellectual disability. Often, the mother becomes the spokesperson for the family as a whole, and the informant about the person with intellectual disabilities. Clearly, there are good reasons for this approach: in most families, the mother is the primary caregiver for the member who has intellectual disability, and is the family member who has the most contact with the educational and service systems (Barnett & Boyce, 1995; Heller, Hsieh & Rowitz, 1997; Roach, Orsmond & Barratt, 1999; Essex, Seltzer & Krauss, 2001).

However, there are pitfalls in relying on maternal reports. Research shows that there are large gender differences in many of the variables included in studies of families with a member who has intellectual disabilities. In general, women tend to report lower levels of marital adjustment, more behavior problems for children, and higher levels of depression and anxiety than men (Cleary, 1987), whereas men report more financial stress, higher rates of drug and alcohol abuse, and more frequent antisocial personality disorder (Aneshensel, Rutter & Lachenbruch, 1991). Among parents of children with intellectual disabilities, mothers experience more depression and stress than fathers (Bristol, Gallagher & Schopler, 1988; Shonkoff, Hauser-Cram, Krauss & Upshur, 1992). In addition, mothers express more need for family and social support than do fathers (Bailey et al., 1992). Hence, mixing reports from mothers and fathers has the potential of introducing considerable measurement error. If we collect data from mothers only, gender is held constant, and the effect of the child with the disability on the parents' well-being can be detected.

Data from mothers also yield a different picture of the parent–child relationship than reports from fathers. For example, Krauss (1993) reported that fathers experienced more stress than mothers with respect to their feelings of attachment to and reinforcement from their toddler with a developmental disability. Observations of mothers and fathers show that mothers in particular are highly directive and involved with children who have intellectual disabilities (Floyd & Phillippe, 1993), whereas in some circumstances, such as when fathers are unhappy with their marriages, the fathers may withdraw from confrontations with the child (Floyd, Gilliom & Costigan, 1998). Studying considerably older families, Essex, Seltzer & Krauss (1999) compared married couples who had an adult son or daughter with intellectual disabilities, and found that mothers' self-reported feelings of closeness with their adult children were significantly higher than fathers' self-reports on the same measure.

Siblings, too, present a different perspective on the family context. In studies of young children, observational data that include the nondisabled siblings enrich the assessment of the family context (Costigan, Floyd, Harter & McClintock, 1997). In studies of older families, adult siblings can provide a distinct point of view about the functioning of the family, the intergenerational transmission of caregiving responsibility, and the effects of having a brother or sister with a disability on their own development during childhood, adolescence, and adulthood. Gordon, Essex, Seltzer and Krauss (1995) reported that adult siblings' ratings of the family environment differed significantly from parental ratings, with siblings rating the family as less cohesive, more conflictual, and more controlling than their parents. These data suggest that reliance on maternal report would underestimate siblings' concerns about the family.

Thus, the source of data within the family—the mother, the father, or siblings—has been shown to influence (or bias) the conclusions that are reached about families who have a child with intellectual disabilities. How should this be remedied? First, when only one family member can provide data, it is important to use the same member in all families in order to reduce measurement error variance due to source differences. Otherwise, the source effects should be controlled for or systematically investigated. As we discuss later concerning measurement, it would be ideal to combine multiple sources of data within each family to provide the most comprehensive picture possible of family life. However, it is certainly not reasonable to expect family studies to collect data routinely from the mother, the father, and siblings, all in the interest of characterizing the family context completely and accurately. Studies that take a more restricted approach need to recognize the limitations that are imposed by having a singular source of data about as complex a social system as a family. Investigators also should not generalize findings beyond the specific source of the data. For example, in studying mothers, but not fathers, generalizations to "parents" of children with disabilities may be unfounded. Similarly, the literature is replete with studies of putative "family stress" that more accurately should be characterized as studies of mothers' stress.

Examining Similarities to and Differences from Normative Families

Although the literature on families who have children with intellectual disabilities frequently refers to the special needs of these families (Turnbull et al., 1993), relatively few studies have actually *compared* these families with those whose children are unaffected by disability or chronic health problems. Such comparative studies are valuable because they potentially reveal both quantitative and qualitative effects of caregiving for families, or alternatively, how families are able to maintain normative functioning. Most studies with a normative comparison group that were conducted in the 1980s or earlier concluded that mothers and fathers of children with disabilities have higher levels of distress than their counterparts whose children are developing typically (e.g., Dyson & Fewell, 1986; Bristol et al., 1988). However, in a recent study, we examined whether the stresses of caregiving possibly lead to different life-course patterns for parents of children with intellectual disabilities as compared to parents with only typically developing children (Seltzer et al., 2001). This research involved parents of adults, rather than children, and the parents' well-being was assessed in midlife. Across most outcomes, the parents of adults with intellectual disabilities did not differ from a normative comparison group, including parental health status, depressive symptoms, or alcohol symptoms. Furthermore, they did not have a higher divorce rate than the norm. However, parents of adults with intellectual disabilities—particularly the mothers—were less likely to be employed, and they were less likely to spend time socializing with friends. It is possible that there is life-course variation in the extent of distress and the nature of functioning that is characteristic of parents of children with intellectual disabilities in comparison with parents of children who develop typically, with elevated distress evident during the childhood years, but less so after the person with intellectual disabilities reaches adulthood. Given this possible life-course variation, broad generalizations across the life course about the special needs or different level of functioning of these families should be avoided.

Comparison to normative functioning may be impeded in some circumstances by problems with the comparability of variables, tasks, or measures across the groups. For example, there are aspects of caregiving stress for families of children with intellectual disability, such as limitations on family activities or worries about lifelong care, that simply are not relevant to other families. Comparison to normative samples on measures that assess these unique forms of stress are not useful for advancing our understanding of family functioning (Stoneman, 1989). Conversely, some aspects of family life, such as rules about curfew, may be less relevant to families of children who have intellectual disabilities. A more subtle concern is when measures have different meanings across groups. For example, Marfo (1990) points out that the typical laboratory "play" session used to assess mother–child interactions may be interpreted by mothers of children with intellectual disabilities as an opportunity to teach or demonstrate the child's competencies, rather than an opportunity to play per se. The higher rates of directiveness and intrusiveness frequently seen in these mothers, as opposed to mothers of children without disabilities, could be attributed to the different meanings the mothers assign to the task.

An alternative to normative comparisons is to contrast families of children with intellectual disabilities to families who are also dealing with some of the same concerns that are associated with intellectual disabilities. Appropriate comparison groups might include, for example, children who have language impairments, are socially isolated, have physical disabilities or chronic health problems, or exhibit maladaptive behaviors. Stoneman (1989) argues that theoretically grounded selection of comparison groups is a key to understanding the causal mechanisms that account for differences between families of children with intellectual disabilities and other families. For example, a study comparing families of children with intellectual disabilities, children with chronic illnesses (such as diabetes or asthma), and children with behavior problems found that the parents of children with intellectual disabilities experienced greater stress only in specific domains, such as concerns about limited independent functioning for the child (Floyd & Gallagher, 1997). The presence of significant behavior problems for the child, irrespective of disability status, was a relatively more important source of most forms of stress for the parents in all groups, a finding which suggests that it is the behavior problems associated with intellectual disabilities that cause widespread stress for parents.

Modeling Within-Sample Heterogeneity

The considerable heterogeneity within the population of families who have a child with intellectual disabilities is frequently linked to the specific diagnosis of the child. One common comparison is between families who have a child with Down syndrome and families who have a child with autism. In an early study, Holroyd and McArthur (1976) reported that mothers of children with autism scored significantly higher than those with Down syndrome with respect to parenting stress. More recently, it has been confirmed that parents (both mothers and fathers) of children with autism have greater parenting stress than parents of children with Down syndrome (Fisman, Wolf & Noh, 1989; Dumas, Wolf, Fisman & Culligan, 1991), cystic fibrosis (Bouma & Schweitzer, 1990), or mental retardation (Kasari & Sigman, 1997). Another common comparison is between parents of children and adults with Down syndrome and parents of individuals with heterogeneous groups of other types of intellectual disabilities. Almost uniformly, parents whose child has Down syndrome have been found to have better well-being and family functioning (Mink, Nihira & Meyers, 1983; Goldberg, Marcovitch, MacGregor & Lojkasek, 1986; Erickson & Upshur, 1989; Hodapp, Dykens, Evans & Merighi, 1992; Seltzer, Krauss & Tsunematsu, 1993).

These diagnostic-group differences may result from the specific caregiving demands posed by children with different syndromes or disabilities, differences in public familiarity with and support for each disability, differences in the course or trajectory of various types of disabilities, and differences in their causes and consequences. Whatever the source, there are several points relevant to research design here. First, the family context is affected by the specific nature of the child's disability; thus, studies based on samples that are heterogeneous with respect to the etiology of the child's disability may not reveal the diagnosis-specific effects that have been documented for autism, Down syndrome, and other diagnostic subgroups. For this reason, it is risky to generalize across diagnostic groups with respect to the family context. On the other hand, for the majority of individuals with intellectual disabilities, there is no known etiology of their disabilities. Thus, it is impossible to disaggregate fully the population with intellectual disabilities in order to carry out focused studies of the family context for different subgroups. Therefore, recognition of the variability of the family context in part as a result of the nature of the child's disability is an important cautionary consideration.

Apart from the nature and cause of the child's disability, many characteristics of family psychosocial climate and psychosocial resources account for heterogeneity among families. In a seminal theoretical and review paper in 1983, Crnic, Friedrich and Greenberg focused on the family's coping resources, social supports, and ecological environments that mediate and moderate the family's response to the stress of parenting a child with a disability. During the same period, groundbreaking empirical work on the heterogeneity of family contexts was published by Nihira, Mink and their colleagues (Mink et al., 1983; Nihira, Mink & Meyers, 1985). These studies showed how characteristics of family psychosocial environment, such as family cohesiveness and conflict, parenting practices, and cognitive stimulation in the home, are bidirectionally associated with the adjustment of children with developmental disabilities over time. Together, these conceptually important contributions had a substantial influence on subsequent within-group studies of families who have a child with a disability, as reflected in a special issue of the *American Journal on Mental Retardation* (November, 1989) devoted to family research. Since then, many important studies have drawn upon the broader family ecology, family systems, and stress and coping framework to investigate heterogeneity among families who have a child with an intellectual disability. For example, in a study of families of adults who have intellectual disabilities, Seltzer, Krauss and colleagues have shown that the use of problem-focused coping can buffer the stresses of parenting an adult with intellectual disabilities for mothers, but not for fathers (Seltzer, Greenberg & Krauss, 1995; Essex et al., 1999). They also found that mothers of adults with intellectual disabilities benefit from having large and diverse social support networks (Greenberg, Seltzer, Krauss & Kim, 1997), further accounting for the heterogeneity in the well-being of families of persons with intellectual disabilities.

An additional source of within-group heterogeneity derives from family sociodemographic characteristics, which may interact with and condition the caregiving experience. As argued by Pearlin (Pearlin, Mullan, Semple & Skaff, 1990), the position in the social structure occupied by family caregivers (with respect to key variables such as socioeconomic status, race, gender, and age) has been shown to lead to different patterns of coping with stress. The research by Borkowski and colleagues (Mylod, Whitman & Borkowski, 1997; O'Callaghan, Borkowski, Whitman, Maxwell & Keogh, 1999) illustrates this point well. Their longitudinal study of children born to teenaged mothers shows how low levels of education, poverty, and young age at the birth of the child contribute to a family context in which the child is at risk of developing cognitive and behavioral disabilities. In contrast, the research of Hauser-Cram et al. (1999), with a largely middle-class sample (mean years of maternal education = 14.1 years), demonstrates that when the family context is characterized by high levels of cohesion and a strong mother–child relationship, children with Down syndrome show growth in communication, daily living skills, and socialization skills.

In addition to the direct effects of social class on child development in families who have a child with intellectual disabilities, there are indirect effects, mediated by barriers to service utilization. A number of studies have shown that rates of service utilization, including use of residential services, are lower among members of ethnic minority groups than among European-Americans who have a child with intellectual disabilities, and that levels of unmet service needs are consequently higher (McCallion, Janicki & Grant-Griffin, 1997; Hatton, in press; Magana, Seltzer & Krauss, 2002). Lower levels of access to needed services for the family member with intellectual disabilities is an individual difference variable that can lead to suboptimal development, compounding the direct effects of poverty.

Individual differences are also the result of variation in the quality of the parents' marriage and their ability to work together as a coparenting team. Specifically, good marital adjustment characterized by cohesiveness and effective problem-solving skills leads to the development of effective coparenting alliances, which are associated with greater confidence for parents as well as fewer negative interactions with children who have disabilities (Floyd & Zmich, 1991). Furthermore, these factors predict decreases in hostile exchanges over time between parents and school-age children who have intellectual disabilities (Floyd et al., 1998).

Another factor contributing to heterogeneity in the family context is whether the child was the biological offspring of the parent or adopted (Glidden, 1989; Glidden, Kiphart, Willoughby & Bush, 1993). Glidden and colleagues have shown that parents who knowingly adopt a child with an intellectual disability are less vulnerable to distress during the early years of parenting than biological parents, possibly because of the subjective interpretation of the caregiving situation as willingly chosen versus out of the family's control. Glidden's research suggests that it is not the objective challenge of parenting a child with an intellectual disability that contributes to family well-being; rather, there is an interaction between these objective demands and the subjective interpretation that families bring to this challenge that determines parental adaptation patterns and the family context.

Collectively, these studies suggest that the family context is a function of macrosocial factors, the interpersonal relationships within the family, the characteristics of the child with the disability, the resources on which parents can draw, and the subjective interpretation that parents bring to the challenge of parenting a child with intellectual disabilities. Thus, studies of the family context would profit by attending to sources of within-group variation, as well as by conducting comparative analyses of distinct subgroups within the population with intellectual disabilities.

Studying Change in Families Over Time

The life course of families of children with intellectual disabilities is characterized by trajectories of change (Gath, 1993). It has been well documented that the early years following the diagnosis of disability in a child are extremely taxing for families, who must realign their hopes and expectations for family life (Blacher, 1984). Middle childhood brings a different set of challenges, including dealing with the educational and social service systems, advocating for inclusive services, and acquiring fostering skills (Turnbull et al., 1986). Adolescence brings yet other stresses, such as the struggle for autonomy and independence, issues of sexuality, and the anticipation of the end of educational services (Mellon, Wilgosh, McDonald & Baine, 1993). In adulthood, families are challenged to think about where the son or daughter should ultimately live, develop long-range plans for care and support, and offer opportunities for independence and autonomy (Heller et al., 1997; Krauss & Seltzer, 1999).

To track even small segments of this life-course trajectory, longitudinal designs are advantageous. Factors that promote adaptation at one point in the life course might lose their significance in later years, while other factors might retain their predictive power across life stages, a possibility which would not be evident without repeated measures taken on the same sample of parents. Only with longitudinal studies can patterns of constancy and change be elucidated. An example of constancy comes from Blacher and Baker's (1994) two-year longitudinal analysis of family involvement following placement of a child with intellectual disabilities in an out-of-home setting. They found convincing evidence that family members remain highly attached to the children across time. In an example of change over time, Floyd, Costigan and Phillippe (1997) conducted a longitudinal analysis of parent–child interactions over an 18- to 24-month period. They found that both positive and negative exchanges decrease over time as children with intellectual disabilities become older, and these changes only partially overlap with patterns found in cross-sectional comparisons of age groups. Moreover, despite group-level changes, there was considerable within-group stability over time, suggesting that styles of interacting are consistent over time within families.

Another reason to use longitudinal designs concerns the challenge of identifying the specific unfolding influences on the family context. There are three types of designs that are particularly useful here: designs that examine the influence of earlier features of the family context on later development of the child, designs that investigate events or transitions in the child's life and how they affect the family, and designs that seek to determine the bidirectional influences of parent on child and child on parent over time.

An example of the first type of design (that is, the influence of earlier features of the family environment on subsequent child development) is the longitudinal study of Hauser-Cram and colleagues (1999), who tracked 54 children with Down syndrome and their families over a 5-year period. Using hierarchical linear modeling, measures of the family environment taken when the child with Down syndrome averaged 3.4 months of age predicted growth in the child's communication, daily living, and social skills over the subsequent 5 years. The specific aspects of the family environment that predicted gains in these adaptive skills included maternal education, family cohesion, maternal sensitivity and responsiveness to the child with Down syndrome, and maternal fostering of social-emotional and cognitive development. Thus, the family environment when the child was an infant was a powerful predictor of change in adaptive behavior during the toddler and preschool years.

The second type of longitudinal design concerns events or transitions in the child's life and their effects on the family. Individuals with intellectual disabilities experience a series of transitions throughout their life course that may have an effect on the family as a whole. Beginning with entry into early intervention programs and then continuing through the school years with services mandated by Federal legislation, individuals with intellectual disabilities leave school later (at age 22) than their peers without disabilities and face a more challenging transition to adult roles, including the move to non-family living. Each of these transitions has the potential to renew feelings of family stress that may have been dormant during periods of stability in the child's life (Wikler, 1986). Longitudinal studies can track the short- and long-term effects of these transitions in the life of the child on the well-being of individual family members and on family functioning. One example of this type of design is a study of continuity or discontinuity of family involvement after adults with intellectual disabilities move away from the parental home (Seltzer et al., 2001). In this study, families were studied before and at three points after an adult child moved away from home, with the post-relocation study period spanning 3 years. The findings indicated stability in some indices of family involvement (such as emotional involvement) and change in other indices (such as declining worries about the future and increasing sibling contact) during the points of data collection after the residential transition.

The third type of longitudinal design seeks to identify the bidirectional influences of families on their children and, conversely, children on their families. In this type of design, repeated assessments are made of both the child and the family members to evaluate mutual patterns of influence. Keogh, Garnier, Bernheimer and Gallimore (2000) used this approach to evaluate the transactional nature of family accommodations to children with disabilities and the development of child competencies between ages 3 and 11 years. The findings support a child-driven model in which changes in family accommodations are responsive to child characteristics, but not vice versa. Interestingly, the opposite pattern was indicated in an example from Seltzer, Hong and Krauss (1997) in a 6-year study of adults with intellectual disabilities and their aging mothers. The study examined whether maternal psychological distress was related to behavior problems manifested by adults with intellectual disabilities and, reciprocally, whether adult behavior problems were related to maternal psychological distress. The findings indicated that among adults *who lived in the parental home throughout the study period*, maternal distress predicted changes in the behavior problems of the adult with retardation, such that mothers with initially high levels of distress had sons or daughters who had increasing behavior problems over the 6-year study period, whereas mothers who had initially low levels of distress had sons or daughters whose behavior problems decreased over the study period. The direction of effects thus flowed from the mother to the adult child. The reverse pattern was not evident (that is, the initial level of behavior problems of the adult son or daughter did not predict changes in maternal distress over the study period). However, among adults *who were placed out of the home during the study period*, the reverse direction of effects was evident: high initial levels of behavior problems predicted increasing maternal distress over the study period and low initial levels of behavior problems predicted decreasing maternal distress over time. The direction of effects, in this subsample, flowed from the adult child to the mother, but the reverse pattern was not evident (that is, the initial level of the mother's psychological distress did not predict changes in the adult child's behavior problems). Together, these studies underscore the importance of the interplay between the parent and the individual with intellectual disabilities in creating the family context, and also show that patterns of mutual effects may vary depending on the specific constructs assessed, the stage in the life course evaluated, and social context factors.

Cohort Effects

In addition to longitudinal research, there is a great need for cross-sequential designs in order to evaluate possible cohort effects in research on families and intellectual disabilities. It is likely that cohort effects are more pronounced in these families than in the general population. Ongoing changes in governmental legislation, the nature of educational placements and interventions for persons with intellectual disabilities, changes in community support services for these individuals and their families, and changes in diagnostic criteria and sophistication can alter the family context and its influence on the member with intellectual disabilities. Earlier research that showed considerable stress and disruption for families (Farber, 1959; Byrne & Cunningham, 1985) is inconsistent with more recent reports of positive family adaptation (e.g., Glidden, 1989; Wilson, Blacher & Baker, 1989; Krauss & Seltzer, 1999), possibly due to these historical changes.

Experimental Designs

In family research, experimental designs are restricted to studies of the effectiveness of family-based interventions. In most cases, a subset of families is randomly assigned to receive an intervention, and other subsets receive either no intervention or some form of alternative or placebo control; and measurements are taken before and after the intervention to evaluate changes in functioning. While primarily focused on the identification and refinement of useful family services, these studies also illuminate the nature of family life and factors that affect family adaptation. For example, Baker's (1989) demonstrations of the effectiveness of teaching parents to conduct skills training and manage behavior problems for children with developmental disabilities reveal how parenting practices influence the adjustment of the children. Nixon and Singer's (1993) successful cognitive restructuring intervention for parents of children with severe disabilities supports their model concerning the role of guilt and self-blame as cognitive factors that lead to depression and poor adjustment for parents of children with disabilities. Keltner and colleagues (Keltner, Finn & Shearer, 1995) evaluated a supportive intervention designed to enhance the self-esteem and parenting skills of mothers with intellectual disabilities. Improvements in parent–child interactions relative to an alternative intervention reveal how the mothers' sense of competency can affect their role functioning. In addition to group designs such as these, the use of single-case experimental designs to evaluate either the factors that influence families or the impact of the family context on individual family members is a promising, but less explored, avenue for future work.

SAMPLING

The low prevalence of intellectual disabilities makes sampling a particular challenge for all research in the field, including research on the family context. It is impractical and untenable to sample randomly from the population in order to obtain a sufficiently large sample of persons who have intellectual disabilities, particularly if the investigator focuses on a narrow age group or type of disability. Therefore, most researchers rely on some form of convenience sampling. Common approaches include recruiting samples via media announcements, or from disability assessment centers (Mink et al., 1983), special education classes (Floyd & Phillippe, 1993), family and disabilities service agencies (Bristol et al., 1988; Shonkoff et al., 1992), family support groups, and snowball sampling where participants nominate acquaintances to participate. Many studies use several or all of these recruitment strategies (Krauss & Seltzer, 1999). Because the source of participants and the sampling procedures can greatly affect the nature of the sample and the type of data obtained, investigators need to be aware of how their findings might be influenced by the sampling scheme. The extent and nature of family stress, the quality of family relationships and family adaptation, and the use of services and other resources all could be affected by, for example, whether the families were recruited from service agencies as opposed to schools or community groups.

A sampling problem with almost all family research is self-selection effects caused by the fact that all participants specifically choose to volunteer for the research. Although these effects might be relatively minor in situations where brief surveys are administered to a captive sample, self-selection is particularly pronounced in studies that involve lengthy protocols with multiple family members. For example, in recruiting a sample for extensive, in-home observations conducted on multiple occasions, Floyd and Phillippe (1993) found that only approximately 10% of mailed solicitations to families of students in special education were responded to, and another 25% of initial respondents were unable or unwilling to follow through with all procedures. Because families who volunteer for research clearly are a select subset of the relevant population of families, investigators need to estimate how selection effects may bias the data they obtain. At the same time, it is important to implement procedures that may make participation attractive to a wider range of families (e.g., Hogue, Johnson-Leckrone & Liddle, 1999). Some practices might include conducting research sessions in convenient locations or in the home, providing monetary incentives, giving families feedback about their data, and providing referral services. For longitudinal research, it is also important to implement tracking procedures and incentives to keep participants engaged in the study over time (cf. Ribisl et al., 1996).

Alternatively, a promising strategy both for obtaining sufficiently large samples and for avoiding self-selection biases is to conduct secondary data analyses of population-based or representative random samples. Fujiura (Fujiura & Yamaki, 1997; Fujiura, 1998) has selected families with members who have developmental disabilities from respondents to the Survey of Income and Program Participation conducted by the US Census Bureau. Seltzer et al. (2001) identified parents of children with developmental disabilities who participated in the Wisconsin Longitudinal Study, an ongoing investigation of a random sample of 10 000 young adults who graduated from Wisconsin high schools in 1957 and selected siblings. In both cases, the samples were not recruited because of the presence of a family member with disabilities, and, thus, any self-selection related to this situation does not influence the data. Nevertheless, any recruitment or selection criteria for samples such as these (such as families with telephones, or parents who completed high school) must be taken into consideration when interpreting the findings.

Stoneman's (1989) analysis of design issues related to the use of comparison groups in research on families of children with intellectual disabilities raises several important points about sampling. Most notably, researchers should measure and control for important demographic factors that have been shown to be related to family functioning, including race/ethnicity, socioeconomic status, parent age and education, family composition, and family size. The need to control for these variables is underscored by the fact that, as noted earlier, these factors tend to differ for samples of families with members who have developmental disabilities as opposed to the general population. In addition, important child characteristics to control or match for include age, gender, level of intellectual abilities, and birth order. Comparison samples should also be at similar stages of the family life cycle to the families of children with intellectual disabilities (thus, matching with normative groups based on child mental age is usually inappropriate except when the children are infants). Stoneman (1989) describes other variables that may be relevant for matching groups when studying siblings or studying parents who have intellectual disabilities. She also notes that it is important to ensure that comparison groups are recruited from the same population as the families of children who have intellectual disabilities in order to avoid possible confounds associated with different family ecology across groups.

MEASUREMENT ISSUES

Levels of Measurement and Analysis

Families are complex, multifaceted systems, and thus measurement of the family context involves selecting among the array of components that comprise the system. A highly salient dimension of measurement is the extent to which the measurement focuses on individual versus systemic level variables. A complete picture of the family context would require sampling measures from various levels within the family system (Ryff & Seltzer, 1995).

Individual Level

Clearly, most research that addresses the family context focuses on individual-level variables, that is, variables that relate to the functioning of individual family members. Typical variables include mothers' and fathers' attitudes, stress, and well-being (e.g., Frey, Greenberg & Fewell, 1989), and sibling attitudes and childcare responsibilities (e.g., McHale & Gamble, 1989). The attitudes and adjustment of individual family members should have implications for the lives of other members within the family (Pruchno, Blow & Smyer, 1984). Thus, individual-level variables can reflect important features of the family context for children with intellectual disabilities. For example, Glidden (1991) found that mothers' depression, prior attitudes and experience with handicapping conditions, and religious beliefs predicted the success of adoption placements for children with intellectual disabilities. In turn, the effects of having a family member with intellectual disabilities are often experienced on the individual level, with responses such as stress and burden (e.g., Warfield, Krauss, Hauser-Cram, Upshur & Shonkoff, 1999), dissatisfaction, guilt, and depression (Nixon & Singer, 1993).

Family Dyads

The next level of analysis concerns the nature of dyadic relationships within the family system. Relevant dyads include parent–child dyads, the marital dyad, and sibling dyads, all of which have received considerable attention in previous research.

As noted earlier, parent–child dyads (usually mother–child dyads) are the most common foci for family studies, the majority of which use observational methods to examine factors associated with sensitive parenting and child responsiveness. Drawing from a common approach in child-development research, mothers and young children are usually observed in a research playroom as they complete various instructional, problem-solving, or play tasks. This paradigm has been extremely productive in demonstrating the ways in which mother–child interactions differ for children with intellectual disabilities as opposed to typically developing children, including relatively high levels of mother intrusiveness, directiveness, and control during play tasks (see Floyd & Costigan, 1997, for a review). Father–child interactions have received relatively less attention. A challenge for research with fathers is to identify measures that tap relevant domains of father–child relationships. That is, measures of direct childcare may be inappropriate for fathers who perform few childcare tasks separately from the mother. Factors such as the type and amount of support that fathers provide may be more appropriate (Essex et al., 2002). Also relevant to parent–child dyads are self-report measures of parenting attitudes and practices, including the Parenting Style Survey (Saetermoe, Widaman & Borthwick-Duffy, 1991), which was validated for use with parents of children with intellectual disabilities.

Regarding the marital dyad, frequently used measures include marital status and duration as well as the quality of the marital relationship. For example, single/unmarried status is associated with high levels of stress and service utilization among mothers of children with intellectual disabilities (Floyd & Gallagher, 1997). Ethnicity may interact with marital status to explain divergent processes in these groups. For example, single Latina mothers with a child with intellectual disabilities show lower levels of caregiving burden than their married counterparts (Magana, Seltzer, Krauss, Rubert & Szapocznik, 2002), perhaps because of traditional gender roles that are characteristic of some Latina married mothers (that is, obligations to serve the husband as well as to care for the child with disabilities). Among marital quality variables, marital adjustment is an important summary construct that incorporates spouses' satisfaction with the relationship along with indices of the amount of agreement, conflict, and affection in the relationship. For example, Willoughby and Glidden (1995) found that parents of children with intellectual disabilities reported higher levels of marital adjustment when they shared childcare responsibilities. Furthermore, marital adjustment is a consistent predictor of other individual and family outcomes, such as behavior problems for children (Gath & Gumley, 1986) and participation in early intervention programs (Gavidia-Payne & Stoneman, 1997). Another relevant domain of marriage concerns the couples' alliance as a coparenting team. Similar to other couples, the quality of the parenting alliance for parents of children with mild and moderate intellectual disabilities is correlated with the quality of parent–child relationships concurrently (Floyd & Zmich, 1991) and predicts changes in these relationships over time (Floyd et al., 1998).

Among sibling dyads, three features have received the most attention: the nature and structure of sibling roles, the quality of sibling emotional bonds, and the amount and type of caregiving provided by siblings to the family member with intellectual disabilities. Regarding sibling roles, a series of elegant observational studies by Stoneman, Brody and their colleagues (see Stoneman & Brody, 1993, for a review) documents role asymmetries among disabled and nondisabled siblings, wherein both older and younger siblings take on more dominant roles in relation to the sibling with intellectual disabilities. Research on emotional bonds generally focuses on sibling-report measures of warmth/affection, companionship, and conflict. For example, one study indicates that siblings of children with intellectual disabilities report less warmth and closeness, but also less conflict than other siblings, and that both positive and negative emotional bonds are described as less intense when siblings who have intellectual disabilities are placed out of the home (Eisenberg, Baker & Blacher, 1998).

Finally, considerable research documents relatively high levels of caregiving by siblings toward the child with intellectual disabilities both in childhood (e.g., McHale & Gamble, 1989) and adulthood (Seltzer, Greenberg, Krauss, Gordon & Judge, 1997), which includes activities such as supervision of the sibling and assisting with personal care. In addition to activities, it is important to evaluate siblings' attitudes toward these responsibilities. Although, in some cases, childcare responsibilities may be resented and are associated with negative outcomes, such as more hostile sibling relationships (Stoneman & Brody, 1993) or poor adjustment for the sibling (McHale & Gamble, 1989), many siblings seem to value their childcare roles. For example, studies indicate that siblings of children with disabilities are more likely to intervene in parent conflicts with the child who has disabilities (Nixon & Cummings, 1999), and have stronger feelings of responsibility for the sibling (Wilson et al., 1989) than do other siblings.

The Family Unit

The family systems framework posits that each family is an interpersonal system that can be characterized by a variety of qualities such as implicit and explicit rules and values, power dynamics, equilibrium maintenance mechanisms, cohesiveness, and boundaries, among others (Cox & Paley, 1997). The system is both reactive to environmental events that threaten its equilibrium, and exerts pressure on individual family members to behave in ways that maintain its integrity. Furthermore, the principle of wholeness proposes that the functioning of the system is more than the sum of the parts. Thus, measurement of the family context should also address characteristics of the family unit as a system. Available measures of family-level variables address the physical characteristics of the home (e.g., Bradley, Caldwell, Brisby & Magee, 1992) as well as the social climate among family members (e.g., Moos & Moos, 1981). These measures have been used extensively in studies of families of children and adults with intellectual disabilities to characterize complex patterns of family system functioning (e.g., Mink et al., 1983; Floyd & Saitzyk, 1992).

The family unit also exists within a larger network of social systems. As noted earlier, the links between the family system and other social systems may be particularly relevant for families with a member who has intellectual disabilities because of the need for special supports and services. For example, Frey et al. (1989) found that the quality of family social networks was associated with both family adjustment and the psychological well-being of fathers. Floyd and Gallagher (1997) found that single mothers of children with intellectual disabilities were more likely than other families to use formal services of various types, especially if the child had significant behavior problems, suggesting that the formal service system is a particularly important source of support for these families.

SPECIAL CONTENT AREAS

The family context for persons with intellectual disabilities involves several areas of functioning that are unique to the circumstances of intellectual disabilities. Most notably, families must cope with chronic stress associated with the disability. Thus, a commonly used measure of stress associated with disability, the Questionnaire on Resources and Stress (Holroyd, 1974), emphasizes family-level stress associated with the ongoing demands of disability (Friedrich, Greenberg & Crnic, 1983). Extensive research has focused on the nature and extent of various coping strategies employed by parents (Seltzer et al., 1995; Essex et al., 1999), disability-specific family coping patterns (Hodapp & Dykens, 1991), and how cognitive coping strategies might be uniquely effective in coping with uncontrollable aspects of living with a family member who has intellectual disabilities (Turnbull et al., 1993). Gallimore and colleagues (Gallimore, Coots, Weisner, Garnier & Guthrie, 1996) examine the accommodations that families make in adapting to disabilities, which are alterations in everyday routines that serve to enhance family "sustainability". Bailey et al. (1992)

developed the Family Needs Survey to identify the types of supports and services families require in coping with disability. In addition to these disability-specific measures, it is important to recognize how measures that are commonly used with other families may take on different meanings with families of persons with intellectual disabilities. For example, the earlier discussion of mother–child play interactions illustrates how a "play" procedure takes on a different meaning, and thus assesses different constructs with these mother–child dyads. Similarly, self-evaluations of coping effectiveness or family adaptation may be influenced by the types of expectations family members hold when a member has intellectual disabilities, and, thus, might not be directly comparable to scores from other families.

Ethnic and Cultural Diversity

Since culture is transmitted primarily through the family, it is likely that cultural variations are most evident in family contexts. Accordingly, cultural variations seem to be relevant to family responses to disabilities. For example, Latina mothers of children with intellectual disabilities report higher levels of depression than other mothers (Blacher, Lopez, Shapiro & Fusco, 1997; Blacher, Shapiro, Lopez & Diaz, 1997). Nihira, Webster, Tomiyasu and Oshio (1988) demonstrated that associations between family affect and the developmental functioning of children with mild intellectual disabilities differed for Japanese as opposed to American families. Heller and Factor (1988) found that African-American families in the USA are less interested in obtaining out-of-home placements as their children grow older than are white families, and Hatton (in press) confirmed this pattern among ethnic minority families in the UK as well as the USA.

In order to understand the mechanisms by which cultural factors influence family outcomes, it is important to measure the cultural variables themselves, rather than relying on ethnicity or race alone as a proxy for putative cultural effects (Keogh, Gallimore & Weisner, 1997). For example, Pruchno, Patrick and Burant (1997) found that measures of sociocultural, situational, and other variables that are correlated with race accounted for the effects of race on caregiver burden and satisfaction for mothers of children with disabilities. Understanding the impact of specific cultural variables provides a clearer understanding of the nature of cultural effects. To date, limited research has been conducted to address specifically cultural diversity and its implications for the family context of intellectual disabilities. Mink (1997) suggests an agenda for future research that accounts for differences in definitions of atypicality across cultures, conceptual and measurement equivalence across groups, and the impact of poverty for ethnic minorities.

Multiple Perspectives and Multiple Methods

The complexity of the family context requires the collection of data from multiple family members and multiple methods of measurement. Clearly, individual family members have unique perspectives on family life, the impact of intellectual disabilities on the family, and their own roles within the family. Although family members often show high levels of agreement, as described earlier, there are many inconsistencies as well. Multiple methods of measurement are important for any research endeavor in order to control for and, when possible, partial out the effects of method variance. Multiple methods are particularly relevant to family research because various domains of family functioning may be relatively accessible to various forms of measurement. For example, self-report questionnaires or interview measures from siblings are essential in understanding their mixed feelings toward their brother or sister with intellectual disabilities. Specifically, observations may not capture these sentiments because it may be difficult for the siblings to express affection or hostility, either because of the child's lack of emotional reciprocity or the parents' prohibition of expressions such as hitting when angry (Gamble & Woulbroun, 1993). However, observations of siblings together may be needed in order to understand how sentiments translate to actions toward the sibling.

CONCLUSIONS

Study of the family context offers both opportunities and challenges to researchers investigating intellectual disabilities. Primary among the opportunities is the rich heterogeneity of families of children with intellectual disabilities, as intellectual disabilities cut across social and demographic lines, and thus offer a microcosm of society in which research can be carried out. Primary among the challenges is determining how to isolate the effects of intellectual disability from the effects of the multitude of other characteristics that define these families.

As compared with 20 years ago, when studies of families of children with intellectual disabilities were sparse, the contemporary literature is rich in research on the family context. Thus, new investigators and new investigations can build on a firmer foundation of knowledge about how families who have a child with intellectual disabilities function, what their special challenges are, and where they show patterns of resiliency. Moreover, the marked level of heterogeneity within this group of families is now well documented, whereas in the past this group was viewed as homogeneous and experiencing great stress.

However, much remains unknown, and thus there is ample room and substantial need for new lines of investigation of the family context. Among the many possible items on this agenda for future research are the following.

Studies of Ethnic and Racial Diversity in Families of Children with Intellectual Disabilities

We have only scratched the surface in investigating how distinct ethnic groups differ in the family context of intellectual disabilities. Important lines of investigation include influences of ethnicity versus acculturation, differences in the meaning and acceptance of disability across ethnic groups, examination of how diverse family routines and rituals affect the child with intellectual disabilities, and barriers to service utilization as experienced by ethnic families.

Studies of Parents with Intellectual Disabilities

Among those with mild intellectual disabilities, parenthood is not an uncommon role. Yet the challenges of parenting for these individuals should not be underestimated. In addition to studying the types of supports needed by parents with intellectual disabilities to foster the growth and development of their children and to prevent disability, there is a need to examine how all of the factors raised in this chapter might be different in families headed by a parent with intellectual disabilities. For example, sources of data and appropriateness of measures and tasks would warrant re-examination. The roles of siblings may be distinct from their roles in other families, especially siblings whose intellectual abilities might exceed the parents'. The selection of appropriate comparison groups would necessitate a distinct set of considerations, just to name a few examples.

Studies of the Pathways to Resiliency and Vulnerability

It is now known that most parents of children with intellectual disabilities are resilient even in the face of lifelong parenting challenges and with a life course that takes a divergent path. Yet there is little understanding of the processes and mechanisms that lead to this outcome of resilience or the factors that differentiate the resilient from the vulnerable among such families. We know, for example, that resilient parents use more adaptive coping strategies than vulnerable families, but is the better coping the cause or the result of the resilience? Similarly, we have seen that parents make accommodations to their family organization and rituals in response to having a child with intellectual disabilities. But do these accommodations in turn lead to better social and psychological adjustment among the parents and better development for the child? Digging deeper into the sources of family resilience would elucidate important processes and mechanisms that might be relevant to all families, not just those who have a child with intellectual disabilities.

Studies of the Effects of Services and Interventions on Families

Families are increasingly exposed to services and interventions directed at their children and at their family as a unit. Beginning with early intervention during the years after the identification and diagnosis of the child's disability, followed by multiple educational and therapeutic interventions during the long stretch of school years, and then by services for adults with disabilities after the child transitions out of the school context, parents interact with a host of service systems, all aimed at improving the skills and quality of life of their child with intellectual disabilities. Although these service systems and their proximal effects have been described in the literature, there is a need for a fresh look at the cumulative effects of this level of exposure of families to the public sector. The family serves as a boundary between the child and the service system, optimally deciding which interventions and programs are best for the child, advocating for unavailable services, partnering with professionals, and brokering among agencies. However, the long-range effects of these roles on families have not been studied. Under what circumstances does this unique constellation of family responsibilities deplete family well-being and when does it build family resilience? What educational, financial, social, and psychological resources do families need to develop mastery over the demands of the service system? How do families develop teamwork, as opposed to adversarial associations, with schools and service agencies?

These are just a few promising lines of investigation that can be taken by scholars of the family context of a child with intellectual disabilities. The research methods described in this chapter and the approaches taken in prior studies point to strategies and avenues of investigation that have the potential to expand our understanding of how the family context influences the development of children and adults with intellectual disabilities, and, in turn, how these individuals affect their families.

ACKNOWLEDGMENTS

Support for the preparation of this chapter was provided by grants from the National Institute of Aging to the first author (R01 AG08768) and from the National Institute of Child Health and Human Development to the second author (R01 HD24205 and R01 HD 35988).

REFERENCES

Abbot, D.A. & Meredith, W.H. (1986). Strengths of parents with retarded children. *Family Relations*, **35**, 371–375.

Aneshensel, C.S., Rutter, C.M. & Lachenbruch, P.A. (1991). Social structure, stress, and mental health: competing conceptual and analytic models. *American Sociological Review*, **56**, 166–178.

Bailey, D.B., Blasco, P.M. & Simeonsson, R.J. (1992). Needs expressed by mothers and fathers of young children with disabilities. *American Journal on Mental Retardation*, **97**, 1–10.

Baker, B.L. (1989). *Parent Training and Developmental Disabilities*. Washington, DC: American Association on Mental Retardation.

Barnett, W.S. & Boyce, G.C. (1995). Effects of children with Down syndrome on parents' activities. *American Journal on Mental Retardation*, **100**, 115–127.

Beavers, J., Hampson, R.B., Hulgus, Y.F. & Beavers, W.R. (1986). Coping in families with a retarded child. *Family Process*, **25**, 365–378.

Benson, B.A. & Gross, A.M. (1989). The effect of a congenitally handicapped child upon the marital dyad: a review of the literature. *Clinical Psychology Review*, **9**, 747–758.

Blacher, J. (1984). Sequential stages of parental adjustment to the birth of a child with handicaps: fact or artifact? *Mental Retardation*, **22**, 55–68.

Blacher, J. & Baker, B.L. (1994). Family involvement in residential treatment of children with retardation: is there evidence of detachment? *Journal of Child Psychology and Psychiatry and Allied Disciplines*, **35**, 505–520.

Blacher, J., Lopez, S., Shapiro, J. & Fusco, J. (1997). Contributions to depression in Latina mothers with and without children with retardation: implications for caregiving. *Family Relations: Interdisciplinary Journal of Applied Family Studies*, **46**, 325–334.

Blacher, J., Shapiro, J., Lopez, S. & Diaz, L. (1997). Depression in Latina mothers of children with mental retardation: a neglected concern. *American Journal on Mental Retardation*, **101**, 483–496.

Bouma, R. & Schweitzer, R. (1990). The impact of chronic childhood illness on family stress: a comparison between autism and cystic fibrosis. *Journal of Clinical Psychology*, **46**, 722–730.

Braddock, D. (1999). Aging and developmental disabilities: demographic and policy issues affecting American families. *Mental Retardation*, **37**, 155–161.

Braddock, D., Emerson, E., Felce, D. & Stancliffe, R.J. (2001). Living circumstances of children and adults with mental retardation or developmental disabilities in the United States, Canada, England and Wales, and Australia. *Mental Retardation and Developmental Disabilities Research Reviews*, **7**, 115–121.

Bradley, R.H., Caldwell, B.M., Brisby, J. & Magee, M. (1992). The HOME Inventory: a new scale for families of pre- and early adolescent children with disabilities. *Research in Developmental Disabilities*, **13**, 313–333.

Bristol, M.M., Gallagher, J.J. & Schopler, E. (1988). Mothers and fathers of young developmentally disabled and nondisabled boys: adaptation and spousal support. *Developmental Psychology*, **24**, 441–451.

Byrne, E.A. & Cunningham, C.C. (1985). The effects of mentally handicapped children on families—a conceptual review. *Journal of Child Psychology and Psychiatry*, **26**, 847–864.

Carter, E.A. & McGoldrick, M. (1980). *The Family Life Cycle: A Framework for Family Therapy*. New York: Gardner.

Cleary, P.D. (1987). Gender differences in stress-related disorders. In R.C. Barnett, L. Biener & G.K. Baruch (Eds) *Gender and Stress* (pp. 39–72). New York: Free Press.

Costigan, C.L., Floyd, F.J., Harter, K.S.M. & McClintock, J.C. (1997). Family process and adaptation to children with mental retardation: disruption and resilience in family problem-solving interactions. *Journal of Family Psychology*, **11**, 515–529.

Cox, M.J. & Paley, B. (1997). Families as systems. *Annual Review of Psychology*, **48**, 243–267.

Crnic, K.A., Friedrich, W.N. & Greenberg, M.T. (1983). Adaptation of families with mentally retarded children: a model of stress, coping and family ecology. *American Journal of Mental Deficiency*, **88**, 125–138.

Dumas, J.E., Wolf, L.C., Fisman, S.M. & Culligan, A. (1991). Parenting stress, child behavior problems, and dysphoria in parents of children with autism, Down syndrome, behavior disorders, and normal development. *Exceptionality*, **2**, 97–110.

Dyson, L.L. (1996). The experiences of families of children with learning disabilities: parental stress, family functioning, and sibling self-concept. *Journal of Learning Disabilities*, **29**, 280–286.

Dyson, L. & Fewell, R.R. (1986). Stress and adaptation in parents of young handicapped and nonhandicapped children: a comparative study. *Journal of the Division for Early Childhood*, **10**, 25–34.

Eisenberg, L., Baker, B.L. & Blacher, J. (1998). Siblings of children with mental retardation living at home or in residential placement. *Journal of Child Psychology and Psychiatry and Allied Disciplines*, **39**, 355–363.

Erickson, M. & Upshur, C.C. (1989). Caretaking burden and social support: comparison of mothers of infants with and without disabilities. *American Journal on Mental Retardation*, **94**, 250–258.

Essex, E.L. (1998). Parental caregivers of adults with mental retardation: the experience of older mothers and fathers. Doctoral dissertation, University of Wisconsin–Madison. *Dissertation Abstracts International*, 59-08.

Essex, E.L., Seltzer, M.M. & Krauss, M.W. (1999). Differences in coping effectiveness and well-being among aging mothers and fathers of adults with mental retardation. *American Journal on Mental Retardation*, **104**, 545–563.

Essex, E.L., Seltzer, M.M. & Krauss, M.W. (2001). Fathers as caregivers for adult children with mental retardation. In B.J. Kramer & E.H. Thompson (Eds) *Men as Caregivers: Theory, Research, and Service Implications*. New York: Springer.

Farber, B. (1959). Effects of a severely mentally retarded child on family integration. *Monographs of the Society for Research in Child Development*, **24** (Serial No. 71).

Fisman, S., Wolf, L. & Noh, S. (1989). Marital intimacy in parents of exceptional children. *Canadian Journal of Psychiatry*, **34**, 519–525.

Floyd, F.J. & Costigan, C.L. (1997). Family interactions and family adaptation. In N.W. Bray (Ed.) *International Review of Research in Mental Retardation*, vol. 20 (pp. 47–74). New York: Academic Press.

Floyd, F.J., Costigan, C.L. & Phillippe, K.A. (1997). Developmental change and consistency in parental interactions with school-aged children with mental retardation. *American Journal on Mental Retardation*, **101**, 579–594.

Floyd, F.J. & Gallagher, E.M. (1997). Parental stress, care demands, and use of support services for school-age children with disabilities and behavior problems. *Family Relations*, **46**, 359–371.

Floyd, F.J., Gilliom, L.A. & Costigan, C.L. (1998). Marriage and the parenting alliance: longitudinal prediction of change in parenting perceptions and behaviors. *Child Development*, **69**, 1461–1479.

Floyd, F.J. & Phillippe, K.A. (1993). Parental interactions with children with and without mental retardation: behavior management, coerciveness, and positive exchange. *American Journal on Mental Retardation*, **97**, 673–684.

Floyd, F.J. & Saitzyk, A. (1992). Social class and parenting children with mild and moderate mental retardation. *Journal of Pediatric Psychology*, **17**, 607–631.

Floyd, F.J. & Zmich, D.E. (1991). Marriage and the parenting partnership: perceptions and interactions of parents with mentally retarded and typically developing children. *Child Development*, **62**, 1434–1448.

Frey, K.S., Greenberg, M.T. & Fewell, R.R. (1989). Stress and coping among parents of handicapped children: a multidimensional approach. *American Journal on Mental Retardation*, **94**, 240–249.

Friedrich, W.N., Greenberg, M.T. & Crnic, K.A. (1983). A short form of the Questionnaire on Resources and Stress. *American Journal on Mental Deficiency*, **87**, 606–613.

Fujiura, G.T. (1998). Demography of family households. *American Journal on Mental Retardation*, **103**, 225–235.

Fujiura, G.T. & Yamaki, K. (1997). An analysis of ethnic variations in developmental disability: prevalence and household economic status. *Mental Retardation*, **35**, 286–294.

Gallimore, R., Coots, J., Weisner, T., Garnier, H. & Guthrie, D. (1996). Family responses to children with early developmental delays. II. Accommodation intensity and activity in early and middle childhood. *American Journal on Mental Retardation*, **101**, 215–232.

Gamble, W.C. & Woulbroun, E.J. (1993). Measurement considerations in the identification and assessment of stressors and coping strategies. In Z. Stoneman & P. Waldman Berman (Eds) *The Effects of Mental Retardation, Disability, and Illness on Sibling Relationships* (pp. 287–319). Baltimore, MD: Brookes.

Gath, A. (1993). Changes that occur in families as children with intellectual disability grow up. *International Journal of Disability, Development and Education*, **40**, 167–174.

Gath, A. & Gumley, D. (1986). Family background of children with Down's syndrome and of children with a similar degree of mental retardation. *British Journal of Psychiatry*, **149**, 161–171.

Gavidia-Payne, S. & Stoneman, Z. (1997). Family predictors of maternal and paternal involvement in programs for young children with disabilities. *Child Development*, **68**, 701–717.

Glidden, L.M. (1989). *Parents for Children, Children for Parents: The Adoption Alternative*. Washington, DC: American Association on Mental Retardation.

Glidden, L.M. (1991). Adopted children with developmental disabilities: post-placement family functioning. *Children and Youth Services Review*, **13**, 363–377.

Glidden, L.M., Kiphart, M.J., Willoughby, J.C. & Bush, B.A. (1993). Family functioning when rearing children with developmental disabilities. In A.P. Turnbull, J.M. Patterson, S.K. Behr, D.L. Murphy, J.G. Marquis & M.J. Blue-Banning (Eds) *Cognitive Coping, Families, and Disability* (pp. 183–194). Baltimore, MD: Brookes.

Goldberg, S., Marcovitch, S., MacGregor, D. & Lojkasek, M. (1986). Family responses to developmentally delayed preschoolers: etiology and the father's role. *American Journal of Mental Deficiency*, **90**, 610–617.

Gordon, R.M., Essex, E.A., Seltzer, M.M. & Krauss, M.W. (1995). Mothers', fathers', and adult siblings' perceptions of family well-being. Paper presented at the 119th annual conference of the American Association on Mental Retardation, San Francisco, CA.

Greenberg, J.S., Seltzer, M.M., Krauss, M.W. & Kim, H. (1997). The differential effects of social support on the psychological well-being of aging mothers of adults with mental illness or mental retardation. *Family Relations*, **46**, 383–394.

Hatton, C. (in press). People with intellectual disabilities from ethnic minority communities in the US and the UK. *International Review of Research in Mental Retardation*, **25**.

Hauser-Cram, P., Warfield, M.E., Shonkoff, J.P., Krauss, M.W., Upshur, C.C. & Sayer, A. (1999). Family influences on adaptive development in young children with Down syndrome. *Child Development*, **70**, 979–989.

Heller, T. & Factor, A. (1988). Permanency planning among black and white family caregivers of older adults with mental retardation. *Mental Retardation*, **26**, 203–208.

Heller, T., Hsieh, K. & Rowitz, L. (1997). Maternal and paternal caregiving of persons with mental retardation across the life span. *Family Relations*, **46**, 407–415.

Hodapp, R.M. & Dykens, E.M. (1991). Toward an etiology-specific strategy of early intervention with handicapped children. In K. Marfo (Ed.) *Early Intervention in Transition: Current Perspectives on Programs for Handicapped Children* (pp. 41–60). New York: Praeger.

Hodapp, R.M., Dykens, E.M., Evans, D.W. & Merighi, J.R. (1992). Maternal emotional reactions to young children with different types of handicaps. *Journal of Developmental and Behavioral Pediatrics*, **13**, 118–123.

Hogue, A., Johnson-Leckrone, J. & Liddle, H.A. (1999). Recruiting high-risk families into family-based prevention and prevention research. *Journal of Mental Health Counseling*, **21**, 337–351.

Holroyd, J. (1974). The Questionnaire on Resources and Stress: an instrument to measure family responses to a handicapped member. *Journal of Community Psychology*, **2**, 92–94.

Holroyd, J. & McArthur, D. (1976). Mental retardation and stress on the parents: a contrast between Down's syndrome and childhood autism. *American Journal of Mental Deficiency*, **80**, 431–436.

Kasari, C. & Sigman, M. (1997). Linking parental perceptions to interactions in young children with autism. *Journal of autism and Developmental Disorders*, **27**, 39–57.

Keltner, B., Finn, D. & Shearer, D. (1995). Effects of family intervention on maternal–child interaction for mothers with developmental disabilities. *Family and Community Health*, **17**, 35–49.

Keogh, B.K., Gallimore, R. & Weisner, T. (1997). A sociocultural perspective on learning and learning disabilities. *Learning Disabilities Research and Practice*, **12**, 107–113.

Keogh, B.K., Garnier, H.E., Bernheimer, L.P. & Gallimore, R. (2000). Models of child–family interactions for children with developmental delays: child-driven or transactional? *American Journal on Mental Retardation*, **105**, 32–46.

Krauss, M.W. (1993). Child-related and parenting stress: similarities and differences between mothers and fathers of children with disabilities. *American Journal on Mental Retardation*, **97**, 393–404.

Krauss, M.W. & Seltzer, M.M. (1999). An unanticipated life: the impact of lifelong caregiving. In H. Bersani (Ed.) *Responding to the Challenge: International Trends and Current Issues in Developmental Disabilities.* Brookline, MA: Brookline Books.

Magana, S., Seltzer, M.M. & Krauss, M.W. (2002). Service utilization patterns of adults with intellectual disabilities: a comparison of Puerto Rican and non-Latino white families. *Journal of Gerontological Social Work*, **37**, 65–86.

Magana, S., Seltzer, M.M., Krauss, M.W., Rubert, M. & Szapocznik, J. (2002). Well-being and family role strains among Cuban-American and Puerto Rican mothers of adults with mental retardation. *Journal of Human Behavior in the Social Environment*, **5**, 31–55.

Marfo, K. (1990). Maternal directiveness in interactions with mentally handicapped children: an analytical commentary. *Journal of Child Psychology and Psychiatry*, **31**, 531–549.

McCallion, P., Janicki, M.P. & Grant-Griffin, L. (1997). Exploring the impact of culture and acculturation on older families' caregiving for persons with developmental disabilities. *Family Relations*, **46**, 347–357.

McHale, S.M. & Gamble, W.C. (1989). Sibling relationships of children with disabled and nondisabled brothers and sisters. *Developmental Psychology*, **25**, 421–429.

Mellon, S., Wilgosh, L., McDonald, L. & Baine, D. (1993). Transition to adulthood: stresses experienced by families of young people with severe disabilities. *Developmental Disabilities Bulletin*, **21**, 34–45.

Mink, I.T. (1997). Studying culturally diverse families of children with mental retardation. *International Review of Research in Mental Retardation*, **20**, 75–98.

Mink, I.T., Nihira, K. & Meyers, C.E. (1983). Taxonomy of family lifestyles. I. Homes with TMR children. *American Journal of Mental Retardation*, **87**, 484–497.

Moos, R.H. & Moos, B.S. (1981). *Family Environment Scale Manual.* Palo Alto, CA: Consulting Psychologists Press.

Mylod, D.E., Whitman, T.L. & Borkowski, J.G. (1997). Predicting adolescent mothers' transition to adulthood. *Journal of Research on Adolescence*, **74**, 457–478.

Nihira, K., Mink, I.T. & Meyers, C.E. (1985). Home environment and development of slow-learning adolescents: reciprocal relations. *Developmental Psychology*, **21**, 784–794.

Nihira, K., Webster, R., Tomiyasu, Y. & Oshio, C. (1988). Child–environment relationships: a cross-cultural study of educable mentally retarded children and their families. *Journal of Autism and Developmental Disorders*, **18**, 327–341.

Nixon, C.D. & Singer, G.H.S. (1993). A group cognitive behavioral treatment for excessive parental self-blame and guilt. *American Journal of Mental Retardation*, **97**, 665–672.

Nixon, C.L. & Cummings, E.M. (1999). Sibling disability and children's reactivity to conflicts involving family members. *Journal of Family Psychology*, **13**, 274–285.

O'Callaghan, M.F., Borkowski, J.G., Whitman, T.L., Maxwell, S.E. & Keogh, D. (1999). A model of adolescent parenting: the role of cognitive readiness to parent. *Journal of Research on Adolescence*, **9**, 203–225.

Orsmond, G.I. & Seltzer, M.M. (2000). Brothers and sisters of adults with mental retardation: the gendered nature of the sibling relationship. *American Journal on Mental Retardation*, **105**, 486–508.

Pearlin, L.I., Mullan, J.T., Semple, S.J. & Skaff, M.M. (1990). Caregiving and the stress process: an overview of concepts and their measures. *Gerontologist*, **30**, 583–594.

Pruchno, R.A., Blow, F.C. & Smyer, M.A. (1984). Life events and interdependent lives: implication for research and intervention. *Human Development*, **27**, 31–41.

Pruchno, R.A., Patrick, J.H. & Burant, C.J. (1997). African-American and white mothers of adults with chronic disabilities: caregiving burden and satisfaction. *Family Relations: Interdisciplinary Journal of Applied Family Studies*, **46**, 335–346.

Ribisl, K.M., Walton, M.A., Mowbray, C.T., Luke, D.A., Davidson, W.S. & Bootsmiller, B.J. (1996). Minimizing participant attrition in panel studies through the use of effective retention and tracking strategies: review and recommendations. *Education and Program Planning*, **19**, 1–25.

Roach, M.A., Orsmond, G.I. & Barratt, M.S. (1999). Mothers and fathers of children with Down syndrome: parental stress and involvement in childcare. *American Journal on Mental Retardation*, **104**, 422–436.

Ryff, C.D. & Seltzer, M.M. (1995). Family relations and individual development in adulthood and aging. In R. Blieszner & V.H. Bedford (Eds) *Handbook of Aging and the Family* (pp. 95–113). Westport, CT: Greenwood.

Saetermoe, C.L., Widaman, K.F. & Borthwick-Duffy, S. (1991). Validation of the Parenting Style Survey for parents of children with mental retardation. *Mental Retardation*, **29**, 149–157.

Seltzer, M.M., Greenberg, J.S., Floyd, F.J., Pettee, Y. & Hong, J. (2001). Life course impacts of parenting a child with a disability. *American Journal on Mental Retardation*, **106**, 265–286.

Seltzer, M.M., Greenberg, J.S. & Krauss, M.W. (1995). A comparison of coping strategies of aging mothers of adults with mental illness or mental retardation. *Psychology and Aging*, **10**, 64–75.

Seltzer, M.M., Greenberg, J.S., Krauss, M.W., Gordon, R.M. & Judge, K. (1997). Siblings of adults with mental retardation or mental illness: effects on lifestyle and psychological well-being. *Family Relations*, **46**, 395–405.

Seltzer, M.M., Hong, J. & Krauss, M.W. (1997). Behavior problems in adults with mental retardation and maternal well-being. Paper presented at the 30th Annual Gatlinburg Conference on Research and Theory in Mental Retardation, Riverside, CA.

Seltzer, M.M. & Krauss, M.W. (1994). Aging parents with co-resident adult children: the impact of lifelong caregiving. In M.M. Seltzer, M.W. Krauss & M.P. Janicki (Eds) *Life Course perspectives on Adulthood and Old Age* (pp. 3–18). Washington, DC: American Association on Mental Retardation.

Seltzer, M.M., Krauss, M.W., Hong, J. & Orsmond, G.I. (2001). Continuity or discontinuity of family involvement following residential transitions of adults with mental retardation. *Mental Retardation*, **39**, 181–194.

Seltzer, M.M., Krauss, M.W. & Tsunematsu, N. (1993). Adults with Down syndrome and their aging mothers: diagnostic group differences. *American Journal on Mental Retardation*, **97**, 464–508.

Seltzer, M.M. & Ryff, C.D. (1994). Parenting across the life span: the normative and nonnormative cases. In D.L. Featherman, R.M. Lerner & M. Perlmutter (Eds) *Life Span Development and Behavior*, vol. 12 (pp. 1–40). Hillsdale, NJ: Erlbaum.

Shonkoff, J.P., Hauser-Cram, P., Krauss, M.W. & Upshur, C.C. (1992). Development of infants with disabilities and their families: implications for theory and service delivery. *Monographs of the Society for Research in Child-Development*, **57** (6).

Stoneman, Z. (1989). Comparison groups in research on families with mentally retarded members: a methodological and conceptual review. *American Journal on Mental Retardation*, **94**, 195–215.

Stoneman, Z. (1997). Mental retardation and family adaptation. In W.E. MacLean Jr (Ed.) *Ellis' Handbook of Mental Deficiency Psychology Theory* (pp. 405–437). Mahwah, NJ: Erlbaum.

Stoneman, Z. & Berman, P.W. (Eds) (1993). *The Effects of Mental Retardation, Disability, and Illness on Sibling Relationships: Research Issues and Challenges*. Baltimore, MD: Brookes.

Stoneman, Z. & Brody, G.H. (1993). Sibling relations in the family context. In Z. Stoneman & P.W. Berman (Eds) *The Effects of Mental Retardation, Disability, and Illness on Sibling Relationships: Research Issues and Challenges* (pp. 3–30). Baltimore, MD: Brookes.

Todd, S., Shearn, J., Beyer, S. & Felce, D. (1993). Careers in caring: the changing situations of parents caring for an offspring with learning difficulties. *Irish Journal of Psychology*, **14**, 130–153.

Turnbull, A.P., Brotherson, M.J. & Summers, J.A. (1986). Family life cycle: theoretical and empirical implications and future directions for families with mentally retarded members. In

J.J. Gallagher & P.M. Vietze (Eds) *Families of Handicapped Persons: Research, Programs, and Policy issues* (pp. 45–66). Baltimore, MD: Brookes.

Turnbull, A.P., Patterson, J.M., Behr, S.K., Murphy, D.L., Marquis, J.G. & Blue-Banning, M.J. (Eds) (1993). *Cognitive Coping, Families, and Disability*. Baltimore, MD: Brookes.

Warfield, M.E., Krauss, M.W., Hauser-Cram, P., Upshur, C.C. & Shonkoff, J.P. (1999). Adaptation during early childhood among mothers of children with disabilities. *Journal of Developmental and Behavioral Pediatrics*, **20**, 9–16.

Wikler, L.M. (1986). Periodic stresses of families of older mentally retarded children: an exploratory study. *American Journal of Mental Deficiency*, **90**, 703–706.

Willoughby, J.C. & Glidden, L.M. (1995). Fathers helping out: shared child care and marital satisfaction of parents of children with disabilities. *American Journal on Mental Retardation*, **99**, 399–406.

Wilson, J., Blacher, J. & Baker, B.L. (1989). Siblings of children with severe handicaps. *Mental Retardation*, **27**, 167–173.

CHAPTER 12

Quality of Life and Subjective Well-Being: Conceptual and Measurement Issues

Robert L. Schalock
Hastings College, USA
and
David Felce
Welsh Centre for Learning Disabilities, UK

OVERVIEW

Developments in a number of research areas are beginning to coalesce into a clearer understanding of the concepts of quality of life and subjective well-being (SWB). However, despite the clearer understanding, there are still at least two basic questions that need to be resolved. First, what does one define as quality of life? Is it SWB or one or more quality-of-life-related scores from scales that have items that are a mixture of subjective appraisal and objective responses? Second, are the assessments of quality of life that one frequently finds in the literature measures of SWB or objective circumstances and personal experiences? The intent of this chapter is to address these two unresolved questions and suggest guidelines regarding the measurement and interpretation of SWB and objective quality-of-life indicators. To that end, the chapter is divided into four sections:

(1) an overview of the concept of quality of life, including its use, domains, person-referenced outcomes, and principles regarding its conceptualization, measurement, and application
(2) an overview of the area of SWB, including its two major components of happiness and personal satisfaction
(3) a summary of four recent studies that reflect the importance of being careful when discussing research on "perceived quality of life" to emphasize whether research measures relate to SWB *or* objective life circumstances and experiences
(4) a discussion of four measurement issues in quality-of-life and SWB research that set the stage for the next phase of research in the area of quality of life.

The International Handbook of Applied Research in Intellectual Disabilities. Edited by E. Emerson, C. Hatton, T. Thompson and T.R. Parmenter ISBN 0-471-49709-6.

The chapter concludes with a reaffirmation of our basic premise and suggested guidelines.

We approach our task from a number of perspectives. First, we have both been involved in the area of quality of life for a number of years and have published widely in its conceptualization, measurement, and application. Second, we have also been contributors to an international consensus document (Schalock et al., 2002) that summarizes current approaches and principles regarding the conceptualization, measurement, and application of the concept of quality of life. Third, we both subscribe to a systems perspective on quality of life that focuses on the individual (microsystem), the community (mesosystem), and the larger society (macrosystem) (Bronfenbrenner, 1979; Schalock & Verdugo-Alonso, 2002). And fourth, we stress the need to employ a methodological pluralism approach to the measurement of quality of life that focuses on both personal appraisal and person-referenced functional assessment (Schalock, 2001).

The basic premise of the chapter is that one needs to be careful in considering empirical results relating to quality of life to distinguish whether the assessments used measure SWB or objective life circumstances and experiences. Additionally, two guidelines reflect our approach to the topic: (a) if we want to determine whether people with mental retardation/intellectual disabilities are as satisfied with life as other population subgroups, we should assess SWB and compare; (b) if we want to evaluate environmental design or service programs in a sensitive way, we should use objective indicators of personal experiences and circumstances.

OVERVIEW OF QUALITY OF LIFE

Uses of the Term

Although there are numerous definitions of "quality of life" (for example, see Goode, 1994), the current consensus is that quality of life is a multidimensional construct that has a number of different "meanings" depending on its use. Indeed, throughout the world, the concept of quality of life is being used as the following:

- a *sensitizing notion* that gives one a sense of reference and guidance from the individual's perspective, focusing on the person and the individual's environment. As a sensitizing notion, "quality" makes us think of the excellence associated with human characteristics and positive values, such as happiness, success, wealth, health, and satisfaction, whereas "of life" indicates that the concept concerns the very essence or essential aspects of human existence (Lindstrom, 1992; Schalock et al., 2002).
- a *social construct* that is used as an overriding principle to evaluate person-referenced outcomes and to improve and enhance a person's perceived quality of life. In that regard, the concept is affecting program development, service delivery, management strategies, and evaluation activities in the areas of education, disabilities, mental health, and aging (Schalock, 2001).
- a *unifying theme* that provides a systematic framework for understanding and applying the concept of quality of life. This systematic framework includes conceptualizing, measuring, and applying the concept of quality of life from a systems perspective: microsystem—the immediate social setting, including the person, family, and/or advocates; mesosystem—the neighborhood, community, or organization providing

education and habilitation services and supports; and macrosystem—the overarching patterns of culture, society, larger populations, country or sociopolitical influences (Keith & Schalock, 2000; Schalock & Verdugo-Alonso, 2002).

- a *motivational construct* that stresses three motivational aspects of the concept: (a) the end states represented by each quality-of-life domain represent desired human conditions and therefore result in incentives that underlie the motivational process; (b) the person-centered nature of the concept and its application results in an increase in one's internal locus of control, enhanced self-regulation, autonomy, self-determination, personal control, and expectancy of success; and (c) the ecological nature of quality-of-life enhancement techniques augments the positive effects of mediated learning experiences and thereby increases one's intrinsic motivation (Schalock, in press).

Quality-of-Life Core Domains

Historically, attempts to conceptualize and measure quality of life encompassed two perspectives: social indicators and psychological indicators. Social indicators refer to external, environmentally based conditions such as health, social welfare, friendships, standard of living, education, public safety, housing, neighborhood, and leisure. These indicators are usually defined as a statistic of direct normative interest that facilitates concise, comprehensive, and balanced judgments about the conditions of major aspects of society (Andrews & Whithey, 1976). In distinction, psychological indicators focus on a person's subjective reactions to life experiences. Two different approaches were used to measure these subjective evaluations: psychological well-being and personal satisfaction/happiness. An example of the psychological well-being approach was the work of Flanagan (1982), who attempted to conceptualize and operationalize life domains associated with psychological well-being. On the basis of a review of 6500 critical incidents collected from nearly 3000 people of various ages and demographic conditions, he identified 15 factors defining quality of life. He then grouped these 15 categories into five general dimensions of quality of life: physical and material well-being; relations with other people; social, community, and civic activities; personal development and fulfillment; and recreation. An example of the personal satisfaction/happiness approach is reflected in the work of Campbell, Converse and Rogers (1976), who completed national (US) studies of satisfaction and dissatisfaction in a variety of life domains such as family, leisure, income, social relations, and health.

Based on this historical work, the current emphasis in quality-of-life research, application, and evaluation is to approach quality of life as a multidimensional construct, with both subjective and objective components. The acceptance of the multidimensionality of a life of quality has led to considerable work in identifying and evaluating what are referred to as the "core domains" in the areas of person-centered, family-centered, and health-related quality of life. A listing of these domains, with author references, is found in Table 12.1.

As shown in Table 12.1, there is considerable consistency in the core quality-of-life domains. Throughout the current literature, one finds reference to the critical role that factors such as emotional well-being, interpersonal relationships, material well-being, personal development, physical well-being, self-determination, social inclusion, and rights play in a life of quality.

Table 12.1 Quality-of-life core domains

Person-centered domains:
Cummins (1994): safety, health, intimacy, material things, productivity, emotional well-being, and place in society
Felce (1997): physical well-being, material well-being, social well-being, productive well-being, emotional well-being, and civic well-being
Schalock (2000): emotional well-being, interpersonal relationships, material well-being, personal development, physical well-being, self-determination, social inclusion, and rights
Health-related domains:
Coulter (1996): general satisfaction and feelings of well-being, physiological state/symptoms of illness, neuropsychological functioning, interpersonal relationships, performance of social skills, and economic and employment status
Family-centered domains:
Poston et al. (2003): daily family life, family interactions, financial well-being, parenting, advocacy, emotional well-being, health, physical environment, productivity, and social well-being

Person-Referenced Outcomes

Although quality of life can be assessed from the perspective of one's larger society (as it has been historically), this section of the chapter focuses on the two most commonly used *individual-referenced assessment strategies* that result in person-referenced quality-of-life outcomes: personal appraisal and functional assessment.

Personal Appraisal

As discussed later in the chapter in reference to satisfaction, outcomes based on personal appraisal address the subjective nature of quality of life, typically by asking individuals how satisfied they are with the various aspects of their lives. For example, one can ask, "How satisfied are you with the skills and experiences you have gained or are gaining from your job?", or "How happy are you with your home or where you live?" Although individuals' responses are subjective, their responses can be measured in psychometrically sound ways (Schalock, 2001). Measures of happiness are also used in personal appraisal methodology, although the current measurement instruments are being fine-tuned, and standard methodological concerns (for example, validity, response bias, factor purity, correlation to other measures, and social desirability issues) should be addressed before wider use is advocated (Helm, 2000).

Functional Assessment

This person-referenced outcome category addresses the objective nature of quality of life and focuses on personal experiences and circumstances. The most typical formats used in functional assessment include rating scales, direct observation, and questionnaires. Each attempts to document a person's functioning across one or more core quality-of-life domains.

Most instruments employ some form of an ordinal rating scale to yield a profile of the individual's functioning to accomplish this. A number of specific behavioral indicators can also be used in functional assessment, including:

- engagement in everyday activities such as domestic activity, leisure and personal activity, and social interaction (Felce, 2000)
- self-determination skills and personal control (Stancliffe, 2000; Wehmeyer & Schalock, 2001)
- activities and instrumental activities of daily living (Schalock, 2001)
- role (education, employment, and living) status (Schalock, 2001).

Conceptualization, Measurement, and Application Principles

Over the last 20 years, a number of principles have emerged regarding the conceptualization, measurement, and application of the concept of quality of life. Table 12.2 summarizes a number of these principles that are discussed more fully in Schalock et al. (2002).

Table 12.2 Conceptualization, measurement, and application of quality-of-life principles

Conceptualization principles: quality of life:

(1) Is composed of those same factors and relationships for people with intellectual disabilities that are important to those without disabilities.
(2) Is experienced when people's needs are met and when they have the opportunity to pursue life enrichment in major life settings.
(3) Has both subjective and objective components, but it is primarily the perception of the individual that reflects the quality of life he/she experiences.
(4) Is based on individual needs, choices, and control.
(5) Is a multidimensional construct influenced by personal and environmental factors.

Measurement principles: quality of life:

(1) Measures the degree to which people have meaningful life experiences they value.
(2) Measurement enables people to move toward a meaningful life they enjoy and value.
(3) Measures the degree to which life domains contribute to a full and interconnected life.
(4) Measurement is undertaken within the context of environments that are important to people: where they live, work, and play.
(5) Measurement for individuals is based upon both common human experiences and unique, individual life experiences.

Application principles: quality of life:

(1) The primary purpose for applying the concept of quality of life is to enhance an individual's well-being.
(2) Quality of life needs to be applied in light of the individual's cultural and ethnic heritage.
(3) The aims of any quality-of-life-oriented program should be to collaborate for change at the personal, program, community, and national levels.
(4) Quality-of-life applications should enhance the degree of personal control, and individual opportunity exerted by people in relation to their activities, interventions, and environments.
(5) Quality of life should occupy a prominent role in gathering evidence, especially in identifying the significant predictors of a life of quality and the impact of targeting resources to maximize positive effects.

OVERVIEW OF SUBJECTIVE WELL-BEING (SWB)

SWB refers to people's evaluation of their lives, and includes evaluations that are both affective and cognitive. Four separable components of SWB have been identified (Diener, 1984; 2000): life satisfaction (global judgments of one's life), satisfaction with important domains (for example, work satisfaction), positive affect (that is, experiencing many pleasant emotions and moods), and low levels of negative affect (that is, experiencing few unpleasant emotions and moods).

Considerable research involving the predictors of SWB has been done by Myers and his colleagues (Myers & Diener, 1996; Myers, 2000), who have aggregated data from 916 surveys of 1.1 million people in 45 nations, calibrating SWB on a 0–10 scale (where 0 is the low extreme, such as very unhappy or completely dissatisfied with life, 5 is neutral, and 10 the high extreme). Across these 1.1 million respondents, the average response is 6.75 (Myers & Diener, 1996), a conclusion similar to that reached by Cummins' (1998) review. Major generalizations from the survey findings include the following:

- People are happier than one might expect, and happiness does not appear to depend significantly on external circumstances, since happiness cuts across almost all demographic classifications of age, economic class, race, and education level.
- Predictors of SWB include a combination of personal characteristics and sociocultural factors such as extroversion, meeting intellectual challenges, social belonging and social support, health, religiosity, personal freedom, and being reasonably affluent (although in most nations, the correlation between income and happiness is negligible).

Two concepts are embedded in the research on SWB: happiness and satisfaction. Although these concepts are closely related, clarity is not always maintained between them. To quote Cummins (1998, p. 308),

> There remains little certainty and no agreed upon rules for the operationalization of this construct (SWB). Most commonly, it is considered to be some combination of happiness, or positive effect, and life satisfaction. But while such a view has intuitive appeal and face validity, closer inspection reveals very different ideas on the nature of the component parts and almost no information on how the components combine. Some authors simply declare happiness and life satisfaction to be synonymous, but this view is not supported by a considerable body of literature. Measures of happiness and satisfaction share a maximum of 50–60 common variance. These data confirm the view expressed by others that while happiness and satisfaction may indeed form part of the SWB construct, it is heuristically useful to measure and analyze them separately.

For the purposes of this chapter, the following distinctions can be made:

- Happiness represents one component of satisfaction, and reflects the positive and negative affects of positive or negative emotions and moods. Happiness tends to be more transitory than satisfaction (Helm, 2000).
- Satisfaction represents the global judgments about one's life, including subdomains such as work or health satisfaction. Satisfaction demonstrates a trait-like stability over time, and (a) has little relationship to objective indicators; and (b) is not predicted by environmental situations or personal characteristics such as skills or challenging

behaviors (Cummins, 1996, 1997; Edgerton, 1996; Diener, 2000; Schalock, Bonham & Marchand, 2000).

Happiness

A recent issue of the *American Journal on Mental Retardation* was devoted to the topic of happiness, with special reference to its measurement (Carver, 2000; Helm, 2000), application to health-services research (Meyers, 2000), and treatment goals (Szymanski, 2000). In the introduction to this issue, Crocker (2000) makes the following five summary statements about his review of the happiness literature:

(1) Happiness is more accessible and prevalent than had been earlier supposed.
(2) Many external factors do not correlate well with happiness.
(3) There are significant internal or personal factors that do relate importantly to happiness.
(4) We have been neglectful in the study of happiness.
(5) Studies need to be conducted in which investigators examine happiness in persons with developmental disabilities.

As with SWB, studies (as summarized in Helm, 2000) have begun to show that happiness is related to or correlates with social competence, social skills and cooperativeness, satisfaction with relationships with others, and participation in work and leisure activity. It is interesting that investigators have found that wealth, good looks, and good physical health account for only a small variance of being happy (p. 330).

Satisfaction

This component of SWB addresses the subjective nature of quality of life, typically by asking individuals how satisfied they are with the various aspects of their lives. Increasingly, a person's measured level of satisfaction is a commonly used dependent measure in evaluating quality-of-life domains and life experiences (Cummins, 1996, 1998).

Two recent studies have begun to delineate what is satisfaction and its importance in the area of quality-of-life research. In one study (Bonham et al., in press), the relationships between measured satisfaction to each of the eight core quality-of-life domains listed in Table 12.1 were determined in a group of 1050 adult service recipients in the State of Maryland (USA). Measured satisfaction was related significantly only to measured emotional well-being and material well-being. This result is quite consistent with the work of Cummins in Australia (Cummins, 1998), who found that material wealth and individualism are outstanding in their ability to predict life satisfaction and account for about 35% of the variance in his international studies of measured satisfaction.

The advantages of adopting satisfaction as the main dependent measure of quality of life are that it is a commonly used measure, either as a global assessment or an aggregate of individual life domains, and demonstrates a trait-like stability over time; there is an extensive body of research on level of satisfaction across populations and service delivery recipients; and it allows one to assess the relative importance of individual quality-of-life domains and thereby assign value to the respective domains (Cummins, 1996, 1998). The major disadvantages of using only satisfaction as a dependent measure of quality of life include the reported low or no correlation between subjective and objective measures of quality of life, its limited utility for smaller group comparison, its tendency to provide only a global measure of perceived well-being, and its discrepancy with other dependent measures of the multidimensional nature of quality of life (Schalock, 2001). Thus, both personal appraisal (that is, satisfaction or happiness measures) and functional assessments of personal experiences and circumstances are suggested as appropriate dependent, person-referenced, quality-of-life measures. Examples of each will be found in the following section that summarizes four studies that reflect the importance of being careful in discussing the predictors of quality of life to emphasize whether the predictors measure SWB or objective circumstances and experiences.

SUMMARY OF RECENT QUALITY-OF-LIFE STUDIES

Four recent studies that the authors have been involved with reflect the importance of distinguishing clearly between whether one is using an SWB (usually satisfaction) measure *or* one based on objective life circumstances or experiences. These studies have been done in England and Wales and the USA, and have involved well over 1000 individuals.

Role of Subjective and Objective Measures on Outcomes

Perry, Felce and Lowe (2000) employed a variety of subjective and objective measures of three quality-of-life-related outcomes: choice, constructive activity, and social and community affiliation. Their study involved 154 individuals living in a random sample of community-based group homes for six or fewer people in south Wales and southwest England. The study explored whether objective and subjective measures were correlated with each other, and whether personal characteristics (for example, adaptive behavior and challenging behavior) or setting variables (for example, setting size, provider agency, home-likeness, degree of physical integration, staff : resident ratio, environmental milieu, working methods, and staff–resident interaction) predicted significant levels of variation in either objective or subjective outcome. The results of the study suggested strongly that satisfaction is a trait-like entity which: (1) correlates little with objective indicators; (2) is not predicted by personal characteristics such as adaptive behavior levels; (3) is not predicted by environmental characteristics; and (4) produces scores around the expected 70–75% mark, consistent with the reviewed literature reported above. In contrast, personal and environmental characteristics explained significant proportions of the variation in the objective measures of the three outcomes: choice, constructive activities, and social and community affiliation.

Consumer-Based Quality-of-Life Assessment

A recent participatory action research study (Schalock et al., 2000) evaluated the impact of 32 predictor variables on assessed satisfaction levels in a group of 237 service recipients.

The study involved training self-advocates to evaluate other self-advocates on a 50-item quality-of-life questionnaire whose five factors were satisfaction (the dependent measure used in the analyses), dignity (or respect), independence, integration, and work. The results of a path analysis conducted on the person-referenced outcomes indicated that perceived dignity and work contributed the most to perceived life satisfaction, with the degree of independence consumers felt, and the degree of their integration into the community, indirectly affecting measured satisfaction. Consumer abilities (as measured by intelligence tests) or characteristics such as age, communication problems, and walking difficulties had no effect, either directly or indirectly, on assessed life satisfaction.

Environmental Factors and Assessed Quality of Life

A multistudy line of research has involved using hierarchical regression analysis to determine significant predictors of assessed quality of life. In both studies summarized below, the total score for the Schalock–Keith *Quality of Life Questionnaire* (Schalock & Keith, 1993) was the dependent variable. It is important to point out that the *Questionnaire* contains a mixture of subjective appraisal and objective functional assessment. In the analyses, predictor variables were entered in the analysis in three blocks: personal factors, environmental variables, and care-provider characteristics. The first study (Schalock, Lemanowicz, Conroy & Feinstein, 1994) sample included 715 persons with mental retardation who were members of the 1984 *CARC v Thorne* consent agreement in Pennsylvania, and who were living in community-based programs at the time of the study. The second study (Faulkner, 1995) sample consisted of 162 individuals with mental retardation living either in a community setting (67%) or more structured environment (33%). Across these two studies, the following personal characteristics, environmental variables, and care-provider characteristics were significant predictors of the *Quality of Life Questionnaire* total score:

- personal characteristics: health status, adaptive behavior index, and maladaptive/ challenging behavior index
- environmental variables: perceived social support, type of current residential setting, number of household activities participated in, earnings, and integrated activities
- care-provider characteristics: worker stress score, satisfaction in working with the client, and job satisfaction.

Relationship Among Quality-of-Life Domains

The fourth study is an extension of the "consumer-based quality-of-life assessment" study discussed previously. The study (Bonham et al., in press) involved reassessing the same consumers on a newly developed quality-of-life scale that is composed of the eight core domains proposed by Schalock (2000, 2001). Each of the eight subscales is composed of six items that are answered (see Schalock et al., 2000, for a description of the survey methodology) on a three-point Likert scale reflecting personal appraisal responses. Pearson product-moment correlations were computed between each of the "old" subscales (satisfaction, work, dignity, community integration, and independence) and the "new" subscales (emotional well-being, material well-being, physical well-being, interpersonal relations, personal development, social inclusion, self-determination, and rights). Significant correlations were found between:

- satisfaction and emotional well-being (0.47) and material well-being (0.24)
- work and emotional well-being (0.35), material well-being (0.61), physical well-being (0.35), interpersonal relations (0.34), and personal development (0.39)
- dignity and physical well-being (0.47), interpersonal relations (0.58), and personal development (0.35)
- community integration and personal development (0.21), social inclusion (0.69), and self-determination (0.32)
- independence and self-determination (0.49) and rights (0.69).

Collectively, these four studies indicate clearly that what one measures should be consistent with—and aligned to—the purpose of the study. We feel that the mistake that happens frequently in quality-of-life research is failure to be clear on the purpose of the evaluation and whether or not one is measuring SWB or objective circumstances and experiences. Thus, our two guidelines:

(1) If one wants to find out whether people with mental retardation/intellectual disabilities are as satisfied with life as are other population subgroups, one should assess SWB and compare. If the scores are about the same, satisfaction is normative. If not, one needs to look for personal or environmental factors that might explain such a difference. However, the expectation that SWB will be a sensitive indication of good environmental design and service programs has yet to be demonstrated.

(2) If one wants to evaluate environmental design or service programs in a sensitive way, one should use objective indicators of life experiences and circumstances. This guideline follows Edgerton's (1990, 1996) recommendations of divorcing objective and subjective appraisal.

Thus, a civilized society should offer all people the experiences and circumstances it deems good, but people strive for SWB on their own. Furthermore, what one measures should be consistent with the purpose of the evaluation/study. It is a mistake to mix subjective and objective measures and try to reach a sensitive evaluation of environmental design and services programs by using measures of SWB.

MEASUREMENT ISSUES IN QUALITY-OF-LIFE AND SWB RESEARCH

Based on the two guidelines just presented and on our experiences obtained from those perspectives and the material summarized in the three preceding sections, we suggest four future issues that will set the stage for the next phase of research in the areas of quality of life and SWB: (1) respondent variables; (2) research design; (3) methodological pluralism; and (4) participatory action research.

Respondent Variables

Issues regarding two types of respondent variables will frame the future: response bias and the use of proxies.

Response Bias

Response bias occurs when the respondent always answers similarly, even in the face of receiving contradictory information (Heal & Sigelman, 1996; Matikka & Vesala, 1997). For example, people may answer "yes" or "no" to both of two oppositely worded statements. Alternatively, they may select alternative answers based on the order of presentation rather than on their meaning. This is an important issue that needs to be addressed in all research purporting to represent user views, for if a user's view is deemed important, it is equally important to determine that one has obtained a true opinion rather than a response which follows an arbitrary rule or social convention. There is evidence that response bias is widespread among people who have limited intellectual ability and that the likelihood of response bias increases with level of intellectual disability (Heal & Sigelman, 1996).

This view has been challenged from both sociolinguistic theory and participatory action research (PAR). For example, Rapley (2000) has stated that:

> the widespread, uncritical acceptance of the phenomenon of "acquiescence" has inadvertently, perhaps, tended to discredit the views of service recipients. People with mental retardation have, in effect, been rendered incompetent to comment on their own feeling states. (p. 164)

According to Rapley (2000) and Psathas (1995), close examination of the actual exchange of talk between people with mental retardation and professionals in quality-of-life assessments reveals that while certain responses might look acquiescent on a superficial reading, closer inspection shows these instances to be clearly interpretable as an interplay of a range of respondents' conversation-management strategies and interviewer demands. Furthermore, there is no single thread that ties all the strategies together, since they are all taken from the normal repertoire of conversational management. Thus, it might be easy, according to these authors, for an analyst looking only at their surface appearance of inconsistency and agreement to categorize them all as "acquiescent".

Similarly, the presence of acquiescence in persons with intellectual disabilities is being challenged on the basis of data resulting from PAR studies. For example, in the PAR study discussed above (Schalock et al., 2000), in which self-advocates were trained as interviewers of other persons with intellectual disabilities, a simplification of wording and the use of pictorial flashcards enabled 81% of the consumers to respond for themselves; 93% of those who responded verbally for themselves; and 54% of those with severe language problems to respond. Equally important, an analysis of potential acquiescence indicated that only 2.5% of the people answered more than 90% of the questions with the most positive response, and only 5.5% answered 10% or fewer questions with the most positive response. The median was 42% of questions answered with the most positive response, with the overall pattern resembling a bell curve, slightly skewed toward 33%, since all questions had three possible answers.

However, one should stress that questioning whether response bias has or has not been correctly interpreted in the past is not the same as demonstrating that it is not the issue which it has been thought to be. Perry et al. (2000) sought to establish how many people in their random sample of community residences responded without response bias and how such responding related to assessed adaptive behavior and language level. They used the questions incorporated within the Comprehensive Quality of Life Scale (ComQol) (Cummins, 1997) and the Choice Questionnaire (CQ) (Stancliffe & Parmenter, 1999) to screen for acquiescence and recency biases. They found that all members of their sample with rank Adaptive Behavior Scale (ABS) (Nihira, Leland & Lambert, 1993) scores in the bottom quartile did not respond to the questions on either the CQ or the ComQol. Eighty-three percent of the second quartile group also did not respond, and all of the remainder showed acquiescence bias and most showed recency bias. Response bias affected between a half and two-thirds of the remaining respondents with ABS scores in the two deciles between 51–60 and 61–70, but it was shown by only a minority above this level. Occurrence of response bias was significantly inversely correlated with total rank ABS scores, the ABS language development domain scores, and British Picture Vocabulary Scale (BPVS) (Dunn, Dunn, Whetton & Burley, 1997) scores. The mean BPVS score among those not showing response bias (62) converts to an equivalent language age of 9 years 4 months. These results suggest that ongoing attention to the phenomenon is merited.

Use of Proxies

As discussed by Stancliffe (2000), beyond the fact that consumers and proxies sometimes agree and sometimes do not, little is known about consumer–proxy concordance and its relation to the nature and content of interview questions, to the characteristics of self-report and proxy respondents, or to situational factors in the interview. As a result, it is difficult to predict the likely level of agreement between proxies and self-reports.

One common method of evaluating consumer–proxy agreement is to compare proxy responses about consumers who can respond for themselves with self-reports from these same consumers. This approach has produced mixed results (for example, Schalock & Keith, 1993; Wehmeyer & Metzler, 1995; Rapley, Ridgway & Beyer, 1998; Stancliffe, 1999). In light of such mixed results, the use of proxies needs to be investigated by one or more of the following four alternative strategies (Stancliffe, 2000):

(1) Analyze only the self-report data and discard the proxy data. This approach has the advantage of maximizing the face validity of data by relying solely on self-reports. The disadvantage is that individuals who cannot respond for themselves are disenfranchised, and the generality of the research is limited.
(2) Obtain proxy data for all participants and ignore self-reports. The advantage of this alternative is that it includes all participants, but fails to address the validity of proxy data, and does not focus on consumers' own views.
(3) Analyze self-report data and proxy data separately. This approach has been used successfully (see, for example, Stancliffe, 1997), especially where both self-report and proxy data are available for all participants.
(4) Correct statistically for the influence of proxies. For example, Heal and Chadsey-Rusch (1985) included an acquiescence subscale in the *Lifestyle Satisfaction Scale*. The

subscale consisted of paired questions for which responding "yes" to both would constitute self-contraction and indicate acquiescence. By multiple-regression techniques, lifestyle satisfaction scores were then corrected for acquiescence. In the Schalock et al. (2000) study, a variable for proxies was included in the path analysis. Statistically, inclusion of this variable in the multivariate analysis should "correct" for differences between proxies and self-reports, so that any effect of proxies is held constant while evaluating the influence of other variables. In this study, it was found that proxies are more likely than consumers to report both greater availability of transportation and greater dignity.

Perry et al. (2000) found good concordance between proxy-reported and self-reported data for the CQ (Stancliffe & Parmenter, 1999), but not the satisfaction or importance items of the ComQoL (Cummins, 1997). They suggested that the difference may be related to the nature of the information being elicited, as the CQ asks about potentially verifiable fact (that is, the extent of choice exercised in various aspects of life) and the ComQoL items address subjective opinion. The possibility that proxies may provide more valid information about objective lifestyle than service user views is worthy of further investigation.

Research Design

The primary issue here is the focus of quality-of-life-related comparisons: should the comparison be the individual and changes over time within the person, or should one person's assessed quality of life be compared with another's? Over the last decade, we have seen a significant shift from a "between" to a "multivariate/within" approach to quality-of-life research designs. Historically, the study of quality of life was approached from a between-groups (or between-conditions) perspective; hence, investigators sought to find factors such as socioeconomic status and large demographic population descriptors that could discriminate between those persons or countries with a higher and those with a lower quality of life. This "between" mentality spilled over to our early work in quality of life in subtle ways, as reflected in the need to have different measures or indices of quality of life for those who are higher functioning and for those who are either nonverbal or lower functioning.

Shifting to a multivariate research design has a number of heuristic and practical advantages. Among the more important, multivariate research designs allow us to:

- focus more on the correlates and predictors of a life of quality rather than comparing quality-of-life scores or status
- determine the relationship among a number of measured predictor variables and one's perceived quality of life
- make programmatic changes and implement quality-enhancement techniques based on the identified variables to enhance a person's quality of life
- understand better the complexity of the concept of quality of life and the role that a number of contextual variables play in the perception of a life of quality
- shift the focus of our thinking and intervention from personal to environmental factors as major sources of quality-of-life enhancement.

Although there are definite advantages to a multivariate approach, two research design issues will probably frame the future. First, how do we incorporate a "within-person focus and emphasis" into a "between-groups mentality" wherein funders, service providers, policy makers, and consumers are all interested in programs, services, and supports that enhance a person's quality of life? Second, how do we identify, isolate, and measure the essential personal characteristics and sociocultural variables that significantly affect a life of quality?

Methodological Pluralism

Research strategies and evaluation theory have undergone tremendous changes over the last 30 years. Two concepts denote the change: the postmodernist approach and social constructivism. The postmodernist approach is characterized by minimizing the role of science-based, quantitative research methodology and maximizing a qualitative, methodological pluralism approach. Social constructivism emphasizes the pragmatic evaluation design, ideographic research, context-specific knowledge, decision-oriented evaluation, and the use of methodological pluralism (Schalock, 2001). These two concepts have significantly affected the methodological pluralism approach to quality-of-life assessment and its use of personal-appraisal and functional-assessment strategies.

The use of methodological pluralism is reflected well in the work of Heal (Heal & Sigelman, 1996) and Felce (2000), who collectively suggest four alternatives to obtain meaningful information about a person's quality of life. First, identify optimally effective questioning techniques. Based on extensive research, Heal and Sigelman (1996) suggest that (a) either/or questions (or objective multiple-choice questions with three or four options accompanied by pictures) are a very promising approach to questioning; and (b) factual multiple-choice questions offering discrete options (for example, ways to get to school or one's job) work well—much better than multiple-choice questions presenting happy and sad faces or quantitative options such as "a lot", "sometimes", "not much", and "never".

Second, correct statistically for response bias. This second alternative was discussed previously with regard to acquiescence.

Third, use proxies for measures ascertaining objective information about lifestyle. Given the concerns expressed earlier about proxy respondents, a possible variant of using complete proxy responses is to devise a screening interview that can be used to determine whether the individual or someone else should provide the data. Such a screening interview might assess responsiveness to questions, determine the validity of responses to basic questions whose answers are known, and gauge susceptibility to responses biases that might compromise the validity of answers to the full interview (Heal & Sigelman, 1996).

Fourth, employ more behaviorally based quality-of-life indicators. Felce (2000), for example, has developed an observational framework for residential services that includes two primary observational categories: resident behavior and staff or supporter behavior. Indicators for resident behavior include engagement in typical activities in the home, social interaction, and challenging behavior, along with disengagement or nonpurposeful engagement with the environment. Indicators for staff or support behavior include interaction with the resident, praise, restraint, and conversation, along with processing (care without resident participation). Similarly, Schalock (2000) has identified exemplary indicators (which are states of existence and/or circumstances that have developed over time or have a sense of enduring beyond the immediate activity of the moment) for each of his proposed core quality-of-life domains. For emotional well-being, for example, behavioral indicators include spirituality, freedom from stress, and content; for interpersonal relationships, family, friendships, and supports; for material well-being, ownership, financial security, employment, and possessions; for personal development, skills, competence, and advancement; for physical well-being, health and nutrition; for self-determination, autonomy, choices, and personal control; for social inclusion, acceptance, status, and roles; and for rights, access, ownership, and privacy.

A useful guideline regarding these four alternatives is presented by Heal and Sigelman (1996).

> Ultimately, researchers might do best to adopt a blend of these approaches. For example, they might rely on either-or or multiple-choice questions accompanied by pictures whenever feasible; build into their interview schedules checks for response bias that can later be used to adjust scores to remove the effects of response bias; and turn to information gathering techniques other than client interviews when those alternative techniques are likely to yield the most valid data. (p. 100)

Participatory Action Research (PAR)

PAR has its roots in the work of Lewin, who coined the phrase "action research". As discussed by Whitney-Thomas (1997), PAR is neither a qualitative nor a quantitative approach to research; rather, it is a paradigm that maximizes the involvement and participation of the consumer of the research in the research process and outcome.

Participatory research is an emerging approach to research, problem solving, and social change that is particularly suited to issues of quality of life for persons with intellectual disabilities. As currently undertaken, the PAR process involves three phases: problem identification and planning, action/data gathering, and analysis/synthesizing. A careful consideration of four factors will enhance the successful implementation of PAR (McTaggart, 1991; Whitney-Thomas, 1997):

- Validity is increased by defining constructs carefully, crafting appropriate data-collection instruments, and specifying clearly the context in which the research is conducted.
- Reliability is increased by carefully designing and using data-collection techniques, consistently implementing any treatments or interventions, and describing clearly the context in which the research occurs.
- PAR assumes that the participants identify issues and research questions from their own lives; thus, an outside perspective is impossible.
- Successful PAR can be maximized by following three critical processes (Whitney-Thomas, 1997, p. 194): ensure ongoing, genuine, and negotiated participation in all phases of the process; acknowledge and build upon the diversity of opinions, values, and experiences within the working group; and consider mutual ownership and benefit as the best compensation for participation.

In summary, future research directions regarding the clarification of respondent variables, the use of multivariate research designs and analyses, the use of methodological pluralism, and the incorporation of PAR strategies will provide answers to—and thereby help resolve—those concerns expressed earlier in the chapter about the need to clarify what one is measuring and how one uses that information to describe either levels of personal satisfaction or predictors of a life of perceived quality. For example, as the objective indicators of life conditions that might well be used as predictors of a life of quality are increasingly identified and better understood, the issue of evaluating the impact of quality-enhancement techniques on one's perceived quality of life should be understood better. Moreover, a better understanding of assessment strategies should reduce the problems discussed regarding quality-of-life assessment, especially for persons with limited communication skills. Finally, as consumers are increasingly included in the design and implementation of quality-of-life-oriented issues regarding research designs, appropriate comparisons, and a within-groups focus, the use of quality-of-life data should be significantly enhanced.

CONCLUSION

In conclusion, researchers and evaluators have an obligation to be clear about what they are measuring and the soundness of their measures. Throughout the chapter, we have stressed three important points. First, there is a need to be careful when discussing the predictors of quality-of-life scores to emphasize whether they measure SWB (that is, personal appraisal such as satisfaction) or objective circumstances and experiences (that is, functional assessment of objective indicators of life experiences or conditions). Second, we have suggested that SWB is a trait-like factor that does not relate greatly to objective measures of experience, personal skills, or environmental circumstances; on the other hand, personal characteristics, environmental variables, and care-provider characteristics might be potentially significant predictors of assessed life experiences and conditions and their impact on one's perceived quality of life. Third, we have proposed two guidelines regarding the use of either personal-appraisal or functional-assessment data: (1) if we want to determine whether people with mental retardation/intellectual disabilities are as satisfied with life as other population subgroups, we should assess SWB and compare; and (2) if we want to evaluate environmental design or service programs in a sensitive way, we should use objective indicators of personal experience and circumstances.

REFERENCES

Albin Dean, J.E. & Mank, D.M. (1997). Continuous improvement and quality of life: lessons from organizational management. In R.L. Schalock (Ed.) *Quality of Life*, vol. II. *Application to Persons with Mental Retardation* (pp. 165–179). Washington, DC: American Association on Mental Retardation.

Andrews, F.R. & Whithey, S.B. (1976). *Social Indicators of Well-Being: Americans' Perceptions of Life Quality*. New York: Plenum.

Antaki, C. & Rapley, M. (1996). Questions and answers to psychological measurement: hidden troubles in "quality of life" interviews. *Journal of International Disabilities Research*, **40**, 421–437.

Bonham, G.S., Basehart, S., Schalock, R.L., Marchand, C.B., Kirchner, N. & Rumenap, J.M. (in press). Consumer-based quality of life assessment: the Maryland Ask Me! Project. *Mental Retardation*.

Bronfenbrenner, U. (1979). *The Ecology of Human Development*. Cambridge, MA: Harvard University Press.

Campbell, A., Converse, P.E. & Rogers, W.L. (1976). *The Quality of American Life: Perceptions, Evaluations, and Satisfaction*. New York: Russell Sage Foundation.

Carver, C.S. (2000). On the continuous calibration of happiness. *American Journal on Mental Retardation*, **105**, 336–341.
Coulter, D.L. (1996). Prevention as a form of support. *Mental Retardation*, **34**, 108–116.
Crocker, A.C. (2000). Introduction: the happiness in all our lives. *American Journal on Mental Retardation*, **105**, 319–325.
Cummins, R.A. (1994). The Comprehensive Quality of Life Scale: instrument development and psychometric evaluation. *Educational and Psychological Measurement*, **54**, 372–382.
Cummins, R.A. (1996). The domains of life satisfaction: an attempt to order chaos. *Social Indicators Research*, **38**, 303–328.
Cummins, R.A. (1997). Assessing quality of life. In R.I. Brown (Ed.) *Assessing Quality of Life for People with Disabilities* (pp. 116–130). Cheltenham: Stanley Thornes.
Cummins, R.A. (1998). The second approximation to an international standard for life satisfaction. *Social Indicators Research*, **43**, 307–334.
Diener, E. (1984). Subjective well-being. *Psychological Bulletin*, **95**, 542–575.
Diener, E. (2000). Subjective well-being: the science of happiness and a proposal for a national index. *American Psychologist*, **55**, 34–43.
Dunn, L., Dunn, L., Whetton, C. & Burley, J. (1997). *The British Picture Vocabulary Scale, Second Edition*. Windsor: NFER-Nelson.
Edgerton, R. (1990). Quality of life from a longitudinal research perspective. In R. Schalock (Ed.) *Quality of Life Perspectives and Issues* (pp. 149–160). Washington, DC: American Association on Mental Retardation.
Edgerton, R.B. (1996). A longitudinal-ethnographic research perspective on quality of life. In R.L. Schalock (Ed.) *Quality of Life*, vol. I. *Conceptualization and Measurement* (pp. 83–90). Washington, DC: American Association on Mental Retardation.
Faulkner, E.H. (1995). Quality of life: a comparative study of institutional and community-based care for adults with mental retardation. Unpublished doctoral dissertation. Lincoln, NE: Graduate College in the University of Nebraska.
Felce, D. (1997). Defining and applying the concept of quality of life. *Journal of Intellectual Disability Research*, **41**, 126–143.
Felce, D. (2000). Engagement in activity as an indicator of quality of life in British research. In K.D. Keith & R.L. Schalock (Eds) *Cross-Cultural Perspectives on Quality of Life* (pp. 173–190). Washington, DC: American Association on Mental Retardation.
Flanagan, J.C. (1982). Measurement of quality of life: current state of the art. *Archives of Physical Medicine and Rehabilitation*, **63**, 56–59.
Gilbert, T.E. (1978). *Engineering Worthy Performance*. New York: McGraw-Hill.
Goode, D.A. (Ed.) (1994). *Quality of Life for Persons with Disabilities: International Perspectives and Issues*. Boston, MA: Brookline Books.
Heal, L.W. & Chadsey-Rusch, J. (1985). The Lifestyle Satisfaction Scale (LSS): assessing individuals' satisfaction with residence, community setting, and associated services. *Applied Research in Mental Retardation*, **6**, 475–490.
Heal, L.W. & Sigelman, C.K. (1996). Methodological issues in quality of life measurement. In R.L. Schalock (Ed.) *Quality of Life*, vol. I. *Conceptualization, Measurement, and Application* (pp. 91–104). Washington, DC: American Association on Mental Retardation.
Helm, D.T. (2000). The measurement of happiness. *American Journal on Mental Retardation*, **105**, 326–335.
Keith, K.D. & Schalock, R.L. (2000). *Cross-Cultural Perspectives on Quality of Life*. Washington, DC: American Association on Mental Retardation.
Lindstrom, B. (1992). Quality of life: a model for evaluating health for all. *Sozial- und Praventivmedizin*, **37**, 301–306.
Lobley, J. (2000). Quality of life and organization change leadership. In K.D. Keith & R. L. Schalock (Eds) *Cross-Cultural Perspectives on Quality of Life* (pp. 135–154). Washington, DC: American Association on Mental Retardation.
Matikka, L.M. & Vesala, H.T. (1997). Acquiescence in quality-of-life interviews with adults who have mental retardation. *Mental Retardation*, **35**, 75–82.
McTaggart, R. (1991). Principles for participatory action research. *Adult Education Quarterly*, **41**, 168–187.

Meyers, A.R. (2000). From function to felicitude: physical disability and the search for happiness in health services research. *American Journal on Mental Retardation*, **105**, 342–351.

Myers, D.G. (2000). The funds, friends, and faith of happy people. *American Psychologist*, **55**, 56–67.

Myers, D.G. & Diener, E. (1996). The pursuit of happiness: new research uncovers some anti-intuitive insights into how many people are happy and why. *Scientific American*, **156**, 70–72.

Nihira, K., Leland, H. & Lambert, N. (1993). *AAMR Adaptive Behavior Scale—Residential and Community* (2nd edn). Austin, TX: Pro-Ed.

O'Brien, J. (1987). A guide to lifestyle planning: using the Activities Catalog to integrate services and natural support systems. In B. Wilcox & G.T. Bellamy (Eds) *The Activity Catalog: An Alternative Curriculum Design for Youth and Adults with Severe Disabilities* (pp. 104–110). Baltimore, MD: Brookes.

Perry, J,, Felce, D. & Lowe, K. (2000). *Subjective and Objective Quality of Life Assesment: Their Interrelationship and Determinants*. Cardiff: Welsh Centre for Learning Disabilities, University of Wales College of Medicine.

Poston, D., Turnbull, A., Park, J., Mannan, H., Marquis, J. & Wang, W. (2003). Family quality of life: a qualitative inquiry. *Mental Retardation*, **41**, 313–328.

Psathas, G. (1995). *Conversation Analysis: The Study of Talk-in-Interaction*. Thousand Oaks, CA: Sage.

Rapley, M. (2000). The social construction of quality of life: the interpersonal production of well-being revisited. In K.D. Keith & R.L. Schalock (Eds) *Cross-Cultural Perspectives on Quality of Life* (pp. 155–172). Washington, DC: American Association on Mental Retardation.

Rapley, M., Ridgway, J. & Beyer, S. (1998). Staff : staff and staff : client reliability of the Schalock and Keith (1993) Quality of Life Questionnaire. *Journal of Intellectual Disabilities Research*, **42**, 37–42.

Schalock, R.L. (2000). Three decades of quality of life. In M.L. Wehmeyer & J.R. Patton (Eds) *Mental Retardation in the 21st Century* (pp. 335–358). Austin, TX: Pro-Ed.

Schalock, R.L. (2001). *Outcome-Based Evaluation* (2nd edn). New York: Kluwer Academic/Plenum.

Schalock, R.L. (in press). Quality of life from a motivational perspective. In H. Switzky (Ed.) *International Review of Research in Mental Retardation: Current Perspectives on Individual Differences in Personality and Motivation in Persons with Mental Retardation and Other Developmental Disabilities*.

Schalock, R.L., Bonham, G.S. & Marchand, C.B. (2000). Consumer based quality of life assessment: a path model of perceived satisfaction. *Evaluation and Program Planning*, **23**, 77–88.

Schalock, R.L., Brown, I., Brown, R., Cummins, R.A., Felce, D., Matikka, L., et al. (2002). Conceptualization, measurement, and application of quality of life for persons with intellectual disabilities: report of an international panel of experts. *Mental Retardation*, **40**, 457–470.

Schalock, R.L. & Keith, K.D. (1993). *Quality of Life Questionnaire*. Worthington, OH: IDS Publishing.

Schalock, R.L., Lemanowicz, J.A., Conroy, J.W. & Feinstein, C.S. (1994). A multivariate investigative study of the correlates of quality of life. *Journal on Developmental Disabilities*, **3**, 59–73.

Schalock, R.L. & Verdugo-Alonso, M.A. (2002). *Handbook on Quality of Life for Human Service Practitioners*. Washington, DC: American Association on Mental Retardation.

Stancliffe, R.J. (1997). Community living-unit size, staff presence, and resident's choice-making. *Mental Retardation*, **35**, 1–9.

Stancliffe, R.J. (1999). Proxy respondents in the reliability of the Quality of Life Questionnaire empowerment scale. *Journal of Intellectual Disabilities Research*, **43**, 185–193.

Stancliffe, R.J. (2000). Proxy respondents and quality of life. *Evaluation and Program Planning*, **23**, 89–93.

Stancliffe, R.J., Abery, B.H. & Smith, J. (2000). Personal control and the ecology of community living settings: beyond living-unit size and type. *American Journal on Mental Retardation*, **105**, 431–454.

Stancliffe, R.J., Abery, B.H., Springborg, H. & Elkin, S. (2000). Substitute decision-making and personal control: implications for self-determination. *Mental Retardation*, **38**, 407–421.

Stancliffe, R.J. & Parmenter, T. (1999). The Choice Questionnaire. A scale to assess choices exercised by adults with intellectual disability. *Journal of Intellectual and Developmental Disability Research*, **24**, 107–132.

Szymanski, L.S. (2000). Happiness as a treatment goal. *American Journal on Mental Retardation*, **105**, 352–362.

Wehmeyer, M.L. & Metzler, C.A. (1995). How self-determined are people with mental retardation? The national consumer survey. *Mental Retardation*, **33**, 111–119.

Wehmeyer, M.L. & Schalock, R.L. (2001). Self-determination and quality of life: implications for special education services and supports. *Focus on Exceptional Children*, **33**, 1–16.

Wehmeyer, M.L. & Schwartz, M. (1998). The relationship between self-determination, quality of life, and life satisfaction for adults with mental retardation. *Education and Training in Mental Retardation and Developmental Disabilities*, **33**, 3–12.

Whitney-Thomas, J. (1997). Participatory action research as an approach to enhancing quality of life for individuals with disabilities. In R.L. Schalock (Ed.) *Quality of Life*, vol. II. *Application to Persons with Disabilities* (pp. 181–198). Washington, DC: American Association on Mental Retardation.

CHAPTER 13

Investigating Inclusion: A Review of Research Methods for Individuals with Intellectual Disability

Samuel L. Odom
Indiana University, USA
Katherine Klingerman
Indiana University, USA
and
Mark Jakowski
Indiana University, USA

Should school systems include students with intellectual disabilities (ID) in classes with nondisabled peers? Is inclusion effective for individuals with ID? Are individuals with ID well integrated into the community? How do we measure the positive (or negative) outcomes of inclusion? These and many other questions surface when individuals with ID are placed in childcare settings, public-school settings, and community settings with individuals who do not have disabilities. These practical questions, and also more theoretical ones, provide impetus for an accelerating program of research on inclusion. The purpose of this chapter is to describe the methods of research and evaluation used to study inclusion of individuals with ID in school and community settings. We begin this chapter with a brief examination of the concept of inclusion and offer a working definition. In any type of research, it is essential to understand the instrumentation or techniques used to assess the outcomes of inclusion, and in this chapter we review measurement approaches related to attitudes, social competence and relationships, and students'/individuals' academic skills and adaptive behavior. A second set of research has examined the process of inclusion with the intent of describing how inclusion is implemented or conducted, and we review different approaches for assessing implementation. A third set of research issues relates to methodology that researchers have used to investigate the impact of inclusion on individuals with ID.

The International Handbook of Applied Research in Intellectual Disabilities. Edited by E. Emerson, C. Hatton, T. Thompson and T.R. Parmenter ISBN 0-471-49709-6.

A DEFINITION OF INCLUSION

Current conceptualizations of inclusion emerged out of the movement away from the selective secondary education service in several European countries (Organization for Economic Cooperation and Development [OECD], 1995), increased visibility and influence of the principles of normalization originating in Scandinavia (Nirje, 1969, 1985), and the reshaping of those principles to fit the human service and educational systems in the USA and Canada (Wolfensberger, 1972). As a working definition, we will define inclusion as the participation of individuals with ID in school and community settings typical of and involving individuals without disabilities.

A dilemma faced by researchers investigating inclusion has been the use of different terms to refer to services or contexts. The preferred terminology sometimes differs depending on whether the activity is examined in school settings or outside the school context. When examining inclusion in educational settings, researchers and consumers have used terms such as "mainstreaming", "integration", "inclusive education", and "least restrictive environment". For example, in their study of educational programs around the world, the Centre for Research and Innovation of the OECD used the term "integration" to denote "that process which maximizes the interaction between disabled and non-disabled pupils" (OECD, 1995, p. 13). In the USA, the term "natural environments" is used to refer to the requirement that early intervention services be provided in family and community settings such as ones in which young children without disabilities would naturally participate (that is, a concept very similar to normalization). The term "community integration" is also often used to describe the participation or inclusion of individuals with ID in typical community setting and activities. All of these terms would be subsumed under our working definition of inclusion.

OUTCOMES OF INCLUSION

A primary interest of researchers investigating inclusion is related to outcomes. The selection of outcomes measures is, hopefully, tied closely to the research questions addressed. Such questions may arise from a theoretical/conceptual orientation (such as normalization or ecological systems theory), emerge from a program of research that addresses applied questions (such as the effects of using individual transition plans), respond to pressing policy issues of the day (Hegarty, 1993), or reflect the needs and perspectives of individuals with disabilities (Wehmeyer & Metzler, 1995).

Attitudes

Researchers have often investigated the attitudes of parents, teachers, and peers toward individuals with ID in inclusive settings. They frequently use survey methodology in these studies. In survey research, Likert-scales methodology (Likert, 1932) is employed most often. These scales are characterized as self-reporting instruments in that participants respond to a series of statements by indicating their extent of agreement.

Although researchers often design surveys to address their specific research questions, survey research methodology is amenable to analysis of the psychometric qualities of the instrument. For example, Henry, Keys, Jopp and Balcazar (1996) evaluated the internal consistency, test–retest reliability, and construct validity of the Community Living Attitudes Scale, Mental Retardation Form. They found the instrument to be psychometrically sound and useful in their study of attitudes toward individuals with ID. Furthermore, an advantage to survey research is its compatibility with the statistical analysis of the data collected. Krajewski and Flaherty (2000) used multivariate analysis of variance (MANOVA) and univariate analysis of variance (ANOVA) to analyze data collected with the Mental Retardation Attitude Inventory–Revised in their study assessing the impact of certain variables on the attitudes of high-school students toward students with ID. They were also able to point to a psychometric study (Antonak & Larrivee, 1995) that showed the inventory to be reliable. Both Ward, Center and Bochner (1994) and Forlin (1995) have used survey methodology to examine the attitudes of teachers, other staff, and administrators toward inclusion in Australia.

Although self-reporting surveys are used widely to assess the attitudes of parents, teachers and older students, verbal interviewing is used more frequently with younger students. This procedure is advantageous because of its flexibility and the depth of responses that an informant might provide. For example, when interviewing a parent or teachers, the researcher may base questions upon the previous observations or answers given by participants and probe further to gain greater insight (Fraenkel & Wallen, 2000). In his study of attitudes, Schnorr (1990) used interviewing along with observation to assess the perspectives of typical first graders regarding the part-time inclusion of a student with ID.

The effects of inclusion on typically developing or nondisabled individuals in the inclusive setting is of interest to researchers, teachers, and parents. A primary outcome often identified is the impact of inclusion on the attitudes of children in inclusive settings (Farrell, 1997). One measure of this is through sociometric methodology, discussed in a subsequent paragraph. In other studies, researcher-created surveys, in which children and adolescents provide written responses, assess the general attitude toward disabilities that may have been affected by experiences in inclusive classrooms (Voeltz, 1980; Whittaker, 1994; Hastings & Graham, 1995). For preschool and kindergarten children, accommodations to the methodology are needed to assess attitudes reliably. For example, Favazza and Odom (1996) adapted the Acceptance Scale (Voeltz, 1980) for kindergarten children by using graphic representations (such as a happy face or a sad face) and by administering the scale to small groups of children. They found the scale to be reliable and sensitive to differences in treatments related to inclusion (Favazza & Odom, 1997). For preschool children, Diamond, Hestenes, Carpenter and Innes (1997) used small dolls of the same gender as the individual child assessed in order to provide visual cues and to lessen cognitive-processing demands. Three dolls with varying forms of disabilities were used, while one doll was presented without an apparent disability. A rating-scale measure and semistructured interviews were both administered to participants. As with other studies cited in this chapter, the validity and reliability of the rating scales were assessed and found acceptable.

A number of scales with solid psychometric qualities have been developed to measure attitudes toward the inclusion of students with a wide range of disabilities. These scales may also be useful for the study of inclusion for students with ID. These measures include the updated version of the Opinions Relative to Mainstreaming scale constructed by Larrivee and Cook (Antonak & Larrivee, 1995), the Scale of Attitudes Toward Disabled Persons (Yuker & Block, 1986), the Attitudes Toward Mainstreaming Scale–Revised (Berryman, Neal & Berryman, 1989), and the Attitudes Toward Inclusive Education Scale (Wilczenski, 1992).

Social-Competence and Social-Relationships Outcomes

One set of frequently assessed outcomes of inclusion is the social competence that individuals with ID display in inclusive settings, the social acceptance and rejection of children with ID and individuals without disabilities, and perceptions of the social skills and loneliness of individuals with ID.

Social Competence

Social competence may be defined as the use of social behaviors in an effective (for reaching one's social goals) and appropriate (for the social context) manner (Odom, McConnell & McEvoy, 1992). Research methodology for assessing the competent use of social behavior in inclusive contexts consists of rating scales of social skills and observational measures of children's behavior. Several rating scales have been developed to assess the social skills of children and youth. The Social Skills Rating System (SSRS) (Gresham & Elliott, 1990) is one of the most frequently used and psychometrically sound instruments. It consists of Likert-scale items to which a teacher, parent, or student responds (that is, different forms have different numbers of items). The scale has been used in studies of individuals with ID in the USA (Margalit, 1991, 1993) and Israel (Heiman & Margalit, 1998). The Teacher Rating of Social Skills (TRSS) (Clark, Gresham & Elliott, 1985) is a similar but older Likert-type rating scale, available only in a teacher rating form, that has strong evidence of reliability and validity when used with individuals with ID and other disabilities (Gresham, Elliott & Black, 1987). It is also common for traditional, norm-referenced measures of adaptive behavior to have subscales that measure social abilities of individuals with ID. For example, the Vineland Adaptive Behavior Scale (VABS) (Balla, Cicchetti & Harrison, 1985), one of the psychometrically strongest scales, has a socialization subscale that could be used to assess outcomes related to inclusion.

Direct observation methodology, containing behavioral categories and a quantitative measurement system, has often been used to assess the social behavior of individuals with ID in inclusive settings. Unlike other forms of measurement, standard observational systems (that is, an identical system used in different studies) have not been established, and researchers tend to design observational systems to address their specific research questions. However, categories developed to assess social behavior, at least in young children, have similar definitions (Odom & Ogawa, 1992). The important qualities of observational methodology have been described in Chapter 8 in this text and in other texts (Thompson, Felce & Symons, 2000), to which we refer the reader.

Sophisticated, computer-based observational systems, such as the Observer (Noldus Information Technology, 1993), MOOSES (Tapp & Wehby, 2000), and PROCODER (Tapp & Walden, 2000) are available for analysis of social behavior in inclusive settings, although, to date, there has been limited use of this methodology. With preschool children, Guralnick and colleagues (Guralnick, Gottman & Hammond, 1996; Guralnick, 1999) have conducted an extensive program of research on inclusion, using a revised form of the Parten (1932) scale of social participation, Smilansky's play scale (1968), and individual categories of social and pragmatic behaviors. In intervention-oriented and descriptive work, other researchers have examined the initiation of social interaction, responses, and duration of interactions

(Strain & Timm, 1974; Odom et al., 1999). For example, to assess social interaction in inclusive and noninclusive settings for children with severe disabilities, Hunt, Farron-Davis, Beckstead, Curtis and Goetz (1994) used the Educational Assessment of Social Interaction system, in which observers watched children for 15-second intervals and recorded the first communicative initiation of social behavior and the response to the initiation in a subsequent 15-second recording interval. Data were collected in 10-minute samples that were distributed across multiple days. Similar observational systems have been used for assessing the social interaction of middle-school (Haring & Breen, 1992; Siperstein & Leffert, 1997) and high-school students (Gaylord-Ross, Haring, Breen & Pitts-Conway, 1984; Mu, Siegel & Allinder, 2000). In all of these studies, researchers met the basic requirement of establishing a satisfactory level of interobserver agreement (see Hartmann & Wood, 1990).

Social Acceptance and Rejection

Sociometric and peer-rating techniques are the primary methodologies used for assessing social relationships of individuals with disabilities in inclusive settings (McConnell & Odom, 1986). With peer-nomination sociometric methodology, individuals from the classroom or other contexts in which an individual with ID participates list peers who fit a specified criterion, with positive (such as "best friend") and negative (such as "do not like at all", and "dislike") criteria being employed in some systems. The numbers of nominations per individual in the setting are summed, and popularity or unpopularity may be established by the positive and negative nominations an individual receives. Peer-nomination sociometrics have been often used to establish the relative popularity or rejection of individuals with ID (e.g., Siperstein, Leffert & Widaman, 1996).

In an elaboration of the peer-nomination technique that is sometimes described as peer assessment, Pearl et al. (1998) had elementary-aged children nominate three classmates on eight different criteria (such as "cooperative", "leader", and "starts fights") and used the information to examine the social integration of students with ID in inclusive classrooms. These researchers also used a social-cognitive mapping procedure, which allowed them to analyze the peer social network in the classroom. Although social-network analysis (Scott, 1991) is potentially an effective technique for assessing social outcomes of inclusion, the Pearl et al. study has been one of the few to use this approach.

Peer-rating assessments differ from peer nominations in that all individuals from a setting assign a rating to all other members of the setting, and average ratings are computed for each individual. Such ratings may then be summarized to establish the relative social acceptance or rejection in the setting. This form of assessment also differs from peer nomination in that it provides information about social acceptance, while peer-nomination methodology provides information about popularity. Like peer nominations, researchers have also used peer ratings to examine social acceptance in inclusive settings (Gresham & Reschley, 1987; Heiman & Margalit, 1998).

A critical feature of this methodology is the characteristics of the nominators or assessors. When researchers compare inclusive and noninclusive settings, individuals with different characteristics constitute the peer group (that is, typically developing individuals in the inclusive settings and individuals with disabilities in the noninclusive settings). This has two implications for research on inclusion. First, social acceptance or rejection in a peer group of individuals with ID and a peer group of typically developing individuals may mean different things (for example, different behaviors may affect social acceptance) and therefore may not be comparable sources of information. Second, in the two settings, informants may have different abilities, and assessment techniques may have to be modified for individuals with disabilities or for classes in which children are young (that is, preschool and kindergarten). Researchers (McCandless & Marshall, 1957; Asher, Singleton, Tinsley & Hymel, 1979) have adapted these techniques, using pictures of peers (that is, rather than children responding to written names of children), and found them to be reliable for children as young as four years of age.

Other Outcomes

Individuals' self-assessment of social skills, feelings about their participation in inclusive settings, or feelings of loneliness are also possible outcomes of participation in inclusive programs, and researchers have designed or selected measures to assess these outcomes. For example, the SSRS (Gresham & Elliott, 1990) has a self-rating form that individuals with ID could use to appraise their own social skills. To assess the depression of children with ID in different education settings, Heiman and Margalit (1998) used the elementary and high-school form of the Childhood Depression Inventory (Kovacs & Beck, 1977). Loneliness, as a construct distinct from depression, has also been assessed. Asher and colleagues have developed an assessment of loneliness (Williams & Asher, 1992) that researchers have used to assess children and adolescents with ID in inclusive and noninclusive settings (Taylor, Asher & Williams, 1987; Luftig, 1988; Margalit & Ronen, 1993).

Self-Determination Outcomes

Self-determination refers to the ability of and opportunity for individuals to make choices about key features of their life (Wehmeyer, 1996). Researchers have used a variety of methods to assess self-determination. A primary methodology is through self-report. For example, Wehmeyer (1996) developed the Arc's Self-Determination Scale, normed it on 500 adolescents with and without ID, and provided convincing evidence of reliability and validity. Other researchers have also used other self-report measures (Wehmeyer & Bolding, 1999), survey methodology (Nowak, Laitinen, Stowitschek & Affleck, 1995), interview approaches (Field & Hoffman, 1994), qualitative research methods (Serna & Lau-Smith, 1995), and a combination of methodologies (Emerson et al., 2001). Researchers have used these measures to examine the differences in self-determination for students with ID in inclusive and noninclusive classrooms (Zhang, 2001), the effects of a curriculum model designed to support self-determination of students with ID (Agran, Blanchard & Wehmeyer, 2000), and the amount of choice or self-determination occurring for individuals with ID in different types of residential and vocational settings (Wehmeyer & Bolding, 1999; Stancliffe, Abery & Smith, 2000; Emerson et al., 2001).

Individual Performance Outcomes

Performance outcomes for individuals in inclusive and noninclusive settings vary by the age of the child, the type of inclusive settings in which individuals are placed, and the goals of the inclusive placement. Generally, these outcomes may be grouped into academic performance outcomes, which are usually related to inclusion in school settings, and adaptive behavior outcomes, which may apply to school or community settings.

Academic Outcomes

Outcomes related to academics may be thought of as either *summative* or *formative* in nature. Summative outcomes reflect the effects of an individual's participation in an inclusive and/or noninclusive placement. To quantify the results or end products of students' learning, researchers often measure student academic achievement. Measures in this type of study are usually standardized and norm-referenced, allowing students to be compared with national averages. In their review of 36 studies of outcomes for children with mental retardation in general and special education settings, Freeman and Alkin (2000) found that researchers used a range of measures to assess academic attainment. Many psychometrically sound measures are available and may be selected to fit the researchers' questions. For example, in their study of inclusion, Saint-Laurent and Lessard (1991) used the KeyMath Revised: A Diagnostic Inventory of Essential Mathematics (Connolly, 1981) and the Peabody Picture Vocabulary Test–Revised (Dunn, Dunn, Robertson & Eisenberg, 1981; 3rd edn, Dunn & Dunn, 1997). In their study of the inclusion of children with Down syndrome, Casey, Jones, Kugler and Watkins (1988) were interested in language, numeracy, and reading, so they employed the Reynell Developmental Language Scales (Reynell & Gruber, 1990), McCarthy Scales of Children's Abilities (McCarthy, 1972), and the Neale Analysis of Reading Ability Revised British Edition assessment (Neale, Christopher & Whetton, 1989—revised normative update). Other high-quality norm-referenced assessment tools that could be used to assess overall academic or developmental outcomes are (for school-aged children) the Woodcock-Johnson Psychoeducational Battery–Revised (Woodcock, Johnson, Mather, McGrew & Werder, 1991) and (for young children) the Battelle Developmental Inventory (Newborg, Stock, Wnek, Guidubaldi & Svinicki, 1984).

Formative assessment is collected on an ongoing basis, rather than in the "pre-post" fashion of summative assessment, and is used to adapt teaching to meet students' needs (Klingerman, Washburn & Cole, 2001). This assessment information is often collected informally by teachers (as in daily or weekly quizzes), but systematic procedures for conducting formative assessment have been developed. An early formative assessment approach was the application of precision teaching techniques (White & Haring, 1980) to academic instruction, which could occur in inclusive or mainstreamed settings (White, 1986). In a related procedure called curriculum-based measurement (CBM) (Deno, 1985), students complete short probes that assess their progress in relation to a preselected area of the curriculum. CBM has been used in investigations of instructional approaches occurring in inclusive classes (Fuchs, Fuchs, Hamlett, Phillips & Karns, 1995). The current generation of this approach, as applied to early literacy, is the development of the Dynamic Indicators of Basic Early Literacy Skills (DIBELS) by Good, Kaminski and colleagues at the University of Oregon (website http://dibels.uoregon.edu/).

Other measures include teacher- or student-completed reports or checklists, which may serve to inform the researcher of students' academic performance. Furthermore, researchers might analyze special education documents that record students' educational plans and school goals and objectives. For example, Hunt, Goetz and Anderson (1986) designed an Individualized Educational Program (IEP) evaluation instrument that assessed the quality of IEP objectives by seven indicators of best practice. In a subsequent study, Hunt et al. (1994) used the evaluation instrument to analyze students' IEP to determine the quality and curricular content of students' objectives in inclusive and segregated settings.

Adaptive Behavior Outcomes

Studies of outcomes in inclusive settings sometimes measure the adaptive behavior of individuals with ID in inclusive settings. Adaptive behavior skills are those that center on students' abilities to take care of themselves and fully participate in the community and school settings. Researchers might assess students' independent living, community participation, daily living skills, communication skills, motor skills, and employment as a way to measure their functional performance. Researchers use adaptive behavior scales to measure these domains. The VABS (Balla et al., 1985), mentioned previously, is one such measure that is commonly used. It is norm-referenced, technically adequate, and is designed to provide a general assessment of adaptive behavior. The domains measured are communication, daily living skills, socialization, and motor skills. For example, Ittenbach, Bruininks, Thurlow and McGrew (1993) used the VABS to assess the adjustment of young adults with mental retardation in community settings. Other measurement tools available include the AAMR Adaptive Behavior Scale–School, Second Edition (Lambert, Nihira & Leland, 1993), the Developmental Assessment for the Severely Handicapped (Dykes, 1980), and the Adaptive Behavior Evaluation Scale–Second Edition (McCarney, 1995).

Implementation

Researchers are sometimes interested in describing or analyzing how inclusion is implemented in educational and community contexts. Both quantitative and qualitative methodologies have been developed to examine the "process variables" operating in inclusive settings. Some researchers may then ask the further question of how the process variables relate to the types of outcomes noted previously.

Quantitative approaches to assessing implementation usually employ observational methodology. Through observation, the researchers attempt to capture the physical and social "ecology" of the setting (Odom & Bailey, 2001). For elementary-age children with ID, Greenwood and colleagues (Kamps, Greenwood & Leonard, 1991) developed an observational coding system entitled the Code for Instructional Structure and Academic Response–Mainstream Version (MS–CISSAR). The MS–CISSAR contains behavioral categories that assess the physical ecology of the classroom (such as activity), teachers' behaviors (such as questions), and the students' behaviors (such as writing). The most current version of the MS–CISSAR is available in a multisystem, computer-based package, the Ecobehavioral Assessment Systems Software (Greenwood, Carta, Kamps & Delquadri, 1997). Researchers have used the MS–CISSAR to examine the instructional and social characteristics in inclusive settings and their relationships to students' academic behaviors (Marston, Deno, Kim, Diment & Rogers, 1995; McDonnell, Thorson, McQuivey & Kiefer-O'Donnell, 1997). For preschool children, Odom, Favazza, Brown and Horn (2000) adapted the technology originated by the Greenwood, Carta group of researchers to design a system called the Code for Active Student Participation and Engagement–Revised (CASPER). They have used the

CASPER to examine inclusion of preschool children with ID in a range of early childhood settings (Brown, Odom, Li & Zercher, 1999).

Researchers have also employed qualitative methodology to examine the implementation of inclusion. Elsewhere in this text, authors have described qualitative methods (such as participant observation, interviewing, and case-study analysis), so only examples of their use will be provided in this chapter. To learn about the adoption of inclusion as a service model, Janey, Snell, Beers and Raynes (1995) interviewed personnel from 10 schools in Virginia, conducted a content analysis of the interviews, and identified four sets of recommendations that could be useful for school-system personnel considering inclusion as a service option. On a larger scale, Baker and Zigmond (1995) published five case studies of inclusion of students with learning disabilities based on observations, interviews, and analysis of documents. They then identified themes common to the implementation of inclusion across sites. At the foundation level, Salisbury, Palombaro and Hollowood (1993) documented the implementation of a full inclusion model for elementary-aged students. At the preschool level, Odom et al. (1999) employed participant observation, interviews, and document analysis, as well as quantitative methodology, to create case studies that were then analyzed to yield descriptions of how inclusion was implemented in different organizational contexts and through different individualized services delivery models.

Effects of Inclusion

A primary question in the research on inclusion of individuals with ID is about the impact of this form of service or placement relative to placement or services in noninclusive settings. Again, both quantitative and qualitative research methodologies may address this question, although there are issues necessary to consider when using either approach.

One quantitative experimental methodology is single-subject design (Kazdin, 1982). Researchers have created single-subject methodology, such as those of alternating treatment, simultaneous treatment, and multiple treatment, that is specifically designed to compare treatments (Holcombe, Wolery & Gast, 1994). In these designs, a small number of individuals participate in different forms of treatment (such as participation in inclusive and noninclusive settings). Usually, researchers use these designs to assess the effects of different intervention or instructional approaches, although they have occasionally been used to investigate the effects of placements in inclusive or noninclusive settings or conditions (Strain, 1983; Robertson & Weismer, 1997). The feasibility of assigning individuals to rapidly alternating conditions is sometimes a difficulty with this methodology if the larger question about the effects of inclusive placements across time is the focus of the research. Moreover, with treatment-comparison designs, the threat of multiple treatment interference (for example, individuals learn skills in one setting that they use in the other setting) exists.

Traditional group experimental design methodology is a second approach researchers may use to examine the effects of inclusion. The most rigorous form of this methodology would require random assignment to inclusive and noninclusive settings (Campbell & Stanley, 1966), and there may be legal and/or ethical limitations (Farrell, 1997). For example, in the USA, the current law stipulates that the least restrictive environment (that is, inclusion) be the first placement considered for individuals with disabilities, a fact which may preclude random assignment to noninclusive settings. Researchers have often solved this problem by using quasi-experimental design (Cook & Campbell, 1979), which may produce useful information if proper controls are employed (such as evidence that groups are comparable). For example, Casey et al. (1988) examined the performance of children with Down syndrome enrolled in inclusive and noninclusive settings across a two-year period. They were able to demonstrate that the groups were comparable on dependent measures at the beginning of the study and found differences, favoring the inclusive group, across the five points at which they collected data. As mentioned previously, Freeman and Alkin (2000) reviewed a large number of studies that compared academic and social attainment in inclusive and noninclusive settings. The studies primarily employed group experimental designs or quasi-experimental designs and generally revealed that children with ID received lower social acceptance scores than typically developing peers in inclusive setting but higher academic and social outcomes in inclusive than noninclusive settings.

Qualitative research on inclusion has increased dramatically in the last decade, although its roots extend further back. Perhaps the best example of the application of qualitative and ethnographic methodology to the study of inclusion is the classic program of research conducted by Edgerton and his colleagues (Edgerton, 1967; 1984). A wide range of more recent studies has documented the effects of inclusive settings for single or small groups of individuals (e.g., Baker & Zigmond, 1995; Ryndak, Morrison & Sommerstein, 1999; Walker, 1999). Qualitative research rarely compares different types of intervention or conditions but rather describes the effects of inclusion on individuals. Therefore, a basis for comparing inclusive and noninclusive settings does not exist in many qualitative studies—indeed, such comparison is not the goal of many qualitative studies. The exception to this general rule is when individuals with ID make a transition from one type of setting or experience to another (e.g., Edgerton, 1967; Ryndak et al., 1999), in which case the experiences of the same individual(s) may be compared in inclusive and noninclusive contexts.

CONCLUSION

Individuals with ID of all ages are being included in preschool, public school, and community settings. In this chapter, we have reviewed research instruments and techniques that researchers have used to investigate inclusion. The most active research literature appears to be the examinations of attitudes of individuals (teachers, parents, individuals) about inclusion and the social status of individuals with ID in inclusive settings. With the current sophistication and access to observational methodology, assessments of classroom ecologies and the effects of classroom variables may well increase in the future. The potential for qualitative research to contribute to our understanding of inclusion or to embellish the quantitative information collected (that is, through multimethod research approaches) also clearly exists and may be a trend in future research.

REFERENCES

Agran, M., Blanchard, C. & Wehmeyer, M.L. (2000). Promoting transition goals and self-determination through student self-directed learning: the self-determination learning model of instruction. *Education and Training in Mental Retardation and Developmental Disabilities*, **35**, 351–364.

Antonak, R.F. & Larrivee, B. (1995). Psychometric analysis and revision of the opinions relative to mainstreaming scale. *Exceptional Children*, **62**, 139–149.

Asher, S.R., Singleton, L.C., Tinsley, B.R. & Hymel, S. (1979). A reliable sociometric measure for preschool children. *Developmental Psychology*, **15**, 443–444.

Baker, J.M. & Zigmond, N. (1995). The meaning and practice of inclusion for students with learning disabilities: themes and implications from the five cases. *Journal of Special Education*, **27**, 163–172.

Balla, D.A., Cicchetti, D.V. & Harrison, P.L. (1985). *Vineland Adaptive Behavior Scale (Interview Edition, Expanded Form).* Circle Pines, MN: American Guidance Service.

Berryman, J.D., Neal, W.R. & Berryman, C. (1989). *Attitudes Toward Mainstreaming Scale—Revised.* Athens, GA: University of Georgia.

Brown, W.H., Odom, S.L., Li, S. & Zercher, C. (1999). Ecobehavioral assessment in early childhood programs: a portrait of preschool inclusion. *Journal of Special Education*, **33**, 138–153.

Campbell, D.T. & Stanley, J.C. (1966). *Experimental and Quasi-experimental Designs for Research on Teaching*. Chicago: Rand McNally.

Casey, W., Jones, D., Kugler, B. & Watkins, B. (1988). Integration of Down's syndrome children in the primary school: a longitudinal study of cognitive development and academic attainments. *British Journal of Educational Psychology*, **58**, 279–286.

Clark, L., Gresham, F.M. & Elliott, S.N. (1985). Development of a social skills assessment measure: the TROSS-C. *Journal of Psychoeducational Assessment*, **4**, 347–356.

Connolly, A.J. (1981). *KeyMath Revised: A Diagnostic Inventory of Essential Mathematics*. Circle Pines, MN: American Guidance Service.

Cook, T.D. & Campbell, D.T. (1979). *Quasi-experimentation: Design and Analysis for Field Settings.* Chicago: Rand McNally.

Deno, S.L. (1985). Curriculum-based measurement: the emerging alternative. *Exceptional Children*, **52**, 219–232.

Diamond, K.E., Hestenes, L.L., Carpenter, E.S. & Innes, F.K. (1997). Relationships between enrollment in an inclusive class and preschool children's ideas about people with disabilities. *Topics in Early Childhood Special Education*, **17**, 520–536.

Dunn, L.M. & Dunn, L.M. (1997). *Peabody Picture Vocabulary Test, Third Edition*. Circle Pines, MN: American Guidance Service.

Dunn, L.M., Dunn, L.M., Robertson, G.J. & Eisenberg, J.L. (1981). *Peabody Picture Vocabulary Test, Revised.* Circle Pines, MN: American Guidance Service.

Dykes, M.K. (1980). *Developmental Assessment for the Severely Handicapped.* Austin, TX: Exceptional Resources.

Edgerton, R. (1967). *The Cloak of Competence: Stigma in the Lives of the Retarded.* Berkeley, CA: University of California Press.

Edgerton, R. (1984). *Lives in Process: Mildly Retarded Adults in a Large City.* Washington, DC: American Association on Mental Deficiency.

Emerson, E., Robertson, J., Gregory, N., Hatton, C., Kessissoglou, S., Hallan, A., et al. (2001). Quality and costs of supported living residences and group homes in the United Kingdom. *American Journal on Mental Retardation*, **106**, 401–416.

Farrell, P. (1997). The integration of children with severe learning difficulties: a review of the recent literature. *Journal of Applied Research in Intellectual Disabilities*, **10**, 1–14.

Favazza, P. C. & Odom, S.L. (1996). Use of the Acceptance Scale to measure attitudes of kindergarten-age children: a preliminary investigation. *Journal of Early Intervention*, **20**, 232–249.

Favazza, P.C. & Odom, S.L. (1997). Promoting positive attitudes of kindergarten-age children toward individuals with disabilities. *Exceptional Children*, **63**, 405–422.

Field, S. & Hoffman, A. (1994). Development of a model for self-determination. *Career Development for Exceptional Individuals*, **17**, 159–169.

Forlin, C. (1995). Educators' beliefs about inclusive practices in Western Australia. *British Journal of Special Education*, **22**, 179–186.

Fraenkel, J. & Wallen, N. (2000). *How to Design and Evaluate Research in Education* (4th edn) (pp. 509–515). New York: McGraw-Hill.

Freeman, S.F. & Alkin, M.C. (2000). Academic and social attainments of children with mental retardation in general education and special education settings. *Remedial and Special Education*, **21**, 3–18.

Fuchs, L.S., Fuchs, D., Hamlett, C.L., Phillips, N.B. & Karns, K. (1995). General educator's specialized adaptation for students with learning disabilities. *Exceptional Children*, **61**, 440–459.

Gaylord-Ross, R.J., Haring, T.G., Breen, C. & Pitts-Conway, V. (1984). The training and generalization of social interaction skills with autistic youth. *Journal of Applied Behavior Analysis*, **17**, 611–621.

Greenwood, C.R., Carta, J.J., Kamps, D. & Delquadri, J. (1997). *Ecobehavioral Assessment Systems Software (EBASS)*. Kansas City, KS: University of Kansas, Juniper Gardens Children's Project.

Gresham, F.M. & Elliott, S.N. (1990). *Social Skills Rating System*. Circle Pines, MN: American Guidance Service.

Gresham, F.M., Elliott, S.N. & Black, F.L. (1987). Factor structure, application, and bias investigation of the Teacher Rating of Social Skills. *Journal of School Psychology*, **25**, 81–92.

Gresham, F.M. & Reschley, D.J. (1987). Sociometric differences between mildly handicapped and nonhandicapped black and white students. *Journal of Educational Psychology*, **79**, 195–197.

Guralnick, M.J. (1999). The nature and meaning of social integration for young children with mild developmental delays in inclusive settings. *Journal of Early Intervention*, **22**, 70–86.

Guralnick, M.J., Gottman, J.M. & Hammond, M.A. (1996). Effects of social setting on the friendship formation of young children differing in developmental status. *Journal of Applied Developmental Psychology*, **17**, 625–651.

Haring, T.G. & Breen, C.G. (1992). A peer-mediated social network intervention to enhance the social integration of persons with moderate and severe disabilities. *Journal of Applied Behavior Analysis*, **25**, 319–335.

Hartmann, D.P. & Wood, D.D. (1990). Observational methods. In A. Bellack, M. Hersen & A. Kazdin (Eds) *International Handbook of Behavior Modification and Therapy* (pp. 107–138). New York: Plenum.

Hastings, R. & Graham, S. (1995). Adolescents' perceptions of young people with severe learning difficulties: the effects of integration schemes and frequency of contact. *Educational Psychology*, **15**, 149–159.

Hegarty, S. (1993). Reviewing the literature on integration. *European Journal of Special Needs*, **8**, 194–200.

Heiman, T. & Margalit, M. (1998). Loneliness, depression, and social skills among students with mild mental retardation in different educational settings. *Journal of Special Education*, **32**, 154–163.

Henry, D., Keys, C., Jopp, D. & Balcazar, F. (1996). The Community Living Attitudes Scale, Mental Retardation Form: development and psychometric properties. *Mental Retardation*, **34**, 149–158.

Holcombe, A., Wolery, M. & Gast, D.L. (1994). Comparative single-subject research: description of designs and discussion of problems. *Topics in Early Childhood Special Education*, **14**, 119–145.

Hunt, P., Farron-Davis, R., Beckstead, S., Curtis, D. & Goetz, L. (1994). Evaluating the effects of placement of students with severe disabilities in general education versus special classes. *Journal of the Association for Persons with Severe Handicaps*, **19**, 200–214.

Hunt, P., Goetz, L. & Anderson, J. (1986). The quality of IEP objectives associated with placement in integrated versus segregated school sites. *Journal of the Association for Persons with Severe Handicaps*, **11**, 125–130.

Ittenbach, R.F., Bruininks, R.H., Thurlow, M.L. & McGrew, K.S. (1993). Community integration of young adults with mental retardation: a multivariate analysis of adjustment. *Research in Developmental Disabilities*, **14**, 275–290.

Janey, R.E., Snell, M.E., Beers, M.K. & Raynes, M. (1995). Integrating students with moderate and severe disabilities into general education classes. *Exceptional Children*, **61**, 425–439.

Kamps, D., Greenwood, C.R. & Leonard, B. (1991). Ecobehavioral assessment in classrooms serving children with autism and developmental disabilities. In R.J. Prinz (Ed.) *Advances in Behavioral Assessment of Children and Families: A Research Annual*, vol. 5 (pp. 203–237). London: Jessica Kingsley.

Kazdin, A.E. (1982). *Single Case Research Designs: Methods for Clinical and Applied Settings*. New York: Oxford University Press.

Klingerman, K., Washburn, S. & Cole, C. (2003). *Formative Assessment in Inclusive Classrooms: A Descriptive Study*. Submitted for publication.

Kovacs M. & Beck, A.T. (1977). An empirical clinical approach toward a definition of childhood depression. In J. Schlterbrant & A. Raskin (Eds) *Depression in Childhood: Diagnosis, Treatment, and Conceptual Models* (pp. 56–67). New York: Raven Press.

Krajewski, J. & Flaherty, T. (2000). Attitudes of high school students toward individuals with mental retardation. *Mental Retardation*, **38**, 154–162.

Lambert, N., Nihira, K. & Leland, H. (1993). *AAMR Adaptive Behavior Scale—School* (2nd edn). Austin, TX: Pro-Ed.

Likert, R. (1932). A technique for the measurement of attitudes. *Archives of Psychology*, **140**, 55.

Luftig, R.I. (1988). Assessment of the perceived school loneliness and isolation of mentally retarded and nonretarded students. *American Journal on Mental Retardation*, **92**, 472–475.

Margalit, M. (1991). Promoting classroom adjustment and social skills for students with mental retardation within an experimental and control group design. *Exceptionality*, **2**, 195–204.

Margalit, M. (1993). Social skills and classroom behavior among adolescents with mild mental retardation. *American Journal on Mental Retardation*, **97**, 685–691.

Margalit, M. & Ronen, T. (1993). Loneliness and social competence among preadolescents and adolescents with mental retardation. *Mental Handicap Research*, **6**, 97–111.

Marston, D., Deno, S.L., Kim, D., Diment, K. & Rogers, D. (1995). Comparison of reading intervention approaches for students with mild disabilities. *Exceptional Children*, **2**, 20–37.

McCandless, B.R. & Marshall, H.R. (1957). A picture sociometric technique for preschool children and its relation to teacher judgments of friendship. *Child Development*, **28**, 139–147.

McCarney, S.B. (1995). *Adaptive Behavior Evaluation Scale, Revised Second Edition.* Columbia, MO: Educational Services.

McCarthy, D. (1972). *McCarthy Scales of Children's Abilities.* Cleveland, OH: Psychological Corporation.

McConnell, S. & Odom, S.L. (1986). Sociometrics: peer-referenced measures and the assessment of social competence. In P. Strain, M. Guralnick & H. Walker (Eds) *Children's Social Behavior: Development, Assessment, and Modification* (pp. 215–284). New York: Academic Press.

McDonnell, J., Thorson, N., McQuivey, C. & Kiefer-O'Donnell, R. (1997). Academic engaged time of students with low-incidence disabilities in general education classes. *Mental Retardation*, **35**, 18–26.

Mu, K., Siegel, E.B. & Allinder, R.M. (2000). Peer interactions and sociometric status of high school students with moderate or severe disabilities in general education classrooms. *Journal of the Association for Persons with Severe Handicaps*, **25**, 142–152.

Neale, M.D., Christopher, U. & Whetton, C. (1989). *Neale Analysis of Reading Ability, Revised British Edition.* London: NFER-Nelson.

Newborg, J., Stock, J.R., Wnek, L., Guidubaldi, J. & Svinicki, J. (1984). *Battelle Developmental Inventory.* Austin, TX: DLM Teaching Resources.

Nirje, B.A. (1969). A Scandinavian visitor looks at US institutions. In W. Wolfensberger & R. Kugel (Eds) *Changing Patterns in Residential Services for the Mentally Retarded* (pp. 51–58). Washington, DC: President's Commission on Mental Retardation.

Nirje, B.A. (1985). The basis and logic of the normalization principle. *Australian and New Zealand Journal of Developmental Disabilities*, **11**, 65–68.

Noldus Information Technology (1993). *The Observer.* Sterling, VA: Author.

Nowak, R., Laitinen, R., Stowitschek, J. & Affleck, J. (1995). Advocates and adults with developmental disabilities: shared and unshared perceptions of self-determination opportunities and impact. *Journal of Vocational Rehabilitation*, **5**, 307–317.

Odom, S.L. & Bailey, D.B. (2001). Inclusive preschool programs: ecology and child outcomes. In M. Guralnick (Ed.) *Early Childhood Inclusion: Focus on Change* (pp. 253–276). Baltimore, MD: Brookes.

Odom, S.L., Favazza, P.C., Brown, W.E. & Horn, E.M. (2000). Approaches to understanding the ecology of inclusive early childhood settings for children with disabilities. In T. Thompson, D. Felce & F. Symons (Eds) *Behavioral Observation: Innovations in Technology and Application in Developmental Disabilities* (pp. 193–214). Baltimore, MD: Brookes.

Odom, S.L., Horn, E.M., Marquart, J., Hanson, M.J., Wolfberg, P., Beckman, P.J., et al. (1999). On the forms of inclusion: organizational context and individualized service delivery models. *Journal of Early Intervention*, **22**, 185–199.

Odom, S.L., McConnell, S.R. & McEvoy, M.A. (1992). Peer-related social competence and its implications for young children with disabilities. In S. Odom, S. McConnell & M. McEvoy (Eds) *Social Competence of Young Children with Disabilities* (pp. 3–36). Baltimore, MD: Brookes.

Odom, S.L., McConnell, S.R., McEvoy, M.A., Peterson, C., Ostrosky, M., Chandler, L.K., et al. (1999). Relative effects of interventions for supporting the social competence of young children with disabilities. *Topics in Early Childhood Special Education*, **19**, 75–91.

Odom, S.L. & Ogawa, I. (1992). Direct observation of preschool children's social interaction: a methodological review. *Behavioral Assessment*, **14**, 407–442.

Organization for Economic Cooperation and Development (1995). *Integration of Students with Special Needs into Mainstream Schools*. Paris: Author.

Parten, M.B. (1932). Social participation among preschool children. *Journal of Abnormal and Social Psychology*, **27**, 243–269.

Pearl, R., Farmer, T.W., Van Acker, R., Rodkin, P.C., Bost, K.K., Coe, M., et al. (1998). The social integration of students with mild disabilities in general education classrooms: peer group membership and peer-assessed social behavior. *Elementary School Journal*, **99**, 167–185.

Reynell, J.K. & Gruber, C.P. (1990). *Reynell Developmental Language Scales* [US edn]. Los Angeles, CA: Western Psychological Services.

Robertson, S.B. & Weismer, S.E. (1997). The influence of peer models on the play scripts of children with specific language impairment. *Journal of Speech, Language, and Hearing Research*, **40**, 49–61.

Ryndak, D.L., Morrison, A.P. & Sommerstein, L. (1999). Literacy before and after inclusion in general education settings: a case study. *Journal of the Association for Persons with Severe Handicaps*, **24**, 5–23.

Saint-Laurent, L. & Lessard, J. (1991). Comparison of three educational programs for students with moderate mental retardation integrated in regular schools: preliminary results. *Education and Training in Mental Retardation*, **26**, 370–380.

Salisbury, C.L., Palombaro, D. & Hollowood, A. (1993). On the nature and change of an inclusive elementary school. *Journal of the Association for Persons with Severe Handicaps*, **18**, 75–84.

Schnorr, R.F. (1990). "Peter? He comes and goes...": First graders' perspectives on a part-time mainstream student. *Journal of the Association for Persons with Severe Handicaps*, **14**, 231–240.

Scott, J. (1991). *Social Network Analysis*. Newbury Park, CA: Sage.

Serna, L. & Lau-Smith, J. (1995). Learning with purpose: self-determination skills for students who are at risk for school and community failure. *Intervention in School and Clinic*, **30**, 142–146.

Siperstein, G.N. & Leffert, J.S. (1997). Comparison of socially accepted and rejected children with mental retardation. *American Journal on Mental Retardation*, **101**, 339–351.

Siperstein, G.N., Leffert, J.S. & Widaman, K. (1996). Social behavior and the social acceptance and rejection of children with mental retardation. *Education and Training in Mental Retardation and Developmental Disabilities*, **31**, 271–281.

Smilansky, S. (1968). *The Effects of Sociodramatic Play on Disadvantaged Preschool Children*. New York: Wiley.

Stancliffe, R.J., Abery, B.H. & Smith, J. (2000). Personal control and the ecology of community living settings: beyond living-unit size and type. *American Journal on Mental Retardation*, **105**, 431–454.

Strain, P.S. (1983). Generalization of autistic children's social behavior change: effects of developmentally integrated and segregated settings. *Analysis and Intervention in Developmental Disabilities*, **3**, 369–382.

Strain, P.S. & Timm, M.A. (1974). An experimental analysis of social interaction between a behaviorally disordered preschool child and her classroom peers. *Journal of Applied Behavior Analysis*, **7**, 583–590.

Tapp, J. & Walden, T.A. (2000). PROCODER: a system for collection and analysis of observational data from videotape. In T. Thompson, D. Felce & F. Symons (Eds) *Behavioral Observation: Innovations in Technology and Application in Developmental Disabilities* (pp. 61–70). Baltimore, MD: Brookes.

Tapp, J. & Wehby, J.H. (2000). Observational software for laptop computers and optical bar code readers. In T. Thompson, D. Felce & F. Symons (Eds) *Behavioral Observation: Innovations in Technology and Application in Developmental Disabilities* (pp. 71–82). Baltimore, MD: Brookes.

Taylor, A.R., Asher, S.R. & Williams, G.A. (1987). The social adaptation of mainstreamed mildly retarded children. *Child Development*, **58**, 1321–1334.

Thompson, T., Felce, D. & Symons, F. (Eds) (2000). *Behavioral Observation: Innovations in Technology and Application in Developmental Disabilities*. Baltimore, MD: Brookes.

Voeltz, L.M. (1980). Children's attitudes toward handicapped peers. *American Journal of Mental Deficiency*, **84**, 455–464.

Walker, P. (1999). From community presence to sense of place: community experiences of adults with developmental disabilities. *Journal of the Association for Persons with Severe Handicaps*, **24**, 23–32.

Ward, J., Center, Y. & Bochner, S. (1994). A question of attitudes: integrating children with disabilities into regular classrooms. *British Journal of Special Education*, **21**, 34–39.

Wehmeyer, M.L. (1996). Student self-report measure of self-determination for students with cognitive disabilities. *Education and Training in Mental Retardation and Developmental Disabilities*, **31**, 282–293.

Wehmeyer, M.L. & Bolding, N. (1999). Self-determination across living and working environments: a matched-samples study of adults with mental retardation. *Mental Retardation*, **37**, 353–363.

Wehmeyer, M.L. & Metzler, C.A. (1995). How self-determined are people with mental retardation? National Consumer Survey. *Mental Retardation*, **33**, 111–119.

White, O.R. (1986). Precision teaching, precision learning. *Exceptional Children*, **52**, 522–534.

White, O.R. & Haring, N.G. (1980). *Exceptional Teaching* (2nd edn). Columbus, OH: Merrill.

Whittaker, P. (1994). Mainstream students talk about integration. *British Journal of Special Education*, **21**, 13–16.

Wilczenski, F.L. (1992). Reevaluating the factor structure of the Attitudes Toward Mainstreaming Scale. *Educational and Psychological Measurement*, **52**, 499–504.

Williams, G.A. & Asher, S.R. (1992). Assessment of loneliness at school among children with mild mental retardation. *American Journal on Mental Retardation*, **96**, 373–385.

Wolfensberger, W. (1972). *The Principles of Normalization in Human Services*. Toronto: National Institute on Mental Retardation.

Woodcock, R.W., Johnson, M.B., Mather, N., McGrew, K.S. & Werder, J.K. (1991). *Woodcock-Johnson Psychoeducational Battery–Revised*. Chicago: Riverside.

Yuker, H.E. & Block, J.R. (1986). *Research with the Attitude Toward Disabled Persons Scales (ATDP) 1960–1985*. Hofstra University.

Zhang, D. (2001). Self-determination and inclusion: are students with mild mental retardation more self-determined in regular classrooms? *Education and Training in Mental Retardation and Developmental Disabilities*, **35**, 357–362.

CHAPTER 14

Research on Social Relationships

Craig H. Kennedy
Vanderbilt University, USA

Many researchers have noted that social relationships are a fundamental dimension of human psychology (Gewirtz & Petrovich, 1983; Maccoby, 1998), and an important element in how people define their life quality (Gottlieb & Leyser, 1996; Barrera, 2000). As more and more people with intellectual disabilities live in the community, attend public schools, and join the regular workforce, a greater range of outcomes are coming to the forefront for researchers to investigate. Among those outcomes are an improved social life (Haring, 1991; Staub, Peck, Gallucci & Schwartz, 2000). It is not surprising that co-occurring with an increased presence in the community for people with disabilities is an increased interest in social outcomes.

Having people in your life who provide companionship and provide social support has been identified as among the most important variables in predicting people's happiness (e.g., Friedland, Renwick & McColl, 1996; Caron, Tempier, Mercier & Leouffre, 1998). Because positive personal relationships correlate with lower stress levels and improved health, their presence is an important determinant of life quality (e.g., Avery, Speare & Lawton, 1989; Wineman, 1990). Our relationships with others provide key access to tangible resources, as well as providing a source of psychological well-being. Clearly, social relationships are an important element to consider when identifying critical variables for support providers to facilitate and enhance. This is particularly true for people with intellectual disabilities who, by the nature of their disability, require ongoing support from other people to maximize their life quality.

The field of social-relationship research has seen a substantial increase in published studies during the past decade. This increase in activity, at least in part, reflects the increased demand by research consumers for new and valid approaches to facilitating and maintaining social relationships. The increase in research activity also reflects some key changes in the experimental questions, measures, and designs researchers are using to explore this topic.

This chapter provides a selective review of recent developments in the research literature on social relationships. The primary foci will be on research studies using single-case experimental designs and qualitative research employing a variety of techniques. In addition, the chapter focuses primarily on research on school-age populations, rather than adults. A focus on these areas should provide the reader with a contemporary review of the most active

The International Handbook of Applied Research in Intellectual Disabilities. Edited by E. Emerson, C. Hatton, T. Thompson and T.R. Parmenter ISBN 0-471-49709-6.

areas of research on social relationships for people with intellectual disabilities, although this approach limits its scope.

One trend that has emerged over the past 10 years is an increase in the complexity of experimental questions being posed by researchers (Kennedy & Shukla, 1995). Thirty years ago, research focused on questions such as how to teach a person with a disability to say "Hello" to another person. In contrast, contemporary research is studying interventions that often incorporate not only whole classrooms or work settings, but the entire school or business that encapsulates these entities.

Not surprisingly, with this increase in intervention complexity, there has been a concomitant interest in what is being measured. By current standards, the measurement of discrete occurrences of a greeting response presents few technical challenges. However, consider the complexities involved in defining and measuring, in a valid and reliable manner, such constructs as friendship, happiness, and life quality.

The types of experimental designs being used by researchers are also increasing in sophistication. Research designs capable of documenting the functional properties of social interactions are emerging as a means of understanding why people choose to interact. At the same time, research designs are also becoming increasingly eclectic, incorporating elements of single-case analyses and ethnographic approaches.

RESEARCH METHODOLOGY

The remainder of this paper will provide a discussion of these emerging trends in social-relationship research. The discussion will focus on three fundamental aspects of experimental analyses: the nature of (a) independent variables, (b) dependent measures, and (c) experimental designs. The goal is to provide the reader with a foundation in contemporary issues influencing this area of research, and some prescriptive suggestions regarding future issues and directions for researchers.

Independent Variables

The move toward interventions that facilitate a person's inclusion into regular school, work, and living situations is resulting in increasingly complex independent variables. This trend has been emerging over the past decade, with current interventions containing as many as 10–15 individual components (e.g., Hunt, Alwell, Farron-Davis & Goetz, 1996; Janney & Snell, 1996; Staub, Spaulding, Peck & Gallucci, 1996; Werts, Wolery, Snyder & Caldwell, 1996; Werner, Horner & Newton, 1997; Kamps, Dugan, Potucek & Collins, 1999; Shukla, Kennedy & Cushing, 1999; Mu, Siegel & Allinder, 2000; Odom, 2000).

The reason for this complexity is a shift in the focus of interventions. Although interventions continue to focus on dyadic (or small-group) interactions between people with and without disabilities, these discrete interactions are taking place in different settings. For example, Mu et al. (2000) developed an intervention to include students with intellectual disabilities into general education classrooms to facilitate social interactions with peers without disabilities. The intervention included elements of

(1) formal and informal agreements between general and special education teachers regarding roles and responsibilities
(2) recruitment of students with disabilities who met specific behavioral requirements

(3) sociometric analyses of peers without disabilities and subsequent recruitment of interaction partners
(4) establishing group activities within the general education curriculum for students with and without disabilities
(5) strategies for facilitating task engagement and social interactions for all students involved
(6) consultation with university personnel.

As the foregoing example illustrates, researchers are testing independent variables that require coordinating the activities of a dozen or more individuals for each person with a disability, and the implementation of several layers of support activities. It appears that this increase in intervention complexity is not simply an effort to increase the complexity of independent variables, but is a response to the demands of including people with disabilities in typical settings. That is, inclusive school, work, and home settings require more comprehensive interventions to achieve success. This increase in the complexity of independent variables, however, raises some concerns that researchers and consumers of research need to be aware of.

Operationalizing Independent Variables

One issue relates to the adequacy of current attempts to operationalize interventions. Operationalization in this context is important for the following reasons:

(1) Defining key aspects of an intervention allows researchers and consumers to be aware of what specifically constitutes an intervention.
(2) Operationalizing the variables that constitute the independent variable is a necessary, but not sufficient, set of prerequisites for monitoring intervention fidelity.
(3) Adequately specifying the elements of an intervention, both intended and unintended, is a critical step toward allowing replication of experimental outcomes by other researchers.

Given the multifaceted dimensions of current social-relationship interventions, this is not an easy task. There is an inherent tension between what an experimenter believes his or her independent variable may be, and what actually occurs. Comprehensively defining all the elements of an independent variable has historically required experimenters to specify, a priori, what constitutes an intervention. The nature of current independent variables designed to facilitate social relationships may violate this dictum. Researchers must

(1) a priori define what they believe to be the elements of an intervention (being aware that this specification may be incomplete)
(2) monitor the fidelity of those components (being aware that in application some components may be implemented at greater or lesser levels than planned)
(3) continually check for the possibility that additional events have emerged as influential variables (being aware that serendipitous aspects of any intervention may be functionally important and difficult to predict).

An awareness of these issues suggests that future research should carefully attend to the nature of independent variables and the importance of capturing various facets of the intervention, both experimenter-specified and serendipitous. Such efforts require a substantive reallocation of the resources used to conduct research.

Ineffective Intervention Elements

A second challenge for researchers imposed by the complexity of social-relationship interventions is the identification of ineffectual or superfluous elements. This is a difficult undertaking for several reasons. Indeed, even beginning the process of identifying, studying, and removing ineffective interventions requires precise operationalization of independent variables (as was just discussed).

Once the specification of elements is satisfactorily accomplished, experimenters need to contend with a recurrent problem when conducting research that is part of the psychological nature of experimentation (Sidman, 1960). That is, what an experimenter believes to be a critical variable in his or her intervention (or, conversely, what is an unimportant variable) may lead him or her not to analyze critically specific variables because of implicit assumptions. For example, a researcher may assume that a reinforcement contingency for peers without disabilities to participate in a peer-support program is necessary and, hence, fail to consider this variable a necessary element for analysis. This interesting psychological phenomenon, which is understudied, can cause an experimenter to assume the importance (or unimportance) of certain elements, and not critically assess their viability as part of an intervention. Perhaps the only remedy for this concern is the constant and critical appraisal of a researcher's activities. A researcher should be loath to impose his or her own esthetics regarding how something works when studying how systems actually function.

Another concern with identifying ineffective elements of independent variables is less abstract—some elements of social-relationship interventions may be ethically or practically impossible to manipulate. Because of the necessity of manipulating (that is, withdrawing, presenting, comparing, and/or parametrically varying) intervention components to study their influence on behavior, researchers need to contend with what can (and cannot) be systematically varied within an intervention. For example, in one of our research studies (Shukla et al., 1999), a journal review team criticized the experimental design because it did not provide an exhaustive test of the two-by-two factorial nature of the independent variable. However, the missing combination of variables would have meant placing an adolescent with profound disabilities in a general education classroom with no adult or peer support, something that we were unwilling to do, even for a brief period of time. Researchers should be aware that not all elements or combinations of elements can be experimentally analyzed. Such a reality imposes further complexities on how to test for ineffectual intervention components. Perhaps the best that can be accomplished in these situations is for researchers explicitly to acknowledge and discuss these issues when they arise, and provide a forthright elucidation of the potential ramifications for interpreting experimental findings.

Effective Intervention Elements

A final challenge that needs to be addressed by contemporary research on social-relationship interventions is how to identify key elements of interventions. Although in many respects this is a reciprocal of identifying ineffective intervention elements, there are some aspects of studying effective elements that warrant a separate treatment. Simply identifying ineffectual intervention components is not an adequate demonstration that the other components of an intervention are effective or necessary. The identification of effective intervention variables cannot be accomplished by default, but, instead, must be systematically analyzed to identify how their presence may influence specific outcomes.

In addition, researchers may want to consider establishing "function curves" for key elements of interventions. This entails parametric variations in the level or amount of some element of an intervention to study its effect on the dependent variables. Function curves allow for the establishment of how varying levels of an independent variable influence the occurrence or nonoccurrence of specific behaviors. Not only is this good scientific practice, but it also has practical implications. Because of the complexity of contemporary social-relationship interventions, issues of cost and feasibility will inevitably arise from funders and distal consumers. In an era when researchers are increasingly attending to the dictum that the outcomes of research need to be "faster, better, cheaper", a defensible analysis of "how much is enough" may be an important experimental outcome.

Summary

It goes without saying that an independent variable is an important part of a research study. Of course, this implies that careful scrutiny be given to interventions. However, it could be argued that researchers pursuing enhanced social outcomes for people with intellectual disabilities have paid more attention to experimental outcomes than the precise nature of the independent variable. Although it is laudable that researchers have been so focused on improving social outcomes, there is an increasing need for greater attention to the nature of independent variables.

Dependent Measures

The measurement of social relationships is plagued by difficulties (Barker, 1978; Argyle, 1993). The fundamental problem with measuring social relationships is definitional—What is a social relationship? Like other constructs, social relationships mean different things to different people. At a broad level, people agree that social relationships are affiliations among people, but, when more specific definitions are focused on, it becomes clear that there is a wide divergence of opinion on what constitutes interpersonal relationships. Indeed, most terms of interest to researchers focusing on social relationships—friendship, reciprocity, membership, and belonging—are almost indefinable constructs.

There are several prerequisites of an adequate measurement system (Johnston & Pennypacker, 1994). First, the measurement categories need to be valid indicators of the events of interest (even if it is only face validity). Second, the measurement system needs to estimate accurately the occurrence of events in specific categories. Third, if events are not being mechanically recorded, multiple individuals using the measurement system need to record consistently and independently the occurrence and nonoccurrence of events. At first contact, these prerequisites may seem quite simple. However, even for social responses such as responding to another person, researchers have found the measurement of social events difficult (Storey, 1993). These problems have been compounded as researchers have moved toward studying more complex forms of social interaction, such as social relationships.

Measuring Multiple Events

The problem of operationalizing constructs is often acknowledged in research on social relationships, and there seems to have developed a general strategy for dealing with this limitation (Duck, 1992). That is, researchers have typically used multiple measures of various events that seem plausibly related to the definition of social relationships. For example, Staub et al. (2000) have focused their measurement system on three levels of variables related to social interactions: (a) relationships, (b) membership, and (c) skills. Relationships in the Staub et al. conceptual system refer to interactions among people and their perceptions of those interactions. Membership refers to a person's social embeddedness among a group of people. Finally, skills refer to behaviors that occur during social interactions that relate to social competence. Similarly, Kennedy (2001a) used a conceptual system that focused on social interactions, social networks, and social-support behaviors.

What these and other recently developed conceptual systems focus on is the use of multiple measures to capture discrete aspects of social relationships that can be estimated and compared. The result is a "mosaic" of structural and process variables relating to social relationships that allow researchers to compare various patterns of social affiliation (Pennington, Gillen & Hill, 1999). For example, researchers can document the number of times two people interact in a particular week, what they did, what types of behaviors were exchanged during the interaction, who else might have been involved, and how those various people tended to interact with each other. Although this approach has its limitations—for example, it is analogous to the strategy that if it quacks like a duck, walks like a duck, and looks like a duck, it is a duck—it has provided researchers with consistent estimates of events related to social relationships, even if no single measure is definitive of the construct.

Different Measurement Approaches

Co-occurring with the emergence of a multiple-measure approach to capturing social relationships is the use of eclectic measurement approaches. Traditionally, researchers have used measurement systems derived from applied behavior analysis (Bijou, Peterson & Ault, 1968) or social psychology (Argyle, 1993). Behavior-analytic approaches have focused on observable events that can be discretely defined and measured. Approaches derived from social psychology have focused on capturing events that reflect underlying processes of outcome variables. There is currently a trend toward including additional types of information in this area of research. The goal of using differing measurement approaches, like the goal of using multiple measures, is to capture for review and analysis as many different facets of events relating to social relationships as possible.

An important area from which measurement approaches are being drawn is that of ethnography. Qualitative research has risen in visibility during the 1990s, and some aspects of this catchment of methods are being used by researchers interested in social relationships. Indeed, there are a range of approaches within the constellation of qualitative methods that are of potential interest in understanding social relationships. Measurement approaches used in qualitative research range from archival review of records to descriptive field notes to in-depth interviews with individuals or small groups (Ferguson, 1993). What these approaches share, and makes them distinct from those discussed in the previous section, is a focus on interpreting events to synthesize meaning. Often, but certainly not exclusively, the focus of these measures is to capture the gist of events and the context they occur in, without the focus on internal validity or objectivity that behavioral measures require as prerequisites.

Currently, these measures are being used across a continuum of approaches to integrate objective and interpretative strategies. For example, some studies have relied primarily on ethnographic data with supplemental objective measures (e.g., Schnorr, 1997) or vice versa (e.g., Kennedy, Shukla & Fryxell, 1997), while other analyses have attempted to balance and integrate the two approaches to measurement (e.g., Wolfberg et al., 1999). Perhaps of most interest to the readers of this chapter are research strategies that aim to blend or mix measurement approaches (discussed in the next section).

Summary

As researchers have increased the complexity of experimental questions and interventions, measurement systems are also evolving in complexity. That researchers are attempting to define, measure, and understand such variables as friendship, belonging, membership, and popularity is an important phenomenon for research relating to people with intellectual disabilities. It may be that the innovations in measuring complex constructs and the diverse measures and approaches used in social-relationship research will have implications for other research areas (e.g., Kennedy, 2002). Whatever the eventuation, this research topic is one of the most dynamic and debated areas of scholarly inquiry in the field of disability studies.

Experimental Designs

As independent and dependent variables have become more complex, so have the experimental designs used to investigate causal regularities between these variable sets. Although multiple measures do not necessarily require more sophisticated analytical tactics, the change in the types of interventions being studied does require more sophisticated designs. If we cast the literature of social-relationship intervention in light of Sidman's classic work on inductive research (1960), we can suggest several ways in which research in this area is evolving.

Predominately, researchers have been interested in design approaches that allow the testing of new behavioral techniques (see Sidman, 1960, Chapter 1). In social relationship research, this has focused on new ways to include people in school, work, and community environments to gain access to and facilitate interactions between people with and without intellectual disabilities. However, since Sidman's treatment of why research is conducted, there has been an increasing trend toward investigations of new behavioral processes and the parameters of those processes. Researchers are beginning to explore what behavior–environment relations that are derived from basic research may be influencing social-affiliation patterns, and how those basic behavioral processes may be synthesized in applied research (Kennedy, in 2001b).

Single-Case Designs

A design that has been dominant in social-relationship research has been the multiple baseline across participants design. Considered by many methodologists as the weakest form of $N = 1$ designs and not actually a single-case design (Kazdin, 1984; Johnston & Pennypacker, 1993; Kennedy & Thompson, 2000), this approach has nonetheless been the predominant analytical method. Perhaps the reason for its prolific use is that the multiple baseline across participants design requires the least amount of independent variable manipulation of any single-case design. In this design type, each participant receives exposure to only a single baseline followed by an intervention.

Several analytical concerns are raised by the use of multiple baseline across participant designs. First, it provides only single baseline-intervention comparisons for a particular participant. Another concern with this design type is that, by necessity, one person is kept in a prolonged baseline condition as a control technique, with baselines sometimes lasting months to achieve experimental control. Finally—and this concern is not specific to multiple baseline across participant designs—is the issue of "sham" baselines to establish dependent-variable levels prior to an intervention. In the contemporary literature on social relationships, baseline measures typically show either ceiling effects (of undesired behaviors) or basal effects (of desired behaviors) during baseline. Such arrangements constitute very poor comparison (and, hence, control) techniques.

However, there are signs that researchers are opting for single-case designs that allow more analytical flexibility and more stringent control. Increasingly, researchers are using ABAB withdrawal or multielement designs for studying behavioral processes. For example, Shukla et al. (1999) used the ABAB withdrawal design and an embedded component analysis to study how teachers versus peers without disabilities influenced the types of support that students with intellectual disabilities received. Such arrangements allow for a more flexible treatment of how a particular intervention affects a person's social life and provides an opportunity to study other aspects of the intervention.

Similarly, the use of more sophisticated $N = 1$ designs may allow researchers to study the parametric levels of specific interventions to establish function curves between interventions and behavior change. For example, the amount of time that an instructional aide spends directly monitoring a dyad of students with and without disabilities could be conducted to analyze when there is a differential impact on academic and social behaviors.

Overall, there are signs of a shift in the types of single-case designs used to study social-relationship processes. Importantly, this shift appears to be related to the testing of more elaborate experimental questions. An evolution from initial comparisons of previous support strategies and newly developed strategies for more typical environments is requiring greater analytical flexibility. As researchers seek to conduct component and parametric analyses better to understand influential behavioral processes affecting social relationships, design alternatives to the multiple baseline across participants design are emerging.

Mixed-Method Designs

Although there may be some future integration of group comparison designs with either single-case or interpretivist approaches, it is largely the integration of these last two design types that is attracting the attention of contemporary researchers. However, at present, the integration of these designs is largely in the area of conceptual discussions and the potential that these design approaches possess.

At its best, the integration of single-case and qualitative research methods will allow for a more complete investigation of social processes. Although single-case designs provide the researcher with tools for inductive exploration of behavioral processes operating on people's social activities, there are some limitations in what this design type can explore in terms of social context and the interpretation of social meaning. As noted earlier, single-case designs focus on precise operational definitions of events being studied. However, this focus on precision has sometimes prevented single-case researchers from exploring less easily defined processes (Wolf, 1978; Schwartz & Baer, 1991). The study of social relationships can be viewed as a case in point regarding the difficulties in operationalizing events that are primarily socially constructed. Although the point of this chapter is not to discuss a constructivist perspective on social relationships, it is important to note that the phenomena we refer to as friendships, belonging, and so on, are largely defined by social context.

Hence, the promise of mixed methodologies. If researchers can use single-case designs to analyze precisely and experimentally to control key variables that may influence social relationships, then qualitative methods could be used to explore less tangible or less accessible aspects of the social context in which behaviors are changing. Indeed, because both design types are known for their ability to be used as flexible and inductive research tools, the possibility of more completely understanding what are currently poorly understood processes is intriguing. For example, Wolfberg et al. (1999) used both objective measures (which child played with whom) and interpretative measures (interviews with children and their teachers). The goal was to arrive at an understanding of which children chose to interact, or not interact, why those choices were made, and how the educational setting influenced those choices and affiliation patterns. Efforts like the Wolfberg et al. study may be a primary area for growth in social-relationship research, and these blended methodologies hold much promise.

However, the promise of mixed methodologies is currently largely a promise. With a few notable exceptions, research to date that has used mixed methodologies has not yet realized the potential of this approach. Contemporary research using mixed methodologies could be summarized as being in either of two categories: (a) single-case designs that add some element of a qualitative approach to the analysis, or (b) qualitative approaches that add some element of a single-case design to the analysis. That is, it is rare to see a mixed-methods study that is innovative in both its qualitative and quantitative components. Of particular note is that not only do the two design approaches need to be ably conducted, but, at its best, they need to be integrated into an analysis so that they complement and support each other. However, the promising mixed methodologies, at this point in time, will have to await future development before the efficacy of this approach to systematic inquiry can be evaluated in the area of social-relationship research.

Summary

As has been the case with the review of research methodology relating to independent and dependent variables, the use of experimental designs to study social relationships is in a transitional period. At least part of what has caused this transition in research practices is an interest in more complex social processes (for example, facilitating friendship development versus increasing social initiations). In the area of research designs, the demand for increasingly sophisticated analytical approaches has had two effects. First, single-case designs are becoming increasingly sophisticated in terms of establishing meaningful and sensitive baselines, and in the use of more complex design tactics to analyze social processes. Second, researchers are beginning to explore how to combine single-case designs with qualitative designs to study experimental questions at multiple levels. What is exciting about these trends in social-relationship research is the potential for new methodological innovations to emerge.

CONCLUSION

Self-advocates, family members, and support providers are requesting a greater focus on social relationships as a focus of interventions. This trend is occurring across the life span (Kennedy & Itkonen, 1995) and globally (Fisher, Kennedy & Buswell, 2000). During the past 30 years, researchers have focused on academically oriented issues for people with intellectual disabilities, particularly the development of life skills. Indeed, if one peruses textbooks focusing on teacher training in the area of severe disabilities, there is almost a complete omission of curricular and instructional issues pertaining to facilitation of social relationship. However, the field's tendency not to focus on social development is showing signs of changing in terms of research and personnel preparation (e.g., Snell & Brown, 2000; Kennedy & Horn, 2004; Ryndak & Alper, in press).

However, this shift in focus toward social, as well as academic, development is forcing researchers to develop new methods. This chapter has surveyed trends in three areas integral to the research process: independent variables, dependent measures, and experimental designs.

- As researchers strive to achieve broader outcomes relating to social relationships, interventions are becoming proportionally more complex. Because social relationship interventions are multicomponent in nature, researchers need to strive to identify what are and are not effective intervention elements. To accomplish this goal, researchers will need to develop more effective methods for operationalizing and monitoring the implementation of independent variables.
- Correspondingly, the research designs being used to analyze social relationships are becoming increasingly sophisticated in at least two ways. First, rather than simple documentation or description of the nature of independent variables, there is an emerging trend toward analyzing the behavioral processes responsible for intervention effects in more inclusive support settings. Second, the types of designs used to analyze social processes are becoming multifaceted. This trend is shown in the increased sophistication of single-case designs and the use of mixed designs that integrate elements of single-case and ethnographic approaches.
- Finally, the broader outcomes that researchers are pursuing also require better specification of what is being measured as outcome variables. A trend is emerging that suggests that researchers are using multiple measures, often from a range of methodological traditions, that encompass social phenomena from discrete exchanges of behavior to long-term patterns of social affiliation. Although no definitive system currently exists

for studying the social relationships of people with intellectual disabilities, current approaches are striving to capture as many relevant dimensions of this, and its associated constructs, as possible.

The growth of experimental activity relating to social relationships is an encouraging sign of the health and diversity of intellectual disability research. On the one hand, it demonstrates that researchers can be responsive to demands from self-advocates, family members, and practitioners to focus on areas that are of immediate concern to them and the life quality of people with intellectual disabilities. On the other hand, this growth in research is invigorating research methodology by forcing researchers to grapple with new approaches to conducting research to answer new questions.

As a whole, the state of research relating to social relationships and people with disabilities is in a transitional period. Initial efforts to study new independent variables that can result in more inclusive outcomes have produced promising results. At the same time, researchers are striving to understand better how these interventions work through refinement of experimental methodologies. The next decade of research on social relationships is promising because it is likely to produce improved outcomes for people with intellectual disabilities and innovations in experimental methodology.

REFERENCES

Argyle, M. (1993). *Experiments in Social Interaction.* Brookfield, VT: Dartmouth.

Avery, R., Speare, A. & Lawton, L. (1989). Social support, disability and independent living of elderly persons in the United States. *Journal of Aging Studies*, **3**, 279–293.

Barker, R.G. (1978). *Habitats, Environments, and Human Behavior.* San Francisco, CA: Jossey-Bass.

Barrera, M. Jr (2000). Social support research in community psychology. In J. Rappaport & E. Seidman (Eds) *Handbook of Community Psychology* (pp. 215–245). New York: Plenum.

Bijou, S.W., Peterson, R.F. & Ault, M.H. (1968). A method to integrate descriptive and experimental field studies at the level of data and empirical concepts. *Journal of Applied Behavior Analysis*, **1**, 175–191.

Caron, J., Tempier, R., Mercier, C. & Leouffre, P. (1998). Components of social support and quality of life in severely mentally ill, low income individuals and a general population group. *Community Mental Health Journal*, **34**, 459–475.

Duck, S. (1992). *Human Relationships* (2nd edn). London: Sage.

Ferguson, D.L. (1993). Something a little out of the ordinary: reflections on becoming an interpretivist researcher in special education. *Remedial and Special Education*, **14**, 35–43, 51.

Fisher, D., Kennedy, C.H. & Buswell, B. (2000). *1999 TASH Conference Yearbook.* Baltimore, MD: Brookes.

Friedland, J., Renwick, R. & McColl, M. (1996). Coping and social support as determinants of quality of life in HIV/AIDS. *AIDS Care*, **8**, 15–31.

Gewirtz, J.L. & Petrovich, S.B. (1983). Early social and attachment learning in the frame of organic and cultural evolution. In T.M. Field, A. Huston, H.C. Quay, L. Troll & G.E. Finley (Eds) *Review of Human Development* (pp. 3–19). New York: Wiley.

Gottlieb, J. & Leyser, Y. (1996). Attitudes of public school parents toward mainstreaming: changes over a decade. *Journal of Instructional Psychology*, **23**, 257–264.

Haring, T.G. (1991). Social relationships. In L.H. Meyer, C.A. Peck & L. Brown (Eds) *Critical Issues in the Lives of People with Severe Disabilities* (pp. 195–217). Baltimore, MD: Brookes.

Hunt, P., Alwell, M., Farron-Davis, F. & Goetz, L. (1996). Creating socially supportive environments for fully included students who experience multiple disabilities. *Journal of the Association for Persons with Severe Handicaps*, **21**, 53–71.

Janney, R.E. & Snell, M.E. (1996). How teachers use peer interactions to include students with moderate and severe disabilities in elementary general education classes. *Journal of the Association for Persons with Severe Handicaps*, **21**, 72–80.

Johnston, J.M. & Pennypacker, H.S. (1994). *Strategies and Tactics of Behavioral Research* (2nd edn). Hillsdale, NJ: Erlbaum.

Kamps, D.M., Dugan, E., Potucek, J. & Collins, A. (1999). Effects of cross-age peer tutoring networks among students with autism and general education students. *Journal of Behavioral Education*, **9**, 97–115.

Kazdin, A.E. (1984). *Single-Case Research Designs.* New York: Oxford University Press.

Kennedy, C.H. (2001a). Promoting social-communicative interactions in adolescents. In H. Goldstein, L. Kaczmarek & K.M. English (Eds) *Promoting Social Communication: Children with Developmental Disabilities from Birth to Adolescence* (pp. 307–330). Baltimore, MD: Brookes.

Kennedy, C.H. (2001b). Social interaction interventions for youth with severe disabilities should emphasize interdependence. *Mental Retardation and Developmental Disabilities Research Reviews*, **7**, 122–127.

Kennedy, C.H. (2002). Toward a socially valid understanding of problem behavior. *Education and Training of Children*, **25**, 142–153.

Kennedy, C.H. & Horn, E. (2004). *Including of Students with Severe Disabilities.* Boston, MA: Allyn & Bacon.

Kennedy, C.H. & Itkonen, T. (1995). Social relationships, influential variables, and change across the life span. In L. Kern-Koegel, R.L. Koegel & G. Dunlap (Eds) *Positive Behavioral Support: Including People with Difficult Behavior in the Community* (pp. 287–304). Baltimore, MD: Brookes.

Kennedy, C.H. & Shukla, S. (1995). Social interaction research for people with autism as a set of past, current, and emerging propositions. *Behavioral Disorders*, **21**, 21–36.

Kennedy, C.H., Shukla, S. & Fryxell, D. (1997). Comparing the effects of educational placement on the social relationships of intermediate school students with severe disabilities. *Exceptional Children*, **64**, 31–47.

Kennedy, C.H. & Thompson, T. (2000). Health conditions contributing to problem behavior among people with mental retardation and developmental disabilities. In M. Wehmeyer & J. Patten (Eds) *Mental Retardation in the 21st Century* (pp. 211–231). Austin, TX: Pro-Ed.

Maccoby, E.E. (1998). *The Two Sexes: Growing Up Apart, Coming Together.* Cambridge, MA: Harvard University Press.

Mu, K., Siegel, E.B. & Allinder, R.M. (2000). Peer interactions and sociometric status of high school students with moderate to severe disabilities in general education classrooms. *Journal of the Association for Persons with Severe Handicaps*, **25**, 142–152.

Odom, S.L. (2000). Preschool inclusion: what we know and where we go from here. *Topics in Early Childhood Special Education*, **20**, 20–27.

Pennington, D.C., Gillen, K. & Hill, P. (1999). *Social Psychology.* London: Arnold.

Ryndak, D.L. & Alper, S. (in press). *Curriculum Content for Students with Moderate or Severe Disabilities in Inclusive Settings* (2nd edn). Boston, MA: Allyn & Bacon.

Schnorr, R.F. (1997). From enrollment to membership: "belonging" in middle and high school classes. *Journal of the Association for Persons with Severe Handicaps*, **22**, 1–15.

Schwartz, I.S. & Baer, D.M. (1991). Social validity assessments: is current practice state of the art? *Journal of Applied Behavior Analysis*, **24**, 189–204.

Shukla, S., Kennedy, C.H. & Cushing, L.S. (1999). Supporting intermediate school students with severe disabilities in general education classrooms: a comparison of two approaches. *Journal of Positive Behavior Interventions*, **1**, 130–140.

Sidman, M. (1960). *Tactics of Scientific Research: Evaluating Experimental Data in Psychology.* New York: Free Press.

Snell, M.E. & Brown, F. (2000). *Instruction of Students with Severe Disabilities* (5th edn). New York: Merrill.

Staub, D., Peck, C.A., Gallucci, C. & Schwartz, I. (2000). Peer relationships. In M.E. Snell & F. Brown (Eds) *Instruction of Students with Severe Disabilities* (5th edn) (pp. 381–408). New York: Merrill.

Staub, D., Spaulding, M., Peck, C.A. & Gallucci, C. (1996). Using nondisabled peers to support the inclusion of students with disabilities at the junior high school level. *Journal of the Association for Persons with Severe Handicaps*, **21**, 194–205.

Storey, K. (1993). A proposal for assessing integration. *Education and Training of the Mentally Retarded*, **28**, 279–287.

Werner, K., Horner, R.H. & Newton, J.S. (1997). Reducing structural barriers to improve the social life of three adults with severe disabilities. *Journal of the Association for Persons with Severe Handicaps*, **22**, 138–150.

Werts, M.G., Wolery, M., Snyder, E.D. & Caldwell, N.K. (1996). Supports and resources associated with inclusive schooling: perceptions of elementary school teachers about need and availability. *Journal of Special Education*, **30**, 187–203.

Wineman, N.M. (1990). Adaptation to multiple sclerosis: the role of social support, functional disability, and perceived uncertainty. *Nursing Research*, **39**, 294–299.

Wolf, M.M. (1978). Social validity: the case for subjective measurement or how applied behavior analysis is finding its heart. *Journal of Applied Behavior Analysis*, **11**, 203–214.

Wolfberg, P.J., Zercher, C., Lieber, J., Capell, K., Matias, S., Hanson, H., et al. (1999). "Can I play with you?" Peer culture in inclusive preschool programs. *Journal of the Association for Persons with Severe Handicaps*, **24**, 69–84.

CHAPTER 15

Sexuality Research and Persons with Intellectual Disabilities

Dorothy M. Griffiths
Brock University, Canada
Shelley L. Watson
University of Alberta, Canada
Tanya Lewis
Brock University, Canada
and
Karen Stoner
Brock University, Canada

Historically, the sexuality of persons with developmental disabilities has been ignored, repressed, and punished. At the beginning of the last century, the eugenics movement was responsible for segregating, institutionalising, and sterilising persons with intellectual disabilities because of fear of procreation. The eugenics movement created erroneous impressions of people with intellectual disabilities as sexually dangerous to the future of society. It was a movement founded on flawed research (that is, Goddard's research on the Kallikak dynasty) (Scheerenburger, 1983). Today, attitudes and understanding of the sexuality of people with intellectual disability have evolved. There is an ever-emerging acceptance of the sexuality of persons with intellectual disabilities and an awareness of healthy sexuality as part of mental wellness (Griffiths, Richards, Fedoroff & Watson, 2002). However, empirical research in this area has been slow in emerging.

In the remainder of this chapter, the authors will explore four topics of sexuality and the challenges in design and measurement faced when exploring this sensitive area of research. The four topics are sexual attitudes of and towards people with intellectual disabilities, sexuality education, sexual abuse and prevention, and sexual offence. The chapter will conclude with a discussion of ethical considerations for research in this area.

The International Handbook of Applied Research in Intellectual Disabilities. Edited by E. Emerson, C. Hatton, T. Thompson and T.R. Parmenter © 2004 John Wiley & Sons, Ltd. ISBN 0-471-49709-6.

SEXUAL ATTITUDES OF/TOWARDS PEOPLE WITH INTELLECTUAL DISABILITIES

There is considerable literature on attitudes towards the sexuality of persons with intellectual disabilities (Jurkowski & Amado, 1993; Pendler, 1993; Wendell, 1996; Griffiths, 1999), but surprisingly little *empirical* research, other than survey data. The existing studies focus on the attitudes of the following:

- parents towards sexuality (Hall, Morris & Barker, 1973; Fischer & Krajicek, 1974)
- staff in community settings (Adams, Tallon & Alcorn, 1982; Brantlinger, 1983; Hingsburger, 1993; Murray & Minnes, 1994; Szollos & McCabe, 1995)
- staff in institutional settings (Mitchell, Doctor & Butler, 1978; Coleman & Murphy, 1980; Adams et al., 1982; Brantlinger, 1983)
- individuals or staff of institutions compared with staff in community settings (Hall et al., 1973; Hall & Morris, 1976; Edmonson, McCombs & Wish, 1979; Brantlinger, 1983)
- staff compared to college or university students (Adams et al., 1982; Szollos & McCabe, 1995; McCabe & Cummins, 1996; McCabe, 1999)
- staff and professionals from past to present (Hingsburger, 1993; Griffiths & Lunsky, 2000)
- staff over time and in correlation to age, gender, religious affiliation, status, and type of facility (Heshusius, 1982; Trudel & Desjardins, 1992)
- parents and their children (Hall et al., 1973; Fischer & Krajicek, 1974)
- individuals who have intellectual disabilities (Hall & Morris, 1976; Edmonson et al., 1979; Timmers, Ducharme & Jacob, 1981; Heshusius, 1982; McCabe & Schreck, 1992; McCarthy, 1993; Thompson, 1994; Szollos & McCabe, 1995; Konstantareas & Lunsky, 1997).

Research on the attitudes of persons with intellectual disabilities has been gaining increased momentum in recent years. The research on "consumers" represents some of the more sophisticated research in the sexual-attitudes literature and has produced the most informative findings (i.e., McCarthy, 1993; Thompson, 1994). The composite research literature demonstrates increasingly positive staff and parental attitudes, in contrast to the more negative attitudes towards sexuality expressed by persons with intellectual disabilities.

Design and Measurement

There are two main research approaches that have been used: questionnaires and interviews.

Questionnaires

Survey research (questionnaires) is the predominant method of attitude data collection for this topic (i.e., Hall et al., 1973; Fischer & Krajicek, 1974; Hall & Morris, 1976; Mitchell et al., 1978; Coleman & Murphy, 1980; Timmers et al., 1981; Adams et al., 1982; Brantlinger, 1983; Hingsburger, 1993; Murray & Minnes, 1994; Griffiths & Lunsky, 2000).

The questionnaire research has primarily addressed limited areas of investigation, such as masturbation, heterosexual activity, and homosexual activity (Mitchell et al., 1978; Coleman & Murphy, 1980; Adams et al., 1982; Hingsburger, 1993; Murray & Minnes, 1994). The issue of permission for sexual activity was rarely included (McCarthy, 1993; Thompson, 1994).

"With the relationship between attitudes and behaviours being well documented, the development of reliable and valid attitude scales is important to the further investigation of this relationship, and as a basis for planning sexuality and human relationship education programmes" (Patton & Mannison, 1995, p. 269). However, for the most part, sexuality-attitude questionnaires regarding persons with intellectual disabilities have not been subject to the standard of reliability and validity. One exception is Brantlinger's (1983) Sexuality and Mental Retardation Attitude Inventory. This inventory is a 40-item Likert-type rating scale in which individuals respond according to their degree of agreement with the item. The inventory includes five subscales, namely, general attitudes towards sex, sexuality education, sexual rights of the retarded, rights of minors, and stereotyping of sexuality of retarded persons. The scale was field-tested with 232 parents and staff from a variety of locations. High degrees of internal consistency and test–retest reliability on this instrument were reported (Brantlinger, 1992).

Interviews

Interviews were also used by some researchers to gather attitude data and sexual experience information directly from persons with intellectual disabilities. McCabe, Cummins and Reid (1994) compared the level of sexual knowledge and experience of sexual abuse between individuals with intellectual disabilities and a nondisabled comparison group. McCarthy (1993) conducted semistructured interviews with men and women with intellectual disabilities living in institutional settings about their sexual experiences in the context of an AIDS awareness educational programme. Thompson (1994) talked to men with intellectual disabilities about their experiences of sex with men in public places; the men had been referred to a sexuality-education team to address their sexually abusive behaviour. Owen, Griffiths, Sales, Feldman and Richards (2000) interviewed individuals with intellectual disabilities living in residential services and their staff regarding their attitudes towards personal boundaries within the caregiving relationship.

In qualitative research, interviews are a major strategy for data collection, or are employed in conjunction with participant observation, document analysis, or other techniques (Bogdan & Biklen, 1992). The attitude studies on the topic of sexuality were rarely triangulated with other methods, such as participant observations, consumer reports, archival data, or interviews. For example, Adams et al. (1982) determined staff opinion on public and private sexual activity but did not distinguish its relationship to actual practice. Additional qualitative research methods could validate whether the sexual attitudes demonstrated through interviews or questionnaires had social validity in practice. Evidence of positive attitudes towards the sexuality of persons with intellectual disabilities (Coleman & Murphy, 1980; Adams et al., 1982; Brantlinger, 1983; Hingsburger, 1993; Murray & Minnes, 1994) does not predict whether the attitudes influence interactions in the natural environment. For example, Brantlinger (1983) found that, although the sexuality of persons with intellectual disabilities was considered acceptable to staff, it was rarely encouraged.

Several researchers have raised fundamental questions regarding the environmental and cultural influence on the sexuality of persons with intellectual disabilities (i.e., McCarthy, 1993; Thompson, 1994; Thompson, Clare & Brown, 1997; Owen et al., 2000). For example, Thompson (1994) reported that men with disabilities exchanged sex for small moments of social acceptance, McCarthy (1993) observed that women are unable to exercise choice over sex, and Owen et al. (2000) and Thompson et al. (1997) found blurred boundaries in staff–consumer roles and attitudes towards appropriate sexuality. While the objective of attitude research is largely practical, the questions underlying this type of research often fail to address the systemic issues through which people with intellectual disabilities are profoundly devalued.

In general, attitude research has several limitations. Very few studies clearly define the nature of the disability or evaluate sexuality among different disability groupings. Konstantareas and Lunsky (1997) and Lunsky and Konstantareas (1998) are a notable exception. They compared the attitudes of persons with intellectual disability to persons labelled with autistic disorder. Many of the attitude studies are limited in sample size (16–25) (i.e., Fischer & Krajicek, 1974; Timmers et al., 1981; Szollos & McCabe, 1995), by geographical area (i.e., Konstantareas & Lunsky, 1997; Lunsky & Konstantareas, 1998), or by non-representative samples (i.e., Hall et al., 1973; Hall & Morris, 1976; Timmers et al., 1981).

Very few studies examined cross-cultural differences in attitude. Different countries have their cultural research. A partial list includes Australia (McCabe & Schreck, 1992; Szollos & McCabe, 1995; McCabe & Cummins, 1996), Canada (Trudel & Desjardins, 1992; Murray & Minnes, 1994; Konstantareas & Lunsky, 1997; Lunsky & Konstantareas, 1998), the UK (McCarthy, 1993; Thompson, 1994), and the USA (Hall et al., 1973; Fischer & Krajicek, 1974; Hall & Morris, 1976; Mitchell et al., 1978; Edmonson et al., 1979; Timmers et al., 1981; Adams et al., 1982; Heshusius, 1982; Brantlinger, 1983). Hingsburger (1993) is one of the few researchers to evaluate data from different countries. He compared attitude questionnaires from Canada (Ontario) and the USA (Louisiana and Texas) and found that there was great similarity in the two populations (Canada and the USA), although there was no statistical analysis presented.

Summary of Sexuality Attitude Research

Research in the area of sexual attitudes and intellectual disability, notably parental and societal attitude research, is growing but limited. The research is largely narrow in focus and lacking rich qualitative analysis to demonstrate the social validity of the results, although more recent qualitative studies (i.e., McCarthy, 1993; Thompson, 1994; Thompson et al., 1997; Owen et al., 2000) provide much promise and have valued the contribution from "consumer" interviews.

Future directions in research need to explore the contextual nature of attitudes. For example, although the sexuality attitudes of caregivers are reportedly more liberal, the attitudes of individuals with intellectual disabilities continue to be more negative and disempowered (i.e., McCarthy, 1993; Thompson, 1994). The practice in the field often reflects a more conservative and often suppressive approach to sexual issues. The gaps in attitude and practice can provide a context for realistically researching the experiences of persons with intellectual challenges.

SEXUALITY EDUCATION

The field has been inundated with sexuality-education programmes for persons with intellectual disabilities. However, sexuality-education programmes have generally been unevaluated (Whitehouse & McCabe, 1997). Coleman and Murphy (1980) reported that one-third of the institutions surveyed lacked evaluation of their sexuality-education programmes. The remaining two-thirds evaluated their programmes by a variety of measures, including surveys of staff reactions, pre-post questionnaires, or behavioural measures of the residents. However, 79% of the evaluation results were unavailable, rendering the reliability of the evaluation methods questionable.

In teaching sexuality education, it is important to assess the participant's skills before instruction to determine where to begin with sociosexual training (Edmonson et al., 1979). Testing should also occur during and after the intervention as a means of evaluating progress (Lumley & Miltenberger, 1997). Minimally, Griffiths (1999) advocates the use of a pre- and post-evaluation of sexual knowledge and attitudes.

Although considerable clinical evidence exists, there is little empirical support to demonstrate that persons with intellectual disabilities benefit from sexuality-education programmes (Lindsay, Bellshaw, Culross, Staines & Michie, 1992; Whitehouse & McCabe, 1997). For example, Whitehouse and McCabe (1997) noted that, although studies such as that of Hamre-Nietupski and Ford (1981) claim to evaluate efficacy, they failed to produce data to support their claim.

Design and Measurement Issues

Measurements

The Socio-Sexual Knowledge and Attitudes Test (SSKAT) (Wish, McCombs & Edmonson, 1980) and the Sexual Knowledge, Experience, Feelings, and Needs Scale (SexKen-ID) (McCabe, 1994) are two of the evaluative tools that measure change in both knowledge and attitude. These measures provide an individually administered evaluation using a picture book, to which participants answer minimally verbally demanding questions. Less complicated questionnaires than the SSKAT and the SexKen-ID exist (i.e., Timmers et al., 1981). However, psychometric evaluation of the simpler measures is lacking (McCabe, Cummins & Deeks, 1999).

The most comprehensive sociosexual assessment was the SSKAT. However, it has been criticised because it is time-consuming, requires a high level of skill to administer, is overly complicated in parts but not exhaustive in others, contains many value-laden items, and does not discuss the sexual experiences of the individual (Edmonson et al., 1979; McCabe et al., 1999).

The SSKAT was revised and renamed as the Socio-Sexual Knowledge and Attitude Assessment Tool (SSKAAT-R) (Griffiths & Lunsky, 2003). The SSKAAT-R was field-tested in Canada and the USA with 276 adolescents and adults with intellectual disabilities. The sample included individuals from diverse settings: institutions, group homes, semi-independent living situations, and family homes. The SSKAAT-R produced high internal consistency (0.81–0.92 using a Cronback alpha), high test–retest reliability (0.78–0.96), and high internal reliability (0.89–0.96). The new measure demonstrated reasonable validity

Table 15.1 Design and outcome measures of sexuality-education research

Reference	Participants	Design/assessment	Findings	Limitations	Comments
Bennett, Vockell & Vockell (1972)	10 young F; only 7 at post-test. IQs ranged from 58 to 81	Pre/post Sex Information Inventory for Girls	Increased knowledge depends on pre-test knowledge. More permissive attitudes expressed after instruction	Quantitative data not reported No control group	Women who had some basic knowledge learned more than those with no prior knowledge
Foxx, McMorrow, Storey & Rogers (1984)	6 F with moderate to mild IQ deficiency	Multiple baseline design across groups. Social/sexual skills game used for assessment of skills. Generalisation test designed	Appropriate social responses to sexually related situations increased during training	Small sample size Only females No control group	
Penny & Chataway (1982)	21 F and 28 M with mild and moderate ID	Pre/post measure using sexual vocabulary test (SVT), constructed by researchers; 6 teaching sessions	Increase in vocabulary at post-test and further at further post-test No change in attitude	No control group or generalisation reported	No validity or reliability of SVT Discuss "experimenter effect"
Robinson (1984)	83 adults with ID aged $16^{1}/_{2}$ to 52 years. IQs ranged from 50 to 80	Control group Pre/post SSKAT	Quantitative analysis of knowledge post-test is positive	Attitudes reported as changed, but no data to support this	No gender analysis
Shapiro & Sheridan (1985)	1 female with mild ID, 30 years old	Assessment designed by researchers Training—multiple probe design across skill areas	Knowledge generalised and maintained over 3 weeks	Limited information about client's history Single-case design Limited follow-up time	Instruction on breast assessment, pap tests, pelvic examinations
Lindsay, Bellshaw, Culross, Staines & Michie (1992)	Mild or moderate ID Training group ($n = 46$) Control group ($n = 14$)	Pre/post-follow-up questionnaire (body parts, masturbation, intercourse, STD, pregnancy, and contraception)	On all measures, group receiving education programme improved their knowledge significantly and maintained to a 3-month follow-up	Generalisation to daily life not addressed	No discussion of attitude change

Lawrence & Swain (1993)	12 M and 5 F, aged 19–22. No evaluation of IQ or language skills	Semistructured interview—students interviewed before and after training. Analysis of transcripts of sex education sessions	Open communication seems to be vital in evaluating the effectiveness of sex education	Unclear whether students increased sexual knowledge or developed more positive feelings towards sexuality	Reliability of transcript analysis as a method of evaluation not established No pre/test or control group
Scotti, Speaks, Masia, Boggess & Drabman (1996)	31 persons with severe to mild ID at a sheltered workshop (61% F)	One group pre/post-test design AIDS Risk Knowledge Test and Sexuality Survey	Participants with mild ID improved significantly pre to post, whereas scores for those with moderate disability remained unchanged	Persons with severe disability excluded from the research No control group	5-week AIDS-risk information training (18–20 years old)
Scotti et al. (1997)	13 persons (7 F and 6 M) with mild ID	Pre, post, and follow-up using Modified AIDS Risk Knowledge Test (MARKT), sexual history questionnaire, role-play, sexual knowledge test	Increase of knowledge at post-test and follow-up. Statistically significant improvement in performance on all role-plays	Need for revision of several test items and further reliability and validity analyses of measure Small sample size No control group	
Bambury, Wilton & Boyd (1999)	18 adults (15 M and 3 F) aged 17–46 years. Mild ID (50–70 IQ)	Pre/post SSKAT Slide and video-based sex education and attitude programme compared to control group	Those who received slide or video increased significantly in knowledge compared to control group Attitude change was not significant	Gender imbalance No follow-up or generalisation	

ID = intellectual disability; M = male; F = female.

when examined against the SSKAT and the Sex-Ken ID and as a pre/post measure for sex education.

The SexKen-ID is a comprehensive evaluation of the sexual knowledge, experience, feelings, and needs of people with intellectual disabilities and provides a much more updated version for assessment. The method of test construction adds to the validity of the items included in the measure. McCabe et al. (1999) report high levels of internal consistency for the subscales of the SexKen-ID, with the exception of the needs and feeling subscales and reliable test–retest results. This assessment differs from the SSKAT and SSKAAT-R because it also requests information about experiences. Whitehouse and McCabe (1997) state that future programmes need to consider the use of checklists and transcript analysis to cover the more accurate but more limited assessment of sexual facts as well as the more complex analysis of feelings and attitudes. However, for the purpose of evaluating educational knowledge and attitudes, clinical information regarding experiences may not be appropriate.

Design

Sexuality-education research has several methodological flaws, including a lack of adequate measures, a lack of control comparisons, and limited follow-up evaluation of maintenance or generalisation (Whitehouse & McCabe, 1997). Of the research that has reported evaluation data, none reported the effectiveness of sexuality education in relation to increasing sexual knowledge and enhancing positive attitudes towards sexuality (Whitehouse & McCabe, 1997).

As shown in Table 15.1, few data-based studies exist. In the limited sample found, most studies employed an AB (pre–post) design (Bennett, Vockell & Vockell, 1972; Penny & Chataway, 1982; Robinson, 1984; Scotti, Speaks, Masia, Boggess & Drabman, 1996; Katz, 1998). Most studies lacked concrete descriptions of participants or the nature of their intellectual challenge other than IQ. Few studies employed control groups, conducted follow-up for maintenance, or assessed generalisation. When assessment of generalisation was done, it was often informal and anecdotal, or based on simulations (i.e., Katz, 1998; Foxx, McMorrow, Storey & Rogers, 1984, respectively).

Generalisation is one of the most important issues specific to sexuality education research. To be effective, a therapeutic change must occur over time, persons, and settings. Moreover, the effects of the change should spread to a variety of related behaviours (Stokes & Baer, 1977). Edmonson and Wish (1975) found that a test of anatomy terminology is not equivalent to inferential comprehension of sexual activity. It is more important to measure the skills the individual actually employs in a target situation (Lumley & Miltenberger, 1997). Pitceathly and Chapman (1985) cautioned that, although research may demonstrate that people with intellectual disability can learn positive attitudes and appropriate sociosexual knowledge, this does not predict the implementation of these skills on a routine basis. Outcome should be measured by an increase in actual behaviours and skills rather than merely an increase in knowledge (Lumley & Miltenberger, 1997).

Sexuality education also involves learning the social skills to form relationships with others. However, general social skills research for persons with intellectual disabilities has been fraught with challenges in generalisation (Griffiths, 1995). Many of the programmes teaching social skills focus on training about discrete social skills (that is, eye contact and social distance). An example of this is the CATCH programme (Sheppard, Pollock & Rayment, 1983). Jupp and Looser (1988) cautioned that, although skills may increase during training, programming may not generalise outside the training environment. This was noted by Valenti-Hein, Yarnold and Mueser (1994). They found that, although sociosexual skills were successfully taught during training, when the participants were faced with situations outside training, anxiety mediated their responses. The learned skills did not transfer to real-life situations. Similarly, Foxx and his associates demonstrated that sociosexual skills learned in training generalised to *simulated* role-play situations (Foxx et al., 1984), but not to the natural environment (Foxx, McMorrow, Bittle & Ness, 1986a). Foxx and his associates chose simulated generalisation probes because of the issues of privacy regarding sociosexual issues. However, there is little empirical evidence that generalisation to the natural environment will occur unless there are sufficient generalisation strategies built into the programme (i.e., Griffiths, Feldman & Tough, 1997).

A final research area involves training of sexuality educators. Our literature search failed to discover studies that evaluated the training or competency of sexuality teachers. However, there is evidence that special education teachers do not feel they are sufficiently trained to teach sexuality education (Brantlinger, 1992; Foley, 1995; May & Kundert, 1996). Foley and Kittleson (1993) and Evans, Melville and Cass (1992) found that special educators reported that they lacked competencies in many areas, such as topics associated with HIV/AIDS.

Summary of Sexuality Education Research

People with intellectual disabilities are being taught, and therefore are *assumed* to have acquired knowledge and skills about sexuality. However, there is little empirical evidence that persons with intellectual disabilities acquire training knowledge or that the knowledge or skills are maintained and generalised to their daily lives. There are few data regarding which participants will benefit most from a general sexuality-education course (Lindsay et al., 1992), or whether different methods of instruction are more effective with different participants. Without empirical evidence of pre- and post-training evaluation, control-group comparison, and generalisation data, the assumption that knowledge has been acquired may be both erroneous and dangerous. Future research would benefit from empirical validation of sexuality education, assessing improved knowledge, skill generalisation and maintenance, and the social validity of the training. The context of training and consistency with the experiences of persons with intellectual disabilities is an area of further research. Additionally, sexuality-education programmes may need to be assessed and adapted to the differential learning needs of the heterogeneous group of persons labelled as intellectually disabled.

SEXUAL ABUSE AND ABUSE PREVENTION

Sobsey and Doe (1991) conservatively estimate that sexual abuse of persons with intellectual disabilities occurs at $1\frac{1}{2}$ times the rate for the general population. Although more girls than boys experience higher rates of abuse (62% to 38%), boys with intellectual disabilities experience higher rates of abuse than boys with no known disability (Sobsey, Randall & Parrila, 1997). Depending on the definition and methodology used, the statistics vary greatly across studies.

Design and Measurement Issues

Research on sexual abuse is fraught with difficulty. Abuse presents challenges of repressed memory (Herman, 1992), denial, shame, fear, and dependency (Bass & Davis, 1988). In addition, people with intellectual disabilities exhibit communication difficulties and lack of sexual knowledge.

There are several methodological approaches to research on sexual abuse within the lives of people with intellectual disabilities. First, researchers have reviewed existing literature to enhance public education and to describe potential interventions (Tharinger, Horton & Millea, 1990; Baladerian, 1991; Muccigrosso, 1991).

Second, researchers have examined reports of abuse of people with intellectual disabilities. For example, Sobsey and Doe (1991) requested reports from sexual assault centres and disability advocacy groups, asking people with intellectual disabilities and their advocates to fill out a report. Sobsey et al. (1997) examined substantiated cases of child maltreatment. However, data from public reports of abuse do not reflect the experiences of individuals whose sexual abuse goes undetected, nor the impact of the abuse from the perspective of the survivor, nor the context within which the abuse takes place.

Third, researchers have interviewed people about their experiences or perceptions (i.e., McCarthy, 1993; Thompson, 1994). Although they offer valuable descriptive data, the interviews do not provide insight into the underlying experiences and teachings that give rise to the current attitudes expressed by individuals with intellectual disabilities within this research. Without this information, researchers attempt to connect the data to their knowledge of the isolating and devaluing circumstances in which people with intellectual disabilities live. A major challenge in this area of research is to overcome the communication barriers (some of which may be related to the dependence of individuals on caregivers) in order to understand the experience of sexual abuse from the perspective of people with intellectual disabilities.

Fourth, researchers have made deductions based on the correlation between experiences of abuse and other relevant life experiences. For example, Hard (cited in Senn, 1988) examined the correlation between rates of abuse and sexuality education and found a high correlation between experiences of abuse and lack of sexuality education. However, these data must be interpreted with caution because correlation may not necessarily demonstrate causality.

Sexual Abuse Prevention Training

Sexual abuse prevention programmes have been designed to address abuse risk factors associated with a lack of sexual knowledge, learned compliance, and communication difficulties (Haseltine & Miltenberger, 1990; Collins, Schuster & Nelson, 1992; Lumley, Miltenberger, Long, Rapp & Roberts, 1998). Recent directions include increasing access to effective sexuality education as a first step in preventing sexual abuse. Sexual abuse prevention programmes (Walker-Hirsch & Champagne, 1986; Kempton, 1987; O'Day, 1988) are some of the most popular and widespread resources; however, the programmes generally fail to report evaluation data. In fact, although conceptually sound, there is little empirical evidence to show that sexuality education does decrease the vulnerability of people with disabilities to sexual abuse (Whitehouse & McCabe, 1997).

One of the major challenges in evaluating sexual abuse prevention research is determining the validity of the training. Generalisation and social validity of sexual abuse training have been applied on what Stokes and Baer (1977) call a train-and-hope approach; typically, programme developers and researchers have assessed knowledge change, but not whether there is transfer of skills to the natural environment. Generalisation of training has presented a challenge in the social skills training of persons with intellectual disabilities (Griffiths, 1995). However, in situ probes in the natural environment have demonstrated generalisation in social skills training when sufficient generalisation strategies have been employed at all stages of training (i.e., Griffiths et al., 1995). Using similar in situ probes following an abuse prevention programme, Lumley et al. (1998) demonstrated generalisation to the natural environment. However, the use of in situ probes for high-risk behaviours has been considered ill-advised by some abuse researchers (i.e., Sobsey, 1994). As a result, other researchers have employed potentially less reliable probes, using simulated situations (i.e., Griffiths et al., 1996).

Generalisation poses two critical and competing ethical challenges. First, does training provide a false sense of security that allows caregivers to reduce supervision and unknowingly leave a person at risk if acquisition and generalisation of skills have not been established? Second, does effective assessment of generalisation (that is, potentially invasive, albeit contrived, assessment strategies such as "in situ" evaluation, as evidenced in Lumley et al., 1998) pose a greater risk to the individual than the train-and-hope approach of most researchers in this area?

Summary of Abuse Research

The research in the area of sexual abuse and intellectual disability has a twofold focus: (a) addressing the particular risk factors that people with intellectual disabilities face, and (b) teaching strategies that may address their particular vulnerabilities (Sobsey, 1994). The use of qualitative approaches to research that portray the survivor's experiences and the subtle contextual dynamics within which the sexual abuse occurred may redress this balance. Communication barriers create a significant difficulty in developing this work. Additionally, safe and confidential environments need to be established that allow the stories of survivors to emerge. Research critics have suggested that disability researchers need to ensure that the perspectives and contributions of consumer groups and advocates are included in the research (Ward & Flynn, 1994).

Sobsey (1994) noted that there was an increased surge in research on violence and abuse in the lives of persons with developmental disabilities. However, there are two major areas of future research. First, the conditions that increase risk and those that improve safety have not yet been fully explored, including how to identify and screen for offenders (Sobsey, 1994). Second, validated prevention and intervention programmes are also required (Sobsey, 1994), with special consideration of options for evaluating generalisation.

SEXUAL OFFENCE

Among charged sexual offenders, 15–33% are intellectually challenged (Steiner, 1984; Shapiro, 1986). There is a great disparity in the prevalence of sexual offending behaviour in persons with intellectual disabilities. The disparity appears to depend on how the data were gathered. Most of the data are based on prison data or arrest/conviction rates. This over-representation may not necessarily provide evidence of higher rates of sexual offence among this population, but, rather, higher rates of arrest, confession, and conviction (Brown & Courtless, 1971; Santamour & West, 1978; Murphy, Coleman & Haynes, 1983a; McGee & Menolascino, 1992). Day (1994) cautioned that the current offence data do not include situations where persons with intellectual disabilities were not charged or incarcerated for their offence but diverted to residential care facilities.

Prior to the 1980s, few programmes offered specialised treatment for persons with intellectual disabilities who demonstrated sexually challenging behaviour (Coleman & Murphy, 1980). The treatment that was then available was largely behavioural suppression (Foxx, Bittle, Bechtel & Livesay, 1986b). In the past two decades, an increasingly rich body of clinical intervention literature has emerged (i.e., Murphy et al., 1983a; Griffiths, Quinsey & Hingsburger, 1989; Haaven, Little & Petre-Miller, 1990; Lund, 1992; Ward et al., 1992). More recently, the treatment focus has shifted from behavioural suppression to include promotion of adaptive "alternative" coping and sociosexual behaviours (i.e., Griffiths et al., 1989; Haaven et al., 1990; Ward et al., 1992; Nezu, Nezu & Dudeck, 1998). Specialised treatment providers have reported (often anecdotally) that sex offenders with intellectual disabilities, particularly those individuals who have mild and moderate disabilities, have been surprisingly responsive to treatment (Lackey & Knopp, 1989). However, to date, there is minimal empirical demonstration of treatment effectiveness.

Research Design and Measurement

Most of what is known about the presentation of sexual offence symptoms in the population of persons with intellectual disabilities is based on reviews of clinical records (i.e., Day, 1994; 1997) and extrapolation from research conducted on non-disabled offenders (i.e., Murphy, Coleman & Abel, 1983b). The research on non-disabled offenders has generally been conducted with great scientific rigour. Extrapolation to this population is in most cases logical. However, differences in the experience of persons with intellectual disability give rise to some caution. For example, an important challenge for mental health professionals charged with the assessment and treatment of people with intellectual delay is the accurate assessment of risk of violent or sexual offences. Typical interviewing and testing procedures (such as phallometric testing) require adaptation and caution when used with this population (Murphy et al., 1983b). The research on differential evaluation procedures is largely unavailable for this population. Moreover, direct application of some testing procedures to this population may pose potential challenges. For example, one of the best-researched risk assessments for non-disabled sex offenders is the Sex Offender Risk Appraisal Guide (SORAG) (Quinsey, Harris, Rice & Cormier, 1998). This assessment is based on actuarial data that provide a base on which to predict recidivism. However, persons with intellectual disabilities may score uniformly higher or lower on various measures of the score by virtue of the experiences afforded them in life because of the disability label. In a matched group of offenders (non-disabled and developmentally disabled), Fedoroff, Smolewska, Selhi, Ng and Bradford (2001) found that although both groups of offenders had equal numbers of victims, people with developmental disabilities scored significantly higher on the SORAG and produced significant differences on three items (lived with both biological parents to age 16, marital status, and number of previous offence convictions).

Design

Many of the treatment studies that are reported in the literature are simple, single-case studies, often lacking the rigour of accepted single-subject experimental design. For an analysis of the research prior to 1986, readers are referred to Foxx et al. (1986b). Many studies were remiss in providing pre-treatment measures or generalisation probes. Most single-case studies employed a pre-post (AB) design (i.e., Rivenq, 1974; Luiselli, Helfen, Pemberton & Reisman, 1977; Shaw & Walker, 1979), although several single-case studies conducted during the 1970s and 1980s used more complex behavioural design strategies. Lutzker (1974) presents one of the few studies that employed an ABCD (baseline, intervention 1, intervention 2, intervention 1) design, to allow for comparison between procedures. Although these treatment conditions showed treatment effects, when multiple-baseline designs across settings were employed, there was little stimulus generalisation to non-treatment settings (Polvinale & Lutzker, 1980; Barmann & Murray, 1982). Generalisation may require explicit training to produce independence of the response and setting (Foxx et al., 1986b).

Since the early 1980s, the literature on persons with intellectual disabilities who demonstrate sexually inappropriate behaviour has been expanding rapidly. However, for the most part, the literature represents programmatic descriptions or outcome data rather than empirical treatment-evaluation data. For example, Nolley, Muccigrosso and Zigman (1996) and Swanson and Garwick (1990) reported post-treatment gain in skills and positive behaviours as indication of success. Other studies have provided post-treatment programme-evaluation data as evidence of treatment effectiveness (i.e., Haaven et al., 1990; Lund, 1992; Day, 1994), without benefit of pre-treatment comparison data. The challenge for research clinicians appears to rest in determining reliable baseline measures of relevant behavioural indicators in a field where the key variable being assessed is recidivism. This challenge is explored more in the following discussion on measures.

Measures

In recent years, a major paradigm shift in research has occurred in the treatments employed for sexual offences for those with intellectual disabilities. Initial treatments often attempted to suppress inappropriate behaviour through punishment. For example, in early studies, researchers employed overcorrection (Luiselli et al., 1977; Polvinale & Lutzker, 1980), an aversive contingency plan (slaps, ignore, or contingent squirts of lemon juice) (Cook, Altman, Shaw & Blaylock, 1978), and facial screening (Barmann & Murray, 1982) to treat masturbation. Although their methods were empirically validated, these procedures, by today's standards, would be considered highly intrusive, and not representative of current clinical practice.

State-of-the-art intervention for sexual offences involves multicomponent treatment and evaluation (Griffiths, 2002), although there are few studies that have evaluated multicomponent treatment. Some exceptions are Lund (1992) and Nolley et al. (1996). Lund (1992) described an evaluation of 16 males described as having serious sexual behaviour problems. The participants received individual counselling, sociosexual training, and personal behavioural programmes for sexual issues within a home programme atmosphere. Each participant received an individual programme plan of treatment. Lund (1992) was able to demonstrate positive changes with a multimodal teaching approach. Although his intervention was not designed as research, he reports treatment outcome. Treatment outcome was based on a number of dimensions, including discharge to the community or less restrictive setting, reduction in restrictive procedures, and a change in targeted maladaptive behaviours. He reports both generalisation and maintenance for a mean length of 2.1 years for six of the discharged individuals. Because the components of treatment were presented simultaneously, there can be no causality demonstrated between specific aspects of the intervention plan and enhanced functioning. Additionally, specific skill development, although targeted, was not measured.

Current programmes would benefit from evaluation of not just the reduction in the challenging behaviour, but also a concurrent demonstration of increased coping and skill development and an improvement in quality of life. Attention is drawn to the application of functional assessment to the treatment of the sexual offender population (i.e., Fredericks & Nishioka-Evans, 1999). They demonstrated that functional assessment was beneficial in training staff to identify the thinking errors and precursors of sexual offending behaviour and the setting events, antecedents, and functional sociosexual skill deficits.

Foxx et al. (1986a) reviewed the range of dependent measures to assess treatment effectiveness in offenders employed prior to 1986. They found that researchers relied on rates of institutional readmission (i.e., Dial, 1968), self-report (i.e., Rosenthal, 1973), anecdotal information (i.e., Kolvin, 1967), direct observation of precursor behaviours (i.e., Wong, Gaydos & Fuqua, 1982), frequency of occurrence (i.e., Polvinale & Lutzker, 1980), and response latency (i.e., Shaw & Walker, 1979). Much of the research, with few exceptions (i.e., Barmann & Murray, 1982), failed to demonstrate the reliability of the measures.

Based on the above measures, claims of effectiveness could be open to scrutiny (Foxx et al., 1986a). For example, the use of self-report as a sole dependent variable raises questions of reliability and intervening influences (for example, escape from the aversive condition if change is self-reported). Additionally, there may be cause to challenge the accuracy of monitoring readmission rates as a dependent measure. For example, Swanson and Garwick (1990) evaluated a group-therapy programme, using as measures of effectiveness (a) the attainment of personal goals, and (b) rearrest records. The use of personal goals was not described nor demonstrated to relate to recidivism. Moreover, although recidivism rates are often used as a dependent measure of treatment success (Haaven et al., 1990; Lund, 1992; Day, 1994), these data rely on reconviction or detection, which may differ from re-offence rates.

The use of direct observation across individuals and settings in the natural environment, such as by Polvinale and Lutzker (1980), appears to provide increased levels of confidence in the results. However, for low-frequency or more dangerous behaviours, researchers have tended to rely on analogue research that produces fewer degrees of confidence for validity and treatment generalisation. Foxx et al. (1986a) suggest that when analogue settings are used it is important to employ behavioural referents for change in the target behaviour. However, some offence behaviour is dependent on the presence of a triggering event. Depending on the nature of the triggering event, it may not be practically or ethically presentable in treatment (for example, a child of a certain age and sex). As a result, researchers cannot witness the actual event but must rely on precursor behaviours as both targets of intervention and dependent measures of change (i.e., Wong et al., 1982). This procedure has applicability, both clinically and empirically. Foxx et al. (1986a) have suggested that although the empirically based studies suggest effective ways of dealing with certain behaviours when conditions are circumscribed (such as behavioural observation in the natural setting), there is a need for greater emphasis on establishing valid measures.

The statistics on recidivism vary for programmes in locked residential or institutionally based populations (i.e., Haaven et al., 1990) and in the community (i.e., Nolley et al., 1996). Demetral (as cited in Nolley et al., 1996) reported a recidivism rate of less than 2% within a community programme; Haaven et al. (1990) indicated a rate of recidivism of 23% for their population of institutionalised offenders. In such comparative data, there is always the temptation to assume the difference in the two populations to be (a) a lack of rigour of follow-up observation in the community, or (b) unequally challenging populations. However, Nolley and associates (1996) suggest that treatment outcome in the community may be enhanced by the use of qualified facilitators, increased social opportunities for persons with intellectual disabilities, the enlistment of natural support systems, and teaching about culturally acceptable ways of sexual expression. Although no systematic study has been conducted to analyse the multiple components of a successful relapse-prevention programme, the limited data available appear to link to the same areas of generalisation found to be critical in all areas of sociosexual training.

There are two alternative approaches to evaluated treatment:

(1) Fredericks and Nishioka-Evans (1999) provide the framework for developing alternative dependent measures for treatment effectiveness, based on a triangulation of observation, self-report, and other reports. These dependent measures are definable target behaviours that are operationally defined in terms of triggering events (setting events, people, and schedules) and precursor behaviours. The application of solid, applied behaviour-analysis principles may provide the foundation for developing researchable objectives for behavioural change in this area of study.

(2) Page (1991) recommends a self-regulation approach to determining programme effectiveness. This includes training in skill development, including the ability to distinguish situations in which sexual behaviours are appropriate, and the self-evaluation of success in these areas. He reiterates that programming begins with a functional analysis of behaviour and baseline assessment.

Furthermore, in comparison to the traditional quantitative research, recent qualitative approaches have been emerging which shed light on the context of sexually offending behaviour. Thompson et al. (1997) explored with staff the boundaries of what is considered acceptable sexual behaviour and how breaches of this are responded to within services. This type of qualitative research study directs the focus from the individual to the interactions and systemic issues that influence the behaviours, and directly to intervention at a systems rather than individual level. This is an important and yet grossly neglected area of research. However, this type of systems or contextual research would benefit from quantitative methodology as well.

Summary of Sexual-Offence Research

In the past three decades, the field of intellectual disabilities has gained increased clinical understanding of sexually inappropriate behaviour. Early research tended to be more rigorous, but the applicability to current practice is limited. Recent research has been largely descriptive and anecdotal. The application of applied behavioural analysis procedures, such as functional assessment, may add greatly to the development of empirical research in this area. Systematic research is needed to determine the relative value of the components for successful relapse prevention.

In contrast to the quantitative research, recent qualitative research studies, such as that of Thompson et al. (1997), provide considerable promise for expanding the knowledge base and identifying the unique qualities of the experience of persons with intellectual disabilities who sexually offend.

Ethical Considerations

Sexuality as a research topic is fraught with research ethical challenges. These challenges become more exaggerated when exploring the sexuality of persons who have intellectual disabilities. In the section that follows, the six key ethical issues (consent, privacy, abuse and re-traumatisation, legal implications, programme evaluation, and contextual relevance) will be briefly explored.

Consent

When studying persons with intellectual disability, communication and comprehension limitations make it more difficult and yet vitally important to ensure that the individual understands what is being asked and why. The devaluing of people with disabilities and their dependence has led to a history of compliance with those in authority or in care-taking roles. Capacity to give consent in the legal sense may also be unclear. When it comes to research in such a personal area of human experience, ensuring informed consent becomes critically important and for the above reasons difficult to achieve. Dinerstein (1999) has suggested that "Those seeking to obtain the consent of the person with mental retardation must seek out ways to enhance the person's knowledge, and they must take extra care to communicate effectively. Those seeking consent must not confuse the person's informational poverty with his or her decisional capacity" (p. 3). When learning and communication are so difficult, best practice needs to be the standard. For additional information on this topic, see Herr, O'Sullivan and Dinerstein (1999).

Privacy

Thompson (1994) suggests that people with intellectual disabilities have come to expect their lives to be matters of public discussion. For example, Thompson et al. (1997) gathered information from staff on the role of women support staff in relation to men with intellectual disabilities who have sexually difficult behaviour. In doing so, they asked the staff to reflect on the behaviour of the persons they support. Although the individuals were not the subjects of the research, Thompson et al. (1997) questioned whether the individuals with intellectual disabilities would have elected to be the topic of this research if permission had been requested. In a follow-up on this dilemma, Brown and Thompson (1997) explored the ethics of research with persons with intellectual disabilities who sexually offend, and posed a dilemma for researchers. On the one hand, they contend that persons with intellectual disabilities may not be able to or choose not to consent to be a party to research; on the other hand, they question whether those who have sexually offended have lost some rights to exclude themselves from research intended to reduce abuse. Research ethics would dictate that their right to choose to participate in research is not withdrawn because of their offence histories and must still be protected.

Re-traumatisation

Given the rates of sexual abuse and learned compliance with authority figures, talking with persons with intellectual disabilities about sexuality may bring researchers quickly into the realm of abuse disclosure. Because of the very real possibility that abuse may be uncovered during the research, there is an ethical responsibility to act and to establish a protocol as part of the research proposal. When one conducts research with vulnerable populations, it must be carefully designed to minimise the risk of re-traumatisation, and supports should be planned for assisting individuals to process the information if they choose to do so.

Legal Implications

When one deals with issues of sexual offence or abuse, the disclosed information may also have complex legal issues. Disclosures of abuse or abusive behaviour may require legal reporting. Research participants need to be informed that this type of information cannot be protected by confidentiality. Additionally, the process by which researchers handle such disclosures may be very important to the legal process. Therefore, a plan for reporting this information needs to be clearly identified within a research protocol.

Programme Evaluation

Fifth, a key issue within many sexuality research studies is determination whether an intervention is successful, whether it is abuse-prevention training, sexuality training, or alternative skill training for offenders. In effect, researchers want to know whether training effectively reduces abuse, leads to responsible and healthy sexual practices, and/or reduces offending behaviour. However, researchers are often challenged to find ethical ways of assessing effectiveness. The validity and reliability of the measures have been discussed throughout the chapter. However, the evaluation of treatment outcomes and generalisation also offers a very real and complex ethical challenge.

Becker, Harris and Sales (1993) have argued that treatment-outcome research on offenders needs to demonstrate the value of treatment components by comparing outcomes for persons who receive and do not receive various treatments. Although withholding treatment can be seen as unethical, Becker et al. (1993) argue that until treatment effectiveness is known, an argument cannot be made that effective treatment is being withheld.

Similarly, generalisation evaluation has been fraught with ethical dilemmas. In situ evaluation has been recommended as a highly reliable means of evaluating generalisation; in situ assessment involves evaluating the response of individuals to a contrived situation in a naturalistic environment without their awareness (Haseltine & Miltenberger, 1990; Collins et al., 1992; Lumley et al., 1998). As Lumley and Miltenberger (1997) discuss, the use of in situ probes are likely to be effective in evaluating sexuality-education programmes, whereas attempts to assess the acquisition of skills by interview or paper-and-pencil measures can not evaluate how an individual will actually respond in a situation. Assessment probes occur in environments with which the participants are familiar (Haseltine & Miltenberger, 1990; Collins et al., 1992). Due to ethical concerns, these role-plays do not portray sexually explicit situations, but use authoritative, general, or incentive lures to measure whether people with disabilities can apply what they have learned in training within everyday settings (Haseltine & Miltenberger, 1990).

The ethical issues surrounding the use of in situ evaluation are so significant that most researchers choose not to use this method. The decision not to use this type of assessment is based on the potential psychological distress or harm that could be caused by exposing an individual to seemingly real, albeit simulated, sexually risky situations. However, does failure to evaluate generalisation put the individual at the same risk or at greater risk than not knowing? The relative risks or benefits of using in situ generalisation tests for this population pose an interesting ethical question. Is not testing worse than testing?

Content

Social science research often focuses on individuals in isolation from the environment in which they live. This perspective often results in the individuals being seen as "at fault" for their life circumstances. When people have been profoundly marginalised in all aspects of their life and lack a basic education, they may be limited in their capacity to understand and articulate their life experiences, particularly when communication is an issue. Research might benefit from examining the work of action researchers, in which research is embedded in the realities of individuals' lives and responds to the issues raised by the research. Some action researchers might argue that there is an ethical obligation to place research findings in a critical analytical framework in which the marginalisation of individuals can be seen and understood. Action research in sexuality may be employed to create change at the level of action on the part of service providers and families, as well as generate knowledge and, as such, be part of a political project to raise issues of marginalisation and, wherever possible, to develop research projects that will increase the capacity of individuals to understand their life experience. However, the age-old problem of research application continues: research results can be used by others to foster their own political agenda.

CONCLUSION AND FUTURE DIRECTIONS

Our review of sexuality research (attitudes, education, abuse, and offence) uncovered two general themes. First, there is a dearth of empirical evidence for the ideas and practice in this field. Second, when research has been conducted, it often lacked the scientific rigour that has come to be accepted as the common research standard. Notably, the studies lack demographic information regarding participants, fail to employ accepted research designs that can demonstrate causality, and often do not assess instrument reliability and validity, maintenance, generalisation, or the social validity of the outcomes.

Sexuality is an important but neglected research area in the field of intellectual disability. Research is needed on many fronts. Without research, practitioners and teachers are unaware of the most effective strategies to impart knowledge and ensure generalisation of that knowledge. Knowledge of sexuality and abuse prevention is logically linked to enhanced functioning and reduction of maltreatment; however, the cause–effect relationship between the two phenomena is not empirically strong at this time. In addition to explanatory or evaluative research in this area, there is also a need for more exploratory and descriptive research. The patterns of sexual behaviour of persons with developmental disabilities, including those of an abusive or offending nature, are beginning to emerge in the literature. Further exploration with regard to the complexity of factors that intersect biomedically, socially, and psychologically to influence the sexuality of persons with intellectual disabilities is greatly needed. The sexual life experiences of different persons with disabilities vary due to genetic or biomedical factors, life experience, and factors related to their own strengths or vulnerabilities. The biopsychosocial complexity of this area has only begun to be explored.

The lack of scientific exploration of the sexuality of persons with intellectual disabilities to date may speak to the value or lack thereof that researchers place on this topic. However, our review has demonstrated a strong and emerging interest in this field by practitioners. The challenge may therefore be the dichotomy between research and practice. The implication of our review is that practitioners need to become closely linked to researchers to ensure that *practice* is evaluated and empirically demonstrated as effective. Additionally, there is a growing trend to develop research that incorporates the perspectives and contributions of persons with disabilities (Ward & Flynn, 1994). Partnerships of researchers, practitioners, consumers, and their advocates promise to yield research that results in empirically supported and practical outcomes.

REFERENCES

Adams, G.L., Tallon, R.J. & Alcorn, D.A. (1982). Attitudes toward the sexuality of mentally retarded and nonretarded persons. *Education and Training of the Mentally Retarded*, **17**, 307–312.

Baladerian, N. (1991). Sexual abuse of people with intellectual disabilities. *Sexuality and Disability*, **9**, 323–335.

Bambury, J., Wilton, K. & Boyd, A. (1999). Effects of two experimental educational programmes on the socio-sexual knowledge and attitudes of adults with mild intellectual disability. *Education and Training in Mental Retardation and Developmental Disabilities*, **34**, 207–211.

Barmann, B.C. & Murray, W.J. (1982). Suppression of inappropriate sexual behavior by facial screening. *Behavior Therapy*, **12**, 730–735.

Bass, E. & Davis, L. (1988). *The Courage to Heal: A Guide for Women Survivors of Sexual Abuse*. New York: Harper & Row.

Becker, J.V., Harris, C.D. & Sales, B.D. (1993). Juveniles who commit sexual offenses: a critical review of the research. In G.C. Nagayama Hall, R. Hirschman, J.R. Graham & M.S. Zaragoza (Eds) *Sexual Aggression: Issues in Etiology, Assessment and Treatment* (pp. 215–228). Bristol, PA: Taylor & Francis.

Bennett, B., Vockell, E. & Vockell, K. (1972). Sexuality education for EMR adolescent girls: an evaluation and some suggestions. *Journal for Special Educators of the Mentally Retarded*, **9**, 3–7.

Bogdan, R.C. & Biklen, S.K. (1992). *Qualitative Research for Education: An Introduction to Theory and Methods*. Boston, MA: Allyn & Bacon.

Brantlinger, E. (1992). Sexuality education in the secondary special education curriculum: teachers' perceptions and concerns. *Teacher Education and Special Education*, **15**, 32–40.

Brantlinger, F.A. (1983). Measuring variation and change in attitudes of residential care staff toward the sexuality of mentally retarded persons. *Mental Retardation*, **21**, 17–22.

Brown, B.S. & Courtless, R.F. (1971). *Mentally Retarded Offender*. Washington, DC: National Institute of Mental Health, Center for Studies of Crime and Delinquency.

Brown, H. & Thompson, D. (1997). The ethics of research with men who have learning disabilities and abusive sexual behaviour: a minefield in a vacuum. *Disability and Society*, **12**, 695–707.

Coleman, E.M. & Murphy, W.D. (1980). A survey of sexual attitudes and sex education programs among facilities for the mentally retarded. *Applied Research in Mental Retardation*, **1**, 269–279.

Collins, B.V., Schuster, J.W. & Nelson, C.M. (1992). Teaching a generalized response to the lures of strangers to adults with severe handicaps. *Exceptionality*, **3**, 67–80.

Cook, H.W., Altman, K., Shaw, J. & Blaylock, M. (1978). Use of contingent lemon juice to eliminate public masturbation by a severely retarded boy. *Behavior Research and Therapy*, **16**, 131–134.

Day, K. (1994). Male mentally handicapped sex offenders. *British Journal of Psychiatry*, **165**, 630–639.

Day, K. (1997). Clinical features and offence behaviour of mentally retarded sex offenders: a review of research. In R.J. Fletcher & D. Griffiths (Eds) *Congress Proceedings—International Congress II on the Dually Diagnosed* (pp. 95–99). New York: NADD.

Dial, K.B. (1968). A report of group work to increase social skills of females in a vocational rehabilitation program. *Mental Retardation*, **6**, 11–14.

Dinerstein, R.D. (1999). Introduction. In R.D. Dinerstein, S.S. Herr & J.L. Sullivan (Eds) *A Guide to Consent* (pp. 3–6). Washington, DC: American Association on Mental Retardation.

Edmonson, B., McCombs, K. & Wish, J. (1979). What retarded adults believe about sex. *American Journal of Mental Deficiency*, **84**, 11–18.

Edmonson, B. & Wish, J. (1975). Sexual knowledge and attitudes of moderately retarded males. *American Journal of Mental Deficiency*, **80**, 172–179.

Evans, E.D., Melville, G.A. & Cass, M.A. (1992). AIDS: special educators' knowledge and attitudes. *Teacher Education and Special Education*, **15**, 300–306.

Fedoroff, J.P., Smolewska, K., Selhi, Z., Ng, E. & Bradford, J. (2001). Assessment of violence and sexual offense risk using the "VRAG" and "SORAG" in a sample of men with developmental delay and paraphilic disorders: a case controlled study. *International Academy of Sex Research, 27th Annual Meeting Abstracts*, **17**.

Fischer, H.L. & Krajicek, M. (1974). Sexual development of the moderately retarded child: level of information and parental attitudes. *Mental Retardation*, **12**, 28–30.

Foley, R.M. (1995). Special educators' competencies and preparation for the delivery of sex education. *Special Services in the Schools*, **10**, 95–112.

Foley, R.M. & Kittleson, M.J. (1993). Special educators' knowledge of HIV transmission: implications for teacher education programs. *Teacher Education and Special Education*, **16**, 342–350.

Foxx, R.M., Bittle, R.G., Bechtel, D.R. & Livesay, J.R. (1986b). Behavioral treatment of the sexually deviant behavior of mentally retarded individuals. *International Review of Research in Mental Retardation*, **14**, 291–317.

Foxx, R.M., McMorrow, M.J., Bittle, R.G. & Ness, J. (1986a). An analysis of social skills generalization in two natural settings. *Journal of Applied Behavior Analysis*, **19**, 299–311.

Foxx, R.M., McMorrow, M.J., Storey, K. & Rogers, B.M. (1984). Teaching social/sexual skills to mentally retarded adults. *American Journal of Mental Deficiency*, **89**, 9–15.

Fredericks, B. & Nishioka-Evans, V. (1999). Functional assessment of a sex offender population. In A.C. Repp & R.H. Horner (Eds) *Functional Analysis of Problem Behavior: From Effective Assessment to Effective Support* (pp. 279–304). Belmont, CA: Wadsworth.

Griffiths, D. (1995). Teaching for generalization of social skills with persons who have intellectual disabilities. *Intellectual Disabilities Bulletin*, **23**, 43–58.

Griffiths, D. (1999). Sexuality and people with developmental disabilities: myth conceptions and facts. In I. Brown & M. Percy (Eds) *Developmental Disabilities in Ontario* (pp. 443–451). Toronto: Front Porch.

Griffiths, D. (2002). Sexual aggression. In W.I. Gardner (Ed.) *Aggression and Other Disruptive Behavioural Challenges: Biomedical and Psychosocial Assessment and Treatment* (pp. 325–398). New York: National Association for Dual Diagnosis.

Griffiths, D., Baxter, J., Haslam, T., Richards, D., Stranges, S. & Vyrostko, B. (1996). Building healthy boundaries: considerations for reducing sexual abuse. *NADD 13th Annual Conference Proceedings* (pp. 114–118). Kingston, NY: NADD.

Griffiths, D., Feldman, M. & Tough, S. (1997). Programming generalization when teaching social skills to adults with mental retardation: effects on generalization, social validity and self-report. *Behavior Therapy*, **28**, 253–269.

Griffiths, D. & Lunsky, Y. (2000). Changing attitudes towards the nature of socio-sexual assessment and education for persons with developmental disabilities: a twenty-year comparison. *Journal of Developmental Disabilities*, **7**, 16–33.

Griffiths, D. & Lunsky, Y. (2003). *Socio-sexual Knowledge and Attitude Assessment Tool (SSKAAT-R)*. Wood Dale, IL: Stoelting Company.

Griffiths, D.M., Quinsey, V.L. & Hingsburger, D. (1989). *Changing Inappropriate Sexual Behavior: A Community Based Approach for Persons with Intellectual Disabilities*. Baltimore, MD: Brookes.

Griffiths, D., Richards, D., Fedoroff, P. & Watson, S. (2002). Sexuality and mental health in persons with developmental disabilities. In D. Griffiths, C. Stavrakaki & J. Summers (Eds) *An Introduction to the Mental Health Needs of Persons with Developmental Disabilities* (pp. 419–454). Ontario: Habilitative Mental Health Resource Network.

Haaven, J., Little, R. & Petre-Miller, D. (1990). *Treating Intellectually Disabled Sex Offenders: A Model Residential Program*. Orwell, VT: Safer Society.

Hall, J. & Morris, H. (1976). Sexual knowledge and attitudes of institutionalized and noninstitutionalized retarded adolescents. *American Journal of Mental Deficiency*, **80**, 382–387.

Hall, J., Morris, H. & Barker, H. (1973). Sexual knowledge and attitudes of mentally retarded adolescents. *American Journal of Mental Deficiency*, **77**, 706–709.

Hamre-Nietupski, S. & Ford, A. (1981). Sexuality education and related skills: a series of programs implemented with severely handicapped students. *Sexuality and Disability*, **4**, 179–193.

Haseltine, B. & Miltenberger, R.G. (1990). Teaching self-protection skills to persons with mental retardation. *American Journal on Mental Retardation*, **95**, 188–197.

Herman, J.L. (1992). *Trauma and Recovery*. New York: Basic Books.

Herr, S.S., O'Sullivan, J.L. & Dinerstein, R.D. (1999). Consent to participate in research trials. In R.J. Dinerstein, S.S. Herr & J.L. O'Sullivan (Eds) *A Guide to Consent* (pp. 111–114). Washington, DC: American Association on Mental Retardation.

Heshusuis, L. (1982). Sexuality, intimacy and persons we label mentally retarded: what they think—what we think. *Mental Retardation*, **20**, 164–168.

Hingsburger, D. (1993). Staff attitudes, homosexuality and intellectual disability: a minority within a minority. *Canadian Journal of Human Sexuality*, **2**, 19–21.

Jupp, J.J. & Looser, G. (1988). The effectiveness of the "CATCH" social skills training program with adolescents who are mildly and intellectually disabled. *Australia and New Zealand Journal of Developmental Disabilities*, **14**, 135–145.

Jurkowski, E. & Amado, A. (1993). Affection, love, intimacy and sexual relationships. In A. Amado (Ed.) *Friendships and Community Connections Between People With and Without Developmental Disabilities* (pp. 129–151). Baltimore, MD: Brookes.

Katz, G. (1998). Sexuality groups for adolescents with intellectual disabilities. *Journal on Developmental Disabilities*, **6**, 73–88.

Kempton, W. (1987). *Life Horizons*. Santa Monica, CA: James Stanfield.

Kolvin, I. (1967). "Aversive imagery" treatment in adolescents. *Behavior Research and Therapy*, **5**, 245–248.

Konstantareas, M.M. & Lunsky, Y. (1997). Sociosexual knowledge, experience, attitudes and interests in individuals with autistic disorder and intellectual delay. *Journal of Autism and Intellectual Disorders*, **27**, 397–413.

Lackey, L.B. & Knopp, F.H. (1989). A summary of selected notes from the working sessions of the First National Training Conference on the Assessment and Treatment of Intellectually Disabled Juvenile and Adult Sexual Offenders. In F. Knopp (Ed.) *Selected Readings: Sexual Offenders Identified as Intellectually Disabled*. Orwell, VT: Safer Society.

Lawrence, P. & Swain, J. (1993). Sexuality education programmes for students with severe learning difficulties in further education and the problem of evaluation. *Disability, Handicap, and Society*, **8**, 405–421.

Lindsay, W.R., Bellshaw, E., Culross, G., Staines, C. & Michie, A. (1992). Increases in knowledge following a course of sex education for people with intellectual disabilities. *Journal of Intellectual Disability Research*, **36**, 531–539.

Luiselli, J.K., Helfen, C.S., Pemberton, B.W. & Reisman, J. (1977). The elimination of a child's in-class masturbation by overcorrection and reinforcement. *Journal of Behavior Therapy and Experimental Psychiatry*, **8**, 201–204.

Lumley, V.A. & Miltenberger, R.G. (1997). Sexual abuse prevention for persons with mental retardation. *American Journal on Mental Retardation*, **101**, 459–472.

Lumley, V.A., Miltenberger, R.G., Long, E.S., Rapp, J.T. & Roberts, J.A. (1998). Evaluation of a sexual abuse prevention program for adults with mental retardation. *Journal of Applied Behavior Analysis*, **31**, 91–101.

Lund, C.A. (1992). Long-term treatment of sexual behavior in adolescent and adult intellectually disabled persons. *Annals of Sex Research*, **5**, 5–21.

Lunsky, Y. & Konstantareas, M.M. (1998). The attitudes of individuals with autism and mental retardation towards sexuality. *Education and Training in Mental Retardation and Developmental Disabilities*, **33**, 24–33.

Lutzker, J.R. (1974). Social reinforcement control of exhibitionism in a profoundly retarded adult. *Mental Retardation*, **12**, 46–47.

May, D.C. & Kundert, D.K. (1996). Are special educators prepared to meet the sexuality education needs of their students? A progress report. *Journal of Special Education*, **29**, 433–441.

McCabe, M.P. (1994). *Sexual Knowledge, Experience, Feelings and Needs Scale for People with Intellectual Disability (SexKen-ID)* (4th edn). Burwood, Australia: Deakin University.

McCabe, M. (1999). Sexual knowledge, experience and feelings among people with disabilities. *Sexuality and Disability*, **17**, 157–170.

McCabe, M. & Cummins, R. (1996). The sexual knowledge, experience, feelings and needs of people with mild intellectual disability. *Education and Training in Mental Retardation and Intellectual Disabilities*, **31**, 13–21.

McCabe, M.P., Cummins, R.A. & Deeks, A.A. (1999). Construction and psychometric properties of sexuality scales: sex knowledge, experience, and needs scales for people with intellectual disabilities (SexKen-ID), people with physical disabilities (SexKen-PD), and the general population. *Research in Developmental Disabilities*, **20**, 241–254.

McCabe, M.P., Cummins, R.A. & Reid, S.B. (1994). An empirical study of the sexual abuse of people with intellectual disability. *Sexuality and Disability*, **12**, 297–305.

McCabe, M. & Schreck, A. (1992). Before sexuality education: an evaluation of the sexual knowledge, experience, feelings and needs of people with mild intellectual disabilities. *Australia and New Zealand Journal of Developmental Disabilities*, **18**, 75–82.

McCarthy, M. (1993). Sexual experiences of women with learning difficulties in long-stay hospitals. *Sexuality and Disability*, **11**, 277–286.

McGee, J. & Menolascino, F.J. (1992). The evaluation of defendants with mental retardation in the criminal justice system. In R.W. Conley, R. Luckasson & G.N. Bouthilet (Eds) *The Criminal Justice System and Mental Retardation: Defendants and Victims* (pp. 55–78). Baltimore, MD: Brookes.

Mitchell, L., Doctor, R. & Butler, D. (1978). Attitudes of caretakers toward the sexual behavior of mentally retarded persons. *American Journal of Mental Deficiency*, **83**, 289–296.

Muccigrosso, L. (1991). Sexual abuse prevention strategies and programmes for persons with intellectual disabilities. *Sexuality and Disability*, **9**, 261–271.

Murphy, W.D., Coleman, E.M. & Abel, G.G. (1983b). Human sexuality in the mentally retarded. In J.L. Matson & F. Andrasik (Eds) *Treatment Issues and Innovations in Mental Retardation* (pp. 581–643). New York: Plenum.

Murphy, W.D., Coleman, E.M. & Haynes, M. (1983a). Treatment and evaluation issues with the mentally retarded sex offender. In J. Greer & I. Stuart (Eds) *The Sexual Aggressor: Current Perspectives on Treatment* (pp. 22–41). New York: Van Nostrand Reinhold.

Murray, J. & Minnes, P. (1994). Staff attitudes towards the sexuality of persons with intellectual disability. *Australia and New Zealand Journal of Developmental Disabilities*, **19**, 45–52.

Nezu, C.M., Nezu, A.M. & Dudeck, J. (1998). A cognitive behavioural model of assessment and treatment for intellectually disabled sexual offenders. *Cognitive and Behavioral Practice*, **5**, 25–64.

Nolley, D., Muccigrosso, L. & Zigman, E. (1996). Treatment successes with mentally retarded sex offenders. *Sex Offenders' Treatment: Biological Dysfunction, Intrapsychic Conflict, Interpersonal Violence* (pp. 125–141). Haworth, UK: Haworth Press.

O'Day, B. (1988). *Preventing Sexual Abuse of Persons with Disabilities: A Curriculum for the Hearing Impaired, Physically Disabled, Blind and Mentally Retarded Students*. Santa Cruz, CA: CA Network.

Owen, F., Griffiths, D., Sales, C., Feldman, M. & Richards, D. (2000). Perceptions of acceptable boundaries by persons with developmental disabilities and their caregivers. *Journal of Developmental Disabilities*, **7**, 34–49.

Page, A.C. (1991). Teaching developmentally disabled people self-regulation in sexual behaviour. *Australia and New Zealand Journal of Developmental Disabilities*, **17**, 81–88.

Patton, W. & Mannison, M. (1995). Sexuality attitudes: a review of the literature and refinement of a new measure. *Journal of Sex Education and Therapy*, **21**, pp. 268–295.

Pendler, B. (1993). Opening Pandora's box: a parent's perspective on friendship and sexuality. In A. Amado (Ed.) *Friendships and Community Connections Between People With and Without Intellectual Disabilities* (pp. 229–240). Baltimore, MD: Brookes.

Penny, R.E.C. & Chataway, J.E. (1982). Sex education for mentally retarded persons. *Australia and New Zealand Journal of Developmental Disabilities*, **8**, 204–212.

Pitceathly, A.S. & Chapman, J.W. (1985). Sexuality, marriage and parenthood of mentally retarded people. *International Journal for the Advancement of Counseling*, **8**, 173–181.

Polvinale, R.A. & Lutzker, J.R. (1980). Elimination of assaultive and inappropriate behavior by reinforcement and social-restitution. *Mental Retardation*, **18**, 27–30.

Quinsey, V.L., Harris, G.T., Rice, M.E. & Cormier, C.A. (1998). *Violent Offenders: Appraising and Managing Risk*. Washington, DC: American Psychological Association.

Rivenq, B. (1974). Behavioural therapy of phobias: a case of gynecomastia and mental retardation. *Mental Retardation*, **12**, 44–45.

Robinson, S. (1984). Effects of a sexuality education program on intellectually handicapped adults. *Australia and New Zealand Journal of Intellectual Disabilities*, **10**, 21–26.

Rosenthal, T.L. (1973). Response-contingent versus fixed punishment in aversion conditioning of pedophilia: a case study. *Journal of Nervous and Mental Disease*, **156**, 440–443.

Santamour, W. & West, B. (1978). *The Mentally Retarded Offender and Corrections*. Washington, DC: US Department of Justice.

Scheerenburger, R.C. (1983). *The History of Mental Retardation*. Baltimore, MD: Brookes.

Scotti, J.R., Nangle, D.W., Masia, C.L., Ellis, J.T., Ujcich, K.J., Giacoletti, A.M., et al. (1997). Providing an AIDS education skills training program to persons with mild intellectual disabilities. *Education and Training in Mental Retardation and Developmental Disabilities*, **32**, 113–128.

Scotti, J.R., Speaks, L.V., Masia, C.L., Boggess, J.T. & Drabman, R.S. (1996). The educational effects of providing AIDS risk information to persons with developmental disabilities: an exploratory study. *Education and Training in Mental Retardation and Developmental Disabilities*, **3**, 115–122.

Senn, C.Y. (1988). *Vulnerable: Sexual Abuse and People with Intellectual Handicap*. Downsview, Ontario: Roeher Institute.

Shapiro, S. (1986). Delinquent and disturbed behavior within the field of mental deficiency. In A.V.S. deReuck & R. Porter (Eds) *The Mentally Abnormal Offender*. New York: Grune & Stratton.

Shapiro, E.S. & Sheridan, C.A. (1985). Systematic assessment and training of sex education for a mentally retarded woman. *Applied Research in Mental Retardation*, **6**, 307–317.

Shaw, W.J. & Walker, C.E. (1979). Use of relaxation in the short-term treatment of fetishistic behavior: an exploratory case study. *Journal of Pediatric Psychology*, **4**, 403–407.

Sheppard, J.L., Pollock, J.M. & Rayment, S.M. (1983). *Catch Project Social Skills Kit*. Sydney: Cumberland College of Health Sciences.

Sobsey, D. (1994). *Violence and Abuse in the Lives of People with Disabilities: The End of Silent Acceptance?* Baltimore, MD: Brookes.

Sobsey, D. & Doe, T. (1991). Patterns of sexual abuse and assault. *Sexuality and Disability*, **9**, 243–259.

Sobsey, D. & Mansell, S. (1990). The prevention of sexual abuse of people with developmental disabilities. *Developmental Disabilities Bulletin*, **18**, 55–66.

Sobsey, D., Randall, W. & Parrila, R.K. (1997). Gender differences in abused children with and without disabilities. *Child Abuse and Neglect*, **21**, 707–720.

Steiner, J. (1984). Group counselling with retarded offenders. *Social Work*, **29**, 181–182.

Stokes, T.F. & Baer, D.M. (1977). An implicit technology of generalization. *Journal of Applied Behavior Analysis*, **9**, 31–40.

Swanson, C.K. & Garwick, F.B. (1990). Treatment for low functioning sex offenders: group therapy and interagency cooperation. *Mental Retardation*, **28**, 155–161.

Szollos, A.A. & McCabe, M. (1995). The sexuality of people with mild intellectual disability: perceptions of clients and caregivers. *Australia and New Zealand Journal of Developmental Disabilities*, **20**, 205–222.

Tharinger, D., Horton, C.B. & Millea, S. (1990). Sexual abuse and exploitation of children and adults with mental retardation and other handicaps. *Child Abuse and Neglect*, **14**, 301–312.

Thompson, D. (1994). The sexual experiences of men with learning disabilities having sex with men—issues for HIV prevention. *Sexuality and Disability*, **12**, 221–242.

Thompson, D., Clare, I. & Brown, H. (1997). Not such an "ordinary" relationship: the role of women support staff in relation to men with learning disabilities who have difficult sexual behaviour. *Disability and Society*, **12**, 573–592.

Timmers, R.L., Ducharme, P. & Jacob, G. (1981). Sexual knowledge, attitudes and behaviours of intellectually disabled adults living in a normalized apartment setting. *Sexuality and Disability*, **4**, 27–39.

Trudel, G. & Desjardins, G. (1992). Staff reactions toward the sexual behaviours of people living in institutional settings. *Sexuality and Disability*, **10**, 173–188.

Valenti-Hein, D.C., Yarnold, P.R. & Mueser, K.T. (1994). Evaluation of the dating skills program for improving heterosocial interactions in people with mental retardation. *Behavior Modification*, **18**, 32–36.

Walker-Hirsch, L. & Champagne, M.P. (1986). *Circles: Stop Abuse*. Santa Monica, CA: James Stanfield.

Ward, L. & Flynn, M. (1994). What matters most: disability, research and empowerment. In M.H. Rioux & M. Bach (Eds) *Disability Is Not Measles: New Research Paradigms in Disability*. Toronto: Roeher Institute.

Ward, K.M., Heffern, S.J., Wilcox, D.A., McElwee, B.S., Dowrick, P., Brown, M.J., et al. (1992). *Managing Inappropriate Sexual Behavior: Supporting Individuals with Developmental Disabilities in the Community*. Anchorage, AK: Alaska Specialized Training Services.

Wendell, S. (1996). *The Rejected Body: Feminist Philosophical Reflection on Disability*. New York: Routledge.

Whitehouse, M.A. & McCabe, M.P. (1997). Sex education programmes for people with intellectual disability: how effective are they? *Education and Training in Mental Retardation and Developmental Disabilities*, **32**, 229–240.

Wish, J., McCombs, K. & Edmonson, B. (1980). *Socio-Sexual Knowledge and Attitudes Test*. Wood Dale, IL: Stoelting.

Wong, S.E., Gaydos, G.R. & Fuqua, R.W. (1982). Operant control of pedophilia: reducing approaches to children. *Behavior Modification*, **6**, 73–84.

CHAPTER 16

Choice

Chris Hatton
Lancaster University, UK

INTRODUCTION

The exercise of choice by people with intellectual disabilities is becoming increasingly central to legislation and policy. For example, in the UK, the most recent policy statement *Valuing People* (Department of Health, 2001) puts choice as one of its four key principles, alongside legal and civil rights, independence, and inclusion:

> Choice: Like other people, people with learning disabilities [the official UK term, synonymous with "intellectual disabilities" internationally] want a real say in where they live, what work they should do and who looks after them. But for too many people with learning disabilities, these are currently unattainable goals. We believe that everyone should be able to make choices. This includes people with severe and profound disabilities who, with the right help and support, can make important choices and express preferences about their day to day lives. (Department of Health, 2001, p. 24)

Major policy and practice initiatives promoting self-determination among people with intellectual disabilities, including components concerning choice, are also taking place in the USA (Ward, 1996; Nerney, 1998). Clearly, the issue of choice is becoming central in policy-relevant research with people with intellectual disabilities, and several reviews have noted a rapid growth in the number of research studies investigating various aspects of choice-making among people with intellectual disabilities (Kern et al., 1998; Lohrmann-O'Rourke & Browder, 1998; Stalker & Harris, 1998; Algozzine, Browder, Karvonen, Test & Wood, 2001; Stancliffe, 2001). As with any relatively new field of inquiry, diversity in definitions, measures, populations, and research questions is prominent, although common strands of research have been emerging since the 1980s. This chapter will provide an overview of some of the major strands of research concerning choice among people with intellectual disabilities, focusing on conceptual and methodological issues relevant to those considering research in this area. In particular, the chapter will focus on the following issues:

(1) defining choice, particularly in relation to self-determination
(2) research assessing the capacity of people with intellectual disabilities to demonstrate preferences and choice-making behaviour

The International Handbook of Applied Research in Intellectual Disabilities. Edited by E. Emerson, C. Hatton, T. Thompson and T.R. Parmenter ISBN 0-471-49709-6.

(3) research assessing the degree to which people with intellectual disabilities make choices in their lives, including the degree to which their environments support choice-making
(4) research evaluating interventions designed to improve the capacity of people with intellectual disabilities to make choices
(5) research evaluating the promotion of choice-making among people with intellectual disabilities as a vehicle for promoting other valued lifestyle outcomes, such as reductions in challenging behaviour.

Cross-cutting themes relevant to all these issues, such as the validity of obtaining information from proxy respondents, will be addressed throughout the chapter.

DEFINING CHOICE

Although choice has become an important component of government policy concerning people with intellectual disabilities in many countries, both policy statements and research studies have rarely defined choice. In particular, the terms "choice", "control", and "self-determination" have frequently been used as synonyms. However, theoretical formulations of self-determination (see Stancliffe, 2001; Wehmeyer, 2001, for reviews) emphasise that choice is only one component of the much broader construct of self-determination. The term "self-determination" can be used in two distinct ways; firstly, concerning the collective self-determination of a group, and, secondly, concerning the personal self-determination of an individual (Wehmeyer, 2001). Collective self-determination refers to a group of people having the right to self-governance; such a meaning of self-determination is often used to refer to the rights of people with intellectual disabilities collectively (see Nerney, 1998). Personal self-determination refers to individuals determining the course of their own life without compulsion from others, or "acting as the primary causal agent in one's life and making choices and decisions regarding one's quality of life free from undue external influence or interference" (Wehmeyer, 1996a, p. 24).

Although different theories of personal self-determination among people with intellectual disabilities place different emphasis on personal self-determination skills (see Wehmeyer, 2001) versus ecological factors helping or hindering personal self-determination (see Abery & Stancliffe, 1996), they all include choice as one component of self-determination. For example, the functional model of self-determination locates personal choice-making skills as one of 12 component elements of self-determined behaviour (Wehmeyer, 2001). The ecological model of self-determination similarly locates choice-making skills as one of 16 individual competencies needed for self-determination, embedded within ecosystems that are more or less supportive of self-determination (Abery & Stancliffe, 1996). However, it is important not to over-emphasise the importance of choice as a component of self-determination; as Wehmeyer (2001) notes, "Making choices is only one aspect of being self-determined, and to take it out of the broader context can be problematic" (p. 8).

Compared to personal self-determination, choice has a relatively restricted definition: "Making an unforced selection of a preferred alternative from two or more options" (Stancliffe, 2001, p. 92). As Stancliffe (2001) emphasises, this definition very much specifies the minimum requirements for choice, although it does emphasise the importance of choice-making as an active process. This definition also does not regard choice as synonymous with personal control. Control is usually more far-reaching than choice (for example, control over which options are available to choose from or control over when choices can be exercised), and in certain circumstances people with control may cede choice over certain aspects of their life (for example, choice of what dosage of anaesthetic medications are to be used during a surgical procedure).

These definitional issues should be fundamental to researchers investigating choice among people with intellectual disabilities. For many researchers, investigating choice may be too limiting if they are interested in self-determination, which would properly involve the investigation of a complex set of constructs including problem-solving skills, internal locus of control, and self-awareness (see Wehmeyer, Kelchner & Richards, 1996). Researchers also need to consider whether they are interested in choice per se or in more far-reaching aspects of personal control, and ensure that the methodologies they use reflect the construct of interest.

Broader theories of self-determination also raise other questions for researchers interested in choice, which will have important consequences for research designs and research methods including choice. First, is choice a valued end in itself, or is choice a vehicle through which other positive lifestyle outcomes can be achieved? Second, is choice-making largely a function of the skills of the person with intellectual disabilities, or is choice-making largely a function of supportive or restrictive environments? Third, who is in the best position to assess the choices exercised by people with intellectual disabilities; the person with intellectual disabilities (through self-report or direct observation) or an informant? Different answers to these research questions have resulted in the distinct strands of research on choice-making to be discussed below.

ASSESSING THE CAPACITY TO MAKE CHOICES

Given the cognitive limitations of people with intellectual disabilities, a substantial strand of research has been devoted to investigating the capacity of people with intellectual disabilities to make choices. The vast majority of this research has been conducted with people with severe or profound intellectual disabilities, using the framework of applied behaviour analysis to investigate whether people make behavioural responses demonstrating a stable preference for a particular alternative. The typical research strategies adopted have been single-case experimental designs. Research in this paradigm shows great diversity in the number and type of preference alternatives used, the procedures used to assess preference alternatives, the settings within which preference alternatives are presented, and how a behavioural response indicating a preference is established. A systematic examination of all the dimensions of this methodological diversity is beyond the scope of this chapter (see Lohrmann-O'Rourke & Browder, 1998, for a systematic review), which will focus on some of the major methodological issues for researchers interested in assessing the capacity to make choices.

How Many Alternatives to Present

Although there are many procedural variants, researchers investigating preference assessment have presented stimuli in one of the following three ways:

(1) *Presenting individual stimuli sequentially, and comparing behavioural responses for each stimulus (for example, duration of manipulation of the stimulus object;*

approaching the stimulus object) to determine preference (e.g., Green, Reid, Canipe & Gardner, 1991; Green, Middleton & Reid, 2000). It could be argued that these procedures do not meet Stancliffe's (2001) minimum definition of choice, although preferences are in fact being demonstrated among alternative options distributed temporally rather than spatially, as in the following procedures.

(2) *Presenting stimuli in pairs, and evaluating the stability of behavioural responses demonstrating a preference for one of the two stimuli in the pair* (e.g., Sigafoos, Laurie & Pennell, 1995; Carey, O'Reilly, Walsh & Lancioni, 1996). Studies comparing individual and paired stimulus presentation procedures have reported that paired presentation procedures may allow for greater differentiation among stimuli and may also provide more information on non-preferred stimuli (e.g., Fisher et al., 1992), although the position of presented stimuli must be counterbalanced to examine whether participants are selecting stimuli on the basis of position (such as the stimulus on the right).

(3) *Presenting stimuli in groups, and evaluating the stability of behavioural responses demonstrating a preference for one of the stimuli in the group* (e.g., Nozaki & Mochizuki, 1995; Higbee, Carr & Harrison, 2000). Studies comparing paired and group presentation of stimuli vary in their findings concerning the relative reliability of the two approaches (Windsor, Piche & Locke, 1994; DeLeon & Iwata, 1996), although the differences are relatively small. In addition, group-stimulus presentation methods, particularly if presented in formats where non-preferred alternatives are not replaced in later rounds, may allow for the development of preference hierarchies (DeLeon & Iwata, 1996; Higbee et al., 2000).

What Type of Alternatives to Present

Most preference-assessment studies have used tangible objects as stimuli, such as food items or items designed for sensory stimulation or leisure activity (e.g., Fisher et al., 1992; DeLeon & Iwata, 1996). Such stimulus objects are non-symbolic, in that they allow for direct engagement rather than being representations of other constructs. However, a small number of studies have used less tangible stimulus materials, including microswitches (e.g., Dattilo, 1986), representations of activities in a person's individualised educational plan (Foster-Johnson, Ferro & Dunlap, 1994), vocational preferences (e.g., Mithaug & Hanawalt, 1978), and verbal presentations of alternatives (Cohen-Almeida, Graff & Ahearn, 2000). For some of these stimuli, it is unclear whether participants are responding to the sensory characteristics of the stimulus presented rather than activities represented by the stimulus. While there is research suggesting that symbolic stimulus materials may be effective for some participants (Parsons, Harper, Jensen & Reid, 1997; Cohen-Almeida et al., 2000), pre-training to demonstrate understanding of symbolic stimuli needs to be a routine feature of preference assessments using such stimuli (Lohrmann-O'Rourke & Browder, 1998).

Although there is consistent evidence that highly preferred objects can act as reliable reinforcers (DeLeon & Iwata, 1996; Piazza, Fisher, Hagopian, Bowman & Toole, 1996; Higbee et al., 2000), it is important to consider the impact of using different classes of stimulus materials in preference assessments. For example, presented with stimulus materials representing both food and non-food items, participants show a high preference for the food items, even though apparently non-preferred non-food items can be highly preferred in other stimulus arrays and can act as reinforcers (DeLeon, Iwata & Roscoe, 1997; Bojak

& Carr, 1999; Taravella, Lerman, Contrucci & Roane, 2000). With preference assessments using mixed stimulus arrays, additional assessments of apparently non-preferred stimuli are recommended (Taravella et al., 2000).

However, it is worth noting that few studies have allowed participants greater control than simply selecting from a predetermined stimulus array, such as giving participants the option to select or change the stimulus array (Kennedy & Haring, 1993) or end the testing session (Nozaki & Mochizuki, 1995).

What Behavioural Responses Indicate a Preference?

Researchers have defined behavioural responses indicating a preference in a number of ways, although most of these involve responding to a set of predetermined stimuli rather than self-initiated access to stimulus materials. Behavioural responses used to indicate a preference include approaching and making physical contact with an object (e.g., Foxx, Faw, Taylor, Davis & Fulia, 1993), duration of contact with the object (e.g., Piazza et al., 1996), functional engagement with the object (e.g., Parsons & Reid, 1990), use of microswitches (e.g., Dattilo, 1986), and selection of one stimulus object from an array (e.g., Higbee et al., 2000). Some studies have also evaluated behaviours indicating a non-preferred option, such as refusal (e.g., Sigafoos & Dempsey, 1992). However, no evidence currently exists on the relative merits of different definitions of behavioural response.

What Settings to Use When Conducting the Preference Assessment

Researchers have generally used two procedures to conduct preference assessments. The first involves massed trials of stimulus arrays under experimental conditions (e.g., Hanley, Iwata & Lindberg, 1999); the second involves embedding preference assessments within the participant's routine (e.g., Dattilo & Mirenda, 1987; Green et al., 2000). Embedded preference assessments have disadvantages in terms of convenience and experimental control, but have advantages in terms of ecological validity, and the two approaches seem to yield similar results (Green et al., 2000). Other aspects of the settings of preference-assessment protocols have been little investigated, such as the person presenting the stimulus materials and physical aspects of the setting (Lohrmann-O'Rourke & Browder, 1998).

How Often Should Preference Assessments Be Repeated?

Most preference-assessment studies have used very limited periods of time to conduct a preference assessment (typically three days or less) (Lohrmann-O'Rourke & Browder, 1998), although research studies over longer periods of time have demonstrated considerable variability in the selection of preferences at different time points (e.g., Mason, McGee, Farmer-Dougan & Risley, 1989; Zhou, Iwata, Goff & Shore, 2001). At present, such data are interpreted as demonstrating that participants change their preferences quite rapidly, illustrating the need for repeated preference assessments (Lohrmann-O'Rourke & Browder, 1998). However, it may also be possible that a measure of stability in personal preference is expected, in which case the validity of current preference-assessment protocols needs to be critically evaluated. One possibility is that preferences will be more or less stable at different levels of generality; for example, a vegetarian might select very different menu options upon repeated restaurant visits, but would never select a meat dish. A further possibility with some empirical support is that the preferences of people with severe intellectual disabilities may become more stable as they experience more opportunities to sample from stimulus arrays (Lim, Browder & Bambara, 2001).

Can Preference Data Be Gathered from Proxy Respondents?

Some studies have investigated agreement between the findings of direct preference assessments and the views of a proxy respondent, typically a member of staff working with the person. Research has generally reported relatively poor concurrence between direct preference assessments and proxy views (e.g., Parsons & Reid, 1990; Windsor et al., 1994), although the use of highly structured interview schedules with proxy respondents may improve agreement (Fisher, Piazza, Bowman & Amari, 1996). It is also worth noting that considerable inconsistencies have been noted between the preferences of people with profound multiple disabilities identified through person-centred plans and the preferences identified through systematic preference assessment (Reid, Everson & Green, 1999; Green et al., 2000; Reid & Green, 2002). While a reinforcer choice assessment scale has been developed for staff working with people with severe or profound intellectual disabilities (Matson et al., 1999), this measure has not yet been validated against direct preference-assessment procedures.

These behavioural paradigms of preference assessment have not generally been used with people with mild or moderate intellectual disabilities, the assumption being that these groups do have the capacity to make choices. Although some self-report, self-determination measures for people with intellectual disabilities do include subscales concerning skills related to the capacity to make choices, such as interpersonal problem-solving and self-efficacy (for example, the Self-Determination Scale) (Wehmeyer et al., 1996; Wehmeyer & Bolding, 1999, 2001), they do not assess choice-making ability directly. Only one study has described a 16-item, self-report measure designed to assess choice-making competence among people with intellectual disabilities (Taal, Wessels & van der Molen, 2001), with some preliminary evidence of the scale's reliability and concurrent validity. Other studies have used semistructured interviews with people with intellectual disabilities to discuss personal lifestyle preferences (e.g., Neumayer & Bleasdale, 1996) and detailed procedures to establish residential preferences (e.g., Davis & Faw, 2002), although extensive validation of these methods has not been conducted. Instead, a major focus of research with people with mild and moderate intellectual disabilities has been the extent to which people with intellectual disabilities make choices in their lives, and the degree to which environments support people in making choices.

ASSESSING CHOICE-MAKING IN THE LIVES OF PEOPLE WITH INTELLECTUAL DISABILITIES

Research concerning choice-making in the lives of people with intellectual disabilities has generally used very different methods form the behavioural designs underpinning preference-assessment studies. For investigating choice-making, studies have typically used relatively structured interviews and questionnaires. These measures have varied along two dimensions; firstly, whether they are conducted with people with intellectual disabilities or with an informant, typically a carer supporting the person, and, secondly, whether they are assessing the choices that people with intellectual disabilities make or the procedures in the person's environment that promote or hinder choice-making. All these measures assess a number of domains of choice-making, from routine everyday choices (such as meals) to major life choices (such as where and whom to live with). Table 16.1 presents selected information on some measures of choice-making in the lives of people with intellectual disabilities. General quality-of-life measures are not included here, as either they do not include a choice component (Cummins, 1997) or they embed a small number of choice items within scales representing broader constructs, such as empowerment and independence (e.g., Schalock & Keith, 1993).

Several measures have been developed for use with people with intellectual disabilities directly, typically concerning the extent to which people report having choices in their lives. These measures are typically structured interviews between a researcher and a person with intellectual disabilities (Kishi, Teelucksingh, Zollers, Park-Lee & Meyer, 1988; Stancliffe & Parmenter, 1999). Many interviews contain initial checks for response bias, including acquiescence and recency checks (Stancliffe & Parmenter, 1999) and a "lie" item assessing understanding of the concept of choice (Kishi et al., 1988). Although some scales have reported successful use with people with severe intellectual disabilities who have verbal skills (Stancliffe & Parmenter, 1999), it is crucial that researchers systematically evaluate sources of response bias when interviewing people with intellectual disabilities (see Chapter 5, this volume).

To avoid such potential response bias from people with intellectual disabilities, and to enable the collection of data on choice-making concerning people with intellectual disabilities across the whole ability range, some measures have also been developed for use by staff (Kearney, Durand & Mindell, 1995; Kearney, Bergan & McKnight, 1998; Stancliffe & Parmenter, 1999; Hatton et al., in press). As with the self-report measures, most of these measures also assess the extent to which people with intellectual disabilities make choices about their lives, although there is potential for a social desirability response bias among staff informants inflating scores on choice-making measures. One measure has attempted to minimise the impact of staff social desirability response bias by asking staff to produce specific examples of how a person with intellectual disabilities is supported to make choices in a particular domain; these examples are then independently rated by the interviewer (Hatton et al., in press).

Researchers are paying increasing attention to investigating the reliability and validity of choice-making measures. While many authors have demonstrated the internal reliability of choice scales, it can be argued that choice-making may not be a unitary construct and therefore internal consistency of choice-making items within a choice scale may not be expected. It is also unclear whether choice-making scales are most meaningfully scored at the level of individual items, subscales, or a total choice-making score. Reasonable test–retest reliability and/or interrater reliability between staff informants have been established for several scales (Kearney et al., 1995, 1998; Stancliffe & Parmenter, 1999; Hatton et al., in press), although studies have varied in the extent of agreement reported in using people with intellectual disabilities and staff as informants on choice-making (e.g., Stancliffe & Parmenter, 1999; Chapter 5, this volume).

In terms of the validity of choice-making scales, several scales have reported concurrent validity with related measures, such as self-determination (e.g., Wehmeyer, 1996b;

Table 16.1 Measures of choice-making and environmental support for choice-making

Measure	Construct	Informant	Procedure	Scoring
Resident Choice Scale (Robertson et al., 2001; Hatton et al., in press)	Environmental support for choice-making in residential settings	Staff	26-item largely structured interview Examples of supportive procedures given by informant, rated by interviewer (1 = no supports mentioned to 4 = support for resident to have final say unless inappropriate/ dangerous)	Item scores 8 subscale scores Total score
Resident Choice Assessment Scale (Kearney et al., 1995; 1998)	Choice-making in residential settings	Staff	25-item questionnaire Rating made by informant (1 = never to 7 = always)	Item scores Mean item score (total)
Life Choices Survey (Kishi et al., 1988)	Choice-making in residential settings	Person with ID, supplemented by staff	10-item structured interview 1 "lie" item Rating made by person with ID (1 = this choice does not seem appropriate to me/this choice is not available to me to 4 = I can make this choice whenever I want to)	Item scores
Choice Questionnaire Version 2 (Stancliffe & Parmenter, 1999)	Choice-making in residential settings	Parallel versions for people with ID and staff informants	Structured interview for person with ID, including 4 screening items for response bias (recency and acquiescence) Questionnaire for staff, 26 items Rating made by person with ID or informant (3-point scales individually worded for each item)	Item scores Total score

ID: intellectual disabilites.

Wehmeyer & Schwartz, 1998), different choice-making scales (e.g., Stancliffe & Parmenter, 1999), and satisfaction with choice-making expressed by people with intellectual disabilities (Hatton et al., in press). Furthermore, studies report robust associations between living environment and choice-making, with choice-making increasing as living environments become less restrictive (for example, institution versus group homes versus supported living)

(Kearney et al., 1995, 1998; Stancliffe, 1997; Stancliffe & Abery, 1997; Heller, Miller & Factor, 1999; Wehmeyer & Bolding, 1999; Robertson et al., 2001). However, the choices of people with intellectual disabilities, particularly concerning major life decisions such as where and whom to live with, are still very limited in all settings (e.g., Stancliffe & Abery, 1997; Kishi et al., 1988; Robertson et al., 2001).

Studies using choice-making scales also consistently report that greater choice-making is strongly associated with greater ability on the part of people with intellectual disabilities (Stancliffe, 1997; Stancliffe & Abery, 1997; Kearney et al., 1998; Heller et al., 1999; Robertson et al., 2001). It is difficult to disentangle potential explanations for this robust association; for example, whether greater ability is a necessary skill for choice-making, living environments are biased towards providing greater choices for more able people with intellectual disabilities, or choice-making measures are biased in their content towards more able people with intellectual disabilities.

Given the robust associations found between choice-making, living environment, and ability, it is vital that researchers using choice-making scales also assess potentially relevant characteristics of the person with intellectual disabilities and the person's living environment to use as covariates in analyses of choice. There is also considerable room for development in choice-making measurement, both in terms of content (such as choice-making for people with intellectual disabilities living with family members; choice-making in work settings) and in terms of method (such as qualitative interviews with people with intellectual disabilities concerning choice-making; non-participant or participant observations of choice-making in everyday life).

IMPROVING CHOICE-MAKING SKILLS

As mentioned earlier, theories of self-determination regard choice-making as one of several fundamental skills required for self-determined behaviour on the part of people with intellectual disabilities (see Stancliffe, 2001; Wehmeyer, 2001). On this basis, several studies have attempted to intervene to improve choice-making skills among people with intellectual disabilities. A recent systematic review (Algozzine et al., 2001) thoroughly examines the research literature concerning interventions to promote self-determination for people with a range of disabilities; this chapter will focus on some salient issues when evaluating interventions designed to promote choice-making skills among people with intellectual disabilities.

Research evaluating interventions to improve choice-making skills among people with intellectual disabilities has largely been conducted with two different intervention and evaluation paradigms. First, interventions with people with severe and profound intellectual disabilities have been largely single-participant designs designed to increase choice-making behaviour in everyday settings. Areas of intervention have included choosing between different foods or drinks (Parsons & Reid, 1990; Sigafoos, Roberts, Couzens & Kerr, 1993; Belfiore, Browder & Mace, 1994), choosing preferred leisure activities (Nietupski et al., 1986; Sigafoos et al., 1993; Parsons et al., 1997; Browder, Cooper & Lim, 1998), choosing preferred work activities (Parsons, Reid, Reynolds & Bumgarner, 1990), choosing food in fast-food restaurants (Cooper & Browder, 1998), assessing the availability of preferred lifestyle options (Foxx et al., 1993), and expressing choices during social interactions (Kennedy & Haring, 1993). Although conducted with very small samples, these studies have consistently demonstrated socially significant and generalised improvements in choice-making behaviour (Algozzine et al., 2001).

The second paradigm has been to evaluate teaching interventions designed to improve choice-making skills as a component of self-determination, largely conducted in groups with people with mild/moderate intellectual disabilities. These have typically reported pre/post intervention improvements in choice-making and control (e.g., Abery, Rudrud, Arndt, Schauben & Eggebeen, 1995; Ezell, Klein & Ezell-Powell, 1999). More specific group interventions concerning choice over employment options and person-centred planning strategies have produced similar improvements in choice-making (Cross, Cooke, Wood & Test, 1999). Single-participant designs evaluating the teaching of choice-making skills have also reported success in improving and generalising choice-making skills among children and adults with intellectual disabilities (Rietveld, 1983; Schleien & Larson, 1986). Finally, some studies have reported training programmes for staff that resulted in increased choices being made available by staff to people with intellectual disabilities (e.g., Salmento & Bambara, 2000; McKnight & Kearney, 2001).

While these studies have involved larger numbers of participants, there are a number of challenges for researchers wanting to develop and evaluate teaching interventions to improve choice-making skills. First, most of the interventions discussed have been self-determination interventions, where the training of choice-making skills is a relatively small component of a multicomponent intervention. More detailed evaluation of the effectiveness of specific components is a potential future avenue for research in this area. Second, many of the outcome measures used in evaluations have been self-report assessments of self-determination, again with choice-making as a small component. Third, few studies have attempted to evaluate the extent to which choice-making skills learned during interventions generalise to everyday settings (e.g., Abery et al., 1995), a result that is clearly crucial if interventions are to be effective. Finally, studies have typically used pre-/post-intervention designs; more powerful designs including comparison groups or multiple baselines are needed.

IMPROVING CHOICE AS A LIFESTYLE INTERVENTION

The research discussed so far in this chapter has largely concerned choice as a valued end in itself. However, a body of research has used choice as an independent variable in intervention studies using choice-making as a vehicle to improve lifestyle. Once again, a relatively recent systematic review is available concerning increasing choice-making as an intervention to improve behaviour (Kern et al., 1998), with the bulk of research adopting a behavioural, single-participant design with people with severe or profound intellectual disabilities. Under conditions of greater choice for the person with intellectual disabilities, these studies have demonstrated the following:

(1) greater on-task behaviour during academic, vocational, or domestic tasks (e.g., Rice & Nelson, 1983; Parsons et al., 1990; Dunlap, Kern-Dunlap, Clarke & Robbins, 1991; Harding, Wacker, Cooper, Millard & Jensen-Kovolan, 1994; Bambara, Ager & Koger, 1994; Bambara, Koger, Katzer & Davenport, 1995; Seybert, Dunlap & Ferro, 1996; Umbreit & Blair, 1996; Dibley & Lim, 1999)
(2) greater leisure activities and social behaviour (Dattilo & Rusch, 1985; Peck, 1985; LaMore & Nelson, 1993)

(3) reduced challenging behaviours (Dyer, Dunlap & Winterling, 1990; Dunlap et al., 1991; Harding et al., 1994; Vaughn & Horner, 1995, 1997; Seybert et al., 1996; Umbreit & Blair, 1996; Graff, Libby & Green, 1998; Dibley & Lim, 1999).

However, it is unclear whether choice-making is the active ingredient in improving behaviour; for example, the presence of a high-preference stimulus in the absence of choice (Fisher, O'Connor, Kurtz, DeLeon & Gotjen, 2000; Parsons et al., 1990; Bambara et al., 1995; Umbreit & Blair, 1996; Vaughn & Horner, 1997) or the presence of novel stimuli (Toro-Zambrana, Lee & Belfiore, 1999) may be sufficient in themselves to improve behaviour. Larger group surveys of people with intellectual disabilities across a wider range of ability report less consistent associations between choice-making and challenging behaviour (see Stancliffe, 1997; Stancliffe, Abery & Smith, 2000; Robertson et al., 2001).

Clearly, behavioural interventions have demonstrated that improving choice can have a socially significant impact on the lives of people with severe or profound intellectual disabilities. Perhaps the next challenge is to demonstrate the applicability of such interventions to routine practice; can such interventions be effectively used for larger numbers of people, in a wider range of settings, with staff groups in routine service settings? The lack of systematically evaluated interventions designed to improve choice-making for more able people with intellectual disabilities as a vehicle to improve lifestyle is perhaps surprising. Given the lack of choice-making in all settings where people with intellectual disabilities live, such interventions may have a significant impact on the frequently impoverished lifestyles of people with intellectual disabilities across the ability range.

CONCLUSIONS

Research concerning choices in the lives of people with intellectual disabilities has burgeoned over the past 20 years, with a number of significant strands of research beginning to produce exciting findings and, more importantly, meaningful changes in people's lives.

(1) Researchers investigating choice need to work to a clear definition of choice, and ensure that their assessment procedures reflect this definition. In particular, researchers need to build on current models of self-determination to delineate more precisely the location of choice within models of self-determination; how distinct is choice from related constructs in self-determination models, such as decision-making, and where does choice fit in a causal theory of self-determination?

(2) For researchers working with people with severe or profound intellectual disabilities and using a preference-assessment paradigm, sophisticated and validated methods have been developed. Possible future directions for this paradigm may include:
- more research investigating the long-term stability of individual preferences, and factors which influence preference stability
- the extension of the preference-assessment paradigm from tangible objects to more symbolic objects representing bigger life choices
- investigating further how preference assessments can be embedded into routine practice, particularly into the routine practice of staff regularly working with people with intellectual disabilities and into new developments such as person-centred planning

- the investigation of preference-assessment procedures with larger numbers of people with intellectual disabilities across a broader ability range.

Perhaps surprisingly, very little work has focused on assessing choice-making ability among more able people with intellectual disabilities, and there is considerable potential here for the development of measures of choice-making competencies.

(3) Considerable effort has been put into research concerning choice-making in the lives of people with intellectual disabilities. Self-report measures of choice-making are improving in terms of reliability and concurrent validity, although their application will always be limited to a restricted range of people with intellectual disabilities. Some informant-report measures also report satisfactory reliability and concurrent validity, and can be used for all people with intellectual disabilities, although caution must be used with such measures due to the likely social desirability response bias of many informants. There is certainly scope for greater methodological diversity in the investigation of choice-making in the lives of people with intellectual disabilities, including the use of qualitative interview and analysis methods and observational methods.

(4) As with preference-assessment studies, behavioural interventions evaluating interventions to improve choice-making skills among people with severe and profound intellectual disabilities have demonstrated considerable sophistication and report very encouraging findings. The major challenges for researchers in this field concern demonstrating the generalisability of the behavioural interventions used to a greater range of settings, to a larger number of people, and into routine service settings. Teaching interventions designed to improve the choice-making skills of people with intellectual disabilities also hold a number of challenges for researchers, including more rigorous study designs, more systematic investigations of the active components of self-determination interventions, and a greater focus on the social validity of any improvements found.

(5) Finally, as with behavioural interventions to improve choice-making behaviours, interventions using choice-making as a vehicle to improve lifestyle could profitably pay greater attention to generalisability issues, as well as systematically evaluating the impact of choice per se versus the availability of preferred items on lifestyle outcomes. There appears to be very little research systematically evaluating the impact of choice-making on the lifestyles of more able people with intellectual disabilities; given the low levels of choice-making reported by people with intellectual disabilities in all settings, effective interventions could have a substantial impact on the lives of more able people with intellectual disabilities.

REFERENCES

Abery, B., Rudrud, L., Arndt, K., Schauben, L. & Eggebeen, A. (1995). Evaluating a multicomponent program for enhancing the self-determination of youth with disabilities. *Intervention in School and Clinic*, **30**, 170–179.

Abery, B.H. & Stancliffe, R.J. (1996). The ecology of self-determination. In D.J. Sands & M.L. Wehmeyer (Eds) *Self-Determination Across the Life Span: Independence and Choice for People with Disabilities* (pp. 111–145). Baltimore, MD: Brookes.

Algozzine, B., Browder, D., Karvonen, M., Test, D.W. & Wood, W.M. (2001). Effects of interventions to promote self-determination for individuals with disabilities. *Review of Educational Research*, **71**, 219–277.

Bambara, L.M., Ager, C. & Koger, F. (1994). The effects of choice and task preference on the work performance of adults with severe disabilities. *Journal of Applied Behavior Analysis*, **27**, 555–556.

Bambara, L.M., Koger, F., Katzer, T. & Davenport, T.A. (1995). Embedding choice in the context of daily routines: an experimental case study. *Journal of the Association for Persons with Severe Handicaps*, **20**, 185–195.

Belfiore, P.J., Browder, D.M. & Mace, C. (1994). Assessing choice making and preference in adults with profound mental retardation across community and center-based settings. *Journal of Behavioral Education*, **4**, 217–225.

Bojak, S.L. & Carr, J.E. (1999). On the displacement of leisure items by food during multiple-stimulus preference assessments. *Journal of Applied Behavior Analysis*, **32**, 515–518.

Browder, D.M., Cooper, K.J. & Lim, L. (1998). Teaching adults with severe disabilities to express their choice of settings for leisure activities. *Education and Training in Mental Retardation and Developmental Disabilities*, **33**, 228–238.

Carey, Y., O'Reilly, M., Walsh, P.N. & Lancioni, G. (1996). Identifying preferred activities for a student with severe and multiple disabilities. *Irish Journal of Psychology*, **17**, 251–257.

Cohen-Almeida, D., Graff, R.B. & Ahearn, W.H. (2000). A comparison of verbal and tangible stimulus preference assessments. *Journal of Applied Behavior Analysis*, **33**, 329–334.

Cooper, K.J. & Browder, D.M. (1998). Enhancing choice and participation for adults with severe disabilities in community-based instruction. *Journal of the Association for Persons with Severe Handicaps*, **23**, 252–260.

Cross, T., Cooke, N.L., Wood, W.M. & Test, D.W. (1999). Comparison of the effects of MAPS and ChoiceMaker on student self-determination skills. *Education and Training in Mental Retardation and Developmental Disabilities*, **34**, 499–510.

Cummins, R.A. (1997). *Comprehensive Quality of Life Scale-Intellectual/Cognitive Disability: Fifth Edition (ComQol-I5)*. Melbourne: School of Psychology, Deakin University.

Dattilo, J. (1986). Computerized assessment of preference for severely handicapped individuals. *Journal of Applied Behavior Analysis*, **19**, 445–448.

Dattilo, J. & Mirenda, P. (1987). An application of a leisure preference assessment protocol for persons with severe handicaps. *Journal of the Association for Persons with Severe Handicaps*, **12**, 306–311.

Dattilo, J. & Rusch, F. (1985). Effects of choice on leisure participation for persons with severe handicaps. *Journal of the Association for Persons with Severe Handicaps*, **10**, 194–199.

Davis, P. & Faw, G. (2002). Residential preferences in person-centered planning: empowerment through the self-identification of preferences and their availability. In S. Holbourn & P.M. Vietze (Eds) *Person-Centered Planning: Research, Practice, and Future Directions* (pp. 203–221). Baltimore, MD: Brookes.

DeLeon, I.G. & Iwata, B.A. (1996). Evaluation of a multiple-stimulus presentation format for assessing reinforcer preferences. *Journal of Applied Behavior Analysis*, **29**, 519–534.

DeLeon, I.G., Iwata, B.A. & Roscoe, E.M. (1997). Displacement of leisure reinforcers by food during preference assessments. *Journal of Applied Behavior Analysis*, **30**, 475–484.

Department of Health (2001). *Valuing People: A New Strategy for Learning Disability for the 21st Century*. London: Stationery Office.

Dibley, S. & Lim, L. (1999). Providing choice making opportunities within and between daily school routines. *Journal of Behavioral Education*, **9**, 117–132.

Dunlap, G., Kern-Dunlap, L., Clarke, S. & Robbins, F.R. (1991). Functional assessment, curricular revision, and severe behavior problems. *Journal of Applied Behavior Analysis*, **24**, 387–397.

Dyer, K., Dunlap, G. & Winterling, V. (1990). Effects of choice making on the serious problem behaviors of students with severe handicaps. *Journal of Applied Behavior Analysis*, **23**, 515–524.

Ezell, D., Klein, C.E. & Ezell-Powell, S. (1999). Empowering students with mental retardation through portfolio assessment: a tool for fostering self-determination skills. *Education and Training in Mental Retardation and Developmental Disabilities*, **34**, 453–463.

Fisher, W.W., O'Connor, J.T., Kurtz, P.F., DeLeon, I.G. & Gotjen, D.L. (2000). The effects of noncontingent delivery of high- and low-preference stimuli on attention-maintained destructive behavior. *Journal of Applied Behavior Analysis*, **33**, 79–83.

Fisher, W.W., Piazza, C.C., Bowman, L.G. & Amari, A. (1996). Integrating caregiver report with a systematic choice assessment to enhance reinforcer identification. *American Journal on Mental Retardation*, **101**, 15–25.

Fisher, W.W., Piazza, C.C., Bowman, L.P., Hagopian, L.P., Owen, J.C. & Slevin, I. (1992). A comparison of two approaches for identifying reinforcers for persons with severe and profound disabilities. *Journal of Applied Behavior Analysis*, **25**, 491–498.

Foster-Johnson, L., Ferro, J. & Dunlap, G. (1994). Preferred curricular activities and reduced problem behaviors in students with intellectual disabilities. *Journal of Applied Behavior Analysis*, **27**, 493–504.

Foxx, R.M., Faw, G.D., Taylor, S., Davis, P.K. & Fulia, R. (1993). "Would I be able to . . .?" Teaching clients to assess the availability of their community lifestyle preferences. *American Journal on Mental Retardation*, **98**, 235–248.

Graff, R.B., Libby, M.E. & Green, G. (1998). The effects of reinforcer choice on rates of challenging behavior and free operant responding in individuals with severe disabilities. *Behavioral Interventions*, **13**, 249–268.

Green, C.W., Middleton, S.G. & Reid, D.H. (2000). Embedded evaluation of preferences sampled from person-centered plans for people with profound multiple disabilities. *Journal of Applied Behavior Analysis*, **33**, 639–642.

Green, C.W., Reid, D.H., Canipe, V.S. & Gardner, S.M. (1991). A comprehensive evaluation of reinforcer identification process for persons with profound multiple handicaps. *Journal of Applied Behavior Analysis*, **24**, 537–552.

Hanley, G.P., Iwata, B.A. & Lindberg, J.S. (1999). Analysis of activity preferences as a function of differential consequences. *Journal of Applied Behavior Analysis*, **32**, 419–435.

Harding, J., Wacker, D.P., Cooper, L.J., Millard, T. & Jensen-Kovolan, P. (1994). Brief hierarchical assessment of potential treatment components with children in an outpatient clinic. *Journal of Applied Behavior Analysis*, **27**, 291–300.

Hatton, C., Emerson, E., Robertson, J., Gregory, N., Kessissoglou, S. & Walsh, P.N. (in press). The Resident Choice Scale: a measure to assess opportunities for self-determination in residential settings. *Journal of Intellectual Disability Research.*

Heller, T., Miller, A.B. & Factor, A. (1999). Autonomy in residential facilities and community functioning of adults with mental retardation. *Mental Retardation*, **37**, 449–457.

Higbee, T.S., Carr, J.E. & Harrison, C.D. (2000). Further evaluation of the multiple-stimulus preference assessment. *Research in Developmental Disabilities*, **21**, 61–73.

Kearney, C.A., Bergan, K.P. & McKnight, T.J. (1998). Choice availability and persons with mental retardation: a longitudinal and regression analysis. *Journal of Developmental and Physical Disabilities*, **10**, 291–305.

Kearney, C.A., Durand, V.M. & Mindell, J.A. (1995). Choice assessment in residential settings. *Journal of Developmental and Physical Disabilities*, **7**, 203–213.

Kennedy, C.H. & Haring, T.G. (1993). Teaching choice making during social interactions to students with profound multiple disabilities. *Journal of the Association for Persons with Severe Handicaps*, **11**, 28–38.

Kern, L., Vorndran, C.M., Hilt, A., Ringdahl, J.E., Adelman, B.E. & Dunlap, G. (1998). Choice as an intervention to improve behavior: a review of the literature. *Journal of Behavioral Education*, **8**, 151–169.

Kishi, G., Teelucksingh, B., Zollers, N., Park-Lee, S. & Meyer, L. (1988). Daily decision-making in community residences: a social comparison of adults with and without mental retardation. *American Journal on Mental Retardation*, **92**, 430–435.

LaMore, K.L. & Nelson, D. (1993). The effects of options on performance of an art project in adults with mental disabilities. *American Journal of Occupational Therapy*, **47**, 397–401.

Lim, L., Browder, D.M. & Bambara, L. (2001). Effects of sampling opportunities on preference development for adults with severe disabilities. *Education and Training in Mental Retardation and Developmental Disabilities*, **36**, 188–195.

Lohrmann-O'Rourke, S. & Browder, D.M. (1998). Empirically based methods to assess the preferences of individuals with severe disabilities. *American Journal on Mental Retardation*, **103**, 146–161.

Mason, S.A., McGee, G.G., Farmer-Dougan, V. & Risley, T.R. (1989). A practical strategy for ongoing reinforcer assessment. *Journal of Applied Behavior Analysis*, **22**, 171–179.
Matson, J.L., Bielecki, J., Mayville, E.A., Smalls, Y., Bamburg, J.W. & Baglio, C.S. (1999). The development of a reinforcer choice assessment scale for persons with severe and profound mental retardation. *Research in Developmental Disabilities*, **20**, 379–384.
McKnight, T.J. & Kearney, C.A. (2001). Staff training regarding choice availability for persons with mental retardation: a preliminary analysis. *Journal of Developmental and Physical Disabilities*, **13**, 1–10.
Mithaug, D.E. & Hanawalt, D.A. (1978). The validation of procedures to assess prevocational task preferences in retarded adults. *Journal of Applied Behavior Analysis*, **11**, 153–162.
Nerney, T. (1998). Self-determination for people with developmental disabilities. Doing more with less: rethinking long-term care. *AAMR News and Notes*, **11**, 10–12.
Neumayer, R. & Bleasdale, M. (1996). Personal lifestyle preferences of people with an intellectual disability. *Journal of Intellectual and Developmental Disability*, **21**, 91–115.
Nietupski, J., Hamre-Nietupski, S., Green, K., Varnum-Teeter, K., Twedt, B., LePera, D., et al. (1986). Self-initiated and sustained leisure activity participation by students with moderate/severe handicaps. *Education and Training of the Mentally Retarded*, **21**, 259–264.
Nozaki, K. & Mochizuki, A. (1995). Assessing choice making of a person with profound disabilities: a preliminary analysis. *Journal of the Association for Persons with Severe Handicaps*, **20**, 196–201.
Parsons, M.B., Harper, V.N., Jensen, J.M. & Reid, D.H. (1997). Assisting older adults with severe disabilities in expressing leisure preferences: a protocol for determining choice-making skills. *Research in Developmental Disabilities*, **18**, 113–126.
Parsons, M.B. & Reid, D.H. (1990). Assessing food preferences among persons with profound mental retardation: providing opportunities to make choices. *Journal of Applied Behavior Analysis*, **23**, 183–195.
Parsons, M.B., Reid, D.H. & Green, C.W. (1998). Identifying work-based preferences prior to supported work for an individual with multiple severe disabilities including deaf-blindness. *Journal of the Association for Persons with Severe Handicaps*, **23**, 329–333.
Parsons, M.B., Reid, D.H., Reynolds, J. & Bumgarner, M. (1990). Effects of chosen versus assigned jobs on the work performance of persons with severe handicaps. *Journal of Applied Behavior Analysis*, **23**, 253–258.
Peck, C. (1985). Increasing opportunities for social control by children with autism and severe handicaps: effects of student behavior and perceived classroom climate. *Journal of the Association for Persons with Severe Handicaps*, **10**, 183–194.
Piazza, C.C., Fisher, W.W., Hagopian, L.P., Bowman, L.G. & Toole, L. (1996). Using a choice assessment to predict reinforcer effectiveness. *Journal of Applied Behavior Analysis*, **29**, 1–10.
Reid, D.H., Everson, J.M. & Green, C.W. (1999). A systematic evaluation of preferences identified through person-centered planning for people with profound multiple disabilities. *Journal of Applied Behavior Analysis*, **32**, 467–477.
Reid, D.H. & Green, C.W. (2002). Person-centered planning with people who have severe multiple disabilities: validated practices and misapplications. In S. Holbourn & P.M. Vietze (Eds) *Person-Centered Planning: Research, Practice, and Future Directions* (pp. 183–202). Baltimore, MD: Brookes.
Rice, M. & Nelson, D. (1983). Effect of choice making on a self-care activity in mentally retarded adult and adolescent males. *Occupational Therapy Journal of Research*, **8**, 176–185.
Rietveld, C.M. (1983). The training of choice behaviors in Down's syndrome and non-retarded preschool children. *Australia and New Zealand Journal of Developmental Disabilities*, **9**, 75–83.
Robertson, J., Emerson, E., Hatton, C., Gregory, N., Kessissoglou, S., Hallam, A., et al. (2001). Environmental opportunities and supports for exercising self-determination in community-based residential settings. *Research in Developmental Disabilities*, **22**, 487–502.
Salmento, M. & Bambara, L.M. (2000). Teaching staff members to provide choice opportunities for adults with multiple disabilities. *Journal of Positive Behavior Interventions*, **2**, 12–21.
Schalock, R.L. & Keith, K.D. (1993). *Quality of Life Questionnaire*. Worthington, OH: IDS Publishing.
Schleien, S.J. & Larson, A. (1986). Adult leisure education for the independent use of a community recreation center. *Journal of the Association for Persons with Severe Handicaps*, **11**, 39–44.

Seybert, S., Dunlap, G. & Ferro, J. (1996). The effects of choice-making on the problem behaviors of high school students with intellectual disabilities. *Journal of Behavioral Education*, **6**, 49–65.

Sigafoos, J. & Dempsey, R. (1992). Assessing choice making among children with multiple disabilities. *Journal of Applied Behavior Analysis*, **25**, 747–755.

Sigafoos, J., Laurie, S. & Pennell, D. (1995). Preliminary assessment of choice making among children with multiple disabilities. *Journal of Applied Behavior Analysis*, **25**, 747–755.

Sigafoos, J., Roberts, D., Couzens, D. & Kerr, M. (1993). Providing opportunities for choice-making and turn taking to adults with multiple disabilities. *Journal of Developmental and Physical Disabilities*, **5**, 297–310.

Stalker, K. & Harris, P. (1998). The exercise of choice by adults with intellectual disabilities: a literature review. *Journal of Applied Research in Intellectual Disabilities*, **11**, 60–76.

Stancliffe, R.J. (1997). Community living-unit size, staff presence, and residents' choice-making. *Mental Retardation*, **35**, 1–9.

Stancliffe, R.J. (2001). Living with support in the community: predictors of choice and self-determination. *Mental Retardation and Developmental Disabilities Research Reviews*, **7**, 91–98.

Stancliffe, R.J. & Abery, B.H. (1997). Longitudinal study of deinstitutionalization and the exercise of choice. *Mental Retardation*, **35**, 159–169.

Stancliffe, R.J., Abery, B.H. & Smith, J. (2000). Personal control and the ecology of community living settings: beyond living-unit size and type. *American Journal on Mental Retardation*, **105**, 431–454.

Stancliffe, R.J. & Parmenter, T.R. (1999). The Choice Questionnaire: a scale to assess choices exercised by adults with intellectual disability. *Journal of Intellectual and Developmental Disability*, **24**, 107–132.

Taal, M., Wessels, M. & van der Molen, M. (2001). Choice making, competence and well-being of persons with mild mental retardation or borderline intelligence. *Developmental Disabilities Bulletin*, **29**, 49–60.

Taravella, C.C., Lerman, D.C., Contrucci, S.A. & Roane, H.S. (2000). Further evaluation of low-ranked items in stimulus-choice preference assessments. *Journal of Applied Behavior Analysis*, **33**, 105–108.

Toro-Zambrana, W., Lee, D.L. & Belfiore, P.J. (1999). The effects of response effort and choice on productivity. *Journal of Developmental and Physical Disabilities*, **11**, 287–293.

Umbreit, J. & Blair, K.-S. (1996). The effects of preference, choice, and attention on problem behavior at school. *Education and Training in Mental Retardation and Developmental Disabilities*, **31**, 151–161.

Vaughn, B.J. & Horner, R.H. (1995). Effects of concrete versus verbal choice systems on problem behavior. *Augmentative and Alternative Communication*, **11**, 89–92.

Vaughn, B.J. & Horner, R.H. (1997). Identifying instructional tasks that occasion problem behaviors and assessing the effects of student versus teacher choice among these tasks. *Journal of Applied Behavior Analysis*, **30**, 299–312.

Ward, M.J. (1996). Coming of age in the age of self-determination: a historical and personal perspective. In D.J. Sands & M.L. Wehmeyer (Eds) *Self-Determination Across the Life Span: Independence and Choice for People with Disabilities* (pp. 1–16). Baltimore, MD: Brookes.

Wehmeyer, M.L. (1996a). Self-determination as an educational outcome. Why is it important for individuals with disabilities? In D.J. Sands & M.L. Wehmeyer (Eds) *Self-Determination Across the Life Span: Independence and Choice for People with Disabilities* (pp. 17–36). Baltimore, MD: Brookes.

Wehmeyer, M.L. (1996b). Student self-report measure of self-determination for students with cognitive disabilities. *Education and Training in Mental Retardation and Developmental Disabilities*, **31**, 282–293.

Wehmeyer, M.L. (2001). Self-determination and mental retardation. *International Review of Research in Mental Retardation*, **24**, 1–48.

Wehmeyer, M.L. & Bolding, N. (1999). Self-determination across living and working environments: a matched-samples study of adults with mental retardation. *Mental Retardation*, **37**, 353–363.

Wehmeyer, M.L. & Bolding, N. (2001). Enhanced self-determination of adults with intellectual disabilities as an outcome of moving to community-based work or living environments. *Journal of Intellectual Disability Research*, **45**, 371–383.

Wehmeyer, M.L., Kelchner, K. & Richards, S. (1996). Essential characteristics of self-determined behavior of individuals with mental retardation. *American Journal on Mental Retardation*, **100**, 632–642.

Wehmeyer, M. & Schwartz, M. (1998). The relationship between self-determination and quality of life for adults with mental retardation. *Education and Training in Mental Retardation and Developmental Disabilities*, **33**, 3–12.

Windsor, J., Piche, L.M. & Locke, P.A. (1994). Preference testing: a comparison of two presentation methods. *Research in Developmental Disabilities*, **15**, 439–455.

Zhou, L., Iwata, B.A., Goff, G.A. & Shore, B.A. (2001). Longitudinal analysis of leisure-item preferences. *Journal of Applied Behavior Analysis*, **34**, 179–184.

CHAPTER 17

Research on Engagement in Activity

David Felce
University of Wales College of Medicine, UK
and
Eric Emerson
Lancaster University, UK

This chapter is concerned with the evaluation of activity levels and/or "engagement" as an indicator of the quality of life of people with intellectual disabilities and, indirectly, the support that they receive. First, we provide a rationale for evaluating engagement in activity. Second, we discuss key issues that need to be addressed when quantifying engagement. These include the definition of observational categories, training observers, minimising reactivity and observer fatigue, the implications of the influence of personal characteristics on engagement in activity for the design of comparative evaluations, and recent developments in observational technology and analysis. Third, we present a number of research applications that have arisen from this field of enquiry. In this section, we review research that has evaluated outcome in different residential service models or that has explored environmental predictors of outcome. We also illustrate the emerging application of sequential analysis to the understanding of challenging behaviour and the evaluation of staff training. Finally, we conclude by discussing the continued utility of engagement in activity as a quality-of-life indicator and the conclusions which can be drawn to date about residential arrangements which promote engagement in activity.

RATIONALE FOR RESEARCH IN ENGAGEMENT IN ACTIVITY

Interest in evaluating the patterns of activity has its roots in the exposure during the 1960s of the abusive and degrading nature of life in long-stay institutions for people with intellectual disabilities. Journalistic exposés, photographic essays, research reports, and the results of government-led enquiries all highlighted the time people habitually spent being socially isolated, unduly passive, or engaging in repetitive, apparently purposeless behaviour (Blatt & Kaplan, 1966; Morris, 1969; Oswin, 1971; Scheerenberger, 1983; Martin, 1984). The concern expressed about prolonged disengagement or inactivity pointed to the significance

The International Handbook of Applied Research in Intellectual Disabilities. Edited by E. Emerson, C. Hatton, T. Thompson and T.R. Parmenter ISBN 0-471-49709-6.

which many people feel is attached to constructive interaction with their material and social worlds. Except for a small minority who choose the contemplative life, interaction with the environment characterises people's existence unless they are traumatised, ill, chronically depressed or withdrawn, or in some other way incapacitated. Curiosity or an innate inclination to interact with the environment may well have become integral to the human condition through its survival value. Moreover, selection on a different timescale is also implied by socialisation. Although cultures tolerate enormous variety in individual behaviour, they typically shape conformity among citizens to certain norms. Sustaining a level of occupation consistent with one's age is an expectation and an indicator of status in many cultures.

In addition, the level of physical activity is an important determinant of physical and mental health. Research undertaken on people who do not have intellectual disabilities suggests that physical activity prevents the development of a wide range of age-related impairments in older people (Blain, Vuillemin, Blain & Jeandel, 2000) and that there are clear links between activity levels and low mood, including depression (Sallis, Prochaska & Taylor, 2000; van Gool et al., 2003). Indeed, the link between activity levels and mood is such that there is evidence to suggest that increasing activity levels may be effective in reducing depression and problem behaviours among clinical and non-clinical populations (Allison, Faith & Franklin, 1995; Lawlor & Hopker, 2001; Brosse, Sheets, Lett & Blumenthal, 2002). The importance of physical activity for people with intellectual disabilities is outlined by Messent, Cooke and Long (1999), who note that the poor cardiovascular fitness of people with intellectual disabilities may be one of the main contributing factors for the high mortality rate among those with intellectual disabilities.

The application of non-participant observational techniques to the measurement of engagement in activity derives from the work of Todd Risley and his colleagues (see Risley & Cataldo, 1973; Jones, Risley & Favell, 1983) and from parallel ecological research using direct observation by Sackett and Landesman-Dwyer (1977). Within this tradition, although the persons with intellectual disabilities and their activity are the focus of observation, the persons themselves are not being evaluated. Rather, the focus of evaluation is the adequacy of the environment in providing the opportunities, antecedent and concurrent support, and motivation necessary for people with intellectual disabilities to spend their time involved in constructive and worthwhile pursuits. If the level of activity is significantly below that which is usual, the implication drawn is that environmental arrangements are not well matched to the needs of the service users and should be changed. Risley and Cataldo (1973) encapsulated this position:

> The direction and extent of engagement with the physical and social environment appears to be an almost universal indication of the quality of a setting for people. Those familiar with educational settings often evaluate a particular activity area or an entire classroom at almost a glance, without even knowing the curriculum or the goals of the program, and they usually agree with each other's independent evaluations. They are simply assessing how many of the children are looking at and/or physically interacting with materials or people at any moment in time, or, in other words, what proportion of his time each child spends appropriately engaged with his environment. (first paragraph of preface, page unnumbered)

Although we have suggested that engagement in activity is a normal state for most people going about their daily affairs, there have been few comparative studies that have examined the activity patterns of people with and without intellectual disabilities. The extent and range of ordinary people's typical engagement in activities has been assumed rather than demonstrated. One exception, which evaluated change in the activities undertaken by 27 people with intellectual disabilities following deinstitutionalisation, showed that people with intellectual disabilities engaged in less general, family role, social, outside, independent, and recreation activity, on average, than non-disabled people (O'Neill, Brown, Gordon & Schonhorn, 1985). Similarly, Robertson et al. (2000) reported that levels of physical activity were markedly lower among a sample of 500 people with intellectual disabilities in supported accommodation than among the English adult population (see also Flynn & Hirst, 1992).

QUANTIFYING ENGAGEMENT IN ACTIVITY

Various authors have characterised the activities undertaken by service users by rating the activities undertaken in a typical time period (such as a week or a month) on a scale or checklist (O'Neill, Brown, Gordon, Schonhorn & Greer, 1981; Kennedy, Horner, Newton & Kanda, 1990; Raynes, Wright, Shiell & Pettipher, 1994). However, quantification of constructive activity has generally been achieved through direct non-participant observation of behaviour. The principal dimensions of engagement in activity with this method are extent and quality. Extent refers to the time spent doing particular activities relative to the total time available (that is, the percentage duration of each form of activity). Quality includes the nature of activity (social interaction, leisure, household, etc.) and other salient aspects, such as whether it was self-initiated (that is, voluntary), functional, or age-appropriate. The most flexible method for constructing an ecological record is time-anchored qualitative description, using the full breadth and subtlety of language to describe events. However, there are advantages both for summarising large quantities of data and for comparing across situations if activity is coded in some standard way and its duration measured systematically.

Defining Observational Categories

Defining what is constructive activity is of course problematic and may depend on the purposes or goals of a particular environment of interest. Coding schemes and category definitions can, in principle, reflect more or less fine-grain distinctions in the quality of different forms of activity together with cultural, age-group, and setting expectations, depending on the complexity of what can be achieved in practice. For example, Felce, de Kock and Repp (1986), Beyer, Kilsby and Willson (1995), and Saxby, Thomas, Felce and de Kock (1986) employed different operationalisations of the underlying concept to observe engagement in the home, workplace, and community. However, generally in our research, we have not been overly restrictive in whether activities are included as constructive, simply seeking to distinguish any meaningful social interaction or adaptive pursuit from challenging behaviour, apparently purposeless, repetitious acts, and inactivity. Other coding schema have recorded engagement that is functional and/or age-appropriate (Hatton, Emerson, Robertson, Henderson & Cooper, 1995; Ferro, Foster-Johnson & Dunlap, 1996).

Time-sampling procedures have made multiple-category observation in the natural environment feasible for some time; now, small, portable computers have permitted real-time data capture on the same basis (Emerson, Reeves & Felce, 2000a). Exploiting the full capacity for multiple-category recording means that environmental conditions and events experienced by the person can be recorded at the same time as the activity of the person being

Table 17.1 Behavioural observation codes

Subject	Observational category
Staff behaviour	*Verbal instruction:* spoken or signed instruction to perform an activity or corrective feedback containing an instruction. *Prompting/demonstration:* gestural or physical prompting to perform an activity, presenting materials in the context of an activity, providing a demonstration, or corrective feedback containing a prompt or demonstration. *Physical guidance:* guiding the motor coordination of a participant to do an activity, manipulating the materials being used by a participant to help him or her do an activity, or corrective feedback containing guidance. *Praise:* verbal, gestural, or physical appreciation of participant activity. *Restraint:* physical or verbal disapproval without correction or physically preventing activity. *Other conversation:* all other spoken or signed interactions neither encouraging nor discouraging of activity. *Processing/feeding:* seeing to the self-care and feeding needs of participants without their participation.
Participant behaviour	*Social engagement:* speech, sign, gesture, or other attempt to gain or retain the attention of another person (except by challenging behaviour) or the giving of attention, as evidenced by eye contact or orientation of the head, to another person who is reciprocally interacting. *Non-social engagement—domestic:* getting ready for, doing, or clearing away a household or gardening activity. *Non-social engagement—personal:* getting ready for, doing, or clearing away a self-help or personal activity. *Non-social engagement—leisure and other:* getting ready for, doing, or clearing away a recreational activity or educational activity, the content of which could not be coded under the two codes above. *Challenging behaviour (five categories): self-injury, aggression against other, damage to property, stereotypy, other inappropriate behaviours.* *Disengagement:* all other behaviour, including no activity, passively holding materials, walking when not part of an engagement activity, smoking, and unpurposeful activity such as manipulating materials to no apparent purpose.

observed. Social interaction can thus be recorded and the reciprocity of relationship established. Moreover, the observation of social interaction of others encompasses staff, carer, or supporter activity. This, in conjunction with observation of the person's engagement in activity, can determine the initiation and level of independence of activity. Table 17.1 gives brief details of a typical set of definitions.

Ensuring Data Quality

The "reliability" of data collected through non-participant observation is typically assessed through the determination of levels of interobserver agreement (cf. Suen & Ary, 1989). That is, do two observers simultaneously and independently observing the same events produce similar records? Ensuring acceptable levels of interobserver agreement is dependent on providing appropriate pre-observation training for observers, implementing an observational protocol that minimises observer fatigue, and incorporating ongoing quality checks.

Observer training will typically involve the following:

(1) observer familiarisation with the coding scheme and recording apparatus through demonstration, discussion, and private study
(2) guided practice in simulated conditions (such as from video or role-play)
(3) guided practice in situ.

Pre-observation training should be continued until observers attain a level of interobserver agreement superior to that considered "acceptable" on the index of interobserver agreement to be employed in the study.

Maintaining acceptable levels of interobserver agreement can be aided by implementing an observational protocol that minimises observer fatigue, and by incorporating ongoing quality checks. Observer fatigue is a function of the complexity of the coding scheme, the length and structure of the observational session, and the observational sampling procedure (such as momentary time sampling, partial interval recording, or real-time multiple-category recording). In particular, real-time, multiple-category recording in the natural environment places considerable demands on observers. We have, however, maintained acceptable levels of interobserver agreement by using relatively detailed coding schema in real-time, multiple-category recording in the natural environment for observation sessions lasting 3–4 hours, split into separate 20-minute blocks. At the end of each block, the observer saves the data on the hand-held computer and completes any written notes (for example, to note the occurrence of potentially salient uncoded events or events that were difficult to code).

Within non-participant observational research, "reliability" is not seen as an inherent characteristic of the measurement tool (such as a questionnaire), but as a function of the observational process. As such, ongoing quality checks are essential in determining the level of interobserver agreement and may also be used to provide feedback to observers on the quality of their observation.

Minimising Reactivity

The "validity" of non-participatory behavioural observation is dependent in part on the extent to which the process of observation influences what is being observed. While the literature on participant reactivity suggests that the effects of being observed are relatively transient and small (Harris & Lahey, 1982), even among care staff (Orlowska, 1990) and families (Jacob, Tennenbaum, Seilhamer & Bargiel, 1994; Gittelsohn, Shankar, West, Ram & Gnywali, 1997), a number of simple steps can be taken to minimise these "observer effects". These include developing explicit protocols about how observers deal with enquiries from participants during observation sessions, dressing to "blend in" with the setting, and positioning observers in quiet areas of public spaces. The reported transience of reactivity effects also allows for the possibility of assessing reactivity within observational studies and, if necessary, discarding data collected at the beginning of observational sessions.

Designing Comparative Evaluations: Taking Personal Characteristics into Account

Measures of developmental status, such as mental-age assessments or normed scales of adaptive behaviour, characterise the skills which individuals possess to meet the demands of the environment. It would not be surprising, therefore, if the extent and range of activities undertaken by people in any environment were strongly related to their assessed skills. There is now a sizeable body of evidence in research on residential services that engagement in activity is significantly and positively related to adaptive behaviour among the following groups:

(1) cross-sections of people with intellectual disabilities (Felce & Perry, 1995; Thompson, Robinson, Dietrich, Farris & Sinclair, 1996; Felce et al., 1999)
(2) people with severe and multiple disabilities (Emerson et al., 2000b)
(3) people with severe or profound intellectual disabilities and very severe challenging behaviour (Felce et al., 1998)
(4) people with intellectual disabilities and sensory impairments (Hatton et al., 1996).

In addition, similarly strong associations have been found between adaptive behaviour and observational or scale assessment of participation in domestic tasks (Felce et al., 1998, 1999; Perry, Felce & Lowe, 2000) or social interaction (Perry et al., 2000).

The level of challenging behaviour has been found to be inversely associated with observed engagement in activity and scaled measures of participation in domestic tasks (Felce, Lowe & Jones, 2002). However, levels of adaptive and challenging behaviour were confounded by a significant inverse correlation. Associations between ability and outcome were stronger than those between level of challenging behaviour and outcome. Challenging behaviour was not a significant predictor in a multivariate regression analysis of either outcome when entered with adaptive behaviour. In keeping with this, no significant association between activity levels and assessed challenging behaviour was reported by Emerson et al. (2000b), Felce, Lowe, Beecham and Hallam (2000a), or Perry et al. (2000). However, Thompson et al. (1996) found that level of challenging behaviour on admission predicted level of inactivity.

As Stancliffe, Emerson and Lakin (Chapter 23, this volume) report, a pervasive problem of internal validity arises in comparative studies, as service users are not assigned to different types of service models at random (e.g., Lakin, Bruininks, Hill, Chen & Anderson, 1993; Emerson et al., 2000b; Stancliffe, Abery & Smith, 2000). Given the strong association between ability or adaptive behaviour and engagement, it will nearly always prove necessary either to treat ability as a covariate or match for levels of ability in comparative studies that examine levels of engagement across different models of service provision.

Recent Developments in Observational Technology

As noted above, the ready availability of powerful palm-top computers has for the first time made real-time multiple-category data collection in the natural environment practically possible (Emerson et al., 2000a). This, in turn, has opened up opportunities for the analysis of conditional and sequential relationships within observational data (Hall & Oliver, 2000; Quera & Bakeman, 2000; Yoder & Feurer, 2000; Chapter 8, this volume) That is, the use of simple statistical procedures on real-time, multiple-category data allows us to identify the environmental conditions under which engagement becomes more or less likely and the environmental precursors and consequences of engagement (see below).

RESEARCH APPLICATIONS

Comparison of Engagement Across Residential Service Models

Direct observation of the extent of engagement in activity has been the most frequently used outcome measure in British deinstitutionalisation research since 1980 (Emerson & Hatton, 1994). In an updated review, Hatton and Emerson (1996) considered 118 publications reporting the findings of 70 separate British research studies since the same date. Seventy-seven publications based on 47 studies provided evidence of the participation of residents in everyday activity, including indicators of participation in domestic activities (e.g., Raynes et al., 1994), observed engagement in a range of constructive activities (e.g., Felce & Perry, 1995), and participation in social pursuits with friends and relatives (e.g., de Kock, Saxby, Thomas & Felce, 1988). The majority of these publications (44 of 77) and studies (27 of 47) concerned directly observed engagement in activity. The percentage of time residents were engaged in activity was generally greater in community houses (mean, 48%; range, 8–74%) than in intermediate community settings (mean, 25%; range, 6–54%) or institutions (mean, 14%; range, 2–23%). The majority of individual studies were consistent with this differentiation in engagement, and there is some, albeit limited, evidence that improved levels of engagement in activity within community houses are maintained over time (Saxby, Felce, Harman & Repp, 1988; Rapley & Beyer, 1998). The results of direct observational research are supported by evaluations that have used rating scales or inventory approaches to assess activity both between institutions and intermediate community settings and between institutions and community houses.

Research from other countries has reached similar conclusions. Cummins, Polzin and Theobold (1990) reported increases in participation in active leisure and social interaction after resettlement from institutional living to community houses in Australia. Two studies evaluating moves from institutions to community houses in the USA (O'Neill et al., 1981; 1985) showed increases in the extent of activity undertaken. Moreover, these and the Australian study provided further evidence that improved participation in activity may maintain over time.

Environmental Predictors of Engagement in Residential Research

Hatton and Emerson (1996) emphasise the variation in engagement that is discernible between ostensibly similar service models and suggest that parameters by which service models have been categorised, such as size, location, architectural design, or administrative arrangement, exert an incomplete influence on outcome. Statistical analysis has been used to identify the impact of service design and operational variables more closely.

Residence Size (Number of Residents per Setting)

Evidence supporting the positive advantage of small resident groupings may be inferred from the deinstitutionalisation literature, but it is generally not possible to conclude that reduced size is a causal influence, due to the number of confounded differences between service types. A number of studies of engagement in activity within residential settings have *not* found smaller size to predict more positive outcome within the sometimes constrained range of residential groupings studied (Emerson et al., 2000b; Felce et al., 2000a; 2002; Perry et al., 2000). Felce et al. (2000a) distinguished institutional and community residential services for people with severe intellectual disabilities and very severe challenging behaviour by cluster analysis of a number of quantifiable setting descriptors, and treated the resulting distinction of service model as a dichotomous variable within a multivariate regression analysis of service costs and outcome. The service model dummy variable and residence size were significantly intercorrelated. However, the dichotomous service model variable provided as much explanatory power as more finely grained setting size across a number of outcomes, including participation in domestic tasks. They discussed the possibility that setting size may be a proxy for service model when size differences are large, but that, consistent with the findings above, outcome may be insensitive to small variations within models. In support of this line of argument, setting size may exert an indirect effect on outcome by being closely associated with other variables which affect outcome more directly, such as the homelikeness of the building (Thompson, Robinson, Graff & Ingenmey, 1990), or the pattern of staff : resident groupings within the setting (Felce, Repp, Ager & Blunden, 1991; Holland & Meddis, 1993).

Architectural Design, Furnishings, and Material Enrichment

Again, evidence supporting the positive advantage of normative architectural design, furnishings, and material enrichment may be inferred from the deinstitutionalisation literature, but with equal uncertainty, due to the number of confounded differences between service models. A number of studies directly implicate homelikeness in design and furnishings, access to the normal functional areas within homes, and material enrichment as influences on participation in domestic tasks and engagement in activity in general. Felce, Thomas, de Kock, Saxby and Repp (1985) observed the activity of residents who moved from relatively barren, architecturally non-normative institutional settings to relatively enriched, architecturally normative community houses. They showed that engagement in activities involving use of materials, furnishings, or equipment was greater in the latter, and that a high proportion of the additional activity was undertaken in the kitchen and laundry room areas of the houses, two functional spaces which were not part of or accessible within the institutional living spaces.

After controlling for subject and setting characteristics, Thompson et al. (1996) found that residents in more homelike community settings were more likely to engage in household tasks and other individual activities, whereas those in less homelike community settings were more likely to be inactive or engaged in repetitive, stereotyped movements. They also found that homelikeness and the orientation of staff (vis à vis supporting resident choice and participation in activities) were intertwined, so it is possible that homelikeness was both an influence on and influenced by the orientation of staff. These results are consistent with those of Perry et al. (2000), who found that the extent of attention residents received from staff was the main predictor of resident engagement in activity after resident characteristics had been taken into account. Homelikeness of the setting was the main predictor of the extent of attention residents received.

Staff: Resident Ratio and Staff: Resident Groupings

Higher staff: resident ratios have *not* been found to predict higher resident engagement in activity or participation in domestic tasks in a number of regression or correlational analyses (Hatton, Emerson, Robinson, Henderson & Cooper, 1996; Thompson et al., 1996; Emerson et al., 2000b; Felce et al., 2000a; 2002; Perry et al., 2000). Consistent with this, Stancliffe and Keane (2000) found greater participation in domestic tasks in partially staffed community houses (that is, semi-independent living) than fully staffed community houses in a matched-ability comparison.

While number of staff in relation to number of residents at the facility level has not been associated with activity participation, the size of staff: resident groupings within settings, has. Felce et al. (1991) observed resident engagement in activity and the attention residents received from staff in institutions, intermediate community settings, and community houses, recording simultaneously the numbers of staff and residents in the room occupied by the person being observed. The extents of attention residents received and their engagement in activity were then analysed for different staff: resident group sizes. In general, neither quantity increased greatly when the number of staff to a given size of resident group was increased from one through two, three, or four. Arithmetically identical staff: resident ratios were not associated with similar activity patterns. In every case, the larger staff: resident group was associated with lower resident activity. The condition associated with the highest participation in activity was when one member of staff worked alone with a small resident group. This occurred more frequently in the community houses and rarely in the other two service models, where larger resident groups predominated.

Staff Procedures and Performance

Among people who do not organise and undertake their activity independently, one might expect that what staff do to support resident activity participation would be important. A growing body of evidence demonstrates the strength of association between engagement in activity and the receipt of some form of attention from staff. Felce et al. (2000a) and Perry et al. (2000) demonstrated that extent of attention from staff was the strongest predictor of resident engagement in activity after taking account of resident adaptive behaviour. Felce et al. (2002) and Emerson et al. (2000b) demonstrated associations between the level of assistance residents received from staff (instruction, prompting, demonstration, and physical guidance to do an activity) and their engagement in activity, and Felce et al. (1999) reported an association between receipt of assistance and resident engagement in domestic activity. Emerson et al. (2000b) and Hatton et al. (1996) reported significant associations between engagement in activity and receipt of praise from staff.

It should not be surprising that such relationships are found, given the depth of experimental research within applied behaviour analysis demonstrating the impact of antecedent, concurrent, and consequent attention on functioning. However, staff do not necessarily interact in ways which effectively support activity. Repp, Barton and Brulle (1981) found that staff rarely used the form of instruction most likely to help residents respond correctly (non-verbal instruction either with or without physical assistance) and usually employed the form of instruction (verbal instruction) which most likely led to non-response. Various studies have demonstrated the beneficial impact of training or supervising staff to provide assistance or praise for participation, schedule activity, and organise their responsibilities for supporting resident activity (e.g., Porterfield, Blunden & Blewitt, 1980; Parsons, Cash & Reid, 1989; Harchik, Sherman, Sheldon & Strouse, 1992; Anderson, Sherman, Sheldon & McAdam, 1997; Jones et al., 1999, 2001).

Holland and Meddis (1993) concluded that people who spent more time engaged in household activities lived in community houses which had procedures to encourage participation, such as schedules of household tasks and staff actively supporting people to undertake them. The presence of procedures for planning or organising activities was also identified as a significant predictor of engagement in activity by Emerson et al. (2000a) and Hatton et al. (1996). Such emphasis is consistent with the findings of Thompson et al. (1996) regarding programme orientation. However, a recent replication study of training staff to organise activities and provide effective assistance and praise for participation (Jones et al., 2001), while reporting positive results, also showed that the intervention was most appropriate for persons with more severe intellectual disabilities, and was not appropriate for people with greater abilities. Taken together with the research by Stancliffe and Keane (2000) showing that people with mild and moderate intellectual disabilities living in semi-independent accommodation participated in domestic activities more than people in fully staffed group homes, these results indicate the importance of matching staffing arrangements and staff training and performance to the needs of residents.

Research Using Conditional and Sequential Analysis

As noted above, recent development in computer technology has opened up opportunities for the analysis of conditional and sequential relationships within observational data, including the identification of the environmental conditions under which engagement becomes more or less likely (such as different forms of staff contact) and contextual variables that act to moderate the impact of these effects. Emerson, Hatton, Robertson, Henderson and Cooper (1999), for example, calculated the odds ratios for engagement under different forms of staff contact (practical support, other contact, or no contact) for 36 people with severe intellectual disabilities and sensory impairments. They reported that, for the 29 participants for whom complete data were available, the staff states under which engagement was most likely were practical support for 22 participants and no contact for the remaining seven. They also reported that the effectiveness of staff support in facilitating engagement was related to a range of contextual variables, including the extent of institutional routines in the setting, the number of scheduled activities, participant age and ability, service cost, staffing ratios, rates of staff sickness and turnover, and staff age.

Smith, Felce, Jones and Lowe (2002a) and Felce et al. (2000b) used a similar approach to investigate the extent to which staff training changed the effectiveness with which staff assistance facilitated participant engagement. In both studies, training was associated with significant increases in participant responsiveness (as measured by Yule's Q) to assistance provided by staff. No such changes were found in a control group (Smith et al., 2002a). However, Smith et al. (2002a) reported that these effects were apparent only for participants with more severe intellectual disabilities who neither showed challenging behaviour nor had mental health problems. Finally, Smith et al. (2002b) reported that reduction of antipsychotic medication was not associated with an increased responsivity to staff assistance among 26 people who completed or partially completed a drug-reduction programme.

DISCUSSION

Engagement in activity as a quality-of-life indicator can be understood on two levels. First, it may be considered as a reasonably important quality-of-life indicator in its own right. People experience boredom as unpleasant. It is associated with waiting for something to do. It is often felt in environments designed for purposes other than the occupation of the person concerned. For example, being in hospital or waiting for travel connections are essentially situations to be endured for this reason. Both may be made more bearable by personally arranging a sufficient means of occupation to pass the time. For most people, such circumstances are transient. As we set out in the introduction, the problem, and the relevance of engagement in activity as a quality measure, occurs when people inhabit environments which habitually do not provide them with sufficient stimulation or interest. Lifelong under-occupation is wasteful of human potential.

Second, engagement in activity may be considered as a fundamental aspect of life which underpins other quality-of-life outcomes. An international consensus report has recently put forward eight core domains of quality of life: emotional well-being, interpersonal relationships, material well-being, personal development, physical well-being, self-determination, social inclusion, and rights (Schalock et al., 2002). We cited evidence for the relationship between activity and both mood and health in the introduction to this chapter. It is hard to conceive that it would be possible to gain or sustain interpersonal relationships, employment or income, personal development, the exercise of choice and personal control, or community participation without fairly extensive engagement in activity. Therefore, engagement in activity may be regarded as a building block to seven of the eight core quality-of-life domains (one might hope that a civilised society would confer rights on all citizens irrespective of their degree of participation). That is not to say that engagement in activity needs to be a constant state for these other outcomes to follow, or that more is necessarily better. The focus of concern is again when the level is so low as to jeopardise achievement of such accomplishments.

Activity indicators have been widely used in evaluating the adequacy of service environments and supports for people with intellectual disabilities. Even with the inclusive definitions of engagement in activity typically used, the studies referred to above have repeatedly demonstrated levels of constructive occupation among people with intellectual disabilities low enough to be of concern. The problem is particularly acute when the people being considered have severe or profound intellectual disabilities. Such extreme under-occupation is not an inevitable consequence of the severity of intellectual disability, as has been shown by staff-training studies (e.g., Jones et al., 1999). Low engagement in activity points to a deficiency in the environment, an absence of sufficient support or assistant environmental technology which would enable individuals to take a more active part in ordering their affairs. We believe that it will remain a relevant measure until the quality of environmental prosthesis and support is routinely considerably better than it is today, even in our better services.

The measurement of engagement in activity has been achieved with adequate interobserver reliability in a considerable number of studies. One can therefore conclude that there is a robust methodology for such measurement, one which now has the added advantage of computerised data capture, summary, and analysis. Advances in observational technology have permitted a breadth of measurement consistent with an ecological understanding of behaviour and the sequential analysis of behavioural patterns and behaviour–environment interactions. While acknowledging these developments, it is also true to say that worthwhile research can also still be undertaken by traditional time-sampling and recording techniques.

Finally, the evaluation literature which has used measures of engagement in activity has made a contribution to our understanding about how to design better environments for people with intellectual disabilities. The following broad conclusions can be drawn from the literature on residential supports:

- Community provision using ordinary housing stock is to be preferred.
- Normative architecture, decor, furnishings, standards of material enrichment, and access to the various functional spaces usual within a home are to be preferred.
- The use of normative housing constrains group living to a relatively small scale (that is, within the range of the number of people who typically live together in family homes). However, there is little evidence that smaller size within this range is to be preferred to larger size.
- There is little evidence to suggest that higher staff : resident ratios lead to uniformly better outcome. Research suggests that staffing levels need to be matched to the support needs of residents, and that either overstaffing or understaffing may constrain outcome.
- Staff orientation, working methods, and performance are important influences on outcome. They have not received the attention they merit. There is some evidence that greater "resident-orientation", an orientation towards offering choice and opportunities to participate, and more thorough planning of opportunities are associated with greater household activity. There is also evidence that the extent and nature of the attention residents receive from staff influences outcome, and that training staff can have a beneficial effect. However, training and staff performance need to be matched to the support needs of residents.

Beyond these conclusions, it is clear that the environmental determinants of engagement in activity are incompletely understood. Therefore, in this regard, it is important that more attention is given to reaching an international consensus about the important variables to be described when doing service research, so that relationships between environmental characteristics and outcome can be identified with greater confidence. It is understandable that evaluation in such a policy-related area as this should highlight loosely described, poorly operationalised service "models". However, generality of understanding would be enhanced if a more generic classification and measurement of setting characteristics was developed and applied.

REFERENCES

Allison, D.B., Faith, M.S. & Franklin, R.D. (1995). Antecedent exercise in the treatment of disruptive behavior—a metaanalytic review. *Clinical Psychology—Science and Practice*, **2**, 279–303.

Anderson, M.D., Sherman, J.A., Sheldon, J.B. & McAdam, D. (1997). Picture activity schedules and engagement of adults with mental retardation in a group home. *Research in Developmental Disabilities*, **18**, 231–250.

Beyer, S., Kilsby, M. & Willson, C. (1995). Interaction and engagement of workers in supported employment: a British comparison between workers with and without learning disabilities. *Mental Handicap Research*, **8**, 137–155.

Blain, H., Vuillemin, A., Blain, A. & Jeandel, C. (2000). Preventative effects of physical activity in older adults [English abstract]. *Presse Medicale*, **29**, 1240–1248.

Blatt, B. & Kaplan, F. (1966). *Christmas in Purgatory: A Photographic Essay on Mental Retardation*. New York: Allyn & Bacon.

Brosse, A.L., Sheets, E.S., Lett, H.S. & Blumenthal, J.A. (2002). Exercise and the treatment of clinical depression in adults—recent findings and future directions. *Sports Medicine*, **32**, 741–760.

Cummins, R.A., Polzin, U. & Theobold, T. (1990). The deinstitutionalization of St Nicholas Hospital. III. Four-year follow-up of life-skill development. *Australia and New Zealand Journal of Developmental Disabilities*, **16**, 219–232.

de Kock, U., Saxby, H., Thomas, M. & Felce, D. (1988). Community and family contact: an evaluation of small community homes for severely and profoundly mentally handicapped adults. *Mental Handicap Research*, **1**, 127–140.

Emerson, E. & Hatton, C. (1994). *Moving Out: Relocation from Hospital to Community*. London: HMSO.

Emerson, E., Hatton, C., Robertson, J., Henderson, D. & Cooper, J. (1999). A descriptive analysis of the relationships between social context, engagement and stereotypy in residential services for people with severe and complex disabilities. *Journal of Applied Research in Intellectual Disabilities*, **12**, 11–29.

Emerson, E., Reeves, D. & Felce, D. (2000a). Palm-top computer technologies for behavioral observation research. In T. Thompson, D. Felce & F. Symons (Eds) *Computer-Assisted Behavioral Observation in Developmental Disabilities*. Baltimore, MD: Brookes.

Emerson, E., Robertson, J., Gregory, N., Kessissoglou, S., Hatton, C., Hallam, A., et al. (2000b). The quality and costs of community-based residential supports and residential campuses for people with severe and complex disabilities. *Journal of Intellectual and Developmental Disability*, **25**, 263–279.

Felce, D., Bowley, C., Baxter, H., Jones, E., Lowe, C. & Emerson, E. (2000b). The effectiveness of staff support: evaluating active support training using a conditional probability approach. *Research in Developmental Disabilities*, **21**, 243–255.

Felce, D., de Kock, U. & Repp, A. (1986). An eco-behavioural analysis of small community-based houses and traditional large hospitals for severely and profoundly mentally handicapped adults. *Applied Research in Mental Retardation*, **7**, 393–408.

Felce, D., Lowe, K., Beecham, J. & Hallam, A. (2000a). Exploring the relationships between costs and quality of services for adults with severe intellectual disabilities and the most severe challenging behaviours in Wales: a multivariate regression analysis. *Journal of Intellectual and Developmental Disability*, **25**, 307–326.

Felce D., Lowe, K. & Jones, E. (2002). Association between the provision characteristics and operation of supported housing services and resident outcomes. *Journal of Applied Research in Intellectual Disabilities*, **15**, 404–418.

Felce, D., Lowe, K., Perry, J., Jones, E., Baxter, H. & Bowley, C. (1999). The quality of residential and day services for adults with learning disabilities in eight local authorities in England: objective data gained in support of a Social Services Inspectorate inspection. *Journal of Applied Research in Intellectual Disabilities*, **12**, 273–293.

Felce, D., Lowe, K., Perry, J., Jones, E., Hallam, A. & Beecham, J. (1998). Service support to people with severe intellectual disabilities and the most severe challenging behaviours in Wales: processes, outcomes and costs. *Journal of Intellectual Disability Research*, **42**, 390–408.

Felce, D. & Perry, J. (1995). The extent of support for ordinary living provided in staffed housing: the relationship between staffing levels, resident dependency, staff : resident interactions and resident activity patterns. *Social Science and Medicine*, **40**, 799–810.

Felce, D., Repp, A.C., Ager, A. & Blunden, R. (1991). The relationship of staff : client ratios, interactions and residential placement. *Research in Developmental Disabilities*, **12**, 315–331.

Felce, D., Thomas, M., de Kock, U., Saxby, H. & Repp, A. (1985). An ecological comparison of small community-based houses and traditional institutions for severely and profoundly mentally handicapped adults. II. Physical settings and the use of opportunities. *Behaviour Research and Therapy*, **23**, 337–348.

Ferro, J., Foster-Johnson, L. & Dunlap, G. (1996). Relation between curricular activities and problem behaviors of students with mental retardation. *American Journal of Mental Retardation*, **101**, 184–194.

Flynn, M. & Hirst, M. (1992). *This Year, Next Year, Sometime . . .? Learning Disability and Adulthood.* London: National Development Team/Social Policy Research Unit.

Gittelsohn, J., Shankar, A.V., West, K., Ram, R.M. & Gnywali, T. (1997). Estimating reactivity in direct observation studies of health behavior. *Human Organization*, **56**, 182–189.

Hall, S. & Oliver, C. (2000). An alternative approach to the sequential analysis of behavioral observations. In T. Thompson, D. Felce & F. Symons (Eds) *Computer-Assisted Behavioral Observation in Developmental Disabilities*. Baltimore, MD: Brookes.

Harchik, A.E., Sherman, J.A., Sheldon, J.B. & Strouse, M.C. (1992). Ongoing consultation as a method of improving performance of staff members in a group home. *Journal of Applied Behavior Analysis*, **25**, 599–610.

Harris, F.C. & Lahey, B.B. (1982). Subject reactivity in direct observational assessment; a review and critical analysis. *Clinical Psychology Review*, **2**, 523–538.

Hatton, C. & Emerson, E. (1996). *Residential Provision for People with Learning Disabilities: A Research Review*. Manchester: Hester Adrian Research Centre, Manchester University.

Hatton, C., Emerson, E., Robertson, J., Henderson, D. & Cooper, J. (1995). The quality and costs of services for adults with multiple disabilities: a comparative evaluation. *Research in Developmental Disabilities*, **16**, 439–460.

Hatton, C., Emerson, E., Robertson, J., Henderson, D. & Cooper, J. (1996). Factors associated with staff support and user lifestyle in services for people with multiple disabilities: a path analytic approach. *Journal of Intellectual Disability Research*, **40**, 466–477.

Holland, A. & Meddis, R. (1993). People living in community homes: the influences on their activities. *Mental Handicap Research*, **6**, 333–345.

Jacob, T., Tennenbaum, D., Seilhamer, R.A. & Bargiel, K. (1994). Reactivity effects during naturalistic observation of distressed and non-distressed families. *Journal of Family Psychology*, **8**, 354–363.

Jones, E., Felce, D., Lowe, K., Bowley, C., Pagler, J., Gallagher, B., et al. (2001). Evaluation of the dissemination of Active Support training in staffed community residences. *American Journal on Mental Retardation*, **106**, 344–358.

Jones, E., Perry, J., Lowe, K., Felce, D., Toogood, S., Dunstan, F., et al. (1999). Opportunity and the promotion of activity among adults with severe mental retardation living in community residences: the impact of training staff in Active Support. *Journal of Intellectual Disability Research*, **43**, 164–178.

Jones, M.L., Risley, T.R. & Favell, J.E. (1983). Ecological patterns. In J.L. Matson & S.E. Breuning (Eds) *Assessing the Mentally Retarded*. New York: Grune & Stratton.

Kennedy, C.H., Horner, R.H., Newton, J.S. & Kanda, E. (1990). Measuring the activity patterns of adults with severe disabilities using the Resident Lifestyle Inventory. *Journal of the Association for Persons with Severe Handicaps*, **15**, 70–85.

Lakin, K.C., Bruininks, R.H., Hill, B.K., Chen, T.H. & Anderson, D.J. (1993). Personal characteristics and competence of people with mental retardation living in foster homes or small group homes. *American Journal on Mental Retardation*, **97**, 616–627.

Lawlor, D.A. & Hopker, S.W. (2001). The effectiveness of exercise as an intervention in the management of depression: systematic review and meta-regression analysis of randomised controlled trials. *British Medical Journal*, **322**, 763–767.

Martin, J.P. (1984). *Hospitals in Trouble*. Oxford: Blackwell.

Messent, P., Cooke, C. & Long, J. (1999). What choice: a consideration of the level of opportunity for people with mild and moderate learning disabilities to lead a physically active lifestyle. *British Journal of Learning Disabilities*, **27**, 73–77.

Morris, P. (1969). *Put Away*. London: Routledge and Kegan Paul.

O'Neill, J., Brown, M., Gordon, W. & Schonhorn, R. (1985). The impact of deinstitutionalization on activities and skills of severely/profoundly mentally retarded multiply-handicapped adults. *Applied Research in Mental Retardation*, **6**, 361–371.

O'Neill, J., Brown, M., Gordon, W., Schonhorn, R. & Greer, E. (1981). Activity patterns of mentally retarded adults in institutions and communities: a longitudinal study. *Applied Research in Mental Retardation*, **2**, 367–379.

Orlowska, D. (1990). Staff reactivity to observation. *British Journal of Mental Subnormality*, **36**, 125–131.

Oswin, M. (1971). *The Empty Hours*. London: Allen Lane.

Parsons, M.B., Cash, V.B. & Reid, D.H. (1989). Improving residential treatment services: implementation and norm-referenced evaluation of a comprehensive management system. *Journal of Applied Behavior Analysis*, **22**, 143–156.

Perry, J., Felce, D. & Lowe, K. (2000). *Subjective and Objective Quality of Life Assessment: Their Interrelationship and Determinants*. Cardiff: Welsh Centre for Learning Disabilities, University of Wales College of Medicine.

Porterfield, J., Blunden, R. & Blewitt, E. (1980). Improving environments for profoundly handicapped adults: using prompts and social attention to maintain high group engagement. *Behavior Modification*, **4**, 225–241.

Quera, V. & Bakeman, R. (2000). Quantification strategies in behavioral observation research. In T. Thompson, D. Felce & F. Symons (Eds) *Computer-Assisted Behavioral Observation in Developmental Disabilities*. Baltimore, MD: Brookes.

Rapley, M. & Beyer, S. (1998). Daily activity, community participation and quality of life in an ordinary housing network: a two-year follow-up. *Journal of Applied Research in Intellectual Disability*, **11**, 34–43.

Raynes, N., Wright, K., Shiell, A. & Pettipher, C. (1994). *The Cost and Quality of Community Residential Care*. London: David Fulton.

Repp, A.C., Barton, L.E. & Brulle, A.R. (1981). Correspondence between effectiveness and staff use of instructions for severely retarded persons. *Applied Research in Mental Retardation*, **2**, 237–245.

Risley, T.R. & Cataldo, M.F. (1973). *Planned Activity Check: Materials for Training Observers*. Lawrence, KS: Center for Applied Behavior Analysis.

Robertson, J., Emerson, E., Gregory, N., Hatton, C., Turner, S., Kessissoglou, S., et al. (2000). Lifestyle related risk factors for poor health in residential settings for people with intellectual disabilities. *Research in Developmental Disabilities*, **21**, 469–486.

Sackett, G.P. & Landesman-Dwyer, S. (1977). Toward an ethology of mental retardation. In P. Mittler (Ed.) *Research to Practice in Mental Retardation*, vol. II. *Education and Training* (pp. 27–37). Baltimore, MD: University Park Press.

Sallis, J.F., Prochaska, J.J. & Taylor, W.C. (2000). A review of correlates of physical activity of children and adolescents. *Medicine and Science in Sports and Exercise*, **32**, 963–975.

Saxby, H., Felce, D., Harman, M. & Repp, A. (1988). The maintenance of client activity and staff : client interaction in small community houses for severely and profoundly mentally handicapped adults: a two-year follow-up. *Behavioural Psychotherapy*, **16**, 189–206.

Saxby, H., Thomas, M., Felce, D. & de Kock, U. (1986). The use of shops, cafes and public houses by severely and profoundly mentally handicapped adults. *British Journal of Mental Subnormality*, **32**, 69–81.

Schalock, R.L., Brown, I., Brown, R., Cummins, R.A., Felce, D., Matikka, L., et al. (2002). Conceptualization, measurement, and application of quality of life for persons with intellectual disabilities: report of an international panel of experts. *Mental Retardation*, **40**, 457–470.

Scheerenberger, R.C. (1983). *A History of Mental Retardation*. Baltimore, MD: Brookes.

Smith, C., Felce, D., Ahmed, Z., Fraser, W.I., Kerr, M., Kiernan, C., et al. (2002b). Sedation effects on responsiveness: evaluating the reduction of antipsychotic medication in people with intellectual disability using a conditional probability approach. *Journal of Intellectual Disability Research*, **46**, 464–471.

Smith, C., Felce, D., Jones, E. & Lowe, K. (2002a). Responsiveness to staff support: evaluating the impact of individual characteristics on the effectiveness of active support training using a conditional probability approach. *Journal of Intellectual Disability Research*, **46**, 594–604.

Stancliffe, R.J., Abery, B.H. & Smith, J. (2000). Personal control and the ecology of community living settings: beyond living-unit size and type. *American Journal on Mental Retardation*, **105**, 431–454.

Stancliffe, R.J. & Keane, S. (2000). Outcomes and costs of community living: a matched comparison of group homes and semi-independent living. *Journal of Intellectual and Developmental Disability*, **25**, 281–305.

Suen, H.K. & Ary, D. (1989). *Analyzing Quantitative Behavioral Observation Data*. Hillsdale, NJ: Erlbaum.

Thompson, T., Robinson, J., Dietrich, M., Farris, M. & Sinclair, V. (1996). Interdependence of architectural features and program variables in community residences for people with mental retardation. *American Journal on Mental Retardation*, **101**, 315–327.

Thompson, T., Robinson, J., Graff, M. & Ingenmey, R. (1990). Home-like architectural features of residential environments. *American Journal on Mental Retardation*, **95**, 328–341.

Van Gool, C.H., Kempen, G., Pennix, B., Deeg, D., Beekman, A. & van Eijk, J. (2003). Relationship between changes in depressive symptoms and unhealthy lifestyles in late middle aged and older persons. *Age and Ageing*, **32**, 81–87.

Yoder, P.J. & Feurer, I.D. (2000). Quantifying the magnitude of sequential association between events or behaviors. In T. Thompson, D. Felce & F. Symons (Eds) *Computer-Assisted Behavioral Observation in Developmental Disabilities*. Baltimore, MD: Brookes.

CHAPTER 18

Adaptive Behavior: Its Conceptualization and Measurement

Robert L. Schalock
Hastings College, USA

OVERVIEW

The last three decades have seen considerable research and interest in the concept of adaptive behavior, including its assessment and application in the field of intellectual disabilities. While the conceptual and operational use of adaptive behavior is continually changing, the concept of adaptive behavior has remained central to identifying, classifying, and supporting people with intellectual disabilities. This chapter, which reflects primarily the approach taken to adaptive behavior in the USA, provides a brief historical overview of the concept and use of adaptive behavior, followed by a more in-depth discussion of two current trends and three future research directions that emerge from these two trends. The chapter concludes with a discussion of three implications for the field of intellectual disabilities of the trends and future research directions outlined.

At the outset, it is important to stress four issues regarding the conceptualization and measurement of adaptive behavior:

(1) Adaptive behavior must be seen as a cultural-specific construct.
(2) Everyone has a unique cultural heritage.
(3) Reliable and valid assessment of cultural similarities and differences in adaptive behavior is in its infancy.
(4) The cultural basis of adaptive behavior requires that investigators be clear about the purpose of their investigation and the comparison group, their attempt to control for and minimize test bias, and how they will integrate a number of guidelines for culturally competent assessment into their work.

Approaches that investigators might use to overcome these four issues are discussed throughout the chapter.

The International Handbook of Applied Research in Intellectual Disabilities. Edited by E. Emerson, C. Hatton, T. Thompson and T.R. Parmenter ISBN 0-471-49709-6.

Throughout the chapter, adaptive behavior is defined as a multidimensional construct that reflects the effectiveness and degree with which people meet the standard of personal independence and social responsibility expected of their age and cultural groups. Thus, the concept stresses everyday coping and refers to what people do to take care of themselves and relate to others in daily living, rather than to the abstract potential implied by intelligence (Grossman, 1983; Harrison, 1989).

A HISTORICAL OVERVIEW OF ADAPTIVE BEHAVIOR

Although adaptive behavior has a long philosophical, literary, and medical history, its inclusion in the field of intellectual disabilities/mental retardation began in 1959 when the American Association on Mental Deficiency (now AAMR) included the concept in the definition of mental retardation (Heber, 1959). In a recent review of the history of adaptive behavior, Nihira (1999) summarized the history in the USA of the concept since 1960.

- *1960s decade*. The concept of adaptive behavior provided the basis for describing a person's competencies in specific behavioral terms. Adaptive behavior assessment offered a technical basis for implementing deinstitutionalization and community rehabilitation. Thus, the concept provided socially relevant goals for treatment and intervention efforts. It was during this decade that the Behavioral Checklist was developed that later became the predecessor of the AAMR Adaptive Behavior Scales.
- *1970s decade*. The principles of normalization and mainstreaming became dominant during this decade, with assessment and training of adaptive behavior integral to these principles. To that end, considerable research efforts were devoted to the identification of the skills needed for successful integration into community-based environments. A corollary to this effort was the need to develop assessment instruments and testing procedures that ensured nondiscriminatory assessment, since by the end of the decade adaptive behavior measures were used administratively as a diagnostic tool for identifying and labeling schoolchildren.
- *1980s decade*. During the 1980s, the controversies over IQ, adaptive behavior, and school classification moved in the USA from the courtrooms to research (Reschly, 1988). This movement resulted in: (a) developing a proliferation of adaptive behavior instruments for either programming, treatment, or identification/labeling; (b) developing instructional programs to prepare individuals for living in less restrictive environments and to structure transitional programs; (c) investigating the factor structure of adaptive behavior; (d) investigating the convergent and discriminant validities of different adaptive behavior scales; (e) determining developmental trends in adaptive behavior through longitudinal and cross-cultural studies.
- *1990s decade*. In the 1992 AAMR *Mental Retardation: Diagnosis, Classification, and Systems of Supports* manual (Luckasson et al., 1992), the term "adaptive skills" replaced the older concept of adaptive behavior. In an effort to define the term operationally, 10 adaptive skill areas were included in the definition: communication, self-care, home living, social skills, community use, self-direction, health and safety, functional academics, leisure, and work. In addition, the 1992 AAMR definition expanded the conception of adaptive behavior in a number of other significant ways: (a) the 10 adaptive skill areas are considered central to successful life functioning and relate to the need for supports; (b) since the relevant skills within each adaptive skill area may vary with chronological

age, assessment should be referenced to the person's chronological age; (c) practical and social intelligence are seen as acting in concert to sustain the development of adaptive skills; (d) the adaptive difficulties in intellectual disabilities/mental retardation derive from limitations in practical and social intelligence.

- In the 2002 AAMR *Diagnosis, Classification and Systems of Support* manual (Luckasson et al., 2002) adaptive behaviour was defined as the collection of conceptual, social and practical skills that have been learned by people to function in their everyday lives (p. 73).

In summary, although the concept of adaptive behavior is included currently in all the major classification systems (including those of the AAMR, the *Diagnostic and Statistical Manual of Mental Disorders* [American Psychiatric Association, 1994], and the *International Classification of Diseases* [World Health Organization, 1993]), there is still no universal agreement on the factor structure of adaptive behavior, the best method to assess it, the role that adaptive behavior or skill deficits should play in the definition and diagnosis of intellectual disabilities/mental retardation, and the relationship between the concepts of intelligence and adaptive behavior (Nihira, 1999). Two current trends in the research on adaptive behavior reflect potentially useful and productive efforts to resolve these issues: (1) the functional and structural characteristics of adaptive behavior; (2) the merging of the concepts of intelligence and adaptive behavior.

CURRENT TRENDS IN ADAPTIVE BEHAVIOR RESEARCH

The Functional and Structural Characteristics of Adaptive Behavior

Despite a relatively high level of agreement in defining adaptive behavior from a functional perspective, until recently, there has been little consensus regarding its structure. With the introduction of factor analysis and the use of more standardized factor-analytical procedures (that will be discussed later in the chapter), the factor structure is becoming clearer. Table 18.1 summarizes the results of a number of seminal review articles summarizing the factor structure of adaptive behavior. These results provide the basis for the following three statements regarding a clearer understanding of the functional and structural characteristics of adaptive behavior:

(1) Adaptive behavior is a multidimensional construct that most likely includes five adaptive factors (personal independence, responsibility, cognitive/academic performance, physical/developmental competencies, and vocational/community skills), and two maladaptive factors (personal and social punitiveness).
(2) Hierarchical models can be used to denote the relationships among the multiple dimensions. For example, Widaman, Borthwick-Duffy and Little (1991) suggest that the four adaptive behavior factors identified in their review (motor development, independent living skills, cognitive competencies, and social competencies) can be related to a higher-order independence factor, and that the two maladaptive factors (personal and social punitiveness) can be related to a higher-order general maladaptive factor.
(3) The concept of personal competence can be used as an overarching framework to encompass adaptive behavior within an ever-larger conceptual framework that includes what we know about intelligence and adaptive behavior. For example, Thompson,

Table 18.1 Dimensions of adaptive and maladaptive behavior

Meyers, Nihira and Zetlin (1979)
- Adaptive behavior: autonomy (personal independence and self-sufficiency) and responsibility (interpersonal skills and competencies)
- Maladaptive behavior: personal and social punitiveness

McGrew and Bruininks (1989)
- Adaptive behavior: personal independence, responsibility, functional academic/cognitive, vocational/community, and physical development

Widaman, Borthwick-Duffy and Little (1991)
- Adaptive behavior: motor development, independent living skills, cognitive competence, social competence
- Maladaptive behavior: social and personal

Widaman and McGrew (1996)
- Adaptive behavior: motor and physical competence, independent/daily living skills, cognitive competence and communication, and social competence

Thompson, McGrew and Bruininks (1999)
- Adaptive behavior: personal independence, responsibility, cognitive/academic, physical/developmental, and vocational/community
- Maladaptive behavior: personal and social punitiveness

McGrew and Bruininks (1999) used Greenspan's model of personal competence (McGrew, Bruininks & Johnson, 1996; Greenspan & Driscoll, 1997; Greenspan, 1999) to show the hierarchical arrangements among physical competence and physical/developmental skills; conceptual intelligence and cognitive/academic skills; practical intelligence and personal independence and vocational/community skills; and social intelligence and social responsibility, emotional competence, and personal and social punitiveness.

In summary, these three statements based on samples in the USA reflect significant progress over the last 25 years in understanding the functional and structural characteristics of adaptive behavior. As just discussed, there is an emerging consensus in the literature that adaptive behavior is a multidimensional construct, that hierarchical models can be used to denote the relationship among the multiple dimensions, and that the concept of personal competence can be used as an overarching framework to show the relationship between intelligence and adaptive behavior. This "merging of intelligence and adaptive behavior" is discussed next.

The Merging of the Constructs of Intelligence and Adaptive Behavior

The concept of intelligence can best be defined as (Arvey et al., 1994):

> a very general mental capability that, among other things, involves the ability to reason, plan, solve problems, think abstractly, comprehend complex ideas, learn quickly, and learn from experience. It is not merely book learning, a narrow academic skill, or test taking smarts. Rather, it reflects a broader and deeper capacity for comprehending our surroundings—catching on, making sense of things, or figuring out what to do. (p. B1)

As reflected in this definition, the concept of intelligence is also a multidimensional phenomenon. As with adaptive behavior, considerable factor-analytical work has been done over the last five decades in an effort to develop a taxonomy of cognitive abilities (Thurstone, 1947; Carroll, 1993, 1997). Two examples of this trend are reflected in the work on multiple intelligences and personal-social competence.

Multiple Intelligences

Thurstone (1938) argued that intelligence involves seven distinct factors: word fluency, verbal comprehension, spatial ability, perceptual speed, numerical ability, inductive reasoning, and memory. More recently, Gardner (1993) has proposed a theory of multiple intelligence that postulates seven distinct types: linguistic (reading, writing, and receptive language), logical (mathematical: solving problems and logical reasoning), spatial (getting from one place to another; sequential activities), musical (expressive and receptive musical behaviors), bodily and kinesthetic (dancing, playing ball, running, and throwing), interpersonal (relating to other people; interacting with others), and intrapersonal (understanding the self).

Similarly, Sternberg (1988) has proposed three fundamental aspects of intelligence—analytical, creative, and practical. In analytical thinking, one tries to solve familiar problems by using strategies that manipulate the elements of a problem or the relationships among the elements. In creative thinking, one tries to solve new kinds of problems that require one to think about the problem and its elements in a new way. In practical thinking, one tries to solve problems that apply what we know to everyday contexts. According to this triarchic theory, people differ in how well they apply their intelligence to different kinds of problems. For example, some people may be more intelligent when they face academic problems, whereas others may be more intelligent when they face practical problems.

Personal-Social Competence

The personal and social competence approach to intelligence is not new. In fact, a tripartite model of intelligence comprising social, practical, and conceptual components was originally proposed by E.L. Thorndike in 1920. As generally understood, the personal-social competence model of intelligence involves three components, conceptual intelligence, practical intelligence, and social intelligence, as follows:

- *Conceptual intelligence*, which is also referred to as academic or analytical, involves the ability to solve abstract "intellectual" problems and to use and understand symbolic processes, including language. It includes the traditional notion of intelligence quotient and school-related competencies (Sternberg, 1997). Nesser (1976), for example, describes academic intelligence tasks (that are common in the classroom and on intelligence tests) as formulated by others, often of little or no intrinsic interest, having all needed information available from the beginning, disembedded from an individual's ordinary experience, and having but one correct answer.
- *Practical intelligence* involves the ability to deal with the physical and mechanical aspects of life, including self-maintenance, daily living competencies, and vocational activities. It can be viewed as people's ability to adapt successfully to the real-world environments in which they find themselves and to exercise at least some significant degree of mastery over their environment (Sternberg & Wagner, 1986). It also includes

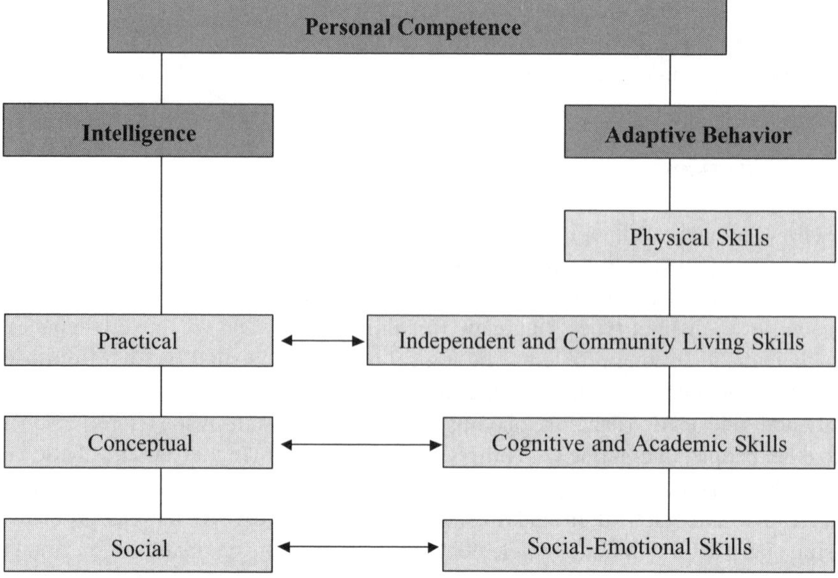

Figure 18.1 Integration of the constructs of intelligence and adaptive behavior

the ability to solve the ill-defined problems that arise in daily life, for which there may be no clear-cut answers (Wagner, 1994). Nesser (1976) describes practical intelligence tasks as often unformulated or in need of reformulation, of personal interest, lacking in information necessary for a solution, related to everyday experience, poorly defined, and characterized by multiple "correct" solutions, each with liabilities as well as assets.

- *Social intelligence* involves the ability to understand and deal effectively with social and interpersonal objects and events, including the ability to act wisely in human relations, to exhibit appropriate social skills, be empathetic and self-reflective, and achieve desired interpersonal outcomes (Greenspan, 1979; Cantor & Kihlstrom, 1987; Taylor & Cadet, 1989; Bennett, 1993). The concept of emotional intelligence is sometimes subsumed under this broader concept of social intelligence (Goleman, 1995), as it is in this chapter.

The concepts of multiple intelligences and personal-social competence have many common elements as follows: they reflect a multidimensional approach to understanding and measuring intelligence, indicate a significant difference between conceptual and other types of intelligences (such as practical and social), propose that human intelligence can best be understood from a contextual perspective, and suggest that intelligence can be subsumed under a broader framework of personal competence that is reflected in adaptive behaviors exhibited when dealing with environmental demands. A model that integrates these common elements is shown graphically in Figure 18.1, the left side of which depicts the multidimensional aspects of intelligence just described.

The right portion of Figure 18.1 reflects the multidimensionality of adaptive behavior described in the preceding section. By way of review,

- *Physical skills* involve gross and fine motor skills, and ambulating.
- *Independent and community living skills* involve household chores, personal care, community access and use, and vocational skills.
- *Cognitive and academic skills* involve receptive and expressive language, reading and writing, and handling money.
- *Social-emotional skills* involve friendship (formation and maintenance), interaction with others, social participation, comprehension, social reasoning, and self-control (that encompasses maladaptive behavior).

The parallelness of these multidimensional adaptive behavior factors to those suggested earlier for intelligence is shown in the right portion of Figure 18.1. The reader should note especially the *conceptual similarity* between the taxonomies of cognitive ("intellectual") abilities and adaptive skills, and the *specific similarities* between practical intelligence and adaptive behaviors involving independent and community living skills, conceptual intelligence and cognitive and academic skills, and social intelligence and social-emotional skills. As noted before, the concept of maladaptive behavior is subsumed under social-emotional skills.

The heuristic model shown in Figure 18.1 is based heavily on the work of Nesser (1976); Widaman, Gibbs and Geary (1987); Sternberg (1988); Greenspan and Granfield (1992); Ittenbach, Speigel, McGrew and Bruininks (1992); Mathia and Nettelbeck (1992); Sternberg, Wagner, Williams and Horvath (1995); Greenspan, Switzky and Granfield (1996); McGrew et al. (1996); Widaman and McGrew (1996); and Thompson et al. (1999).

In summary, not only is there a better understanding of the functional and structural characteristics of adaptive behavior (Table 18.1), but there is also reason to assume that the two concepts can be merged (Figure 18.1). Results from these two current trends in adaptive behavior research provide the basis for suggesting three future research issues and directions: (1) validating the factor structure of adaptive behavior, (2) developing conceptual models, and (3) understanding better the cultural correlates of adaptive behavior.

FUTURE RESEARCH ISSUES AND DIRECTIONS

Validate the Factor Structure of Adaptive Behavior

The factor-analytical studies of adaptive behavior summarized in Table 18.1 provide a strong base for the first future research issue: validating the factor structure of adaptive behavior. This validation will require reaching consensus on a standard approach to factor-analytical studies. Factor analysis is based on the premise that there are variables of theoretical interest that cannot be directly observed. Information concerning unobservable variables, typically referred to as latent factors or common factors, must be obtained indirectly by examining their effects on observed variables, such as items or subscales on an adaptive behavior instrument. Factor-analytical studies are completed by collecting data on a sample population and by applying a sequential series of statistical procedures to the data to identify variables that cluster together (that is, are highly correlated with one another). A good factor model is parsimonious and accounts for a significant proportion of the covariance among the variables comprising a data set (Thompson et al., 1999, p. 20).

Factor analysis is typically divided into exploratory and confirmatory procedures. Exploratory methods, which provide a means by which to investigate the underlying factor structure when there is little basis for hypothesizing the parameters or structure of a model, are especially valuable in the early stages of theory building and measurement development. The weakness of exploratory methods stems from the wide range of models that can be obtained, since there are no constraints placed on model parameters. This atheoretical limitation can be overcome through the application of confirmatory methods that require researchers to specify any or all of four restrictions prior to the analysis: which pairs of common factors are correlated, which observed variables are affected by which common factors, which observed variables are affected by a unique factor, and which pairs of unique factors are correlated (Thompson et al., 1999).

McGrew and Bruininks (1989) concluded that much of the variability found in the adaptive behavior studies they reviewed was due to the measurement level of the factored variables. As discussed by these authors and Thompson et al. (1999), three levels of measurement have been used in studies to date: *item level*, where individual items are the unit of measurement; *parcel studies*, where factored composite variables comprise five or fewer items; and *subscale studies*, where multivariate variables that average six or more items per unit of analysis were used. Subscale studies have thus far produced the most robust results.

Given this overview and general summary of factor analysis, it seems reasonable to propose that a standard approach to validating the factor structure of adaptive behavior should be based on the subscale level of measurement, and on confirmatory factor-analytical methods driven by conceptual models and frameworks.

Develop Conceptual Models

The next generation of research in the area of adaptive behavior will undoubtedly be based on results from the two research trends discussed earlier: the functional and structural characteristics of adaptive behavior, and the merging of the constructs of intelligence and adaptive behavior. Once the factor structure of adaptive behavior is validated, it is anticipated that a second future research issue will be to develop conceptual models of adaptive behavior and intelligence (Thompson et al., 1999).

Figure 18.2, which is an extension of Figure 18.1, shows one such conceptual model. As shown in Figure 18.2, personal competence is used as the overarching framework for integrating the four performance domains of physical competence, practical intelligence, conceptual intelligence, and social-emotional intelligence. Each performance domain is defined operationally by a number of maximum and typical performance indicators. The hierarchical structural model shown in Figure 18.2 is based on:

- The integration and synthesis of current literature in the areas of adaptive behavior and intelligence that indicate the utility of a hierarchical model where specific factors ("typical performance indicators") are subsumed by narrow factors ("maximum performance indicators"), which, in turn, are subsumed by broader factors ("domains"). This structure has a direct parallel in Carroll's (1993; 1997) three-stratum theory of cognitive abilities, and Widaman and McGrew's (1996) integration of the research on adaptive and maladaptive behavior and the broader models of personal competence.

Table 18.2 Exemplary maximum and typical performance indicators

Maximum performance indicators	Typical performance
Physical competence	
Strength	Locomotion
Flexibility	Ambulation
Gross and fine motor	Fine motor
Stamina	Mobility
Speed	
Control precision	
Practical intelligence	
Currently lacking	Activities/instrumental activities of daily living
	Community living skills
	Vocational skills
Conceptual intelligence	
Fluid intelligence	Receptive/expressive language
Crystalized intelligence	Reading and writing skills
WAIS-R and WISC-III Verbal and performance subscales	Money management
	Nonverbal communication
Social-emotional intelligence	
Personality traits (neuroticism, extraversion openness, agreeableness, conscientiousness)	Cooperation
	Assertion
Social awareness (social inference, social comprehension, psychological insight, moral judgment)	Responsibility
	Empathy
	Emotional integration

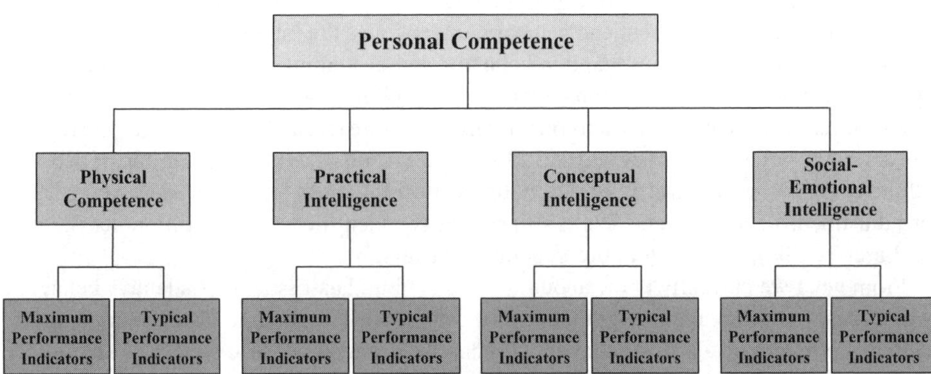

Figure 18.2 Intelligence and adaptive behavior hierarchical structure model

- The distinction between measures of maximum and typical performance (Cronbach, 1984; Widaman & McGrew, 1996). In this distinction, measures of maximum performance (such as intelligence tests) focus on the optimal or potential level of performance, whereas typical performance measurement focuses more on the observable behavior people display when responding to challenges in their environment. An initial listing of maximum and typical performance indicators is found in Table 18.2. This list is based on the work of Costa and McCrae (1992), Greenspan and Granfield (1992), Schalock

(1999), and Thompson et al. (1999). Although it is beyond the scope of this chapter to identify specific standardized assessments for each indicator, such is possible.

- The focus on a person's performance across domains, rather than treating adaptive behavior as an independent construct. As discussed by Thompson et al. (1999), proponents of this focus argue for a movement away from continued attempts to identify the nature or characteristics (that is, factors) of the identity or trait of adaptive behavior toword delineating those skills or achievements in the major domains of personal competence.
- The operational definitions of the four domains. Physical competence involves gross and fine motor skills along with locomotion and ambulation; practical intelligence involves the ability to deal with the physical and mechanical aspects of life, including self-maintenance, daily living competencies, and vocational activities; conceptual intelligence involves the ability to solve abstract "intellectual" problems and to use and understand symbolic processes including language; and social-emotional intelligence involves the ability to understand and deal effectively with social and interpersonal objects and events.
- The inclusion of emotional intelligence (Goleman, 1995) and maladaptive behavior within the broader domain of social-emotional intelligence.

Understand the Cultural Correlates of Adaptive Behavior

Cultural and demographic comparisons of adaptive behavior reflect mixed results and lack of a clear purpose (Bryant, Bryant & Chamberlain, 1999; Craig & Tasse, 1999). This finding should not surprise anyone, since people live in a variety of systems that influence the development of their values, beliefs, attitudes, and behavior. The current ecological focus in the field of intellectual disabilities/mental retardation, with its emphasis on describing the many contexts of development and behavior, underscores the importance that one's culture plays in defining the role of adaptive behavior and evaluating the importance placed on specific behaviors the person exhibits or does not exhibit (Craig & Tasse, 1999). Five terms are important to keep in mind when considering this future research direction: culture (the set of values and beliefs that is learned and adopted as a result of living with a group of people), ethnicity (a unique ancestral, religious, or linguistic group), moderator variable (a correction or adjustment of assessment results to account for identified cultural differences), emic (culture-specific), and etic (culture-general or universal).

From what we currently know about the cross-cultural assessment of adaptive behavior, we suggest the following five guidelines for future work in the area of understanding the cultural correlates of adaptive behavior: (1) adaptive behavior needs to be seen as a culturally specific construct; (2) instrument developers and publishers have significant responsibilities; (3) test bias needs to be controlled and minimized; (4) translation equivalence needs to be established; (5) investigators need to develop cross-cultural competence.

Adaptive Behavior as a Culturally Specific Construct

Heal and Tasse (1999) suggest that since everyone has a unique cultural heritage, the assessment of adaptive behavior requires an individually focused assessment system. Furthermore, investigators need to be sensitive to a number of factors that can account for differences in adaptive profiles across language-national-cultural groups including language, test content, test bias, normative sample characteristics, age, gender, socioeconomic status, acculturation, geographical region, and family structure (Bryant et al., 1999; Craig & Tasse, 1999). Thus, the assessment of adaptive behavior within a cultural context requires a number of evaluation actions, including the following (Lynch & Hanson, 1992):

- Select valid instruments for the language and culture of the individual and the family.
- Use a trained interpreter proficient in the language and cultural cues.
- Conduct the assessment at a time when people important to the family can be present.
- Conduct the assessment at a location comfortable for the family.
- Collect information in areas of family concern.
- Explain every step and purpose of the assessment.

Test Developer and Publisher Responsibilities

In 1996, a set of guidelines was proposed by the International Test Commission (Van de Vijver & Hambleton, 1996). The most relevant of these guidelines for this chapter are that instrument developers or publishers should:

- ensure the translation or adaptation process takes full account of linguistic and cultural differences among the populations for whom the translated or adapted versions of the instrument are intended
- provide evidence that the testing techniques, item formats, test conventions, and procedures are familiar to all intended populations
- provide evidence that the item content and stimulus materials are familiar to all intended populations
- implement systematic judgmental evidence, both linguistic and psychological, to improve the accuracy of the translation or adaptation process and compile evidence on the equivalence of all language versions
- provide information on the evaluation of the validity in all target populations for whom the translated or adapted versions are intended.

Control for or Minimize Test Bias

A test can be considered biased if its content, procedures, or use results in a systematic advantage or disadvantage to members of certain groups over other groups, and if the basis of this differentiation is irrelevant to the test purpose (Brown, 1983). Key steps to control or minimize test bias include the following (Hammill, Pearson & Wiederholt, 1996): (1) describe the content of tests in terms of potential bias; (2) include targeted demographic groups (that is, identifiable groups that differ from the "mainstream" population in normative samples) in the same proportion as the groups occur at each age level in the most recent census data; (3) provide separate reliability and validity information for the targeted groups; (4) show that test items are as appropriate for the targeted groups as for the mainstream population.

Establish Translation Equivalence

As discussed by Tasse and Craig (1999), adaptive behavior scales sometimes need to be adapted when cultural expectations differ, even when the language of the scale remains unchanged. Thus, translating a phrase or text requires more than merely transcribing words into another language; it requires an attempt to reproduce the meaning of the item, and not to render a mere literal translation. Currently, the preferred approach to ensure the linguistic or cultural equivalence of two versions of a translated or adapted scale is the "back-translation approach" that involves one person (or bilingual committee) translating from the original language to the other language, and a second person (or committee) blindly (without having seen the original document) translating the test back to the original language.

Develop Cross-Cultural Competence

Cross-cultural (or ethnic) competence is becoming an increasingly important concept in studying the cultural basis of adaptive behavior. This competency includes an awareness of one's own cultural limitations; an openness, appreciation, and respect for cultural differences; the ability to interact and communicate in a sensitive fashion; a view of intercultural interactions as learning opportunities; the ability to use cultural resources in the assessment process; an acknowledgment of the integrity and value of all cultures; and the ability to reach consensus regarding the appropriate adjustments that should be made in adaptive behavior assessment findings when clear evidence exists of a strong cultural difference among groups (Lynch & Hanson, 1992; Schalock, 1999).

It is anticipated that a better understanding of the cultural correlates of adaptive behavior will have a significant impact on the conceptualization, understanding, and assessment of adaptive behavior. Research in this area points out that adaptive behavior needs to be understood within the context of the individual's personal and social environment, that the cross-cultural understanding of adaptive behavior must be considered within the emic and etic meaning of the term, and that the cross-cultural assessment of adaptive behavior involves a number of guidelines and procedures to minimize test bias and maximize cross-cultural equivalence. This increased understanding will also have three significant implications for the field of intellectual disabilities related to (1) the concept of disability, (2) the definition of intellectual disabilities/mental retardation, and (3) the focus of assessment.

IMPLICATIONS FOR THE FIELD OF INTELLECTUAL DISABILITIES

Concept of Disability

As with the constructs of intelligence and adaptive behavior, the concept of disability is also undergoing significant changes. For example, in 1980, the World Health Organization defined a handicap or disability as "arising from failure or inability to conform to the expectations or norms of the individual's universe ... and characterized by a discordance between the individual's performance or status and the expectations of the individual himself or the particular group of which he is a member" (WHO, 1980, p. 183). More recently, Bradley (1995) and the World Health Organization (1999) stress that since one's disability results from an interaction between disease and one's physical and social environment and resources, one needs to focus on the impairment of functional skills/adaptive behaviors and the environmental supports that lessen the impairment and thereby enhance personal competence. This concept of disability has a number of implications:

- Disability is neither fixed nor dichotomized; rather, it is fluid, continuous, and changing, depending upon the person's functional limitations and the supports available within a person's environment.
- One lessens functional limitations (and hence a person's disability) by providing interventions or services and supports that focus on prevention, adaptive behaviors, and role status.
- Evaluation focuses on the extent to which the functional limitations have been reduced, and the person's adaptive behavior and role status has been enhanced.

Definition of Intellectual Disabilities/Mental Retardation

Defining intellectual disabilities/mental retardation as characterized by limitations in practical, conceptual, and social-emotional performance skills is a continuation of our attempts to understand better this important construct. The personal competence models outlined in Figures 18.1 and 18.2 suggest the need to reconceptualize (and potentially redefine) the construct of intellectual disabilities/mental retardation to be consistent with the notion of personal competence and functional limitations in the performance domains of practical, conceptual, and social-emotional intelligence. This suggestion is consistent with a number of recent attempts (for example, Greenspan & Granfield, 1992; Greenspan, 1997; Haywood, 1997; Schalock, 1999) to reformulate the construct of intellectual disabilities/mental retardation within the context of the multidimensional approach to intelligence and adaptive behavior described in this chapter.

Focus of Assessment

If disability is defined as functional limitations in personal competence, and if intellectual disabilities/mental retardation is defined as limitations in practical, conceptual, and social performance skills, the focus of assessment (and by inference diagnosis) should be on the maximum and typical performance indicators summarized in Figure 18.2 and Table 18.2. As shown in the model, personal competence is defined operationally on the basis of the three *performance domains* of practical, conceptual, and social-emotional intelligence, which are further defined in terms of maximum and typical performance *indicators* that can be assessed via a combination of *measures*, including standardized instruments and functional assessments (Kamphaus, 1987; Schalock, 2001).

CONCLUSION

As the reader is aware, the field of intellectual disabilities is in a state of transition characterized by:

(1) a transformed vision of what constitutes the life possibilities of persons with intellectual disabilities

(2) an emphasis on self-determination, strengths and capabilities, inclusion, provision of individualized support systems, enhanced adaptive behavior and role status, and equity
(3) a supports paradigm that focuses on supported living and employment and inclusive education
(4) an interfacing of the concept of quality of life with quality enhancement, quality assurance, quality management, and outcome-based evaluation
(5) a changing conception of disability, moving away from a focus on pathology to a contextual perspective in which a person's disability results from an interaction between functional limitations and the person's social and physical environment.

As important as this transition is to both persons with intellectual disabilities and workers in the field, its success and future unfolding cannot be separated from our current efforts to understand the concept of adaptive behavior and intelligence. As discussed in this chapter, we have made significant progress over the last few decades in understanding the functional and structural characteristics of adaptive behavior and seeing how the constructs of intelligence and adaptive behavior may be merged into an overall framework of personal competence.

We are not there yet, but the future research on validation, conceptual model development, and cross-cultural understanding of the concept of adaptive behavior will continue to move us in a very different direction from our not-too-distant past. How the future plays out is anyone's guess; but a safe bet is that the concept of adaptive behavior will increasingly be integrated into conceptual models of personal competence; be used as the basis for diagnosis, intervention, and supports provision; and be viewed from a multidimensional perspective. It is a bright future.

REFERENCES

American Psychiatric Association (1994). *Diagnostic and Statistical Manual for Mental Disorders* (4th edn). Washington, DC: Author.

Arvey, R.D., Bourchard, T.J., Carroll, J.B., et al. (1994). Mainstream science on intelligence. *Wall Street Journal*, 5th August, B1, B3.

Bennett, M. (Ed.) (1993). *The Development of Social Recognition*. New York: Guilford.

Bradley, E. (1995). The ICIDH: format, application in different settings, and distinction between disability and handicap. *International Disability Studies*, **9**, 122–125.

Brown, F.G. (1983). *Principles of Educational Psychology* (3rd edn). New York: Holt, Rinehart and Winston.

Bryant, B.R., Bryant, D.P. & Chamberlain, S. (1999). Examination of gender and race factors in the assessment of adaptive behavior. In R.L. Schalock (Ed.) *Adaptive Behavior and Its Measurement: Implications for the Field of Mental Retardation* (pp. 141–160). Washington, DC: American Association on Mental Retardation.

Cantor, N. & Kihlstrom, J.F. (1987). *Personal and Social Intelligence*. Englewood Cliffs, NJ: Prentice-Hall.

Carroll, J.B. (1993). *Human Cognitive Abilities: A Summary of Factor Analytic Studies*. New York: Cambridge University Press.

Carroll, J.B. (1997). The three-stratum theory of cognitive abilities. In D.P. Flanagan, J.L. Genshaft & P.L. Harrison (Eds) *Contemporary Intellectual Assessment: Theories, Tests, and Issues* (pp. 122–130). New York: Guilford.

Costa, P.T. Jr & McCrae, R.R. (1992). Four ways five factors are basic. *Personality and Individual Differences*, **13**, 653–655.

Craig, E.M. & Tasse, M.J. (1999). Cultural and demographic group comparisons. In R.L. Schalock (Ed.) *Adaptive Behavior and Its Measurement: Implications for the Field of Mental Retardation* (pp. 119–138). Washington, DC: American Association on Mental Retardation.

Cronbach, L.J. (1984). *Essentials of Psychological Testing* (4th edn). New York: Harper & Row.

Gardner, H. (1993). *Multiple Intelligences: The Theory in Practice*. New York: Basic Books.

Goleman, D. (1995). *Emotional Intelligence*. New York: Bantam.

Greenspan, S. (1979). Social intelligence in the retarded. In N. Ellis (Ed.) *Handbook of Mental Deficiency: Psychological Theory and Research* (2nd edn) (pp. 483–531). Hillsdale, NJ: Erlbaum.

Greenspan, S. (1997). Dead manual walking? Why the 1992 AAMR definition needs redoing. *Education and Training in Mental Retardation and Developmental Disabilities*, **32**, 179–190.

Greenspan, S. (1999). A contextualist perspective on adaptive behavior. In R.L. Schalock (Ed.) *Adaptive Behavior and Its Measurement: Implications for the Field of Mental Retardation* (pp. 61–80). Washington, DC: American Association on Mental Retardation.

Greenspan, S. & Driscoll, J. (1997). The role of intelligence in a broad model of personal competence. In D.P. Flanagan, G. Genshaft & P.L. Harrison (Eds) *Contemporary Intellectual Assessment: Theories, Tests, and Issues* (pp. 131–150). New York: Guilford.

Greenspan, S. & Granfield, J.M. (1992). Reconsidering the construct of mental retardation: implications of a model of social competence. *American Journal on Mental Retardation*, **96**, 442–453.

Greenspan, S., Switzky, H.N. & Granfield, J.M. (1996). Everyday intelligence and adaptive behavior: a theoretical framework. In J.W. Jacobson & J.A. Mulick (Eds) *Manual of Diagnosis and Professional Practice in Mental Retardation* (pp. 127–135). Washington, DC: American Psychological Association.

Grossman, H.J. (Ed.) (1983). *Classification in Mental Retardation*. Washington, DC: American Association on Mental Retardation.

Hammill, D.D., Pearson, N. & Wiederholt, J.L. (1996). *Comprehensive Test of Nonverbal Intelligence*. Austin, TX: Pro-Ed.

Harrison, P.L. (1989). Adaptive behavior: research to practice. *Journal of School Psychology*, **23**, 301–313.

Haywood, H.C. (1997). Global perspectives on mental retardation. Keynote address, 121st Annual Meeting of the American Association on Mental Retardation, New York City, 28 May.

Heal, L.W. & Tasse, M.J. (1999). The culturally individualized assessment of adaptive behavior: an accommodation to the 1992 AAMR definition, classification and systems of support. In R.L. Schalock (Ed.) *Adaptive Behavior and Its Measurement: Implications for the Field of Mental Retardation* (pp. 185–206). Washington, DC: American Association on Mental Retardation.

Heber, R. (1959). *A Manual on Terminology and Classification in Mental Retardation. American Journal of Mental Deficiency*, **64** (Monograph Suppl.).

Ittenbach, R.F., Speigel, A.N., McGrew, K.S. & Bruininks, R.H. (1992). A confirmatory factor analysis of early childhood ability measures within a model of personal competence. *Journal of School Psychology*, **30**, 307–323.

Kamphaus, R.W. (1987). Conceptual and psychometric issues in the assessment of adaptive behavior. *Journal of Special Education*, **21**, 27–35.

Luckasson, R., Coulter, D.L., Polloway, E.A., Reiss, S., Schalock, R.L., Snell, M.E., et al. (1992). *Mental Retardation: Definition, Classification, and Systems of Supports*. Washington, DC: American Association on Mental Retardation.

Luckasson, R., Borthwick-Duffy, S., Buntix, W.H.E., Coulter, D.L., Craig, E.M., Recue, A. et al. (2002). *Mental Retardation: Definition, Classification, and Systems of Support*. Washington, DC: American Association on Mental Retardation.

Lynch, E.W. & Hanson, M.J. (Eds) (1992). *Developing Cross-Cultural Competence*. Baltimore, MD: Brookes.

Mathia, J.L. & Nettelbeck, T. (1992). Validity of Greenspan's models of adaptive and social intelligence. *Research in Developmental Disabilities*, **13**, 113–129.

McGrew, K.S. & Bruininks, R.H. (1989). The factor structure of adaptive behavior. *School Psychology Review*, **18**, 64–81.

McGrew, K.S., Bruininks, R.H. & Johnson, D.R. (1996). Confirmatory factor analytic investigation of Greenspan's model of personal competence. *American Journal on Mental Retardation*, **100**, 535–545.

Meyers, C., Nihira, K. & Zetlin, A. (1979). The measurement of adaptive behavior. In N.R. Ellis (Ed.) *Handbook of Mental Deficiency: Psychological Theory and Research* (2nd edn) (pp. 431–481). Hillsdale, NJ: Erlbaum.

Nesser, U. (1976). General, academic, and artificial intelligence. In L. Resnick (Ed.) *Human Intelligence: Perspectives on Its Theory and Measurement* (pp. 179–189). Norwood, NJ: Ablex.

Nihira, K. (1999). Adaptive behavior: a historical overview. In R.L. Schalock (Ed.) *Adaptive Behavior and Its Measurement: Implications for the Field of Mental Retardation* (pp. 7–14). Washington, DC: American Association on Mental Retardation.

Reschly, D.J. (1988). Assessment issues, placement litigation, and the future of mild mental retardation classification and programming. *Education and Training in Mental Retardation*, **23**, 285–301.

Schalock, R.L. (1999). Adaptive behavior and its measurement: setting the future agenda. In R.L. Schalock (Ed.) *Adaptive Behavior and Its Measurement: Implications for the Field of Mental Retardation* (pp. 209–222). Washington, DC: American Association on Mental Retardation.

Schalock, R.L. (2001). *Outcome-Based Evaluation* (2nd edn). New York: Kluwer Academic/Plenum.

Sternberg, R.J. (1988). *The Triarchic Mind*. New York: Viking.

Sternberg, R.J. (1997). The concept of intelligence and its role in lifelong learning and success. *American Psychologist*, **52**, 1030–1037.

Sternberg, R.J. & Wagner, R.K. (1986). *Practical Intelligence: Nature and Origins of Competence in the Everyday World*. Cambridge: Cambridge University Press.

Sternberg, R.J., Wagner, R.K., Williams, W.M. & Horvath, J.A. (1995). Testing common sense. *American Psychologist*, **50**, 912–927.

Tasse, M.J. & Craig, E.M. (1999). Critical issues in the cross-cultural assessment of adaptive behavior. In R.L. Schalock (Ed.) *Adaptive Behavior and Its Measurement: Implications for the Field of Mental Retardation* (pp. 161–183). Washington, DC: American Association on Mental Retardation.

Taylor, E.H. & Cadet, J.L. (1989). Social intelligence: a neurological system? *Psychological Reports*, **64**, 423–444.

Thompson, J.R., McGrew, K.S. & Bruininks, R.H. (1999). Adaptive and maladaptive behavior: functional and structural characteristics. In R.L. Schalock (Ed.) *Adaptive Behavior and Its Measurement: Implications for the Field of Mental Retardation* (pp. 15–42). Washington, DC: American Association on Mental Retardation.

Thorndike, E.L. (1920). Intelligence and its uses. *Harper's Magazine*, **140**, 227–235.

Thurstone, L.L. (1938). *Primary Mental Abilities*. Psychometric Monographs (No. 1). Chicago: University of Chicago Press.

Thurstone, L.L. (1947). *Multiple Factor Analysis: A Development and Expansion of the Vectors of Mind*. Chicago: University of Chicago Press.

Van de Vijver, F. & Hambleton, R.K. (1996). Translating tests: some practical guidelines. *European Psychologist*, **1**, 89–99.

Wagner, R.K. (1994). Practical intelligence. In R.J. Sternberg (Ed.) *The Encyclopedia of Human Intelligence*, vol. II (pp. 821–828). New York: Macmillan.

Widaman, K.F., Borthwick-Duffy, S. & Little, T.D. (1991). The structure and development of adaptive behavior. In N.W. Bray (Ed.) *International Review of Research in Mental Retardation*, vol. 17 (pp. 1–54). New York: Academic Press.

Widaman, K.F., Gibbs, K.W. & Geary, D.C. (1987). Structure of adaptive Behavior. I. Replication across fourteen samples on nonprofoundly mentally retarded people. *American Journal on Mental Retardation*, **91**, 348–360.

Widaman, K.F. & McGrew, K.S. (1996). The structure of adaptive behavior. In J.W. Jacobson & J.A. Mulick (Eds) *Manual of Diagnosis and Professional Practice in Mental Retardation* (pp. 97–110). Washington, DC: American Psychological Association.

World Health Organization (1980). *International Classification of Impairments, Disabilities and Handicaps*. Geneva, Switzerland: Author.

World Health Organization (1999). *ICIDH-2 (Beta 2) International Classification of Functioning and Disability*. Geneva: Author.

CHAPTER 19

Communication and Language: Research Design and Measurement Issues

Steven F. Warren
University of Kansas, USA
Nancy C. Brady
University of Kansas, USA
and
Marc E. Fey
University of Kansas, USA

INTRODUCTION

The fundamental role of communication and language in social and cognitive functioning is painfully evident when these critical domains fail to develop as expected. Delayed and/or disordered communication and language development are implicit aspects of our definitions of intellectual disabilities (Rosenberg & Abbeduto, 1993) and autism (Lord & Risi, 2000). Furthermore, underlying communication disorders often contribute to the development of challenging behaviors, including aggression and self-injury (Fox, Dunlap & Buschbacher, 2000). Communication- and language-related disorders also affect the vast majority of individuals with milder forms of intellectual disabilities (Abbeduto, 1991). Irrespective of whether people are members of a first-world or a third-world society, communication and language abilities will affect their employment prospects, their social and educational opportunities, and, in many cases, their overall quality of life. Individuals who fail to acquire complex language repertoires will almost invariably endure lives of undue dependency, social isolation, and restriction.

The central contribution of communication and language development to intellectual and social functioning has been recognized for centuries (Itard, 1962). However, serious scientific inquiry into the relationship of communication and language development to cognitive and social development and intellectual disabilities has been underway for less than 50 years. Researchers in the 1960s and 1970s were polarized (and, to some extent,

The International Handbook of Applied Research in Intellectual Disabilities. Edited by E. Emerson, C. Hatton, T. Thompson and T.R. Parmenter ISBN 0-471-49709-6.

paralyzed) by the great nature–nurture debate fueled by the conflicting views of theorists such as Skinner (1957) and Chomsky (1965). Fortunately, this debate began to recede in the 1970s due in part to a renewed emphasis on the social bases of language (e.g., Bruner, 1975), which created some common ground for researchers from seemingly divergent theoretical perspectives (e.g., Golinkoff & Hirsh-Pasek, 1990). This common ground expanded throughout the 1990s with the increasing evidence of the critical and at times inseparable roles played by both "nature" and "nurture" (Elman et al., 1996; Abbeduto, Evans & Dolan, 2001). The drive to understand how genes and environments interact over time to build and support human tools such as language remains one of the great quests of the life sciences. While there remain plenty of contentious issues to keep everyone busy, contemporary theories of communication and language development are increasingly driven by "the data", a reflection of the substantial progress of empirical research in the past two decades.

Over the past 15 years, there have also been important advances in research on the relation of communication and language research and intellectual disabilities. For example, advances have been made in conceptual models of understanding both the atypical development (e.g., Abbeduto et al., 2001) and intervention (e.g., Warren & Yoder, 1997a); in determining the behavioral phenotype of a wide range of genetically influenced disorders, such as fragile X syndrome (Bailey, Hatton & Skinner, 1998); in the role of the environment in influencing relative differences in language development (Hart & Risley, 1995); in the relation of language and cognitive development (Mervis, Morris, Bertrand & Robinson, 1999); in our understanding of communication and aberrant behavior (Reichle & Wacker, 1993); in the development of valid assessments (Cole, Dale & Thal, 1996); and in the provision of increasingly effective early intervention approaches (Warren & Walker, in press). Recent reviews of these and other developments include those by Adamson and Romski (1997), Tager-Flusberg (1999), Reichle and Wacker (1993), and Wetherby, Warren and Reichle (1998).

Despite substantial progress, many of the fundamental research questions identified nearly 30 years ago (Schiefelbusch & Lloyd, 1974) remain at least partially unanswered. For example, we still do not know the extent to which early intervention can substantially alter the long-term communication and language development of children with intellectual disabilities. To move forward on these and other critical questions, investigators need to understand fully the strengths and weaknesses of various research designs and measures. Therefore, the goal of the present chapter is to address methodological issues central to the study of communication and language development, and intervention with individuals with intellectual disabilities. The chapter consists of major sections on research design and on measurement issues. Future research directions are briefly addressed in a concluding discussion.

RESEARCH DESIGN

In this section, we provide an overview of research design issues central to the study of communication and language development, and intervention. We begin with a discussion of some of the challenges inherent in this area of inquiry. Next we characterize the literature on development and intervention from the perspective of present limitations and potential solutions to these.

Challenges

Systematic research on communication and language development with children with intellectual disabilities has been underway for more than a half-century. Throughout this period, the designs used in research have been constrained by several inherent problems that reflect both the population under study (individuals with intellectual disabilities) and the target of inquiry (communication and language development). Four inherent challenges are the following:

(1) the large amount of developmental and behavioral variability in the population
(2) the difficulty and expense in recruiting sufficient numbers of participants, particularly of any specific etiology
(3) difficulties in establishing and demonstrating experimental control over measures that are undergoing development at the time of intervention
(4) the complex nature of communication and language development, which makes both the conceptualization and measurement of dependent and independent variables particularly challenging.

The first two challenges affect virtually all research on intellectual disabilities and primarily reflect the fact that intellectual disabilities encompass a large number of specific etiologies, each of which itself subsumes substantial variation. The third and fourth challenges are particularly problematic with children.

The Problem of Variability

There is substantial evidence that various etiologies manifest unique patterns or characteristics in terms of communication and language development. For example, research indicates that children with Down syndrome generally display relative strengths in visuospatial skills and relative weaknesses in auditory verbal tasks, such as memory for nonwords (Marcell & Armstrong, 1982; Laws, 1998) and sentences and the use of grammatical morphology (Eadie, Fey, Douglas & Parsons, 2002). Even within the realm of language, there are typical asymmetries, with special strengths in vocabulary relative to grammar and in comprehension compared to production (Chapman, 1995; Eadie et al., 2002). However, there is substantial variability within the population of individuals with Down syndrome, even when developmental and chronological age is controlled for (Chapman & Hesketh, 2000). Unique phenotypes with substantial within-phenotype variability have also been reported for most etiologies and syndromes that have been studied in depth with large numbers of cases (Tager-Flusberg, 1999). These problems can be magnified when "mixed etiology" samples are used in descriptive or intervention studies and can complicate both the analysis and interpretation of results in these studies (Wachs, 2000).

The Problem of Sufficient Sample Size

With typically developing children, the problem of variability is usually addressed by recruiting a sufficiently large sample. However, recruiting large sample sizes of individuals with intellectual disabilities can be extraordinarily challenging. For example, to conduct descriptive studies of the language development of children with fragile X syndrome, the most common inherited cause of intellectual disabilities, researchers with the Carolina Fragile X Project at the University of North Carolina have had vigorously to recruit participants from several southeastern states and often travel hundreds of miles to collect a single "data point" on a child's development (Roberts, Mirrett, Anderson, Burchinal & Neebe, 2002). Other researchers studying fragile X syndrome have flown participants to their laboratories from all over the USA (D. Bailey, personal communication, 22 April 2002). The unique patterns of language development reportedly associated with the very rare disorder of Williams syndrome (1 in 20 000 live births) have required researchers to recruit throughout the USA as well (C. Mervis, personal communication, 2 May 2002). One indicator of the difficulty in recruiting specific etiology samples is the fact that we have far more knowledge of relatively common disorders, such as Down syndrome, which is arguably the most common cause of moderate to severe intellectual disabilities, and autism spectrum disorders (for which no definitive diagnostic test exists) than other etiologies. Our knowledge of many specific etiologies is restricted to case studies, and most of the literature on intervention has used mixed etiology samples at the same general developmental level (Hodapp & Dykens, Chapter 9, this volume).

The Problem of Development

Young children spend most of their waking hours engaged in "language learning" of one type or another (Bates, Bretherton & Snyder, 1988; Chapman et al., 1992; Hart & Risley, 1999). This fact does not present a particular challenge to descriptive research. However, it provides a potentially daunting challenge for intervention studies. The typical prescription to overcome this problem is to compare two randomly assigned, matched groups, one that receives intervention, and one that does not. Then the "developmental trajectory" of the non-treatment group can be compared (that is, subtracted) from the developmental trajectory of the intervention group to estimate the amount of growth added by the intervention (Yoder, Kaiser & Alpert, 1991; Yoder & Warren, 1998). However, to date, most of the intervention studies conducted with children with intellectual disabilities have used single-subject designs (Warren & Yoder, 1997b), which are more susceptible to the confound of development (Warren & Bambara, 1989). That is, "development" can affect baseline and intervention performance. In theory, multiple-baseline designs control for this in that baselines prior to intervention need to be stable to allow a demonstration of the effects of intervention separate from "development". However, when short baselines and long intervention conditions are used, multiple-baseline designs can effectively hide and confound whatever portion of growth might be due to factors other than the intervention itself.

The Problem of Complexity

Human language is an extraordinarily powerful tool and an extraordinarily complex one as well. Language development and use draw on fine motor skills, auditory skills, high-level cognitive and social skills, and much more. Development proceeds simultaneously along a number of dimensions that come together, resulting in increasingly sophisticated communication. But these dimensions can also be decoupled such that, for example, a child may develop excellent receptive language, demonstrate good oral motor development and hearing, and yet be unable to speak. Furthermore, the language system requires knowledge of word production and meaning, morphology and syntax, pragmatics, and more. This complexity adds further challenges to investigators in this area, as discussed later in the section on "measurement". For interventionists, it raises a deceptively complicated question: is your intervention actually affecting what you think it is affecting? For example, is the intervention enhancing the actual acquisition of new language, or simply the use (generalization) of already acquired language to the intervention context? Or is an intervention enhancing productive skills, but not receptive skills? Or elicited imitation, but not spontaneous imitation? Or vocabulary, but not syntax? Or syntax, but not pragmatics?

As a reflection of these challenges, the literature in this area includes a large number of small N descriptive and case studies, a large number of single-subject design intervention studies, and relatively few longitudinal descriptive or intervention studies (Warren & Yoder, 1997b). The use of random assignment in intervention studies has been particularly rare. However, there is also clear evidence that some researchers are addressing the challenges of this area with well-designed studies that have strong internal and external validity. In the next section, we will overview research-design issues in terms of descriptive research, and follow this with a discussion of intervention research.

Descriptive Research

By descriptive research, we mean all research other than clinical intervention studies. These include correlational and observational studies aimed at understanding how children develop or behave in various contexts or over time, as well as experimental manipulations with well-controlled hypothesis testing (Chapman, Seung, Schwartz & Kay-Raining Bird, 1998; Eadie et al., 2002). There are a number of compelling reasons for the continuation of this line of research. These include the following:

(1) determining the behavioral phenotype of genetically influenced disorders
(2) understanding how specific disorders and "the environment" (such as maternal responsivity) interact over time to result in varied outcomes among individuals with the same etiology
(3) understanding how language relates to other domains such as cognitive, sensory, and social development
(4) understanding how the brain adapts to disorders in specific neurological and sensory functions via studies that employ neuroimaging or evoked potentials
(5) determining skills that may be most appropriate as intervention targets and those for which intervention may achieve the greatest overall impact.

Finally, many researchers interested in understanding what drives and supports typical communication and language development continue to study impaired populations for insights relevant to the process of normal acquisition and growth.

There are several obvious trends in the descriptive research when one takes a broad view of the past two decades. First, there is a trend away from mixed etiology studies and a closely related trend toward the study of specific etiologies (Brady & Warren, 2003;

Hodapp & Dykans, Chapter 9, this volume). Often two or more etiologies are compared. For example, children with Down syndrome might be compared to children with fragile X syndrome (Sudhalter, Choen, Silverman & Wolf-Schein, 1990), and children with fragile X syndrome to children with autism (Bailey, Hatton, Mesibov, Ament & Skinner, 2000). This tactic is employed as a means of determining what is truly unique about certain etiologies and where overlaps may occur due to a general level of intellectual disabilities. Thus, researchers are no longer just asking how children with Down syndrome differ from children developing typically, but also how children with Down syndrome differ from those with fragile X syndrome and other developmental disabilities, including specific language impairment (Chapman et al., 1998; Eadie et al., 2002).

Another trend is toward longitudinal studies and away from single-data-point studies or cross-sectional comparisons. This trend has allowed the use of structural equation modeling approaches (such as hierarchical linear modeling) to compare the developmental trajectories or "growth curves" of various measures over time. Hierarchical linear modeling requires at least three longitudinal data points, and becomes increasingly powerful in terms of modeling development with five or more data points per subject or group (Goldstein, 1979). Because major changes in language development often take many months or years, even in typically developing children, these studies increasingly cover at least one year of a child's life and often two or more (Yoder & Warren, 2001b). This adds substantially to the cost of such work, as does the need to recruit over large geographical areas (such as many states) or across very large metropolitan areas (such as southern California) to constitute etiology-specific samples of disorders other than Down syndrome and autism.

The use of control groups remains of central importance to the design of descriptive studies. The "ideal" design controls for both history and present developmental level when the goal is to ferret out unique phenotypic differences. However, this is also among the most expensive designs to conduct because it typically requires two control groups—one that is age-matched and another that is developmentally matched. There is also a clear place for studies that do not employ a control or comparison group per se. For example, a study of the variability in the fragile X phenotype might compare fragile X syndrome participants with other fragile X syndrome participants at the same age (Roberts et al., 2002). Longitudinal growth curve modeling is particularly useful for such comparisons.

Intervention Research

A large number of small N intervention studies aimed at enhancing or modifying some aspect of communication and language development or use by individuals with intellectual disabilities have been reported over the past four decades (Yoder & Warren, 1993). These studies have formed part of the foundation for the development over time of a comprehensive model of communication and language intervention (Warren & Yoder, 1997b). Although this research has some inherent limitations, as noted above, it also has a number of virtues. First, the internal validity of the multiple-baseline design (the primary design used), applied either across specific communication targets with a single individual or across three or more individuals (McReynolds & Kearns, 1983), has typically been strong. Published studies have usually demonstrated experimental control while utilizing reliable measures of both the independent and dependent variables. Furthermore, the multiple-baseline design has been the design of choice because of the operating assumption that "developmental processes" and/or important communication skills should not be "reversed" via experimental manipulation. Thus, single-subject designs that use "return to baseline" reversal conditions to demonstrate experimental control are extremely rare in this literature.

Second, single-subject studies have allowed researchers to develop specific techniques (such as time delay, mand-model, and recasting) aimed at specific communication and language targets (such as expressive vocabulary, requests, comments, and two-term semantic relations) or developmental markers (such as mean length of utterance above 2.0 morphemes) relatively inexpensively. As a result, the development of procedures for enhancing and facilitating communication and language development has been substantial. In fact, we have reached the point where innovations in terms of specific intervention techniques are becoming increasingly rare.

Although single-subject designs have been very useful in developing intervention techniques and conducting relatively short-term tests of their efficacy, they are inappropriate for demonstrating either efficacy or effectiveness of broader, more comprehensive communication interventions such as those often employed in educational or clinical settings. The ideal design for addressing questions of this nature is the "longitudinal experimental design" with random assignment to a treatment and control group, or, alternatively (and increasingly), to one of two contrasting treatments. These designs allow direct comparisons of relative effectiveness and also control for potential confounds in the samples. However, they do not necessarily control for "development outside intervention" unless they include a true "no treatment" control. They typically require at least 40 or more participants (the specific number of subjects should be determined by a power analysis) randomly assigned to two or more conditions to ensure sufficient power to allow analyses for aptitude by treatment interactions as well as main effects. Nevertheless, the results of just a few well-executed longitudinal experiments (or randomized clinical trials) have the potential to fill important gaps left by the relatively large number of single-subject design studies that have been conducted over the past three decades.

The difficulty in recruiting sufficient sample sizes is magnified in intervention research because of the necessity to work directly with participants for extended periods of time. This is, no doubt, another reason for the relative popularity of small N designs. Most intervention studies, whether they have used small N designs or longitudinal experimental designs with random assignment, have used mixed etiology samples at similar developmental levels. The main exception to this has been in the area of autism (Yoder et al., 1991).

However, even intervention studies that include only participants with Down syndrome are rare, and no communication intervention study has yet been published with fragile X syndrome participants, despite the fact that it is the most common inherited cause of intellectual disabilities. The logistical difficulty in recruiting subjects even for mixed etiology studies has been further increased by the success of educational and social "inclusion" practices in early intervention and education in recent years. That is, centers or schools with lots of children with intellectual and developmental disabilities are now all but nonexistent, at least in the USA and Canada. As a result, researchers (the authors of this chapter being prime examples) must budget for substantial amounts of staff time and travel expense to reach participants in their homes or schools for screening, assessment, and intervention activities. This side effect of inclusion increases both the cost and complexity of conducting intervention research on anything but a small scale.

Two other weaknesses in intervention research deserve note. First, the length and intensity of interventions in most studies can best be described as "short" and "low". This is not much of a problem when the study addresses one or a small set of highly specific language targets to evaluate the short-term effects of a specific procedure. However, it becomes a substantial problem when researchers wish to assess the efficacy or effectiveness of more comprehensive packages of procedures that address children's communication problems more broadly. Children engage in the process of communication and language acquisition throughout their waking hours, every day, 365 days a year. For example, the babbling infant lying in bed is actually working on the fine motor and auditory skills necessary to produce clear speech. Children receive all sorts of incidental language input, and they make use of their communicative skills from the time they arise in the morning until going to sleep at night (Chapman et al., 1992; Hart & Risley, 1999). Yet, researchers have commonly presumed that 20 minutes of targeted intervention a few times a week for a few months should be sufficient to change the trajectory of a child's development.

There are two possible solutions to this shortcoming. One is to program intervention for a substantial portion of a child's day and for a substantial length of time, such as two years. This is the model associated with the Lovaas approach to intervention with young children with autism (Lovaas, 1987). An alternative approach, typified by the research of Yoder and Warren on prelinguistic communication intervention (Warren & Yoder, 1998; Yoder & Warren, 2001a), is to intervene with the child directly to teach certain pivotal communication functions. This is then accompanied by training caregivers to be highly responsive communication partners capable of noticing, supporting, and consequating relatively small increments in their children's communication skills (Warren & Yoder, 1998). There is evidence that such an approach can lead to long-term increases in children's language development (Yoder & Warren, 2001b). The ultimate efficacy of these models remains to be demonstrated. However, the need to address length and intensity of treatment in the conceptualization, design, and implementation of communication and language intervention research is a necessary prerequisite for this area of inquiry to move forward in the future.

A second design problem concerns how to study intervention with specific etiologies other than the relatively frequent conditions of Down syndrome and autism. For example, although fragile X syndrome is the most common inherited cause of intellectual disabilities (the estimated prevalence ranges from 1 in 4000–6000 births [Mazzocco, 2000]), it would be prohibitively expensive (we estimate it would probably cost at least a million dollars per year) to conduct just one longitudinal experimental intervention study with 40 or more children with fragile X syndrome, and it would be a logistical nightmare as well. Thus, it is difficult to imagine such a study being conducted in the near term, at least if it requires frequent and sustained contact between clinician and child, as most intervention studies do. Even a multiple-baseline design across subjects presents formidable problems with logistics, although such a study is conceivable within a very large metropolitan area. So how could the relative efficacy of an intervention that appears to be particularly well suited for the unique phenotypic characteristics of fragile X syndrome be studied? A possible answer to this question is portrayed in Figure 19.1.

Figure 19.1 shows the growth curves for a large number of young children with fragile X syndrome. The development of most of these children is being studied longitudinally over several years, and no systematic, experimental intervention is being conducted with them. However, a small group of the children, those indicated by dark lines, received an intensive communication and language intervention for one year between ages 2 and 3.

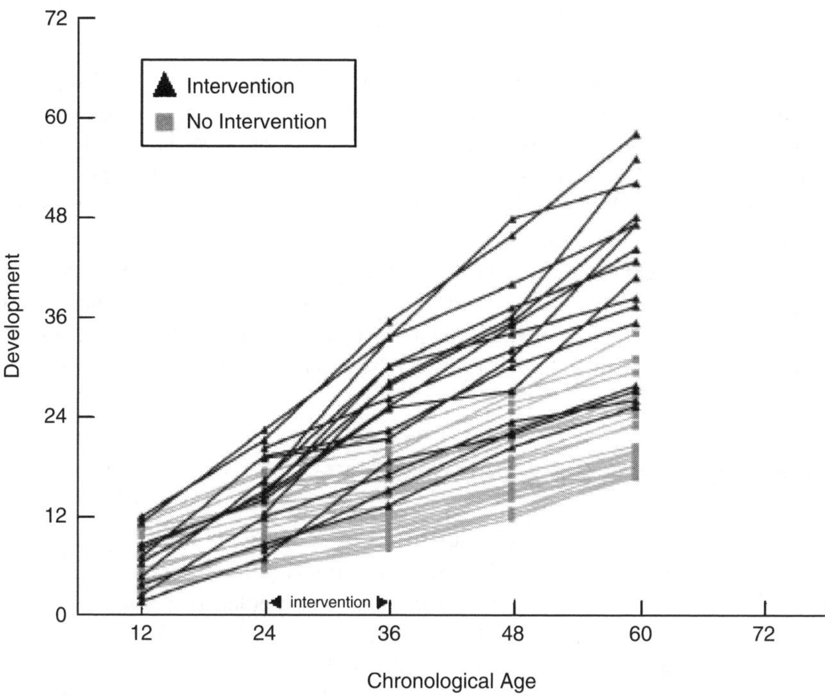

Figure 19.1 The hypothetical growth curves for very young children with fragile X syndrome. The dark lines represent the growth curves of those children who receive intensive early intervention between 24 and 36 months. The light lines represent the growth curve of children who receive only those services typically provided in their communities

The growth curves of these 10 children are then compared to the growth curve of the much larger group of children who did not receive this intervention.

A study of this nature might be "built" over time. Random assignment might even be used with the proposed design, assuming it is possible to recruit at least 20 children at a relatively early age, say, 2–3 years. Ten of these 20 children would be selected at random to receive the experimental early intervention. The 10 additional children would be assigned to the nontreatment control group. For analytical purposes, this group of children could be joined at later points by additional subjects identified later in development (say, at age 3). These children would still be part of a longitudinal comparison in which their development would be compared to the "intensive early intervention" subjects and other control subjects at ages 4, 5, and so on. This would allow questions such as the following: "Do fragile X syndrome children who receive an intensive intervention between ages 2 and 3 differ significantly at age 4 from other fragile X syndrome children at age 4 who did not receive this intervention?"

It is unclear what the minimum number of subjects is for the intervention condition in order for a design like this to provide reliable, valid data. In any case, designs like this may provide a reasonable if less than ideal way to study the relative efficacy of various intervention approaches with relatively rare disorders.

MEASUREMENT ISSUES

Language measures often serve as primary dependent variables, but may also provide essential information when the focus of research is other than language. For example, it may be helpful to provide readers with a comprehensive description of the sample population, including language skills. In this section, we will describe measures often used to quantify various aspects of language and communication in research on children with intellectual disabilities. We will provide a guideline for which measures, or types of measures, are most appropriate for various research purposes, including identification of participants, matching language characteristics of participants, providing phenotypic descriptions of language characteristics, and measuring changes due to development or intervention. A summary of the various measures discussed in the following section is provided in Table 19.1.

Identification and Description of Participants

The language and communication characteristics of children are often key variables used in identifying participants for research, particularly intervention research. The general aim of most intervention research is to demonstrate that a particular intervention was effective in some way for *a given population*. It is therefore necessary to specify the similarity of participants' language and communication skills with appropriate measures. Results from standardized tests, as well as descriptive profiles and rating scales, are typically used for this purpose.

Standardized Tests

Results from standardized tests can inform readers that participants fall within a certain range on particular aspects of language development. For example, Cole, Coggins and Vanderstoep (1999) compared intervention outcomes for two groups of students—one group was delayed in both language and cognition, and the second group was delayed in language but had relatively good cognitive scores. Language delay was demonstrated by scores of at least one standard deviation below the mean for the normative sample on two language tests, the Peabody Picture Vocabulary Test III (Dunn & Dunn, 1997) and the Test of Early Language Development (Hresko, Reid & Hammill, 1981). Cognitive levels were measured with the McCarthy Scales of Children's Abilities General Cognitive Index (McCarthy, 1972). Standardized tests have also been used to describe language comprehension and grammatical production in older children and adolescents (Facon, Tacon-Bollengier & Grubar, 2002; Miolo, Chapman & Sindberg, in press).

Describing participants' range of abilities in language and communication is important when intervention is targeted at a specific range of skills. Yoder and Warren (2001b) reported results from an intervention intended specifically for prelinguistic children. In addition to documenting that all children had vocabularies of less than five words, the authors reported that participants' scores on the Communication Development Inventory (Fenson et al., 1991), a standardized, parent-report, vocabulary measure, were below the 10th percentile.

Table 19.1 The advantages and disadvantages of different methods for measuring communication and language development

Measure	Advantages	Disadvantages	Example/sources
Standardized tests	• Provides numerical description of how study population compares to a normative sample • Provides global indices of change • Tests with subtests of language (e.g., vocabulary, auditory processing) may yield information for profiles or matching participant groups	• May not represent members of diverse populations • May lack ecological validity • Scores may not reflect changes after intervention • May be too global for identification or evaluation of specific skills • Age of normative sample may be inappropriate for some individuals with intellectual disabilities	• Peabody Picture Vocabulary Test III (Dunn & Dunn, 1997) • Communication and Symbolic Behavior Scales (Wetherby & Prizant, 1990) • Test for Auditory Comprehension of Language (Carrow-Woolfolk, 1999) • Reynell Developmental Language Scale (Reynell & Gruber, 1990)
Rating scales	• Time efficient • Indicates relative import of behavior to others • Socially valid indicators of change	• Raters may have skewed expectations for individuals with disabilities, leading to limited range of scores • Empirical evidence of validity is often unavailable	• Intelligibility scales (e.g., Romski & Sevcik, 1996; Konst, Weersink-Braks, Rietveld & Paeters, 2000)
Parent report measures	• Time efficient • Capitalize on experiences of knowledgeable informants	• May show little correspondence to language observed by others	• The Language Development Survey (Rescorla, 1989) • Receptive, Expressive, Emergent Language Scale (Bzoch & League, 1991)
Probes	• Assess specific behaviors of interest to researchers • Sensitive to intervention • Measure participants' responses to independent variables • May be ecologically valid	• Difficult to compare outcome to others (participants and nonparticipants) • Often requires individualized construction of measure	• Structured Communication Assessments (e.g., McLean, McLean, Brady & Etter, 1991) • Sentence Comprehension Task (Miolo et al., in press)
Language sample measures	• Measures language development within and across participants of same culture/language • Indicates actual language use in context • Computerized calculation tools available	• Time required to collect, transcribe, and analyze sample • Test–retest reliability may be relatively low	• Mean length of utterance (MLU) • Lexical diversity

Scores from some standardized tests, such as the Sequenced Inventory of Communication Development (SICD) (Hedrick, Prather & Tobin, 1984), are presented as language-age equivalents. Tannock, Girolametto and Siegel (1992) reported the results of an intervention for children with delayed language. Receptive language-age equivalents, according to the SICD, were between 12.5 and 18 months, compared to a chronological age range of 24.8–40.3. Similarly, Warren, Gazdag, Bambara and Jones (1994) reported participants' receptive and expressive language ages from the SICD, both before and after participating in milieu language intervention. Age-equivalent scores can be useful for communicating relative abilities to readers. However, caution is needed in interpreting age-equivalent scores, because they form only an ordinal scale, and they should not be construed to indicate similarities between participants and much younger children.

The use of standardized tests is complicated when participants are from a variety of cultures and/or live in homes where English is not the primary language. Standardized tests should be free from biases associated with particular cultures in order to verify that test differences between participants are not due to differences in culture or native language. Several older versions of tests have been found to be biased against African-American children in the USA in particular (Washington & Craig, 1992; Scheffner-Hammer, Pennock-Roman, Rzasa & Tomblin, 2002). Tests that were standardized on a sample of English-speaking children cannot be merely translated into another language either, because acquisition of the constructs tested (such as verb tenses) differs across languages. Finding standardized assessments that are free from cultural bias and that do not unduly penalize nonnative English speakers can be extremely difficult. These are just some of the reasons why it is beneficial to use other measures in addition to standardized tests to identify and describe participants for language research.

Rating Scales, Parent Report, and Probes

In addition to standardized tests, researchers use rating scales, parent-report measures, and specific probes of particular aspects of language to identify and describe participants in language research. For example, children's intelligibility of speech is often reported in terms of rating scales. Ratings have been used to indicate the amount of change in children's speech after some type of intervention (Konst, Weersink-Braks, Rietveld & Paeters, 2000; Allen, Nikolopoulos, Dyar & O'Donoghue, 2001). Similarly, the intelligibility of children's use of sign language and other forms of augmentative communication systems has been measured with rating scales (Powell & Clibbens, 1994; Romski & Sevcik, 1996). Typically, naive listeners rate how well they can understand the speech or nonspeech communication on a Likert-type scale.

Parent-report measures provide valuable indices of children's speech and language development, especially for infants, young children, and difficult-to-test children. Several parent-report measures have been standardized (Rescorla, 1989; Fenson et al., 1991), and results from these tests can be used in much the same way as other standardized test results. A major advantage of parent-report measures is that they are relatively efficient in terms of administration time. For young children or children with disabilities who may not respond readily to unfamiliar assessors, parent report may also yield more valid measures than other strategies. Conditions that lead to the most accurate parent reporting of language behaviors have been studied and described (Dale, 1991, 1996; Thal, O'Hanlon, Clemmons & Fralin,

1999). In general, parent reports are most accurate when the parent is asked to provide information about current behavior, and a recognition format is used. For example, parents are asked to indicate current vocabulary understanding and production with the Macarthur Communication Development Inventory (MCDI) (Fenson et al., 1991), by marking listed vocabulary (that is, a recognition format).

The usefulness of parent report may be limited to certain types of behaviors. For example, Thal et al. (1999) reported nonsignificant correlations between observed gesture use and parent reports of gesture use on the MCDI (Fenson et al., 1991). This may be because parents are not as accustomed to observing gestures as they are to listening for words. However, Brady and Kruger (2000) reported significant correlations between gestures reported on the MCDI, and those observed during the Communication and Symbolic Behavior Scales (CSBS) assessment. These authors concluded that the MCDI is a valuable index of gesture use in communicative contexts (in addition to expressive and receptive vocabulary).

The utility of parent report has also been questioned for children with developmental disabilities (Dale, 1996). According to Dale, parents of children with identified intellectual disabilities may not expect as much from their children, and hence be less attuned to behaviors assessed through parent report. However, in our own clinical and research work, we have noted many occasions in which parent report (as with the MCDI) turned out to be more accurate over time than what we directly observed in a time-limited assessment.

Researchers often want to describe a specific aspect of communication and language, in addition to a range of scores. Specific probes are useful for this purpose. For example, the number of communication acts produced during a structured communication probe has been reported by several researchers studying communication in prelinguistic children and adults (Wetherby & Prutting, 1984; Brady, 2000; Calandrella & Wilcox, 2000; Yoder & Warren, 2001a). Similarly, a description of how children communicate during such structured probes (for example, with gestures, speech, or augmentative modes of communication) can be helpful for conveying participants' actual communication skills to readers.

Matching Participants by Group Membership

In order to demonstrate that members of a targeted group are not different on key variables from control-group participants, some form of matching is often used. Children may be matched according to chronological age, or mental or language characteristics. Chronological and mental-age matches are used to demonstrate that a group differs specifically in terms of language performance. Matching of language performance is used to demonstrate that a particular characteristic is not merely a manifestation of concomitant language impairment. For example, in a study by Boucher, Lewis and Collis (1998), face and voice recognition skills in children with autism were compared to a control group matched according to their verbal mental-age scores on the Action Picture Test Information scale (Renfrew, 1972). Results showing poorer performance by children with autism confirmed the authors' hypotheses regarding specific impairments in children with autism that were not solely attributable to language differences. Such designs have been used to compare differences associated with specific etiologies such as Down syndrome and autism (Sigman & Ruskin, 1999).

A commonly used measure for matching participants is mean length of utterance (MLU). For example, Levy, Tennenbaum and Ornov (2000) compared the spontaneous language of eight children with congenital neurological syndromes and cognitive impairments to a group of eight typically developing children matched to the subjects according to MLU. The results showed that language profiles of participants with neurological impairments and control participants were similarly distributed. Other aspects of MLU will be discussed in the section on *Measures of change due to development or intervention.*

An obvious problem in using language-matched controls for children with intellectual disabilities is that the control children will usually be much younger than the participants with disabilities. Plante, Swisher, Kiernan and Restrepo (1993) advised researchers to interpret differences between target participants and language-matched controls with caution because the differences could be due to differences in underlying language constructs associated with age. MLU may be particularly susceptible to this age variable because of dissociations between MLU and other aspects of language at particular developmental periods. In addition, Mervis and Robinson (1999) suggest that language-"matched" controls may in fact differ from target-group participants, even if there is not a statistically significant difference in language measures. An alternative approach to characterizing differences uniquely associated with particular disorders is the use of profiling.

Describing Characteristic Profiles

All of the measures discussed thus far may contribute to the identification of profiles of communication and language associated with particular etiologies or developmental levels. Profiling strategies rely on measuring across many different areas and looking for relative strengths and deficits within an individual. For example, Mervis and colleagues (1999) used standardized test results to construct a profile of relative strengths and weaknesses in children with Williams syndrome. Various aspects of cognition and language were measured in 110 individuals with Williams syndrome, a genetic disorder characterized by intellectual disabilities or learning difficulties and unique cognitive and personality profiles. The characteristic cognitive profile showed relative strengths in auditory short-term memory and language abilities, and relative weakness in visuospatial skills. Delineation of this profile was accomplished through comparison of various standardized test results. The accuracy of the profile was gauged according to the degree of sensitivity; how many children known to have Williams syndrome showed the pattern and specificity, and how many children with different etiologies did not show this pattern.

An example of an assessment that allows for profiling communication strengths and weaknesses in young children is the Communication and Symbolic Behavior Scales (CSBS) (Wetherby & Prizant, 1990). This test is unique because it combines the advantage of norms with those of behavioral observation, by assessing children in a set of predetermined play-like interactions. The CSBS consists of several observational "probes": communicative temptations, symbolic play, constructive play, and language comprehension. Raw scores from each of these sections are clustered within the following areas: communicative functions, gestural communication, vocal communication, social-affective skills, and symbolic behavior. Standard scores are derived for each cluster and can be based on children's language stage, rather than chronological age, if the child is older than 24 months of age. Language stages range from prelinguistic through multiword use, and each stage is defined within the manual. A profile of relative strengths and weaknesses can be obtained by comparing the standard scores obtained on each cluster. For example, a child may have relatively strong skills in using gestures, a variety of communicative functions, and social-affective skills, but relatively weak vocal communication and symbolic behavior (Wetherby & Prizant, 1992).

Specific profiles emerge when the children's performance is compared to that of typical children at similar stages of language development. These profiles may be characteristic of specific disorders (Wetherby & Prutting, 1984; Wetherby, Yonclas & Bryan, 1989; Mervis et al., 1999). For example, Wetherby and colleagues (1989) showed that four out of four children with Down syndrome tested with the CSBS had similar profiles to children without disabilities who were at the same language stage. In contrast, four out of four children with specific language impairment had scores that were equal to or better than language-matched children on every cluster except syllable shape. Three out of three children with autism had poorer skills than children at the same language stage in every cluster except rate of communication and syllabic shape.

Results from probes can also be used to construct profiles of strengths and weaknesses. McLean, McLean, Brady and Etter (1991) presented communication profiles associated with various types of gestures used by adults with severe to profound intellectual disabilities. Probes similar to the CSBS, but adapted to be age appropriate, were administered to two groups of adults—those who used contact gestures, such as giving and showing, and those who pointed in addition to the contact gestures. Group differences in communicative functions and initiations were recorded in response to the structured probes. For more verbal participants, responses to specific grammatical and syntactic probes may yield key deficits relative to other areas of language.

Measures of Change Due to Development or Intervention

All of the measures described above can be helpful in characterizing the communication and language skills of children undergoing change. In intervention studies, results from specific probes and rating scales may be more indicative of changes directly due to independent variables, while changes in standardized test scores or MLU seem to suggest broader changes in language.

Probes are particularly useful for describing changes in language and communication research because there are so many types of language deficits that may be addressed through intervention. For example, even if we exclude reading and writing problems, language and communication disorders include an array of problems in producing intelligible speech; using words appropriately and creatively; formulating grammatical sentences; producing coherent, well-organized, and cohesive narration; and managing language use in pragmatically appropriate ways. In addition to disorders in these areas of language production, comprehension in each of these areas also may be affected. That is, language comprehension also can be broken down into understanding of speech sounds, words, grammar, sentences and longer units of text, discourse, and social aspects (Bishop, 1997). Intervention studies have often targeted one of these aspects of language; hence, change may best be reflected with specific probes of the targeted aspect. For example, to determine whether children learned specific vocabulary targeted in a book-reading intervention, Senechal (1997) constructed a 10-item picture vocabulary test that was administered before and after intervention.

Measures obtained from standardized tests and communication sampling provide more global indices of changes in language and communication. For example, in addition to specific probes for comprehension of semantic relations, Yoder and Warren (2001b) also presented data from the Reynell Developmental Language Scale (Reynell & Gruber, 1990), a broad-based assessment of children's skills in language comprehension and production, before and after a six-month language intervention.

Analyses of communication samples can yield many valuable measures, including MLU, measures of lexical diversity and density, and grammatical information. In language or communication sampling, a verbatim transcript is created of the child's communication. This transcript is then analyzed to describe the child's current language/communication use. The obvious advantage of this strategy is that children's actual communication in real-life contexts is reflected. Considerations in language sampling include determining the length of the sample, the collection method, communication partners, and the sampling context.

The length of the sample may affect outcome measures. For children who talk, one of the primary outcomes of a language sample may be an estimate of the child's MLU. MLU was introduced by Brown (1973) and has been described by Miller (1996) as one of the most innovative measures developed to describe language progress. MLU can be used to describe grammatical development over time and across children. It has been used more than any other metric to describe developmental progress in language and can also be a sensitive measure of disordered performance (Miller, 1996).

MLU is calculated by dividing the number of different morphemes (both free morphemes which have meaning standing alone, such as "ball", and bound morphemes that have meaning only when attached to a free morpheme, such as the plural "s") by the total number of utterances in a sample. Differences in MLU may be obtained when different numbers of utterances are analyzed (Eisenberg, Fersko & Lundgren, 2001). The recommended number of utterances for a language sample is at least 50 (Miller, 1996). However, Eisenberg et al. (2001) point out that poor test–retest reliability results if samples of fewer than 100 utterances are used. In addition, the appropriateness of MLU as an index of grammatical complexity above MLUs of 3 or 4 becomes minimal.

In addition to MLU, measures of lexical diversity can be obtained from a communication sample. The number of different words used by a child within a sample, or the lexical density, indicates a child's skill in conveying diverse meanings through different words or word approximations (Yoder & Warren, 2001b). Such measures provide an indirect estimate of the child's development in vocabulary (Goffman & Leonard, 2000). Lexical density is preferable to the type-token ratio (number of different words divided by total number of words spoken) because the type-token ratio does not change over development in most children (Richards, 1987). Lexical density is calculated by counting the number of nonimitatively produced word roots spoken or signed by a child during a communication sample of a set number of utterances or length of time. A word root refers to the unbound morpheme of a word. For example, "ball" and "ball/s" would be counted as the same word root. Lexical density has been reported as a sensitive outcome measure for young children with intellectual disabilities (Yoder & Warren, 2001b), as well as in adolescents with Down syndrome (Chapman, Seung, Schwartz & Bird, 2000) and children with specific language impairment (Goffman & Leonard, 2000). Calculation of lexical density (number of different words), MLU, and other indices of sentence complexity (such as developmental sentence scoring) (Lee, 1974), can be facilitated with computer programs such as the Systematic Analysis of Language Transcripts (SALT) (Miller & Chapman, 1985) and Computerized Profiling (Long & Fey, 1993).

CONCLUSION

A cursory review of published research over the past decade reveals two emerging trends in research on communication and language development in individuals with intellectual disabilities. One trend is the steadily increasing effort to determine the communication and language phenotype associated with specific disorders (fragile X syndrome, Prader-Willi syndrome, Down syndrome, autism, etc.), as well as how these specific phenotypes compare to each other. That is, how Down syndrome is like and different from fragile X syndrome, or fragile X syndrome is like or different from autism (Hodapp & Dykens, Chapter 9, this volume). A second trend is the move beyond small N intervention studies toward longitudinal-experimental studies with random assignment to two or more experimental conditions. These two trends might be viewed as reflecting the leading edge of knowledge generation in the field.

A major challenge, and possibly a major downside, of these two trends is that they implicitly necessitate expensive, complex, large-scale, logistically daunting studies. That is, for the field to move ahead and grow beyond its historic reliance on small N and/or mixed etiology studies, it will have to rely on the knowledge generated by a relatively small number of well-funded researchers engaged in a relatively small number of complicated, longitudinal studies. However, small N studies will continue to play an important role. Given the expense of longitudinal research in both time and money, the role of small N pilot research becomes even more critical. Furthermore, there are a large number of relatively rare syndromes that have been, at best, poorly characterized. Small N studies will continue to play a crucial role in this type of research. Finally, various new "hybrid treatments" (such as pharmacological treatment plus intensive communication intervention) await initial testing via small N designs. Consequently, it will be necessary for researchers to continue to be skilled in both small N and large N studies. Likewise, since large-scale studies are likely to employ a variety of measures, yet have little tolerance for inappropriate measures, knowledge of the pros and cons of the many measurement issues implicit in human language will remain at a premium.

How should an investigator select the most appropriate design and measures for a study? The answer to this question will always depend on the purpose of the research and the specific questions to be investigated. These issues should determine the design and the measures, not the other way around. However, the complexity of communication and language acquisition and use will continue to require that researchers are deeply knowledgeable, highly resourceful, and creative.

REFERENCES

Abbeduto, L. (1991). Development of verbal communication in persons with moderate to mild mental retardation. In N. Bray (Ed.) *International Review of Research in Mental Retardation*, vol. 17 (pp. 91–115). New York: Academic Press.

Abbeduto, L., Evans, J. & Dolan, T. (2001). Theoretical perspectives on language and communication problems in mental retardation and developmental disabilities. *Mental Retardation and Developmental Disabilities Research Reviews*, **7**, 45–55.

Adamson, L.B. & Romski, M.A. (1997). *Communication and Language Acquisition.* Baltimore, MD: Brookes.

Allen, C., Nikolopoulos, T.P., Dyar, D. & O'Donoghue, G. (2001). Reliability of a rating scale for measuring speech intelligibility after pediatric cochlear implantation. *Otology Neurotology*, **22**, 631–633.

Bailey, D.B., Hatton, D.D., Mesibov, G., Ament, N. & Skinner, M. (2000). Early development, temperament, and functional impairment in autism and fragile X syndrome. *Journal of Autism and Developmental Disorders*, **30**, 49–59.

Bailey, D.B., Hatton, D.D. & Skinner, M. (1998). Early developmental trajectories of males with fragile X syndrome. *American Journal of Mental Retardation*, **103**, 29–39.

Bates, E., Bretherton, I. & Snyder, L. (1988). *From First Words to Grammar.* New York: Cambridge University Press.

Bishop, D. (1997). *Uncommon Understanding.* Hove, UK: Psychology Press.

Boucher, J., Lewis, V. & Collis, G. (1998). Familiar face and voice matching and recognition in children with autism. *Journal of Child Psychology and Psychiatry*, **39**, 171–181.

Brady, N. (2000). Improved comprehension of object names following voice output communication aid use: two case studies. *Augmentative and Alternative Communication*, **16**, 197–204.

Brady, N. & Kruger, S. (2000). Measures of gesture development: correspondence between parent report and observation. Paper presented at the American Speech Language Hearing Association Annual Meeting, Washington, DC.

Brady, N.C. & Warren, S.F. (2003). Language intervention for children with mental retardation. In L. Abbeduto (Ed.) *International Review of Research in Mental Retardation*, vol. 27 (pp. 231–254). San Diego, CA: Academic Press.

Brown, R. (1973). *A First Language: The Early Stages.* Cambridge, MA: Harvard University Press.

Bruner, J.S. (1975). The ontogenesis of speech acts. *Journal of Child Language*, **2**, 1–19.

Bzoch, K. & League, R. (1991). *Receptive-Expressive Emergent Language Scale–Second Edition.* Austin, TX: Pro-Ed.

Calandrella, A.M. & Wilcox, M.J. (2000). Predicting language outcomes for young prelinguistic children with developmental delay. *Journal of Speech, Language, and Hearing Research*, **43**, 1061–1071.

Carrow-Woolfolk, E. (1999). *Test for Auditory Comprehension of Language–3rd Edition.* Austin, TX: Pro-Ed.

Chapman, R., Seung, H., Schwartz, S. & Bird, E. (2000). Predicting language production in children and adolescents with Down syndrome: the role of comprehension. *Journal of Speech, Language, and Hearing Research*, **43**, 340–350.

Chapman, R.S. (1995). Language development in children and adolescents with Down syndrome. In P. Fletcher & B. MacWhinney (Eds) *The Handbook of Child Language* (pp. 641–663). Cambridge, MA: Blackwell.

Chapman, R.S. & Hesketh, L.J. (2000). Behavioral phenotype of individuals with Down syndrome. *Mental Retardation and Developmental Disabilities Research Reviews*, **6**, 84–95.

Chapman, R.S., Seung, H.K., Schwartz, S.E. & Kay-Raining Bird, E. (1998). Language skills of children and adolescents with Down syndrome. II. Production deficits. *Journal of Speech, Language, and Hearing Research*, **41**, 861–873.

Chapman, R.S., Streim, N., Crais, E., Salmon, D., Strand, E. & Negri, N.A. (1992). Child talk: assumptions of a development process model for early language learning. In R.S. Chapman (Ed.) *Child Talk: Process in Language Acquisition and Disorders* (pp. 3–19). St Louis, MO: Mosby Year-Book.

Chomsky, N. (1965). *Aspects of the Theory of Syntax.* Cambridge, MA: MIT Press.

Cole, K., Coggins, T. & Vanderstoep, C. (1999). The influence of language/cognitive profile on discourse intervention outcome. *Language, Speech and Hearing Services in Schools*, **30**, 61–67.

Cole, K.N., Dale, P.S. & Thal, D.J. (Eds) (1996). *Assessment of Communication and Language*, vol. 6. Baltimore, MD: Brookes.

Dale, P. (1996). Parent report assessment of language and communication. In K.N. Cole, P.S. Dale & D.J. Thal (Eds) *Assessment of Communication and Language* (pp. 161–182). Baltimore, MD: Brookes.

Dale, P.S. (1991). The validity of a parent report measure of vocabulary and syntax at 24 months. *Journal of Speech and Hearing Research*, **34**, 565–571.

Dunn, L.M. & Dunn, L.M. (1997). *Peabody Picture Vocabulary Test–III* (3rd edn). Circle Pines, MN: American Guidance Service.

Eadie, P.A., Fey, M.E., Douglas, J.M. & Parsons, C.L. (2002). Profiles of grammatical morphology and sentence imitation in children with specific language impairment and Down syndrome. *Journal of Speech, Language, and Hearing Research*, **45**, 720–732.

Eisenberg, S., Fersko, T.M. & Lundgren, C. (2001). The use of MLU for identifying language impairment in preschool children: a review. *American Journal of Speech-Language Pathology*, **10**, 323–342.

Elman, J., Bates, E., Johnson, M., Karmiloff-Smith, A., Parisi, D. & Plunkett, K. (1996). *Rethinking Innateness: A Connectionist Perspective on Development.* Cambridge, MA: MIT/Bradford Books.

Facon, B., Tacon-Bollengier, T. & Grubar, J. (2002). Chronological age, receptive vocabulary, and syntax comprehension in children and adolescents with mental retardation. *American Journal of Mental Retardation*, **107**, 91–98.

Fenson, L., Dale, P., Reznick, S., Thal, D., Bates, E., Hartung, J., et al. (1991). *Technical Manual for the MacArthur Communicative Development Inventories.* San Diego, CA: San Diego State University.

Fox, L., Dunlap, G. & Buschbacher, P. (2000). Understanding and intervening with children's challenging behavior: a comprehensive approach. In M. Wetherby, A. Prizant & B. Prizant (Eds) *Autism Spectrum Disorders: A Transactional Developmental Perspective*, vol. 9 (pp. 307–331). Baltimore, MD: Brookes.

Goffman, L. & Leonard, J. (2000). Growth of language skills in preschool children with specific language impairment: implications for assessment and intervention. *American Journal of Speech-Language Pathology*, **9**, 151–161.

Goldstein, H. (1979). *The Design and Analysis of Longitudinal Studies.* New York: Academic Press.

Golinkoff, R.M. & Hirsh-Pasek, K. (1990). Let the mute speak: what infants can tell us about language acquisition. *Merrill-Palmer Quarterly*, **36**, 67–92.

Hart, B. & Risley, T. (1995). *Meaningful Differences in the Everyday Experience of Young American Children.* Baltimore, MD: Brookes.

Hart, B. & Risley, T. (1999). *Social World of Children Learning to Talk.* Baltimore, MD: Brookes.

Hedrick, D.E., Prather, E.M. & Tobin, A.R. (1984). *Sequenced Inventory of Communication Development–Revised.* Seattle, WA: University of Washington Press.

Hresko, W., Reid, D. & Hammill, D. (1981). *Test of Early Language Development.* Austin, TX: Pro-Ed.

Itard, J.M.G. (1962). *The Wild Boy of Aveyron* (G. Humphrey & M. Humphrey, Trans.). Englewood Cliffs, NJ: Prentice-Hall.

Konst, E.M., Weersink-Braks, H., Rietveld, T. & Paeters, H. (2000). An intelligibility assessment of toddlers with cleft lip and palate who received and did not receive presurgical infant orthopedic treatment. *Journal of Communication Disorders*, **33**, 483–499.

Laws, G. (1998). The use of nonword repetition as a test of phonological memory in children with Down syndrome. *Journal of Child Psychology and Psychiatry*, **39**, 1119–1130.

Lee, L. (1974). *Developmental Sentence Analysis.* Evanston, IL: Northwestern University Press.

Levy, Y., Tennenbaum, A. & Ornov, A. (2000). Spontaneous language of children with specific neurological syndromes. *Journal of Speech and Hearing Research*, **43**, 1119–1130.

Long, S. & Fey, M. (1993). *Computerized Profiling.* Ithaca, NY: Steven Long.

Lord, C. & Risi, S. (2000). Diagnosis of autism spectrum disorders in young children. In A.M. Wetherby & B. Prizant (Eds) *Autism Spectrum Disorders: A Transactional Developmental Perspective*, vol. 9 (pp. 11–30). Baltimore, MD: Brookes.

Lovaas, O.I. (1987). Behavioral treatment and normal educational and intellectual functioning in young autistic children. *Journal of Consulting and Clinical Psychology*, **55**, 3–9.

Marcell, M.M. & Armstrong, V. (1982). Auditory and visual sequential memory of Down syndrome and nonretarded children. *American Journal of Mental Deficiency*, **87**, 86–95.

Mazzocco, M. (2000). Advances in research on the fragile X syndrome. *Mental Retardation and Developmental Disabilities Research Reviews*, **6**, 96–106.

McCarthy, D. (1972). *Manual for the McCarthy Scales of Children's Abilities.* New York: Psychological Corporation.

McLean, J.E., McLean, L.K.S., Brady, N.C. & Etter, R. (1991). Communication profiles of two types of gesture using nonverbal persons with severe to profound mental retardation. *Journal of Speech and Hearing Research*, **34**, 294–308.

McReynolds, L.V. & Kearns, K.P. (1983). *Single-subject experimental designs in communicative disorders.* Baltimore, MD: University Park Press.

Mervis, C. & Robinson, B. (1999). Methodological issues in cross-syndrome comparisons: matching procedures, sensitivity (Se), and specificity (Sp). *Monographs of the Society for Research in Child Development*, **64**, 115–139.

Mervis, C.B., Morris, C.A., Bertrand, J. & Robinson, B.F. (1999). Williams syndrome: findings from an integrated program of research. In H. Tager-Flusberg (Ed.) *Neurodevelopmental Disorders* (pp. 65–110). Cambridge, MA: MIT Press.

Miller, J.F. (1996). Progress in assessing, describing, and defining Child Language Disorder. In K.N. Cole, P.S. Dale & D.J. Thal (Eds) *Assessment of Communication and Language*, vol. 6 (pp. 309–325). Baltimore, MD: Brookes.

Miller, J.F. & Chapman, R.S. (1985). *Systematic Analysis of Language Transcripts.* Madison, WI: Waisman Center on Mental Retardation and Human Development, University of Wisconsin.

Miolo, G., Chapman, R. & Sindberg, H. (in press). Sentence comprehension in adolescents with Down syndrome. *Journal of Speech, Language, and Hearing Research.*

Plante, E., Swisher, L., Kiernan, B. & Restrepo, M.A. (1993). Language matches: illuminating or confounding? *Journal of Speech and Hearing Research*, **36**, 772–776.

Powell, G. & Clibbens, J. (1994). Actions speak louder than words: signing and speech intelligibility in adults with Down's syndrome. *Down Syndrome: Research and Practice*, **2**, 127–129.

Reichle, J. & Wacker, D.P. (Eds) (1993). *Communicative Alternatives to Challenging Behavior: Integrating Functional Assessment and Intervention Strategies.* Baltimore, MD: Brookes.

Renfrew, C. (1972). *The Action Picture Test.* London: Sage.

Rescorla, L. (1989). The language development survey: a screening tool for delayed language in toddlers. *Journal of Speech and Hearing Disorders*, **54**, 587–599.

Reynell, J.K. & Gruber, C.P. (1990). *The Manual for the Reynell Developmental Language Scales, US Edition.* Los Angeles, CA: Western Psychological Services.

Richards, B. (1987). Type/token ratios: what do they really tell us? *Journal of Child Language*, **14**, 201–209.

Roberts, J.E., Mirrett, P., Anderson, K., Burchinal, M. & Neebe, E. (2002). Early communication profiles of young males with fragile X syndrome. *American Journal of Speech-Language Pathology*, **11**, 295–304.

Romski, M.A. & Sevcik, R.A. (1996). *Breaking the Speech Barrier: Language Development Through Augmented Means.* Baltimore, MD: Brookes.

Rosenberg, S. & Abbeduto, L. (1993). *Language and Communication in Mental Retardation: Development, Processes, and Intervention.* Hillsdale, NJ: Erlbaum.

Scheffner-Hammer, C., Pennock-Roman, M., Rzasa, S. & Tomblin, J.B. (2002). An analysis of the Test of Language Development-Primary for Item Bias. *American Journal of Speech-Language Pathology*, **11**, 274–284.

Schiefelbusch, R.L. & Lloyd, L.L. (Eds) (1974). *Language Perspectives: Acquisition, Retardation, and Intervention.* Baltimore, MD: University Park Press.

Senechal, M. (1997). The differential effect of storybook reading on preschoolers' acquisition of expressive and receptive vocabulary. *Journal of Child Language*, **24**, 123–138.

Sigman, M. & Ruskin, E. (1999). Continuity and change in the social competence of children with autism, Down syndrome, and developmental delays. *Monographs of the Society for Research in Child Development*, **64**, v-114.

Skinner, B.F. (1957). *Verbal Behavior.* East Norwalk, CT: Appleton-Century-Crofts.

Sudhalter, V., Cohen, I.L., Silverman, W. & Wolf-Schein, E.G. (1990). Conversational analyses of males with fragile X, Down syndrome, and autism: comparison of the emergence of deviant language. *American Journal of Mental Retardation*, **94**, 431–441.

Tager-Flusberg, H. (Ed.) (1999). *Neurodevelopmental Disorders.* Cambridge, MA: MIT Press.

Tannock, R., Girolametto, L. & Siegel, L.S. (1992). Language intervention with children who have developmental delays: effects of an interactive approach. *American Journal of Mental Retardation*, **97**, 145–160.

Thal, D.J., O'Hanlon, L., Clemmons, M. & Fralin, L. (1999). Validity of a parent report measure of vocabulary and syntax for preschool children with language impairment. *Journal of Speech, Language, and Hearing Research*, **42**, 482–496.

Wachs, T.D. (2000). *Necessary But Not Sufficient: The Respective Roles of Single and Multiple Influences on Individual Development.* Washington, DC: American Psychological Association.

Warren, S., Gazdag, G., Bambara, L. & Jones, H. (1994). Changes in the generativity and use of semantic relationships concurrent with milieu language intervention. *Journal of Speech and Hearing Research*, **37**, 924–934.

Warren, S.F. & Bambara, L.M. (1989). An experimental analysis of milieu language intervention: teaching the action-object form. *Journal of Speech and Hearing Disorders*, **54**, 448–461.

Warren, S.F. & Walker, D. (in press). Fostering early communication and language development. In D.M. Teti (Ed.) *Handbook of Research Methods in Developmental Psychology.* Oxford: Blackwell.

Warren, S.F. & Yoder, P.J. (1997a). Communication, language, and mental retardation. In W.E. MacLean (Ed.) *Ellis' Handbook of Mental Deficiency, Psychological Theory and Research* (3rd edn) (pp. 379–403). Hillsdale, NJ: Erlbaum.

Warren, S.F. & Yoder, P.J. (1997b). Emerging model of communication and language intervention. *Mental Retardation and Developmental Disabilities Research Reviews*, **3**, 358–362.

Warren, S.F. & Yoder, P.J. (1998). Facilitating the transition to intentional communication. In A.M. Wetherby, S.F. Warren & J. Reichle (Eds) *Transitions in Prelinguistic Communication*, vol. 7 (pp. 365–385). Baltimore, MD: Brookes.

Washington, J. & Craig, H. (1992). Performances of low-income, African-American preschool and kindergarten children on the Peabody Picture Vocabulary Test–Revised. *Language, Speech, and Hearing Services in the Schools*, **23**, 329–333.

Wetherby, A. & Prizant, B. (1990). *Communication and Symbolic Behavior Scales Manual (CSBS).* San Antonio, TX: Special Press.

Wetherby, A. & Prizant, B. (1992). Profiling young children's communicative competence. In J. Reichle (Ed.) *Causes and Effects in Communication and Language Intervention*, vol. 1 (pp. 217–255). Baltimore, MD: Brookes.

Wetherby, A. & Prutting, C. (1984). Profiles in communicative and cognitive-social abilities in autistic children. *Journal of Speech and Hearing Disorders*, **27**, 364–377.

Wetherby, A., Yonclas, D. & Bryan, A. (1989). Communicative profiles in preschool children with handicaps: implications for early identification. *Journal of Speech and Hearing Disorders*, **54**, 148–158.

Wetherby, A.M., Warren, S.F. & Reichle, J. (1998). Introduction. In A.M. Wetherby, S.F. Warren & J. Reichle (Eds) *Transitions in Prelinguistic Communications* (pp. 1–14). Baltimore, MD: Brookes.

Yoder, P.J., Kaiser, A.P. & Alpert, C.L. (1991). An exploratory study of the interaction between language teaching methods and child characteristics. *Journal of Speech and Hearing Research*, **34**, 155–167.

Yoder, P.J. & Warren, S.F. (1993). Can developmentally delayed children's language development be enhanced through prelinguistic intervention? In A.P. Kaiser (Ed.) *Enhancing Children's Communication: Research Foundations for Intervention. Communication and Language Intervention Series*, Vol. 2 (pp. 35–61). Baltimore, MD: Brookes.

Yoder, P.J. & Warren, S.F. (1998). Maternal responsivity predicts the extent to which prelinguistic intervention facilitates generalized intentional communication. *Journal of Speech, Language, and Hearing Research*, **41**, 1207–1219.

Yoder, P.J. & Warren, S.F. (2001a). Intentional communication elicits language-facilitating maternal responses in dyads with children who have developmental disabilities. *American Journal of Mental Retardation*, **106**, 327–335.

Yoder, P.J. & Warren, S.F. (2001b). Relative treatment effects of two prelinguistic communication interventions on language development in toddlers with developmental delays vary by maternal characteristics. *Journal of Speech, Language, and Hearing Research*, **44**, 224–237.

Yoder, P.J., Warren, S.F. & Bigger, H.A. (1997). Stability of maternal reports of lexical comprehension in very young children with developmental delays. *American Journal of Speech-Language Pathology*, **6**, 59–65.

CHAPTER 20

Mental Health

Sally-Ann Cooper
Gartnavel Royal Hospital, UK

INTRODUCTION

Recent decades have seen a growing interest in and understanding of the mental health needs of people with intellectual disabilities. However, the evidence base in this area is limited, with few published large-scale research projects, and even fewer published projects with findings that are generalisable. This is demonstrated in the learning disabilities chapter recently published as one of the *Health Evidence Bulletins Wales: Learning Disabilities (Intellectual Disability)* (National Assembly for Wales, 2001). Of the existing literature, it is often difficult to draw comparisons between studies, due to differences in methodologies. Key methodological issues for comparison between studies include the method of sampling to recruit study participants (to avoid sample bias), the method of assessment used to collect information, and diagnostic procedures such as diagnostic criteria (so that results are valid and of maximal reliability). This chapter will consider these issues. The chapter will focus on adults with intellectual disabilities, rather than children or young people.

Mental health needs are considered to be common in adults with intellectual disabilities, although a definitive large-scale epidemiological study has yet to be undertaken. Of existing studies, such work has focused on the prevalence of mental health needs (the number of adults within the population who have such needs), rather than incidence (the number of adults in the population who newly acquire such needs in a given time period). Some studies fail to distinguish between point prevalence (the proportion of adults who currently have mental ill health) and lifetime prevalence (the proportion of adults who have current mental ill health, or who are currently well but have a past history of mental ill health, such as a person with bipolar affective disorder who is currently euthymic). Failure to distinguish between point and lifetime prevalence complicates the interpretation of studies. There is only a limited understanding of factors which increase vulnerability to mental health needs, or protect against such needs: one area which has been examined in this context is the relationship between people's level of ability and their mental health.

Penrose (1938) was one of the first researchers to consider the mental health of people with intellectual disabilities. He drew attention to the high prevalence of mental health needs in an institutionalised population of over 1000 people. Several further studies of people living in institutions have found the prevalence of mental health needs to range from 6%

The International Handbook of Applied Research in Intellectual Disabilities. Edited by E. Emerson, C. Hatton, T. Thompson and T.R. Parmenter ISBN 0-471-49709-6.

(Heaton-Ward, 1977) to 80% (Ballinger, Ballinger, Reid & McQueen, 1991). Similarly, a wide discrepancy in prevalence rates has been reported by more recent studies of community service users, such as individuals referred to community teams (Eaton & Menolascino, 1982; Bouras & Drummond, 1992) or attending day centres (Ballinger & Reid, 1977; Reiss, 1990). These differences may be attributed to methodological differences between the studies. Some studies used brief screens to select a sample for further assessment (Heaton-Ward, 1977; Wright, 1982), whereas others assessed whole or random samples of institutional populations (Glue, Webb & Surgenor, 1988; Ballinger et al., 1991). Some studies did not employ interviewing schedules or instruments, whereas others did. Several studies do not describe the diagnostic criteria they employed, or they state that they have used modified standard criteria without describing the modifications. Where modifications are described, these differ from one study to another. Some studies do not include the full range of possible types of mental health need, thereby reducing the overall detected total prevalence rate. The samples of participants also differ. Studies of populations referred for clinical assessment and intervention are likely to yield higher prevalence rates of mental health needs than would be found in the whole population of people with intellectual disabilities. Individuals living in institutions are not representative of the whole population of adults with intellectual disabilities, particularly since the policy of closure of institutions has been introduced, leading to highly selective admission into institutions and resettlement of people into the community (possibly with individuals without mental health needs being resettled earlier than those with greater needs).

More recent studies from the USA have reported low rates of mental health needs in adults with intellectual disabilities. These studies have analysed information on known clinical diagnoses held on administrative databases (Borthwick-Duffy & Eyman, 1990; Jacobson, 1990). However, as not everyone included in the database had had a mental health assessment, these figures will inevitably be an underestimation of need.

Of the studies which included both (a) individual assessments undertaken with all study participants, and (b) participants recruited in a population-based way (to avoid sample bias), some similarities are seen. Corbett (1979) studied 402 adults living in Camberwell, London, using an initial screen of behavioural disturbance or a case-note history of psychiatric diagnosis to trigger psychiatric assessment. He found a 46% lifetime prevalence of psychiatric disorder (excluding dementia) as defined by the *International Classification of Diseases* (Eighth Revision) (World Health Organisation, 1968). He included a category of "behaviour disorder" within the 46% prevalence rate. Lund (1985) studied a random sample of 302 Danish adults with intellectual disabilities, and found a lower total prevalence rate of 28% with psychiatric disorders, as defined by (undescribed) modifications from Feighner et al. (1972) and the *Diagnostic and Statistical Manual of Mental Disorders* (Third Edition) (American Psychiatric Association, 1980). The lower prevalence rate might be accounted for by the checklist used to assess psychopathology, that is, a checklist of psychiatric symptoms that had been derived from only 38 institutionalised individuals. The checklist is unlikely to have encompassed the full range of potential psychopathology.

Patel, Goldberg and Moss (1993) assessed a total population of 105 adults with moderate to profound intellectual disabilities, aged 50 years or over, using the PAS-ADD (Moss et al., 1993). They found 11.4% to have mental health needs and 11.4% to have dementia. They did not include problem behaviours, autism, or obsessive-compulsive disorder within their assessment of mental health needs, which they defined by the criteria of the *Diagnostic and Statistical Manual of Mental Disorders* (Third Edition Revised) (American Psychiatric

Association, 1987). They commented that schizophrenia was not detected by the PAS-ADD instrument. Cooper (1997a) individually assessed a total population of 134 people with intellectual disabilities aged 65 years and over, and a random sample of 73 people aged 20–64 years. She used the PPS-LD (Cooper, 1997b) to measure psychopathology, which was classified according to the modified *Diagnostic Criteria for Research* (DCR) (World Health Organisation, 1993). She found 47.9% of the younger and 68.7% of the older cohort to have a mental health need (lifetime prevalence). This equated to a point prevalence of 43.8% for the younger and 61.9% for the older cohort. The older cohort had a higher prevalence of dementia, and some increase in anxiety disorders, with similar prevalences of most other disorders, when compared with the younger cohort. Lifetime prevalence of psychiatric disorders for the total adult population was found to be 49% with a point prevalence of 40% (Cooper & Bailey, 2001).

When the prevalence rates for specific types of mental health needs, such as depressive episode or generalised anxiety disorder, are compared, the rates of the studies of Corbett (1979), Patel et al. (1993), and Cooper (1997a) are broadly comparable, despite the difference in overall prevalence, which is accounted for by the differences in included categories. The trend across the studies is that mental health needs are prevalent in adults with intellectual disabilities. This also can be inferred from the study by Gostason (1985), who demonstrated significantly greater rates of mental health needs in adults with severe intellectual disabilities than in comparison groups of individuals from the general population. A recent, large-scale UK study conducted by the Office of Population Censuses and Surveys (Meltzer, Gill, Pettigrew & Hinds, 1995) determined the prevalence of mental ill health in the general population. Although there are methodological differences, comparison of the findings of Meltzer et al. (1995) with those from intellectual disabilities populations suggests that schizophrenia and anxiety disorders are particularly more common in adults with intellectual disabilities, in addition to problem behaviours, autism, and dementia.

While there are many possible explanations for the high rates of mental health needs among adults with intellectual disabilities, which may be considered along biological–psychological–social–developmental dimensions, few such hypotheses have been scientifically tested.

Some studies, but not all, have demonstrated an association between increasing severity of intellectual disabilities and mental health needs. However, methodological problems affect the interpretation of much of this work. Studies with institutional populations have shown the association of increased rates of psychiatric disorder with milder (rather than more severe) intellectual disabilities (Penrose, 1938; Williams, 1971; Glue et al., 1988; Crews, Bonaventura & Rowe, 1994). Some studies of community populations have supported this finding (Iverson & Fox, 1989; Borthwick-Duffy & Eyman, 1990; Jacobson, 1990; Bouras & Drummond, 1992). Of the population-based studies, results differ. Corbett (1979) found similar rates of psychiatric disorders in adults with severe and mild intellectual disabilities. Conversely, mental health needs have been reported to be more common in adults with more severe intellectual disabilities (Gostason, 1985; Lund, 1985; Cooper & Bailey, 2001). Studies of children (rather than adults) have also shown higher rates of mental health needs in those with more severe intellectual disabilities (Borthwick-Duffy, 1994).

As some of the biological, psychological, social, and developmental factors that might increase a person's risk of mental health needs are likely to affect people with more severe intellectual disabilities to a greater extent, there are possible explanations to account for the association. People with more severe intellectual disabilities are more likely to have a genetic factor or other identified factor affecting brain structure or function, as a cause of their disabilities. Some genetic causes of intellectual disabilities are associated with specific mental health needs as part of the behavioural phenotype of the syndrome; for example, Down's syndrome is associated with dementia and depressive episode (Collacott, Cooper & McGrother, 1992; Holland & Oliver, 1995); Prader-Willi syndrome with (possibly affective) psychosis (Beardsmore, Dorman, Cooper & Webb, 1998; Clarke et al., 1998); and Smith-Magenis syndrome with self-injury (Clarke & Boer, 1998; Dykens & Smith, 1998; Smith, Dykens & Greenberg, 1998). Epilepsy/birth injury has been demonstrated to increase a person's vulnerability to schizophrenia and possibly other psychiatric disorders (O'Dwyer, 1997). People with severe intellectual disorders may also be at greater risk of experiences in childhood which lead to a psychological predisposition to mental health needs in adult life. Examples may include lack of consistent parental figures, with frequent moves within residential/institutional settings, and abuse. Such factors are thought to be aetiologically important, but require scientific testing (Hollins, 2003; Lindsey, 1997). Social disadvantages may also be contributory, as may developmental factors such as limited communications skills.

There is an absence of convincing studies exploring treatments or interventions and supports for adults with intellectual disabilities and mental health needs. There are some case reports and small case series, such as those of the beneficial use of antidepressant and mood-stabilising drugs for people with depressive episode or bipolar affective disorder (Pilkington, 1962; Naylor, Donald, Le Poidevin & Reid, 1979; Rivinus & Harmatz, 1979; Field, Aman, White & Vaithianathan, 1986; Aman, White, Vaithianathan & Teehan, 1986; Kadambari, 1986; Kerebeshian, Burd & Fisher, 1987; Glue, 1989; Sovner, 1989; Howland, 1992; Langee & Conlon, 1992; Sovner, Fox, Lowry & Lowry, 1993; Bhaumik, Collacott & Ghandi, 1994). However, randomised controlled trials have not been undertaken, even for different types of antipsychotic drugs used to reduce the symptoms of schizophrenia (Duggan & Brylewski, 1999). In clinical practice, at present, such decisions are currently based on extrapolations from the general population, consensus opinion, and individual preferences.

DESIGN AND MEASUREMENT ISSUES

The design of any study needs to take into account the research question. However, there are some particular design and measurement issues that often need to be considered when one researches the mental health of adults with intellectual disabilities.

Sampling

The population which is most appropriate for identification of study participants will depend upon the nature of the research question. This is one of the first methodological issues to consider. In order for results from *descriptive studies* to be generalisable, study participants must be representative of the population. This presents the issue of case ascertainment rate (the prevalence of people with intellectual disabilities within the local general population).

Where case ascertainment for a database has been comprehensive, the population of people with moderate/profound learning disabilities is likely to be fairly fully identified.

This is because such individuals are likely to require additional support from services due to their intellectual disabilities. However, this is unlikely to be the case for people with mild intellectual disabilities. Some people with mild intellectual disabilities require additional educational support during childhood, but go on to acquire the skills to lead an independent life, perhaps holding down paid employment, marrying, and raising a family. As such, they are unlikely to be using or in contact with special services or organisations. Those individuals with mild intellectual disabilities who have additional health needs, such as mental health needs, are more likely to be using services, and hence more likely to be identified. Hence, those people with mild disabilities included on administrative database are not likely to be representative of the whole population with mild intellectual disabilities. This point is important, for example, if one is undertaking epidemiological studies of mental health needs. The difference between the population prevalence of intellectual disabilities on administrative databases and the "true" prevalence can be about 10-fold. The normal distribution of intelligence quotient (IQ) implies that about 2% of the population have an IQ more than two standard deviations from the mean at both tails (that is, an IQ of less than 70 at the left-hand tail), although the prevalence of intellectual disabilities is probably higher than this, due to genetic and traumatic factors increasing the risk of an IQ less than 50, in addition to the normal distribution. This compares with identified populations on administrative databases of around 0.2–0.7 (Farmer, Rohde & Sacks, 1993; Cooper, 1997b; Mulvany, 2001).

Selecting samples in other ways may also introduce bias. For example, people attending psychiatric outpatient clinics, or on the caseloads of other intellectual disabilities professionals, are accessing those services for a reason. People living in hospitals or institutions may have a higher level of additional health problems than those who do not. People using a particular day centre may also not necessarily be representative of the whole population with intellectual disabilities.

A *case-control* design for mental health studies can be useful—for example, to determine vulnerability or protective factors for particular types of mental health needs, or to explore the pattern of psychiatric disorders in one particular group of individuals compared with the whole population of people with intellectual disabilities. Where case-control studies are employed, it is important that the matching of control individuals takes into account other factors which might affect the research question under examination. For example, it is likely that mental health needs are more prevalent in people with more severe than milder levels of intellectual disabilities, there being a difference in types of psychiatric disorders. The clinical presentation of specific psychiatric disorders (that is, the psychopathology within disorders) also differs at differing levels of ability. Hence, matching control individuals to the same level of intellectual disabilities as the study participants will be important for many mental health research questions. In the general population, certain psychiatric disorders, such as depression, are more common in women than men, and so control individuals will require matching for gender in some studies. Age also influences vulnerability to mental health needs, particularly dementia, in people with intellectual disabilities (Cooper, 1997a), and so some case-control studies will require age matching. Many mental health needs seen in adult life are uncommon in children. Many children with intellectual disabilities experience developmental disorders or problem behaviours, which often (though not always) persist to adult life. Consequently, whether or not to include children together with adults as participants will depend upon the research question. Depending upon the research question, other factors may also require consideration, such as living environment and social networks.

Randomised treatment/intervention outcome studies can provide useful information, where individuals are randomised into either a group receiving the new treatment under study, or a group receiving no treatment or the standard treatment. With such an approach, however, it is important that study individuals are typical or representative of those individuals for whom the treatment is designed or intended. For example, if there are many exclusion criteria as to whom is randomised into the study, the results of the study might not be generalisable to the usual population that might seek such treatment. Non-randomised naturalistic approaches, concerning effects over a period of time, provide an alternative research approach and can also provide useful research information to evaluate treatments and interventions.

Consent

It is always important to provide enough information, and answer all questions potential study participants might have, such that they can make an informed choice as to whether or not they wish to participate in the study. The way that information is communicated should be considered, as this will affect the extent to which participants may understand. Their understanding may be impaired by their intellectual disabilities, but also by mental health problems, which can affect factors such as concentration. Hence, attention needs to be paid to all aspects of communication, including verbal language, gesture, intonation, and environment. Some people may find pictorial information helpful, or tape-recorded information which they can replay.

Consent to participate in the study should always be obtained, as far as possible. People may not be able to understand the full ramifications of a study, but may still have an opinion on whether or not they wish to participate. Some people may have difficulty in understanding the concept of altruistic research, but will be able to consider whether or not they wish to spend time answering questions, and such opinions and wishes must be respected.

Researchers may have protocols or guidelines local to their geographical area with instructions on procedures to follow for people who cannot give full consent due to their ability level or mental health needs. One approach is always to obtain assent from people's relatives or key support workers in addition to taking consent from the people themselves, as far as they have capacity to consent. In Scotland, for example, there is a requirement to act in this way, as legislated in the Adults with Incapacity Act (Scottish Executive, 2001). More detailed information on ethical issues is provided in Chapter 3 in this book.

Relapsing–Remitting Disorders

When designing a mental health research project, the type of mental health need being studied may also indicate the need for special considerations. Some psychiatric disorders naturally follow a relapsing and remitting course, as in bipolar affective disorder; and many psychiatric disorders, such as schizophrenia and depression, respond beneficially to treatments or interventions. Other disorders, such as autism, anxious personality, and dementia, tend to follow a more chronic and persistent course. Consequently, a study with people with depression requires clarity as to whether participants should be those who are currently depressed (for example, if exploring the clinical presentation of depression and the pathoplastic effect of level of ability on symptomatology or presentation, or intervention outcome studies), or whether the study may include people who have ever been depressed (for example, if exploring factors associated with depression). In the latter case, there would still be a requirement for adequate documentation or currently available history to confirm the previous diagnosis of depression. The relapsing–remitting nature of some types of mental health needs is particularly pertinent to research aimed at developing rating scales and assessment tools, where measurement of repeat test reliability may be affected.

Assessment and Diagnosis

Psychopathology

Measurement of psychopathology requires careful attention. The concept of diagnostic overshadowing is important (Reiss, Levitan & Szyszko, 1982; Reiss & Szyszko, 1983): the significance of emotional symptoms and other psychopathology may be overlooked because of the extent of people's intellectual disabilities and their consequent associated needs. If the person has autistic spectrum disorder or long-standing problem behaviours, the needs associated with these may also dominate the clinical picture, with other psychopathology being less apparent, or ascribed to the person's developmental disorder.

In clinical practice, the extent to which symptoms are recognised and therefore presented for professional advice will depend upon how well and for how long support workers have known the person, how much time they spend with the person, and how effectively information is communicated within the support team. Recognition of symptoms may also depend on symptom type. If people exhibit aggressive behaviour against others or themselves, this may be more immediately apparent than symptoms such as social withdrawal, withdrawal from activities, or lethargy. Consequently, all such symptoms must be specifically enquired about, rather than relying upon support workers to volunteer such information. The number of people known to have a mental illness is likely to be only a proportion of the total, with some symptoms not having been recognised, and the significance of other recognised symptoms not having been realised or acted upon (Patel et al., 1993).

This means that research assessments must be thorough in order to identify those individuals with mental health needs, and, if a control group is to be included, to make sure that they are free from the mental health need in question. Relying upon known diagnoses is inadequate, unless past assessments have been comprehensive and are clearly documented.

In order to establish that the person has a psychiatric disorder, a full range of symptomatology must be enquired about: not just those symptoms and issues that the person and the relative or support worker spontaneously describe. This requires a structured approach where, after the person and relative or support worker volunteer any problems, each potential symptom is asked about in turn. It is also important to distinguish between long-standing problems and change, that is, a symptom. For example, if a person has long-standing or lifelong difficulties with sleep, this would be conceived of as a problem behaviour or sleep disorder, and not a symptom of depression. However, if a person who usually sleeps well has recently had problems getting to sleep, waking early in the morning, or waking during the night, this is significant as a new symptom and may be due to a depressive episode (if the person also has other associated symptomatology). If a long-standing or lifelong difficulty with sleep changes in its nature—for example, becomes more severe—that also may indicate a psychiatric disorder, as a diagnosis of psychiatric disorder relies on establishing a pattern of associated symptoms, and then the timescale of each symptom. It is always important to include a relative or support worker in each assessment, as well as the person with intellectual disabilities, to attempt to maximise the amount of available information and its accuracy. Ideally, the informant should have known the person well for many years. It is also important not to make assumptions, and to recognise that there may be gaps of unknown information.

Diagnostic Criteria

A decision will also be required as to the definition of psychiatric disorders to be used in the study—that is, the diagnostic criteria. "Pathoplasticity" is the term used to describe how pathology is altered by specific factors. It is recognised that intellectual disability has a pathoplastic affect on psychopathology, the presentation of mental illness (Sovner, 1986; Sovner & DesNoyers Hurley, 1986). Numerous researchers have commented that standard general population diagnostic criteria are not appropriate without modification, particularly for people with more severe intellectual disabilities (Pawlarcyzk & Beckwith, 1987; Szymanski, 1988; Sovner & Lowry, 1990; Reiss, 1993; Cooper & Collacott, 1994; Einfield & Aman, 1995; Sturmey, 1995; Cooper & Collacott, 1996; Charlot, 1997; Davis, Judd & Herrman, 1997; Marston, Perry & Roy, 1997; Einfield & Tonge, 1999; Clarke & Gomez, 1999; Cooray & Tyrer, 2000). Indeed, Sturmey (1995) points out that all studies with adults with intellectual disabilities modify the standard diagnostic criteria in some way, a fact which indicates serious limitations on their use with this population.

Classification systems are generally either categorical or dimensional. The advantages and disadvantages of these approaches are considered by Cantwell and Rutter (1994). Psychiatric clinical decisions tend to be categorical; hence, in practice, there are advantages to this approach. Categorical classification is widely used with the general population, and has advantages for persons in clinical management, and also research and service planning, which outweigh the disadvantages of inappropriate stigmatisation. Further information can be found in Rutter and Gould (1985) and Einfeld and Aman (1995).

After we establish a person's symptomatology, a categorical approach would be to classify it by the diagnostic criteria adopted for the study. In view of the confusion in the existing literature on this point, clarity is important. While some researchers have described the diagnostic criteria which they have employed, others have not. In the latter case, it is not possible for other researchers to replicate studies or build upon them. Possible approaches include using existing standard diagnostic criteria designed for use with the general population, such as the *Diagnostic and Statistical Manual of Mental Disorders* (Fourth Edition) (DSM-IV: American Psychiatric Association, 1994) and DCR (World Health Organisation, 1993). With this approach, the limitations of DSM-IV and DCR should be recognised (that is, that the individuals with disorders fitting these criteria are unlikely to be representative of all people with intellectual disabilities who have that type of psychiatric disorder). If the research is specifically addressing people with mild intellectual disabilities who have mental health needs, DSM-IV or DCR is recommended. Alternatively, *Diagnostic Criteria for Psychiatric Disorders for Use with Adults with Learning Disabilities/Mental Retardation* (DC-LD: Royal College of Psychiatrists, 2001) provides criteria which have been specifically developed for use with adults with intellectual disabilities. DC-LD provides operationalised criteria, and so is suitable for research use. DC-LD was derived by pooling information from currently published research, and consensus opinion from practising psychiatrists who specialise in working with adults with intellectual disabilities. The criteria were piloted across England, Northern Ireland, the Republic of Ireland, Scotland, and Wales prior to publication. However, DC-LD has not yet been more widely used, and international opinion regarding its utility is not yet available. Alternatively, researchers could use diagnostic criteria or modifications which other researchers have developed, utilised, and published (Hucker, Day, George & Roth, 1979; Sovner, 1986; Gedye, 1992; Cooper & Collacott, 1996; Davis et al., 1997; Clarke & Gomez, 1999; Cooper & Bailey, 2001), or devise their own modifications. However, in view of the existence of DC-LD, this latter approach is not now recommended unless further limitations of DC-LD become apparent.

DC-LD provides diagnostic categories for problem behaviours as well as mental illness, bringing both together, along with developmental disorders, under the broad heading of mental disorder. The utility of diagnostic labels and arbitrary delineation into caseness or non-case for problem behaviours is controversial. Problem behaviours can have many causes—they may be a symptom of mental illness; may have a genetic cause (a behavioural phenotype); may be long-standing patterns of behaviour that have evolved from early life experiences; may have a communicative function, such as reflecting poverty or inappropriateness of social environment; or may be best understood by developmental models. There may be a combination of factors resulting in the problem behaviour. A diagnostic label is therefore not explanatory of aetiology, nor prognostic, and so could be viewed as of limited value, or even stigmatising. It is descriptive of type of problem behaviour and frequency or severity. A converse view is that the prevalence of problem behaviours, our need better to understand aetiology and to develop effective interventions, and the need for population data for service planning, means that categorical classification is beneficial. The same considerations are relevant to mental illness, and Einfeld and Tonge (1999) have argued that there is no practical distinction between problem behaviours and mental illness.

Differential Diagnosis

Differential diagnosis is a further important consideration in the diagnostic assessment. Many disorders can mimic mental health needs by causing a similar symptom profile, and some symptoms occur in several different types of mental illness. So, if the study requires clarity as to type of disorder, this must be determined. An example would be a drug treatment trial being undertaken. In this case, as well as a full assessment of symptoms that can occur in all types of mental disorders, physical illness must also be excluded, by completing a medical assessment, routine investigations, and special investigations where indicated by the assessment findings.

Screening and Diagnostic Tools

Various assessment tools have been developed to detect or measure psychiatric disorder in adults with intellectual disabilities. All have their limitations. The Reiss Screen (Reiss, 1988) and PIMRA (Matson, 1988) include a limited range of items which may be helpful as a preliminary screening tool. The DASH (Matson, Gardner, Coe & Sovner, 1991) covers a little more ground. The PPS-LD (Cooper, 1997b) and the three versions of the PAS-ADD (Moss et al., 1993, 1998; Prosser et al., 1998) have been used with large cohorts of adults with intellectual disabilities, and have published results regarding their reliability and validity. However, these instruments do not contain the full range of possible mental illness, and although the PAS-ADD provides detail on communicating with adults with intellectual disabilities, such as use of an anchor event, its symptomatology profile does not accommodate the pathoplastic effect of severity of intellectual disabilities. (It was designed for use with standard general population diagnostic criteria.)

While the published rating scales have had reliability studies conducted with them, the results of such studies will depend upon the investigators' understanding of psychopathology, and their training and clinical skills in eliciting symptoms, and not just the design of the instrument. Validity is at least equally important, with the diagnostic categories generated from the assessment tool needing to be meaningful, that is, to reflect the way that each disorder actually manifests itself clinically in this population.

At present, there is no assessment instrument which gathers information that can then be classified by DC-LD. While such an instrument would be useful, the lack of one should not be a barrier to conducting research. In the absence of an off-the-peg rating scale, options include supplementing existing ones with additional symptoms to cover more comprehensively the range seen, or designing checklists from DC-LD to supplement a clinical assessment.

For large-scale epidemiological work, involving a high volume of assessments, there is some advantage in having a screening instrument that might be employed in the first instance, with high scorers then undergoing a second-stage, more complete assessment. The PAS-ADD checklist (Moss et al., 1998) has been designed to provide for this intention: it is quick to complete, can be completed by a relative or support worker, and, while being short, manages to cover key areas of psychopathology.

Measures of Severity of Symptoms

Some tools are not diagnostic instruments as they do not consider a full range of psychopathology or differential diagnosis, but are designed to measure severity of symptoms. Such tools are designed for use in monitoring progression of a disorder over time. For example, once caseness is determined, people could be randomly allocated to one of two treatment groups, in order to compare outcome of two different types of treatments. This requires a comparison of severity of symptoms in both groups at preset time intervals. The Beck Depressive Inventory (Beck, Ward, Mendleson, Mock & Erbaugh, 1961) is an example and has been used with adults with mild intellectual disabilities, although it is less appropriate for persons with severe intellectual disabilities (in view of pathoplasticity which affects the validity of the items included on the scale). The Aberrant Behaviour Checklist is another tool measuring severity of symptoms—in this case, problem behaviours.

CONCLUSIONS

Interest in the mental health of adults with learning disabilities is growing, and this is demonstrated by an increasing volume of published research. However, many questions are yet to be answered. One could argue that there is still ambiguity in our knowledge of the following areas. How common are psychiatric disorders? How does a person's level of intellectual disabilities affect quantity, quality, type, and presentation of psychiatric disorder? What factors increase vulnerability to psychiatric disorder and how might these be modified? What factors are protective against psychiatric disorder, and, of these, which might be developed for people in the population with intellectual disabilities who are currently at risk? Which are the most beneficial treatments and interventions when a person develops mental health needs? What is the long-term outcome of psychiatric disorder? What information is most helpful for people with mental health needs? What are the most useful ways to provide support for people with mental health needs and their relatives and support workers? How can services be planned and coordinated to provide the most responsive, flexible, and effective supports and interventions for people with intellectual disabilities who have psychiatric disorders? These questions are of practical importance, as health affects people's well-being, employment, family, social networks, and those they live with, and may affect inclusion in community participation and integration.

There is some background research which would usefully facilitate research work. In particular, the development of a range of diagnostic rating scales with valid diagnostic categories would simplify research. Given the publication of DC-LD, further fieldwork to explore the validity of its diagnostic categories at all levels of intellectual disability might be a starting point. Alternatively, other innovative research to describe the presentation of specific types of psychiatric disorders at different ability levels could help to give valid diagnostic categories. There is also a need for the development of rating tools which appropriately measure the severity of different types of psychiatric disorders, and so can be used (alongside other measurements such as skills level) to follow the progress of an illness, or measure the outcome of a treatment or intervention. In order to determine the items to be usefully included on such scales, a better understanding of clinical presentation/diagnostic categories is a prerequisite.

It seems essential that this basic background work is undertaken, if research into a range of mental health issues is to be accelerated.

ACKNOWLEDGEMENT

I am grateful for secretarial support from Mrs Eileen Green in preparing this chapter.

REFERENCES

Aman, M.G., White, A.J., Vaithianathan, C. & Teehan, C.J. (1986). Preliminary study of imipramine in profoundly retarded residents. *Journal of Autism and Developmental Disorders*, **16**, 263-273.

American Psychiatric Association (1980). *Diagnostic and Statistical Manual of Mental Disorders* (3rd edn). Washington, DC: American Psychiatric Association.

American Psychiatric Association (1987). *Diagnostic and Statistical Manual of Mental Disorders* (3rd edn, revised). Washington, DC: American Psychiatric Association.

American Psychiatric Association (1994). *Diagnostic and Statistical Manual of Mental Disorders* (4th edn). Washington, DC: American Psychiatric Association.

Ballinger, B.R., Ballinger, B.C., Reid, A.H. & McQueen, E. (1991). The psychiatric symptoms diagnoses and care needs of 100 mentally handicapped patients. *British Journal of Psychiatry*, **158**, 251–254.

Ballinger, B.R. & Reid, A.H. (1977). Psychiatric disorder in an adult training centre and a hospital for the mentally handicapped. *Psychological Medicine*, **7**, 525–528.

Beardsmore, A., Dorman, T., Cooper, S.-A. & Webb, T. (1998). Affective psychosis and Prader-Willi syndrome. *Journal of Intellectual Disability Research*, **42**, 463–471.

Beck, A.T., Ward, C.H., Mendleson, M., Mock, J.E. & Erbaugh, J.K. (1961). An inventory for measuring depression. *Archives of General Psychiatry*, **4**, 561–571.

Bhaumik, S., Collacott, R.A. & Ghandi, D. (1994). A study in the use of antidepressants in adults with mental retardation and affective disorders. *Neuropsychopharmacology*, **10**, 1625.

Borthwick-Duffy, S.A. (1994). Epidemiology and prevalence of psychopathology in people with mental retardation. *Journal of Consulting and Clinical Psychology*, **62**, 17–27.

Borthwick-Duffy, S.A. & Eyman, R.K. (1990). Who are the dually diagnosed? *American Journal on Mental Retardation*, **94**, 586–595.

Bouras, N. & Drummond, C. (1992). Behaviour and psychiatric disorders of people with mental handicaps living in the community. *Journal of Intellectual Disability Research*, **36**, 349–357.

Cantwell, D. & Rutter, M. (1994). Classification. In M. Rutter, E. Taylor & L. Hersov (Eds) *Child and Adolescent Psychiatry; Modern Approaches* (3rd edn) (pp. 3–21). Oxford: Blackwell Scientific.

Charlot, L.R. (1997). Irritability, aggression and depression in adults with mental retardation: a developmental perspective. *Psychiatric Annals*, **27**, 190–197.

Clarke, D.J. & Boer, H. (1998). Problem behaviours associated with deletion Prader-Willi, Smith-Magenis and cri du chat syndromes. *American Journal on Mental Retardation*, **103**, 264–271.

Clarke, D.J., Boer, H., Webb, T., Scott, P., Frazer, S., Vogels, A., et al. (1998). Prader-Willi syndrome and psychotic symptoms. I. Case descriptions and genetic studies. *Journal of Intellectual Disability Research*, **42**, 440–450.

Clarke, D.J. & Gomez, G.A. (1999). Utility of modified DCR-10 criteria in the diagnosis of depression associated with intellectual disability. *Journal of Intellectual Disability Research*, **43**, 413–420.

Collacott, R.A., Cooper, S.-A. & McGrother, C. (1992). Differential rates of psychiatric disorders in adults with Down's syndrome compared to other mentally handicapped adults. *British Journal of Psychiatry*, **161**, 671–674.

Cooper, S.-A. (1997a). Epidemiology of psychiatric disorders in elderly compared with younger adults with learning disabilities. *British Journal of Psychiatry*, **170**, 375–380.

Cooper, S.-A. (1997b). The Epidemiology of Psychiatric Disorders Amongst Elderly People with Learning Disabilities. MD Thesis, University of London.

Cooper, S.-A. & Bailey, N.M. (2001). Psychiatric disorders amongst adults with learning disabilities—prevalence and relationship to ability level. *Irish Journal of Psychological Medicine*, **18**, 45–53.

Cooper, S.-A. & Collacott, R.A. (1994). Clinical features and diagnostic criteria of depression in Down's syndrome. *British Journal of Psychiatry*, **165**, 399–403.

Cooper, S.-A. & Collacott, R.A. (1996). Depressive episodes in adults with learning disabilities. *Irish Journal of Psychological Medicine*, **13**, 105–113.

Cooray, S.E. & Tyrer, P. (2000). Utility of an ICD-10/DSM-IV based multi-axial classificatory system for people with developmental disabilities. In *Best Practices in Dual Diagnosis: Proceedings NADD International Congress IV* (pp. 114–119). New York: NADD Press.

Corbett, J.A. (1979). Psychiatric morbidity and mental retardation. In F.E. James & R.P. Snaith (Eds) *Psychiatric Illness and Mental Handicap* (pp. 11–25). London: Gaskell.

Crews, W.D., Bonaventura, S. & Rowe, F. (1994). Dual diagnosis: prevalence of psychiatric disorders in a large state residential facility for individuals with mental retardation. *American Journal on Mental Retardation*, **98**, 724–731.

Davis, J.P., Judd, F.K. & Herrman, H. (1997). Depression in adults with intellectual disability. II. A pilot study. *Australian and New Zealand Journal of Psychiatry*, **31**, 243–251.

Duggan, L. & Brylewski, J. (1999). Effectiveness of antipsychotic medication in people with intellectual disability and schizophrenia. A systematic view. *Journal of Intellectual Disability Research*, **43**, 94–105.

Dykens, E.M. & Smith, A.C. (1998). Distinctiveness and correlates of maladaptive behaviour in children and adolescents with Smith-Magenis syndrome. *Journal of Intellectual Disability Research*, **42**, 481–489.

Eaton, L. & Menolascino, F.J. (1982). Psychiatric disorders in the mentally retarded: types, problems, and challenges. *American Journal of Psychiatry*, **139**, 1297–1303.

Einfield, S.L. & Aman, M. (1995). Issues in the taxonomy of psychopathology in mental retardation. *Journal of Autism and Developmental Disorders*, **25**, 143–167.

Einfield, S.L. & Tonge, B.J. (1999). Observation on the use of the *ICD-10 Guide for Mental Retardation. Journal of Intellectual Disability Research*, **43**, 408–412.

Farmer, R., Rohde, J. & Sacks, B. (1993). *Changing Services for People with Learning Disabilities.* London: Chapman & Hall.

Feighner, J.P., Robins, E., Guze, S.B., Woodruff, R.A., Winokur, G. & Munoz, R. (1972). Diagnostic criteria for use in psychiatric research. *Archives of General Psychiatry*, **26**, 57–63.

Field, C.J., Aman, M.G., White, A.J. & Vaithianathan, C. (1986). A single subject study of imipramine in a mentally retarded woman with depressive symptoms. *Journal of Mental Deficiency Research*, **30**, 191–198.

Gedye, A. (1992). Recognising obsessive-compulsive disorder in clients with developmental disabilities. *The Habilitative Healthcare Newsletter*, **11**, 11.

Glue, P. (1989). Rapid cycling affective disorders in the mentally retarded. *Biological Psychiatry*, **26**, 250–256.

Glue, P., Webb, O.J. & Surgenor, L. (1988). Psychopathology in adult mental handicapped hospital patients. *Australian and New Zealand Journal of Psychiatry*, **22**, 312–315.

Gostason, R. (1985). *Psychiatric Illness Among the Mentally Retarded—A Swedish Population Study. Acta Psychiatrica Scandinavica*, **71** (Suppl.), 1–117.

Heaton-Ward, A. (1977). Psychosis in mental handicap. The Tenth Blake Marsh Lecture delivered before the Royal College of Psychiatrists, 2 February 1976. *British Journal of Psychiatry*, **130**, 525–533.

Holland, A.J. & Oliver, C. (1995). Down's syndrome and the links with Alzheimer's disease. *Journal of Neurology, Neurosurgery and Psychiatry*, **59**, 111–115.

Hollins, S. (2003). Counselling and psychotherapy. In W. Fraser & M. Kerr (Eds) *Seminars in the Psychiatry of Learning Disabilities* (pp. 186–200). London: Gaskell Press.

Howland, R.H. (1992). Fluoxetine treatment of depression in mentally retarded adults. *Journal of Nervous and Mental Disease*, **180**, 202–205.

Hucker, S.J., Day, K.A., George, S. & Roth, M. (1979). Psychosis in mentally handicapped adults. In F.C. James & R.P. Snaith (Eds) *Psychiatric Illness and Mental Handicap* (pp. 27–35). London: Gaskell.

Iverson, J.C. & Fox, R.A. (1989). Prevalence of psychopathology among mentally retarded adults. *Research in Developmental Disabilities*, **10**, 77–83.

Jacobson, J.W. (1990). Do some mental disorders occur less frequently among persons with mental retardation? *American Journal on Mental Retardation*, **94**, 596–602.

Kadambari, S.R. (1986). Manic depressive psychosis in a mentally handicapped person: diagnosis and management. *British Journal of Psychiatry*, **148**, 595–596.

Kerebeshian, J., Burd, L. & Fisher, W. (1987). Lithium carbonate in the treatment of two patients with infantile autism and atypical bipolar symptomatology. *Journal of Clinical Psychopharmacology*, **7**, 401–405.

Langee, H.R. & Conlon, M. (1992). Predictors of response to antidepressant medications. *American Journal on Mental Retardation*, **97**, 65–70.

Lindsey, M. (1997). Emotional, behavioural and psychiatric disorders in children. In O. Russell (Ed.) *Seminars in the Psychiatry of Learning Disabilities* (pp. 81–104). London: Gaskell.

Lund, J. (1985). The prevalence of psychiatric disorder in mentally retarded adults. *Acta Psychiatrica Scandinavica*, **72**, 563–570.

Marston, G.W., Perry, D.W. & Roy, A. (1997). Manifestations of depression in people with intellectual disability. *Journal of Intellectual Disability Research*, **41**, 476–480.

Matson, J.L. (1988). *Psychopathology Inventory for Mentally Retarded Adults Test Manual.* Orland Park, IL: International Diagnostic Systems.

Matson, J., Gardner, W., Coe, D. & Sovner, R. (1991). A scale for evaluating emotional disorders in severely and profoundly mentally retarded persons: development of the Diagnostic Assessment for the Severely Handicapped (DASH) Scale. *British Journal of Psychiatry*, **159**, 404–409.

Meltzer, H., Gill, B., Pettigrew, M. & Hinds, K. (1995). *The Prevalence of Psychiatric Morbidity Among Adults Living in Private Households.* OPCS: Survey of Psychiatric Morbidity in Great Britain, Report 1. London: HMSO.

Moss, S., Patel, P., Prosser, H., Goldberg, D., Simpson, N., Rowe, S., et al. (1993). Psychiatric morbidity of older people with moderate and severe learning disability. I. Development and reliability of the patient interview (PAS-ADD). *British Journal of Psychiatry*, **163**, 471–480.

Moss, S., Prosser, H., Costello, H., Simpson, N., Patel, P., Rowe, S., et al. (1998). Reliability and validity of the PAS-ADD Checklist for detecting psychiatric disorders in adults with intellectual disability. *Journal of Intellectual Disability Research*, **42**, 173–183.

Mulvany, F. (2001). *National Intellectual Disability Database. Annual Report, 2000.* Health Research Board: Dublin.

National Assembly for Wales. (2001). *Health Evidence Bulletins Wales: Learning Disabilities (Intellectual Disability).*

Naylor, G.J., Donald, J.M., Le Poidevin, D. & Reid, A.H. (1979). A double blind trial of long-term lithium therapy in mental defectives. *British Journal of Psychiatry*, **124**, 52–57.

O'Dwyer, J.M. (1997). Schizophrenia in people with learning disability: the role of pregnancy and birth complications. *Journal of Intellectual Disability Research*, **41**, 238–251.

Patel, P., Goldberg, D. & Moss, S. (1993). Psychiatric morbidity in older people with moderate and severe learning disability. II. The prevalence study. *British Journal of Psychiatry*, **163**, 481–491.

Pawlarcyzk, D. & Beckwith, B.E. (1987). Depressive symptoms displayed by persons with mental retardation: a review. *Mental Retardation*, **25**, 325–330.

Penrose, L.S. (1938). *A Clinical and Genetic Study of 1280 Cases of Mental Defect (the Colchester Survey). Medical Research Council Special Report 229.* Reproduced by the Institute for Research into Mental and Multiple Handicap: London (1975).

Pilkington, T.L. (1962). A report on "tofranil" in mental deficiency. *American Journal on Mental Deficiency*, **66**, 729–732.

Prosser, H., Moss, S.C., Costello, H., Simpson, N., Patel, P. & Rowe, S. (1998). Reliability and validity of the mini PAS-ADD for assessing psychiatric disorders in adults with intellectual disability. *Journal of Intellectual Disability Research*, **42**, 264–272.

Reiss, S. (1988). *Reiss Screen for Maladaptive Behaviour Test Manual.* Orland Park, IL: International Diagnostic Systems.

Reiss, S. (1990). Prevalence of dual diagnosis in community based day programs in the Chicago metropolitan area. *American Journal of Mental Retardation*, **94**, 578–585.

Reiss, S. (1993). Assessment of psychopathology in persons with mental retardation. In J.L. Matson & R.P. Barrett (Eds) *Psychopathology in the Mentally Retarded* (2nd edn) (pp. 17–40). Boston, MA: Allyn & Bacon.

Reiss, S., Levitan, G.W. & Szyszko, J. (1982). Emotional disturbance and mental retardation: diagnostic overshadowing. *American Journal of Mental Deficiency*, **86**, 567–574.

Reiss, S. & Szyszko, J. (1983). Diagnostic overshadowing and professional experience with mentally retarded persons. *American Journal of Mental Deficiency*, **87**, 396–402.

Rivinus, T.M. & Harmatz, J.S. (1979). Diagnosis and lithium treatment of affective disorders in the retarded: 5 case studies. *American Journal of Psychiatry*, **136**, 551.

Royal College of Psychiatrists (2001). *DC-LD [Diagnostic Criteria for Psychiatric Disorders for Use with Adults with Learning Disabilities/Mental Retardation].* London: Gaskell.

Rutter, M. & Gould, M. (1985). Classification. In M. Rutter & L. Hersov (Eds) *Child and Adolescent Psychiatry: Modern Approaches* (pp. 304–321). Oxford: Blackwell Scientific.

Smith, A.C., Dykens, E. & Greenberg, F. (1998). Behavioural phenotype of Smith-Magenis syndrome (del 17p11.2). *American Journal of Medical Genetics*, **81**, 179–185.

Sovner, R. (1986). Limiting factors in the use of DSM-III criteria with mentally ill/mentally retarded persons. *Psychopharmacology Bulletin*, **22**, 1055–1059.

Sovner, R. (1989). The use of valproate in the treatment of mentally retarded persons with typical and atypical bipolar disorders. *Journal of Clinical Psychiatry*, **50** (Suppl.), 40–43.

Sovner, R. & DesNoyers Hurley, A.D. (1986). Four factors affecting the diagnosis of psychiatric disorders in mentally retarded persons. *Psychiatric Aspects of Mental Retardation Reviews*, **5**, 45–48.

Sovner, R., Fox, C.J., Lowry, M.J. & Lowry, M.A. (1993). Fluoxetine treatment of depression and associated injury in two adults with mental retardation. *Journal of Intellectual Disability Research*, **37**, 301–311.

Sovner, R. & Lowry, M.A. (1990). A behavioural methodology for diagnosing affective disorders in individuals with mental retardation. *The Habilitative Mental Healthcare Newsletter*, **9**, 55–61.

Sturmey, P. (1995). DSM-IIIR and persons with dual diagnosis: conceptual issues and strategies for future research. *Journal of Intellectual Disability Research*, **39**, 357–364.

Szymanski, L.S. (1988). Integrative approach to diagnosis of mental disorders in the mentally retarded. In J.A. Stark, F.J. Menolascino, M.A. Albarelli & V.C. Gray (Eds) *Mental Retardation and Mental Health: Classification, Diagnosis, Treatment, Services* (pp. 124–139). New York: Springer-Verlag.

Williams, C.E. (1971). A study of the patients in a group of mental subnormality hospitals. *British Journal of Subnormality*, **17**, 29–41.

World Health Organisation (1968). *Eighth Revision of the International Classification of Diseases: Glossary of Psychiatric Disorders*. Geneva: WHO.

World Health Organisation (1993). *The ICD-10 Classification of Mental and Behavioural Disorders: Diagnostic Criteria for Research*. Geneva: WHO.

Wright, E.C. (1982). The presentation of mental illness in mentally retarded adults. *British Journal of Psychiatry*, **141**, 496–502.

CHAPTER 21

Challenging Behavior: Research Design and Measurement Issues

Edward G. Carr
State University of New York (SUNY) at Stony Brook, USA
John Innis
SUNY at Stony Brook, USA
Audrey Blakeley-Smith
SUNY at Stony Brook, USA
and
Shawn Vasdev
SUNY at Stony Brook, USA

The purpose of this chapter is to provide an overview of research design and measurement issues pertinent to the assessment and remediation of challenging behaviors. Such behaviors include, but are not limited to, aggression, self-injury, property destruction, and tantrums. We begin by briefly describing a general paradigm for understanding challenging behavior, noting seminal studies and key outcome literature (meta-analyses). We then overview research design issues relevant to assessment, specifically, functional analysis and its alternatives, followed by an overview of research design issues relevant to intervention, specifically, validity aspects of multiple-baseline designs, long-term evaluation, and multicomponent strategies. Next, we discuss measurement issues with respect to independent variables—namely, systems factors, setting events, discriminative stimuli, and consequences—as well as dependent variables—namely, challenging behavior and quality of life. We close the chapter by highlighting critical gaps in the field that merit future attention from researchers.

The International Handbook of Applied Research in Intellectual Disabilities. Edited by E. Emerson, C. Hatton, T. Thompson and T.R. Parmenter ISBN 0-471-49709-6.

A GENERAL PARADIGM FOR UNDERSTANDING CHALLENGING BEHAVIOR

Challenging behavior is affected by both antecedent and consequent variables (O'Neill et al., 1997), whose influence can be conceptualized according to a general paradigm:

Systems factors → setting events → discriminative stimuli → challenging behavior → consequences

We can illustrate and define the elements of this paradigm by means of a concrete example. Consider the aggressive behavior displayed by a young man. Discriminative stimuli are discrete, proximal antecedents that trigger episodes of aggressive behavior because, in the past, such behavior has been useful in the presence of those stimuli. For example, a task demand ("Clean your room") might trigger aggression, because, in the past, that behavior was useful in extricating the man from having to perform the task. Setting events include those variables that alter ongoing discriminative stimulus-challenging behavior relationships. For example, a task demand (discriminative stimulus) may be more likely to evoke aggression when the man is ill (setting event present) than when he is healthy (setting event absent). The final class of antecedents, systems factors, refers to molar aspects of the environment, such as rules, regulations, and policies, that influence the nature and magnitude of setting events. For example, a service agency whose policy mandates flu shots and uncrowded living conditions may minimize the likelihood of certain illness-related setting events, thereby indirectly reducing the level of aggressive behavior. Finally, on the consequence side, a variety of stimuli that follow aggression may help strengthen (reinforce) such behavior by providing outcomes that are useful (functional) for the man. For example, aggression may help the man to terminate an aversive demand situation (that is, an escape function), attract attention from others (that is, an attention-seeking function), obtain desired tangible items such as snacks (that is, a tangible-seeking function), or generate desired sensory stimuli (that is, a sensory reinforcing function). Setting events, in turn, influence the strength of these functions. Thus, when the man is ill, a particular discriminative stimulus (such as task demands) may become more aversive; therefore, the escape function becomes more potent, with the result that any aggressive behavior that extricates the man from having to perform task demands will be strengthened (reinforced). The paradigm just articulated has proven to be a useful guide in the assessment of and intervention for problem behavior.

SEMINAL STUDIES AND KEY OUTCOMES

Over the past four decades, assessment and intervention strategies have evolved within the context of the general paradigm just described. Conceptual (Carr, 1977) and procedural (Iwata, Dorsey, Slifer, Bauman & Richman, 1982) papers on assessment have articulated a framework for identifying specific classes of antecedent and consequent stimuli that elucidate the many functions (such as escape versus attention-seeking) and subfunctions (such as escape from task demands versus escape from negative feedback) of challenging behavior. Many effective intervention strategies for reducing the level of challenging behavior have been developed. These include replacing challenging behavior with communicative behavior that serves the same function (functional communication training), thereby rendering challenging behavior unnecessary (Carr & Durand, 1985); interspersing difficult task demands with easy ones to reduce noncompliance with the former demands (Mace et al., 1988); increasing opportunities for making choices (Dunlap et al., 1994); redesigning aspects of the academic curriculum (Dunlap, Kern-Dunlap, Clarke & Robbins, 1991); strengthening self-management skills (Koegel, Koegel, Hurley & Frea, 1992); and manipulating setting events (Horner, Vaughn, Day & Ard, 1996).

The seminal studies just cited have helped fuel the evolution of an effective technology for dealing with challenging behavior, as documented in several recent meta-analyses and research syntheses (e.g., Didden, Duker & Korzilius, 1997; Carr et al., 1999). The main results of these outcome evaluations are as follows:

(1) There has been a steady growth over time in the use of functional assessment as a basis for intervention planning.
(2) Typically, for 50% or more of the cases of severe challenging behavior studied, substantial reductions in such behaviors (90% or more reduction from baseline) are observed following intervention.
(3) The success rate of interventions based on functional assessment information is approximately double that obtained with interventions not based on such assessment.

Clearly, although an effective technology exists, there are also many instances in which only limited success has been achieved. The focus of the remainder of this chapter concerns how researchers might best address design and measurement issues further to advance inquiry into the nature and remediation of challenging behavior in developmental disabilities.

DESIGN ISSUES

The fundamental purpose of research design is to ensure that the study methods used to investigate a problem are adequate for answering the questions posed. With respect to challenging behavior, the key questions are as follows:

(1) How does one identify the controlling variables for the behavior?
(2) How does one evaluate the impact of intervention?

ASSESSMENT: IDENTIFYING CONTROLLING VARIABLES

The major goal of assessment design is to employ methods that are adequate for identifying the variables that control challenging behavior so that such information can be used in the design of subsequent interventions.

Functional Analysis: The Basic Strategy

One of the most common methods used in the assessment of challenging behavior is functional analysis. Functional analysis involves the experimental manipulation of the antecedents and consequences of the behavior in order to identify the purpose (function) of the behavior. Typically, a withdrawal design (Hersen & Barlow, 1976) is used in which specific variables are presented and withdrawn to determine whether they affect the occurrence of challenging behavior. For example, consider the general paradigm described earlier. If one wished to determine whether a specific discriminative stimulus (such as task demands) had an impact, one would systematically present and withdraw the discriminative stimulus (demands). If aggression, for example, was more frequent in the presence of task demands than in their absence, one would conclude that task demands constitute a discriminative stimulus for aggression. If one wished to determine whether a specific reinforcing consequence (such as escape from demands as a negative reinforcer) had an impact, one would systematically present and withdraw the reinforcer, either by withdrawing demands contingent on the display of aggressive behavior or by not withdrawing demands while aggressive behavior was occurring. If aggression was more frequent when escape from demands was permitted than when it was not, one would conclude that negative reinforcement was a maintaining variable (consequence) for aggression. Finally, if one wished to determine whether a specific setting event (such as crowding) had an impact, one would systematically introduce an individual into a situation where there were many people present versus a situation in which there were few people present. If aggression was more frequent during the time period when the individual was in a crowded situation and less frequent when the individual was in a situation in which there were few people, one would conclude that crowding was a setting event for aggression.

Functional analysis can be a powerful tool when used as an assessment strategy involving withdrawal designs. Because the variables hypothesized to control challenging behavior (setting events, discriminative stimuli, and reinforcing consequences) are experimentally manipulated, those variables can be more conclusively identified. The designs we have described have substantial internal validity. However, limitations are also apparent, particularly as one attempts to study challenging behavior in the less controlled environment of the community.

Limitations of Functional Analysis

There is a rich history in the field of conducting functional analyses in highly controlled settings to enhance our ability to make causal statements (internal validity). However, as we have moved our efforts into the community, new issues have come to light that force changes in our study-design strategy. In this section, we review these issues, and in the subsequent section, suggest some adjuncts and alternatives to functional analysis.

First, since functional analysis involves manipulating putative controlling variables, there is a question of how we would know in advance what is worth manipulating. In a community setting, numerous potential setting events, discriminative stimuli, and reinforcing consequences may be present over time. Which of these are most worth focusing on to advance our understanding of challenging behavior? There is no a priori way of answering this question. Good study design requires assessment tools beyond the sole use of functional analysis. A related issue concerns whether the conditions eventually chosen for study in the analog or simulation assessment situation are those that the person with developmental disabilities actually encounters in the natural environment. If not, then the conditions may be irrelevant to understanding challenging behavior and subsequently designing useful interventions.

Second, in the community (school, home, neighborhood, or workplace), one often identifies numerous problem situations that evoke challenging behavior. It is not practical to submit each to a thorough, time-consuming functional analysis. Furthermore, not every community has people with the expertise to design carefully an appropriate functional analysis.

Third, functional analysis is often socially unacceptable in the community. If one suspects that crowding, for example, is a setting event for aggression, it is unlikely that one would conduct a functional analysis in a crowded movie theater or supermarket.

Fourth, conducting a functional analysis in an analog simulation of the natural environment may create problems of ecological validity. For example, one might create a laboratory analog of a crowded supermarket by systematically manipulating the presence versus absence of people in a private, controlled setting resembling a supermarket. Since the setting is both controlled and outside the view of the public, the issue of community acceptability would be lessened. However, one would not know whether the simulation successfully included all the important variables present in the community setting. Crowding may not be the relevant variable; rather, noise level, or the presence of specific people, the configuration of the aisles, or certain odors, may contribute to challenging behavior. Laboratory analogs may fail to capture the ecology of the community, providing a misleading picture of the critical controlling variables.

Fifth, functional analysis can raise ethical questions. Since functional analysis involves evoking challenging behavior, the design procedure may temporarily worsen an individual's behavior. Severe head-banging or eye-gouging may be too dangerous to submit to repeated functional analysis.

Sixth, functional analytical design typically involves repeated measurement of challenging behavior that occurs reliably in brief time periods, often only 10–15 minutes in duration. Yet, in naturalistic environments, it is common to encounter low-frequency challenging behavior that is clinically significant due to its intensity. Thus, a child may bite another child or adult only once or twice a month, but the bite may be of such intensity that deep wounds requiring sutures are produced. While this behavior would be important to assess, it would be hard to do so within the context of standard functional analysis. Relatedly, challenging behavior often arises as a result of prolonged intermittent exposure to specific aversive or painful conditions. Thus, a brief functional analysis may be inadequate for identifying the cumulative impact of these long-term conditions.

Seventh, although the literature on functional analysis shows considerable success in identifying discriminative and reinforcing stimuli for challenging behavior, and some success in identifying setting events, there are no well-developed design models for identifying systems variables. Although, in principle, one might be able to manipulate, in a withdrawal design, a systemic variable such as an agency's policy on living arrangements, it is doubtful, as a practical matter, whether many agencies would permit repeated manipulation of such a complex and costly variable.

Adjuncts and Alternatives to Functional Analysis

To address the limitations just described, investigators often include other assessment approaches—most commonly, interview and direct observation. At its core, functional analysis is an experiment, that is, a procedure that involves the systematic manipulation of the variables of interest. In contrast, interview and direct observation are descriptive rather than manipulative. Challenging behavior and its context are described indirectly (interview) or directly (direct observation), and relevant associations between behavior and environment are noted. The interview represents a relatively quick way to gather information on behavior characteristics as well as on environmental factors that appear to evoke and maintain the behaviors of interest. However, such indirect measurement raises validity issues since the value of the gathered information depends on the ability of the interviewee to provide accurate descriptions.

Direct observation, though more time-consuming than interviews, helps compensate for some of the validity issues inherent in interviews because data collection requires that episodes of challenging behavior be measured directly, along with environmental events that precede and follow the behavior. Nonetheless, the fact that aggression, for example, is reliably observed to follow difficult demands does not mean that the latter is caused by the former but, merely, that the two events are closely associated with one another. Thus, one must be cautious about asserting that the relevant controlling variables have been definitely identified. In sum, each of the three approaches to assessment has strengths and limitations, suggesting that good research design ought to combine several strategies rather than relying on only one (Carr et al., 1994).

How does the addition of interview and direct observation to the design of a study help compensate for the limitations inherent in functional analysis? The answer to this question parallels the seven limitations noted earlier. First, detailed interview combined with direct observation generates a rich source of data that can be screened for promising correlations between behavior and environment. Variables of potential significance can therefore be identified and subsequently manipulated in a functional analysis, should one be warranted. Second, strong correlations suggest variables that might be important to attend to when building interventions. Should the subsequent intervention be successful, one would not have to carry out a multitude of potentially time-consuming functional analyses; interview and direct observation would have proven to be sufficient. Third, since interview and direct observation do not entail evoking challenging behavior, the problem of assessments that are socially unacceptable in the community (that is, that generate high rates of challenging behavior) is avoided. Fourth, since both interview and direct observation do not involve the use of analog situations that merely simulate the community environment, assurance of ecological validity is less of an issue. Fifth, there is no ethical problem involving the purposeful creation of situations that evoke challenging behavior, since such a strategy is not part of either interview or direct observation. Sixth, low-frequency, high-intensity behaviors may be identified by interview, since this method of assessment does not require repeated measures of challenging behavior that occur at high rates in short time periods. Seventh, given appropriate interview questions, one may identify broad systems variables that do not easily lend themselves to assessment via experimental manipulation (that is, functional analysis).

Best practice suggests that a thorough and systematic initial interview should be followed by direct observation to corroborate the major variables identified by the interview. Interventions that reflect the variables identified through the two types of assessment can then be constructed. If such intervention is not successful, one could consider the more expensive and time-consuming method of functional analysis as a way of generating more definitive information concerning critical variables. However, clinical experience and recent data (Cunningham & O'Neill, 2000; Yarbrough & Carr, 2000) suggest that it may not always be necessary to do a functional analysis in order to generate accurate and useful assessment data. Sometimes, interview and/or direct observation suffice.

INTERVENTION: EVALUATION OF IMPACT

Carefully constructed research designs allow one to evaluate whether assessment-based intervention strategies positively affect quality of life and reduction of challenging behavior.

Why Group Designs Are Uncommon

The typical scientific strategy for evaluating intervention impact involves randomly assigning participants to an experimental group (that receives the intervention) or a control group (that does not receive the intervention) and then comparing outcomes statistically. Random sampling, successfully executed, helps ensure the external validity (generalizability) of the results due to the plausible assumption that those individuals in the general population who are similar (with respect to age, gender, diagnosis, IQ, and type of problem behavior) to the research participants will respond to the intervention in much the same way. Although group designs have been employed to study the effects of intervention on challenging behavior in people with developmental disabilities, they are much less common here than for other clinical populations.

There are three reasons why group designs are infrequently used: ethical, practical, and conceptual. It is ethically unacceptable to have, for example, a control group of people who bang their heads and whose treatment is deferred to ensure a more powerful scientific demonstration. Moreover, it is often practically difficult to locate, at a given site, a sufficiently large sample of participants who are relatively homogeneous with respect to age, gender, diagnosis, IQ, and type of problem behavior, and who can, therefore, legitimately be compared with one another. Finally, at a conceptual level, meaningful comparisons can generally be made only when there is assurance that participants are also matched with respect to motivational variables. That is, if an intervention is designed to address escape-motivated challenging behavior, all participants must show behavior that is based on avoidance or escape factors. Otherwise, one may be evaluating an intervention that is relevant only to other maintaining variables (such as attention, tangible reinforcement, sensory reinforcement, and so on), a circumstance which would produce an inaccurate estimate of intervention effectiveness. Of course, the necessity of ensuring motivational equivalence across groups, as well as equivalence with respect to demographic variables, puts a further strain on an investigator's ability to generate a large enough sample size for statistical purposes. For all these reasons, investigators have most commonly employed within-subject designs rather than between-group designs.

Multiple-Baseline Design: Internal and External Validity Issues

The most common design for evaluating intervention is the multiple-baseline design (see Hersen & Barlow, 1976, for a detailed exposition of the generic technical aspects associated with implementing multiple-baseline designs). This within-subject design uses baselines of different lengths as a method of ensuring internal validity. A functional relationship between changes in environmental conditions (the independent variable) and changes in the level of challenging behavior (the dependent variable) is demonstrated if the level of the behavior is altered when, and only when, the independent variable is introduced or withdrawn. For example, in evaluating intervention effects for three individuals with challenging behavior, one could introduce the intervention sequentially so that each individual had a different length of baseline. If challenging behavior then decreased when, and only when, the intervention was introduced for each individual, in turn, that would suggest that the behavioral change was due to the intervention rather than some other time-dependent but extraneous variable (such as maturation). This type of design is referred to as a multiple baseline across individuals. Of course, the same logic and design could be applied to study sequentially the effects of intervention on a number of different behaviors (such as tantrums, self-injury, or aggression), in which case we would have a multiple baseline across behaviors, or we could also use this design across behavior in a number of different settings (such as home, school, or neighborhood), in which case we would have a multiple baseline across settings. In all instances, the design is robust with respect to internal validity.

Because multiple-baseline designs involve a small number of participants and lack random assignment to an intervention condition, concerns may arise regarding the external validity (generalizability) of successful intervention. Typically, these concerns are addressed through systematic replication (Sidman, 1960). Consider a multiple-baseline design across individuals that demonstrates the effectiveness of an intervention involving functional communication training (described earlier) in controlling the aggressive behavior of three kindergarten-age boys with autism who exhibit a moderate level of mental retardation. Is the intervention also applicable to other individuals who differ demographically from the original sample? Here, systematic replication would involve repeating the multiple baseline for other individuals who differed from the original sample with respect to age, gender, diagnosis, and IQ. Conducting such a systematic replication would demonstrate that the intervention has some measure of external validity and can, therefore, be recommended for individuals beyond those represented in the original sample of three boys.

Linkage with Assessment: An Essential Design Feature

Historically, assessment and intervention often represented two discrete, unconnected activities. One might have assessed an individual's IQ, but the assessment information often had little relationship to subsequent intervention. In contrast, the strategies we have described involve a direct linkage between functional assessment and intervention design. Best practice dictates that interventions reflect information derived from assessment.

For example, consider the three boys with autism mentioned earlier. If assessment indicated their aggressive behavior was escape motivated, one could plausibly use a multiple-baseline design to evaluate an intervention, such as functional communication training (FCT), specifically focused on escape motivation. The boys could be taught to request help (for example, "This puzzle is too hard. Help me."), a strategy designed to reduce frustration and failure, thereby mitigating escape motivation and associated challenging behavior. On the other hand, if assessment indicated attention-seeking as the motivation for challenging behavior, a different variant of FCT would be evaluated (for example, the child might be taught appropriate attention-seeking through a statement such as, "Look what I drew!").

Finally, if tangible-seeking was identified through assessment as an important motivational variable, a different variant of FCT would be evaluated (such as requesting the relevant tangible item, as in "I want a sandwich"). The important point is that the multiple baseline is not used to evaluate a "one size fits all" intervention strategy; it is used to study the impact of a function-based intervention whose specific properties are dictated by the assessment results. It is necessary to emphasize that evaluation efforts are not, for the most part, driven by consideration of traditional demographic or topographical categories. That is, one does not evaluate the impact of an intervention by assuming that individuals of a certain age, gender, diagnosis, or level of cognitive ability ought to receive a certain intervention. Nor is it true that one should assume that a certain topography of problem behavior (tantrums versus aggression versus property destruction) ought to receive a certain intervention. Rather, it is the behavior functions, not personal demographic characteristics or behavior topographies, that typically dictate the selection of one intervention over another for systematic evaluation of impact. However, there may be some instances in which an individual's diagnostic label provides information useful to assessment and subsequent intervention. For example, a high percentage of individuals with Cornelia de Lange syndrome suffer from gastroesophageal reflux disease (Bohmer, 1996). Painful acid reflux could conceivably elicit problem behavior. Additionally, many individuals with Williams syndrome experience hypersensitivity to sound and recurrent otitis media (middle-ear infection). It may be useful to focus on these correlated conditions when studying problem behavior in people with Williams syndrome (O'Reilly, 1997). These and other examples suggest that future assessment and intervention research studies could profitably attend to biological, cognitive, and affective conditions associated with specific diagnoses as a rich source of hypotheses concerning the control of problem behavior.

Design Issues Pertinent to Long-Term Evaluation

There are numerous well-controlled demonstrations in the research literature of single-component, assessment-based interventions reducing challenging behavior. However, these demonstrations often involve short durations (10- to 15-minute sessions) in circumscribed venues (for example, a medical clinic or a segregated institution such as a developmental center). In the last 15 years, however, research efforts have moved increasingly into the community and have emphasized behavior change over the long term. Investigators may focus their efforts over a period of several years, often in complex, difficult-to-control settings such as supermarkets, job sites, neighborhood schools, and the ever-changing venue of the home. In these circumstances, one finds that the setting events, discriminative stimuli, and reinforcing consequences for challenging behavior are not static; they are in constant flux. Design strategies that involve a single initial functional assessment followed by a single assessment-based intervention are often inadequate. In such cases, we have learned that best design practice has two key features: repeated assessment over time, and the use and evaluation of multicomponent intervention (Horner et al., 1996; Carr et al., 1999).

Design modifications within long-term evaluations should be triggered by the occurrence of behavior deterioration and regression, as measured by follow-up probes, over protracted periods of time. Typically, this deterioration manifests itself when there have been significant changes in the individual's life, such as in work, social, recreational, academic, or family settings. Such change is normative, in the long term, for these types of settings. Deteriorating probe data should trigger a new wave of functional assessments designed to identify new setting events, discriminative stimuli, and related functions (reinforcers) for challenging behavior. These assessment data, in turn, should be used to generate new interventions that can be evaluated via multiple-baseline design. Because community venues are multidimensional (for example, they involve many setting events and discriminative stimuli), multiple functions and subfunctions of challenging behavior demand the use of several strategies combined (that is, multicomponent intervention). One may need to evaluate a multicomponent intervention (such as FCT plus choice plus self-management plus setting event change) by means of the multiple-baseline design. The logic of the design, articulated earlier, remains unchanged, but now a package of strategies is evaluated rather than a single one.

Evaluating Multicomponent Intervention: Issues of Internal Validity and Fidelity

Multicomponent intervention is common in community-based approaches for dealing with challenging behavior. This type of intervention often involves combining many different interventions to produce an effective package. A multiple-baseline design can demonstrate that behavior change is closely associated with the package (that is, internal validity is demonstrated). However, one cannot attribute behavior change to one or more specific components of the package because all components are implemented concurrently. Practically, this fact is not a problem for two reasons. First, our main concern is whether the package as a whole reduces challenging behavior. The multiple-baseline design can answer this question. Second, each of the individual components has an associated research literature demonstrating clinical effectiveness (often using multiple-baseline designs) with similar populations, displaying similar behavior challenges. However, should components be incorporated into the package that have not been separately evaluated in previous research (such as specialized diets and idiosyncratic sensory stimulation), one would not know whether these components were making any contribution to intervention effectiveness. Even if the package as a whole were successful, one could not recommend, with any confidence, that these unevaluated components be routinely incorporated into future intervention efforts.

Intervention fidelity refers to the degree to which the various components making up the intervention were actually implemented. If this circumstance cannot be demonstrated, one cannot say with any certainty that successful outcomes were due to the intervention rather than other unspecified factors. Fidelity is relatively easy to demonstrate in laboratory simulations involving single interventions applied repeatedly over short time periods. However, research has now moved from the laboratory to complex, multidimensional community settings where large numbers of intervention components are applied, often for protracted periods of time. Direct observation and detailed monitoring of the fidelity of many intervention variables over many months (or longer) is often impossible. Some way must be found to evaluate fidelity so that we can have confidence that our success is due to intervention variables, rather than extraneous and unspecified factors. Ultimately, the utility of our design strategies depends on the measurement tools we employ to study behaviors of interest.

MEASUREMENT ISSUES

We will examine two issues:

(1) What are the most critical variables to measure?
(2) What are the best ways to measure these variables?

WHAT IS WORTH MEASURING?

Throughout this chapter, we have discussed four independent variables (systems factors, setting events, immediate antecedents, and consequences) and two dependent variables (challenging behavior and quality of life) that have proven to be critical to measure in order to achieve meaningful assessment, as well as a clear evaluation of intervention impact. Published measurement strategies have tended to group immediate antecedents, challenging behavior and consequences together. Setting events and systems factors have usually been a distinct but related focus. Finally, quality of life has typically been a measurement target that is both separate from the others and relatively uncommon. We will discuss means of measurement using this grouping format.

WHAT ARE THE BEST WAYS TO MEASURE?

Antecedents, Challenging Behavior, and Consequences

The two basic approaches to measurement involve informant assessment (indirect observation) and descriptive analysis (direct observation). Direct observation alone poses practical problems. Given the enormous number of settings in which challenging behavior might occur and the large number of stimulus variables present within each setting, where should one begin to observe, and what stimuli, both antecedent and consequent, are worth measuring? This task could be prohibitively time-consuming. Investigators typically begin with interview and/or rating scales. These measurement tools help narrow the focus to a manageable number of settings and relevant stimulus variables. For example, the Functional Assessment Interview Form (FAIF) (O'Neill et al., 1997) is a structured interview that asks informants questions related to the following:

(1) discriminative stimuli/immediate antecedents, such as time of day, settings, people present, and relevant activities, that are most likely/least likely to evoke challenging behavior
(2) consequences/outcomes that maintain challenging behavior, including attention, desired tangible items, sensory reinforcement, and escape/avoidance of activities/people
(3) dimensions of the challenging behavior itself, such as topography, frequency, duration, and intensity.

The interview allows an investigator to focus subsequent direct observation efforts specifically on stimulus and response variables that have a high likelihood of revealing important information about the control of challenging behavior. The interview is an initial tool for identifying putative relationships that can be a basis for subsequent intervention planning. The interview can more readily identify low-frequency/high-intensity behaviors that would be impractical to detect with more time-consuming and expensive direct-measurement strategies. Relatedly, the Motivation Assessment Scale (MAS) (Durand & Crimmins, 1992) can also be used to identify the situations in which challenging behavior can occur. This measurement tool is a rating scale in which informants fill out a series of 7-point Likert scales pertaining to judgments of the likelihood that challenging behavior will occur in various circumstances.

Once the universe of plausible antecedents, behaviors, and consequences has been narrowed by indirect observation, it becomes more practical to use direct observation measures to confirm the accuracy of the interview/rating scale measures. As the name implies, direct observation does not involve the use of intermediaries; rather, selected people (such as staff, teachers, parents, and researchers) observe environment–behavior relationships as they occur. Two of the most prominent direct observation strategies are antecedent–behavior–consequence (ABC) charts, and structured recording of environment–behavior sequences.

ABC charts (e.g., Pyles & Bailey, 1990; Carr et al., 1994; O'Neill et al., 1997) allow the observer to write down simple narrative descriptions of behavior as it occurs and then to describe the stimulus events immediately preceding (discriminative stimuli) and following (maintaining consequences/functions) the behavior of interest. For example, informant assessment may have indicated that aggressive behavior was common for a specific individual and that it was most likely to occur in a few situations (for example, during math; or while being teased); therefore, one might profitably focus ABC measurement on those situations. The observer (such as a teacher) waits for the individual to enter the situation of interest (such as math) and then begins narrative recording. When aggressive behavior is observed, the immediate antecedents (such as demands, transitions, and interruptions) and consequences (such as peer comments, task withdrawal, and presentation of desired tangible items) are noted.

Although ABC charts may provide an indication of important environment–behavior sequences, the narrative nature of such measures does not precisely describe moment-to-moment changes. To accomplish this goal, one may have to resort to variations of time sampling (e.g., Lalli, Browder, Mace & Brown, 1993) or real-time recording (e.g., Emerson et al., 1996). Most commonly, measurement consists of either frequency counts (that is, counting the number of episodes of challenging behavior in a block of time) or time sampling (for example, dividing a period of time, say, 60 minutes, into a period of, say, 10-second time samples, noting the presence/absence of behavior at any point in each time sample, and then cumulating the total number of time samples in which the behavior is present, a method referred to as partial-interval time sampling). In fact, there are several variations of time sampling that can be used (Thompson, Symons & Felce, 2000). In addition to partial-interval sampling, just described, there is whole-interval sampling (the behavior must be observed during the entire interval) and momentary sampling (the behavior must be observed at a prespecified single point in time during the interval). Structured recording methods provide precise time-based information on antecedent–behavior–consequence sequences as they occur. These may be summarized either as percent time samples in which the events of interest have occurred (Lalli et al., 1993) or as specific conditional probabilities existing between environmental and behavioral events (e.g., Emerson et al., 1996). Although these measurement methods are costly in terms of required time and personnel, they are often the most precise and reliable tools available for analyzing challenging behavior and the factors that appear to be controlling it. This type of measurement can raise issues of social acceptability or danger to self and others. Time sampling severe self-injury and aggression in a supermarket or movie theater would be problematic in that the community would not tolerate such behavior (social acceptability), nor would such measurement be safe because of the risks posed to the person with disabilities and others (danger to self/others). Fortunately, these issues can be dealt with, when warranted, by using latency and/or percent task completion measures. If a man with autism began to bite himself or others upon entering the supermarket, the time elapsed between entering the supermarket and the first episode of challenging behavior would be recorded (latency to challenging behavior). The man would then be removed, thereby protecting him and others from future harm. Such limited exposure to the behavior minimizes issues of social acceptability and danger. Once intervention is implemented and the man's behavior slowly improves, one could also measure the extent to which he completed the "tasks" (for example, tally the number of the following task steps that were completed before the challenging behavior occurred: enter store; get shopping cart; get items 1, 2, 3, etc.; go to check-out line; place items on counter; pay; pick up bags of items; return to car). An increasing number of task steps completed in the absence of challenging behavior is an indication that challenging behavior has been brought under control. Latency and task steps completed have been successfully used as measurement tools in community settings such as supermarkets (Carr & Carlson, 1993) and employment sites (Kemp & Carr, 1995).

Setting Events and Systems Factors

The measurement of setting events can often most efficiently begin with indirect observation (for example, checklists/interviews) and then proceed, if necessary and feasible, to direct observation (for example, scatter plots or frequency/time sampling). With respect to indirect observation, three measurement instruments are especially useful: the Setting Event Checklist (Gardner, Cole, Davidson & Karan, 1986), the Multimodal Functional Diagnostics Worksheet (Gardner & Sovner, 1994), and the Functional Assessment Interview Form (O'Neill et al., 1997). All three instruments ask that significant others (such as parents, teachers, and residential staff) recall whether exemplars of specific setting-event categories occurred during time periods preceding incidents of challenging behavior. Although the wording of each instrument varies, setting events are defined in terms of three generic categories: physical events (such as temperature, noise, and architecture), social events (such as presence/absence of specific people, previously occurring social interactions characterized by either a positive or negative valence), and physiological events (such as illness, hunger, fatigue, and drug status).

One can design interventions based solely on indirect observation. However, typically, direct observation is used to verify informant reports. Scatter-plot analysis (Touchette, MacDonald & Langer, 1985) is a useful direct observation measure for identifying setting events. This measurement strategy involves the use of a grid divided into time intervals that cover each day of observation, resulting in a table of squares (for example, the entire day may be broken into half-hour blocks of time). High and low levels of challenging behavior are operationally defined and recorded (for example, zero episodes of challenging behavior are indicated by a blank square, two or fewer episodes constitute "low" levels and are indicated by a "/" mark in the appropriate square, and three or more episodes constitute a "high" level and are indicated by a filled-in square). In this manner, the scatter plot provides a visual pattern indicating what particular time blocks (and their associated stimulus variables) are more/less likely to be associated with high/low levels of challenging behavior over many days. Patterns of responding may reveal those setting events that reliably occur at particular times of day (such as presence/absence of specific people, a unique class of activities, and a specific social situation).

Scatter plots can provide a global picture of the relationship between setting events and challenging behavior over time. To obtain a more detailed analysis of moment-to-moment relationships, one would need continuous monitoring of challenging behavior throughout the day. This type of measurement is both costly and rare. Nonetheless, Horner and colleagues (1996) demonstrated that such detailed measurement was possible, as they conducted frequency counts of challenging behavior, continuously, for 45 individuals across 17 712 hours while simultaneously noting whether specific setting events were present. These data permitted the calculation of conditional probabilities (that is, likelihood of challenging behavior given the presence/absence of specific setting events). This type of measurement approach yields the most precise data concerning the impact of setting events. However, for practical purposes, it is best reserved for those instances in which one desires to demonstrate that a specific setting event affects challenging behavior over a circumscribed time period.

While the measurement of setting events in relation to challenging behavior is only in the early stages of development, the measurement of broader systems factors is even less well developed. At this point, what the field has to offer is a description of generic categories of systems factors that are logically but, for the most part, only anecdotally related to challenging behavior. A particularly useful schema, based on principles of organizational behavior management, has been described by Knoster, Villa and Thousand (2000). These authors note several systems categories that may merit measurement: agency policies ("vision"); adequacy of training for support people; incentives for caregivers to engage in problem solving; distribution of resources (temporal, physical, and human); presence/absence of action plans that define roles, responsibilities, and monitoring; and methods for correcting new or ongoing deficiencies. In principle, each of these systems variables could be measured; in practice, specific instruments for measuring their impact on challenging behavior have yet to be fully developed. Nonetheless, the authors' schema does, at least, provide guidelines concerning where it might be profitable to focus measurement efforts.

Quality of Life

Recall that the ultimate goal of assessment and intervention is not simply to reduce challenging behavior; rather, it is to produce comprehensive lifestyle change that improves quality of life not only for persons with disabilities, but also for those who support them. Therefore, on the dependent-variable side, researchers need to use measurement instruments that can capture broad lifestyle changes. There is some controversy in the literature concerning how best to conceptualize quality of life. Some investigators emphasize an individualistic approach that focuses on subjective experiences, whereas other investigators emphasize a population-based perspective in which objective indices are used to compare the lifestyles of those with and without disabilities (Felce & Emerson, 2000). Generic guidelines as well as specific strategies for measuring quality-of-life changes are available (e.g., Schalock, 1990) and are discussed in detail in Chapter 12 of this volume. Therefore, for present purposes, we simply note the need for researchers to measure the multiple dimensions that define quality of life (Hughes, Hwang, Kim, Eisenman & Killian, 1995), including improvements in social relationships (such as friendship formation), employment (such as productivity and a good job match), personal satisfaction (such as self-confidence and happiness), recreation and leisure (such as good quality of activities), self-determination (such as personal control and choice of living arrangements), community integration (such as school inclusion), and community adjustment (such as survival skills).

One issue worthy of consideration concerns whether quality of life is related to challenging behavior as an independent or dependent variable. For example, researchers have presented highly suggestive data demonstrating that meaningful and interesting employment and recreation activities may function as an independent variable to reduce the level of challenging behavior (Allen, 1994). In all likelihood, however, quality-of-life variables probably function as both dependent and independent variables contingent on the specifics of how an intervention is implemented. Thus, initially, one might reduce challenging behavior directly by means of communication training, with the result that social relationships are gradually facilitated and become easier to maintain (quality of life as a dependent variable). Such improvement opens a path for caregivers actively to program a greater depth and variety of social opportunities that, in turn, produce further reductions in challenging behavior (quality of life as an independent variable). Given the plausibility of this scenario, it would make sense to measure quality-of-life factors irrespective of whether they are conceptualized as independent or dependent variables; the measurement strategies discussed by Schalock and Felce (Chapter 12 of this volume) facilitate achievement of this goal.

Reliability and Validity Issues

The psychometric properties of many of the measurement tools we have discussed have not been fully examined. Therefore, researchers need to exercise caution in interpreting data derived from these measurement methods with respect to both reliability and validity issues.

Regarding reliability, the key questions concern:

(1) interobserver reliability (that is, the degree to which the measure remains consistent irrespective of who is doing the measuring)
(2) test–retest reliability (for example, whether a function identified at one point in time remains the same at a different point in time).

Three issues are worth noting. First, interobserver reliability is relatively straightforward for direct observation since observer records can be compared and level of agreement precisely calculated; however, the situation is more complex for indirect measurement. For example, some data suggest that the reliability of the Motivation Assessment Scale (MAS) is good (Durand & Crimmons, 1988), whereas other data suggest it is not (Zarcone, Rodgers, Iwata, Rourke & Dorsey, 1991). Indirect measurement can sometimes be influenced by psychosocial factors that affect the judgment of the rater or interviewee thereby producing a distorted estimate of the level of problem behavior (Thompson et al., 2000). Second, most investigators (including those who developed the MAS) suggest that best measurement practice should always involve the use of at least two instruments related to the target of interest, an especially prudent suggestion given the paucity of reliability data for most instruments. This multimethod approach allows a better estimate of how confident one should be about the reliability of the data. Third, test–retest reliability in complex community environments is likely to be poor, particularly if the testing points are widely separated in time. Setting events and systems factors often change in community venues over time. These variables could alter behavioral functions, making it likely that the set of functions identified at time 1 are not isomorphic with the set of functions identified at time 2. In the natural environment, one should assume that functions are most likely not stable over time. The problem of test–retest reliability, therefore, needs to be addressed by making repeated functional assessments over the course of intervention with a view to redesigning interventions as behavioral functions change.

Regarding validity, the key questions concern:

(1) content validity (for example, are the conditions in the assessment environment sufficiently similar to those in the community environment to allow one to make generalizations across the two environments?)
(2) predictive validity (for example, do the results of the assessment lead to effective interventions?).

Again, since systematic data on validity are not available for most of the measurement tools we have described, best measurement practice should involve the use of more than one instrument to measure the same variables of interest. To avoid content validity problems, one should avoid, whenever possible, the exclusive use of analog assessments and, instead, assess in the natural environment itself, thereby minimizing generalization concerns. However, if this strategy is not possible, one needs to compare the degree to which the assessment environment captures the main features of the natural community environment so that one can at least estimate the degree of confidence about generalizing from the former environment to the latter. Finally, with respect to predictive validity, the field has not, as yet, compared different measurement tools. There is, however, one guiding principle that is especially relevant to this issue, namely, that interventions based on accurate identification of behavioral function produce better outcomes than those not based on such information (Carr et al., 1999). This fact suggests that predictive validity is best addressed by using measurement tools that yield detailed information on behavioral function.

FUTURE ISSUES IN RESEARCH METHODS

The research methods applied to the study of challenging behavior are in a state of flux because the analysis of and intervention for such behavior has increasingly moved from the highly controlled settings of the past (such as segregated institutions, clinics, and laboratory simulations) to the much less controlled community settings of the present (such as community residences, neighborhood schools, and the workplace). Arguably, our discussion in this chapter leads to the conclusion that, with respect to design and measurement issues, future research efforts might profitably be focused on the following initiatives:

(1) We need to develop user-friendly assessments that are valid. That is, we need to determine what nonexperimental methods under what circumstances yield data comparable to those obtained using rigorous experimental methods (functional analysis).

Without such methodological studies, we will always be in the position of relying on time-consuming, often impractical methods that require high levels of expertise. This situation would impede developing an understanding of challenging behavior in the complex, natural environment of the community. However, it is also important to acknowledge that some important information about problem behavior (such as the role of complex biological factors) may be obtainable only through assessments that prove to be laborious and costly. Thus, research may demonstrate that user-friendliness is an important criterion, but not the only one.

(2) We need to evaluate and strengthen the psychometric properties (reliability and validity) of measurement tools pertinent to evaluating the role of setting events and systems factors. Without serious advances in these areas, we will be less effective in understanding the role that molar variables play in the control and remediation of challenging behavior.

(3) We need to develop algorithms that permit investigators to link, in a systematic manner, the design of interventions with multidimensional assessment data (that is, involving systems factors, setting events, discriminative stimuli, and reinforcing consequences). Without efforts to build and articulate a heuristic set of decision rules, the linkage between assessment data and intervention design will often be unclear, and the advantages of a rational, prescriptive approach to intervention will be minimized.

In sum, as we have noted elsewhere (Carr et al., 2002), as we enter a new era emphasizing community-based approaches for dealing with challenging behavior, much flexibility and innovation will be required with respect to both research design and measurement strategies.

ACKNOWLEDGMENT

Preparation of this paper was supported by Cooperative Agreement H133B98005 from the National Institute on Disabilities and Rehabilitation Research, "Rehabilitation Research and Training Center on Positive Behavioral Support".

Correspondence concerning this chapter can be sent to Edward Carr, Department of Psychology, State University of New York, Stony Brook, NY 11794-2500, USA.

REFERENCES

Allen, D. (1994). Towards meaningful daytime activity. In E. Emerson, P. McGill & J. Mansell (Eds) *Severe Learning Disabilities and Challenging Behaviours* (pp. 157–178). London: Chapman & Hall.

Bohmer, C.J.M. (1996). *Gastro-Oesophageal Reflux Disease in Intellectually Disabled Individuals.* Amsterdam: VU University Press.

Carr, E.G. (1977). The motivation of self-injurious behavior: a review of some hypotheses. *Psychological Bulletin*, **84**, 800–816.

Carr, E.G. & Carlson, J.I. (1993). Reduction of severe behavior problems in the community using a multicomponent treatment approach. *Journal of Applied Behavior Analysis*, **26**, 157–172.

Carr, E.G., Dunlap, G., Horner, R.H., Koegel, R.L., Turnbull, A.P., Sailor, W., et al. (2002). Positive behavior support: evolution of an applied science. *Journal of Positive Behavior Interventions*, **4**, 4–16, 20.

Carr, E.G. & Durand, V.M. (1985). Reducing behavior problems through functional communication training. *Journal of Applied Behavior Analysis*, **18**, 111–126.

Carr, E.G., Horner, R.H., Turnbull, A.P., Marquis, J., Magito McLaughlin, D., McAtee, M.L., et al. (1999). *Positive Behavior Support for People with Developmental Disabilities: A Research Synthesis*. Washington, DC: American Association on Mental Retardation.

Carr, E.G., Levin, L., McConnachie, G., Carlson, J.I., Kemp, D.C. & Smith, C.E. (1994). *Communication-Based Intervention for Problem Behavior. A User's Guide for Producing Positive Change*. Baltimore, MD: Brookes.

Cunningham, E. & O'Neill, R.E. (2000). Comparison of results of functional assessment and analysis methods with young children with autism. *Education and Training in Mental Retardation and Developmental Disabilities*, **35**, 406–414.

Didden, R., Duker, P.C. & Korzilius, H. (1997). Meta-analytic study on treatment effectiveness for problem behaviors with individuals who have mental retardation. *American Journal on Mental Retardation*, **101**, 387–399.

Dunlap, G., dePerczel, M., Clarke, S., Wilson, D., Wright, S., White, R., et al. (1994). Choice making and proactive behavioral support for students with emotional and behavioral challenges. *Journal of Applied Behavior Analysis*, **27**, 505–518.

Dunlap, G., Kern-Dunlap, L., Clarke, S. & Robbins, F.R. (1991). Functional assessment, curricular revision, and severe behavior problems. *Journal of Applied Behavior Analysis*, **24**, 387–397.

Durand, V.M. & Crimmins, D.B. (1988). Identifying the variables maintaining self-injurious behavior. *Journal of Autism and Developmental Disorders*, **18**, 99–117.

Durand, V.M. & Crimmins, D.B. (1992). *The Motivation Assessment Scale (MAS) Administration Guide*. Topeka, KS: Monaco.

Emerson, E., Reeves, D., Thompson, S., Henderson, D. & Robertson, J. (1996). Descriptive analysis of severe challenging behaviour: the application of lag-sequential analysis. *Journal of Intellectual Disability Research*, **40**, 260–274.

Felce, D. & Emerson, E. (2000). Observational methods in assessment and quality of life. In T. Thompson, D. Felce & F.J. Symons (Eds) *Behavioral Observation: Technology and Applications in Developmental Disabilities* (pp. 159–174). Baltimore, MD: Brookes.

Gardner, W.I., Cole, C.L., Davidson, D.P. & Karan, O.C. (1986). Reducing aggression in individuals with developmental disabilities: an expanded stimulus control, assessment, and intervention model. *Education and Training of the Mentally Retarded*, **21**, 3–12.

Gardner, W.I. & Sovner, R. (1994). *Self-Injurious Behaviors*. Willow Street, PA: Vida.

Hersen, M. & Barlow, D.H. (1976). *Single Case Experimental Designs*. New York: Pergamon.

Horner, R.H., Close, D.W., Fredericks, H.D.B., O'Neill, R.E., Albin, R.W., Sprague, J.R., et al. (1996). Supported living for people with profound disabilities and severe problem behaviors. In D.H. Lehr & F. Brown (Eds) *People with Disabilities Who Challenge the System* (pp. 209–240). Baltimore, MD: Brookes.

Horner, R.H., Vaughn, B.J., Day, H.M. & Ard, W.R. (1996). The relationship between setting events and problem behavior. In L.K. Koegel, R.L. Koegel & G. Dunlap (Eds) *Positive Behavioral Support* (pp. 381–402). Baltimore, MD: Brookes.

Hughes, C., Hwang, B., Kim, J.H., Eisenman, L.T. & Killian, D.J. (1995). Quality of life in applied research: a review and analysis of empirical measures. *American Journal on Mental Retardation*, **99**, 623–641.

Iwata, B.A., Dorsey, M.F., Slifer, K.J., Bauman, K.E. & Richman, G.S. (1982). Toward a functional analysis of self-injury. *Analysis and Intervention in Developmental Disabilities*, **2**, 3–20.

Kemp, D.C. & Carr, E.G. (1995). Reduction of severe problem behavior in community employment using an hypothesis-driven multicomponent intervention approach. *Journal of the Association for Persons with Severe Handicaps*, **20**, 229–247.

Knoster, T.P., Villa, R.A. & Thousand, J.S. (2000). A framework for thinking about systems change. In R.A. Villa & J.S. Thousand (Eds) *Restructuring for Caring and Effective Education* (pp. 93–128). Baltimore, MD: Brookes.

Koegel, L.K., Koegel, R.L., Hurley, C. & Frea, W.D. (1992). Improving social skills and disruptive behavior in children with autism through self-management. *Journal of Applied Behavior Analysis*, **25**, 341–353.

Lalli, J.S., Browder, D.M., Mace, F.C. & Brown, D.K. (1993). Teacher use of descriptive analysis data to implement interventions to decrease students' problem behaviors. *Journal of Applied Behavior Analysis*, **26**, 227–238.

Mace, F.C., Hock, M.L., Lalli, J.S., West, B.J., Belfiore, P., Pinter, E., et al. (1988). Behavioral momentum in the treatment of noncompliance. *Journal of Applied Behavior Analysis*, **21**, 123–141.

O'Neill, R.E., Horner, R.H., Albin, R.W., Sprague, J.R., Storey, K. & Newton, J.S. (1997). *Functional Assessment and Program Development for Problem Behavior*. Pacific Grove, CA: Brooks/Cole.

O'Reilly, M.F. (1997). Functional analysis of episodic self-injury correlated with recurrent otitis media. *Journal of Applied Behavior Analysis*, **30**, 165–167.

Pyles, D.A.M. & Bailey, J.S. (1990). Diagnosing severe behavior problems. In A.C. Repp & N.N. Singh (Eds) *Perspectives on the Use of Nonaversive and Aversive Interventions for Persons with Developmental Disabilities* (pp. 381–401). Sycamore, IL: Sycamore.

Schalock, R.L. (Ed.) (1990). *Quality of Life*, vol. 1. *Conceptualization and Measurement*. Washington, DC: American Association on Mental Retardation.

Sidman, M. (1960). *Tactics of Scientific Research*. New York: Basic Books.

Thompson, T., Symons, F.J. & Felce, D. (2000). Principles of behavioral observation: assumptions and strategies. In T. Thompson, D. Felce & F.J. Symons (Eds) *Behavioral Observation: Technology and Applications in Developmental Disabilities* (pp. 3–16). Baltimore, MD: Brookes.

Touchette, P.E., MacDonald, R.F. & Langer, S.N. (1985). A scatter plot for identifying stimulus control of problem behavior. *Journal of Applied Behavior Analysis*, **18**, 343–351.

Yarbrough, S.C. & Carr, E.G. (2000). Some relationships between informant assessment and functional analysis of problem behavior. *American Journal on Mental Retardation*, **105**, 130–151.

Zarcone, J.R., Rodgers, T.A., Iwata, B.A., Rourke, D.A. & Dorsey, M.F. (1991). Reliability analysis of the Motivation Assessment Scale. *Research in Developmental Disabilities*, **12**, 349–360.

SECTION IV

Researching the Impact of Support Systems and Services

CHAPTER 22

Educational Supports

Robert E. O'Neill
University of Utah, USA
and
Lora Tuesday Heathfield
University of Utah, USA

This chapter will provide a review and analysis of design and measurement issues in research on educational interventions and supports for persons with intellectual disabilities. We will focus primarily on instructional and skill-training issues in the educational context, as the area of interventions and supports for managing problem behaviors is dealt with in other chapters in this volume. The existing technology of systematic instructional and support strategies has come out of the applied behavior analysis (ABA) tradition. This is because ABA has been and continues to be the primary foundation for effective practices for persons with intellectual and developmental disabilities (Horner, 1991; Remington, 1991). This emphasis will be reflected in our discussion. Finally, the chapter will focus on quantitative experimental research methods, and will not delve into other approaches (such as qualitative or interpretivist research).

A RICH HISTORY: WHERE WE HAVE BEEN AND WHERE WE ARE NOW

Instructional interventions and supports for persons with intellectual disabilities in educational settings have been the focus of empirical research and evaluation efforts for several decades (Westling & Fox, 2000; McDonnell, Hardman & McDonnell, 2003). Beginning in the late 1950s and early 1960s, much of the initial work was done by researchers applying principles and procedures of operant conditioning (e.g., Wolf, Risley & Mees, 1964; Hewett, 1965; Lovaas, Berberich, Perloff & Schaeffer, 1966). These early studies documented that a variety of systematic instructional techniques could teach a wide range of positive skills and behaviors to children and adults with developmental disabilities. For example, early research by Bijou and colleagues demonstrated that systematic instructional procedures in classroom settings could result in improvements in acquisition of preacademic and academic skills (such as reading and mathematics) and improvements in social behavior. These procedures included systematically analyzed and sequenced curricular materials, direct teaching of

The International Handbook of Applied Research in Intellectual Disabilities. Edited by E. Emerson, C. Hatton, T. Thompson and T.R. Parmenter ISBN 0-471-49709-6.

academic and related skills, a token/point system for motivation, and evaluation of ongoing performance data (Birnbrauer, Wolf, Kidder & Tague, 1965; Bijou, Birnbrauer, Kidder & Tague, 1966).

Experimental Methodology

These studies established models for rigorous measurement methodology and structured experimental manipulations to demonstrate functional relationships between interventions and behavioral and educational outcomes (Bijou & Baer, 1966; 1967). Measurement primarily consisted of direct observation and recording of various classes of ongoing student behavior and associated permanent products (such as worksheets) (Bijou et al., 1966). For example, in a paper which has been widely cited and used as a methodological springboard in a multitude of subsequent research studies, Bijou, Peterson and Ault (1968) described a methodology for direct observation and recording applicable to a broad variety of behaviors and skills in educational and other settings. Such approaches emphasize detailed and valid definition of behavior classes of interest, effective methods for recording, and data accuracy and integrity through assessment of interobserver agreement and other methods (Suen & Ary, 1989; Iwata, Neef, Wacker, Mace & Vollmer, 2000; Thompson, Felce & Symons, 2000). The earlier and subsequent research largely hewed to experimental design principles fundamental to ABA. These include repeated presentations of baseline and intervention conditions and replication of effects within and/or across participants, using withdrawal and multiple-baseline designs, among others (Kazdin, 1982).

Development of a Technology of Instruction

These early demonstrations were followed in the ensuing decades by a large number of studies documenting the acquisition of academic and social skills and reductions in problem behavior in a range of educational settings (Sailor, Wilcox & Brown, 1980; Horner, Meyer & Fredericks, 1986; Iwata et al., 1996). This research empirically delineated a body of instructional techniques and strategies for students with intellectual disabilities. While not exhaustive, a list of the primary components of effective instruction is presented in Table 22.1.

Curricular Content and Programming Location: The Interaction Between Practice and Research

Along with the empirical development of an instructional technology, the last three decades also saw an evolution with regard to curricular focus and content; that is, *what* was being taught. Initial curricular content was often developmental in nature, with students being taught skills that were considered to be motor or cognitive prerequisites to more advanced academic and functional skills (for example, fine motor manipulation of pegs in a pegboard) (Westling & Fox, 2000). Through the 1970s and 1980s, the emphasis shifted away from developmental progressions to a focus on teaching behaviors and skills that would be of direct and immediate use to students in the current and future environments in which they functioned (such as self-care, job skills, and functional academics) (Snell & Brown, 2000).

Table 22.1 Main components of instructional techniques and strategies for students with intellectual disabilities

(1) Selecting, sequencing, and presenting instructional stimuli and curricular materials (Horner, McDonnell & Bellamy 1986)
(2) Using and fading a wide variety of verbal, gestural, and written prompts (Wolery, Ault & Doyle, 1992)
(3) Systematically selecting and using stimuli as reinforcing consequences (Piazza, Fisher, Roane & Hilker, 1999)
(4) Combining strategies into intervention packages to facilitate self-direction and self-management by students in educational settings (Koegel, Harrower & Koegel, 1999)
(5) Collecting and analyzing performance data to make instructional decisions (Brown & Snell, 2000).

This curricular shift was accompanied by changes in where students spent their time. A greater percentage of time was spent in nonschool community settings, in order to allow students to acquire relevant skills in the environments in which they would actually be used (Horner, McDonnell & Bellamy, 1986). The last 15 years have seen movement toward serving students in more inclusive regular education settings, producing yet another shift in curricular content focus. More time and effort is being spent on attempting to identify and meet important student goals within the general curriculum followed in regular education settings (Ryndak & Alper, 1996).

These shifts in curricular content and service locations have been reflected in the research literature. Much of the early and subsequent research on curricular and instructional strategies was conducted in special education settings. That is, the students involved in the research spent the majority of their time in classrooms and school settings with peers with disabilities. As mentioned above, in the last 10–15 years, there has been a major philosophical and programmatic shift in educational service systems toward serving students with intellectual disabilities in regular education settings to the greatest extent possible (Vaughn, Bos & Schumm, 2003). There are, however, interesting data indicating that during this same time there has been a relatively modest but consistent decline in the overall frequency and proportion of research studies focused on curricular and instructional methods, particularly studies targeting immediately functional life and academic skills (Nietupski, Hamre-Nietupski, Curtin & Shrikanth, 1997). Nietupski et al. documented a concomitant increase in studies targeting social interaction/integration skills. There are many possible explanations for these observed trends. One possibility is that the emphasis has shifted away somewhat from more functional life skills that cannot be as easily addressed in the regular classroom to skill areas such as social interaction that are very important for inclusive settings (Nietupski et al., 1997).

These data are a good illustration of the important interplay between research, philosophical values, and applied programming in the area of educational supports. For example, early research documenting the success of systematic instructional methods probably contributed to changes in policy in the USA leading to greater access to educational programs for children with disabilities (for example, PL 94-142/Individuals with Disabilities Education Act) (Westling & Fox, 2000). In more recent years, advocacy based on philosophical values of normalization and regular community participation has played a major role in the shift toward more inclusive programming for many students. This has occurred even though the empirical research base for successfully supporting students in regular education settings has only recently begun to develop to an appreciable degree (Hunt & Goetz, 1997).

The above snapshot provides an outline of where the field currently stands, and how we have arrived there. This provides the foundation for discussing current critical challenges and strategies in conducting research in this area.

RESEARCH DESIGN ISSUES AND STRATEGIES

Early Emphasis on Single-Subject Design Strategies

As mentioned above, much of the early research on educational interventions was conducted by persons coming from a behavior analytic tradition (Kratochwill & Williams, 1988). Indeed, children and adults with disabilities were one of the primary populations focused upon as researchers moved from laboratory settings and began applying behavioral principles and procedures to affect socially important behavior (Iwata et al., 1996). This resulted in studies employing design elements and procedures typical in behavior analytical research, such as the establishment of baseline performance and repeated presentation of experimental conditions to demonstrate replication of effects within and/or across participants. For example, a common design is known as a withdrawal design, and involves (1) establishing a stable level of baseline performance, (2) implementing a given intervention or instructional strategy and assessing its impact, (3) withdrawing the intervention in a return to baseline phase, and (4) reimplementing the intervention to replicate initial effects (see Figure 22.1) (Baer et al., 1968). This and other design approaches, such as multiple-baseline, changing-criterion, and alternating treatment designs were eventually systematized via ongoing research and written guidelines and texts (Kazdin, 1982; Barlow & Hersen, 1984; Tawney & Gast, 1984; Iwata et al., 2000).

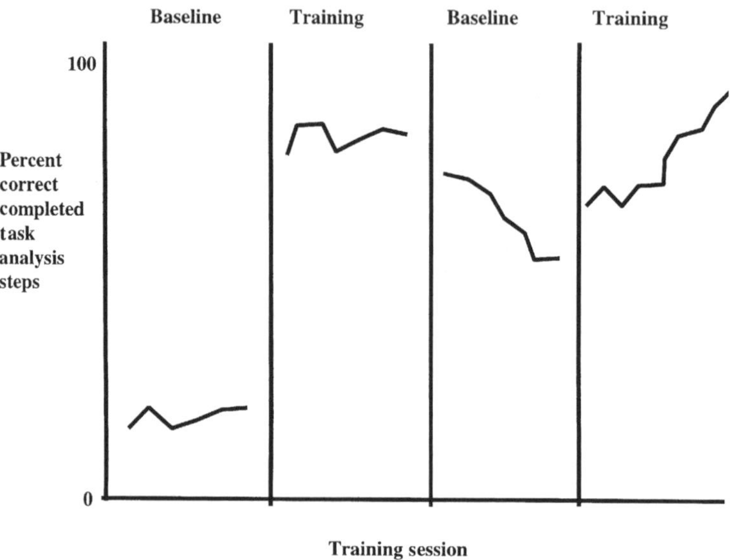

Figure 22.1 Hypothetical example of data from a withdrawal design

Factors Affecting Design Choice

Difficulties in Employing Group Comparison Designs

Other issues have contributed to the reliance on single-subject designs in this area. Design variations involving randomly assigned treatment and control groups pose significant challenges with regard to individuals with developmental disabilities. First, the populations available from which to draw research participants are relatively small and fairly heterogeneous. Epidemiological data indicate that mental retardation occurs in less than 3% of the general population. Additionally, the manifestation of mental retardation can vary significantly across individuals in terms of etiology, severity, age of onset, and presence or absence of a host of concomitant complications, including mental illness. Researchers are thus hard pressed to identify a substantial number of individuals with developmental disabilities in the general population to include in a group-design research study, let alone a group of individuals that share similar characteristics. A related issue is the ethical limitations inherent in randomized group designs. Determining which individuals receive the identified instructional strategy (treatment group) and which individuals do not (control group) creates a myriad of ethical quandaries, including the possible denial of appropriate services to those in need.

Individual Programming Needs of Individuals with Intellectual Disabilities

Other factors that can contribute to choice of research design are the legal mandates and individual needs guiding the delivery of special education services to persons with disabilities. Beginning with the Education for All Handicapped Children Act in 1975 (in the USA) through today's mandates based on the 1997 IDEA amendments, instruction of individuals who qualify for special education services must include an individualized education plan (IEP). Inherent in the concept of the IEP is that instruction for students who qualify for services must be tailored to meet their individual educational needs. Because individuals with developmental disabilities have complex learning needs, any particular instructional strategy will probably not meet the needs of all individuals in this population. The need for individualized instructional strategies argues for the use of single-subject design methodology to assess a particular instructional intervention's effectiveness. IEP goals are supposed to include observable, measurable criteria, which fit well with the data collection and data-based decision making that are some of the primary features of single-subject design methodology.

Characteristics of Targeted Behaviors/Skills

In much, if not most, instructional research, the targeted behaviors/skills will be such that they will be influenced by acquisition processes. That is, once students begin to learn part or all of the steps or components of a skill, their performance probably will not return to baseline (pretraining) if training is stopped. This issue puts some constraints on the types of experimental designs that can be used. Reversal or withdrawal designs will not

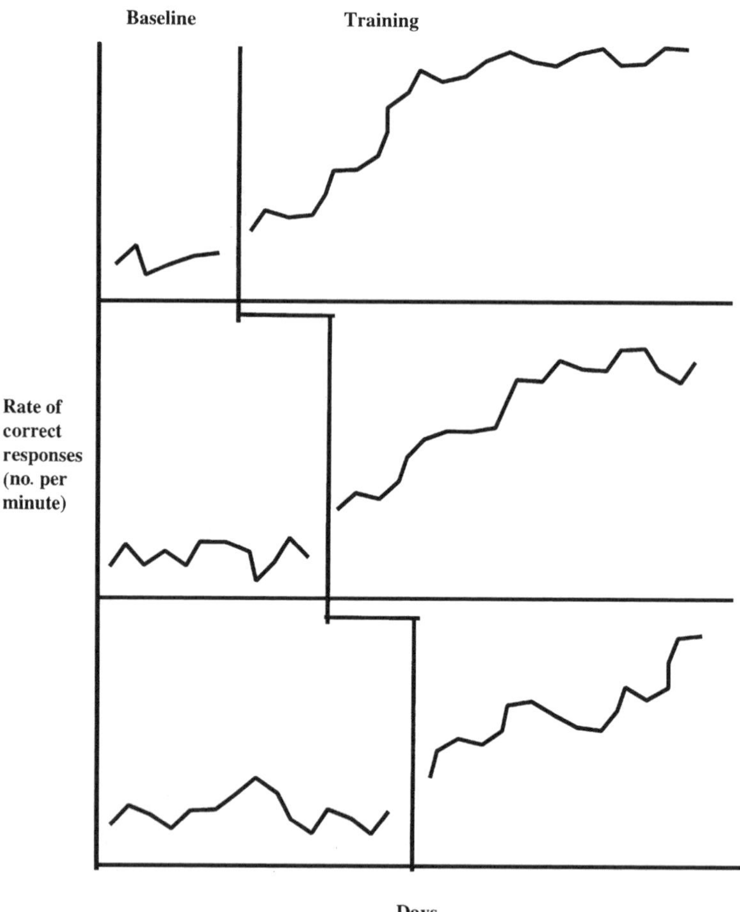

Figure 22.2 Hypothetical example of data from a multiple-baseline design

be suitable since they rely on behavioral performance returning to baseline levels during withdrawal phases in order to demonstrate experimental control. These kinds of concerns explain why multiple-baseline designs are very common in instructional research. In such approaches, baseline performance data are gathered across multiple persons, or multiple behaviors and/or settings for an individual. Training or intervention is then implemented in a staggered fashion (that is, at successively later points in time) across the baselines (see Figure 22.2) (Tawney & Gast, 1984). Experimental control is demonstrated when behavior change occurs only when the training has been implemented (Kazdin, 1982). For example, Cuvo and Klatt (1992) reported a study in which they compared the effectiveness of different methods of teaching community-referenced sight words to students with intellectual disabilities. They conducted baseline measurement of student reading of groups of sight words. Different training strategies (flashcards, video presentation, and community signs) were then implemented with different groups of words to allow a within-subject comparison of the effectiveness of the different methods. However, training was implemented in a multiple-baseline fashion across the participating students. Positive changes in student

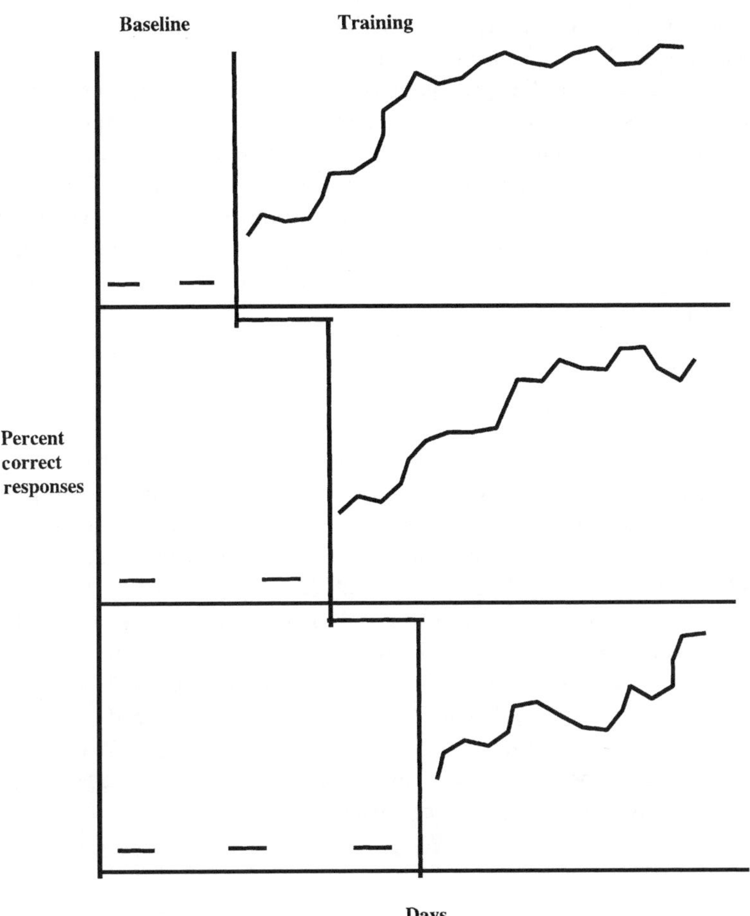

Figure 22.3 Hypothetical example of data from a multiple-probe design

performance occurred only with the onset of training, providing evidence that the training was responsible for these outcomes.

The multiple-probe design, a variation of the standard multiple-baseline design, is useful in situations in which frequent multiple exposures to baseline performance assessment situations may lead to reactive behavior change (see Figure 22.3) (Horner & Baer, 1978). For example, consider a student who is going to be taught how to do laundry. If the student has frequent opportunities to be in relevant situations with access to task materials, it is possible that the student could begin to demonstrate correct performance on some steps or parts of the task through exposure and "trial and error". This could lead to variable or otherwise problematic baseline performance levels (Kazdin, 1982). The multiple-probe design attempts to minimize such problems simply by conducting fewer intermittent baseline assessment probes, as opposed to more typical frequent ongoing measurement. For example, baseline performance data might be gathered once every 2–3 weeks instead of the more typical daily or every other day measurement. As with the multiple-baseline design, training is introduced in a staggered fashion across the multiple-probe baselines.

An example of this design strategy was provided by Schuster, Gast, Wolery and Guiltinan (1988), who assessed the effectiveness of a constant time-delay procedure (providing a request followed by a controlling prompt to respond) in teaching chains of food-preparation skills to adolescent students with moderate mental retardation. Each student was trained in three different food-preparation routines (sandwich preparation, boil-in-a-bag, and canned biscuits). A multiple-probe design was implemented across the three skills for each student. Following a few initial probes, intermittent baseline probes (every 3–4 days) continued to be conducted for some skills while others were in training. This helped avoid problems with students beginning to demonstrate performance of skill steps due to frequent repeated opportunities to respond.

Ethical Issues

A common concern with reversal/withdrawal designs is the issue of having to withdraw and reimplement training or intervention to demonstrate experimental control. Such a reversal or withdrawal may result in a decline in performance (that is, a return to baseline). While providing a convincing demonstration of experimental control, this is obviously an undesirable outcome from an educational or applied perspective (Voeltz & Evans, 1983). A multiple-baseline or probe design helps to avoid such problems. The only drawback is that such designs involve students in nontraining or baseline conditions, which may last from several days to multiple weeks, depending on the situation (Kazdin, 1982). It is very important for researchers to make clear to students, teachers, parents, and others what will be occurring or not occurring during all phases of a planned study, and provide a rationale for why certain things will be done in a certain way. This will help avoid later disappointment or otherwise negative reactions from participants.

Summary

There are a number of experimental design options for conducting studies of educational interventions and supports. Each has its own advantages and disadvantages. Researchers need to consider the issues described above ("reversibility" of behaviors and ethical issues) in choosing the most appropriate design to answer the particular questions in which they are interested. Some of the most pressing issues have to do with identification of effective instructional strategies in inclusive settings, and approaches for achieving generalized behavior change across settings (Westling & Fox, 2000).

MEASUREMENT ISSUES AND STRATEGIES

Factors Affecting the Choice of Dependent Variables

Social Validity and Other Characteristics of Target Behaviors

As described above, over the years there have been changes in the curricular focus of instructional programs for students with intellectual disabilities, with an increasing emphasis on skills and behaviors that will be relevant to students in a variety of current and postgraduation school and community settings (Snell & Brown, 2000). Therefore, researchers need to focus on target behaviors that will have social validity. That is, they will be viewed by students, teachers, parents, and other caregivers as being important and relevant to the students involved in research (Kazdin, 1977; Wolf, 1978). The types of target behaviors selected will, in part, drive the choice of dependent variables and the measurement strategies used to assess them. Whether frequency, duration, topography, or other aspects are important will depend on the context and characteristics of the targeted behaviors. For example, in teaching students job-related skills for use in employment settings (such as food preparation and component assembly), correct performance and speed (accuracy and frequency/rate) would probably be important to measure and report. However, these could be measured via a variety of dependent variables, such as number of completed items per session, the percentage of correctly completed items, or the rate of performance (such as number of items completed per minute). As in any research, it is important that dependent variables and measurement procedures are chosen that provide a valid and accurate assessment of the targeted skills or behaviors.

Resource Issues

Another major factor affecting the choice of dependent variables and measurement strategies is the resources available for data collection. If a researcher is going to be dependent upon teachers or other school personnel to collect data, this may affect its consistency and validity, and present various logistical barriers (such as time needed for training and interference with other teacher activities). It may also be difficult to arrange for such things as multiple simultaneous observers to assess interobserver agreement on observational data (Bailey & Burch, 2002). Care must be taken to ensure that such persons actually have the time and ability to collect valid and accurate data. The researcher may need to be creative in making such arrangements work (Maruyama & Deno, 1992). For example, data collection may be scheduled only for those classroom periods during which the teacher or teaching assistant is able to devote time to it, or other school personnel (such as the school psychologist or guidance counselor) may be recruited periodically to assist. The researcher may also be able to provide some time from outside personnel (such as university students) to supplement the data-collection process so that the entire burden does not fall on school or classroom staff. Of course, an ideal resource solution would be to be able to provide all needed resources from external sources, such as research staff supported by grant monies (but see Context/Setting and Measurement Reactivity below). However, obviously, this may not be available in many situations.

Another approach that can be helpful is to focus on low-effort measurement strategies, such as relying on permanent products to the greatest extent possible. Such products might include academic worksheets, assembled items or objects (such as a food item or folded laundry), or other results of behavior (such as a completed telephone call to a friend or a completed computer activity). Such products can be assessed and data recorded at more varied times that are more workable for both school and research staff.

Context/Setting and Measurement Reactivity

The movement toward supporting students in more inclusive settings has implications for research procedures, particularly measurement strategies. In the past, students were often primarily served in more segregated schools and classrooms. In such settings, it is not unusual to have a variety of teaching personnel, related services staff, parents or other family members, and other visitors and observers coming and going. This made the presence of research staff involved in data collection less of an issue. Students and others often became accustomed to a variety of persons coming in and out, observing and collecting a variety of information.

In more integrated or regular education settings, the presence of outside observers collecting data becomes more problematic for a variety of reasons. Teachers and students who are less accustomed to the presence of a variety of persons may be very curious, inquisitive, and/or intimidated. This may in turn affect their behavior in various ways, potentially influencing the measurement and resulting data. A teacher may be nervous about being observed and either increase or decrease his or her interactions with a target student. This may influence the student's behavior in an undesirable manner. Similarly, if students recognize that observers are focusing on a particular classmate, they may alter their interactions with that classmate, thereby again possibly influencing the resulting data in a problematic manner.

There are multiple strategies that can help minimize such reactivity effects. As mentioned above, researchers can attempt to identify and use measures based on permanent product evaluation that do not require the ongoing presence of observers. If observers are necessary, researchers should, if possible, take advantage of observation windows (such as one-way windows), although these are unlikely to be available in most typical general education settings. For in-room observations, researchers should plan on having observers in the setting for an initial acclimation or "desensitization" period prior to collecting useable data. This will allow time for reactivity effects to diminish to some degree (Barlow & Hersen, 1984). Other strategies can minimize the obtrusiveness of such persons. They can attempt to sit in less visible locations, avoid continuous eye contact with particular students, and minimize attention-getting stimuli. For example, teaching staff or observers can record data with 3 × 5 cards, Post-it notes, quiet wrist or key-chain counters, or abacus beads, instead of larger, more noticeable data sheets (often typically accompanied by the inevitable clipboard) (Brown & Snell, 2000). To the extent that observers are also able to participate in some typical activities during data collection (such as helping students with classroom tasks), they may come to be viewed as a less obtrusive part of the environment.

Ethical Issues

It is perhaps best to acknowledge that such reactivity effects are almost unavoidable. While some things can be done to minimize them, researchers should proceed on the assumption that they are almost always influencing data to some extent. This does not render such data useless, but these potential influences must always be kept in mind and acknowledged. As ethical standards have evolved over the years, there has been increasing emphasis on informed consent and informing participants about the rationale for and procedures involved in research activities (Sprague, 1994). This includes informing children and obtaining their assent for study participation. In some cases, researchers conducting minimal risk studies may obtain permission to avoid obtaining assent to minimize reactivity effects. However, some researchers have recommended providing a clear rationale to participants to reduce uncertainty and the likelihood of such reactivity (Barlow & Hersen, 1984). For example, the first author remembers an incident in which he was involved in collecting observational data on playground interactions of elementary-age students at risk of developing antisocial behavior patterns. These students had been informed of the rationale and procedures of the research. While stationed on the playground, he was approached by a student, who asked, "Are you here to watch us be violent?" Being caught off guard and somewhat flustered, he managed to respond in some vague manner that he was interested in how children play together, etc. While reactivity was clearly an issue, there was no real choice, from an ethical perspective, other than to inform the students to some extent about what was going on. Again, however, the possible reactive effects must be acknowledged and taken into account in analyzing the data and discussing it.

Along with potential effects on experimental procedures and data, reactivity also encompasses possible negative social or emotional effects on students. Awareness that particular students are being observed or involved in training activities that seem out of the ordinary may lead to undue attention being called to the students, with resultant stigmatizing effects (Brown & Snell, 2000). Research staff can attempt to minimize such problems via the strategies discussed above. In addition, they need to stay in constant contact with teaching staff to keep abreast of such problems and plan how to prevent or minimize them should they occur. It is important for investigators to keep in mind that school staff may not always eagerly welcome research activities and personnel with open arms. Therefore, it is incumbent on research staff to do all that they can to make their presence and involvement as unobtrusive and considerate as possible (Maruyama & Deno, 1992).

FUTURE DIRECTIONS

The past three decades saw the development of an empirically based technology of instruction and support for students with intellectual disabilities. While producing very effective strategies, much of this research was carried out in special education settings, and was therefore shaped by characteristics of those settings. Current social and programmatic trends are pushing researchers into new settings and directions, with resulting influence on when, where, and how research will be carried out.

An obviously important issue is the movement toward supporting students in more inclusive regular education settings. Since this has been, to some extent, a philosophically driven trend, there is a great need for ongoing research to document the instruction and support strategies that will allow students to succeed in such settings (Hunt & Goetz, 1997). One concern has been that, to date, much work in inclusive settings has primarily focused on social interactions and outcomes (Kennedy & Itkonen, 1994; Nietupski et al., 1997). There is a great need for studies that can empirically identify instructional strategies that will (1) result in acquisition of academic and other functional skills, and (2) not radically affect or disrupt the routines of regular education students and settings (Cushing & Kennedy, 1997). For example, recent research by McDonnell and colleagues (e.g., McDonnell, Mathot-Buckner, Thorson & Fister, 2001) demonstrates the effectiveness of instructional strategies that are embedded within more typical classroom routines and activities. Additional work in these areas will be critical to help equip teachers and school staff with effective techniques, and assuage concerns of parents and other groups about the outcomes that are possible in inclusive programs.

Along with the implementation of instructional strategies themselves, working in inclusive settings poses some unique challenges in areas such as data collection. As discussed above, issues of reactivity and student stigmatization become more salient as researchers move out from more segregated settings. Investigators need to work more closely with school staff and students and parents to develop data-collection strategies that will be comprehensive, valid, and accurate, but will also not be obtrusive and disruptive (Maruyama & Deno, 1992).

While developing less obtrusive measures is critical, it is also important for researchers simultaneously to keep abreast of exciting new developments in data-collection technology. In recent years, a number of computer-based systems have been developed for gathering observational and other types of data in applied settings (Kahng & Iwata, 2000). These systems typically operate on either laptop or palmtop devices, and offer a range of sophisticated options for data acquisition, calculation, graphing, and analysis (Thompson et al., 2000). Studies reporting data acquired by such systems have been a relatively small but consistent and growing part of the literature (Emerson, Reeves & Felce, 2000). Computer-based systems hold incredible promise for facilitating and improving the data-collection and analysis process. However, the experience of the authors and various colleagues has demonstrated that such systems also can pose substantial challenges. They may be relatively costly to purchase and install on multiple devices. They also typically require personnel with a substantial level of computer and data analytical expertise to keep them running smoothly, troubleshoot the inevitable glitches and problems, and transfer data into suitable formats for analysis by other programs (such as SPSS). As discussed above, the presence of an observer with a laptop computer may also provide stimuli-provoking substantial reactivity, particularly on the part of children and others in naturalistic classroom settings. Hopefully, as the available technology continues to develop and improve, and effective devices become smaller and less obtrusive, such issues will be minimized. It is interesting and fun to speculate on how easy and effective the data-collection process of the future will be like, but we are not there yet!

Behavioral research on educational interventions and supports for persons with intellectual disabilities has been a unique interplay among values, philosophies, and empirical research strategies. Powerful strategies have been developed in the service of socially valid and important outcomes for students and their families. We encourage researchers who have not yet participated to consider joining in the effort both to implement empirically proven practices and to develop and refine those practices to be even more effective in the future.

REFERENCES

Baer, D.M. (1991). The future of applied behavior analysis for people with severe disabilities: commentary II. In L.H. Meyer, C.A. Peck & L. Brown (Eds) *Critical Issues in the Lives of People with Severe Disabilities* (pp. 613–615). Baltimore, MD: Brookes.

Bailey, J.S. & Burch, M.R. (2002). *Research Methods in Applied Behavior Analysis.* Newbury Park, CA: Sage.

Barlow, D.H. & Hersen, M. (1984). *Single Case Experimental Designs: Strategies for Studying Behavior Change* (2nd edn). Boston, MA: Allyn & Bacon.

Bijou, S.W. & Baer, D.M. (1966). Operant methods in child behavior and development. In W. Honig (Ed.) *Operant Behavior: Handbook of Research and Application* (pp. 333–404). New York: Appleton-Century-Crofts.

Bijou, S.W. & Baer, D.M. (Eds) (1967). *Child Development: Readings in Experimental Analysis.* New York: Appleton-Century-Crofts.

Bijou, S.W., Birnbrauer, J.S., Kidder, J.D. & Tague, C. (1966). Programmed instruction as an approach to the teaching of reading, writing, and arithmetic to retarded children. *Psychological Record*, **16**, 505–522.

Bijou, S.W., Peterson, R.F. & Ault, M.H. (1968). A method to integrate descriptive and experimental field studies at the level of data and empirical concepts. *Journal of Applied Behavior Analysis*, **1**, 175–191.

Birnbrauer, J.S., Wolf, M.M., Kidder, J.D. & Tague, C. (1965). Classroom behavior of retarded pupils with token reinforcement. *Journal of Experimental Child Psychology*, **2**, 219–235.

Brown, F. & Snell, M.E. (2000). Measurement, analysis, and evaluation. In M.E. Snell & F. Brown (Eds) *Instruction of Students with Severe Disabilities* (5th edn) (pp. 173–206). Columbus, OH: Merrill.

Cushing, L.S. & Kennedy, C.H. (1997). Academic effects of providing peer support in general education classrooms on students without disabilities. *Journal of Applied Behavior Analysis*, **30**, 139–150.

Cuvo, A.J. & Klatt, K.P. (1992). Effects of community-based, videotape, and flash-card instruction of community-referenced sight words on students with mental retardation. *Journal of Applied Behavior Analysis*, **25**, 499–512.

Emerson, E., Reeves, D.J. & Felce, D. (2000). Palmtop computer technologies for behavioral observation research. In T. Thompson, D. Felce & F.J. Symons (Eds) *Behavioral Observation: Technology and Applications in Developmental Disabilities* (pp. 47–59). Baltimore, MD: Brookes.

Hewett, F.M. (1965). Teaching speech to autistic children through operant conditioning. *American Journal of Orthopsychiatry*, **34**, 927–936.

Horner, R.D. & Baer, D.M. (1978). Multiple probe technique: a variation of the multiple baseline, *Journal of Applied Behavior Analysis*, **11**, 189–196.

Horner, R.H. (1991). The future of applied behavior analysis for people with developmental disabilities: commentary I. In L.H. Meyer, C.A. Peck & L. Brown (Eds) *Critical Issues in the Lives of People with Severe Disabilities* (pp. 607–611). Baltimore, MD: Brookes.

Horner, R.H., McDonnell, J.J. & Bellamy, G.T. (1986). Teaching generalized skills: general case instruction in simulation and community settings. In R.H. Horner, L.H. Meyer & H.D.B. Fredericks (Eds) *Education of Learners with Severe Handicaps: Exemplary Service Strategies* (pp. 289–314). Baltimore, MD: Brookes.

Horner, R.H., Meyer, L.H. & Fredericks, H.D.B. (Eds) (1986). *Education of Learners with Severe Handicaps: Exemplary Service Strategies*. Baltimore, MD: Brookes.

Hunt, P. & Goetz, L. (1997). Research on inclusive educational programs, practices, and outcomes for students with severe disabilities. *Journal of Special Education*, **31**, 3–29.

Iwata, B.A., Bailey, J.S., Neef, N.A., Wacker, D.P., Repp, A.C. & Shook, G.L. (Eds) (1996). *Behavior Analysis in Developmental Disabilities* (3rd edn). Lawrence, KS: SEAB.

Iwata, B.A., Neef, N.A., Wacker, D.P., Mace, F.C. & Vollmer, T.R. (Eds) (2000). *Methodological and Conceptual Issues in Applied Behavior Analysis* (2nd edn). Lawrence, KS: SEAB.

Kahng, S. & Iwata, B.A. (2000). Computer systems for collecting real-time observational data. In T. Thompson, D. Felce & F.J. Symons (Eds) *Behavioral Observation: Technology and Applications in Developmental Disabilities* (pp. 35–45). Baltimore, MD: Brookes.

Kazdin, A.E. (1977). Assessing the clinical or applied significance of behavior change through social validation. *Behavior Modification*, **1**, 427–452.

Kazdin, A.E. (1982). *Single Case Research Designs: Methods for Clinical and Applied Settings*. New York: Oxford University Press.

Kennedy, C.H. & Itkonen, T. (1994). Some effects of regular class participation on the social contacts and social networks of high school students with severe disabilities. *Journal of the Association for Persons with Severe Handicaps*, **19**, 1–10.

Koegel, L.K., Harrower, J.K. & Koegel, R.L. (1999). Support for children with developmental disabilities in full inclusion classrooms through self-management. *Journal of Positive Behavior Interventions*, **1**, 26–34.

Kratochwill, T.R. & Williams, B.L. (1988). Perspectives on pitfalls and hassles in single-subject research. *Journal of the Association for Persons with Severe Handicaps*, **13**, 147–154.

Lovaas, O.I., Berberich, J.P., Perloff, B.F. & Schaeffer, B. (1966). Acquisition of imitative speech in schizophrenic children. *Science*, **151**, 705–707.

Maruyama, G. & Deno, S. (1992). *Research in Educational Settings.* Newbury Park, CA: Sage.

McDonnell, J.J., Hardman, M.L. & McDonnell, A.P. (2003). *An Introduction to Persons with Severe Disabilities* (2nd edn). Boston, MA: Allyn & Bacon.

McDonnell, J., Mathot-Buckner, C., Thorson, N. & Fister, S. (2001). Supporting the inclusion of students with severe disabilities in typical junior high school classes: the effects of class wide peer tutoring, multi-element curriculum, and accommodations. *Education and Treatment of Children*, **24**, 141–160.

Nietupski, J., Hamre-Nietupski, S., Curtin, S. & Shrikanth, K. (1997). A review of curricular research in severe disabilities from 1976 to 1995 in six selected journals. *Journal of Special Education*, **31**, 36–55.

Piazza, C.C., Fisher, W.W., Roane, H.S. & Hilker, K. (1999). Predicting and enhancing the effectiveness of reinforcers and punishers. In A.C. Repp & R.H. Horner (Eds) *Functional Analysis of Problem Behavior: From Effective Assessment to Effective Intervention* (pp. 57–77). Belmont, CA: Wadsworth.

Remington, B. (Ed.) (1991). *The Challenge of Severe Mental Handicap: A Behaviour Analytic Approach.* Chichester: Wiley.

Ryndak, D.L. & Alper, S. (1996). *Curriculum Content for Students with Moderate and Severe Disabilities in Inclusive Settings.* Boston, MA: Allyn & Bacon.

Sailor, W., Wilcox, B. & Brown, L. (1980). *Methods of Instruction for Severely Handicapped Students.* Baltimore, MD: Brookes.

Schuster, J.W., Gast, D.L., Wolery, M. & Guiltinan, S. (1988). The effectiveness of a constant time-delay procedure to teach chained responses to adolescents with mental retardation. *Journal of Applied Behavior Analysis*, **21**, 169–178.

Snell, M.E. & Brown, F. (Eds) (2000). *Instruction of Students with Severe Disabilities* (5th edn). Columbus, OH: Merrill.

Sprague, R.L. (1994). Ethics of treatment evaluation: balancing efficacy against other considerations. In T. Thompson & D.B. Gray (Eds) *Destructive Behavior in Developmental Disabilities: Diagnosis and Treatment* (pp. 293–311). Thousand Oaks, CA: Sage.

Suen, H.K. & Ary, D. (1989). *Analyzing Quantitative Behavioral Observation Data.* Hillsdale, NJ: Erlbaum.

Tawney, J.W. & Gast, D.L. (1984). *Single Subject Research in Special Education.* Columbus, OH: Merrill.

Thompson, T., Felce, D. & Symons, F.J. (Eds) (2000). *Behavioral Observation: Technology and Applications in Developmental Disabilities.* Baltimore, MD: Brookes.

Vaughn, S., Bos, C.S. & Schumm, J.S. (2003). *Teaching Exceptional, Diverse, and At-Risk Students in the General Education Classroom.* Boston, MA: Allyn & Bacon.

Voeltz, L.M. & Evans, I.M. (1983). Educational validity: procedures to evaluate outcomes in programs for severely handicapped learners. *Journal of the Association for Persons with Severe Handicaps*, **8**, 3–15.

Westling, D.L. & Fox, L. (2000). *Teaching Students with Severe Disabilities* (2nd edn). Columbus, OH: Merrill.

Wolery, M., Ault, M.J. & Doyle, P.M. (1992). *Teaching Students with Moderate to Severe Disabilities.* New York: Longman.

Wolf, M.M. (1978). Social validity: the case for subjective measurement or how applied behavior analysis is finding its heart. *Journal of Applied Behavior Analysis*, **11**, 203–214.

Wolf, M.M., Risley, T.R. & Mees, H. (1964). Application of operant conditioning procedures to the behavior problems of an autistic child. *Behavior Research and Therapy*, **1**, 305–312.

CHAPTER 23

Residential Supports

Roger J. Stancliffe
University of Sydney, Australia
Eric Emerson
Lancaster University, UK
and
K. Charlie Lakin
University of Minnesota, USA

INTRODUCTION

Residential supports have a major influence on shaping the life experiences of those who receive them. Provision of residential supports constitutes the greatest single sector of expenditure within current service systems for people with intellectual disabilities (Black & Maples, 1998; Kavanagh & Opit, 1998). The past 150 years have involved the creation and partial dissolution of large-scale institutions for people with intellectual disabilities across North America, Europe, and Australia (Ryan & Thomas, 1987; Trent, 1994; Braddock, Emerson, Felce & Stancliffe, 2001).

Deinstitutionalisation has been intensively researched (Emerson & Hatton, 1996; Young, Sigafoos, Suttie, Ashman & Grevell, 1998; Kim, Larson & Lakin, 2001). Initially, studies tended to approach deinstitutionalisation as a policy that may be appropriate for *some* people with intellectual disabilities, and attempted to identify the characteristics of those people who "succeeded" or "failed" in the community. This approach was superseded by one that sought to evaluate the impact of deinstitutionalisation, and early studies within this tradition focused almost exclusively on evaluating changes in adaptive and challenging behaviour. However, the growing importance of notions of normalisation, social inclusion, civil rights, and consumerism led to the expansion of the range of outcomes of deinstitutionalisation investigated to include such variables as expressed satisfaction of the person and their relatives; income and personal possessions; involvement in community activities; choice and self-determination; and, more recently, health status (Emerson & Hatton, 1996; Young et al., 1998; Kim et al., 2001).

In recent years, an increasing number of "post-deinstitutionalisation" studies have appeared. These have investigated the impact of different approaches to providing community-based residential supports, either by comparing outcomes of different models of support or

The International Handbook of Applied Research in Intellectual Disabilities. Edited by E. Emerson, C. Hatton, T. Thompson and T.R. Parmenter ISBN 0-471-49709-6.

by identifying variables associated with variation in outcomes of a particular model (Burchard, Hasazi, Gordon & Yoe, 1991; Anderson, Lakin, Hill & Chen, 1992; Lakin, Bruininks, Hill, Chen & Anderson, 1993; Conroy, 1996; Howe, Horner & Newton, 1998; Wehmeyer & Bolding, 1999; Emerson et al., 2000; Stancliffe, Abery & Smith, 2000; Stancliffe & Keane, 2000; Emerson et al., 2001).

Comparison of different models of residential support has been motivated primarily by the strong interest in knowing which models are more effective and/or more cost-effective in achieving desired outcomes. These comparisons also enable researchers to examine more complex issues, such as the relations among classes of variables, such as the following:

- *consumer characteristics* (such as adaptive and challenging behaviour, age, and demographic variables)
- *service inputs* (such as staffing levels, features of the living environment, expenditure on services, and funding arrangements)
- *process variables* (such as staff working practices, household social climate, amount of staff support of individual consumers, and amount of training received by individual consumers)
- *service outcomes* (consumer outcomes such as self-determination, community participation, and change in functional skills).

Studying the relations among these variables enables identification of factors that are functionally related to outcomes of interest. This knowledge provides the basis for effective ways to improve outcomes and efficiency within existing service models (see Jones et al., 1999). It can also contribute to policies regarding the use or non-use of particular models and/or service inputs or processes.

In the remainder of this chapter, we will address methodological and measurement issues related to three areas: (1) specifying the characteristics of residential support services; (2) taking account of resident characteristics when making comparisons between models of residential supports; and (3) measuring outcomes.

DESCRIBING AND MEASURING THE CHARACTERISTICS OF RESIDENTIAL SUPPORT SERVICES

Descriptions of different forms of residential supports are notoriously imprecise. While the term "institution" is commonly associated with segregated settings housing large numbers of people with intellectual disabilities, it has also been used to describe services supporting as few as four people (Tøssebro, 1995). The terminology associated with community-based residential supports is similarly imprecise, reflecting national systems of administrative classification (such as "residential care home" in the UK; "Intermediate Care Facility—Mentally Retarded [ICF-MR]" in the USA) and poorly defined "models" of support (such as "supported living" and "group homes") that often contain elements relating to both the structural characteristics of settings (such as number of cohabitants), tenancy arrangements (such as residence owned or leased by consumers), and internal processes for delivering support (such as the emphasis on self-determination in supported living).

Replicability requires that researchers describe, in detail, potentially salient characteristics of the residential supports. Measurement of such characteristics also provides an opportunity for analyses that attempt to isolate the impact of the specific structural and procedural characteristics of residential supports on outcomes (e.g., Emerson et al., 2000, 2001; Stancliffe et al., 2000).

The importance of analysing the impact of the characteristics of residential supports is illustrated by recent research on supported living (Howe et al., 1998; Emerson et al., 2001). Howe et al. compared the quality and costs of the residential supports provided to adults in supported living with a matched sample of adults living in "traditional" residential services in Oregon, USA. While costs were similar, participants in supported living experienced a greater variety and frequency of community-based and social activities than participants in "traditional" services. Unfortunately, the comparison confounded the effects of model of provision (supported living versus traditional) with facility size (mean 1.6 cohabitants for supported living and 6.9 for traditional services). More recently, Emerson et al. (2001) have demonstrated that the benefits in the domain of social relationships reported by Howe et al. may be attributable to variations in facility size, rather than the supported living model per se.

Table 23.1 provides a preliminary list of potentially salient characteristics of residential support services and, where applicable, examples of measurement instruments and/or related resources (reviews or research articles). Because instruments of this type are comparatively rare, we have erred on the side of inclusiveness by listing scales with little or no current psychometric support. Information in several of these domains is also necessary for constructing facility-specific costs of residential support (see Chapter 30).

The extent to which the psychometric properties of the instruments listed in Table 23.1 have been investigated varies widely. The development of measures of the characteristics of residential supports has lagged significantly behind the assessment of resident characteristics and outcomes (see below). There is a clear need for further research in this area.

Varying amounts of research have examined the relations between these characteristics and outcomes. The relation between size of living unit (that is, number of cohabitants) and outcomes has attracted considerable interest (cf. Balla, 1976; Baroff, 1980; Tøssebro, 1995; Stancliffe, 1997), but very little attention indeed has been paid to the impact of organisational culture on outcomes (see Gillett, 2000).

At present, only tenuous relations have been found between measures of basic resources (structural characteristics, size, and staffing ratios) and the outcomes experienced by residents (Emerson, 1999), suggesting that internal management practices may play an important moderating role in ensuring effective and efficient use of available resources. Indeed, internal management procedures have been associated with increased levels of engagement in everyday activities (Jones et al., 1999); more effective, equitably distributed staff support (Jones et al., 1999; Felce et al., 2000); larger and more varied social networks (Robertson et al., 2001a); increased opportunities for self-determination (Robertson et al., 2001b); and higher levels of expressed satisfaction among residents (Gregory, Robertson, Kessissoglou, Emerson & Hatton, 2001).

PERSONAL CHARACTERISTICS AND COMPARISONS AMONG MODELS OF RESIDENTIAL SUPPORT

A pervasive problem of internal validity arises when comparing residential models, because service users are not assigned to models at random. Studies have reported systematic

Table 23.1 Selected characteristics of residential supports and related resources

Domain/Characteristic	Resource
The physical setting	
External and internal aspects of architectural design	• Architectural Features Scale (Thompson, Robinson, Graff & Ingenmey, 1990) • North Princeton Evaluation Environment Assessment (Apgar, Cook & Lerman, 1997)
Domestic equipment and furnishings	• Felce, Thomas, de Kock, Saxby and Repp (1985)
Type of neighbourhood (e.g., level of social deprivation, and local crime and accident rates)	• Halpern, Close and Nelson (1986a)
Proximity to community resources and public transport	• Halpern et al. (1986a)
Household composition	
Number of cohabitants (size)	
Level and range of abilities and needs of cohabitants	• See Adaptive behaviour, challenging behaviour, and psychiatric symptoms in Table 23.3
Administrative status of service and tenancy arrangements	
Administrative status of service (e.g., ICF-MR, residential care home, or nursing home) and funding arrangements	• See Larson, Lakin and Bruininks (1998)
Characteristics of managing organisation(s) (e.g., organisational size, status, and philosophy)	• See Larson et al. (1998)
Tenancy status of cohabitants	
Staffing and support arrangements	
Management arrangements for provision of personal support staff (weekly hours of staff support and staff schedules)	• See Larson et al. (1998)
Number, age, gender, ethnicity, marital status, dependents, qualifications, remuneration, and employment conditions of direct support staff and of indirect support staff	• See Larson et al. (1998)
Staff roles, coping styles, satisfaction, morale, turnover, absenteeism, and sick leave	• See Larson et al. (1998); Buckingham and Coffman (1999); Hatton et al. (2001) for a range of instruments
Internal working practices (e.g., individual planning and support to staff)	• Residential Services Working Practices Scale (Felce, Lowe & Emerson, 1995)
Presence of "institutional" routines	• Group Home Management Interview (Pratt, Luszcz & Brown, 1980)
Organisational climate	• Organisational Culture Inventory (Cooke & Lafferty, 1989) • See Larson et al. (1998)
Observational measures of staff activity	• See Felce and Emerson (2000) for a range of examples

Some of the assessment instruments listed in Table 23.1 currently have unknown psychometric characteristics.

differences in personal characteristics by residence type (Burchard et al., 1991; Lakin et al., 1993; Stancliffe et al., 2000; Emerson et al., 2000, 2001). Personal characteristics, such as level of intellectual ability and adaptive behaviour, are also strongly related to consumer outcomes, including choice, quality of life, engagement in activities, and community participation (Anderson et al., 1992; Schalock & Keith, 1993; Stancliffe, 1997; Stancliffe & Lakin, 1998; Felce & Emerson, 2001). Expenditure on services has been shown to relate to resident characteristics in some studies (Raynes, Wright, Shiell & Pettipher, 1994; Campbell & Heal, 1995; Emerson et al., 2001), but not in others (Hatton, Emerson, Robertson, Henderson & Cooper, 1995; Felce et al., 1998; Stancliffe & Lakin, 1998).

Without adequate control of variation in residents' personal characteristics, observed differences between living arrangements may be due to environmental factors *or* to residents' personal characteristics. Therefore, to compare meaningfully residential service types, differences in personal characteristics need to be held constant. Methods of achieving this include: (a) random assignment to living arrangements, (b) matching, (c) statistical control (using covariance and regression), and (d) longitudinal crossover studies of individuals who move from one type of residential setting to another.

Random Assignment

Random assignment controls bias by averaging out *all* systematic effects on the dependent variable due to participants' personal characteristics, regardless of whether these biasing effects are known to the researcher or not. Given the probabilistic nature of randomisation, group differences sometimes occur *by chance*. Therefore, when one uses random assignment, it is prudent to check whether group differences on important personal characteristics are evident despite randomisation.

The primary limitations of randomisation are ethical and practical. Informed consent is a fundamental requirement of ethical research. Too much is known about the relative effects of different settings, personal interest in the way people live is too strong, and legal protections of the right to the "most integrated" lifestyle are too clearly articulated to engender the suspension of judgement needed to consent to random assignment. If research on living arrangements relied solely on randomisation, almost no research would occur. We located only three studies involving random assignment to living arrangements (Close, 1977; MacEachron, 1983; Landesman, 1987), representing a tiny proportion of the overall research effort in this field.

Matching

Matching involves a sampled participant from one group being matched with an individual from another group on specific quantitative (such as adaptive behaviour) or categorical (such as gender) variables.

Several recent comparisons of models of residential support used matching based on one or more of the following characteristics: adaptive behaviour, challenging behaviour, age, gender, level of intellectual disability, or IQ (Conroy, 1996; Howe et al., 1998; Wehmeyer & Bolding, 1999; Stancliffe & Keane, 2000). Matching typically results in groups that do not differ significantly on the matching variables, but this is by no means inevitable. If differences between matched participants are small, but predominantly favour one group, the groups may differ significantly. Consequently, it is good practice to check whether significant differences remain between groups on the matching variables.

Matching is easily understood and intuitively appealing, and typically requires straightforward statistics such as *t*-tests or chi-square. One disadvantage is loss of participants because no suitable matching individuals are available. The larger the number of matching variables employed, and the more stringent the criterion for matching on each variable, the more difficult it is to find a match, and the greater is the likely loss of participants.

The personal characteristics on which participants are matched should have a demonstrable relation with the dependent variable(s). Matching by adaptive behaviour will often be preferred because adaptive behaviour has been shown to be strongly related to a wide range of consumer outcomes (Emerson & Hatton, 1996; Stancliffe & Lakin, 1998; Felce & Emerson, 2001). However, this depends on the particular outcomes under examination, because some outcomes (such as social network) may also be related to other characteristics, such as challenging behaviour or age (Robertson et al., 2001a).

Randomisation should control systematic bias related to *any* personal characteristic, but matching controls only bias associated with the matching variables. Matched groups may still differ on *unmatched* characteristics, so if the groups are not matched on important variables, the problem for internal validity posed by uncontrolled differences between the groups remains.

Regression Towards the Mean

Regression towards the mean may threaten the internal validity of matched-comparison studies in certain limited circumstances. This issue arises when participants are matched on the basis of a *pretest* score on a particular variable, and then compared at *post-test* on that same variable.

Consider two living arrangements, types A and B, where the population in type A has significantly higher adaptive behaviour scores than residents of type B. In selection of matches for a sample of individuals from type B (group B), the type A matches (group A) will tend to have substantially lower adaptive behaviour scores than the average for all type A residents. Scores towards the lower margin of a distribution tend to be underestimates relative to the true score. Likewise, scores selected from the upper range tend to overestimate. Upon *retest*, scores tend to regress somewhat towards their population mean. In the preceding example, group A's retest scores would *improve*, on average, due to regression towards the mean, giving group A an unfair advantage over group B at post-test. The higher the test's reliability and the smaller the difference between the group and population means, the smaller the regression effect. For example, Inventory for Client and Agency Planning (ICAP) (Bruininks, Hill, Weatherman & Woodcock, 1986) adaptive behaviour scores have a test–retest reliability of $r = 0.91$ for adults with intellectual disability. If groups A and B were matched on pretest ICAP adaptive behaviour scores, and if group A had adaptive behaviour scores that were 0.5 of a standard deviation *below* the population A mean, then regression towards the mean should result in a $(1–0.91) \times 0.5 = 0.045$ standard deviation units *increase* in average adaptive behaviour scores for subgroup A on reassessment with the ICAP. That is, regression effects may be relatively modest.

Regression effects threaten internal validity most seriously when the matched groups regress in *opposite* directions (that is, one group improves, and the other declines), so that these effects *both* unfairly favour one group. Heifetz (1998, p. 230) noted, "where *both* comparison groups are regressing in the *same direction*, any regression artefact is likely to be rather small, or even insignificant". In circumstances where the reliability of the test and the population means are known, it is possible to estimate the size of the regression effect and to take this into account when making group comparisons at post-test.

Statistical Control

Methods such as analysis of covariance (ANCOVA) and multiple or logistic regression provide statistical methods to control the effect of biasing variables (the covariates) (see Stancliffe et al., 2000). These techniques also reduce error variance, making statistical comparisons between residential models more precise and capable of detecting smaller differences. To be effective, the covariate(s) must have a relation with the dependent variable. Nothing is gained from using a covariate that is uncorrelated with the dependent variable. Unlike matching, covariance analyses proceed using data from *all* available participants.

ANCOVA and regression, like matching, effect statistical control *only* for the characteristics that the researcher controls explicitly. Other *unassessed* personal characteristics may also be important predictors of the dependent variable. If important personal characteristics are not controlled statistically, the study's internal validity may be compromised and the claimed differences between residential settings may not be valid. Readers must decide how credible the statistical controls selected by the researcher are at counteracting bias. Adaptive behaviour is correlated with a wide variety of consumer outcomes (Emerson & Hatton, 1996; Stancliffe & Lakin, 1998; Felce & Emerson, 2001) and so will frequently be an important covariate. Previous research and theoretical considerations will help identify potential covariates for particular dependent variables of interest.

Longitudinal Crossover Studies

Longitudinal crossover comparisons involve repeated assessments, following the same participants over time as they move from one type of living arrangement to another. There may or may not be a contrast group whose living arrangements remain unchanged. This approach eliminates problems with differences in personal characteristics between living arrangements, because persons are compared with themselves. A second advantage is that, if changes in outcomes *follow* the transfer to a different residence type, a stronger case can be made that this new environment *caused* the change in outcomes, because one criterion for establishing causation is temporal precedence.

Longitudinal studies are more expensive because they involve repeated assessments over an extended period. They also require a sample of individuals who will, after initial data collection in one type of setting, actually move to another. Almost all longitudinal crossover studies have been of groups leaving large institutions and moving to the community as part of predictable implementation of public policy. Therefore, longitudinal crossover comparisons of community residence types are rare. We located some longitudinal crossover comparisons involving relocation from a community hostel (a non-domestic scale community dwelling housing up to 15 people) to group homes in ordinary community houses (e.g., Conneally, Boyle & Smyth, 1992; see review by Emerson & Hatton, 1996).

Analytical techniques for longitudinal data are currently undergoing substantial development (Willett, Singer & Martin, 1998; Little, Schnabel & Baumert, 2000). C*hange scores*, calculated by subtracting pretest scores from post-test scores, have been the subject of considerable controversy (Willett, 1988). Use of ANCOVA, with post-test scores serving as the dependent variable and pretest scores as the covariate, means that change scores are not required. However, current analytical approaches to longitudinal data emphasise obtaining *multiwave* data rather than simply using two time points, and undertaking individual growth modelling by using *hierarchical linear models* (also known as mixed models), which offer many advantages over more traditional analyses (Willett et al., 1998; Little et al., 2000). Similarly, *survival analysis* (also known as hazard modelling) may be applied to longitudinal data where the dependent variable is binary (for example, admission to an out-of-home residential placement) to analyse whether and when the event occurred (Willett et al., 1998). Use of these techniques has not been prominent in the intellectual disability literature to date.

Hierarchical linear models are also useful in dealing with *nested* data in cross-sectional studies. In residential services, individuals are often nested within living units that are in turn nested within organisations, with data available about personal, living-unit, and organisational characteristics. Hierarchical models take the hierarchical (nested) data structure into account and appropriately incorporate variables from each level.

Another issue associated with longitudinal crossover studies is that change over time may be attributable to predicable human development. One way of controlling for maturation is to have a contrast group who remain in the original setting and help estimate what might have been expected to change among "movers" if they had stayed behind. Efforts to establish randomly assigned or matched control groups are affected by the randomisation and matching issues described previously. Matching is further complicated by the likelihood of movement out of a setting by members of the matched contrast group notionally designated as "stayers". It is also possible to evaluate the effect of time/maturation by use of repeated measures in an AB design in which evidence for the impact of the change in residential setting is provided by a difference in level and/or slope from baseline to "intervention".

In longitudinal crossover studies, informant characteristics may differ systematically by setting. In deinstitutionalisation research, informants typically are institution staff prior to relocation and community staff thereafter. If these informant groups differ (as in differences in tolerance of challenging behaviours), observed outcome changes may be partly due to these differences rather than true change in consumer outcomes. The effect of this issue can partly be gauged by using direct observation or consumer self-reports—data-collection methods that do not involve changes of informants over time. If longitudinal trends are similar in informant data and observational data or self-reports, then the effect of differences in informant characteristics is probably minimal.

Variation Within a Single Model of Residential Support

Research on residential supports does not always require that different models be compared. One solution to the confounding of living arrangements and consumer characteristics is to study relations among important variables such as consumer outcomes and environmental characteristics *within* a single residential support model (e.g., Felce & Perry, 1995). A possible problem with this approach is that there may be insufficient variability in consumer outcomes and environmental characteristics within a single model for the underlying links between variables to be detected.

Other Issues

This discussion has focused on internal validity problems associated with differences in resident characteristics when comparing models of residential support. Other issues involving (a) sampling and the generalisability of research findings; (b) the reliability and validity of research instruments; (c) the sensitivity of assessments to the degree of change in lifestyle, skill, or behaviour for individuals with more severe disability; and (d) the extent to which research findings are replicated all also have important repercussions for the utility of community living research.

OUTCOMES OF RESIDENTIAL SERVICES

Identifying Outcomes

A key element of research involving residential services is to identify and assess relevant outcomes. Community living is complex and conceptualisations of quality and outcomes include a number of different components (Lakin, Hayden & Abery, 1994). Much contemporary research on residential services now uses multiple outcome measures in an attempt to capture the complexity of community living (Burchard et al., 1991; Conroy, 1996; Stancliffe & Lakin, 1998; Stancliffe & Keane, 2000; Emerson et al., 2000, 2001). It is important to obtain a *comprehensive* picture of the outcomes of different models of community living so that information guiding public policy, programme development, and individual decisions about living arrangements portrays the richness and complexity of community life. Table 23.2 provides a list of important *consumer* outcomes that should be considered by community-living researchers. We have focused on consumer outcomes because they embody the goals and purposes of residential services and are therefore the primary focus of research.

Assessing Outcomes

Despite some notable exceptions, there has been limited progress in developing an array of readily available, valid, and reliable assessment instruments to measure the varied outcomes of community living. This is in contrast to the measurement of adaptive behaviour. Researchers and practitioners around the world can readily access commercially available adaptive behaviour assessments with satisfactory psychometric properties. There has been no equivalent development in the evaluation of outcomes of community living. By default, researchers frequently develop their own assessments, and these instruments often have unknown psychometric characteristics and limited replication and refinement. Table 23.3 presents a list of consumer outcome assessments that have been developed or adapted for use with persons with intellectual disability, that are published, and that report at least basic

Table 23.2 Consumer outcomes related to research on residential services

Consumer outcomes
• Community participation, independent community participation, participation in preferred community activities, use of mainstream services, community assimilation and acceptance, sense of community
• Domestic participation, engagement in domestic activities; hygiene, appearance, and personal care
• Quality of life, choice, self-determination, satisfaction, happiness, control of services, participation in individual planning
• Social network, family contact, social contact, social participation, engagement in social activities, social integration, living companion turnover, natural support, loneliness, compatibility with fellow residents
• Leisure/recreation participation, participation in preferred leisure/recreation activities, leisure/recreation integration
• Rights, safety, abuse, risk, dignity, access
• Physical health, exercise, mental health, stress, well-being
• Adaptive behaviour, challenging behaviour, skill acquisition

psychometric data. We do not claim to have a comprehensive list. In addition, we have listed related resources, such as review articles and research studies, that may be useful in locating or developing assessments.

Large-Scale Outcome Assessments

In addition to the scales listed in Table 23.2, a number of assessments have been developed expressly to have widespread or national applicability, such as the National Health Interview Survey—Disability Supplement (NHIS—D). These scales also may have associated large-scale databases that are accessible to researchers. These data sets can be useful not only for primary descriptive purposes but also as points of comparison for smaller-scale studies.

Most research into living arrangements has not included people living with families or in their own homes (see Larson, Lakin, Anderson & Kwak, 2001a). Likewise, it is uncommon for studies to incorporate comparison data from populations without disabilities (see Sands & Kozleski, 1994). Data from such comparison populations helps place research findings in a broader societal framework and can facilitate a focus on variables such as poverty, marital status, or access to health services that may be overlooked in the intellectual disability literature. Likewise, using items or scales drawn from national surveys such as NHIS—D enables researchers to make comparisons with extant, population-based survey data (see Larson et al., 2001a,b).

We now briefly describe two major US assessments and associated databases: (a) the Core Indicators Project, and (b) National Health Interview Survey—Disability Supplement.

Core Indicators Project

The Core Indicators Project began in 1997. Its purpose is to develop nationally recognised individual service performance indicators based on the kinds of outcomes identified in

Table 23.3 Examples of published consumer outcome assessment instruments and additional resources

Domain	Resources	Instruments
Adaptive behaviour	Chapter 18*	• Adaptive Behavior Scale—Residential and Community (Nihira, Leland & Lambert, 1993) • Inventory for Client and Agency Planning (Bruininks et al., 1986) • Scales of Independent Behaviour (Bruininks, Woodcock, Weatherman & Hill, 1984)
Challenging behaviour	Reviews by Aman (1991); Emerson (in press), Chapter 21	• Aberrant Behavior Checklist (Aman, Burrow & Wolford, 1995) • Adaptive Behavior Scale—Residential and Community (Nihira et al., 1993) • Inventory for Client and Agency Planning (Bruininks, et al., 1986) • Scales of Independent Behaviour (Bruininks et al., 1984)
Psychiatric symptoms	Review by Aman (1991); Chapter 20	• PAS-ADD Checklist (Moss, Prosser, Costello, Simpson & Patel, 1996; Moss et al., 1998) • Reiss Screen (Reiss, 1988) • Psychopathology Instrument for Mentally Retarded Adults (PIMRA) (Matson, Kazdin & Senatore, 1984; Swiezy, Matson, Kirkpatrick-Sanchez & Williams, 1995)
Quality of life/Satisfaction	Chapter 12; review by Cummins (1997b)	• Comprehensive Quality of Life Scale—Intellectual/Cognitive Disability (5th edn) (ComQol-I5) (Cummins, 1997a) • Quality of Life Questionnaire (Schalock & Keith, 1993)
Choice	Review by Stancliffe (2001); Chapter 16	• Choice Questionnaire (Stancliffe & Parmenter, 1999) • The Choices Scale (Hatton, Robertson & Emerson, 2001)
Loneliness		• Loneliness Questionnaire (Chadsey-Rusch, DeStefano, O'Reilly, Gonzalez & Collet-Klingenberg, 1992)
Stress		• Lifestress Inventory (Bramston & Bostock, 1994; Bramston & Fogarty, 1995; Fogarty, Cummins & Bramston, 1997)
Self-determination	Review by Stancliffe (2001)	• The Arc's Self-Determination Scale (Wehmeyer, 1996)
Community participation		• Index of Community Involvement (Raynes et al., 1994) • Guernsey Community Participation and Leisure Assessment (Baker, 2000)
Domestic participation		• Index of Participation in Domestic Life (Raynes et al., 1994)
Social network	Dagnan & Ruddick (1997); Halpern et al. (1986a); Krauss & Erickson (1988); Robertson et al. (2001a); Chapter 14	
Leisure/Recreation participation	Halpern et al. (1986a)	• Guernsey Community Participation and Leisure Assessment (Baker, 2000)
Health outcomes	Beange, Lennox & Parmenter (1999)	• The Health Survey for England 1993 (Bennett, Dodd, Flatley, Freeth & Bolling, 1995)
Safety	Halpern et al. (1986a)	

* Chapters refer to present volume.

Table 23.2. The project enabled developmental disabilities policy makers to benchmark the performance of their state or different state programmes against other states or programmes, and/or to track system performance and outcomes from year to year on a consistent basis (Human Services Research Institute and National Association of State Directors of Developmental Disabilities Services, 2001). Initially, seven states worked together to develop 61 "indicators" for a consumer survey and a survey of families with an adult family member at home. Field-testing assessed utility and reliability. A family/guardian survey has also been added when an adult family member receives residential supports outside the family home. In 2001, 15 states were participating to some extent. A substantial limitation of the comparability of the outcome data gathered is the absence of data on important individual characteristics for use in statistical control when comparing outcomes.

In Australia, adapted versions of instruments from the Core Indicators Project were used in a nationally representative satisfaction survey of clients of disability services (E-QUAL & Donovan Research, 2000).

National Health Interview Survey—Disability Supplement

In 1994 and 1995, the National Health Interview Survey had a supplement focused specifically on persons with disabilities. The questions within the Disability Supplement primarily addressed physical and health-related conditions, service use, and satisfaction with services. A significant problem with the survey is that only one person per household responded to questions about all household members. This survey includes only persons living in non-institutional households. Larson et al. (2001a,b) analysed data from the NHIS—D and produced nationally representative data on personal and demographic characteristics and service use among people with intellectual/developmental disabilities who live in their own homes or with family members.

Interpreting Outcome Data: Dimensions of Community Adjustment

Widely accepted theoretical models of community living have yet to emerge to provide a conceptual framework within which to organise available data. The multiplicity of outcomes and process variables to be evaluated can create a bewildering array of variables that are difficult to synthesise into a coherent picture of community living. For example, Emerson et al. (2000; 2001) examined the relations among a large number of outcome indicators. After they controlled for adaptive and challenging behaviour, only a small proportion of the indicators were significantly related to one another. They concluded that there was little empirical support for an overall index of quality outcomes for residential services.

There have been several empirically based attempts to bring greater conceptual order to community-living data. Halpern, Nave, Close and Nelson (1986b) used factor analysis to identify *four* dimensions of community adjustment: (a) occupation, (b) residential environment, (c) social/support/safety, and (d) client satisfaction. Each factor incorporated several composite variables that were made up of a number of individual items. For example, the residential environment factor related to the cleanliness and state of repair of the person's home, the upkeep and safety of the neighbourhood, and the person's access to the community.

Any such analysis of latent variables reflects the initial data on which the analyses are based. More recent research, based on different sources of raw data, has identified up to *eight* dimensions of community adjustment: (a) recreation/leisure integration, (b) social network integration, (c) residential integration, (d) employment/economic integration, (e) employment stability, (f) personal satisfaction, (g) community assimilation and acceptance, and (h) need for social support services (Bruininks, Chen, Lakin & McGrew, 1992; McGrew, Bruininks, Thurlow & Lewis, 1992; McGrew & Bruininks, 1994).

On the basis of these studies' findings, two conclusions may be proposed. First, it is feasible to identify dimensions of community adjustment that combine scores from a number of scales or items. Second, there are *multiple* dimensions of community adjustment, so any attempt to reduce community adjustment to a single construct is contradicted by available empirical evidence.

Importance of Various Outcomes

Given the large number of outcomes that could be evaluated, it makes sense to focus on the most important outcomes. There are marked variations in the features of living environments that are considered most important by different individuals (Foxx, Faw, Taylor, Davis & Fulia, 1993). One approach to resolving this dilemma was put forward by Gardener, Nudler and Chapman (1997), who advocate that the individual consumer is the ultimate referent and often the ultimate judge of outcomes. The Council on Quality and Leadership, for which they work, has identified 24 outcome realms of consistent importance to a large proportion of people with disabilities. Individual outcomes within those realms are established according to each individual's particular interests and preferences. A difficulty with such approaches in a research context is that it is hard to make valid comparisons across individuals and groups. Furthermore, such an approach is inaccessible to a number of people with more severe disabilities except through a proxy respondent.

Satisfaction

Consumer satisfaction with services has considerable appeal as a potentially overarching outcome because it puts the consumer at the centre of quality determination. However, there are a number of important issues to be considered when obtaining and interpreting such information.

Respondents with and without intellectual disability tend to report being satisfied with living arrangements they are familiar with, regardless of their objective quality (Larson & Lakin, 1991; Donnelly et al., 1994; Hatton, 1998; Emerson el al., 2000). Emerson et al. found very high ratings of satisfaction and almost no differences in satisfaction between residents of two different residential service models, despite significant differences in service inputs and consumer outcomes. Likewise, Donnelly et al. found high levels of reported satisfaction across all types of residential services. Satisfaction is generally unrelated to objective indices of quality (Hatton, 1998). Consequently, objective quality indicators should also be used when obtaining satisfaction data regarding residential services.

Research involving the general population also shows that overall life satisfaction and subjective well-being are stable characteristics of individuals that may show the short-term impact of major life events, but revert to dispositional levels in the longer term (Hatton, 1998). Thus, interventions that are intended to improve long-term satisfaction or subjective well-being may be doomed to make no long-term difference by virtue of the way in which the impact of intervention is measured. However, Heller, Factor, Hsieh and Hahn (1998) evaluated satisfaction before and after transfer from nursing homes to community settings, and found that movers showed a significant increase in satisfaction after an average of two years' community living, whereas non-movers showed no change. Similarly, Emerson and Hatton (1996) reviewed seven UK studies of satisfaction with services or with life in general, and found that most studies reported an improvement in satisfaction associated with movement from institutions to community living.

Taken together, such findings suggest that (a) the *absolute* level of satisfaction expressed about current living arrangements may be misleading, so *cross-sectional* comparisons of living arrangements based on satisfaction should be treated with considerable caution; (b) when satisfaction ratings are generally high, individual expressions of *dis*satisfaction are especially notable and should result in very serious efforts to improve the situation; and (c) *relative* level of satisfaction evaluated *longitudinally* (that is, *change* in satisfaction levels) may be an important indicator of the impact of change in living arrangements (but this issue requires further research).

One important facet of satisfaction data concerns *when* questions about satisfaction are asked. Larson and Lakin (1991) found that parental attitudes about institutional and community living showed a pattern of high satisfaction with institutional placements *before* moving to the community, high levels of satisfaction with community placements *after* transfer from the institution, but lower *retrospective* levels of satisfaction with the institution when this question was asked *after* relocation. These findings suggest that (a) *retrospective* satisfaction ratings (satisfaction with previous living arrangements), *prospective* satisfaction (regarding future living arrangements not yet experienced directly), and ratings of satisfaction with *current* circumstances should be compared with considerable caution; and (b) satisfaction ratings are influenced by the basis for comparison available to the individual (for example, whether the person has had direct experience of alternatives to current living arrangements).

Hatton (1998, p. 108) suggested that "subjective well-being . . . is clearly not a methodologically or conceptually appropriate research tool for evaluating the quality of services". We believe there is insufficient evidence to reach such a conclusion at present. The fact that satisfaction is frequently unrelated to objective indicators of quality is consistent with factor analytical studies that have identified satisfaction as a separate dimension of community adjustment (Halpern et al., 1986b; McGrew & Bruininks, 1994). As noted, there are multiple independent dimensions of community adjustment. This finding has not led to a call for the elimination of some of these outcomes as quality indicators. Rather it has led to recognition that community adjustment requires multiple outcome indicators if it is to be evaluated adequately. Therefore, we consider that assessment of consumer and family satisfaction should be retained, but with careful consideration of the methodological and interpretative difficulties we have highlighted, and concurrent use of objective quality indicators.

Two other issues require consideration. First, studies sometimes equate family satisfaction with consumer satisfaction, particularly when family proxies respond for individuals considered unable to respond for themselves. Without clear evidence to the contrary, family satisfaction and individual satisfaction should be seen as representing different perspectives and should be evaluated separately (Cummins, 2002). Second, efforts need to continue to be made to enhance the validity and reliability of individual responses and to enable more people with severe disabilities to respond for themselves. Such efforts include simplification of question wording and use of response aids such as pictures.

CONCLUSIONS

Inevitably, our examination of issues concerning research on residential supports for people with intellectual disability has been incomplete. For example, we have not considered qualitative research, simply because it is an area in which we lack significant expertise. Nevertheless, a number of conclusions arise from the issues discussed.

First, there is an evident need to conceptualise and describe more clearly a consistent set of salient characteristics of residential supports, including both structural characteristics and support delivery processes, and to develop satisfactory assessment instruments to evaluate these features. This approach should lead to a clearer understanding of important differences between models and to a better explanation of variation in outcomes between and within these models.

Second, researchers consistently need to use appropriate research design and data analytical techniques to control for threats to internal validity associated with systematic differences in personal characteristics of service users.

Third, research should continue to focus on a wide variety of outcomes, including health, safety, and subjective data such as satisfaction, with appropriate caution being applied to the collection and interpretation of satisfaction data. Substantial efforts are needed to develop further and make widely available valid and reliable assessment instruments to evaluate the full range of outcomes, including endeavours to enable more people with severe disabilities to respond for themselves, and to enhance the validity and reliability of self-reports. Understanding the relation between proxy data and self-reports requires continued attention to both objective and subjective measures.

Fourth, further development of theoretical models of community living is needed to provide an adequate framework within which to organise and understand the available research data.

Fifth, researchers should make use of recently developed statistical methods, such as hierarchical linear models, to analyse longitudinal and nested data (Willett et al., 1998; Little et al., 2000). Nested data are particularly common in residential research.

Sixth, just as research has moved beyond evaluation of deinstitutionalisation, studies need to focus not only on formal residential support services, but also on people living with family or in their own home. Newer approaches, such as supported living and the Robert Wood Johnson Foundation "self-determination" projects, also need to be examined in published research. More serious efforts at obtaining relevant comparison data regarding community members without disabilities are also needed.

These issues have the potential to contribute to the understanding and achievement of high-quality residential supports. In an era increasingly characterised by public disquiet about the quality of community residential services (American Association on Mental Retardation, 2000), this is both important and timely.

REFERENCES

Aman, M.G. (1991). *Assessing Psychopathology and Behavior Problems in Persons with Mental Retardation: A Review of Available Instruments*. Rockville, MD: US Department of Health and Human Services, Public Health Service, Alcohol, Drug Abuse, and Mental Health Administration, National Institutes of Mental Health.

Aman, M.G., Burrow, W.H. & Wolford, P.L. (1995). Aberrant Behavior Checklist—Community: factor validity and effect of subject variables for adults in group homes. *American Journal on Mental Retardation*, **100**, 283–292.

American Association on Mental Retardation (2000). Disability quality coalition formed. *American Association on Mental Retardation, News and Notes*, **14**, 1, 14, 20.

Anderson, D.J., Lakin, K.C., Hill, B.K. & Chen, T.H. (1992). Social integration of older persons with mental retardation in residential facilities. *American Journal on Mental Retardation*, **96**, 488–501.

Apgar, D.H., Cook, S. & Lerman, P. (1997). *The North Princeton Evaluation Environment Assessment* [short form]. Newark, NJ: New Jersey Institute of Technology, Center for Architecture and Building Science Research.

Baker, P.A. (2000). Measurement of community participation and use of leisure by service users with intellectual disabilities: the Guernsey Community Participation and Leisure Assessment (GCPLA). *Journal of Applied Research in Intellectual Disabilities*, **13**, 169–185.

Balla, D. (1976). Relationship of institution size to quality of care: a review of the literature. *American Journal of Mental Deficiency*, **81**, 117–124.

Baroff, G. (1980). On size and the quality of residential care: a second look. *Mental Retardation*, **18**, 117–124.

Beange, H., Lennox, N. & Parmenter, T.R. (1999). Health targets for people with an intellectual disability. *Journal of Intellectual and Developmental Disability*, **24**, 283–297.

Bennett, N., Dodd, T., Flatley, J., Freeth, S. & Bolling, K. (1995). *The Health Survey for England 1993.* London: HMSO.

Black, K. & Maples, J. (1998). *Disability Support Services Provided Under the Commonwealth/State Disability Agreement: National Data 1997.* Canberra: Australian Institute of Health and Welfare (AIHW Cat. No. DIS 12).

Braddock, D., Emerson, E., Felce, D. & Stancliffe, R.J. (2001). The living circumstances of children and adults with MR/DD in the United States, Canada, England and Wales, and Australia. *Mental Retardation and Developmental Disabilities Research Reviews*, **7**, 115–121.

Bramston, P. & Bostock, J. (1994). Measuring perceived stress in people with intellectual disabilities: the development of a new scale. *Australia and New Zealand Journal of Developmental Disabilities*, **19**, 149–157.

Bramston, P. & Fogarty, G.J. (1995). Measuring stress in the mildly intellectually handicapped: the factorial structure of the subjective stress scale. *Research in Developmental Disabilities*, **16**, 117–131.

Bruininks, R.H., Chen, T.H., Lakin, K.C. & McGrew, K.S. (1992). Components of personal competence and community integration for persons with mental retardation in small residential programs. *Research in Developmental Disabilities*, **13**, 463–479.

Bruininks, R.H., Hill, B.K., Weatherman, R.F. & Woodcock, R.W. (1986). *Examiner's Manual. ICAP Inventory for Client and Agency Planning.* Allen, TX: DLM Teaching Resources.

Bruininks, R.H., Woodcock, R.W., Weatherman, R.F. & Hill, B.H. (1984). *Scales of Independent Behaviour*. Allen, TX: DLM Teaching Resources.

Buckingham, M. & Coffman, C. (1999). *First, Break All the Rules: What the World's Greatest Managers Do Differently*. New York: Simon and Schuster.

Burchard, S.N., Hasazi, J.E., Gordon, L.R. & Yoe, J. (1991). An examination of lifestyle and adjustment in three community residential alternatives. *Research in Developmental Disabilities*, **12**, 127–142.

Campbell, E.M. & Heal, L.W. (1995). Prediction of cost, rates, and staffing by provider and client characteristics. *American Journal on Mental Retardation*, **100**, 17–35.

Chadsey-Rusch, J., DeStefano, L., O'Reilly, M., Gonzalez, P. & Collet-Klingenberg, L. (1992). Assessing the loneliness of workers with mental retardation. *Mental Retardation*, **30**, 85–92.

Close, D.W. (1977). Community living for severely and profoundly retarded adults: a group home study. *Education and Training of the Mentally Retarded*, **12**, 256–262.

Conneally, S., Boyle, G. & Smyth, F. (1992). An evaluation of the use of small group homes for adults with a severe or profound mental handicap. *Mental Handicap Research*, **5**, 146–168.

Conroy, J.W. (1996). The small ICF/MR program: dimensions of quality and cost. *Mental Retardation*, **34**, 13–26.

Cooke, R.A. & Lafferty, J.C. (1989). *Organizational Culture Inventory*. Plymouth, MI: Human Synergistics.

Cummins, R.A. (1997a). *Comprehensive Quality of Life Scale—Intellectual/Cognitive Disability* (5th edn) (ComQol-I5). Melbourne, Australia: Deakin University, School of Psychology. This document may also be retrieved from http://acqol.deakin.edu.au/instruments/com_scale.htm.

Cummins, R.A. (1997b). Self-rated quality of life scales for people with an intellectual disability: a review. *Journal of Applied Research in Intellectual Disabilities*, **10**, 199–216.

Cummins, R.A. (2002). Proxy responding for subjective well-being: a review. *International Review of Research in Mental Retardation*, **25**, 183–207.

Dagnan, D. & Ruddick, L. (1997). The social networks of older people with learning disabilities living in staffed community based homes. *British Journal of Developmental Disabilities*, **43**, 43–53.

Donnelly, M., McGilloway, S., Mays, N., Perry, S., Knapp, M., Kavanagh, S., et al. (1994). *Opening New Doors: An Evaluation of Community Care for People Discharged from Psychiatric and Mental Handicap Hospitals*. London: HMSO.

Emerson, E. (1999). Residential supports for people with intellectual disabilities: questions and challenges from the UK. *Journal of Intellectual and Developmental Disability*, **24**, 309–319.

Emerson, E. (in press). Challenging behaviour. In J. Hogg (Ed.) *Assessing Adults with Intellectual Disability*. London: Blackwell.

Emerson, E. & Hatton, C. (1996). Deinstitutionalization in the UK and Ireland: outcomes for service users. *Journal of Intellectual and Developmental Disability*, **21**, 17–37.

Emerson, E., Robertson, J., Gregory, N., Hatton, C., Kessissoglou, S., Hallam, A., et al. (2000). Quality and costs of community based residential supports, village communities, and residential campuses in the United Kingdom. *American Journal on Mental Retardation*, **105**, 81–102.

Emerson, E., Robertson, J., Gregory, N., Hatton, C., Kessissoglou, S., Hallam, A., et al. (2001). Quality and costs of supported living residences and group homes in the United Kingdom. *American Journal on Mental Retardation*, **106**, 401–415.

E-QUAL & Donovan Research (2000). *National Satisfaction Survey of Clients of Disability Services*. A report prepared for the Steering Committee for the Review of Commonwealth/State Service Provision and the National Disability Administrators. Canberra, ACT: AusInfo. This document may also be retrieved at www.pc.gov.au/gsp/nsscds/index.html.

Felce, D., Bowley, C., Baxter, H., Jones, E., Lowe, C. & Emerson, E. (2000). The effectiveness of staff support: evaluating active support training using a conditional probability approach. *Research in Developmental Disabilities*, **21**, 243–255.

Felce, D. & Emerson, E., (2000). Observational methods in the assessment of quality of life. In T. Thompson, D. Felce & F. Symons (Eds) *Behavioral Observation: Technology and Applications in Developmental Disabilities*. Baltimore, MD: Brookes.

Felce, D. & Emerson, E. (2001). Living with support in a home in the community: predictors of behavioral development and household and community activity. *Mental Retardation and Developmental Disabilities Research Reviews*, **7**, 75–83.

Felce, D., Lowe, K. & Emerson, E. (1995). *Residential Services Working Practices Scale*. Cardiff: Welsh Centre on Learning Disabilities Applied Research Unit.

Felce, D., Lowe, K., Perry, J., Baxter, H., Jones, E., Hallam, A., et al. (1998). Service support to people in Wales with severe intellectual disability and severe challenging behaviours: processes, outcomes, and costs. *Journal of Intellectual Disability Research*, **42**, 390–408.

Felce, D. & Perry, J. (1995). The extent of support for ordinary living provided in staffed housing: the relationship between staffing levels, resident dependency, staff : resident interactions and resident activity patterns. *Social Science and Medicine*, **40**, 799–810.

Felce, D., Thomas, M., de Kock, U., Saxby, H. & Repp, A. (1985). An ecological comparison of small community-based houses and traditional institutions for severely and profoundly mentally handicapped adults. II. Physical settings and the use of opportunities. *Behaviour Research and Therapy*, **23**, 337–348.

Fogarty, G.J., Cummins, R.A. & Bramston, P. (1997). Validation of the Lifestress Inventory for people with a mild intellectual disability. *Research in Developmental Disabilities*, **18**, 435–456.

Foxx, R.M., Faw, G.D., Taylor, S., Davis, P.K. & Fulia, R. (1993). "Would I be able to . . .?" Teaching clients to assess the availability of their community living lifestyle preferences. *American Journal on Mental Retardation*, **98**, 235–248.

Gardener, J.F., Nudler, S. & Chapman, M.S. (1997). Personal outcomes as measures of quality. *Mental Retardation*, **35**, 295–305.

Gillett, L. (2000). Can organisational culture account for the difference in quality of life in small community-based residential services for people with intellectual disabilities? Paper presented at BPS Annual Conference, Winchester.

Gregory, N., Robertson, J., Kessissoglou, S., Emerson, E. & Hatton, C. (2001). Predictors of expressed satisfaction among people with intellectual disabilities receiving residential supports. *Journal of Intellectual Disability Research*, **45**, 279–292.

Halpern, A.S., Close, D.W. & Nelson, D.J. (1986a). *On My Own: The Impact of Semi-independent Living Programs for Adults with Mental Retardation*. Baltimore, MD: Brookes.

Halpern, A., Nave, G., Close, D. & Nelson, D. (1986b). An empirical analysis of the dimensions of community adjustment for adults with mental retardation in semi-independent living programs. *Australia and New Zealand Journal of Developmental Disabilities*, **12**, 147–157.

Hatton, C. (1998). Whose quality of life is it anyway? Some problems with the emerging quality of life consensus. *Mental Retardation*, **36**, 104–115.

Hatton, C., Emerson, E., Rivers, M., Mason, H., Swarbrick, R., Mason, L., et al. (2001). Factors associated with intended staff turnover and job search behaviour in services for people with intellectual disability. *Journal of Intellectual Disability Research*, **45**, 258–271.

Hatton, C., Emerson, E., Robertson, J., Henderson, D. & Cooper, J. (1995). The quality and costs of services for adults with multiple disabilities: a comparative evaluation. *Research in Developmental Disabilities*, **16**, 439–460.

Hatton, C., Robertson, J. & Emerson, E. (2001). The Choices Scale. Lancaster, UK: Institute for Health Research, Lancaster University.

Heifetz, L.J. (1998). Break the data bank with Monte Carlo? Statistical problems in the dispute between Conroy (1996) and Crinella, McCleary, and Swanson (1998). *Mental Retardation*, **36**, 227–236.

Heller, T., Factor, A.R., Hsieh, K. & Hahn, J.E. (1998). Impact of age and transitions out of nursing homes for adults with developmental disabilities. *American Journal on Mental Retardation*, **103**, 236–248.

Howe, J., Horner, R.H. & Newton, J.S. (1998). Comparison of supported living and traditional residential services in the state of Oregon. *Mental Retardation*, **36**, 1–11.

Human Services Research Institute and National Association of State Directors of Developmental Disabilities Services (2001, May). *Consumer Survey: Phase II Technical Report. Core Indicators Project*. Cambridge, MA: Author [this report can be retrieved from www.hsri.org/cip/cipresults.html].

Jones, E., Perry, J., Lowe, K., Felce, D., Toogood, S., Dunstan, F., et al. (1999). Opportunity and the promotion of activity among adults with severe mental retardation living in community residences: the impact of training staff in Active Support. *Journal of Intellectual Disability Research*, **43**, 164–178.

Kavanagh, S. & Opit, L. (1998). *The Cost of Caring: The Economics of Providing for the Intellectually Disabled*. London: Politeia.

Kim, S., Larson, S.A. & Lakin, K.C. (2001). Behavioral outcomes of deinstitutionalization for people with intellectual disabilities: a review of US studies conducted between 1980 and 1999. *Journal of Intellectual and Developmental Disability*, **26**, 15–34.

Krauss, M.W. & Erickson, M. (1988). Informal support networks among aging persons with mental retardation: a pilot study. *Mental Retardation*, **26**, 197–201.

Lakin, K.C., Bruininks, R.H., Hill, B.K., Chen, T.H. & Anderson, D.J. (1993). Personal characteristics and competence of people with mental retardation living in foster homes or small group homes. *American Journal on Mental Retardation*, **97**, 616–627.

Lakin, K.C., Hayden, M.F. & Abery, B.H. (1994). An overview of the community living concept. In M.F. Hayden & B.H. Abery (Eds) *Challenges for a Service System in Transition: Ensuring Quality Community Experiences for Persons with Developmental Disabilities* (pp. 3–22). Baltimore, MD: Brookes.

Landesman, S. (1987). The changing structure and function of institutions: a search for optimal group care environments. In S. Landesman & P.M. Vietze (Eds) *Living Environments and Mental Retardation* (pp. 79–126). Washington, DC: American Association on Mental Retardation.

Larson, S.A. & Lakin, K.C. (1991). Parent attitudes about residential placement before and after deinstitutionalization: a research synthesis. *Journal of the Association for Persons with Severe Handicaps*, **16**, 25–38.

Larson, S.A., Lakin, K.C., Anderson, L. & Kwak, N. (2001a, April). Characteristics of and service use by persons with MR/DD living in their own homes or with family members: NHIS-D analysis. *MR/DD Data Brief, 3(1)* [available from Publications Office, Institute on Community Integration, University of Minnesota, 109 Pattee Hall, 150 Pillsbury Drive SE, Minneapolis, MN 55455, USA].

Larson, S.A., Lakin, K.C., Anderson, L. & Kwak, N. (2001b, June). Demographic characteristics of persons with MR/DD living in their own homes or with family members: NHIS-D analysis. *MR/DD Data Brief, 3(2)* [available from Publications Office, Institute on Community Integration, University of Minnesota, 109 Pattee Hall, 150 Pillsbury Drive SE, Minneapolis, MN 55455, USA].

Larson, S.A., Lakin, K.C. & Bruininks, R.H. (1998). *Staff Recruitment and Retention: Study Results and Intervention Strategies* [D. Braddock, Ed.]. Washington, DC: American Association on Mental Retardation.

Little, T.D., Schnabel, K.U. & Baumert, J. (2000). *Modeling Longitudinal and Multilevel Data*. Mahwah, NJ: Erlbaum.

MacEachron, A.E. (1983). Institutional reform and adaptive functioning of mentally retarded persons: a field experiment. *American Journal of Mental Deficiency*, **88**, 2–12.

McGrew, K.S. & Bruininks, R.H. (1994). A multidimensional approach to the measurement of community adjustment. In M.F. Hayden & B.H. Abery (Eds) *Challenges for a Service System in Transition: Ensuring Quality Community Experiences for Persons with Developmental Disabilities* (pp. 65–79). Baltimore, MD: Brookes.

McGrew, K.S., Bruininks, R.H., Thurlow, M. & Lewis, D. (1992). An empirical analysis of multidimensional measures of community adjustment of young adults with retardation. *American Journal on Mental Retardation*, **96**, 475–487.

Matson, J.L., Kazdin, A.E. & Senatore, V. (1984). Psychometric properties of the Psychopathology Instrument for Mentally Retarded Adults. *Applied Research in Mental Retardation*, **51**, 81–89.

Moss, S.C., Prosser, H., Costello, H., Simpson, N. & Patel, P. (1996). *PAS-ADD Checklist*. Manchester: University of Manchester, Hester Adrian Research Centre.

Moss, S.C., Prosser, H., Costello, H., Simpson, N., Patel, P., Rowe, S., et al. (1998). Reliability and validity of the PAS-ADD Checklist for detecting psychiatric disorders in adults with intellectual disabilities. *Journal of Intellectual Disability Research*, **42**, 173–183.

Nihira, K., Leland, H. & Lambert, N. (1993). *Adaptive Behavior Scale—Residential and Community* (2nd edn). Austin, TX: Pro-Ed.

Pratt, M.W., Luszcz, M.A. & Brown, M.E. (1980). Measuring the dimensions of the quality of care in small community residences. *American Journal on Mental Deficiency*, **85**, 188-194.

Raynes, N.V., Wright, K., Shiell, A. & Pettipher, C. (1994). *The Cost and Quality of Community Residential Care: An Evaluation of the Services for Adults with Learning Disabilities*. London: David Fulton.

Reiss, S. (1988). *The Reiss Screen Test Manual*. Orland Park, IL: International Diagnostic Systems.

Robertson, J., Emerson, E., Gregory, N., Hatton, C., Kessissoglou, S., Hallam, A., et al. (2001a). Social networks of people with intellectual disabilities in residential settings. *Mental Retardation*, **39**, 201–214.

Robertson, J., Emerson, E., Hatton, C., Gregory, N., Kessissoglou, S., Hallam, A., et al. (2001b). Environmental opportunities for exercising self-determination in residential settings. *Research in Developmental Disabilities*, **22**, 487–502.

Ryan, J. & Thomas, F. (1987). *The Politics of Mental Handicap*. London: Free Association Books.

Sands, D.J. & Kozleski, E.B. (1994). Quality of life differences between adults with and without disabilities. *Education and Training in Mental Retardation and Developmental Disabilities*, **29**, 90–101.

Schalock, R.L. & Keith, K.D. (1993). *Quality of Life Questionnaire.* Worthington, OH: IDS Publishing.

Stancliffe, R.J., (1997). Community living-unit size, staff presence, and residents' choice-making. *Mental Retardation*, **35**, 1–9.

Stancliffe, R.J. (2001). Living with support in the community: predictors of choice and self-determination. *Mental Retardation and Developmental Disabilities Research Reviews*, **7**, 91–98.

Stancliffe, R.J., Abery, B.H. & Smith, J. (2000). Personal control and the ecology of community living settings: beyond living-unit size and type. *American Journal on Mental Retardation*, **105**, 431–454.

Stancliffe, R.J. & Keane, S. (2000). Outcomes and costs of community living: a matched comparison of group homes and semi-independent living. *Journal of Intellectual and Developmental Disability*, **25**, 281–305.

Stancliffe, R.J. & Lakin, K.C. (1998). Analysis of expenditures and outcomes of residential alternatives for persons with developmental disabilities. *American Journal on Mental Retardation*, **102**, 552–568.

Stancliffe, R.J. & Parmenter, T.R. (1999). The Choice Questionnaire: a scale to assess choices exercised by adults with intellectual disability. *Journal of Intellectual and Developmental Disability*, **24**, 107–132.

Swiezy, N.B., Matson, J.L., Kirkpatrick-Sanchez, S. & Williams, D.E. (1995). A criterion validity study of the schizophrenia subscale of the Psychopathology Instrument for Mentally Retarded Adults (PIMRA). *Research in Developmental Disabilities*, **16**, 75–80.

Thompson, T., Robinson, J., Graff, M. & Ingenmey, R. (1990). Home-like architectural feature of residential environments. *American Journal on Mental Retardation*, **95**, 328–341.

Tøssebro, J. (1995). Impact of size revisited: relation of number of residents to self-determination and deprivatization. *American Journal on Mental Retardation*, **100**, 59–67.

Trent, J.W. (1994). *Inventing the Feeble Mind: A History of Mental Retardation in the United States.* Berkeley, CA: University of California Press.

Wehmeyer, M.L. (1996). Student self-report measure of self-determination for students with cognitive disabilities. *Education and Training in Mental Retardation and Developmental Disabilities*, **32**, 282–293.

Wehmeyer, M.L. & Bolding, N. (1999). Self-determination across living and working environments: a matched samples study of adults with mental retardation. *Mental Retardation*, **37**, 353–363.

Willett, J.B. (1988). Questions and answers in the measurement of change. In L.L. Rothkoph (Ed.) *Review of Research in Education, 15* (pp. 345–422). Washington, DC: American Education Research Association.

Willett, J.B., Singer, J.D. & Martin, N.C. (1998). The design and analysis of longitudinal studies of development and psychopathology in context: statistical models and methodological recommendations. *Developmental Psychopathology*, **10**, 395–426.

Young, L., Sigafoos, J., Suttie, J., Ashman, A. & Grevell, P. (1998). Deinstitutionalisation of persons with intellectual disabilities: a review of Australian studies. *Journal of Intellectual and Developmental Disability*, **23**, 155–170.

CHAPTER 24

Interaction with the Criminal Justice System

Susan Hayes
University of Sydney, Australia

INTRODUCTION

Research focusing on people with intellectual disabilities and the criminal justice system is sparse, and tends to concentrate on prevalence and correlational studies, as recent key reviews indicate (Hayes, 1996a, 2000). While these aspects of research are important in establishing the magnitude of the problems, thus allowing resource planning, the emphasis now needs to move towards examination of causative factors, prevention of offending behaviour, and effectiveness of treatment programmes. A small number of controlled studies of factors contributing to offending behaviour and outcomes of intervention programmes exists (Lindsay, Marshall, Neilson, Quinn & Smith, 1998a; Lindsay, Neilson, Morrison & Smith, 1998b), but few utilise large samples (Hayes, 2000; Law, Lindsay, Quinn & Smith, 2000), and research design is rarely longitudinal. Comparisons with non-disabled offenders with similar characteristics, or with non-offenders who have an intellectual disability, are rare (Brown & Stein, 1997). Definitional problems muddy the research waters. Ethical issues abound, with informed consent to interventions and placements, and behaviour-management plans that may infringe civil rights, constituting two of the most vexing areas (Lindsey & Luckasson, 1991; Grubb-Blubaugh, Shire & Balser, 1994). The aims of this chapter are, first, to highlight the sampling and methodological decisions that researchers have to make when proposing to conduct research into this area, and, second, to outline the important ethical and design factors that need to be taken into account.

THEORETICAL BASIS FOR RESEARCH

Research in this area of criminology is seldom based on theoretical concepts, possibly owing to the sometimes confusing plethora of psychological, educational, sociological, and criminological theories which can be applied. Nevertheless, the lack of theoretical underpinning has a pervasive effect on the value of research outcomes, generalisability of results, and the translation of results into clinical and preventative applications. In the

The International Handbook of Applied Research in Intellectual Disabilities. Edited by E. Emerson, C. Hatton, T. Thompson and T.R. Parmenter © 2004 John Wiley & Sons, Ltd. ISBN 0-471-49709-6.

absence of a theoretical underpinning, research becomes simply descriptive, and adds little to an understanding of the causal factors leading to over-representation of this group in the justice system, and to the identification of the most effective interventions, at societal, institutional, and individual levels. Therefore, a researcher needs not only to state clearly, "I want to find this out", but also to add, "because, on the basis of Z theory, I hypothesise that X may be influencing Y".

Social psychology and environmental theories of crime offer important concepts to researchers studying crime and victims and offenders with intellectual disabilities, and also provide insight into the complementary question of why many people with intellectual disabilities do not become offenders. Sociological theories place emphasis upon the social environment rather than the individual, learning theories emphasise the acquisition of criminal behaviour, the rational choice perspectives consider the role of decision processes, and role theories relate role performance to situational demands (for further discussion of these theories, a key reference is Blackburn, 1993). In addition to examining whether a particular intervention is effective, it is important to attempt to understand why it is so.

Blackburn (1993) states that classification of crimes and criminals is important for three major reasons:

(1) *management decisions* in the correctional system, which can include internal and external security reasons, and promotion of the safety of the community and the smooth running of the institution with minimal danger to staff and inmates
(2) *treatment decisions,* allocating inmates to units where they can receive appropriate treatment or rehabilitation programmes
(3) *theoretical understanding*, to assist in constructing causal theories for particular classes of offence or offender.

While such classifications may appear to be objective and clear, they may disguise flaws. For example, in a study of sex offenders, the aim of research could be to compare the characteristics of paedophiles with those who offend against adults. The confounding factors include the fact that those accused only of crimes against adults may nevertheless have committed crimes against children which are unknown; charges for crimes against children may have been dropped because there was little chance of obtaining a conviction; and charges of sexual assault may have been changed to common assault, as a consequence of plea bargaining. Thus, a prisoner may be classified as being of low risk, having committed "only" common assault, when, in fact, the nature of the crime against child victims, if known to other inmates, could place the individual at risk in the mainstream of the prison, thus posing a management dilemma. In addition, if the "true" nature of the crime is not known to correctional managers, the prisoner is likely not to be allocated to specialist rehabilitation units for sex offenders, rendering treatment decisions invalid. A major limitation of criminological research is the reliance upon the charges or convictions as recorded, despite all the possible hidden background information.

SAMPLING ISSUES

Definitions of Intellectual Disability

The interface between the law and the disciplines relevant to intellectual disability is problematical. Definitional difficulties play a significant part in the problems experienced by workers at this interface, owing to the following factors:

- In some jurisdictions, intellectual disability is included under legal concepts of mental illness.
- The cut-off points for operationally defining intellectual disability may vary by up to 15–20 points between jurisdictions, a fact which clearly affects prevalence rates. Furthermore, cut-off scores for intellectual disability can be used to limit access to available community-based resources and services, and therefore allow more "offenders" to be dealt with in the criminal justice system rather than community and welfare systems.
- Correctional services may define intellectual disability differently from community/welfare services in the same jurisdiction, and this can create problems of excluding clients from one service while including them in another, or result in lack of follow-up after release from custody.
- Legal definitions of intellectual disability are not necessarily similar to accepted definitions in professional intellectual disability arenas (a key reference related to the criminal law and offenders with intellectual disability is Hayes & Craddock, 1992).
- The differentiation between intellectual disability and mental illness, a hard-won distinction for the two disciplines in service provision, may be blurred in the legal system; people with intellectual disabilities may receive appropriate protections offered by the criminal justice system only at the price of receiving a label of "insanity", "defect of mind", "not guilty by reason of insanity", or any one of a number of other inappropriate terms used in statutes (Hayes, 1997).
- Where people with an intellectual disability suffer from a dual diagnosis, having a psychiatric diagnosis in addition to their intellectual disability, they may fall through the gap between intellectual disability services and mental health services. Sentencing, placement, and intervention options might exist in the mental health arena, but a parallel system usually does not exist for people with intellectual disabilities, thus forcing them into inappropriate services, or into prisons.
- The term "recidivism" needs to be defined carefully if replication of research is to be facilitated. The term may be used variously to include participants who reoffend within the follow-up time of the research; those who engage in behaviour which is similar to their previous offending behaviour, but who are not charged or convicted; and those who are reconvicted of similar or completely different offences.

These definitional problems pose hurdles for a researcher in terms of case-finding within the legal and correctional settings, including or excluding possible research participants, and comparing research results between studies. Negative consequences for researchers can arise, including the inability of other investigators to undertake further research. Furthermore, government agencies that have participated in research have the opportunity to dismiss the research results when they realise the controversial nature of the findings, citing definitional "discrepancies" as an effective method of discrediting research outcomes.

Recorded Crime or Antisocial Behaviour

The first challenge in undertaking research in the area of criminology is to decide the subject matter of the study. Many crimes are not detected or reported, giving rise to bias in statistics about crime rates, prevalence of various types of offences, and rates of prosecution and conviction. In the former "whole of life" institutions for people with intellectual disabilities, most crime went unreported and was dealt with within the institution. Now that many people with intellectual disabilities reside in the community, apparent "increases" in crimes by and against people with intellectual disabilities may to some extent arise from increased reporting to police, and increased numbers of court appearances. Differences in diversionary options among jurisdictions can result in some people being diverted out of the criminal justice system prior to being charged in one jurisdiction, whereas they will be charged, appear before the court, and be sentenced in another jurisdiction. Diversion out of the criminal justice system at any of these stages can affect crime statistics derived from courts and correctional settings. In one jurisdiction, therefore, a person with an intellectual disability who commits a certain act may be adjudicated as "criminal", whereas that same label may not pertain elsewhere. The provision of services for clients with intellectual disability can affect the disposition of offenders—such factors might include the following:

- availability of residential and secure facility options
- opportunities for diversion from the criminal justice system to treatment programmes
- policies of community welfare organisations actively to seek prosecution of clients who exhibit antisocial behaviours or who damage property
- the adequacy of funding for disability support services
- availability of behaviour-management programmes to address challenging behaviour through early intervention.

These factors are entirely unrelated to "true" crime rates, yet they can significantly affect the numbers of people with intellectual disability involved with the criminal justice system as either offenders or victims of crime. Researchers, therefore, must decide whether to study crime as legally defined, or whether to study behaviour which is antisocial and possibly harmful, but which may not be legally defined as crime (Blackburn, 1993). Sociologists and psychologists argue that rule-breaking and law-breaking are similar in the sense that the individual knows that there are rules or laws, and that to break them attracts a penalty or punishment (Blackburn, 1993). However, this concept may not apply to some individuals with intellectual disability who lack the moral and cognitive reasoning skills to comprehend such concepts. Therefore, to extend the study of illegal acts to include antisocial acts begs the question of whether an act is antisocial if the actor does not realise that it is; in this instance, the judgement of "antisocial" is being made by the observer or researcher, and may be value laden.

The measurement of crime can be derived from official statistics of reported crimes, self-reports of criminal behaviour, crime surveys of communities that ask about the experience of being the victim of a crime, and court statistics concerning charges and convictions. The limitations of each of these methods are legion. Bias occurs because citizens do not bother to report some forms of petty crime, or are unwilling to report more serious interpersonal crimes such as child abuse or sexual assault. Similarly, self-reports of criminal acts are limited by the wariness of the participant. Court statistics are affected by plea bargaining (in which a client pleads guilty to a lesser charge), the policies of police or prosecutors that may result in cases proceeding only when there is a good chance of a conviction, variation in rates of acquittal, and the availability of legal aid (Hayes, 1996c). Sentencing statistics can be influenced in turn by the politics of the day emphasising variously stern punishment, community sentencing options, and mental health/disability law. The personal characteristics of the accused, including race, gender, perceptions that they suffer from a "mental disorder", socio-economic status, and stable family, work, and community ties may have a strong influence on the outcome of legal proceedings, including bail or community-based sentences (Blackburn, 1993; Hayes, 1996a). Measurement of crime and court outcomes is not an exact science.

Offenders with an intellectual disability resemble rather than differ from their non-disabled counterparts—both groups are likely to have low socio-economic backgrounds, be unemployed, be concentrated in younger age categories, be male, have fragmented family backgrounds, be poorly educated, and have literacy deficits. Behavioural problems in the preschool years translate into later delinquency, with low intellectual functioning being a risk factor and high functioning being a protective factor (White, Moffitt & Silva, 1989). Approaching the issue from the other perspective, longitudinal research indicates that people with intellectual disabilities tend to be charged at a rate greater than their non-disabled peers in a birth cohort (Hodgins, 1992). Correlation is not explanation, as any student of statistics knows, yet there is a dearth of research which assists in understanding the aetiology of offending behaviour in persons with an intellectual disability, and which can therefore be used to design preventative programmes.

Offender, Accused Person, or Victim

As noted above, many research studies cannot be compared with other studies or replicated because of inadequately defined and confusing terminology. The distinction between an accused person and an offender is an example. While the legal and police professions tend to be scrupulous in abiding by this distinction, criminological, sociological, and psychological researchers are less so. The importance of obtaining a sample of adequate size can lead a researcher to include different categories of participants, such as the following:

- those who engage in behaviour that could lead to their being charged, or which is "antisocial"
- those who engage in socially unacceptable behaviour, but who are unlikely to be charged, possibly because of difficulties with the prosecution case and proof
- those who were charged and later found not guilty
- juvenile and adult offenders
- those found not guilty by reason of mental illness
- individuals who were charged and diverted out of the criminal justice system, with the result that the charge is effectively dropped
- prisoners, a group that may include remandees and sentenced prisoners
- individuals who may have been found guilty, but an offence has not been recorded against them for a variety of legal and judicial reasons
- offenders who have been found guilty and sentenced, receiving a custodial or non-custodial sentence, including a suspended sentence or a "good behaviour" bond.

In some studies, the distinction between groups may not be important, depending on the variables studied, while in other research, the different categories may have a strong bearing on the conclusions. Researchers must specify clearly the criteria for inclusion, and if the study includes participants from many of the categories described above, this design needs to be justified.

Sampling difficulties occur with victim groups also, and include the following issues:

- Are individuals regarded as victims on the basis of self-report alone, or must there be other evidence that a crime has been committed against them?
- Is the person a victim if the crime has not been reported to police?
- People with intellectual disabilities may not be able to describe their victimisation, and evidence that a crime has been committed against them might have to be derived from third-party sources such as staff or family members.
- Crime statistics find that the incidence of crime victimisation reported during surveys of individuals is higher than reported crime rates—for example, many more women admit to being the victim of sexual assault than actually report the assault to police. Therefore, crime rates may be quite different, depending on the method used to identify victims.
- The limited verbal capabilities of people with intellectual disabilities may reduce the information that can be obtained about crimes against them, and the impact of the crime.

DESIGN ISSUES

Understanding and investigating the involvement of people with intellectual disability in crime, and their interactions with the criminal justice system, is a subspecialisation that poses special challenges within each of the disciplines of sociology, psychiatry, psychology, and criminology.

Research Design

True experiments, quasi-experiments, observational studies, and correlational research are quantitative research methods, whereas qualitative research "emphasises meaningful issues, rather than measurement" (Berglund, 2001, p. 8). Details of general issues surrounding research designs are available elsewhere; this chapter will focus upon specific issues of research design and measurement in criminological settings.

Participants

The restricted range of the subject populations that are sampled is an ongoing concern in psychological, criminological, and medical research, where studies rely heavily upon available populations. Clinical and correctional populations are typically enticed into participation by personal, interpersonal, and environmental incentives, giving rise to the question as to whether the results can be generalised to wider samples, especially when matching the sample with a control or comparison group is difficult. If there is no apparent bias in selection, and no targeting of special minority groups or units within the criminal justice system, there can be greater reliance on generalisations made on the basis of research results.

A further complicating issue is volunteer status. While the issue of possible bias from a volunteer sample is difficult for much research into intellectual disability (see above), drawing volunteers from among an offender population, especially in prison, has even more pitfalls. Generally, in community-based psychological research, volunteers tend to be younger, better educated, have higher occupational status, be higher in intelligence, and have a greater need for social approval while being more sociable, desirous of stimulation, less conventional in their behaviour, less authoritarian, more self-disclosing, and more maladjusted (Kazdin, 1992). This profile does not provide encouragement for researchers who hope that offenders with intellectual disabilities will volunteer for research. On the other hand, the demographic factors associated with being an offender are themselves atypical—offenders tend to be of low socio-economic status and intelligence, to be under-educated and illiterate young males, and to be disproportionately from some minority ethnic groups (Aboriginal in Australia, and black in the USA and UK) (Blackburn, 1993). The sample in any criminological research is therefore likely not to be representative of the community, and it is important that crime statistics about offenders with an intellectual disability not be extrapolated to this community group. Offenders with an intellectual disability tend to resemble other offenders more than they resemble non-offenders with an intellectual disability. The problems of sampling and obtaining participants should not be allowed to prohibit research, however. Important information can be obtained from samples, provided the limitations of extrapolation are recognised, and introduced bias is avoided. For example, prison studies of the prevalence of intellectual disability where participants are referred by correctional staff or prison psychologists, or the sample is from clinic patients within the prison, are clearly likely to be biased. Better sampling methods can include a reception sample of prisoners as they arrive at prison or a random sample called up from the prisoner list. In the latter design, even if an individual prisoner declines participation, the process goes randomly onto the next person, without introduced bias. While prisoners low in intelligence may be less likely to volunteer because they are reluctant to enter a study where their intellectual deficits are revealed, if they are called up on a "next-in-line" or random basis, there may be no differences in rates of participation. There is no clear evidence either way that proper sampling procedures, even though bedevilled by all of the limitations of volunteer participants, tend to increase or decrease the numbers of prisoners with intellectual disabilities who will participate.

Potential biases can be introduced by some methods of recruiting prisoners, however. Notices placed around the prison asking for volunteers will possibly disenfranchise those with an intellectual disability who cannot read. If the "true" purpose of a study is revealed, people with an intellectual disability may not want to participate—ethics committees may approve a slight obfuscation of the actual intent, by allowing information for prospective participants to describe the study as pertaining to educational background, for example. Announcements about the research over the loudspeaker system in a prison are likely to exclude prisoners with an intellectual disability, because they are more likely to have hearing impairment, or experience difficulty processing the verbal information and instructions about how to enrol in the study. Generally, prisoners are suspicious of research and want to know about the advantages (if any) to them of participation. Collaboration with a prisoner representative committee may be useful in motivating participants, and so may small rewards, agreed upon with the prison authorities and ethics committee, such as chocolate bars or personal toiletries.

Control and Comparison Groups

The types of control and comparison groups found in human research are legion—no-treatment, waiting-list, no-contact, placebo and attention-placebo, clinical trials, and non-randomly assigned groups, for example. In criminal justice settings, assigning individuals to the usual control conditions may not be ethical or feasible. Assigning participants to prison, hospital, or community-based sentence is the responsibility of the criminal justice system, not the researcher. Research design can employ comparison groups—for example, in comparing a new treatment with a standard treatment. Ethically, this is sound because all groups receive treatment, and the research design is not compromised to the point where results become meaningless or uninterpretable. Accurate description of both conditions is essential if the research is to meet that other important criterion, ability to be replicated. Too often, the description of the actual treatment or intervention is vague, "gilds the lily", or is dependent on the charisma and motivation of a single staff member.

Research in the criminal justice system often involves a group of special interest, such as murderers, or sex offenders with an intellectual disability. Other groups may be selected as comparison groups, and this is nearly always difficult—the decision has to be taken whether to compare the interest group with other offenders with an intellectual disability, with non-offenders with an intellectual disability, or with non-disabled offenders who have committed similar offences. The hypotheses to be tested, previous research findings, and practical and ethical constraints determine the characteristics of the comparison group.

Attrition is an important factor in determining the size of the groups. Not surprisingly, many participants are lost to follow-up in criminological research. Furthermore, ethical constraints can affect how energetic the follow-up can be. A participant may leave prison and get a job, and be unwilling to jeopardise this employment and living situation by participating in further data collection. Careful attention must be given to prediction of attrition and enrolment of a sufficiently large initial sample.

Sample Characteristics

Special difficulties can arise in criminological samples, such as the inclusion or exclusion of non-English-speaking participants. In an ideal research design, the tests and interviews should be administered in every participant's first language. Practical considerations mean that many psychometric tests are not available in different languages. Even non-verbal tests or subtests need some explanation, and cannot be administered to a totally non-English speaker without an interpreter. Non-verbal tests may not be completely culture-fair, and the culture-bias of tests is especially problematic when using instruments to assess adaptive behaviour. Research design has to be adapted to the requirements of a maximum-security institution in some instances. Furthermore, the logistics and costs of having interpreters in a prison setting are real barriers, especially when many languages may be spoken. Even in indigenous groups such as Australian Aborigines, there are many tribal languages and very few interpreters; therefore, compromises in research design have to be made. Exclusion of non-English speakers from research is a risky strategy, however, especially since lack of proficiency in English can disguise the presence of intellectual disability.

Gender balance is a perennial problem in criminological research because of the imbalance between males and females at every stage of the criminal justice system. Nevertheless, where possible, it is important to obtain a sample of women because their psychological (they are more likely to have a dual diagnosis, for example) and offence characteristics tend to differ significantly from their male counterparts (Hayes & McIlwain, 1988). Women with an intellectual disability can suffer dual discrimination. For example, women with an intellectual disability tend to be over-represented in "care" proceedings in children's courts, and receive differentially harsh outcomes. Children are more likely to be removed from these parents and made state wards (McConnell, Llewellyn & Ferronato, 2000). (No studies have been located of criminal charges of child neglect against women with an intellectual disability.) Women offenders are an under-investigated group, and more research needs to be directed towards women victims and offenders with an intellectual disability.

Lack of homogeneity of participants can limit interpretation of results and the ability to generalise from research findings. The subject group designated "intellectually disabled" may contain individuals with conditions of varying aetiologies, and is also likely to contain participants with dual diagnosis (see, for example, Keating, 2000), factors that can influence the response to interventions and the likelihood of recidivism.

ETHICAL ISSUES

Ethics in Criminological Research

Any criminological research is fraught with ethical dilemmas, exacerbated by the difficulties of conducting research involving people with intellectual disabilities. The limitations of the volunteer nature of the sample are discussed further below, yet non-volunteer participation is rare, except possibly in some health surveys where the health of the whole population (say, a prison survey of hepatitis) is important. Another important issue is informed consent to participation. Offenders with intellectual disability may be unable to participate in a study because they cannot understand the information given to them about the research, or provide informed consent themselves, and there is no legal guardian or parent who can give consent on their behalf. Those who might benefit most from participation in a study could be excluded because of the lack of consent. In some jurisdictions (most Australian states, Canada, and the USA, for example) a guardianship tribunal can consent on behalf of a person with an intellectual disability, provided the research is in the participant's best interests and unlikely to be harmful. The principles of beneficence, respect for persons, and justice are the basic ethical principles that ethics committees use in evaluating decisions about research proposals (Berglund, 2001).

Complex issues face researchers in this field. A participant may be in a relationship of potential dependency on the researcher or the institution, introducing an element of real or perceived coercion or inducement. If the researcher conducts the sole available programme for offenders with an intellectual disability, it can be difficult for the individual to refuse to participate in research evaluating the programme. The privacy and confidentiality of research data can be compromised if the researcher belongs to the staff of the service offering support to the individual, or if the researcher also performs a treatment role. The possibility of the participant's data being identified becomes real, if small groups or institutions are involved. Research in custodial environments is always fraught with the fear on the part of the participants that their personal data will be revealed to custodial staff, complemented by a desire on the part of the custodial staff to be apprised of any information that could be relevant to a breach of security or the behaviour of the inmate. The participant may reveal other offences to the researcher. These competing pressures render it difficult for the staff of a custodial institution to play the dual role of researcher, and yet they may be the only professionals who are able to collect research data in the circumstances. Research projects in custodial environments should be overseen by outside, independent research committees if they are to be untainted by privacy and confidentiality issues. Vulnerable subject populations can be exploited or at least over-researched. If the results of the research are to be applied to general community groups, the ethics and practical issues of using "convenient" institutional samples must be questioned (Berglund, 2001). Accurate analysis, careful interpretation of research findings, and publication of results form part of the element of justice in research, yet researchers in government agencies, particularly sensitive agencies such as corrective services, juvenile justice, police, and welfare, may be reluctant to publish findings that are thought to reflect negatively on that agency or government. The importance of collaboration with independent research units cannot be underestimated. If people with intellectual disabilities, offenders or victims of crime, are to be the subjects of study, at least they and their guardians and lobbyists should see the results of that research, and be able to use and learn from the results. Fair distribution of the outcomes of research is imperative.

Social Control

Criminal courts and prisons are institutions for social control; services for people with intellectual disability, once considered to have a social-control function, are now not designed so. When the two social agencies meet, one may take on the roles and values of the other; therefore, professionals and researchers in the field of intellectual disability must be vigilant in preserving their caring rather than controlling roles. Psychiatric nursing in prison reels under accusations of social control rather than caring (Polczyk-Przybyla & Gournay, 1999); secure hospitals debate the custodial versus the treatment role (Travers, 1997). Just as the role of the practitioner may be confused or difficult, so may the researcher's role. A desire to control the flow of information and social interactions, and to monitor the environment for potentially negative or disruptive consequences, may result in staff or researchers creating a "protective cocoon" around the clients with intellectual disability, and limiting risks (Todd, 2000). Social-control issues may also arise in relation to the following circumstances:

- research pertaining to medication and other interventions for behavioural control
- the effectiveness of treatment plans
- sole-gender residences or programmes
- antilibidinal medication and other methods of "controlling" sexual expression
- predictions of recidivism
- assessments of dangerousness
- making value judgements on behalf of clients about lifestyle issues (for example, that a secure hospital is preferable to prison, or that working is better than being unemployed).

The outcomes for clients must be balanced against the outcomes for the community generally. If a client faces the choice between imprisonment or participation in a research study on offending behaviour while residing in a group home, the latter may be the best option; however, the client may also make an informed decision that imprisonment is preferable to indeterminate detention in a secure hospital, or placement in a brutal institution where medication is used as a method of behavioural control.

An important issue is the labelling of the participants. After psychometric testing, a participant may receive a diagnosis of intellectual disability, whereas before he or she may have been regarded by others as, and had a self-image of being, a non-disabled person. Despite the advantages which may be available to them in the justice system—special police-interviewing precautions, issues of evidence during the trial, mitigation in sentencing, admission to treatment programmes, and legal protections for people with an intellectual disability in the criminal justice system—they may choose to eschew the label "intellectually disabled". The concept of "dignity of risk" must allow them this choice, even when researchers, carers, and lawyers feel that it is not in their best interests.

MEASUREMENT ISSUES

As with any rigorous research design, the measures chosen must be valid, reliable, and sensitive. Investigators are advised to use established psychometric instruments whose characteristics are established and standardised. Developing new measures may be essential in this field, however, because of the paucity of appropriate instruments; nevertheless, researchers need to remember that developing a properly normed and standardised instrument is a lengthy research project in itself. Self-report, observer ratings, and objective testing are three of the most widely used modalities; within these categories, the characteristics to be considered include the depth and breadth of the variables to be measured; stable or transient characteristics; direct or indirect measures; obtaining new information or using existing information or records, including medical records; and the format in which the data will be obtained. These measurement issues are common to most investigations of human behaviour. This section will discuss some of the specialist issues relevant to the study of offenders with an intellectual disability.

Response Characteristics

The accuracy of participants' responses during criminological research is often questioned; they may be suspected of "faking good" to present themselves in a better light or in an attempt to present a better picture of themselves in a court case, or "faking bad" to obtain a poor result because of some perceived advantage, such as being considered not responsible for their actions, or to obtain mitigation in sentencing. Although research may not bear directly upon any of these outcomes, the participants might think otherwise. Personality tests usually incorporate a scale that specifically assesses the degree to which clients are faking good or bad, along parameters such as agreeing with an item because of a desire to present themselves in a favourable light (such an item may be "I never lie"), the consistency of people's responses (to ensure that they are paying attention and not randomly responding), and agreeing with fictitious items (for example, indicating that a fictitious author is their favourite). Some self-report attitude and personality tests do not have validity scales, however; furthermore, personality assessment of people with intellectual disabilities is difficult owing to their verbal deficits and limited self-insight.

Faking bad consistently on an intelligence test is a more difficult undertaking than faking on a self-report instrument, with the participant requiring a comprehensive knowledge of the developmental stages of tasks such as hand–eye coordination, verbal skills, concentration span, sequencing ability, memory, and vocabulary in order to be consistent. In addition, the level of assumed limitation must be maintained throughout a fairly lengthy and demanding interview, and in each of the subtests and other confirmatory tests; furthermore, the participant would need access to the manual and to know the age-appropriate test norms (Hayes, 1997). In a research study, frequently used sources for verification of a client's history, such as school reports or reports from a general practitioner or other health worker, parents and siblings, former employers (if any), church workers, and welfare agencies, may not be available.

The question of whether non-disabled participants who were asked deliberately to "fake bad" could be distinguished from those with genuinely low intelligence was examined with the Gudjonsson Suggestibility Scale (GSS) (Smith & Gudjonsson, 1986). Those subjects who were asked to fake low ability on the GSS tended to give themselves away because they lacked knowledge about how the scale worked and what was expected. Fakers could produce false results fairly accurately when the aim of the subtest was clear, but when they did not know what was being assessed, they tended to give extremely low-level responses which were very different from the other subtests, and from the genuine low-ability participants. For the investigator attempting to detect faking, therefore, discrepancies between performances on different sections of the test would be an indicator that further confirmatory assessment procedures should be undertaken. Where possible, therefore, measurement instruments whose immediate purpose is not obvious should be selected, and confirmatory tests should be administered.

Apart from deliberate distortion, response bias on personality or attitude scales (especially sexual attitudes scales) can occur when participants answer in a socially desirable manner, or have a high need for social approval. Projective techniques can resolve many of the limitations of self-report scales, by measuring characteristics indirectly, but these tests (such as the Rorschach) may not be appropriate for use with participants of low intelligence, and they tend to be time-consuming to administer and score. Other measures that are less open to distortion include objective third-party behavioural assessments (many adaptive behaviour scales fall into this category), neuropsychological assessments, and psychophysiological measurements of state of arousal. The goals of the research and the practical issues of time, cost, and access to the sample population will influence the choice of instruments, and investigators must be able to justify their choice, and indicate the advantages and limitations of their chosen measurement tools.

Minimising the Effect of the Intervention

A major difficulty in criminological research is that the participants usually have an unstated motivation to participate, and may perceive, sometimes erroneously, that the research is going to affect them in some way. This situation can create unknown sources of bias. The prisoner's motivation may be as elementary as a desire to have contact with someone from outside the prison system, or for stimulation to break the boredom of the normal prison day. Even such a simple motive can affect the responses—prisoners may slow down their responses or exaggerate reactions in order to prolong the interaction with the researcher, thus affecting test results. On the other hand, they might minimise their problems to present themselves in the best possible light. If their performance is altered by awareness of the purpose of the study and the measures (and most consent forms will have to state the purpose of the research clearly, at the insistence of ethics committees), the problem of *reactivity* is occurring and must be addressed (Kazdin, 1992). Reactivity can be reduced by using a number of ways of measuring the same variables, some more apparent in their purpose than others. If the research aims allow, two different research settings can be used, where the motivation of the participants is different.

The influence of the investigator, while always an important feature of research with "vulnerable" populations, is especially important in criminological research—the investigator's age, gender, race, and ability to establish rapport can be critical. Unobtrusive observation is almost impossible in a custodial environment where the inmates know all the custodial staff, and where a stranger who is observing and making notes may be regarded with great suspicion. To minimise bias generated by the investigator's personal characteristics, a single investigator could be used; when multiple researchers are involved, each individual's results should be examined to ensure there is no consistent bias. Of critical importance is the training given to the researchers to ensure that they administer tests reliably, and respond consistently to questions from participants. The informal gossip network in an offender environment quickly spreads the word about discrepancies.

Observational studies are useful where a measure of a participant's baseline behaviour is essential, prior to intervention. Noting outbursts of anger, the frequency and type of social interaction, and reactions in certain situations can be of interest to the investigator, and a valuable research tool. Ethical issues surrounding consent to the observation have to be addressed with the participants or their legal guardian.

Archival research provides opportunities for long-term research on trends in incarceration and a wealth of other information that may be useful to the researcher in the field of intellectual disability in the criminal justice system. Researcher bias or reactivity to the researcher is not a factor. Potential pitfalls, however, are the change in terminology and diagnostic classifications over time, as well as the limitations of the original data. For example, records may note that a patient is "mentally retarded", yet offer no information about how that diagnosis was arrived at, and whether it was an impressionistic view of a staff member unqualified to offer such a diagnosis, or whether it was based on psychometric assessment. Similarly, categories of offence can change over time; rates of arrest for certain categories of crime and rates of reporting some crimes can also vary as a consequence of sociological and political factors. Consideration must be given to the reasons why some information was recorded and other information was ignored—there is a strong selectivity bias in all recorded data.

A significant and almost insoluble problem in research on offenders is that the behaviour of interest might not occur in the particular environment of a secure hospital or prison; a paedophile will not have access to children while in prison, and therefore the effectiveness of intervention programmes is impossible to assess directly. Indirect "markers", including self-esteem, denial, empathy, psychopathy, and problem-solving ability in a risk situation, can be utilised, but the relationship between these and the offending behaviour may be unclear. Longitudinal studies are important to follow up participants once they leave a supervised environment (Lindsay, Olley, Baillie & Smith, 1999). Nevertheless, non-recurrence of an offence may mean that the offender is better at covering his or her tracks and avoiding apprehension, and may not necessarily indicate that the participant no longer engages in the behaviour of interest.

PRACTICAL ISSUES RELATED TO CONDUCTING RESEARCH IN THE CRIMINAL JUSTICE SYSTEM

Cooperation with Criminal Justice Agencies

The major issues for investigators collaborating with government agencies are the following:

- time delays in obtaining ethical approval and implementing research projects
- lack of "real" cooperation in the following areas:
  (1) access to participants
  (2) privacy and confidentiality of participants' data
  (3) ownership of data
  (4) the right to publish research findings in academic journals.

Unless these issues are addressed at the time of initiation of the project, investigators may spend years undertaking research which is then not publishable within the academic community, and therefore is unavailable to the wider research community, and to those interested in the plight of people with intellectual disabilities in the criminal justice system. The issue of justice to the participants who gave their time must also be considered.

Research into offenders with an intellectual disability almost always requires some level of cooperation and negotiation with criminal justice organisations, even when the researcher works within the organisation. The organisation may welcome research, but may try to impose restrictions on the publication of results (see the section "Ethics in criminological research", above). Another issue is time investment. Working with corrective services, police, or courts, for example, can be time-consuming for the researcher, first, because several ethics committees have to approve the project, and, secondly, because the researcher has limited control over recruitment of participants and the rate of recruitment. Not surprisingly, research in custodial environments is particularly difficult. Once a project has been approved by the government agency, the research has to be implemented in a practical sense, and the researcher can find that the initial stages of implementation raise unexpected problems and limitations that have to be addressed without compromising ethics, research design, and confidentiality of participants' information. Frequently, the most vital cooperation must come from lower-level staff who are in charge of space allocation for the project or access to participants, and who may have least awareness of the importance of research to the organisation generally.

An example is a research study which was conducted in six magistrates' courts in New South Wales, Australia. The study is one of very few court cohort studies to have been undertaken; logistical difficulties are possibly a major reason for the paucity of research in the area. After approval was obtained from two ethics committees, each with slightly different requirements, magistrates gave permission for the study to be conducted in "their" courthouses. Levels of cooperation by court staff varied—in some courthouses, the researchers were allocated a private room for interviewing participants; in others, a corner of the foyer was made available. The practical problems of enrolling participants were enormous; on a day of great trauma and personal anguish, the day of their court appearance, people who were charged with offences were asked to participate in research and to provide some personal details. The personal characteristics, skills, and knowledge of the researchers at each courthouse were of paramount importance. Where the researchers were reticent or did not establish adequate rapport, participation rates plunged. In two courts where the researchers were known to participants in previous roles as indigenous support workers, participation rates neared 100%, and missing data rates were almost zero. An effective inducement was found to be offering participants the opportunity to have the results sent to their solicitor, so that the solicitor could organise a full-scale psychological or psychiatric assessment if the research results indicated the possibility of a mental abnormality or condition that required follow-up.

CONCLUSION

Research into the *prevalence* of people with an intellectual disability who come into contact with the criminal justice system continues to be an important area, because statistics are currently sparse, and there is a dearth of data allowing comparisons between different jurisdictions. The prevalence of suspects with an intellectual disability in police stations, rate of diversion out of the criminal justice system, rate of intellectual disability among persons appearing before courts, proportion of accused persons found unfit to be tried, case outcomes, utilisation of custodial and community-based sentences, types of crime committed, rates of recidivism, the significance of dual diagnosis, and gender differences are just some of the areas which require further research effort.

Outcome research concerning the *effectiveness of interventions* needs greater emphasis. Many studies have small participant groups, and lack the specific detail which allows replication in other populations. Following the model used by medical researchers undertaking clinical trials, investigators must cooperate internationally and between institutions, share their knowledge and expertise about interventions, design programmes that are carefully documented and can be implemented by others, and allow for long-term follow-up. In this way, participant numbers can be increased, allowing better analyses of within-group differences (gender, race, age, type of offence, dual diagnosis, and type of intervention). Longitudinal studies tracking factors contributing to subsequent involvement in the criminal justice system are vital, and can assist in establishing the effectiveness of early intervention programmes (key references are the sequence of papers reporting longitudinal outcomes for a birth cohort) (e.g., White et al., 1989).

In addition to creating bigger databases, with comparable variables and information, future research needs to concentrate upon investigating *theoretical explanatory concepts*, which can inform the design and implementation of preventative measures across a range of services including education, health and mental health, accommodation, and family support.

The ethical and practical dilemmas and problems are legion, yet the advantages of further research to the population of people with intellectual disabilities in contact with the criminal justice system are enormous, for the participants, as well as their families and carers, and for society in general.

REFERENCES

Berglund, C.A. (2001). *Health Research*. Melbourne: Oxford University Press.

Blackburn, R. (1993). *The Psychology of Criminal Conduct. Theory, Research and Practice*. Chichester: Wiley.

Brown, H. & Stein, J. (1997). Sexual abuse perpetrated by men with intellectual disabilities: a comparative study. *Journal of Intellectual Disability Research*, **41**, 215–224.

Grubb-Blubaugh, V., Shire, B.J. & Balser, M.L. (1994). Behavior management and offenders with mental retardation: the jury system. *Mental Retardation*, **32**, 213–217.

Hayes, S.C. (1996a). Recent research on offenders with learning disabilities. *Tizard Learning Disability Review*, **1**, 7–15.

Hayes, S.C. (1996b). Minorities—as victims and offenders. In K.M. Hazlehurst (Ed.) *Crime and Justice: Australian Textbook in Criminology* (pp. 317–348). Sydney: Law Book Information Services.

Hayes, S.C. (1996c). *People with an Intellectual Disability and the Criminal Justice System: Two Rural Courts* (5). New South Wales Law Reform Commission.

Hayes, S.C. (1997). Intellectual disability. In I. Freckelton & H. Selby (Eds) *Expert Evidence* (pp. 6-1351–6-1477). Melbourne: Law Book Co.

Hayes, S.C. (2000). *Hayes Ability Screening Index (HASI) Manual*. Sydney: Behavioural Sciences in Medicine, University of Sydney.

Hayes, S.C. & Craddock, G. (1992). *Simply Criminal* (2nd edn). Sydney: Federation Press.

Hayes, S.C. & McIlwain, D. (1988). *The Prevalence of Intellectual Disability in the New South Wales Prison Population: An Empirical Study*. Canberra: Criminology Research Council.

Hodgins, S. (1992). Mental disorder, intellectual deficiency, and crime. Evidence from a birth cohort. *Archives of General Psychiatry*, **49**, 476–483.

Kazdin, A. (1992). *Research Design in Clinical Psychology*. Boston, MA: Allyn & Bacon.

Keating, T.P. (2000). RESPECT-super (TM): a 7 step system to treat pedophiles who are mentally retarded, have mental illness, and physical handicaps. *Journal of Psychology and Human Sexuality*, **11**, 89–114.

Law, J., Lindsay, W., Quinn, K. & Smith, A. (2000). Outcome evaluation of 161 people with mild intellectual disabilities who have offending or challenging behaviour [Abstract]. *Journal of Intellectual Disability Research*, **44** (3 and 4), 360–361.

Lindsey, P. & Luckasson, R. (1991). Consent Screening Interview for community residential placement: report on the initial pilot study data. *Mental Retardation*, **29**, 119–124.

Lindsay, W., Marshall, I., Neilson, C., Quinn, K. & Smith, A. (1998a). The treatment of men with a learning disability convicted of exhibitionism. *Research in Developmental Disabilities*, **19**, 295–316.

Lindsay, W., Neilson, C., Morrison, F. & Smith, A. (1998b). The treatment of six men with a learning disability convicted of sex offences with children. *British Journal of Clinical Psychology*, **37** (Part 1), 83–98.

Lindsay, W.R., Olley, S., Baillie, N. & Smith, A.H.W. (1999). Treatment of adolescent sex offenders with intellectual disabilities. *Mental Retardation*, **37**, 201–211.

McConnell, D., Llewellyn, G. & Ferronato, L. (2000). *Parents with a Disability and the New South Wales Children's Court*. University of Sydney.

Polczyk-Przybyla, M. & Gournay, K. (1999). Psychiatric nursing in prison: the state of the art? *Journal of Advanced Nursing*, **30**, 893–900.

Smith, K. & Gudjonsson, G. (1986). Investigation of the responses of "fakers" and "non-fakers" on the Gudjonsson Suggestibility Scales (GSS). *Medicine, Science and the Law*, **26**, 66–71.

Todd, S. (2000). Working in the public and private domains: staff management of community activities for and the identities of people with intellectual disabilities. *Journal of Intellectual Disability Research*, **44** (Part 5), 600–620.

Travers, R.F. (1997). The future of Britain's high security hospitals. Primacy of patient care must be re-established as sole reason for hospitals' existence [Letter]. *British Medical Journal*, **314** (7094), 1622.

White, J.L., Moffitt, T.E. & Silva, P.A. (1989). A prospective replication of the protective effects of IQ in subjects at high risk for juvenile delinquency. *Journal of Consulting and Clinical Psychology*, **57**, 719–724.

CHAPTER 25

Emerging Trends in Methods for Research and Evaluation of Behavioral Interventions

J. Stephen Newton
University of Oregon, USA
and
Robert H. Horner
University of Oregon, USA

In a prescient article commemorating the twentieth anniversary of the *Journal of Applied Behavior Analysis*, Baer, Wolf and Risley (1987) described the continuing relevance of applied behavior analysis, and considered how the discipline might evolve over the next 20 years. As they noted, the hallmark of any applied discipline should be its effectiveness. Their discussion of intervention effectiveness as a dimension of applied behavior analysis touched on issues at the heart of current discussions about behavioral interventions in the field of intellectual disabilities, beginning with a recognition that definitions of effectiveness change over time, as do society's notions about the small- and large-scale social problems that should constitute the "applied" in applied behavior analysis.

Today, researchers who develop behavioral interventions on behalf of individuals with intellectual disabilities are being challenged as never before to adopt higher standards of effectiveness—for example, by demonstrating not only "small-scale" changes in behavior (such as reduction in the frequency, rate, and severity of an individual's challenging behavior), but also, as Baer et al. (1987) detailed, (a) involvement of consumers in identifying their personal goals before interventions are designed, (b) improvement in the consumer's overall quality of life, (c) adherence to social validity criteria, (d) achievement of acceptable cost-benefit ratios, (e) generalized outcomes, and (f) maintenance of intervention effects. This broadening perspective on intervention effectiveness has been accompanied by a call for—indeed, a *necessity* for—researchers to develop a technology of multicomponent, system-wide interventions capable of addressing this broader range of outcomes.

Thus, the mandate that researchers be *applied*, *technological*, *effective*, and capable of producing *generalized* outcomes has considerably broadened in its meaning; at the same

The International Handbook of Applied Research in Intellectual Disabilities. Edited by E. Emerson, C. Hatton, T. Thompson and T.R. Parmenter ISBN 0-471-49709-6.

time, the injunctions that they also be rigorously *behavioral*, *analytical*, and *conceptual* have remained steadfast (Baer, Wolf & Risley, 1968; 1987).

Broadly considered, this challenging agenda foretold four currently emerging trends in behavioral intervention. The purposes of this chapter are to describe these trends and to outline their implications for research and evaluation questions, measurement, design, and future directions.

EMERGING TRENDS IN BEHAVIORAL INTERVENTION

Behavioral interventions traditionally have focused on reduction of challenging behavior as the primary outcome. This focus led to research and evaluation emphasizing operational measures of problem behavior (Thompson, Symons & Felce, 2000), clarification of the behavioral mechanisms affecting behavior (Catania, 1992), and research designs documenting application of these mechanisms to produce socially important reductions in challenging behavior (Gersten, Schiller & Vaughn, 2000). While these emphases have been useful in defining basic principles of behavior and implementing successful interventions, they have not met the growing need for broad social impact. Too often behavioral interventions have produced reduction in challenging behavior without enhancing the broader living and learning options for an individual (Carr et al., 1999a).

More recently, some advocates and clinicians have looked to behavioral interventions to adopt a broader perspective, and their work has molded a technology of positive behavior support characterized by four trends that are reshaping the design of interventions. These trends are characterized by (a) incorporation of personally valued outcomes, (b) attention to behavioral and biological science, (c) development and implementation of comprehensive interventions, and (d) focus on organizational systems.

Personally Valued Outcomes

Among the most important themes affecting behavioral interventions, as well as the methods needed for research and evaluation of behavioral interventions, is the expansion of the outcomes used to define intervention success. Behavioral interventions are needed because problem behaviors, such as self-injury, aggression, property destruction, disruption, and defiance, create threats to basic safety and barriers to community-based learning and living. Any behavioral intervention deemed to be a success must, of course, demonstrate a reduction in the frequency and/or intensity of challenging behaviors. But reduction in problem behavior alone is insufficient. As the notion of "behavioral intervention" has given way to that of "behavioral support", expectations have expanded to include the organization of environments that not only result in reduction in problem behaviors, but also seek to foster (a) acquisition of adaptive skills, (b) maintenance of health and safety, and (c) access to activities and settings that uniquely define a reasonable quality of life for a person. The outcomes of behavioral interventions are now inexorably tied to the personal values of the person receiving support and his or her advocates. While everyone may agree that self-biting is bad for an individual, agreement about what replacement behaviors and alternative activities would be appropriate to support a rich living and learning opportunity will be personally defined by the individual and his or her family and advocates.

This expansion of the outcomes associated with behavioral intervention links the social values of those receiving support with the technical skills of those providing support. Not only has the range of outcome measures for an intervention been expanded, but the breadth of measures for problem behaviors has also increased. Reduction of problem behavior continues to be essential. But this becomes socially important only when the reduced level (a) allows access to other activities, (b) ensures safety, (c) generalizes across the full range of settings and conditions that affect the person's life, and (d) is maintained beyond the brief periods studied in most research reports to the years that mark the life of an individual.

Change in the outcomes used to assess behavioral interventions is forcing (a) inclusion of those receiving support into the selection of outcomes, (b) expansion in the array of outcomes expected, and (c) greater precision in the attention to issues of generalization and maintenance. Each of these influences has dramatic importance for future research and evaluation efforts.

Behavioral and Biological Science

As the language and outcomes of behavioral interventions are extended to discussions of support that result in "lifestyle impact" (Carr et al., 1999a; Reeve & Carr, 2000), care will be needed to ensure that the technology remains grounded in empirical science. Behavioral interventions should be the direct result of applying principles of human behavior to the social needs of citizens. Given the range and intensity of current behavioral needs, however, a tendency to proffer unproven interventions will continue. The need for ongoing research and evaluation will be essential both to document those procedures and approaches that can be empirically validated, and to identify interventions that cannot be validated.

As the outcomes of behavioral interventions have expanded, so, too, has the array of scientific sources of input. Among the most important are the roles of biological and health variables that affect problem behaviors (Cataldo & Harris, 1982; Carr & Smith, 1995; Kennedy & Thompson, 2000; Reiss, 2000). Future research will be expected to define better the interaction effects of biological variables on behavioral interventions, and to document the impact of psychopharmacology on problem behavior (both independently and in concert with behavioral interventions). These expectations have direct relevance to the measures and designs that will be needed to meet future needs.

Comprehensive Interventions

Early demonstrations of behavioral interventions were exciting because they documented that systematic application of behavioral principles, such as reinforcement, punishment, and stimulus control, was linked to change in behavior (Bijou, Peterson & Ault, 1968; Catania, 1992). Recent demonstrations have focused on the need for "comprehensive" interventions (Durand, 1990; Carr et al., 1994; Koegel, Koegel & Dunlap, 1996; Horner & Carr, 1997). Comprehensive behavioral interventions (a) address all problem behaviors that pose challenges to an individual, (b) address all times of day where problem behaviors are a barrier, and (c) incorporate multiple intervention procedures (such as environmental redesign, curricular revision, instruction on functionally equivalent appropriate behaviors, extinction of problem behaviors, and reinforcement of appropriate behaviors). The emphasis on comprehensive interventions is not new, but it has received renewed focus (Horner & Carr, 1997). The current commitment to reducing problem behaviors through preventive strategies (Carr et al., 1994; Koegel & Koegel, 1995; Carr et al., 1999a; Scotti & Meyer, 1999) not only expands the procedures in behavioral interventions beyond the use of programmed consequences, but also requires a much more complete focus on intervention design with multiple behavioral (and biobehavioral) elements.

Behavioral interventions in the twenty-first century will continue to be based on the science of behavioral and biobehavioral theory. It is more likely, however, that interventions will include procedures for changing the physical setting, activity patterns, social interaction patterns, instruction of new skills, and the traditional changes in consequences. This meshing of procedures will make it more difficult to conduct the kind of research that carefully documents the effects of a single-variable intervention. Research on behavioral interventions will need to become much more adept at documenting packages of procedures, teasing out the effects of package elements, and assessing the interaction effects associated with elements of multicomponent interventions (Carr et al., 1999a; Reeve & Carr, 2000).

Organizational Systems

Historically, research on behavioral interventions has emphasized the analysis of the behavioral mechanisms (and interventions based on the mechanisms) that affect problem behavior. This has been, and will continue to be, an important component of behavioral intervention research. However, we believe that behavioral interventions will not achieve social relevance until better attention is given to the "systems" variables that affect use of effective interventions (Colvin, Kame'enui & Sugai, 1993; Lewis & Sugai, 1999).

We now know that the use of a functional assessment is directly related to the improved effects of behavioral interventions (Scotti, Ujcich, Weigle, Holland & Kirk, 1996; Didden, Duker & Korzilius, 1997; Marquis et al., 2000). But it is much less clear what relevance this has for schools, communities, and workplaces. Recent research suggests that functional assessment information has little impact on the design of behavior-support plans if support personnel do not have training in behavioral theory (Hsiao & Albin, 2000; Mitachi & Albin, 2001). If a technology of behavioral interventions is to be complete, attention must be given to the variables that will make that technology available to families, children, adults, and communities in need. Organizational variables, such as (a) adequate personnel, (b) personnel who are trained in behavioral theory, (c) time for teams to meet and design plans, (d) expectation that behavioral assessment will precede behavioral intervention, (e) reporting of outcome measures, and (f) active supervision, will determine the extent to which proven behavioral interventions will be available in our society. Too little research has addressed the organizational systems needed to nurture and maintain the use of effective behavioral interventions. The assumption should not be made that behavioral procedures will be used in applied contexts simply because research evidence documents the effectiveness of the interventions.

In addition, behavioral interventions are being proposed beyond the traditional scope of a single individual. Discussion of "school-wide" interventions emphasizes procedures for teaching appropriate behavior without (a) waiting for documentation of problem behaviors or (b) conducting functional assessments. It must always be remembered that organizations do not "behave"; individuals behave. However, if behavioral interventions are to have the impact on society that they promise, the unit of behavioral interventions (and behavior analysis) must expand to include schools, communities, and workplaces (Biglan, 1995).

Understanding the systems variables that influence use of proven behavioral procedures and understanding how behavioral interventions can be applied to the social ecologies that make up schools, communities, and workplaces will be a daunting task. These efforts, however, hold the key to transforming behavioral interventions into a technology of broad impact across society. The challenge to define research and evaluation methods responsive to these broad perspectives will be a worthy endeavor.

We propose that research and evaluation methods addressing behavioral interventions will need to respond to these four emerging trends. The remainder of this chapter addresses the measurement and design implications that stem from these trends.

MEASUREMENT ISSUES ASSOCIATED WITH EMERGING TRENDS

Personally Valued Outcomes

The trend toward personally valued outcomes will require researchers to continue focusing on "technical" measures that demonstrate functional relationships between "small-scale" dependent variables (such as the frequency or rate of a challenging behavior) and the independent variables designed to affect them. However, researchers will also be called upon to gather measures that demonstrate the degree to which generalized outcomes and maintenance of intervention effects are achieved, both for these small-scale dependent variables and for the "personal", large-scale outcomes that define intervention effectiveness from the perspective of the consumer.

Personal Measures of Intervention Effectiveness

Perhaps the foremost issue in developing a behavioral intervention is the question of *what* to measure, because judgments about the effectiveness of an intervention will be based on its impact on the chosen dependent variables. Traditionally, in the case of individuals with severe challenging behaviors, identifying and defining measures (that is, the dependent variables) has rarely been an issue; indeed, developing operational definitions of challenging behaviors and identifying antecedent stimulus conditions under which the behaviors do, and do not, occur are universally accepted, essential features of the functional analysis or functional assessment process (Iwata, Dorsey, Slifer, Bauman & Richman, 1982; O'Neill et al., 1997; Carr, Langdon & Yarbrough, 1999b). After operational definitions have been developed, antecedent stimulus conditions have been identified, and an hypothesis about the function of the challenging behavior has been established (that is, the reinforcing stimuli have been tentatively identified), the veracity of the hypothesis can be tested by gathering direct observation measures of the challenging behavior under the relevant antecedent stimulus conditions. Or, in the case of functional analysis, the hypothesis can be tested by actually manipulating the antecedent and consequent stimulus conditions, and collecting direct observation measures of the targeted behavior under the manipulated conditions.

The trend toward personally valued outcomes, however, makes the issue of identifying and defining what to measure (or what *else* to measure) more complex. Researchers are being asked to broaden further the range of dependent variables to include not only challenging behaviors, but also aspects of a person's "quality of life", under the assumption that, ultimately, the effectiveness of an intervention should be judged not just in terms of reductions in challenging behavior, but also in terms of improvements in overall quality of life.

Person-Centered Planning and Quality-of-Life Measures

The focus on quality of life has resulted in people with disabilities, their families and social network members, and professionals working to create new processes and contexts in which a person's desired lifestyle can be identified and support for achieving lifestyle changes can be rallied. For example, the many varieties of "person-centered planning" (O'Brien, 1987; Mount & Zwernik, 1988; Vandercook, York & Forest, 1989; Smull & Harrison, 1992; Butterworth et al., 1993; Pearpoint, O'Brien & Forest, 1993) are designed to ensure that the person and those closest to the person define a high-quality lifestyle from their personal perspectives, and discuss and develop broad strategies that can create the conditions under which that desired future could be achieved.

Researchers developing behavioral interventions on behalf of individuals with challenging behaviors can honor the personal quality-of-life aspirations of individuals by incorporating quality-of-life measures into their research endeavors. There are at least two approaches to doing so. In cases where the research involves someone with whom person-centered planning has been done, the researcher can create dependent variables and measures that operationally define the "desired future" voiced by participants in the person-centered planning process. In cases where no such planning has been done, the researcher could solicit the services of someone trained in conducting person-centered planning to facilitate a meeting with the person and the person's family and friends. Such approaches could serve as informative precursors to a traditional functional assessment process by providing socially validated "secondary" dependent variables that complement the more traditional dependent variables (that is, challenging behaviors).

At present, few studies—particularly studies involving adults with challenging behavior—have included measures derived from a person-centered planning process. In a study that included students, Flannery and her colleagues with the Oregon Transition Systems Change project (Flannery et al., 2000) provided inservice training workshops on person-centered planning for educators, parents of individuals with disabilities, rehabilitation personnel, paraprofessionals, and case managers. The training consisted of: (a) description of the key features of person-centered planning; (b) description and modeling of an actual instance of one particular method of person-centered planning, Personal Futures Planning (Mount & Zwernik, 1988); (c) description and practice sessions using four other person-centered planning processes/tools; and (d) role-play of Personal Futures Planning to practice facilitation and recording skills.

Eight teachers and transition specialists who had participated in the training agreed to participate in a study examining the effects of the training. Likewise, 10 of the students served by these educators agreed to participate, along with their family members. Results obtained from the educators indicated that the individualized education program (IEP) meetings they conducted after the training were significantly more likely to include six of the nine key features of person-centered planning; data from students/families indicated that they found seven of the nine features were significantly more likely to be present after training. In responding to a satisfaction questionnaire, both educators and students/families indicated that they were significantly more satisfied with the post-training IEP meetings and the content of the IEPs. Finally, responses to a plan questionnaire demonstrated significant differences in the pretraining and post-training IEPs. More nonschool personnel (such as family members and community members) were involved in delivering IEP-related support to the student during implementation of the post-training IEP. In addition, IEP-related support was more likely to be provided in the evenings and on weekends during implementation of the post-training IEP. A significant drawback to the study, however, was the lack of data concerning whether the outcomes defined in the person-driven IEP were actually achieved.

Measures of Social Validity

Closely linked to the issue of quality-of-life measures is the matter of social validity. Wolf (1978) suggested that the acceptability of a behavioral intervention will be judged on the perceived social significance of its goals, the social appropriateness of its procedures, and the social importance of its effects. Schwartz and Baer (1991) have argued that social validity assessments/measures should be a standard part of any applied research methodology, and that such assessments should be conducted (a) prospectively, (b) throughout an intervention, and (c) at the end of the intervention.

Given that the purpose of a social validity assessment is to gather feedback from consumers regarding the acceptability of an intervention so that the intervention can be modified as necessary to increase its "survival value" (e.g., Albin, Lucyshyn, Horner & Flannery, 1996), it appears likely that developing interventions that include measures of improved quality of life—as defined by the consumer in, for example, a person-centered planning process—would improve the consumers' assessment of the social significance of the intervention's goals. And, to the extent that a functional relationship can be established between the intervention and an increase in the behaviors that define aspects of an improved quality of life for the consumer, one would also expect consumers' social validity assessment of the social importance of the intervention's effects to be favorable. That is, one would expect a high, positive correlation between measures of the degree to which a successful intervention is referenced to a consumer's definition of a desired future, and measures of a consumer's judgment of the social validity of the intervention's goals and results (Kazdin, 1977).

Quality-of-Life Frameworks and "Generic" Measures of Quality of Life

Some general frameworks have been developed for ensuring that the planning, implementation, and evaluation of services for individuals with developmental disabilities are referenced to measurable outcomes generally valued by society (such as community presence, community participation, and independence). Within this framework, outcomes and activities personally preferred by an individual (such as experiencing the outcome of "community presence" by attending a baseball game, experiencing the outcome of "community participation" by having one's best friend over for dinner, or experiencing the outcome of increased independence by learning to order and pay for a meal at a favorite restaurant) can be identified and supported (e.g., Meyer & Evans, 1989; Newton, Ard, Jr, Horner & Toews, 1996; Risley, 1996; Council on Quality and Leadership in Supports for People with Disabilities, 2000). These approaches, like those identified as "official" person-centered planning processes (O'Brien & Lovett, 1998), can be used to target and measure the degree to which individuals experience the lifestyle outcomes and activities they value. For example, Newton and Horner (1995) conducted a descriptive analysis that involved 33 participants with developmental disabilities from 18 residential programs whose staff had been taught to use the Residential Outcomes System (Newton et al., 1996), a system designed to increase the likelihood that residential services are developed, delivered, and evaluated according to the activities and outcomes personally valued by participants. The study was undertaken to determine what effect, if any, staff members' use of the system had on actual outcomes experienced by participants. Results demonstrated that after implementation of the system, participants experienced, on average, more community-based activities per week, had more activities with individuals other than (or in addition to) paid staff per week, and had larger social networks made up of more people identified as "friends" than before the implementation of the Residential Outcomes System.

A final approach to gathering measures of quality of life should be noted. It is not surprising that the ongoing discussion about quality of life in the field of developmental disabilities (e.g., Knoll, 1990; Goode, 1994; Hughes, Hwang, Kim, Eisenman & Killian, 1995; Schalock, 2000) has produced some standardized measurement instruments (Heal, Harner, Amado & Chadsey-Rusch, 1993; Schalock & Keith, 1993; Wehmeyer, 1995) that focus on these broad variables. Researchers working with individuals who have not participated in a person-centered planning process, and who are not receiving services within a framework that naturally incorporates a specific quality-of-life approach that includes a measurement component, might consider incorporating some "generic" measures of quality of life, derived from standardized instruments, into their work. For example, in a follow-up study of 85 individuals who 15 years before had moved from a rural community-based program (the mid-Nebraska program) to more independent housing and competitive employment settings, Schalock and Genung (1993) used (among other instruments) the Quality of Life Questionnaire (Schalock & Keith, 1993) to assess the individuals' current levels of independence, productivity, and community integration. Findings indicated that individuals who were no longer receiving formal MR/DD services (due in part to their higher functioning level and long-term placement success) were experiencing higher levels of independence and productivity than were the individuals who continued to receive such services. Individuals from the two groups did not experience significantly different levels of community integration.

"Technical" Measures of Intervention Effectiveness

Personal measures are, by definition, identified and defined by the consumer as indices of intervention effectiveness from his or her perspective. From the researcher's perspective, however, there are also "technical" measures that are important for evaluating both the internal validity of the intervention and the *extent* of its effectiveness. This technical focus includes gathering measures of generalized outcomes and maintenance of intervention effects.

Generalized Outcomes and Maintenance of Intervention Effects

In their seminal review of the generalization literature and categorization of its implied technology, Stokes and Baer (1977), for their purposes, defined generalization as "the occurrence of relevant behavior under different, nontraining conditions (that is, across subjects, settings, people, behaviors, and/or time) without scheduling of those same events in those conditions as had been scheduled in the training conditions" (p. 350). Although this pragmatic notion of generalization has been followed by calls to examine the actual behavioral principles that underlie generalized outcomes (Engelmann & Carnine, 1982; Horner, Bellamy & Colvin, 1984; Kirby & Bickel, 1988), the quest remains the same: implementing behavioral interventions in a manner that will result in an individual's emitting targeted adaptive behaviors—and omitting targeted challenging behaviors—across the range of nontraining settings, people, etc., that he or she typically encounters in daily home and community life. In light of the emerging trend that defines intervention effectiveness in terms of improvements in personally defined quality of life, researchers will be challenged to program their interventions so as to produce generalization (Albin & Horner, 1988; Dunlap, 1993), and to document their results via measures of generalized outcomes associated with adaptive behavior (e.g., Sprague & Horner, 1984; Doyle, Goldstein, Bourgeois & Nakles, 1989) and challenging behavior (e.g., Shore, Iwata, Lerman & Shirley, 1994). For example, O'Neill, Horner, O'Brien and Huckstep (1991) implemented assessment and intervention strategies based on a competing stimulus control framework (Horner & Billingsley, 1988) to address the problem behavior of grabbing eyeglasses exhibited by a young man with severe mental retardation. Results demonstrated that the frequency of eyeglass-grabbing behavior was reduced in both the classroom training setting and in nontraining, generalization probe settings (that is, work and community).

The issues of maintenance of intervention effects (that is, response maintenance) and generalized outcomes are closely linked. Indeed, response maintenance has often been referred to as "generalization across time" (e.g., Drabman, Hammer & Rosenbaum, 1979). There is continuing disagreement as to whether response maintenance involves (a) the complete withdrawal of "contrived" intervention contingencies (Boyce & Geller, 2001; Malott, 2001), (b) the formal "institutionalization" of intervention contingencies after researchers have withdrawn from the setting (e.g., Fox, Hopkins & Anger, 1987), or (c) the effect of natural contingencies that support the maintenance of responding in the community (Baer & Wolf, 1970). Regardless of how researchers conceptualize response maintenance, emerging trends will necessitate a focus on its programming and maintenance (Foxx & Livesay, 1984; Carr et al., 1999a). When the goal of an intervention is not only to demonstrate a functional relationship between independent and dependent variables but also to improve quality of life through achievement of large-scale personally valued outcomes, evidence for long-term response maintenance assumes great importance. Jensen, McConnachie and Pierson (2001) adopted such a long-term approach in their case study, which reported—over a 63-month period—reductions in the self-injury, assault, and property destruction behaviors of a 35-year-old man with autism and moderate mental retardation.

BEHAVIORAL AND BIOLOGICAL SCIENCE

Although the trend toward incorporating personally valued outcomes will call upon researchers to develop and implement new measurement strategies at the macrolevel, the trend toward attending to behavioral and biological science will ensure that researchers continue to focus their measurement efforts at the microlevel. At this point in the history of applied behavior analysis, procedures for operationally defining challenging behaviors and gathering measures of a behavior's frequency, rate, and severity are well understood (Cooper, Heron & Heward, 1987).

What is not so well understood, however, is how and when to gather measures that allow for investigating the relationship between biological conditions and challenging behavior, an area with great research potential. There is some research demonstrating that biological conditions may function as setting events for challenging behaviors (Carr & Smith, 1995; Kennedy & Meyer, 1996). O'Reilly (1997), for example, examined the possibility that otitis media might function as a biological setting event for the episodic self-injury of a 26-month-old girl with moderate developmental disabilities. Functional analyses conducted on days when otitis media was diagnosed as being present, and again on days when it was diagnosed as being absent, revealed that no self-injury occurred on the absent days.

It has been speculated that if challenging behavior is reliably predicted by physiological states, today's technology may make it possible to monitor and prevent such behavior via a feedback process (Romanczyk & Matthews, 1998). And there are undoubtedly many instances in which individuals with developmental disabilities who also experience psychiatric disorders are receiving both psychopharmacological treatments and behavioral interventions, but little research has been done to investigate the possibility of additive or synergistic effects being achieved by combining the two approaches (Lewis, Aman, Gadow, Schroeder & Thompson, 1996).

The most immediate measurement implication for this trend perhaps resides in the range of variables to be considered in the functional assessment process. As previously noted, the practice of functional assessment (and/or a functional analysis) is now recognized as a necessary precursor to development of an intervention, and manuals that may aid in the process of conducting a functional assessment are beginning to appear (Dunlap & Kincaid, 2001). One such manual (O'Neill et al., 1997) emphasizes the range of physical, social, and biological variables that may be worth probing in the functional assessment process, including an individual's medications, medical/physical conditions, sleeping patterns, and diet. Typically, this information is gathered in an interview. Although gathering such information may not, strictly speaking, constitute "measurement", the process is useful in scheduling subsequent direct observation and measurement for times when a possible setting event (and thus, possibly, the challenging behavior) is present.

COMPREHENSIVE INTERVENTIONS AND ORGANIZATIONAL SYSTEMS

The trends toward development and implementation of comprehensive interventions and the focus on organizational systems will likewise have an impact on measures gathered by researchers. Potentially relevant measures include those focused on the issues of (a) treatment integrity and contextual fit, and (b) cost-benefit.

Treatment Integrity and Contextual Fit

In a recent chapter, Gresham (1997) reminded readers that legitimate claims of a functional relationship between an experimenter-manipulated independent variable and subsequent change in a dependent variable are possible only when the intervention is implemented with accuracy and consistency. However, in summarizing reviews of the literature to determine the degree to which measures of treatment integrity had been included in 1237 journal articles published between 1968 and 1990 (Peterson, Homer & Wonderlich, 1982; Moncher & Prinz, 1991; Gresham, Gansle & Noell, 1993; Gresham, Gansle, Noell, Cohen & Rosenblum, 1993), Gresham noted that only 17.2% of the studies included such measures. In concluding his chapter, he recommended that researchers consistently include clear operational definitions of their independent variables, and gather and report direct observation measures of implementation (with, perhaps, supplemental measures of implementation gathered via self-monitoring, self-report, behavior rating scales, or behavioral interviews). Furthermore, he recommended that reviewers consider the issue of treatment-integrity data when making publication decisions.

Treatment integrity may be influenced by "contextual fit" (Albin et al., 1996) and "organizational culture" (e.g., Hatton et al., 1999). In cases where there is a poor fit between the elements of an intervention and (a) the person for whom the intervention is designed, (b) the people responsible for long-term implementation of the intervention, and/or (c) the "culture" within which service providers and service recipients interact, the fidelity of implementation may be poor. Thus, measures of treatment integrity are useful not only for documenting functional relationships between independent and dependent variables, but also for identifying and remedying poor treatment integrity, perhaps stemming from poor contextual or organizational fit.

There are at least two strategies that might improve the integrity with which an independent variable is implemented, either of which could be subjected to tests for empirical validation via measures of treatment integrity. First, it could prove wise to gather survey measures of contextual fit *prior to* implementation of a proposed intervention in order to gauge the likelihood that the intervention will be implemented as designed (Sandler, 2001). Behavioral interventions that are technically sound but unlikely to be implemented with fidelity are unlikely to produce the targeted small- or large-scale outcomes. Alternatively, it could prove beneficial to include individuals with disabilities, families, and support providers as active participants in the research enterprise, an approach often referred to as "participatory action research" (Vaughn, Dunlap, Fox, Clarke & Bucy, 1997; Meyer, Park, Grenot-Scheyer, Schwartz & Harry, 1998). Participants who were involved—from the beginning—in discussions of research questions; research methods; data collection; summarization, analysis, and interpretation of findings; and formulation of conclusions might be more likely to implement an intervention with fidelity.

Finally, as a prelude to designing an intervention—or as an area of research in its own right—some researchers may find it profitable to undertake an explicit examination of contingencies that govern staff behavior (e.g., Hastings & Remington, 1994; Mansell & Elliot, 2001), or of the organizational culture within which services are provided. For example, in conducting a study of the organizational cultures of five community residential programs serving individuals with developmental disabilities in the UK, Hatton et al. (1999) gathered questionnaire data from staff concerning their perceptions of the "actual" organizational culture (that is, the culture within which they currently provided services) and the "ideal" organizational culture. A comparison of data derived from the two questionnaires demonstrated that the greatest mismatches between staff ratings of actual and ideal organizational culture occurred with two of the nine organizational culture factors: rewarding staff for good performance and managing/resolving conflict within the organization, with the ideal organizational culture outperforming the actual in both cases. A further examination of the relationship between person–organization fit (that is, the degree of mismatch between staff members' ratings of their actual and ideal organizational cultures) and staff outcomes demonstrated that (for example) the poorest ratings of "fit" for each of the nine organizational culture factors were strongly associated with staff members' feelings of being trapped in the organization. The researchers speculate that these findings may indicate that the behavior of support staff may be more readily improved by developing a productive organizational culture than by attempting to alter the values of individual staff members.

Given the trends toward development and implementation of comprehensive interventions and a focus on the organizational systems within which interventions are embedded, researchers seeking to satisfy Gresham's appeal for detailed operational definitions of independent variables, accompanied by measures of the degree to which those variables are implemented with integrity, may find the documentation effort to be complex. It could prove daunting—but worthwhile—to document (a) individual elements of a comprehensive treatment package, (b) any intervention-related changes in the structure of the organization responsible for continued implementation of the intervention (such as an increased staff-to-participant ratio or a special program for familiarizing new staff with a participant's preferences, dislikes, and personally valued outcomes), and (c) innovations in the service delivery system. For example, as federal and state systems serving individuals with developmental disabilities make formal efforts to become more person-centered, behavioral interventions may be implemented in the context of service brokerage models, individualized funding, and increased levels of natural support (Roeher Institute, 1991; Howe, Horner & Newton, 1998; Ohtake & Chadsey, 2001; Simon-Rusinowitz et al., 2001). In the interest of providing information that addresses the issue of external validity, researchers will want to describe, if not measure, organization and system variables that may influence the effectiveness of a comprehensive intervention. This issue will become particularly important in cases where researchers have an opportunity to work with pilot programs whose outcomes may foreshadow a broad systems-change "rollout".

Cost-benefit

In all likelihood, measures of financial cost-benefit will assume importance only as secondary dependent variables (Kee, 1994; Schalock, 2001). But given the trend toward attending to comprehensive interventions and organizational systems, such measures may become more prominent. For example, although few administrators will raise questions about the "cost-benefit" associated with implementing a small-scale intervention that employs, say, differential reinforcement of incompatible behavior (DRI), almost all administrators will raise questions about adopting an intervention that necessitates changing staffing patterns (for example, adding additional staff so that a person has guaranteed access to community-based activities at least three evenings each week).

Of course, questions about cost-benefit are secondary to demonstrations of functional relationships, but once an intervention has proven to be effective, it is relevant to ask questions such as, "How much does it cost to produce this outcome?", "How much would it cost to implement this intervention on a more widespread basis?", and "What are the financial implications of permanently maintaining this intervention?" Researchers or evaluators working in the program- and systems-change arenas will do well to attend not only to traditional evaluation foci, such as context, input, process, and products (Stufflebeam, 1983), but also to the cost-benefit associated with an intervention (Conley, Rusch, McCaughrin & Tines, 1989; Howe et al., 1998; Rudolph, Lakin, Oslund & Larson, 1998). For example, Knobbe, Carey, Rhodes and Horner (1995) conducted a cost-benefit analysis that involved an examination of the public program costs (and lifestyle benefits) incurred by 11 individuals with severe/profound mental retardation and significant problem behaviors at two points in time: (a) at the time the individuals lived in a large, state-run institution and (b) after the same individuals had moved to small, community-based homes. Results from the analysis demonstrated that the community-based alternative produced a slight savings in public program costs and significant changes in lifestyle benefits for the participants (such as larger social networks and increased community activities).

DESIGN ISSUES ASSOCIATED WITH EMERGING TRENDS

The four emerging trends have implications for experimental design, because in some cases they present technical challenges to the mandate that behavior analysis remain rigorously *behavioral*, *analytical*, and *conceptual*. A researcher's deployment of experimental designs is, of course, concerned with the second and third of these dimensions: creating a context in which there is the opportunity to demonstrate convincingly that a dependent variable is functionally related—in a way that makes sense conceptually—to the manipulation of an independent variable. It is probable that the trend toward continuing to focus on behavioral science while incorporating attention to the biological sciences will present the least challenge to remaining analytical and conceptual within the context of traditional single-case experimental designs. Such designs have served behavior analysis well (e.g., Hersen & Barlow, 1976), including the analysis of challenging behavior associated with biological/physiological setting events (O'Reilly, 1997; O'Reilly, Lacey & Lancioni, 2000).

Issues Complicating the Use of Traditional Single-Case Designs

Bigger challenges will arise, however, as researchers confront the macrolevel issues associated with the other major trends (personally valued outcomes, development and implementation of comprehensive interventions, and focus on organizational systems), which strain the conventions of single-case designs. Baer et al. (1987) recognized the potentially limiting effect of traditional single-case research designs, noting that over time they have become codified with rigid sets of rules. Baer et al. (1987) concluded their reflection on the issue by stating, "Perhaps the important point is that convincing designs should be more important than 'proper' designs" (p. 320).

Of course, one approach to dealing with the emerging trends would be for researchers to continue using "proper" single-case designs to search for functional relationships between microlevel independent and dependent variables, while regarding the macrolevel independent variables as potentially important but (a) unmanipulable, and therefore (b) not amenable to analysis, and, thus, (c) beyond the reach of behavior analysis. For example, Risley (1996) has suggested that conditions for individuals with developmental disabilities could be improved—and problem behaviors reduced—if one provided support that began with flexible funding, cooperation from a team of significant others, and the use of "life arrangement" strategies that addressed an individual's personally valued outcomes. Researchers who work in situations where such macrolevel variables have been employed, but who regard them as intractable to analysis, could simply address an individual's "residual" challenging behaviors at the microlevel via traditional behavior analysis, deploying single-case designs. There may be a certain wisdom in adopting this approach, given that the trend toward comprehensive interventions may result in the development of packages of independent variables that include both setting events and large-scale organizational or systems variables seemingly not amenable to analysis via traditional, fast-paced multielement designs (Hains & Baer, 1989; Kennedy & Itkonen, 1993; Horner, Vaughn, Day & Ard, Jr, 1996; Vollmer & Van Camp, 1998). Note, however, that despite such difficulties, Carr et al. (1999) have implemented comprehensive, multicomponent interventions consisting of building rapport, providing functional communication training, building tolerance for delay of reinforcement, embedding "demands" in a positive context, and providing choices; and they have analyzed such interventions within the context of a multiple-probe design (Horner & Baer, 1978). Larger challenges may await researchers who also incorporate broad "systems change" variables into their multicomponent approaches (e.g., Emerson, McGill & Mansell, 1994).

There is a further problem associated with analyzing macrolevel variables: when intervention effectiveness is measured in terms of generalized outcomes and longitudinal maintenance of personally valued outcomes, there will probably be a "scaffolding" of interventions over time, with one intervention being built on another, each perhaps producing an effect that may be improved upon by the next. This arrangement naturally introduces the problem of multiple-treatment interference (Barlow & Hersen, 1984). Of course, at some level, researchers are also likely to agree that multiple treatment interference is simply a fact of life to be controlled pragmatically, as best one can. In effect, anyone with a behavioral history is a beneficiary (or a victim) of multiple treatment interference, and implementation of any programmed intervention always takes place against that backdrop.

How Could We Proceed?

Naturally, the application of a research design presupposes precise, operationally defined measures stemming from accurate descriptions and observations of relevant variables. The foregoing discussion suggests that the emerging trends will test researchers' abilities to remain precise as they are called upon to deal with macrolevel independent and dependent variables. Although controversial, researchers may need to consider the possibility that our ability to describe accurately and (potentially) manipulate large-scale independent variables could profit from an initial application of longitudinal case-study designs (US General Accounting Office, 1990; Yin, 1994; Kazdin, 1998). For example, it may be important to develop accurate descriptions of the implementation of large-scale variables such as (a) individualized funding, (b) social-support networks, and (c) person-centered planning, rather than treating them as background variables against which a microlevel intervention targeted at challenging behavior could be implemented and assessed.

Accurate description of such variables could lead to development of more precise operational definitions and measurement strategies that would subsequently allow the variables to be examined within the context of conventional research designs. For example, Holburn and his colleagues have argued that research and practice would benefit from a better description of the process and outcomes of person-centered planning (Holburn, 1997; Holburn, Jacobson, Vietze, Schwartz & Sersen, 2000). The scaffolding of a comprehensive intervention that incorporated person-centered planning might proceed by initially treating it as a dependent variable and manipulating an independent variable (such as training) designed to result in the team of person-centered planners engaging in the behaviors, and producing the permanent products, that constitute "true" person-centered planning. Next, person-centered planning would be treated as the independent variable and could be manipulated (accompanied by measures of treatment fidelity) to determine whether the target person with developmental disabilities more frequently engages in the behaviors that operationally define his or her personally valued outcomes. Perhaps such a strategy could also be employed to examine other macrolevel independent variables, such as implementation of support brokerages, individualized funding, and the use of natural support. Although cumbersome and time-consuming, accurate description of large-scale variables, followed by an examination of their "scaffolding", could possibly be accommodated within the context of conventional multiple-baseline designs.

As interventions become more comprehensive, the units of analysis may expand, and researchers may find themselves focusing on changing "cultural practices", with dependent variables being measured in terms of the incidence or prevalence of target behaviors (Biglan, 1995). When this is the case, researchers may have to consider the possibility of using "old-fashioned", quasi-experimental, interrupted time-series designs (Campbell, 1969; Cook & Campbell, 1979). In some cases, even when the unit of analysis is still the individual person but the focus is longitudinal, researchers may even consider adopting "new-fangled" designs incorporating, for example, hierarchical linear modeling (Bryk & Raudenbush, 1992; Dunst & Trivette, 1994). Although the work will still be behavioral, the goal will still be the prediction and influence of behavior, and the measures will still be gathered and analyzed at the level of the single case (albeit, perhaps, a *large* single case), analysis per se may have left the realm of applied behavior analysis as we currently know it. The question is: Will the analysis be convincing, even if it is not "proper"?

SUMMARY

Researchers working in the area of behavioral interventions for individuals with intellectual disabilities are being challenged to adopt higher standards of intervention effectiveness. These new standards stem, in part, from four emerging trends: (a) incorporation of personally valued outcomes, (b) attention to both the behavioral and biological sciences, (c) development and implementation of comprehensive interventions, and (d) a focus on organizational systems. These trends have implications for both measurement and design.

Demonstrations of intervention effectiveness will be required to focus on personal and technical measures associated with both small- and large-scale variables. With regard to personal measures, researchers will be called upon to demonstrate that an intervention produces not only a reduction in challenging behavior, but also an increase in the behaviors that define an individual's personally valued outcomes (that is, quality of life). Technical measures will be required to demonstrate that an intervention achieves generalized outcomes and beneficial effects that are maintained. For purposes of improving the implementation of an intervention in a given setting, and for purposes of improving external validity, measures of treatment integrity and contextual fit will become increasingly important.

The design of research will also be affected. Although traditional single-case designs (such as multiple baselines) will continue to be instrumental in demonstrating the internal validity of an intervention at the "small scale", implementation of comprehensive interventions and the increasing focus on organizational systems may induce researchers to consider an initial use of case-study and quasi-experimental designs to improve description and to hone measures. The "scaffolding" of interventions to produce improvements in a person's overall quality of life may require several iterations of design and intervention, making it difficult to interpret effectiveness. This is likely to force researchers to exercise new creativity in the design of research.

The behaviors and outcomes that are now considered socially important differ in scale from those of two decades ago. The precision that is a hallmark of behavior analysis has never been more challenged by, or more important to, how intervention effectiveness is currently to be defined and confirmed.

ACKNOWLEDGMENT

The development of this chapter was supported in part by Grant No. H326S980003 and Grant No. H133B980005-00 funded by the US Department of Education, Office of Special Education Programs. Opinions expressed herein do not necessarily reflect the position of the US Department of Education, and such endorsements should not be inferred.

REFERENCES

Albin, R.W. & Horner, R.H. (1988). Generalization with precision. In R.H. Horner, G. Dunlap & R.L. Koegel (Eds) *Generalization and Maintenance: Life-Style Changes in Applied Settings* (pp. 99–120). Baltimore, MD: Brookes.

Albin, R.W., Lucyshyn, J.M., Horner, R.H. & Flannery, K.B. (1996). Contextual fit for behavioral support plans: a model for "goodness of fit". In L.K. Koegel, R.L. Koegel & G. Dunlap (Eds) *Positive Behavioral Support: Including People with Difficult Behavior in the Community* (pp. 81–98). Baltimore, MD: Brookes.

Baer, D.M. & Wolf, M.M. (1970). The entry into natural communities of reinforcement. In R. Ulrich, T. Stachnik & J. Mabry (Eds) *Control of Human Behavior*, vol. 2. *From Cure to Prevention* (pp. 319–324). Glenview, IL: Scott Foresman.

Baer, D.M., Wolf, M.M. & Risley, T.R. (1968). Some current dimensions of applied behavior analysis. *Journal of Applied Behavior Analysis*, **1**, 91–97.

Baer, D.M., Wolf, M.M. & Risley, T.R. (1987). Some still-current dimensions of applied behavior analysis. *Journal of Applied Behavior Analysis*, **20**, 313–327.

Barlow, D.H. & Hersen, M. (1984). *Single Case Experimental Designs: Strategies for Studying Behavior Change* (2nd edn). New York: Pergamon.

Biglan, A. (1995). *Changing Cultural Practices: A Contextualist Framework for Intervention Research.* Reno, NV: Context Press.

Bijou, S.W., Peterson, R.F. & Ault, M.H. (1968). A method to integrate descriptive and experimental field studies at the level of data and empirical concepts. *Journal of Applied Behavior Analysis*, **1**, 175–191.

Boyce, T.E. & Geller, E.S. (2001). Applied behavior analysis and occupational safety: the challenge of response maintenance. *Journal of Organizational Behavior Management*, **21**, 31–60.

Butterworth, J., Hagner, D., Heikkinen, B., Faris, S., DeMello, S. & McDonough, K. (1993). *Whole Life Planning: A Guide for Organizers and Facilitators.* Boston, MA: Institute for Community Inclusion, Children's Hospital.

Byrk, A.S. & Raudenbush, S.W. (1992). *Hierarchical Linear Models: Applications and Data Analysis Methods.* Newbury Park, CA: Sage.

Campbell, D.T. (1969). Reforms as experiments. *American Psychologist*, **24**, 409–429.

Carr, E.G., Horner, R.H., Turnbull, A.P., Marquis, J.G., Magito McLaughlin, D., McAtee, M.L., et al. (1999a). *Positive Behavior Support for People with Developmental Disabilities: A Research Synthesis.* Washington, DC: American Association on Mental Retardation.

Carr, E.G., Langdon, N.A. & Yarbrough, S.C. (1999b). Hypothesis-based intervention for severe problem behavior. In A.C. Repp & R.H. Horner (Eds) *Functional Analysis of Problem Behavior: From Effective Assessment to Effective Support* (pp. 9–31). Belmont, CA: Wadsworth.

Carr, E.G., Levin, L., McConnachie, G., Carlson, J.I., Kemp, D.C. & Smith, C.E. (1994). *Communication-Based Intervention for Problem Behavior: A User's Guide for Producing Positive Change.* Baltimore, MD: Brookes.

Carr, E.G., Levin, L., McConnachie, G., Carlson, J.I., Kemp, D.C., Smith, C.E., et al. (1999). Comprehensive multisituational intervention for problem behavior in the community: long-term maintenance and social validation. *Journal of Positive Behavior Interventions*, **1**, 5–25.

Carr, E.G. & Smith, C.E. (1995). Biological setting events for self-injury. *Mental Retardation and Developmental Disabilities Research Reviews*, **1**, 94–98.

Cataldo, M.F. & Harris, J. (1982). The biological basis of self-injury in the mentally retarded. *Analysis and Intervention in Developmental Disabilities*, **7**, 21–39.

Catania, C. (1992). *Learning*. Englewood Cliffs, NJ: Prentice-Hall.

Colvin, G., Kame'enui, E.J. & Sugai, G. (1993). Reconceptualizing behavior management and school-wide discipline in general education. *Education and Treatment of Children*, **16**, 361–381.

Conley, R.W., Rusch, F.R., McCaughrin, W.B. & Tines, J. (1989). Benefits and costs of supported employment: an analysis of the Illinois supported employment project. *Journal of Applied Behavior Analysis*, **22**, 441–447.

Cook, T.D. & Campbell, D.T. (1979). *Quasi-Experimentation: Design and Analysis Issues for Field Settings.* Boston, MA: Houghton Mifflin.

Cooper, J.O., Heron, T.W. & Heward, W.L. (1987). *Applied Behavior Analysis.* Columbus, OH: Merrill.

Council on Quality and Leadership in Supports for People with Disabilities (2000). *Personal Outcome Measures: 2000 Edition.* Towson, MD: Author.

Didden, R., Duker, P.C. & Korzilius, H. (1997). Meta-analytic study on treatment effectiveness for problem behaviors with individuals who have mental retardation. *American Journal on Mental Retardation*, **101**, 387–399.

Doyle, P.J., Goldstein, H., Bourgeois, M.S. & Nakles, K.O. (1989). Facilitating generalized requesting behavior in Broca's aphasia: an experimental analysis of a generalization training procedure. *Journal of Applied Behavior Analysis*, **22**, 157–170.

Drabman, R.S., Hammer, D. & Rosenbaum, M.S. (1979). Assessing generalization in behavior modification with children: the Generalization Map. *Behavioral Assessment*, **1**, 203–219.

Dunlap, G. (1993). Promoting generalization: current status and functional considerations. In R. Van Houten & S. Axelrod (Eds) *Behavior Analysis and Treatment* (pp. 269–296). New York: Plenum.

Dunlap, G. & Kincaid, D. (2001). The widening world of functional assessment: comments on four manuals and beyond. *Journal of Applied Behavior Analysis*, **34**, 365–377.

Dunst, C.J. & Trivette, C.M. (1994). Methodological considerations and strategies for studying the long-term effects of early intervention. In S.L. Friedman & H.C. Haywood (Eds) *Developmental Follow-Up: Concepts, Domains, and Methods* (pp. 277–313). San Diego, CA: Academic Press.

Durand, V.M. (1990). *Severe Behavior Problems: A Functional Communication Training Approach.* New York: Guilford.

Emerson, E., McGill, P. & Mansell, J. (Eds) (1994). *Severe Learning Disabilities and Challenging Behavior: Designing High Quality Services.* London: Chapman & Hall.

Engelmann, S. & Carnine, D. (1982). *Theory of Instruction: Principles and Applications.* New York: Irvington.

Flannery, K.B., Newton, J.S., Horner, R.H., Slovic, R.B., Blumberg, R. & Ard, W.R. Jr (2000). The impact of person centered planning on the content and organization of individual supports. *Career Development for Exceptional Individuals*, **23**, 123–137.

Fox, D.K., Hopkins, B.L. & Anger, W.K. (1987). The long-term effects of a token economy on safety performance in open-pit mining. *Journal of Applied Behavior Analysis*, **20**, 215–224.

Foxx, R.M. & Livesay, J. (1984). Maintenance of response suppression following overcorrection: a 10-year retrospective examination of eight cases. *Analysis and Intervention in Developmental Disabilities*, **4**, 65–79.

Gersten, R., Schiller, E.P. & Vaughn, S. (Eds) (2000). *Contemporary Special Education Research: Syntheses of the Knowledge Base on Critical Instructional Issues.* Mahwah, NJ: Erlbaum.

Goode, D. (Ed.) (1994). *Quality of Life for Persons with Disabilities: International Perspectives and Issues.* Cambridge, MA: Brookline Books.

Gresham, F.M. (1997). Treatment integrity in single-subject research. In R.D. Franklin, D.B. Allison & B.S. Gorman (Eds) *Design and Analysis of Single-Case Research* (pp. 93–117). Mahwah, NJ: Erlbaum.

Gresham, F.M., Gansle, K. & Noell, G. (1993). Treatment integrity in applied behavior analysis in children. *Journal of Applied Behavior Analysis*, **26**, 257–263.

Gresham, F.M., Gansle, K., Noell, G., Cohen, S. & Rosenblum, S. (1993). Treatment integrity of school-based behavioral intervention studies: 1980–1990. *School Psychology Review*, **22**, 254–272.

Hains, A.H. & Baer, D.M. (1989). Interaction effects in multielement designs: inevitable, desirable, and ignorable. *Journal of Applied Behavior Analysis*, **22**, 57–69.

Hastings, R.P. & Remington, B. (1994). Rules of engagement: toward an analysis of staff responses to challenging behavior. *Research in Developmental Disabilities*, **15**, 279–298.

Hatton, C., Rivers, M., Mason, H., Mason, L., Emerson, E., Kiernan, C., et al. (1999). Organizational culture and staff outcomes in services for people with intellectual disabilities. *Journal of Intellectual Disability Research*, **43**, 206–218.

Heal, L.W., Harner, C., Amado, A.R.N. & Chadsey-Rusch, J. (1993). *The Lifestyle Satisfaction Scale.* Worthington, OH: IDS Publishing.

Hersen, M. & Barlow, D.H. (1976). *Single Case Experimental Designs: Strategies for Studying Behavior Change.* New York: Pergamon.

Holburn, S. (1997). A renaissance in residential behavior analysis? A historical perspective and a better way to help people with challenging behavior. *Behavior Analyst*, **20**, 61–85.

Holburn, S., Jacobson, J.W., Vietze, P.M., Schwartz, A.A. & Sersen, E. (2000). Quantifying the process and outcomes of person-centered planning. *American Journal on Mental Retardation*, **105**, 402–416.

Horner, R.D. & Baer, D.M. (1978). Multiple-probe technique: a variation of the multiple baseline. *Journal of Applied Behavior Analysis*, **11**, 189–196.

Horner, R.H., Bellamy, G.T. & Colvin, G.T. (1984). Responding in the presence of nontrained stimuli: implications of generalization error patterns. *Journal of the Association for Persons with Severe Handicaps*, **9**, 287–295.

Horner, R.H. & Billingsley, F.F. (1988). The effect of competing behavior on the generalization and maintenance of adaptive behavior in applied settings. In R.H. Horner, G. Dunlap & R.L. Koegel (Eds) *Generalization and Maintenance: Life-Style Changes in Applied Settings* (pp. 197–220). Baltimore, MD: Brookes.

Horner, R.H. & Carr, E.G. (1997). Behavioral support for students with severe disabilities: functional assessment and comprehensive intervention. *Journal of Special Education*, **31**, 84–109.

Horner, R.H., Vaughn, B.J., Day, H.M. & Ard, W.R. Jr (1996). The relationship between setting events and problem behavior: expanding our understanding of behavioral support. In L.K. Koegel, R.L. Koegel & G. Dunlap (Eds) *Positive Behavioral Support: Including People with Difficult Behavior in the Community* (pp. 381–401). Baltimore, MD: Brookes.

Howe, J., Horner, R.H. & Newton, J.S. (1998). A comparison of supported living and traditional residential services in the State of Oregon. *Mental Retardation*, **36**, 1–11.

Hsiao, Y. & Albin, R. (2000). The effect of functional assessment information on the behavioral support recommendations for school personnel. In T. Lewis-Palmer (Chair), *Functional Behavioral Assessment in Schools*. Symposium conducted at the 26th annual convention of the Association for Behavior Analysis, Washington, DC.

Hughes, C., Hwang, B., Kim, J., Eisenman, L.T. & Killian, D.J. (1995). Quality of life in applied research: a review and analysis of empirical measures. *American Journal on Mental Retardation*, **99**, 623–641.

Iwata, B.A., Dorsey, M.F., Slifer, K.J., Bauman, K.E. & Richman, G.A. (1982). Toward a functional analysis of self-injury. *Analysis and Intervention in Developmental Disabilities*, **2**, 3–20.

Jensen, C.C., McConnachie, G. & Pierson, T. (2001). Long-term multicomponent intervention to reduce severe problem behavior: a 63-month evaluation. *Journal of Positive Behavior Intervention*, **3**, 225–236.

Kazdin, A.E. (1977). Assessing the clinical or applied importance of behavior change through social validation. *Behavior Modification*, **1**, 427–452.

Kazdin, A.E. (1998). *Research Design in Clinical Psychology* (3rd edn). Boston, MA: Allyn & Bacon.

Kee, J.E. (1994). Benefit-cost analysis in program evaluation. In J.S. Wholey, H.P. Hatry & K.E. Newcomer (Eds) *Handbook of Practical Program Evaluation* (pp. 456–491). San Francisco, CA: Jossey-Bass.

Kennedy, C.H. & Itkonen, T. (1993). Effects of setting events on the problem behavior of students with severe disabilities. *Journal of Applied Behavior Analysis*, **26**, 321–327.

Kennedy, C.H. & Meyer, K.A. (1996). Sleep deprivation, allergy symptoms, and negatively reinforced problem behavior. *Journal of Applied Behavior Analysis*, **29**, 133–135.

Kennedy, C.H. & Thompson, T. (2000). Health conditions contributing to problem behavior among people with mental retardation and developmental disabilities. In M.L. Wehmeyer & J.R. Patton (Eds) *Mental Retardation in the 21st Century* (pp. 211–231). Austin, TX: Pro-Ed.

Kirby, K.C. & Bickel, W.K. (1988). Toward an explicit analysis of generalization: a stimulus control interpretation. *Behavior Analyst*, **11**, 115–129.

Knobbe, C.A., Carey, S.P., Rhodes, L. & Horner, R.H. (1995). Benefit-cost analysis of community residential versus institutional services for adults with severe mental retardation and challenging behaviors. *American Journal on Mental Retardation*, **99**, 533–541.

Knoll, J.A. (1990). Defining quality in residential services. In V.J. Bradley & H.A. Bersani (Eds) *Quality Assurance for Individuals with Developmental Disabilities: It's Everybody's Business* (pp. 235–261). Baltimore, MD: Brookes.

Koegel, L.K. & Koegel, R.L. (1995). Motivating communication in children with autism. In E. Schopler & G.B. Mesibov (Eds) *Learning and Cognition in Autism* (pp. 73–87). New York: Plenum.

Koegel, L.K., Koegel, R.L. & Dunlap, G. (Eds) (1996). *Positive Behavioral Support: Including People with Difficult Behavior in the Community*. Baltimore, MD: Brookes.

Lewis, M.H., Aman, M.G., Gadow, K.D., Schroeder, S.R. & Thompson, T. (1996). Psychopharmacology. In J.W. Jacobson & J.A. Mulick (Eds) *Manual of Diagnosis and Professional Practice in Mental Retardation* (pp. 323–340). Washington, DC: American Psychological Association.

Lewis, T.J. & Sugai, G. (1999). Effective behavior support: a systems approach to proactive school-wide management. *Focus on Exceptional Children*, **31**, 1–24.

Malott, R.W. (2001). Occupational safety and response maintenance: an alternate view. *Journal of Organizational Behavior Management*, **21**, 85–102.

Mansell, J. & Elliot, T. (2001). Staff members' prediction of consequences for their work in residential settings. *American Journal on Mental Retardation*, **106**, 434–447.

Marquis, J.G., Horner, R.H., Carr, E.G., Turnbull, A.P., Thompson, M., Behrens, G.A., et al. (2000). A meta-analysis of positive behavior support. In R. Gersten, E.P. Schiller & S. Vaughn (Eds) *Contemporary Special Education Research: Syntheses of Knowledge Base on Critical Instructional Issues*. Mahwah, NJ: Erlbaum.

Meyer, L.H. & Evans, I.M. (1989). *Nonaversive Intervention for Behavior Problems: A Manual for Home and Community*. Baltimore, MD: Brookes.

Meyer, L.H., Park, H.-S., Grenot-Scheyer, M., Schwartz, I. & Harry, B. (1998). Participatory research: new approaches to the research to practice dilemma. *Journal of the Association for Persons with Severe Handicaps*, **23**, 165–177.

Mitachi, M. & Albin, R.W. (2001). The effect of functional assessment information on the behavioral support recommendations for school personnel. In T. Lewis-Palmer (Chair), *Applications of Functional Assessment in Schools*. Symposium conducted at the 27th annual convention of the Association for Behavior Analysis, New Orleans, LA.

Moncher, F. & Prinz, R. (1991). Treatment fidelity in outcome studies. *Clinical Psychology Review*, **11**, 247–266.

Mount, B. & Zwernik, K. (1988). *It's Never Too Early, It's Never Too Late.* St Paul, MN: Minnesota Governor's Council on Developmental Disabilities.

Newton, J.S., Ard, W.R. Jr, Horner, R.H. & Toews, J.D. (1996). Focusing on values and lifestyle outcomes in an effort to improve the quality of residential services in Oregon. *Mental Retardation*, **34**, 1–12.

Newton, J.S. & Horner, R.H. (1995). Feedback to staff on resident lifestyle. *Behavior Modification*, **19**, 95–118.

O'Brien, J. (1987). A guide to life-style planning: using the Activities Catalogue to integrate services and natural support systems. In G.T. Bellamy & B. Wilcox (Eds) *A Comprehensive Guide to the Activities Catalogue: An Alternative Curriculum for Youth and Adults with Severe Disabilities* (pp. 175–189). Baltimore, MD: Brookes.

O'Brien, J. & Lovett, H. (1998). Finding a way toward everyday lives: the contribution of person-centered planning. In J. O'Brien & C.L. O'Brien (Eds) *A Little Book About Person Centered Planning* (pp. 113–132). Toronto: Inclusion Press.

Ohtake, Y. & Chadsey, J.G. (2001). Continuing to describe the natural support process. *Journal of the Association for People with Severe Handicaps*, **26,** 87–95.

O'Neill, R.E., Horner, R.H., Albin, R.W., Sprague, J.R., Storey, K. & Newton, J.S. (1997). *Functional Assessment and Program Development for Problem Behavior: A Practical Handbook* (2nd edn). Pacific Grove, CA: Brooks/Cole.

O'Neill, R.E., Horner, R.H., O'Brien, M. & Huckstep, S. (1991). Generalized reduction of difficult behaviors: analysis and intervention in a competing behaviors framework. *Journal of Development and Physical Disabilities*, **3**, 5–21.

O'Reilly, M.F. (1997). Functional analysis of episodic self-injury correlated with recurrent otitis media. *Journal of Applied Behavior Analysis*, **30**, 165–167.

O'Reilly, M.F., Lacey, C. & Lancioni, G.E. (2000). Assessment of the influence of background noise on escape-maintained problem behavior and pain behavior in a child with Williams syndrome. *Journal of Applied Behavior Analysis*, **33**, 511–514.

Pearpoint, J., O'Brien, J. & Forest, M. (1993). *PATH: A Workbook for Planning Positive Possible Futures and Planning Alternative Tomorrows with Hope for Schools, Organizations, Business, and Families* (2nd edn). Toronto: Inclusion Press.

Peterson, L., Homer, A. & Wonderlich, S. (1982). The integrity of independent variables in behavior analysis. *Journal of Applied Behavior Analysis*, **15**, 477–492.

Reeve, C.E. & Carr, E.G. (2000). Prevention of severe behavior problems in children with developmental disabilities. *Journal of Positive Behavioral Interventions*, **2**, 144–160.

Reiss, S. (2000). Psychopharmacology and mental retardation. In M.L. Wehmeyer & J.R. Patton (Eds) *Mental Retardation in the 21st Century* (pp. 197–209). Austin, TX: Pro-Ed.

Risley, T. (1996). Get a life! Positive behavioral intervention for challenging behavior through life arrangement and life coaching. In L.K. Koegel, R.L. Koegel & G. Dunlap (Eds) *Positive Behavioral Support: Including People with Difficult Behavior in the Community* (pp. 425–437). Baltimore, MD: Brookes.

Roeher Institute (1991). *The Power to Choose: An Examination of Service Brokerage and Individualized Funding as Implemented by the Community Living Society.* North York, Ontario, Canada: Author.

Romanczyk, R.G. & Matthews, A.L. (1998). Physiological state as antecedent. In J.K. Luiselli & M.J. Cameron (Eds) *Antecedent Control: Innovative Approaches to Behavioral Support* (pp. 115–138). Baltimore, MD: Brookes.

Rudolph, C., Lakin, K.C., Oslund, J.M. & Larson, W. (1998). Evaluation of outcomes and cost-effectiveness of a community behavioral support and crisis response demonstration project. *Mental Retardation*, **36**, 187–197.

Sandler, L. (2001). Goodness-of-fit and the viability of behavioral support plans: a survey of direct care adult residential staff. Unpublished dissertation. University of Oregon, Eugene, OR.

Schalock, R.L. (2000). Three decades of quality of life research. In M.L. Wehmeyer & J.R. Patton (Eds) *Mental Retardation in the 21st Century* (pp. 335–356). Austin, TX: Pro-Ed.

Schalock, R.L. (2001). *Outcome-Based Evaluation* (2nd edn). New York: Kluwer Academic/Plenum.

Schalock, R.L. & Genung, L.T. (1993). Placement from a community-based mental retardation program: a 15-year follow-up. *American Journal on Mental Retardation*, **98**, 400–407.

Schalock, R.L. & Keith, K.D. (1993). *Quality of Life Questionnaire*. Worthington, OH: IDS Publishing.

Schwartz, I. & Baer, D.M. (1991). Social validity assessments: is current practice state of the art? *Journal of Applied Behavior Analysis*, **24**, 189–204.

Scotti, J.R. & Meyer, L.H. (1999). *Behavioral Interventions: Principles, Models and Practices*. Baltimore, MD: Brookes.

Scotti, J.R., Ujcich, K.J., Weigle, K.L., Holland, C.M. & Kirk, K.S. (1996). Interventions with challenging behaviors of persons with developmental disabilities: a review of current research practices. *Journal of the Association for Persons with Severe Handicaps*, **21**, 123–134.

Shore, B.A., Iwata, B.A., Lerman, D.C. & Shirley, M.J. (1994). Assessing and programming generalized behavioral reduction across multiple stimulus parameters. *Journal of Applied Behavior Analysis*, **27**, 371–384.

Simon-Rusinowitz, L., Mahoney, K.J., Shoop, D.M., Desmond, S.M., Squillace, M.R. & Sowers, J.A. (2001). Consumer and surrogate preferences for a cash option versus traditional services: Florida adults with developmental disabilities. *Mental Retardation*, **39**, 87–103.

Smull, M. & Harrison, S. (1992). *Supporting People with Severe Reputations in the Community.* Alexandria, VA: National Association of State Mental Retardation Program Directors.

Sprague, J.R. & Horner, R.H. (1984). The effects of single instance, multiple instance, and general case training on generalized vending machine use by moderately and severely handicapped students. *Journal of Applied Behavior Analysis*, **17**, 273–278.

Stokes, T.F. & Baer, D.M. (1977). An implicit technology of generalization. *Journal of Applied Behavior Analysis*, **10**, 349–367.

Stufflebeam, D.L. (1983). The CIPP model for program evaluation. In G.F. Madaus, M. Scriven & D.L. Stufflebeam (Eds) *Evaluation Models: Viewpoints on Educational and Human Services Evaluation* (pp. 117–141). Boston, MA: Kluwer-Nijhoff.

Thompson, T., Symons, F.J. & Felce, D. (2000). Principles of behavioral observation: assumptions and strategies. In T. Thompson, D. Felce & F.J. Symons (Eds) *Behavioral Observation: Technology and Applications in Developmental Disabilities*. Baltimore, MA: Brookes.

US General Accounting Office (November, 1990). *Case Study Evaluations.* (GAO/PEMD-91-10.1.9). Washington, DC: Author.

Vandercook, T., York, J. & Forest, M. (1989). The McGill action planning system (MAPS): a strategy for building the vision. *Journal of the Association for Persons with Severe Handicaps*, **14**, 205–215.

Vaughn, B.J., Dunlap, G., Fox, L., Clarke, S. & Bucy, M. (1997). Parent-professional partnership in behavioral support: a case study of community-based intervention. *Journal of the Association for Persons with Severe Handicaps*, **22**, 186–197.

Vollmer, T.R. & Van Camp, C.M. (1998). Experimental designs to evaluate antecedent control. In J.K. Luiselli & M.J. Cameron (Eds) *Antecedent Control: Innovative Approaches to Behavioral Support* (pp. 87–111). Baltimore, MD: Brookes.

Wehmeyer, M.L. (1995). *The Arc's Self-Determination Scale.* Arlington, TX: The Arc National Headquarters.

Wolf, M.M. (1978). Social validity: the case for subjective measurement, or how behavior analysis is finding its heart. *Journal of Applied Behavior Analysis*, **11**, 203–214.

Yin, R.K. (1994). *Case Study Research: Design and Methods* (2nd edn). Thousand Oaks, CA: Sage.

CHAPTER 26

Research Issues in Cognitive Therapy

Dave Dagnan
University of Northumbria at Newcastle, UK
and
William R. Lindsay
University of Abertay, UK

INTRODUCTION

People with intellectual disabilities have traditionally been seen as unable to benefit from cognitive and other talking therapies (Kroese, 1997). However, it is well established that the cognitive and behavioural problems for which cognitive therapies are commonly used with people without intellectual disabilities are at least as prevalent in people with intellectual disabilities (e.g., Borthwick-Duffy, 1994), and it has been shown that many of the cognitive processes that mediate psychological and mental health problems in people without intellectual disabilities are also present in people with intellectual disabilities (e.g., Nezu, Nezu, Rothenberg & Dellicarpini, 1995; Dagnan & Sandhu, 1999). A small number of reviews of single-case studies and other interventions suggest that cognitive approaches can be effective for some people with intellectual disability (e.g., Martin, Burger, Elia-Burger & Mithang, 1988; Lindsay, 1999b).

This chapter will consider research issues in cognitive approaches to working with people with intellectual disabilities. We will present a brief overview of research in this area and identify a number of themes that may usefully be considered in the future development of research in this area.

THE CLINICAL APPLICATION OF COGNITIVE THERAPY

There are a number of therapeutic approaches for people without intellectual disabilities that can be considered to be "cognitive". Some "cognitive" therapies have been developed for particular client groups (e.g., Ronen, 1997), while others can be used with a range of client groups and problems (e.g., Ellis, 1977). Dagnan and Chadwick (1997) identify two distinct approaches to cognitive therapy that have been used with people with intellectual

The International Handbook of Applied Research in Intellectual Disabilities. Edited by E. Emerson, C. Hatton, T. Thompson and T.R. Parmenter © 2004 John Wiley & Sons, Ltd. ISBN 0-471-49709-6.

disabilities. The first is based within a "deficit" model that assumes that emotional and behavioural difficulties are due to a lack of cognitive skills (e.g., Whitman, 1990). Whitman (1990) suggests that people with intellectual disabilities do not easily transfer skills learned in one situation to other similar situations, and that this difficulty is primarily related to the development of language skills. Intervention approaches associated with the "deficit" model include self-regulation (Rachlin, 1974; Kanfer, 1975; Nelson & Hayes, 1981) and self-instruction approaches (Meichenbaum & Goodman, 1971). Although these approaches have different theoretical histories, a number of reviews in this area consider them as a broad single class of intervention. For example Harchick, Sherman and Sheldon (1992) review 59 case studies using "self-management" procedures where "self-management" is defined as "everything a person does to influence his or her own behaviour" (p. 212).

The second approach to cognitive therapy for people with intellectual disabilities is concerned with "cognitive distortion" and has developed from a psychotherapeutic tradition. In the clinical models developed by therapists such as Beck, Rush, Shaw and Emery (1979) and Ellis (1977), unhelpful or irrational emotions and behaviours are considered to be the products of "distorted" cognitions (such as beliefs, attributions, inferences, or evaluations). Cognitive therapy, then, aims to help people examine and test the usefulness of the meanings they generate. There is relatively little work describing this approach to cognitive therapy with people with intellectual disabilities (Kroese, Dagnan & Loumidis, 1997).

Self-Management Approaches

Harchick et al. (1992) identify self-monitoring and subsequent self-evaluation and self-reinforcement as a particular strategy within their broad definition of self-management. The core process within this approach is the monitoring of one's own behaviour, which in certain circumstances will be reactive, leading to behaviour change. There are a number of different theoretical perspectives on the observed reactivity (Rachlin, 1974; Kanfer, 1975; Nelson & Hayes, 1981); however, the approach has been widely applied and can be effective with people with more severe disabilities (e.g., Hughes & Agran, 1993). Most of the interventions using self-monitoring reviewed by Harchick et al. (1992) and other similar reviews (e.g., Martin et al., 1988) are concerned with functional-academic or vocational tasks.

Self-instructional approaches require people to "make directive verbal statements about their own behaviour" (Harchick et al., 1992, p. 213). As with self-monitoring, the use of self-instruction with people with intellectual disabilities has most frequently been in the area of adaptive and vocational skills. However, this approach has also been used as the basis of interventions for emotional and behavioural disorders. In these approaches, alternative, helpful, or maintaining self-instructions are offered to replace irrational, unhelpful, or inhibiting cognitions. One of the first therapists to consider a cognitive analysis and intervention of this type that would be relevant to people with intellectual disabilities was Meichenbaum (Meichenbaum & Goodman, 1971; Meichenbaum, 1977). Meichenbaum's self-instruction programme was based within a Vygotskian account (Vygotsky, 1962) of how children develop self-control through a process of internalising the external verbal control of others. Although developed for children, the technique is eminently suitable for adaptation for clients with mild and moderate intellectual disabilities. Meichenbaum (1999) has subsequently developed self-instruction training and cognitive-behaviour therapy to include more subtle assessment and analysis of strengths and weaknesses for people with intellectual disabilities.

Self-instruction training can be used both to offer specific self-statements in response to specific situations and to provide structured, problem-solving techniques that are applicable to a variety of situations. Self-instruction can also be used in clinical situations where the individual has a repertoire of skills that are appropriate to the situation but is unable to use them because of interfering cognitions. For example, Lindsay and Kasprowicz (1987) report social skills training programmes where participants achieved only marginal changes in skill acquisition, but showed considerable change in the self-statements used when going into social situations and in their sociability and self-confidence in social situations.

Although self-instruction can be used in isolation, it is more frequently used as part of a treatment package that teaches other behavioural and cognitive skills, as in anger management (e.g., Benson, Rice & Miranti, 1986; Black & Novaco, 1993; Benson, 1994; Lindsay, Overend, Allen, Williams & Black, 1998a; Rose, West & Clifford, 2000); social skills and social problem-solving training (Castles & Glass, 1986; Loumidis & Hill, 1997a,b); and treatment programmes for offenders with intellectual disabilities (e.g., Lindsay, Neilson, Morrison & Smith, 1998b; Lindsay, Olley, Baillie & Smith, 1999).

Cognitive Therapy

Since the initial effectiveness of interventions within the theoretical framework provided by Meichenbaum (1977), clinicians have explored other cognitive-therapy models for a range of problems experienced by people with intellectual disabilities. Beck's (Beck et al., 1979) cognitive therapy has been revised and simplified so that it is appropriate for a variety of problem areas and presentations within the intellectual disability population (e.g., Dagnan & Chadwick, 1997; Hare, 1997; Lindsay, Neilson & Lawrenson, 1997; Lindsay, 1999b).

One of the first problems to receive attention was that of depression. Matson (1982) and Matson, Dettling and Senatore (1987) describe a series of case studies using a social skills training programme with cognitive elements, for the treatment of depression. Lindsay, Howells and Pitcaithly (1993) retained the structure and process of therapy described by Beck et al. (1979). They included the essential principles and components of cognitive treatment and report two successful case studies. Dagnan and Chadwick (1997), Lindsay and Olley (1998), and Lindsay (1999a) have all described successful case illustrations employing cognitive therapy for depression.

Problems of anxiety in people with intellectual disabilities have received more attention, although, in general, treatments have been more behavioural and physiological in focus (Lindsay & Olley, 1998). Lindsay et al. (1997) reported two successful case studies employing Beck's cognitive therapy for anxiety. In both cases, anxiety remained stable and low at 18-month follow-up. Lindsay (1999b) reports a cohort of 15 individuals with clinically significant levels of anxiety. Treatment lasted an average of 23 sessions and resulted in a statistically significant reduction in self-report measures of anxiety; improvements were maintained at 6-month follow-up.

CRITIQUE OF COGNITIVE-THERAPY RESEARCH

Design Issues

Models for evidence-based approaches to clinical practice (e.g., Roth & Fonagay, 1996) often identify a hierarchy of research methods based upon a design's potential for external validity and greater potential to infer causality (e.g., Cook & Campbell, 1979). The hierarchy usually identifies case studies and single-case experimental designs as less externally valid designs, and between-group hypothesis-testing methods as more externally valid designs. Case studies may be presented in a highly structured manner (e.g., Fishman, 1999), but usually describe cases selected because of unique or theoretically important presentations, innovative interventions, or unusual outcomes. At its simplest, the single-case design consists of multiple measures at baseline and post-intervention, with participants acting as their own controls, although most published designs are more sophisticated (Hersen & Barlow, 1976). More externally valid designs include the controlled clinical trial and the randomised control trial. These designs allocate participants to groups receiving different treatments in an effort to achieve a design where it can be concluded that the presence of an intervention is the sole or main cause of any subsequently observed difference in outcome between groups. In practice, in small populations, even randomly generated groups tend to differ systematically on potentially confounding variables, and appropriate statistical control may still be necessary (Hamilton, 1974).

Most published cognitive-therapy interventions for people with intellectual disabilities are single-case experimental designs or case studies. There are a small number of controlled trials, most of these being of structured group-based interventions, such as anger-management training (Rose et al., 2000) and social problem solving (e.g., Loumidis & Hill, 1997a). Clearly, there is a need for carefully constructed controlled trials in areas of cognitive therapy for people with intellectual disabilities where treatment protocols are now well established. However, Dagnan (1999) identifies a number of factors that may have limited the development of controlled studies in this area, and it is important to note that there is also considerable scope for exploring a more systematic use of the single-case experimental design and case-study approach. For example, multiple-baseline designs both between and within participants and across settings (Hersen & Barlow, 1976) can be used to demonstrate the specific relationship between intervention, setting, and cognitive change. Similarly, case studies can be presented in highly structured and systematic format to facilitate comparison across cases (e.g., Fishman, 1999).

There is a significant literature examining the relationship between research evidence and clinical practice (e.g., Clegg, 1998). Within this literature, there is an emerging critique of the simple hierarchy of evidence quality judged on the criterion of external validity. For example, within reflective models of clinical practice, it is possible to see the more externally valid research designs as offering a broad framework for clinical intervention, but to suggest that clinical problem solving integrates a wider range of evidence and experience (e.g., Schon, 1983; Dagnan, 1999). From this perspective, the single-case experimental design and descriptive case study remain important contributions to evidence-based practice.

Many of the best-established cognitive behavioural interventions are integrative in their approach. For example, anger-management training offers a combination of cognitive and behavioural strategies, including arousal reduction (relaxation), education about emotion, education about the appraisal of anger-provoking situations, and change in the individual's cognitive appraisal of provoking situations (Black & Novaco, 1993). In most studies, it is difficult to determine which of these therapeutic components has the most significant effect, or, indeed, whether they work only in combination. Therefore, while it is commendable that there are controlled studies in this field, the relative effectiveness of the cognitive component is uncertain. There are, as yet, no studies that attempt a component analysis of the various elements within intervention approaches of this type, although studies of this type have been carried out for people without intellectual disabilities (e.g., Kelly, Scott, Preve & Rychtarik, 1985).

Measurement Issues

There are a number of excellent reviews of measurement issues in gaining information from people with learning disabilities (e.g., Prosser & Bromley, 1998; Finlay & Lyons, 2001). In this section, we will consider some of the issues that arise in using standardised self-report scales with particular emphasis on the assessment of depression.

A number of self-report questionnaires for measuring depression and anxiety have been reported in the literature. Although a small number of studies use scales in the same format as they would be used with people without learning disabilities (for example, the unmodified Zung Depression Scales and Beck Depression Inventory used by Prout & Schaefer, 1985), it is more usual that some degree of adaptation of wording and response format is applied to scales. For example, the Zung Depression Scale (Zung, 1965) is the most widely used depression self-report scale for people with learning disabilities (e.g., Kazdin, Matson & Senatore, 1983; Helsel & Matson, 1988; Lindsay, Michie, Baty, Smith & Miller, 1994; Lindsay et al., 1997; Dagnan & Sandhu, 1999). The changes made to the scale are minimal: the response options may be changed from an ordinal scale to "yes/no" format, and the item regarding satisfaction with sexual activity is often left out. Similarly, the Beck Depression Inventory has also been used in an unmodified (e.g., Prout & Shaeffer, 1985) and modified form (Kazdin et al., 1983; Helsel & Matson, 1988; Nezu et al., 1995). The potential difficulties in questionnaire adaptation are highlighted in a number of studies examining the various question formats, wording, and response formats that would be suitable for working with people with learning disabilities. Finlay and Lyons (2001) make a number of valuable points in this area. In particular, they note that it might be unreasonable to expect one format of a questionnaire to be suitable to all people with learning disabilities, given the wide variation in communicative and cognitive abilities within the population.

As questionnaires have been adapted and are being used with groups for which they have not previously been standardised, special attention should be paid to the psychometric properties of any adapted questionnaires used with people with learning disabilities. The tendency for clinical studies in this area to be single-case or small-group designs has resulted in a relatively small number of studies that describe the psychometric properties of outcome measures. Even when group studies have adapted measures and reported psychometric properties, the group size is often insufficient for the analysis to be anything other than tentative (e.g., Dagnan & Sandhu, 1999). However, a number of studies have demonstrated that adapted scales, such as the Zung Depression Scales (Zung, 1965; Kazdin et al., 1983) and the Beck Depression Inventory (Beck, Ward, Mendelshon, Mock & Erbaugh, 1961), have good concurrent validity with other scales measuring similar concepts (e.g., Helsel & Matson, 1988; Lindsay et al., 1994; Nezu et al., 1995; Dagnan & Sandhu, 1999). The concurrent and predictive validity of commonly used self-report depression scales is reviewed in detail by Finlay and Lyons (2001). A number of interesting issues have been highlighted in these studies. In particular, a small number of studies have compared self-report questionnaires with observer-rated scales of mental health difficulties, with many studies finding relatively poor correlations between scales (e.g., Rojahn, Lederer & Tasse, 1995). Moreover, given the general finding of different levels of mental health difficulty across the range of ability, there are few examples of correlations having been found between ability measures and levels of self-reported distress (e.g., Finlay & Lyons, 2001).

Other studies have also used scales adapted for use with people with intellectual disabilities. For example, Dagnan and Sandhu (1999) used an adapted version of the Rosenberg Self-Esteem Scale (Rosenberg, Schooler & Schoenbach, 1989) and the Gilbert and Allen (1994) Social Comparison Scale, in a study of the impact of social comparison and self-esteem on depression in people with mild intellectual disabilities. Their paper reports the psychometric analysis of these scales, indicating a factor structure that is consistent with that of the original scales when used with people without intellectual disabilities, and a good level of internal and test–retest reliability. However, as stated above, the numbers involved in this study are small and the analysis should be treated with caution. Nezu et al. (1995) used the revised version of the Beck Depression Inventory (Kazdin et al., 1983) to demonstrate the applicability of Beck's cognitive model of depression with 107 adults with mild intellectual disabilities. They found that depressed subjects were significantly differentiated from non-depressed subjects on feelings of hopelessness and rates of self-reinforcement. However, the study does not report the psychometric details of the scales used.

There are a wide range of studies that show that people with mild and moderate intellectual disabilities are reliable in their use of sophisticated and individualised measures of belief intensity and frequency. For example, researchers have used response formats ranging from a dichotomous yes/no response to three- or four-point or continuous analogue scales and personal questionnaires (e.g., Dagnan & Ruddick, 1995; Dagnan & Chadwick, 1997; Lindsay et al., 1997). The range of response formats reported in the literature is useful from a clinical perspective where it offers opportunity to adapt methods to suit the individual client. However, from a research perspective, some degree of standardisation of response format within scales is essential. For example, the Zung scales (1965; 1971) have been used with a four-point analogue response (Helsel & Matson, 1988; Kazdin et al., 1983; Lindsay et al., 1994) and a nominal two-point response (Lindsay et al., 1994; Dagnan & Sandhu, 1999). There are also little data available on the baseline levels of anxiety and depression in the intellectual disability population with the standard measures identified above. In his original studies, Zung (1965; 1971) published information on several reference groups, so that one could judge the extent to which a specific score fell within various client categories. Similar work could be done for groups of people with intellectual disabilities by giving reference data for people in day services, residential services, or living at home; those referred for anxiety or depression difficulties; those with a diagnosed mental illness; those with challenging behaviour; and those with offending behaviour.

In conclusion, although scales generally need to be adapted for use with people with intellectual disabilities, it is likely to be more productive to use adapted scales than to create entirely new scales for this group. There is a considerable literature examining the models of depression reflected within particular scales (e.g., Dunbar, Ford, Hunt & Der, 2000), and the opportunity to replicate work of this type is most easily offered when scales are minimally adapted. There is a need for considerable further standardisation of scales used with people with intellectual disabilities. Both the psychometric properties and the standardised scores for various groups need further examination; in particular, there is a relatively small literature validating self-report scales against external observation and clinical diagnosis. Further work is also needed on appropriate methods of screening performance on scales. It is inevitable that some people with intellectual disabilities will at times find answering certain types of question difficult (Finlay & Lyons, 2001). Identifying which items are suited to particular ranges of ability and what types of rephrasing and presentation best suit particular people will enable the appropriate use of scales in both a research and clinical context.

POTENTIAL AREAS FOR FUTURE RESEARCH

Therapy Process Issues

In therapy for people without intellectual disabilities, there is a significant literature examining factors within therapies that contribute to the change process (e.g., Llewelyn & Hardy, 2001). For example, Greenberg (1986) identifies three levels of process contributing to change within therapy, the speech act (for example, the verbal responses occurring between therapist and client) (e.g., Stiles, Shapiro & Firth-Cozens, 1988), the change episodes or events (for example, resolution of a conflict for the client or gaining new insight) (e.g., Greenberg, 1986), and the nature of the therapeutic relationship (e.g., Lambert, 1983). Greenberg (1986) also notes that outcomes are equally hierarchical, ranging from within-session changes that result from a particular intervention to "extra-sessional" intermediate changes that may be robust enough to become a final therapy outcome. There is a significant literature that has examined the link between process variables and therapy outcomes across different types of therapy (e.g., Shapiro, Barkham, Hardy & Morrison, 1990). The literature concerning therapy process for people without intellectual disabilities has significantly contributed to a broader understanding of therapy and its effectiveness (Roth & Fonagay, 1996; Llewelyn & Hardy, 2001).

This type of research has considerable potential to contribute to an increased understanding of therapy processes for people with intellectual disabilities. There is little systematic consideration of the therapeutic process and interaction for this client group. This is of particular interest, given the general finding that language is used to control and reduce the opportunities available to people with intellectual disabilities in many other types of interaction (e.g., Rapley & Antaki, 1996). In therapy for people without intellectual disabilities, the study of therapy process has contributed considerably to the development of therapy technique and theory (Roth & Fonagay, 1996) and should be explored in relation to people with intellectual disabilities.

Predictors of Outcome in Therapy

Many therapies have developed pretherapy assessments of the core activities required within the therapeutic approach. For example, Davanloo (1980) describes an approach to trial interpretations during a pretherapy interview as an assessment of suitability for short-term psychotherapy. Safran, Segal, Vallis, Shaw and Samstag (1993) describe an assessment of predictors of outcome in interpersonal cognitive therapy that was used in a study of 42 people without intellectual disabilities attending a clinic for anxiety and depression. The functioning assessed was in the areas of the cognitive-therapy process (such as accessibility of automatic thoughts, awareness and differentiation of emotions, and compatibility with the cognitive rationale); relationship formation (evidence gathered from within session and evidence from other aspects of the person's life; maintenance of a problem focus in sessions); and other aspects, such as acceptance of personal responsibility for change, the chronicity of problems, and the presence of security operations. The study found that the indicators could be reliably rated and were significantly associated with a positive outcome in short-term interpersonal cognitive therapy.

A similar approach has been developed and explored by Dagnan and colleagues (Dagnan & Chadwick, 1997; Dagnan, Chadwick & Proudlove, 2000) for people with intellectual disabilities. This approach is based upon the processes used in cognitive therapy to identify mediating cognitions. Safran, Vallis, Segal & Shaw (1986) suggest that within therapy the path to identifying mediating cognitions involves first identifying the emotional or behavioural consequence, moving back to the antecedent event, and then identifying the mediating cognition. Thus, the assessment process for people with intellectual disabilities first involves assessing the person's ability to identify emotions (Rojahn et al., 1995). While there is considerable literature on the nature of emotion recognition for people with intellectual disabilities, the features of the various stimuli available to clinicians for this process are less well known. There is also discussion in the research literature concerning the nature of the tasks that have previously been used in research (Rojahn et al., 1995; Moore, 2001). Moore (2001) suggests that, if the verbal components of the tasks are reduced, people with intellectual disabilities perform as well as people without intellectual disabilities. He goes on to suggest a number of research strategies to test this hypothesis. The approach then assesses the person's ability to link emotions with activating events. The assessment used is based upon that of Reed and Clements (1989). Finally, the assessment explores the person's ability to link emotions, activating events, and mediating cognitions. Two methods have been suggested; the first uses an open-ended response format (Dagnan & Chadwick, 1997), and the second uses a structured response format (Dagnan et al., 2000). There is considerable room to develop these assessments and to determine their relationships with other factors within the assessment process.

The degree to which these assessments predict outcome in particular forms of cognitive therapy and their use as assessments of suitability for different forms of cognitive therapy has not yet been established. It is self-evident that certain people with severe and profound intellectual disabilities will be unable to engage in cognitive therapy, or indeed any other talking therapy. However, if we view assessment in a constructional manner, these approaches may be used to determine whether people have areas of skill that might be amenable to a prosthetic or skill-based intervention that will enable them to benefit more fully from a particular cognitive approach (e.g., Ludwig & Hingsburger, 1989; Clements, 1997). For example, it is possible that a person who can identify basic emotions and can describe simple events, but who cannot yet link events and emotions, would be able to work within a self-monitoring framework. The person who can link emotions and events, but who cannot identify mediating cognitions, may be able to use a self-instructional approach, the assumption being that people who can link emotions and events will be able to interpose cognition based upon a simple understanding of the antecedents of their own emotions. Finally, the person who can identify mediating cognitions and shows some signs of being able to modify cognitions based upon emotional change may have the ability to work within a hypothesis-testing cognitive framework. There is considerable further work that could be carried out to explore the skills associated with the various types of cognitive therapy and to develop further assessment and training approaches associated with each approach.

An examination of the Safran paper suggests a number of other areas where further research would develop assessment processes. Although not specific to cognitive therapy, many of the factors identified as important in predicting outcome in therapy are factors that we could expect to be of difficulty for people with intellectual disabilities.

The Development of Models of Cognitive Therapy

In cognitive therapy with people without intellectual disabilities, there is a considerable integration between cognitive information-processing approaches (e.g., Williams, Watts, MacLeod & Mathews, 1988), cognitive models of emotions (e.g., Teasdale & Barnard, 1993; Power & Dalgleish, 1997), and cognitive-therapy intervention (e.g., Blackburn & Twaddle, 1996). In cognitive therapy for people with intellectual disabilities, there is a significant body of theoretical research in verbal self-regulation and self-instruction (e.g., Rachlin, 1974; Kanfer, 1975; Nelson & Hayes, 1981) that explores some of the fundamental assumptions of the nature of the change processes (such as reactivity) in these approaches. Developmental theorists (e.g., Vygotsky, 1962) clearly indicate that positive developmental pathways are dependent upon environments that enable and encourage the use of self-control and independent decision making (Jones, Williams & Lowe, 1993; Williams & Jones, 1997). Cognitive researchers and theoreticians also describe models that emphasise the social-developmental history of the individual in the development of schema and representations of the world (e.g., Power & Dalgleish, 1997). Within the study of intellectual disabilities, the literature that can be drawn upon to understand the interaction between social experience and cognitive structures is diverse, ranging from literature on personality development (e.g., Zigler, Bennet-Gates & Cohen, 1999) to information-processing accounts of particular emotional problems, such as anger and aggression (e.g., Fuchs & Benson, 1995).

Studies of cognitive models of distress in people with intellectual disabilities have explored relationships between constructs such as hopelessness (Nezu et al., 1995), self-esteem and social comparison (Dagnan & Sandhu, 1999), levels of social support (Reiss & Benson, 1985), awareness of disadvantage (Reiss & Benson, 1984), self-concept (Benson & Ivins, 1992), and psychological distress in people with intellectual disabilities. However, although there is a beginning literature in this area, the number of studies that have properly established links between variables such as self-esteem and self-concept and psychological distress and mental health problems is small in comparison to the literature for people without intellectual disabilities. There is a general assumption that people with intellectual disabilities are exposed to higher rates of environmental disadvantage and adverse life events, and that this partly accounts for the raised rates of mental health problem in them. However, it is notable that the fundamental research that identifies links between these environmental factors and subsequent psychological distress is missing.

There is a beginning literature that directly examines the effects of negative social experience on the self-concept and other psychological processes of people with intellectual disabilities. Such studies begin to support the assertion that it is important to formulate the psychological distress of people with intellectual disabilities in the context of their social experiences, with particular emphasis on the devalued construction of people with intellectual disabilities (Jahoda, Pert, Squire & Trower, 1998; Dagnan & Sandhu, 1999; Pert, Jahoda & Squire, 1999). The systematic study and development of such models remains an important clinical and research activity, as it is through the careful exploration of how the social experiences of people with intellectual disabilities affect their cognitive processes that we may develop sensitive cognitive interventions that take into account the social context of people with intellectual disabilities.

Currently, the cognitive approaches have been applied only to broad classes of psychological problem. For example, there have been a number of interventions reported for anxiety (Lindsay, 1999b). However, DSM-IV (American Psychiatric Association, 1994) describes specific subtypes of anxiety disorder, each with its own diagnostic criteria. Many of these have been discussed in relation to people with intellectual disabilities (e.g., Khreim & Mikkelsen, 1997), and most have distinct forms of cognitive therapy associated with them for people without intellectual disabilities (e.g., Salkovskis, 1985; Clark, 1986). While there are case examples of psychological treatments of people with intellectual disabilities with specific anxiety problems, such as phobia (King, Ollendick, Guillone, Cummins & Josephs, 1990), obsessive-compulsive disorder (Matson, 1982), and post-traumatic problems (Ryan, 1994), most studies describe behavioural or generalised therapeutic approaches. The newer and established cognitive treatments for people without intellectual disability involve presentation-specific cognitive-behavioural models and treatments. There are no accounts of these models having been applied to people with intellectual disabilities, and there is much to be gained from exploring these interventions with this population.

CONCLUSIONS

A number of areas of research development have been considered in this chapter. First of all, it is clear that the outcomes research in some areas is limited. There is a need for more controlled outcome studies, but also for the use of more sophisticated single-case designs. The often limited research that is carried out in the area of cognitive therapy of people with intellectual disabilities is further hampered by a lack of clarity regarding the forms of therapy used and the use of a wide range of different outcome measures which prevent easy comparison across papers. Many of the areas suggested for future research are areas where there is a significant body of research in mainstream cognitive therapy. There is a clear message concerning the benefits of taking models, processes, and predictors that have been explored and applied to people without intellectual disabilities, and considering their adaptation and exploration for people with intellectual disabilities.

REFERENCES

American Psychiatric Association (1994). *Diagnostic and Statistical Manual of Mental Disorders*. Washington, DC: American Psychiatric Association.

Beck, A.T., Rush, A.J., Shaw, B.F. & Emery, G. (1979). *Cognitive Therapy of Depression*. New York: Wiley.

Beck, A.T., Ward, C.H., Mendelshon, M., Mock, J. & Erbaugh, J. (1961). An inventory for measuring depression. *Archives of General Psychiatry*, **4**, 561–571.

Benson, B.A. (1994). Anger management training: a self-controlled programme for persons with mild mental retardation. In N. Bouras (Ed.) *Mental Health in Mental Retardation: Recent Advances and Practices* (pp. 224–232). Cambridge: Cambridge University Press.

Benson, B.A. & Ivins, J. (1992). Anger, depression and self-concept in adults with mental retardation. *Journal of Intellectual Disability Research*, **36**, 169–175.

Benson, B.A., Rice, C.J. & Miranti, S.V. (1986). Effects of anger management training with mentally retarded adults in group treatment. *Journal of Consulting in Clinical Psychology*, **54**, 728–729.

Black, L. & Novaco, R.W. (1993). Treatment of anger with a developmentally handicapped man. In R.A. Wells & V.J. Geinnetti (Eds) *Casebook of the Brief Psychotherapies* (pp. 33–52). New York: Plenum.

Blackburn, I. & Twaddle, V. (1996). *Cognitive Therapy in Action*. Souvenir Press.

Borthwick-Duffy, S. (1994). Epidemiology and prevalence of psychopathology in people with mental retardation. *Journal of Consulting and Clinical Psychology*, **62**, 17–27.

Castles, E.E. & Glass, C.R. (1986). Training in social and interpersonal problem solving skills for mildly and moderately mentally retarded adults. *American Journal of Mental Retardation*, **91**, 35–42.

Clark, D.M. (1986). A cognitive approach to panic. *Behaviour Research and Therapy*, **24**, 461–470.

Clegg, J. (1998). *Critical Issues in Clinical Practice*. London: Sage.

Clements, J. (1997). Sustaining a cognitive psychology for people with learning disabilities. In B.S. Kroese, D. Dagnan & K. Loumidis (Eds) *Cognitive Behaviour Therapy for People with Learning Disabilities* (pp. 162–181). London: Routledge.

Cook, T.D. & Campbell, D.T. (1979). *Quasi-Experimentation: Design And Analtsis Issue for Field Seeting*. Chicago: Rand McNally.

Dagnan, D. (1999). Evidence based practice in learning disabilities. *Clinical Psychology Forum*, **134**, 10–12.

Dagnan, D. & Chadwick, P. (1997). Cognitive behaviour therapy for people with learning disabilities: assessment and intervention. In B.S. Kroese, D. Dagnan & K. Loumidis (Eds) *Cognitive Behaviour Therapy for People with Learning Disabilities* (pp. 110–123). London: Routledge.

Dagnan, D., Chadwick, P. & Proudlove, J. (2000). Towards an assessment of suitability of people with mental retardation for cognitive therapy. *Cognitive Therapy and Research*, **24**, 627–636.

Dagnan, D. & Ruddick, L. (1995). The use of analogue scales and personal questionnaires for interviewing people with learning disabilities. *Clinical Psychology Forum*, **79**, 21–24.

Dagnan, D. & Sandhu, S. (1999). Social comparison, self-esteem and depression in people with learning disabilities. *Journal of Intellectual Disability Research*, **43**, 372–379.

Davanloo, H. (Ed.) (1980). *Short-Term Dynamic Psychotherapy*. New York: Aronson.

Dunbar, M., Ford, G., Hunt, K. & Der, G. (2000). A confirmatory factor analysis of the Hospital Anxiety and Depression Scale: comparing empirically and theoretically derived structures. *British Journal of Clinical Psychology*, **39**, 79–94.

Ellis, A. (1977). The basic clinical theory of rational emotive therapy. In A. Ellis & R. Grieger (Eds) *Handbook of Rational-Emotive Therapy* (pp. 10–37). New York: Springer-Verlag.

Finlay, W.M. & Lyons, E. (2001). Methodological issues in interviewing and using self-report questionnaires with people with mental retardation. *Psychological Assessment*, **13**, 319–335.

Fishman, D.B. (1999). *The Case for Pragmatic Psychology*. New York: New York University Press.

Fuchs, C. & Benson, B. (1995). Social information processing by aggressive and non-aggressive men with mental retardation. *American Journal on Mental Retardation*, **100**, 244–252.

Gilbert, P. & Allen, S. (1994). Assertiveness, submissive behaviour and social comparison. *British Journal of Clinical Psychology*, **33**, 295–306.

Greenberg, L.S. (1986). Change process research. *Journal of Consulting and Clinical Psychology*, **54**, 4–9.

Hamilton, K.E. & Dobson, K.S. (2002). Cognitive therapy of depression: pre-treatment patient predictors of outcome. *Clinical Psychology Review*, **22**, 875–893.

Hamilton, M. (1974). *Lectures on the Methodology of Clinical Research*. Edinburgh: Churchill Livingstone.

Harchick, A.E., Sherman, J.A. & Sheldon, B. (1992). The use of self-management procedures by people with developmental disabilities: a brief review. *Research in Developmental Disabilities*, **13**, 211–217.

Hare, D.J. (1997). The use of cognitive behavioural therapy with people with Asperger syndrome: a case study. *Autism*, **1**, 215–225.

Helsel, W.J. & Matson, J.L. (1988). The relationship of depression to social skills and intellectual functioning in mentally retarded adults. *Journal of Mental Deficiency Research*, **32**, 411–418.

Hersen, M. & Barlow, D.H. (1976). *Single Case Experimental Designs: Strategies for Studying Behaviour Change*. New York: Pergamon.

Hughes, C. & Agran, M. (1993). Teaching persons with severe disabilities to use self-instruction in community settings: an analysis of applications. *Journal of the Association of Persons with Severe Handicaps*, **18**, 261–274.

Jahoda, A., Pert, C., Squire, J. & Trower, P. (1998). Facing stress and conflict: a comparison of the predicted responses and self-concepts of aggressive and non-aggressive people with intellectual disabilities. *Journal of Intellectual Disability Research*, **42**, 360–369.

Jones, R.S., Williams, W.H. & Lowe, C.F. (1993). Verbal self-regulation. In I. Fleming & B. Kroese (Eds) *People with Learning Disability and Severe Challenging Behaviour: New Developments in Services and Therapy* (pp. 17–32). Manchester: Manchester University Press.

Kanfer, F.H. (1975). Self-management methods. In F.H. Kanfer & A.P. Goldstein (Eds) *Helping People Change* (pp. 309–355). New York: Pergamon.

Kazdin, A.E., Matson, J.L. & Senatore, V. (1983). Assessment of depression in mentally retarded adults. *American Journal of Psychiatry*, **140**, 1040–1043.

Kelly, M.L., Scott, W.O.M., Preve, D.M. & Rychtarik, R.G. (1985). A component analysis of problem-solving skills training. *Cognitive Therapy and Research*, **9**, 429–441.

Khreim, I. & Mikkelsen, E. (1997). Anxiety disorders in adults with mental retardation. *Psychiatric Annals*, **27**, 175–181.

King, N.J., Ollendick, T.H., Guillone, E., Cummins, R.A. & Josephs, A. (1990). Fears and phobias in children and adolescents with intellectual disabilities: assessment and intervention strategies. *Australia and New Zealand Journal of Developmental Disabilities*, **16**, 97–108.

Kroese, B.S. (1997). Cognitive behaviour therapy for people with learning disabilities: conceptual and contextual issues. In B.S. Kroese, D. Dagnan & K. Loumidis (Eds) *Cognitive Behaviour Therapy for People with Learning Disabilities* (pp. 1–15). London: Routledge.

Kroese, B.S., Dagnan, D. & Loumidis, K. (Eds) (1997). *Cognitive Behaviour Therapy for People with Learning Disabilities*. London: Routledge.

Lambert, M. (1983). *Psychotherapy and Patient Relationship*. New York: Dorsey.

Lindsay, W.R. (1999a). Pitching it right. *New Therapist*, **6**, 30–34.

Lindsay, W.R. (1999b). Cognitive therapy. *Psychologist*, **12**, 238–241.

Lindsay, W.R., Howells, L. & Pitcaithly, D. (1993). Cognitive therapy for depression with individuals with intellectual disabilities. *British Journal of Medical Psychology*, **66**, 135–141.

Lindsay, W.R. & Kasprowicz, M. (1987). Challenging negative cognitions: developing confidence in adults by means of cognitive therapy. *Mental Handicap*, **15**, 159–162.

Lindsay, W.R. & Michie, A.M. (1988). Adaptation of the Zung self-rating anxiety scale for people with mental handicap. *Journal of Mental Deficiency Research*, **32**, 485–490.

Lindsay, W.R., Michie, A.M., Baty, F.J., Smith, A.H.W. & Miller, S. (1994). The consistency of reports about feelings and emotions from people with intellectual disability. *Journal of Intellectual Disability Research*, **38**, 61–66.

Lindsay, W.R., Neilson, C. & Lawrenson, H. (1997). Cognitive behaviour therapy for anxiety in people with learning disabilities. In B.S. Kroese, D. Dagnan & K. Loumidis (Eds) *Cognitive Behaviour Therapy for People with Learning Disabilities* (pp. 124–140). London: Routledge.

Lindsay, W.R., Neilson, C.Q., Morrison, F. & Smith, A.H.W. (1998b). The treatment of six men with a learning disability convicted of sex offences with children. *British Journal of Clinical Psychology*, **37**, 83–98.

Lindsay, W.R. & Olley, S. (1998). Psychological treatment for anxiety and depression for people with learning disabilities. In W. Fraser, D. Sines & M. Kerr (Eds) *Hallas' The Care of People with Intellectual Disabilities* (9th edn) (pp. 235–252). Oxford: Butterworth Heinemann.

Lindsay, W.R., Olley, S., Baillie, N. & Smith, A.H.W. (1999). The treatment of adolescent sex offenders with intellectual disability. *Mental Retardation*, **37**, 320–333.

Lindsay, W.R., Overend, H., Allen, R., Williams, C. & Black, L. (1998a). Using specific approaches for individual problems in the management of anger and aggression. *British Journal of Learning Disabilities*, **26**, 44–50.

Llewelyn, S. & Hardy, G. (2001). Process research in understanding and applying psychological therapies. *British Journal of Clinical Psychology*, **40**, 11–21.

Loumidis, K.S. & Hill, A. (1997a). Training social problem solving skill to reduce maladaptive behaviours in intellectual disability groups: the influence of individual difference factors. *Journal of Applied Research in Intellectual Disabilities*, **10**, 217–237.

Loumidis, K. & Hill, A. (1997b). Social problem solving groups for adults with learning disabilities. In B.S. Kroese, D. Dagnan & K. Loumidis (Eds) *Cognitive Behaviour Therapy for People with Learning Disabilities* (pp. 86–109). London: Routledge.

Ludwig, S. & Hingsburger, D. (1989). Preparation for counselling and psychotherapy: teaching about feelings. *Psychiatric Aspects of Mental Retardation Review*, **8**, 1–7.

Martin, J.E., Burger, D.L., Elia-Burger, S. & Mithang, D.E. (1988). Applicating self-control strategies to facilitate independence in vocational and instructional settings. *International Review of Research in Mental Retardation*, **15**, 155–194.

Matson, J. (1982). Treating obsessive-compulsive behaviour in mentally retarded adults. *Behaviour Modification*, **6**, 551–567.

Matson, J.L., Dettling, J. & Senatore, V. (1987). Treating depression of a mentally retarded adult. *British Journal of Subnormality*, **26**, 86–89.

Meichenbaum, D. (1977). *Cognitive Behaviour Modification: An Integrative Approach*. New York: Plenum.

Meichenbaum, D. (1999). Goal setting procedures: a cognitive behavioural approach. Paper presented to the 20th Annual International Conference on M.R./D.D., Y.A.I., New York City.

Meichenbaum, D. & Goodman, J. (1971). Training impulsive children to talk to themselves: a means of developing self-control. *Journal of Abnormal Psychology*, **77**, 115–126.

Moore, D.G. (2001). Reassessing emotion recognition performance in people with mental retardation: a review. *American Journal of Mental Retardation*, **106**, 481–502.

Nelson, R.O. & Hayes, S. (1981). Theoretical explanation for reactivity in self-monitoring. *Behavioral Modification*, **5**, 3–14.

Nezu, C.M., Nezu, A.M., Rothenberg, J.L. & Dellicarpini, L. (1995). Depression in adults with mild mental retardation: are cognitive variables involved? *Cognitive Therapy and Research*, **19**, 227–239.

Pert, C., Jahoda, A. & Squire, J. (1999). Attribution of intent and role taking: cognitive factors as mediators of aggression with people who have mental retardation. *American Journal on Mental Retardation*, **104**, 399–409.

Power, M. & Dalgleish, T. (1997). *Cognition and Emotion from Order to Disorder.* Hove: Psychology Press.

Prosser, H. & Bromley, J. (1998). Interviewing people with intellectual disabilities. In E. Emerson, C. Hatton, J. Bromley & A. Caine (Eds) *Clinical Psychology and Intellectual Disabilities* (pp. 99–113). Chichester: Wiley.

Prout, H.T. & Schaefer, B.M. (1985). Self-reports of depression by community based mildly mentally retarded adults. *American Journal of Mental Deficiency*, **90**, 220–222.

Rachlin, H. (1974). Self-control. *Behaviorism*, **2**, 94–104.

Rapley, M. & Antaki, C. (1996). A conversational analysis of acquiescence of people with learning disabilities. *Journal of Community and Clinical Psychology*, **6**, 207–227.

Reed, J. & Clements, J. (1989). Assessing the understanding of emotional states in a population of adolescents and young adults with mental handicaps. *Journal of Mental Deficiency Research*, **33**, 229–233.

Reiss, S. & Benson, B. (1984). Awareness of negative social conditions among mentally retarded, emotionally disturbed outpatients. *American Journal of Psychiatry*, **141**, 88–90.

Reiss, S. & Benson, B. (1985). Psychosocial correlates of depression in mentally retarded adults. I. Minimal social support and stigmatization. *American Journal of Mental Deficiency*, **89**, 331–337.

Rojahn, J., Lederer, M. & Tasse, M.J. (1995). Facial emotion recognition by persons with mental retardation: a review of the experimental literature. *Research in Developmental Disabilities*, **16**, 393–414.

Ronen, T. (1997). *Cognitive Developmental Therapy with Children*. Chichester: Wiley.

Rose, J. (1996). Anger management: a group treatment programme for people with mental retardation. *Journal of Physical and Developmental Disabilities*, **8**, 133–150.

Rose, J., West, C. & Clifford, D. (2000). Group interventions for anger and people with intellectual disabilities. *Research in Developmental Disabilities*, **21**, 171–181.

Rosenberg, M., Schooler, E. & Schoenbach, C. (1989). Self-esteem and adolescent problems: modelling reciprocal effects. *American Sociological Review*, **54**, 1004–1016.

Roth, A. & Fonagay, P. (1996). *What Works for Whom? A Critical Review of Psychotherapy Research*. London: Guilford.

Ryan, R. (1994). Posttraumatic stress disorder in persons with developmental disabilities. *Community Mental Health Journal*, **30**, 45–54.

Safran, J.D., Segal, Z.V., Vallis, T.M., Shaw, B.F. & Samstag, L.W. (1993). Assessing patient suitability for short-term cognitive therapy with an interpersonal focus. *Cognitive Therapy and Research*, **17**, 23–38.

Safran, J.D., Vallis, T.M., Segal, Z.V. & Shaw, B.F. (1986). Assessment of core cognitive processes in cognitive therapy. *Cognitive Therapy and Research*, **10**, 509–526.

Salkovskis, P. (1985). Obsessive compulsive problems: a cognitive behavioural analysis. *Behavior Research and Therapy*, **23**, 571–583.

Schon, D. (1983). *The Reflective Practitioner*. New York: Basic Books.

Senatore, V., Matson, J.L. & Kazdin, A.E. (1985). An inventory to assess psychopathology in mentally retarded adults. *American Journal of Mental Retardation*, **89**, 459–466.

Shapiro, D.A., Barkham, M., Hardy, G. & Morrison, L.A. (1990). The 2nd Sheffield Psychotherapy Project—rationale, design and preliminary outcome data. *British Journal of Medical Psychology*, **63**, 97–108.

Stiles, W.B., Shapiro, D.A. & Firth-Cozens, J.A. (1988). Verbal response mode use in contrasting psychotherapies: a within subjects comparison. *Journal of Consulting and Clinical Psychology*, **56**, 727–733.

Teasdale, J. & Barnard, P. (1993). *Affect, Cognition and Change*. Hove: Psychology Press.

Vygotsky, L. (1962). *Thought and Language*. Cambridge, MA: MIT Press.

Whitman, T.L. (1990). Self-regulation and mental retardation. *American Journal on Mental Retardation*, **94**, 347–362.

Williams, H. & Jones, R.S.P. (1997). Teaching cognitive self-regulation of independence and emotion control skills. In B.S. Kroese, D. Dagnan & K. Loumidis (Eds) *Cognitive Behaviour Therapy for People with Learning Disabilities* (pp. 67–85). London: Routledge.

Williams, J.M.G., Watts, F.N., MacLeod, C. & Mathews, A. (1988). *Cognitive Psychology and Emotional Disorders*. Chichester: Wiley.

Zigler, E., Bennet-Gates, D. & Cohen, D. (Eds) (1999). *Personality Development in Individuals with Mental Retardation*. Cambridge: Cambridge University Press.

Zung, W.K. (1965). A self-rating depression scale. *Archives of General Psychiatry*, **12**, 63–70.

Zung, W.K. (1971). A rating instrument for anxiety disorders. *Psychosomatics*, **12**, 371–379.

CHAPTER 27

Methodology, Design, and Evaluation in Psychotherapy Research with People with Intellectual Disabilities

Nigel Beail
Barnsley Psychological Health Care and University of Sheffield, UK

The term "psychotherapy" covers a wide range of approaches to the treatment of psychological problems. According to Kazdin (1996), hundreds of forms of psychotherapy are available. However, the treatment literature concerning people with intellectual disabilities largely concerns the application of behavioural approaches to manage behavioural problems (Scotti, Evans, Meyer & Walker, 1991; Whittaker, 1993; Nezu & Nezu, 1994; Didden, Duker & Korzilius, 1997; Prout & Nowak-Drabik, 2003). During the latter part of the twentieth century, a literature has emerged concerning the use of cognitive and psychodynamically based treatments with people with intellectual disabilities.

In the previous chapters, the behavioural and cognitive approaches have been reported. This chapter will focus on the psychotherapies derived from psychoanalytic ideas. These include psychoanalysis, and psychoanalytic and psychodynamic psychotherapy. Throughout the chapter, I will use the generic term "psychodynamic psychotherapy".

Reviews of the provision of psychodynamic psychotherapy for people with intellectual disability reveal decades of inactivity (Nezu & Nezu, 1994; Beail, 1995). The application of psychoanalytic ideas to the field of intellectual disability dates back to the 1930s (Nezu & Nezu, 1994; Butz, Bowling & Bliss, 2000). But, as Sinason (1992) points out, this mainly amounts to a "few moments of curiosity". Bender's (1993) review charts a "history of therapeutic disdain" dating back to the beginning of the twentieth century and the early days of psychoanalysis. Other writers have commented on the enduring professional negative biases against the use of verbal psychotherapies with people with intellectual disabilities (Nezu & Nezu, 1994; Hurley, Pfadt, Tomasulo & Gardner, 1996).

During the 1980s, case reports concerning the psychodynamic treatment of people with intellectual disabilities began being published with increasing regularity (see Beail, 1995, for a review). At the same time, several papers were published drawing attention to the

The International Handbook of Applied Research in Intellectual Disabilities. Edited by E. Emerson, C. Hatton, T. Thompson and T.R. Parmenter © 2004 John Wiley & Sons, Ltd. ISBN 0-471-49709-6.

lack of provision and calling for research (Hurley, 1989; Nezu & Nezu, 1994). The first attempts to evaluate a series of cases were subsequently reported (Beail & Warden, 1996; Beail, 1998, 2001). This has occurred within the context of major changes in the way services are organised and delivered to people with intellectual disabilities. The philosophy of social-role valorisation has enabled previous views regarding the inappropriateness of providing psychodynamic psychotherapy to people with intellectual disabilities to be challenged. Services have moved from institutions to community bases. Reviews of treatments provided for people with intellectual disabilities reveal that studies have concerned behaviour treatments with recipients with high-frequency problem behaviour living in institutional settings. Most commentators draw attention to the closure of these institutions and their impact on the lives of those who lived within them. However, we often forget that the staff who worked within them were also relocated to community bases and consequently had to start delivery services differently.

Deliverers of psychological interventions faced new challenges—would their methods work in the community? (Whittaker, 1993). Certainly, the provision of psychodynamic and cognitive psychotherapy has grown with the change from inpatient to outpatient services. Other issues which seem to have contributed to the growth of psychotherapy services are the growing recognition of the mental health needs of people with intellectual disabilities (Bouras, 1994) and the recognition of sexual abuse as a significant issue requiring a treatment response (Brown, Stein & Turk, 1995).

EVALUATING PSYCHODYNAMIC PSYCHOTHERAPY

In order to evaluate psychotherapy, decisions need to be made concerning what questions need to be answered. The nature and extent of the evaluation will be a function of whom, or for what purpose, the questions are being asked. This chapter considers four main areas of evaluation: (a) service audit; (b) quality assurance; (c) effectiveness; and (d) cost-benefits, cost-efficiency, and cost-effectiveness. The methods described can be used to evaluate any psychotherapeutic intervention. However, the focus of this chapter is on psychodynamic approaches.

Service Audit

A service audit aims to find out who uses a service and how resources are allocated, and it comprises systematic data collection and analysis. An audit would involve the collection of socio-demographic information such as age, gender, geographical allocation, and occupation. Information on referring agent and range of presenting problems would be particularly relevant. Everyone referred to the service could also be assessed on measures of psychological well-being. Such a database enables services to have basic information on their service users. This facilitates the production of reports for service managers and purchasers as well as service-evaluation projects (e.g., Newman, Kellett & Beail, 2003).

Quality Assurance

Quality assurance focuses on the process by which psychotherapy is delivered and involves the setting and monitoring of standards of performance. In quality assurance, practitioners evaluate the quality of their service and devise and implement strategies for improving it. What can be achieved depends on the resources available. Maxwell (1984) has put forward six dimensions by which the quality and success of a service can be assessed—relevance, equity, accessibility, acceptability, effectiveness, and efficiency.

Service providers should ask whether psychodynamic psychotherapy matches the needs of the people referred to them. At the same time, they need to consider whether their service is equitable. Services can be made inequitable by unwarranted exclusion criteria. Clearly, "at least average intelligence" has been an unwarranted exclusion criterion, as it is without empirical foundation. Service providers need to ensure that their service is accessible. People with intellectual disabilities are often dependent on someone else to take them to outpatient appointments or teach them how to get there.

Service providers need to monitor whether or not their service is acceptable to their recipients. A consumer-satisfaction survey of users of a psychotherapy service for adults with intellectual disabilities found generally favourable responses. Recipients felt helped by the service and felt better after treatment. However, some respondents reported feeling confused sometime during treatment. There was also a difference between users' views and therapists' views on how therapy was ended (Brownlee, 1996).

Evaluating Effectiveness and Efficacy

The development of new therapeutic approaches calls for formal evaluation of their efficacy (the results the treatment achieves in the setting of a research trial) and their clinical effectiveness (the outcome of the treatment in routine clinical practice). Salkovskis (1995) describes a process of development he calls the "hourglass" model. In practice, what usually happens first is the reporting of case studies concerning theory and practice. This is followed by exploratory studies such as single-case designs or studies of a series of recipients in which technical standards of design and implementation are relatively relaxed. This kind of exploratory analysis then allows a narrowed focus on key effects. Here there is a requirement for research that conforms to the most rigorous standards of enquiry—equivalent to the pinch in the hourglass. This involves a fuller range of control groups, more stringent measures and statistical techniques, and careful specification of recipients to ensure replicability. Paradoxically, the designs of these studies can limit the clinical applicability of the research, as internal validity takes priority. However, issues concerning generalisability can be answered in a subsequent phase of research, which returns to an externally valid form of enquiry.

Enquiry in the psychoanalytic world has been dominated by theoretical discussion and illustrative case reports. This tradition can be clearly identified in the emerging literature on psychodynamic psychotherapy with people with intellectual disabilities. Reviews published in the 1990s found only narrative or anecdotal case reports with very few attempts at measuring outcome (Nezu & Nezu, 1994; Beail, 1995). Psychodynamic psychotherapists have also argued that the effects of treatment are not measurable or that the process of measurement would damage the therapeutic relationship and the treatment's effect. For example, Denman (1995) states that there is a "widespread criticism that the investigations that research requires (tapes of sessions and reports from patients during therapy) contaminate therapy and may adversely alter its course". However, Denman points out that claims of cure or outcome cannot be insulated from calls for validation or refutation. Despite objections, psychodynamic psychotherapy has been subject to extensive evaluation in the field of adult mental health (Bergin & Garfield, 1994; Roth & Fonagy, 1996). Roth and Fonagy's (1996) major review of psychotherapy research concluded that, in relation to major mental health conditions, psychological therapies have been found to achieve symptom reduction and improve social adjustment and work relationships. They found more evidence of cognitive-behavioural therapy than psychodynamic therapy and little evidence of "eclectic therapy". They concluded that all therapies appear to be dependent on a therapeutic alliance (good relationship and congruence about goals and methods). They found some evidence of specificity in relation to some conditions and some evidence of therapist skilfulness. With regard to people with intellectual disabilities, they state "although there are reports of effective psychodynamic treatment (e.g., Sinason, 1992), systematic outcome research has focused on behavioural training techniques (Target & Fonagy, 1996)". In fact, Sinason provides narrative case studies and does not address effectiveness.

Single-Case Evaluation of Treatment Outcome

Case reports of psychodynamic psychotherapy with people with intellectual disabilities including outcome measures are rare (Beail, 1995; Prout & Nowack-Drabik, 2003). The applications of single-case experimental designs are notably absent. In contrast, the treatment literature concerning people with intellectual disabilities is dominated by single-case experimental designs (Scotti et al., 1991; Whittaker, 1993; Didden et al., 1997). However, philosophical objections aside, there is no reason why these approaches could not be used to evaluate the outcome of psychodynamic psychotherapy.

Pre-Post Measurement

The simplest way to evaluate the outcome of treatment is to measure the symptoms, behaviour, or well-being of recipients before they undergo the treatment and again when treatment is complete. In long-term treatments, measurements may also be taken at intervals. We may also wish to see how the recipient did after treatment, and so follow-up measurements may also be taken.

Mr D was referred for aggressive behaviour. He agreed to undergo a course of psychotherapy to help him explore the reasons for his behaviour and help him control it. He attended 16 sessions of individual psychodynamic psychotherapy. To illustrate outcome, the results of his scores on the Hostility Scale and the General Severity Index (GSI) of the Symptom Checklist 90—Revised (SCL-90-R) at intake, 8 weeks (interval), 16 weeks (post), and 3-month follow-up are shown in Figure 27.1.

The results show reductions in symptomatology over the course of treatment, which were maintained at follow-up. However, the results may be open to competing explanations, and this reduces their value and informativeness. Mr D could have got better anyway. This is referred to as spontaneous remission. On the other hand, longitudinal studies have found considerable stability in the presence of behavioural difficulties in people with intellectual disabilities (Eyman, Borthwick & Miller, 1981; Kiernan et al., 1997).

If Mr D's scores had not changed at all, the conclusion could be drawn that the treatment was ineffective. However, alternatively, the treatment may have stemmed a deteriorating course. Issues such as these have led to the use of no-treatment control methods. Thus, evaluating a period of no treatment prior to treatment is one option in evaluating a single case. This is a common procedure in single-case experimental designs.

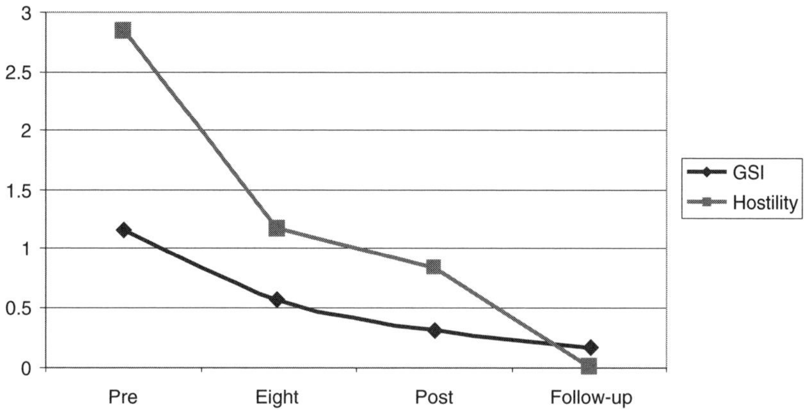

Figure 27.1 Mr D's GSI and hostility scores on the SCL-90-R

Single-Case Experimental Designs

Single-case experimental designs have been extensively employed to evaluate behavioural treatments with people with intellectual disabilities (see Chapter 21). It is not surprising, therefore, to find this approach being employed to evaluate cognitive-behavioural treatment with people with intellectual disabilities. Single-case experimental design reports of psychodynamic psychotherapy with non-disabled people are rare (Turpin, 2000; see Kellett & Beail, 1997, for an example) and non-existent for people with an intellectual disability. However, Dyson and Beail (2001) have utilised an A/B multiple-baseline, time-series design to evaluate the effectiveness of outpatient psychodynamic psychotherapy with a woman with intellectual disabilities. The recipient was displaying chronic somatisation about pains in her legs, and aggressive and obstructive behaviours at home.

The method involves two conditions, baseline or no-treatment (A) and intervention (B), which consists of a series of observations of target behaviours on a daily basis. Target behaviours are identified that reflect the nature and degree of the recipient's current problems, and these are coupled with positive alternative behaviours that are expected as a consequence of therapy. Obtaining descriptions of events from carers at the recipient's home identified target and alternative behaviours. These were corroborated with daily incident records kept by her carers, clinical observation, and interviews with the recipient.

To illustrate this approach to outcome, the target behaviour "somatisation" (states she is unwell, poorly, and in pain) and alternative behaviour of "engaging in activities without prompts" will be used. Carers recorded whether or not the behaviours occurred within 1-hour periods throughout the day. Data were collected for 21 days of baseline, 70 days during treatment, and 21 days of follow-up. Although the data were collected on an hourly basis, the results are presented in Figures 27.2 and 27.3 as weekly totals in order to facilitate visual inspection.

Visual inspection of the graphs in Figures 27.2 and 27.3 shows a decrease in somatisation and an increase in those willing to engage. Statistical tests can be applied to these data; however, this is possible only if the data are not correlated in time. Therefore, for each measure, a test of serial dependency/autocorrelation was carried out for baseline, intervention, and follow-up. These were all non-significant; therefore, trend lines and summaries of central tendency were calculated.

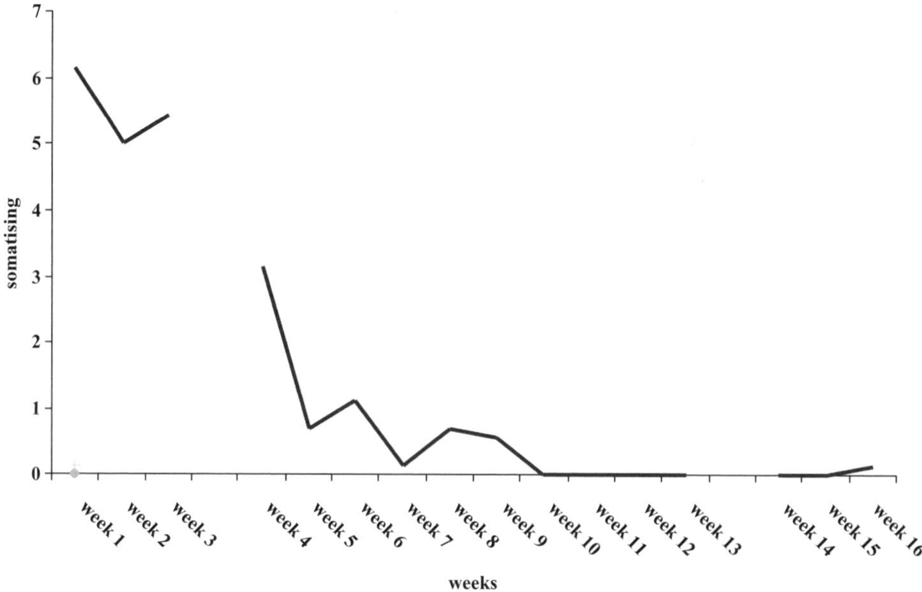

Figure 27.2 Weekly mean somatisations at baseline (weeks 1–3), treatment (weeks 4–13), and follow-up (weeks 14–16)

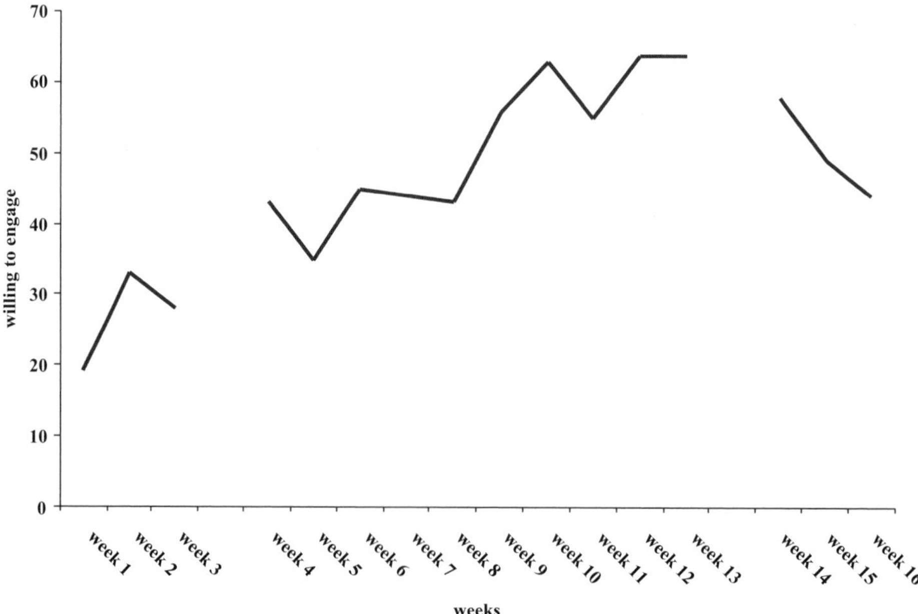

Figure 27.3 Weekly numbers "willing to engage" at baseline (weeks 1–3), treatment (weeks 4–13), and follow-up (weeks 14–16)

Table 27.1 Measures of central tendency for somatising and willingness to engage during baseline, intervention, and follow-up phases of psychodynamic psychotherapy with a woman with an intellectual disability

	Baseline		Intervention		Follow-up	
	M	SD	M	SD	M	SD
Somatising	36.7	13.3	5.2	6.7	0.3	0.6
Willing to engage	30.3	14.5	51.2	10.5	50.4	7.1

Note: M = mean; SD = standard deviation

The regression trend-line equations were significant within the treatment phases for somatising (Y = −1.802 × +15.101; r = .004) and willingness to engage (Y = 3.102 × +34.137; r = .0004). The measures of central tendency in Table 27.1 confirm visual impression and regression trends.

The effects remained once treatment was withdrawn, as no differences were apparent between treatment and follow-up. However, the differences between no-treatment and treatment phases are very clear.

Roth and Fonagy (1996) point out that single-case studies have a number of attractive features. They can be carried out in routine clinical practice, do not require the facilities associated with larger-scale research, and can be conducted fairly quickly. They also have a number of limitations. Results are difficult to generalise; however, over time studies can be subjected to meta-analytic techniques, as in the case of behavioural interventions (Scotti et al., 1991; Didden et al., 1997). For the evaluation of psychodynamic psychotherapy, the method is limited to A/B and follow-up, as this treatment is concerned to demonstrate lasting effects. Thus, reversal or withdrawal designs are not appropriate. The method may also have limitations, as many people with intellectual disability would not be able to keep daily records of their own thoughts, feelings, and behaviour. Thus, this approach may be more appropriate where others can record observable behaviours.

Group Designs

Open Trials

Open trials usually involve the evaluation of a series of recipients of treatment by pre- and post-measures. Entry to treatment may be governed by some criteria, but there is no control group. Such designs reflect a more naturalistic treatment protocol. Salkovskis (1995) states that, at this stage of the hourglass model, resources are often limited (often small numbers or solitary clinicians engaged in routine service provision), recipient sizes are small, and measures are unsubtle.

To date, research reports concerning the outcome of psychodynamic psychotherapy with people with intellectual disabilities have been open-trial designs. Beail (1998) reported the outcome of weekly outpatient psychodynamic psychotherapy for 20 men with intellectual disabilities who presented with a behaviour problem or had offended. The frequency of the behaviour problem was measured before and after treatment and at 6-month follow-up. For the offenders, the index offence was used as the outcome measure. The study involved a solitary clinician engaged in normal clinical practice with a small number of recipients. In line with Salkovskis' comments, the measures were also unsubtle. However, in most cases, the problem behaviour was eliminated, and this was maintained at 6-month follow-up.

Beail (2000) and Beail and Warden (1996) conducted a further study of 20 recipients who presented with psychological distress. In this study, they employed three outcome measures frequently used in psychotherapy outcome studies. The SCL-90-R (Derogatis, 1983) is often employed as a measure of symptom change. The Inventory of Interpersonal Problems (IIP-32) (Barkham, Hardy & Startup, 1996) and the Rosenberg Self-Esteem Inventory (Rosenberg, 1965) were also used. The study involved two clinicians working in routine clinical practice. However, this time, graduate psychologists were employed to carry out all the measurement, through an assisted completion format of the measures (see Kellett, Beail, Newman & Mosely, 1999, for an example of this procedure). The therapists were also kept blind to the results until after treatment. The study found significant reductions in symptoms, improvements in interpersonal functioning, and increases in self-esteem.

Beail (2001) reports a study of recidivism rates after psychodynamic psychotherapy among male offenders with intellectual disabilities. The recipients were 18 men who had been diverted from the criminal justice system. Thirteen participated in treatment and five refused. Of the 13 who completed treatment, two reoffended. The rest remained offence free at 4-year follow-up. The five who refused treatment all reoffended within 2 years.

These pre-post group designs suffer from the same difficulties as pre-post single-case reports. They also examine the truth of the null hypothesis—that is, that psychotherapy has no effect. The convention is to report statistical significance in terms of a confidence level of $P < .05$. However, demonstration of statistical effects may not be equivalent to clinically significant change. One alternative is to compare recipients' pre- and post-treatment scores with clinical and non-clinical population norms on outcome measures. Unfortunately, very few normative data have been collected to enable such analyses. In the absence of such data, Beail and Warden (1996) compared the outcome scores of their recipients with the non-patient norms for the SCL-90-R. This showed that recipients had scores well above the criterion for clinical caseness prior to treatment and fell below this at outcome and follow-up.

These pre-post uncontrolled exploratory analyses allow a narrowed focus on key effects, progressively moving towards more rarefied research. In the area of psychodynamic psychotherapy and outcome, that progress to date has been very slow.

Randomised-Control Trials (RCTs)

The blind, randomised-control trial (RCT) gives the clearest indication of the efficacy of treatment. The RCT asks questions about the comparative benefit of two or more treatments. The design permits active treatments to be compared with no treatment, waiting list, or placebo. Carr and colleagues (Chapter 21) and Dagnan and Lindsay (Chapter 26) report little progress with this approach to evaluating behavioural and cognitive therapies. In the area of psychodynamic psychotherapy, no progress has been made. However, some argue that, when possible, group designs with random assignment and adequate control groups should be standard (Nezu & Nezu, 1994; Whittaker, 2001).

In the RCT, participants are randomly allocated to the different conditions. A high degree of control is exercised over factors such as demographic variables, symptomatology and its severity, and level of functioning. The length of treatment is controlled, therapist experience is standardised, the treatments are manualised, and therapist adherence is monitored.

There are three basic research designs employed to evaluate treatments. For information on a wider range of approaches, see Kazdin (1994).

Treatment Versus No-Treatment or Waiting-List Control

In these studies, recipients are randomly assigned to treatment or no-treatment groups. Thus, spontaneous remission and impact of the passage of time is controlled for. Any change in the control group provides an estimate of what would have happened to the treatment group if they had not undergone treatment. It is assumed that the groups comprise individuals who are comparable in their personal characteristics and circumstances.

Treatment Versus Placebo Control

It may be that people improve when they undergo treatment due to the expectation that they will do so, rather than due to the treatment. In psychotherapy research, this design is beset by the difficulty of finding an activity which could be guaranteed to have no therapeutic element, which controls for the effect of attention, and which is viewed by recipients as being as credible as the active intervention (Roth & Fonagy, 1996).

Although ideal designs would involve contrasting treatment with no treatment and/or a placebo treatment, this is rarely possible either ethically or practically. In the field of psychotherapy outcome research with non-disabled recipients, researchers have restricted themselves to the comparison of active treatments.

Comparative Outcome Design

In this design, recipients are randomly assigned to one of several active treatments. As all treatments share the non-specific benefit arising from participants' belief in their value, this design reduces the need for a placebo condition. This also improves the ethical status of the design, as everyone is given active treatment.

Issues When Considering an RCT with Recipients with Intellectual Disabilities

Participant Characteristics, Numbers, and Recruitment

Nezu and Nezu (1994) argue that "samples should be homogeneous with regard to (a) level of intellectual disability, (b) psychiatric diagnosis, and (c) age". Additional factors not mentioned by them, but which are requirements of the RCT, include control over length of treatment, manualisation of treatment, control of therapist experience, and monitoring of therapist adherence to treatment. Studies meeting these criteria have not been carried out, and there are major issues that need to be addressed when considering such designs.

RCTs are usually restricted to the evaluation of treatment of one psychological problem. The requirement for one RCT to evaluate a treatment or treatments for, say, depression would require strict specification of recipient inclusion criteria. Such criteria would include level of intellectual disability (such as 55–70); meeting DSM-IV diagnostic criteria for depression; scoring above the cut-off level for severe depression on a measure of depression; being, say, between 18 and 35 years of age; not experiencing any other mental health problems; and exhibiting no behaviour disorder. Furthermore, the researchers would have to specify treatment length, therapist experience, and manualise the treatment. A system of therapist adherence to the treatment manual would also need to be established. A set of outcome measures would be needed, and the frequency of administration set.

A major issue in psychotherapy outcome research is the extent to which a study can detect differences between groups when differences exist in the population. This notion is referred to as statistical power, and it reflects the probability that the test will lead to the rejection of the null hypothesis. Power is a function of the criteria for statistical significance, sample size, and effect size (the difference that exists between groups). Thus, researchers need to determine whether the design of the evaluation is sufficiently powerful to detect meaningful differences.

In psychotherapy research, issues of power might emerge as a function of the different types of comparison that are made and the different effect sizes the comparisons are likely to yield. To compare psychodynamic psychotherapy with no treatment, it is reasonable to expect a large effect around one standard deviation unit (that is, the mean of the treated group one standard deviation better than the mean of the untreated group). To detect such an effect, a sample size of approximately 20–30 recipients in each condition is needed (Kraemer, 1981). When we compare two treatments, however, considerably larger groups are required because the average effect sizes obtained in such studies are only one-half of a standard deviation (Kazdin & Bass, 1989). Thus, around 60–70 recipients completing each treatment would be required. All recipients would also have to meet the studies selection criteria. These figures are minimums, as several times as many participants are usually needed in studies of non-disabled recipients, due to attrition.

Consent

Participants in RCTs concerning treatment have to give their consent to treatment and to being a research participant. Consent involves an ability to list the benefits, risks, and alternatives and to understand the consequences of having and not having treatment. They need to be able to retain, believe, and comprehend the information; weight it in the balance; and arrive at a choice. After their consent to treatment is obtained, the researcher needs to obtain their consent to being a research participant. Arscott, Dagnan and Kroese (1998) found that adults with mild intellectual disabilities appeared to understand the nature of an interview-only research study but had a limited understanding of the risks and benefits of being involved or their right to refuse to participate, or to drop out of the study. The decision concerning consent to an RCT is more complex than suggested by the investigation by Arscott et al. (1998). In addition to being interviewed, prospective participants would need to make a decision regarding randomisation and its implications for them. This may be difficult to comprehend. However, being allocated to one of two treatments that may benefit the participant would be a sounder option. Still, the capacity of people with intellectual disabilities to weigh in the balance the risks and benefits of alternate treatments in order to arrive at a choice, as well as their understanding of their right to refuse or opt out, makes obtaining informed consent difficult.

Treatment Length

Currently, there is no research with people with intellectual disabilities that could indicate how long treatment should be. The open trials reported by Beail (1998; 2000) did not place a time limit on treatment. In one study, treatment varied in length from 3 to 43 months (Beail, 1998); in the other, the range was 5–48 sessions (Beail, 2000).

Generalisation

RCTs rarely monitor the outcome of psychological therapies in routine clinical practice. In order to satisfy the demands of internal validity, the results of RCTs can fail to generalise to normal clinical practice.

The Future of RCTs in the Evaluation of Psychotherapy with People with Intellectual Disabilities

There are considerable obstacles to mounting an RCT to evaluate the outcome of psychodynamic psychotherapy with people with intellectual disabilities. Ensuring adequate numbers of participants to meet the stringent requirements of internal validity is fraught with difficulties.

Roth and Fonagy (1996) identify the problem for psychotherapy researchers in the tension between satisfying the demands of internal and external validity when developing research strategies. They argue that current designs have to reach a compromise between these factors by building a bridge between scientific rigour on the one hand and generalisability on the other hand. There is clearly a lot of scope for further research on psychodynamic psychotherapy with people with intellectual disabilities. We need a further stage of clinical development before the pinch of the hourglass. Alternatively, we could accept that the volumes of research on psychotherapy with non-disabled populations have established their efficacy (Roth & Fonagy, 1996), and move on to explore the generalisability of these approaches with people with intellectual disabilities.

Some more ethical ways forward would include the use of non-random waiting-list control groups or wider use of single-case designs that include baseline periods. Roth and Fonagy (1996) favour single-case experimental designs, as external validity is not an inherent problem in designs of this type. They state that, when replicated randomly across sampled cases, these designs have considerable generalisability. They argue that they can be employed to answer most questions that concern researchers, such as the appropriateness of a particular form of treatment, the length of the treatment required for good outcome, the relative impact of the treatment on a particular problem, or the relevance of particular components of treatment. This approach needs to be further explored in the evaluation of psychodynamic psychotherapy with people with intellectual disabilities. The decisions involved in obtaining consent are less complex, and no-treatment control is built in. The drawbacks are the high demands on monitoring outcome, the fact that few people with intellectual disabilities would be able to keep their own diaries, and the fact that therapist factors are difficult to study.

Process Research

An alternative to outcome research is process research. This involves the study of what goes on within the therapy sessions. The only example of this research model being applied to the study of psychodynamic psychotherapy with people with intellectual disabilities is that of Newman and Beail (2002). They used the Assimilation of Problematic Experiences Scale (APES) (Stiles et al., 1990) to see whether adults with intellectual disabilities could assimilate their problematic experience during the course of treatment. This design involved tape-recording sessions. After these tapes were transcribed, one problematic experience was identified. The transcript was edited to contain only episodes of dialogue concerning the problematic experience.

Evaluators trained in the use of the APES then rated each episode on the scale. Newman and Beail (2002) found increases in the recipients' level of assimilation of their problematic experience during treatment sessions and across sessions.

Cost-Benefit, Cost-Efficiency, and Cost-Effectiveness

A cost-benefit analysis aims to evaluate the costs and benefits of a treatment in solely monetary terms. A cost-efficiency study involves a comparison between two or more treatments in terms of the cost of achieving a specified outcome. A cost-effectiveness study defines outcomes in more substantive or unspecified terms (for example, psychological health) and aims to find out which treatment obtains the best result for the cost input. Here, only the cost of treatment implementation is expressed in monetary terms. An example might involve the comparison between providing individual versus group psychodynamic psychotherapy for six people. The outcome on measures of psychological distress, behaviour, or interpersonal functioning may show individual psychotherapy to have better outcomes. However, the difference between the treatments might not warrant the additional cost in terms of therapist time or clients' waiting time. Such studies have not yet been conducted with recipients with intellectual disabilities.

Measuring Outcome

In the past, attempts at measuring outcome in psychodynamic psychotherapy relied on projective devices such as the Rorschach and the Thematic Apperception Test (TAT). Lambert and Hill (1994) state that these methods have been largely discarded because of their poor psychometric qualities, reliance on inference, and reflection of orientations that emphasise unconscious processes. However, their preference by some psychodynamic researchers remains. Bichard, Sinason and Usiskin (1996) have employed projective techniques to evaluate long-term individual and group psychodynamic psychotherapy with children and adults with intellectual disabilities. While they report significant improvements, the measures employed do not have wide acceptance outside the psychodynamic field. Moreover, their reliability and validity have not been established.

In general, psychotherapy outcome research measures should be drawn from the following:

- differing symptom domains (such as feelings, thoughts, and behaviour)
- differing domains of functioning (such as social, interpersonal, and adaptive)
- differing perspective (such as those of the recipient, a close relative, carer, or independent observer).

There is little consensus on the precise measures to be employed—for a discussion of these issues in psychotherapy research in general, see Lambert and Hill (1994) and Roth and Fonagy (1996).

In the field of intellectual disability research, there are no well-established methods or measures of psychotherapy outcome (see Aman, 1994; Caine & Hatton 1998; Sturmey, Reed & Corbett 1991, for reviews). The literature concerning the assessment of people with intellectual disabilities is historically laden with instruments that solely measure skills or behaviours with little attention paid to the assessment of mental health problems (Newman & Beail, 1994). There has been an assumption that people with intellectual disabilities are generally unable to give an accurate report of their mental state. Consequently, standardised interviews and checklists of mental health problems in people with an intellectual disability are a rarity (Caine & Hatton, 1998). A few screening instruments have been developed, but the majority are informant-based rather than self-report. However, such information provided by carers has been found to be of questionable reliability and validity (Nadarajah, Roy, Harris & Corbett, 1995; Prosser & Bromley, 1998).

Behavioural outcome studies have largely consisted of single-case experimental designs in which individualised outcome measures are developed. Researchers employing such designs to evaluate psychodynamic psychotherapy would need to take this approach. However, psychotherapy research has traditionally employed a range of checklists. Most of these are in a self-report format requiring at least average reading ability. Despite this, researchers evaluating psychotherapy with people with intellectual disabilities have been employing self-report measures for evaluating change in presenting problems (Nezu, Nezu & Arien, 1991; Beail & Warden, 1996; Beail, 2000).

A number of single-trait measures, such as the Zung Anxiety Scale and the Beck Depression Inventory, have been modified for people with intellectual disabilities and are administered in an interview format. Unfortunately, evaluations of their reliability and validity are sparse (Sturmey et al., 1991). Several multitrait measures have been developed specifically for use with people with intellectual disabilities. However, these are largely diagnostic scales rather than outcome measures. The Reiss Screen (Reiss, 1988) has 36 items administered to an informant regarding the recipient. The scale has adequate psychometric properties, but data concerning the validity of the eight subscales are questionable (Sturmey, Jamieson, Burcham, Shaw & Bertman, 1996). The Psychopathology Instrument for Mentally Retarded Adults (PIMRA) (Matson, Kazdin & Senatore, 1984) has 56 items divided into seven subscales. It has both self-report and informant versions. The PIMRA has been found to be less psychometrically robust than the Reiss Screen, and the validity of its subscales has been called into question.

The PAS-ADD Checklist and the Mini-PAS-ADD were developed to screen for and then assess a person's mental health problems on seven dimensions. Untrained carers can complete the checklist, but mental health professionals should complete the Mini-PAS-ADD. Findings concerning their reliability and validity are encouraging (Moss et al., 1998). While these instruments were not developed as an outcome measure, this could be explored.

In their studies, Beail and Warden (1996) and Beail (2000) used the SCL-90-R (Derogatis, 1983). This checklist is widely used in general psychotherapy outcome studies to monitor changes in symptomatology. Kellett et al. (1999) have evaluated the utility of the SCL-90-R in indexing psychological distress with people with intellectual disabilities when administered in an assisted-completion format. They found the global indices and nine symptom scales to have good internal consistency, split half reliability, and discriminative validity. These finding have been replicated with the Brief Symptom Inventory (Derogatis, 1993), which is a shorter version of the SCL-90-R (Kellett, Beail, Newman & Frankish, 2003).

If the presenting problem is of a behavioural nature, measures such as the Aberrant Behaviour Checklist (Aman, Singh, Stewart & Field, 1985) could be used. This was developed as a measure of drug treatment outcome in institutional settings. However, some questions have been modified for its use with community populations (Aman, Burrow & Wolford, 1994).

Measures of interpersonal relationships and functioning have recently been introduced into psychotherapy outcome studies. The most widely used has been the Inventory of Interpersonal Problems (IIP) (Horowitz, Rosenberg, Baer, Ureno & Villasenor, 1988). The original inventory has 127 items, but short forms are available. Beail and Warden (1996) and Beail (2000) used a 32-item version of the IIP (Barkham et al., 1996) in their study. However, work concerning its reliability and validity when used with people with intellectual disabilities remains to be carried out.

Nezu and Nezu (1994) argue that generalisation effects, especially with regard to changes in adaptive functioning, should be assessed. Thus measures of adaptive behaviour could also be used.

Overall, approaches to the assessment of outcome are in the early stages of development. To date, some attention has been paid to the reliability and validity of extant and new measures when used with people with intellectual disabilities. However, recent developments are encouraging.

CONCLUSION

Psychotherapy research has a long history, and reports on outcome run into volumes. However, people with intellectual disabilities have been excluded from these endeavours. This chapter provides an overview of the current state of research on psychodynamic psychotherapy with people with intellectual disabilities. In terms of the hourglass model, the results suggest we are still in the very early stages. Consideration of research issues concerning the more rigorous research at the pinch of the hourglass reveal major issues which need thought, examination, and debate. Considerable effort also needs to be focused on methods of outcome measurement, especially reliability and validity.

The principal aim of this chapter has been to inform practitioners providing psychotherapy services to people with intellectual disabilities about evaluation. The methods described will enable them to incorporate evaluation techniques into their routine clinical practice. Increased attention to evaluation will also enable practitioners and researchers to find a way forward on the issues that more rarefied research would entail.

REFERENCES

Aman, M.G. (1994). Instruments for assessing treatment effects in developmentally disabled populations. *Assessment in Rehabilitation and Exceptionality*, **1**, 1–20.

Aman, M.G., Burrow, W.H. & Wolford, P.L. (1994). The Aberrant Behaviour Checklist–Community: factor validity and effect of subject variables for adults in group homes. *American Journal of Mental Retardation*, **100**, 283–292.

Aman, M.G., Singh, N.N., Stewart, A.W. & Field, C.J. (1985). The Aberrant Behaviour Checklist: a behaviour rating scale for assessment of treatment effects. *American Journal of Mental Deficiency*, **89**, 485–491.

Arscott, K., Dagnan, D. & Kroese, B.S. (1998). Consent to psychological research by people with an intellectual disability. *Journal of Applied Research in Intellectual Disabilities*, **11**, 77–83.

Barkham, M., Hardy, G. & Startup, M. (1996). The IIP32: a short version of the Inventory of Interpersonal Problems. *British Journal of Clinical Psychology*, **35**, 21–36.

Beail, N. (1995). Outcome of psychoanalysis, psychoanalytic and psychodynamic psychotherapy with people with intellectual disabilities. *Changes*, **13**, 186–191.

Beail, N. (1998). Psychoanalytic psychotherapy with men with intellectual disabilities: a preliminary outcome study. *British Journal of Medical Psychology*, **71**, 1–11.

Beail, N. (2000). An evaluation of out-patient psychodynamic psychotherapy for adults with intellectual disabilities. Paper presented at the 11th World Congress of the International Association for the Scientific Study of Intellectual Disabilities, Seattle. *Journal of Intellectual Disability Research*, **44**, 204.

Beail, N. (2001). Recidivism following psychodynamic psychotherapy amongst offenders with intellectual disabilities. *British Journal of Forensic Practice*, **3**, 33–37.

Beail, N. & Warden, S. (1996). Evaluation of a psychodynamic psychotherapy service for adults with intellectual disabilities: rationale, design and preliminary outcome data. *Journal of Applied Research in Intellectual Disabilities*, **9**, 223–228.

Bender, M. (1993). The unoffered chair: the history of therapeutic disdain towards people with a learning difficulty. *Clinical Psychology Forum*, **54**, 7–12.

Bergin, A.E. & Garfield, S.L. (Eds) (1994). *Handbook of Psychotherapy and Behaviour Change* (4th edn). New York: Wiley.

Bichard, S., Sinason, V. & Usiskin, J. (1996). Measuring change in mentally retarded clients in long-term psychoanalytic psychotherapy. *National Association for the Dually Diagnosed Newsletter*, **13**, 6–11.

Bouras, N. (Ed.) (1994). *Mental Health in Mental Retardation: Recent Advances and Practices*. Cambridge: Cambridge University Press.

Brown, H., Stein, J. & Turk, V. (1995). Report of a two-year incidence survey on the reported sexual abuse of adults with learning disabilities: 1991 and 1992. *Mental Handicap Research*, **1**, 1–22.

Brownlee, Z. (1996). Consumer satisfaction of a psychotherapy service. Unpublished report. Clinical Psychology Unit, Department of Psychology, University of Sheffield, UK.

Butz, M.R., Bowling, J.B. & Bliss, C.A. (2000). Psychotherapy with the mentally retarded: a review of the literature and the implications. *Professional Psychology: Research and Practice*, **31**, 42–47.

Caine, A. & Hatton, C. (1998). Working with people with mental health problems. In E. Emerson, C. Hatton, J. Bromley & A. Caine (Eds) *Clinical Psychology and People with Intellectual Disabilities* (pp. 210–230). Chichester: Wiley.

Denman, C. (1995). Questions to be answered in the evaluation of long-term therapy. In M. Aveline & D.A. Shapiro (Eds) *Research Foundations for Psychotherapy* (pp. 175–190). Chichester: Wiley.

Derogatis, L.R. (1983). *SCL-90-R; Administration, Scoring and Procedures: Manual II*. Towson, MD: Clinical Psychometric Research.

Derogatis, L.R. (1993). *Brief Symptom Inventory: Administration, Scoring and Procedures Manual* (3rd edn). Minneapolis, MN: National Computer Systems.

Didden, R., Duker, P.C. & Korzilius, H. (1997). Meta-analytic study on treatment effectiveness for problem behaviors with individuals who have mental retardation. *American Journal of Mental Retardation*, **101**, 387–399.

Dyson, G. & Beail, N. (2001). Single case experimental design evaluation of psychodynamic psychotherapy with a woman with severe intellectual disabilities. Paper presented at the Third European Congress on Mental Health in Mental Retardation, Berlin.

Eyman, R., Borthwick, S. & Miller, C. (1981). Trends in maladaptive behaviour of mentally retarded persons placed in community settings and institutional settings. *American Journal of Mental Deficiency*, **85**, 473–477.

Horowitz, L.M., Rosenberg, S.E., Baer, B.A., Ureno, G. & Villasenor, V.S. (1988). Inventory of Interpersonal Problems: psychometric properties and clinical applications. *Journal of Consulting and Clinical Psychology*, **56**, 885–892.

Hurley, A.D. (1989). Individual psychotherapy with mentally retarded individuals: a review and call for research. *Research in Developmental Disabilities*, **10**, 261–275.

Hurley, A.D., Pfadt, A., Tomasulo, D. & Gardner, W.I. (1996). Counselling and psychotherapy. In J.W. Jacobson & J.A. Mulick (Eds) *Manual of Diagnosis and Professional Practice in Mental Retardation* (pp. 371–378). Washington, DC: American Psychological Association.

Kazdin, A.E. (1994). Methodology, design, and evaluation in psychotherapy research. In A.E. Bergin & S.L. Garfield (Eds) *Handbook of Psychotherapy and Behaviour Change* (4th edn) (pp. 19–71). New York: Wiley.

Kazdin, A.E. (1996). Forward. In A. Roth & P. Fonagy (Eds) *What Works for Whom: A Critical Review of Psychotherapy Research* (pp. v–vii). New York: Guilford.

Kazdin, A.E. & Bass, D. (1989). Power to detect differences between alternative treatments in comparative psychotherapy outcome research. *Journal of Consulting and Clinical Psychology*, **57**, 138–147.

Kellett, S.C. & Beail, N. (1997). The treatment of chronic post-traumatic nightmares using psychodynamic interpersonal psychotherapy: a single case study. *British Journal of Medical Psychology*, **70**, 35–49.

Kellett, S., Beail, N., Newman, D.W. & Frankish, P. (2003). Utility of the Brief Symptom Inventory in the assessment of psychological distress. *Journal of Applied Research in Intellectual Disabilities*, **16**, 127–134.

Kellett, S., Beail, N., Newman, D.W. & Mosley, E. (1999). Indexing psychological distress in people with intellectual disabilities: use of the Symptom Checklist-90-R. *Journal of Applied Research in Intellectual Disabilities*, **12**, 323–334.

Kiernan, C., Reeves, D., Hatton, C., Alborz, Z., Emerson, E., Mason, H., et al. (1997). *The Hester Adrian Research Centre Challenging Behaviour Project. Report 1: The Persistence of Challenging Behaviour*. Hester Adrian Research Centre: University of Manchester.

Kraemer, H.C. (1981). Coping strategies in psychiatric clinical research. *Journal of Consulting and Clinical Psychology*, **49**, 309–319.

Lambert, M.J. & Hill, C.E. (1994). Assessing psychotherapy outcomes and processes. In A.E. Bergin & S.L. Garfield (Eds) *Handbook of Psychotherapy and Behaviour Change* (4th edn) (pp. 72–113). New York: Wiley.

Matson, J.L., Kazdin, A.E. & Senatore, V. (1984). Psychometric properties of the Psychopathology Instrument for mentally retarded adults. *Applied Research in Mental Retardation*, **5**, 881–889.

Maxwell, R.J. (1984). Quality assessment in health. *British Medical Journal*, **288**, 1470–1472.

Moss, S., Prosser, H., Costello, H., Simpson, N., Patel, P., Rowe, S., et al. (1998). Reliability and validity of the PAS-ADD Checklist for detecting psychiatric disorders in adults with intellectual disability. *Journal of Intellectual Disability Research*, **42**, 173–183.

Nadarajah, J., Roy, A., Harris, T.O. & Corbett, J.A. (1995). Methodological aspects of life events research in people with learning disabilities: a review and initial findings. *Journal of Intellectual Disability Research*, **39**, 47–56.

Newman, D.W. & Beail, N. (1994). The assessment of need: a psychological perspective on people with learning disabilities. *Clinical Psychology Forum*, **71**, 21–25.

Newman, D.W. & Beail, N. (2002). Monitoring change in psychotherapy with people with intellectual disabilities: the application of the Assimilation of Problematic Experiences Scale. *Journal of Applied Research in Intellectual Disabilities*, **15**, 48–60.

Newman, D.W., Kellett, S. & Beail, N. (2003). From research and development to practice based evidence. Clinical governance initiatives in a service for adults with mild intellectual disabilities and mental health needs. *Journal of Intellectual Disability Research*, **47**, 68–74.

Nezu, C.M. & Nezu, A.M. (1994). Outpatient psychotherapy for adults with mental retardation and concomitant psychopathology: research and clinical imperatives. *Journal of Consulting and Clinical Psychology*, **62**, 34–42.

Nezu, C.M., Nezu, A.M. & Arien, P. (1991). Assertiveness and problem-solving therapy for mild mentally retarded persons with dual diagnosis. *Research in Developmental Disabilities*, **12**, 371–386.

Prosser, H. & Bromley, J. (1998). Interviewing people with intellectual disabilities. In E. Emerson, C. Hatton, J. Bromley & A. Caine (Eds) *Clinical Psychology and People with Intellectual Disabilities* (pp. 99–113). Chichester: Wiley.

Prout, H.T. & Nowak-Drabik, K.M. (2003). Psychotherapy with people who have mental retardation: an evaluation of effectiveness. *American Journal of Mental Retardation*, **108**, 82–93.

Reiss, S. (1988). *Reiss Screen for Maladaptive Behaviour*. Worthington, OH: IDS Publishing.

Rosenberg, M. (1965). *Society and the Adolescent Self Esteem*. Princeton: Princeton University Press.

Roth, A. & Fonagy, P. (1996). *What Works for Whom: A Critical Review of Psychotherapy Research*. New York: Guilford.

Salkovskis, P.M. (1995). Demonstrating specific effects in cognitive and behavioural therapy. In M. Aveline & D.A. Shapiro (Eds) *Research Foundations for Psychotherapy* (pp. 191–228). Chichester: Wiley.

Scotti, J.R., Evans, I.M., Meyer, L.H. & Walker, P. (1991). A Meta-analysis of intervention research with problem behaviour: treatment validity and standards of practice. *American Journal of Mental Retardation*, **96**, 233–256.

Sinason, V. (1992). *Mental Handicap and the Human Condition: New Approaches from the Tavistock*. London: Free Association.

Stiles, W.B., Elliot, R., Llewelyn, S.P., Firth-Cozens, J.A., Margison, F.R., Shapiro, D.A., et al. (1990). Assimilation of problematic experiences by clients in psychotherapy. *Psychotherapy*, **27**, 411–420.

Sturmey, P., Jamieson, J., Burcham, J., Shaw, B. & Bertman, L. (1996). The factor structure of the Reiss Screen for Maladaptive Behaviours in institutional and community populations. *Research in Developmental Disabilities*, **17**, 285–291.

Sturmey, P., Reed, J. & Corbett, J. (1991). Psychometric assessment of psychiatric disorders in people with learning difficulties (mental handicap): a review of measures. *Psychological Medicine*, **21**, 143–155.

Target, M. & Fonagy, P. (1996). The psychological treatment of child and adolescent psychiatric disorders. In A. Roth & P. Fonagy (Eds) *What Works for Whom: A Critical Review of Psychotherapy Research* (pp. 263–320). New York: Guilford.

Turpin, G. (2000). Single case methodology and psychotherapy evaluation: from research to practice. In C. Mace, S. Moorey & B. Roberts (Eds) *Evidence in the Psychological Therapies: A Critical Guide for Practitioners* (pp. 91–113). London: Brunner-Routledge.

Whittaker, S. (1993). The reduction of aggression in people with learning difficulties: a review of psychological methods. *British Journal of Clinical Psychology*, **32**, 1–37.

Whittaker, S. (2001). Anger control for people with learning disabilities: a critical review. *Behavioural and Cognitive Psychotherapy*, **29**, 277–293.

CHAPTER 28

Methodological Issues in Psychopharmacology for Individuals with Intellectual and Developmental Disabilities

Travis Thompson
Minnesota Autism Center, Minneapolis, USA
Jennifer Zarcone
University of Kansas Medical Center, USA
and
Frank Symons
University of Minnesota, USA

Although many people with intellectual and related disabilities learn the necessary life skills to participate in integrated educational, vocational, residential, and recreational settings, a significant minority do not, instead leading restrictive lives because they injure themselves or others, or they destroy property. Such destructive behavior limits the full participation of people with intellectual disabilities in community settings (Intagliata & Willer, 1981; Vitello, Atthowe & Cadwell, 1983; Davidson et al., 1996).

The most common forms of behavioral challenges include aggressive assault, self-injury, and property destruction. Schroeder, Rojahn and Oldenquist (1991) reported that the prevalence of aggressive behavior in people with mental retardation and developmental disabilities was approximately 9–23%, and property destruction was reported in 4–14% of this population. More recent surveys reveal similar, if not higher, prevalence rates of destructive behavior, including self-injury (Bruininks, Olson, Larson & Lakin, 1994). Some destructive behavior is of special concern because of its pervasiveness and high frequency, and the possibility of tissue damage (such as repetitive skin-picking), whereas other challenging behaviors are significant because of the immediate harm caused by even a few instances (such as physical assault and self-biting). The consequences of such challenging behavior

The International Handbook of Applied Research in Intellectual Disabilities. Edited by E. Emerson, C. Hatton, T. Thompson and T.R. Parmenter ISBN 0-471-49709-6.

can include disfigurement and chronic application of mechanical restraints (for example, self-mutilation in Lesch-Nyhan syndrome). The difficulties of treatment are especially problematic because our understanding of behavior disorders and mental health or psychiatric disorders among people with mental retardation is imprecise, a fact which can result in applying the same treatments to behavior problems that outwardly appear similar but, in fact, are not related.

In the past, treatments for severe destructive behaviors have included intrusive procedures that are generally not socially accepted, and their use has been the object of considerable debate (Repp & Singh, 1990). Positive behavioral intervention procedures using more socially acceptable methods have been designed to reduce the challenging behaviors of people with intellectual disabilities by teaching them functional skills to control events in their surroundings (Horner et al., 1990). Positive behavioral interventions often involve modifying setting events (e.g., Zarcone, Iwata, Smith, Mazaleski & Lerman, 1994; Horner, Vaughn, Day & Ard, 2001), increasing functional alternative communication skills (e.g., Carr & Durand, 1985; Reichle & Wacker, 1993), and increasing reinforcement contingent on appropriate adaptive skills and social behavior (e.g., Mirenda, MacGreger & Kelly-Keough, 2002).

The most widely researched interventions were reviewed critically over a decade ago as part of a US National Institutes of Health (NIH) Consensus Development Conference on Destructive Behavior in Developmental Disabilities (NIH, 1991). The report concluded that many behavior problems appear to involve both biological and environmental components. And, although several types of treatments produce temporary reductions in challenging behavior, the challenging behavior resumes, in many cases, after treatment is reduced or stopped. Treatments typically have been designed on the basis of the assumption of a single type of cause for the challenging behavior (most often *either* biological or environmental, but rarely combined). Many of the most difficult to treat behavioral challenges, however, are probably regulated by factors in the person's social environment, as well as by biological or biochemical factors. Because of this dual control, our assessment and treatment efforts need to consider the possibility of both behavioral and biomedical treatments. In this chapter, our purpose is to focus on psychotropic medication when treating the destructive behavior of persons with intellectual disabilities; however, we do so in the context of environmental factors.

PSYCHOTROPIC MEDICATIONS AND CHALLENGING BEHAVIOR

Over the past three decades, numerous investigators have reviewed the effects of psychotropic medications on behavior problems in intellectual disability (Lipman, 1970; Sprague & Werry, 1971; Aman & Singh, 1991; Napolitano et al., 1999). The purpose of administering psychotropic treatments is to improve a person's functioning by modifying the way in which he or she typically responds to naturally occurring events in the environment. By doing so, challenging behavior is made unnecessary and improbable. Effective use of psychotropic medications enables the person to respond to daily environmental events in a more normalized manner. If pharmacological interventions are successful, they may make it possible for the person to adjust successfully to a wider range of typical settings that do not or are not able to provide environmental supports or modifications.

What Is Being Treated?

A very common mistake in using psychotropic medications is to assume that a medication is used to treat a unitary, underlying psychopathological disorder that is responsible for the signs and symptoms being observed. "What is the most effective medication for treating self-injury in autism?" seems on the surface to be a reasonable question. But this question begins with the erroneous assumption that autism is a unitary condition and that the signs and symptoms exhibited by people with autism occur for a single reason. There are large individual differences among individuals with autism, including the degree of expression of the three groups of cardinal diagnostic features. Self-injury in autism may occur because the person has obsessive-compulsive disorder (which involves serotonergic abnormalities), because self-injury produces the release of beta-endorphin binding to the brain's opiate receptors that reinforces self-injury, because the person suffers from major depression (a serotonin-norepinephrine imbalance), or because self-injury leads to escape from or avoidance of nonpreferred activities, and verbally compromised people have no way of communicating their needs or wants. In short, there is no "best" medication to treat behavior problems associated with autism, although there are effective medications to treat some of the more common behavioral challenges associated with autism, given a proper functional diagnosis.

A woman with learning disability and Asperger's syndrome may strike out against a staff member who requests that she enter her workplace, because she is frightened of the prospect of entering a room that includes several strangers. That may indicate that she suffers from a social anxiety disorder. The person's need to avoid social anxiety-producing situations is presumed to be regulated by a neurochemical abnormality (as in the brain serotonin system) underlying the social phobia. If that neurochemical abnormality is treated with a selective serotonin reuptake inhibitor (SSRI) medication, social situations may become less anxiety producing, thereby obviating the need to avoid them by striking out aggressively. An adolescent with Cornelia de Lange syndrome and severe intellectual disability repeatedly bites her hand, and she does so with or without social interactions. While hand-biting may be more frequent when she is unoccupied for an extended interval, the self-destructive behavior may be present across many situations. Hand-biting causes the release of beta-endorphin, the body's natural reaction to pain, which in turn binds to opiate receptors in the brain, the same chemical receptors to which morphine or heroin binds. By blocking those receptors with a medication that prevents the beta-endorphin from binding to them, the opiate receptor-mediated reinforcing effect is terminated, and eventually hand-biting diminishes and may stop.

In both of the foregoing cases, a brain chemical mechanism is being treated that contributes to the challenging behavior. However, much of the time, people with severe intellectual disabilities exhibit problem behavior, such as aggression or self-injury, and we have no generally recognized way of identifying the underlying psychopathology or the neurochemical consequences of the behavior that may be contributing to its continuation. Indeed, in many instances, there may be no underlying psychopathology. Instead, the challenging behavior may be a maladaptive coping attempt by an individual with limited communication and other skills. A systematic approach is needed to identify likely environmental contributions (or rule them out), and to investigate possible neuropsychopathological mechanisms that may contribute to challenging behavior.

Functional Interpretations of Challenging Behavior

A functional approach to behavioral assessment and treatment identifies factors associated with and controlling the person's challenging behavior (Carr, 1977; Iwata, Dorsey, Slifer, Bauman & Richman, 1994a; Repp & Karsh, 1994; O'Neill et al., 1997). These factors typically include environmental events immediately preceding or following the challenging behavior, as well as features of specific settings in which the challenging behavior occurs. If hitting a staff member reliably results in attention from other staff, and if attention is something the client values, then staff attention may eventually reinforce hitting and make future instances of hitting more likely. Behavior motivated by access to staff attention is said to be attention-motivated. Events prior to the occurrence of behavior problems (that is, antecedents) can also gain control over destructive behavior (such as task demands). A client with no spoken language may bite his hand when staff ask him to brush his teeth. It is likely the staff person will stop asking the client to participate in dental hygiene when biting occurs and, furthermore, may clean his teeth for him. If dental hygiene activities are difficult for the client or are an activity he dislikes, he is more likely to bite himself in the future when he is asked to clean his teeth; thus, he escapes or avoids having to brush his own teeth. Biting is an escape-motivated or negatively reinforced behavior. In both previous examples, the challenging behavior was not random. Nor did it necessarily indicate the presence of a psychiatric disorder, but instead was predictably related to the functions the behavior served in managing the person's environment. Much of the destructive behavior of people with developmental disabilities comes under the control of both antecedent and consequent events, and understanding the function of a challenging behavior is important in designing habilitative or educational programs to promote alternative adaptive behaviors while reducing the challenging behaviors (Baumeister & Sevin, 1990; Iwata et al., 1994b).

Biochemical Interpretations of Challenging Behavior

There are other cases, however, in which destructive behavior is neither purely attention- nor escape-motivated. People with intellectual disabilities are subject to the same mental health problems as other, typically developing people, including major depressive disorder, anxiety disorders, and schizophrenia. Recently, Emerson (2003) evaluated the incidence of psychiatric disorders in children and adolescents with intellectual disabilities as compared to a group of children without disabilities. He found that individuals with intellectual disabilities were more likely to be diagnosed with conduct disorder, anxiety disorder, and pervasive developmental disorders than nonintellectually disabled children, and that the prevalence of depression, eating disorders, and psychosis was about the same in the two groups.

Three theories suggest that biological or biochemical factors may be implicated in such severe challenging behavior involving the neurochemical transmitters dopamine, serotonin, and the neuropeptide opioids. The dopamine theory was proposed following the observation that patients with Lesch-Nyhan syndrome who exhibit very severe self-mutilation have markedly lower levels of dopamine in the central nervous system than people without the syndrome (Lloyd et al., 1981). It has been suggested that the self-injury exhibited by these individuals may result from the dopamine receptors being very sensitive to even small amounts of the neurotransmitter dopamine (referred to as dopamine supersensitivity), particularly involving the D1 dopamine receptor (e.g., Goldstein et al., 1986). Receptors are specialized proteins located in the cell membrane of nerve cells. Neurotransmitter molecules fit into the receptors like keys into locks. When neurotransmitters attach to the receptors on the cells surface (that is, when there are enough keys in enough locks), the nerve cells are activated.

The opioid receptor theory was proposed following the observation that painful stimulation causes release of naturally occurring (endogenous) substances referred to as opioids, which bind or connect with opioid receptors in the brain (Willer, Dehen & Cambier, 1981). Either by modulating normal pain sensation or because of the rewarding effects of the opioid molecules binding to opiate receptors (e.g., Cataldo & Harris, 1982; Stein & Belluzi, 1989), the self-injurious behavior (SIB) producing self-inflicted pain becomes repetitive.

The serotonin theory is based on several observations. First, about one-third of children with autism display elevated blood serotonin levels (Ritvo et al., 1970). Moreover, there is a relation between serotonin blood levels and the amount of disturbed behavior exhibited by persons with autism (Schain & Freedman, 1961; Campbell et al., 1975; Coleman & Gillberg, 1985). Another line of evidence indicates that some antidepressant drugs bind to the receptors that transport serotonin from the spaces between nerve cells back up into the presynaptic cells so the serotonin can be reused. The SSRIs are often effective in reducing symptoms of obsessive-compulsive behavior in autism (McDougle, 1997) and Prader-Willi syndrome (Stein, Keating, Zar & Hollander, 1994). Finally, serotonin agonists reduce aggression in animals (Miczek, Mos & Olivier, 1989; White, Kucharik & Moyer, 1991) as well as in humans. Impulsive aggression related to DSM-III personality disorder was reduced by the serotonin agonist buspirone (Coccaro, Gabriel & Siever, 1990).

Other neurochemical mechanisms are almost certainly involved as well, including the relative balance of serotonin, dopamine, norepinephrine, and gamma-aminobutyric acid. Individuals with repetitive stereotyped behavior and aggressive outbursts may well be experiencing such an imbalance. There also are reasons to believe that depressive disorder may be more common among people with developmental disabilities than is generally appreciated (McBrien, 2003), and the neurochemical mechanisms of depression are well understood (Lowry, 1998). In subsequent sections, we will discuss medications targeted at specific neurochemical systems and the presumed associated psychopathology.

Behavioral Mechanisms of Drug Action

Choosing an effective behavioral treatment depends on the results of a functional assessment of the antecedent conditions preceding and consequent events typically following destructive behavior. This procedure is seldom used in clinical applications or even research projects designed to evaluate the effectiveness of pharmacological treatments (Cerutti & Thompson, 1990; Schaal & Hackenberg, 1994). A functional analysis strategy has been described elsewhere as an element in the analysis of behavioral mechanisms of drug action (Thompson, 1984; Thompson, Egli, Symons & Delaney, 1994a). A functional diagnostic approach attempts to evaluate the most probable behavioral and biological variables that may be contributing to the behavior of concern.

For example, Mace and Mauk (1995) proposed a biobehavioral diagnostic and treatment model to classify different subtypes of SIB. The authors recommended conducting a functional analysis prior to treatment. Based on the outcome of the functional assessment, a medication, behavioral intervention, or both can then be selected.

The idea that medication can have specific effects on the efficacy of reinforcement is not new. For example, there is evidence that methylphenidate can result in decreased sensitivity to reinforcement in children with attention-deficit disorder (ADD) versus typical children (Murray & Kollins, 2000). In addition, methylphenidate appears to affect the strength of reinforcement as well (Wilkinson, Kircher, McMahon & Sloane, 1995). Antipsychotics may modulate or reduce the effects of stimuli such as negative reinforcers or punishers by making these events less effective or aversive (Janssen et al., 1988). Antipsychotics may also affect avoidance (and perhaps escape) responding by reducing the tendency to initiate an avoidance response (Ellenbroek, 1993; Arnt & Skarsfeldt, 1998).

The manner in which psychotropic medications often are prescribed to alter the challenging behavior of people with intellectual disabilities seldom takes these behavioral mechanisms into account. Practitioners and family members are often under the theoretical misconception that drugs alter brain chemical or physiological processes and cause behavior to change independently of the environmental circumstances within which the person functions. It is true that the brain's neurochemistry and the body's physiology set the limits at which external environmental processes and events exert their effects, but this is not achieved in a vacuum. In some circumstances, a medication may have one kind of behavioral effect, whereas under different circumstances the same medication may have a different behavioral effect. To understand better the neurobehavioral mechanisms of action of psychotropic medications in persons with intellectual disabilities, we must better understand the individual's behavioral and medical history as well as the current circumstances influencing his or her behavior (for example, whether the challenging behavior is maintained by positive or negative reinforcement). These variables create the foundations upon which medications are able to produce their behavioral effects.

If the choice of behavioral treatments is based on a functional assessment of the environmental conditions controlling behavior problems, a similar approach should also be adopted to select appropriate pharmacotherapies. Few physicians would pharmacologically treat a patient with an inflamed throat without first measuring body temperature, palpating the neck for signs of enlarged and tender lymph glands, otoscopically examining the eardrum, obtaining a white blood count, and taking an appropriate personal history. Yet, psychotropic medications are routinely prescribed to treat the challenging behavior of people with intellectual disabilities without the comparable information required for an adequate functional diagnosis. By adopting a functional diagnostic approach (Thompson, et al., 1994a), we can identify influential environmental factors, and a behaviorally active medication that will improve the person's ability to function independently. The goal is to treat the underlying behavioral and biological mechanisms, not just the appearance of the challenging behavior.

ASSUMPTIONS UNDERLYING THE ASSESSMENT OF BEHAVIORAL EFFECTS OF MEDICATION

Choosing What to Measure

Certain types of behavior are inherently of concern because of their practical importance. The number of words read correctly per minute during special education reading instruction by a child with dyslexia, the number of potatoes sliced per hour in a fast-food job setting, or the number of assaults against other people in a residential setting are all inherently significant. At other times, instances of a given type of activity (such as making verbal threats against others) may be viewed as important, not because of the threats per se, but because they are viewed as members of a larger class of aggressive behavior, some of which eventually cause bodily harm to others. It is assumed that threats are correlated with the probability of occurrence of other members of the broader functional class, namely, behavior intended to harm or cause submission by others.

"Dispositional clusters" or "response classes" involve behaviors that may appear very different in form, but which share common controlling variables and serve similar functions (Thompson & Lubinski, 1986). It is seldom possible to predict with accuracy which member of a dispositional cluster or response classes will actually occur on a given occasion, but the fact that one member of a class will occur can often be stated with considerable accuracy. The number of responses defining a dispositional cluster can be determined only by observing a person's behavior over an extended period of time, under a wide range of circumstances. When we say, "He seems very aggressive" after he has made a verbal threat, we are subjectively estimating the likelihood the individual will strike a peer, pinch his mother, or scratch his teacher, all of which actions are viewed as being members of a single dispositional response class.

Indirect Behavioral Measurement Approaches

In many clinical settings, medication effects are monitored and documented via clinical notes and medical records made by the medical professionals who are overseeing the clinical care of each individual. Medical records are useful because they are often required in all clinical settings to document not only medication effects, but also changes in medication status and dosage, and frequency of contacts. These documents may be primarily for billing purposes and may allow medical professionals to provide a continuity of service in a format that is easy to interpret and review. For some medications, there are therapeutic levels in the blood that can be monitored regularly to aid in evaluating medication effectiveness. Laboratory values also can be useful to monitor physiological side effects, such as red and white blood count levels, thyroid deficiencies, and endocrine function. Unfortunately, most medical records are inconsistent with regard to their content, as medical notes are taken for a variety of reasons, not just to document medication response. In addition, with the exception of laboratory values, most medical records are not objective or quantifiable. In addition, laboratory values, particularly therapeutic levels, can be very helpful in determining an adequate dose and to avoid levels that may be potentially harmful to a patient.

An alternative to using clinical measures to evaluate medication effects, rating scales completed by caregivers can also be used to estimate response dispositions. Using such a Likert-like rating scale, the caregivers estimate the relative frequency and intensity of behavioral events they might have observed over a specific time period, under a wide array of circumstances. Ratings may be based on an estimate of the strength or the probability of the occurrence of members of a cluster of responses by observing the individual, by talking with others (such as parents or teachers) who interact with the individual, and by reviewing documents, all of which shape a rating. The rater may infrequently observe the individual being rated, and may witness only one or two instances of the cluster of responses in question. Nonetheless, the rater will make an estimate of the strength of a cluster of response tendencies. Ratings are powerfully influenced by recency effects, and they undervalue events that have occurred over several days or a longer interval (Schwartz, 1999). The rating of an individual's aggressive behavior over the past week may be determined largely by the outburst that led to a staff injury earlier the same morning, though the individual may have displayed few instances of aggression for the previous week. Rating scales are often used because norms may be available for various groups of individuals (such as typically developing children or adult psychiatric patients). These ratings are especially useful because they show how the response tendencies of groups of people being studied differ from a reference group. In addition, they reveal how those tendencies change over time or in response to medication or educational procedure.

Several rating scales have been developed to (1) evaluate medication effects, and/or (2) evaluate behavior problems in individuals with intellectual disabilities; but they do not often do both. Schroeder, Rojahn and Reese (1997) evaluated the reliability and validity of several instruments for assessing psychotropic medication effects in the treatment of SIB. The authors found quite a bit of variability across test–retest ratings, interrater reliability, and ratings of internal consistency across tests. The authors also found that while it is difficult to compare directly across subscales, there was considerable consistency across scales that included items on mood, emotionality, and irritability.

One of the most common rating scales used to measure medication effects in developmentally disabled individuals is the Aberrant Behavior Checklist (ABC). The ABC is a 58-item, standardized rating scale developed to measure the effects of medication on challenging behavior in individuals with intellectual disabilities (Aman, Singh, Stewart & Field, 1985a). The items are broken down into five subscales: irritability, lethargy/social withdrawal, stereotypic behavior, hyperactivity/noncompliance, and inappropriate speech. The scale has been experimentally validated across a wide variety of intellectual disability populations (Freund & Reiss, 1991; Rojahn & Helsel, 1991; Marshburn & Aman, 1992; Aman, Burrow & Wolford, 1995). In addition, it has been evaluated for internal consistency and test–retest reliability (Aman, Singh, Stewart & Field, 1985b), and it has a high degree of validity and consistency with ratings on other adaptive behavior scales and objective observations of behavior (Aman et al., 1985b). Given its widespread use and acceptance, it is considered to be one of the "best" measures of medication effects with people with intellectual disabilities. Other measures of challenging behavior in individuals with intellectual disabilities include the Emotional Problems Scales: Behavior Rating Scales (BRS) and Self-Report Inventory (SRI), the former being a lengthy rating scale that is used with informants, while the SRI can be used directly with individuals with disabilities who are able to self-report emotional problems (Strohmer & Prout, 1991). While the BRS has strong psychometric properties and may be a useful diagnostic instrument, there are currently no empirical studies using this scale to evaluate the effects of medication on individuals with intellectual disabilities.

The Reiss Screen for Maladaptive Behavior and the Nisonger Child Behavior Rating Form (NCBRF) are well-standardized instruments that have been used primarily with higher functioning individuals, but have not been used to evaluate medication effects (Aman, Tasse, Rojahn & Hammer, 1995). Finally, the Self-Injurious Behavior Questionnaire (SIBQ) has been used to address challenging behavior in adults with disabilities such as SIB, aggression, stereotyped behavior, destruction, tantrums, and attention and emotional/mood problems (Gualtieri & Schroeder, 1989). It can be used to measure behavior in a wide range of individuals at varying functioning levels, and it is based on the frequency and severity of explicit challenging behaviors; however, it is not very sensitive to low-frequency, low-intensity behavior, and it has not been psychometrically standardized.

Other rating scales have been developed to measure specific types of disorders such as obsessive-compulsive disorder (for example, the Yale-Brown Obsessive Compulsive Scale) (Goodman et al., 1989a,b), and have been used extensively to evaluate medication effects (Brodkin, McDougle, Naylor, Cohen & Price, 1997; McDougle et al., 1995, 1998). Other scales have been used with individuals with intellectual disabilities, but not for the purposes of evaluating treatment effects (for example, the Compulsive Behavior Checklist [Gedye, 1992] and the Repetitive Behavior Scale [Bodfish, Symons & Lewis, 1999]).

Finally, measuring anxiety and depression in individuals with intellectual disabilities may be difficult, but two scales have been developed that may prove useful. The Glasgow Anxiety Scale for People with Intellectual Disabilities (GAS-ID) was recently developed by Mindham and Espie (2003) as a self-report scale that can be used for assessing anxiety level in individuals with intellectual disabilities. The Clinical Behavior Checklist for Persons with Intellectual Disabilities (CBCPID) was developed as a broad screening measure of a variety of potential symptoms of depression in people with intellectual disabilities (Marston, Perry & Roy, 1997). Additionally, the use of global impression scales (such as the Clinical Global Impressions Scale [CGI] [Guy, 1976]) and diagnostic tools (such as the Diagnostic Assessment for the Severely Handicapped [Matson, Coe, Gardner & Sovner, 1991]) may also be useful in evaluating medication effects.

Direct Behavioral Measurement Approaches

In direct observational approaches, verbal descriptions of each type of behavior being recorded are agreed upon by all people doing the observations. Each behavioral description is referred to as a behavioral *code*, and the process of recording such instances (for example, in vivo or from a videotaped recording) is called *coding*. Without carefully specified criteria for determining when a particular type of behavior is or is not a member of the class in question, considerable variability can result. For example, aggression means many things to different people, depending on personal experience and social background. An observer who had previously worked as a counselor in a correctional facility may have a very high threshold for considering an action aggressive. Another individual may consider a socially insensitive remark about another person's physical appearance an aggressive comment. Operational definitions are *always* a part of direct observational systems.

Direct behavioral observations use behavior of the individual within an environmental context as the unit of analysis. Change in the frequency or probability of the behavior as a result of the intervention usually involves a measure of central tendency and variability based on repeated measures of the behavioral variable. Having measured change scores for individuals, these values may be averaged across individuals for certain purposes. It may be useful to use a standardized rating scale to characterize several children with attention-deficit hyperactivity disorder before beginning treatment with a new medication to facilitate comparison of populations across studies. It does not necessarily follow that changes in scores on that same test will necessarily be most useful in determining whether and in what way those children benefited from treatment or which side effects emerged. Key target responses having educational or clinical face validity can be more useful in determining whether a child profited from treatment and in what ways.

Several studies have been conducted by direct observation of target behaviors to measure the effects of medication. The study of stimulant medications has probably received the most attention in this area. Studies of the effects of medication by direct observations are often combined with rating-scale measures such as Conners ratings scales (Conners, 1990). Many of these studies have focused not only on off-task or disruptive behavior, but also academic performance and other positive behaviors (e.g., Schell et al., 1986; Pelham et al., 1993; Stoner, Carey, Ikeda & Shinn, 1994; Kayser et al., 1997). For example, Johnson, Handen, Lubetsky and Sacco (1994) studied the effects of methylphenidate on both fidgety and disruptive behavior as well as on-task and task accuracy performance in three children with ADD—hyperactive type. Several studies have also compared the separate and combined effects of medication to other forms of interventions, specifically behavioral intervention. For example, in the study by Johnson et al. (1994) described above, the effects of methylphenidate were compared alone and in combination with a token economy system and the token economy combined with reinforcement for task accuracy. Methylphenidate reduced fidgetiness and disruption across conditions, but task accuracy improved only when the medication was combined with the reinforcement contingency. While most of these studies have focused on typically developing children with ADD, several studies have included children with intellectual disabilities and similar results have been found; methylphenidate and other stimulant medications appear to reduce the negative behaviors, but only when they are combined with behavioral interventions are there positive effects on academic performance and other adaptive behaviors (e.g., Handen et al., 1992; Blum, Mauk, McComas & Mace, 1996; Handen, Feldman, Lurier & Murray, 1999).

Although direct observation measures have been used primarily in studies with children with ADD, additional studies have evaluated the effects of medication, primarily on severe behavior problems, by direct observation measures. Often the focus of the studies was on evaluating a behavioral intervention combined with medication (e.g., Durand, 1982; Burgio, Page & Capriotti, 1985; Luiselli, 1991). Only a few of these studies evaluated the interventions separately, however. For example, Luiselli (1986) evaluated the effects of haloperidol on the SIB of an individual with intellectual disabilities in combination with differential reinforcement of other behavior (DRO) and timeout. Many of these studies, however, were single-case studies that were not well controlled. Finally, Smith et al. (2002) used direct observations to measure the effects of staff responsiveness after withdrawal of long-term antipsychotic treatment and found no difference between before and after the withdrawal of medication.

More controlled studies have evaluated the effects of naltrexone in the treatment of SIB by using naturalistic observations (Sandman et al., 1993). Thompson, Hackenberg, Cerutti, Baker and Axtell (1994b) conducted a double-blind, placebo-controlled study of nine self-injurious individuals to evaluate the effects of naltrexone. The authors collected 5-minute samples of behavior nine times across the day, during baseline, placebo, and treatment with two different doses. The results showed that naltrexone reduced head-banging and self-biting, but not other SIB (such as throat-poking). Sandman et al. (2000) collected direct observation data on 15 individuals with SIB who participated in a double-blind, multiple-dose, placebo-controlled trial of naltrexone. Initially, participants were treated over a 10-week period, followed by a 1-year hiatus, followed by an 18-month, placebo-controlled, long-term study. Three 15-minute observations were collected each week in the individuals' homes. The results of the study demonstrated mixed findings for the participants; some individuals demonstrated long-term effects of the medication, even after the hiatus, while for others those effects diminished over time.

Finally, several controlled studies have evaluated the effects of atypical antipsychotics by a variety of rating-scale measures (e.g., McDougle et al., 1998; Aman, De Smedt, Derivan, Lyons & Findling, 2002; Research Units on Pediatric Psychopharmacology Autism Network, 2002). Only a few have combined rating scales with direct observation measures; however, Hammock, Schroeder and Levine (1995) evaluated the effects of clozapine on the SIB of an adult with profound intellectual disabilities. The authors demonstrated that clozapine was effective in a double-blind, placebo-controlled, crossover trial using the Aberrant Behavior Checklist as well as observations of the individual for 60 minutes per day. Zarcone et al. (2001) also used ratings scales (such as the ABC, the Nisonger Child Behavior Rating Form, and the CGI) combined with direct observations to measure the effects of risperidone on 20 individuals with challenging behavior. Results of the study showed that, overall, based on ABC score, risperidone was effective in reducing challenging behavior by approximately 40% during the blind phase, and almost 50% in the open, follow-up phase. Direct observation of five of the participants showed reductions in challenging behavior in all but one individual. Finally, Valdovinos et al. (2002), in a further investigation of the Zarcone et al. (2001) risperidone trial, specifically compared the more subjective ratings made by caregivers and the clinical team to direct observations made by direct care staff throughout the day, brief naturalistic observations, and analog functional analysis sessions made by the research team. These observations were made with only two individuals during the course of the double-blind study, but demonstrated the degree to which different methods of data collection can correspond to each other. The results of the study demonstrated that for the most part, the different measures agreed that there was a significant effect of risperidone in reducing challenging behavior across environmental conditions. In other words, there was not a selective effect of the risperidone for these two individuals under any specific reinforcement condition, setting, or environmental situation.

There have been only a few studies in which a functional analysis was conducted concurrent with a medication evaluation. Fisher, Piazza and Page (1989) examined the effects of haloperidol on psychotic speech and disruptive behavior via functional analysis sessions throughout the medication trial. Although the haloperidol appeared to reduce the frequency of psychotic speech, the authors demonstrated that a behavioral intervention was even more effective in reducing both challenging behavior and psychotic speech.

In a more experimentally controlled series of studies, Northup and his colleagues examined the role of environmental versus medication variables affecting disruptive behavior in children with ADD using double-blind, placebo-controlled studies of methylphenidate (Northup, Fusilier, Swanson, Roane & Borrero, 1997a; Northup et al., 1997b; Northup et al., 1999). For example, Northup et al. (1999) demonstrated that environmental variables such as peer and teacher attention, reprimands, and timeout modulated the behavioral effects of methylphenidate. In fact, there appeared to be environmental antecedents and consequences that overrode the treatment effects of the medication (for example, when no teacher was

Table 28.1 Time line for the occurrences and observations of self-injurious behaviors across a day of placebo (PL) and the last day of treatment (Rx)

Time	8:00	9:00	10:00	11:00	12:00	13:00	14:00	15:00	16:00	17:00	18:00	19:00	20:00	21:00	22:00
PL		3		1			5				2	8		1	
	OB			OB						OB				OB	
Rx		2		1		1		2			2	3		1	
			OB					OB		OB				OB	

present or when timeout was used). Finally, Garcia and Smith (1999) conducted functional analyses during a double-blind, placebo-controlled trial of naltrexone in the treatment of SIB in two women with intellectual disabilities. The authors demonstrated that naltrexone had a differential impact on SIB based on topography and function for two individuals whose SIB occurred across several conditions during a premedication functional analysis. Specifically, naltrexone reduced head-slapping during the escape condition for one individual, but had no effect on head-banging during any of the other conditions.

In a recent study of effects of the atypical antipsychotic, risperidone, on challenging behavior, a functional analysis was conducted prior to and concurrent with a double-blind, placebo-controlled trial with 17 individuals (Zarcone et al., in press). The goal of the study was to determine not only whether challenging behavior was reduced by the medication, but also how challenging behavior was differentially affected by the medication under common environmental conditions. The results showed that risperidone effectively decreased all challenging behavior to zero or near zero levels for five individuals (62.5%) across functional assessment conditions. For individuals for whom we obtained a differentiated functional analysis during the premedication sessions, risperidone appeared to decrease the escape-maintained challenging behavior more than behavior maintained by other reinforcers.

Measuring medication treatment effects on challenging behavior can be methodologically difficult. For example, self-injury is often episodic. Some individuals may self-injure 10–20 times per day, while others do so far more often. Usually, self-injurious bouts are separated by intervals with no self-injury. Rating-scale or observational strategies that do not take the base rate and overall pattern of self-injury into consideration may be insensitive to treatment effects. Measuring baseline or placebo rates at one point in time, followed by a second comparable measurement after treatment, is especially prone to missing treatment effects. An individual may strike his head with his hand 20 times per 15-hour period, with 1–8 head hits per bout. By time-sampling randomly four times per day for 10 minutes each, it is very likely self-injury bouts will be missed.

Suppose, for example, we observe an individual for 1 day during placebo administration (PL) and for 1 day at the end of active medication treatment (Rx) (Table 28.1). For any given hour, the likelihood is 1 in 6 ($P = .167$) that the period during which one is observing will coincide with a bout of self-injury. For example, if one observed on the placebo day at 8:00, 11:00, 17:00, and 21:00, selecting the 10-minute observation (OB) period randomly out of 60 minutes, one would conclude that the baseline rate of self-injury was yielding a total of 7.5 instances of self-injury per 15 hours (15-hour period $\times$ 2 instances of self-injury observed, divided by 4 actual observation periods—estimated 7.5 instances). Similar random time-sampling on the second day at the conclusion of treatment would lead to the conclusion that self-injury had increased to 53%. In reality, the baseline rate under placebo was 20 times during the 15-hour period and dropped to 13 times, or a reduction of 35%, after treatment. This would be a possible indication of a positive treatment effect given data from a larger sample. The probability of error in measurement is amplified when one considers that the probability of observing self-injury that is actually occurring is 1/6, or .167.

The problem is not solved by using rating scales, since attempting to arrive at an overall impression of the amount of severity of self-injury over an 8- or 15-hour period is fraught with error due not only to the same observational sampling problems, but also to recency effects, with the episodes that occur shortly before ratings are made unduly influencing overall ratings. An especially severe instance of self-injury observed during the 19:00 hour of treatment assessment (with ratings being made at 20:00 hours) may lead to an overall higher rating for the entire day than more frequent, but less severe, self-injury during the entire day of placebo treatment. The solution lies in evaluating baseline rates and patterns of self-injury prior to devising an observational schedule for measuring medication effects (Thompson, Symons & Felce, 2000).

APPROPRIATE AND INAPPROPRIATE CIRCUMSTANCES FOR USE OF DIRECT BEHAVIORAL OBSERVATIONAL METHODS

Practical considerations militate against using direct behavioral observational methods to measure treatment effects when it may be unsafe or unethical to do so. Behavior such as setting fires, sexual assault, or severe self-injury (as in the Lesch-Nyhan syndrome) cannot be allowed to occur and simply be recorded to assess frequency, prior to, during, and subsequent to intervention. There may be circumstances under which the behavior of concern cannot be observed for ethical reasons. Attempting to observe intimate sexual interactions, personal hygiene activities, illicit drug use, or confidential conversations would all pose significant ethical problems. Some behavior, such as theft, is surreptitious and fleeting, and therefore does not lend itself to direct observational assessment methods. The behavior of stealing personal items from fellow residents in a community residential program for adults with developmental delays is rarely observable. The theft is discovered when the personal items are missing, and at a later time the pilfered item is found among the perpetrator's possessions hidden in a drawer or closet. The stealing, as such, is not observable. Behavior that is infrequent, with any occurrences of serious concern (such as suicide attempts), is not appropriate for measurement and evaluation by direct behavioral observational methods.

Other psychological events cannot be directly observed, but behavior associated with those processes may be observable at times. The hallucinations of an individual with schizophrenia are not observable, but the person with schizophrenia who is seen seeming to talk to someone that no one else sees, or who is seen picking insects off a wall, when no one else in the room sees insects on the wall, is observable, and these actions can be recorded. Similarly, delusional thinking cannot be directly observed, but delusional statements (for example, "God wants me to punish sinners!") can be observed and recorded. Affective states cannot be observed, but behavior associated with those states, such as crying, making self-deprecating statements, making comments of a discouraged and depressive nature, and sighing repeatedly, can be observed and recorded. Hand-wringing, skin-picking, twirling hair, jiggling one's knee in an agitated fashion, pacing, and spontaneous self-statements about "feeling nervous" or "worried" can all be recorded as behavioral measures correlated with the presumed mood state of anxiety (Thompson, Symons & Felce, 2000).

MEDICATIONS USED TO TREAT MENTAL HEALTH AND BEHAVIORAL CHALLENGES IN INTELLECTUAL DISABILITIES

Medications used to treat mental health problems among the general population are also used to treat people with intellectual disabilities. Medications have been categorized according to their therapeutic functions, mechanisms of action, and chemical structures. Haloperidol may be described as an antipsychotic, a dopamine antagonist, and a butyrophenone, according to its therapeutic function, its putative mechanism of action, and its chemical class. All of the medications used for treating mental health problems and challenging behavior exert effects on the nervous system, though their original therapeutic purposes may not correspond to their application in challenging behavior in developmental disabilities. Propanalol was developed as a medication for hypertension; however, in some individuals with developmental disabilities, it appears to reduce symptoms of anxiety and reduce aggressive outbursts. For the purposes of this discussion, we present a mixed classification scheme; five major groups of medications will be discussed according to their therapeutic functions: antipsychotics, antidepressives, mood-disorder medications, antianxiety medications, and attention-hyperactivity medications. Within a given class (such as antidepressives), they are subcategorized according to their brain chemical mechanisms (such as antidepressives that are serotonin reuptake inhibitors). Two groups of medications will be presented according to their chemical mechanisms (that is, autonomic adrenergic drugs and opiate antagonists).

Evidence for Effectiveness

People receiving medication should be assured that what they are consuming is effective and safe. A medication is effective if it produces desired or claimed outcomes. Minimum evidence for the effectiveness of any medication is based on commonly established procedures used throughout medical science, but these kinds of studies are rarely done with individuals with intellectual disabilities (Matson et al., 2000). The following standards are based on procedures developed over the past 50 years regarding scientific evidence.

Appropriate Diagnosis

All of the people receiving a test treatment that is being evaluated must have the same condition or illness. In some poorly controlled studies, the people being treated are not properly diagnosed. As a result, the people receiving the test treatment include a heterogeneous mix of different conditions, some of which may be appropriate for the test medication, and others inappropriate. On conclusion of the study, there will be no way to know whether the failure to observe a consistent treatment effect is because the treatment was not effective, or because some of the people receiving the medication had conditions that were not appropriate for the treatment being tested.

Experimental Control

Several different designs can be used that include elements of experimental control. For example, one group of people is given the test medicine and a second matched group is given an identical appearing pill or liquid not containing the medicine (a placebo) in a parallel-group design. An alternative design involves switching each parallel group to the opposite treatment (for example, the placebo group receives an active medication, and the drug group is switched to placebo) in a crossover design. Alternatively, a reversal design can be used during which a person takes the active medicine during one period of time, while during a second interval, he or she takes a placebo. Sometimes, for ethical reasons, rather than comparing a test medication with an inert placebo, a comparison is made between a standard treatment and the medication rather than a placebo.

Measures of Treatment Effects

Someone other than the person receiving the medicine or placebo must determine whether there is any difference in the person's condition before or after treatment, or if the two groups of people (one receiving the medicine, the other taking a placebo) really differ in outcome. If people receiving the medicine have an intellectual disability, they may not be capable of safely administering their own medication; in such cases, usually, a parent or caregiver administers the medication. If the persons giving the medicine are aware of when the person is receiving the active medicine and when the inert pill or liquid, they cannot evaluate the medication's effects without bias. Their hopes and beliefs about the medication's effects may prejudice their ratings; therefore, an independent person with no stake in the outcome must evaluate any changes. Only when the person giving the medication to the person with the disability is truly unaware of treatment phases (that is, is "blind" to the treatment condition) can such a person also be the one who rates the outcome.

Medication Effects

The medication must be consistent in quality and composition; dosages must be appropriate and must be taken consistently according to established guidelines, and for long enough periods of time to have the opportunity to be effective. Some nonprescription preparations (such as dietary supplements) vary greatly from batch to batch and from one manufacturer to another. Some medications must be taken in gradually increasing dosages over days and weeks before stabilization occurs. Other medications require 4–8 weeks to reach their optimal therapeutic effect.

Drug Interactions

Other medications may interfere with a test medication's effects, and, as a result, usually only one medication is given at a time. In some cases where another medication has been given for an extended period for another reason (for example, to control a seizure disorder), the second medication may be continued. Some medication combinations can be dangerous or even fatal and must be evaluated before the new medication is started.

Other Interventions

It is best if other treatments may not be started or stopped during the period the test medication is being evaluated. Psychological treatments, diet, or educational programs that may also change the person's behavior or mental health condition should be held constant through the entire period the test medication is being evaluated, or it will be difficult to determine whether the treatment in question is effective.

Standardized Measures

Standardized ways of evaluating a person's behavioral and/or psychological condition must be used before and during treatment; usually, a combination of direct behavioral observation methods and standardized rating scales is best (see discussion above). Both the frequency and severity of challenging behavior are often relevant to evaluating accurately medication effects. Many behavioral challenges occur in bouts within and across days or weeks. As a result, measures at two brief points in time (such as one occasion before and once after treatment) are often insensitive to gradual changes in episodic challenging behavior.

Sample Size

Finally, enough people have to be tested with the treatment for us to be confident that the results observed in one or two cases were not an idiosyncratic response. Failure to obtain the similar outcomes for most of the people tested does not deny the reality of the positive outcome for a minority subset that genuinely improved. Such variability in response to a treatment alerts researchers to the possibility that not everyone diagnosed with the same condition (such as Asperger's syndrome) will profit equally.

Safety

Government and international agencies have developed procedures for evaluating prescription medications through established testing procedures before a medication can be prescribed to the general public. The World Health Organization Essential Drugs and Medicines (EDM) <www.who.int/medicines/default.shtml> agency coordinates medication evaluation and monitoring procedures throughout the world. The European Medicines Evaluation Agency, in cooperation with the European Commission Pharmaceuticals (Enterprise DG) program, coordinates uniform policies among European Commission member countries. In the UK, the Medicines Control Agency (MCA) <www.mca.gov.uk> is the executive agency of the Department of Health safeguarding public health by ensuring that all medicines on the UK market meet appropriate standards of safety, quality, and efficacy.

In the USA, a four-stage Food and Drug Administration (FDA) <www.fda.gov> approval process ensures that medications that reach the market place do not produce obvious damage, at least during short-term treatment. In the first phase, a small sample of typical volunteers are given the medication under laboratory conditions, and physiological and biochemical measures are taken to ensure safety of the drug. In a second phase, a small sample of the large population (such as people with autism and aggression) are given low-to-moderate dosages of the medication under carefully controlled conditions, and the possible side effects and basic pharmacological actions are closely monitored for safety and possible efficacy. In the third phase, a large random sample of the target population and a matched control group are given the medication and placebo under typical clinical circumstances, and efficacy and safety are monitored intermittently. Only after passing the three foregoing phases is the medication released for use in general practice. Over the next several years, reports of adverse effects are obtained from practitioners and treated individuals through a process called "pharmacovigilance". Problems that arise with approved medications during this final (fourth) phase usually become apparent only with long-term treatment. The often rare individuals with vulnerabilities that were not previously recognized gradually become apparent.

In the following section, each general category of medication will be discussed in relation to treatment of challenging behavior in individuals with intellectual disabilities.

Antipsychotics

Antipsychotics are some of the most widely used drugs to treat the serious behavioral challenges of people with intellectual and related developmental disabilities (Aman & Madrid, 1999). The factors determining choice among antipsychotics grow out of differences in side effects. Antipsychotics are categorized two ways, as traditional low-potency versus typical high-potency antipsychotics, and as typical versus atypical antipsychotics. Typical or traditional low-potency antipsychotics, such as chlorpromazine and thioridazine, produce fewer extrapyramidal reactions, more sedation, more postural hypotension (dizziness when rising to a standing position), and greater risk of seizures. In addition, low-potency antipsychotics are more likely to produce cardiovascular problems, as well as occasional liver toxicity and damage to white blood cells. High-potency antipsychotics, such as haloperidol, cause more frequent extrapyramidal movement (dystonic) reactions, usually less sedation and less postural hypotension, and have less effect on seizure threshold. Moreover, high-potency antipsychotics produce less cardiovascular toxicity and fewer anticholinergic effects (such as blurred vision and constipation), but they also cause occasional antipsychotic malignant syndrome, a very dangerous and potentially fatal side effect.

The three most widely used *typical antipsychotics* in treating people with intellectual disabilities are chlorpromazine, thioridazine, and haloperidol. They have been used to treat the behavior problems of people with intellectual and related developmental disabilities for over four decades. There is evidence that these medications have no specific effects in the treatment of challenging behavior (Brylewski & Duggan, 1999). In addition, they all produce sedative effects and have considerable risk of movement-disorder side effects, including tardive dyskinesia. Tardive dyskinesia is a late-onset disorder that involves involuntary movements of various body parts, beginning with the mouth and hands, but may include the limbs, neck, and trunk. It is estimated that in approximately one-third of cases, the movement disorder does not completely remit when the medication is discontinued, potentially causing lifelong disability (Gualtieri, Schroeder, Hicks & Quade, 1986). In controlled studies, typical antipsychotics have *few selective effects* on self-injury or aggression apart from sedation. They are primarily used today for crisis management to sedate individuals with intellectual and related developmental disabilities who are violent and dangerously out of control.

The typical antipsychotics have largely been replaced by the *atypical antipsychotics*. The first atypical antipsychotic was clozapine, patented in 1960. Clozapine seldom produces extrapyramidal dysfunction and rarely produces tardive dyskinesia, and is therefore tolerated better by most patients. It does, however, produce other side effects, including mild restlessness (akathisia), sedation, orthostatic hypotension, nausea and vomiting, and weight gain (*Physician's Desk Reference*, 2002). More serious side effects include seizures and damage to the body's ability to manufacture white blood cells (agranulocytosis 1%) that can lead to a fatal inability to fight infection even after long-term use of clozapine (Patel, Dorson & Bettinger, 2002). Individuals treated with clozapine must have white blood cell counts every 2 weeks, which is inconvenient and costly (Baldessarini & Frankenburg, 1991).

There have been a few case studies of the use of clozapine in individuals with intellectual disabilities (e.g., Buzan, Dubovsky, Firestone & Dal Pozzo, 1998; Antonacci & de Groot, 2000); however, only one study has used a double-blind. Hammock and colleagues (1995) treated a man with profound intellectual disability and severe visual handicap with unremitting self-injury with clozapine, using a double-blind reversal design. Clozapine reduced self-injury in a dose-dependent fashion; however, at dosages that stopped self-injury, seizures occurred. While some psychiatrists prescribe clozapine regularly, especially to individuals with schizophrenia who have been unresponsive to other antipsychotics, it is used infrequently to treat individuals with intellectual and related disabilities.

There have been few well-controlled studies with atypical antipsychotics among people with intellectual and related developmental disabilities, though what evidence has emerged indicates that risperidone has promise in treating aggression and self-injury while keeping extrapyramidal side effects low (Lemmens, Brecher & Van Baelen, 1999). McDougle and colleagues (1997; 1998) and the Research Units on Pediatric Psychopharmacology Autism Network (2002) have shown risperidone to be effective in reducing challenging behavior in children and adults with autism, and several recent studies indicate that risperidone reduces the disruptive behavior of children with intellectual disabilities (Aman et al., 2002; Snyder et al., 2002). In one of the more thorough studies, Zarcone et al. (2001) evaluated risperidone in treating aggression and self-injury in 20 individuals with various intellectual disabilities, using a crossover, double-blind design, including a 6-month follow-up. They used a combination of validated rating scales and direct observations, as well as measures of learning ability, reporting that at least 50% of participants improved significantly while receiving risperidone. Risperidone has several side effects, including sedation and weight gain (Research Units on Pediatric Psychopharmacology Autism Network, 2002). Numerous open-label reports have been published with other atypical antipsychotics such as olanzapine (e.g., Krishnamoorthy & King, 1998; McDonough, Hillery & Kennedy, 2000; Williams, Clarke, Bouras, Martin & Holt, 2000), with mixed results. Thorough clinical trials of other atypical antipsychotics have not been conducted with individuals with intellectual disabilities.

Antidepressants

Antidepressant medications with antianxiety effects are among the second most widely used class of psychotropic medications to treat the behavioral challenges of individuals with intellectual disabilities (Sovner, 1989). While people with intellectual disabilities suffer from depressive and anxiety disorders, as do others in the general population, diagnosing these conditions in the former groups is often very difficult. As a result, antidepressants are often used symptomatically among people with aggression, self-injury, and other aberrant behavior, whether or not they present clear signs of depressive or anxiety disorder, on the assumption that those underlying psychopathological conditions exist. It should not be surprising that results are often unpredictable and less than impressive. The monoamine oxidase inhibitors (MAOIs) were among the first antidepressants developed in the 1960s. Though they are effective antidepressants, the MAOIs (phenelzine and tranylcypromine) are used infrequently today because of the risk of dangerous side effects if the person taking the medication consumes aged cheeses, brine from pickled herring, beer, wine, liver, yeast extract, dry sausages, or fava beans. These substances can lead to dangerously high blood pressure and possibly a stroke, due to high levels of the chemical tyramine.

Tricyclic antidepressants (TCAs) are the most studied group of antidepressants because they have been in use longer. Dry mouth, blurred vision, constipation, weight gain, drowsiness, and dizziness are among the most troubling side effects of amitriptyline, clomipramine, doxepin, imipramine, and trimipramine. Amoxapine, desipramine, nortriptyline, and protriptyline generally cause less sedation and less dry mouth and visual or other side effects. *TCAs must not be taken with monoamine oxidase inhibitors* and should be used with caution with a number of other drugs.

Several studies with imipramine, clomipramine, and trazadone have yielded mixed results in treating individuals with developmental disabilities. In controlled, small-sample studies with imipramine, Aman, White, Vaithianathan and Teehan (1986) treated 10 adults with profound intellectual disability with imipramine or placebo. Five were described as having depressive symptoms, and five had "acting-out behavior" but lacked major depressive signs. No differential, favorable behavioral effects were found. The acting-out group became more active, and the depressed group became less active. Field, Aman, White and Vaithianathan (1986) treated a woman with moderate intellectual disability who exhibited screaming, crying, agitation, irritability, and weight loss. Imipramine (100 mg/day) increased food consumption, decreased screaming and crying, and stabilized sleep. Several well-controlled, double-blind trials with clomipramine using validated rating scales have reported reliable decreases in obsessive-compulsive behavior and repetitive stereotypies, and some reductions in aggression and SIB in severe/profound intellectual disability and autism (Lewis, Bodfish, Powell, Parker & Golden, 1996).

Since the 1990s, the drugs of choice for many people for the treatment of major depressive disorder have been the SSRIs (fluoxetine, paroxetine, sertraline, and citalopram), because they have favorable safety profiles and lack many of the unpleasant side effects of the older tricyclic and atypical antidepressants (such as trazadone). SSRIs are approved for treatment of major depression, unipolar affective disorder, obsessive disorder, and panic disorder, with secondary approvals for agoraphobia and social phobia and aggressive-impulsive behavior. The side effects of SSRIs are generally not as unpleasant as those of the older antidepressants. Nausea, common during the first week, usually wanes as the tolerance to the drug develops. Because insomnia can be a problem, these activating antidepressants are usually administered in the morning. Sexual dysfunction is common with SSRIs, including difficulty in achieving an erection among men and orgasm among women.

Numerous case reports of individuals with intellectual disability who exhibited compulsive disorder and depression, and some of whom exhibited challenging behavior, claim positive results with fluoxetine (e.g., Branford, Bhaumik & Naik, 1998) and paroxetine (Masi, Marcheschi & Pfanner, 1997; Davanzo, Belin, Widawski & King, 1998). Most have been open-label trials, with several studies using validated objective behavioral observations, but not blind raters. Several reports claim improvement in weight, sleep, and depression rating-scale scores. McDougle et al. (1996) conducted a double-blind, placebo-controlled study with fluvoxamine in 19 pairs of adolescents and young adults with autism; half were treated with placebo. Significant improvements in compulsive behavior and other symptoms of psychopathology were reported over 3 months compared with placebo participants, who showed no improvement. While small-sample, open-label trials with sertraline (e.g., Hellings, Kelley, Gabrielli, Kilgore & Shah, 1996) and other SSRIs with developmentally disabled populations have been published, most have not been well controlled. Antidepressants acting on other brain chemical systems (such as buproprion, trazodone, mitazapine, venlataxine, and maprotiline) are used at times to treat individuals with intellectual disabilities who have behavioral challenges, but there is very little evidence from controlled clinical studies of their specificity, effectiveness, or safety.

Antiepileptics (Mood Stabilizers)

Antiepileptic medications have been increasingly used to treat challenging behavior among people with developmental disabilities. How the presence of epilepsy affects the occurrence of challenging behavior is unclear. In the past, behavioral outbursts were sometimes linked to psychomotor seizures or other types of epileptic activity. There is evidence that the use of anticonvulsant medications in the treatment of epilepsy in people with intellectual disabilities is basically the same as for other patients with epilepsy (see Alvarez, Besag & Iivanainen, 1998, for a review), and that it is diagnosed and treated with the same types of antiepileptics used with nondisabled individuals. There is evidence, however, that anticonvulsants may affect challenging behavior, regardless of whether the individual has epilepsy.

Among psychiatric patients who do not have intellectual disabilities, numerous controlled studies have reported that some antiepileptics reduce signs and symptoms of psychopathology among individuals with bipolar disorder, especially rapid cycling disorder (e.g., Bennett, Goldman & Suppes, 1997; Young, Robb, Patelis-Siortis, MacDonald & Joffe, 1997). In a review of case studies of patients with rapid cycling bipolar disorder, and intellectual disability, Vanstraelen and Tyrer (1999) found that lithium, carbamazepine, and valproate were the most frequently used medications, with valproate being the most effective treatment. Among people with intellectual disabilities, however, it is extremely difficult to determine whether the behavioral and associated features presented by individuals with behavioral challenges truly satisfy the diagnostic criteria for bipolar disorder or other mood disorders (Cain et al., 2003).

Although there have been several case studies evaluating the effect of antiepileptic medications, there have not been any double-blind, placebo-controlled studies with intellectually disabled individuals (Lindenmayer & Kotsaftis, 2000). One antiepileptic that has often been used as a mood stabilizer is divalproex and its liquid formulation, valproic acid. Ruedrich, Swales, Fossaeeca, Tolliver & Rutkowski (1999) recently demonstrated in a retrospective study that divalproex treatment resulted in reduced Clinical Global Impression (CGI) scores in 28 individuals with intellectual disability and chronic severe challenging behavior. Other open clinical trials of divalproex have also shown significant improvement in mood disorders in individuals with intellectual disability (Sovner, 1989; Kastner, Finesmith & Walsh, 1993). In addition, participants in the Kastner et al. (1993) study also demonstrated decreases in aggression and self-injury as well as manic symptoms. Lindenmayer and Kotsaftis (2000) reviewed the effects of valproic acid in the treatment of aggressive behaviors in nonbipolar patients. Overall, they found that a 50% reduction in target behavior was demonstrated for 77% of the participants.

Over the past 10 years, several newer anticonvulsants have been developed that appear to have some potential for the treatment of mood disorders, particularly manic symptoms, but also challenging behavior in individuals with intellectual disability. For example, gabapentin has been approved as an add-on therapy to augment treatment in cases of partial response to other anticonvulsants, particularly in the treatment of bipolar disorder; however, all studies to date have been with typical populations (Bennett et al., 1997; Young et al., 1997). Lamotrigine is another anticonvulsant that has shown some promise with typical populations in the treatment of bipolar disorders, although there are some reports that it may exacerbate aggressive behavior in individuals with intellectual disabilities (Beran & Gibson, 1998). In an open-label study of lamotrigine and gabapentin in individuals with intellectual disability and seizure disorder, both medications were effective in reducing seizure activity, but gabapentin also improved sleep, general health, and attention (Crawford, Brown & Kerr, 2001). Other reports indicate that treatment of epilepsy with lamotrigine may result in lessened irritability and hyperactivity (Ettinger et al., 1998), improved quality-of-life ratings (Meador & Baker, 1997), and decreased SIB, agitation, and fearfulness (Davanzo & King, 1996). Other agents that have potential as mood stabilizers are topiramate and tigabine, which may also be effective with individuals with intellectual disabilities, but, again, there have been no controlled studies conducted at this time.

Finally, lithium carbonate and lithium citrate have historically been one of the most common treatments for mood disorders, particularly bipolar disorders, and the term "mood stabilizer" was initially applied to lithium salts to describe its behavioral effect (Poindexter et al., 1998). The use of lithium in people with intellectual disabilities indicates that lithium is effective in the treatment of challenging behavior. Naylor, Donald, LePoidevin and Reid (1974) reported equivocal results from a double-blind trial of long-term lithium treatment of 14 institutionalized adults with intellectual disabilities, a variety of functioning levels, and a variety of comorbid diagnoses. Results showed that the number of individual episodes was about the same from placebo to treatment, but that the number of weeks ill during the lithium phase was significantly less than during the placebo phase, although the differences were not statistically significant. Worrall, Moody and Naylor (1975) also conducted a double-blind, placebo-controlled study with eight aggressive, nonmanic-depressive women with intellectual disabilities, and also found mixed results. Finally, Craft et al. (1987) demonstrated that out of 42 individuals treated with lithium or placebo, 73% of people in the lithium-treated group showed a reduction in both frequency and severity of aggression.

Opioid Antagonists

The primary opiate antagonist used to treat severe behavior disorders among individuals with intellectual and developmental disorders is naltrexone hydrochloride. Although their study is now dated, O'Brien, Greenstein, Mintz and Woody (1975) reviewed the literature and concluded that very few side effects were observed under naltrexone. When side effects have been reported in heroin addicts, they have most commonly been gastrointestinal discomfort and skin rash. The most serious side effect associated with naltrexone is a temporary increase in liver enzymes, which can indicate malfunctioning of the liver.

Opiate antagonists, particularly naltrexone, have been studied primarily as a form of treatment for SIB among individuals with intellectual disabilities (White & Schultz, 2000). In the opiate model of SIB (Cataldo & Harris, 1982), individuals are presumed to be "addicted" to the endorphin release that is likely to follow a bout of severe self-injury (that is, drug self-administration) (Thompson, Symons, Delaney & England, 1995), or to have either a congenital or acute dysfunction in endogenous opioid production that results in altered pain thresholds (Sandman, 1988). Controlled treatment trials of the opiate antagonist naltrexone have demonstrated positive effects in the treatment of SIB (Buzan, Thomas, Dubovsky & Treadway, 1995; Symons, Fox & Thompson, 1998; Sandman, Spence & Smith, 1999). Positive long-term effects (~1 year) of naltrexone on self-injury have been reported (Crews, Bonaventura, Rowe & Bonsie, 1993; Casner, Weinheimer & Gualtiere, 1996), but predicting who is most likely to be a long-term responder is complex and may be, in part, dependent on the initial response to acute naltrexone treatment mediated by individual differences in sensitivity to opiate antagonists (Sandman et al., 2000). Two groups have reported differential effects of naltrexone depending on self-injury site (Herman et al., 1987; Thompson et al., 1994b). These findings suggest that naltrexone appears to have different effects depending on the form and/or location of the SIB. Though approximately 30–50% of individuals with intractable self-injury have been reported to show substantial improvement, some people with similar appearing challenging behavior are not responsive to naltrexone (Barrera, Teodoro, Selmeci & Madappuli, 1994; Bodfish, et al., 1994).

Stimulants/Impulsivity and Hyperactivity Treatment

Stimulants are one of the most commonly prescribed and studied psychotropic medications for children both with and without intellectual disabilities, particularly for the treatment of ADD (Arnold, Gadow, Perason & Varley, 1998). Stimulants are generally quickly absorbed, cross the blood–brain barrier easily, and are rapidly metabolized, reaching peak plasma levels 1.5–3 hours after ingestion. Although there is essentially no life-threatening toxicity, there are some common side effects. The primary side effects for stimulant medications are insomnia and anorexia (loss of appetite), with similar incidence for children with and without intellectual disabilities (Gadow, 1982). Other side effects include changes in mood, suppression of spontaneity, withdrawal or symptoms of depression, lethargy/apathy, tics or involuntary movements, and cardiovascular effects. In very rare cases, hallucinations, symptoms of psychosis, and epilepsy have emerged after stimulant use. Finally, there also appears to be a dose-dependent effect on cognitive tasks, with higher doses associated with children being overfocused and very low doses associated with poor performance (Dyme, Sahakian, Golinko & Rabe, 1982).

A review of stimulant use with individuals with intellectual or pervasive developmental disabilities from 1971 to 1996 showed that over 27 double-blind studies of the effects of stimulant medication have been conducted (Arnold et al., 1998). The data reviewed indicate that it is effective in treating disruptive and other challenging behaviors in a variety of settings and applications. Recently, Handen et al. (1999) demonstrated the efficacy of methylphenidate in 11 preschool children with intellectual disabilities and ADD. The results showed significant improvement in hyperactivity and inattention, as well as decreased activity level and improved compliance, to be associated with the medication. Aman et al. (1997) compared methylphenidate to fenfluramine in a child with intellectual disabilities and ADD. Teacher and parent ratings demonstrated that fenfluramine might have resulted in more significant improvements, but with greater side effects.

Although there do not appear to be significant adverse effects with long-term use of stimulant medication, with the possible exception of slowed growth and weight gain, long-term studies with methylphenidate have also demonstrated mixed effects. Aman, Pejeau, Osborne, Rojahn and Handen (1996) did a 2- to 4-year follow-up with children from a medication study, and found that most children were still experiencing significant challenging behaviors, as assessed by parent and teacher ratings. Many of the children required additional interventions, such as more psychotropic medications or nonmedical treatment, in an effort to reduce continued problems. Handen, Janosky and McAuliffe (1997) also followed up 52 children who had previously participated in a clinical trial. They found that while 72% of the children showed continued improvement, over two-thirds still had very high Conners scores. In fact, 22% received inpatient psychiatric treatment prior to follow-up. These findings may indicate that the long-term effects of the medication may not be as positive, particularly for children with intellectual disabilities, comorbid conduct disorders, and severe symptoms of ADD.

CONCLUSION

Many people with intellectual disabilities who are currently treated with psychotropic medications may not require such medications. Their behavioral challenges are often related to the nature of their intellectual ability (such as poor communication skills) and their inability to cope with the environmental demands (unpleasant and unreasonable demands) placed upon them. Suppressing their behavioral signs and symptoms only delays identifying the causes of their challenging behavior through appropriate functional environmental and behavioral assessments.

At the same time, other people with intellectual disabilities who have bona fide psychopathological problems reflecting underlying neurochemical abnormalities are appropriate recipients of psychotropic medications. Which people exhibit behavioral challenges for environmental and skill reasons and which do so because of underlying psychopathology is currently difficult to determine. We would not expect a given instructional method to be equally effective in teaching reading to a heterogeneous group of 5- to 7-year-olds who present with a mixture of hearing problems, poor vision, phonemic awareness difficulties, and motivational difficulties. Yet, a similar expectation often guides routine practice and some clinical research in prescribing psychotropic medications to people with developmental disabilities who share a common behavioral challenge, such as aggression. We must do a better job of identifying putative causal mechanisms and tailor treatments specifically to individuals.

Promising developments have begun to occur in using a combination of standardized psychiatric diagnostic strategies (e.g., Royal College of Psychiatrists, 2001) and direct observational functional assessment methods (e.g., Zarcone et al., in press) to disentangle which people are which. It would be premature to suggest the diagnostic problem has been solved. However, recognizing that there are diagnostic problems is a prerequisite to their solution. There is a tendency among practitioners to view behavioral challenges as integral characteristics of the developmental disability (such as autism) rather than as reflecting an underlying, neurochemically based psychopathological disorder, in a problem known as diagnostic overshadowing (Reiss, Levitan & Szyszko, 1982).

Evaluating medication effects assumes that other exacerbating factors have been considered. Gastrointestinal and sleep disorders are very common among people with some developmental disabilities (Kennedy & Thompson, 2000). Such episodic, undiagnosed co-occurring health problems can cause inexplicable variability in response to treatment. Sex differences and ethnic and racial differences can yield variable results during clinical drug trials. It is known, for example, that antipsychotic medications, particularly risperidone, may disrupt the female menstrual cycle (Compton & Miller, 2002), which, in turn, may cause differences in mood and challenging behavior over time in people treated with antipsychotics. Depending on when during the menstrual cycle assessments are done, different results may be yielded. Liver enzyme systems metabolize some drugs differently among racial groups, yielding different effective blood levels of drugs of interest (Zhou & Liu, 2000).

Ethical issues in medication evaluation are ever present. Psychotropic medications should not be substituted for humane and developmentally appropriate living, learning, and vocational conditions. While it may be less expensive to administer a psychotropic medication than to correct inadequate living conditions and provide more appropriate staffing, that is unacceptable practice. Decisions regarding risk-benefit ratios are often difficult. People with mild intellectual disability and schizophrenia who have been unresponsive to other antipsychotics may profit greatly from the atypical antipsychotic, clozapine, enabling them to lead a relatively stable life in a community setting rather than a restricted psychiatric facility. However, the remote risk of potentially fatal agranulocytosis must be balanced against quality of life.

Some behavioral and social scientists and educators prefer environmental interventions rather than medications for challenging behavior due to concern about side effects. However, there are circumstances in which this bias may inadvertently deny appropriate effective treatment. A person with intellectual disability and schizophrenia who is experiencing a florid period of hallucinations and thought disorder, and who has previously been responsive to antipsychotic medication, or an individual with bipolar disorder in the midst of a manic episode who had been shown to be responsive to lithium, should not be deprived of effective medication treatment on philosophical grounds. Withholding an antipsychotic or an effective mood-disorder medication purely on the basis of a bias against the use of psychotropic medications is ethically questionable. We are beginning to take a more informed, mature approach to the use of psychotropic and other behaviorally active medications in treating individuals with developmental disabilities who have behavioral challenges. There is little question these medications can be highly effective for some people displaying behavioral challenges. The use of molecular genetic diagnostic methods combined with newer brain-imaging methods may further improve our ability to distinguish among subsets of individuals requiring treatment. However, in the meantime, practitioners and researchers must be vigilant in using these medications and view their promise as a work in progress.

REFERENCES

Alvarez, N., Besag, F. & Iivanainen, M. (1998). Use of antiepileptic drugs in the treatment of epilepsy in people with intellectual disability. *Journal of Intellectual Disability Research*, **45**, 139–145.

Aman, M.G., Burrow, W.H. & Wolford, P.L. (1995). The Aberrant Behavior Checklist–Community: factor validity and effect of subject variables for adults in group homes. *American Journal of Mental Deficiency*, **100**, 283–292.

Aman, M.G., De Smedt, G., Derivan, A., Lyons, B. & Findling, R.L. (2002). Double-blind, placebo-controlled study of risperidone for treatment of disruptive behavior in children with subaverage intelligence. *American Journal of Psychiatry*, **159**, 1337–1346.

Aman, M.G., Kern, R.A., Osborne, P., Tumuluru, R., Rojahn, J. & del Medico, V. (1997). Fenfluramine and methylphenidate in children with mental retardation and borderline IQ: clinical effects. *American Journal of Mental Retardation*, **101**, 521–534.

Aman, M.G. & Madrid, A. (1999). Atypical antipsychotics in persons with developmental disabilities. *Mental Retardation and Developmental Disabilities Research Reviews*, **5**, 253–263.

Aman, M.G., Pejeau, C., Osborne, P., Rojahn, J. & Handen, B. (1996). Four-year follow-up of children with low intelligence and ADHD. *Research in Developmental Disabilities*, **17**, 417–432.

Aman, M.G. & Singh, N.N. (1991). Psychopharmacological intervention: an update. In J.L. Matson & J.A. Mulick (Eds) *Handbook of Mental Retardation* (pp. 347–372). Oxford: Pergamon.

Aman, M.G., Tasse, M.J., Rojahn, J. & Hammer, D. (1995). The Nisonger CBRF: a child behavior rating form for children with developmental disabilities. *Research in Developmental Disabilities*, **17**, 41–57.

Aman, M.G., White, A.J., Vaithianathan, C. & Teehan, C.J. (1986). Preliminary study of imipramine in profoundly retarded residents. *Journal of Autism and Developmental Disorders*, **16**, 263–273.

Aman, M.R., Singh, N.N., Stewart, A.W. & Field, C.J. (1985a). The Aberrant Behavior Checklist: a behavior rating scale for the assessment of treatment effects. *American Journal of Mental Deficiency*, **89**, 485–491.

Aman, M.R., Singh, N.N., Stewart, A.W. & Field, C.J. (1985b). Psychometric characteristics of the Aberrant Behavior Checklist. *American Journal of Mental Deficiency*, **89**, 492–502.

Antonacci, D.J. & de Groot, C.M. (2000). Clozapine treatment in a population of adults with mental retardation. *Journal of Clinical Psychiatry*, **61**, 22–25.

Arnold, L.E., Gadow, K., Pearson, D.A. & Varley, C.K. (1998). Stimulants. In S. Reiss & M.G. Amen (Eds) *Psychotropic Medications and Developmental Disabilities: The International Consensus Handbook* (pp. 229–243). Columbus, OH: Ohio State University Nisonger Center.

Arnt, J. & Skarsfeldt, T. (1998). Do novel antipsychotics have similar pharmacological characteristics? A review of the evidence. *Neuropsychopharmacology*, **18**, 63–101.

Baldessarini, R.J. & Frankenburg, F.R. (1991). Clozapine—a novel antipsychotic agent. *New England Journal of Medicine*, **324**, 746–754.

Barrera, F.J., Teodoro, J.M., Selmeci, T. & Madappuli, A. (1994). Self-injury, pain, and the endorphin theory. *Journal of Developmental and Physical Disabilities*, **6**, 169–192.

Baumeister, A.A. & Sevin, J.A. (1990). Pharmacologic control of aberrant behavior in the mentally retarded: toward a more rational approach. *Neuroscience and Biobehavioral Reviews*, **14**, 253–262.

Bennett, J., Goldman, W.T. & Suppes, T. (1997). Gabapentin for treatment of bipolar and schizoaffective disorder. *Journal of Clinical Psychopharmacology*, **17**, 141–142.

Beran, R.G. & Gibson, R.J. (1998). Aggressive behaviour in intellectually challenged patients with epilepsy treated with lamotrigine. *Epilepsia*, **39**, 280–282.

Blum, N.J., Mauk, J.E., McComas, J.J. & Mace, F.C. (1996). Separate and combined effects of methylphenidate and behavioral intervention on disruptive behavior in children with mental retardation. *Journal of Applied Behavior Analysis*, **29**, 305–309.

Bodfish, J.W., McCuller, W.R., Madison, J.M., Register, M., Mailman, R.B. & Lewis, M.H. (1994). Placebo, double-blind evaluation of long-term naltrexone treatment effects for adults with mental retardation and self-injury. *Journal of Developmental and Physical Disabilities*, **9**, 135–152.

Bodfish, J.W., Symons, F.J. & Lewis, M.H. (1999). *Repetitive Behavior Scales Manual*. Morganton, NC: Human Development Research and Training Institute.

Branford, D., Bhaumik, S. & Naik, B. (1998). Selective serotonin re-uptake inhibitors for the treatment of perseverative and maladaptive behaviours of people with intellectual disability. *Journal of Intellectual Disability Research*, **42**, 301–306.

Brodkin, E.S., McDougle, C.J., Naylor, S.T., Cohen, D.J. & Price, L.H. (1997). Clomipramine in adults with pervasive developmental disorders: a prospective open-label investigation. *Journal of Child and Adolescent Psychopharmacology*, **7**, 109–121.

Bruininks, R.H., Olson, K.M., Larson, S.A. & Lakin, K.C. (1994). Challenging behaviors among persons with mental retardation in residential settings: implications for policy, research, and practice. In T. Thompson & D.B. Gray (Eds) *Destructive Behavior in Developmental Disabilities: Diagnosis and Treatment* (pp. 24–48). Thousand Oaks, CA: Sage.

Brylewski, J. & Duggan, L. (1999). Antipsychotic medication for challenging behaviour in people with intellectual disability: a systematic review of randomized controlled trials. *Journal of Intellectual Disability Research*, **43**, 91–98.

Burgio, L.D., Page, T.J. & Capriotti, R.M. (1985). Clinical behavioral pharmacology: methods for evaluating medications and contingency management. *Journal of Applied Behavior Analysis*, **18**, 45–59.

Buzan, R.D., Dubovsky, S.L., Firestone, D. & Dal Pozzo, E. (1998). Use of clozapine in 10 mentally retarded adults. *Journal of Neuropsychiatry and Clinical Neurosciences*, **10**, 93–95.

Buzan, R.D., Thomas, M., Dubovsky, S.L. & Treadway, J. (1995). The use of opiate antagonists for recurrent self-injurious behavior. *Journal of Neuropsychiatry and Clinical Neuroscience*, **7**, 437–444.

Cain, N.N., Davidson, P.W., Burhan, A.M., Andolsek, M.A., Baxter, J.T., Sullivan, L., et al. (2003). Identifying bipolar mood disorders in individuals with intellectual disability. *Journal of Intellectual Disability Research*, **47**, 31–38.

Campbell, M., Friedman, E., Green, W.H., Collins, P.J., Small, A.M. & Breuer, H. (1975). Blood serotonin in schizophrenic children: a preliminary study. *International Pharmacopsychiatry*, **10**, 213–221.

Carr, E.G. (1977). The motivation of self-injurious behavior: a review of some hypotheses. *Psychological Bulletin*, **84**, 800–816.

Carr, E.G. & Durand, V.M. (1985). Reducing behavior problems through functional communication training. *Journal of Applied Behavior Analysis*, **26**, 157–172.

Casner, J.A., Weinheimer, B. & Gualtiere, C.T. (1996). Naltrexone and self-injurious behavior: a retrospective population study. *Journal of Clinical Psychopharmacology*, **16**, 389–394.

Cataldo, M.F. & Harris, J. (1982). The biological basis for self-injury in the mentally retarded. *Analysis and Intervention in Developmental Disabilities*, **2**, 21–39.

Cerutti, D. & Thompson, T. (1990). Drug therapy in mental retardation: "artificial hibernation" evolved [Review of M. Aman's & N.H. Singh's *Psychopharmacology of the Developmental Disabilities*]. *Contemporary Psychology*, **35**, 1148–1150.

Coccaro, E.F., Gabriel, S. & Siever, L.J. (1990). Buspirone challenge: preliminary evidence for a role for central 5-HT 1a receptor function in impulsive aggressive behavior in humans. *Psychopharmacology Bulletin*, **26**, 393–405.

Coleman, M. & Gillberg, C. (1985). *The Biology of the Autistic Syndromes*. New York: Praeger.

Compton, M.T. & Miller, A.H. (2002). Antipsychotic-induced hyperprolactinemia and sexual dysfunction. *Psychopharmacology Bulletin*, **36**, 143–164.

Conners, C.K. (1990). *Manual for Conners' Rating Scales*. North Tonawanda, NY: Multi-Health Systems.

Craft, M., Ismail, I.A., Krishnamurti, D., Matthews, J., Regan, A., Seth, R.V., et al. (1987). Lithium in the treatment of aggression in mentally handicapped patients: a double-blind trial. *British Journal of Psychiatry*, **150**, 685–689.

Crawford, P., Brown, S. & Kerr, M. (2001). A randomized open-label study of gabapentin and lamotrigine in adults with learning disability and resistant epilepsy. *Seizure, the Journal of the British Epilepsy Association*, **10**, 107–115.

Crews, W.D., Bonaventura, S., Rowe, F.B. & Bonsie, D. (1993). Cessation of long-term naltrexone therapy and self-injury: a case study. *Research in Developmental Disabilities*, **14**, 331–340.

Davanzo, P.A., Belin, T.R., Widawski, M.H. & King, B.H. (1998). Paroxetine treatment of aggression and self-injury in persons with mental retardation. *American Journal of Mental Retardation*, **102**, 427–437.

Davanzo, P.A. & King, B.H. (1996). Open trial lamotrigine in the treatment of self-injurious behavior in an adolescent with profound mental retardation. *Journal of Child and Adolescent Psychopharmacology*, **6**, 273–279.

Davidson, P.W., Cain, N.N., Sloane-Reeves, J.E., Giesow, V.E., Quijano, L.D. & Houser, K.D. (1996). Factors predicting re-referral following crisis intervention for community-based persons with developmental disabilities and behavioral and psychiatric disorder. *American Journal on Mental Retardation*, **101**, 109–117.

Durand, V.M. (1982). A behavioral/pharmacological intervention for the treatment of severe self-injurious behavior. *Journal of Autism and Developmental Disorders*, **12**, 243–254.

Dyme, I.Z., Sahakian, B.J., Golinko, B.E. & Rabe, E.F. (1982). Perseveration induced by methylphenidate in children. *Progress in Neuropsychopharmacology*, **6**, 269–273.

Ellenbroek, B.A. (1993). Treatment of schizophrenia: a clinical and preclinical evaluation of antipsychotic drugs. *Pharmacology*, **57**, 1–78.

Emerson, E. (2003). Prevalence of psychiatric disorders in children and adolescents with and without intellectual disability. *Journal of Intellectual Disability Research*, **47**, 51–58.

Ettinger, A.B., Weisbrot, D.M., Saracco, J., Dhoon, A., Kanner, A. & Devinsky, O. (1998). Positive and negative psychotropic effects of lamotrigine in patients with epilepsy and mental retardation. *Epilepsia*, **39**, 874–877.

Field, C.J., Aman, M.G., White, A.J. & Vaithianathan, C. (1986). A single-subject study of impramine in a mentally retarded woman with depressive symptoms. *Journal of Mental Deficiency Research*, **30**, 191–198.

Fisher, W., Piazza, C. & Page, T.J. (1989). Assessing independent and interactive effects of behavioral pharmacological interventions for a client with dual diagnoses. *Journal of Behavior Therapy and Experimental Psychiatry*, **20**, 241–250.

Freund, L.S. & Reiss, A.L. (1991). Rating problem behaviors in outpatients with mental retardation: use of Aberrant Behavior Checklist. *Research in Developmental Disabilities*, **12**, 435–451.

Gadow, K.D. (1982). School involvement in pharmacotherapy for behavior disorders. *Journal of Special Education*, **16**, 385–399.

Garcia, D. & Smith, R.G. (1999). Using analog baselines to assess the effects of naltrexone on self-injurious behavior. *Research in Developmental Disabilities*, **20**, 1–21.

Gedye, A. (1992). Recognizing obsessive-compulsive disorder in clients with developmental disabilities. *Habilitative Mental Healthcare Newsletter*, **11**, 73–77.

Goldstein, M., Kuga, S., Kusano, N., Meller, E., Dancis, J. & Schwarcz, R. (1986). Dopamine agonist induced self-mutilative biting behavior in monkeys with unilateral ventromedial tegmental lesions of the brainstem: possible pharmacological model for Lesch-Nyhan syndrome. *Brain Research*, **367**, 114–119.

Goodman, W.K., Price, L.H., Rasmussen, S.A., Mazure, C., Delgado, P., Henigner, G.R., et al. (1989b). The Yale-Brown Obsessive Compulsive Scale (Y-BOCS). II. Validity. *Archives of General Psychiatry*, **46**, 1012–1016.

Goodman, W.K., Price, L.H., Rasmussen, S.A., Mazure, C., Fleishmann, R., Hill, C., et al. (1989a). The Yale-Brown Obsessive Compulsive Scale (Y-BOCS). I. Development, use, and reliability. *Archives of General Psychiatry*, **46**, 1006–1011.

Gualtieri, C.T. & Schroeder, S.R. (1989). Pharmacotherapy for self-injurious behavior: preliminary tests of the D2 hypothesis. *Psychopharmacology Bulletin*, **25**, 364–371.

Gualtieri, C.T., Schroeder, S.R., Hicks, R.E. & Quade, D. (1986). Tardive dyskinesia in young mentally retarded individuals. *Archives of General Psychiatry*, **43**, 335–340.

Guy, W. (1976). *Assessment Manual for Psychopharmacology*. Washington, DC: US Government Printing Office.

Hammock, R.G., Schroeder, S.S. & Levine, W.R. (1995). The effect of clozapine on self-injurious behavior. *Journal of Autism and Developmental Disorders*, **25**, 611–626.

Handen, B.L., Breaux, A.M., Janosky, J., McAuliffe, S., Feldman, H. & Gosling, A. (1992). Effects and noneffects of methylphenidate in children with mental retardation and ADHD. *Journal of American Academy of Child and Adolescent Psychiatry*, **31**, 455–461.

Handen, B.L., Feldman, H.M., Lurier, A. & Murray, P.J. (1999). Efficacy of methylphenidate among preschool children with developmental disabilities and ADHD. *Journal of the American Academy of Child and Adolescent Psychiatry*, **38**, 805–812.

Handen, B.L., Janosky, J. & McAuliffe, S. (1997). Long-term follow-up of children with mental retardation/borderline intellectual functioning and ADHD. *Journal of Abnormal Child Psychology*, **25**, 287–295.

Hellings, J.A., Kelley, L.A., Gabrielli, W.F., Kilgore, E. & Shah, P. (1996). Sertraline response in adults with mental retardation and autistic disorder. *Journal of Clinical Psychiatry*, **57**, 333–336.

Herman, B.H., Hammock, M.K., Egan, J., Arthur-Smith, A., Chatoor, I., Werner, A., et al. (1987). Naltrexone decreases self-injurious behavior. *Annals of Neurology*, **22**, 550–552.

Horner, R.H., Dunlap, G., Koegel, R.L., Carr, E.G., Sailor, W., Anderson, J., et al. (1990). Toward a technology of "nonaversive" behavioral support. *Journal of the Association for Persons with Severe Handicaps*, **15**, 125–132.

Horner, R.H., Vaughn, B.J., Day, H.M. & Ard, W.R. (2001). The relationship between setting events and problem behavior: expanding our understanding of behavioral support. In L.K. Koegel, R.L. Koegel & G. Dunlap (Eds) *Positive Behavior Support: Including People with Difficult Behavior in the Community* (pp. 381–402). Baltimore, MD: Brookes.

Intagliata, J. & Willer, B. (1981). Reinstitutionalization of mentally retarded persons successfully placed into family-care and group homes. *American Journal of Mental Deficiency*, **87**, 34–39.

Iwata, B.A., Dorsey, M.F., Slifer, K.J., Bauman, K.E. & Richman, G.S. (1994a). Toward a functional analysis of self-injury. *Journal of Applied Behavior Analysis*, **27**, 197–209 (reprinted from *Analysis and Intervention in Developmental Disabilities*, **2**, 3–20, 1982).

Iwata, B.A., Pace, G.M., Dorsey, M.F., Zarcone, J.R., Vollmer, T.R., Smith, R.G., et al. (1994b). The functions of self-injurious behavior: an experimental-epidemiological analysis. *Journal of Applied Behavior Analysis*, **27**, 215–240.

Janssen, P.A.J., Neimegeers, C.J.E., Awouters, F., Schellekens, K.H.L., Meegens, A.A.H.P. & Meert, T.F. (1988). Pharmacology of risperidone (R 64 766), a new antipsychotic with serotonin-S2 and dopamine-D2 antagonistic properties. *Journal of Pharmacology and Experimental Therapy*, **244**, 685–693.

Johnson, C.R., Handen, B.L., Lubetsky, M.J. & Sacco, K.A. (1994). Efficacy of methylphenidate and behavioral intervention on classroom behavior in children with ADHD and mental retardation. *Behavior Modification*, **18**, 470–487.

Kastner, T., Finesmith, R. & Walsh, R. (1993). Long-term administration of valproic acid in the treatment of affective symptoms in people with mental retardation. *Journal of Clinical Psychopharmacology*, **13**, 448–451.

Kayser, K.H., Wacker, D.P., Derby, K.M., Andelman, M.S., Golonka, Z. & Stoner, E.A. (1997). A rapid method for evaluating the necessity for both a behavioral intervention and methylphenidate. *Journal of Applied Behavior Analysis*, **30**, 177–180.

Kennedy, C.H. & Thompson, T. (2000). Health conditions contributing to problem behavior among people with mental retardation and developmental disabilities. In M.L. Wehmeyer & J.R. Patton (Eds) *Mental Retardation in the 21st Century* (pp. 211–231). Austin, TX: Pro-Ed.

Krishnamoorthy, J. & King, B.H. (1998). Open-label olanzapine treatment in five preadolescent children. *Journal of Child and Adolescent Psychopharmacology*, **8**, 107–113.

Lemmens, P., Brecher, M. & Van Baelen, B. (1999). A combined analysis or double-blind studies with risperidone vs. placebo and other antipsychotic agents: factors associated with extrapyramidal symptoms. *Acta Psychiatrica Scandinavica*, **99**, 160–170.

Lewis, M.H., Bodfish, J.W., Powell, S.B., Parker, D.E. & Golden, R.N. (1996). Clomipramine treatment for self-injurious behavior in individuals with mental retardation: a double-blind comparison with placebo. *American Journal on Mental Retardation*, **100**, 654–665.

Lindenmayer, J.P. & Kotsaftis, A. (2000). Use of sodium valproate in violent and aggressive behaviors: a critical review. *Journal of Clinical Psychiatry*, **61**, 123–128.

Lipman, R.S. (1970). The use of psychopharmacological agents in residential facilities for the retarded. In F.J. Menolascino (Ed.) *Psychiatric Approaches to Mental Retardation* (pp. 387–398). New York: Basic Books.

Lloyd, K.G., Hornykiewicz, O., Davidson, L., Shannak, K., Farley, I., Goldstein, M., et al. (1981). Biomedical evidence of dysfunction of brain neurotransmitters in the Lesch-Nyhan syndrome. *New England Journal of Medicine*, **305**, 1106–1111.

Lowry, M.A. (1998). Assessment and treatment of mood disorders in persons with developmental disabilities. *Journal of Developmental and Physical Disabilities*, **10**, 387–406.

Luiselli, J.K. (1986). Behavior analysis of pharmacological and contingency management interventions for self-injury. *Journal of Behavior Therapy and Experimental Psychiatry*, **17**, 275–284.

Luiselli, J.K. (1991). A non-aversive behavioral-pharmacological intervention for severe self-injury in an adult with dual sensory impairment. *Journal of Behavior Therapy and Experimental Psychiatry*, **22**, 233–238.

Mace, F.C. & Mauk, J.E. (1995). Bio-behavioral diagnosis and treatment of self-injury. *Mental Retardation and Developmental Disabilities Research Reviews*, **1**, 104–110.

Marshburn, E.C. & Aman, M.G. (1992). Factor validity and norms for the aberrant behavior checklist in a community sample of children with mental retardation. *Journal of Autism and Developmental Disorders*, **22**, 357–373.

Marston, G.M., Perry, D.W. & Roy, A. (1997). Manifestations of depression in people with intellectual disabilities. *Journal of Intellectual Disability Research*, **41**, 476–480.

Masi, G., Marcheschi, M. & Pfanner, P. (1997). Paroxetine in depressed adolescents with intellectual disability: an open label study. *Journal of Intellectual Disability Research*, **41**, 268–272.

Matson, J.L., Bamburg, J.W., Mayville, E.A., Pinkston, J., Bielecki, J., Kuhn, D., et al. (2000). Psychopharmacology and mental retardation: a 10 year review (1990–1999). *Research in Developmental Disabilities*, **21**, 263–296.

Matson, J.L., Coe, D.A., Gardner, W.I. & Sovner, R. (1991). A factor analytic study of the diagnostic assessment for the severely handicapped scale. *Journal of Nervous and Mental Disease*, **179**, 553–557.

McBrien, J.A. (2003). Assessment and diagnosis of depression in people with intellectual disability. *Journal of Intellectual Disability Research*, **47**, 1–13.

McDonough, M., Hillery, J. & Kennedy, N. (2000). Olanzapine for chronic, stereotypic self-injurious behaviour: a pilot study in seven adults with intellectual disability. *Journal of Intellectual Disability Research*, **44**, 677–684.

McDougle, C.J. (1997). Psychopharmacology. In D.J. Cohen & F.R. Volkmar (Eds) *Handbook of Autism and Pervasive Developmental Disorders* (2nd edn) (pp. 707–729). New York: Wiley.

McDougle, C.J., Holmes, J.P., Bronson, M.R., Anderson, G.M., Volkmar, F.R., Price, L.H., et al. (1997). Risperidone treatment of children and adolescents with pervasive developmental disorders: a prospective, open-label study. *Journal of American Adolescent Psychiatry*, **36**, 685–693.

McDougle, C.J., Holmes, J.P., Carlson, D.C., Pelton, G.H., Cohen, D.J. & Price, L.H. (1998). A double-blind, placebo-controlled study of risperidone in adults with autistic disorder and other pervasive developmental disorders. *Archives of General Psychiatry*, **55**, 633–641.

McDougle, C.J., Kresch, L., Goodman, W.K., Naylor, S.T., Volkmar, F.R., Choen, D.J., et al. (1995). A case-controlled study of repetitive thoughts and behavior in adults with autistic disorder and obsessive-compulsive disorder. *American Journal of Psychiatry*, **152**, 772–777.

McDougle, C.J., Naylor, S.T., Cohen, D.J., Volkmar, F.R., Heninger, G.R. & Price, L.H. (1996). A double-blind, placebo-controlled study of fluvoxamine in adults with autistic disorder. *Archives of General Psychiatry*, **53**, 1001–1008.

Meador, K.J. & Baker, G.A. (1997). Behavioral and cognitive effects of lamotrigine. *Journal of Child Neurology*, **12**, S44–47.

Miczek, K.A., Mos, J. & Olivier, B. (1989). Serotonin, aggression, and self-destructive behavior. *Psychopharmacology Bulletin*, **25**, 399–403.

Mindham, J. & Espie, C.A. (2003). Glasgow Anxiety Scale for people with an intellectual disability (GAS-ID): development and psychometric properties of a new measure for use with people with mild intellectual disability. *Journal of Intellectual Disability Research*, **47**, 22–30.

Mirenda, P., MacGregor, T. & Kelly-Keough, S. (2002). Teaching communication skills for behavioral support in the context of family life. In J.M. Lucyshyn, G. Dunlap & R.W. Albin (Eds) *Families and Positive Behavior Support: Addressing Problem Behavior in Family Contexts* (pp. 185–207). Baltimore, MD: Brookes.

Murray, L.K. & Kollins, S.H. (2000). Effects of methylphenidate on sensitivity to reinforcement in children diagnosed with attention deficit hyperactivity disorder: an application of the matching law. *Journal of Applied Behavior Analysis*, **33**, 573–591.

Napolitano, D.A., Jack, S.L., Sheldon, J.B., Williams, D.C., McAdam, D.B. & Schroeder, S.R. (1999). Drug–behavior interactions in persons with mental retardation and developmental disabilities. *Mental Retardation and Developmental Disabilities Research Reviews*, **5**, 322–334.

National Institutes of Health (1991). Treatment of destructive behavior in persons with developmental disabilities (NIH Publication No. 91-2410). Bethesda, MD: Department of Public Health and Human Services.

Naylor, G.J., Donald, J.M., LePoidevin, D. & Reid, A.H. (1974). A double-blind trial of long-term lithium therapy in mental defectives. *British Journal of Psychiatry*, **124**, 42–57.

Northup, J., Fusilier, I., Swanson, V., Huete, J., Bruce, T., Freeland, J., et al. (1999). Further analysis of the separate and interactive effects of methylphenidate and common classroom contingencies. *Journal of Applied Behavior Analysis*, **32**, 35–50.

Northup, J., Fusilier, I., Swanson, V., Roane, H. & Borrero, J. (1997a). An evaluation of methylphenidate as a potential establishing operation for some common classroom reinforcers. *Journal of Applied Behavior Analysis*, **30**, 614–626.

Northup, J., Jones, K., Broussard, C., DiGiovanni, G., Herring, M., Fusilier, I., et al. (1997b). A preliminary analysis of interactive effects between common classroom contingencies and MPH. *Journal of Applied Behavior Analysis*, **30**, 121–125.

O'Brien, C.P., Greenstein, R.A., Mintz, J. & Woody, C.E. (1975). Clinical experience with naltrexone. *American Journal of Drug and Alcohol Abuse*, **2**, 365–377.

O'Neill, R.E., Horner, R.H., Albin, R.W., Sprague, J.R., Storey, K. & Newton, J.S. (1997). *Functional Assessment and Program Development for Problem Behavior*. Pacific Grove, CA: Brooks/Cole.

Patel, N.C., Dorson, P.G. & Bettinger, T.L. (2002). Sudden late onset of clozapine-induced agranulocytosis. *Annals of Pharmacotherapy*, **36**, 1012–1015.

Pelham, W.E., Carlson, C., Sams, S.E., Vallano, G., Dixon, M.J. & Hoza, B. (1993). Separate and combined effects of methylphenidate and behavior modification on boys with attention deficit–hyperactivity disorder in the classroom. *Journal of Consulting and Clinical Psychology*, **61**, 506–515.

Physician's Desk Reference (2002). Montvale, NY: Medical Economics Co.

Poindexter, A.R., Cain, N., Clarke, D.J., Cook, E.H. Jr, Corbett, J.A., Levitas, A. (1998). Mood stabilizers. In S. Reiss & M.G. Amen (Eds) *Psychotropic Medications and Developmental Disabilities: The International Consensus Handbook* (pp. 215–227). Columbus, OH: Ohio State University Nisonger Center.

Reichle, J. & Wacker, D. (1993). *Communication and Language Intervention*, vol. 3. *Communicative Alternatives to Challenging Behavior: Integrating Functional Assessment and Intervention Strategies*. Baltimore, MD: Brookes.

Reiss, S. (1988). *The Reiss Screen Test Manual*. Orland Park, IL: International Diagnostic Systems.

Reiss, S., Levitan, G.W. & Szyszko, J. (1982). Emotional disturbance and mental retardation: diagnostic overshadowing. *American Journal of Mental Deficiency*, **86**, 567–574.

Repp, A.C. & Karsh, K.G. (1994). Hypothesis-based interventions for tantrum behaviors of persons with developmental disabilities in school settings. *Journal of Applied Behavior Analysis*, **27**, 21–31.

Repp, A.C. & Singh, N.N. (1990). *Perspectives on the Use of Nonaversive and Aversive Interventions for Persons with Developmental Disabilities*. Sycamore, IL: Sycamore.

Research Units on Pediatric Psychopharmacology Autism Network (2002). Risperidone in children with autism and serious behavioral problems. *New England Journal of Medicine*, **347**, 314–321.

Ritvo, E.R., Yuwiler, A., Geller, E., Ornitz, E.M., Saeger, K. & Plotkin, S. (1970). Increased blood serotonin and platelets in infantile autism. *Archives of General Psychiatry*, **23**, 566–572.

Rojahn, B. & Helsel, W.J. (1991). The Aberrant Behavior Checklist with children and adolescents with dual diagnosis. *Journal of Autism and Developmental Disorders*, **21**, 17–28.

Royal College of Psychiatrists (2001). *DC-LD: Diagnostic Criteria for Psychiatric Disorders for Use with Adults with Learning Disabilities (Mental Retardation)*. London: Gaskell.

Ruedrich, S., Swales, T.P., Fossaeeca, C., Tolliver, J. & Rutkowski, A. (1999). Effect of divalproex sodium on aggression and self-injurious behaviour in adults with intellectual disability: a retrospective review. *Journal of Intellectual Disability Research*, **43**, 105–111.

Sandman, C.A. (1988). Beta-endorphin dysregulation in autistic and self-injurious behavior: a neurodevelopmental hypothesis. *Synapse*, **2**, 193–199.

Sandman, C.A., Hetrick, W., Taylor, D.V., Barron, J.L., Touchette, P., Lott, I., et al. (1993). Naltrexone reduces self-injury and improves learning. *Experimental and Clinical Psychopharmacology*, **1**, 242–258.

Sandman, C.A., Hetrick, W., Taylor, D.V., Marion, S.D., Touchette, P., Barron, J.L., et al. (2000). Long-term effects of naltrexone on self-injurious behavior. *American Journal on Mental Retardation*, **105**, 103–117.

Sandman, C.A., Spence, M.A. & Smith, M. (1999). Proopiomelanocortin (POMC) dysregulation and response to opiate blockers. *Mental Retardation and Developmental Disabilities Research Reviews*, **5**, 314–321.

Schaal, D.W. & Hackenberg, T. (1994). Toward a functional analysis of drug treatment of behavior problems of people with developmental disabilities. *American Journal on Mental Retardation*, **99**, 123–140.

Schain, R. & Freedman, D. (1961). Studies of 5-hydroxindol metabolism in autistic and other mentally retarded children. *Journal of Pediatrics*, **58**, 315–320.

Schell, R.M., Pelham, W.E., Bender, M.E., Andree, J.A., Law, T. & Robbins, F.R. (1986). The concurrent assessment of behavioral and psychostimulant interventions: a controlled case study. *Behavioral Assessment*, **8**, 373–384.

Schroeder, S.R., Rojahn, J. & Oldenquist, A. (1991). Treatment of destructive behaviors among people with mental retardation and developmental disabilities: an overview of the problem. In *Treatment of Destructive Behaviors in Persons with Developmental Disabilities* (pp. 125–172) (NIH Publication No. 91-2410). Bethesda, MD: National Institute of Health.

Schroeder, S.R., Rojahn, J. & Reese, R.M. (1997). Brief report: reliability and validity of instruments for assessing psychotropic medication effects on self-injurious behavior in mental retardation. *Journal of Autism and Developmental Disorders*, **27**, 89–102.

Schwartz, N. (1999). Self-reports: how the questions shape the answers. *American Psychologist*, **54**, 93–105.

Smith, C., Felce, D., Ahmed, Z., Fraser, W.I., Kerr, M., Kiernan, C., et al. (2002). Sedation effects on responsiveness: evaluating the reduction of antipsychotic medication in people with intellectual disability using a conditional probability approach. *Journal of Intellectual Disability Research*, **46**, 464–471.

Snyder, R., Turgay, A., Aman, M., Binder, C., Fisman, S. & Carrolle, A. (2002). Effects of risperidone on conduct and disruptive behavior disorders in children with subaverage IQs. *Journal of American Academy of Child and Adolescent Psychiatry*, **41**, 1026–1036.

Sovner, R. (1989). The use of valproate in the treatment of mentally retarded persons with typical and atypical bipolar disorders. *Journal of Clinical Psychiatry*, **50**, 40–43.

Sprague, R.L. & Werry, J.S. (1971). Methodology of psychopharmacological studies with the retarded. In N.R. Ellis (Ed.) *International Review of Research in Mental Retardation*. New York: Academic Press.

Stein, D.J., Keating, J., Zar, H.J. & Hollander, E. (1994). A survey of the phenomenology and pharmacology of compulsive and impulsive-aggressive symptoms in Prader-Willi syndrome. *Journal of Neuropsychiatry*, **6**, 23–29.

Stein, L. & Belluzi, J.D. (1989). Cellular investigations of behavioral reinforcement. *Neuroscience and Biobehavioral Reviews*, **13**, 69–80.

Stoner, G., Carey, S.P., Ikeda, M.J. & Shinn, M.R. (1994). The utility of curriculum-based measurement for evaluating the effects of methylphenidate on academic performance. *Journal of Applied Behavior Analysis*, **27**, 101–113.

Strohmer, D.C. & Prout, H.T. (1991). *The Emotional Problems Scales*. Odessa, FL: Psychological Assessment Resources.

Symons, F.J., Fox, N.D. & Thompson, T. (1998). Functional communication training and naltrexone treatment of self-injurious behavior: an experimental case report. *Journal of Applied Research in Intellectual Disabilities*, **11**, 273–292.

Thompson, T. (1984). Behavioral mechanisms of drug dependence. In T. Thompson, P.B. Dews & J.E. Barrett (Eds) *Advances in Behavioral Pharmacology* (pp. 2–45). Orlando, FL: Academic Press.

Thompson, T., Egli, M., Symons, F. & Delaney, D. (1994a). Neurobehavioral mechanisms of drug action in developmental disabilities. In T. Thompson & D.B. Gray (Eds) *Destructive Behavior in Developmental Disabilities: Diagnosis and Treatment* (pp. 133–188). Thousand Oaks, CA: Sage.

Thompson, T., Hackenberg, T., Cerutti, D., Baker, D. & Axtell, S. (1994b). Opioid antagonist effects on self-injury in adults with mental retardation: response form and location as determinants of medication effects. *American Journal on Mental Retardation*, **99**, 85–102.

Thompson, T. & Lubinski, D. (1986). Units of analysis and kinetic structure of behavioral repertoires. *Journal of the Experimental Analysis of Behavior*, **46**, 219–242.

Thompson, T., Symons, F.J., Delaney, D. & England, C. (1995). Self-injurious behavior as endogenous neurochemical self-administration. *Mental Retardation and Developmental Disabilities Research Reviews*, **1**, 137–148.

Thompson, T., Symons, F.J. & Felce, D. (2000). Principles of behavioral observation: assumptions and strategies. In T. Thompson, D. Felce & F.J. Symons (Eds) *Behavioral Observation: Technology and Applications in Developmental Disabilities* (pp. 3–16). Baltimore, MD: Brookes.

Valdovinos, M.G., Napolitano, D.A., Zarcone, J.R., Hellings, J.A., Williams, D.C. & Schroeder, S.R. (2002). Multimodel evaluation of risperidone for destructive behavior: functional analysis, direct observations, rating scales, and psychiatric impressions. *Experimental and Clinical Psychopharmacology*, **10**, 268–275.

Vanstraelen, M. & Tyrer, S.P. (1999). Rapid cycling bipolar affective disorder in people with intellectual disability: a systematic review. *Journal of Intellectual Disability Research*, **43**, 349–359.

Vitello, S.J., Atthowe, J.M. & Cadwell, J. (1983). Determinants of community placement of institutionalized mentally retarded persons. *American Journal of Mental Deficiency*, **87**, 539–545.

White, S.M., Kucharik, R.F. & Moyer, J.A. (1991). Effects of serotonergic agents on isolation-induced aggression. *Pharmacology, Biochemistry and Behavior*, **39**, 729–736.

White, T. & Schultz, S.K. (2000). Naltrexone treatment for a 3-year-old boy with self-injurious behavior. *American Journal of Psychiatry*, **157**, 1574–1582.

Wilkinson, P.C., Kircher, J.C., McMahon, W.M. & Sloane, H.N. (1995). Effects of methylphenidate on reward strength in boys with attention-deficit hyperactivity disorder. *Journal of American Academy of Child and Adolescent Psychiatry*, **34**, 897–901.

Willer, J.C., Dehen, H. & Cambier, J. (1981). Stress induced analgesia in humans. *Science*, **212**, 680–691.

Williams, H., Clarke, R., Bouras, N., Martin, J. & Holt, G. (2000). Use of the atypical antipsychotics olanzapine and risperidone in adults with intellectual disability. *Journal of Intellectual Disability Research*, **44**, 164–169.

Worrall, E.P., Moody, J.P. & Naylor, G.J. (1975). Lithium in non-manic depressives: antiaggressive effects and red blood cell lithium values. *British Journal of Psychiatry*, **126**, 464–468.

Young, L.T., Robb, J.C., Patelis-Siortis, I., MacDonald, C. & Joffe, R.T. (1997). Acute treatment of bipolar depression with gabapentin. *Biological Psychiatry*, **42**, 851–853.

Zarcone, J.R., Hellings, J.A., Crandall, K., Reese, R.M., Marquis, J., Fleming, K., et al. (2001). Effects of risperidone on aberrant behavior of persons with developmental disabilities. I. A double-blind crossover study using multiple measures. *American Journal on Mental Retardation*, **106**, 525–538.

Zarcone, J.R., Iwata, B.A., Smith, R.G., Mazaleski, J.L. & Lerman, D.C. (1994). Reemergence and extinction of self-injurious escape behavior during stimulus (instructional) fading. *Journal of Applied Behavior Analysis*, **27**, 307–316.

Zarcone, J.R., Lindauer, S.E., Morse, P.S., Crosland, K.A., Valdovinos, M.G., McKerchar, T.L., et al. (in press). Effects of risperidone on destructive behavior of persons with developmental disabilities. IV. Functional analysis. *American Journal on Mental Retardation*.

Zhou, H.H. & Liu, Z.Q. (2000). Ethnic difference in drug metabolism. *Clinical Chemistry and Laboratory Medicine*, **38**, 899–903.

CHAPTER 29

Researching Staff

Chris Hatton
Lancaster University, UK
John Rose
University of Birmingham, UK
and
David Rose
Psychology Department, Ridge Hill, UK

INTRODUCTION

Despite widespread changes in the ideology and organisation of supports over the past 30 years, staff continue to hold a central place in the lives of people with intellectual disabilities. Support staff are ever present throughout the lifespan of many people with intellectual disabilities, from family support, through education, to housing, supported employment, and health services. Furthermore, staff often constitute the largest single component of service revenue expenditure (e.g., Hallam et al., 2002).

A substantial international research literature now exists concerning staff in services for people with intellectual disabilities. This chapter will review some of the conceptual, design, and methodological issues involved in researching staff. Gaps in the existing research literature and recommendations for future research will also be outlined.

CONCEPTUAL ISSUES

The research literature concerning staff in services for people with intellectual disabilities has investigated diverse constructs and has used a plethora of research methods, often involving parallel research traditions with little reference to each other. To place this fragmented research literature within a common conceptual framework, a simple diagram of the core constructs of staff research and some hypothesised links between them is presented in Figure 29.1.

This diagram does not attempt to represent the complexities of hypothesised mediator or moderator relationships between core constructs. Instead, it represents the core assumptions

The International Handbook of Applied Research in Intellectual Disabilities. Edited by E. Emerson, C. Hatton, T. Thompson and T.R. Parmenter ISBN 0-471-49709-6.

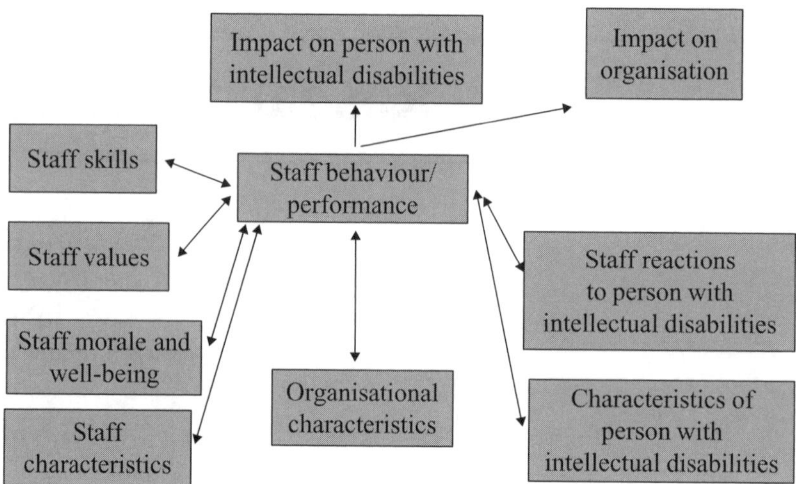

Figure 29.1 Core constructs and hypothesised links between them

of staffing research across the following research traditions:

(1) Staff behaviour has a direct causal influence on the lives of people with intellectual disabilities, through interactions between staff and people with intellectual disabilities.
(2) Staff behaviour has an indirect causal influence on the lives of people with intellectual disabilities, through aspects of staff behaviour that affect the organisation's capacity to deliver support (principally sick leave and turnover).
(3) Staff behaviour is multiply determined by factors associated with service users (such as service-user characteristics and behaviours, and the cognitive and emotional reactions of staff to those characteristics and behaviours), factors associated with staff (such as staff characteristics, skills, values, morale, and well-being), and characteristics of the organisation (such as organisational resources, salaries, and management support).

This chapter will examine the methods used to research these core constructs of staff research: staff behaviour and performance, the cognitive and emotional reactions of staff to people with intellectual disabilities, factors associated with staff working in support services, and the characteristics of organisations within which staff are working. Both measurement and design issues will be addressed when considering these core constructs and assumptions.

STAFF BEHAVIOUR AND PERFORMANCE

Staff behaviour measures are concerned with what staff actually do, whereas staff performance measures evaluate staff behaviour against criteria of competence or appropriateness. Given the centrality of these constructs for staffing research, there is surprisingly little research attempting to investigate directly staff behaviour or staff performance in services for people with intellectual disabilities. There may be several reasons for this relative lack of attention:

(1) A lack of clarity concerning which aspects of staff behaviour are important in promoting positive lifestyles for people with intellectual disabilities (that is, which staff behaviours are relevant to assessing staff performance). Different ideologies of service provision emphasise different aspects of staff performance, such as technically skilled staff behaviour or staff behaviour based on respect and empathy. Furthermore, different stakeholders (such as managers, direct support staff, families, and people with intellectual disabilities) may emphasise different and possibly conflicting aspects of staff performance.
(2) The diversity of support services and staff roles. As yet, there is little research investigating staff behaviour across different types of support service and across different staff roles; are the crucial dimensions of staff performance similar across diverse service types and staff roles, or do several specific measures of staff performance need to be developed?
(3) Design issues in assessing the validity of measures of staff performance. The lack of an obvious indicator of "productivity" for staff working in human services makes the validation of any measure of staff performance difficult. The lifestyle of people with intellectual disabilities experiencing the service would be the most socially valid "productivity" indicator. However, a lack of association between a staff performance measure and an indicator of service-user lifestyle could bear a number of interpretations:
    (a) The measure of staff performance is invalid.
    (b) The aspects of staff performance measured do not have an influence on the aspects of user lifestyle measured.
    (c) As staff and users frequently work in groups, a direct association between an individual staff member's performance and an individual user's lifestyle is not to be expected.

    Similarly, an association between indicators of staff performance and user lifestyle could be interpreted as evidence for the concurrent validity of the staff performance measure, or as evidence that unmeasured aspects of the service influence both staff behaviour and user lifestyle. The complexity of establishing the social validity of staff performance measures may have inhibited research in this area.

Research concerning staff in services for people with intellectual disabilities has generally been more focused on staff behaviour than staff performance. For example, there is a substantial behaviourally based research literature which has used direct non-participant observation to observe interactions between staff and people with intellectual disabilities (see below). Some self-report measures of staff activity have also been developed (see below). Research concerning the evaluation of staff performance with explicit reference to competence criteria is rare, despite the widespread use of such methods throughout organisational psychology generally (Anderson & Herriot, 1997; Gatewood & Feild, 1998). In research concerning staff in services for people with intellectual disabilities, proxy measures of staff performance, such as staff absenteeism, turnover, and intended turnover, are more commonly used. Although these are more properly considered as indicators of the impact of staff on the organisation, they will be reviewed in this section.

OBSERVATION OF STAFF BEHAVIOUR

The most common method of observing staff behaviour has been non-participant quantitative observation (see Thompson, Felce & Symons, 2000). The methodology of non-participant observation is covered in detail in Chapter 8 of this volume. This section will outline the methodological and design issues pertinent to conducting non-participant observation involving staff.

The first fundamental decision for the non-participant observer to make is what to observe. While there are a wealth of technologies for non-participant observation available (Thompson et al., 2000), the decision about which behaviours to operationalise and observe depends on the specific research question being asked. Many researchers use non-participant observation as part of general evaluations of service quality; thus, fairly general categories of staff behaviour are recorded, such as no interaction, assistance, processing/care, praise, social interaction, negative interaction, and restraint (e.g., Felce et al., 1998; Emerson, Hatton, Robertson, Henderson & Cooper, 1999). Such general coding systems can be adapted for specific purposes; for example, to examine the most effective types of staff assistance (for example, verbal, non-verbal, and physical prompting) (Felce et al., 2000; Jones et al., 2001) or social interactions between service users and staff (Clegg, Standen & Cromby, 1991a,b). Although any aspects of staff behaviour can, in principle, be coded, as long as they have validity and interobserver reliability, researchers using non-participant observation have tended to focus on behavioural aspects of staff behaviour rather than affective aspects of staff interactions with people with intellectual disabilities (but see Hogg, Reeves, Roberts & Mudford, 2001). This strand of research thus implies a particular model of which factors are important for effective staff performance. Attempts to use non-participant observation to investigate affective dimensions of staff behaviour could add valuable insights into relationships between staff and service users. Background variables (such as staff ratios, number of staff and service users in the setting, location, activity, and time of day) may also be relevant to non-participant observers (e.g., Emerson et al., 1999).

For researchers using non-participant observation involving staff, the second fundamental decision is whom to observe. Many studies have focused on observing the behaviour of people with intellectual disabilities, with additional codes for staff presence and staff interaction (e.g., Hatton et al., 1995b; Felce et al., 1998; Emerson et al., 1999; Jones et al., 1999). This tells us how much of a person's time is spent in different types of interactions with staff, and lag-sequential analysis (see Chapter 8, this volume) can also provide information concerning functional relationships between the behaviour of the person with intellectual disabilities and staff members (e.g., Emerson et al., 1999; Hall & Oliver, 2000). However, staff interaction codes typically do not differentiate between individual members of staff. Furthermore, such an approach does not provide information about the efficiency of staff working in the service, such as what proportion of staff time is spent directly engaging with a person with intellectual disabilities. A further decision for non-participant observers to make is whether to observe one person for a protracted period of time (e.g., Hatton et al., 1995b), sequentially observe all people in the setting (e.g., Felce et al., 1998), or devise group-observation protocols (see Saunders & Saunders, 2000).

A less-used option has been to observe staff directly (e.g., Orlowska, McGill & Mansell, 1991), including their interactions with people with intellectual disabilities in the service. The advantages and disadvantages of observing staff mirror those involved in observing people with intellectual disabilities; information on the activities undertaken by staff is available through this method, although data on the activities of people with intellectual disabilities are not obtainable and lag-sequential analyses may be more difficult to interpret.

A third fundamental question is how to observe the behaviours the researcher wishes to capture. Improvements in non-participant observation technologies (see Thompson et al., 2000) are leading researchers to observe behaviour in real time by some form of continuous time-sampling. This records both the frequency and duration of behaviours and preserves relationships between behaviours in real time (for example, that an episode of staff assistance began 5 seconds before the onset of constructive activity by a person with intellectual disabilities). Momentary time-sampling is also possible, where all behaviours occurring at particular, regularly separated time points (such as every 20 seconds) (Mansell, McGill & Emerson, 2001) are recorded. This yields information on the likely probability that a behaviour will occur, but allows for less sophisticated analysis and may miss infrequent or short-duration behaviours such as staff interaction with a person with intellectual disabilities.

Finally, practical issues in non-participant observation must be considered. Questions here include: How intrusive and ethical will it be to observe staff in small service settings and community locations? How can reactivity in observed staff be minimised? Is it feasible to conduct non-participant observations in some settings? How many codes can an observer realistically use, while ensuring interobserver reliability?

Qualitative participant observation approaches (see Chapter 7, this volume), despite their potential for revealing the phenomenology of staff experience, appear to have been little used with staff working with people with intellectual disabilities (Todd & Shearn, 1999; Todd, 2000). Such research has highlighted issues neglected in quantitative research to date, such as the management of stigma in public settings and the conflicting demands of different roles (such as friend, parent, and skilled worker) staff feel are required of them.

SELF-REPORT MEASURES OF STAFF ACTIVITY

Rather than adopting the labour-intensive approach of observing staff behaviour, an alternative option is to ask staff to report on the extent and nature of their workplace activity. Basic self-report information on staff activity may include: job title; contracted and actual hours worked in a specified period of time (such as in the last week or month); and the length, timing, and nature of work shifts (e.g., Larson, Lakin & Bruininks, 1998; Hatton et al., 1999c). More detailed self-report measures of staff activity may ask staff to rate the extent of their activity across a number of dimensions (e.g., Allen, Pahl & Quine, 1990; Hatton et al., 1998). While such measures do differentiate staff across different job titles, they are also prone to social desirability biases (Hatton et al., 1998), and their validity compared to observed behaviour is questionable (Rose, 1998).

A different approach pursued in a very small literature has been to ask staff about their relationships with the people with intellectual disabilities they work with. Such research has established a typology of relationships (such as provider, meaning maker, mutual, and companion) (Clegg, Standen & Jones, 1996), although associations between such reported relationships and other aspects of staff and user lifestyles have not been investigated.

MEASURES OF STAFF PERFORMANCE

Measures of staff performance (that is, staff behaviour against clear competence criteria) appear to be virtually absent in published research concerning staff in services for people with intellectual disabilities (Hall & Hall, 2002). In their recent review, Hall and Hall (2002) identified a number of studies in institutions in the 1950s that used supervisor ratings of job performance, but the validity of these ratings was questionable, and they do not seem to have been used in more recent research concerning staff (but see Cope, Grossnickle, Covington, Durham & Zaharia, 1987). However, within the general organisational psychology literature, there are well-validated procedures for establishing measures of staff performance, involving analysis of the core components of the job (or the worker required for the job); deriving behavioural anchors for unacceptable, acceptable, and superior job performance on each component; and producing job performance scales to be completed by multiple respondents (see Anderson & Herriot, 1997; Gatewood & Feild, 1998). Such organisational psychology procedures could be profitably employed to examine the core competencies of staff in services for people with intellectual disabilities from the perspective of different stakeholder groups, such as staff themselves, managers, people with intellectual disabilities, and family members.

PROXY ORGANISATIONAL INDICATORS OF STAFF PERFORMANCE

Although more properly considered as indicators of the impact of staff on an organisation, a body of research has used staff absenteeism, turnover, or intended turnover as proxy indicators of staff performance. Staff absenteeism (time absent from work) is usually measured as the number of days absent in a period of time (usually between 1 month and 1 year), although the number of episodes of absence in a period of time can also be recorded (e.g., Hatton et al., 1999b). Typically, total time absent from work is used as the measure of absenteeism, although this may include other forms of absence than sick leave (for example, leave due to the death of a relative of the staff member). Different sources of information also pose different threats to validity. Self-reports of absenteeism may be underestimates or unreliable over retrospective time periods; organisational records may also underestimate actual absenteeism, and are likely to be inconsistent across organisations in their recording systems and the diligence with which sickness data are collected. The validity of absenteeism as a proxy indicator of staff performance is unknown.

The issue of staff turnover in services for people with intellectual disabilities has received substantial research attention (e.g., Larson, Lakin & Bruininks, 1998; Hatton et al., 2001; Hall & Hall, 2002). Staff turnover is usually assessed in terms of annual turnover:

$$\frac{\text{Number of employees leaving the organisation between time 1 and time 2}}{\text{Mean number of employees at time 1 and time 2}}$$

However, for researchers interested in preventable staff turnover, different reasons for staff leaving the organisation must be analysed separately; typical categories are voluntary turnover (resigning) and involuntary turnover (retirement, death, long-term sickness, or being fired) (Larson et al., 1998). Such research has established very high annual turnover rates among staff in services for people with intellectual disabilities in the USA (typically 50–70% (Braddock & Mitchell, 1992), and lower rates of 10–30% in the UK (Hatton et al., 1995a). Although turnover is typically assessed by service records, exit interviews with leavers may also be useful in deciding which category of turnover the staff member falls into, and also leavers' perceptions of the causes of their turnover (e.g., Larson et al., 1998).

For obvious reasons, a strand of research has also attempted to identify factors associated with staff turnover in services for people with intellectual disabilities. Methodological issues to consider here are:

(1) Are we trying to predict staff turnover levels across different services (for example, why does house X have a higher level of turnover than house Y?), or trying to predict individual staff members' decisions to leave the organisation (for example, why has one member of staff left the organisation while another has remained?) (see Larson & Lakin, 1992)? Service-level predictors (for example, average levels of service-user challenging behaviour in the house) can be investigated only by using services (for example, houses) as the unit of analysis, although studies adopting this approach have generally produced models less predictive of turnover than studies using the individual staff member as the unit of analysis (Larson & Lakin, 1992).

(2) Is there a theoretical rationale underlying the choice of predictor variables, and are all obvious potential predictor variables included? General models of staff turnover consistently highlight similar predictive factors, such as younger age, shorter tenure in the organisation, lower expectations of the job, lower job satisfaction, lower organisational commitment, greater perceived opportunities for alternative employment, and greater intention to leave (e.g., Arnold & Feldman, 1982; Bluedorn, 1982; Michaels & Spector, 1982). Much research concerning services for people with intellectual disabilities either makes little reference to general turnover theory and research, or omits potentially crucial predictor variables (such as perceived opportunities for alternative employment), limiting the scope of the empirically derived models produced.

(3) To achieve the greatest predictive validity of a turnover model, it is best to have an approximately equal number of leavers and stayers (Larson et al., 1998). Depending on the annual turnover within the service, this will affect the optimal length of time at which to assess turnover.

As mentioned above, intention to leave a job, perhaps unsurprisingly, is a strong predictor of actual staff turnover. Intention to leave has typically been assessed by brief, self-report rating scales (e.g., Allen et al., 1990; Razza, 1993; Hatton et al., 2001), despite consistent social desirability biases (e.g., Hatton et al., 2001). Self-reported job search behaviour (such as the number of jobs applied for in the past 3 months) has also been used as an indicator of intention to quit (Hatton et al., 2001). Although intention to leave is consistently associated with actual staff turnover, predictors of intention to leave and actual staff turnover may not be identical, suggesting that intention to leave may not be a wholly reliable proxy indicator of actual staff turnover. It is also important to assess the perceived ease of gaining alternative employment (e.g., Hui, 1988), as this is robustly associated with intended and actual turnover in services for people with intellectual disabilities (Larson et al., 1998; Hatton et al., 2001).

FACTORS ASSOCIATED WITH PEOPLE WITH INTELLECTUAL DISABILITIES

As mentioned above, research concerning staff in services for people with intellectual disabilities has been based largely on the assumption that staff behaviour is multiply determined. These putative determinants of staff behaviour include factors associated with people with intellectual disabilities using the service. Many studies have investigated various characteristics of service users thought to have an influence on staff behaviour. A second set of studies has investigated the cognitive and emotional reactions of staff to people with intellectual disabilities. This section will outline the measures used to investigate service user characteristics and staff reactions, together with a discussion of the methodological issues arising from current research work investigating these issues.

Service User Characteristics

Relatively little research has directly investigated relationships between service user characteristics and staff behaviour. Observational research has consistently demonstrated relationships between service user characteristics such as adaptive behaviour, personal appearance, and challenging behaviour (all measured by non-participant observation or rating scales, see Chapter 21, this volume), and levels of staff positive contact, assistance, and negative contact (e.g., Grant & Moores, 1977; Woods & Cullen, 1983; Carr, Taylor & Robinson, 1991; Hatton et al., 1995b).

A greater volume of research has investigated the relationship between the characteristics of people with intellectual disabilities and staff morale (see below) (e.g., Stenfert, Kroese & Fleming, 1992; Rose, 1993; Hatton et al., 1995a; Jenkins, Rose & Lovell, 1997). The characteristics of service users most frequently assessed are basic demographic characteristics, such as age and gender; adaptive behaviour/skills; and challenging behaviours, typically by standardised scales rated by an informant, often the member of staff. A fuller discussion of these rating scales is provided in Chapters 18, 19, and 21 of this volume. For researchers interested in staff behaviour, a major design problem in relating service user characteristics and staff morale or staff behaviour is the unit of analysis. Unless individual staff members work exclusively with individual service users, the unit of analysis will be a grouping of staff and service users, such as a staffed house. Using these larger units of analysis will involve larger-scale studies and some possible weakening of associations between service user characteristics and staff behaviour or morale.

To enable individual staff to remain the unit of analysis, some researchers have asked staff to rate how stressful they find service user characteristics, such as lack of skills or challenging behaviours, alongside a range of other potential stressors (e.g., Bersani & Heifetz, 1985; Corrigan, 1993; Razza, 1993; Hatton et al., 1999a,c; Rose, 1999). It is worth noting that, although univariate associations are often found between user characteristics measured in this way and staff morale (e.g., Hatton et al., 1995a; 1999a,c), these associations usually drop out when multivariate analyses are conducted that include organisational factors (see Hastings, 2002). These findings highlight the importance of including a comprehensive set of factors when attempting to account for staff behaviour or morale. Finally, it is important to note that most studies investigating relationships between service user characteristics and staffing have used cross-sectional survey designs with correlational analyses; stronger research designs enabling the building of causal models are clearly required.

Staff Cognitive and Emotional Reactions to People with Intellectual Disabilities

As mentioned above, one of the basic assumptions of staffing research is that staff responses to a person with intellectual disabilities will be mediated by the cognitions and emotions of staff members (see Hastings & Remington, 1994a,b). A substantial body of research literature has explored this assumption, typically involving some variant of attribution theory.

Attribution theory (Heider, 1958; Kelly, 1967; Fenwick, 1995) assumes that people are motivated to find causes for events, and that these attributions of cause influence behaviour (Fenwick, 1995). At its most basic, attribution theory proposes that people tend to make two types of causal attribution for interpersonal behaviour, an internal attribution (the behaviour is located within the person) or an external attribution (the behaviour is located outside the person) (Aronson, Wilson & Akert, 1997). Attribution theory has increasingly been applied in research concerning staff reactions to people with challenging behaviour—for example, whether staff attribute challenging behaviour to internal causes, such as severity of intellectual disability, or to external causes, such as the environment (e.g., Berryman, Evans & Kalbag, 1994; Bromley & Emerson, 1995; Hastings, 1995; Hastings, Remington & Hopper, 1995).

More recently, more elaborated theoretical models, combining both cognitive and emotional reactions to service users, have been applied to staff in services for people with intellectual disabilities, most commonly Weiner's (1980; 1986) cognitive-emotional models of helping behaviour. These models suggest that attributions determine emotional responses, which then determine staff behaviour (e.g., Dagnan, Trower & Smith, 1998; Stanley & Standen, 2000). Specifically, if the cause of people's challenging behaviour is seen as internal, controllable (that is, part of their characteristics and under their control), and stable (that is, the cause is the same each time they exhibit challenging behaviour), it will determine whether the staff member reacts emotionally with anger or sympathy. This then determines the level of staff help.

While there is a large body of research concerning staff cognitive and emotional reactions to people with intellectual disabilities, the following methodological issues need to be considered by researchers applying such models to staff in services for people with intellectual disabilities.

Measuring Attributions

In measuring attributions, the most fundamental question is whether to investigate staff descriptions of causes of the service user's behaviour, or to assess staff attributions for the behaviour along causal attributional dimensions. Several studies have used either free-response formats or lists of causes based on pilot studies (e.g., Berryman et al., 1994; Bromley & Emerson, 1995; Hastings, 1995; Hastings et al., 1995) to elicit staff descriptions of causes such as environmental elicitation, stimulation, attention requesting, frustration, abnormal stress, communication/biology, and mood. The CHABA is probably the most fully investigated of these measures (Hastings, 1997). While such measures may have ecological validity, how such causal descriptions map on to attributional dimensions (such as internal/external) is unclear and little investigated.

An alternative is to use rating scales with staff to map their cognitive responses along a number of attributional dimensions, such as internal/external, global/specific, stable/unstable, and controllable/uncontrollable. A frequently used measure among researchers working with staff in services for people with intellectual disabilities is the Attributional Style Questionnaire (ASQ) (Peterson et al., 1982; Peterson & Villanova, 1988). This measure was initially developed for people with depression, and measures the dimensions of internality, globality, stability, and controllability. Adaptations for staff working with people with intellectual disabilities (e.g., Dagnan et al., 1998; Stanley & Standen, 2000) have demonstrated some evidence of adequate psychometric properties and concurrent validity, although more stringent validity criteria have not been applied.

Measuring Emotions

As mentioned above, researchers have only recently begun to investigate the emotional reactions of staff to the behaviour of people with intellectual disabilities, principally challenging behaviour (Bromley & Emerson, 1995; Dagnan et al., 1998; Stanley & Standen, 2000). These measures have tended to use self-report rating scales for a number of positive and negative emotions, which are then either analysed individually or combined into positive and negative emotion scales, although the emotions selected may not be the emotions most commonly reported by carers (Mitchell & Hastings, 1998). Some studies have also measured an additional construct of staff optimism about the behaviour of the service user, hypothesised to mediate the relationship between staff attributions/emotions and staff behaviour, by single-item rating scales (e.g., Dagnan et al., 1998; Stanley & Standen, 2000). While studies using these measures of emotions find associations between staff emotional reactions and staff attributions, optimism, and willingness to help (see below), staff responses are highly skewed towards highly positive emotions, suggesting a pervasive social desirability effect. Some attempts have been made to reduce the likely impact of social desirability—for example, by asking about the emotional responses of respondents' colleagues rather than the emotional responses of respondents themselves (Bromley & Emerson, 1995). General measures of positive and negative affect with demonstrated validity and reliability, such as the PANAS scale, may be more useful (Watson, Clark & Tellegen, 1988; Watson & Tellegen, 1985).

Characteristics of Service Users and Staff Associated with Attributions

The vast bulk of research in this area has concerned staff responses to challenging behaviour on the part of service users, with research finding differential but inconsistent patterns of staff responses depending on the topography of the challenging behaviour (e.g., Bromley & Emerson, 1995; Hastings, Reed & Watts, 1997). Some of these inconsistencies may be accounted for by variations in the instructions given to staff; for example, whether staff are asked to select the most likely cause of the behaviour and complete attributional ratings accordingly (e.g., Dagnan et al., 1998) or are asked to rate their response to the behaviour as a whole (e.g., Stanley & Standen, 2000). Given that all these factors may have an impact on staff attributions, researchers need at least to record and preferably investigate systematically these factors when assessing staff attributions. Furthermore, it is worth noting that challenging behaviour has been the almost exclusive focus of attention; staff cognitive and emotional reactions to positive dimensions of service user behaviour are unexplored.

Using Stimulus Materials

Most research concerning staff cognitive and emotional responses to challenging behaviour has used either written (e.g., Dagnan et al., 1998) or simulated video (e.g., Mossman, Hastings & Brown, 2002) vignettes of a person with intellectual disabilities, rather than exploring staff reactions to actual behaviours. While there are advantages to vignettes in terms of standardisation of the stimulus and ease of systematic manipulation of the stimulus, there is currently no research evidence demonstrating the validity or generalisability of staff responses to a vignette to actual staff reactions to a person with intellectual disabilities.

Measuring Staff Behaviour

Research in this area has largely focused on describing the cognitive and emotional reactions of staff to challenging behaviour, and aspects of service users and staff associated with different patterns of cognitive and emotional response. Surprisingly little research has attempted to link staff cognitive and emotional reactions to staff behaviour. The most common method has been to assess staff self-ratings of their willingness to help the person with intellectual disabilities (e.g., Dagnan et al., 1998; Stanley & Standen, 2000). However, staff responses on these measures are highly skewed towards maximum willingness to help, suggesting a pervasive social desirability bias. Furthermore, helping behaviour is undefined by these measures, and may include counter-habilitative staff behaviours (Jones & Hastings, 2003).

FACTORS ASSOCIATED WITH STAFF WORKING IN SERVICES FOR PEOPLE WITH INTELLECTUAL DISABILITIES

As mentioned at the beginning of this chapter, staff behaviour is hypothesised to be multiply determined; by factors associated with service users, factors associated with staff, and organisational factors. Quite a substantial strand of research has investigated factors associated with staff in services for people with intellectual disabilities, although this strand of research has been conducted largely independently of research concerning staff behaviour or staff cognitive and emotional reactions to people with intellectual disabilities (but see Mitchell & Hastings, 2001; Hastings & Brown, 2002). Research investigating factors associated with staff can be categorised into four broad areas: staff morale and well-being, staff values, staff skills, and staff characteristics. These areas will be outlined in turn.

Staff Morale and Well-Being

A substantial volume of research has focused on the morale and well-being of staff in services for people with intellectual disabilities. The rationale for this is that staff well-being is likely to be an important determinant of staff behaviour, although research directly investigating this hypothesis is virtually absent (but see Rose, Jones & Fletcher, 1998a,b). Typically, researchers have focused on some aspect of staff distress, using a wide range of constructs and measures.

Although definitions of distress vary widely (Aldwin, 1994; Payne, 1999), researchers in the intellectual disability field have tended implicitly or explicitly to endorse the construct of distress taken from stress and coping theory (see Rose et al., 1998a,b), namely, that distress occurs when the demands placed upon a staff member exceed their perceived resources and ability to cope with these demands (Lazarus & Folkman, 1984; Lazarus, 1966, 1999; Cox, 1993; Firth-Cozens & Payne, 1999). As with the models reviewed above concerning staff cognitive and emotional reactions to service users, it is the cognitive appraisals and coping strategies of individual staff that are hypothesised to mediate the relationship between external demands and internal perceptions of distress.

Measures of distress used by researchers vary widely. These include short checklists designed to measure general distress or psychopathology, such as the General Health Questionnaire (Goldberg, 1978; Hatton et al., 1999a) or the Malaise Inventory (Rutter, Tizard & Whitmore, 1970; Hatton & Emerson, 1993). Other studies have used more specific checklists assessing anxiety and/or depression, such as the Thoughts and Feelings Index (Fletcher, 1989; Rose, 1995). The advantages of such measures are that they are well validated on general populations and normative data are readily available. However, measures of distress specifically associated with the job may be more relevant in determining workplace factors associated with staff distress (Hatton et al., 1995a, 1999c).

A second common indicator of staff distress is burnout. Burnout is typically defined as having three components (Maslach & Jackson, 1981, 1986):

> A psychological syndrome of emotional exhaustion, depersonalisation, and reduced personal accomplishment that can occur among individuals who work with other people in some capacity. (p. 20)

The dimension of emotional exhaustion refers to a feeling of a lack of emotional resources, similar to general distress (Cordes & Dougherty, 1993). This is accompanied by depersonalisation, which refers to the development in the staff of negative attitudes that comprise a loss of concern, positive feelings or sympathy, or respect for the service users they are working with. The third component, reduced personal accomplishment, refers to a loss of a sense of satisfaction or achievement in the job. Thus, burnout consists of the distress construct plus additional components specifically associated with the workplace. The Maslach Burnout Inventory is the most commonly used measure of burnout (Maslach & Jackson, 1986), and has been successfully used with staff in services for people with intellectual disabilities (e.g., Caton, Grossnickle, Cope, Long & Mitchell, 1988; Aitken & Schloss, 1994; Blumenthal, Lavender & Hewson, 1998; Ito, Kurita & Shiiya, 1999). Both the construct and measure of burnout appear to have considerable promise for investigating staff morale in services for people with intellectual disabilities.

A third class of staff distress measures concern job strain, typically again involving brief checklists (e.g., Aitken & Schloss, 1994; Hatton et al., 1995a, 1999c). Research has shown that workplace factors explain more of the variance in job strain scores than general distress scores (Hatton et al., 1995a, 1999c), and may be more strongly associated with intended turnover and job search behaviour than general distress measures (Hatton et al., 2001). However, relationships between job strain and burnout have been little investigated in services for people with intellectual disabilities (but see Aitken & Schloss, 1994).

In contrast to distress measures, a strand of studies has also assessed work satisfaction, often using standard scales from organisational psychology (e.g., Borrill et al., 1996; Hatton et al., 1999a, 2001). Organisational psychology research has demonstrated that work satisfaction and distress are independent constructs (Arnold, Cooper & Robertson, 1995), and studies with staff in services for people with intellectual disabilities have both replicated this finding (e.g., Hatton et al., 1999a) and demonstrated important roles for both distress and work satisfaction in predicting intended turnover (e.g., Razza, 1993; Hatton et al., 2001).

As with other strands of research concerning staff in services for people with intellectual disabilities, research concerning staff morale and well-being generally displays a number of methodological limitations, which future researchers will need to take into account:

(1) A sound theoretical basis must be used for the selection of measures and the design of the study. Such theoretical frameworks are becoming more clearly elaborated within organisational psychology generally.
(2) Studies need to be conducted that link staff morale and well-being to actual staff behaviour and performance, taking into account issues discussed earlier regarding the measurement of staff behaviour.
(3) Studies to date have been largely cross-sectional surveys with correlational analytical strategies; stronger designs allowing causal model-building are required.
(4) Qualitative strategies have rarely been applied to the investigation of staff stress and morale. Such approaches may yield some insight into important issues as yet uninvestigated by quantitative methods.

Staff Values

According to several prevalent service ideologies, the values of staff should be crucial determinants in job performance. One study has reported linking staff attitudes to workplace characteristics and organisational culture (Jacobson & Ackerman, 1992). Several self-report measures of attitudes towards people with intellectual disabilities have included staff, including measures of attitudes towards community living (e.g., Henry, Keys, Jopp & Balcazar, 1996), sexuality (e.g., Johnson & Davies, 1989; Oliver, Anthony, Leimkuhl & Skillman, 2002), and training (e.g., Knowles & Landesman, 1986). Studies in this area have also included a broader range of staff, such as general medical practitioners and primary health-care workers (e.g., Kerr, Dunstan & Thapar, 1996; Bond, Kerr, Dunstan & Thapar, 1997; Stein, 2000; Gill, Stenfert Kroese & Rose, 2002;). However, it is only recently that attention has been given to the reliability and validity of questionnaires used in this type of research (Gill et al., 2002). Psychological models of attitude measurement also provide an opportunity to link attitudes with expressed behavioural intention (e.g., Fishbein & Ajzen, 1975; Fishbein, 1998), although there is little evidence for the effective application of such models in the research literature to date.

More recent studies have generally reported increasingly positive attitudes among staff, but there is a high likelihood of social desirability biases, and more innovative approaches to evaluating staff attitudes, such as participation observation or ethnography, may be indicated here. There appear to have been no attempts to examine directly the relationship between staff values and staff performance. On occasions where staff attitudes have been changed as a result of a training intervention, no evidence has been provided of a resultant change in staff behaviour (Rose & Holmes, 1991).

Staff Skills and Training

Given the lack of consensus of the core competencies of staff in services for people with intellectual disabilities and the lack of research activity concerning staff performance, it is perhaps unsurprising that little research attention has been devoted to staff skills and how these can be improved (cf. Ziarnik & Bernstein, 1982). The best-defined approaches to defining, measuring, and training in staff skills have been developed within behavioural frameworks, largely concerning staff working with people with severe or profound intellectual disabilities and/or challenging behaviours. Studies have evaluated the impact of training on reactive strategies used by staff in response to challenging behaviours (Allen, McDonald, Dunn & Doyle, 1997; Allen & Tynan, 2000), strategies to increase choice-making behaviours (Parsons, McCarn & Reid, 1993; McKnight & Kearney, 2001), strategies to improve communication (McNaughton & Light, 1989), strategies to increase constructive engagement and user skills (Burch, Reiss & Bailey, 1987; Felce et al., 2000; Jones et al., 2001; Saloviita & Lehtinen, 2001), and strategies to increase community integration (Smalley, Certo & Goetz, 1997).

Researchers investigating staff skills and training need to pay attention to the following three issues:

(1) *Defining and operationalising relevant staff skills*. Without clear definitions and operationalisations of staff skills, a relevant training programme or method of directly assessing staff skills cannot be developed.
(2) *Design issues*. Many of the studies outlined above have been case studies, with relatively few studies involving control groups (e.g., Saloviita & Lehtinen, 2001) or more sophisticated multiple-baseline designs (e.g., Felce et al., 2000; Jones et al., 2001). Designs allowing causal interpretation are required.
(3) *Assessing the impact of training*. Measures to assess the impact of training can relate directly to staff skills (have such skills improved?) or more broadly to some aspect of the lifestyle of service users designed to be improved through increased staff skills. Careful selection of relevant measures is needed here.

Staff Characteristics

As staff performance is multiply determined, many characteristics of staff in services for people with intellectual disabilities have been investigated, largely in terms of relationships between staff characteristics and staff morale and/or staff turnover. While a myriad of constructs and self-report measures have been assessed, some of the more common staff characteristics assessed include the following:

(1) Basic demographic characteristics of staff, such as age, gender, ethnicity, marital status, caring for dependants at home, and education (e.g., Larson & Lakin, 1992; Larson et al., 1998; Hatton et al., 1999b, 2001). Younger age and staff having a higher education have been reliably associated with increased staff turnover. It is worth noting that, due to the relative ethnic homogeneity of staff groups in services (that is, almost all white and English-speaking in the USA and the UK), the impact of staff ethnicity on working relationships with persons of colour with intellectual disabilities remains largely uninvestigated (see Hatton, Chapter 2, this volume).
(2) The interface between work and home (e.g., Hatton et al., 1995a, 1999a; Rose, 1995), with greater work–home conflict associated strongly with general distress but less strongly with job strain (Hatton et al., 1995a).
(3) Coping strategies used by staff in the workplace, such as practical coping and wishful thinking (Hatton & Emerson, 1995a), with reliable associations found between wishful thinking and staff distress and intended turnover (e.g., Hatton et al., 1999a; 2001).
(4) Staff commitment to the organisation or the type of work (e.g., Penley & Gould, 1988), with alienative commitment (feeling trapped in the organisation) robustly associated with staff distress and intended turnover (e.g., Hatton & Emerson, 1993; Larson et al., 1998; Hatton et al., 1999a, 2001).

While all these measures have been investigated in various studies, few studies have attempted to include a comprehensive range of measures to allow for multivariate analysis based on theoretical foundations (e.g., Razza, 1993; Larson et al., 1998; Hatton et al., 1999a, 2001). It is also important to note that characteristics of the staff member within the organisation overlap conceptually with organisational factors, which are discussed in the next section.

FACTORS ASSOCIATED WITH ORGANISATIONS

The final group of factors hypothesised to determine staff behaviour concerns factors associated with the organisations within which staff work, although, again, few studies have investigated relationships between organisational factors and staff behaviour or performance. As with factors associated with staff, a plethora of constructs and measures have been investigated, with little coherence between studies. If we use general organisational psychology theories as a framework, organisational factors can be grouped into the following areas: organisational resources, characteristics of the job, social support, organisational roles and demands, working practices, and organisational structure and climate.

Organisational Resources

Studies investigating organisational resources tend to fall into two distinct strands. The first strand has investigated organisational resource factors associated with observed staff and service user behaviour (see Felce & Emerson, 2001, for a review), focusing on resources such as staff: user ratios, costs of care packages for service users, and physical characteristics of residential settings. Few associations have been found between such organisational resources and staff behaviour, although it should be noted that these measures of organisational resource are often collected at a service rather than individual staff level, weakening the potential for significant associations.

The second strand of research is collected via self-report from individual staff members, and has largely involved measures of income or satisfaction with income (e.g., Bersani & Heifetz, 1985; Larson & Lakin, 1992; Hatton & Emerson, 1993; Mitchell & Braddock, 1993). Measuring income may be particularly important for staff in deregulated services, where rates of pay are frequently at poverty-line levels (Mitchell & Braddock, 1993).

Characteristics of the Job

Many basic characteristics of the job have been investigated by single-item self-report methods, such as length of time the staff member has worked in the service (Larson & Lakin, 1992; Razza, 1993), contracted and actual hours worked (e.g., Larson et al., 1998; Hatton et al., 1999a,b), the length and timing of shifts (e.g., Power & Sharp, 1988; Razza, 1993; Rose, 1993), job variety (e.g., Allen et al., 1990), and whether staff are working on fixed-term or permanent contracts (e.g., Allen et al., 1990; Hatton et al., 1999a,b).

Social Support

Various self-report rating scales have been used to investigate the social support staff receive from others in the workplace. Such scales can include perceived practical and emotional support from colleagues, supervisors, and managers (e.g., Razza, 1993; Rose, 1993, 1995; Hatton et al., 1995a, 1999a,b, 2001; Rose & Schelewa-Davies, 1997; Dyer & Quine, 1998; Harris & Rose, 2002) and the extent and nature of feedback received from supervisors on job performance (e.g., Hatton & Emerson, 1993). Although reliable and robust associations are found between social support and staff distress, work satisfaction, and turnover, more sophisticated measures of social support grounded in current social support theory are indicated, including the development of measures which allow for negative as well as positive perceptions of support (Rose, 1993).

Organisational Roles and Demands

A number of brief, self-report measures of the role of staff members in the organisation have been used, the most common being a brief measure of role ambiguity, or a lack of staff clarity about what the job entails (e.g., Blumenthal et al., 1998; Dyer & Quine, 1998; Hatton et al., 1999a,b, 2001). Other self-report measures have included various ways of investigating the demands placed on staff members by the organisation within which they work. Such measures at their simplest assess perceived work overload (e.g., Power & Sharp, 1988; Razza, 1993; Rose, 1993). Slightly more complex measures assess perceptions of conflicting demands being placed on the staff member, or perceptions that staff are being asked to do their jobs with inadequate resources (e.g., Razza, 1993; Dyer & Quine, 1998; Hatton et al., 1999). Finally, some studies have assessed mismatches between staff expectations of the job and what the job actually entails (e.g., Hatton et al., 1999a,b; Larson & Lakin, 1992). Role ambiguity, role conflict, and work overload all appear to be important determinants of staff morale, although stronger causal designs are required.

It is also worth noting here that general self-report measures of job stressors and supports covering several domains of working with people with intellectual disabilities have been developed (e.g., Bersani & Heifetz, 1985; Thompson, 1987; Rose, 1993, 1999; Hatton et al., 1995a, 1999a,b; Harris & Rose, 2002). Unsurprisingly, such measures show robust associations with staff morale, although their relationship to staff behaviour or staff performance is unknown.

Working Practices

As mentioned earlier, behavioural research has reported few associations between service resources and staff behaviour. The working practices of a service, such as how tasks are allocated among staff members, assessed at a service level through interviews with staff, may be an important mediator between service resources and staff performance (e.g., Emerson et al., 2000; Felce & Emerson, 2001).

Organisational Structure and Climate

The impact of service-level factors, such as the structure and climate of organisations, on staff has been little investigated, although some measures indicate the potential of these constructs for models of staff performance. First, simple, self-report rating scales of job control and participation in service-level decision making (e.g., Allen et al., 1990; Hatton & Emerson, 1993; Blumenthal et al., 1998; Dyer & Quine, 1998; Hatton et al., 1999a) have reported consistent associations with staff morale. Second, measures of team climate (Rose & Schelewa-Davies, 1997) and organisational culture (Hatton et al., 1999d) have been used in services for people with intellectual disabilities.

CONCLUSIONS

As this chapter has hopefully demonstrated, there is a wealth of research activity concerning staff in services for people with intellectual disabilities. There is, however, much important research work still to be done. This final section will briefly outline some issues for future researchers to address:

(1) *Theory*. Much current research concerning staff in services for people with intellectual disabilities is atheoretical or certainly not firmly grounded in mainstream psychological and organisational theories. Future research activities should be firmly grounded in relevant theoretical frameworks and should test the applicability of these frameworks to staff in services for people with intellectual disabilities.

(2) *Staff performance*. Surprisingly little research activity has directly assessed staff behaviour or developed valid and reliable measures of staff performance. Such measures of staff behaviour and staff performance are fundamental if researchers are to

investigate factors associated with "productivity" directly, rather than assessing factors associated with proxy measures of staff performance.

(3) *Variation.* Current research activity has paid little attention to variation across job titles, service types, or geographical areas. Future research endeavours need to investigate such variations systematically.

(4) *Design.* Much research involves survey designs and correlational analyses. Future research designs need to allow stronger causal interpretations if more robust models of staff behaviour and staff performance are to be developed. A further design issue concerns the comprehensiveness of the measures used; if staff behaviour is multiply determined, as many as possible of the relevant determinants need to be included. Finally, the unit of analysis (individual staff member, individual service user, or service) needs to be decided upon, as this will have ramifications for the measures used and the size and sample required.

(5) *Measurement.* As described throughout the chapter, there are several problems with many of the measurement strategies currently used by researchers. First, there is a reliance on proxy measures of staff performance and vignettes, rather than measuring actual staff performance with people with intellectual disabilities. Second, there is a reliance on self-report measures from staff. While most of these measures can be defended on theoretical grounds (that is, the staff perception is the crucial factor), pervasive social desirability biases exist. Third, there is little consistency in the measures used across studies and little evaluation of the reliability and validity of measures. All these issues need to be attended to by future researchers.

(6) *Qualitative research.* Very little research utilising qualitative approaches appears to exist concerning staff in services for people with intellectual disabilities. Such approaches, including semistructured interviews, participant observation, and ethnography, could yield important insights into topics as yet uninvestigated, and could also help in building theoretical models of staff behaviour grounded in data.

(7) *Integration.* Finally, it has been noted throughout this chapter that separate strands of research concerning staff in services for people with intellectual disabilities have been conducted largely independently of each other. Future research should be directed at integrating these separate strands of research, both theoretically and methodologically.

REFERENCES

Aitken, C.J. & Schloss, J.A. (1994). Occupational stress and burnout amongst staff working with people with an intellectual disability. *Behavioural Interventions*, **9**, 225–234.

Aldwin, C.M. (1994). *Stress, Coping and Development*. London: Guilford.

Allen, D., McDonald, L., Dunn, C. & Doyle, T. (1997). Changing care staff approaches to the prevention and management of aggressive behaviour in a residential treatment unit for persons with mental retardation and challenging behaviour. *Research in Developmental Disabilities*, **18**, 101–112.

Allen, D. & Tynan, H. (2000). Responding to aggressive behavior: impact of training on staff members' knowledge and confidence. *Mental Retardation*, **38**, 97–104.

Allen, P., Pahl, J. & Quine, L. (1990). *Care Staff in Transition*. London: HMSO.

Anderson, N. & Herriot, P. (Eds) (1997). *International Handbook of Selection and Assessment*. Chichester: Wiley.

Arnold, H.J. & Feldman, D.C. (1982). A multivariate analysis of the determinants of job turnover. *Journal of Applied Psychology*, **67**, 350–360.

Arnold, J., Cooper, C.L. and Robertson, I.T. (1995). *Work Psychology* (2nd edn). London: Pitman.

Aronson, E., Wilson, T.D. & Akert, R.M. (1997). *Social Psychology* (2nd edn). New York: Longman.

Baumeister, A. & Zaharia, E.S. (1987). Withdrawal and commitment of basic-care staff in residential programmes. In S. Landesman and P. Vietze (Eds) *Living Environment and Mental Retardation.* Washington: American Association for Mental Deficiency.

Berryman, J., Evans, I.M. & Kalbag, A. (1994). The effects of training in nonaversive behaviour management on the attitudes and understanding of direct care staff. *Journal of Behaviour Therapy and Experimental Psychiatry*, **25**, 241–250.

Bersani, H.A. & Heifetz, L.J. (1985). Perceived stress and satisfaction of direct-care staff members in community residences for mentally retarded adults. *American Journal of Mental Deficiency*, **90**, 289–295.

Bluedorn, A.C. (1982). The theories of turnover: causes, effects, and meaning. *Research in the Sociology of Organizations*, **1**, 75–128.

Blumenthal, S., Lavender, T. & Hewson, S. (1998). Role clarity, perception of the organisation and burnout amongst support workers in residential homes for people with intellectual disability: a comparison between a National Health Service trust and a charitable company. *Journal of Intellectual Disability Research*, **42**, 409–417.

Bond, L., Kerr, M., Dunstan, F. & Thapar, A. (1997). Attitudes of general practitioners towards health care for people with intellectual disability and the factors underlying these attitudes. *Journal of Intellectual Disability Research*, **41**, 391–400.

Borrill, C., Wall, T.D., West, M.A., Hardy, G.E., Shapiro, D.A., Carter, A., et al. (1996). *Mental Health of the Workforce in NHS Trusts: Phase 1 Final Report.* Sheffield: Institute of Work Psychology.

Braddock, D. & Mitchell, D. (1992). *Residential Services for Persons with Developmental Disabilities in the United States: A National Study of Staff Compensation, Turnover, and Related Issues.* Washington, DC: American Association on Mental Retardation.

Briner, R.B. (1997). Improving stress assessment: toward an evidence-based approach to organisational stress interventions. *Journal of Psychosomatic Research*, **43**, 61–71.

Bromley, J. & Emerson, E. (1995). Beliefs and emotional reactions of care staff working with people with challenging behaviour. *Journal of Intellectual Disability*, **39**, 341–352.

Buckhalt, J.A., Marchetti, A. & Bearden, L.J. (1990). Sources of job stress and job satisfaction reported by direct care staff of large residential mental retardation facilities. *Education and Training in Mental Retardation*, **25**, 344–351.

Burch, M.R., Reiss, M.L. & Bailey, J.S. (1987). A competency-based "hands-on" training package for direct-care staff. *Journal of the Association for Persons with Severe Handicaps*, **12**, 67–71.

Carr, E.G., Taylor, J.C. & Robinson, S. (1991). The effects of severe behavior problems in children on the teaching behavior of adults. *Journal of Applied Behavior Analysis*, **24**, 523–535.

Caton, D.J., Grossnickle, W.F., Cope, J.G., Long, T.E. & Mitchell, C.C. (1988). Burnout and stress among employees at a state institution for mentally retarded persons. *American Journal on Mental Retardation*, **93**, 300–304.

Clegg, J.A., Standen, P.J. & Cromby, J.J. (1991a). Interactions between adults with profound intellectual disability and staff. *Australia and New Zealand Journal of Developmental Disabilities*, **17**, 377–389.

Clegg, J.A., Standen, P.J. & Cromby, J.J. (1991b). The analysis of talk sessions between staff and adults with profound intellectual disability. *Australia and New Zealand Journal of Developmental Disabilities*, **17**, 391–400.

Clegg, J., Standen, P. & Jones, G. (1996). Striking the balance: a grounded theory analysis of staff perspectives. *British Journal of Clinical Psychology*, **35**, 249–264.

Cohen, J. (1988). *Statistical Power Analysis for the Behavioural Sciences* (2nd edn). Hillsdale, NJ: Erlbaum.

Cope, J., Grossnickle, W., Covington, K., Durham, T. & Zaharia, E. (1987). Staff turnover as a function of performance in a public residential facility. *American Journal of Mental Deficiency*, **92**, 151–154.

Cordes, C.L. & Dougherty, T.W. (1993). A review and an integration of research on job burnout. *Academy of Management Review*, **18**, 621–656.

Corrigan, P.W. (1993). Staff stressors at a developmental center and state hospital. *Mental Retardation*, **31**, 234–238.

Cox, T. (1990). The recognition and measurement of stress: conceptual and methodological issues. In J.R. Wilson & N. Corlett (Eds) *Evaluation of Human Work*. London: Taylor & Francis.

Cox, T. (1993). Stress research and stress management: putting theory to work. HSE Contract Research Report No. 61/1993. London: Health and Safety Executive/ HMSO.

Cox, T., Kuk, G. & Leiter, M.P. (1993). Burnout, health, work stress and organisational healthiness. In W. Schaufeli & C. Maslach (Eds) *Professional Burnout: Recent Developments in Theory and Research*. New York: Hemisphere.

Cox, T. & Leiter, M. (1992). The health of health care organisations. *Work and Stress*, **6**, 219–227.

Dagnan, D., Trower, P. & Smith, R. (1998). Care staff responses to people with learning disabilities and challenging behaviour: a cognitive-emotional analysis. *British Journal of Clinical Psychology*, **37**, 59–68.

Dyer, S. & Quine, L. (1998). Predictors of job satisfaction and burnout among the direct care staff of a community learning disability service. *Journal of Applied Research in Intellectual Disabilities*, **11**, 320–332.

Emerson, E. (1995). *Challenging Behaviour: Analysis and Intervention in People with Learning Disabilities*. Cambridge: Cambridge University Press.

Emerson, E. (1998). Working with people with challenging behaviour. In E. Emerson, C. Hatton, J. Bromley & A. Caine (Eds) *Clinical Psychology and People with Intellectual Disabilities* (pp. 127–153). Chichester: Wiley.

Emerson, E. & Bromley, J. (1995). The form and functioning of challenging behaviours. *Journal of Intellectual Disability Research*, **39**, 388–398.

Emerson, E. & Hatton, C. (1994). *Moving Out: Relocation from Hospital to Community*. London: HMSO.

Emerson, E., Hatton, C., Robertson, J., Henderson, D. & Cooper, J. (1999). A descriptive analysis of the relationships between social context, engagement and stereotypy in residential services for people with severe and complex disabilities. *Journal of Applied Research in Intellectual Disabilities*, **12**, 11–29.

Emerson, E., Reeves, D., Thompson, S., Henderson, D. & Robertson, J. (1996). Time-based lag sequential analysis in the functional assessment of severe challenging behaviour. *Journal of Intellectual Disability Research*, **40**, 260–274.

Emerson, E., Remington, B., Hatton, C. & Hastings, R.P. (Eds) (1995). Special issue on staffing. *Mental Handicap Research*, **8**, 215–339.

Emerson, E., Robertson, J., Gregory, N., Kessissoglou, S., Hatton, C., Hallam, A., et al. (2000). The quality and costs of community-based residential supports and residential campuses for people with severe and complex disabilities. *Journal of Intellectual and Developmental Disability*, **25**, 103–119.

Etzion, D. (1984). Moderating effect of social support on the stress–burnout relationship. *Journal of Applied Psychology*, **69**, 615–622.

Felce, D., Bowley, G., Baxter, H., Jones, E., Lowe, K. & Emerson, E. (2000). The effectiveness of staff support: evaluating Active Support training using a conditional probability approach. *Research in Developmental Disabilities*, **21**, 243–255.

Felce, D. & Emerson, E. (2001). Living with support in a home in the community: predictors of behavioural development and household and community activity. *Mental Retardation and Developmental Disabilities Research Reviews*, **7**, 75–83.

Felce, D., Lowe, K., Perry, J., Baxter, H., Jones, E., Hallam, A., et al. (1998). Service support to people in Wales with severe intellectual disabilities and the most severe challenging behaviours: processes, outcomes and costs. *Journal of Intellectual Disability Research*, **42**, 390–408.

Fenwick, A. (1995). On attribution theory: challenging behaviour and staff beliefs. *Clinical Psychology Forum*, May, **79**, 29–31.

Firth-Cozens, J. & Payne, R. (Eds) (1999). *Stress in Health Professionals*. Chichester: Wiley.

Fishbein, M. (1998). Changing behavior to prevent STDs/AIDS. *International Journal of Gynecology and Obstetrics*, **63**, 175–181.

Fishbein, M. & Ajzen, I. (1975). A theory of reasoned action. In I. Ajzen & M. Fishbein (Eds) *Understanding Attitudes and Predicting Social Behaviour* (pp. 4–11). Englewood Cliffs, NJ: Prentice-Hall.

Fletcher, B.(C.) (1989). *The Cultural Audit: An Individual and Organisational Investigation.* Cambridge: PSI Publications.

Gardner, B.J. (2002). The role of primary and secondary appraisal in work related stress. University of Birmingham: Unpublished thesis.

Gatewood, R.D. & Feild, H.S. (1998). *Human Resource Selection* (4th edn). Orlando, FL: Harcourt Brace.

Gill, F., Stenfert Kroese, B. & Rose, J. (2002). General practitioners' attitudes and emotions associated with patients who have a learning disability. *Psychological Medicine*, **32**, 1445–1455.

Goldberg, D. (1978). *General Health Questionnaire (GHQ)-12.* Oxford: NFER–Nelson.

Grant, G.W. & Moores, B. (1977). Resident characteristics and staff behavior in two hospitals for mentally retarded adults. *American Journal of Mental Deficiency*, **82**, 259–265.

Hall, P.S. & Hall, N.D. (2002). Hiring and retaining direct-care staff: after fifty years of research, what do we know? *Mental Retardation*, **40**, 201–211.

Hall, S. & Oliver, C. (2000). An alternative approach to the sequential analysis of behavioural interactions. In T. Thompson, D. Felce & F.J. Symons (Eds) *Behavioral Observation: Technology and Applications in Developmental Disabilities* (pp. 335–348). Baltimore, MD: Brookes.

Hall, S., Oliver, C. & Murphy, G. (2001). The early development of self-injurious behaviour: an empirical study. *American Journal on Mental Retardation*, **106**, 189–199.

Hallam, A., Knapp, M., Jarbrink, K., Netten, A., Emerson, E., Robertson, J., et al. (2002). Costs of village community, residential campus and dispersed housing provision for people with intellectual disability. *Journal of Intellectual Disability Research*, **46**, 394–404.

Harris, P. & Rose, J. (2002). Measuring staff support in services for people with intellectual disability: the Staff Support and Satisfaction Questionnaire, Version 2. *Journal of Intellectual Disability Research*, **46**, 151–157.

Hastings, R. (1995). Understanding factors that influence staff responses to challenging behaviours: an exploratory interview study. *Mental Handicap Research*, **8**, 296–320.

Hastings, R.P. (1997). Measuring staff perceptions of challenging behaviour: the Challenging Behaviour Attributions Scale (CHABA). *Journal of Intellectual Disability Research*, **41**, 495–501.

Hastings, R.P. (2002). Do challenging behaviours affect staff psychological well-being?: issues of causality and mechanism. *American Journal on Mental Retardation*, **107**, 455–467.

Hastings, R.P. & Brown, T. (2002). Coping strategies and the impact of challenging behaviors on special educators' burnout. *Mental Retardation*, **40**, 148–156.

Hastings, R.P., Reed, T.S. & Watts, M.J. (1997). Community staff causal attributions about challenging behaviours in people with intellectual disabilities. *Journal of Applied Research in Intellectual Disabilities*, **10**, 238–249.

Hastings, R.P. & Remington, B. (1994a). Staff behaviour and its implications for people with learning disabilities and challenging behaviours. *British Journal of Clinical Psychology*, **33**, 423–438.

Hastings, R.P. & Remington, B. (1994b). Rules of engagement: towards an analysis of staff responses to challenging behaviour. *Research in Developmental Disabilities*, **14**, 279–298.

Hastings, R.P. & Remington, B. (1995). The emotional dimension of working with challenging behaviours. *Clinical Psychology Forum*, **79**, 11–16.

Hastings, R.P., Remington, B. & Hopper, G.M. (1995). Experienced and inexperienced health care workers' beliefs about challenging behaviours. *Journal of Intellectual Disability Research*, **39**, 474–483.

Hatton, C., Brown, R., Caine, A. & Emerson, E. (1995a). Stressors, coping strategies and stress-related outcomes among direct care staff in staffed houses for people with learning disabilities. *Mental Handicap Research*, **8**, 252–271.

Hatton, C. & Emerson, E. (1993). Organisational predictors of staff stress, satisfaction and intended turnover in a service for people with multiple disabilities. *Mental Retardation*, **31**, 388–395.

Hatton, C. & Emerson, E. (1995a). Staff in services for people with learning disabilities: an overview of current issues. *Mental Handicap Research*, **8**, 215–219.

Hatton, C. & Emerson, E. (1995b). The development of a shortened "ways of coping" questionnaire for use with direct care staff in learning disability services. *Mental Handicap Research*, **8**, 237–251.

Hatton, C., Emerson, E., Rivers, H., Mason, H., Mason, L., Swarbrick, C., et al. (1999a). Factors associated with staff stress and work satisfaction in services for people with intellectual disability. *Journal of Intellectual Disability Research*, **43**, 253–267.

Hatton, C., Emerson, E., Rivers, M., Mason, H., Swarbrick, R., Mason, L., et al. (2001). Factors associated with intended staff turnover and job search behaviour in services for people with intellectual disability. *Journal of Intellectual Disability Research*, **45**, 258–270.

Hatton, C., Emerson, E., Robertson, J., Henderson, D. & Cooper, J. (1995b). The quality and costs of residential services for adults with multiple disabilities: a comparative evaluation. *Research in Developmental Disabilities*, **16**, 439–460.

Hatton, C., Emerson, E., Robertson, J., Henderson, D. & Cooper, J. (1996). Factors associated with staff support and user lifestyle in services for people with multiple disabilities: a path analytic approach. *Journal of Intellectual Disability Research*, **40**, 466–477.

Hatton, C., Rivers, M., Emerson, E., Kiernan, C., Reeves, D., Alborz, A., et al. (1999b). Staff characteristics, working conditions and outcomes in services for people with intellectual disabilities: results of a staff survey. *Journal of Applied Research in Intellectual Disabilities*, **12**, 340–347.

Hatton, C., Rivers, M., Mason, H., Kiernan, C., Emerson, E., Alborz, A., et al. (1998b). *Staff in Services for People with Learning Disabilities*. Manchester: Hester Adrian Research Centre.

Hatton, C., Rivers, M., Mason, H., Mason, L., Emerson, E., Kiernan, C., et al. (1999d). Organizational culture and staff outcome in services for people with intellectual disabilities. *Journal of Intellectual Disability Research*, **43**, 206–218.

Hatton, C., Rivers, M., Mason, H., Mason, L., Kiernan, C., Emerson, E., et al. (1999c). Staff stressors and staff outcomes in services for adults with intellectual disabilities: the staff stressor questionnaire. *Research in Developmental Disabilities*, **20**, 269–285.

Health and Safety Executive (1997). *Stress at Work: A Guide for Employers*. Norwich: HMSO.

Health and Safety at Work Act (1974). London: HMSO.

Heider, F. (1958). *The Psychology of Interpersonal Relations*. New York: Wiley.

Henry, D., Keys, C., Jopp, D. & Balcazar, F. (1996). The Community Living Attitudes Scale, Mental Retardation Form: development and psychometric properties. *Mental Retardation*, **34**, 149–158.

Heyman, B., Swain, J. & Gilman, M. (1998). A risk management dilemma: how day care centre staff understand challenging behaviour. *Disability and Society*, **13**, 163–182.

Hogg, J., Reeves, D., Roberts, J. & Mudford, O.C. (2001). Consistency, context and confidence in judgements of affective communication in adults with profound intellectual and multiple disabilities. *Journal of Intellectual Disability Research*, **45**, 18–29.

Hui, C.H. (1988). Impact of objective and subjective labour market conditions on employee turnover. *Journal of Occupational Psychology*, **61**, 211–219.

Ito, H., Kurita, H. & Shiiya, J. (1999). Burnout amongst direct-care staff members of facilities for persons with mental retardation in Japan. *Mental Retardation*, **37**, 477–481.

Jacobson, J.W. & Ackerman, L.J. (1992). Staff attitudes and the group home as a workplace. In J. Jacobson & S.N. Burchard (Eds) *Community Living for People with Developmental and Psychiatric Disabilities* (pp. 232–243). Baltimore, MD: Johns Hopkins University Press.

Jenkins, R., Rose, J. & Lovell, C. (1997). Psychological well-being of staff working with people who have challenging behaviour. *Journal of Intellectual Disability Research*, **41**, 502–511.

Johnson, P.R. & Davies, R. (1989). Sexual attitudes of members of staff. *British Journal of Mental Subnormality*, **35**, 17–21.

Jones, C. & Hastings, R.P. (2003). Staff reactions to self-injurious behaviours in learning disability services: attributions, emotional responses and helping. *British Journal of Clinical Psychology*, **42**, 189–203.

Jones, E., Felce, D., Lowe, K., Bowley, C., Pagler, J., Gallagher, B., et al. (2001). Evaluation of the dissemination of active support training in staffed community residences. *American Journal on Mental Retardation*, **106**, 344–358.

Jones, E., Perry, J., Lowe, K., Felce, D., Toogood, S., Dunstan, F., et al. (1999). Opportunity and the promotion of activity among adults with severe mental retardation living in community residences: the impact of training staff in active support. *Journal of Intellectual Disability Research*, **43**, 164–178.

Kelly, H.H. (1967). Attribution theory in social psychology. In E. Aronson, T.D. Wilson & R.M. Akert (Eds) *Social Psychology* (2nd edn). New York: Longman.

Kerr, M., Dunstan, F. & Thapar, A. (1996). Attitudes of general practitioners to caring for people with learning disability. *British Journal of General Practice*, **46**, 92–94.

Knowles, M. & Landesman, S. (1986). National survey of state-sponsored training for residential direct-care staff. *Mental Retardation*, **24**, 293–300.

Larson, S.A. & Lakin, K.C. (1992). Direct-care staff stability in a national sample of small group homes. *Mental Retardation*, **30**, 13–22.

Larson, S.A., Lakin, K.C. & Bruininks, D. (1998). *Staff Recruitment and Retention: Study Results and Intervention Strategies*. Washington, DC: American Association on Mental Retardation.

Lazarus, R.S. (1966). *Psychological Stress and the Coping Process*. New York: McGraw-Hill.

Lazarus, R.S. (1999). *Stress and Emotion: A New Synthesis*. London: Free Association Books.

Lazarus, R.S. & Folkman, S. (1984). *Stress, Appraisal and Coping*. Berlin: Springer-Verlag.

Leiter, M.P. (1991). Coping patterns as predictors of burnout: the function of control and escapist coping patterns. *Journal of Organizational Behaviour*, **12**, 123–144.

Lowe, K. & Felce, D. (1994). Challenging behaviour: the effectiveness of specialist support teams. *Journal of Intellectual Disability Research*, **40**, 336–347.

Machin, C.D. (1998). The roles of cognition and emotion in carers' responses to challenging behaviour: review and treatment considerations. University of Birmingham: Unpublished thesis.

Mansell, J., McGill, P. & Emerson, E. (2001). Development and evaluation of innovative residential services for people with severe intellectual disability and serious challenging behaviour. *International Review of Research in Mental Retardation*, **24**, 245–298.

Maslach, C. & Jackson, S.E. (1981). *The Maslach Burnout Inventory*. Research edn. Palo Alto, CA: Consulting Psychologists Press.

Maslach, C. & Jackson, S.E. (1986). *The Maslach Burnout Inventory*. Manual (2nd edn). Palo Alto, CA: Consulting Psychologists Press.

Maslach, C., & Pines, A. (1977). The burnout syndrome in the day care setting. *Child Care Quarterly*, **6**, 100–113.

Mason, J.W. (1975). A historical view of the stress field. *Journal of Human Stress*, **1**, 6–27.

McKnight, T.J. & Kearney, C.A. (2001). Staff training regarding choice availability for persons with mental retardation: a preliminary analysis. *Journal of Developmental and Physical Disabilities*, **13**, 1–10.

McNaughton, D. & Light, J. (1989). Teaching facilitators to support the communication skills of an adult with severe cognitive disabilities: a case study. *Augmentative and Alternative Communication*, **5**, 35–41.

Michaels, C.E. & Spector, P.E. (1982). Causes of employee turnover: a test of the Mobley, Griffeth, Hand, and Meglino model. *Journal of Applied Psychology*, **67**, 53–59.

Mitchell, D. & Braddock, D. (1993). Compensation and turnover of direct-care staff in developmental disabilities residential facilities in the United States. I. Wages and benefits. *Mental Retardation*, **31**, 429–437.

Mitchell, G. & Hastings, R.P. (1998). Learning disability care staff's emotional reactions to aggressive challenging behaviours: development of a measurement tool. *British Journal of Clinical Psychology*, **37**, 441–449.

Mitchell, G. & Hastings, R.P. (2001). Coping, burnout and emotion in staff working in community services for people with challenging behaviours. *American Journal on Mental Retardation*, **106**, 448–459.

Mossman, D.A., Hastings, R.P. & Brown, T. (2002). Mediators' emotional responses to self-injurious behavior: an experimental study. *American Journal on Mental Retardation*, **107**, 252–260.

Murray, G.C., Sinclair, B., Kidd, G.R., Quigley, A. & McKenzie, K. (1999). The relationship between staff sickness levels and client assault levels in a health service unit for people with an intellectual disability and severely challenging behaviour. *Journal of Applied Research in Intellectual Disabilities*, **12**, 263–268.

Newton, T.J. (1989). Occupational stress and coping with stress: a critique. *Human Relations*, **42**, 441–461.

Oliver, M.N., Anthony, A., Leimkuhl, T.T. & Skillman, G.D. (2002). Attitudes toward acceptable socio-sexual behaviors for persons with mental retardation: implications for normalization and community integration. *Education and Training in Mental Retardation and Developmental Disabilities*, **37**, 193–201.

Orlowska, D., McGill, P. & Mansell, J. (1991). Staff–staff and staff–resident verbal interactions in a community-based group home for people with moderate and severe mental handicaps. *Mental Handicap Research* **4**, 3–19.

Parsons, M.B., McCarn, J.E. & Reid, D.H. (1993). Evaluating and increasing meal-related choices throughout a service setting for people with severe disabilities. *Journal of the Association for Persons with Severe Handicaps*, **18**, 253–260.

Payne, R. (1999). Stress at work: a conceptual framework. In J. Firth-Cozens & R. Payne (Eds) *Stress in Health Professionals* (pp. 3–16). Chichester: Wiley.

Penley, L.E. & Gould, S. (1988). Etzioni's model of organizational involvement: a perspective for understanding commitment to organizations. *Journal of Organizational Behavior*, **9**, 43–59.

Peterson, C., Semmel, A., von Bayer, C., Abramson, L.Y., Metalsky, G.I. & Seligman, M.E.P. (1982). The attributional style questionnaire. *Cognitive Therapy and Research*, **6**, 287–299.

Peterson, C. & Villanova, P.A. (1988). The expanded attributional style questionnaire. *Journal of Abnormal Psychology*, **97**, 87–89.

Power, K.G. & Sharp, G.R. (1988). A comparison of sources of nursing stress and job satisfaction among mental handicap and hospice nursing staff. *Journal of Advanced Nursing*, **13**, 726–732.

Quick, J.C., Murphy, L.R. & Hurrell, J.J. (1992). *Stress and Well-Being at Work: Assessments and Interventions for Occupational Mental Health*. Washington, DC: American Psychological Association.

Razza, N.J. (1993). Determinants of direct-care staff turnover in group homes for individuals with mental retardation. *Mental Retardation*, **31**, 284–291.

Rice, D.M. & Rosen, M. (1991). Direct-care staff: a neglected priority. *Mental Retardation*, **29**, iii–iv.

Robson, C. (1993). *Real World Research*. Oxford: Blackwell.

Rose, J. (1993). Staff stress in residential settings: the move from hospital to the community. *Mental Handicap Research*, **6**, 312–332.

Rose, J. (1995). Stress and residential staff: towards an integration of existing research. *Mental Handicap Research*, **8**, 220–236.

Rose, J. (1997). Stress and stress management. *Tizard Learning Disability Research*, **43**, 268–278.

Rose, J. (1998). Measuring quality: the relationship between diaries and direct observation of staff. *British Journal of Developmental Disabilities*, **44**, 30–37.

Rose, J. (1999). Stress and residential staff who work with people who have an intellectual disability: a factor analytic study. *Journal of Intellectual Disability Research*, **43**, 268–278.

Rose, J. & Holmes, S. (1991). Changing staff attitudes to the sexuality of people with mental handicaps: an evaluative comparison of one and three day workshops. *Mental Handicap Research*, **4**, 67–79.

Rose, J., Jones, F. & Fletcher, B. (1998a). Investigating the relationship between stress and worker behaviour. *Journal of Intellectual Disability Research*, **42**, 163–172.

Rose, J., Jones, F. & Fletcher, B. (1998b). The impact of a stress management programme on staff well-being and performance at work. *Work and Stress*, **12**, 112–124.

Rose, J. & Schelewa-Davies, D. (1997). The relationship between staff stress and team climate in residential services. *Journal of Learning Disabilities for Nursing, Health and Social Care*, **1**, 19–24.

Rutter, M., Tizard, J. & Whitmore, K. (1970). *Education, Health and Behaviour*. Harlow: Longman.

Saloviita, T. & Lehtinen, U. (2001). Paraprofessional staff teaching adults with mental retardation. *Education and Training in Mental Retardation and Developmental Disabilities*, **36**, 103–106.

Saunders, R.R. & Saunders, J.L. (2000). Monitoring staff and consumer behavior in residential settings. In T. Thompson, D. Felce & F.J. Symons (Eds) *Behavioral Observation: Technology and Applications in Developmental Disabilities* (pp. 115–142). Baltimore, MD: Brookes.

Sharrock, R., Day, A., Qazi, F. & Brewin, C.R. (1990). Explanations by professional care staff, optimism and helping behaviour: an application of attribution theory. *Psychological Medicine*, **20**, 849–855.

Smalley, K.A., Certo, N.J. & Goetz, L. (1997). Effect of a staff training package on increasing community integration for people with severe disabilities. *Education and Training in Mental Retardation and Developmental Disabilities*, **32**, 42–48.

Stanley, B. & Standen, P.J. (2000). Carers' attributions for challenging behaviour. *British Journal of Clinical Psychology*, **39**, 157–168.

Stein, K. (2000). Caring for people with learning disability: a survey of general practitioners' attitudes in Southampton and south-west Hampshire. *British Journal of Learning Disabilities*, **28**, 9–15.

Stenfert Kroese, B. & Fleming, I. (1992). Staff's attitudes and working conditions in community-based group homes of people with mental handicaps. *Mental Handicap Research*, **5**, 82–91.
Stoter, D. (1992). The culture of care. *Nursing Times*, **88**, 30–31.
Thompson, S. (1987). Stress in staff working with mentally handicapped people. In R. Payne & J. Firth-Cozens (Eds) *Stress in Health Professionals*. Chichester: Wiley.
Thompson, T., Felce, D. & Symons, F.J. (2000). *Behavioral Observation: Technology and Applications in Developmental Disabilities*. Baltimore, MD: Brookes.
Timmins, N. (1996). *The Five Giants: A Biography of the Welfare State*. London: HarperCollins.
Todd, S. (2000). Working in the public and private domains: staff management of community activities for and the identities of people with intellectual disability. *Journal of Intellectual Disability Research*, **44**, 600–620.
Todd, S. & Shearn, J. (1999). *Creating Home: The Work of Staff in Four Welsh Staffed Houses for People with Learning Disabilities*. Cardiff: Welsh Centre for Learning Disabilities Applied Research Unit, University of Wales College of Medicine.
Wanless, L. (2001). Staff responses towards people with mild to moderate intellectual disabilities who engage in aggressive behaviour: a cognitive emotional analysis. Conference Abstracts: Centenary Annual Conference, BPS, Glasgow.
Watson, D., Clark, L.A. & Tellegen, A. (1988). Development and validation of brief measures of positive and negative affect: the PANAS scales. *Journal of Personality and Social Psychology*, **54**, 1063–1070.
Watson, D. & Tellegen, A. (1985). Toward a consensual structure of mood. *Psychological Bulletin*, **98**, 219–235.
Weiner, B. (1980). A cognitive (attribution)-emotion-action model of helping behaviour: an analysis of judgements of help giving. *Journal of Personality and Social Psychology*, **39**, 1142–1162.
Weiner, B. (1985). An attributional theory of achievement, motivation and emotion. *Psychological Review*, **92**, 547–573.
Weiner, B. (1986). *An Attributional Theory of Motivation and Emotion*. Berlin: Springer-Verlag.
Woods, P. & Cullen, C. (1983). Determinants of staff behaviour in long-term residential care. *Behavioural Psychotherapy*, **11**, 4–17.
Ziarnik, J.P. & Bernstein, G.S. (1982). A critical examination of the effect of inservice training on staff performance. *Mental Retardation*, **20**, 109–114.

CHAPTER 30

The Economics of Intellectual Disability

Angela Hallam
Health and Community Care Research Team, Edinburgh, UK
and
Martin Knapp
Institute of Psychiatry, UK

INTRODUCTION

A range of formal and informal health and social care services is likely to be required during the lifetime of a person with intellectual disability. In addition to deficits in intellectual functioning, present from birth, individuals often have physical and/or sensory disabilities and may present a complex range of challenging behaviours. They may also be more prone than the rest of the population to chronic health problems, including epilepsy, dementia, and hepatitis. Arrangements for the care and support needed over the life cycle could have major resource implications for the government, the independent sectors, and the wider society.

Economics is primarily concerned with those resource implications; in particular, how resources are allocated and the associated consequences. Every care system in the world operates under conditions of scarcity, and always has, but questions concerning the best use of scarce resources appear to be more frequently voiced today, reflecting the more widespread recognition of scarcity and greater willingness to target services where needs are assessed to be greatest. (McCrone, 1998, provides a useful introduction to the issues of rationing and prioritisation.)

In responding to these resource allocation questions, economists have pursued cost-effectiveness and similar analysis, as we discuss in this chapter. However, responding to scarcity also requires examination of patterns of employment, the forces of demand and supply, the roles of markets in resource and treatment allocation, and the incentives and disincentives to better practice. These are among the broad range of topics addressed by economists, but most are beyond the scope of this chapter, whose primary aim is to describe economic evaluation, how it might be undertaken or interpreted, and what might be learned from some completed studies.

The International Handbook of Applied Research in Intellectual Disabilities. Edited by E. Emerson, C. Hatton, T. Thompson and T.R. Parmenter ISBN 0-471-49709-6.

The next section introduces a conceptual framework from which to hang economic evaluations. The third section then details the different modes of evaluation: when they can be used, what they do, and some examples from recent research. The fourth section discusses the accurate measurement of service use and cost and some of the most common associated problems. The fifth section considers cost variations and service patterns. The concluding section looks to future directions for research and touches on a few design challenges which should be addressed to improve the quality of economic evaluations. One challenge facing economic studies is that their results do not always travel well from one care system to another. Here we use empirical examples from the UK to illustrate our arguments, and towards the end of the chapter discuss the issue of international relevance and transferability.

CONCEPTUAL FRAMEWORK AND CRITERIA

Performance Criteria

In the early 1980s, the then Conservative UK government announced its Financial Management Initiative (FMI) and established the Audit Commission. These linked events heralded the arrival in the public sector of what had become known in management jargon as the "three Es": economy, efficiency, and effectiveness. These are obviously candidate criteria for service or resource allocation, but there is a need to include at least a fourth E: *equity*, or distributive justice. Other criteria might also be used to evaluate a service or policy, such as the extent of participation of service users in decision making.

What do these various performance criteria mean? In this chapter, our focus is on economic evaluation, and so we concentrate our attention on the four criteria in Box 30.1.

Box 30.1 Economy, effectiveness, efficiency, and equity

- *Economy* is the saving of resources. The pursuit of economy requires detailed and accurate cost information but, in a strict sense, pays no heed to the impact of lower spending upon people with intellectual disability, their families, or the wider society.
- Improving *effectiveness*, on the other hand, means enhancing health or quality of life or moving a providing or commissioning agency closer to its chosen operational objectives. Strictly speaking, the promotion of effectiveness pays no particular regard to costs, and many of its most important facets are especially hard to gauge.
- *Efficiency* combines the resource and effectiveness sides: the pursuit of efficiency could mean reducing the cost of producing a stated level of outcome or effectiveness, or improving the level of effectiveness or the volume and quality of outcomes achieved under fixed budgets.
- *Equity* refers to the fairness of an allocation. It is particularly associated with the targeting of services on needs.

It is helpful for the discussion of performance criteria to locate them within an appropriate conceptual framework. A useful structure for the job is the *production of welfare* approach, summarised in simplified outline form in Figure 30.1 (Davies & Knapp, 1981,

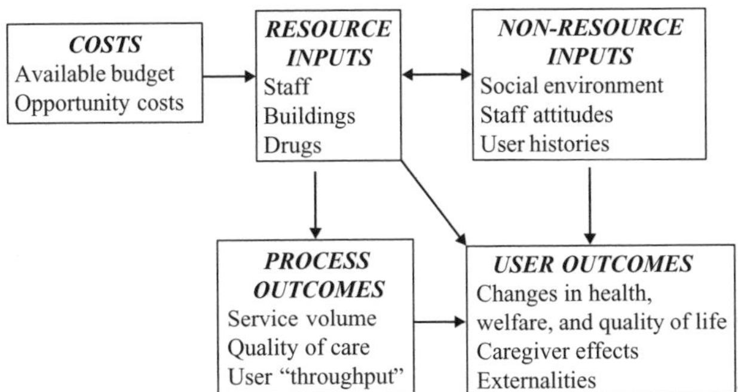

Figure 30.1 The production of welfare

1988; Knapp, 1984). The framework distinguishes the key elements in the provision of services, particularly as follows:

- the *resource inputs* to care (mainly staff, capital, and consumables)
- the *costs* of those resource inputs expressed in monetary terms
- the so-called *non-resource inputs* to the care process, which are influences on the achievement of outcomes which do not have an identifiable price or are not currently marketed—such as the social milieu of a service setting, staff attitudes, and service user histories
- the *intermediate or process outcomes*, which are the volumes of service output and/or the quality of care, perhaps weighted in some way for user characteristics, produced from combinations of the resource and non-resource inputs
- the *final or user outcomes*, which are changes over time in the health, welfare, and quality of life of users and their carers.

We can see from Figure 30.1 that it is possible, for instance, to define effectiveness as the achievement of either service-related ("process") or user-related goals. Efficiency and equity can also be defined and measured in terms of component elements within the framework (singly or in combination). It is usually a combination of factors which determines the level of effectiveness, efficiency, or equity. The production-of-welfare approach—which encapsulates an economist's perspective on the organisation and allocation of services and user-level achievements—is thus a summary of the myriad and complex linkages between services and achievements and the resource and non-resource inputs that make them possible. It is obviously also a platform on which to build an evaluation. The various influences on outcomes—the inputs—are often highly intercorrelated, but the conceptual and practical approaches should be capable of disentangling these interconnections.

There is nothing peculiar or particular about the production-of-welfare framework, nor the economist's approach to resource allocation in general from which it is derived. The approach is simply an ordered collection of likely (hypothesised) and proven (evidence-based) causal connections between the factors within the control of decision makers, staff, and carers (and perhaps also of users), and the achievements they make possible, either at a service level or in terms of improvements in the welfare of people.

The approach offers a theoretical framework within which to locate many of the current views on the organisation and delivery of services. Because it suggests clear hypotheses about the links between the availability of different resources, personnel activities, user preferences, and identifiable changes in circumstances and characteristics, the framework is testable. If it is carefully constructed and responsively restructured, the framework can embody the results of empirical research. There are, for example, many assumed and some corroborated causal relationships between aspects of care, carers, and users. While the approach cannot contain all the perspectives put forward, it provides a coherent conceptual framework in which to locate and examine interrelationships. What is more, the approach suggests which relationships should be examined and how these may be interpreted. We shall draw on the production-of-welfare framework as we introduce and illustrate the modes of economic evaluation in the next section.

MODES OF EVALUATION

An economic evaluation must fulfil two basic requirements:

- It measures both costs and outcomes.
- It compares two or more interventions.

Consequently, comparing the costs of one care setting with another, without any evidence on the outcomes of settings for users or quality of care, is generally *not* an economic evaluation. It might be an interesting cost comparison and the costs might be calculated with considerable skill, but it does not provide enough information to assist decision makers facing the choice between the two treatment options, or two service arrangements, for it tells them nothing about the outcome consequences of choosing one level of expenditure over another. Similarly, calculating the costs and outcomes of a single service could be very interesting, but is *not* evaluative unless those costs and outcomes are compared with equivalent data for another service (or even compared with the option of "doing nothing").

Economists have developed a number of evaluation tools, and those developed by health economists to evaluate services, treatments, and policies provide a sound baseline for work in the field of intellectual disabilities. Textbooks such as those by Drummond, O'Brien, Stoddart and Torrance (1997) and Gold, Siegal, Russell and Weinstein (1996) provide excellent, accessible accounts of these approaches.

Cost comparisons

Cost-offset and *cost-minimisation analyses* are the simplest of procedures and are concerned only with costs. By the definition that we have just offered, these cannot be seen as economic evaluations per se. They assume either that health and quality-of-life outcomes have been well established from other research, or that outcomes are (currently) not measurable because of conceptual difficulties or research funding limitations. A cost-minimisation approach often proceeds in the knowledge that previous research has shown outcomes to be identical in the two or more treatment or policy alternatives being examined (in which case it could be seen as an "interrupted economic evaluation"). Its principal aim is to look for the lowest cost alternative. A cost-offset analysis compares costs incurred with (other) costs saved, and is sometimes conducted as part of a fuller evaluation such as a cost-effectiveness study (see below).

Economic Evaluations

Other modes of economic evaluation are more informative, but correspondingly more complex. The best known, but most rarely conducted, is the *cost-benefit analysis (CBA)*. This approach is unique among economic evaluations in that it addresses the extent to which a treatment or policy is socially worthwhile in the broadest sense, with all costs and benefits valued in the same monetary units. If benefits exceed costs, the evaluation would recommend providing the treatment, and vice versa. With two or more alternatives, the evaluation would recommend the one with the greatest net benefit as the most efficient. CBAs are intrinsically attractive, but conducting them would certainly be problematic in the intellectual disabilities field because of the difficulties associated with valuing all outcomes in monetary terms. However, methodologies are being developed by economists working in other fields which aim to obtain direct valuations of health outcomes by users, relatives, or the general public, such as "willingness-to-pay" techniques, where people state the amount they would be prepared to pay (hypothetically) to achieve a given health state or health gain (see Olsen & Smith, 2001, for a review of studies in health care generally).

Cost-effectiveness analysis (CEA) is concerned with ensuring that the resources allocated to (say) the intellectual disabilities sector are used to best effect. CEA is usually employed to help decision makers choose between alternative interventions available to or aimed at specific user groups. If two care options are of equal cost, which of them provides the greater effectiveness? Or if two options have been found to be equally effective in terms of reduced symptoms, improved functioning, or enhanced quality of life, which is less costly? In the strict sense, CEA looks at a single effectiveness dimension and often constructs a cost-effectiveness ratio.

A generalisation of CEA to multiple outcomes is *cost-consequences analysis* (a label not widely used), which produces a number of ratios of outcome to costs, rather than one single ratio. This has the ability to evaluate policies and practices in a way that comes much closer to everyday reality. As with the results from any evaluation, the findings from a cost-consequences analysis would need to be reviewed by decision makers, and the different outcomes weighed up and compared with costs. The decision calculus may be more complicated than when using cost-effectiveness ratios or monetary measures of cost-benefit differences, but decision-makers elsewhere in health-care systems—from strategic policy-makers to individual professionals—make these kinds of decisions every day.

Cost-utility analysis (CUA) is a technique now quite widely employed in health-care evaluations. It is similar to CEA but measures the impact of an intervention in terms of improvements in health-related quality of life. The value of the quality-of-life improvement is measured in units of "utility", expressed by a combined index of the mortality and quality-of-life effects of an intervention (the Quality Adjusted Life Year [QALY] is the best-known index). This is in contrast to CBA, which uses monetary values, and also in contrast to CEA and cost-consequences analysis, which rely on the kinds of measure conventionally found in clinical evaluations (symptom scores, behaviour ratings, and so on). CUAs avoid the potential ambiguities with multidimensional outcomes but are obviously more general than the single-outcome CEA. The result is a series of cost-utility ratios (such as the cost per QALY gained) upon which health-care resource allocation priorities might be based. They can be applied to choices across a range of treatments or diagnoses, and they can compare one health-care area to another. The transparency of the methods used to derive utility scores is a particular strength, but the currently available measures (which are intended for use across the widest diagnostic range) may not be sensitive enough to the kinds of changes usually found in interventions (services) for people with intellectual disabilities to provide the sole indicator of impact (cf. Chisholm, Healey & Knapp, 1997, for an analagous discussion in the mental health context).

A review of economic evaluations of care for people with intellectual disability conducted in the UK found no CBA or CUA (Kavanagh & Opit, 1998). This absence is not at all surprising given the practical difficulties of doing these kinds of evaluations.

Cost-of-Illness Studies

Another technique employed by some health economists is the *cost-of-illness study (COI)*. To gauge the overall resource impact of intellectual disability, the diverse economic impacts (such as health service utilisation, other formally delivered services, lost employment and productivity, and family and caregiver impacts) need to be transformed into a single cost-based measure. For example, a recent study estimated the economic consequences of autism in the UK, on the basis of published evidence and the reanalysis of data held at the Centre for the Economics of Mental Health. With an assumed prevalence of 5 per 10 000, the annual societal cost was estimated to exceed £1 billion sterling. The lifetime cost for a person with autism exceeded £2.4 million, with the main costs associated with living support and day activities (Järbrink & Knapp, 2001).

COIs are helpful because they allow comparisons with other illnesses and draw attention to what could be a major societal impact. By expressing a diversity of impacts in a single (monetary) unit, such aggregate measures can be drawn to the attention of decision makers, who might otherwise not be familiar with the effects of intellectual disability. However, aggregate cost measures may oversimplify the complexity of the real world. In addition, COI calculations are *not* evaluative exercises: they do not say anything about how to improve efficiency or reduce inequity. A high-cost illness is not necessarily amenable to treatment or may not have cost-effective treatments available (Byford, Torgerson & Raftery, 2000). Another difficulty is attribution. An individual with intellectual disability, psychotic episodes, and epilepsy is likely to be a heavy service user, but are the associated costs to be attributed to intellectual disability, psychosis, epilepsy, or all three?

Outcomes

On the resource side, each of the above evaluation types measures costs according to widely accepted procedures, as we shall discuss in the next section. Where they differ is in respect to their measurement of outcomes. We do not discuss outcome measurement here, as the topic is well covered in other chapters.

COST MEASUREMENT

Economic evaluations require accurate cost information. When people with intellectual disabilities were cared for in traditional institutions, such as the old "mental handicap hospitals" in the UK, most of the services they received were located on site and funded by the health service. The institution provided board and lodging, the services of health and social care professionals, medication, and day activities. As services moved into the community, funding responsibilities passed from the health sector to a mix of public and independent sector agencies. Professionals from a variety of agencies and organisations may provide housing, education, and health and social care. Making sensible comparisons of hospital and community services therefore requires computation of all the services these individuals use. The same need for comprehensiveness arises in many other contexts. In order to evaluate whether services are provided cost-effectively, it is usually necessary to consider *all* cost implications.

Measuring Service Utilisation

The Client Service Receipt Inventory (CSRI) (Beecham & Knapp, 1992, 2001) was developed to collect details of the service package received by individual people with health or social care needs; it serves as the basis for costing. The CSRI may be adapted for the specific requirement of each evaluation and has been used widely in the field of intellectual disability research in the UK since 1986 (e.g., Knapp et al., 1992; Cambridge, Hayes, Knapp, Gould & Fenyo, 1994; Donnelly et al., 1994; Felce et al., 1999; Emerson et al., 2000; Hallam et al., 2003).

The CSRI collects information about every aspect of the service user's life which has an actual or an implied cost to an agency or individual: background socio-demographic characteristics, accommodation arrangements, employment and income details, and all recent or regular service receipt. The CSRI is a flexible instrument, and may be adapted to meet the needs of a specific evaluation or context. In addition, to avoid duplication, some or all of its elements may be incorporated into other data-collection instruments. The schedule has also continued to develop over time: expansion of the socio-demographic section for use in a cross-cultural comparison of mental health service utilisation and cost (CSSRI) (Chisholm et al., 2000) allowed a more sophisticated level of information to be collected in the third evaluation of the experiences of participants in the Care in the Community demonstration programme, 12 years after leaving institutional care in the UK (Hallam et al., 2003).

CSRI data are usually collected by a researcher at interview with study participants, their key worker, or their main carer. If the person is supported in specialised accommodation, however, the informant should be, or have access to, a manager, or a representative from the provider organisation. This person should be prepared to supply information relating to staff and financial arrangements with the commissioning authority.

Measuring Unit Costs

The completed CSRI provides a description of a person's circumstances and service arrangements. It may indicate the fee charged to the commissioning agency for that person's support, but it does not record the costs of provision. The calculation of costs should encompass the resource implications of all elements of a service, even though service planners may be interested primarily in the cost to their own agencies. Cost calculation should also take account of differences caused by input factors, such as the variation in land and property values from one region of the country to another.

Economic theory advocates basing cost measures on *long-run marginal opportunity costs.* Marginal cost reflects the addition to total cost attributable to the inclusion of one more service user; opportunity costs reflect the resource implications of opportunities forgone rather than amounts spent. In particular, capital investment in one area of service development represents a major, long-term, financial commitment that precludes year-by-year expansion in other ways. Short-run marginal costs are inappropriate for most costing tasks, as they include only revenue costs and do not take account of the full costs of creating new services. However, knowledge about the present time is more certain than knowledge of the future, so the convention is to use short-run average costs, which include both revenue and capital elements as an approximation of long-run marginal costs. (See Knapp, 1993, for more detail on long-run marginal opportunity costs.)

Whether facility-specific or nationally applicable data are used in the calculation of costs usually depends upon the focus of the individual study. However, contact with peripatetic staff such as nurses and social workers is unlikely to make up a large part of the total cost of supporting a person with intellectual disability, so it is rarely worth calculating costs from first principles for all service professionals with whom contact has been recorded. In the UK, a publication compiled annually by researchers at the Personal Social Services Research Unit (PSSRU) brings together average unit cost information for a number of health and social care professionals, day services, and types of accommodation facility (Netten & Curtis, 2000). These costs may be weighted to reflect regional differences or (in some instances) levels of disability. The appropriate unit cost (for an occupational therapist, for example) is then multiplied by the amount of contact made with the service by the study participant in order to reach a figure which represents the costs of occupational therapy in that particular service package.

Facility-Specific Costing

In the field of intellectual disability research, many studies are primarily concerned with the evaluation of building-based services, where cost may be affected by a number of factors. The size, location, and managing agency of the facility, the number and qualifications of staff and the type of support they provide, and the service users' characteristics and level of needs are some of the elements likely to influence the costs (and, ultimately, the cost-effectiveness) of support within that service. For this reason, it is usually necessary to calculate a cost specific to the individual facility, and this requires more detailed information about the service than can be collected with the CSRI.

It is usually necessary to take a "top-down" approach at the level of the organisation responsible for providing care, in order to capture elements of the cost of providing the service which might not be visible at the level of the individual study participant. For example, while the CSRI collects information about care staff, it is not able to track the input of human resources departments, the staff's line management arrangements, or the work of finance departments, all of which clearly have a role in the overall cost of supporting the service user.

Facility-specific costing begins with gaining access to disaggregated, annual revenue accounts relating to that service. The full costs of employing staff, heating and lighting the building, carrying out routine maintenance, and providing food and beverages are all essential pieces of data to collect if two models of residential provision or day-activity services are to be compared on a "like with like" basis. However, these data should be treated with caution.

Annual accounts are produced by organisations to satisfy auditors that budgets have been used wisely, not to provide economists with costs evidence. The following are two of the most common areas where errors can be made:

- Details may relate to the disposal of a budget that may be one of several if, for example, staff salaries come from more than one provider sector.
- Costs may be hidden if, for example, there is a reliance on the input of volunteers, or if the families of users support the service, perhaps by raising funds to buy vehicles for residents' use.

Because information is rarely comprehensive, there is a danger of making inappropriate comparisons between service models or organisations. Although accounts information is extremely useful as a starting point for cost calculation, it is important to have a way to check its validity so that additional elements may be supplemented if necessary.

Deciding on Units of Measurement

Once calculated, costs should be disaggregated to an appropriate unit of measurement close to the level of service user data. People use services in discrete units: for example, hospital service use is counted by the number of inpatient days or outpatient attendances, while contact with community-based service professionals (such as occupational therapists or social workers) is measured in minutes. More complex analyses allow a more detailed level of disaggregation, such as ward-level hospital costs or the disaggregation of residential care costs in recognition of residents' dependency levels (Emerson et al., 2000) (see below).

Informal Care

In many countries, the majority of people with intellectual disabilities live in domestic settings: for example, approximately 60% of adults with intellectual disability in the UK live with their families (Department of Health, 2001). Much of the support these people receive is provided by unpaid family members. The need to reach an accurate estimate of the costs associated with informal care becomes of ever greater importance as survival rates for people with intellectual disability increase. Support provided informally may have to be provided through formal agencies in the future, as parents die or become too frail to support their adult children.

Time is the main input of informal care. Like money, time is a scarce resource that can be put to other valuable uses. Time spent caring for a person with support needs may be time diverted from paid work, unpaid work, or leisure. There is no consensus in the health economics literature on how loss of time should be valued, but methodological debates have centred on a number of issues, including:

- *whether lost time should be included in economic evaluations of health care.* While only costs borne out of pocket may be relevant to the family providing support, from the societal perspective, all costs, including an estimate of the value of lost time, should be included in any CEA (Gold et al., 1996; McDaid, 2001).
- *how time spent on informal care should be measured.* It is inherently difficult to define precisely what activities carried out (say) in the home are occasioned by the disability of a family member.
- *how lost time should be valued.* Health economics literature provides two competing theories of valuing time:
  (1) the *opportunity-cost approach*. Here a wage rate that reflects the cost of the person's time in the next best alternative employment is used. The opportunity costs are the benefits forgone because a resource—in this case, the caregiver's time—is not used in the best possible way.
  (2) the *market-value approach*. This estimates the economic costs of informal caregiving time by using a wage rate for paid employees providing similar services. Here the carer's lost time is valued as the cost of replacing his or her input with that of professional formal carer. The valuation of the informal caregiver's lost time is then based on the cost-savings due to a reduced need for professional time.

Example of Cost Measurement: The Quality and Costs of Residential Supports

A recent project examined the quality and costs of support for people with intellectual disability in independently managed village communities, National Health Service (NHS) residential campuses, and dispersed, community-based housing in the UK (Emerson et al., 2000; Emerson et al., 2001; Hallam et al., 2002). So that a comparison between three very different residential categories could be made, it was important to ensure that data collection was comprehensive. Information was collected, routinely, at three levels: the individual service user, the residential facility, and the managing agency organisation.

In Figure 30.2, all the service settings included in the evaluation are aggregated into the three residential categories. The percentage contribution of each constituent component to the average weekly cost of care of costs is represented in order to demonstrate where some of the variations in cost may appear.

Although the costs of providing support varied a good deal, direct staffing costs contributed most to total cost in each residential category. Within village communities and residential campuses, non-staffing revenue items (such as heat, light, and provisions) were met by budgets within the organisation itself. Costs were covered by the charge made to the commissioning authority on the service user's behalf, leaving the person responsible for the purchase of personal items only. A number of different systems operated in dispersed housing schemes but, in general, the provider organisation was directly responsible for fewer revenue items. CSRI information indicated that study participants often received higher levels of Department of Social Services (DSS) benefits if they were living in dispersed housing, enabling them to pay the bills for utilities and to buy food. (Input percentages can be seen in the "client expenses" layer of the bar chart.)

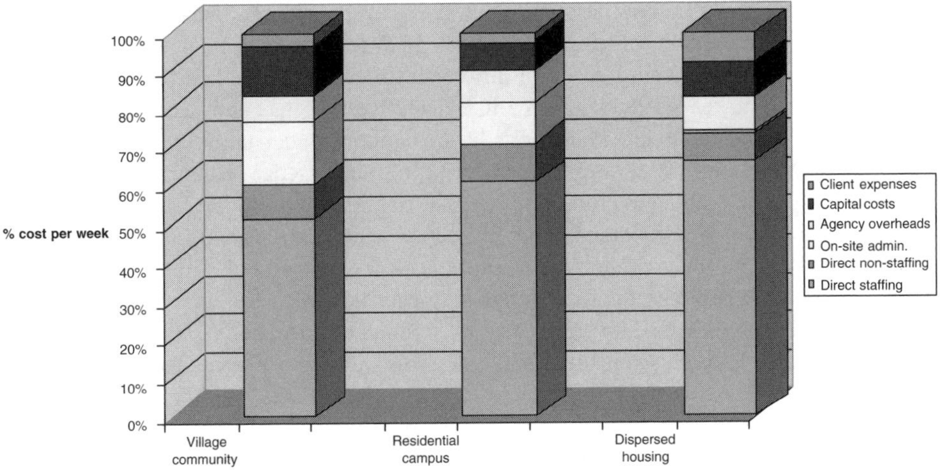

Figure 30.2 Components of the cost of accommodation and associated support

For village communities and residential campuses, complex structures in which housing and shared central facilities were clustered together on single sites, it was possible to identify two distinct strata of costs information relating to agency overheads (such as administration, finance, human resources, and management). Staff were employed at the site itself and at the organisation's central office. Dispersed housing arrangements, on the other hand, comprised small, scattered units and, therefore, input by administration and management staff usually came from company headquarters.

Figure 30.2 relates only to costs associated with residential provision. Although accommodation and associated supports may be expected to make up the greatest proportion of the total cost of care, it is important to ensure that service receipt data collection is comprehensive. Direct staffing costs were lower in the village communities category than in either of the other two service models. While there could be many reasons for this, it was noted that a number of residents participated in full-time day activities. Staff cover within the residential settings during the day would therefore be minimal, and the costs of supporting the residents would fall to the providers of day services. The full service package should be considered to ensure the incorporation of all cost elements.

The study did not attempt to cost informal care. Having ascertained that the support the study participants received was almost entirely provided on a formal basis, the research focused on professional input. Ideally, the care provided by paid and unpaid individuals should be traced and measured, but, inevitably, the emphasis of any evaluation is dictated by resource constraints.

EXPLORING VARIATIONS AND PATTERNS

Cost Variations

One of the inherent difficulties in the calculation and examination of service utilisation and costs data is the variation between individual service users, settings, facilities, and areas. Cost variation is relevant to policy-makers as they seek to provide efficient and equitable community care. For example, does variation in cost between individuals reflect outcome achievements? Do the costs of supporting people in different accommodation settings vary according to residents' needs? Are cost differences between public and independent sector facilities due to the needs of service users, service type or quality, or organisational "efficiency"? Some economic evaluations have sought to understand the causes of these cost variations, and with what implications for policy and practice (Knapp, 1998).

One example of such an exploration of cost variations followed the launch, in the late 1980s, of a programme of demonstration projects to seek general and transferable lessons for the development of community care in the UK (Renshaw et al., 1988). Eleven pilot projects providing services for discharged long-stay hospital residents with intellectual disabilities were studied, and, overall, costs were found to be higher for community-based settings than they had been in institutional care. This study also found links between costs and service user needs, and some evidence of economies of scale within accommodation facilities (Knapp et al., 1992).

As policy interest in many countries has moved from the costs and benefits of community versus institutional provision to a post-reprovision agenda, there has been a belated but vigorous debate about models of community-based provision. A second example of cost-variations analysis was for a random stratified sample of staffed community facilities in England in 1988–89 (Shiell, Pettipher, Raynes & Wright, 1993). Smaller facilities were apparently no more expensive than larger ones, and the independent sector appeared to be providing a quality service at no additional cost. However, the authors advised that their findings should be interpreted with caution. The relationship between agency type and cost was complicated by the interactions between agency, quality of service, and the dependency of the service users. There were distinct differences in the type of resident supported within each of the provider sectors, with public-sector facilities catering for people with highest levels of need, and private- and voluntary-sector providers supporting the most independent.

Earlier in this chapter, an evaluation of various types of residential supports for people with intellectual disability was discussed, in the context of accurate cost measurement. The evaluation, carried out between 1996 and 1998, collected data relating to independent sector village or residential communities; NHS residential campuses built, or converted, to accommodate former long-stay hospital patients; and small, community-based, dispersed housing units (group homes and supported living arrangements). In this study, higher costs were found to be associated with lower levels of ability and with younger users, for whom more costly residential supports and more innovative day programmes were provided (Emerson et al., 2000). Unlike the findings of Shiell et al., there were links between higher cost and smaller facilities; in addition, several indicators of the quality of care affected cost. Generally, more sophisticated procedures (for example, activity planning for residents and individual personal plans) were associated with higher cost. Where less sophisticated procedures existed for staff training and supervision, however, the cost was also higher. This may be because ill-defined internal procedures for training and support of staff result in higher staff turnover, lower morale, and higher levels of staff sickness.

Identifying Patterns of Service Use

The formalisation of decision making about service delivery and funding in health and social care in the UK has taken a particular direction since implementation of the 1990

National Health Service and Community Care Act. Purchasing and provision have been separated, and commissioning of services has become a key activity. The main players in the "quasi-markets" that now structure care systems are looking for approaches, frameworks, or tools to aid their decision making. Although decisions based on the individual service user's needs and preferences are central to community-based care systems, it is also important to seek approaches which, when applied in the aggregate, can simplify the otherwise complex tasks of matching resources to needs and keeping within available budgets.

One approach that has been examined in a number of health-care systems, starting in the USA, has been to develop diagnostic related groups (DRGs). In the UK NHS, the DRG approach has been explored in what has been called the Health Care Framework, which classifies patients' needs by using health benefit groups and classifies interventions by using health-care resource groups (NHS Information Authority, 1999).

- *Health-care resource groups (HRGs)* are sets of activities (procedures or interventions) that are clinically similar and consume similar amounts of resources.
- *Health benefit groups (HBGs)* are sets of patients or users who have similar health-care needs and who are likely to have similar outcomes (given the same packages of care).

There are obviously many differences between services for people with intellectual disabilities and "mainstream" acute health-care interventions. However, a pilot study by Pendaries (1997) showed that it was possible to build "resource groups" which could offer a useful degree of cost prediction in this area, according to individuals' levels of disability and the presence or absence of challenging behaviour. Recently, this approach was further explored in a survey of more than 2000 adults with intellectual disabilities (Comas-Herrera, Knapp, Pendaries, Beecham & Carthew, 2001). Data relating to levels of intellectual disability, challenging behaviour, and service use were collected by the CSRI, and costs were calculated with data relating to specific facilities and nationally applicable unit costs. The feasibility of the approach was established: using cluster analysis, nine benefit groups were created that were meaningful from a practitioner's perspective and 96 resource groups that were coherent in terms of likely care packages.

The exploratory approach to develop "benefit groups" and "resource groups" is intended as an "enabling framework" and should be seen as neither proscriptive nor deterministic. Rather, it is an attempt to identify and describe patterns in a way that might assist purchasers and providers by giving them a framework within which to commission and deliver need-sensitive and preference-responsive services.

CONCLUSIONS: FUTURE DIRECTIONS

There is widespread acknowledgement that the costs of supporting individuals who have intellectual disabilities are often substantial and spread widely between agencies, service users, and families. Policy-makers and those who commission and provide services need to recognise how resources might be better deployed, for example, to achieve improved outcomes from the same level of expenditure. The costs and consequences (outcomes) of the alternatives need to be measured and analysed systematically in order to reach informed decisions.

Long-Term Perspectives

In their review of the economics of providing for the people who are intellectually disabled, Kavanagh and Opit (1998) recommended longitudinal research focusing on pathways through care at key periods in the life cycle (birth, detection and early service use, the teenage years where education services end and adult services responsibility begins, or where parents are ageing). Longitudinal studies are very costly to mount but can obviously serve many purposes; supporting economic evaluations is one of them.

As life expectancy for people with intellectual disability has improved, it has become more important to ensure that the development of age-related disabilities can be prevented or controlled, and that general well-being and quality of life can be maintained (Holland, 2000). A longer lifespan carries major resource implications for service provision even before considering additional impairments associated with the ageing process, since parents will age and die, or become too frail to provide care. Physical age-related diseases such as stroke, cardiovascular disease, and malignancy will also be of growing concern as people with intellectual disability survive to a greater age, and placement in more specialised accommodation may be required in order to provide appropriate care. Interestingly, functional ability has been found to *improve* in later life, due to differential mortality rates leading to a shorter life expectancy for people with more severe intellectual disabilities, and for people with Down's syndrome (Holland, 2000). Research is needed into the resource implications of supporting people in the community in later life, and to a greater understanding of how functional ability in survivors can be maximised while services are targeted on increasing age-related impairments.

Some areas of policy and practice might be seen as in need of priority attention. When people with intellectual disabilities were cared for within institutions, their health needs were catered for by psychiatric specialists. However, major shifts in the balance of care now mean that primary- and community-care professionals are increasingly likely to be responsible for meeting the needs of people with intellectual disabilities. These service professionals will need to respond to complex physical, psychiatric, and developmental problems (Department of Health, 1999). It would be useful, for example, to have more information on the use of primary-care (medical) services by people living in various levels of specialist staffed accommodation and domestic housing, and the cost-effectiveness of service delivery.

Economic Evaluation as Standard Practice

However, a case could probably be made for giving priority evaluative attention to any number of practice or policy areas. The fundamental point is that economic evaluations can make contributions to our understanding in almost every aspect of policy and practice development in the intellectual disability field. In thinking about future directions for research, therefore, one of the most pressing needs is to ensure that more economics studies—of high quality—are undertaken.

Economic Methodologies

If that quality is to be achieved, evaluators need to pay especial attention to cost measurement, outcome conceptualisation and measurement, and research design. Space precludes anything more than a few words on each. Drummond et al. (1997) and Gold et al. (1996) give good accounts of the general issues, although health-economics theory and practice continues to develop apace, so that some parts of these books are already quite out of date.

The measurement of service costs is generally good, but disputes still rage as to the costing of (informal) family care, lost employment and productivity, and (if one wants such a measure) premature mortality. Outcome measurement represents a tougher challenge because—as we argued earlier—different policy questions require different modes of evaluation, in turn generating a need to develop the techniques that would allow the construction of utility scores and/or the monetary valuation of outcomes (the "benefits"). These methodological desiderata are of course on top of the broader need to improve effectiveness measurement in (some) intellectual disability research areas.

This is linked to a third area where researchers should pay attention to research quality: the overall design of their studies, experimental or naturalistic settings, sample size and statistical power, the generalisability of findings, and so on. These are perennial issues in evaluation research but sometimes with a particular application for an economic evaluation. Finally, there is the challenge of international transferability of research results. Economics evidence is closely bound up with the support and care systems within which it is gathered. Unlike evidence on user outcomes, therefore, cost-effectiveness findings do not always travel well from system to system or country to country. What *are* internationally transferable are the evaluation methodologies and the practical lessons in their application.

REFERENCES

Beecham, J. & Knapp, M. (1992). Costing psychiatric interventions. In G. Thornicroft, C. Brewin & J. Wing (Eds) *Measuring Mental Health Needs* (pp. 163–183). London: Gaskell.

Beecham, J. & Knapp, M. (2001). Costing psychiatric interventions (revised). In G. Thornicroft (Ed.) *Measuring Mental Health Needs* (2nd edn). London: Gaskell.

Byford, S., Torgerson, D.J. & Raftery, J. (2000). Cost of illness studies. *British Medical Journal*, **320**, 1335.

Cambridge, P., Hayes, L. & Knapp, M.R.J. with Gould, E. & Fenyo, A. (1994). *Care in the Community: Five Years On*. Aldershot: Ashgate.

Chisholm, D., Healey, A. & Knapp, M.R.J. (1997). QALYs and mental health care. *Social Psychiatry and Psychiatric Epidemiology*, **32**, 68–75.

Chisholm, D., Knapp, M., Knudsen, H.C., Vasquez-Barquero, J.L., Lasalvia, A., Padfield, S., et al. and the EPSILON Study Group (2000). Client Socio-Demographic Service Receipt Inventory–European Version: development of an instrument for international research. *British Journal of Psychiatry*, **177** (Suppl. 39), 28–33.

Comas-Herrera, A., Knapp, M.R.J., Pendaries, C., Beecham, J. & Carthew, R. (2001). Benefit groups and resource groups for adults with intellectual disabilities in residential accommodation. *Journal of Applied Research in Intellectual Disability*, **14**, 120–140.

Davies, B.P. & Knapp, M.R.J. (1981). *Old People's Homes and the Production of Welfare*. London: Routledge & Kegan Paul.

Davies, B.P. & Knapp, M.R.J. (Eds) (1988). The production of welfare approach? Evidence and argument from the PSSRU. *British Journal of Social Work*, **18** (Suppl.).

Department of Health (1999). *Once a Day*. London: NHS Executive.

Department of Health (2001). *Valuing People: A New Strategy for Learning Disability for the 21st Century*. Cmnd. 5086. London: Department of Health.
Department of Health and Social Security (1979). *A Report of the Committee of Enquiry into Mental Handicap Nursing and Care* (Jay Report). Cmnd. 7468. London: HMSO.
Department of Health and Social Security (1983). *Care in the Community*. HC(86)3, LAC(83)5. London: HMSO.
Donnelly, M., McGilloway, S., Mays, N., Perry, S., Knapp, M., Kavanagh, S., et al. (1994). *Opening New Doors: An Evaluation of Community Care for People Discharged from Psychiatric and Mental Handicap Hospitals*. London: HMSO.
Drummond, M., O'Brien, B., Stoddart, G. & Torrance, G. (1997). *Methods for the Economic Evaluation of Health Care Programmes*. Oxford: Oxford University Press.
Emerson, E., Robertson, J., Gregory, N., Hatton, C., Kessissoglou, S., Hallam, A.J., et al. (2000). The quality and costs of village communities, residential campuses and community-based residential supports in the UK. *American Journal of Mental Retardation*, **105**, 81–102.
Emerson, E., Robertson, J., Gregory, N., Hatton, C., Kessissoglou, S., Hallam, A., et al. (2001). The quality and costs of supported living schemes and group homes in the UK. *American Journal of Mental Retardation*, **105**, 401–415.
Felce, D., Lowe, K., Perry, J., Baxter, H., Jones, E., Hallam, A., et al. (1999). Service support to people with severe intellectual disabilities and the most severe challenging behaviours in Wales: processes, outcomes and costs. *Journal of Intellectual Disability Research*, **42**, 390–408.
Gold, M.R., Siegel, J.E., Russell, L.B. & Weinstein, M.C. (Eds) (1996). *Cost-Effectiveness in Health and Medicine*. New York: Oxford University Press.
Goodwin, S. (1997). *Comparative Mental Health Policy*. London: Sage.
Hallam, A.J., Beecham, J.K., Knapp, M.R.J., Carpenter, J., Cambridge, P., Forrester-Jones, R., et al. (2003). Service use and the costs of support for people with learning disabilities. (Submitted for publication.)
Hallam, A.J., Knapp, M.R.J., Järbrink, K., Netten, A., Emerson, E., Robertson, J., et al. (2002). The costs of village community, residential campus and dispersed housing provision for people with intellectual disability. *Journal of Intellectual Disability Research*, **46**, 394–404.
Holland, A.J. (2000). Ageing and learning disability. *British Journal of Psychiatry*, **176**, 26–31.
Järbrink, K. & Knapp, M. (2001). The economic impact of autism in Britain. *Autism*, **5**, 17–22.
Kavanagh, S. & Opit, L. (1998). *The Cost of Caring: the Economics of Providing for the Intellectually Disabled*. London: Politeia.
King's Fund Centre (1980). *An Ordinary Life*. London: King's Fund Centre.
Knapp, M. (1993). Background theory. In J. Beecham & A. Netten (Eds) *Costing Community Care* (pp. 9–24). Aldershot: Ashgate.
Knapp, M. (1998). Making music out of noise—the cost function approach to evaluation. *British Journal of Psychiatry*, **173** (Suppl. 36), 7–11.
Knapp, M., Cambridge, P., Thomason, C., Beecham, J., Allen, C. & Darton, R. (1992). *Care in the Community: Challenge and Demonstration*. Aldershot: Ashgate.
Knapp, M.R.J. (1984). *The Economics of Social Care*. London: Macmillan.
McCrone, P. (1998). *Understanding Health Economics: A Guide for Health Care Decision Makers*. London: Kogan Page.
McDaid, D. (2001). Estimating the costs of informal care for people with Alzheimer's disease: methodological and practical challenges. *International Journal of Geriatric Psychiatry*, **16**, 400–405.
National Health Service Information Authority (1999). *The Healthcare Framework*. Winchester, 1999-1A-57.
Netten, A. & Curtis, L. (2000). *Unit Costs of Health and Social Care 2000*. Canterbury. PSSRU, University of Kent.
Olsen, J.A. & Smith, R.D. (2001). Theory versus practice: a review of "willingness to pay" in health and health care. *Health Economics*, **10**, 39–52.
Pendaries, C. (1997). Pilot study on the development of the learning disability Healthcare Resource Groups. *British Journal of Learning Disabilities*, **25**, 122–126.

Renshaw, J., Hampson, R., Thomason, C., Darton, R.A., Judge, K. & Knapp, M.R.J. (1988). *Care in the Community: The First Steps*. Aldershot: Gower.

Scull, A. (1984). *Decarceration: Community Treatment and the Deviant: A Radical View* (2nd edn). Cambridge: Polity Press.

Shiell, A., Pettipher, C., Raynes, N. & Wright, K. (1993). A cost function analysis of residential services for adults with a learning disability. *Health Economics*, **2**, 247–256.

Walker, A. (1982). *Community Care: The Family, the State and Social Policy*. Oxford: Blackwell.

Wolfensberger, W. (1972). *The Principle of Normalization in Human Services*. Toronto: National Institute on Mental Retardation.

Index

Note*:* *Italic* page references refer to Figures and Tables

Compiled by Indexing Specialists (UK) Limited